COMPUTER APPLICATIONS IN BUSINESS

COMPUTER APPLICATIONS IN BUSINESS

(Including Introduction to Information Technology, MS Office 2010, HTML and Tally ERP 9)

Dr. S. SUDALAI MUTHU

Reader,
Department of Banking Technology,
School of Management
Pondicherry Central University,
Puducherry - 605 014.

Dr. S. ANTHONY RAJ

BBM,MFT,MBA,M.Phil., PGDCA, PGDOM, PGDM, DIM, Ph.D.,
Assistant Professor (SG),
Karunya School of Management,
Karunya University,
Coimbatore - 641 114.

Himalaya Publishing House

ISO 9001:2015 CERTIFIED

First Edition : 2008
Second Revised Edition : 2012
Reprint : 2014, 2015, 2016, 2017
Reprint : 2018, 2019, 2022, 2023
Reprint : 2024

Published by : Mrs. Meena Pandey
for **HIMALAYA PUBLISHING HOUSE PVT. LTD.,**
"Ramdoot", Dr. Bhalerao Marg, Girgaon, Mumbai - 400 004.
Phone: 022-23860170/23863863, Fax: 022-23877178
E-mail: himpub@bharatmail.co.in; **Website:** www.himpub.com

Branch Offices :

New Delhi : "Pooja Apartments", 4-B, Murari Lal Street, Ansari Road, Darya Ganj, New Delhi - 110 002.
Phone: 011-23270392, 23278631; Fax: 011-23256286

Nagpur : Kundanlal Chandak Industrial Estate, Ghat Road, Nagpur - 440 018.
Phone: 0712-2738731, 2721216

Bengaluru : Plot No. 91-33, 2nd Main Road Seshadripuram, Behind Nataraja Theatre,
Bengaluru - 560 020. Phone: 080-41138821, Mobile: 09379847017, 09379847005.

Hyderabad : No. 3-4-184, Lingampally, Besides Raghavendra Swamy Matham, Kachiguda,
Hyderabad - 500 027. Phone: 040-27560041, 27550139

Chennai : No. 34/44, Motilal Street, T. Nagar, Chennai - 600 017. Mobile: 09380460419

Pune : First Floor, "Laksha" Apartment, No. 527, Mehunpura, Shaniwarpeth
(Near Prabhat Theatre), Pune - 411 030. Phone: 020-24496323/24496333; Mobile: 09370579333

Cuttack : Plot No. 5F-755/4, Sector-9, CDA Markat Nagar, Cuttack - 753 014,
Odisha. Mobile: 09338746007

Kolkata : 3, S.M. Bose Road, Near Gate No. 5, Agarpara Railway Station, North 24 Parganas,
West Bengal - 700 109. Mobile: 09674536325

DTP by : Priyanka Mahadik.

Printed at : M/s. Giriraj Printers, Hyderabad. On behalf of HPH.

Dedicated to

our

Parents & Teachers

PREFACE

The whole world is nothing without computers. Computers have changed the trends almost in all fields. The contribution of computers in business is impeccable and invaluable. The business operations with effective usage of computers are inseparable in nature. The operation of these devices needs certain education and skill.

Developing countries like India is rich in human resource and abundance of employment opportunities is seen. And these opportunities are highly available for those who possess computer operating skill. The computers and its components play an important role in the field of business. Today, in the globalized era, without computers and internet we cannot run the business effectively. Computer and computer based network facilities help to do borderless business with minimum cost. Realizing the importance of computers in the field of business, many Universities in India have introduced computer based subjects in the commerce and management curriculum.

Realizing this need, the authors tried to bridge the gap between the skill required and the course curriculum. This second edition of this book is prepared so as to make even an ordinary layman as a computer literate.

This second edition of this book covers MS OFFICE 2010, HTML and TALLY ERP 9, which are considered to be the most important package required for a business. There are many special packages as well as specialised softwares, but MS OFFICE 2010 is BEST in its user friendliness. The approach of authors in handling this subject is as simple as a nutshell.

This second edition of this book covers MS OFFICE 2010,and TALLY ERP 9. This book is very lucid and elaborate. To facilitate the students, practical lists and elucidation of the same were also given at appropriate chapters. Shortcut keys were also given for effective operation.

This book is fragmented into 12 chapters. The following are the ingredients of this book:

- ❖ Basic concepts of computers
- ❖ Software applications
- ❖ Data processing
- ❖ E-Commerce
- ❖ SAD & MIS
- ❖ MS Office 2010 (Word, Powerpoint, Excel, Access & Front Page)

❖ HTML & Web Publishing

❖ E-mail & Internet

❖ Information System Audit

❖ Operating System, and

❖ Tally ERP 9

The above content covers the syllabus of the papers titled "Computer Applications in Business", "Introduction to Information Technology", "Office Automation", "MS-OFFICE 2010", "Web Technology through HTML", "PC Software" and "Tally ERP 9" in the B.Com., B.Com with Computer Applications, B.Com. (E-Commerce), BCS, BBM, BBM with Computer Applications, BBA, M.Com., M.Com. IB, M.Com. with Information Technology, MFC, MIB, MBA etc. courses offered by Bharathiar University, Bharathidasan University, University of Madras, Madurai Kamaraj University, Pondicherry University, Periyar University, Alagappa University, Manonmaniam Sundaranar University, and various Autonomous Institutions in Tamil Nadu, Andhra Pradesh, Karnataka and Kerala.

We hope this book will be handy and helping source to those who pursue it to escalate their computer operating skills in business and its related activities.

Dr. S. SUDALAI MUTHU

Dr. S. ANTHONY RAJ

ACKNOWLEDGEMENT

"...God is the highest altitude;

God is the highest end; and

God is the highest destination...."

Our special thanks to The "GOD ALMIGHTY", the living gods "OUR PARENTS", our "TEACHERS", our "FAMILY MEMBERS" and to our "FRIENDS".

We have made acknowledgement of every idea whose source we have been able to identify, but some writers or authors may have been missed unintentionally. We would like to thank all those who have directly and indirectly helped us in making this publication a successful one.

We wish to express thanks to the members of the Himalaya Publishing House especially **Mr. Niraj Pandey**, whose high performance standards and in-depth knowledge of publishing have been invaluable in the development of the text. We are also thankful to **Ms. Nimisha,** Himalaya Publications and **Dr. A. Anandaraj**, Area Sales Executive Coimbatore for their continuous support in bringing this book in time.

Any constructive comments for improving the contents will be warmly appreciated.

Dr. S. SUDALAI MUTHU
sm_vcas@yahoo.com

Dr. S. ANTHONY RAJ
rajpillaianto@gmail.com

CONTENTS

CHAPTER 1

INTRODUCTION TO COMPUTER

Structure:

1.1 MEANING AND DEFINITION OF COMPUTERS

The term computer is derived from the Latin word compute, which means to calculate. A computer is an electronic machine, devised for performing calculations and controlling operations that can be expressed either in logical or numerical terms. In simple terms, a computer is an electronic device that performs diverse operations with the help of instructions to process the information in order to achieve the desired results. Computer application extends to cover huge area including education, industries, government, medicine, scientific research etc.

A computer is one of the most influential forces available in modern times. Due to its memory, high speed and perfection, its application can be extended to almost infinite levels. Millions of complex calculations can be done in mere fraction of time. Difficult decisions can be made with accuracy for comparatively little cost. Computers are widely seen as instruments for future progress and as tools to achieve substantiality by way of improved access to information by means of video conferencing and e-mail. Indeed computers have left such on impression an modern civilization that we call this era as the information age.

1.2 CHARACTERISTICS OF COMPUTERS

The main characteristics of computers are:

(a) Speed: Computers are capable of carrying out the task with enormous speed. Today's computers, according to their class, can perform from 4 MIPS (Millions of instructions per second) to 100 MIPS. What may take days for manual calculations may take only a few hours for computers to perform. Inside the computer the information signal travels at incredible electronic speed.

(b) Storage: Computers can store enormous quantity of information. It is achieved through its 'Main memory' or 'Primary storage' and through 'auxiliary storage' or 'Secondary storage.' The Hard disks Floppy disk, Compact Disc (CD) and Magnetic Tape storage are examples of secondary storages. These large volumes of storage occupy much lesser space compared to paper documents and this aspect of computers makes them more powerful.

(c) Accuracy: The accuracy of a Computer is consistently high. In fact, this quality of the computers make them indispensable in various fields such as Scientific Research, Space Research, Weather Predictions and many other areas where precision of a high order is required. The accuracy of the computer is best achieved by programming them in the most efficient manner. When it comes to very complex mathematical or scientific problem the computer's accuracy has no substitute.

(d) Versatility: Computers are versatile in that they can perform almost any task, provided they are given the appropriate logical steps. For example, they are capable of performing wide ranging tasks such as construction of a payroll, inventory management in a factory, hotel billing, hospital management, banking applications and any imaginable task in every walk of life.

(e) Automation: The biggest advantage of computers is that it is automatic in its operation. Once a programming logic is initiated the computer performs repeated operations without human interventions until program completion.

(f) Diligence: Computers are machines and that do not get tired or 'lose concentration' like human beings. If a large number of calculations say million calculations are to be performed the resultant output will remain exactly the same even if operations are repeated any number of times. But when a human being is asked to do the same job this consistency cannot be achieved. Thus for those who want consistent and continuous standard output, computer's 'diligence' is of great help.

(g) Power of Remembering: Computer has the power of storing any amount of information or data. Any information can be stored and recalled as long as you require it, for any numbers of years. It depends entirely upon you how much data you want to store in a computer and when to lose or retrieve these data.

(h) No IQ: Computer is a dumb machine and it cannot do any work without instruction from the user. It performs the instructions at tremendous speed and with accuracy. It is you to decide what you want to do and in what sequence. So a computer cannot take its own decision as you can.

(i) No Feeling: It does not have feelings or emotion, taste, knowledge and experience. Thus it does not get tired even after long hours of work. It does not distinguish between users.

1.3 HISTORY OF COMPUTERS

In the early days of mankind, man used to count the head of cattle by putting lines on trees. Slowly these lines changed to numbers. To do calculation on numbers he started inventing machines.

1. Abacus

Abacus was probably the earliest of counting devices. It consists of rectangular wooden frame with two compartments and beads sliding along the steel wires for counting. Multiplication and divisions are done using repeated additions and subtractions. Even today in which cross strings are fixed. Beads are inserted on to the strings. There are a number of rows of beads.

2. Napier's Logs and Bones

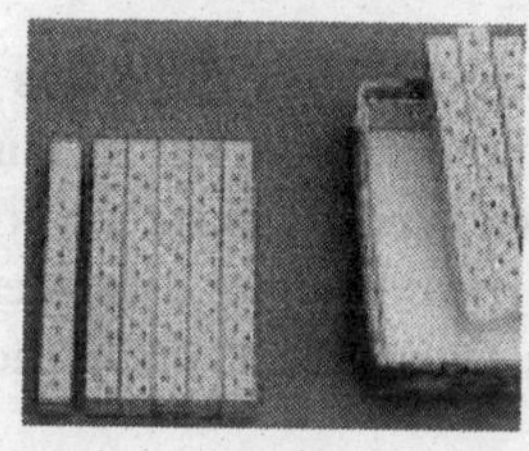

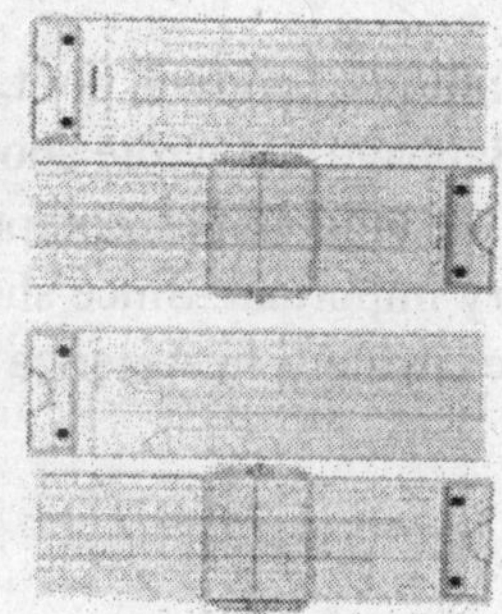

John Napier, a Scottish mathematician invented logarithms. The use of logarithms enabled him to transform multiplications and division problems of addition and subtractions. In the beginning he called logarithms as artificial numbers. But later he named them logarithms.

Napier also invented a computing device consisting of sticks with numbers carved on them. These sticks are called bones as they were made of bones. These bones helped a lot in multiplication involving large numbers.

3. Slide Rule

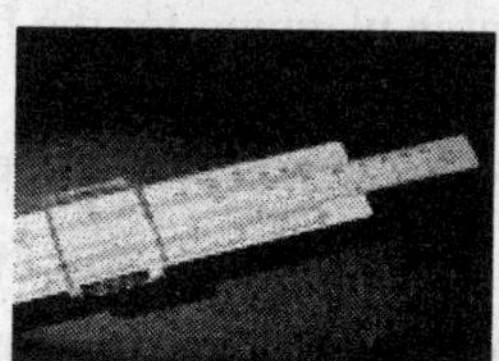

As the name indicates, the slide rule has one scale sliding within the other. Suppose you want to add two numbers 3 and 5, set 3 on the fixed scale and slide the moving scale. So that its "0' coincides with"5" of sliding scale. This is the sum of 3 and 5. The process of reading could be quick if you are trained in the use of slide rule.

4. Calculating Machines and Pascal's Calculator

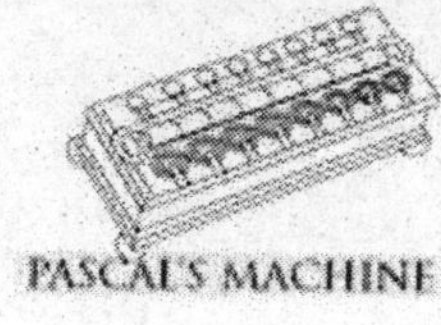

PASCAL'S MACHINE

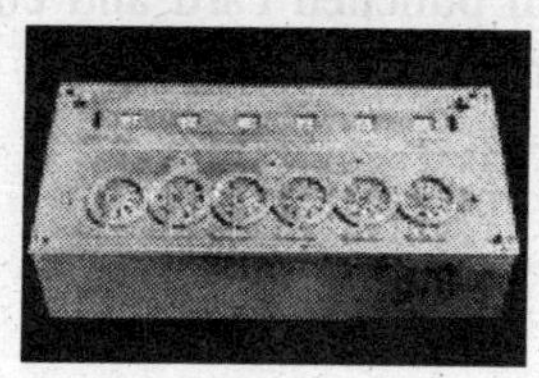

A French mathematician, Blaise Pascal invented a machine based on gear wheels. He was the son of tax collector who had to do lot of calculations as part of his job. Blaise Pascal wanted to make his job easier by inventing a calculator. You might be familiar with gear wheels in use in your bicycle which meshes with a driving chain. He used similar gear wheels with ten teeth for each digit position. He fixed them together so that one wheel drives the other. When the wheel corresponding to units position rotated by ten teeth, it drove the wheel corresponding to the next higher position by one tooth. Thus one could make calculations. Pascal provided dials, which indicated numbers stored on each wheel. He also used suitable "dialing system" to operate the gear wheels. Other people also made a number of such calculators. Computer scientists honoured Pascal by naming a programming language Pascal after him.

5. Babbage Difference and Analytical Engines

Babbage, a British National and the son of a wealthy banker wanted to correct the errors in the logarithm tables being used during his time. In 1822, he made a machine which calculated the successive difference of expressions (X2 + ax + b is an example of an expression) and prepared table which helped him in his calculations. The royal Astronomical society awarded a gold medal to him for his invention and granted a large sum of money to carry out further work. He wanted to make an accurate calculating machine called "Babbage's Analytical Engine." The analytical Engine was supposed to be very accurate. So it needed lot of parts made with precision. Babbage could not make such parts. He conceived that his machine would use input devices, would have a processing part called "mill" where you can perform calculations, would also incorporate.

It consists of rectangular frame in which cross strings are fixed. Beads are inserted on to the strings. There are a number of rows of beads. Since he was about 100 years ahead in his ideas, he could not get parts needed for his machine. This is because there were no tools to make such precision parts. He did lot of work related to making precision parts and spend all the grants (and lot of his money too) but failed in his attempt to make a machine. He ultimately died as a frustrated man.

6. Lady Ada Lovelace

Lovelace is the daughter of the famous English poet Lord Byron. She was a mathematician. She studied the works of Babbage and wrote about them. From her account only, we can see the close resemblance of the modern day computers and Babbage's work. Lady Ada Lovelace's contributions are very important. Since she predicted that computers can be programmed, a language, Ada used widely in America's Department of Defence Computers was named after her.

7. Herman Hollerith's Machine

Governments all over the world collect details about the number of people living in their countries. This information helps the Government in planning for the future, Sometimes you find enumerators (people taking such details) coming to your house with forms to collect such details. This operation is called "census" which is normally done once in 10 years.

In the United States a census was carried out in 1880 and the U S Government was processing the census data. Even as this was going on, the next census was due in 1890. To process the census of 1890 fast, the Government announced a competition.

Dr. Herman Hollerith Produced cards out of special paper pulp designed punching machines to punch holes in the card to count census figures and invented sorting machines to read such punched card and collect data. He could complete the job within three years, achieving a speedup of about three times.

8. Mechanical and Electrical Calculator

In the beginning of 19th century the mechanical calculator was developed to perform all sorts of mathematical calculations. Up to the 1960s it was widely used. Later the rotating part of mechanical calculator was replaced by electric motor. So it was called the electrical calculator.

9. ABC Computer

In 1937, Dr. John Atanstoff with the help of his assistant Berry designed the Atanstoff Berry Computer (ABC). The machine laid the foundation for the development of electronic digital computer.

10. ENIAC — Electronic Numerical Integrator and Calculator

In 1947 John Mauchly and Eckart completed the first large-scale Electronic Digital Computer, ENIAC. In this computer, each time a program was changed, the wiring had to be completely rearranged. It weighed 30 tons, contained 18,000 vacuum tubes and occupied a space of 30^3 50 feet.

11. EDSAC-Electronic Delay Storage Automatic Calculator

Maurice V. Wilkes of Cambridge University completed EDSAC in 1949. EDSAC was the first computer to operate on the stored program concept.

12. UNIVAC-I — Universal Automatic Computers

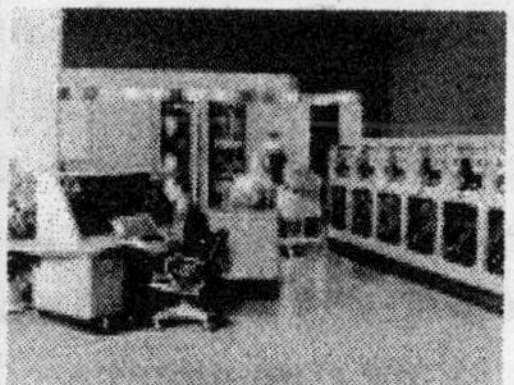

In 1947, after ENIAC became operational Mauchly and Eckart formed their own Company "The Eckart-Mauchly Computer Corporation." Immediately after this they started the design of UNIVAC-I. This was purchased by US bureau of Census. UNIVAC was the first computer dedicated to business applications.

13. Modern Electronic Calculator

The electronic calculator used in 1960s was run with electron tubes, which was quite bulky. Later it was replaced with *transistors* and as a result the size of calculators became too small.

The modern electronic calculator can compute all kinds of mathematical computations and mathematical functions. It can also be used to store some data permanently. Some calculators have in-built programs to perform some complicated calculations.

14. Mainframe Computers

In the year 1960, Gene Amdahl designed IBM system/360 series of Mainframe computers, the first general purpose digital computers to use integrated circuits.

15. Mini Computer

In the year 1963 Olsen with Digital Equipment Corporation produced the PDP-1 (Program Data Processor), the first Mini computer.

16. Micro Computer

In the year 1970 Intel created a memory chip that could store a kilobit of information. A kilobit translates roughly into 25 five letter words. Another innovation at Intel came from Ted Hoff, who has integrated circuit by compressing twelve chips into four. The arithmetic and logic functions of several chips could be contained on one chip, called Microprocessor. Hoff's Microprocessor was called the Intel 4004 ("forty-oh-four").

In the year 1975, H. Edward Roberts, an Electronic Engineer who is now generally known as the "Father of the Micro Computer" designed the first Micro Computer.

In the year 1977, Stephen Wozniak, the technical expert and Steven Jobs designed and built the first **Apple Micro Computer**.

17. Super Computer

Seymour Cray's CRAY-I super computer was delivered to Los Alamos Scientific Laboratory in New Mexico in the year 1976.

18. Personal Computers

In the year 1980, Lower cost computer systems called Personal Computers intended for home use were produced. New program products are also introduced.

1.4 TYPES OF COMPUTER SYSTEMS

Introduction

Our society is being reshaped by rapid advances in information technologies, Computer, Telecommunication networks and other digital systems that have vastly increased our capacity to know, achieve and collaborate. These technologies allow people to transmit information quickly and widely, linking distance places and to create communities that just a decade ago were unimaginable.

It is difficult to appreciate just how quickly information technology is evolving. Five decades ago ENIAC, one of the earliest computers stood ten feet tall and stretched eighty feed wide; while today, one can buy a musical greeting card with a silicon chip that is 100 times faster than ENIAC. This extraordinary phase of information technology is bringing people and cultures together and creating new social dynamics in the process. It is leading to the formation of closely bonded and widely dispersed community of people united by their interest in doing business or in sharing experiences and intellectual pursuits. New forms of knowledge accumulation are developing, as are computer based learning system that opened the way to innovate modes of instruction and learning.

A computer is an electronic machine, operating under the control instructions stored inside its memory. As an aid in problem solving, it accepts data, both numeric and non-numeric, processes and presents it in the desired form.

The following are the various types of computer systems:

Various Types of Computer Systems

1. Analog Computers

Analog is the Greek word, which means similar. So, in analog computers, the similarities between any two quantities are measured by electrical voltages or current. The analog computers operate by measuring instead of counting.

The analog computer works on the supply of continuous electrical signals. The display is also continuous. Its output is in the form of graphs.

Analog Signal: An analog signal is a continuous variable electromagnetic wave. It can consume an infinite number of voltage or current values.

Characteristics of Analog Computer

The analog computer has the following important characteristics:

(a) It operates by measuring.

(b) It requires physical analog.

(c) It functions on continuously varying quantities.

(d) The output is usually represented in the form of graph.

(e) In analog, the calculations are first converted in equation and later converted into electrical signals.

(f) The accuracy of the output is poor.

(g) It has limited memory space.

(h) It is not versatile, i.e., it has limited application.

(i) The speed of analog computer is low.

(j) Not suitable for business and industry.

2. Digital Computers

These computers work with quantities represented as digits. They operate on discrete quantities. In digital computer, both numeric and non-numeric information are represented as strings of digits. These computers use binary codes, 0's and 1's, to represent the information. The information is given to the computer in the form of discrete electrical signals.

The basic operation performed by a digital computer is addition. Hence, the other operations such as multiplication, division, subtraction and exponentiation are first converted into "addition" and then computed.

Characteristics of Digital Computer:

The digital computer has the following characteristics:

(a) It operates by counting.

(b) It functions on discrete numbers.

(c) The calculations are converted into binary numbers, i.e., 1s and 0s.

(d) The output is represented in the form of discrete values.

(e) Its accuracy is good.

(f) It has large memory space.

(g) It is versatile in nature and is suitable for a number of applications.

(h) In digital computers, the numbers, words and symbols can be used.

(i) Its processing speed is high.

(j) It is highly suitable for business application.

Hybrid Computers

Analog	Special purpose Digital
	General purpose digital

3. Hybrid Computers

The computer which possess the features of both analog and digital computers are called hybrid computers. That is, the hybrid computers have the good qualities of both analog and digital computer.

With the hybrid computer the user can process both continuous and discrete data. This computer accepts either digital or analog or both types of input and gives the results as per requirements through special devices. In the hybrid computers a converter is fixed to convert the analog data into digital data and vice versa. These are special purpose devices and are not widely used.

Analog VS Digital Computer

S. No	Analog Computer	Digital Computer
1.	It operates by measuring	It operates by counting
2.	It requires physical analog	It functions on discrete numbers
3.	The calculations are first converted to equations and later converted into electrical signals	The calculations are converted into binary numbers (1s and 0s)
4.	The output is in the form of graph	The output is in the form of discrete values
5.	Less accurate	More accurate
6.	Less speed	High speed
7.	Limited memory is available	More memory is available
8.	Lacks flexibility	Highly flexible
9.	Cannot process alpha-numeric information	Can process alpha number information
10.	Limited application	More number of applications
11.	Not suitable for business applications	Highly suitable for business applications

4. General Purpose Computer

These are designed and constructed to cater almost all the needs of the society. They can perform various operations. In fields of engineering, science, commerce and industry. They are able to perform according to the programs created to meet different needs. The general purpose computer can be used to prepare stores reports, sales reports, payroll, etc. A general purpose computer can solve a much broader class problems, specifically a general purpose digital computer is remarkably versatile.

5. Special Purpose Computers

These computers are designed to solve a particular problem or task, the computers are provided with limited memory and speed necessary for a particular job. The instructions needed to perform the particular task are incorporated into the internal memory of the computer. It does not possess unnecessary options, hence it is economical, e.g., business purpose computers and scientific purpose computers.

What Computer can do?

A Computer is a machine that can solve problems by accepting data, performing certain operations and presenting the results of those operations under the direction of detailed step by step instructions. Such a set of sequenced instructions, which cause a computer to perform particular operations is called a program.

So a computer can:

1. Read a finite ranged value from memory
2. Write a finite ranged value in memory
3. Simulate arithmetic on finite ranged values
4. Based on the results of 1, 2, and 3 (or nothing at all), change the current flow of execution
5. Activate/Deactivate/Control peripheral devices

What Computers cannot do?

Computers are very good at what they do, but there are many tasks that they can't do. They can't do anything unless they are first programmed with specific instructions. Computers can't decide how they are to be programmed or provide their own input: they can't interpret the data they generate: they can't implement any decisions that they suggest: and they can't "think."

Computers can be programmed to store recipes, but they can't decide to fix dinner. They can keep track of scientific data, but they can't conceive or express the ideas for continued research. Their memories can contain the contents of encyclopedias, but only humans can decide what to do with that knowledge.

1.5 CLASSIFICATION OF COMPUTERS ON THE BASIS OF GENERATIONS

Introduction

The history of computer development is often discussed with reference to different generations of computing devices. In computer terminology, the word generation is described as a stage of technological development or innovation. A major technological development that fundamentally changed the way computers operate resulting in increasingly smaller, cheaper, more powerful and more efficient and reliable devices characterize each generation of computers.

Generations of Computers

1. First Generation (1940-1956)

Vacuum Tubes: First generation computers were vacuum tube/thermionic valves-based machines. These computers used vacuum tubes for circuitry and magnetic drums for memory. A magnetic drum is a metal cylinder coated with magnetic iron-oxide material on which data and programs can be stored. Input was based on punched cards and paper tape, and output was displayed on printouts.

First generation computers relied on binary-coded language (language of 0s and 1s) to perform operations and were able to solve only one problem at a time. Each machine was fed with different binary codes and hence were difficult to program. This resulted in lack of versatility and speed. In addition, to run on different types of computers, instructions must be rewritten or recompiled.

Examples: ENIAC, EDVAC, and UNIVAC

➢ **Characteristics of First Generation Computers:**

- These computers were based on vacuum tube technology.
- These were the fastest computing devices of their times (computation time was in milliseconds).
- These computers were very large, and required a lot of space for installation.
- Since thousands of vacuum tubes were used, they generated a large amount of heat. Therefore, air conditioning was essential.
- These were non-portable and very slow equipments.
- They lacked in versatility and speed.
- They were very expensive to operate and used a large amount of electricity.
- These machines were unreliable and prone to frequent hardware failures. Hence, constant maintenance was required.
- Since machine language was used, these computers were difficult to program and use.
- Each individual component had to be assembled manually. Hence, commercial appeal of these computers was poor.

2. Second Generation Computers (1956-1963)

Transistors: In the sixties, there was lot of development in semiconductor field — a field of materials. In vacuum tubes, a filament is heated to emit electrons (the basic component of an atom) that carry current. In 1946, Willam Shockley and a few of his colleagues invented **transistors**, which do not need any heating to liberate electrons in addition to being smaller in size, they saved power due to the absence of heating and hence the cooling needed. the smaller size resulted in smaller distances that the electrons have to travel to transmit information from one part of the computer to another. Hence calculations became faster. The reliability also increased. Today you cannot see any second generation computers.

The smaller size of components saw mass production of computers which became cheaper. Many companies started buying and using them increasing the demand. Computer programming languages developed further to make programming easier and user friendly. yet if you compare today's computers, they were a lot behind. The increased use of computers and the consequent mass production sent the prices crashing down. Computer scientists and electronic engineers were developing more sophisticated computers.

➢ **Characteristics of Second Generation Computers:**

- These machines were based on transistor technology.
- These were smaller as compared to the first generation computers.
- The computational time of these computers was reduced to microseconds from milliseconds.
- These were more reliable and less prone to hardware failure. Hence, such computers required less frequent maintenance.
- These were more portable and generated less amount of heat.
- Assemble language was used to program computers. Hence, programming became more time efficient and less cumbersome.

❖ Second generation computers still required air conditioning.

❖ Manual assembly of individual components into a functioning unit was still required.

3. Third Generation Computers (1964 — early 1970s)

Integrated Circuits: In second generation computers, one could recognize the circuit components such as transistors, resistors and capacitors distinctly. They were physically separate or "discreet." Slowly scientists started integrating these components together so that they are not separate. They were fused into the circuits. People called it large-scale integrated circuits (LSI). Computers using such components were called third generation computers. Since components were packed together more densely, the size of computers became smaller. Programmers also developed more sophisticated software. By 1970, engineers developed a device called microprocessor. Lot of circuits was packed into it. Intel 4004 was one such chip.

➢ **Characteristics of Third Generation Computers:**

❖ These computers were based on integrated circuit (IC) technology.

❖ They were able to reduce computational time from microseconds to nanoseconds.

❖ They were easily portable and more reliable than the second generation.

❖ These devices consumed less power and generated less heat. In some cases, air conditioning was still required.

❖ The size of these computers was smaller as compared to previous computers.

❖ Since hardware rarely failed, the maintenance cost was quite low.

❖ Extensive use of highlevel language became possible.

❖ Manual assembling of individual components was not required, so it reduced the large requirement of labour and cost. However, highly sophisticated technologies were required for the manufacture of IC chips.

❖ Commercial production became easier and cheaper.

4. Fourth Generation Computers (Early 1970s – till date)

Micro Processors: More and more circuits were packed in a microprocessor. The components were integrated further and very large-scale integration (VLSI) technology revolutionized computer field further. Intel Corporation made chips such as 8080 and 8086 to be followed by 80286, 80386, 80486 and now the Pentium processor. These chips perform calculations faster. They are not only used in computers, but also in measuring devices and even in household devices such as washing machines.

Computers using such VLSI chips progressively shrunk in size. Computers using the microprocessors are termed as microcomputers. The software technology also developed further. Programmers developed more sophisticated and user friendly software. In course of time, the cost of these computers have come down so much that even individuals bought them so they came to be known as personal computers.

➢ **Characteristics of Fourth Generation Computers:**

❖ Fourth generation computers are microprocessor-based systems.

❖ These computers are very small.

❖ Fourth generation computers are the cheapest among all the other generations.

❖ They are portable and quite reliable.

- ❖ These machines generate negligible amount of heat, hence they do not require air conditioning.
- ❖ Hardware failure is negligible so minimum maintenance is required.
- ❖ The production cost is very low.
- ❖ GUI and pointing devices enable users to learn to use the computer quickly.
- ❖ Interconnection of computers leads to better communication and resource sharing.

5. Fifth Generation Computers (Present and Beyond)

Artificial Intelligence: Up to fourth generation, the classification was based purely on hardware. Fifth generation computers are classified based on software also. VLSI technology is used in fifth generation computers. They have large main memories. The speed is also high. In addition to all this, Fifth generation computers run software called 'expert systems.'

➢ **Characteristics of Fifth Generation Computers:**

- ❖ **Mega Chips:** Fifth generation computers will use Super Large Scale Integrated (SLSI) chips, which will result in the production of microprocessor having millions of electronic components on a single chip. In order to store instructions and information, fifth generation computers require a great amount of storage capacity. Mega chips may enable the computer to approximate the memory capacity of the human mind.
- ❖ **Parallel Processing:** Most computers today access and execute only one instruction at a time. This is called serial processing. However, a computer using parallel processing accesses several instructions at once and works on them at the same time through use of multiple central processing units.
- ❖ **Artificial Intelligence (AI):** It refers to a series of related technologies that tries to simulate and reproduce human behaviour, including thinking, speaking and reasoning. AI comprises a group of related technologies: expert systems (ES), natural language processing (NLP), speech recognition, vision recognition, and robotics.

First Generation	Second Generation	Third Generation	Fourth Generation	Fifth Generation
Trend: Toward Smaller, Faster, More Reliable, and Less Costly				
Vacuum Tubes	Solid-State	Integrated Circuits	LSI, VLSI Micro-processors	Greater Power, Smaller Footprint
Trend: Toward Easy to Purchase, and Easy to Maintain				

1.6 CLASSIFICATION OF COMPUTERS ON THE BASIS OF SIZE AND SPEED

Although they belong to the fifth generation, they can be divided into different categories depending upon the size, efficiency, memory and number of users. Broadly, they can be divided it to the following categories:

1. Micro Computers

Because of its small size and the use of micro-processor, this computer is called micro computer. All the computers have three units, namely, input, output and central processing unit, (CPU). The entire CPU is contained in a single or a few microchips. When equipped with memory and input/output control circuitry, it is called micro computer. Its storage capacity is low when compared to mini and main frame computers. It is able to accept most of the high level languages. However, it uses an interpreter or complier for running high level languages.

Microchips contain micro electronic circuitries which are very tiny. Large numbers of these can be packed tightly on to a single tiny piece of silicon. Silicon is a material found in sand. The microchip is made by building up a series of very thin layers of silicon and of the tiny components which are held in it.

The Micro computers are small and portable. They are relatively inexpensive; the micro computers have excellent graphic capabilities. The maximum word length varies according to the configuration of the microcomputers.

Kinds of Microchips:

The microchips can be classified as follows:

(a) **Micro Processors:** These are the most powerful kind. They are almost tiny computers in themselves. Each one has a processing Unit, a memory and a special area to handle input and output. Microprocessors are the most important part of the CPU of a modern computer

(b) **Memory Chips:** These are the common form of computer memory. They are used to hold information either temporarily or permanently.

(c) **Input and Output Chips:** In these chip circuits the flow of information is in both directions.

Features of Micro Computers:

(a) Its storage capacity is low.

(b) Its rate of acceptance and transfer of data is limited, i.e., a maximum of 5 lack bytes / second.

(c) It is able to accept most high level languages. However it uses an interpreter when running high level language because most micros do not have sufficiently large memory to support compliers.

(d) The maximum word length it holds is 16-bits.

Advantages

(a) They are small and portable.

(b) They are relatively inexpensive.

(c) They work as soon as they are switched on.

(d) They have excellent graphic capabilities,

(e) They do not occupy much space.

(f) They do not consume much power.

Disadvantages

(a) Micros have a limited storage capacity.

(b) They are relatively slow.

2. Mini Computers

The size of the mini-computer is in between the size of micro and main frame computers. It is more powerful than a micro computer. Mini computers are usually designed to serve multiple users. Today, mini-computers are the popular data processing systems in the field of business and industry. These computers accept all high level languages.

Characteristics

(a) It is a general purpose machine with a smaller CPU than a main frame

(b) Its storage capacity is about 2 mega words

(c) Its word lengths are usually 12, 16, 24, 32 bits.

(d) Its rate of acceptance and transfer of data is a maximum of 4 million bytes/seconds

(e) It can support all high level languages.

(f) It can support many terminals, i.e., more than 20 terminals.

Advantages

(a) It performs almost all the tasks that a mainframe computer does.

(b) It is relatively inexpensive and is within the purchasing power of the small and medium sized business firms.

Disadvantages

(a) They are very expensive

(b) They required large room space.

(c) Their consumption of electricity is very high.

(d) Maintenance coast is also very high.

3. Mainframes

These types of computers are generally 32-bit microprocessors. They operate at very high speed, have very large storage capacity and can handle the work load of many users. They are generally used in centralised databases. They are also used as controlling nodes in Wide Area Networks (WAN). Example of mainframes are DEC, ICL and IBM 3000 series.

4. Workstation

Workstation is a type of computer used for engineering applications (CAD/ CAM), desk top publishing, software development, and other types of applications that required a moderate amount of computing power and relatively high quality graphics capabilities. Workstations generally come with a large, high-resolution graphics screen, at least 64MB (Mega bytes) of RAM, built-in network support, and a graphical user interface. Most workstations also have a mass storage device such as a dish drive, but a special type of workstation, called a diskless workstation, comes without a disk drive. The most common operating systems for workstations are UNIX and Windows NT. In terms of computing power, workstations lie between personal computers and mini-computers, although the line is fuzzy on both ends high-end personal computers are equivalent to low-end workstations. And high-end workstations are equivalent to minicomputers. Like personal computers, most workstations are single-user computers. However, workstations are typically liked together to form a localarea network, although they can also be used as stand-alone systems.

5. Super Computers

The super computers are very costly. Hence it is rarely used. Its capacity is abnormally high, it cannot be compared with any other computers in capacity, function, speed, accuracy, language etc., they have operations done in parallel, rather than sequential. They are employed for specialized applications that require immense amounts of mathematical calculations. The chief difference between a super computer and a main frame computer is that a super computer channels all its power into executing a few programs as fast as possible. But main frame uses its power to execute many programs concurrently. CRAY – 3, Cyber 205, and PARAM are some well known super computers.

Characteristics

(a) They use several processors working simultaneously.

(b) They process at a rapid speed.

(c) The main memory ranges from 8 to 64 megabytes.

(d) They have operations done in parallel, rather than sequentially. They are used in weather forecasting, supersonic aircrafts design and other works that require billions of calculations per second.

(e) They can be used for animated graphics-fluid dynamic calculations etc.,

6. Network Computer

It was used (c. 1996 - c. 2000) by Oracle and an alliance of businesses including Sun and Acorn, to mean a diskless desktop computer — or in some cases a set top box — meeting a particular minimum specification. It was also employed as a marketing term to try to popularise this design of computer within businesses and among consumers (even though the essentials of the concept were not novel).

Due to the buzz created around the term, and the fact that diskless nodes can be used as thin clients, it has also been used more informally to mean simply a diskless desktop computer or a thin client. Because many NCs did not use Intel CPUs or Microsoft software, Microsoft and Intel developed a competing standard called NetPC for the same market, in order to try not to lose too much of their enormous desktop computer market shares to the NC upstarts.

The NC brand was mainly intended to denote a range of desktop computers from various suppliers that — by virtue of their diskless design and use of inexpensive components and software — were supposed to be significantly cheaper and easier to manage than standard fat client PCs. However, due to the PC coming down in price, and due to the increasing availability and popularity of various options for using PCs as diskless nodes, thin clients and hybrid clients, the NC brand never achieved the popularity hoped for by Oracle's CEO Larry Ellison, and was eventually mothballed.

Network Computer Reference Profile (NC reference profle, NCRP): Was a specification for a network computer put forward by Oracle Corporation, endorsed by Sun Microsystems, IBM, Apple Computer, and Netscape, and finalized in 1996.

The first version of this specification was known as the NC1 Reference Profile.

NCRP specified minimum hardware requirements and software protocols. Among the software requirements were support of IP-based protocols (TCP/IP, FTP, etc.), www standards (HTTP, HTML, Java Application Environment), e-mail protocols, multimedia file formats, security standards.

The minimum hardware requirements were

Minimum screen resolution of 640 x 480 (VGA) or equivalent

Pointing device

Text input capability

Audio output

7. Laptop Computer

Laptop computer, simply laptop (notebook computer or notebook), is a small mobile computer, which usually weighs 2-18 pounds (1-6 kilograms), depending on size, materials, and other factors.

Laptops usually run on a single main battery or from an external AC/DC adapter which can charge the battery while also supplying power to the computer itself. Many computers also have a 3 volt cell to run the clock and other processes in the event of a power failure.

As personal computers, laptops are capable of the same tasks as a desktop computer, although they are typically less powerful for the same price. They contain components that are similar to their desktop counterparts and perform the same functions, but are miniaturized and optimized for mobile use and efficient power consumption. Laptops usually have liquid crystal displays and most of them use different memory modules for their random access memory (RAM), for instance, SO-DIMM in lieu of the larger DIMMs. In addition to a built-in keyboard, they may utilize a touchpad (also known as a trackpad) or a pointing stick for input, though an external keyboard or mouse can usually be attached.

Basic Principles of Operation of Digital Computer Anatomy of Digital Computer:

Today, the most commonly used computers in business are digital computers. Even though they may differ in constructional details, the basic principles of operation are almost the same.

A computer is basically a device used for processing of data, it performs the following three operations in sequence:

(a) Receives the data and instruction.

(b) Processes the data as per the instructions.

(c) Output the result, i.e., information.

This cycle of operation of a computer is known as the input process — Output cycle. This can be explained in the following figure:

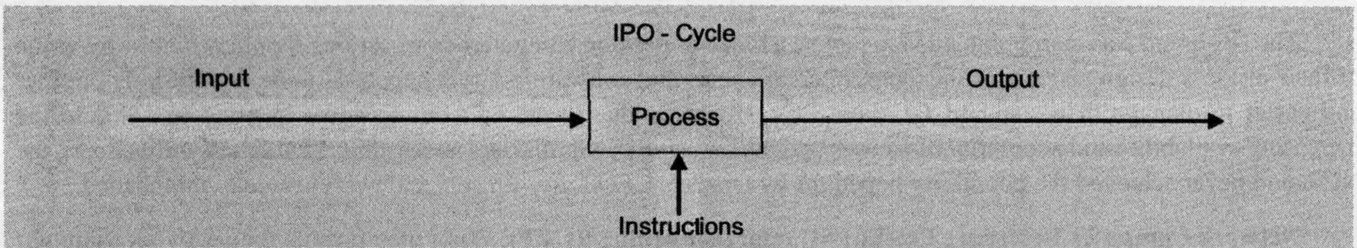

The data are provided to the computer through the input devices. They are encoding in such a way, that the computer can understand. The computer then processes the data with the help of instructions provided to it, then it produces a meaningful and desired output known as information.

The above functions are collectively known as the basic principles of operation of a digital computer. These can be expanded as follows:

(a) Accepting inputs

(b) Memory manipulation

(c) Arithmetic operations

(d) Decision making and

(e) Giving output

Block Diagram of a Computer

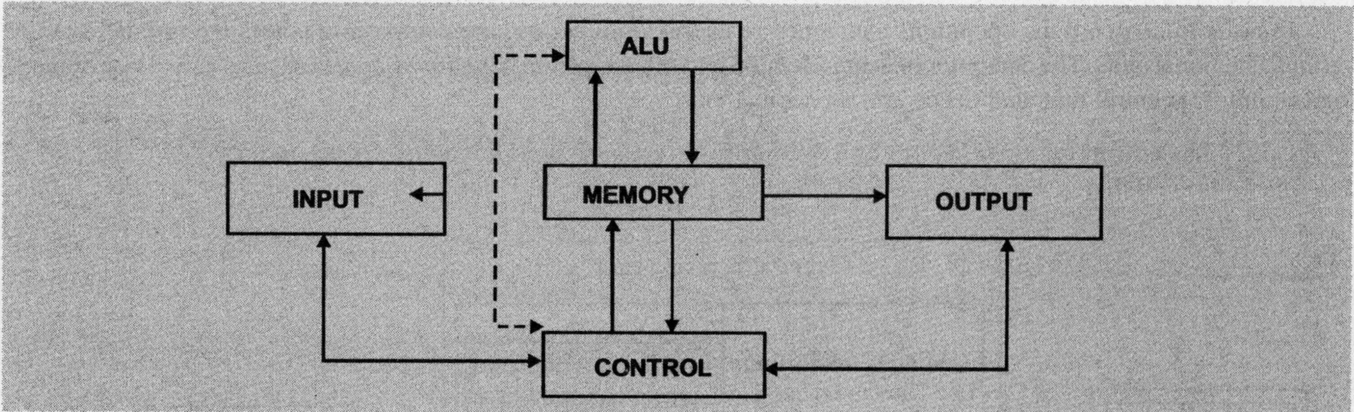

1.7 BASIC COMPUTER OPERATIONS

A computer can perform basically five major operations or functions irrespective of their size and make. These are (1) it accepts data or instructions by way of input, (2) it stores data, (3) it can process data as required by the user, (4) it gives results in the form of output, and (5) it controls all operations inside a computer. We discuss below each of these operations.

1. Input: This is the process of entering data and programs in to the computer system. You should know that computer is an electronic machine like any other machine which takes as inputs raw data and performs some processing giving out processed data. Therefore, the input unit takes data from us to the computer in an organized manner for processing.

2. Storage: The process of saving data and instructions permanently is known as storage. Data has to be fed into the system before the actual processing starts. It is because the processing speed of Central Processing Unit (CPU) is so fast that the data has to be provided to CPU with the same speed. Therefore the data is first stored in the storage unit for faster access and processing. This storage unit or the primary storage of the computer system is designed to do the above functionality. It provides space for storing data and instructions.

The storage unit performs the following major functions:

- All data and instructions are stored here before and after processing.
- Intermediate results of processing are also stored here.

3. Processing: The task of performing operations like arithmetic and logical operations is called processing. The Central Processing Unit (CPU) takes data and instructions from the storage unit and makes all sorts of calculations based on the instructions given and the type of data provided. It is then sent back to the storage unit.

4. Output: This is the process of producing results from the data for getting useful information. Similarly the output produced by the computer after processing must also be kept somewhere inside the computer before being given to you in human readable form. Again the output is also stored inside the computer for further processing.

5. Control: The manner how instructions are executed and the above operations are performed. Controlling of all operations like input, processing and output are performed by control unit. It takes care of step by step processing of all operations inside the computer.

1.8 FUNCTIONAL UNITS OF COMPUTER

In order to carry out the operations mentioned in the previous section the computer allocates the task between its various functional units. The computer system is divided into three separate units for its operation. They are: (1) arithmetic logical unit, (2) control unit, and (3) central processing unit.

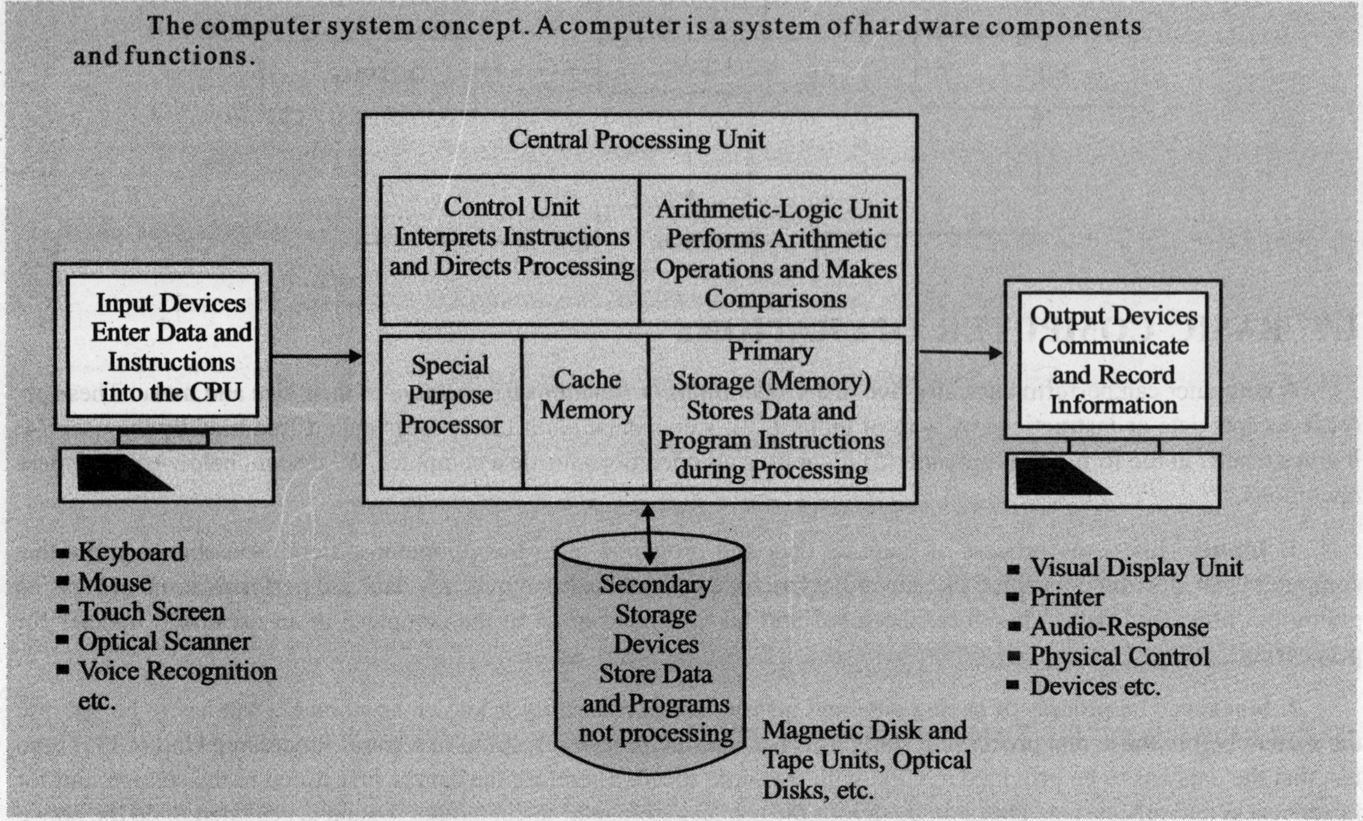

1. Arithmetic Logical Unit (ALU)

After you enter data through the input device it is stored in the primary storage unit. The actual processing of the data and instruction are performed by Arithmetic Logical Unit. The major operations performed by the ALU are addition, subtraction, multiplication, division, logic and comparison. Data is transferred to ALU from storage unit when required. After processing the output is returned back to storage unit for further processing or getting stored.

2. Control Unit (CU)

The next component of computer is the Control Unit, which acts like the supervisor seeing that things are done in proper fashion. The control unit determines the sequence in which computer programs and instructions are executed. Things like processing of programs stored in the main memory, interpretation of the instructions and issuing of signals for other units of the computer to execute them. It also acts as a switch board operator when several users access the computer simultaneously. Thereby it coordinates the activities of computer's peripheral equipment as they perform the input and output. Therefore it is the manager of all operations mentioned in the previous section.

3. Central Processing Unit (CPU)

The ALU and the CU of a computer system are jointly known as the central processing unit. You may call CPU as the brain of any computer system. It is just like brain that takes all major decisions, makes all sorts of calculations and directs different parts of the computer functions by activating and controlling the operations.

The CPU has three Components:

(a) The Control Unit

(b) The Arithmetic Logic Unit and

(c) The Memory Unit.

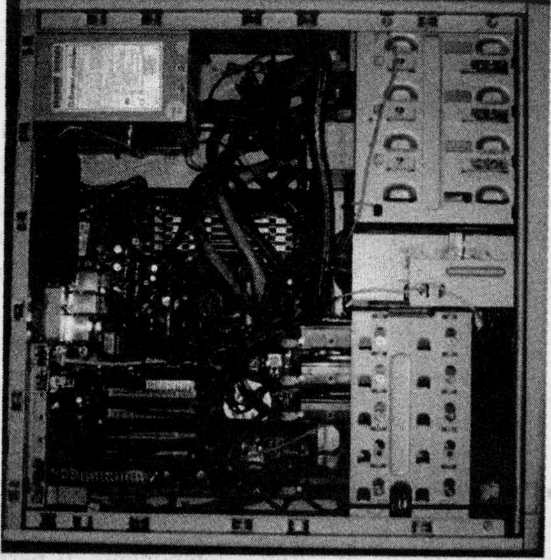

(a) Control Unit: It controls the overall operation of the computer system. It is considered as the heart of the computer system. It controls all the other units, directs them to operate in a proper way and co-ordinates various operations performed.

It instructs the input device to transfer the data and instructions to the main memory and then to the arithmetic and logic unit (ALU). Then, it sends the processed result from ALU to the memory unit for storage and transfers it to the visual display unit or to the printer.

The control unit coordinates the various parts of the computer system — the arithmetic logic unit, the memory unit and the peripheral units. Besides, it controls the flow of data into, from and within the main storage as per the program instructions.

To perform its control operations effectively and quickly, the control unit has four basic components. They are:

(a) Instruction Register

(b) Decoder

(c) Address Register and

(d) Instruction Counter

The instruction register receives one by one the instructions to be executed in the required sequence. Then, the operation code of the instructions is transferred to decoder, which decodes the operation code. And it activates the appropriate circuits of the arithmetic and logic unit to perform the operation. The address register enables the data in the location specified in the instruction to be transferred to a specified accumulator for the arithmetic and logic unit.

(b) Arithmetic and Logic Unit

This unit performs two kinds of operations, the arithmetic processing and logical processing. In arithmetic processing it performs all mathematical operations such as addition, subtraction, multiplication and division. In logical processing, it performs the relational and logical operations such as comparing larger or smaller values, true or false statements, etc.

(c) Memory Unit

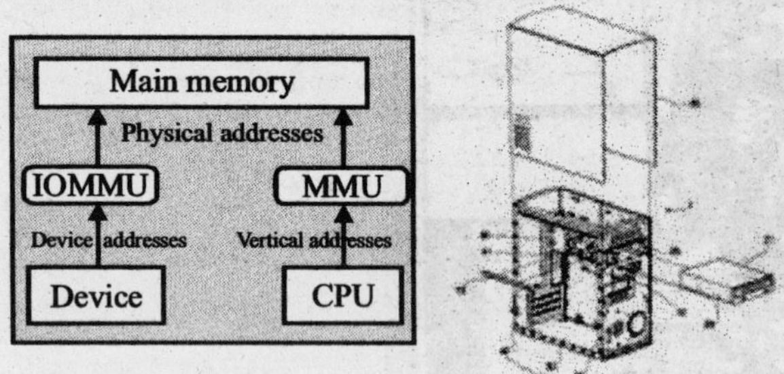

This unit holds the intermediate results during the course of calculations and provides the data as and when required. This internal storage is also called primary memory or main memory. This memory takes the data from an input device and stores it until the computer is ready to process it. It also stores processed data and intermediate results. When the processing is finished, it transfers the results to an output device.

1.9 BASIC COMPONENTS OF COMPUTER

A computer system is a combination of various components. It performs the system functions such as input, processing, output, storage and control. A computer system consists of the following components:

1. Hardware
2. Software
3. Humanware
4. Firmware
5. Bridgeware

1. Hardware

The physical components of the computer, such as electrical, electronics and mechanical unit are known as the hardware of the computer. That is, the input units, output units and CPU are called hardware. Thus hardware is the equipment involved in the function of a computer. It consists of the components that can be physically handled. The function of these components is typically divided into three main categories: input, output, and storage. Components in these categories connect to microprocessors, output and storage. Components in these categories connect to microprocessors, specifically, the computer's central processing unit (CPU), the electronic circuitry that provides the computational ability and control of the computer, via wires or circuitry called a bus.

Components of Hardware

(I) *Input device:* This unit accepts instructions and data.

(II) *Output device:* This unit communicates the results to the user.

(III) *Storage device:* This unit stores temporary and final results.

(IV) *Central Processing Unit (CPU):* This unit performs processing of instructions and data inside the computer.

2. Software

The computer performs operations like addition, subtraction, multiplication and division only when the user instructs it to do so. The user issues instructions and the CPU acts in accordance with the instructions. The sets of instructions, which control the sequence of operations, are known as *programs*, and collectively programs are called **software.** The software can be broadly classified into two types. They are:

(a) System Software: Programs that manage and support the resources and operations of a computer system or network as it performs various information processing tasks.

(b) Application Software: Programs that direct the performance of a particular use, or application, of computers and computer networks to meet the information processing needs of end users.

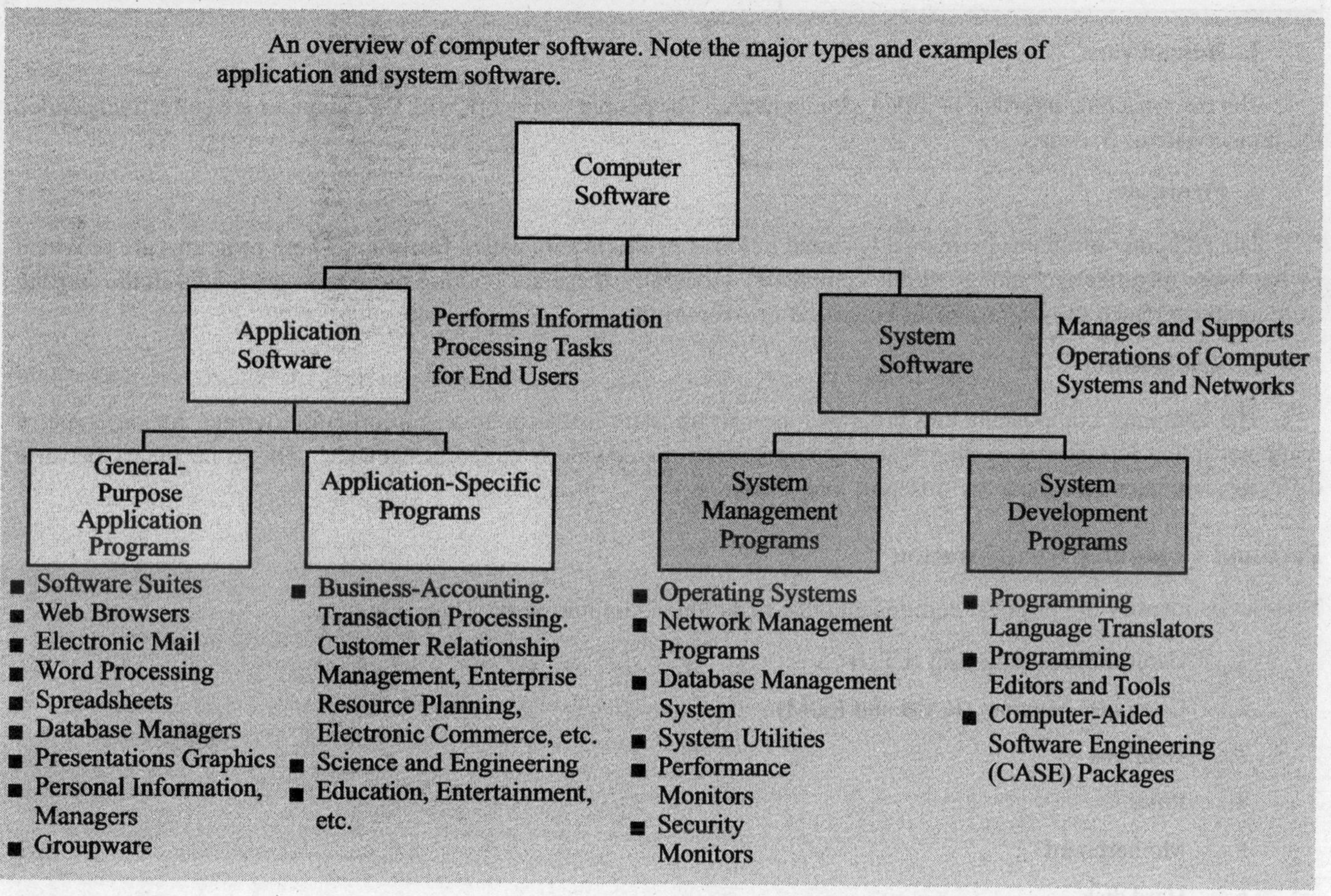

Difference between Hardware and Software

HARDWARE	SOFTWARE
1. It is the physical unit of the computer	1. It is a collection of programs to bring the hardware system into operation
2. It has permanent structure and cannot be altered	2. It has no permanent structure but can be altered and reused
3. It is normally affected by agent like dust, heat, humidity, etc.	3. It is not affected by these agents to some extent
4. Hardware understands only machine language, lower level language or binary	4. It is written by a well versed programmer and language, lower level generally in higher level language which is readable by human being
5. It works with binary code, the presence or absence of Pulses as 1's or 0's.	5. It is represented by the Higher Level Languages such as BASIC, COBOL, etc.,

3. Humanware

The man-machine interface is called a humanware. The people who work with the computer are collectively called the humanware or livewire.

4. Firmware

The computer programs permanently stored in ROM or PROM are called firmware. These programs are provided by hardware manufacturer alongwith the computers. Generally, these are booting programs which help in the starting of a computer. Such programs cannot be erased or overwritten.

5. Bridgeware

The computer components and programs used to translate instructions and information written for one type of computer into a format that another type of computer can understand is called bridgeware. This is necessary because different computers are made by different manufacturers.

Personal Computer Configuration

Now let us identify the physical components that make the computer work. These are:

1. Central Processing Unit (CPU)
2. Computer Memory (RAM and ROM)
3. Data bus
4. Ports
5. Motherboard
6. Hard disk
7. Output Devices
8. Input Devices

All these components are interconnected for the personal computer to work.

1.10 MEMORY SYSTEM IN A COMPUTER

There are two kinds of computer memory: *primary* and *secondary*. Primary memory is accessible directly by the processing unit. RAM is an example of primary memory. As soon as the computer is switched off the contents of the primary memory is lost. You can store and retrieve data much faster with primary memory compared to secondary memory. Secondary memory such as floppy disks, magnetic disk, etc., is located outside the computer. Primary memory is more expensive than secondary memory. Because of this the size of primary memory is less than that of secondary memory. We will discuss about secondary memory later on.

Computer memory is used to store two things: (i) instructions to execute a program and (ii) data. When the computer is doing any job, the data that have to be processed are stored in the primary memory. This data may come from an input device like keyboard or from a secondary storage device like a floppy disk.

As program or the set of instructions is kept in primary memory, the computer is able to follow instantly the set of instructions. For example, when you book ticket from railway reservation counter, the computer has to follow the same steps: take the request, check the availability of seats, calculate fare, wait for money to be paid, store the reservation and get the ticket printed out. The programme containing these steps is kept in memory of the computer and is followed for each request.

But inside the computer, the steps followed are quite different from what we see on the monitor or screen. In computer's memory both programs and data are stored in the binary form. You have already been introduced with decimal number system, that is the numbers 1 to 9 and 0. The binary system has only two values 0 and 1. These are called *bits*. As human beings we all understand decimal system but the computer can only understand binary system. It is because a large number of integrated circuits inside the computer can be considered as switches, which can be made ON, or OFF. If a switch is ON it is considered 1 and if it is OFF it is 0. A number of switches in different states will give you a message like this: 110101...10. So the computer takes input in the form of 0 and 1 and gives output in the form 0 and 1 only. Is it not absurd if the computer gives outputs as 0's & 1's only? But you do not have to worry about. Every number in binary system can be converted to decimal system and vice versa; for example, 1010 meaning decimal 10. Therefore it is the computer that takes information or data in decimal form from you, convert it in to binary form, process it producing output in binary form and again convert the output to decimal form.

The primary memory as you know in the computer is in the form of IC's (Integrated Circuits). These circuits are called Random Access Memory (RAM). Each of RAM's locations stores one *byte* of information. (One *byte* is equal to *8 bits*). A bit is an acronym for *binary digit*, which stands for one binary piece of information. This can be either 0 or 1. You will know more about RAM later. The Primary or internal storage section is made up of several small storage locations (ICs) called cells. Each of these cells can store a fixed number of bits called *word length.*

Each cell has a unique number assigned to it called the address of the cell and it is used to identify the cells. The address starts at 0 and goes up to (N-1). You should know that the memory is like a large cabinet containing as many drawers as there are addresses on memory. Each drawer contains a word and the address is written on outside of the drawer.

Capacity of Primary Memory

You know that each cell of memory contains one character or 1 byte of data. So the capacity is defined in terms of byte or words. Thus, 64 kilobyte (KB) memory is capable of storing 64 × 1024 = 32,768 bytes. (1 kilobyte is 1024 bytes). A memory size ranges from few kilobytes in small systems to several thousand kilobytes in large mainframe and super computer. In your personal computer, you will find memory capacity in the range of 64 KB, 4 MB, 8 MB and even 16 MB (MB = Million bytes).

The following terms related to memory of a computer are discussed below:

1. **Random Access Memory (RAM):** The primary storage is referred to as random access memory (RAM) because it is possible to randomly select and use any location of the memory, directly store and retrieve data. It takes same time to any address of the memory as the first address. It is also called read/write memory. The storage of data and instructions inside the primary storage is temporary. It disappears from RAM as soon as the power to the computer is switched off. The memories, which loose their content on failure of power supply, are known as **volatile** memories. So now we can say that RAM is volatile memory.

2. **Read Only Memory (ROM):** There is another memory in computer, which is called Read Only Memory (ROM). Again it is the ICs inside the PC that form the ROM. The storage of program and data in the ROM is permanent. The ROM stores some standard processing programs supplied by the manufacturers to operate the personal computer. The ROM can only be read by the CPU, but it cannot be changed. The basic input/output program is stored in the ROM that examines and initializes various equipment attached to the PC when the switch is made ON. The memories, which do not lose their content on failure of power supply, are known as **non-volatile** memories. ROM is non-volatile memory.

3. **PROM:** There is another type of primary memory in computer, which is called Programmable Read Only Memory (PROM). You know that it is not possible to modify or erase programs stored in ROM, but it is possible for you to store your program in PROM chip. Once the programmes are written it cannot be changed and remain intact even if power is switched off. Therefore, programs or instructions written in PROM or ROM cannot be erased or changed.

4. **EPROM:** This stands for Erasable Programmable Read Only Memory, which overcome the problem of PROM & ROM. EPROM chip can be programmed time and again by erasing the information stored earlier in it. Information stored in EPROM exposing the chip for some time ultraviolet light and it erases chip reprogrammed using a special programming facility. When the EPROM is in use information can only be read.

5. **Cache Memory:** The speed of CPU is extremely high compared to the access time of main memory. Therefore the performance of CPU decreases due to the slow speed of main memory. To decrease the mismatch in operating speed, a small memory chip is attached between CPU and Main memory whose access time is very close to the processing speed of CPU. It is called CACHE memory. CACHE memories are accessed much faster than conventional RAM. It is used to store programs or data currently being executed or temporary data frequently used by the CPU. So each memory makes main memory to be faster and larger than it really is. It is also very expensive to have bigger size of cache memory and its size is normally kept small.

6. **Registers:** The CPU processes data and instructions with high speed, there is also movement of data between various units of computer. It is necessary to transfer the processed data with high speed. So the computer uses a number of special memory units called *registers*. They are not part of the main memory but they store data or information temporarily and pass it on as directed by the control unit.

7. **Flash Memory:** is non-volatile computer memory that can be electrically erased and reprogrammed. It is a technology that is primarily used in memory cards, and USB flash drives (thumb drives, handy drive, memory stick, flash stick, jump drive) for general storage and transfer of data between computers and other digital products. It is a specific type of EEPROM that is erased and programmed in large blocks; in early flash the entire chip had to be erased at once. Flash memory costs far less than byte-programmable EEPROM and therefore has become the dominant technology wherever a significant amount of non-volatile, solid-state storage is needed. Examples of applications include and laptop computers, digital audio players, digital cameras and mobile phones. It has also gained some popularity in the game console market, where it is often used instead of EEPROMs or battery-powered static RAM (SRAM) for game save data.

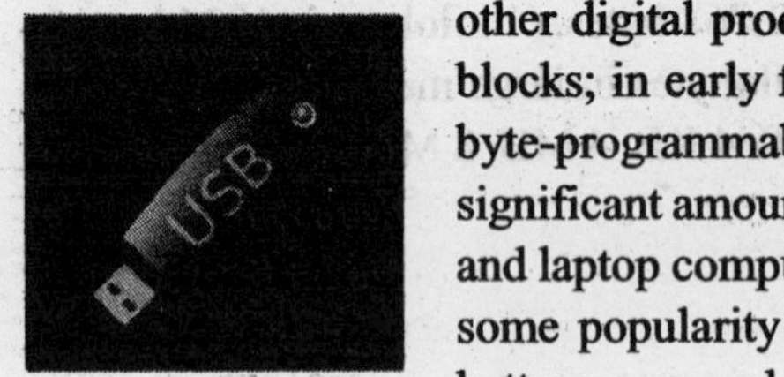

Flash memory is non-volatile, which means that it does not need power to maintain the information stored in the chip. In addition, flash memory offers fast read access times (although not as fast as volatile DRAM memory used for main memory in PCs) and better kinetic shock resistance than hard disks. These characteristics explain the popularity of flash memory for applications such as storage on battery-powered devices. Another feature of flash memory is that when packaged in a "memory card", it is enormously durable, being able to withstand intense pressure, extremes of temperature and immersion in water.

Although technically a type of EEPROM, the term "EEPROM" is generally used to refer specifically to non-flash EEPROM which is erasable in small blocks, typically bytes. Because an erase cycle is slow, the large size of a flash ROM's erase block can make programming it faster than old-style EEPROM.

1.11 PRACTICAL DATA PROCESSING APPLICATIONS IN BUSINESS

The following are some data processing information undertaken by commercial organizations:

1. Process Control: In the production process, a computer is directly connected to some plant to control and monitor it. Here, the computer receives the data directly from the plant. It analyses the input data and initiates action to control the on-going process.

2. Accounting: The Data Processing System can be used to maintain the accounting records and in preparation of final accounts. The general ledger, Accounts Payable, Accounts Receivable, etc., are the examples for the computerized accounting systems followed in most business organizations.

3. Payroll Preparation: In personnel department the data processing system is used to record the operations of the number of employees of different departments in each shifts, leave taken, deductions such as ESI, PF and finally in the preparation of Pay Slips.

4. Sales Analysis: The Data Processing system is highly useful in sales analysis. The sales manager can prepare the sales forecast on the basis of per month's sales reports and subsequent future actions can be taken.

5. Inventory Management: Actually the Data Processing System is a boon to every organization, in respect of inventory management. Data Processing is used to maintain up-to-date information about stock, their costs and to initiate orders when the times are about to be exhausted.

6. Office Automation: The modem offices and business organizations are dependent upon computer based office automation for their competitiveness and better management.

7. Banking and Insurance: Data Processing Systems are highly needed in the Banking sector where the customer satisfaction is the main criteria. To provide quick and perfect service, data processing system is used. Automatic Teller machines are places in big cities and linked to central computers. Hence, the delay in processing is completely avoided.

8. Insurance and Stock Broking: Insurance companies and stock broking firms also use the computerized data processing systems. Large volume of data have to be processed for the preparation of policy statements, interest calculations, renewal notices and in dealing with the securities.

9. Managerial Aid: The Data Processing System is used as a managerial aid in decision-making for solving business problems. It is also very useful in the areas of linear programming, PERT, CPM etc.

Today it appears that the computer is everywhere. Not only the business organization, the other institutions are also using data processing system for their regular use. We cannot think about a situation without a computer. Robotics and Artificial Intelligence are the two promising areas of applications.

1.12 COMPUTER APPLICATIONS IN VARIOUS AREAS OF BUSINESS

Introduction

Computer plays a very important role in each and every aspect of our life, be it banking, insurance or transportation, it is useful for preparing payroll of the employees, maintenance of optimum inventory level, sales order processing, reservation of tickets etc. It processes the transactions very quickly and accurately. So, it finds applications in various stages of business.

Business Applications

The following are some of the areas of business in which computers are applied:

1. Payroll Processing

Business means selling goods and services. To carry out such activities, business management employs people. They have to be paid monthly salaries and the details regarding pay particulars of employees have to be kept track. Business community employs computers for such payroll applications and runs a program consisting of a number of smaller programs or modules. Each module performs a particular function of the payroll. Sometimes we call this set of programs as payroll system.

To calculate the pay of an employee, management normally uses the following details of employees:

(1) Employee number (this is a unique number assigned to the employee to identify him just as your roll number in the school), (2) Name, (3) Basic pay, (4) Allowances (house rent allowance and other allowances), (5) Deductions (example, Provident Fund deduction) and (6) Bank account number. These details the employees do not change but they have to be used every month. So they are entered into a file in a computer storage medium and permanently stored. This file goes with the name master file. The file creation module of the payroll system creates this file once. Before calculation of the pay of employees every month, some figures in the master need changes. For example, if an employee completes a year of service, he normally gets an increment. Such figures are updated using the master update module of the payroll system. After updating, another module of the payroll system reads details from master file and calculates net pay. The program also prints out pay slip for each employee to be handed over to him. A pay slip shows the employee number, name, basic pay, various allowances, various deductions and net pay.

The payroll system also generates a number of statements. It prints out the statement showing employee number, name, bank account number and net pay. This statement is sent to the bank, which transfers the net pay from the company's account to the individual employee's account in the bank. Some companies copy this statement on to a floppy and send to the bank which processes this statement on its computer. The payroll system generates a provident fund deduction statement. This statement shows the employee numbers, names and amount deducted. Another statement showing the names, employee numbers and tax deducted is printed. The company sends it to Income Tax office. Thus we see that a number of statements can be printed from the same master file.

2. Inventory Control

The second application is the use of computers to keep track of the purchase and issues of parts and raw materials needed in an organization. These parts and raw materials are called inventories and the set of programs used to keep track of the purchase and issue of these inventories constitute the inventory control system.

In business, a particularly quantity of each item or raw material has to be stocked. Too less a stock would result in non-availability of these items, when the manufacturing activity needs it. Too much stock of these means, more money in terms of investment in buying the excess stock. Business pays interest on money invested, and the excess interest paid on cost of excess stock is a loss to business. So the business maintains an optimum quantity of material. The inventory control system maintains a file with part number, name, quantity on stock a level of stock at which the company orders for fresh quantity (called reorder level) and the suppliers' addresses. This file is the inventory master.

When an item is issued, the inventory update program updates the inventory master reducing the stock by the quantity issued. If the resultant stock falls below the reorder level, the inventory control program prints out an order to the supplier of the item automatically. It can be mailed to the supplier. When the supplier supplies the item, the inventory control program updates the stock on hand. The inventory control system keeps track of the supplies and issues. So, it can tell the management of the company the usage of these items over a period of time quickly. It also maintains an optimum level of stock of these items.

3. Sales Order Processing

Real-time systems offer the possibility of a greatly prompt service to the customer. His order can be processed within virtually no time. The finished goods inventory file may have data terminals throughout the sales territory. So much that the CRTs can be made to display the invoice on a terminal for the salesman who is in the customer's plant and can input the particulars there and then! The customer would be entered immediately in the general ledger. The invoice can also be posted to the accounts receivable file instantaneously. The selection of warehouse that is closest to the customer can also be made and a copy of the invoice could be displayed at the warehouse terminals. Besides, the following functions can be performed rapidly:

- The inquiries about the customer's accounts status can be answered by the salesman.
- Credit appraisal can be carried out online.
- Sales analysis master file can be updated online. This file provides a ready

  Information to the sales manager regarding sales trends, etc.
- Inventory replenishment order can be determined as a part of the sales order processing.

Online Applications

1. Banking

In banks the customers, present cheques for withdrawing money. The clerk verifies from the register the signature of the customer. (The customer has signed in the application form while opening an account). Then he checks from a ledger the customer's balance. If the customer has sufficient balance to cover the cheque amount, the clerk passes the cheque for payment, and updates the balance.

There are a number of operations that the bank carries out of which the above is an example. We will see how the above operation called personal banking is computerized. Suppose you want to open a bank account. The bank official hands over a form to you. You fill up the details (such as name, address, profession etc.) and sign the application. The bank stores this information in a computer on which banking software runs. The customer's signature is scanned by suitable devices and incorporated in the computer file. If you present a cheque to the clerk in the bank, he can check the signature manually. If he is satisfied with the correctness, he can enter your account number and the cheque amount into the computer which checks your account and updates the amount. The clerk then pays you the money. In the method, the payment is manual and accounting is automatic. There is another way where the checking of you accounts as well as payment is made by computer using an automatic teller machine. Let us study this.

A machine similar to automatic coffee vending machine is installed at selected places. It is connected to the bank's computer. When you open an account, the bank gives you a special type of card. Your name, account number and address are suitably recorded. Your signature is magnetically recorded in that card. All these details are suitably converted and recorded in the computer also. When you want to withdraw money, you go to the teller counter and press a few buttons. You then insert your card in the slot provided in the machine. The machine reads your account number and signature from the card. It sends them to the computer which checks your account number and signature. If they tally, the computer sends a relevant message to the automatic teller machine. It asks you to enter the amount. You may enter the amount through the buttons on the machine. Again the computer checks if you have sufficient balance. If so, it instructs the machine to pay you. The ATM then delivers the cash on the tray fixed in it. You may collect the money.

This is only one example of application of computer in banks. Now large systems installed at the head office of a particular bank are connected to systems installed at its branches all over the country. The computers of different banks are also connected together. By sending suitable messages money can be transferred from one bank to the other. This is called Electronics Funds Transfer.

2. Railway Reservation System

Application of computers in railway reservation has made tremendous impact in India. Before computerizing, there were a number of counters, each counter serving a particular train or a few trains. If you want to make a reservation to, say Delhi, you have to go to the particular counter and join the queue. The clerk had a register in which two or three pages are allotted to each date. He may have two or three more registers for other trains for which he is making reservation.

He puts seat numbers on a page one by one and keeps writing the names of passengers for whom he reserves seats against seat numbers. After some time, if somebody cancels his ticket, he strikes off the name. When the next person reserves for that time and date, the clerk writes his name above the cancelled name. This gives rise to lot of confusions. In a number of situations, two persons used to be allotted the same seat. With the increasing population the Government is increasing the number of trains. Thus the volume of data to be handled has also increased enormously. You can just imagine the confusion this will create if we are still following the manual system of reservation. We just saw how manual system has become unsuitable in the present context. Now let us study how the computerized railway reservation system works.

There is a central computer with a number of terminals connected to it the details of all trains for which reservation is done at the region are stored in the computer. The railway reservation system runs on this computer. The terminals are situated in booking counters. It is possible to install the terminals in a far off place and connect them to the computer through cables. When the passenger presents the reservation form to the booking clerk he enters the train number, date, name, age and other details of the passenger. The program checks availability of seats in that particular train on that particular date. If accommodation is available, the clerk presses a button on the key board and the computer prints out the ticket on the printer connected to the terminal. It also updates the computer file to reflect the new reservation position.

Suppose you wanted the ticket for train number 1, but you get only a waiting list. The clerk tells you your position in the waiting list. If you want you can get a wait listed ticket. If not, you tell the clerk to check for accommodation in a different train to your destination. The clerk only has to re-enter the train number. The computer checks availability, reserves you ticket on that train if a seat is available and prints the ticket. Thus you can go to any booking counter and request for reservation in any train being operated on that station. Also the errors found in the manual reservation method are eliminated.

The reservation system is broader based as follows: Today computers in different cities are connected together. (It is called networking). Suppose you are in Coimbatore. You want to book your journey from Chennai to Coimbatore. You can go to a booking counter (Railways have opened a number of booking counters in the same city) in Coimbatore and reserve your ticket from Chennai to Coimbatore. Thus there is lot of flexibility in reservation. We studied that computers are capable of storing lot of data on the hard disk. They are also capable of retrieving data fast. So the list of passengers for a particular day for a particular train is also printed out very fast.

The reservation data for a number of trains over a period of time is available. By suitable software, the railway authorities can prepare the data regarding passengers traveling in different trains to different places during different periods. This helps them plan for new trains, reschedule the running trains and make lot of analysis regarding passenger traffic.

3. Air lines Reservation System

We saw how computers handle the railway reservation and offer a number of advantages. They can be used also in Airlines reservation. Only difference will be that some booking counters in the reservation network may be situated in different countries.

This means that we have to connect computers across the countries. Such networks are operational now. In the coming years, computerized reservation systems will become very common. Even hotel accommodation reservation systems for major hotels are coming up. If we integrate flight and hotel reservation, it is convenient for the passengers.

4. Real-Time Applications

As we already saw, in real time applications, computers control an on going activity. Let us consider the example of a manufacturing process. A product C is made from raw materials A and B. The quality of C depends upon, among other things, the quality of A and B and their quantities. In big manufacturing processes, raw materials are fed by machineries. Due to problems in machineries, the performances may vary from machine to machine. This affects the quality of final product. Manual inspection of quality and operation of these machineries to control the quantity are slow. This slows the manufacture of C from raw materials A and B. Signals from C are fed to the computer. Suitable sensors are installed in the lines carrying raw materials as well as finished product. These generate signals. The values of these signals for correct proportion of raw materials are stored in the computer. When the process is on signals keep coming from the output line depending up the quality of finished product.

Let us see what happens if either A or B varies in quality. The quality of the finished product also suffers. The sensor in the finished product line senses this. The signals generated by it change in strength. They are sent to the computer. It compares the signals with already stored signals. The difference is used to change the quantity of raw materials A and B.

Manual control of this process is slow. Moreover, if people inspect quality and operate machineries feeding raw materials, they become tired after sometime. But computer does not. So the quality of product is uniform. Moreover, there may be processes where the presence of human beings continuously for hours together will be injurious to their health. In such places computer control avoids such ill-effects.

1.13 COMPUTER RELATED JOBS

Introduction

The fast spread of IT has generated a need for highly trained workers to design and develop new information systems and to integrate new technologies in them. It is creating the need for professional workers who can fulfill the high performance standards in the technology-based industries. The IT professional plan, design, develops, support, and manage the strategies and adopt them to fulfill basic objectives of their firm. The rapidly changing technology requires the employees to have more skills and education. The companies look out for IT professionals who not only have sound technical knowledge of the subject but also have sound interpersonal and communication skills.

Computer Related Jobs

1. Programmer

A programmer is a person who writes the code for a computer program. Computer programs are the instructions given to the computer, telling the computer what to do, which information to identify, access and process. The programmers write programs, depending on the specifications given by the systems analysts and software engineers. After the completion of the design process, the programmer's job is to convert that design into a series of instructions that the computer can follow. These instructions are coded in a programming language such as C, C++, and Java, and then tested to ensure that the instructions are correct and produce the required result. Programmers perform functions such as system designing, and its related services. They are involved in coding of a project and the successful implementation of the developed system.

There are two types of programmers — application programmers and system programmers. The application programmers code programs for a specific task (application) in the organization. On the other hand, the system programmers code programs for controlling and maintaining the computer system software.

2. System Analyst

A system analyst plans, designs, develops, and implements new systems or applies the existing system resources to perform additional operations. Most of the system analysts work with specific type of system like business, accounting, finance, science or engineering and so on. Some systems analysts are also known as system developers or system architects.

A system analyst determines the problem in the system by discussing it with the managers and users before starting an assignment. They study the information needs of the organization to determine the changes that are required to deliver a solution to the problems of users. To design a system, the systems analysts specify the inputs required by the system, plan the processing steps and finalize the output to meet the user's requirements. Next, the system analyst determines the hardware and software needed to set up the system.

System analysts prepare the specifications, flowcharts, and process diagrams for the computer programmers to follow, and then work with the programmers to debut, and to rectify and errors in the system. They also check the initial use of the system and organize tests to check the working of the system to ensure that it works as required or planned. System analyst who perform more intricate testing of products are referred to as software equality assurance analysts. They not only perform tests but also diagnose the problems, suggest solutions and check whether the program requirements have been met or not. The analysts, who design, test and evaluate the Internet, Intranet, local area network (LAN), wide area network (WAN) and other data communication system are called network and data communication analysts.

3. Network Administrator

A network administrator is a person who installs, configures, and supports the local area network, wide area network, the Internet system or the segment of a network system in an organization. Every network in an organization requires at least one network administrator. Network administrators perform the functions such as installation, configuration, maintenance of computers, and networking of equipment. They also check and ensure the availability of network to all the users. They supervise the support of other networks and plan, coordinate and implement network security measures.

4. Database Administrator

A database administrator (DBA) is an individual who is responsible for the storage of data, management of the database, and implementation of the database management system. They work with database management systems software and determine ways to organize and store data. They identify user requirements, set up the computer databases, and test and organize the modifications to the systems. They also ensure the performance of the system in the organization, understand the platform on which the database is running and adds new users to the system. DBA is responsible for maintaining data integrity, back up systems and database security.

5. Web Designers

A web designer is an individual who provides an architectural structure for the effective communication of clients' content by logically organizing the information and making it accessible. With the rapid growth of the Internet, many jobs relating to design, development, and maintenance of the websites and servers have cropped up in the market. The web designer controls all aspects of design and programming of elements of text and visual design. They are responsible for maintaining all technical aspects of a website, including its performance issues such as speed of access and approving the content of the website. Web designers create the artistic feel of the website, facilitate navigation, and make content on the web site accessible to the users.

6. Information Security Analyst

An information security analyst is an individual who performs highly complex analysis and technical tasks involving assignment and co-ordination of measures to provide information assurance, event detection, and rapid response across various environments of the enterprise. Information security analysts design, implement and support integration of information security solutions including security architectures, firewall administration, integrating security products, and developing and coordinating security implementation plans. They provide technical support on security projects that involve a wide range of issues including secure electronic data traffic, network security, platform and data security and privacy. They review and contribute to the security activities of business application and development project plans across all business units.

7. Business Process Outsourcing

Business Processing Outsourcing (BPO) refers to a decision to assign to another party some or all non-core processes. The main motive of BPO is to allow the company to invest more time, money, and human resources into core activities and building strategies, which helps in company growth. The BPO jobs include various sectors like finance, accounts, customer support, IT services, medicines, and many others. Today, the global market is highly competitive and ever changing. A company must focus on improving productivity and even cut down costs. Therefore, many tasks that use precious time, resources and energy, are being outsourced. BPOs or the units to which work is being outsourced are flexible, quicker, and cheaper and very efficient in performance of the work.

Computer Related Jobs

BPO, KPO, LPO etc.	Executive Assistance
Software Development	Office Management
Encryption Techniques	Sales Professionals
Channel Partnership Account Manager	Sales Support Representative
Security support Developers	Technical Support Representative
Sales Employees	Telesales
Marketing Internship	Credit Card Management
Merchant Accounts	Inside Sales
Digital Signature Field	Awareness
Counseling	Business Reprocessing Engineering
Electronic Interchange	Enterprise Messaging
Systems Integration	Network Infrastructure
Program Management	System Analyst
Web Design	Systems Architecture
Java Web Application Development	Software Engineering and Methodologies
Networking and Communication	Computer Graphics
Image Processing	Database Technologies
Distributed Networking	Web Technologies
Office Automation	Multimedia Technologies

QUESTIONS

Short Answer Question

1. What are the components of a computer?
2. Explain EPROM.
3. Explain what is digital computer?
4. Give an example for a super computer?
5. State the number system used in digital computer system.
6. What is digital cash?
7. What is analog computer?
8. Differentiate between digital computer and analog computer.
9. What is Artificial Intelligence?

Long Answer Question

1. What is a computer?
2. State the advantages of Computer.
3. What are the characteristics of computers?
4. What Computer can do? and can't do?
5. What are auxiliary storage devices?
6. Differentiate between digital computer and analog computer.
7. Write the short notes on :

   (a) Micro computer (b) Main frame computer
8. Compare analog, digital and hybrid computers.
9. What is a micro computer?
10. Write short notes on mini and micro computers
11. Explain different types of computers on the basis of memory.
12. How computers are classified on the basis of structure.
13. Explain the classification of digital computer.
14. Explain the development of modern digital computer.
15. What are the special features of fourth generation computer?
16. Describe any six characteristics of digital computer.
17. Explain the features of digital computer and analog computer.

Very long or essay type Question

1. State the application of computers in the various areas of business.
2. Write an essay on history of development of computers.
3. With a block diagram, how a digital computer functions.
4. Explain a different generation of computers.
5. Explain different classifications of computers.
6. Write short notes on:

   (a) Micro computer (b) Mini computer (c) Main frame computer
7. What are the basic principles of operations of digital computers?
8. What are the computer related jobs?
9. Computer plays a key role in the modern technological development. Explain.

CHAPTER 2

COMPONENTS OF A COMPUTER

Structure:

2.1 INTRODUCTION TO COMPUTER MEMORIES

Computer storage is classified into two categories. They are:

1. Primary storage
2. Secondary storage

Major Trends in Primary and Secondary Memories

	First Generation	Second Generation	Third Generation	Fourth Generation	Fifth Generation
PRIMARY STORAGE	Magnetic Drum	Magnetic Core	Magnetic Core	LSI Semiconductor Memory Chips	VLSI Semiconductor Memory Chips
TREND: Toward Large Capacities Using Smaller Microelectronic Circults.					
SECONDARY STORAGE	Magnetic Tape Magnetic Drum	Magnetic Tape Magnetic Disk	Magnetic Disk Magnetic Tape	Magnetic Disk Optical Disk Magnetic tape	Optical Disk Magnetic Disk
TREND: Toward Massive Capacities Using Magnetic and Optical Media					

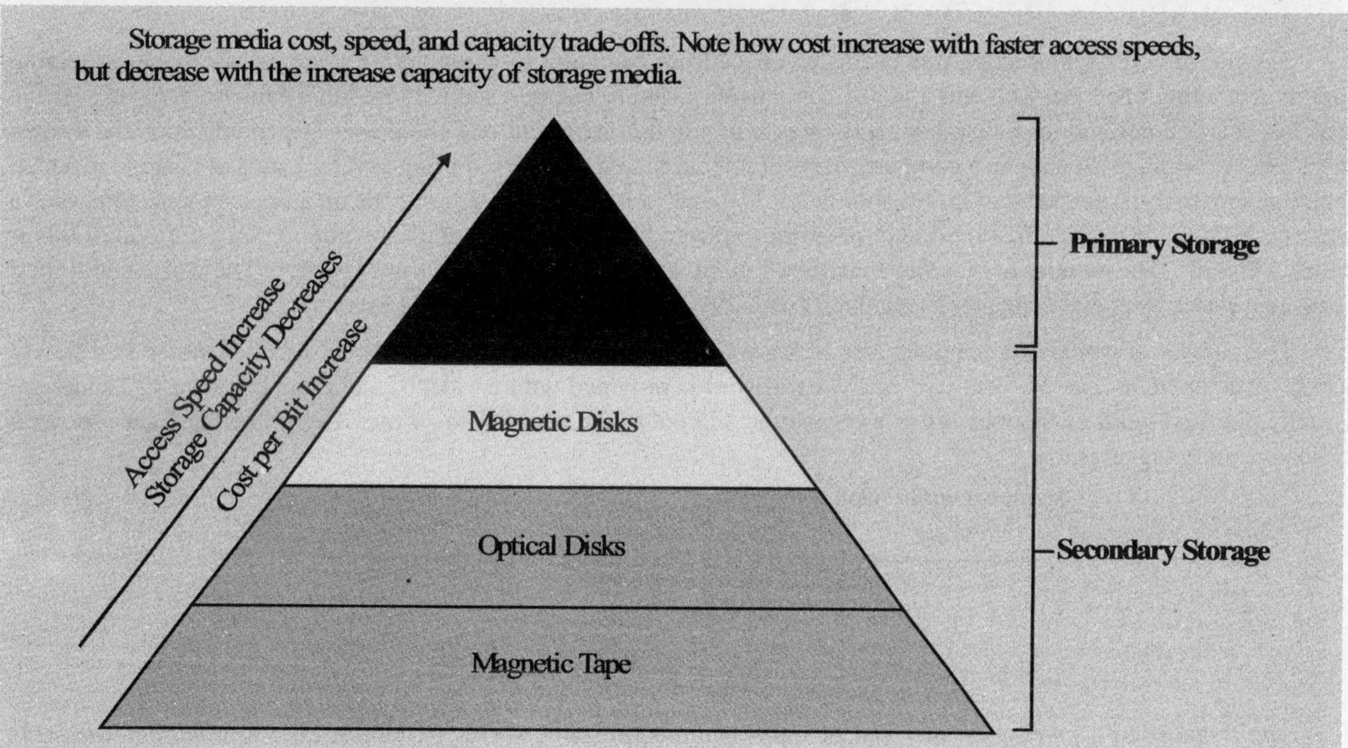

2.2 PRIMARY STORAGE

Primary storage is also called as internal storage (or) main storage. It is internal to the computer, i.e., it lies within the CPU of a computer. There are two primary storage devices popularly used. They are:

1. Magnetic core memory
2. Semi conductor memory

2.2.1 Magnetic Core Memory:

This type of memory was introduced in the year 1955 and was used in computers till 1975. A magnetic core is a small ring of ferromagnetic material. The core has the ability to become magnetized in a few millions of a second and retain it until it is changed. These cores are strong on wires like beads and when electric current is sent through the wire the core becomes magnetized. The direction of the current in the wire determines the polarity (or) direction of the magnetic field of the core.

A sensing wire also passes through each core to detect its polarity. The two directions (polarity) of the core represent data "0" (or) "1".

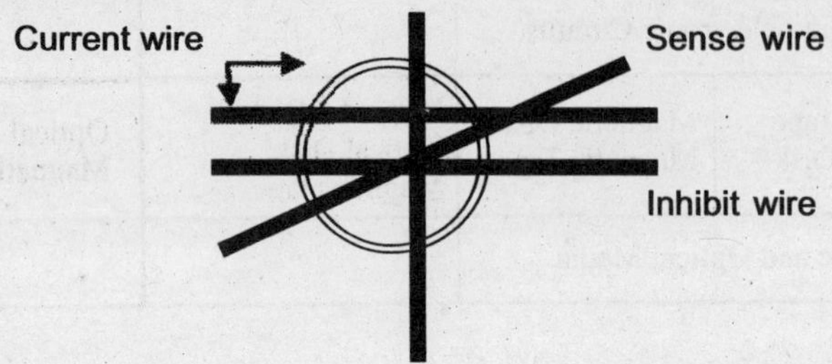

The no. of cores representing one character varies from computer to computer. Each core is capable of storing (or) remembering one binary bit and a no. of cores wired together can be used to store any character. On some of the systems, server cores and in some other eight cores is required to represent one character. Depending upon the system there can be a storage capacity in a computer of several thousand characters requiring several Lakhs of cores to make up their main memory. A single bit of information is hardly handled individually. Instead the memory is organized in such a way that a group of bits can be stored into (or) retrieved from the memory in a single operation. Such a group of bits is called a "word." The number of bits that constitute a word is fixed and is called "word length." The word length for a computer varies from one computer to another. Generally it varies from 8 bits to 64 bits.

The number of words in a computer also varies with the computer. In order that the information stored in different words of the memory can be identified easily, each word is provided with an identifying number called its "address." Usually, the first word of the memory is assigned the address 0, the next 1 and so on. The following figure shows a typical memory organization:

Memory Organization

Address Word

N-1

N- No. of Words

The memory of a given computer can be either word-addressable (or) byte addressable. In a word-addressable computer each word has a distinct address and the smallest addressable unit of memory is a word. On the other hand, in a byte addressable computer each byte has a distinct address. The words in such cases are normally identified by the addresses of the first byte in them.

Word address	Byte address			
0	0	1	2	3
4	4	5	6	7
8	8	9	10	11
12	12	13	14	15
	.	.	.	.
	.	.	.	.
	.	.	.	.

Information stored in a word and the address of the word must be distinguished. The address of a word is fixed and does not change whereas the information in each word can change. Whenever any information is stored in a memory word, the previous contents of the word get destroyed. Note that even if the information is retrieved from a memory word, it will still contain a copy of the information in that word.

The magnetic core memory provides a reliable and fast random access storage though it is expensive.

2.2.2 Semiconductor Memory

All modern computers use semiconductor memory which is faster and cheaper than magnetic core memory. Semiconductor memory is also available in a small board. The only drawback of semi conductor memory is that it is "volatile" and loses its contents in the event of power failure.

Semiconductor memory consists of electronic prepared on silicon chips. The electronic circuit is called a "Flip-Flop." A flip flop circuit can store either 1 (or) 0. A flip flop is also called as "Storage cell." Thousands of these storage cell can be prepared on single silicon of the semiconductor memories is very small.

The basic types of semiconductor memory (or) storage devices are:

RAM - Random Access Memory (can be used for reading and writing)

ROM - Read Only Memory (values are written once by the manufacturer and then can be subsequently read)

PROM - Programmable Road Only Memory (values can be written once by the programmer and then can be subsequently read)

EPROM - Erasable Programmable Read Only Memory (values can be rewritten using special techniques only)

Differences between Magnetic Core and Semiconductor Memories

	Magnetic Core	Semiconductor
1.	Non-volatile	Volatile
2.	Fast access time	Slow access time
3.	Large and heavy	Small and light
4.	High power consumption	Low power consumption
5.	More expensive	Less expensive
6.	Available only in large blocks	Available in a variety of sizes
7.	Best for large memories	Best for small & medium sized memories

2.3 SECONDARY STORAGE/AUXILIARY STORAGE

The size of primary storage (or) main memory in every computer is limited. With this, the computer can only accommodate a limited sized program and data. To carry out big jobs (or) commercial data processing, it becomes essential that data be hold in some expensive form of storage.

This is achieved through secondary storage it is also called as external storage (or) auxiliary storage, and can hold data either sequentially (or) at random. Data in secondary storage is not directly accessible and has to be routed through the main storage for processing.

The commonly used secondary storage devices are:

(a) Magnetic tape

(b) Magnetic Disk and

(c) Magnetic Drum

Comparison of Primary and Secondary Storage

	Characteristic	Primary Storage	Secondary Storage
1.	Location with respect to CPU	With CPU	Outside of but connected to CPU
2.	CPU	Most expensive	Less expensive
3.	Capacity	Low	High
4.	Access time	Fast	Slow
5.	Data can be processed directly from storage	Yes	No, must first be moved to primary storage
6.	Means of storing information	Magnetic core, semiconductor	Magnetic disk, magnetic tape, magnetic drum etc.,

Storage Technology Trend:

	First Generation	Second Generation	Third Generation	Fourth Generation	Fifth Generation
PRIMARY STORAGE	Magnetic Drum	Magnetic Core	Magnetic Core	LSI Sem/conductor Memory chips	VLSI Semiconductor Memory Chips
TREND: Toward Large Capacifos Using Smaller Micrololctronic Circuits.					
SECONDARY STORAGE	Magnetic Tape Magnetic Drum	Magnetic Tape Magnetic Disk	Magnetic Disk Magnetic Tape	Magnetic Disk Optical Disk Magnetic Tape	Optical Disk Magnetic Disk
TREND: Toward Massive Capacibes Using Magnetic and Optical Media.					

Secondary Storage/Auxiliary Storage Devices:

Since, the internal storage capacity of the CPU is not large enough to hold the vast amount of data, secondary storage devices are necessary. The following are popular secondary storage devices:

1. Magnetic Tape
2. Magnetic Disk
3. Floppy Disk
4. Magnetic Drum

Magnetic Tape:

Tapes used for recording / storing data for computer processing are plastic real similar to long lengths of movie film. A tape is usually ½" wide and 2400 feet in length. It is coated with particles of ferric oxide on which data can be recorded magnetically.

The process of reading and writing of data is carried out on a device called Tape Drive. Records on magnetic tape are stored in sequential order. For example, if the payroll file is to be stored on a magnetic tape, the records would likely to be stored in the sequence of employee numbers. Hence magnetic tapes are referred to as sequential access device (or media).

Since magnetic tape is a sequential access device, data recorded on tape cannot be accessed directly and can only be retrieved serially. So if a data item is at the end of a tape, all the earlier parts have to be read before accessing required information.

Magnetic Disk:

Magnetic disk is another type of secondary storage device known as random (direct) access device as it permits direct accessing of data. An individual disk is a circular metal plate coated on both sides by ferrous oxide material. Data is recorded in the form of magnetized spots on the tracks of the disk, a spot representing the presence by "1" & its absence by "0" enabling representation of data in binary.

The surface of the magnetic disk is divided into no. of invisible concentric circles called "tracks". The tracks are further subdivided into "sectors", "blocks" etc. each with its own unique address to facilitate location of data. Disks move on a vertical rotating spindle. Many systems provide for a pack of disks referred to as disk pack to be mounted on the Disk Drive. Reading / writing on the disks is accomplished by means of series of read / write heads which are placed close to the surfaces of the disks.

Data on the magnetic disk can be accessed again and again. It can also be recorded erasing the older information. Magnetic disk drives in which one (or) more disks are permanently mounted to the spindle are termed as fixed disk storage (or) Winchester disk (or) hard disk.

Floppy Disks

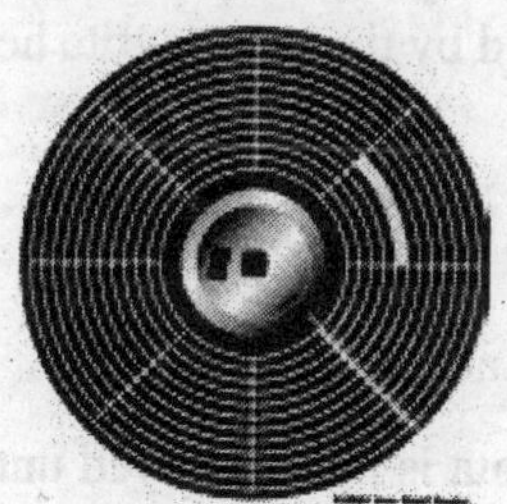

These are also called as flexible disks. These are used in the smallest micro computer systems as well as in minicomputers. Floppy disks have higher storage capacity and offer direct access capability. The floppy disk is permanently sealed in a plastic coated jacket and the whole package is inserted the floppy drive for data recording and retrieval. The jacket of the disk has a small slot to permit the read/write head to contact the disk.

They are 5.25 inch or 3.5 inch in diameter. They come in single or double density and recorded on one or both surface of the diskette. The capacity of a 5.25-inch floppy is 1.2 mega bytes whereas for 3.5 inch floppy it is 1.44 mega bytes. It is cheaper than any other storage devices and is portable. The floppy is a low cost device particularly suitable for personal computer system.

Once data has been recorded, a floppy disk reader can used to enter data into CPU. Again, the disk is loaded and rotated at a constant speed inside its envelope. Tiny magnetic heads in the disk reader access data through the slot in the jacket.

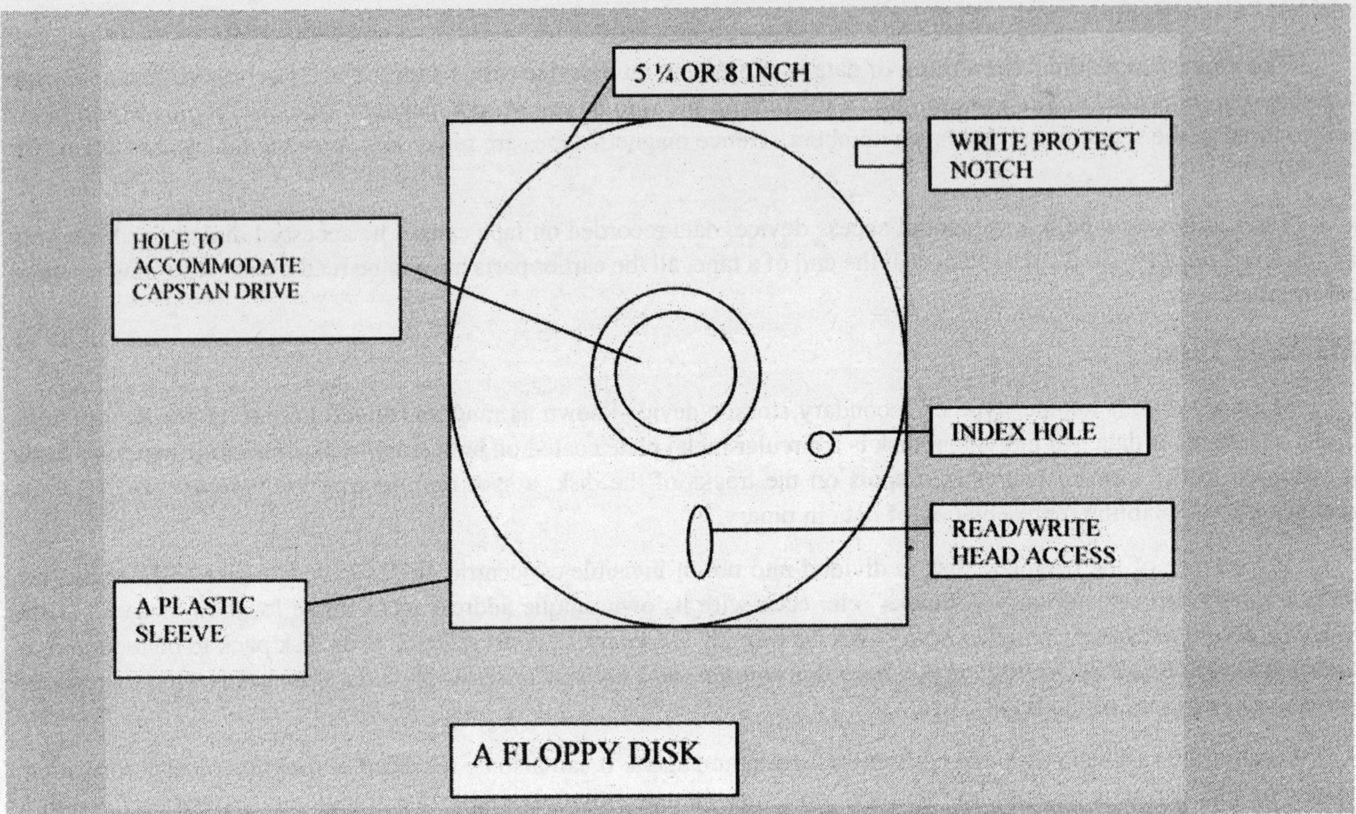

A FLOPPY DISK

Magnetic Drum

It is a metallic cylinder coated with a special magnetic alloy. Data is stored in this surface as minute magnetized spoke arranged in binary form in a series of parallel circular tracks. The drum rotates at a constant speed & data is recorded (or) retrieved by the read / write head. One for each tract. The magnetic drum provides random access storage.

Advantages:

1. Very fast access
2. Random access capability
3. Stored data is not destroyed until new data are written in the same location storage is permanent.

Disadvantages:

1. Drums cannot be removed from the unit & stored or used elsewhere

2. Storage capacity is limited

3. Not humanly readable, requires machine interpretation

Advantages of Magnetic Tapes:

1. **Unlimited length of records:** Any no. of characters can be placed in a record files can be as long as necessary.

2. **Reduced cost:** A tape costs much less than the hundreds of thousand of cards it can replace. Storage space is reduced, and the tape can be reused many times.

3. **Protection against record loss:** In cared system, there is always the danger of losing (or) misplacing one or more cards from a file. The use of magnetic tape is a protection against this danger.

4. **Rapid transfer rate :** The speed of input / output is faster than cards.

Disadvantages of Magnetic Tapes:

1. **Need for machine interpretation:** Since, the magnetized spots are invisible; they cannot be read by humans. A printing operation must be performed if it is necessary to check (or) verify tape data.

2. **Lack of random accessibility:** Because of the sequential nature of tape file processing, it is not generally suitable for jobs that require quick and random access to particular record.

3. **Inflexibility:** The main disadvantage of magnetic tape is its inflexibility. Deletion (or) insertion of records on the tape file are impossible without rewriting the entire file.

4. **Environmental problems :** The dust on a tape can cause an improper reading

Advantages of Magnetic Disks:

1. **Random-access capability** :In magnetic disk, random access processing is possible

2. **Faster updation:** Updating a file of disk records is generally much faster than updating a file of magnetic tape records.

3. Quick & direct inquiry to records is possible.

4. A single input transaction may be used to quickly update records in several related files stored on different disks.

5. Magnetic disks have faster data transfer rates as compared with tape.

Disadvantages of Magnetic Disks:

1. Disks are more expensive than magnetic tapes.

2. Disk packs are bulky. When compared to tape, magnetic disk requires more space.

3. Sequential processing in disks may be slower & less efficient.

Factors Which Determine the Choice of a Storage Device:

(i) **Access Time:** It is the time required to locate & retrieve stored data in the storage device

(ii) **Storage capacity :** It is the amount of data that can be stored on a storage device

(iii) **Cost per bit of storage :** An obvious goal is to minimize the cost.

Hard Disk

A **hard disk drive (HDD)**, commonly referred to as a **hard drive, hard disk** or **fixed disk drive**, is a non-volatile storage device which stores digitally encoded data on rapidly rotating platters with magnetic surfaces. Strictly speaking, "drive" refers to a device distinct from its medium, such as a tape drive and its tape, or a floppy disk drive and its floppy disk. Early HDDs had removable media; however, an HDD today is typically a sealed unit with fixed media.

HDDs were originally developed for use with computers. In the 21st century, applications for HDDs have expanded beyond computers to include digital video recorders, digital audio players, personal digital assistants, digital cameras and video game consoles. In 2005 the first mobile phones to include HDDs were introduced by Samsung and Nokia. The need for large-scale, reliable storage, independent of a particular device, led to the introduction of configurations such as RAID arrays, network attached storage (NAS) systems and storage area network (SAN) systems that provide efficient and reliable access to large volumes of data.

Technology

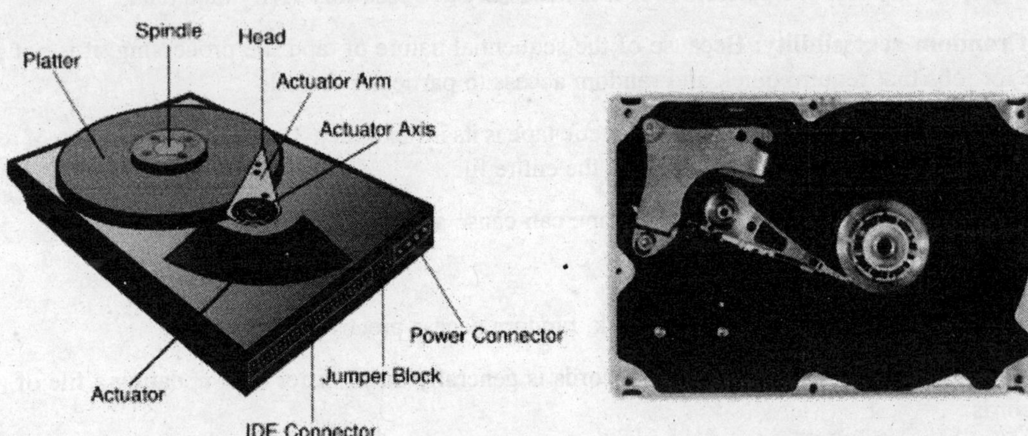

HDDs record data by magnetizing a ferromagnetic material directionally, to represent either a 0 or a 1 binary digit. They read the data back by detecting the magnetization of the material. A typical HDD design consists of a spindle which holds one or more flat circular disks called platters, onto which the data is recorded. The platters are made from a non-magnetic material, usually glass or aluminum, and are coated with a thin layer of magnetic material. Older disks used iron (III) oxide as the magnetic material, but current disks use a cobalt-based alloy.

The platters are spun at very high speeds. Information is written to a platter as it rotates past mechanisms called read-and-write heads that operate very close over the magnetic surface. The read-and-write head is used to detect and modify the magnetization of the material immediately under it. There is one head for each magnetic platter surface on the spindle, mounted on a common arm. An actuator arm (or access arm) moves the heads on an arc (roughly radically) across the platters as they spin, allowing each head to access almost the entire surface of the platter as it spins. The arm is moved using a voice coil actuator or (in older designs) a stepper motor.

The magnetic surface of each platter is divided into many small sub-micrometre-sized magnetic regions, each of which is used to encode a single binary unit of information. In today's HDDs each of these magnetic regions is composed of a few hundred magnetic grains. Each magnetic region forms a magnetic dipole which generates a highly localized magnetic field nearby. The write head magnetizes a magnetic region by generating a strong local magnetic field nearby. Early HDDs used an electromagnet both to generate this field and to read the data by using electromagnetic induction. Later versions of inductive heads included metal in Gap (MIG) heads and thin film heads. In today's heads, the read and write elements are separate but in close proximity on the head portion of an actuator arm. The read element is typically magneto-resistive while the write element is typically thin-film inductive.

In modern drives, the small size of the magnetic regions creates the danger that their magnetic state be lost because of thermal effects. To counter this, the platters are coated with two parallel magnetic layers, separated by a 3-atom-thick layer of the non-magnetic element ruthenium, and the two layers are magnetized in opposite orientation, thus reinforcing each other. Another technology used to overcome thermal effects to allow greater recording densities is perpendicular recording, which has been used in some hard drives as of 2006.

Hard disk drives are sealed to prevent dust and other sources of contamination from interfering with the operation of the hard disk heads. The hard drives are not air tight, but rather utilize an extremely fine air filter, to allow for air inside the hard drive enclosure. The spinning of the disks causes the air to circulate forcing any particulates to become trapped on the filter. The same air currents also act as a gas bearing which enables the heads to float on a cushion of air above the surfaces of the disks.

CD-ROM

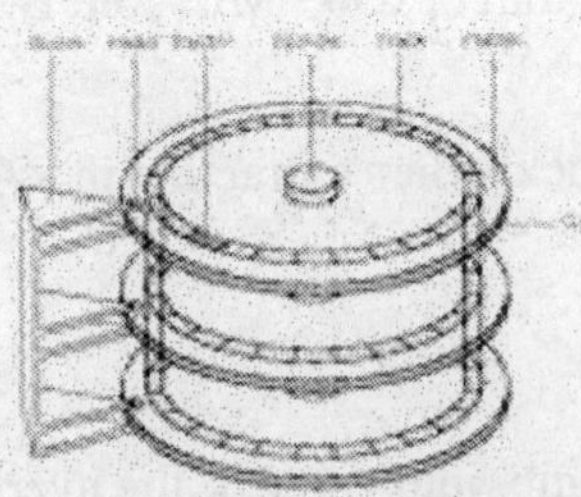

CD-ROM (an abbreviation of "Compact Disc read-only memory") is a Compact Disc that contains data accessible by a computer. While the Compact Disc format was originally designed for music storage and playback, the format was later adapted to hold any form of binary data. CD-ROMs are popularly used to distribute computer software, including games and multimedia applications, though any data can be stored (up to the capacity limit of a disc). Some CDs hold both computer data and audio with the latter capable of being played on a CD player, whilst data (such as software or digital video) is only usable on a computer (such as PC CD-ROMs). These are called Enhanced CDs.

Although many people use lowercase letters in this acronym, proper presentation is in all capital letters with a hyphen between CD and ROM. It was also suggested by some, especially soon after the technology was first released, that CD-ROM was an acronym for "Compact Disc read-only-*media*", or that it was a more 'correct' definition. This was not the intention of the original team who developed the CD-ROM, and common acceptance of the 'memory' definition is now almost universal. This is probably in no small part due to the widespread use of other 'ROM' acronyms such as Flash-ROMs and EEPROMs where 'memory' is the correct term.

CD-ROM format

A CD-ROM *sector* contains 2352 bytes, divided into 98 24-byte frames. The CD-ROM is, in essence, a data disk, which cannot rely on error concealment, and therefore requires a higher reliability of the retrieved data. In order to achieve improved error correction and detection, a CD-ROM has a third layer of Reed-Solomon error correction. A Mode-1 CD-ROM, which has the full three layers of error correction data, contains a net 2048 bytes of the available 2352 per sector. In a Mode-2 CD-ROM, which is mostly used for video files, there are 2336 user-available bytes per sector. The net byte rate of a Mode-1 CD-ROM, based on comparison to CDDA audio standards, is 44.1k/s×4B×2048/2352 = 153.6 kB/s. The playing time is 74 minutes, or 4440 seconds, so that the net capacity of a Mode-1 CD-ROM is 682 MB.

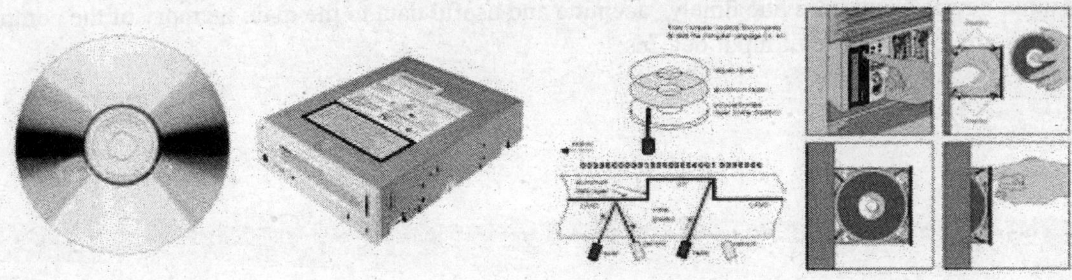

CD sector contents

- A standard 74 min CD contains 333,000 blocks or sectors.
- Each sector is 2352 bytes, and contains 2048 bytes of PC (MODE1) Data, 2336 bytes of PSX/VCD (MODE2) Data, or 2352 bytes of AUDIO.
- The difference between sector size and data content are the Headers info and the Error Correction Codes, that are big for Data (high precision required), small for VCD (standard for video) and none for audio.
- If extracting the disc in RAW format (standard for creating images) always extract 2352 bytes per sector, not 2048/2336/2352 bytes depending on data type (basically, extracting the whole sector). This fact has two main consequences:
    - Recording data CDs at very high speed (40x) can be done without losing information. However, as audio CDs do not contain a third layer of error correction codes, recording these at high speed may result in more unrecoverable errors or 'clicks' in the audio.
    - On a 74 minute CD, one can fit larger images using RAW mode, up to 333,000 × 2352 = 783,216,000 bytes (747~ MiB). This is the upper limit for RAW images created on a 74 min or 650~ MiB Red Book CD. The 14.8% increase is due to the discarding of error correction data.
- Please note that an image size is *always* a multiple of 2352 bytes (the size of a block) when extracting in RAW mode.

Capacity

A standard 120 mm CD-ROM holds 650 or 700 MiB of data. To put this storage capacity into context, the average novel contains 100,000 words. Assume that average word length is 10 letters and that each letter occupies one byte. A novel therefore might occupy 1,000,000 bytes (1000 kB, without layout information). One CD can therefore contain around 700 novels. If each novel occupies at least one centimetre of bookshelf space, then one CD can contain the equivalent of seven metres of bookshelf. However, textual data can be compressed by more than a factor of ten, using compression algorithms, so a CD-ROM can accommodate close to 100 metres of bookshelf space.

2.4 INTRODUCTION TO INPUT/OUTPUT DEVICES

A computer is only useful when it is able to communicate with the external environment. When you work with the computer you feed your data and instructions through some devices to the computer. These devices are called Input devices. Similarly computer after processing gives output through other devices called output devices.

For a particular application one form of device is more desirable compared to others. We will discuss various types of I/O devices that are used for different types of applications. They are also known as peripheral devices because they surround the CPU and make a communication between computer and the outer world.

2.5 INPUT DEVICES

Input devices are necessary to convert our information or data in to a form which can be understood by the computer. A good input device should provide timely, accurate and useful data to the main memory of the computer for processing. Followings are the most useful input devices:

Input Technology Trend:

	First Generation	Second Generation	Third Generation	Fourth Generation	Fifth Generation
INPUT MEDIA METHOD	Punched Cards Paper Tape	Punched Cards	Key to Tape/Disk	Keyboard Data Entry Pointing Devices Optical scanning	Voice Recognition Touch Devices Hardwiring Recognition
TREND: Toward Direct Input Devices That Are More Natural and Easy to Use.					

1. Keyboard

This is the standard input device attached to all computers. The layout of keyboard is just like the traditional typewriter of the type QWERTY. It also contains some extra command keys and function keys. It contains a total of 101 to 104 keys. A typical keyboard used in a computer is shown in Fig. 2.6. You have to press correct combination of keys to input data. The computer can recognise the electrical signals corresponding to the correct key combination and processing is done accordingly.

2. Mouse

Mouse is an input device shown in Fig. 2.7 that is used with your personal computer. It rolls on a small ball and has two or three buttons on the top. When you roll the mouse across a flat surface the screen censors, the mouse in the direction of mouse movement. The cursor moves very fast with mouse giving you more freedom to work in any direction. It is easier and faster to move through a mouse.

3. Scanner

The keyboard can input only text through keys provided in it. If we want to input a picture the keyboard cannot do that. Scanner is an optical device that can input any graphical matter and display it back. The common optical scanner devices are Magnetic Ink Character Recognition (MICR), Optical Mark Reader (OMR) and Optical Character Reader (OCR).

4. Magnetic Ink Character Recognition (MICR)

This is widely used by banks to process large volumes of cheques and drafts. Cheques are put inside the MICR. As they enter the reading unit the cheques pass through the magnetic field which causes the read head to recognise the character of the cheques.

5. Optical Mark Reader (OMR)

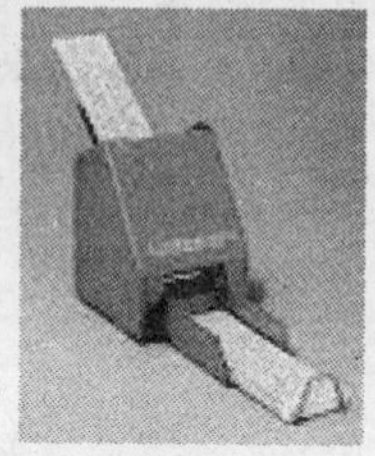

This technique is used when students have appeared in objective type tests and they had to mark their answer by darkening a square or circular space by pencil. These answer sheets are directly fed to a computer for grading where OMR is used.

6. Optical Character Recognition (OCR)

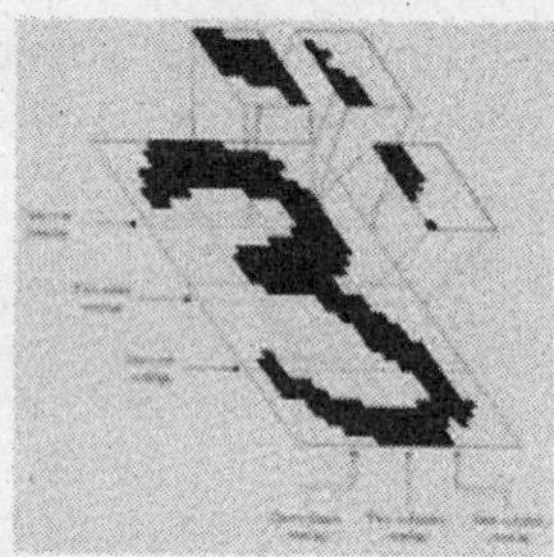

This technique unites the direct reading of any printed character. Suppose you have a set of hand written characters on a piece of paper. You put it inside the scanner of the computer. This pattern is compared with a site of patterns stored inside the computer. Whichever pattern is matched is called a character read. Patterns that cannot be identified are rejected. OCRs are expensive though better than MICR.

7. Digitizing Tablet

It is an input device that enables you to enter drawings and sketches into a computer. A digitizing tablet consists of an electronic tablet and a *cursor* or pen. A cursor (also called a *puck*) is similar to a mouse, except that it has a window with cross hairs for pinpoint placement, and it can have as many as 16 buttons. A pen (also called a *stylus*) looks like a simple ballpoint pen but uses an electronic head instead of ink. The tablet contains electronics that enable it to detect movement of the cursor or pen and translate the movements into digital signals that it sends to the computer.

For digitizing tablets, each point on the tablet represents a point on the display screen in a fixed manner. This differs from mice, in which all movement is relative to the current cursor position. The static nature of digitizing tablets makes them particularly effective for tracing drawings. Most modern digitizing tablets also support a mouse emulation mode, in which the pen or cursor acts like a mouse.

Digitizing tablets are also called digitizers, graphic tablets, touch tablets, or simply tablets.

8. Trackball

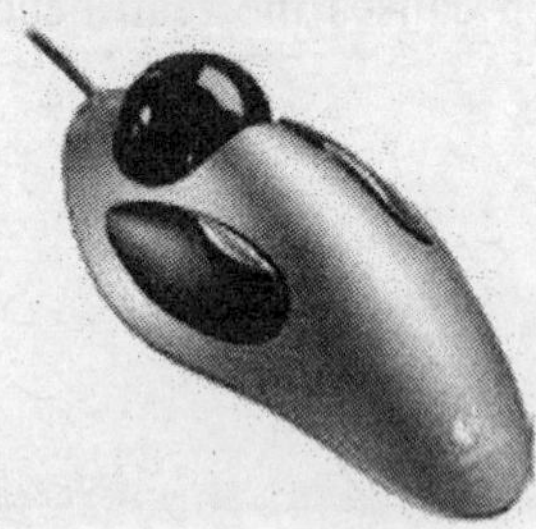

A **trackball** is a pointing device consisting of a ball housed in a socket containing sensors to detect rotation of the ball about two axes — like an upside-down mouse with an exposed protruding ball. The user rolls the ball with the thumb, fingers, or the palm of the hand to move a cursor. Large tracker balls are common on CAD workstations for easy precision. Before the advent of the touchpad, small trackballs were common on portable computers, where there may be no desk space on which to run a mouse. Some small thumbballs clip onto the side of the keyboard and have integral buttons with the same function as mouse buttons. An early example of the trackball, perhaps the earliest, was employed in the Canadian military's DATAR system.

9. Joystick

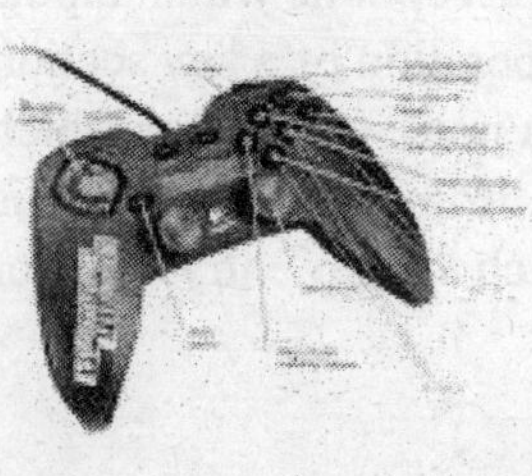

A **joystick** or **control stick** is a personal computer peripheral or general control device consisting of a handheld stick that pivots about one end and transmits its angle in two or three dimensions to a computer.

Joysticks are often used to control video games, and usually have one or more push-buttons whose state can also be read by the computer. The term joystick has become a synonym for game controllers that can be connected to the computer since the computer defines the input as a "joystick input."

Apart from controlling games, joysticks are also used for controlling machines such as aircraft, cranes, trucks, powered wheelchairs and some zero turning radius lawn mowers. More recently miniature joysticks have been adopted as navigational devices for smaller electronic equipment such as mobile phones.

There has been a recent and very significant drop in joystick popularity in the gaming industry. This is primarily due to the shrinkage of the flight simulator genre, and the almost complete disappearance of space-based simulators.

Joysticks can be used within first-person shooter games, but are significantly less accurate than a mouse-keyboard. This is one of the fundamental reasons why multiplayer console games are not compatible with PC versions of the same game. A handful of recent games, including Halo 2 and Shadowrun, have allowed console-PC matchings, but have significantly handicapped PC users by requiring them to use the auto-aim feature.

10. Digital Camera

A **digital camera** is a camera that takes video or still photographs, or both, digitally by recording images on a light-sensitive sensor.

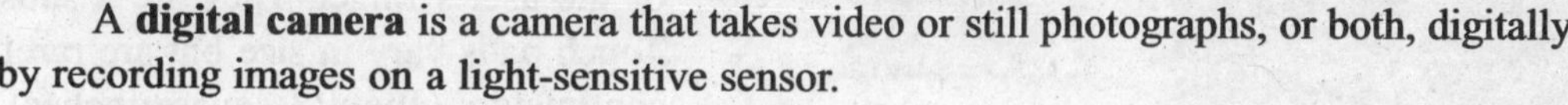

Many compact digital still cameras can record sound and moving video as well as still photographs. In the Western market, digital cameras outsell their 35 mm film counterparts.

Digital cameras can include features that are not found in film cameras, such as displaying an image on the camera's screen immediately after it is recorded, the capacity to take thousands of images on a single small memory device, the ability to record video with sound, the ability to edit images, and deletion of images allowing re-use of the storage they occupied. Digital cameras are incorporated into many devices ranging from PDAs and mobile phones (called camera phones) to vehicles. The Hubble Space Telescope and other astronomical devices are essentially specialised digital cameras.

11. Barcode Reader

A **barcode reader** (or **barcode scanner**) is an electronic device for reading printed barcodes. Like a flatbed scanner, it consists of a light source, a lens and a photo conductor translating optical impulses into electrical ones. Additionally, nearly all barcode readers contain *decoder* circuitry analyzing the barcode's image data provided by the photo conductor and sending the barcode's content to the scanner's output port.

12. Speech Input Devices

A speech input device is provided with a microphone which inputs speech, a key entry detector which detects an operation of a key section which serves as a man-machine interface, and a noise eliminator which eliminates a component of an operation sound from the speech that is input into the microphone within a period in which the key entry detector detects the operation.

13. Touch Screen

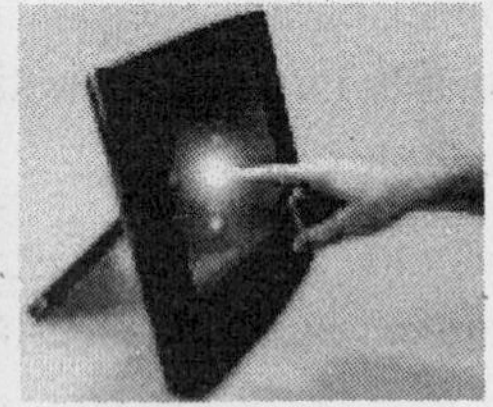

Touch screens are displays which also have the ability to detect the location of touches within the display area. This allows the display to be used as an input device, removing the keyboard and/or the mouse as the primary input device for interacting with the display's content. Such displays can be attached to computers or, as terminals, to networks. Touch screens also have assisted in recent changes in the design of personal digital assistant (PDA), satellite navigation and mobile phone devices, making these devices more usable.

14. Touch Pad

A touch pad (also track pad) is an input device commonly used in laptop computers. They are used to move the cursor, using motions of the user's finger. They are a substitute for a computer mouse. Touch pads vary in size but are rarely made larger than 20 square centimeters (about 3 square inches). They can also be found on personal digital assistants (PDAs) and some portable media players.

Touch pad operates in one of a few different ways, all of which entail sensing the capacitance of a finger, or the capacitance between sensors. This is why they will not sense the tip of a pencil or other similar implement. Gloved fingers may be problematic (such as in a clean room environment) but can sometimes work. Moist, sweaty, or calloused fingers can be problematic for those touch pads that rely on measuring the capacitance between the sensors.

15. Light Pen

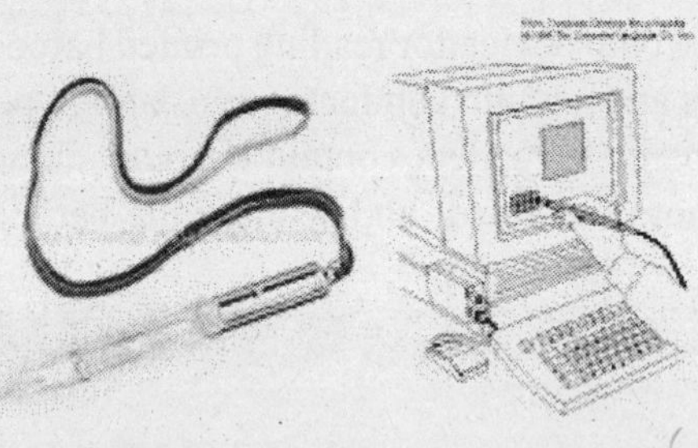

A **light pen** is a computer input device in the form of a light-sensitive wand used in conjunction with the computer's CRT monitor. It allows the user to point to displayed objects, or draw on the screen, in a similar way to a touch screen but with greater positional accuracy. A light pen can work with any CRT-based monitor, but not with LCD screens, projectors and other display devices.

A light pen is fairly simple to implement. The light pen works by sensing the sudden small change in brightness of a point on the screen when the electron gun refreshes that spot. By noting exactly where the scanning has reached at that moment, the X,Y position of the pen can be resolved. This is usually achieved by the light pen causing an interrupt, at which point the scan position can be read from a special register, or computed from a counter or timer. The pen position is updated on every refresh of the screen.

2.6 OUTPUT DEVICES

An **output device** is any piece of computer hardware equipment used to communicate the results of data processing carried out by an information processing system (such as a computer) to the outside world. In computing, input/output, or I/O, refers to the communication between an information processing system (such as a computer), and the outside world. Inputs are the signals or data sent to the system, and outputs are the signals or data sent by the system to the outside.

The most common input devices used by the computer are the keyboard and mouse. The keyboard allows the entry of textual information while the mouse allows the selection of a point on the screen by moving a screen cursor to the point and pressing a mouse button. The most common outputs are monitors, speakers and printers.

Output Technology Trend:

	First Generation	Second Generation	Third Generation	Fourth Generation	Fifth Generation
OUTPUT MEDIA/ METHOD	Punched Cards Printed Reports and Documents	Punched Cards Printed Reports and Documents	Printed Reports and Documents Video Displays	Video Displays Audio Responses Printed Reports and Documents	Video Displays Voice Responses Hyperlinked Multimedia Documents

TREND: Toward Direct Output Methods That Communication Naturally, Quickly, and Clearly

Common Output Devices are:

1. Visual Display Unit or Screen

When a problem is keyed in, the screen (which is similar to a television screen) display the characters. The user can read the problem line by line and make correction before it is stored or printed on a printer. It is also possible to bring to the screen a portion of the program stored in the external storage for editing.

The operator normally uses a cursor to pin-point a particular position on the screen. The cursor can be moved along a line or vertically from one line to another. This facilitates quick and early editing. Screen sizes differ from system to system. The standard size is 24 lines by 80 characters. Most system has provision for scrolling. This facilitates the user to move the text vertically or horizontally on the screen. Thus bringing to the screen to the hidden text. Thus the user can through the entire file either to review or to select a particular portion.

Monitor

The monitor is made up of cathode-ray tube CRT due to which it also called C.R.T. terminal. The screen consists of horizontal and vertical sweep circuits similar to T.V. sets. The screen's inside is coated with dots of phosphor called pixel and can be used for games or graphics or displaying the results of a calculation done by computer. The more the number of pixel or dots in a screen, the better will be the capability of computer to display an information

This capability is known as resolution. The characters typed with the keyboard are displayed on the screen. We can thus verify whether the programs we enter into computer is correct or not.

Tips for Avoiding Computer Vision Syndrome:

Long hours of staring at a computer screen causes dryness and reduces the blinking rate of the eyes. Burning, itchiness and watering of eyes are the common visible syndromes of computer vision syndrome. Often headache is a direct consequence of the glare emitted by the screen.

To avoid the syndrome the following measures are to be taken:

- Make sure that the computer screen is not too close to your face.
- Position the screen so that it is either at eye level, or slightly lower.
- Tilt the monitor slightly to eliminate reflection or glare.
- Make sure that primary light source [such as windows] is not shining into your face or directly on the monitor.
- Frequently look away from the screen and focus on far away objects.
- Reduce the contrast and brightness of the screen by adjusting the controls on the monitor.

2. Sound Cards and Speaker

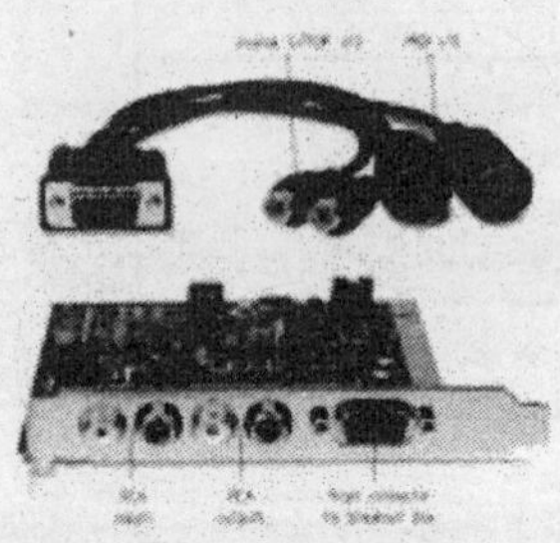

A **sound card** (also known as an audio card) is a computer expansion card that facilitates the input and output of audio signals to/from a computer under control of computer programs. Typical uses of sound cards include providing the audio component for multimedia applications such as music composition, editing video or audio, presentation/education, and entertainment (games). Many computers have sound capabilities built in, while others require additional expansion cards to provide for audio capability

Computer speakers, or **multimedia speakers**, are external speakers, commonly equipped with a low-power internal amplifier. The standard audio connection is a 3.5mm (1/8 inch) stereo jack plugs often colour-coded lime green (following the PC 99 standard) for computer sound cards. A few use an RCA connector for input. There are also USB speakers which are powered from the 5 volts at 200 milliamps provided by the USB port, allowing about 1-watt of output power.

Computer speakers range widely in quality and in price. The computer speakers typically packaged with computer systems are small plastic boxes with mediocre sound quality. Some of the slightly better computer speakers have equalization features such as bass and treble controls, improving their sound quality somewhat.

The internal amplifiers require an external power source, known as a 'wall-wart.' More sophisticated computer speakers may have a 'subwoofer' unit, to enhance bass output, and these units usually include the power amplifiers both for the bass speaker, and the small 'satellite' speakers. Some computer displays have rather basic speakers built-in.

3. Printer

Printer is the most commonly used output device. It is used to prepare permanent documents in human-readable form [hard copy]. There several types of printers that are designed for different types of applications.

Printers are of two types — impact and non impact. Impact printers use the familiar typewriter approach of hammering a typeface against paper and inked ribbon. Non-impact printers do not hit or impact a ribbon to print. They use thermal, electrostatic, chemical and inkjet technologies. Depending on their speed and approach of printing, printers are also classified as character printers, and page printers.

Types of Printers

Printers are available with a variety of printing mechanisms and speed varying quality. The following are the types of printers:

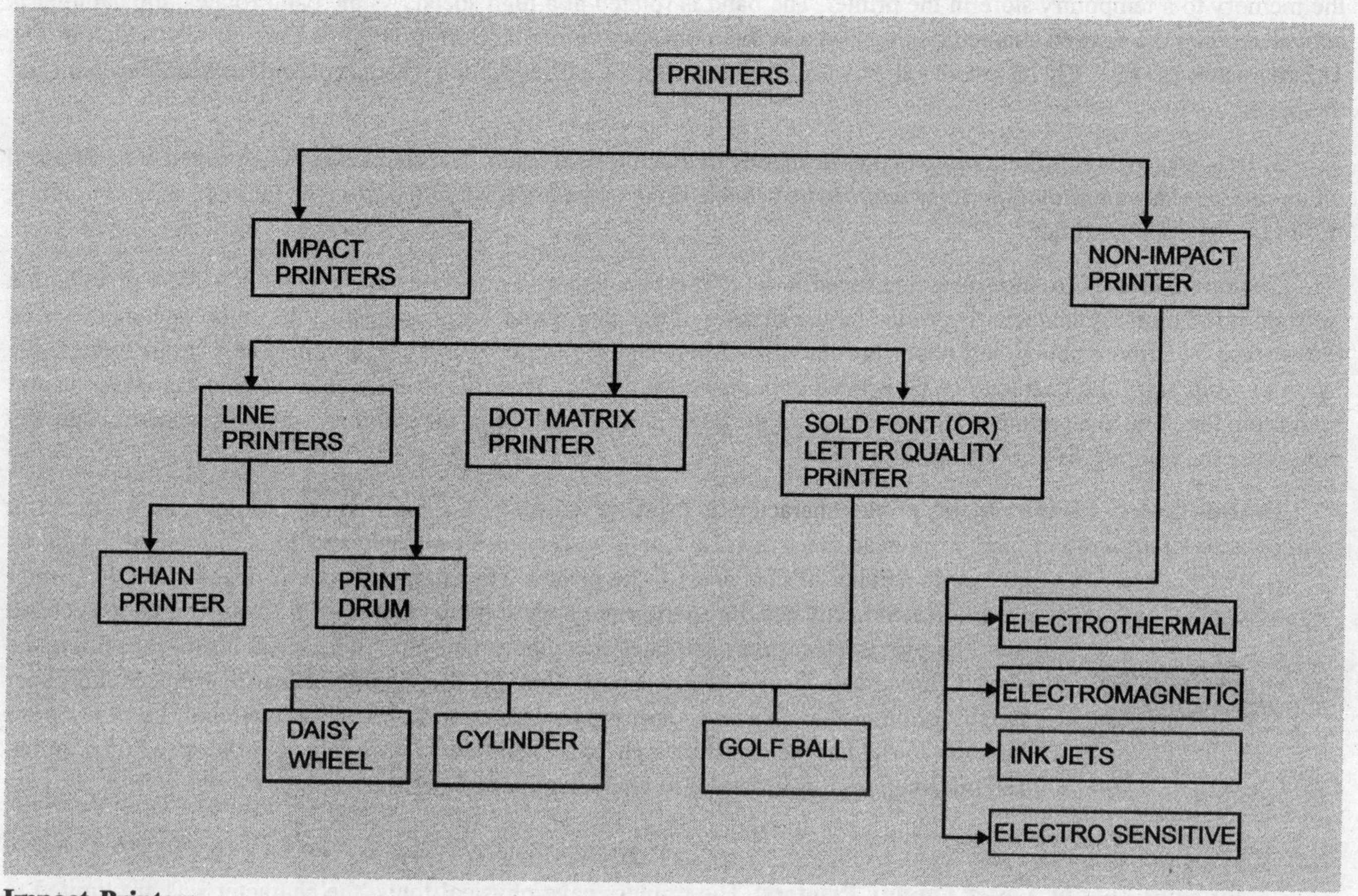

- PRINTERS
  - IMPACT PRINTERS
    - LINE PRINTERS
      - CHAIN PRINTER
      - PRINT DRUM
    - DOT MATRIX PRINTER
    - SOLD FONT (OR) LETTER QUALITY PRINTER
      - DAISY WHEEL
      - CYLINDER
      - GOLF BALL
  - NON-IMPACT PRINTER
    - ELECTROTHERMAL
    - ELECTROMAGNETIC
    - INK JETS
    - ELECTRO SENSITIVE

Impact Printers

In impact printing head strikes a linked ribbon, placed immediately in front of a sheet of paper, leaving an imprint of the print head on the paper. Following are classifications of impact printers:

(a) Line Printer: A line printer which prints an entire rather than a character. Printing speeds vary from 300 lines to 3000 lines per minute with 96 to 160 characters or a 15 inch line. Six to eight lines are printed per vertical inch.

Line printers generally produce only upper case [capital] letters through some have provision for both capital and lower case letters. The quality of printing is poor in terms of style and density for office use. However, they are used for producing large volume of reports on big organizations.

There are two types of line printers:

1. Chain Printers: A chain printer has a steel band on which the character sets are embossed. For a 64 set printer, 4 sets of 64 characters each would be embossed on the band. For printing a line, all the characters in the line are set from the memory to a temporary store in the printer. The band is rotated at a high specd. As the band rotates, the hammer is activated when the desired character as specified in the temporary store comes in front of it. For a printer which prints, 132 characters per line, 132 hammers will be positioned to strike the carbon ribbon which is placed between the chain and the paper.

2. Drum Printers: A drum printer consists mainly of a cylindrical drum. The characters to be printed are embossed on its surface. The codes of all the characters to be printed, on one line are transmitted from the memory of the computer to storage unit in the printer.

The printer drum is rotated on a high speed. A set of print hammers — one for each character in a line - are mounted in front of the drum. A character is printed by the striking of the appropriate hammer against the embossed character on the surface. A carbon ribbon and paper are interposed between the hammer and the drum. As the drum rotates, the hammer waits until the character to be printed appears in front of it. Thus the drum would have to complete on full revolution for a line to be printed. The movement of the drum and the striking of the hammer must synchronize accurately otherwise, the printing will not be uniform

(b) Dot Matrix Printer: In this printer characters to print are made up of a finite number of dots and so, the print head consists of an array of pins. Print head consists of 9*7 or 7*5 array of pins. Characters to be printed are made up of a finite number of dots and so, the printer. The character code is decoded by the printer electronics and activates the appropriate pins in the print head. The character code decoded from the printer electronics activates the appropriate pins in the print head. These pins are moved forward to form a character and they hit the carbon ribbon in front of the paper thereby printing that character. Many dot matrix printers are bi-directional, i.e., they print from left to right as well as from right to left on return. This enhances the speed of printing. The printing speed is around 300 characters per second.

(c) Solid Font or Letter Quality Printers: The printers have physical fonts, the character sets are limited to those by the manufacturers. It includes

1. Daisy Wheel Printer

The daisy wheel is a flat plastic or metal disk on whose rim all the characters are embossed. The daisy wheel is mounted by a carriage which can move from the left to right and can also rotate. Characters to be printed are sent serially to the printer. The movable carriage positions itself at the print position and rotates so that the character to be printed appears in front of the printer ribbon. The carriage now tilts and the embossed character strikes the ribbon and an impression is made on the paper mounted behind the ribbon. The carriage moves one character position to the left and rotates the daisy wheel so that the next character to be printed is positioned correctly and the character is printed. The main advantage of daisy wheel printer is the excellent quality of the print produced by it. Another advantage is the interchangeability of daisy wheels.

2. Cylinder Head Printers

The cylinder head printer has the print symbols embossed on a metal cylinder as shown below:

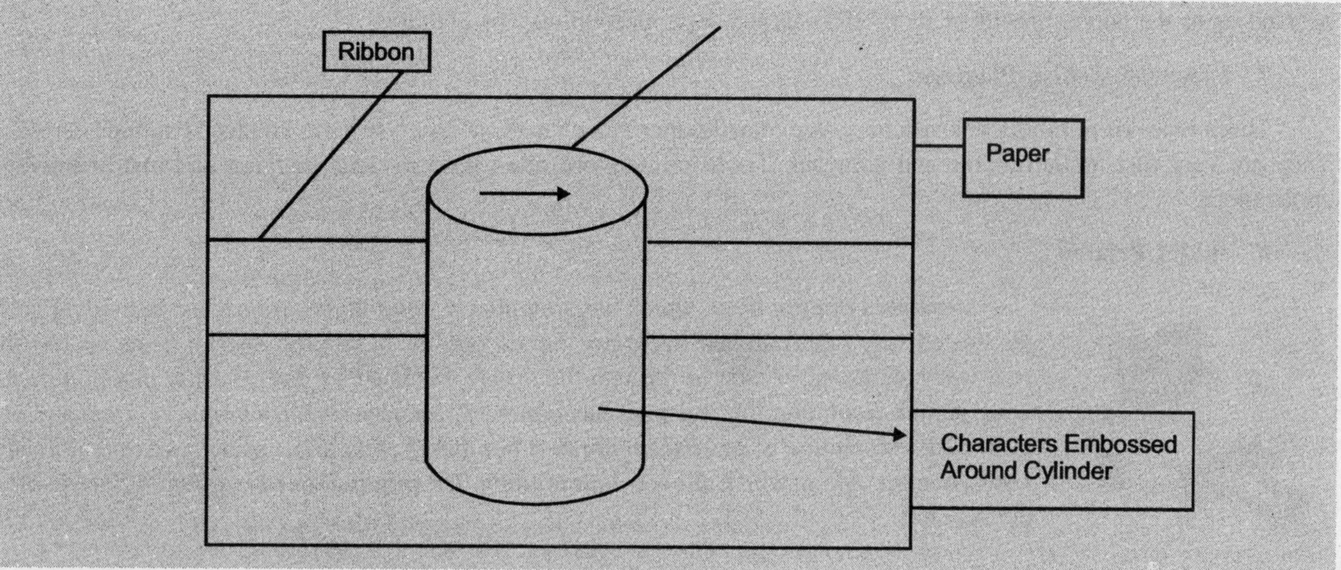

It normally has 4 rows of 16 characters, consisting of upper case alpha-numeric set and other standard symbols. The ribbon and paper are placed in front of the cylinder which has a hammer positioned at the rear. During operation, the head is rotated clockwise or anti-clockwise and moved vertically until the symbol to be positioned next to the ribbon and the paper. Then the hammer strikes the back of the cylinder head. This action forces the head forward, which results in the printing of the character on the paper.

3. Golf Ball Head Printers

It is similar to cylinder head printer, except that their surface area is large and thus allow for greater character set. A character is selected by rotating and then tilting the ball head until the desired character is positioned next to the ribbon and paper. Then the ball is moved forward by a print can which will result in striking the ribbon and the paper. The ball heads may be interchanged thus allowing different character sets to be used.

4. Non-impact Printers

In non-impact printing, the character is formed on the paper by a non-mechanical process, e.g., using heat, laser technology or photographic techniques.These non-impact printers are used only in some special applications, since they are very costly and are produced only by a few manufacturers. The natural limitations of speed in electro mechanical devices and cost considerations have led to development of printers called non-impact printers. These printers are primarily of the following categories:

5. Electrostatic

The print mechanism of electrostatic printers is a line of electric styli or writing nibs. These nibs produce dots of charge corresponding to a latent image on to dielectric paper. Then the paper passes through a toner which contains material with coloured particles carrying an opposite charge to that written by the nibs. As a result, particles adhere to the magnetized areas, forming printed characters. The advantages are high speed and high quality. But the disadvantage is the need for special paper.

6. Electromagnetic Tapes

These Printers use magnetic writing heads [similar to those in tape recorders] to form an image on a magnetic drum surface. This surface is then passed through a magnetic powder, which adheres to the charged areas. The powder is pressed on to the paper. Speeds of up to 250 characters per second may be obtained.

7. Electro-Sensitive Printers

These types of printers use a special silver coated paper that changes colour when the voltage is applied across it. They are very fast, quite reliable and compact. These printers are often used in delta hedging and instrumentation applications.

8. Inkjet Printer

It consists of print head, which has a number of small holes of nozzles. Individual holes are heated very rapidly by an integrated circuit resistor. When the resistor heats up, the ink near it vaporizes and is ejected through the nozzle and makes a dot on paper placed near the head. A high resolution inkjet printer has around 50 nozzles within a height of 7mm and can print with a resolution of more than 300 dots per inch. Latest inkjet printers have multimedia heads, one per colour, which allow colour printing. The printing speed is around 120 characters per second.

9. Electro Photographic Printers

These printers may be direct or indirect devices. Direct electrographic printers use a Zinc-oxide paper that is completely changed or a piece of film. Using a laser, a beam of light is focused through a rotating disc containing a full of characters. This character image is projected on to the paper or film, and the print or negative is developed and fixed in a manner similar to that used for ordinary photographs. This output consists of high letter quality images and hence used for printing book. These laser printers operate at a speed of 21000 lines per minute.

Indirect electro photographic printers use a laser to put a latent image on a photoconductive drum. This light changes the area of an uncharged drum or dissipates charge from a charged drum. Then a toner, which is attracted by the image area is used, to transfer the character on to a plain paper. These types of printers are also called as xerographic printers or page printers [since they may be used to print an entire page at once].

10. Laser Printers:

- In laser printer an electronically controlled laser beam traces out the desired character to be printed on a photo conductive drum.
- The drum attracts an ink toner on to the exposed areas. This image is transferred to the paper, which comes in contact with the drum.
- Very fast printers print 10,000 lines per minute. These printers give excellent outputs and can print a variety of fonts. Low speed laser printers, which can print 4 to 16 pages per minute, are now very popular.

(d) Terminals: It is a very popular interactive input-output unit. It can be divided into two types: hard copy terminals and soft copy terminals. A hard copy terminal provides a printout on paper whereas soft copy terminals provide visual copy on monitor. A terminal when connected to a CPU sends instructions directly to the computer. Terminals are also classified as dumb terminals or intelligent terminals depending upon the work situation.

(e) Plotters: A **plotter** is a vector graphics printing device that connects to a computer. Pen Plotters prints their output by moving a pen across the surface of a piece of paper. This means that plotters are restricted to line art, rather than graphics as with other printers. They can draw complex line art, including text, but do so very slowly because of the mechanical movement of the pens. (Pen Plotters are incapable of creating a solid region of colour; but can hatch an area by drawing a number of close, regular lines.) When computer memory was very expensive, and processor power was very slow, this was often the fastest way to produce colour high-resolution vector-based artwork, or very large drawings efficiently.

QUESTIONS

Short Answer Question

1. What is Primary Storage?
2. What are the Secondary storage devices?
3. What are the types of line printers?
4. Explain EPROM.
5. What is Optical Mark Reader?
6. Any two examples of output devices.
7. Explain Touch Screen.

Long Answer Question

1. What are the primary storage devices? Explain it.
2. Explain secondary storage devices
3. Write short notes on input and output devices.
4. What are the most useful input devices?
5. Explain any threeoutput devices.
6. What are impact printers? Explain.
7. Write short notes on:

   (a) Daisy Wheel Printer (b) Cylinder Head Printers

Very long or essay type Question

1. Explain primary and secondary storage devices.
2. Explain the various types of Printers.
3. Write short notes on:

   (a) Line Printer (b) Inkjet Printer (c) Electro photographic Printers (d) Laser Printers.

3

CHAPTER

SOFTWARE FLOWCHARTS AND PROGRAM DEVELOPMENT

Structure:

3.1 INTRODUCTION TO SOFTWARE

In the previous lesson we discussed about the different parts and configurations of computer. It has been mentioned that programs or instructions have to be fed to the computer to do specific task. So it is necessary to provide sequence of instructions so that your work can be done. We can divide the computer components into two major areas, namely, hardware and software.

What is Software?

As you know computer cannot do anything without instructions from the user. In order to do any specific job you have to give a sequence of instructions to the computer. This set of instructions is called a computer program. Software refers to the set of computer programs, procedures that describe the programs, how they are to be used. We can say that it is the collection of programs, which increase the capabilities of the hardware. Software guides the computer at every step where to start and stop during a particular job. The process of software development is called programming. You should keep in mind that software and hardware are complementary to each other. Both have to work together to produce meaningful result. Another important point you should know that producing software is difficult and expensive.

3.2 SOFTWARE TYPES

Computer software is normally classified into two broad categories:

- Application Software
- System software

Figure given below summarizes the major categories of system and application software. Of course, this is a conceptual illustration. The types of software you will encounter depend primarily on the types of computers and networks you use, and on what specific tasks you want to accomplish.

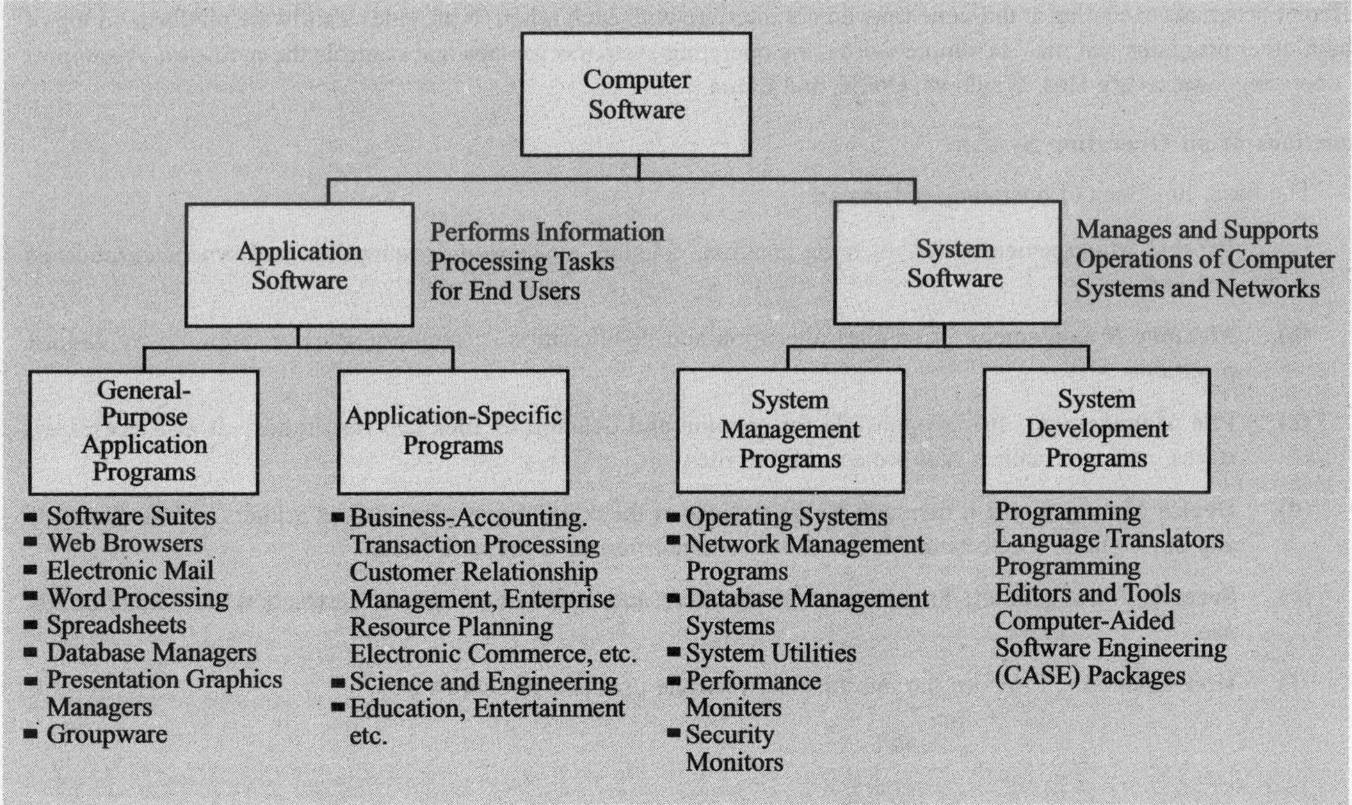

3.3 SYSTEM SOFTWARE

System software consists of several programs, which are directly responsible for controlling, integrating, and managing the individual hardware components of a computer system. You must have noticed that a new computer system is always accompanied by some software, either stored in a floppy or CD, which is supplied by the manufacturer. This software manages and supports the computer system and its information processing activities.

System software is more transparent and less noticed by the users, they usually interact with the hardware or the applications this software provides a programming environment in which programmers can create applications to accommodate their needs. This environment provides functions that are not available at the hardware level and performs the tasks related to the execution of an application program. Hence, system software acts as an interface between the hardware of the computer and the software application.

In simple terms, system software makes the computer functional. They provide basic functionality like file management, visual display, and keyboard input are used by application software to accomplish these functions. Some examples of system software are:

1. Operating system
2. Device drivers
3. Language translators
4. System utilities.

1. Operating System

It is the first layer of software loaded into computer memory when it starts up. As the first software layer, all other software that gets loaded after it depends on it for various common core services. These common core services include disk access, memory management, takes scheduling, and user interfacing. In addition the operating system ensures that different programs executing at the same time do not interfere with each other. It provides a software platform on top of which other programs can run. In simple words, the operating system organizes and controls the hardware. Examples of operating systems are Dos, Windows, UNIX, and Linux.

Functions of an Operating System:

The basic functions of operating systems are:

(a) **Process Management:** It handles the creation, deletion, suspension, resumption, and synchronization of process.

(b) **Memory Management:** It handles allocation and de-allocation of memory space as required by various programs.

(c) **File Management:** It is responsible for creation and deletion of files and directories. It also organizes, stores, retrieves, names, and protects all the files.

(d) **Device Management:** It manages all the devices of the computer system such as printers and modems. If any device fails, it detects the device failure and notifies the same to the user.

(e) **Security Management:** Protects system resources and information against destruction and unauthorized use.

(f) **User Interface:** Provides the interface between the user and the hardware.

3.4 CLASSIFICATION (TYPES) OF OPERATING SYSTEM

These are the different classification (types) of operating system:

(i) DOS (Disk Operating System)

MS-DOS was the widely used operating system before the introduction of the Windows operating system. Even now the MS-DOS commands are used for carrying out many jobs like copying the files, deleting the files etc. The DOS is a set of computer programs. The main functions of DOS are to manage files, allocate system resources according to the requirement. It provides essential features to control hardware devices such a keyboard, screen, disk drives, printers, modems etc. Thus, DOS is a medium through which the user and external devices attached to the system communicate the command with the system. DOS translate communication issued by the computer in the format that is understandable by the computer and instruct computer to work accordingly. It also translates the result and any error message in the format for the user to understand.

➤ **DOS Commands**

We can type all DOS commands in either upper or lower case letters. There are two basic types of DOS commands:

❖ **Internal Commands**

These commands, like COPY, DEL, and TYPE, are stored in computers memory. Many DOS commands fall into this category.

❖ **External Commands**

This group of commands is stored on the disk. To use them, either insert the DOS floppy disk, or change to the directory on hard disk which contains DOS external commands. Examples of external commands include FORMAT, DISKCOPY, and CHKDSK.

Some commands can take several forms. These separate forms are used by including various parameters with the command. Parameters, which will be discussed with each command, are indicated by a / mark. Here is an example of command with an attached parameter:

C:\>DIR/W

[DOS command DIR is attached with parameter W]

All DOS commands must be activated by pressing the <Enter> key after typing the command.

➤ **Features of DOS**

- ❖ Single user system
- ❖ Machine independence
- ❖ Program control
- ❖ Peripheral management
- ❖ Operating with Directories
- ❖ Managing files
- ❖ Processing commands
- ❖ Managing input and output

- Data securing
- Using Batch files
- Managing memory
- Setting up environment
- Command processing — DOS shell (a set of commands which is used to create the programs)
- Operating with Assembler.

➢ **Advantages of DOS**

The DOS provides the following advantages:

- Machine independence
- More security
- User friendly environment
- More useful in commercial applications
- Error finding and recovery is more efficient
- Facilities more graphical user interfaces
- Easy debugging

(ii) Windows Operating System:

Microsoft Windows is the most popular operating system around the world. Even those who are new to computers can use it with a little practice. With the help of Windows, we can operate the computer just by clicking the mouse buttons, Windows 95, Windows 98, Windows 2000 and Windows XP are the various versions of Windows.

Windows is an operating system. It is the extension of the disk operating system. Windows is system software. It requires DOS to run the application programs. The DOS should be loaded into the memory before the window is executed. After the windows is loaded into the memory the windows environment takes all the device controls. It also takes care of the memory management of the programs run by the windows software".

Types of Windows:

There are two types of windows. They are:

(a) **Application windows** displays the executable program in graphical user interface mode.

(b) **Document windows** generated by executable or application program.

1. Windows 98

Windows 98 is the upgraded version of Windows 95. It offers bug fixture and minor enhancements.

➢ **Features of Windows:**

The important features of Windows 98 are as follows:

(a) **Graphical User Interface:** Windows 98 provides user-friendlier interface to work on. Its improved graphical user interface makes learning and using windows 98 more natural and easier for all types of users. It is more powerful, customizable and efficient.

(b) Type of Icons (Small Pictures): There are three types of icons. They are:

(i) **Applications icons:** the minimized version of the currently running application programs. It appears at the bottom of the desktop and can be maximized.

(ii) **Document icons:** the reduced document windows.

(iii) **Program icons:** appear within program manager and clicking on these icons activate the associated applications and also load the related documents or files.

(c) Start Button: Introduction of START button by windows 98 made life much simpler while there is a need to access multiple programs. It is the gateway of accessing most of the functionality available in the computer loaded with windows 98. Just Click on the start button anytime to start any programs, open or find documents, change windows settings, get Help, manage Files, maintain System, much more.

(d) Taskbar: The Task bar provides information and access to the entire task that has been currently activated by windows 98. Using this one can keep a track of what all programs have been activated and switched between them.

(e) Windows Explorer: Windows Explorer more or less acts as File Manager for windows 98, but with lots of new features. It is more efficient, faster and user friendly. Using Explorer one can easily browse through all the drives and network resources available and manage files.

(f) Right Mouse Button: Clicking on the right mouse button activates a pop-up menu in any program so as to help in completing a task efficiently.

(g) Long File Names: As the MS-DOS convention follows, none-of the file used in DOS environment should be more than 8 character of primary name and optimal secondary name (extension) of three characters. However, Windows 98 has broken this barrier. Windows 98 supports long file names maximum of 225 characters. It also allowed space to be used in between file name. This helps to make files and folders (directory/subdirectory) easier to organize and find.

(h) Shortcuts: As the name suggests, SHORTCUTS are the shortest way to access programs, files other resources in Windows 98. Instead of going through the structural process of accessing a program, one can create "shortcuts" to access them. It creates links for easy access to file, programs, folders and more.

(i) Multitasking: Multitasking allows the user to activate and accomplish more than one task at a time. For example, work on a document file WORD programs, which copies file from other computer available in time on the network. With Windows 98, 32 - bit computing environment, the user can do more than one task a time.

(j) Easy Internet Access: Integration of Internet Explorer 4.0 and Active Desktop, which coupled the Internet html hypertext links more tightly to the Windows 98 user interface.

(k) Software Compatibility: Windows 98 provides complete backward compatibility. It is easily compatible with other applications developed for MS-DOS and Windows 3.x environment. It also supports latest 32-bit technology. Most of the latest software packages are now built on Windows 98, operating environment.

(l) Great Gaming Platform: Windows 98 supports rich graphics, high quality audio and video. Software to take advantage of Intel's Multimedia Extensions (MMX) to the IA - 32 instruction set, which are designed to improve the performance of multimedia applications and games developed for windows 98 that uses MMX technology.

(m) Hardware Compatibility: Windows 98 provides greater Hardware compatibility as compared to any other operating environment. It has flexibility of supporting hardware from different vendors.

(n) **Find Utility:** Find Utility of windows 98 allows the user to do searches by partial name, last modified date, or full text. In addition we can save, rename or view files from within the result pane.

(o) **Help:** Windows 98 provides online help to accomplish a task. If the user is not sure how to perform a task, windows 98 Help will provide structured process how to accomplish the task. Simply right-click on any object in the user interface (icon) and he can get relevant description about that object.

(p) **Manage More Numbers of PC's:** Windows 98 can manage up to eight monitors on a single PC. The user can drag and drop resize and move desktop items such as windows, folders, icons, and applications, from one monitor to the next.

(q) **Additional Facilities:** Windows 98 includes additional enhancement of Windows 95 that includes new backup utilities and disk defragmenter capabilities.

2. Windows NT Workstation

Windows NT is a single user; multitasking operating system designed to run on PC workstations and incorporates all latest developments in operating system technology. It was introduced in 1993. It includes the following:

(a) Windows NT workstation
(b) Windows NT server, and
(c) Windows NT enterprise edition

➤ **Features**

(a) **Single User Multitasking:** The main feature is that even through it is meant for a single user environment, provides multitasking. For example, a user may use a word processor, a drawing program, a spreadsheet application to produce a document. Without multitasking, simultaneous use of this will not be possible. They must process with the s/w one by one; provide alignment making changes will be a tedious process. In a multitasking environment, the user may keep all the applications open, prepare the documentation and make necessary change. All of these are possible with increased speed and memory capacity of microprocessors together with the support for virtual memory.

(b) **Ability to Support all Applications:** The power of Windows NT comes form its ability to support applications written for other operating systems. This ability is provided through protected subsystems. The protected subsystems are those parts of NT that interact with the end user.

(c) **Client Server Computing Model:** The way in which the executive, the protected subsystems, and the applications structured in NT is by using the client / server computing model, each server implemented as one or more process. Such process waits for a request from a client for its services, e.g., memory services. A client, which may be an application program or another operating system module, requests a service by sending a message. The message routed through the executive to the appropriate server. The server performs the operation and returns the results or status information by means of another message, which is routed through the executive back to the client.

Client/server architecture has the following advantages:

(i) It simplifies the base operating system, the NT executive.

(ii) It improves reliability. Each server runs on a separate process with its partition of memory, protected from other servers. Also, the servers cannot directly access hardware or modify? memory in which the executive rest, the operating system.

(iii) It provides a natural base for distributed computing.

(d) **Support for Threads:** An important feature of Windows NT is its support for threads within process. A thread is a dispatchable unit of work. It is executed sequentially and may be interrupted so that the processor can turn to other threads. A process is a collection of one or more areas and associated system resources. This is similar to a program in execution. By checking an application into multiple threads, the modularity and the timing of application related events could be maintained.

(e) **Support of Symmetric Multiprocessing (SMP):** In a multiprocessor system, to achieve maximum efficiency and reliability a mode of operation known as symmetric multiprocessing (SMP) is desirable. With SMP, any process or Thread can be assigned to any processor.

(f) **Windows NT uses concepts of object oriented design:** Windows NT uses some concepts of object oriented design. This approach facilitates the sharing of resources and data among processes and the protection of resources from unauthorized access.

➢ **Advantages of Windows NT**

(a) It simplifies the base operating system

(b) It improves reliability

(c) It provides a natural base of distributed computing

(d) Operating-system routines can run on any available processor and different routines can be executed simultaneously on different processors.

(e) NT supports the use of multiple threads of execution within a single process.

(f) NT processes convenient mechanisms for sharing data and resources between processes.

(g) NT provides flexible inter process communication capabilities.

(h) Functionality-NT can communicate with many different types of computers.

(iii) The Unix Operating System

Like DOS and windows, there's another operating system called UNIX. It arrived earlier than the other two, and stayed back like enough to give us the internet. UNIX is a giant operating system and is way ahead of them in sheer power. It has practically everything an operating system should have, and several features which other operating systems never had. Its richness and elegance go beyond the commands and tolls that constitute it, while simplicity permeates the entire system. It runs on practically every hardware and provided motivation to the open source movement.

However, UNIX also makes many demands of the user. It requires a different type of commitment to understand the subject, even when the user is an experienced computer professional. It introduces certain concepts not known to the computing community before, and user numerous symbols whose meaning is anything but clear. It achieves unusual tasks with a few keystrokes, but it takes time to device a sequence of them for a specific task. Often, it doesn't tell you whether you are right or wrong, and doesn't warn you of the consequences of your actions. That is probably the reason why many people still prefer to stay away from UNIX.

➢ **Features of UNIX**

UNIX is an operating system, so it is has all the features an operating system expected to have. However, UNIX also looks at a few things differently and possesses features unique to it. The following section gives a clear idea of the major features of this operating system.

(a) **UNIX: A Multi user System:** From the fundamental point of view, UNIX is a multiprogramming system; it permits multiple programs to run. This can happen in two ways:

Multiple users can run separate jobs.

A single user can also run multiple jobs.

(b) **UNIX: A Multitasking System Too:** A single user can also run multiple tasks at the same time as UNIX is a multitasking system. It is usual for a user to edit a file, print another one on printer, send email to a friend and browse the Word Wide Web — all without leaving any of the application. This kernel is designed to handle a user's multiple needs.

(c) **The UNIX Toolkit:** By one definition, UNIX represents the kernel, but the kernel by itself doesn't do much that can benefit the user. To properly exploit the power of UNIX, you need to use the host of applications that are shipped with every UNIX system. These applications are quite varied in scope. There are general purpose tools, text manipulation utilities (called filters), compilers and interpreters, networked applications and system administration tools.

(d) **Pattern Matching:** UNIX features very sophisticated pattern matching features. UNIX features elaborate pattern matching schemes that use several characters from the Meta character set. The matching isn't confined to filenames only. Some of the most advanced and useful tools also use a special expression called a regular expression that is framed with characters from the set.

(e) **Programming Facility:** The UNIX shell is also a programming language; it was designed for a programmer, not a casual end user. It has all the necessary ingredients, like control structures, loops and variables, that establish it as a powerful programming language in its own right.

(f) **Documentation:** UNIX documentation is no longer the sore point it once was. Even though it is sometimes uneven, at most times the treatment is quite good. The principal online help facility available is the main command, which remains the most important reference for commands and their configuration files. Thanks to O'Reilly & Associates, one can safely say that there's no feature of UNIX on which a separate textbook is not available.

Apart from the online documentation, there's a vast ocean of UNIX resources available on the internet. There are several newsgroups on UNIX where you can fire your queries in case you are stuck with a problem — be it a problem related to shell programming or a network configuration issue. The FAQ (Frequently Asked Questions) a document that addresses common problems is also widely available on the Net. Then there are numerous articles published in magazines and journals and lecture notes available by universities on their Web- sites. UNIX is easily tamed Operating System.

3. Device Drivers

Device drivers are system programs, which are responsible for proper functioning of devices. Every device, whether it is a printer, monitor, mouse or keyboard, has a driver program associated with it for its proper functioning. Whenever a new device is added to the computer system, a new device driver must be installed before the device is used. A device driver is not an independent program; it assists and is assisted by the operating system for the proper functioning of the device.

4. Language Translators

Computers only understand a language consisting of 0s and 1s called machine language. To ease the burden of programming entirely in 0s and 1s, special programming languages called high-level programming languages were developed that resembled natural languages like English. Language translators help in converting programming languages into machine language. To be precise, they convert programming statements into the 0s and 1s that the computer is able to process.

Depending on the programming language used, language translators are divided into three major categories: compilers, interpreter, and assembler.

(a) **Compiler:** The programs written in any high-level programming language (C or Pascal) needs to be converted into machine language. This is achieved by using a complier.

(b) **Interpreter:** An interpreter analyses and executes the source code in line-by-line manner, without looking at the entire program. In other words, an interpreter translates a statement in a program and executes the statement immediately, before translating the next source language statement.

(c) **Assembler:** Compared to all the types of programming languages, assembly language is closest to the machine code. It is fundamentally a symbolic representation of machine code. The assembly language program must be translated into machine code by a separate program called an assembler. The assembler program recognizes the character strings that make up the symbolic names of the various machine operations, and substitutes the required machine code for each instruction. In short, an assembler converts the assembly codes into machine codes, making the assembly program ready for execution.

Typical software generally comprises millions of lines of programming statements or code. The code is divided into logical groups and stored in different independent modules so that the debugging and maintenance of the code becomes easier. Before execution, different object codes resulting from the independent modules have to be linked together to create an executable program. A linker is a system program that links together several objects modules and libraries to form a single, coherent, program (executable program). The part of the operating system that brings an executable file residing on disk into memory and executes it is known as loader. Being responsible for tasks like loading, linking and relocation, loader performs the function of a linked program and then immediately schedules the executable for execution without creating an executable file as an output.

5. System Utility

System utility programs perform day-to-day tasks related to the maintenance of the computer system. They are used to support, enhance, and secure existing programs and data in the computer system. They are generally small programs, having specific tasks to perform:

(a) **File Management:** These utilities make it easier to manage data files. Many programs are written to help users to find the files, create and organize directions, copy, move, and remove files.

(b) **Backup:** It may happen that sometime data files are corrupted, or accidentally deleted. In such a case, data backups become very useful. A backup system utility is essential for those organizations, which want to keep their data intact.

(c) **Data Recovery:** It is the process of retrieving deleted or inaccessible data from failed electronic storage media such as computer hard disk drives, removable media, optical devices, and tape cartridges.

(d) **Virus Protection:** Anti-virus programs are essential system utilities for a computer system functioning in a network. They provide the security to the system from viruses that can damage the computer system.

(e) **Disk Management:** Disk management program includes various system softwares like disk defragmenter, data compressor and disk formatting tools. Defragmentation implies putting fragments of files in a sequential order onto the disk which reduces the time to access the file.

(f) **Firewall:** It is commonly used to protect information such as e-mail and data files within a physical building or organization. Essentially, a firewall is designed to protect a computer from unauthorized access, especially via network.

(g) **Disk Cleanup:** To keep a computer running smoothly, regular maintenance is vital. Therefore, one should use the disk cleanup utility, which easily determines which files on hard drive are no longer needed, then delete those files.

3.5 APPLICATION SOFTWARE

The most often seen software by a user is the application software. It used to accomplish specific tasks rather than just managing a computer system. For a user, the computer system has no specific use without application software. Application software may consist of a single program, such as Microsoft's Note pad (for writing and editing simple text). It may also consist of a collection of programs, often called a software package, which work together to accomplish a task, such as database management software. Application software may also include a larger collection of related but independent programs and packages (a software suite), which have a common user interface or shared data format, such as Microsoft Office suite.

Applications software are dependent on system software. A system software (like operating system) acts as an interface between the user and the computer hardware, while application software performs specific tasks. Applications are pieces of software that perform tasks for the user besides helping the computer operate, which is the tasks of system software. Applications software are controlled by system software, which manages hardware devices and performs background tasks for them. The distinction between the two is important. Without system software, the computer will not run, and without application software, the computer, no matter how powerful, will not be helpful in meeting user requirements. Think of it this way-applications apply the computer's thinking power to business tasks such as tracking the general ledger or billing your customers.

Application software ranges from games, calculators, and word processors (document creating programs), to programs that "paint" images on screen (image editors). Applications represent real world tasks. They can be easily divided by looking at exactly what function they serve. Some of the most commonly used application software is discussed below:

1. Word Processor

A word processor is software used to compose, format, edit, and print electronic documents. Word processing is one of the earliest applications for office productivity and the personal computer. It involves not only typing, but also checking the spelling and grammar of the text and arranging it correctly on the page. A variety of different typefaces is available for a variety of effects. It is possible to include pictures, graphs, charts and many other things within the text of the document. It also allows for changes in margins, fonts, and colour. Nowadays, virtually all personal computers are equipped with a word processing program, which has the same function as a typewriter for writing letters, reports or other documents, and printing. Examples of some well-known word processors are Microsoft Word and Word Perfect.

2. Spreadsheets

One of the first commercial uses of computers was in processing payroll and other financial records, so the programs were designed to generate reports in the standard "spreadsheet" format bookkeepers and accountants used. A spreadsheet application is a rectangular grid, which allows text, numbers, and complex functions to be entered into a matrix of thousands of individual cells. The spreadsheet provides sheets containing cells each of which may contain text and / or numbers. Cells may also contain equations that calculate results from data placed in other cells or series of cells. A simple example might be a column of numbers totalled in a single cell containing an equation relating to that column.

Spreadsheet software are used predominantly for accounting other numerically-based tasks, because financial and mathematical data and analysis are often managed in a tabular style, with columns of financial figures being manipulated and then influencing other data computations. Microsoft Excel and Lotus 1-2-3 are examples of spreadsheet applications.

3. Image Editors

Image editor programs are designed specifically for capturing, creating, editing, and manipulating images. These graphic programs provide a variety of special features for creating and altering images. In addition to offering a host of filters and image transformation algorithms, some image editors also enable the user to create and superimpose layers. Most graphic programs have the ability to import and export one or more graphic file formats. These computer programs enable the user to adjust an image to improve its appearance. With image editing software, one can darken or lighten an image, rotate it, adjust its contrast, crop out extraneous detail, and much more. Examples of these programs are Adobe Photoshop, Adobe Illustrator and Corel Draw.

4. Database Management Systems

Database management software is a collection of computer programs that allow storage, modification, and extraction of information from a database in an efficient manner. It supports the structuring of the database in a standard format and provides tools for data input, verification, storage, retrieval, query, and manipulation. When such software is used, information systems can be changed much more easily as the organization's information requirements change. New categories of data can be added to the database without disrupting the existing system. It also controls the security and integrity of the database from unauthorized access. FoxPro and Oracle are database management systems.

5. Presentation Applications

A presentation is a means of assessment, which requires presentation providers to present their work orally in the presence of an audience. It combines both visual and verbal elements. Presentation software allows the user to create presentations by producing slides or handouts for presentation of projects. Essentially, such computer programs allow users to create a variety of visually appealing electronic slides for presentation. Microsoft PowerPoint is one of the most famous presentation applications.

6. Desktop Publishing Software

The term desktop publishing is usually used to describe the creations of printed documents using a desktop computer. It is a technique of using a personal computer to design images and pages, and assemble type and graphics, then using a laser printer or image-setter to output the assembled pages onto paper, film, or printing plate. These software are used for creating magazines, books, newsletters, and so on. Such software assist in creating sophisticated documents including complicated page designs, detailed illustrations, and camera-ready type faces. Quark Express and Adobe PageMaker are desktop publishing software.

3.6 INTRODUCTION TO PROGRAMMING LANGUAGES

Computers are machines. Unfortunately they cannot understand natural languages, such as Hindi, English, Tamil, etc. that human beings speak and understand. Therefore, to give instructions to computers, different languages have been developed. These languages are called computer languages. To get a particular work done by computers, programmers write instructions using these computer languages. Each computer language has its own vocabulary of a natural language that we speak. Each natural language has its rules and grammar. Similarly, each computer language too has its set of rules that are called as syntax. As computers are not intelligent, we have to use the exact syntax rules of the computer language whenever we write any computer program. Otherwise, the computer will not be able to understand our instructions.

Over the last few decades, several computer languages have developed. Different computer languages are suitable for different applications. For example, COBOL (Common Business Oriented Language) may be more suitable for business applications, whereas FORTRAN may be more suitable for scientific or engineering applications. We can classify all computer languages into three categories.

3.7 TYPES OF PROGRAMMING LANGUAGES

Computer languages are classified into three categories:

1. Machine language
2. Assembly language
3. High level languages

1. Machine Language

The form in which information is denoted or represented by a combination of "1" and "0"s is called machine language. Programs and data are ultimately represented in machine language in memory and other hardware of the computer.

To start with computer programmers used machine language for programming. It was tedious since each operation that the computer has to perform is denoted by a particular combination of"1" s and" 0"s. Also each computer had its own machine language code. One has to remember all these codes to write a program.

While machine language had the drawbacks mentioned above, it was very efficient in using computer circuits. There was no necessity for software to convert since we can directly represent the machine language in the computer circuits without the necessity of conversion.

First Programmer

Lady Lovelace Ada Augusta (officially the first programmer) suggested binary numbers for computer storage instead of decimals. A British mathematician, Alan Mathison Turing, was the first person to recognize that programming in machine language is less time consuming. In 1952, John von Neuman proposed to have new programs loaded from a magnetic tape to read. With differences in magnetic polarities, it can mean either ON of OFF states.

- **Advantages of Machine Language:**

Even though machine languages are not a human friendly language, it offers following advantages.

(a) Translation Free: Machine language is the only language that computers can directly execute without the need for conversion. Even an application using highlevel languages, has to be converted into machine-readable form so that the computer can understand the instructions.

(b) High Speed: Since no conversion is needed, the applications developed using machine languages are extremely fast. It is usually used for complex applications such as space control system, nuclear reactors, and chemical processing.

- **Disadvantages of Machine Language:**

There are many disadvantages in using machine language to develop programs. Some of these are:

(a) Machine Dependent: Every computer type differs from the other, based on its architecture. Hence, an application developed for a particular type of computer may not run on the other type of computer. This may prove costly as well as difficult for the organizations.

(b) Complex Language: Machine language is very difficult to read and write. Since all the data and instructions must be converted to binary code, it is almost impossible to remember the instructions. A programmer must specify each operation, and the specific locations for each piece of data and instructions to be stored. It means that a programmer practically needs to be hardware expert to have proper control over the machine language.

(c) **Error Prone:** Since the programmer has to remember all the opcodes and the memory locations, machine language is bound to be error prone. It requires a super human effort to keep track of the logic of a problem and, therefore, results in frequent programming errors.

(d) **Tedious:** Machine language poses real problems while modifying and correcting a program. Sometimes the programming becomes too complex to modify and the programmer has to rewrite the entire logic again. Therefore, it is very tedious and time-consuming, and since time is a precious commodity, programming using the machine language tends to be costly. Due to its overwhelming limitations, machine language is rarely used nowadays.

2. Assembly Language

As computer field advanced, computer scientists felt the necessity of making computer programming easier. They invented computer languages that are easy to remember and use. These languages called assembly language uses mnemonic codes. for Example: For adding two quantities X and Y, you may code as follows:

ADD X Y

ADD is called operation code that tells the computer what operation it has to perform. X and Y are called operation addresses. These refer to the memory addresses where the quantities you want to add are stored. X refers to the location of first quantity and Y the second quantity. These are called symbolic address, since they do not refer to any fixed address. Software called assembler translates this assembly language program into machine language program which you can load into computer memory and execute.

When the program is loaded into memory for execution the symbolic addresses are automatically converted into actual physical addresses of operands involved in an instruction.

➤ **Assembly language offers the following advantages:**

(a) The assembly language uses mnemonic codes, for programming. So it is easier for the programmer to use assembly language than machine language for programming.

(b) The assemblers, in addition to translating the assembler language program into machine language, list the program statements (called source code) and also the syntax errors that the programmer committed.

➤ **Assembly language has certain disadvantages too**

(a) One has to spend considerable time in writing the assembly language program.

(b) An assembly language program has to be converted into machine language program using assembly.

(c) While it is easier to use than the machine language one still has to remember the operation codes for various operations.

3. High Level Languages

During 1960s computers started to gain popularity and it became necessary to develop languages that were more like natural languages such as English so that a common user could use the computer efficiently. Since assembly language required deep knowledge of computer architecture, it demanded programming as well as hardware skills to use computers. Due to computer's widespread usage, early 1960s saw the emergence of the third generations programming languages (3GL). Languages such as COBOL, FORTRAN, BASIC, and C are examples of 3GLs and are considered high level languages.

High level languages are similar to English language. Programs written using these languages can be machine independent. A single high level statement can substitute several instructions in machine or assembly language. Unlike assembly and machine programs, high level programs may be used with different types of computers with little or no modification, thus reducing the re-programming time.

In highlevel language, programs are written in a sequence of statements to solve a problem. For example, the following BASIC code snippet will calculate the sum of two numbers

```
LET X = 10

LET Y = 20

LET SUM = X + Y     PRINT SUM
```

The first two statements store 10 in variable X (memory locations name) and 20 in variable, Y, respectively. The third statement again creates a variable named SUM, which will store the summation of X and Y value. Finally, the output is printed, that is, the value stored in SUM is printed on the screen.

➤ **Translating High Level Language to Machine Language**

Since computers understand only machine language, it is necessary to convert the high level language programs into machine language codes. This is achieved by using language translators or language processors, generally known as compliers, interpreters or other routines that accepts statements in one language and produces equivalent statements in another language.

(a) **Compiler:** A compiler is a kind of translator that translates a program into another program, known as target language. Usually, the term compiler is used for language translator of highlevel language into machine language. The compiler replaces single high level statement with a series of machine language instructions. A compiler usually resides on a disk or the storage media. When a program is to be compiled, its compiler is loaded into main memory. The compiler stores the entire highlevel program, scans it and translates the whole program into an equivalent machine language program. During the translation process, the compiler reads the source program and checks the syntax (grammatical) errors. If there is any error, the compiler generates an error message, which is usually displayed on the screen. In case of errors, the compiler will not create the object code until all the errors are rectified.

Once the program has been compiled, the resulting machine code is saved in an executable file, which can be run on its own at any time. To be precise, once the executable is generated, there is no need for the actual source code file. Anyway, it is worthwhile to keep the source file(s) because if the source code is modified, it is necessary to recompile the program again to regenerate the executable file containing amendments.

Compilers

Compiler is a program which translates source code written in a particular programming language into computer-readable machine code that can be directly loaded and executed. For each highlevel language, a separate compiler is required. For example, a complier for C language cannot translate a program written in FORTRAN. Hence, to execute both language programs, the host computer must have the compilers of both languages.

(b) **Interpreter:** Unlike compilers, an interpreter translates a statement in a program and executes the statement immediately, before translating the next source language statement. When an error is encountered in the program, the execution of the program is halted and an error message is displayed. Similar to compilers, every interpreted language such as BASIC and LISP has its own interpreters.

Advantages of High Level Languages

High level languages (HLL) are useful in developing complex software, as they support complex data structures. It increases the programmer's productivity (the number of lines of code generated per hour). Unlike assembly language, the programmer does not need to learn the instructions set of each computer being worked with. The various advantages of using high level languages are discussed below:

(a) **Readability:** Since high level languages are closer to natural languages, they are easier to learn and understand. In addition, a programmer does not need to be aware of computer architecture; even a common man can use it without much difficulty. This is the main reason of HLL's popularity.

(b) **Machine Independent:** High level languages are machine independent in the sense that a program created using HLL can be used on different platforms with very little or no change at all.

(c) **Easy Debugging:** High level languages include the support for ideas of abstraction so that programmers can concentrate on finding the solution to the problem rapidly, rather than on low level details of data representation, which results in fewer errors. Moreover, the compilers and interpreters are designed in such a way that they detect and point out the errors instantaneously.

(d) **Easier to Maintain:** As compared to low level languages, the programs written in HLL are easy to modify and maintain because HLL programs are easier to understand.

(e) **Low Development Cost:** High level languages permit faster development of programs. Although a high level program may not be as efficient as an equivalent low level program, but the savings in programmer's time generally outweighs the inefficiencies of the application. This is because the cost of writing a program is nearly constant for each line of code, regardless of the language. Thus, a high level language, where each line of code translates to 10 machine instructions, costs only a fraction as compared to program developed in a low level language.

(f) **Easy Documentation:** Since the statements written in HLL are similar to natural languages, they are easier to understand as compared to low level languages.

Disadvantages of High Level Languages:

The main disadvantages of this language are:

(a) **Poor Control on Hardware:** High level languages are developed to ease the pressure on programmers, so that they do not have to know the intricacies of hardware. As a result, sometimes the applications written in high level languages cannot completely harness the total power available at hardware level.

(b) **Less Efficient:** The HLL applications are less efficient as far as computation time is concerned. This is because, unlike low level languages, high level languages must be created and sent through another processing program known as a compiler. This process of translation increases the execution time of an application. Programs written in high level languages take more time to execute, and require more memory space. Hence, critical applications are generally written in low level languages.

3.8 ALGORITHM

An algorithm is a step by step procedure for solving a problem.

Properties of an Algorithm:

1. It should be simple.
2. It should be clear with no ambiguity.
3. It should lead to a unique solution of the problem.
4. It should involve a finite number of steps.
5. It should have the capability to handle some unexpected situations which may arise during the solution of a problem (e.g., division by zero).

Steps Involved in Developing an Algorithm:

1. Clearly understand the problem.
2. Study the outputs to be generated so that the input can be specified.
3. Design the process which will produce the desired result after taking the input.
4. Refine the process.
5. Test the algorithm by giving the test data and see if the desired output is generated. If not, make appropriate changes in the process and repeat the process.

Advantages of Algorithm:

1. It is very easy to understand.
2. It is easy to first develop an algorithm, then convert it into a flowchart and then into a computer program.
3. It is independent of programming languages.
4. It is easy to debug (correct) as every step has got its own logical sequence.
5. It has got a beginning and an end within which there are definite procedures to produce output(s) within a specified period of time.

Disadvantages of Algorithm:

It is time consuming and difficult as an algorithm is developed first which is converted into a flowchart and then into a computer program.

Problems:

I. The length and width of a rectangle are given. Write an algorithm to find its area.

   1. Read the length and width
   2. Calculate Area = length x width
   3. Print the Area
   4. Stop

II. Sales commission is calculated as 10% of sales amount if it exceeds Rs.10,000, otherwise 5% of sales amount; write an algorithm for this.

   1. Read sales amount
   2. If sales amount > 10,000 then

      Commission = 10000 * 10/100

      else commission = 10000 * 5/100
   3. Print commission
   4. Stop

III. Write an algorithm to calculate the simple interest and compound interest

1. Read P, N, R
2. Calculate simple interest = P*N*R /100
3. Calculate compound interest = $P*(1+R/100)^N - P$
4. Print simple interest, compound interest
5. Stop

3.9 FLOWCHARTS

A flowchart is a diagrammatic (or) pictorial representation of the algorithm (or) the procedure to solve a problem. Flow charts are constructed by using special geometrical symbols. Each symbol represents an activity. The activity may be input / output of data, computation / processing of data, taking a decision, terminating the solution etc. The symbols are joined by arrows to obtain a complete flowchart.

Advantages of using Flowcharts:

1. **Communication:** Flowcharts are a good visual and for communicating the logic of a problem.
2. **Quicker grasp of relationships:** Before any problem could be solved, the relationship that exists among problem elements must be identified. Current and proposed procedures may be understood through the use of flowcharts.
3. **Effective analysis:** The flowchart becomes a model (or) blue print of program (or) system that can be broken down into detailed parts for study.
4. **Proper program documentation:** Flow charts serve as a good program documentation which is needed for the following reasons:
   (a) If programs are modified in future, these flowchart will brief the programmer on what was originally done.
   (b) When staff changes occur, these serve as a training function by helping new employees in understanding the existing programs.
   (c) These will and greatly in future program conversion when new hardware / software packages are acquired.
5. **Efficient coding:** Instructions coded in programming language may be checked against the flowchart to ensure that no steps are omitted.
6. **Orderly debugging and testing of programs:** The flowcharts help in debugging process i.e., it helps in detecting, locating and removing mistakes. The programmer can refer to the flow chart as he re-checks the coding steps and logic of the written instructions.
7. **Efficient program maintenance:** The maintenance of program is facilitated by flowcharts. The chart helps the programmer to concentrate attention on that part of the information flow which is to be modified.

Limitations of Using Flowcharts:

1. **Complex logic:** When the program logic is complex, the flowchart quickly becomes complex.
2. **Alternations & modifications:** If alternations are required; the flowchart may require re-drawing completely.
3. **Reproduction:** As the flowchart symbols cannot be typed, reproduction of flowcharts is often a problem.
4. **No uniform practice:** Is followed for drawing flowcharts as it is used as aid to the program.

5. **Standardization:** Flowcharts, although easy to follow, are not such a natural way of expressing procedures as writing in English.

3.10 TYPES OF FLOWCHARTS

There are two types of flowcharts available, namely:

1. Program Flowcharts
2. System Flowcharts

1. Program Flowchart:

Program Flowchart is a diagrammatic representation of the steps to be performed to solve a problem. Such a diagram provides complete and detailed sequence of operations to be performed in the central processing unit of the computer for executing the program.

These flowcharts display specific operations and decisions and their sequence within the program. Generally the programmer will use these flowcharts to translate the elementary steps of a procedure into a program.

2. System Flowchart:

System Flowchart is designed to present an overview of the data flow through all parts of a data processing system. The system flowchart mainly consists of

(i) The sources from which input data is prepared and the devices used,

(ii) The processing steps (or) sequence of operations involved,

(iii) The final and intermediary outputs prepared and devices used for their storage.

System Flowcharts are usually prepared as an aid to the system analysts to permit them to understand some specific operations and to get an overall view of the operations.

Symbols (conventions) used in Program Flowcharts:

1. Terminal Symbol

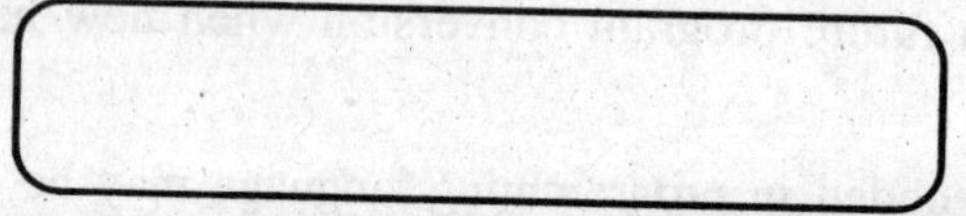

The terminal symbol is used to indicate the point at which a flowchart begins and ends. It is accepted procedure to insert the word START and STOP with the terminal symbol as shown below:

2. Input / Output Symbol

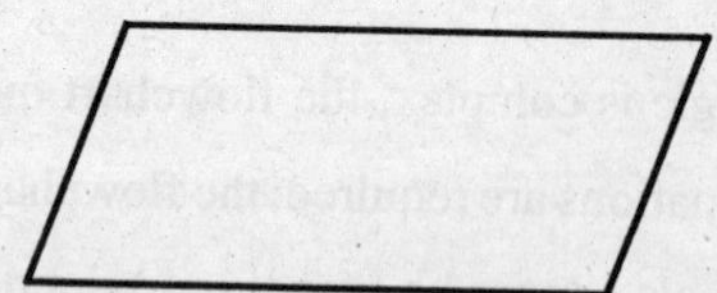

In a program flowchart, the input / output symbol identifies the positioning of input and output operations.

The following figure depicts an input and output operations:

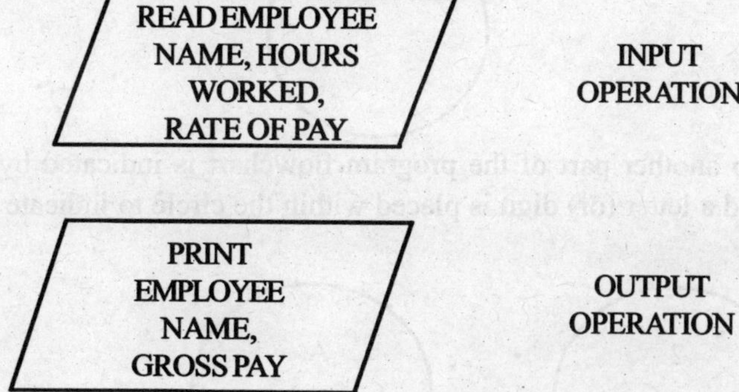

3. **Processing Symbol:**

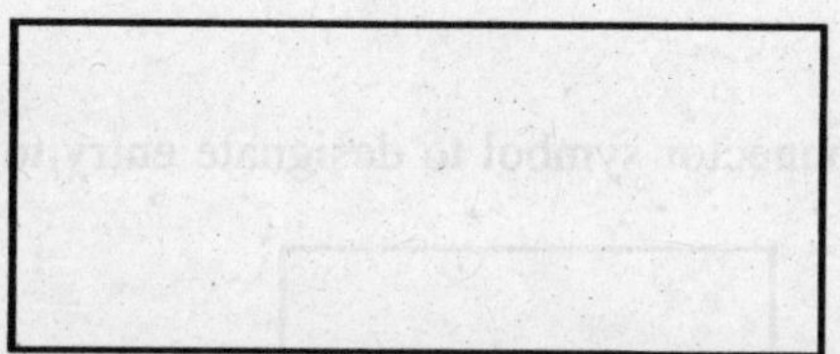

The processing related to all types of data is indicated by the processing symbol. Using this symbol we can define computations, move data from one variable to another variable. The following shows a computation:

COMMISSION = TOTAL SALES * 0.20

4. **Decision Symbol**

To solve business problems, many comparisons (logical operations) are made before selecting the best alternative. Logical operations are indicated in flowcharts through decision symbol.

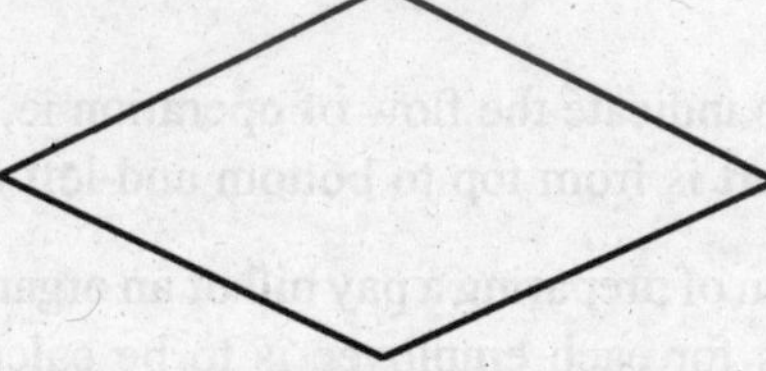

The results of the comparisons are given in terms of YES (OR) NO responses. Note that the YES (OR) NO responses define the only two exits from the decision symbol, e.g.:

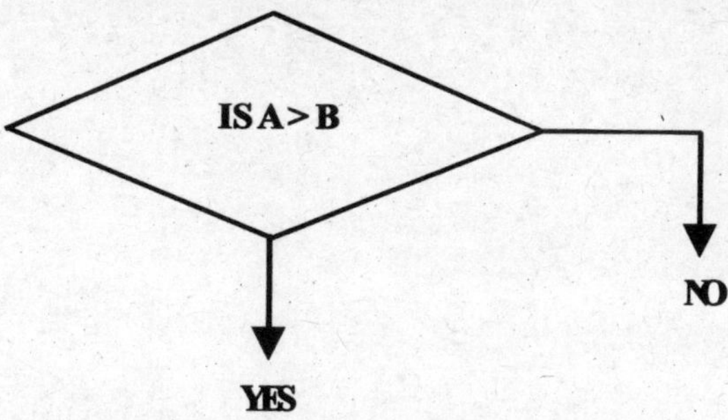

5. Connector

An entry from (or) an exit to another part of the program flowchart is indicated by this symbol. A connector symbol is represented by a circle and a letter (or) digit is placed within the circle to indicate the link.

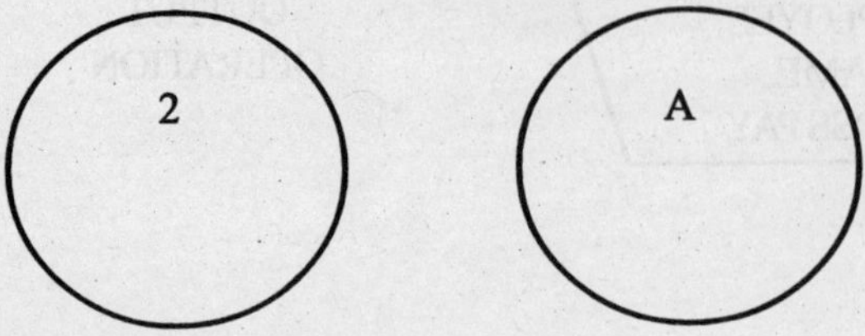

6. Off-page Connector

It is a connector used instead of the connector symbol to designate entry to (or) exit from a page.

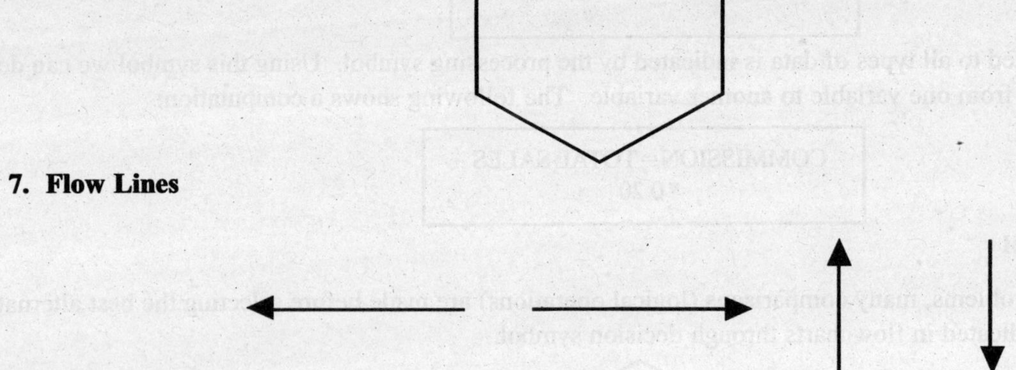

7. Flow Lines

Flow lines with arrow heads are used to indicate the flow of operation ie, exact sequence in which instructions are to be executed. The normal flow of flowchart is from top to bottom and left to right.

For example: Let us consider the problem of preparing a pay bill of an organization. Given the identification number, name, basic pay, allowances and deductions for each employee is to be calculated. Net pay is given as basic pay + allowances – deductions.

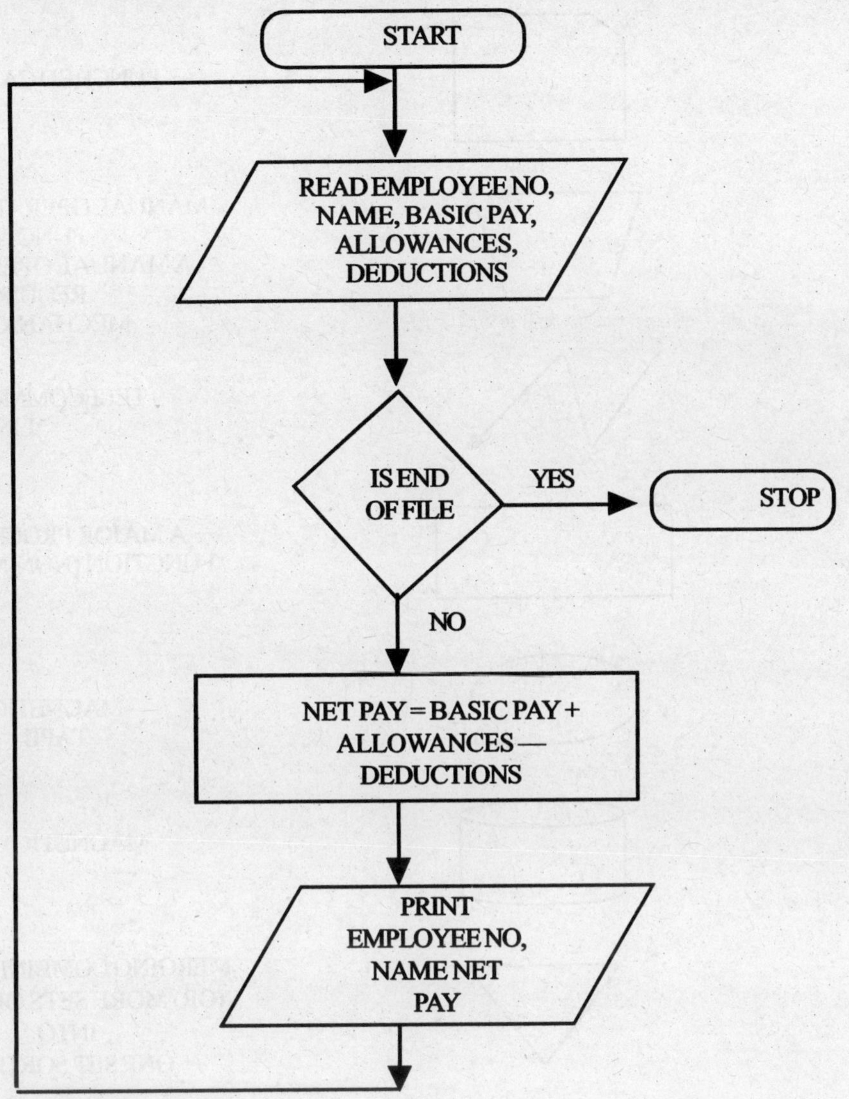

System Flowchart Symbols

No.	Description
4	PUNCHED CARD
5	MANUAL OPERATION AND KEY FUNCTION. A MANUAL OPERATION NOT REQUIRING MECHANICAL AID
6	TELECOMMUNICATION LINK
7	A MAJOR PROCESSING FUNCTION (NON-MANUAL)
8	MAGNETIC TAPE
9	MAGNETIC DISK
10	MERGING COMBINING TWO (OR) MORE SETS OF ITEMS INTO ONE SET SORTING
11	AN OPERATION OF ARRANGING ITEMS IN DESCENDING (OR) ASCENDING ORDER
12	ON LINE STORAGE
13	OFF LINE STORAGE
14	VISUAL DISPLAY

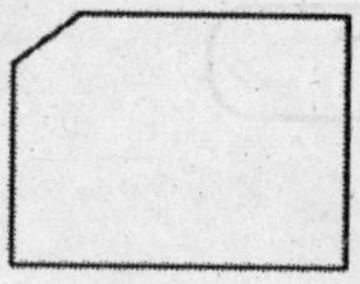

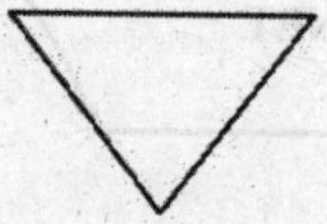

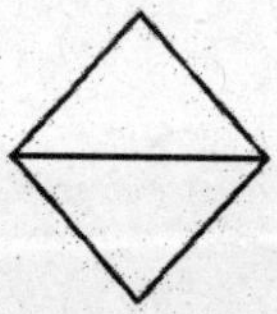

For a System Flowchart

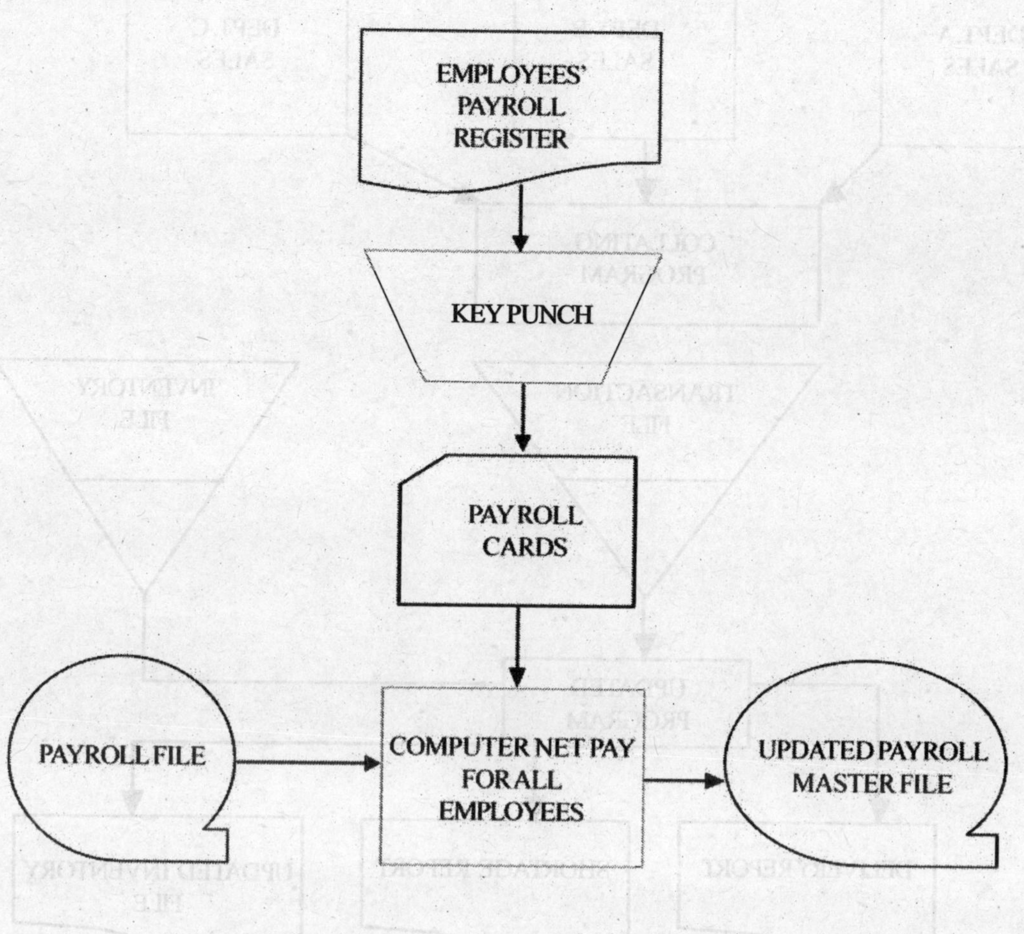

Problem

1. A department store has 3 departments situated in the ground floor, first floor and second floor of a building. The daily transactions of each store are sent to the computer installed in the basement by cables. These transaction reports are collected and put into a transaction file which is then compared with the inventory file. Then the inventory file is updated and daily reports and an invention shortage report are printed. Draw a system flowchart for this problem.

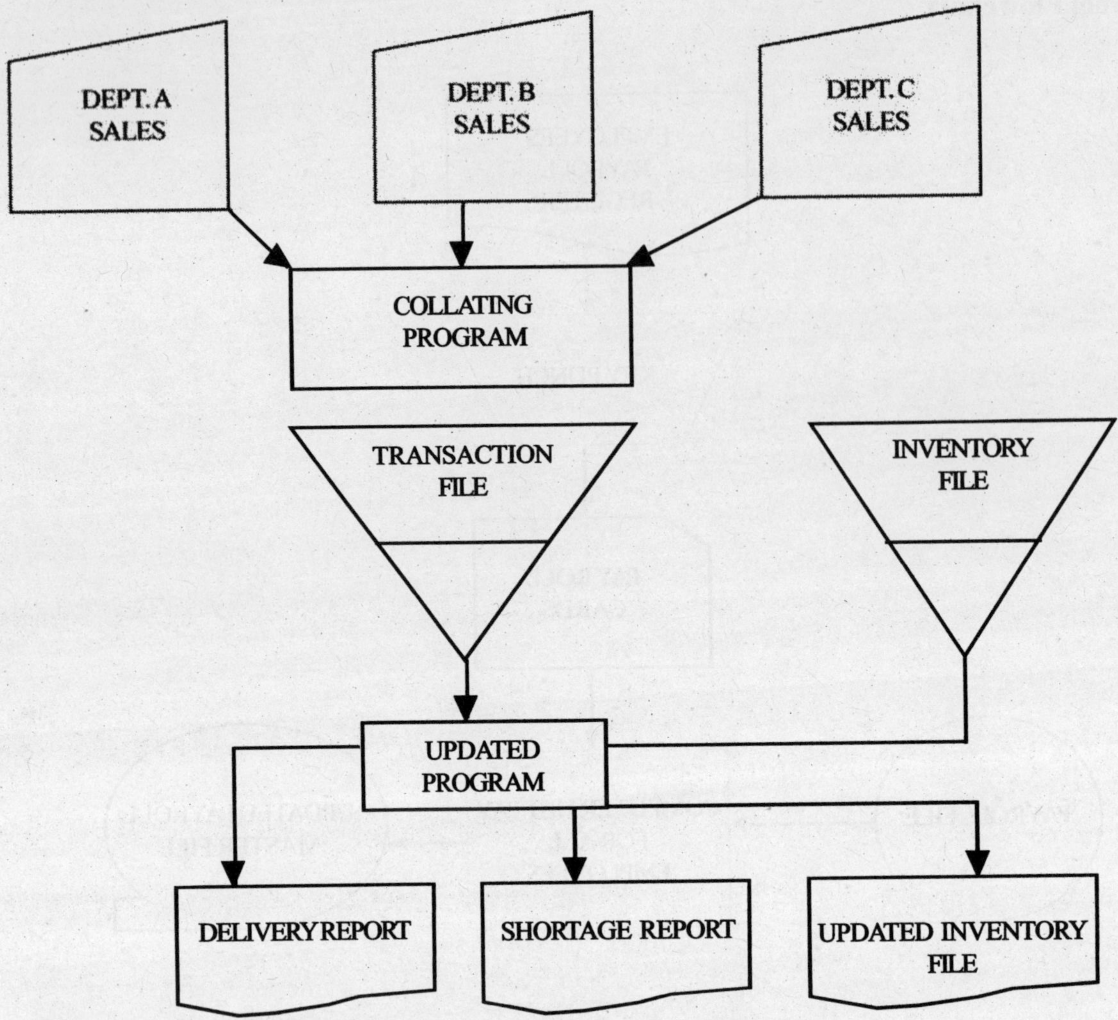

2. Write a system flowchart for the following organizational setup. A company receives orders from customers and sends sales orders to the customers and billing office. The billing office sends a shipping order to the warehouse to find out whether the item is in stock (or) not. The warehouse calls for the old inventory file and if the item is in stock, sends a shipping notice to the customer and to the delivery department . the inventory file is also updated. The delivery office now sends the item to the customer with a bill. The customer signs duplicate copy of the bill, which is sent to the billing office for necessary action. If on the other hand, the item is not found in the inventory a cancellation order is sent to the customer and a copy of it is sent to the billing office, which in turn sends a repayment to the customer.

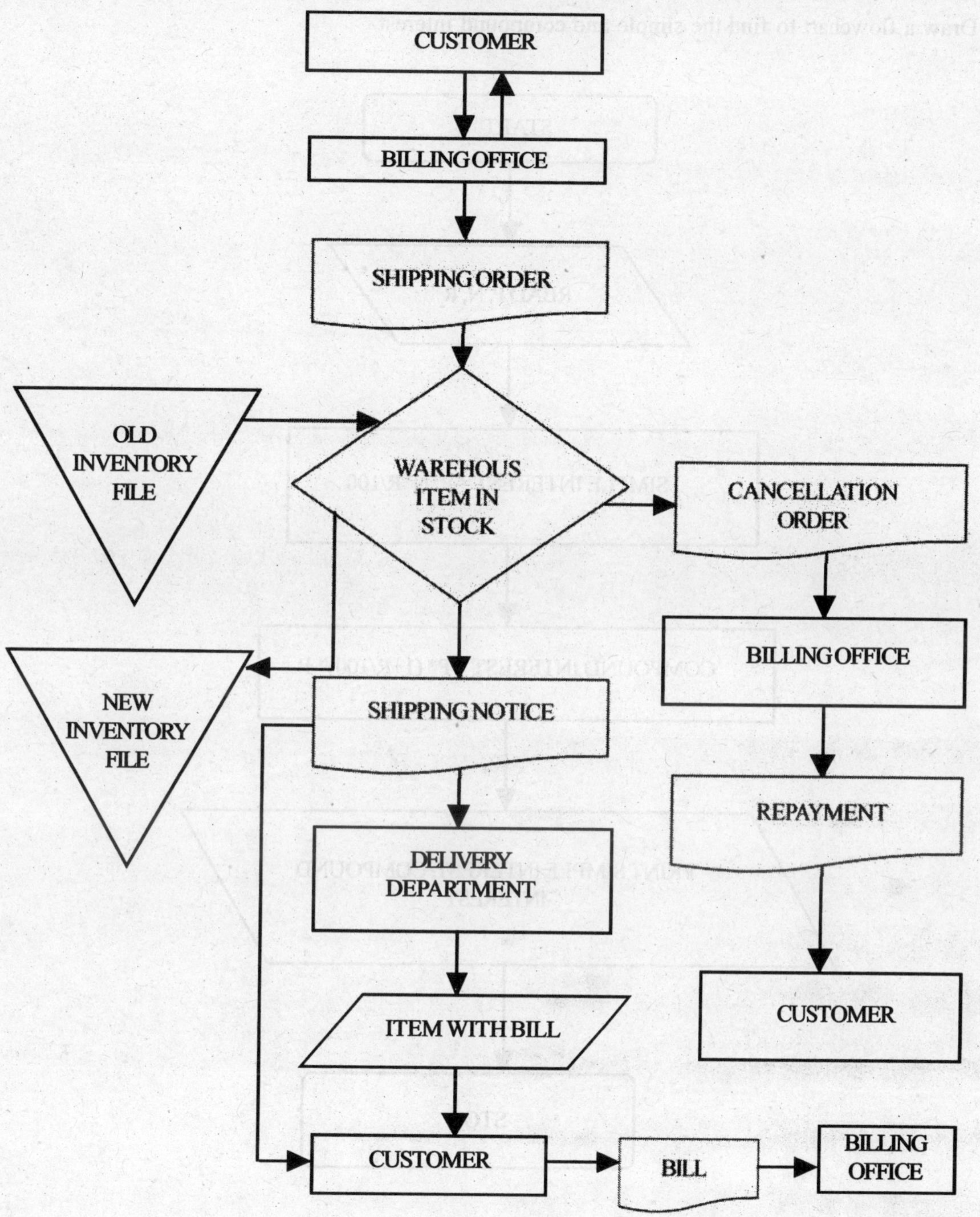
CUSTOMER
BILLING OFFICE
SHIPPING ORDER
OLD INVENTORY FILE
WAREHOUS ITEM IN STOCK
CANCELLATION ORDER
NEW INVENTORY FILE
SHIPPING NOTICE
BILLING OFFICE
REPAYMENT
DELIVERY DEPARTMENT
CUSTOMER
ITEM WITH BILL
CUSTOMER
BILL
BILLING OFFICE

3. Draw a flowchart to find the simple and compound interest

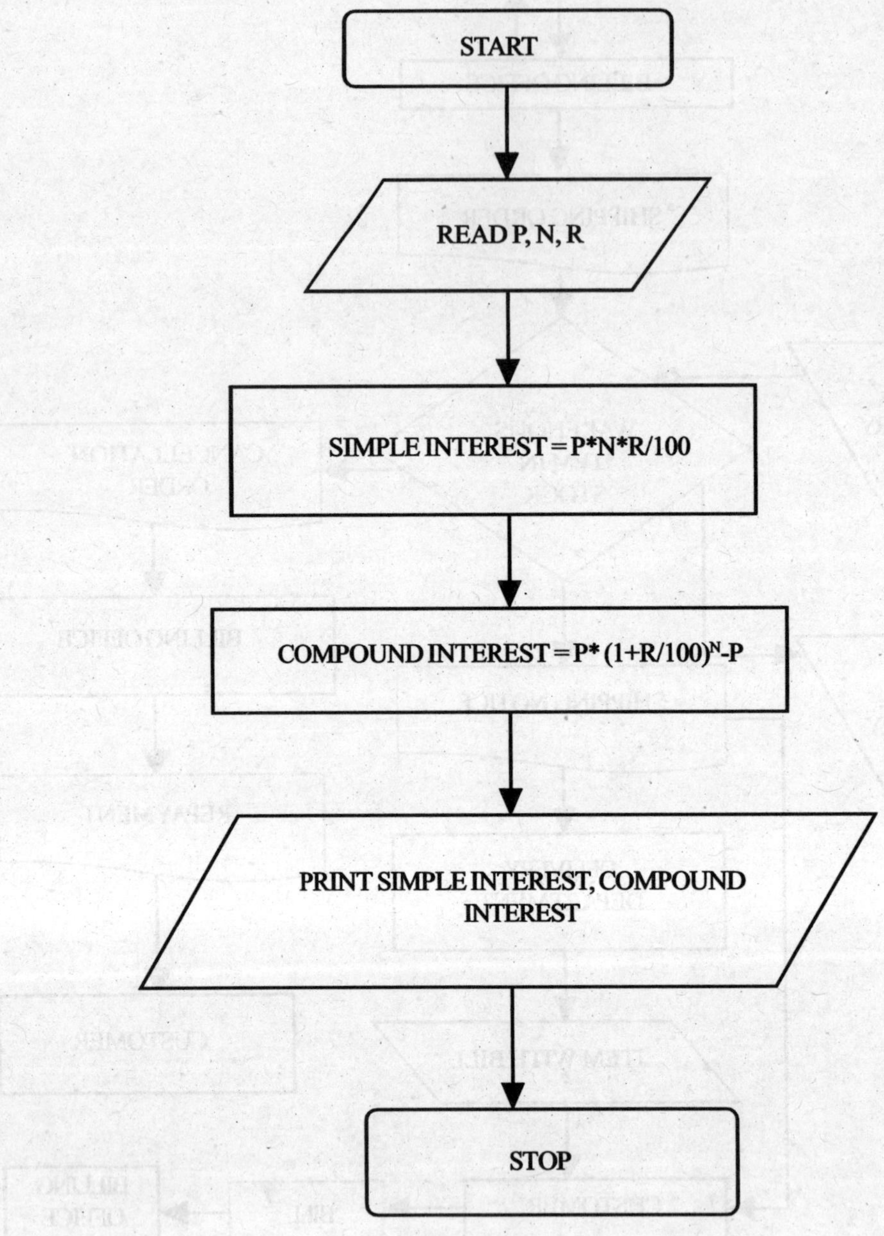

4. **Draw a flowchart to find the largest of given 3 numbers.**

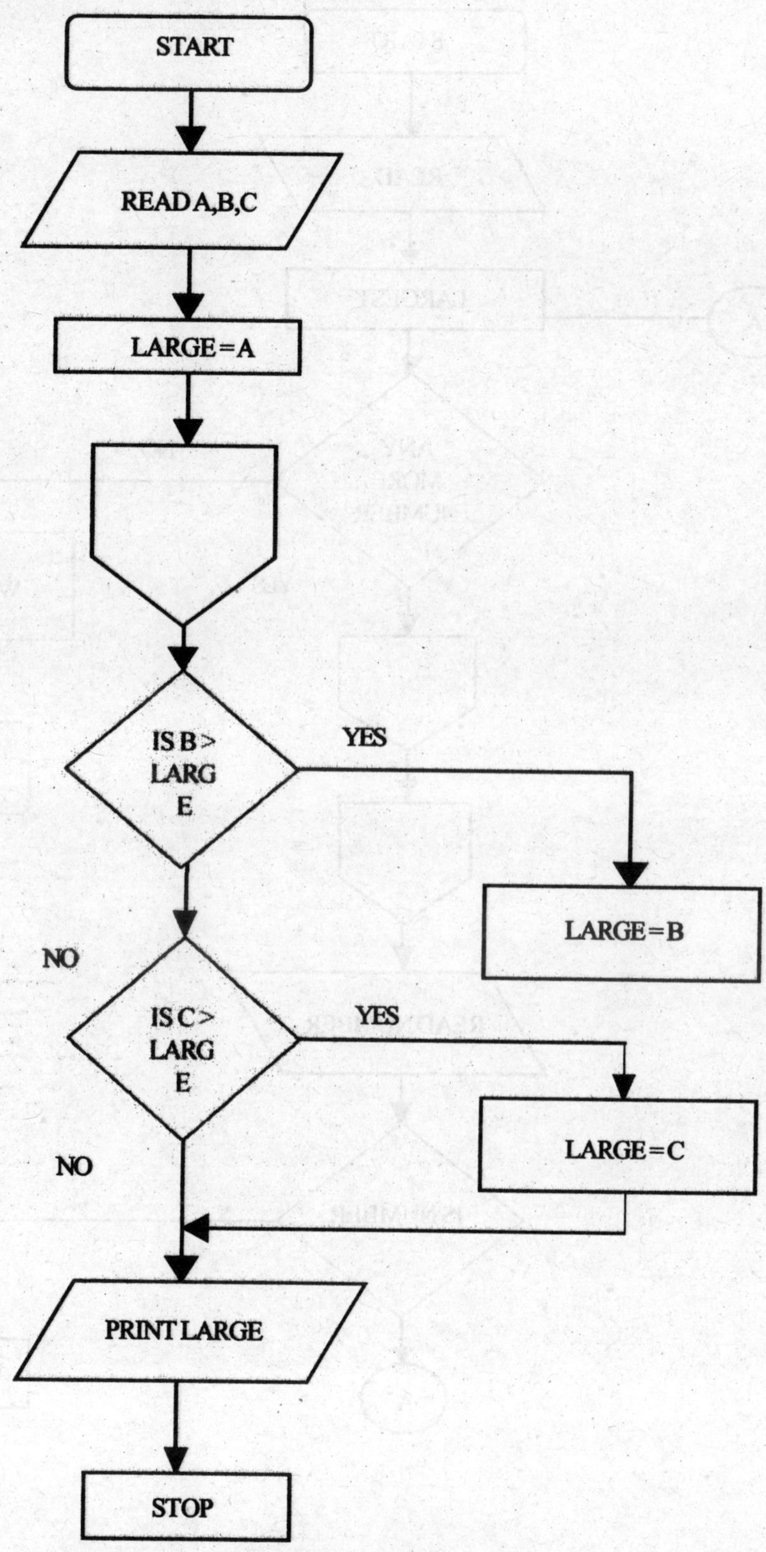

5. Draw a flowchart to pick the largest of a set of numbers.

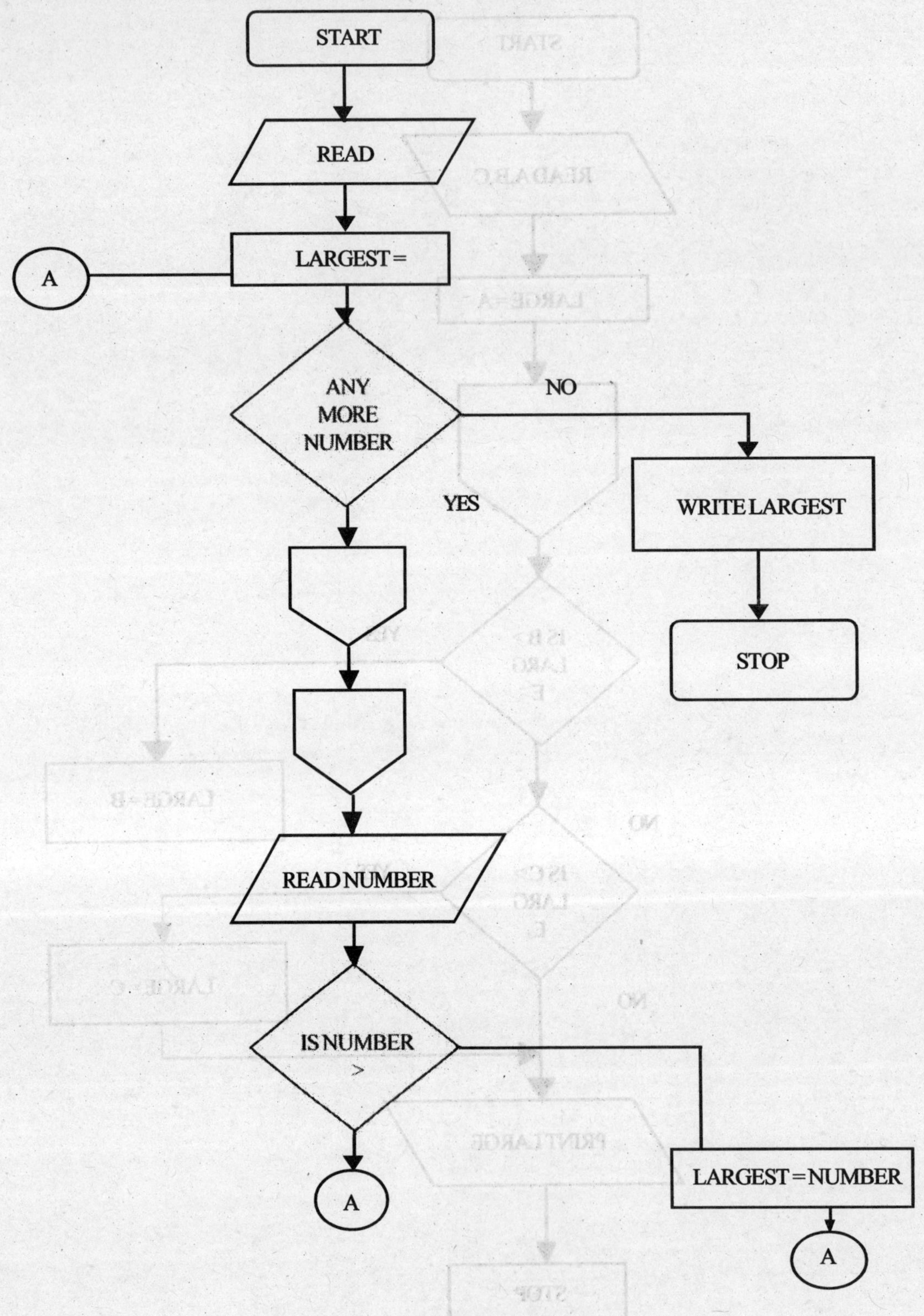

6. **Draw a flowchart to find the mean of (average) given 10 number APR' 94**

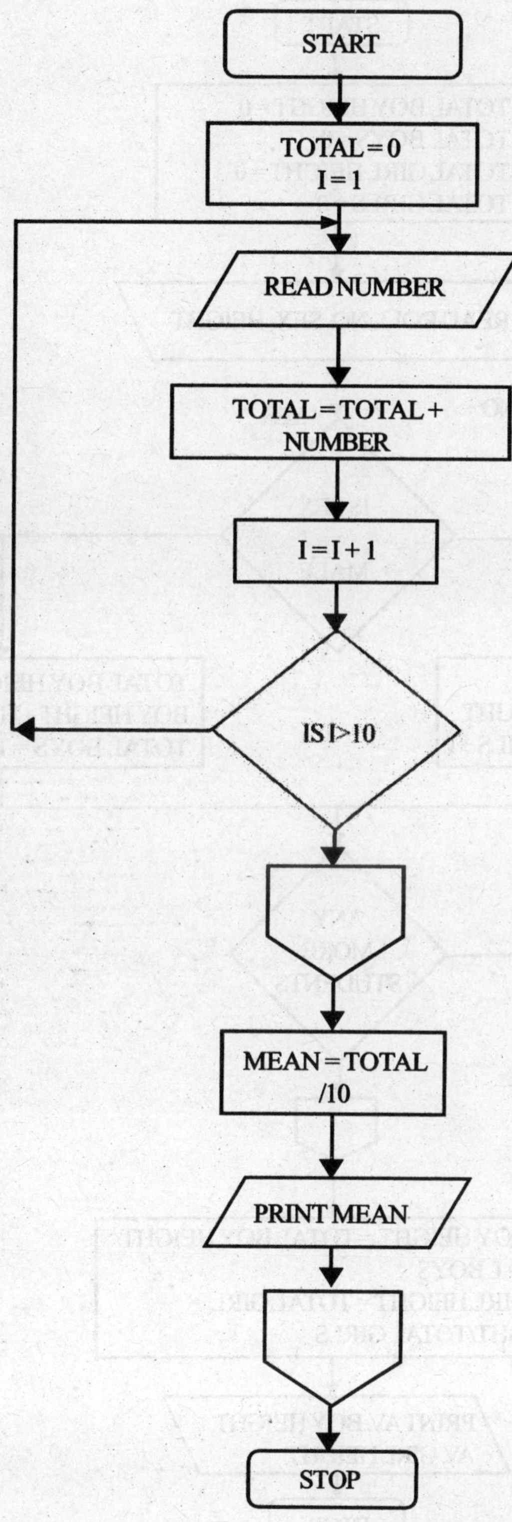

7. Draw a flowchart to find average heights of boys and girls.

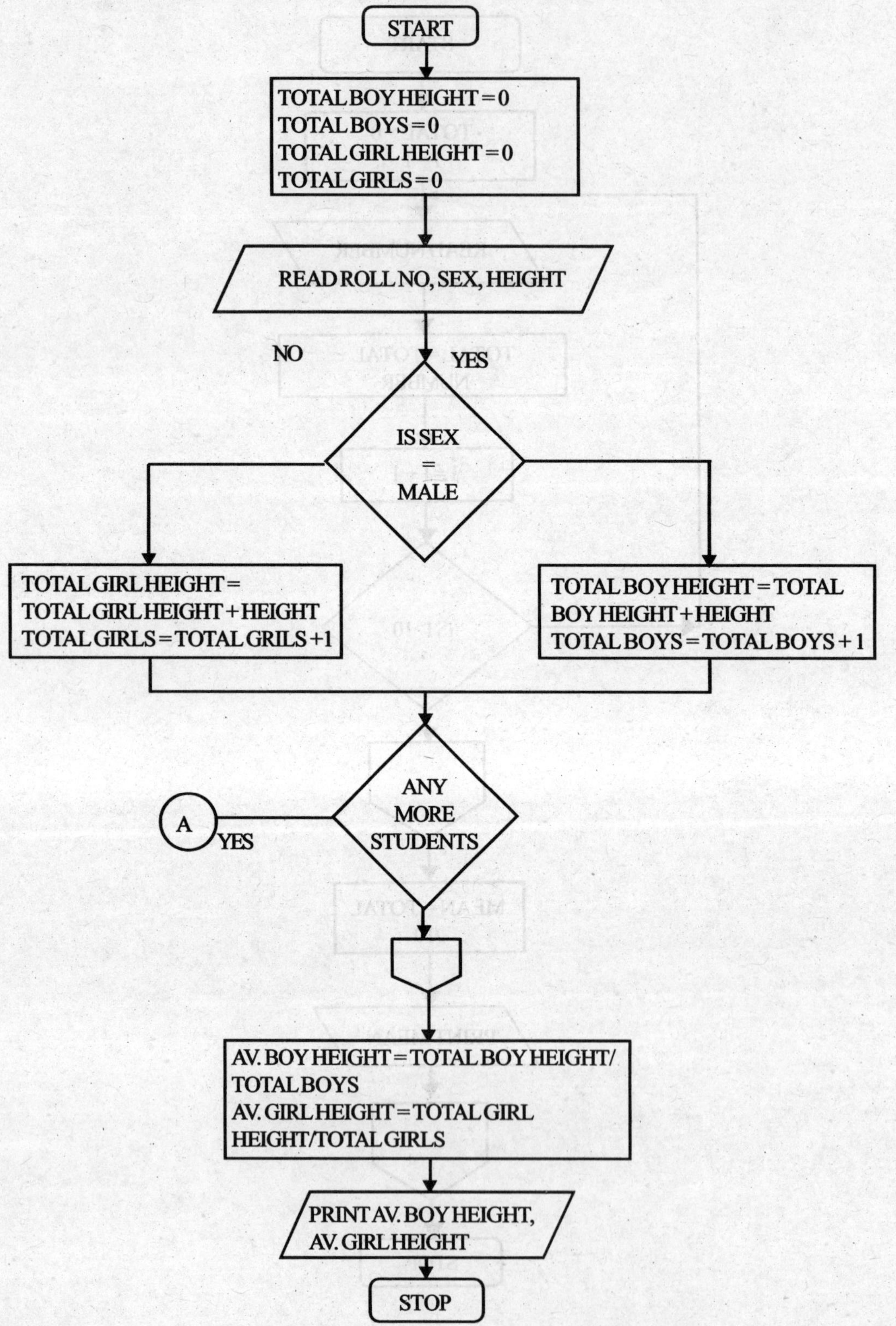

8. Draw a flowchart to examine if the number is positive, zero (or) negative

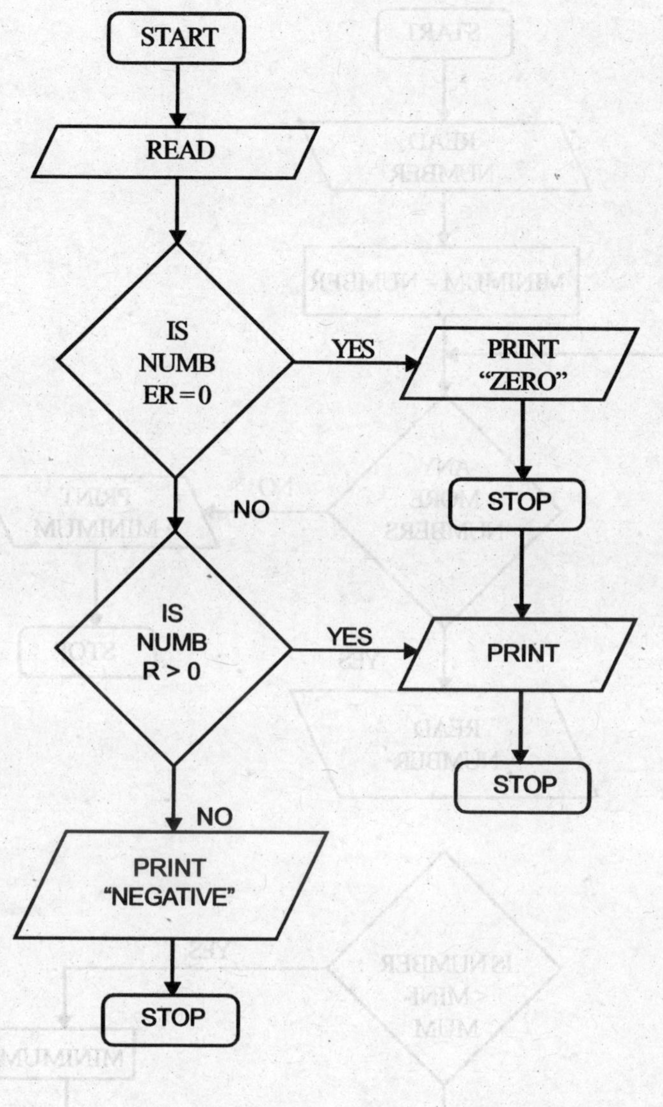

9. Draw a flowchart to find the minimum of given number.

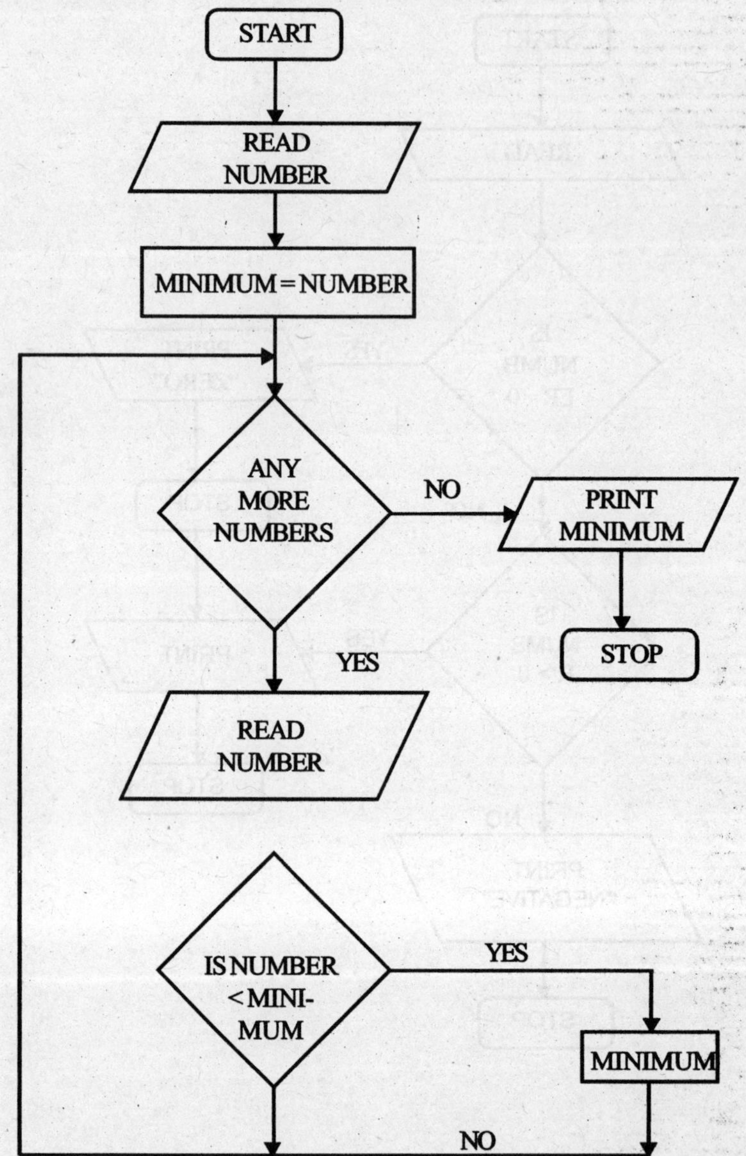

10. **Draw a flowchart to find the sum of given number**

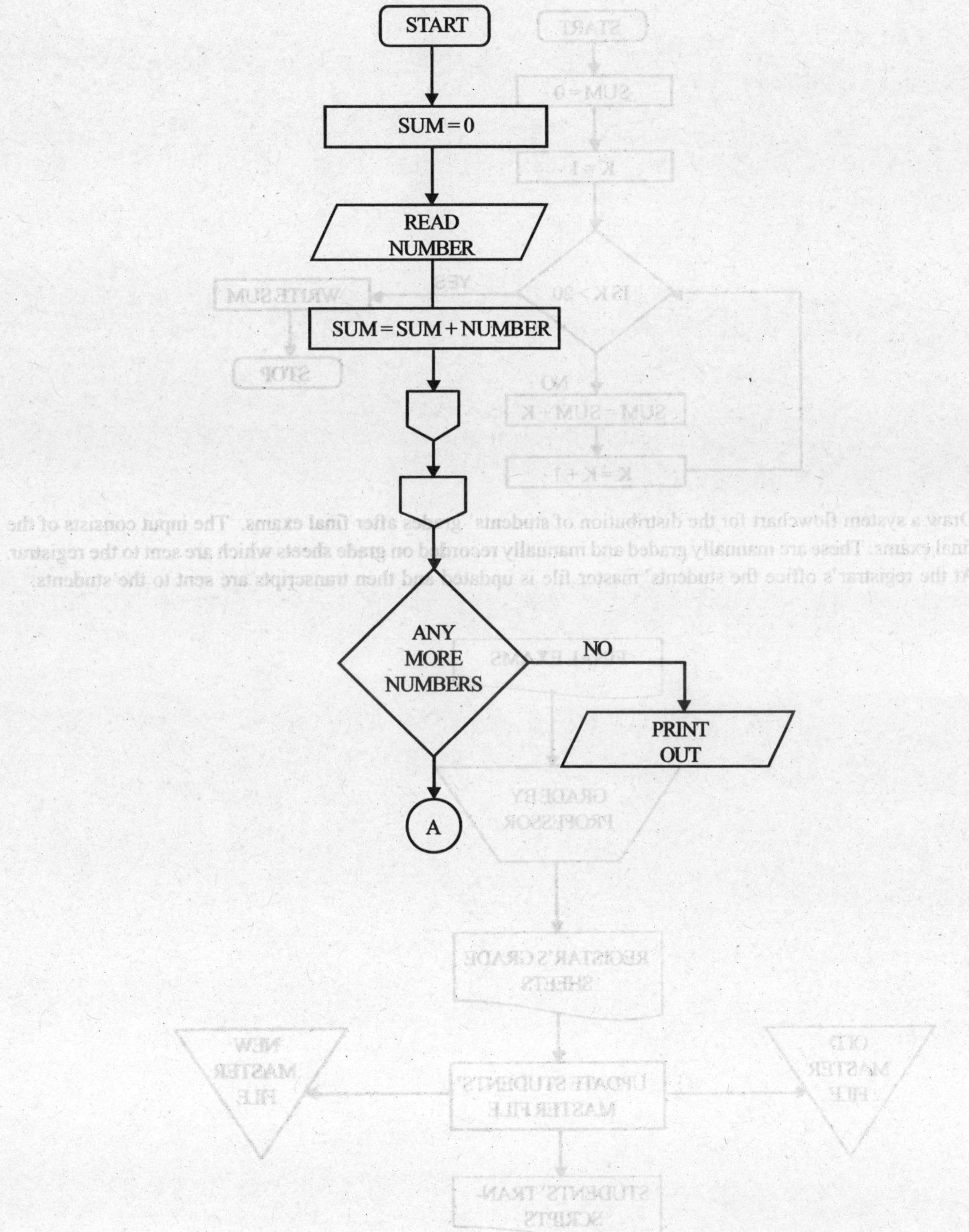

11. **Draw a flowchart to find the sum of first twenty integers**

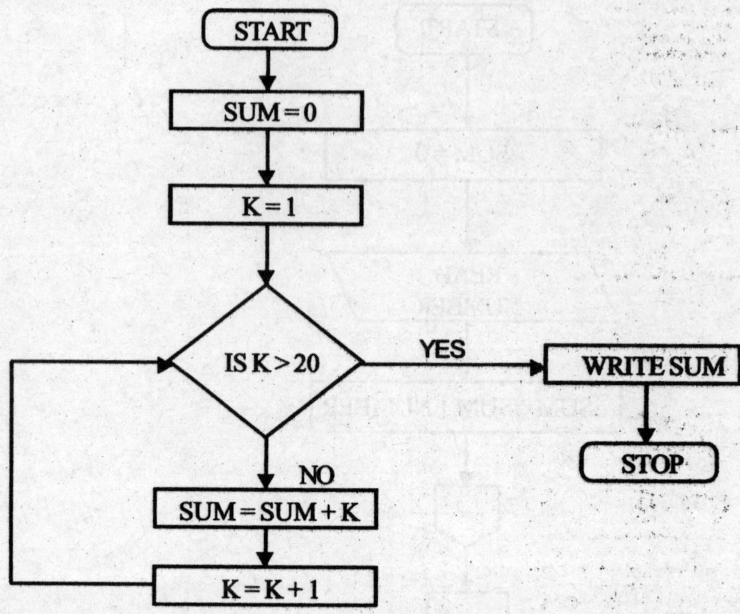

12. **Draw a system flowchart for the distribution of students' grades after final exams. The input consists of the final exams. These are manually graded and manually recorded on grade sheets which are sent to the registrar. At the registrar's office the students' master file is updated and then transcripts are sent to the students.**

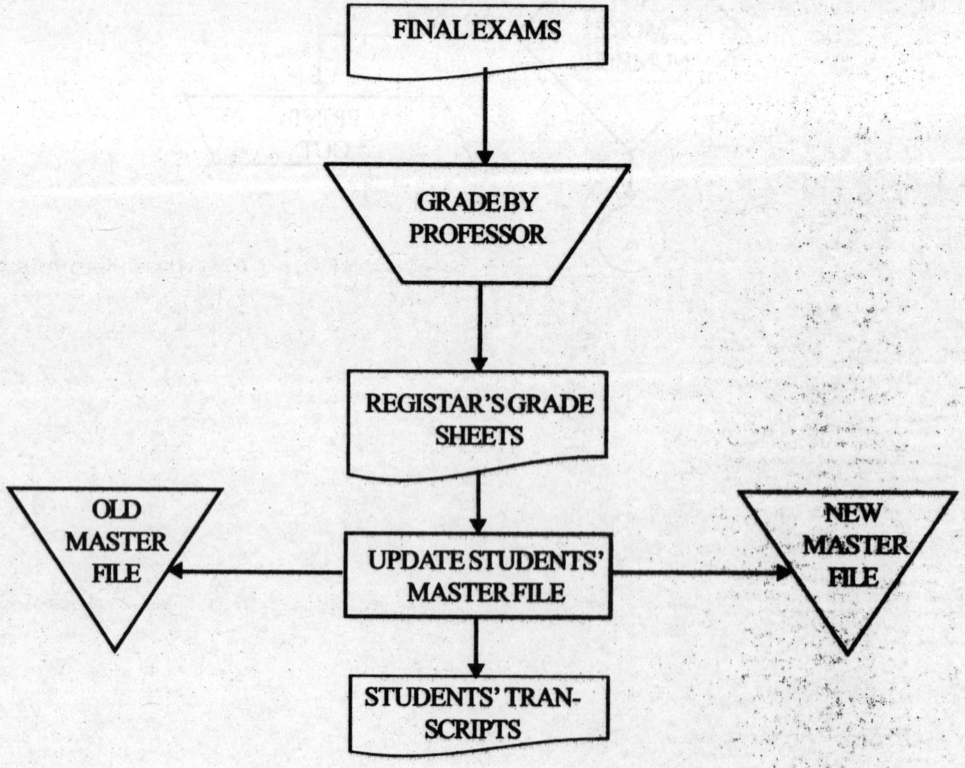

13. Suppose that Rs.5000 is deposited in a savings account in 1980 for fifteen years, and suppose that the bank pays a per cent interest, compounded annually. Draw a flowchart which outputs the YEAR and AMOUNT in the account from 1980 until 1995, when the fifteen years are over.

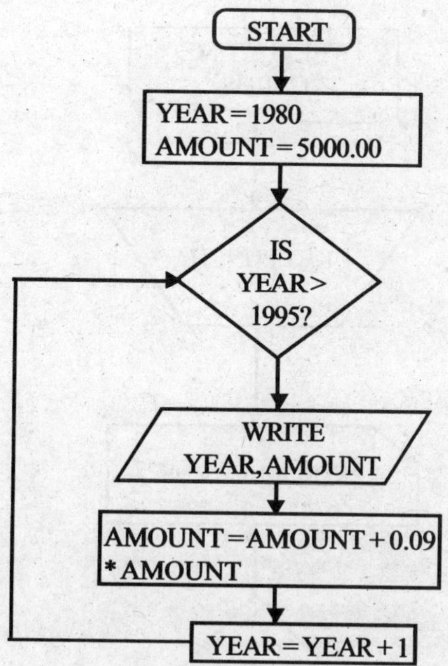

14. Consider the equation $y = x^3 - 8x^2 + 5x - 4$. Draw a flowchart which calculates y for values of x from –4 to 4 in steps of 0.2, and prints each x and its corresponding y.

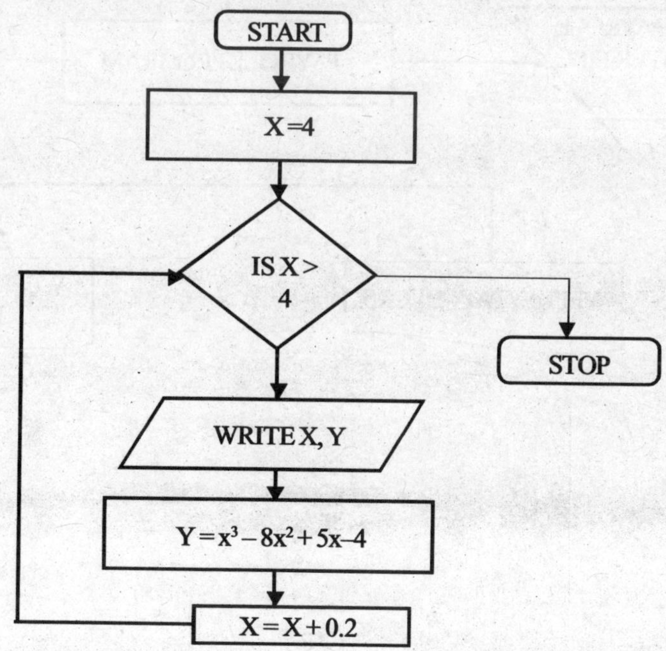

15. Weakly time cards are submitted by the employees. The data are recorded on punched cards, which are then sorted. A payroll program uses these cards together with the master payroll file to output the weekly paychecks for the employees, and a weekly payroll report for the employer. Draw the system flowchart.

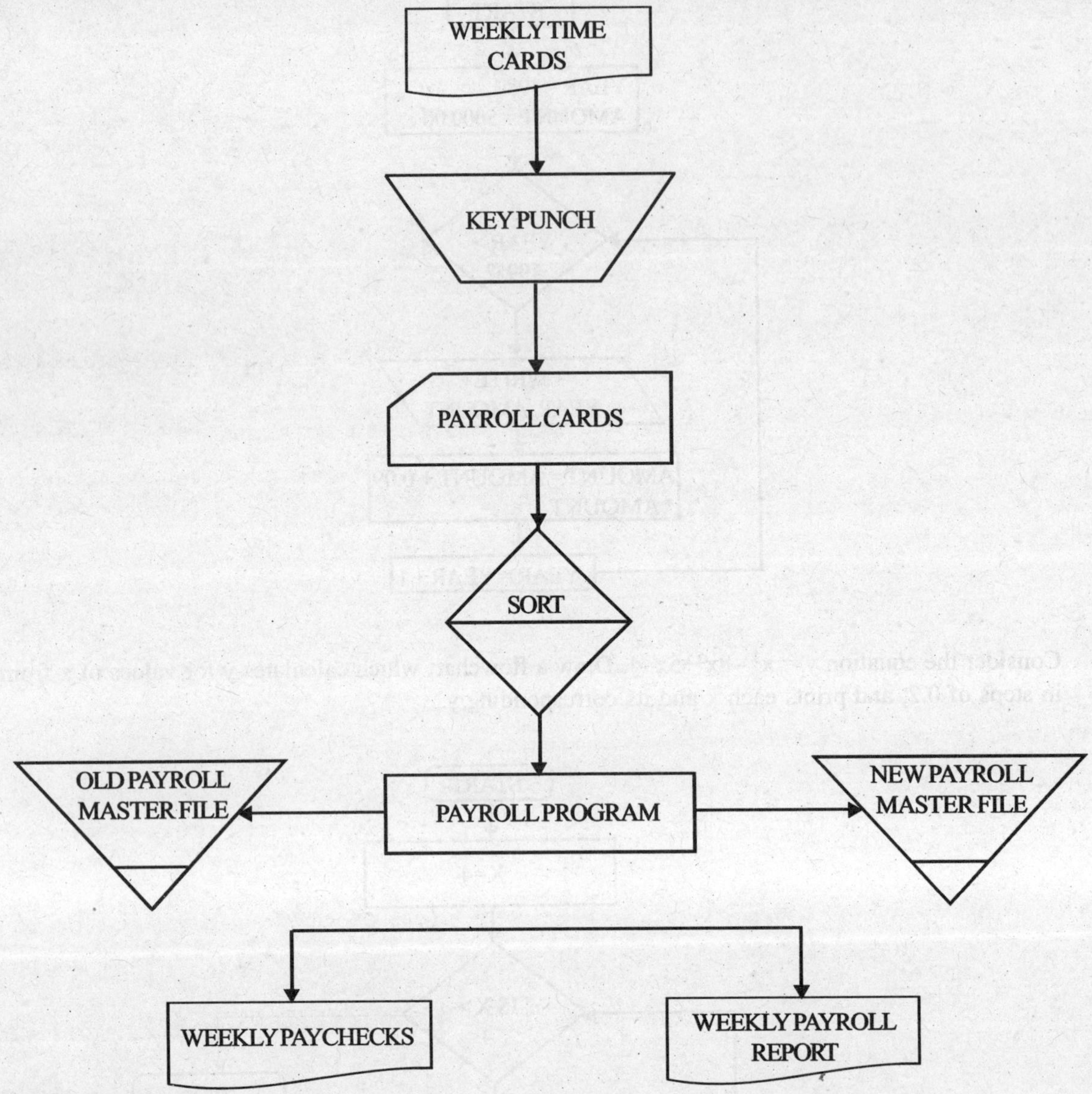

16. A customer requests space on a particular airplane flight. The salesperson sends the request by telecommunication to the central reservations headquarters, where a reservation program checks the request against the master reservations file. Either the "NO SPACE" signal is given to the salesperson, or the "SPACE AVAILABLE" signal is given to the salesperson and the reservations file is updated. In the latter case, the salesperson writes the flight ticket for the customer. Draw the system flowchart.

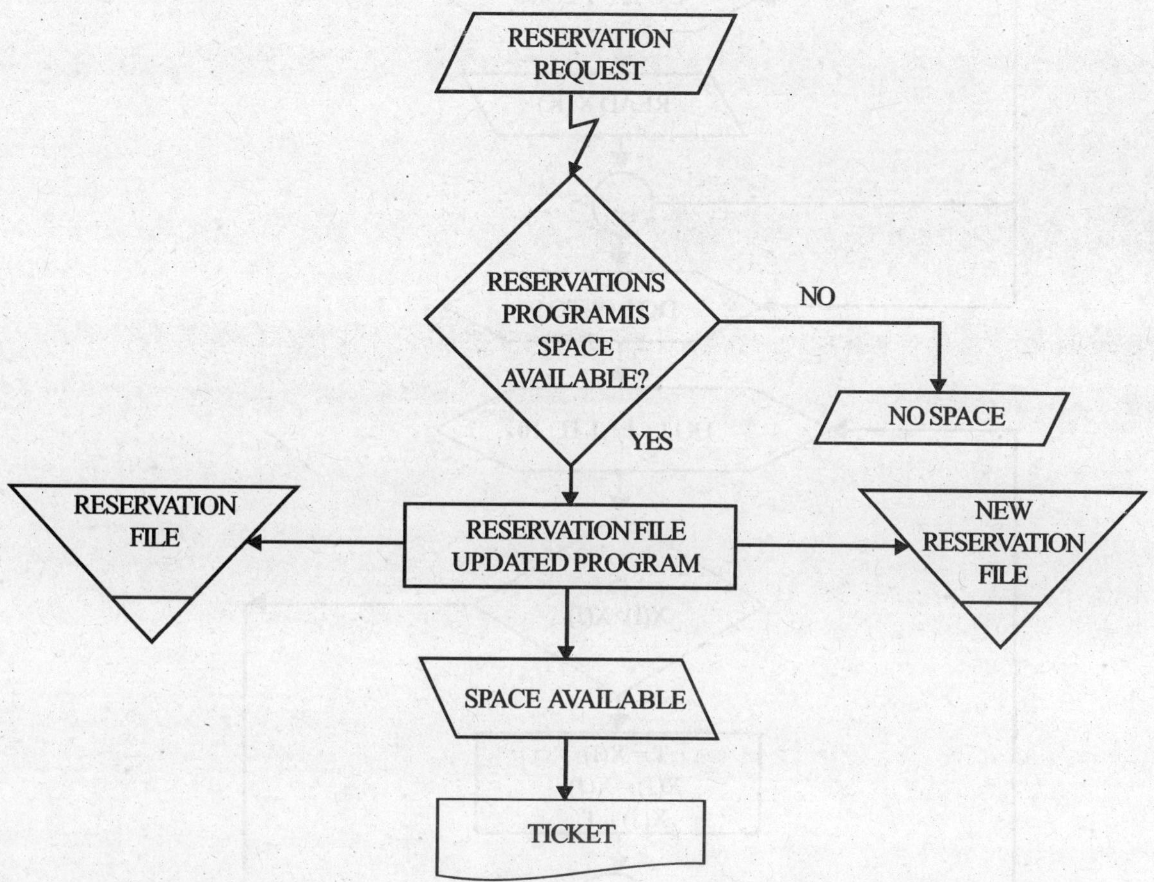

17. Draw a flowchart to sort the given 10 numbers in descending order. APR' 94

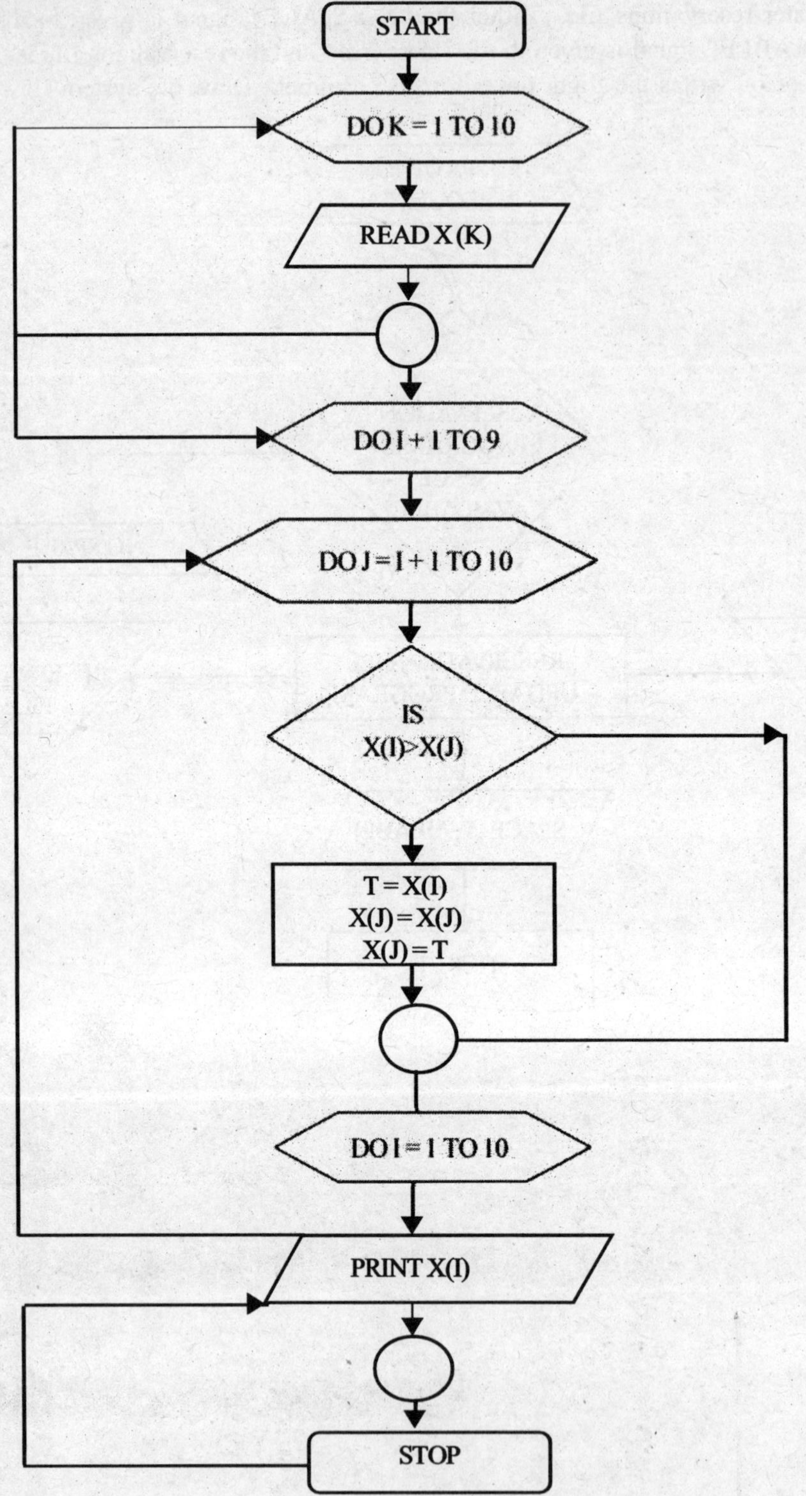

18. Draw a system flowchart for the updating of a banks account records. Observe that the deposits are inputted by means of punched cards and that there is a printed report document showing overdrawn accounts.

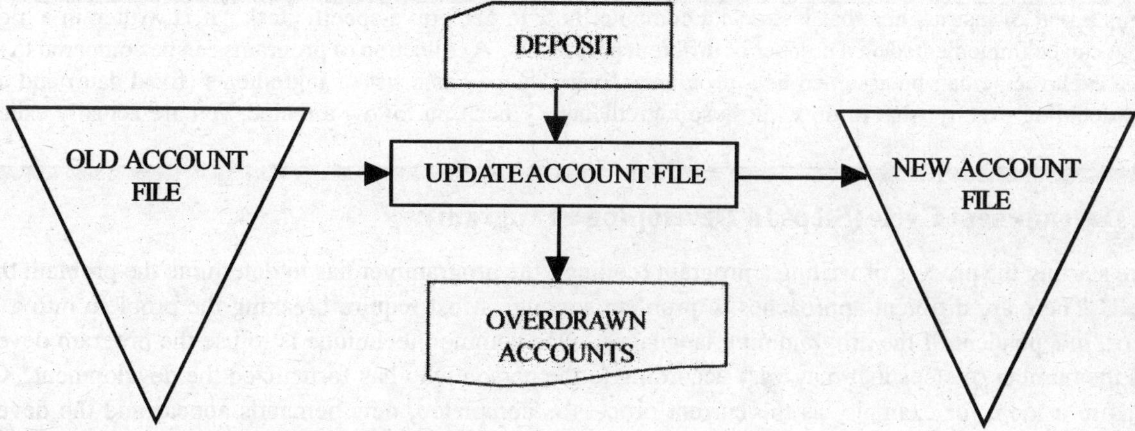

3.11 PROGRAM DEVELOPMENT

The computer has emerged as the most useful machine in recent times. It can perform a variety of tasks like receiving data, processing it, and producing useful results. However, being a machine, the computer cannot perform on its own. A computer needs to be instructed to perform even a simple task like adding two numbers. Computers work on a set of instructions called computer program, which clearly specify the ways to carry out a task. An analogy of this may be thought of as the instructions given by the manager or team leader to its team. The team members follow those instructions and accordingly perform their duties. Similarly, a computer also takes instructions, in the form of computer programs, and carries out the requested task.

Now the question arises how human beings instruct computers. We, as human beings, use natural languages such as English, Spanish, or French to communicate. Similarly, a user communicates with the computer in a language understood by it. Note that human beings cannot interact directly with the computer using natural languages because thus far we have not developed such computers that can comprehend natural languages. Rather the instructions, provided in the form of computer programs, are developed using computer or programming languages. This chapter will provide some of the most prominent concepts related to computer programming and languages.

3.12 DEVELOPING A PROGRAM

A program consists of a series of instructions that a computer processes to perform the required operation. In addition, it also includes some fixed data, required to perform the instructions, and the process of defining those instructions and data. Thus, in order to design a program, a programmer must determine three basic rudiments:

- The instructions to be performed.
- The order in which those instructions are to be performed.
- The data required to perform those instructions.

To perform a task using a program, a programmer has to consider various inputs of the program along with the process, which is required to convert the input into desired output. Suppose we want to calculate the sum of two numbers, A and B, and store the sum in C, here A and B are the inputs, addition is the process, and C is the output of the program.

$$AB \rightarrow C = A + B \rightarrow C$$

Input Processing Output

Development of a Program

A program is a seat of instructions that instructs a computer how to perform a specific task. It is written in a high level language that can be implemented on a number of different processors. A collection of programs can be compared to a recipe book, where each recipe can be assumed as a program. Every recipe has a list of ingredients (fixed data) and a list of instructions detailing exactly what to do with those ingredients. When you follow a recipe, you are actually executing a program.

Program Development Cycle (Steps In Developing a Program):

Before starting the process of writing a program (coding), the programmer has to determine the problem that needs to be solved. There are different approaches to problem solving. Most require breaking the problem into a series of smaller steps, independent of the programming languages. One common technique is to use the program development cycle, with the number of steps that may vary according to the person who has formalized the development. Often the process runs in a loop, for example, as the current process is completed, new demands appear and the development process commences again. Development cycle of a program includes the following phases:

(a) **Analyse/Define the Problem:** Firstly, the problem is analyzed precisely and completely. Based on understanding, the developer knows about the scope within which the problem needs to be developed.

(b) **Task Analysis:** After analyzing the problem, the developer needs to develop various solutions to solve the given problem. From these solutions, the optimum solution (by experimenting with all the solutions) is chosen, which can solve the problem comfortably and economically.

(c) **Developing Algorithm:** After selecting the appropriate solution, algorithm is developed to depict the basic logic of the selected solution. An algorithm depicts the solution in logical steps (sequence of instructions). Further, algorithm is represented by flowcharts and pseudo codes. These tools make program logic clear and they eventually help in coding.

(d) **Testing the Algorithm for Accuracy:** Before converting the algorithms into actual code, it should be checked for accuracy. The main purpose of checking algorithm is to identify major logical errors at an early stage, because logical errors are often difficult to detect and correct at later stages. The testing also ensures that the algorithm is a "true" one and it should work for both normal as well as unusual data.

(e) **Coding:** After meeting all the design considerations, the actual coding of the program takes place in the chosen programming language. Depending upon application domain and available resources, a program can be written by using computer languages of different levels such as machine, assemble or high-level languages.

(f) **Test and Debug the Program:** It is common for the initial program code to contain errors. A program compiler and programmer-designed test data machine tests the code for syntax errors. The results obtained and compared with results calculated manually from this test data. Depending upon the complexity of the program, several rounds of testing may be required.

(g) **Documentation:** Once the program is free from all the errors, it is the duty of the program developers to ensure that the program is supported by suitable documentation. These documents should be supplied to the program users. Documenting a program enables the user to operate the program correctly. It also enables other persons to understand the program clearly so that it may, if necessary, be modified, or corrected by someone other than the original programmer.

(h) **Implementation:** After performing all the above-mentioned steps, the program is installed on the end user's machine. In this stage, users are also provided with all the essential documents so that they can understand how the program works. The implementation can be viewed as the final testing because only after using the program, the user can point out the drawbacks, if any to the developers. Based on the feedback, the programmers can modify or enhance the program.

(i) **Maintenance and Enhancement:** After the program is implemented, it should be properly maintained taking care of the changing requirements of its users and system. The program should be regularly enhanced by adding additional capabilities. This phase is also concerned with detecting and fixing the errors, which were missed in testing phase. Since this step generates user feedback, the programming cycle continues as the program modified or reconstructed to meet the changing needs.

Short Answer Question

1. What is software?
2. What are software components?
3. What is hardware?
4. What is low level language?
5. What is flowchart?
6. Explain the coding.
7. What is algorithm?
8. Explain Connector.
9. What are the types of windows?

Long Answer Question

1. Define software and hardware.
2. Differentiat between hardware and software.
3. Explain the Program Development Cycle.
4. What are the functions of an Operating System?
5. What are the types of system software?
6. What are the Types of Flowcharts?
7. What are the Advantages and disadvantages of Algorithm?
8. Explain UNIX Operating System.
9. Explain Windows Operating System.

Very Long or Essay Typer Question

1. What are the software types? Explain it.
2. Briefly explain flowcharts.
3. Draw a flowchart for the following:
   (a) It is required to tabulate the results of 1000 students who have appeared in an examination. You are given the total marks out of 500.

CHAPTER 4

INTRODUCTION TO DATA PROCESSING

Structure:

4.1 INTRODUCTION TO DATA PROCESSING

Data

Data means any collection of facts. Data can be considered as the raw material of information. The data may be numerical such as payroll, employee Number, etc. or non-numerical like Student names, Product names, etc.

The various types of data are

1. **Numeric Data**
2. **Character Data**
3. **Logical Data**

1. Numeric Data

Numbers are called as numeric data

Roll number of a student

Age of a person

Marks obtained by a student

2. Character Data

A sequence of characters is called a character data. The characters may be numeric, alphabetic and special characters (or) combination of these.

Name of Employee (R.Raja)

Date of Birth (17.03.90)

Address

3. Logical Data

A very important type of data which used by a computer for decision making is called logical data. The logical data involves comparison operation (or) checking operation. It can have either of the values "TRUE" (or) "FALSE"

27 < 10 – TRUE

14 = 20 – FALSE

➢ **Data Processing**

As data is in its raw form it cannot solve any problem. The data needs some processing to make it useful. Data processing is the conversion of data into a more useful form. That is, transmission of data into meaningful information is called data processing.

➢ **Information**

The result obtained by data processing is called information. That is, the processed data is known as information. However, information produced in one data processing step may be used as data in the next data processing step.

Examples of Data and Information

1. **Pay-roll:** Every company (or) factory has to pay salary to its employees by maintaining records of each of them. This record contains name, address, basic pay, allowances etc.... these are data. After processing these data, the pay slips are prepared and these pay slips form the information.

2. **Invoice:** Invoice is a record of details of the items sold on credit. The invoice has the customer's name, address, order number, quantity ordered, price and total amount of items sold. The details of the buyer and the details of the item sold provide data and invoice becomes the information.

3. **Mark Sheet:** The candidate's name, roll numbers and marks obtained form the data and mark sheet which contains the roll numbers in serial order, followed by candidate's name, marks in different subjects is known as information.

Data Versus Information:

The word **data** is the plural of *datum*, though data commonly represents both singular and plural forms. Data are raw facts or observations, typically about physical phenomena or business transactions. For example, a spacecraft launch or the sale of an automobile would generate a lot of data describing those events. More specifically, data are objective measurements of the attributes (the characteristics) of entities (such as people, places, things, and events).

People often use the terms data and *information* interchangeably. However, it is better to view data as raw material resources that are processed into finished information products. Then we can define **information** as data that have been converted into a meaningful and useful context for specific end users. Thus, data are usually subjected to a value-added process (we call data processing or information processing) where

1. Its form is aggregated, manipulated, and organized
2. Its content is analyzed and evaluated
3. It is placed in a proper context for a human user

So, you should view information as processed data placed in a context that gives it value for specific end users.

Data Vs Information

Data	Information
Raw records	Completed One
Unordered	Ordered
Unrefined Data	Refined Data
What prevails?	What is necessary?

4.2 DATA PROCESSING CYCLE

Data Processing consists of six steps. These steps constitute the data processing cycle. The steps are shown in the following figure:

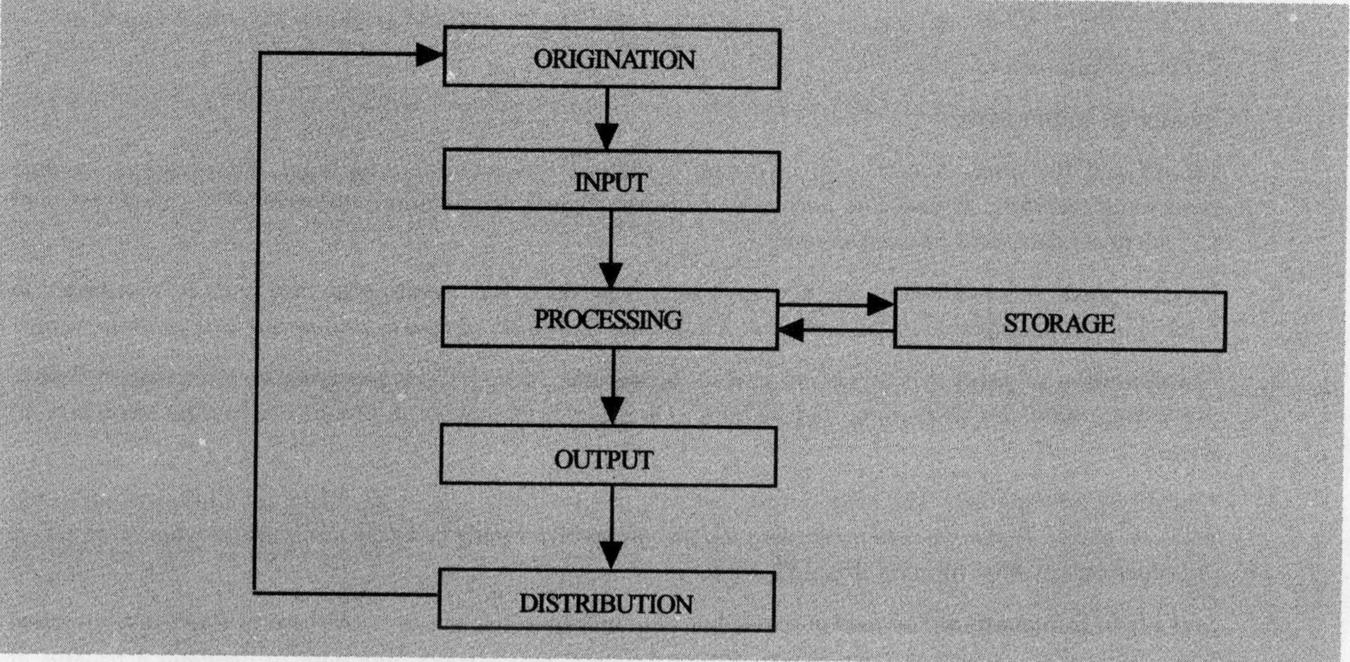

1. **Origination:** This step refers to the process of collecting the original data. An original recording of the data is called a source document, i.e., the document containing the original data. For example, in a mark sheet processing problem, students' test papers are source documents.

2. **Input:** In this step the initial data (or) input data are prepared in some convenient form for processing. The form will depend on the processing machine. For example, if computers are used, the input data could be recorded on any one of several types of input medium such as cards, tapes and so on.

3. **Processing:** In this step, the input data are changed and usually combined with other information to produce data in a more useful form. For example, a summary of sales for the month may be calculated from the sales orders.

4. **Output:** Here the results of the preceding processing step are collected .The particular form of the output data depends on the use of the data. For example, output data may be pay checks for the employees, a printed summary of monthly sales (or) simply data to be stored for further processing at a later date.

5. **Distribution:** This step refers to the distribution of the output data. The documents containing the output data are often called "report documents." For example, the report document of mark sheet problem is the grad sheet.

6. **Storage:** This step is essential in many data processing procedures. Data processing results are frequently placed in storage to be used as input data for further processing at a later date. The two arrows between the processing Box and the storage box indicate the interaction of these two steps.

   The arrow which goes from the distribution box back to the origination box indicates that report documents may become source documents for further data processing.

4.3 STEPS IN DATA PROCESSING

1. Identifying the data.
2. Input of Data.
3. Manipulation of Data.
4. Output of Information.
5. Storage of Information.

1. **Identifying the data:** Accuracy of information depends on accurate data input. The first step in data processing therefore, is to locate necessary facts and figures from source documents. Accurate, relevant and adequate data must be used as input.

2. **Input of data:** After extracting the necessary data from the source documents, they must be transposed in a suitable form acceptable to the computer. Great care should be taken to avoid wrong entries in the forms.

3. **Manipulation of data:** It involves the process of shifting, sorting and rearranging the given input. Before processing, validation procedures may be built in to the code so that input forms do not accept any incorrect data.

4. **Output of information:** The main purpose of data processing is to provide meaningful information to the decision-maker. Hence, in data processing the person involved must be very careful about what information is needed and in what form he likes to have it.

5. **Storage of information:** The data processed need to be kept for future use. All the processed data will need some form of secondary storage. When storing the data, it is always important to maintain a backup. It should be noted that at each and every step the storage might be done.

4.4 DATA PROCESSING OPERATIONS

The data after some processing is transformed into information, which is organized and meaningful. It includes the following operations:

1. Data Generation

Data generates from transactions. A transaction is a business activity. For example, purchasing the raw materials is a transaction. Selling goods for credit is a transaction.

Data generation is also called as origination. This refers to the process of collecting the original data. An original recording of data is called a source document i.e., the document containing the original data. For example, students test paper is a source document.

Examples for Data Generation:

1. Writing a receipt for goods sold to a customer
2. The attendance particulars of a student (or) an employee
3. The electricity consumption for a house in a month.
4. The telephone calls engaged by a subscriber.
5. The books borrowed by a member in a library.

6. The dishes served to a customer in a restaurant.
7. A test conducted by the professor for his students.
8. The money deposited by a customer in a bank.

2. Recording

Here raw data is converted into an acceptable form. That is, the data is transcribed from the source documents on the cards or on some other specified forms and are made readable for the machines. This operation is performed throughout the IPO cycle. The punched cards and paper tapes, magnetic tapes, magnetic disks, tape cassettes, floppy disks, RAM cartridge, charged coupled devices, etc., are used as data recording media.

Recording refers to transfer of data on to some form (or) document. It occurs not only at data generation step but throughout data processing cycle. For example, a professor records the scores of his students in his roll book. At the end of the semester he calculates the final grades and records them in his roll book. He receives the grade sheet from the registrar and records the final grades on it. The registrar then records the grades on the student's file. Each student's grade in the file are recorded on a sheet which is then sent to the student.

Examples for Recording:

1. The sales clerk files out the customer's sales invoice at the time of purchase.
2. A teacher puts absent mark in the attendance register for a student who has not come to the class.
3. A cashier at the Bank make entries in the ledger after paying cash to the customer from his account.
4. The librarian makes entries regarding the member and book before issuing the book to the member.
5. A reservation clerk makes necessary entries before issuing ticket to a passenger.

3. Verification

After the data have been recorded, their accuracy has to be checked. This can be done with the help of another machine called verifier or by re-reading.

4. Classification

Classification of information is the next important operation in which the data is separated into various categories.

5. Sorting

Sorting involves sequencing the data in a pre-determined order to facilitate processing. The order may be either alphabetic or numeric.

6. Merging

It is the operation of combining two or more ordered (sorted) sets of data to form another single ordered set.

7. Calculating

Here calculation of greater magnitude can be processed. Calculation involves solving equations and manipulation of the source data such as addition, subtraction, etc.

8. Recording of Data

Recording refers to transfer of data on to some form (or) document. It occurs not only at data generation step but throughout data processing cycle. For example, a professor records the scores of his students in his roll book. At the end of the semester he calculates the final grades and records them in his roll book. He receives the grade sheet from the registrar and records the final grades on it. The registrar then records the grades on the students file. Each student's grades in the file are recorded on a sheet which is then sent to the student.

Examples for Recording:

1. The sales clerk files out the customer's sales invoice at the time of purchase.

1. A teacher puts absent mark in the attendance register for a student who has not come to the class.
2. A cashier at the Bank make entries in the ledger after paying cash to the customer from his account.
3. The librarian makes entries regarding the member and book before issuing the book to the member.
4. A reservation clerk makes necessary entries before issuing ticket to a passenger.

9. Data Storage and Retrieval

The computer has a program of instructions which specify each step in the processing .These must be held in the storage until ready for execution. Likewise, the data being operated upon must be in storage.

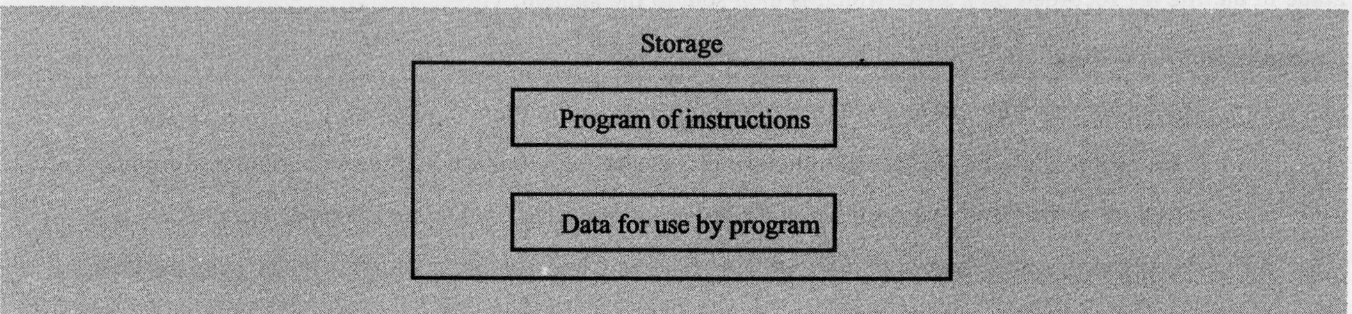

Elements of a Computer File

1. A character is any single number, alphabetic letter (or) special symbol, e.g., X,Y,P,4,0,3,2,+,- etc ....
2. A data field (or) data item is a collection of characters representing specific data element. For example, name of a student, mark etc...
3. A record consists of a group of related data items, e.g., employee's record, customer's record, student's record.
4. A file is a collection of related records ,e.g., employees' file might consist of 1000 individual employees' records.

Hence a file consists of a number of records. Each record is made up of a number of fields and each field consists of a number of characters.

EMPLOYEES' NO.	EMPLOYEE'S NAME	DATE OF BIRTH	SEX	HOURLY PAY RATE
427216	K.S.RAJA	30.4.70	MALE	Rs.100

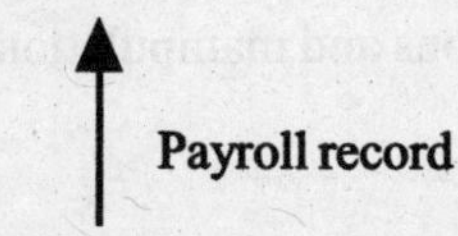

10. Data Retrieving

Data retrieving is the process of searching or locating a data item from the storage. In EDP system, the data is retrieved from the storage device in sequential, indexed sequential or random access mode. The on-line data storage and retrieval is very useful for the proper functioning of a modern business establishment.

11. Reporting

Generally in business data processing, the processing operation comes to an end with the reporting of data. In this operation the results of the data processing are made available to others. The processed information may be reported in a number of ways depending on the use of results. The results may be printed out in the form of pay slips, bills, etc. or in the form of reports as ESI Reports, PF Reports or Sales Reports, etc.

4.5 KINDS OF DATA PROCESSING

The important kinds (or) categories of data processing are as follows:

1. Manual data Processing
2. Semi-manual data processing (Aided by calculator and mechanical devices)
3. Electronic Data Processing

1. Manual Data Processing

It is the most widely used type of data processing. In the manual system, all processing is done by people.

For example, a popular example of manual data processing would be the calculation of an employee's monthly salary by a clerk in an organization, say a factory. The employee's basic pay and other allowances may be available in ledger which is arranged department wise and within a department alphabetically. Similarly deductions for provident fund, insurance, tax and installments for repayment of loans will be available there.

From the employee's department, a report will be received about no., of hours worked in regular shift and no., of hours worked overtime. From his salary hourly rates for both categories are calculated, manipulated by hours worked and added to give total salary. For this deductions are subtracted and net pay calculated.The clerk may write out a cheque for the net amount (or) send a list of payments to the cash department which will pay the employee.

In the above example, similar reports may be received from various departments about sales, purchase etc., by the central office which may prepare consolidated statements of various items and file them for future use.

Disadvantages of Manual Data Processing:

1. Errors : When data is processed manually mistakes are likely to occur.
2. Delay : The manual data processing takes lot of time. If the results are to be used immediately then it becomes difficult to get them in time.
3. Repetition : For each step, the manual work has to be repeated.

2. Electronic Data Processing (or) EDP (or) Computerized Data Processing

Electronic data processing involves the use of computers. The fantastic speed, the accuracy of processing and the capability to store a large amount of data has made computers the most powerful tool for data processing.

The computerized system of data processing involves the following basic steps:

(i) Input

(ii) Manipulating Data (Processing)

(iii) Output

(i) **Input:** Data originating from a transaction is recorded on a source document. Then the transactions are entered in the computer.

(ii) **Manipulating the Data:** The data may be manipulated in the following steps.

(a) Storing (data are stored in memory)

(b) Classifying (if necessary the data are classified)

(c) Sorting (the data is arranged in a desired sequence)

(d) Calculating (arithmetic calculations are done)

(e) Summarizing (the results of all the above operations should be presented in a particular form)

(iii) **Output:** The results obtained by manipulating the data may be printed out as a report and filed (or) it may be stored in a storage medium and retrieved for later reference and use.

A computer is able to perform automatic data processing. Once the input data the instructions are provided, it can process data without human intervention.

Advantages of Electronic Data Processing:

1. **Speed:** The computerization of data processing activities of a business organization helps in processing the data with tremendous speed. The speed of response is more.
2. **Accuracy:** Data processed by using computers is highly accurate. The computer processes data with accuracy provided the input data is accurate.
3. **Flexibility:** The modern digital computers can be used for a variety of purposes.
4. **Storage capacity:** Large volume of data can be conveniently stored, accessed and altered.
5. **Decision-making:** Decision making becomes easier, economical and timely.
6. **Volume:** Number of transactions is increasing steadily and it is becoming difficult to store and process these large volumes of data manually within the desired time. Using computers, it is possible to store large volumes of data and retrieve the desired information quickly. This is particularly useful where a large no., of documents like insurance premium, bills, invoice and bank accounts are handled every day.
7. **Reduction in Paper work:** The use of computers for data processing has helped the management of business organization with the increasing problem of paper handling not only by speeding up the process, but also by eliminating some of the paper needs through the storage of data as computer files.
8. **Reduces cost:** Though the initial investment for installing a computer is high but it substantially reduces the cost of each of its transaction.
9. **Facilitates report preparation:** Data maintained with the help of a computer facilitates the preparation of various type of reports required by organizational executives for the purpose of decision making and control.
10. **Reduces space requirements:** The use of computers for office activities reduces the requirements of office space which otherwise is required.

11. **Reduce the manpower requirement:** The number of persons required for performing various organizational activities will be reduced by using computer system.

3. Semi-manual Data Processing

These Systems utilizes some electro mechanical devices like calculator, adding machine, accounting machine etc., But they need human intervention

Advantages: 1. Speed (Promptness)

2. Accuracy

3. Neatness

4. Effective control

4.6 OBJECTIVES OF DATA PROCESSING

After the industrial revolution, the needs of the mankind increased. Man had to deal with large volume of data. He had to cope up with more and more information. The information collected is to be sorted out, stored and retrieved at short intervals. This necessitated the concept of data processing.

As the complexities of business increased, the number of functions to be performed also increased. The data processing system must be responsible to supply the information when it is needed, so as to make the performance of the organization optimum.

Let us have a look at the general objectives of Data Processing.

1. **Handle Huge Volume of Data**

   The basic objective of data processing is to handle huge data in order to enable the organization to function efficiently.

2. **Qualitative and Quantitative Information**

   The next important want of data processing is to provide qualitative and quantitative information.

3. **Proper and Timely Information**

   Different kinds of information are needed in almost all organizations. Data processing provides correct and timely information.

4. **Storage and Retrieval of Data**

   Through data processing, information can be stored and retrieved as and when necessary.

5. **Helps in Decision-making**

   In every organization various decisions are taken at different levels. Such decisions can be more accurate if effective data processing system is used.

6. **Improves Productivity**

   To improve productivity, various measures are to be identified and implemented. It is possible through the properly designed data processing system.

7. **Maintaining Performance at Optimum Level**

   To maintain the performance of the organization at best possible level various functions at different levels of the organization are to be coordinated. There should be a smooth flow of information among various functional departments. This can be easily achieved through data processing system.

8. Efficient Office Management

In office management also data processing plays a very important role, through which office automation can be done.

4.7 METHODS OF DATA PROCESSING SYSTEMS

The methods of data processing depend upon the following factors:

(a) Volume of data to be processed

(b) Complexity of data processing operations

(c) Computational demands

(d) Processing time constraints and

(e) Economic factors.

Various methods or modes of data processing are given below:

(i) The single user system

(ii) Batch processing

(iii) Multi-programming

(iv) On-line Processing

(v) Real-Time processing

(vi) Time sharing concept

(vii) Distributed processing

Data Processing Systems:

The methods of data processing are explained below:

1. The single user system

It is one-man show and is indicative of one of the earlier stages of computer development. Here only one person can work at a time. Hence, especially if the machine is meant for the use of many persons, much computer time is wasted waiting for one person to finish and debug his program on the machine.

2. Batch Processing

This is an old system but even today it is used for data processing in computing machines, in which the capacity of the CPU is limited. In this system, the data is collected for a predetermined period of time, after which it is accumulated in sequential manner.

In this system the source transaction documents are first collected before being sent to computer room. A batch of transactions is entered onto a computer media by data entry devices. The transactions are validated during data entry and verified with the source documents from the check lists. The validated and verified results on reports are returned to the user departments. In batch processing system the emphasis is on maximizing the computer resource utilization.

In batch processing, the processing cycle called Batch processing cycle repeats itself at every regular interval. The elements of this cycle are given below:

(i) Data capture.

(ii) Data transmission.

(iii) Data transcription, verification and validation.

(iv) Job Processing.

(v) Job assembly putting together the batch for processing.

(vi) Job disassembly (separating out the reports after processing)

(vii) Reports and distribution.

Features

(a) Here, the data is accumulated into batches and processed periodically.

(b) The jobs are processed one after the other without any user interaction.

The concept of Batch Processing is dearly explained with the help of the following diagram:

Concept of Batch Processing

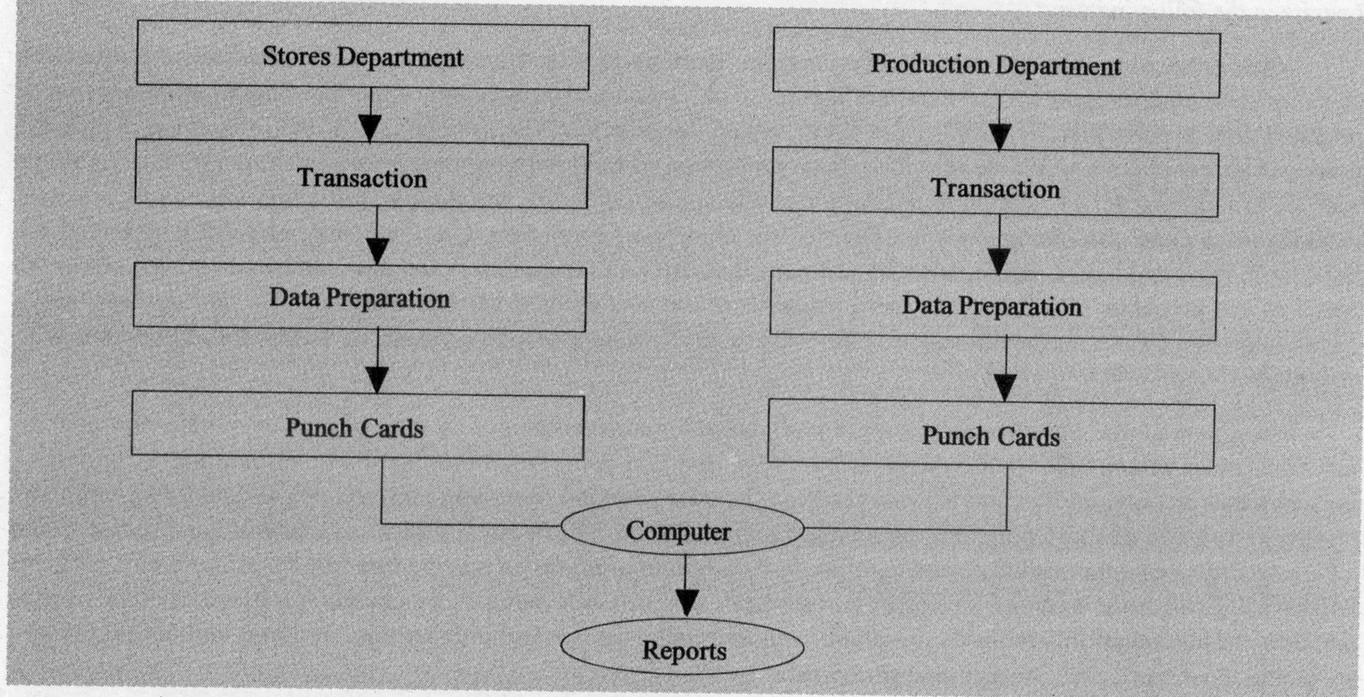

Examples of applications which can use batch processing are:

1. *Payroll Processing:* In payroll processing the data are collected for a stipulated period of time usually one month and processed at regular intervals after which payments are distributed to all the employees.
2. *Telephone Billing:* Here the subscriber does not get a bill for every call he makes. Instead, his calls are recorded at a centralized place and are processed on a predetermined period of time, to prepare his bills.
3. Financial accessing
4. Budgeting and Budgeting control
5. Production planning and control
6. Project planning and control

Drawbacks in Batch Processing:

The following are the drawbacks of batch processing:

1. Time gap between capture of data
2. Time consuming to debug
3. Delay in generating reports

3. Multi-programming

In batch processing, programs are executed one by one. The memory and ALU of the machine are not being fully utilized. To get the maximum use of the machine, multi-programming system is used. "Multi-programming enables to store and execute more than one program in the CPU at the same time." The multi-programming concept is event based. The purpose of multi-programming is to increase utilization of the computer system as a whole.

Multi-programming is defined as execution of two or more program that all reside in primary storage. Since the CPU can execute only one instruction at a time, cannot simultaneously execute instructions from two or more program. However, it can execute instructions from one program, then from second program, then from first again, and so on. This type of processing is referred to as concurrent execution. Using concept of concurrent execution, multi-programming operate in the following way:

When processing is interrupted on our program, perhaps to attend an input or output transfer, the processor switches to another program. This enables all, parts of the system, the processor, input and output peripherals to be operated concurrently thereby utilizing the whole system more fully. When operating on one program at a time the processor or peripherals would be idle for a large proportion, if the total processing time, even though this would be reduced to some extent by buffering. Buffering enables the processor to execute another instruction while input or output is taking place rather than being idle while transfer was completed. Even then, when one program is being executed at a time, basic input and output peripherals such as floppy disk drive and line printers are slow compared with the electronic speed of the processor and this causes an imbalance in the system as a whole. However, in a multi-programming environment the CPU can execute one program's instructions while a second program is waiting for I/O operations to take place.

In a system of multi-programming storage is allocated for each program. The areas of primary storage allocated for individual programs are called 'partitions.' Each partition must have some form of storage protection and priority protection to ensure that program one portion will not accidentally write over and destroy the instructions of another partition and priority (when two or more programs are residing in primary storage) because both programs will need access to the CPU's facilities (e.g., the arithmetic and logic section). A system of priority a method that will determine which program will have first call on the computer's facilities is normally determined by locating the program in specific partitions.Programs that have the highest priority normally are stored in an area called the 'foreground partition.' Program with lowest priority are stored in an area called 'background partition.'

4. Online Processing

Definition of Online Processing

Online processing refers to processing of individual transactions as they occur from their point of origin as opposed to accumulating them into batches. This is made possible by such direct access devices as Magnetic disk and Magnetic Drum and number of terminals connected to, and controlled by a central processor. In this way, various departments in a company can be connected to the process by cables. If operating companies are a number of miles away from the processor then they are linked by means of telegraph or telephone lines. This type of processing provides multi access to information files by terminal users and also enables them to update with transactions' data.

It is a non-sequential process in which data is directly transmitted between input / output device and a computer system via communication links. It is a method of processing where many users have direct access to the same system, and where the file is updated as soon as the transaction is completed.

Special Features

1. In this method data is not accumulated, instead it is entered and executed directly.
2. Quick Processing — by means of direct communication with the computer and continuous flow of input, the delay between transactions and their processing is avoided.
3. This method reduces the data entry errors, because the user who generates, the data is the one who keys it in.
4. This system validates data at various points and ensures that correct data is being entered.
5. Under this method the system performs the whole task in a conversational 'manner helping the data entry process.
6. In online processing, one has the latest update immediately.

Online processing ensures that the records are updated at any time whereas this is so with batch processing say once a week but the fact remains that online processing is usually more costly. Therefore in choosing one of the processing both updating of records and costs are to be considered.

Concept of Online Processing

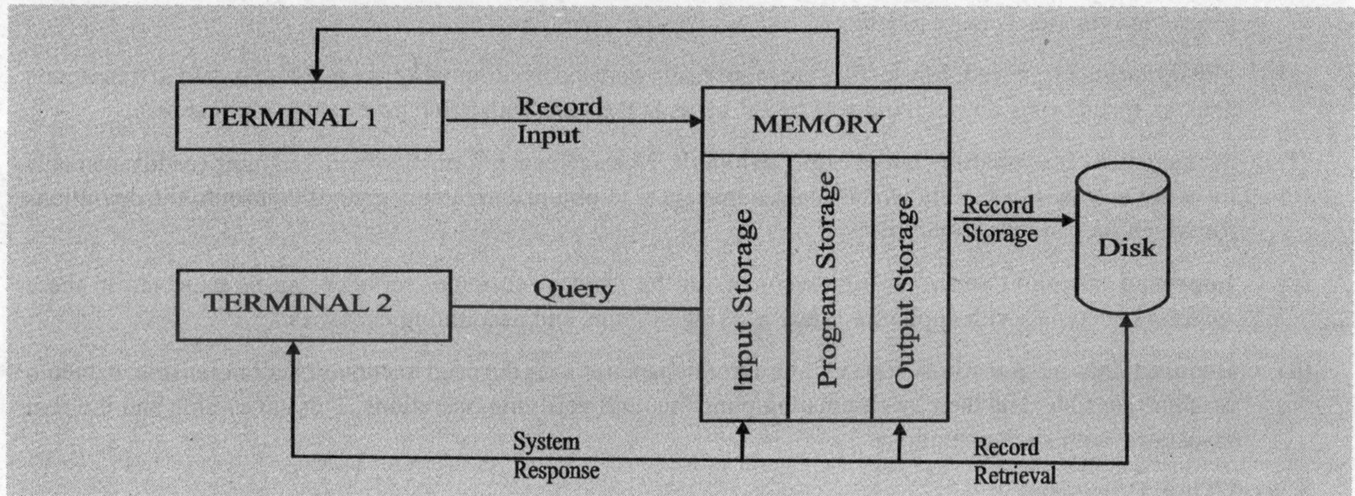

Online Applications:

Systems are being developed and are already in use for a wide range of application in different type of industries described below:

(a) *Electricity and Gas Boards:* By means of terminals situated in showroom it is possible to inform perspective customers of the availability of the appliances in response to their inquiries.

(b) *Banking:* It is possible to inform bank customers of the status of their accounts in response to an inquiry by accessing relevant file using an online terminal.

(c) Tour Operators' Reservation Offices accept telephone inquiries from travel agents regarding the availability of holidays in respect of client's inquiries. By means of terminals, the availability of the required holidays can be checked and booked immediately.

(d) *Stock Exchange:* Terminals located in major stock Exchanges throughout the country and the offices of participating brokerage enable the speedy processing of share dealings.

(e) *Stock Control:* Terminals located in warehouse provide the means for automatic recording of stocks, updating of stock records, reservations, follow-up of outstanding orders and the printing of picking list etc.

Benefits provided by Online Systems: Online systems provide a number of benefits all of which assist in improving administrative efficiency which is essential in today's competitive business environment. A number of benefits are outlined below:

(a) **Integration of clerical work with the computer:** Online systems assist in harnessing activities of clerical staff to the computer by the use of terminals. They can have access to information which they require for the efficient performance of their jobs in dealing with customer enquiries and order processing.

(b) **Elimination of tedious tasks:** Routine clerical tasks are replaced by terminal operations providing a greater degree of job interest, operating efficiency and job satisfaction.

(c) **Reduction in paper work:** Volume of paper work generated by normal clerical system and batch processing system is relatively high. Online systems reduce the volume of print out required for management report since the information can be displayed on terminal screen on demand.

(d) **Improved accuracy:** As terminal messages are checked accuracy before being transmitted to the computer by data validation programs, the quality of formation in a system increases as the input errors are reduced. Hence, information is more reliable.

(e) **File updating improved:** Master files are more easily updated by terminal key board with regard to transaction data, as special runs do not require to be set up as is the case with batch processing applications.

(f) **Management Information more readily available:** Management information becomes more readily available by direct access — a facility which enables managers to obtain a greater degree of control to the operations for which they are responsible.

(g) **Improved customer services:** Improvements in the level of customer services can be expected in these systems concerned with appliance sales, booking systems and accounting enquiries.

(h) **Reduced data preparations cost:** Online system dispense with the need to convert human sensible data into machine sensible data thereby eliminating punching and verifying operations. This saves time and the cost associated with such operations.

5. Real Time Processing

It is also called as interactive mode or Direct mode. This system makes the user to have direct contact with the computer through his terminal. It is an alternative approach to an online processing system. Here the data is processed, the instant it occurs. There is no delay between the time data is available, and the time it is processed.

The term real time refers to the technique of updating file transaction date immediately after the event to which it relates occurs. This is in distinction to batch processing which processes related data to batches of pre-defined periods of time. Real time systems are basically online systems with one specially in inquiry processing. The response of the system to the inquiry itself is used to control the activity. An online production data collection system that simply accepts input and utilises it for payroll and costing purposes cannot be termed realtime, but if, on the other hand, the system is designed to provide immediate information to monitor the production processes, it is a real time system.

Special Features

(a) Program is always under execution.

(b) It produces output to control, direct or affect the outcome of an ongoing activity or process.

(c) In this method, the control is exercised during the actual functioning.

(d) It is meant exclusively to perform one task.

(e) It is like an online system with title constraints on response time availability.

(f) It is called a real time system because it has to give results based on dead lines which are imposed by the real world outside.

(g) The data which has to be produced by the systems has to be in such a less time, that they can influence the external events which are based on this data.

Thus the response of a real time system is one type of feedback control system. The response time would naturally differ from one activity to another. If the example, it is the launching of a space vehicle, the response time should be in split second whereas in business situation even a few minutes of response time may be alright. Online updating in real time usually leads to transaction as a by-product. For example, the updating in real time a customer's order may lead to such transactions as dispatch noted and purchase requests, etc. Real time systems offer accountants and others in business a chance to fulfill the potential of the computer as a tool of management.

Concept of Real Time Processing

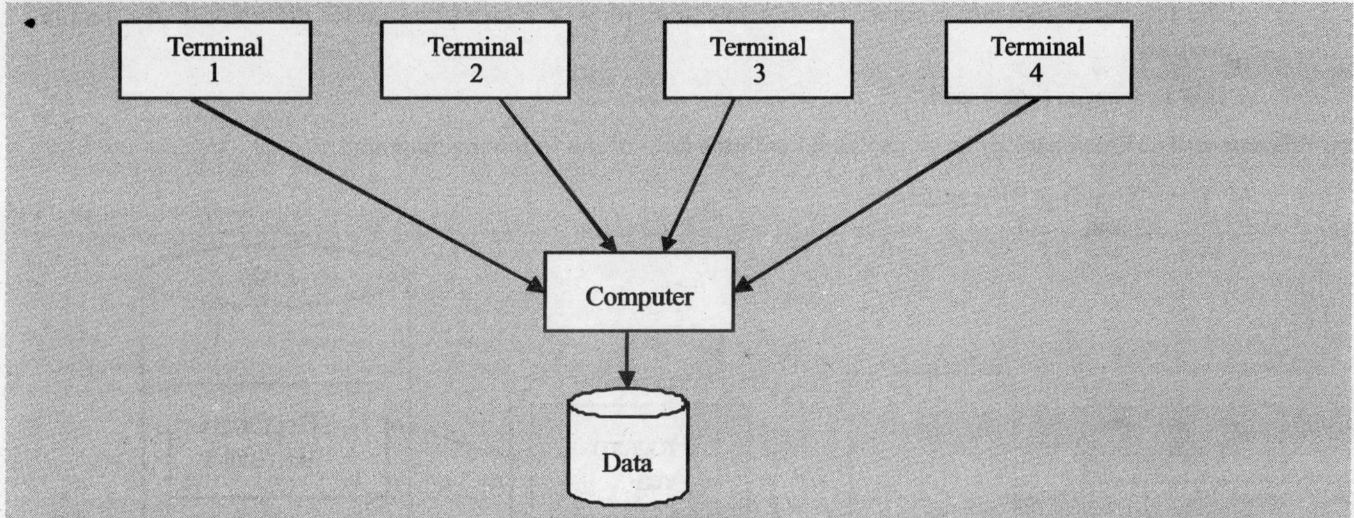

Guided Missile System

Real Time Processing is suitable in the following type of business operations:

- Wholesale supplier and manufacture — Availability of stocks.
- Airline — Flight seat availability.
- Manufacturing — Status of production orders.
- Process Control.
- Space Craft Control.

Real time systems usually operate in multi-programming and multi-processing: This increases both availability and reliability of the system. CPU's in real time system should possess the capability of what is known as program interrupts. These are temporarily stoppage or halts in the execution of a program so that more urgent messages can be handled on priority. It may be worth noting that some computer systems are dedicated to real time operations and others are designed to operate in both batch and real time modes so that they can also serve as stand by unit to each other.

6. Time Sharing

It is a special type of online processing in which several users share the resources of an online computer system to avoid turn about time, especially when results are needed quickly; another system is available, i.e., time sharing system. In this method the individual user has an independent local terminal. The terminal is connected to a main computer, which does all the processing work.

Under this system each person on a terminal has to log into the system. The system then lists him in the order in which he has logged on. Once everybody has logged on, the system will permit the first in the list to run his program. The time given for running the program is generally 10 milliseconds. It is called a time slice or a time slot or a quantum. Starting then, with the first to log on, each user is given his time slice. Once all have made use of it, the system starts all over again, repeating the cycle. The system maintained is called a polling system whereby each terminal is polled on a round robin basis.

All the instructions given by the users are carried to the centrally located main computer system and processed there and retrieve back by the user instantaneously. Since, the centrally located main computer has high-speed processor, users may feel that they are sharing the same computer resources.

Features

1. The processor time is shared between two or more persons.
2. The processor switches from one user's job to another at a rapid rate under the control of a monitor program.
3. This concept is time based.

The concept of time-sharing can be explained with the help of the following diagram:

Concept of Time-Sharing Processing

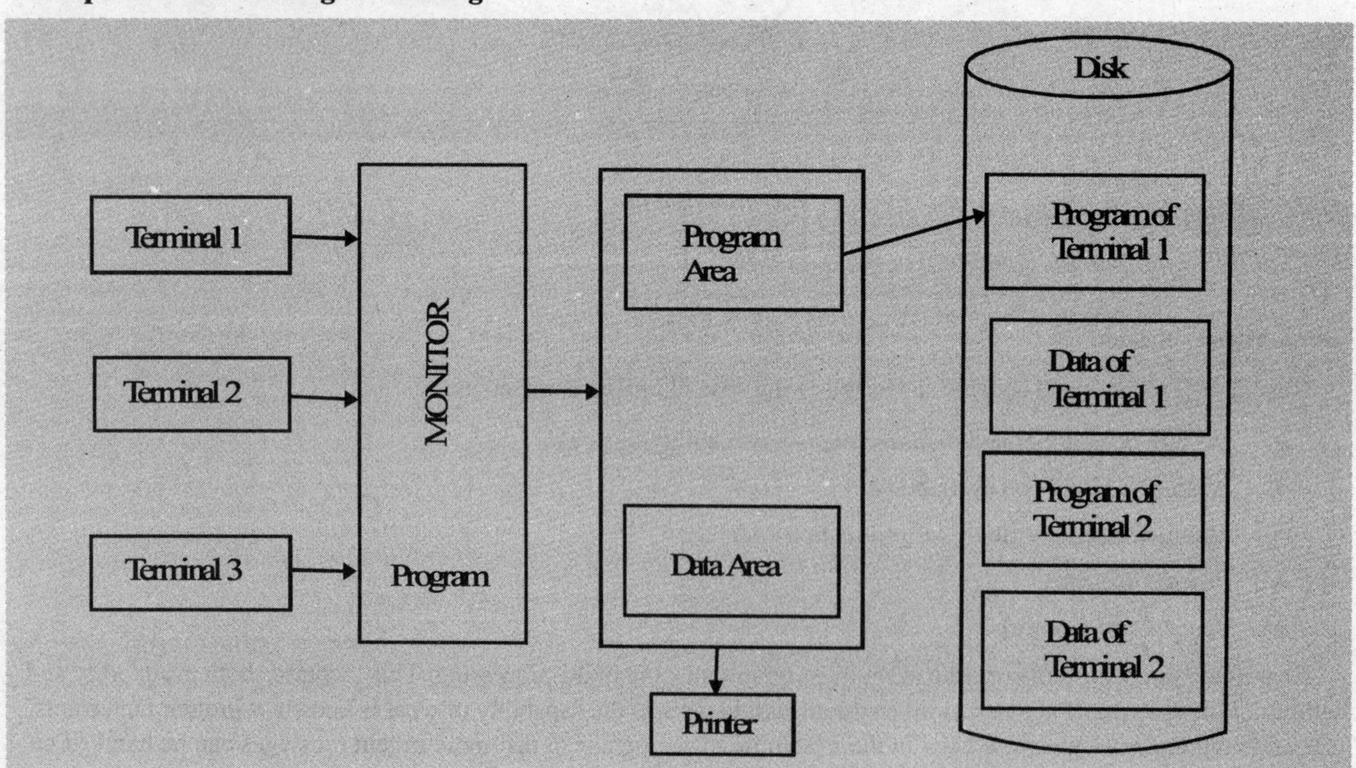

Let us suppose that there are three terminals, each person on a terminal has to log into the system. The system then lists him the order in which he has logged on. Once everyone has logged on, the system will permit the first on the list to run his program. The time given for writing a program is called a time slice or time slot. Starting from the first, each user is given his time slice. Once, all the three users have made use of it, the system starts all over again, repeating the cycle. The sequence maintained is called Polling System. Most time sharing systems respond to user's instructions in milli/ micro seconds.

Advantages of Time-Sharing System:

(1) Simultaneously several users can be served.

(2) All the users have the same priority.

(3) All the users get equal amount of processor time.

(4) The interaction with the running programs is possible.

Time-Sharing Vs Multiprogramming:

The difference between these two methods is that in "time-sharing" the CPU links only one terminal at a time and its total time is shared uniformly by all the users. But in multiprogramming, the CPU links more than one terminal or other peripherals at a time. Therefore, multiprogramming more efficiently utilizes the main memory and the central resources than time sharing. Time sharing is employed only for multi terminal system whereas multiprogramming is meant both for single as well as the multi terminal system.

7. Distributed Processing

In computer science, a form of information processing in which work is performed by separate computers that are linked through a communications network. Distributed processing is usually categorized as either plain distributed processing or true distributed processing. Plain distributed processing shares the workload among computers that can communicate with one another. True distributed processing has separate computers perform different tasks in such a way that their combined work can contribute to a larger goal, such as the transfer of funds from one bank to another. This latter type of processing requires a highly structured environment that allows hardware and software to communicate, share resources, and exchange information freely. At the highest (and most visible) levels, such distributed processing can also require data-transfer mechanisms that are relatively invisible to users but that enable different programs to use and share one another's data.

Distributed data processing system is a network of several computers in remote stations, each of which is linked to a single host computer. The larger, central computer maintains the firm's master data base and system log. Each remote system is a fully independent computer that maintains its own local data base in addition to communication with the master computer. These individual computers are tied together through a high speed communication network. This allows individual computers to communicate with one another in a variety of ways depending on the CIS requirements.

Many small computers (called nodes) are employed as data collection points in several departments. They are connected to a main computer system (called File Server) in a centralized department, which controls the entire database. The processing involved here is known as distributed processing.

The distributed data processing system exists because of the need for large interactive installations with a high degree of reliability and accuracy. Moreover, large number of mini computers can be connected in this system which results in cost reduction.

Features

(a) Decentralized computer system

(b) Interconnected by communication network

(c) More reliable

(d) Since more than one computer is used in the network, it is economical.

Advantages

Distributed Data Processing System has Many Advantages:

(a) Local computers on the network offer immediate response to local needs.

(b) Systems can be expanded in modular fashion as needed because many small computers are used as the system is not dependant on large unit that could shut down the network if it failed.

(c) Equipment operating and managing costs are often lower.

(d) Minicomputers tend to be less complex than large systems; therefore, the system is more useful to local users.

Distributed data processing system — a number of computer systems are linked together. So the facilities available in one computer system can be shared by all. This link is called computer network.

4.8 THE FUNDAMENTAL ROLES OF DATA PROCESSING APPLICATIONS IN BUSINESS

There are three fundamental reasons for all business applications of information technology. They are found in the three vital roles that information systems can perform for a business enterprise.

- Support of its business processes and operations.
- Support of decision-making by its employees and managers.
- Support of its strategies for competitive advantage.

Trends in Information Systems

The roles given to the information systems function have expanded significantly over the years as follows:

- **Data Processing:** 1950s-1960s. Until the 1960s, the role of information systems was simple: transaction processing, record-keeping, accounting, and other electronic data processing **(EDP)** applications.
- **Management Reporting:** 1960s-1970s. As the concept of management information systems **(MIS)** was conceived, another role was added. This new role focused on providing managerial end users with predefined management reports that would give managers the information they needed for decision-making purposes.
- **Decision Support:** 1970s-1980s By the 1970s, it was evident that the prespecified information products produced by such management information systems were not adequately meeting many of the decision-making needs of management. So the concept of decision support systems **(DSS)** was born. The new role for information systems was to provide managerial end users with ad hoc and interactive support of their decision-making processes. This support would be tailored to the unique decision-making styles of managers as they confronted specific types of problems in the real world.

- **Strategic and End User Support:** 1980s-1990s

  ❖ End User Support: In the 1980s, several new roles for information systems appeared. First, the rapid development of microcomputer processing power, application software packages, and telecommunication networks gave birth to the phenomenon of **end user computing**. Now, end users can use their own computing resources to support their job requirements instead of waiting for the indirect support of corporate information services departments.

  ❖ Executive Information Systems: Also in the 1980s it became evident that most top corporate executives did not directly use either the reports of information reporting systems or the analytical modeling capabilities of decision support systems, so the concept of executive information systems **(EIS)** was developed. These information systems attempt to give top executives an easy way to get the critical information they want, when they want it, tailored to the formats they prefer.

  ❖ Expert Systems: Third, breakthroughs occurred in the development and application of artificial intelligence **(AI)** techniques to business information systems. Expert systems **(ES)** and other **knowledge-based systems** forged a new role for information systems. Today, expert systems can serve as consultants to users by providing expert advice in limited subject areas.

  ❖ Strategic Information Systems: An important new role for information systems appeared in the 1980s and continues into the 1990s. This is the concept of a strategic role for information systems, sometimes called strategic information systems **(SIS)**. In this concept, information technology becomes an integral component of business processes, products, and services that help a company gain a competitive advantage in the global marketplace.

- **Electronic Business and Commerce:** 1990s-2000s. Rapid growth of the Internet, intranets, extranets, and other interconnected global networks in the 1990s is dramatically changing the capabilities of information systems in business as we move into the next century. Such enterprise and global internet working is revolutionizing end user, enterprise, and interorganizational computing, communications, and collaboration that supports the business operations and management of successful global enterprises.

4.9 DATA BASE

A database is a collection of interrelated data stored with minimum redundancy to serve many users quickly and effectively. The general objective is to make information access easy, quick, inexpensive and flexible for the user. The smallest unit of data that has no meaning to the user is called a data item. Various data items are grouped together to form a record. Grouping of all records constitute a file. Each of the functional systems in an organization has unique data files, which are used by the sub systems. There are also files which need to be accessed by more than one application and these files to be made available also for general retrieval. These files are organized into what are known are as Data Base. Data Base can be conceived as a repository of information needed for running various functions in an organization. It is a mechanized, formally defined, centrally controlled collection of data in an organization.

Meaning of Database

Database is defined as an integrated collection of data and information which is utilized by several information sub-systems of an organization. It may also be defined as 'super file', which consolidates and integrates data files. Such a database can be organized as an integrated collection of data records into a single 'super file' or it can be organized as an integrated collection of several data files. The organization of common database slows it to be accessed by several information sub-systems and thus eliminates the necessity of duplication in data storage, updating, deletion and protection.

4.10 GENERAL CHARACTERISTICS OF DATABASE

Centralized and integrated data file which consists of all data used by a company.

1. **Organized and structured in a different manner than the conventional sequential file organization.**
2. **Organization is such that duplication of data is minimized if not eliminated entirely.**
3. **Permits access to any or all data quantities by all applications with equal case.**
4. **Emphasies the independence of programs as well as data and application programs and including it as part of the database.**
5. **Stored on a direct access storage device.**
6. **Provides for the definition of logical relationships, which exist between various records in the database.**

Other Characteristics of Database:

1. **It is not possible to construct a database in one single operation. It is usually built up section by section. During this process, it is possible to —**
   - **(a) Add new files of data**
   - **(b) Add new fields to records already present in database.**
   - **(c) Create relationships between the items of data.**
2. **A database requires being stored on large capacity direct-access devices. The usual medium is the magnetic disk.**
3. **Database systems are typically installed and coordinated by an individual called the database administrator who has the overall authority to establish and control data definitions and standards. He is responsible for the design and control of the organization's database in order to preserve its integrity and prevent unauthorized usage or charge.**
4. **Sometimes due to hardware faults data records on direct access storage and destroyed. Such type of problem may be overcome by maintaining a duplicate record of the data on the back-up tape. The original data records may be stored on the back-up tape as well as the direct access storage device. For updating or effecting any change on the direct access it is necessary to record such changes on both direct access storage and back-up storage.**
5. **The problems which are usually observed during the stage of creating a common database in an existing organization is as follows:**
   - **(i) Organizing data in database.**
   - **(ii) Maintenance of database performance.**
   - **(iii) Maintenance of database security.**
   - **(iv) Maintenance of data records and accessibility of database.**

4.11 OBJECTIVES OF DATA BASE

1. **Controlled redundancy**

   Redundant data occupies more space and it is wasteful. A unique aspect of data base design is storing only one data, which controls redundancy and improves system performance. It is often wrongly stated that there is no duplication of data in a database. Data may be duplicated, but it is important to realize that there is no duplication and are minimized and controlled. This is referred to as "Controlled Redundancy."

2. **Data independence**

   An important database objective is changing hardware and storage procedures and adding new data without having to rewrite application programs. The database should be 'tunable' to improve performance without rewriting programs.

3. **More information at low cost**

   The savings attributed to the use of a database result from the computer sharing of records reduced processing times, reduction in the use of software and hardware, more efficient use of data processing personnel, and an overall improvement in the flow of data.

4. **Accuracy**

   One of the benefits of database is the timely and accurate reporting of data to all maintenance centers. The same data is available and distributed to everyone.

5. **Recovery from failure**

   With multi-user access to a database the system must recover quickly from failure with no loss of transactions.

6. **Easy for learning and use**

   A major feature of a user-friendly database package is how easy it is to learn and use.

7. **More information to management**

   Information supplied to managers is more valuable because it is based on a comprehensive collection of data instead of files which contain only the data needed for one application.

8. **Reduce the access style**

   Great deal of programming time is saved because the DBMS handles the construction and processing of files as well as retrieval of data.

9. **Integrity**

   Use of integrity system is greatly facilitates collection of files grouped together as one entity. This collection is tied together by a series of tables and arrays to form one giant, integrated file. The tables and arrays serves as a index to define relationships between records and files maintained in the database.

Disadvantages of a Database:

1. Too much of cost and time required implementing such a system.
2. A database requires the use of a large-scale computer system.
3. The time involved for a project of this scope is a minimum of one to two years.
4. A large full-time staff is also required to design, program and support the implementation of a database.

Data Aggregates:

The database can be sub-divided into levels as follows:

Database: Aggregate of files to meet MIS requirement.

File: Related records or blocks

Blocks: Two or more records retained in a particular storage medium such as a file cabinet or computer tape.

Record: A collection data elements related to a common identifier is such as a person, machine, place, or operation.

Group: Two or more data elements that are logical related and must appear together to form a complete unit of meaning (street number and name, first and last name of a person).

Data element: Sometimes called words, fields or data items is the lowest level of the data structure and the only one with which a specific value may be associated, for example, age, font number, or department number one data elements, as are names or descriptions.

4.12 DATABASE MANAGEMENT SYSTEM

The function of defining, creating, revising and controlling the database is referred as DBMS. DBMS is software, which provides facilities for retrieving data, generating reports, revising data definitions, updating data and building applications. IS has its footing on DBMS. DBMS controls the interaction between the database and application programmers and also between the database and non-programming users.

What is a Database?

Let us begin with the concept 'database' and its management. Database is a collection of information in a structured way. We can say that it is a collection of a group of facts. Your personal address book is a database of names you like to keep track of, such as personal friends and members of your family. Let us look into our earlier example of information on students in NOS. A sample of 5 students is presented in the table below (see, Fig.). We have given 6 items of information on every student, namely, Roll No., Name, Date of Birth, Sex, Postal address and Subjects offered by the student.

Fig. contains required details about each student. There are six pieces of information on each student. They are Roll No, Name, Date of Birth, Sex, Address and Subjects. Each piece of information in database is called a Field. We can define field as the smallest unit in a database. Each field represents one and only one characteristic of an event or item. Thus, there are six fields in this database.

ROLL NO.	NAME	DATE OF BIRTH	SEX	ADDRESS	SUBJECTS
9721001	Subrat Das	21.05.1980	M	C36, Sector 2, Bhubaneswar Orissa	Pol Sc, Eco, History, Eng, Hindi
9721002	Aditya Bhoi	12.06.1981	M	At/Po. Burla, Sambal Pur	Phy, Chem, Biology, Eng, Hindi
9732012	Madhu Jain	03.01.1979	F	A31, Pilani, Rajasthan	Pol Sc, Eco, History, Eng, Hindi
9724004	Ahmad Ali	23.11.1979	M	12A, Sheikh Sarai-I, New Delhi	Phy, Chem, Biology, Eng, Hindi
9715023	C. Suresh	07.09.1980	M	96, Malviya Nagar, Bhopal	Pol Sc, Eco, History, Eng, Hindi

If you take a close look at all these fields, they are not of the same type. Date of birth is *date* type whereas Name is *character* type. In database there can be five categories of fields. They are:

- Numeric
- Character
- Logic
- Memo
- Date

We will discuss about each type of field in detail later on in this lesson. First let us be familiar with another concept that we will use frequently. All the related fields for a particular event is called a **Record**. In the example above, all six fields taken together for a particular student is called a record of that student. Hence, since there are six students there are six records. Thus, we can define record as a collection of logically related fields.

Now we are in a position to define **database** in a formal manner. We can say that it is a collection of logically related records. In other words a database is a collection of database files, and each database file is a collection of records.

The task before us is creation of a database and its management. Data management involves creating, modifying, deleting and adding data in files, and using this data to generate reports or answer queries. The software that allows us to perform these functions easily is called a Data Base Management System (DBMS). Using a DBMS files can be retrieved easily and effectively. There are many DBMS packages available in the market. Some of them are:

- dBASE III Plus
- FoxBASE Plus
- SoftBASE
- Clipper
- Paradox

There are some WINDOWS based database packages available in the market such as MS ACCESS (part of MS OFFICE). In this lesson we will discuss about the package dBASE III + which is a DOS based package. It provides many choices to work with the program. This means you can work through both *assist screen* and *dot prompt*. It allows you to work with both financial figures and text.

Definition

Each database has been defined a system for operating the data base. This system or set of rules and methods, allows for the definition, creation, updating, reading, maintenance and protection of the database. This system is a DBMS.

Impact on Management:

Management can drive some great benefits from proper use of a good DBMS.

- Much more data can be considered when producing information for management decision-making.
- Information can be available to the managers more quickly.
- Business can be transacted more effectively and efficiently, e.g., when customer is made available instantly and, in the case of banks, in whatever branch the customer patronizes.
- Databases from the sources outside the company are available to assist management in decision-making, (e.g., stock information).

Database Management System

A collection of programs required to store and retrieve data from a database is called a database management system (DBMS). It is a complex software system which constructs, expands and maintains the database and also provides the interface between the user and the data in the base.

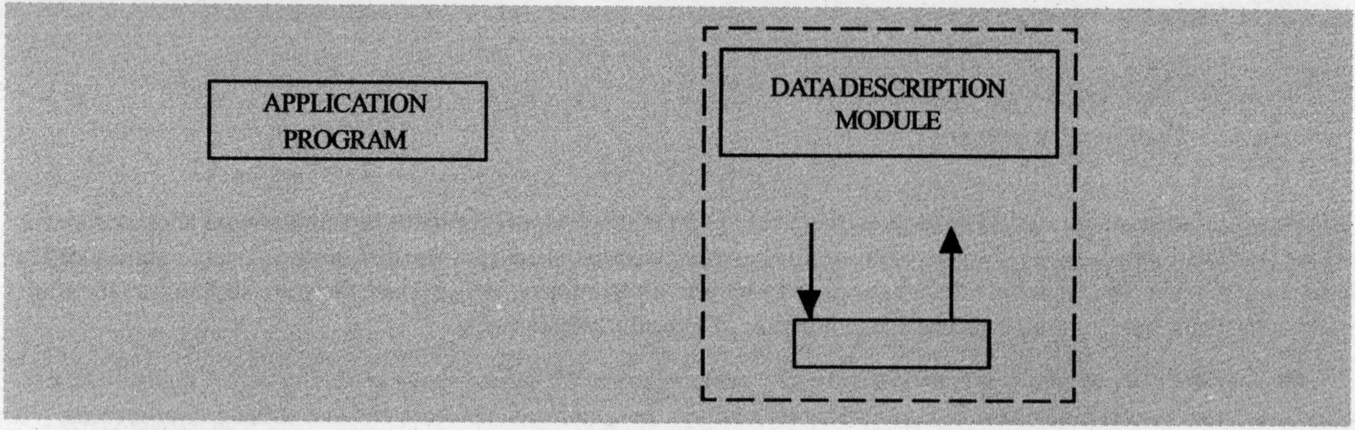

As shown in the above figure, the principle components of a DBMS are a data description module and a data manipulation module. The data description module of the DBMS analyses the data requirements of the application programs and transfers control to the data manipulation module, which retrieves the needed data elements from the database.

4.13 OBJECTIVES OF A DBMS

1. Provide for mass storage of relevant data.
2. Make access to the data easy for the user
3. Provide prompt response to user requests for data.
4. Make the latest modifications to the database available immediately.
5. Eliminate redundant data.
6. Allow multiple users to be active at one time.
7. Allow for Growth in the database system.
8. Protect the data from physical harm.
9. Unauthorized access.

4.14 COMPONENTS OF A DBMS

The following are the five components of a DBMS.

- At least one person who "owns" and is responsible for the data base.
- A set of rules and relationships that defines and governs the interactions among elements of the data base.
- People who put data into the data base.
- People who get data out of the data base.
- The data base itself.

Approaches to defining a database

The following are the three best known approaches to define the database-

- The relational approach
- The hierarchical approach.
- The network approach.

4.15 ACTIVITIES AND FUNCTIONS OF DBMS

The database management system is a sophisticated group of programs that performs the following activities:

(i) Creates the database.

(ii) Maintain the contents in an up-to-date manner.

(iii) Makes the data available to an application, programmes and queries.

(iv) Provides statistics on database.

Functions:

A DBMS is designed to perform six major functions:

1. It organizes data according to the specifications placed in the data definition language by the database administrator (DBA) or system designer in the initial design as well as when the database configuration changes, in the most suitable manner for each application.
2. It orchestrates and integrates data. At the basic element, the field level data is chained, interrelated or linked so that they can be juxtaposed in any desired combination during execution of a designed application program. Thus DBMS is the vehicle to collect, combine and return a part of the available data to the user.
3. Serves as a filter between application programs and data associated with them. The application logic is divorced from the input/output logic that selects the appropriate data elements. It also buffers the logical description and relationships from the way data are physically stored. The database remains secure and in tact even it is processed by different programs describing data in diverse ways and in different languages.
4. Control data appearing as it will as an extension of the operating systems. On data storage requests from programs, it controls where and how data is physically stored, on retrievals, it locates and returns the requested elements of data to the program.
5. Retrieves data (in full or partly) in any desired fashion, serially, in sequence of physical storage, sequentially as desired by the user defined key, randomly, by address, randomly by key, by the structural link.

4.16 ADVANTAGE OF DATA BASE MANAGEMENT

1. **Eliminates data redundancy**

   Under a DBMS, data that are normally stored two or more times are stored only once. This obviously reduces both storage costs and confusion that can occur when data are stored two or more times and are different.

2. **Ability to associate related data**

   The ability to associate related data not only allows data redundancy to be reduced but also provides the ability to process unanticipated requests for data.

3. **Program data independence**

For the DBMS, program can be changed without changing the files, and data files can be changed without changing the programs. The DBMS serves as interface between the programs and the data files so that the programs are concerned only with the logical symbolic names of the data, not, physical storage.

4. **Improvement of the interface between the user and the system**

DBMS provides simple query languages through which the user or the user through an application programming can retrieve information quickly to fill unanticipated needs for information. In addition, these languages enable users to write their own programs to retrieve information periodically.

5. **Increased security and integration of data**

Data contained in a DBMS are lively to be more secure and better integrated than data under traditional file approach because the database administrator's primary function is to provide for the integration, physical storage and security of the data.

QUESTIONS

Short Answer Question

1. Explain the Data and Information
2. Explain data processing.
3. What do you mean by data bank?
4. State the difference between data and information
5. State any two objectives of data processing.
6. Explain DBMS
7. What is a database?
8. Any two drawbacks in Batch Processing.
9. What are the Kinds of Data Processing?

Long Answer Question

1. What is data processing cycle?
2. What are different data types?
3. What is known as data and information?
4. Write short note on data generation.
5. What is data processing? List out various data processing methods.
6. Write short notes on central processing unit.
7. What are the objectives of data processing?
8. Explain any one business data processing
9. Write a note on "updation" in data processing with an example.

10. Write a note on "Reporting" in data processing with an example.
11. What is data structure?
12. What are the functions of data processing?
13. Write short notes on:

    (a) Data (b) Information (c) Data bank and (d) Database
14. What are the advantages of database management system?
15. Explain Online Processing.

Very Long or Essay Type Question

1. What are the roles of data processing applications in business?
2. Explain methods of Data Processing Systems.
3. Distinguish between data processing and data processing system.
4. What are the areas wherein data processing can be used in business?
5. Briefly explain the database management system.
6. Briefly explain:

    (a) Batch processing (b) Online processing

5

CHAPTER

COMPUTER COMMUNICATION

Structure:

5.1 COMMUNICATION AND COMPUTER NETWORK

Today computer is available in many offices and homes and therefore there is a need to share data and programs among various computers with the advancement of data communication facilities. The communication between computers has increased and it thus has extended the power of computer beyond the computer room. Now a user sitting at one place can communicate computers of any remote sites through communication channel. The aim of this chapter is to introduce you the various aspects of computer network.

5.2 DATA COMMUNICATION

We all are acquainted with some sort of communication in our day-to-day life. For communication of information and messages we use telephone and postal communication systems. Similarly data and information from one computer system can be transmitted to other systems across geographical areas. Thus data transmission is the movement of information using some standard methods. These methods include electrical signals carried along a conductor, optical signals along an optical fibers and electromagnetic areas.

Suppose a manager has to write several letters to various clients. First he has to use his PC and Word Processing package to prepare his letter. If the PC is connected to all the clients' PCs through networking, he can send the letters to all the clients within minutes. Thus irrespective of geographical areas, if PCs are connected through communication channel, the data and information, computer files and any other program can be transmitted to other computer systems within seconds. The modern form of communication like *e-mail* and *Internet* is possible only because of computer networking.

Basic Elements of a Communication System:

The following are the basic requirements for working of a communication system.

1. A *sender* (source) which creates the message to be transmitted.
2. A *medium* that carries the message.
3. A *receiver* (sink) which receives the message.

In data communication four basic terms are frequently used. They are:

- **Data:** A collection of facts in raw forms that become information after processing.
- **Signals:** Electric or electromagnetic encoding of data.
- **Signaling:** Propagation of signals across a communication medium.
- **Transmission:** Communication of data achieved by the processing of signals.

Communication Protocols:

You may be wondering how do the computers send and receive data across communication links. The answer is *data communication software*. It is this software that enables us to communicate with other systems. The data communication software instructs computer systems and devices as to how exactly data is to be transferred from one place to another. The procedure of data transformation in the form of software is commonly called *protocol*.

The data transmission software or protocols perform the following functions for the efficient and error free transmission of data.

Data sequencing: A long message to be transmitted is broken into smaller packets of fixed size for error free data transmission.

Data Routing: It is the process of finding the most efficient route between source and destination before sending the data.

Flow control: All machines are not equally efficient in terms of speed. Hence the flow control regulates the process of sending data between fast sender and slow receiver.

Error Control: Error detecting and recovering is the one of the main function of communication software. It ensures that data are transmitted without any error.

Data Transmission Modes

There are three ways for transmitting data from one point to another:

1. **Simplex:** In simplex mode the communication can take place in one direction. The *receiver* receives the signal from the transmitting device. In this mode the flow of information is Uni-directional. Hence it is rarely used for data communication.
2. **Half-duplex:** In half-duplex mode the communication channel is used in both directions, but only in one direction at a time. Thus a half-duplex line can alternately send and receive data.
3. **Full-duplex:** In full duplex the communication channel is used in both directions at the same time. Use of full-duplex line improves the efficiency as the line turn-around time required in half-duplex arrangement is eliminated. Example of this mode of transmission is the telephone line.

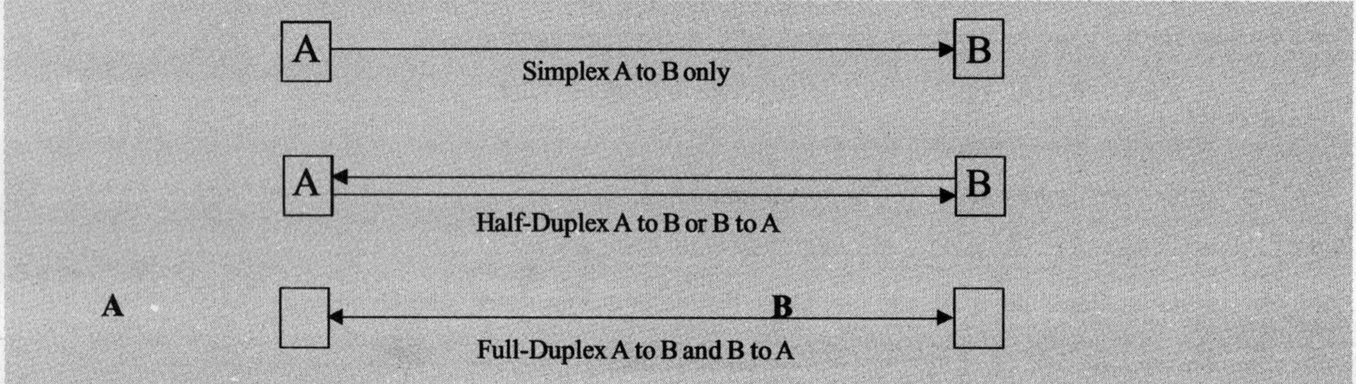

Digital and Analog Transmission:

Data is transmitted from one point to another point by means of electrical signals that may be in digital and analog form. So one should know the fundamental difference between analog and digital signals. In analog signal the transmission power varies over a continuous range with respect to sound, light and radio waves. On the other hand, a digital signal may assume only discrete set of values within a given range. Examples are computer and computer related equipment. Analog signal is measured in *Volts* and its frequency in *Hertz* (Hz). A digital signal is a sequence of voltage represented in *binary form*. When digital data are to be sent over an analog form the digital signal must be converted to analog form. So the technique by which a digital signal is converted to analog form is known as *modulation*. And the reverse process, that is the conversion of analog signal to its digital form, is known as demodulation. The device, which converts digital signal into analog, and the reverse, is known as *modem*.

Analog Signal

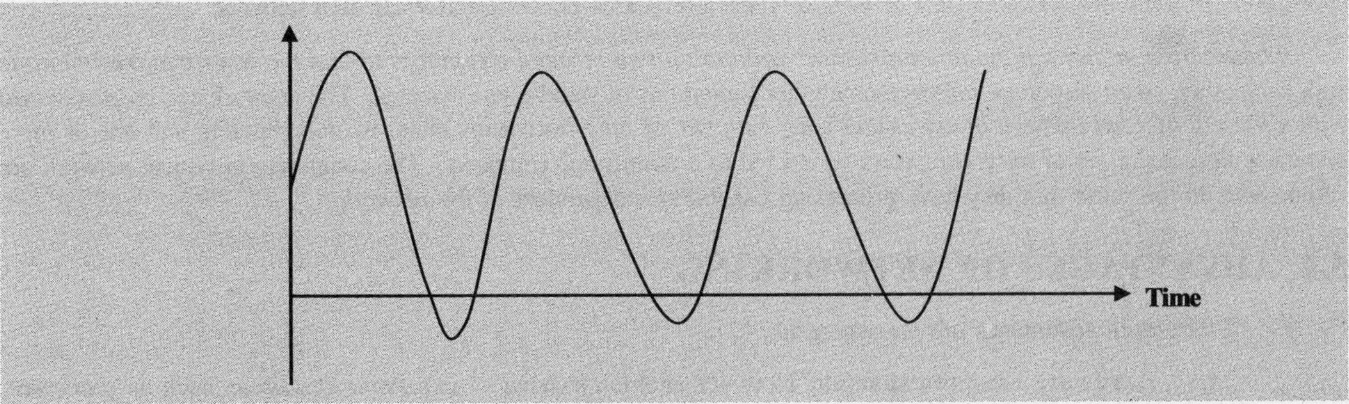

Asynchronous and Synchronous Transmission

Data transmission through a medium can be either asynchronous or synchronous. In asynchronous transmission data is transmitted character by character as you go on typing on a keyboard. Hence there are irregular gaps between characters. However, it is cheaper to implement, as you do not have to save the data before sending. On the other hand, in the synchronous mode, the saved data is transmitted block by block. Each block can contain many characters. Synchronous transmission is well suited for remote communication between a computer and related devices like card reader and printers.

Following are the major communication devices used today.

Wire Pairs: Wire pairs are commonly used in local telephone communication and for short distance digital data communication. They are usually made up of copper and the pair of wires is twisted together. Data transmission speed is normally 9600 bits per second in a distance of 100 meter.

Coaxial Cables: Coaxial cable is groups of specially wrapped and insulted wires that are able to transfer data at higher rate. They consist of a central copper wire surrounded by an insulation over which copper mesh is placed. They are used for long distance telephone lines and local area network for their noise immunity and faster data transfer.

Microwave: Microwave system uses very high frequency radio signals to transmit data through space. The transmitter and receiver of a microwave system should be in line-of-sight because the radio signal cannot bend. With microwave very long distance transmission is not possible. In order to overcome the problem of line of sight and power amplification of weak signal, repeaters are used at intervals of 25 to 30 kilometers between the transmitting and receiving end.

Communication Satellite: The problem of line-sight and repeaters are overcome by using satellites which are the most widely used data transmission media in modern days. A communication satellite is a microwave relay station placed in outer space. INSAT-1B is such a satellite that can be accessible from anywhere in India. In satellite communication, microwave signal is transmitted from a transmitter on earth to the satellite at space. The satellite amplifies the weak signal and transmits it back to the receiver. The main advantage of satellite communication is that it is a single microwave relay station visible from any point of a very large area. In microwave the data transmission rate is 16 giga bits per second. They are mostly used to link big metropolitan cities.

5.3 COMPUTER NETWORK

With standardized hardware and software, the microcomputers provide user-friendly environment. It meets the computing requirements of most users. But, the need for interaction with other computer users and with other computer systems for exchange of data etc., has increased over the years. Networks are increasingly meeting this need. From the users' point of view the networks may be of two types: Local area network and Wide area network.

Computer networking is the process of inter connecting two or more computers so that the users can communicate with each other, share resources and overcome other limitations of stand-alone systems. The network can be established with a variety of combinations of computers such as a net of only microcomputers, microcomputers and one or more minicomputers and a set of microcomputers connected to a mainframe computer. The computers in typical network are autonomous in the sense that they have processing capability independent of the network.

5.4 ADVANTAGES OF NETWORKING

The main advantages of networking are:

(i) **Hardware resource sharing:** Network enables sharing of expensive resources such as processor, storage space and peripherals like modern, fax, and laser printer.

(ii) **Sharing of databases:** The network permits concurrent access to the same data file by many users in the network. Thus, user in the sales department, production department, inventory department etc. share corporate databases.

(iii) **Sharing of Software:** Any user in a network can load and use the software installed on any of the computer of fileserver in the network.

(iv) **Communication between users:** The Network users can communicate between them. E-mail facility can also be used for communication.

(v) **Decentralized data processing:** In a network, the data processing can be decentralized by enabling local offices to capture and store data, and generate information to meet most of their requirements at local level itself.

(vi) **Security of data:** In a networked environment the data is backed up with duplicate storage. Adequate security measures are also put in place to produce the data.

5.5 TYPES OF NETWORK

The networks can be classified into three; local area network (LAN), metropolitan area network (MAN) and wide area network (WAN). They are explained in the following sections:

1. Wide Area Network (WAN)

WAN is made up of number of autonomous computers distributed over a wide geographical area. WANs were originally developed in the late 1960s to enable communication between computer centers and sharing of hardware, software and other communication facilities. WAN can be implemented using private or public networks. In a private network an organization takes on lease telephone lines to connect such sites into a network. It is also possible to connect computers in different locations using microwave or satellite transmission. Public networks are installed by the Government owned telecommunication agencies. WAN spans large geographic distances. It is also called long-haul network. WAN is usually operated at lower speeds then MAN and involves delay.

Most organizations use private networks for communication. Society for Worldwide Inter bank Financial Transactions (SWIFT), a non-profit organization of banks, owns a private network. The network exchanges financial transactions between the participating financial institutions, about 3000 in number in over 60 countries. The terminals of these participating banks are hooked with SWIFT's access centers. The network offers data communication service 24 hours a day, 7 days a week.

INDONET, NICNET, SBINET and WELCOMENET are some of the private networks in India. CMC's INDONET offers e-mail service to customers for a fee. NICNET is a network of National Informatics Center that connects all the district headquarters in the country. SBINET is a private network of State Bank of India and connects its branches across the country. WELCOMNET connects the hotels of the Welcome Group.

Features of Wide Area Network:

A wide area network (WAN) is used to connect LANs and nodes that are separated by great physical distance. Generally speaking it is larger version of LAN with several differences:

1. It operates by means of the international telephone network
2. Unlike LANs which owned by their users, WANs operate on public and leased telephone lines provided by licensed common carriers, or by other means such as satellite and microwave, which are regulated by government agencies.
3. Data transmission is somewhere slower.
4. The WAN compose any of the following system configurations:
5. Single nodes
6. Clusters
7. LANs

Suppose a company has its central headquarters in Coimbatore and the Coimbatore site contains all departments and equipment for product manufacturing and distribution, accounting, and sales. The information pertaining to these operations is tracked by a single centralized database system. As the company becomes more profitable and expands, it establishes additional sales offices in Mumbai and Delhi. Each sales office maintains its own system to record and track customer orders for its region. At the same time the two sites are linked to the mode at corporate headquarters and relay each order shipment and inventory and invoice processing.

➤ Advantages of WAN

The integration of the local nodes into the distributed database linked by the WAN provides the following advantages:

1. The WAN allows access to database at remote sites, enabling exchange of data.
2. If a remote node fails, remaining nodes on the network can still exchange data.
3. If the network fails, the local mode can still access its own database.
4. The data used on daily basis by the sales offices resides at the local site, making it easier to retrieve quickly.
5. The local offices can maintain the data more effectively. The corporate office can access the data as needed.
6. As a site's database grows larger, its system's storage capacity can be easily upgraded without affecting the transfer of data between other nodes on network.

One of the most significant aspects of a wide area network when comparing it with freedom of a local area network is the involvement of a public telecommunications authority. Regardless of whether the network is made up from system, the controlling authority is almost always the public authority. In order to protect their equipment and employees, the authority lays down rules, which must be observed by anyone connecting to their lines. In most countries stringent requirements are also imposed on the characteristics of the data transmissions.

2. Metropolitan Area Network (MAN)

Metropolitan area network covers a wider area than a local area network. Usually MAN covers a large metropolitan city and is a scaled down version of wide area network. It operates at high speeds over distances sufficient for a metropolitan area.

3. Local Area Network (LAN)

A LAN is a system of interconnected microcomputers, sharing common resources like disks, printers etc., and links a number of computer workstations together to allow many people to use the same software and data files. Each user in such a multi-user environment accesses the resources through his microcomputer workstation. The network operating system integrates all the network components and makes operation smooth and transparent. LAN works in restricted geographical area such as within a large building or offices within a few kilometers.

The LAN is an interconnection of computers that need to communicate with each other in a limited geographical area. The network may have other sharable devices attached such as fax, laser printers and copiers. The network includes a central facility with huge storage capacity for the requirements of the organization. It also has a network operating system for managing the network.

➢ Types of LAN

Local area networks are mainly of two types: Client/ Server LAN and Peer-to-Peer LAN.

(a) **Client / Server LAN:** Client, Server LAN has servers and clients. The server is a computer that manages shared resources: hardware as well as software and data. It is usually a powerful computer with large RAM and secondary storage capacity. The LAN has a number of microcomputers, called clients, request the server for services. The LAN may have many servers each specializing in one area of service such as file server, printer server, database server etc. A file server stores program and data files. A database server stores data and a printer server controls printers on the local area network.

(b) **Peer-to-Peer LAN:** In a **Peer-to-Peer LAN:** Every computer is equal in status and functioning. All the computers on the network are capable of communicating independently with any other computer on the network without using a server. Thus, any computer on the network can access data and programs stored on any other computer. The peer-to-peer LAN is less expensive than client/server LAN. But at the same time this LAN may be slower than a client/server LAN.

➢ LAN Topology

The design of network requires selection of a particular topology and architecture for the interconnection of network component. Topology refers to the way the computers are physically connected into the network. The network architecture includes the specifications of the components that can be connected to the network. IBM's Systems Network Architecture (SNA) is an example of vendor developed network architecture. Such network architecture specifies network components such as terminals, workstations, printers, cluster controllers, host computer and communications controllers. There are a number of network topologies. Of them ring, star and bus are popular network topologies.

(a) **Star Topology:** In star network the nodes are connected to a central computer called the host computer. The nodes cannot communicate directly. Each node can communicate with the host computer. The host computer takes the message and routes it to the other node or nodes.

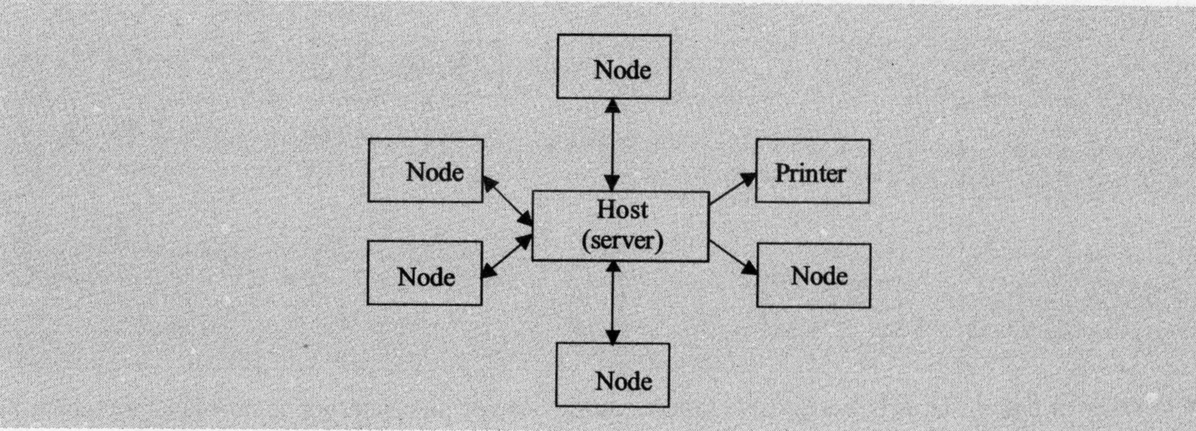

The host is the main computer to which other nodes are connected by communication links. The host computer is responsible for the overall functioning of the network. The node may be a microcomputer, terminal or any other device like storage device, printer etc.,

In a star network centralization of control over the network resources is easy. It is also possible to network minicomputer or mainframe with other microcomputers and dumb terminals. It eliminates single point failure of a common wire. If one of the host computers fails, it does not usually affect the others in the network. But the hub becomes a central point of failure in a ring network. If the host computer breaks down, the entire network breaks down.

(b) Ring Topology: In a ring network the computers can communicate directly with each other and also with the central computer. The nodes are connected to a line that is closed like a loop. The ring network is more reliable than star network. Even if the central computer in the network fails, the other computers can continue to communicate with each other.

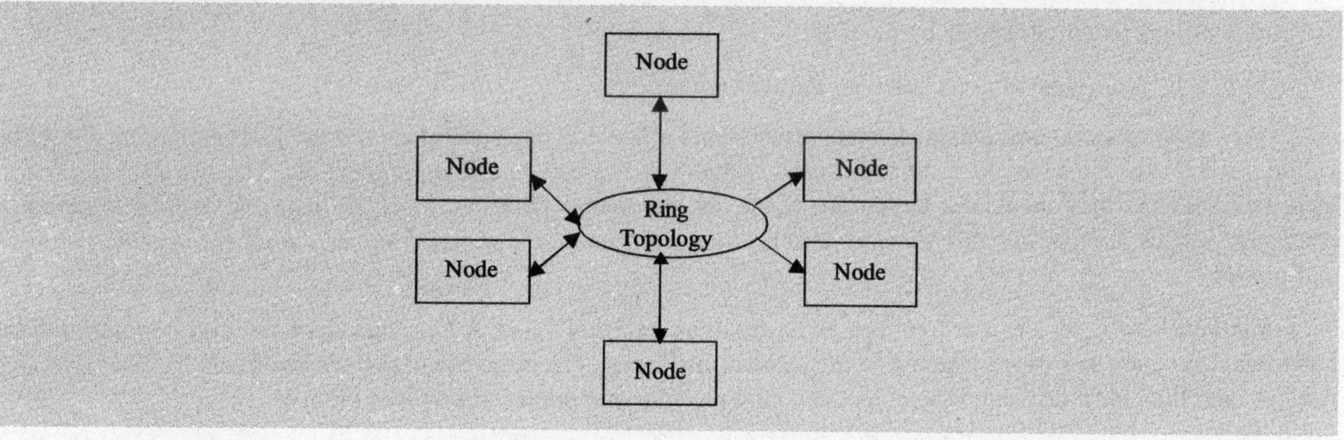

(c) Bus Topology: A bus network configures computers to a single non-looping channel. The computers connected to the network share the same bus or communication channel. Bus wiring is easy and needs much less wring for small segments.

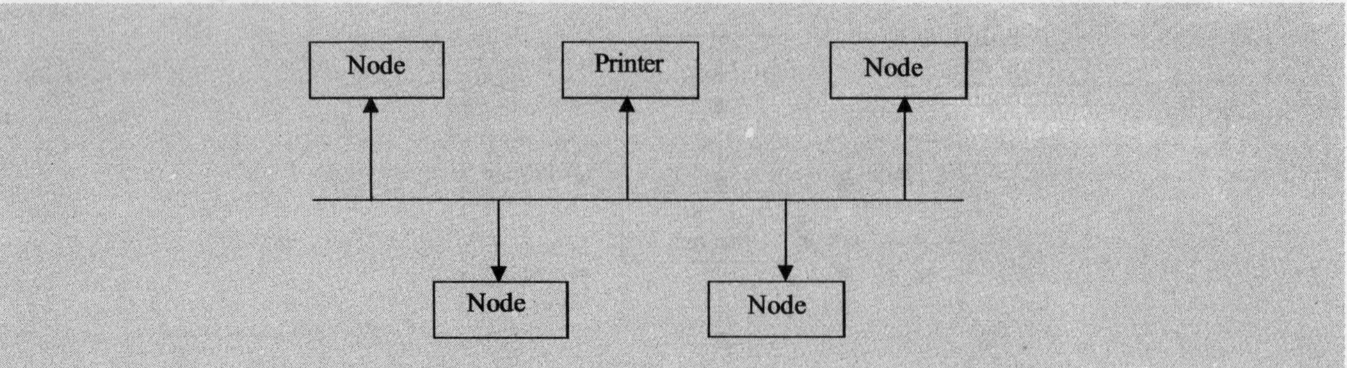

Old Ethernet bus wiring is prone to cable failure. If the bus wiring connection is broken at any point, the entire network fails.

(d) Hybrid Network: In most cases, instead of a single topology, a combination of topologies may be used for greater flexibility and reliability. Hybrid network combines features of Star, Ring and Bus network:

➤ Features of LAN

The features of LAN include the following:

(a) Limited geographical area say within a few kilometers.

(b) Common communication link for sharing information, software and peripheral devices without regard to proximity of user to such resources on the network.

(c) High transmission capability.

(d) Low error rate as the network contains built-in component for detecting for system errors.

(e) Private ownership by the user.

(f) Not subject to regulation by the telecom service.

LAN interconnects computers and components within a limited geographical area. Such LANs are normally set up within a single site can have one or more business complex, a hospital, an office building etc. The site can have one or more buildings but they should not be too far away, say less than 5 kilometers. A LAN can also include a variety of computer systems and devices such as workstations, microcomputers, file servers, plotters, scanners, graphic terminals and printers.

A large personal computer or mini computer serves as the LAN's hub. A high capacity hand disk is attached to the hub as data files and software are stored on the network file server. The users can load the software on the file server and retrieve data files for processing. The output can be directed to the printer attached to the LAN.

Any the communication network that meets most or all of the following characteristics can be classified as LAN:

(a) All the devices on the network share a common transmission medium, that is, the cable and/ or the controller.

(b) The devices connected to the network can operate independent of the network.

(c) Any device connected to it can communicate with any other device on the network, and

(d) The network is capable of supporting heavy data traffic over short distances compared to telecommunication network.

(e) The network covers a limited area usually a few kilometers in radius or a single site like a university campus, an office or a factory.

➤ LAN Components

The components of LAN are File server, workstation, network operating system, LAN cable, Active and Passive hubs etc.

(a) **Workstation:** It is a single-user microcomputer with high power communication facilities. It can exchange message with other workstations or fileserver.

Workstations can be of two types: user workstation and server workstation. User workstation is a microcomputer on the network, which is used to access the network. Service workstation performs service to process other workstations on the network. User workstation normally does not process requests from other workstations. Server workstation makes available all sharable network resources to other workstations. More than one server workstations may be added to the network such as printer server and fileserver. Normally the server workstation is the most powerful workstation. Server workstation may be dedicated or non-dedicated. In case of dedicated workstation, it is not available for other user applications. Non-dedicated server workstation doubles as an individual workstation and at the same time performs network-related functions.

(b) **File Server:** File server is actually a process running on a computer that provides the clients access to files on that computer. The term is loosely applied to mean computer that runs file server software. In this sense, it is a powerful computer with special software to serve files to other workstations on the network. The files, which may be program files or data files, are simultaneously shared by a number of workstations. Novell Netware is a popular network operating system.

(c) **Gateway:** The gateway assists in communicating between LANs. A workstation may be dedicated to serve as gateway. This is required particularly when two networks with different technologies have to communicate with each other. Gateway may also be used to connect LAN with a mainframe computer.

(d) **Network Interface Unit:** The network interface is a printed circuit board installed in the microcomputer. It may be called network card, network adapter or network interface unit. It connects the workstations functionally and physically with the network.

(e) **Active Hub:** Hub is an electronic device to which multiple computers are attached usually using twisted pair cables. Active hub is a powered distribution point with active devices that drive distant nodes up to one kilometer away. It can connect up to eight nodes on the network. The maximum distance carried by an active hub is about 2000 ft.

(f) **Passive Hub:** This hub is a distribution point that does not use power or active devices in a network to connect up to four nodes within a short distance. The maximum distance covered by a passive hub is nearly 300 ft.

(g) **LAN Cable:** LAN requires superior cable capable of transferring data at high speed. Coaxial cables or fibre optic cables may be used for networking computer.

(h) **Network Operating System (NOS):** The NOS integrates all the network components. The NOS facilitates file and print serving along with other functions like communications and e-mail between workstations. In most LANs the NOS exists along with the computer's operating system.The computer's operating system processes the system requests first and processes them if they can be done with the workstation resources. If it is not a local request, meaning that the network resources have to be used, the request is transferred to NOS for carrying out. Thus, the NOS is responsible for controlling access to data, storage space and sharing of other peripheral resources.

(i) **Applications Software:** Another component of LAN is application software. It has to be ensured that the application software works in the multi-user environment.

(j) **Protocols:** Data transmission between devices requires protocol. Protocols are sets of rules and procedures to control the data transmission between computer and other devices. They are common technical guidelines for communication between devices. They specify the order in which signals will be transferred, the signal for completion of transfer etc. Only Devices using the same protocol can communicate directly. Both the sending and receiving devices must use the same protocol for effecting communication. For communication between devices using different protocols requires intermediate interpretation device or software.

The Protocol Performs the Following Functions:

(a) Set up a link with the other device in the communication.

(b) Identify the component to other components in the communication (sending device's channel ID).

(c) Send and interpret the data.

(d) Provide a continuous feedback on data transmission like data is not being received and understood.

(e) Request for retransmission of garbled data.

(f) Engage recovery procedure when error occurs.

(g) Provide an acceptable way of terminating transmission so that all devices have completed the process.

The protocol is embedded in communication software designed to use a particular protocol. The user need not bother about the protocol as the components involved in the communication perform the protocol matching.The data communication protocols are of two main types: asynchronous and synchronous. The synchronous protocol permits continuous data transmission. The devices in communication must be synchronized with the other. The transmission is governed by a time interval and not by start-stop bits. For example, clock, in the modern, sets the time interval.

6

CHAPTER

INTERNET AND E-COMMERCE

Structure:

6.1 INTRODUCTION

Internet is a communication network which bridges all the small computer networks worldwide as a whole. Internet is based upon Internet technology, in particular World Wide Web (WWW), to build Information System within organization or enterprise to accomplish standardization and automation. Fundamentally, it means network computing environments which let the users share the information through the Internet and Web browsers. Ultimately, it allows a certain organization to build a Groupware within Web environment at low cost on top of existing network infrastructure. By doing this, closed organization network would be interconnected with existing worldwide Internet, which results in diverse information that strengthens competitive advantages of the organization. Basically, it runs on top TCP/IP and HTTP and filters out any illegal access through firewall.

Where the Internet connects people and organizations and information sources by using common protocols to link computers on a public and open-to-all basis, an Internet uses the same common protocols for internal company or group purposes. Instead of adopting a common proprietary standard for its communications, information storage and presentation, etc., the company (or any group of people or companies) decides to use Internet standards and methods.

Internet-Meaning

An Internet can be defined as a network connecting an affiliated set of clients using standard Internet protocols, especially. TCP / IP and HTTP or as an IP-based network of nodes behind a firewall, or behind several firewalls connected by secure, possibly virtual, networks.In general, a web is an unstructured client / server network that uses HTTP as its transaction protocol. The World Wide Web comprises all HTTP nodes on the public Internet .An internal web comprises all HTTP nodes on a private network, such as an organization's LAN or WAN. If the organization is a corporation, the internal web is also a corporate web.If a corporate web connects two or more trading partners, it is often referred to as a business-to-business web, or an extranet.

Note that internal webs — also known as intranets — are only logically "internal " to an organization. Physically they can span the globe, as long as access is limited to a defined community of interest.

6.2 HISTORY OF INTERNET

In 1969, the U.S. Defense Department funded a project to develop a network, which can withstand the bombing. Basically the idea was to develop a very secure network which can work even after a nuclear attack. This project was known as ARPANET. The proposed network was not supposed to have a central control — which would be an obvious target. Ten years of research brought Local Area Ethernet Networks (LANs) and workstations were developed to get connected to LAN. These workstations and LANs were then connected to the ARPANET. For next decade the ARPANET grew and its decentralized features helped its rapid expansion. Computers connected to ARPANET used a standard or rule to communicate with each other. This standard used by ARPANET is known as NCP (National Control Protocol). Protocol is a network term used to indicate the standard used by a network for communication. But the passing time and rapid change in information technology suppressed NCP and brought TCP/IP (Transmission Control Protocol/Internet Protocol) in to the world of networking. TCP converts messages into streams of packets at the source, and they are reassembled back into messages at the destination. IP handles the dispatch of these packets. It handles the addressing, and makes sure that a packet reaches its destination through multiple nodes and even across multiple networks with multiple standards. This flexibility of TCP/IP to handle multiple networks with multiple protocols encourages other networks to get connected to ARPANET. Slowly the ARPANET became a massive network of networks and now it is known as 'Internet.'

Internet is termed by some people as the world of largest democracy with no government. It has no state of head to control it. Why do people want to get connected to Internet? May be because of freedom it provides. The Internet is a rare example of a large democracy with no state of head, no official censors, no bosses, no board of directors. Nobody controls the Internet and in principle, any computer can speak to any other computer, as long as it obeys the technical rules of the TCP/IP protocol. This freedom of Internet helped it to move out of its original base in military and research institutions, into elementary and high schools, colleges, public libraries, commercial sectors even into the shop of a vegetable vendor.

6.3 CORE FEATURES OF THE INTERNET

There are some characteristics of the internet that gave it the potential to deliver a special set of business benefits over and above existing IT technologies.

(a) **Simplicity of Use:** The software that is used access the Internet (the web browser software) is comparatively easy to learn and simple to use. It can operate on wide range of operating system platforms and can access any mainstream application like SAP and oracle. The flexibility of the web combined with the simplicity of the browser software has resulted in reduced staff training costs, lower development costs and an increase in the range of users who can have access to the organization.

(b) **Breadth of Access:** The internet is a global network like the telephone network. Its access is not conditioned by geographic boundaries. Unlike the telephone network the cost involved in global connection is not related to the distance involved. No other communication medium has had access to such a large audience and range of people which increases the ability to leverage the value of information to a scale that has never before been possible.

(c) **Synergy with other Media:** Apart from using the existing telecommunication technology, it supports or complements other media. Internet services have demonstrated a high degree of synergy with other media as can be seen from the following:

Example

Book, magazine and newspaper publishers have used the web to supplement and extend their written products. Publishers of CD-ROMs have used the web to maintain the currency of the information they can deliver. Microsoft's encyclopedias CD-ROM, Encarta, allows seamless interface to information accessed from the company's website. Publishers of software and games now deliver their products directly over the internet. Entertainment companies regularly provide extracts of their films and music recordings to promote the real products.

(d) **Low Relative Cost:** The costs involved in conducting a process using internet technology are less than those involving other methods. The internet access requires telephone line for most individual users. The pricing of telephone service is one which is independent of distance. The charge for the usage of telecommunication line is based on local charge rate irrespective of what is sent over the line or how distant the recipient is.

(e) **Extension of Existing IT Resources:** Resource sharing was underlying rationale for the development of the internet. It allows the IT resources to be shared by multiple users in organizations and also with others related to the organization such as trading partners.

(f) **Flexibility of Communication:** The web browsers greatly extend the ways in which individuals can communicate. They support text, voice and multimedia formats and can provide immediate access to shared information. These facilities are available for intra-company communications as those between individuals in separate organizations.

(g) **Security:** Security has been a major issue in internet as any security breach can cause financial loss, leak of sensitive information, etc. Standards for secure electronic transactions have been developed and reasonable security is in place now.

(h) **Speed and Availability:** The transmission speed is very low and it takes a bit too long for downloading files. However, compared to other means of communication, it is indeed fast. It also provides a wide range of communication services that are inexpensive and relatively easy to access for millions of users through a standard set of protocols.

An internet can be as big as a community of interest. Scale is an important factor in web implementation, but it has no bearing on the logical association of clients that make up an intranet. For example, a workgroup with one web server, a company with several hundred web servers, and a professional organization with ten thousand web servers can be considered an intranet.

6.4 INTERNET SOFTWARE

To connect to the Internet, a computer requires mainly three different kinds of software:

(a) **TCP/IP:** TCP/IP, or Transmission Control Protocol / Internet Protocol, is the basic communication protocol of the Internet. It allows programs on user's computer to communicate properly over the internet. Usually, when you are set up with direct access to the Internet, your computer is provided with a copy of the TCP/IP program. Similarly, every other computer that you may send messages to or get information from also has a copy of TCP/IP.

(b) **Dialer Software:** This software is provided by the ISP to instruct the modem to dial the phone number, and identify the user's machine to the access provider's system for access to the network.

(c) **Browser:** To use the Internet, a web browser is essential. This program allows the user to view the information available on the World Wide Web.

6.5 INTERNET APPLICATIONS (OR) SERVICES OF INTERNET

The Internet has grown from a small project to today's biggest network of computers. Due to this colossal growth, the Internet has become the biggest domain of information. Nowadays, an Internet user has access to a wide variety of services such as electronic mail, file transfer, vast information resources, interest group membership, interactive collaboration, multimedia displays, real-time broadcasting, shopping opportunities, and much more. Some of the important services provided by the Internet are briefed in the following few sections:

1. World Wide Web: (WWW)

The World Wide Web (abbreviated as the web or WWW) is one of the most popular services available on Internet. It is a subset of the Internet and it presents text, images, animation, video, sound and other multimedia in a single interface. This greatly enhances the experience of the Internet surfer. Although the World Wide Web is often referred to as the Internet, they are actually two different concepts. The Internet is the decentralized global network of computers that transfer information and the wring that makes all this possible whereas the web is a collection of documents or websites, that users can access using the Internet and a web browser. The web is a part of the Internet and it refers to a system of Internet servers that supports hypertext using a specific Internet protocol called HTTP on a single interface (web browsers). In addition, almost every protocol type available on the Internet is accessible on the web. This includes e-mail, FTP, Telnet, and Usenet News. Since the WWW is a subset of the Internet, it stands to reason that the web could not exist without the Internet. However, the Internet would still be the Internet without the web.

The operation of the web relies primarily on hypertext, as it is a means of information retrieval. Hypertext is a document containing words that connect to other documents. These words are called links, which the user can select. A single hypertext document can contain links to documents and resources throughout the Internet. With the ability of the web to work with multimedia and advanced programming languages, the World Wide Web is the fastest growing and the most interesting part of the Internet. With video conferencing and wireless applications, the Internet is ready to take us to the new realm of communication and information exchange.

2. Electronic Mail (e-mail)

Electronic mail, or e-mail, is a fast, easy, and inexpensive way to communicate with other Internet users around the world. It is one of the basic and earliest services of the Internet and the most used application on the Internet too. E-mail overcomes most of the problems and delays of getting a physical document from one person to another. Rather, it has the dual advantage of not only being faster but cheaper to sue as well.

3. File Transfer Protocol (FTP)

FTP or File Transfer Protocol is a system of rules and a software program that enables a user to log on to another computer and transfer information between it and his/ her computer. It was the first service developed for the Internet so that government and educational institutions could easily exchange files.

FTP allows the user to get access to the files stored in the directory of a remote computer that is connected to the Internet. Using FTP, one can upload and download files from the remote computer (known as FTP servers), if he/she has access permission on the remote machine.

File Transfer Protocol, is an Internet utility software used to upload and download files. It gives access to directories or folders on remote computers and allows software, data and text files to be transferred between different kinds of computers. FTP works on the basis of same principle as that of Client/Server. FTP "Client" is a program running on your computer that enables you to talk to, and get stuff from, remote computers. The FTP client takes FTP commands and sends them as requests for information from the remote computer or known as FTP servers. To access remote FTP server it is required but not necessary to have an account in the FTP server. When the FTP client gets connected, FTP server asks for the identification in terms of User Login name and password of the FTP client. If one does not have an account in the remote FTP server, still he can connect to the server using anonymous login.

Using anonymous login, anyone can login in to a FTP server and can access public file archives, anywhere in the world, without having an account. One can easily Login to the FTP site with the username *anonymous* and e-mail address as password.

The Basic Objectives of FTP are:

- to give flexibility and promote sharing of computer programs, files and data
- to transfer data reliably and more efficiently over network
- to encourage implicit or indirect use of remote computers using Internet
- to shield a user from variations in file storage systems among hosts.

The Basic Steps in an FTP Session are:

- ❖ Start up your FTP client; by typing ftp on your system's command line/'C>' prompt (or, if you are in a Windows, double-click on the FTP icon).
- ❖ Give the FTP client an address to connect to. This is the FTP server address to which the FTP client will get connected
- ❖ Identify yourself to the FTP remote site by giving the Login Name
- ❖ Give the remote site a password
- ❖ Remote site will verify the Login Name/Password to allow the FTP client to access its files
- ❖ Look directory for files in FTP server
- ❖ Change Directories if required

- ❖ Set the transfer mode (optional); Get the file(s) you want; and
- ❖ Quit.

4. Telnet

The word "telnet" is derived from telecommunications and network and is a protocol that allows a user to log on to a remote computer. Telnet is also known as remote login, which means connecting one machine to another in such a way that a person may interact with another machine as if it is being used locally.

Telnet or remote computing is telecommunication utility software, which uses available telecommunication facility and allows you to become a user on a remote computer. Once you gain access to the remote computer, you can use it for the intended purpose. The TELNET works in a very step by step procedure. The commands typed on the client computer are sent to the local Internet Service Provider (ISP), and then from the ISP to the remote computer that you have gained access. Most of the ISP provides facility to TELNET into your own account from another city and check your e-mail while you are traveling or away on business.

The followings steps are required for a TELNET session:

- ❖ Start up the TELNET program;
- ❖ Give the TELNET program an address to connect to (some really nifty TELNET packages allow you to combine steps 1 and 2 into one simple step!);
- ❖ Make a note of what the "escape character" is;
- ❖ Log in to the remote computer;
- ❖ Set the "terminal emulation;"
- ❖ Play around on the remote computer; and
- ❖ Quit.

5. Internet Relay Chat (IRC)

IRC or Internet Relay Chat is a service on the Internet that allows people to communicate in real time and carry on conversations via the computer with one or more people. It provides the user with the facility to engage in simultaneous (synchronous) online "conversation" with other user from anywhere in the world.

6. Chatting and Instant Messaging

Chart programs allow users on the Internet to communicate with each other by typing in real time. They are sometimes included as a feature of a website, where users can log into chat rooms to exchange comments and information about the topics addressed on the site.

7. Internet Telephony

Internet telephone is the use of the Internet rather than the traditional telephone company infrastructure, to exchange spoken or other telephonic information. It consists of hardware and software that enable people to use the Internet as a transmission medium for telephone calls. There are many Internet telephony applications available. Some, such as Cool Talk and NetMeeting, come bundled with popular web browsers.

8. Video Conferencing

Video conferencing uses the same technology as IRC, but also provides sound and video pictures. It enables direct face-to-face communication across networks. A video conferencing system has to more parties in different locations, which have the ability to communicate using a combination of video, audio, and data. A video conference can be person to person (referred to as "point-to-point") or can involve more than two people (referred to as "multipoint") and the video conferencing terminals are often referred to as "endpoints."

The following five elements are common to all video conferencing endpoints:

- **Camera:** The camera captures live images to send across the network.
- **Visual Display:** It displays the images of the people taking part in the video conference.
- **Audio System:** It includes both microphones to capture audio from the endpoint and loudspeakers to play back the audio received from other endpoints across the network connection.
- **Compression:** Videos are very bandwidth-intensive and they take a long time to load. Therefore, video systems include technologies, often referred to as codes, to compress and decompress video and audio data, allowing transmission across a network connection in near-real time.
- **User Interface and Control System:** The user interface allows the users to control interactions for example, placing calls, storing and locating numbers, and adjust environment settings such as volume. The control system handles the underlying communication that takes place between endpoints.

9. Newsgroups (Usenet)

Newsgroups are international discussion groups that focus on a particular topic and helps in gathering information about that topic. The topics discussed here cover all the fields such as politics, computers, technology, and many more. The information or articles that make up the "news" are written by people interested in a specific topic. These articles are posted to the newsgroup so that others can read, reply, and comment on them.

10. Mailing Lists (List Server)

The Internet is home to a large community of individuals who carry out active discussions, organized around topic-oriented forums that are distributed via e-mail. This method of Internet communications is known as mailing list and it enables people with similar interests from all over the world to communicate and share information with each other.

6.6 INTERNET AND WORLD WIDE WEB

World Wide Web (WWW)

WWW is the acronym for the World Wide Web. It is also commonly known as 'The Web.' The WWW is hypertext based information retrieval tool. One can easily surf the Web by jumping from one document to another using the links in those documents. These documents can be in many formats, such as text, graphics, animation, sound and latest is video. They may also be a combination of all these. All the information on Internet are presented to the user as a document or more popularly known as Web Page. All these Web Pages are link to each other or even to section within a Web Page. And these links are known as Hyper Links.

The tool used to view these Web Pages on Internet is known as Internet browser or simply browser. It is a software program specifically developed to extract information on user request from the Internet and present them as a Web Page to the viewer. There are several browsers available in the market. However the most popular are Internet Explorer from Microsoft and Netscape from Netscape Inc. The process of using browser to view information on Internet is known as *Browsing* or *Surfing*.

(a) Internet Address: Just like every house, every office, every location has an address, every page on the Internet has a unique address. This address is used to get the web page for user from Internet. Just as the address of a house or office is known as its postal address, the address on the Internet is known as URL (Uniform Resource Locator). A typical Internet address or URL would look like;

http://www.nos.org/computers/internet/url.htm

The URL locates a particular web Page, among all the computers connected to the Internet. The URL contains the components that specify the protocol, server, and pathname of an item. Let us examine the URL given above (http://www.nos.org/computers/internet/url.htm).

The protocol is followed by a colon (**http:**), the server is preceded by two slashes (**//www.nos.org**), and each segment of the pathname is preceded by a single slash (**/computers/internet/url.htm**). A protocol is set of rules that tells the computer know-how to interpret the information at that address.

The first component, the protocol, defines the manner for interpreting computer information. Many Internet pages use **HTTP** (**H**ypertext **T**ransfer **P**rotocol). Other common Internet protocols that one might come across are **FTP** (File Transfer Protocol), **NEWS** (Usenet news groups protocol), and **GOPHER** (an alternative transfer protocol). Gopher protocol is mostly out of date now.

The second component, the server (**www.nos.edu**), identifies the computer system that stores the information you seek and is always preceded by two slashes. A server is a computer that has information stored on it and sends it to the client, when a request is made. Each server on the Internet has a unique address name whose text refers to the organization maintaining the server.

The last component (**/computers/internet/**), defines the path within the Server where the requested item (**url.htm**) will be found. Most of the Web pages will have **.htm** or **.html** as their secondary or extension name.

(b) How to get connected to Internet: There are various type of connectivity to get hook on to Internet. They all can be broadly classified into following category:

(i) ***Gateway Access:*** Gateway Access is also known as Level-One connection. It is the access to the Internet from a network, which is not on the Internet. The gateway allows the two different types of networks to "talk" to each other. But the users of the Gateway Internet have limited access to the Internet. They might not be able to use all the tools available on Internet. The local Internet Service Provider (ISP) normally defines this limitation.

(ii) ***Dial-up Connection:*** 'Dial-up' connection is also known as Level Two connection. This provides connection to Internet through a dial-up terminal connection. The computer, which provides Internet access is known as 'Host' and the computer that receives the access, is 'Client' or 'Terminal'. The client computer uses modem to access a "host" and acts as if it is a terminal directly connected to that host. So this type of connection is also known as 'Remote Modem Access' connection. And the host to which the client gets connected is actually connected to the Internet by a full time connection (See Leased Connection).

In dial-up connection to Internet, Host carries all the command that are typed on a client machine and forward them to Internet. It also receives the data or information from the Internet on behalf of the 'Client' and passes it to them. The client computer acts as a 'dumb' terminal connected to remote host.

This type of connection can further be divided into two categories.

(iii) ***Shell Connection:*** In this type of Internet Connection, the user will get only textual matter of a Web Page. This connection does not support Graphics display. However, the user will be able to surf the Internet, do FTP, receive mail. Shell Accounts were the only type of Internet access available for many years before the Internet entered in to the world of graphics and became more users friendly.

(iv) ***TCP/IP Connection:*** Today's graphical World Wide Web browsers provide easier access with multimedia sound and pictures. The major difference between Shell and TCP/IP account is that, Shell account can only display text and does not support graphics display, whereas TCP/IP can display both. Hence it is more popular Internet connection. Shell accounts are slowly phasing out from the Internet scenario.

To Access any of these Dial-up Accounts you Need the Following:

- Computer
- Modem
- Telephone Connection
- Shell or TCP/IP account from the ISP
- Internet client software such as Internet browser.

(v) ***Leased Connection:*** Leased connection is also known as direct Internet access or Level Three connection. It is the secure, dedicated and most expensive, level of Internet connection. With leased connection, your computer is dedicatedly and directly connected to the Internet using high-speed transmission lines. It is on-line twenty-four hours a day, seven days a week. Leased Internet connections are limited to large corporations and universities who could afford the cost.

6.7 EXTRANET AND E-MAIL

An Extranet is a private network that uses the internet protocol and the public telecommunication system to securely share part of business information or operations with suppliers, vendors, partners, customers, or other businesses. Through e-mail, documents are prepared and sent electronically. The recipients need not be present at the other end to send the message. The message gets stored in the electronic mailbox of the addressee. The recipient can open the mailbox whenever he is free and can read or print the message.

Extranet

An Extranet can be viewed as part of a company's intranet that is extended to users outside the company. It has also been described as a "state of mind" in which the internet is perceived as a way to do business with other companies as well as to sell products to customers. Extranet extends the intranet from one location to another across the internet by securing data flow, to another intranet to a business partner. In these way intranets of business partners, suppliers, creditors, distributors, customers, and the like are connected to extranets by agreements.

An Extranet requires security and privacy. These require firewall server management, e-issuance and use of digital certificate or similar means of user authentication, encryption of messages, and the use of virtual private networks that tunnel through the public network.

Characteristics of Extranet:

The following are the important characteristics of the Extranet.

(a) It is an extended internet-private business network located outside of the corporate firewall.

(b) It can be referred to an intranet that is partially accessible to authorized outsiders.

(c) It is a network that uses the internet to link businesses with others that share the common goals.

Uses of Extranet:

Companies can use an Extranet to:

(a) Exchange large volumes of data using Electronic Data Interchange.

(b) Share product catalogs exclusively with wholesalers or those in the Trade.

(c) Collaborate with other companies on joint development efforts.

(d) Jointly develop and use training programs with other companies.

(e) Provide or access services provided by one company to a group of other companies, such as an online banking application managed by one company on behalf of affiliated banks.

(f) Share news of common interest exclusively with partner companies.

(g) The manufacturing companies can coordinate the design manufacturing, scheduling and delivery across supply chain.

(h) With extranet the technology firms can support for their customers and partners and make it possible for remote access for employees.

(i) The financial services firms by using extranet can reduce costs of proprietary networks.

(j) With extranet the publishing companies can increase the speed of design and production cycles.

(k) Other benefits:

- Quicker turnaround time
- Improved communication
- Decreased paper flow
- Traceable correspondence
- Better service
- Lower overhead and expenses
- Improved employee morale
- Increased margins
- Flexibility and scalability
- Reduced transitional barriers
- Versatility

A brief list of examples of extranet could include:

- Allowing suppliers' access to relevant inventory levels
- Allowing clients to review their account records
- Allowing students to update address information in real time.

As with intranet, access is granted only where you establish that it is required. User access is controlled by the latest in security technologies, protecting sensitive material from intrusion.

What is the relationship between intranets, Extranets and e-commerce?

The answer has three parts. First, intranets, extranets and e-commerce have in common the use of Internet (predominantly web) protocols to connect business users. Second, intranets are more localized and can therefore move data faster than more distributed extranets. (Bandwidth limitations also apply to e-commerce.) Third, the amount of control that network managers can exert over users is different for the three technologies.

On an Internet, administrators can narrowly prescribe access and policy for a fixed group of users. For example, a company could specify Red Hat Linux as its standard desktop operating system, and Netscape Communicator 5 as its standard browser and mail client. The company could then write intranet workflow applications that leverage the uniform computing environment, over which it exercises strong control.

On a business-to-business Extranet, system architects at each of the participating companies must collaborate to ensure a common interface and consistent semantics (data meanings). Since one company cannot reasonably enforce standards on its trading partners, extranet application developers must take into account a wider range of technologies than is the case for intranets. For example, one company participating in an extranet might be using Microsoft Internet Explorer, another Netscape Navigator 4.5 and another Navigator Gold 3.x. In order to collaborate via extranet, the applications have to perform adequately on all represented platforms.

The same is true, even more, for e-commerce, in which the trading partners may be completely unknown to one another. This is the case when you walk into a supermarket: the common interest in communication is based on the need to transact business, and not necessarily on a long-term trust relationship. Thus, e-commerce applications often support a level of security and transactional integrity (for instance, non-repudiation of orders) not present in intranet or extranet applications.

E-mail

E-mail is an electronic message sent from one computer to another. We can send or receive personal and business-related messages with attachments, such as pictures or formatted documents. We can even send songs and computer programs.

The e-mail communication is incredibly simple. A person with a PC and a modem to connect to the network can communicate with the other(s) so connected to the network. The message can be prepared and sent instantly. The other person finds the e-mail when he checks his mailbox and may replay to the message in the same way. The message sent is private and no other person can read it.

Each user of e-mail service has a user ID or password serving as e-mail address. First thing to do is to get online using modem and communication software. The system requires user-id and password. Now the user can prepare his message in the form of a document using a word processor. The e-mail address of the recipient has to be typed in before the message is sent.

With e-mail each person connected to the system is allotted a mailbox and the software required for sending and receiving e-mail. The mailbox is simply a file into which the e-mail system stores electronic documents. The user can check his mailbox for messages over the network. The sender specifies his identify and that of the recipient. The sender then prepares the document or retrieves the stored document and sends it.

E-mail is a document communication facility. To ensure that the recipient also understands the emotions as well, a set of special symbols is used to convey some non-verbal signals. A few of such symbols are given below.

Symbol	Emotion
:-	Humour
:)	Smile
:(	Frown
:/)	Not funny
p-	Private
: *	Kiss
(: - (	Very sad

E-mail is the transmission of information electronically from terminal to terminal. The document is prepared in a word processor and is mailed electronically. The basic facilities in e-mail include message creation, message transfer and post delivery service. The e-mail service may be traditional mainframe based or minicomputer based or LAN based system with PCS to access from.

How E-Mail Works?

The first thing to be done is to type the message and the e-mail address of the recipient. Once the 'send' button is clicked, this e-mail is sent through the telephone line after its conversion into analog signal by the modem. The e-mail message arrives at our service provider's server. If the server recognizes the e-mail address as valid, the mail will be sent either through the network of the service provider or through internet gateway to the service provider of the recipient.

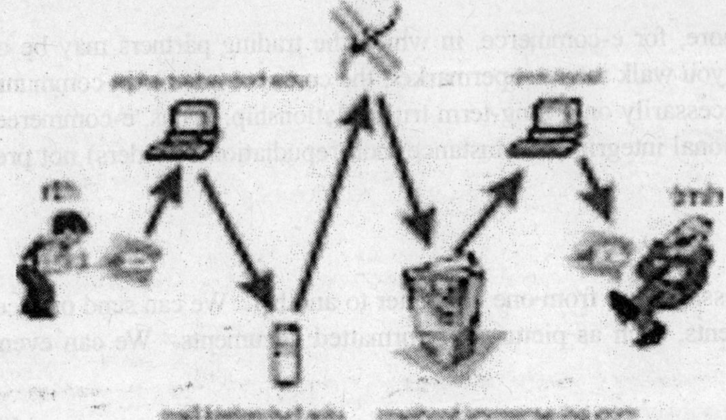

To send e-mail, we need a connection to the internet and access to a mail server that forwards the mail. The standard protocol used for sending internet e-mail is called SMTP, short for Simple Mail Transfer Protocol. It works in conjunction with POP servers. POP stands for Post Office Protocol.

When we send an e-mail message, our computer routes it to an SMTP server. The server looks at the e-mail address (similar to the address on an envelope), then forwards it to the recipient's mail server. Once the message arrives at the destination mail server, It's stored until the addressee retrieves it. We can send e-mail anywhere in the world to anyone who has an e-mail address.

E-mail route

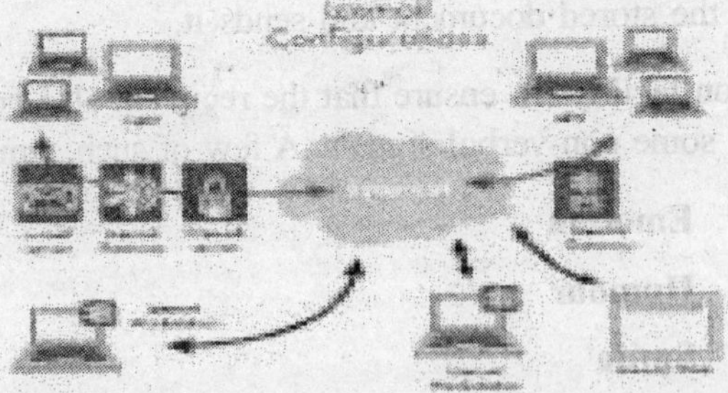

With the advent MIME, which stands for multipurpose Internet Mail Extension, and other types of encoding schemes, we cannot only send messages electronically, but we can also send formatted documents, photos, sound files, and video files.

Infrastructure Requirement for E-Mail

- Personal Computer
- Telephone Connection
- Modem
- Mailing software, viz., Outlook Express or Netscape communicator or Internet Explorer etc.

➤ **Advantages of E-mail**

❖ Messages can be prepared and sent any time convenient for the sender.

❖ Message can be received at the convenience of the recipient.

❖ The transmission takes place instantly and the message gets stored in the mailbox of the recipient.

❖ The system can confirm delivery of message.

❖ Copies of message can be sent to multiple recipients.

❖ It reduces paper work.

➤ **Disadvantages**

❖ Recipients must be having e-mail connectivity. They must have computer terminals, modem and telephone.

❖ They must be subscribing to the same e-mail service provider.

❖ Poor telecommunication affects the quality of message transmitted.

❖ Despite all the disadvantages e-mail is a cheap form of information transmission. INDONET, NICNET, DARTMAIL and ICNET provide this service in India. A user can be a subscriber to such e-mail service providing agencies and use their facility.

E-Mail Addressing Pattern

Internet e-mail addresses typically have two main parts:

ibcocppd@satyammail.com

First there is the user name (ibcocppd) which refers to the recipients mailbox. Then there's an axon sign (@). Next comes the host name (satyammail), also called the domain name. This refers to the mail server, the computer where the recipient has an electronic mailbox. It's usually the name of a company or organization.

The end of the domain name consists of a dot (".") followed by two or three letters (such as .com and .gov) that indicate the top-level domain. This part of the domain name indicates the type of organization or the country where the host server is located.

Components of an E-mail Address

As in the case of normal mail system, e-mail is also based upon the concept of a recipient address. The email address provides all of the information required to get a message to the recipient from anywhere in the world. Consider the e-mail ID john@hotmail.com

In the example above, "john" is the local part, which is the name of a mailbox on the destination computer, where finally the mail will be delivered. Hotmail is the mailserver where the mailbox "john" exists, .com is the type of organisation on net, which is hosting the mail server.

There are six main categories:

com	Commercial institutions or organization
edu	Educational institutions
gov	Government site
mil	Military site
net	Gateways and administrative hosts
org	Private organizations

E-mail Messages

E-mail messages are similar to letters, with two main parts.

The header contains the name and address of the recipient, the name and address of anyone who is being copied, and the subject of the message. Some e-mail programs also display your name and address and the date of the message.

The body contains the message itself. Just like when sending letters, we need the correct address. If we use the wrong address or mistype it, our messages will bounce back with messages like — Return to Sender, Address Unknown routine.

When we receive an e-mail, the header tells us where it came from, how it was sent, and when. It's like an electronic postmark.Unlike a letter, which is sealed in an envelope, e-mail is not as private. It's more like a post card. Messages can be intercepted and read by people who really shouldn't be looking at it. We should therefore avoid including any confidential information unless we have a way to encrypt it.

Usage of Mails

- ❖ Incoming mails can be checked on a daily basis at least 3 times a day.
- ❖ We can use the e-mail facility judiciously and extensively for communicating with Circle Office / Head Office/ Service Branch / Customers.
- ❖ Communicate e-mail id to all domestic and overseas customers and use the facility for passing on information regarding new schemes launched by Bank and other important information to them.
- ❖ Encourage customers to contact branch through e-mail for information regarding their urgent banking requirements.
- ❖ Use the facility as a marketing tool to attract new customers, exchange greetings with existing customers and also inform them about recent happenings in the locality.

6.8 MOBILE COMPUTING

Mobile Computing is a generic term describing your ability to use technology 'un tethered'(wireless), that is not physically connected, or in remote or mobile (non-static) environments. The term is evolved in modern usage such that it requires that the mobile computing activity be connected wirelessly to and through the internet or to and through a private network. This connection ties the mobile device to centrally located information and/or application software through the use of battery powered, portable, and wireless computing and communication devices. This includes devices like laptops with wireless LAN or wireless WAN technology, smart mobile phones, wearable computers and Personal Digital Assistants (PDAs) with Bluetooth or IRDA interfaces.

6.9 TYPES OF MOBILE COMPUTERS

Many types of **mobile computers** have been introduced since the 1990s, including the:

(a) Laptop computer

(b) Sub notebook

(c) Personal digital assistant (PDA)

(d) Portable data terminal (PDT)

(e) Mobile data terminal(MDT)

(f) Tablet personal computer

(g) Smart phone

(h) UMPC

(a) **Laptop Computer:** A laptop computer, simply laptop (notebook computer or notebook), is a small mobile computer, which usually weighs 2-18 pounds (1-6 kilograms), depending on size, materials, and other factors. Laptops usually run on a single main battery or from an external AC/DC adapter which can charge the battery while also supplying power to the computer itself. Many computers also have a 3 volt cell to run the clock and other processes in the event of a power failure.

As personal computers, laptops are capable of the same tasks as a desktop computer, although they are typically less powerful for the same price. They contain components that are similar to their desktop counterparts and perform the same functions, but are miniaturized and optimized for mobile use and efficient power consumption. Laptops usually have liquid crystal displays and most of them use different memory modules for their random access memory (RAM), for instance, SO-DIMM in lieu of the larger DIMMs. In addition to a built-in keyboard, they may utilize a touchpad (also known as a trackpad) or a pointing stick for input, though an external keyboard or mouse can usually be attached.

(b) **Sub Notebook:** A sub notebook is a small and lightweight portable computer, with most of the features of a standard notebook computer but smaller. The term is often applied to systems that run full versions of desktop operating systems such as Windows or Linux. Sub notebooks are smaller than notebook computers but larger than handheld computers and ultra portables. They often have screens that are 10.43 (diagonal) or less, and weigh less than 1 kg; as opposed to full-size laptops with 123 or 153 screens and weighing 2 kg or more. The savings in size and weight are usually achieved partly by omitting ports or having removable media/optical drives; sub notebooks are often paired with docking stations to compensate. Sub notebooks are a niche IT product and rarely sell in large numbers.

(c) **Personal Digital Assistants (PDAs):** Personal Digital Assistants (PDAs) are handheld computers, but have become much more versatile over the years. PDAs are also known as pocket computers or palmtop computers. PDAs have many uses: calculation, use as a clock and calendar, accessing the Internet, sending and receiving E-mails, video recording, typewriting and word processing, use as an address book, making and writing on spreadsheets, scanning bar codes, use as a radio or stereo, playing computer games, recording survey responses, and Global Positioning System (GPS). Newer PDAs also have both colour screens and audio capabilities, enabling them to be used as mobile phones (smart phones), web browsers, or portable media players. Many PDAs can access the Internet, intranets or extranets via Wi-Fi, or Wireless Wide-Area Networks (WWANs). Many PDAs employ touch screen technology.

(d) **Mobile Data Terminal (MDT) :** A mobile data terminal (MDT) is a computerized device used in police cars, taxicabs, courier vehicles, service trucks, commercial trucking fleets, military logistics, fishing fleets, warehouse inventory control, and emergency vehicles to communicate with a central dispatch office.

Mobile data terminals feature a screen on which to view information and a keyboard or keypad for entering information, and may be connected to various peripheral devices. Standard peripherals include two-way radios and taximeters, both of which predate computer assisted dispatching. MDTs may be simple display and keypad units, intended to be connected to a separate black-box or AVL (see below) computer. On the other end of the spectrum, MDTs may contain full, PC-equivalent hardware. The function and programmability of the devices is similarly broad.

(e) **Tablet PC:** A Tablet PC is a notebook or slate-shaped mobile computer. Its touch screen or digitizing tablet technology allows the user to operate the computer with a stylus or digital pen, or a fingertip, instead of a keyboard or mouse.

The form factor offers a more mobile way to interact with a computer. Tablet PCs are often used where normal notebooks are impractical or unwieldy, or do not provide the needed functionality.

(f) **Smart Phone:** A smart phone is a full-featured mobile phone with personal computer like functionality. Most smart phones are cell phones that support full featured e-mail capabilities with the functionality of a complete personal organizer. An important feature of most smart phones is that applications for enhanced data processing and connectivity can be installed on the device, in contrast to regular phones which support sandboxed applications. These applications may be developed by the manufacturer of the device, by the operator or by any other third-party software developer. "Smart" functionality includes any additional interface including a miniature QWERTY keyboard, a touch screen, or even just secure access to company mail, such as is provided by a Blackberry.

(g) **Ultra Mobile PC:** The Ultra Mobile PC (abbreviated UMPC), previously known by its codename Project Origami, is a specification for a small form factor tablet PC. It was developed as a joint development exercise by Microsoft, Intel, and Samsung, among others. Current UMPCs feature the Windows XP Tablet PC Edition 2005, Windows Vista Home Premium Edition, or Linux operating system and low-voltage Intel Pentium or VIA C7-Mprocessors in the 1 GHz range.

6.10 ELECTRONIC COMMERCE

The growth of Internet into a global market place attracts more business firms to use this media for commerce. Business firms may use the Internet initially for communication. Websites are set up to provide information about its products and services. Business firms offer corporate information, product information, marketing related services etc.

The Internet has integrated the fragment markets words over though in a modest way. But this interaction is growing rapidly. The most important advantage of the internet for business firms is that it allows reaching customers at very low costs.

Electronic Commerce — Meaning

Electronic commerce is the process of searching, choosing, buying and selling of product or service on the electronic network; it uses the computer and communication networks for promoting products, selling, delivery, collection and delivery service.

➢ **Electronic Commerce includes:**

(a) Buying and selling on the internet

(b) Making payments electronically

(c) Business transaction in which there is no physical exchange or physical contact.

(d) It is transacting a business over an electronic network without physical contact.

The problems connected with electronic commerce are:

(a) Identity

(b) Authentication

(c) Protection of data

(d) Confidentiality

These Problems Can be Solved by Using:

(a) Secure socket layer and hypertext transfer protocol

(b) Digital signatures

(c) Using public key cryptography

(d) Using digital certificates.

In E-commerce, the parties to a transaction interact electronically. They may be separated by long distances physically, yet the electronic network bring them together not only to complete a transaction but also to get after sales support, E-commerce is not just doing transaction over the Internet, it aims at few other things as well like :

- Web enabling an organization's business so that it can facilitate better customer interaction, handing customer enquiries receiving customer order and payments online.
- Improving customer service capabilities by allowing customers by providing Inert access to it databases containing customer interest information.
- Use the web to gather customer need information and thus to reducing cycle time by responding to customer needs quickly. It enables the firm in coming out with new available product information to customers.
- Raising productivity of all activities in the organization by improving the flow of information in the organization.

Features of E-Commerce

E-Commerce has the following general features:

(a) It is a business strategy to cut down costs, while improving quality and increasing the speed of delivery of goods/services.

(b) It has ability to sell and purchase products/services/information on computer networks.

(c) It is a solution for office automation and quick business transactions.

(d) It is a tool to improve intra business functioning like business re-engineering.

(e) It is tools to improve inter business communication through easy and accurate interaction and information interchange.

6.11 IMPORTANCE OF E-COMMERCE

E-Commerce becomes inevitable because of the following:

(a) Low Setup Cost: Anybody can easily setup a website. In fact there are many organizations and training institutes who help customers in developing and launching websites. To market a product large retail showrooms are not required, just a website showing the characteristics of the product including cost details are sufficient.

(b) **Global Free Market:** Nobody can dominate the global market as presence on the internet is easy not only for global giants, but even small organisations can participate actively at low costs and compete with stiff competition.

(c) **Global Access:** Since more than 200 countries are hooked onto the Internet, anybody who can afford a TV and a telephone can fully access the Internet and gain the information required.

(d) **Availability of Technology:** Since the same technology like web servers, browsers, engines, internet, etc., is used throughout the world therefore business can be easily conducted.

(e) **Multiple Opportunities:** By using E-Commerce multiple activities like selling, renting, purchasing etc. can be performed. In fact a whole variety of transactions can be provided all under one roof.

(f) **Others:** E-commerce systems are being established for automating and enhancing many aspects of communications, publishing, marketing, sales and customer service such as:

- Customer Research;
- Pre-Sales Enquiries;
- Information Publishing and Dissemination;
- Sales;
- Advertising;
- Promotions;
- Public Relations;
- Purchasing;
- Transactions;
- Funds Transfer;
- Production; Delivery;
- After-Sales Service;
- Ongoing Relationship Management; and
- Customer Support.

The benefits of electronic commerce are not just available to large corporations and government departments, but many small to medium businesses are discovering new cost-effective opportunities to use Internet-related technology to help their business operations locally and internationally.

Applications of E-Commerce

E-Commerce Used for:

Sharing of information

Document exchange

Messages despatch

Market and Advertising

Payment transaction

E-Commerce Used in the following fields:

Electronic Auctions

Electronic Banking

Electronic searching

E-Learning

E-Marketing

E-Trading

6.12 TYPES OF ELECTRONIC COMMERCE

Based on the parties involved in electronic transactions, the e-commerce can be classified into the following types:

(a) Business-to-Business (B2B)

(b) Business-to-Consumer (B2C)

(c) Consumer-to-Consumer (C2C)

(a) **Business-to-Business E-Commerce:** This is done between business firms. For example, electronic transactions between a manufacturing firm and its supplier firms are B2B transactions. This segment is the largest and the fastest growing one in electronic, commerce. Here firm use the electronic network for purchasing products, consulting services and paying for them.

(b) **Business-to-Consumer E-Commerce:** Consumers check electronic catalogues to learn about products and compare prices of products sold. They purchase products at the firm's website and may pay electronic cash or other means like credit card.

(c) **Consumer-to-Consumer E-Commerce:** Some sites offer consumers to deal directly with each other. Auction sites are examples. At these auction sites consumers can buy and sell products.

Electronic commerce is useful to both producers and consumers as it helps them overcome the traditional barriers of distance from markets and lack of information about market opportunities. Producers and traders no longer need to maintain physical establishments requiring large capital outlays. Virtual shops and contact points on the Internet may enable storage close to the production site and distribution can be made directly to the consumer. Increased advertising possibilities world wide may help small and medium industries and businesses that traditionally find it difficult to reach the consumer abroad. E- Commerce may also enable such firms to eliminate middlemen while trying to sell their products abroad.

6.13 E-COMMERCE ACTIVITIES

Business firms use the internet platform for communication and commerce. The e-commerce activities can be discussed as follows:

(a) **Direct Marketing and Selling:** Business firms set up websites for direct marketing and selling. Direct selling was one of the earliest forms of e-commerce. For example, Amazon.com, Barnes and noble and Dell computers engaged in direct selling. Gradually firm moved on to one or more complex operations on the web.

(b) **Value Chain Integration:** E-Commerce does not tolerate any kind of delay. Delay in inventory tracking and management can cripple the business. E-Commerce firm use EDI for exchanging transaction data among them so that transactions are automatically processed. Thus suppliers, customers and service providers will use open EDI for integrating their processing systems leading to more efficient operations.

(c) **Corporate Purchasing:** Internet provides opportunities for business firms to reduce cost of purchasing. Suppliers keep their electronic catalogs updated. Comparative price information is also available.

Ordering can be electronically done to reduce the laborious paper work in purchasing. Officers can approve purchase orders electronically. The firm can enforce policies; provide greater services to customers and suppliers.

(d) **Financial and Information Services:** A wide range of financial services are offered on the internet. They include:

- ❖ Online banking
- ❖ Online billing
- ❖ Online securities transactions
- ❖ Secured information distribution

(e) **Mobile Commerce:** Mobile commerce is a part of e-commerce and differs from the latter on the use of mobile telecommunication in place of telecommunication network. M-commerce includes only transactions with a monetary value and it excludes short message services. One condition essential for the success of mobile commerce is large user base of mobile phones. Adequate security for mobile transactions is another condition for its adoption in a big way.

Areas of E-Commerce

1. Website development
2. Online training
3. Shopping
4. Real estate
5. Customer services
6. Medical Consultation
7. Online library
8. Online banking

Software's used in E-Commerce

1. Java language
2. Java Serlet
3. Java Server Pages
4. Enterprise Java beans
5. Remote method invocation
6. XML
7. Weblogic
8. Web Saphere
9. Net Dynamics
10. ASP
11. Corba

CHAPTER 7

SYSTEM ANALYSIS DESIGN AND MANAGEMENT INFORMATION SYSTEM

Structure:

7.1 SYSTEM ANALYSIS AND DESIGN (SAD)

Systems are created to solve problems. One can think of the systems approach as an organized way of dealing with a problem. In this dynamic world, The subject System Analysis and Design (SAD), mainly deals with the software development activities.

Defining A System

A collection of components that work together to realize some objective forms a system. Basically there are three major components in every system, namely, input, processing and output.

In a system the different components are connected with each other and they are interdependent. For example, human body represents a complete natural system. We are also bound by many national systems such as political system, economic system, educational system and so forth. The objective of the system demands that some output is produced as a result of processing the suitable inputs.

System Life Cycle

System life cycle is an organizational process of developing and maintaining systems. It helps in establishing a system project plan, because it gives overall list of processes and sub-processes required for developing a system. System development life cycle means combination of various activities. In other words we can say that various activities put together are referred as system development life cycle. In the System Analysis and Design terminology, the system development life cycle means software development life cycle.

Following are the different phases of software development cycle:

- System study
- Feasibility study
- System analysis
- System design
- Coding
- Testing
- Implementation
- Maintenance

7.2 PHASES OF SYSTEM DEVELOPMENT LIFE CYCLE

Let us now describe the different phases and the related activities of system development life cycle in detail.

(a) System Study

System study is the first stage of system development life cycle. This gives a clear picture of what actually the physical system is? In practice, the system study is done in two phases. In the first phase, the preliminary survey of the system is done which helps in identifying the scope of the system. The second phase of the system study is more detailed and in-depth study in which the identification of user's requirement and the limitations and problems of the present system are studied. After completing the system study, a system proposal is prepared by the System Analyst (who studies the system) and placed before the user. The proposed system contains the findings of the present system and recommendations to overcome the limitations and problems of the present system in the light of the user's requirements.

To describe the system study phase more analytically, we would say that system study phase passes through the following steps:

- Problem identification and project initiation
- Background analysis
- Inference or findings

(b) **Feasibility Study:** On the basis of result of the system study, feasibility study takes place. The feasibility study is basically the test of the proposed system in the light of its workability, meeting user's requirements, effective use of resources and of course, the cost effectiveness. The main goal of feasibility study is not to solve the problem but to achieve the scope. In the process of feasibility study, the cost and benefits are estimated with greater accuracy.

(c) **System Analysis:** Assuming that a new system is to be developed, the next phase is system analysis. Analysis involved a detailed study of the current system, leading to specifications of a new system. Analysis is a detailed study of various operations performed by a system and their relationships within and outside the system. During analysis, data are collected on the available files, decision points and transactions handled by the present system. Interviews, on-site observation and questionnaire are the tools used for system analysis. Using the following steps it becomes easy to draw the exact boundary of the new system under consideration:

- ➢ Keeping in view the problems and new requirements
- ➢ Workout the pros and cons including new areas of the system

All procedures, requirements must be analysed and documented in the form of detailed data flow diagrams (DFDs), data dictionary, logical data structures and miniature specifications. System Analysis also includes sub-dividing of complex process involving the entire system, identification of data store and manual processes.

The main points to be discussed in system analysis are:

- ➢ Specification of what the new system is to accomplish based on the user requirements.
- ➢ Functional hierarchy showing the functions to be performed by the new system and their relationship with each other.
- ➢ Function network, which are similar to function hierarchy but they highlight the functions which are common to more than one procedure.
- ➢ List of attributes of the entities — these are the data items which need to be held about each entity (record).

(d) **System Design:** Based on the user requirements and the detailed analysis of a new system, the new system must be designed. This is the phase of system designing. It is the most crucial phase in the development of a system. Normally, the design proceeds in two stages:

- Preliminary or general design
- Structure or detailed design

Preliminary or general design: In the preliminary or general design, the features of the new system are specified. The costs of implementing these features and the benefits to be derived are estimated. If the project is still considered to be feasible, we move to the detailed design stage.

Structure or Detailed Design

In the detailed design stage, computer oriented work begins in earnest. At this stage, the design of the system becomes more structured. Structure design is a blue print of a computer system solution to a given problem having the same components and inter-relationship among the same components as the original problem. Input, output and processing specifications are drawn up in detail. In the design stage, the programming language and the platform in which the new system will run are also decided.

There are several tools and techniques used for designing. These tools and techniques are:

- Flowchart
- Structured English
- Data flow diagrams (DFDs)
- Decision table
- Data dictionary
- Decision tree

Each of the above tools for designing will be discussed in detail in the next lesson.

(e) **Coding:** After designing the new system, the whole system is required to be converted into computer understanding language. Coding the new system into computer programming language does this. It is an important stage where the defined procedures are transformed into control specifications by the help of a computer language. This is also called the programming phase in which the programmer converts the program specifications into computer instructions, which we refer as programs. The programs coordinate the data movements and control the entire process in a system. It is generally felt that the programs must be modular in nature. This helps in fast development, maintenance and future change, if required.

(f) **Testing:** Before actually implementing the new system into operations, a test run of the system is done removing all the bugs, if any. It is an important phase of a successful system. After codifying the whole programs of the system, a test plan should be developed and run on a given set of test data. The output of the test run should match the expected results.

Using the test data following test run are carried out:

- Unit test
- System test

Unit Test: When the programs have been coded and compiled and brought to working conditions, they must be individually tested with the prepared test data. Any undesirable happening must be noted and debugged (error corrections).

System Test: After carrying out the unit test for each of the programs of the system and when errors are removed, then system test is done. At this stage the test is done on actual data. The complete system is executed on the actual data. At each stage of the execution, the results or output of the system is analyzed. During the result analysis, it may be found that the output are not matching the expected output of the system. In such case, the errors in the particular programs are identified and are fixed and further tested for the expected output. When it is ensured that the system is running error-free, the users are called with their own actual data so that the system could be shown running as per their requirements.

(g) **Implementation:** After having the user acceptance of the new system developed, the implementation phase begins. Implementation is the stage of a project during which theory is turned into practice. During this phase, all the programs of the system are loaded onto the user's computer. After loading the system, training of the user starts. Main topics of such type of training are:

- How to execute the package
- How to process the data (processing details)
- How to enter the data
- How to take out the reports

After the users are trained about the computerized system, manual working has to shift from manual to computerized working. The following two strategies are followed for running the system:

(i) **Parallel run:** In such run for a certain defined period, both the systems, i.e., computerized and manual, are executed in parallel. This strategy is helpful because of the following:

- ❖ Manual results can be compared with the results of the computerized system.
- ❖ Failure of the computerized system at the early stage does not affect the working of the organization, because the manual system continues to work, as it used to do.

(ii) Pilot run: In this type of run, the new system is installed in parts. Some parts of the new system are installed first and executed successfully for considerable time period. When the results are found satisfactory then only other parts are implemented. This strategy builds the confidence and the errors are traced easily.

(h) Maintenance: Maintenance is necessary to eliminate errors in the system during its working life and to tune the system to any variations in its working environment. It has been seen that there are always some errors found in the system that must be noted and corrected. It also means the review of the system from time to time. The review of the system is done for:

- ❖ knowing the full capabilities of the system
- ❖ knowing the required changes or the additional requirements
- ❖ studying the performance.

If a major change to a system is needed, a new project may have to be set up to carry out the change. The new project will then proceed through all the above life cycle phases.

7.3 MANAGEMENT INFORMATION SYSTEM (MIS)

Meaning and Definition

The concept of management information system (MIS) took many years to evolve, borrowing many concepts mainly from fields of managerial accounting, management and computer science. Most significant among them is the system's approach to management.

Management information system is a system, which provides the required information to each level of management at the right time, in the right form, to form the basis of decision-making and control.

In other words "MIS, is a systematic approach of collecting data and processing it into information, storing, retrieving it to obtain timely, accurate and adequate information to the management at various levels of planning, organising, implementing and controlling the various activities within the organization."

Definition

MIS may be defined as: "An integrated man/machine system for providing information to support the planning, controls, organising operating management and decision-making functions in an organization."

MIS is also defined as an assemblage of facilities and personnel for collecting, processing, storing, retrieving and transmitting information that is received by one or more managers in the performance of their functions.

MIS is an integrated, user-machine system for providing information to support operations, management, and decision-making functions in an organization .The system utilizes computer hardware and software, manual procedures, models for analysis, plan control and decision-making, and a database.

The elements of the definition are highlighted. A management information system is:

1. An integrated user-machine system
2. For providing information
3. To support the operations, management, analysis, and decision-making functions.
4. In an organization the system utilizes —

(i) Computer hardware and software

(ii) Manual procedures

(iii) Models for analysis, planning, control and decision-making and

(iv) A database.

7.4 ELEMENTS OF MANAGEMENT INFORMATION SYSTEM

MIS is a system that aids management in making, carrying out and controlling decisions. To understand the concept of management information system clearly, it is necessary to understand its three elements, viz., Management, Information and System.

Management

One of the definitions of management is that it is a process, in the sense of sequence of operations or functions necessary to achieve certain end results. Management is a human and social process, it is also a continuous process to the extent that the cycle of stages or steps is never-ending and is repeated over and over again.

It is generally conceptualized that management process consists of a few inter-related elements, which are also termed as the functions of management.

There are three levels of management:

Top management or systematic management, which concentrates on long-term planning and decision-making.

Middle Management or technical management, which focuses its attention on the planning and decision-making regarding implementation of the policies of the organization.

Lower level Management or Operational management, which is concerned with the decision-making regarding the day-to-day operations of their implementation.

These levels of management require different sets of information. Any system providing information to these levels of management should be such as would cater to their needs.

Information

Information can be defined as the "data that has been processed into a form that is meaningful to the recipient and is of real or perceived value in current or prospective decisions." In other words, information refers to an input of data processing, which is organized and meaningful to the person who received.

For example, data concerning may indicate the name of the salesman. When a large number of such data elements is organized and analyzed, it may provide important information to a marketing director who is attempting to evaluate his sales force.

The terms data and information are commonly used as synonymous. But strictly speaking there exists a difference between the two words. Data are raw facts and figures, unassembled and usually unrelated to one another, not currently being used in a decision process. Files, records and reports not in use are some examples of data.

Levels of Information

In general the information requirements of executing can be categorized into three broad categories, viz.,

➢ Environmental information: It comprises of the following:

1. Government Policies

Information about concessions, benefits, government policies in respect of tax concessions or for any other aspects, which may be useful to an organization in the future period.

2. Factors of Production

Information related with source, cost, location, availability, accessibility and productivity of the major factors of production, viz., (a) labour, (b) material parts and (c) capital.

3. Technological Environment

Forecast of any technological changes in the industry and the probable effect of it on the firm.

4. Economic Trends

It includes information relating to economic indicators like consumer disposable income, employment, productivity, capital investment, etc. Such information is valuable for those firms specially whose outflow is a function of these important variables.

➢ Competitive Information:

It includes the following information —

1. Industry Demand

Demand forecast of industry in respect of the product manufactured and in the area in which the firm would be operative.

2. Firm Demand

Assessment of the firm's product demand in the specified market. It also includes an assessment of firm's capability to meet firm's demand.

3. The Competitive Data

Data of competitive firms for forecasting and decision-making and plans to achieve the forecast.

➢ Internal Information:

It usually includes information about concern's —

(i) Sales forecast

(ii) The financial plan/budget

(iii) Supply factors

(iv) Policies, which are vital for subsidiary planning at all levels in the organization.

Information within an organization can be analyzed into three levels:

(a) **Strategic information:** It is used by senior managers or top management to plan the objectives of the organization, and assess whether objectives are being met in practice.

Such information includes overall profitability, the profitability of the different segments of the business, future market prospects, the availability and cost of raising new funds, total cash needs, total planning levels and capital equipment needs, etc.

(b) **Tactical information:** It is used by middle management to ensure, that the resources of the management are employed to achieve the strategic objectives of the organization.

Such information includes productivity measurement, budgetary control or variance analysis reports and cash flow forecasts etc.

(c) **Operational information:** It is used by operation level of management such as foreman or head clerk to ensure, that specific tasks are planned and carried out properly within a factory or office etc.

System

The word system connotes plan, method, order, and arrangement.

"A system is a regularly interacting or inter-dependant group of items forming a united whole."

A system is thus a set of interacting elements, interacting with each other to achieve a predetermined objective or goal.

A system is schematically represented below:

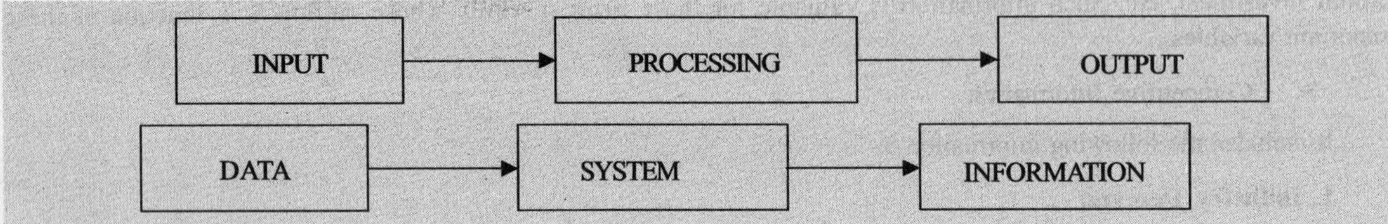

Each system is composed of subsystem, which in turn is made up of other subsystems. Each subsystem is defined through its boundary. Thus every system is a part of larger system.

For example, a finance department is a subsystem of an organization. The organization can be viewed as a subsystem in a particular industry.

The interconnections and interactions between subsystems are called as interfaces. The interface occurs at the boundary of the subsystem through the inputs and outputs.

System

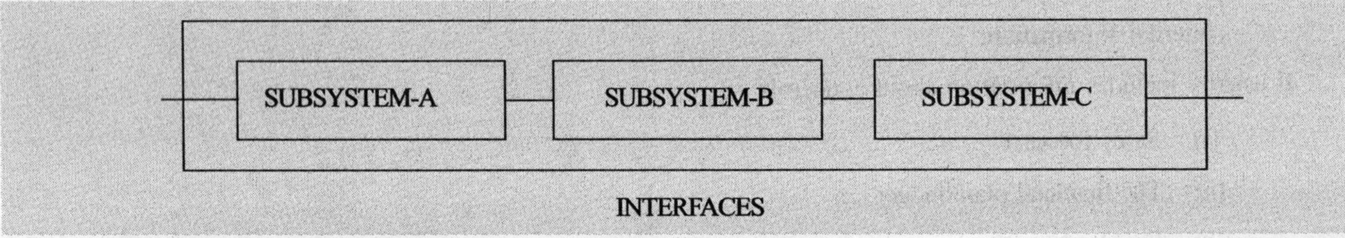

7.5 CHARACTERISTIC FEATURES OF MANAGEMENT INFORATION SYSTEMS

1. An MIS is comprehensive information system. Management information systems are comprehensive in nature. This information system includes all the information.
2. Management information system is coordinated, to get most utility from a management information system; it is necessary that there must be a good coordination between the subsystems.
3. An MIS is a set of information subsystems. The information subsystems jointly make a management information system.
4. An MIS is developed by integrating information subsystems .The integration is done by rationally. It reduces the redundancy in the data and avoids duplication of efforts.
5. An MIS transforms data into information in a variety of ways. The input of an information system usually is raw data and output is information.

6. MIS enhances productivity — it is done in respect of organization, which interacts directly within its customers. For example Banks, Railways etc., by introducing a management information system can enhance their productivity manifold.

7. An MIS is in conformance with manager's styles and characteristics. Every top manager has his own style of doing things. So MIS in organizations are built keeping in view the manager's styles and characteristics.

Value of Information

Information is an organization's resources. Without information business cannot survive. It is said that, a good decision is" 90% information and 10% inspiration."

Information is the catalyst of management and the ingredient that helps the management functions of planning, operating and controlling.

Need for Information

Information is considered as the lifeblood of the business organization. It plays an important and effective role in managing the day-to-day affairs of a business organization. It is in fact highly valuable business resource, both for planning and control.

Business managers at top level and at operational control level are generally confronted with complex problems which are emerging as a result of high rate of growth, change in business size, development in the field of technical know-how, change in consumer's preferences and change in brand loyalties, intensive degree of competition nationally and internationally, and changing government policies and regulations etc.

To overcome the above listed complex problems and to have an effective planning and control system, management in each business organization needs information regarding finance, production, market, environment etc.

There is also need to comply with competition, technological development and changing government policies and legislation. All of these situations require the provision of vital information so that the management can react at the right time at the most suitable strategy.

7.6 REQUIREMENTS OF MANAGEMENT INFORMATIONAL SYSTEM

The nature of the management information system required by an organization depends primarily on the kind of activities performed and the type of decisions to be made by its executives. The information needs of managers/executives tends to vary with the level of the organization because the nature of managerial activities tends to differ at different levels. i.e., top, middle, and supervisory.

I. **Top Management Level:** Top management's main responsibility is in the direction of determining the overall goals and objectives of the business enterprise. It deals mainly with long term plans, policy matters and broad objectives of the company. Also, it establishes a budget under which the various departments operate.

Top management needs information on the trends in the external information on the functioning of the internal organizational subsystems. Apart from historical information top management requires on going current information also which is generated through forecasts of the future.

II. **Middle Management Level:** Middle management is viewed as administrative management in the sense that it is responsible for the elaboration, classification and operationalisation of organizational goals, strategies and policies in terms of action programmes and norms of performance, middle management is concerned with the task of formulating pragmatic operating policies and procedures for the guide of supervisory management.

The nature of information required at this level is less diverse and complex; middle management is fed with information both from top and supervisory management. Information mostly used by this level is internal in nature. Middle management does not require much 'futuristic' information since its decisions are not strategic and long range in nature.

III. **Supervisory Management Level:** At this level, managers are responsible for routine, day-to-day decisions and activities of the organization, which do not require much judgement and discretion.

Supervisory management mostly needs internal information on operational aspects of the functioning of activity units. It, in fact, generates internal information. It also receives information from the middle management level on operational plans and programmes. It tends to be reliable and relatively complete.

7.7 DECISION–MAKING

One of the major roles of managers in organization is processing information and making decision, information systems are developed to help the managers in their decision-making process.

The decision-making process is based on the support of the information systems in the organizations. The managers must be aware of a problem, before a decision can be made. A problem exists when the real situations is different than the expected one. After the problem has been identified, the causes of the existence of the problem must be identified and then the solution to the problem has to be found.

7.8 TYPES OF DECISIONS–MAKING

The decisions can be classified into different categories depending on the management activity. We present here two classifications:

1. Programmed decisions
2. Non-programmed decisions

- Programmed decisions

These decisions are well defined, repetitive and routine in nature. For these, a pre–defined decision rules or algorithms are worked out so that every time the situation occurs, a new analysis is not required.

For example: (i) Office supplies

(ii) Preparation of payroll and disbursement of pay through bank and

(iii) Inventory control.

The necessary guidelines and rules required for taking such decisions are made available, in the form of a procedure manual to users. The important characteristics of programmed decisions are:

1. These decisions can be delegated.
2. The cost of taking such decisions is as high as that of non-programmed ones.
3. These decisions can be made with the help of computer system.

- Non-programmed decisions

These types of decisions are occasional and unique in nature. There is no pre-defined procedure available to solve these problems and a new analysis is required for each occurrence. Production scheduling, advertising, budgets, acquisition of capital projects, i.e., capital budgeting are some examples of non-programmed decisions.

Due to the absence of decision rules, executives make use of problem-solving methodology which itself depends on subjective human judgement. The risk involved in taking decisions to solve the problem in this manner is usually high. The important features of non-programmed decisions are:

1. These decisions cannot be delegated, e.g., the decision regarding purchase of special and scarce material with fluctuating price.
2. The cost of taking such decisions in comparison with programmed decision is quite high.

Distinction Between Programmed and Non-Programmed Decisions

1. Programmed decisions are of repetitive and routine nature whereas both of these features are absent in case of non-programmed decisions. In fact, a non-programmed decision relates to a new situation all together every time.

   For example, the settlement of a bill is a programmed decision, as it can be made in accordance with the set procedure but a decision to manufacture a new product cannot be a new program as it is neither a repetitive nor a routine one and is, thus, a non-programmed one.
2. Programmed decisions are made with the help of pre-decided rules, regulations and procedures laid down by the management for the purpose, whereas non-programmed decisions are mainly based on diverse thinking and deliberations. Besides these factor, judgement experience, expertise and intuition of the manager also play a vital role in taking such decisions.
3. Programmed decisions can be delegated but non-programmed one cannot. For example, the routine purchase of standard material required for manufacture operations is a programmed decision as it can be delegated and thus, it is characterized as non-programmed decision.
4. The cost of taking non-programmed decision is quite high which is contrary to that involved in taking programmed decisions.
5. To solve a problem under programmed approach may use a string of pre-decided rules, regulations and instructions to arrive at its solution. In this way, programmed decision-making helps in the achievement of management information system objective to program more and more decisions.

   On the other hand, under non-programmed approach of decision-making, due to the absence of decision rules, the executives have to fall back upon the general problem solving methodology, which is known as a system's approach to problem solving.

   Programmed decisions can be made with the help of a computer system also but the services of computer cannot be utilized directly in making programmed decisions. However, in this case computer may be used to process huge volume of necessary data.

7.9 DECISION SUPPORT SYSTEM — DSS

Decision support system refers to a class of systems, which support the process of making decisions. DSS allows the decision-maker to retrieve data and test alternative solutions during the process of problem solving.

Need for DSS:

The need for comprehensive decision support system has resulted from three factors:

1. **The importance of information in decision-making:** Information is really a fuel that drives organization. A major work of manager is to convert information into action through the process of decision-making. So the success and effectiveness of an organization is based on information available to its manager.

2. **Mismanagement of current information:** Insufficient and irrelevant information creates confusion and it leads to take wrong decisions. The managers often feel buried by the deluge information and data that comes across their desks. This deluge of information, much of which is not useful, has led to the mismanagement of current information.

   So the DSS is needed for getting sufficient information for taking correct decisions.

3. **Increased use of personal computers:** Personal computers have the capability of increasing both the productivity of managers and the quality of their decisions. The important role of computer is to provide information for decisions and for controlling operations.

   To enable managers to swift and effective decisions, however, present information systems must be developed into more effective computer based decision support system.

Functions of DSS:

Following are the three important functions of DSS:

- Determination of information needs.
- Information gathering and processing and
- Information utilization.

The above functions are clearly explained with the help of the diagram shown below.

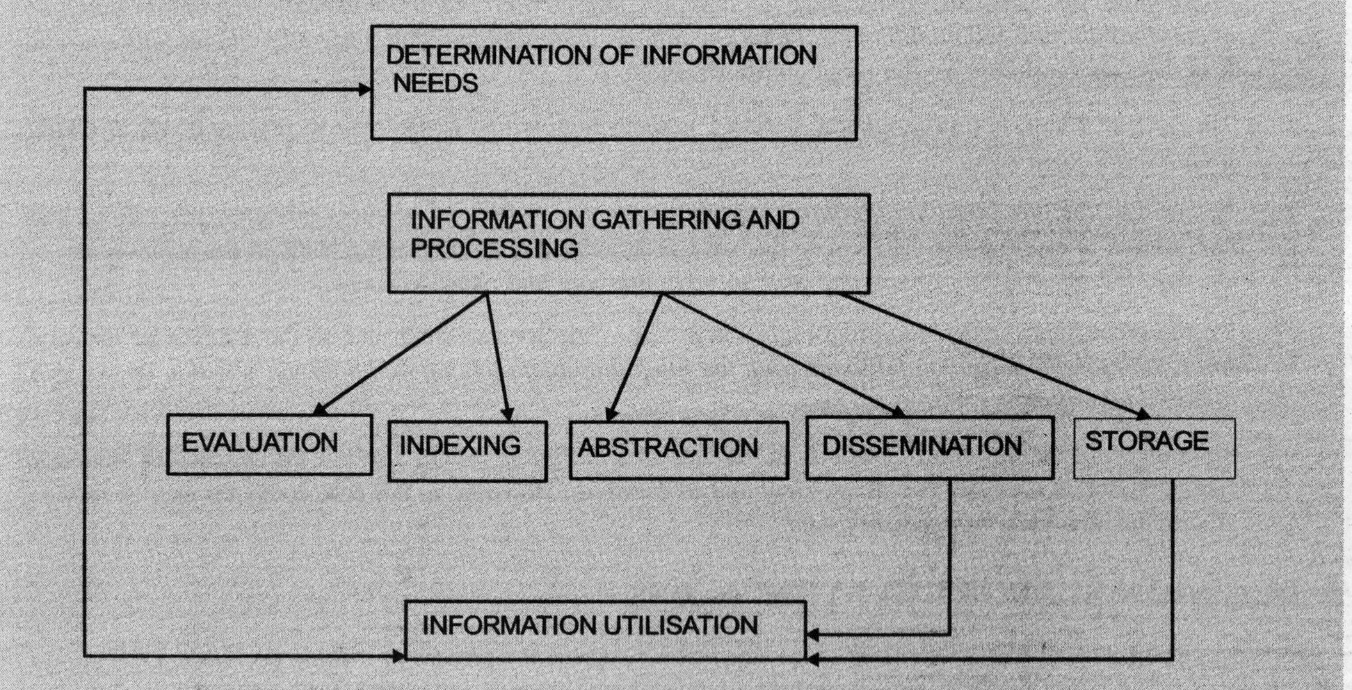

MIS Vs. DSS

Management information system and decision support system are not the same. This could be expressed by using the following figures. In this figure it can be seen that different levels of organizational hierarchy make use of different systems and the focus is entirely different.

An MIS provides information to the management but a DSS shapes that information and provide the same to top level for decision-making and control.

In practice, the general characteristics of MIS are:

- It has an information focus, where the main aim is to supply information to various organizational positions at all levels.
- Its decision is oriented more towards middle managers with emphasis on planning and controlling.
- It ensures an integrated structured information flow throughout the organization.
- It supports only structured and semi-shaped decision-making talks.
- It provides inquiry and report generation facility usually using a database.

The general characteristics of DSS are:

1. DSS generally characterized by decision focus and it provides access to an array of decision and analytical models.
2. Support for unstructured decision-making problems.
3. Its design is oriented for top management function where lots of external information is also used.
4. Presence of comprehensive database and a model base, providing flexibility, adaptability and quick response to the user.
5. Its suitability to the personal decision and styles of individual decision makers.
6. Its capability to stimulate business decisions and mathematically predict the results that will occur from taking one course of action versus another.

7.10 RELEVANCE OF MANAGEMENT INFORMATION SYSTEM

Many of the idea which is part of the management information systems are found in other academic decisions. Following four major academic areas are especially significant to the MIS concept:

1. Management Accounting
2. Operations Research or Management Science
3. Management and Organization Theory
4. Computer Science

Managerial Accounting:

This branch of accounting is concerned with cost analysis and its behaviour which is useful for managerial decisions. Cost analysis is used in managerial accounting to determine the most relevant cost for decision-making. It employs techniques such as capital budgeting, break-even analysis, transfer pricing, etc. It is mainly oriented towards internal management and control and is therefore closely identified with MIS.

Managerial accounting knowledge is of great help in ascertaining the information requirements carrying analysis, in designing forms for procuring and providing information. In fact a managerial accountant has a clear-cut knowledge about the relevant and specific information requirement of executives for performing functions in different departments.

For example, to determine the break-even point the information required is about fixed cost, variable cost and selling price of the product. He also knows the source of information available. All these facts known to managerial accountants were utilized in the evolution of MIS. Thus one can say that is an extension of managerial accounting.

Operations Research

Operation research is the application of scientific method and quantitative analysis technique to management problems. Some of its key concepts are:

- Emphasis on systematic approaches to problem solving.
- Use of mathematical models, mathematical and statistical procedures in analysis.
- Goal of seeking optimal decisions or optimal policy.

Operation research is important relative to management information systems because it has developed procedures for the analysis and computer based solutions of many types of decision problems. The system's approach to problem solving, use of models, and computer-based solution algorithms are generally incorporated in the decision support system component of MIS.

Management and Organization Theory:

There are several management theories — Behavioural, empirical, decision, qualitative and management process. Out of these decision and management are more relevant to us. According to decision theory the most important task of managers is to take decisions.

The second theory known as "Management Process" is the most widespread approach to management. Under this management is defined in terms of what the managers do. According to this management performs the functions of planning, organising, staffing, directing, and controlling.

The knowledge of these management theories enabled the MIS designers to ascertain the type of decisions made and functions performed by executives in various business organizations.

Computer Science:

Computers were not originally planned for processing information but today this is the major use for which they are applied in business situations. The reason for this is their speed of processing, calculating, retrieval of data. In fact, computer technology has been considered as a major factor for MIS development. It has come as a significant tool in information processing and storage.

7.11 STRUCTURE OF MANAGEMENT OF INFORMATION SYSTEM

The structure of MIS is known as comprehensive if it possess the following characteristics:

1. **Flexibility:** All organizations are dynamic and changes occur for a wide range of reasons. A good MIS must be able to adapt to these changes.
2. **Reliability:** Reliability is crucial to performance and can be ensued only by through checking and testing. Good standards help to make the MIS reliable to do validation and security routines.
3. **Simplicity:** Simplicity in design will find the way through the system. Anyone design a system but it takes real skill and experience to design simple systems which are easy to operate and control.
4. **Economy:** The MIS should be cost-effective. There are many hidden costs in the design, and operation of systems the most important of which is the time of the people involved. Cost should be carefully monitored once the system is working and compared with the original plan.
5. **Helpfulness:** Unless the MIS helps for planning, operation and control of the business it is superfluous.
6. **Consistency:** Information system should be consistent. There must be a link between all the data. Data should be collected by the same method and scale and should be presented at equal interval.
7. **Management-oriented:** It means that the development of the information efforts should start from an appraisal of management needs and overall business objectives. Such a system is not necessarily for top

management only it may also meet the information requirements of middle level or operating levels of management as well.

8. **Integrated:** Developed system of information should be integrated one. It means that all the functional and operational information sub-system should be tied together into one entity. An integrated information system has the capability of generating more meaningful information to management.

9. **Common Data Flows:** It means the use of common input, processing and output procedures and media whenever possible. This eliminates duplication in data collection documents and procedures. However, some duplication is necessary in order to ensure effective information systems.

10. **Sub-system Concept:** Even though the information system is viewed as a single entity, it must be broken down into digestible sub-systems, which can be implemented one at a time by developing a phasing plan. The breakdown of MIS into meaningful sub-system sets the stage for this phasing plan.

11. **Common Database:** Database is defined as a "superfile" which consolidates and integrates data records formerly stored in many separate data files. The organization of a database allows it to be accessed by several information subsystems and thus eliminates the necessity of duplication in data storage, updating, deletion and protection.

12. **Computerized:** Computerization of MIS should increase the effectiveness of the system. Computerization will equip the system to handle a wide variety of applications by providing quickly their information requirements.

13. **Relevance:** The information given to each manager should be relevant to his responsibilities and authorities.

14. **Brevity:** Information should not only be clear but should be brief. It means that maximum information should be communicated in minimum words.

15. **Accuracy:** Information should be accurate as far as possible and if not then the level of accuracy should be within limits.

Taking into consideration the above characters the suitable structure of a comprehensive MIS may be a federation of information sub-systems for different functions, viz., production, material management, marketing, finance, engineering and personnel. Each sub-system of information system is supposed to provide information support to executives for operational management control and strategic planning.

The information or data requirements of each sub-system of information system can be met by developing two types of data files, viz., unique and common.

Unique data files meet the specific information requirements of each operational function at different levels of management activity for making programmed and non-programmed decisions.

Common data files stores data/information meant for general use in the decision-making process. The data stored in the data files is usually in the raw form and thus, requires processing. Processing of data may be performed by using software and decision models kept under model base. The use of data, in database, may be controlled by Data Base Management System.

QUESTIONS

Short Answer Question

1. Explain E-commerce.
2. What do you understand by HTTP?
3. What is E-mail?
4. Explain Mobile data terminal (MDT).

5. What are the two benefits of extranet?
6. What is Laptop computer?
7. Explain Tablet PC.
8. Explain the mobile computer.
9. What is extranet?
10. Explain DFD.

Long Answer Question

1. What are the features of e-commerce?
2. What is the importance of e-commerce?
3. Explain World Wide Website.
4. How Internet useful for marketing?
5. Explain Web server and Web browser.
6. Explain HTML.
7. What are the uses of e-mail?
8. How E-Mail Works?
9. What are different types of mobile computers?
10. What are the tools and techniques used for system designing?
11. What is the relationship between intranets, extranets and e-commerce?

Very long or essay type Question

1. Explain Online processing system.
2. Describe the procedure for sending E-mail.
3. Describe the anatomy of E-commerce applications.
4. What is Electronic Mail? Discuss the advantages of E-mail.
5. Write short notes on:
   (a) World Wide Web (WWW)
   (b) Intranet and its importance
   (c) Internet service provider (ISP)
6. What are the uses of Internet?
7. Explain the internet applications.
8. What are the phases of system development life cycle?
9. What is multimedia? What are the different media elements?
10. Explain data Communication and Computer Network.

CHAPTER 8

INFORMATION SYSTEM AUDIT

Structure:

8.1 INTRODUCTION

The developments in Information Technology have a tremendous impact on auditing. Information Technology has facilitated re-engineering of the traditional business processes to ensure efficient operations and improved communication within the organisation and between the organisations and its customers. Auditing in a computerized and networked environment is still at its nascent stage in India and established practices and procedures are evolving. Well planned and structured audit is essential for risk management and monitoring and control of Information Systems in any organisation.

Information Systems (IS) auditing is a systematic independent examination of the information systems and the environment to ascertain whether the objectives, set out to be met, have been achieved. Auditing is also described as a continuous search for compliance. The Auditors may not necessarily examine the entire system. They may examine a part or parts of it only. Auditing covers primarily the following broad major areas of activity:

(a) gathering of information

(b) comparison of information and

(c) asking why

8.2 OBJECTIVES OF INFORMATION SYSTEMS AUDIT

The objectives of IS audit are to identify the risks that an organisation is exposed to in the computerized environment. IS audit evaluates the adequacy of the security controls and informs the Management with suitable conclusions and recommendations. IS audit is an independent subset of the normal audit exercise in an organisation. The overall objectives of the normal audit exercise do not change, when applied to the computerized environment. The major objectives of IS audit include, among others, the following:

(a) Safeguarding of Information System Assets/Resources

(b) Maintenance of Data Integrity

(c) Maintenance of System Effectiveness

(d) Ensuring System Efficiency

Safeguarding of Information System Assets/Resources:

The Information System Assets of the organisation must be protected by a system of internal controls. It includes protection of hardware, software, facilities, people (knowledge), data files, system documentation and supplies. This is because hardware can be damaged maliciously, software and data files can be stolen, deleted or altered and supplies of negotiable forms can be used for unauthorized purposes. Safeguarding of the Information System Assets is a very important function of each organisation.

The term IT infrastructure is a generic one used to describe the physical computer installations, the system software and the Information Systems process that support them. The IS auditor will require to review the physical security over the facilities, the security over the systems software and the adequacy of the internal controls. The IT facilities must be protected against all hazards. The hazards can be accidental hazards or intentional hazards.

Accidental hazards include fire, flood, power failure etc. Fire starts accidentally or is the result of a deliberate attack. All the computer installations should take adequate precautions to ensure that fire can be prevented, detected and extinguished. Flooding can cause extensive damage to the computer systems. The power supply for the computer installation is a vital service need and the uninterrupted availability thereof has to be ensured to facilitate continuity in processing.

Maintenance of Data Integrity :

Data Integrity includes the safeguarding of the information against unauthorized addition, deletion, modification or alteration. This includes items such as accounting records, backup, documentation etc. Information Systems are used to capture, store, process, retrieve and transmit the data in a secure and efficient manner. The emphasis is on the accuracy of the data and its transmission in a secured manner. Data Integrity also implies that during the various phases of electronic processing, various features of the data, viz., Accuracy, Confidentiality, Completeness, Up-to-date status, Reliability, Availability, Timeliness and Effectiveness are not compromised. In other words, data should remain accurate during electronic processing. The desired features of the data are described hereunder:

Accuracy : Data should be accurate. Inaccurate data may lead to wrong decisions and thereby, hindering the business development process.

Confidentiality: Information should not lose its confidentiality. It should be protected from being read or copied by anyone who is not authorized to do so. It also includes protecting the individual pieces of information that may seem harmless by the owner, but can be used to infer other confidential information.

Completeness: Data should be complete. Incomplete data loses its significance and importance.

Up-to-date Status : Data should be updated regularly. If the information is not up-to-date, it presents a false picture of the organization.

Reliability: Data should be reliable because all business decisions are taken on the basis of the current database.

Availability: Data should be available when an authorized user needs it. It should be ensured that the information services are unavailable to the unauthorised users.

Timeliness: Timeliness of the data is very important because if data is not available when required, the very purpose of maintaining the database gets defeated.

Effectiveness: Information should be effective, so that it helps in the process of business development and expansion.

If data integrity is not maintained, an organization loses its true representation. Poor data integrity could lead to loss of competitive advantage. Corruption of data would affect many users in a networked environment. If the data is valuable to a competitor, its loss may undermine an organization's competitive position.

8.3 MAINTENANCE OF SYSTEM EFFECTIVENESS

An effective Information System significantly contributes to the achievement of the goals of an organization. Therefore, one of the objectives of IS audit is to verify system effectiveness. It provides input to decide when, what and how the system should be improved, so that its utility to the management is the maximum.

The main objective of introducing computerization in the organisations in the banking and financial sector is to achieve the goals effectively and efficiently. The IS auditor's responsibility is to examine how the Information Systems assist in the achievement of each organisation's goals. System Effectiveness is a ratio of the actual output to the standard (budgeted) output. If it is more than 100%, effectiveness is achieved; or else, it shall be deemed that ineffectiveness has been introduced in the business process. Major goals and criteria of computerization are:

(a) **Improved Task Accomplishments:** The Information Systems should improve the task accomplishment capacity of its users by enabling them to become more productive.

(b) **Improved Quality:** It should improve overall quality of work and services by increased accuracy of information. It should also reduce the time required for retrieval of information.

(c) **Operational Effectiveness:** The Information System should be operationally effective and easy to use. It should be frequently used and users must be satisfied with its performance.

(d) **Technical Effectiveness:** The Information System should be equipped and upgraded by appropriate hardware and software from time to time.

(e) **Economic Effectiveness:** The Information System should be fully utilized. Benefits derived should exceed the cost of procurement, implementation, operation and maintenance.

8.4 ENSURING SYSTEM EFFICIENCY

The resources used by the Information Systems such as the machines, computer peripherals, software etc. are scarce and costly. Efficient Information Systems use minimum resources to achieve the desired objectives. When computer no longer has excess capacity, system efficiency becomes important. It becomes necessary to know whether the available capacity has been exhausted or the existing allocation of the computer resources are causing the bottlenecks.

The ratio of the output to the input is known as efficiency. If output is more with the same or less actual input, system efficiency is achieved; or else, the system is inefficient. If computerization results in the degradation of efficiency, the effort for making the process automated stands defeated. Hence, the assessment of the capabilities of the hardware and software against the workload of the environment is very essential. The IS auditors are responsible to examine how efficient the application software is in relation to the users and the workload of the environment. The system should assist in management planning and efficient execution thereof. The organisation should get maximum output using minimum resources. In this context, the efficient use of the hardware resources and their upgradation, as per requirements, is very essential. Automation should deliver the planned results with less consumption of computer hardware, software, computerized operations and computer personnel.

8.5 OTHER OBJECTIVES

The following could be, among others, considered the other objectives of IS audit :

(a) Identify the risks that the organisation is exposed to in the existing computerized environment and to prioritize such risks for remedial action.

(b) The implementation of Information Technology in the organisation is as per the parameters laid down in the Security Policy, as approved by the Board of Directors of the organisation.

(c) Verify whether the Information System procedures and policies have been devised for the entire organisation and that the organisation's systems, procedures and practices are adhered to and that due prudence is exercised at all times in accordance with the circulars and instructions for a computerized environment, issued by the management of the organisation.

(d) Verify whether proper security policies/procedures have been formulated and implemented regarding the duties of the system administrators, system maintainers and persons operating the system for daily operations.

(e) Contribute effectively towards the minimization of computer abuses/ crimes by suggesting steps for removing any laxity observed in the physical and logical controls.

(f) Suggest improvements in the security controls for the Information Systems.

(g) Act as an advisor to the management of the organisation for improving security and IT implementation standards.

(h) Adhere to the established norms of ethics and professional standards to ensure quality and consistency of audit work.

8.6 SCOPE OF INFORMATION SYSTEM AUDIT

The IS audit should cover all the computerized departments/offices of the organisation. The scope of IS audit should include the collection and evaluation of evidence/information to determine whether the Information Systems in use safeguard the assets, maintain data security, integrity and availability, achieve the organizational goals effectively and utilize the resources efficiently. The scope of IS audit should also include the processes for the planning and organization of the Information Systems activity, the processes for the monitoring of such activity and the examination of the adequacy of the organization and management of the IS specialist staff and the non-specialists with IS responsibilities to address the exposures of the organisation.

8.7 INFORMATION SYSTEM AUDIT APPROACHES

There are three approaches for conducting Information System Audit, viz., auditing around the computer, auditing through the computer and auditing with the computer.

Auditing around the Computer:

Under this approach, the emphasis is on checking the correctness of the output data/documents with reference to the input of a process without going into the details of the processing involved. This approach is preferred, where auditors themselves do not have the desired level of technical skills to adopt the other approaches. This is also preferred, when high reliance is placed on the users rather than the computer controls to safeguard the assets, maintain data integrity and attain effectiveness and efficiency objectives. The focus is on the procedural controls rather than the computer controls. This approach can be used in the following circumstances :

When an application system is simple, logic is straightforward and clear audit trail exists, this approach can be adopted. The process generates the audit trails such as the generation of exception reports along with the main reports. Such systems have very low inherent risk, i.e., they are unlikely to be susceptible to material errors or irregularities or to be associated with significant ineffectiveness or inefficiencies in operations. Input transactions in such systems is in batch mode and control is maintained using traditional methods like the separation of duties and management supervision. Further, the task environment in such systems is relatively constant and the system itself is rarely modified.

This approach may be used when an application system uses a generalized package that is well tested and used by many users as its software platform. If the package has been provided by a reputed vendor, has received widespread use and appears error free, the auditors may decide to adopt this approach. Auditors should ensure that the organization has not modified the package and adequate controls exist over the source code and documentation to prevent unauthorized modification of the package. When high reliance is placed on the users rather than the computer controls to safeguard the assets, maintain data integrity and attain effectiveness and efficiency objectives, this approach can be adopted.

Auditing around the computer is a simple approach. It does not provide any information about the system's ability to cope with the changes. Systems can be designed and programs can be written in certain ways to inhibit their degradation, when user requirements change. Further, this method cannot be used for complex systems. Otherwise, the auditors might fail to understand some aspects of a system that could have a significant effect on the audit approach.

Auditing through the Computer:

Auditing through the computer requires fair knowledge of the operating system, hardware being used and certain technical expertise in systems development. Under this approach, the computer programs and the data constitute the target of IS audit. Compliance and substantive tests are performed on the computer system, its software (both operating system and application system) and the data. IS auditors can test the application system effectively using this approach. The IS auditors can use computer to test logic and controls existing within the system and also records produced by the system. This approach increases the IS auditor's confidence in the reliability and applicability of the evidence/information collected and evaluated. This approach is time consuming, as it needs understanding of the internal working of an application system. It also needs some technical expertise.

Auditing with the Computer:

Under this approach, the computer system and its programs are used as tools in the audit process. The objective is to perform substantive tests using the computers and its programs. The data from the auditee's computer system are retrieved to an independent environment. Audit interrogation and query is carried out on such data, using special programs designed for the purpose. This method is used where :

(a) Application system consists of a large volume of inputs, producing large volume of outputs and where the direct examination of the inputs/outputs is difficult.

(b) Logic of the system is complex.

(c) There are substantial gaps in the visible trails.

Computers are quite useful in the testing of transactions. Some of the software tools used for this purpose are briefly described hereunder:

Computer Assisted Audit Tools (CAATs) are efficient and effective ways to audit system-generated files, records and documents and to evaluate internal controls of an accounting system in many Information Systems. Computer Assisted Audit Tools are a practical means for conducting audit, wherever the information is available on the magnetic media alone. The technical papers relating to the use of the CAATs should be kept separate from the other audit working papers. The IS audit documentation should contain the description of the CAAT application.

Audit Software: It is a program, used by the auditors, to process data of audit significance from the auditee's accounting system. There are three types of such programs as under :

(a) **Package programs** are designed to perform processing functions, creating data files and reports in a format specified by the auditor.

(b) **Special Purpose Programs** are used to perform the audit tasks in specific circumstances and are prepared by the auditors or an outside programmer, engaged by the auditor.

(c) **Utility Programs** are used to perform common data processing functions such as sorting, creating and printing files.

Test Data Techniques: A sample of data transactions is entered into the auditee's computer system and the results are compared with the predetermined results. CAATs are used to test the details of the sample transactions, the balances of the accounts, to identify unusual fluctuations, if any and general EDP controls like accessing the program libraries.

General Audit Software: It is the most widely used technique in conducting IS audit. Its use is limited by the skills of the personnel conducting the audit. Audit Command Language (ACL) is one such software. It is a tool for data analysis. It has the capabilities for Compliance and Substantive testing.

ACL is used to access, analyze, summarize or report data. Advantages of the ACL are as under:

(a) It creates flexible reports and documents.

(b) Auditors are independent of the technical experts for the data, access and process.

(c) It increases audit coverage.

(d) It saves time, money and effort.

(e) It helps gain control over and confidence in the audit results.

(f) General Audit Software is not useful at application level.

Any Computer Assisted Audit Tool (CAAT) is as good as a data mining tool, which is used for extracting data from a data warehouse for MIS / Audit purposes. The following are a few of the generalized audit software in addition to ACL (ACL Services):

(a) Audex 100 (Arthur and Andersons)

(b) Pan Audit (Pansophic Systems)

(c) Audit Aid (Seymour Schneidman & Co.)

(d) EDP Auditor (Cullinane Corporation)

(e) Probe (Citibank)

8.8 INFORMATION SYSTEM AUDIT METHODOLOGY

8.8.1 Audit Methodology

The IS audit work includes manual procedures, computer assisted procedures and fully automated procedures, depending on whether it is around, through, with or a combination of all these types of audit. In many cases, a combination of these techniques is required. The IS auditors may utilize the manual procedures when they are more effective than the other alternatives or when these procedures cannot be partially or fully automated. He/She should also use computer assisted procedures known as Computer Assisted Audit Tools (CAATs) because they permit the IS auditors to switch from the procedures based on limited, random and statistical samples of records in a file to a procedure that includes every record in a file.

8.8.2 Audit activity is broadly divided into 5 major steps for the convenience and effective conduct of audit

(a) Planning IS Audit

(b) Tests of Controls

(c) Tests of Transactions

(d) Tests of Balances

(e) Completion of Audit

(a) Planning IS audit: Planning is the first step of the IS audit. IS auditors should plan the audit work in a manner appropriate for meeting the audit objectives. As a part of the planning process, IS auditors should obtain an understanding of the auditee department/ office/organisation and its processes. It includes understanding of the objectives to be accomplished in the audit, collecting background information, assigning appropriate staff keeping in mind skills, aptitude etc. and identifying the areas of risk. Risk analysis of the operational system is carried out to identify the system with highest risks, considering the critical nature of the information processed through such system as well as the number and the value of the transactions processed. This is to identify the systems having the highest risk and to decide on the extent of the detailed analysis and testing to be conducted on those systems.

In this phase, IS auditors are required to understand the internal controls used within an organization. Various techniques can be used to understand the internal controls, viz., review of previous audit reports/papers, interview/interaction with the management and Information Systems personnel, observation of activities carried out within the Information Systems function and review of Information Systems documentation.

(b) Tests of Controls: During this phase of IS audit, Internal Controls are tested to evaluate whether they operate effectively. This includes testing of management controls and application controls. The objective is to evaluate the reliability of the controls and find out weaknesses of the controls for meeting the IS audit objectives. IS auditor is required to make recommendations to rectify the weaknesses, observed during the course of an IS audit.

While carrying out tests of controls, the IS auditors should satisfy themselves regarding the following aspects of controls:

Identification: Organization should identify the controls to minimize the occurrence of unlawful events.

Implementation: Identified controls should be implemented.

Existence: Sometimes it happens that controls have been implemented, but in reality they do not exist due to various reasons. For example, the organization may have stipulated that the users should change their passwords every week. But, in reality this may not be happening. Physical existence of the controls is equally important.

Adequacy: IS auditors should examine the adequacy of the controls. They should see that the controls are adequate to cover all possible threats.

Documentation: All controls should be documented to make them effective.

Maintenance: Controls should be maintained intact on a continuous basis. For example, only the provision and installation of the fire extinguishers, smoke detectors, UPS etc. do not solve the problem. These instruments should be properly maintained, so that they serve the purpose, as and when needed.

Monitoring: Controls should be monitored by means of strict supervision, surprise checks, periodic inspection etc.

(c) **Tests of Transactions:** Tests of Transactions are used to evaluate whether erroneous transactions have led to a material misstatement of the financial information and whether the transactions have been handled effectively and efficiently. The objective is to evaluate data integrity. Some of such tests include the tracing of journal entries to their source documents, the examination of the price files, the testing of computational accuracy, the study of the transaction log etc. These tests are used to indicate the database system's effectiveness. CAATs are quite useful to perform these tests.

(d) **Tests of Balances:** During this phase of IS audit, final judgement is made on the extent of the losses or account misstatement that occur when Information Systems fail to safeguard assets, maintain data integrity and achieve system effectiveness and efficiency goals. As regards the safeguarding of assets and data integrity objectives, the typical substantive tests used are confirmation of the receivables, physical verification of inventory and recalculation of depreciation on the fixed assets. Regarding the system effectiveness and system efficiency objectives, the tests to be conducted are in the process of evolution. For example, the shortcomings in the Information Systems Planning may have resulted in the purchase of inappropriate hardware. The system may provide outputs, but not of the required standards to make high quality decisions. During this phase of the IS audit, computer support is often required. General Audit Software can be used to select and print confirmations; expert systems can be used to estimate the likely bad debts and so on.

(e) **Completion of Audit:** This is the final stage of IS audit. Auditors are required to form their opinion, clearly indicating their findings, analysis and recommendations. Potential IS audit findings should be discussed with the appropriate/authorised personnel throughout the course of IS auditing. Preliminary conclusions and the audit findings should be presented to the auditee during an exit conference. All potential findings with sufficient merits and preliminary IS audit recommendations should be included for discussion in the exit conference. The exit meeting should document and include the auditee's comments and questions concerning the preliminary IS audit recommendations. The draft audit report should be the natural extension of the exit conference materials alongwith with the discussions that took place during the exit meeting. Once the auditee's responses have been received, the final audit report should be prepared and submitted to the designated authority/management of the organisation.

Work papers used in the auditing should be well organized, clearly written and address all the areas included in IS audit. IS audit work papers should contain sufficient evidence/information of the tasks performed and the conclusions reached, including the results achieved, issues identified and authorized signatures approving the final opinion.

A typical audit report will include, among others, an introduction to the audit objectives, scope, general approach employed, summary of the critical findings, the data to support the critical findings, potential consequences of the weaknesses, auditee's responses and recommendations to rectify the weaknesses.

8.8.3 Sub-system Factoring

IS audit is generally an exercise dealing with the complex Information Systems. In order to understand the complex system, it is always advisable to break the system into sub-systems. A sub-system is a component of a system that performs some basic functions needed by the overall system to attain its basic objectives. The process of breaking a system into sub-systems is called **factoring.** The process of factoring terminates when it is felt that the system has been broken into sub-systems, small enough to be understood and evaluated. Thus, a complicated system is divided into small sub-systems until it becomes easily understandable.

Once the system has been factored into several easily understandable sub-systems, the task of the IS auditors is :

(a) To evaluate the effectiveness of the controls in each sub-system.

(b) To determine the implications of each sub-system's reliability vis-a-vis the overall reliability/effectiveness of the system.

8.8.4 There are two Main Sets of Systems, which Require to be Further Factored into sub-systems for Conducting IS Audit

Management Systems

Management Systems provide stable and basic infrastructure facility on which the Information Systems can be built and operated on a day-to-day basis. Management Systems can be factored into sub-systems that perform Top-level Management, Information Systems Management, Systems Development Management, Programming Management, Data Administration, Quality Assurance Management, Security Administration and Operations Management.

Top-level Management is responsible for long-term policy decisions on the use of the Information Systems in the organisation.

Information Systems Management is responsible for planning and controlling the Information Systems' activities in the organisation. It provides assistance to the top management for making long-term policies and translates the long-term policies into short-term goals and objectives.

System Development Management designs, implements and maintains the application systems.

Programming Management prepares programs for new systems, maintains old systems and provides general systems support software.

Data Administration addresses the planning and control issues in relation to the use of the database.

Quality Assurance Management ensures that the Information System' development, implementation, operations and maintenance conform to the established quality standards.

Security Administration is responsible for access control and physical security over the Information Systems.

Operations Management plans and controls the day-to-day operations of the Information Systems.

Application Systems

Application Systems undertake basic transactions processing, management reporting and decision support. They can be broken into sub-systems that perform boundary, input, communication, processing, database and output functions.

Boundary Sub-system consists of the components that establish interface between the user and the system.

Input Sub-system comprises the components that capture, prepare and enter commands and data into the system.

Communications Sub-system consists of the components that transmit data among the sub-systems and systems.

Processing Sub-system includes the components that perform decision-making, computation, classification, ordering and summarization of the data in the system.

Database Sub-system comprises the components that define, add, access, modify and delete data in the system.

Output Sub-system consists of the components that retrieve and present data to the users of the system.

8.9 BROAD FRAMEWORK FOR CONDUCTING INFORMATION SYSTEM AUDIT

A broad framework can be formed from the basic objectives of IS audit. In addition to this, IS audit evaluates the organizational set up and quality of administration. It should be noted that IS audit is not limited by laid down procedures. It is also important to keep one's eyes and ears open. The IS auditors should, therefore, analyze what they observe and hear. The main issue involved in IS audit is confidentiality of programs, files, access rights to files and focus on software application packages. The major concerns of the IS audit, as derived from its objectives, are as under:

A. Safeguarding Assets

One of the prime objectives of any audit is to ensure that the assets of the organisation are safeguarded. In the computerized environment, the assets to be safeguarded are hardware, software, data and users. The yardstick to measure the importance of this objective is the expected loss that may be sustained by the organisation if the asset is destroyed, stolen, lying unutilized, service denied or used for unauthorized purposes. The IS auditors should verify that the assets are put to effective use in a secured environment. In order to determine whether the assets of the organisation are duly safeguarded, the IS auditors should inspect, among others, the following areas :

Environmental Security: It is very important for the effectiveness of all other protective measures stipulated or installed at the sites. The server room houses the all-important hardware. Its location should be a strategic one and not easily accessible. The server room should be exclusively for the server itself and the other items, equipment etc. should not be kept there.

Uninterrupted Power Supply : The uninterrupted power systems are meant for supplying conditioned and stabilized power to computer equipments at all times. It also provides stabilized power from battery storage when electricity fails. It is very important that the UPS functions properly when electricity fails. The UPS should be maintained regularly.

Electrical Lines: Electrical cabling and wiring constitute the basic components. Faulty electrical cabling and wiring are responsible for operational failures. There should be a separate and proper earthing for the dedicated electrical line.

Data Cabling: Information Technology experts estimate that 90 per cent of the network problems are cable related. Hence, all possibilities of routing cables, locations of cable closets, sites of Switch, Router installation etc. should be explored before finalizing the plan. Detailed map of the cable lay out including Switches, Routers is very important to guide the hardware service engineer in the event of LAN cable fault. Further, electrical cable and data cable should not cross each other to avoid possible disturbance during data transfer.

Fire Protection: Fire alarm system, smoke detectors and fire extinguishers are very important to deal with the event of fire breaking out. Fire extinguishers are commonly filled with water, carbon dioxide or Halon. Little care is required while operating gas based extinguishers because they replace oxygen and thereby, extinguish the fire. Water is effective. But, it is dangerous to use in proximity to live equipments. Dry powder or foam type extinguishers are not advisable because they leave deposits on the equipments.

Insurance: All critical computer equipments are required to be insured with reputed insurance firm/s to secure the Information System resources/assets of the organisation.

Annual Maintenance Contract: Periodic maintenance of the computers, network etc. is essential to ensure trouble free operations of the equipments. For this purpose, it is required that the annual maintenance contract is awarded and renewed in time. At the same time, it is also essential that the maintenance staff is available in time. There should be a proper record of the activities carried out during maintenance.

Logical Security: It restricts access to the system if the user fails to identify himself/herself to the system correctly. Login name/user ID and password are controls for this security. It is exercised at the operating system level and at the application system level. Logical security at the operating system level ensures the access to the computer system when it is successfully powered on, after its boot operation is completed. Logical security at the application system level gives access rights to specific application software depending on the responsibility and authority of the user. IS auditors should verify the effectiveness of the logical security in place by evaluating its controls. Secrecy and security of the user ID and password, different levels of access rights and their allocation to the users, creation of users, its records, users created for maintenance purpose and their termination on completion of the work, user log in status report, presence of dummy user ID in the system etc. are some of the points which require consideration of the IS auditors.

B. Data Integrity

Data is the most important resource in a computerized environment, which needs to be accurate, complete, consistent, up-to date and authentic. The IS auditors are concerned with the possibility of deviation from the standards. They are required to verify how well data integrity is maintained and find out any laxity therein.

The examination of the following points is very important in respect of data integrity:

Data Input Controls: The largest number of controls is available at the time of data entry in the system. Data Input Controls are error prone because the activities involved in data entry are of routine and monotonous nature. Data entry is also a major area for intentional fraudulent activity. It involves addition, deletion, modification or alteration of the input transactions of data. Hence, the IS auditors should minutely evaluate the effectiveness of the data input controls. The use of the scanner and inputs to the system through floppy should be monitored and controlled.

Data Processing Controls: The application system processes the data online on day-to-day basis. The IS auditors are concerned about the Data Processing Controls. They should examine that only designated/authorized officers perform start-of-day operation. The day end process should be completed with the generation of the prescribed reports. It is also required that proper record is maintained in respect of the corrections made in the database under authentication.

Patch Program: It uses the file structure of the existing database files and is capable of effecting changes in a data file. It bypasses the proper menu access controls provided by the application software system and does not leave any audit trail. It can add, modify, alter and delete the data. The behaviour of the approved programs are known and certified, but it is uncertain in the case of such patch programs. They usually bypass all the safeguards available to the system programs. They conveniently flout all norms to achieve results at any costs. Therefore, the IS auditors should verify that only approved programs are loaded in the system and the application programs are exactly identical with the list of the approved programs in respect of file name, file size, date and time of compilation. It is also necessary that a record be maintained regarding the patch programs used indicating the reasons under authentication.

Purging of Data Files: It is pruning of the data files of the identified past period for which it is no more necessary to store the data in the current system. Before undertaking the purging activity, it is necessary to take a backup of full data directory. The purging of the static data or master particulars is never taken. The IS auditors should examine that the purged data backup media is stacked in chronological order for easy tracing and also is in safe custody. A manual record of purging activity should also be maintained. The access to the purged data should be restricted and controlled to ensure the integrity of the purged data.

Data Backup: Data backup is an essential aspect of all computer operations. Some commonly used computer media include hard disk, floppy disks, tape cartridges, CD-ROMs, DVD ROMs etc. Off-site back-ups are taken on floppies or tape cartridges, while on-site back-up is taken on hard disks. Back-up is one of the measures of the business continuity planning and is also required for archiving of old records. It is necessary that the back-ups are taken regularly. One set of the back-up requires to be stored off-site. The back-ups have to be tested periodically by restoring the data therefrom. The back-up media have to be verified periodically for readability. Back-up media should be properly labled and numbered. This is a very important area and requires proper attention.

Restoration of Data: It is defined as downloading of data afresh from magnetic media, in case of crash of the system, irrecoverable corruption or loss of data, for going back on line. Back-up is taken at a particular point of time like beginning of day operations, end of day operations etc. Thus, restoration of data is dependent on the magnetic media and the data stored thereon. Restoration of the data is required in the event of major corruption of data. In the event of a virus attack or total destruction of a server or the computer site, the only option is to fall back upon the restoration option. Restoration of data helps to obtain a position of data as of a particular date, to establish whether any data tampering has taken place. It assists in conducting system audit as of a previous date and generates ledgers of previous years. Transactions of purged period can also be retrieved.

C. Business Continuity Planning

Disruption of operations can occur because of two types of problems. First, some minor problems like power failure, UPS failure, server failure, inability to read/restore back-ups, cable fault etc. can disrupt the operations. Second type of disruption can occur on account of natural calamities like fire, flood, building collapse or man made calamities like bomb blast, radiation, virus attack, induced data loss etc. Business Continuity Plan is prepared to recover from such kind of interruptions. It relates to a higher level of failure. It is all about anticipating any disastrous event and planning adequately for the business to live through it. The IS auditors should verify the existence and operability of the Business Continuity Plan. They should also examine the awareness of the staff regarding the execution of the plan in a genuine emergency and comment upon its effectiveness. Business Continuity Plan should be documented and tested at regular intervals to assess its effectiveness.

BCP is required to satisfy short, medium and long-term recovery. In the short-term, the essential systems and services are restored. Medium-term plans are for recovering the organisation's systems and services on a temporary basis. Long-term plans are for total recovery of the processing environment.

There are three methods of recovery, namely, cold, warm and hot back-up sites. A cold site is where a computer room is provided in which equipment can be installed when needed. A warm site is a computer room filled with all the required equipment, but onto which all the software and applications must be loaded when it is needed. A hot site is one where the original installation is duplicated and ready to use when disaster occurs.

BCP should outline the responsibilities for all the recovery processes, procedures for reproducing the computer media, location of the back-up media, priorities for recovery, sources of replacement hardware and software and alternative data communication facilities.

Output Reports: One of the basic principles in the computerized environment is known as GIGO, i.e., "Garbage in Garbage out." This means that, if the input to the system is garbage (or meaningless), the output will also be garbage. Reports and printouts are generated in computerized environment to ensure the correctness of the inputs and processing. Reports are also important to ensure that the application system programs serve the needs of the organisation. Any lacunae or bugs in the application software can be located by checking the reports and printouts. The importance of checking the reports can never be over emphasized. The IS auditors should scrutinize output reports on sample basis to identify the trend, the quality of follow up and the control exercised by the management. The audit trail report should generate the user ID of the data entry operator and the authorized official for any addition, change, modification and deletion of transactions effected in the database. It should provide the evidence/information of unauthorized access outside the application menu. The IS auditors should verify whether the audit trail reports are generated and checked by the designated officials. Exceptional transaction report is also a very important report.

Version Control: Data integrity is very much dependent on the version of the software running in the system. Authorized Version of the software can lead to accurate processing. Non-standard programs are potential threat to integrity. A complete listing of the programs loaded in the system should be available on record for verification. The IS auditors should verify that licensed copies of the operating system and the application system software are used for computerized operations.

Virus Protection: Computer virus is a program that is self-replicating and can corrupt or destroy data irretrievably. It resembles biological viruses in behaviour. It may have a dormancy period and gets activated on a certain date. It is potentially disastrous. Anti-virus software is available and is capable of countering against known viruses, malicious programs. Anti-virus software is updated by the manufacturers on a regular basis to counter against the new viruses coming up. It is necessary to keep the anti-virus software updated at all times. All extraneous floppies and other media should be checked/scanned for virus before use.

D. System Effectiveness

It is expected that the Information system should improve the overall quality of work including accuracy and time consumed in performing the tasks. Further, it should be user friendly. The IS auditors should judge how effective the system is in accomplishing the goals with which computerization was introduced.

E. System Efficiency

The IS auditors should examine whether every computer asset is used to its maximum operational capacity.

F. Organization and Administration

Efficiency in computerized operations is dependent on the efficiency of the personnel using the computer resources. Computer personnel should do their work completely, timely, accurately and that too, with minimum resources. They should deliver more output quantitatively and qualitatively. Proper placement of the computer personnel on the basis of their aptitude, skill, knowledge and experience is very important. Computer personnel should be used effectively and efficiently with proper security for the organisation to reap maximum advantages.

Segregation of duties, job description for each level, proper training to the staff, dual control aspect in performing important operations, designated system administrator with suitable back-up arrangement etc., are important points to be considered. Records of work assigned to the staff, rotation, training imparted, login name given etc. are to be checked/ verified by the IS auditors.

8.10 PLANNING OF INFORMATION SYSTEMS AUDIT

The IS auditor will require to plan the information systems audit work to address the audit objectives and to comply with the applicable professional auditing standards. The IS auditor should follow the guidelines, as under, for planning the information systems audit work. These guidelines cover the planning process, the identification of the levels of planning and the documentation of the work to be performed by the IS auditors. These guidelines also set out how the IS auditor should comply with the internationally accepted standards.

Planning: While planning the IS audit work, the IS auditor should consider the following factors :

Knowledge of the Organisation:

Before beginning IS auditing, the IS auditor's work should be planned in a manner appropriate for meeting the audit objectives. As a part of the planning process, the IS auditor should obtain an understanding of the organisation and its processes. In addition to giving the IS auditor an understanding of the organisation's operations and its IS requirements, this will assist the IS auditor in determining the levels of materiality of the IS resources being audited, as they relate to the objectives of the organisation. IS auditors should also establish the scope of the audit and perform a preliminary assessment of the internal controls over the functions being audited.

The extent of the knowledge of the organisation and its processes, required by the IS auditor will be determined by the nature of the organisation and the level at which the audit is being performed. An organisation with unusual or complex operations may require the IS auditor to obtain a greater knowledge of the organisation than a similar organisation without specialised operations. A more extensive knowledge of the organisation and its processes will ordinarily be required when the audit objective involves a wide range of information system functions than when the objectives are for limited functions. For example, an audit with the objective of evaluating controls over an organisation's payroll system would normally require a more thorough understanding of the organisation than an audit with the objective of testing controls over a specific program library system.

The IS auditor should gain an understanding of the types of events, transactions and practices that can have a significant effect on the functions being audited. Knowledge of the organisation should include the business and financial risks facing the organisation as well as the conditions in the organisation's market place. The IS auditor should use this information in identifying potential problems, setting the scope of work, evaluating the audit evidence/information and considering the actions of the management for which the IS auditor should be alert.

Materiality

In the planning process, the IS auditor should normally establish levels of materiality such that the audit work will be sufficient to meet the audit objectives and will use audit resources efficiently. For example, in the review of an existing system, the IS auditor will evaluate materiality of the various components of the system in planning the audit programme for the audit work to be performed.

An assessment of the risks should be made to provide reasonable assurance that the material items will be adequately covered during the audit work. This assessment should identify the areas with relatively high risks of the existence of material problems.

Audit Programme

A preliminary programme for an audit engagement should normally be established by the IS auditor before the start of work. This audit programme should be documented in a manner that will permit the IS auditor to record completion of portions of the audit and identify work that remains to be done. As the work progresses, the IS auditor should evaluate the adequacy of the audit programme, based on the evidence/information being gathered in the process of auditing and indicate the areas that might require extended examination.

In addition to a listing of the work to be done, the IS auditor should prepare a list of the resources required to complete the work, a schedule for the work and a budget.

During the course of the work, the IS auditor should consider changes in the audit programme based on the IS auditor's evaluation of the adequacy of the programme and the IS auditor's preliminary findings. The Management/ Designated Authority of the organisation will require to be communicated all such changes with justification therefor.

Internal Control Evaluation

Most audit engagements should include an evaluation of internal controls either directly as a part of the audit objectives or as a basis for reliance upon information being gathered as a part of the audit. Where the objective is evaluation of internal controls, the IS auditor should distinguish between the types of engagements. When the objective is to assess the effectiveness of the controls over a period of time, the IS auditor should include the procedures appropriate for meeting the audit objectives and these procedures may include compliance testing of controls. When the objective is to identify the control procedures at a point in time, the audit plan could be less extensive.

When the IS auditor evaluates the internal controls for the purpose of placing reliance on the control procedures in support of the information/evidence, information being gathered as part of the audit, the IS auditor should make a preliminary evaluation of the internal controls and develop the audit plan on the basis of this evaluation. During an audit, the IS auditor should consider the appropriateness of this evaluation in determining the extent to which the internal controls can be relied upon during testing. For example, in using computer programs to test data files, the IS auditor should evaluate the controls over the program libraries containing programs, being used for audit purposes, to determine the extent to which these programs are protected from unauthorised destruction/modifications.

Documentation of the Audit Plan

The IS auditor's plan should be documented in audit work papers to the extent necessary for the IS auditor to determine that the steps of the plan have been carried out.

The IS auditor's plan may be documented on paper or in other appropriate and retrievable form.

8.11 STANDARDS AND GUIDELINES FOR INFORMATION SYSTEM AUDIT

The specialised nature of the Information Systems (IS) auditing and the skills necessary to perform such audits require standards that apply specifically to IS auditing. Such standards will require to be internationally accepted standards only. This will ensure that the IS auditor performs auditing, conforming to the minimum level of acceptable performance and meeting the required professional responsibilities.

The IS auditing Standards define the mandatory requirements for IS auditing and reporting. The IS auditing Guidelines provide the guidance for the application of the IS auditing standards. The IS auditor should take care of how to achieve the implementation of the Standards, the use of professional judgement in the application of the Standards and should also be prepared to justify any departure/deviation therefrom in the IS auditing work.

The IS auditor shall prepare the procedure including the information on how to meet the Standards while performing the IS auditing work. However, the procedure shall not set the requirements for IS auditing.

IS auditing should be performed by personnel with the required expertise and skills such as Certified Information Systems Auditor, Certified Information Systems Security Professionals etc.

The profitability and the future viability of the organizations in the banking and financial sector increasingly depend on the continued, secured and uninterrupted operations of the Information Systems. Therefore, it is essential for the IS auditors to be conversant with various aspects of Information Technology and the developments taking place in this area. The role of the IS auditors is to see that the organization's assets are protected and suitable internal controls are in place to protect its information and information resources. IS audit is responsible for providing an organization with independent and objective views on the level of security that should be applied to the Information Systems. Computer Security on the other hand is responsible for implementing security in the computerized environment. The IS auditor will learn to co-exist with the Computer Security function and work together for the benefit of the whole organization ensuring that professional standards are maintained at all times.

Major areas, which will require to be IS audited, are broadly as under:

(a) Safeguarding of Assets

(b) Data Integrity

(c) System Effectiveness

(d) System Efficiency

(e) Organization and Administration

(f) Business Continuity Operations

IS auditing of the above areas at the micro level are as under :

Safeguarding of Assets

The IS auditors will require concentrating on the following areas to ensure that the Information Systems Assets of the organisation are safeguarded:

(a) Environmental Security

(b) Data

(c) Uninterrupted Power Supply

(d) Electrical Lines

(e) Data Cables and Networking Products

(f) Fire Protection

(g) Insurance of Assets

(h) Annual Maintenance Contract

(i) Logical Security and Access Control — Operating System Level

(j) Logical Security and Access Control — Application System Level

The IS auditor shall be required to verify/inspect the following points in respect of the areas mentioned above.

A. Environmental Security

The IS auditors should verify whether:

(a) There is separate room for the server.

(b) Server room has adequate space for operational requirements.

(c) Server room is visible from a distance, but is not easily accessible.

(d) Server room is away from the basement, water/drainage systems.

(e) Server room can be locked and the key being under the custody of the authorized persons (System Administrator) only. Entry doors are protected by biometric/PIN or proximity key card access verification. Any failed attempts or system tampering as also unscheduled movement in restricted areas, glass breakage or the opening of doors will require to be logged and immediately reported to the Control Staff at the site. The biometric system will require to store all attempts at access.

(f) To access any equipment in the Data Centre, one has to pass through (preferably) a minimum of two separate security doors, utilising biometric/PIN and/or proximity key card access verification facilities.

(g) Server is not in close proximity to the UPS room.

(h) Access to server room is restricted to authorized persons and activities in the server room are monitored.

(i) Air-conditioning system provides adequate cooling.

(j) Storage devices to keep stationery and other such items are not kept inside the server room.

(k) All the walls with potential access will require to be heavily reinforced.

(l) Humidity and heat measuring instruments like (Thermometer and Hygrometer) are installed in the server room.

(m) Temperature readings are taken throughout the raised floor and equipment areas, power rooms, basement, diesel fuel storage area, roof, generator, cooling towers, waiting and display areas.

(n) Smoking, eating and drinking are prohibited in the server room to prevent spillage of food or liquid into sensitive computer equipment.

(o) Briefcases, handbags and other packages are restricted from the server room, tape library and other sensitive computer area to prevent unauthorized removal of data held on removable media as also to prevent entry of unacceptable material into the area.

(p) Server room is neat and clean to ensure dust free environment.

(q) Scanners are kept in safe custody and access is restricted.

(r) Floppy disk drives on the nodes can be disabled, if necessary for better security.

(s) Steel bollards to be placed in the front of the building to prevent vehicular ingress.

(t) Data Centre to be so choosen to have police protection and fire prevention services within a very short time, say, 5-10 minutes.

B. Uninterrupted Power Supply

In addition to the availability of the Generator facility at the site, the IS auditor should verify whether:

(a) There is a separate enclosure and locking arrangement for the UPS.

(b) Maintenance agency provides battery service regularly.

(c) There is a regular contract for maintenance of the UPS and the preventive maintenance is carried as per the contract.

(d) The record of the tests undertaken is maintained to verify the satisfactory functioning of the UPS.

(e) UPS cabin has adequate ventilation to take care of acid fumes emitted by the Lead Acid batteries.

(f) Capacity of the UPS system is sufficient to take care of the electricity load required for computers installed.

(g) UPS is free of the electricity load relating to the tube-lights, fans, water coolers etc.

(h) UPS functions properly when electricity fails.

C. Electrical Lines:

The IS auditors should verify whether:

(a) There is a separate dedicated electrical line for the computer equipment.

(b) Power supply to computer equipment is through UPS system only.

(c) The electrical wiring looks concealed and is not hanging from ceiling or nodes.

(d) The circuit breaker switches exist in locked condition only.

D. Data Cables

The IS auditors should verify whether :

(a) A map of the cable layout is kept in a secure place with proper authority. This is helpful in timely and fast repairs of LAN cable faults.

(b) Cabling is properly identified and recorded as fiber optic, co-axial, unshielded twisted pair (UTP) or Shielded Twisted Pair (STP).

(c) Electrical cable and data cable do not cross each other to avoid possible disturbance during data transfer within the network.

E. Fire Protection

The IS auditors should verify whether:

(a) Fire alarm system is installed.

(b) Smoke detectors are provided in the server room and in the other areas of computer installations.

(c) Smoke detectors are tested on a regular basis to ensure that they work.

(d) Gas type (Carbon dioxide, Halogen etc.) fire extinguishers are installed at strategic places like server room, UPS room and near the nodes and printers.

(e) Dry powder or foam type extinguishers should not be used as they tend to leave deposits.

(f) Staff knows how to use the fire extinguishers.

(g) Fire extinguishers are regularly refilled/maintained.

(h) An evacuation plan is documented and rehearsed at regular intervals for taking immediate action in the case of the outbreak of fire.

F. Insurance

The IS auditors should verify whether:

(a) All the computer equipments are covered under the appropriate electronic equipment insurance policy with a reputed insurance firm.

(b) A record of the original policy is maintained with the detailed list of the equipments covered under the policy.

(c) Information regarding shifting of computer equipment to or from or within the department/office is conveyed to the insurance firm.

(d) Adequacy of the insurance cover should be verified as per the policy of the organisation.

G. Annual Maintenance Contract

The IS auditors should verify whether:

(a) Stamped agreements for maintenance contract are executed and available.

(b) Activities carried out during maintenance have been reported in the registers and duly authenticated.

(c) Contract renewal rates are maintained in the register.

(d) Access for maintenance purpose is granted only on verifying the identity of the service person.

(e) The maintenance staff support is available in time.

H. Logical Security and Access Control— Operating System Level

The IS auditors should verify whether:

(a) Access to the systems is only through password protected user IDs.

(b) Operating System (OS) allots unique user identity (ID) for all users.

(c) OS provides for different levels of access rights to volumes, directories and files.

(d) OS prompts for change of the user password after the lapse of specified periods.

(e) OS ensures secrecy and security of the user passwords and the access rights granted to a user.

(f) Unrestricted access to the systems is provided only to the System Administrator.

(g) Administration level access is restricted to authorized and limited persons.

(h) All the security features available in the OS are enabled/taken advantage of as far as possible for ensuring better security.

(i) Administration access should not be available to the officials who are under notice period, retiring shortly, under disciplinary action etc.

(j) OS provides for loading of virus prevention software and is implemented.

(k) Record is maintained and authenticated regarding the installation of the Operating System, its upgradation, reinstallation and maintenance.

(l) A register is maintained in respect of all the OS level users, giving the details such as the date of creation, suspension, cancellation, access rights granted, purpose of creation etc.

(m) Users created for audit/maintenance purpose are disabled immediately after the work is over.

(n) The department reviews the number of the OS level users periodically.

I. Logical Security and Access Control — Application System Level

The IS auditors should verify whether:

(a) System provides for unique user IDs and password for all users.

(b) System provides for different levels of access.

(c) System prompts for change of user password after lapse of specified period.

(d) System ensures secrecy and security of the user passwords and the access rights granted to users.

(e) Unrestricted access to the entire application system menu is provided only to a Super User.

(f) Application makes use of all the security features available at the Application System level.

(g) Super User access in application level is not given to staff who is under notice period, retiring shortly, under disciplinary action etc.

(h) The application system user list is periodically reviewed.

(i) The access privileges granted in the system are in accordance with the designation/duties performed.

(j) None of the staff members has multiple level or duplicate access ID in the system.

(k) Allocation of the suspended, disabled user ID to new users is avoided.

(l) Active user IDs of the transferred, retired, suspended or dismissed employees are not present in the system.

(m) There is no dummy user ID created in the system.

(n) The user ID of staff on long leave, training etc. is suspended.

(o) System logs out automatically if the user is inactive for a specified time (or user consciously logs out when he/she leaves a terminal).

(p) System does not allow concurrent login to a single user ID from different nodes.

(q) Users, created for maintenance purpose, are cancelled on completion of the job.

(r) The system does not allow user to cancel his/her own user ID.

(s) Authority periodically reviews the user login status report.

(t) Users do not share their passwords.

(u) Passwords of alphanumeric characters are used.

(v) Users do not write their passwords on wall, desk diary etc. and are aware of the need for the secrecy of their passwords.

(w) System automatically locks the user ID after unsuccessful login attempts.

(x) User log indicating date, time, node, user ID, transactions performed etc. are generated by the system and evaluated by the System Administrator.

Data Integrity

The IS auditor will require to address, among others, the following areas under IS auditing :

(a) Data Input Controls

(b) Data Processing Controls

(c) Patch Programs

(d) Purging of Data Files

(e) Back-up of data

(f) Restoration of Data

(g) Business Continuity Planning

(h) Output Reports

(i) Version Control

(j) Virus Protection

A. Data Input Controls:

The organisations in the banking and financial sector undertake diverse activities relating to the receipt of deposits, advancement of credit, investment of funds etc. Further, the areas of operation and the level of economic activities could also be different. All these activities, the transactions resulting therefrom, the data inputs required therefor including the data input controls to be in place in the organisation will require to be judiciously addressed. However, illustratively, such data input controls may relate to the following areas of activity and the IS auditors will require to verify the same.

(a) History of signatures scanned is available in the system.

(b) The entire stock of cheque books is fed to the system.

(c) The cheque books issued are entered and confirmed in the system on day-to-day basis.

(d) The data fed in to various accounts including the customer accounts is accurate and correct.

(e) Clear administrative guidelines exist regarding the access to live data.

(f) Clear guidelines exist for online transactions including those put through the INTERNET by the Customers.

(g) Data Administration is a part of System Administration. However, Database Administration is separate from System Administration.

(h) Data Owner (DA) and Database Administrator (DBA) are independent of both the systems development and operational activities.

(i) The roles of DA and DBA are clearly defined in respect of, among others, (i) definition, creation and retirement of data, (ii) database availability to Users, (iii) information and services to Users, (iv) maintenance of database integrity and (v) monitoring and performance.

B. Data Processing Controls

The IS auditor should verify whether:

(a) The designated/authorized officials do start-of-day process.

(b) The operating staff pay attention to the error messages displayed on the screen and initiates corrective action.

(c) Entries are cancelled only by the appropriate authority.

(d) Cash entries are not deleted from the system.

(e) Prescribed reports are generated at the end-of-day process.

(f) Printouts are scrutinized and preserved.

(g) Proper record is maintained in respect of the corrections made in database under authentication.

(h) Master data printouts are preserved carefully.

(i) Input to the system through floppy is monitored and controlled.

(j) Use of the scanner is monitored and controlled.

C. Patch Programs

The IS auditors should verify whether:

(a) The application programs are exactly identical with the standard list of approved programs in respect of file name, file size, date and time of compilation.

(b) Only approved programs have been loaded in the system.

(c) There are programs other than the approved ones.

(d) There is a record of the patch programs used and the reason thereof under authentication.

D. Purging of Data Files

The IS auditors should verify whether:

(a) Purging activity is recorded and maintained in a register.

(b) Purged back-up media is kept properly under safe custody.

(c) Access to purged data is restricted.

E. Back-up of Data

The IS auditors should verify whether:

(a) All the floppies/CDs/tapes, purchased, pertaining to the OS software, application software and utility programs, drivers etc. are recorded in a register and properly stored.

(b) Hardware, software, operating system, printer manuals are properly labelled and maintained.

(c) Latest user manuals of the application software and other end-user packages running on the system are available for guidance.

(d) Daily/weekly/monthly and quarterly back-up of data is taken without fail and is available (as per requirement).

(e) Back-up' tapes are properly labelled and numbered.

(f) Proper storage procedures and facilities are in place for back-up copies.

(g) There is offsite storage of one set of the back-up data.

(h) Back-up tapes are verified/tested periodically by restoring the data and record maintained.

(i) Back-up media is verified periodically for readability.

(j) Record is available in respect of such verification.

(k) Back-up media are phased out of use after a specified period.

(l) Back-up register is maintained wherein all the events pertaining to the back-up including the procedure of back-up are recorded.

(m) Physical and fire protection is provided to back-up media.

F. Restoration of Data

The IS auditors should verify whether:

(a) The instructions for restoration of the back-up data have been compiled.

(b) The data integrity is verified after the restoration work is over.

(c) Activities carried out during the restoration work are recorded indicating date, time, reason for restoration and size of the data restored.

G. Business Continuity Planning (BCP)

The IS auditors should verify whether:

(a) Business continuity plan has been documented.

(b) BCP covers all levels of disaster from pm1ial to total destruction of facilities and contains guidelines to help determine the level of recovery necessary.

(c) A copy of the plan is securely stored off site.

(d) Detailed restart procedure has been documented in the plan.

(e) BCP has been tested and is regularly tested to assess its effectiveness.

(f) There is awareness among the staff members about the BCP and the modalities of its execution in case of an emergency.

(g) Ready or alternate source of hardware/software is there to resume business activity within the shortest possible time after disruption.

(h) A reliable back-up of data and software is available all the times for restoration.

H. Output Reports

The IS auditors should verify whether:

(a) The audit trail report generates the user ID of the operator and the official for any addition / modification / deletion of the transaction data affected in the database.

(b) Audit trail report is generated daily. Entries are scrutinized and verified.

(c) Audit trail report indicates the evidence/information of unauthorized access outside application menu.

(d) List of the cancelled entries is scrutinized and reasons for cancellation are recorded.

I. Version Control

The IS auditors should velify whether:

(a) The computer system has authorized version of an OS, authorized version of anti-vims software with its latest updates.

(b) There exist the documentary evidence/information about the authenticity and the right to use the copy of the OS software, OS system utility, third party software, the runtime system of specified language or database in use and the anti-virus software.

(c) Legally licenced copies of the software are used for computerized operations and the licenses are currently in force.

(d) Changes made to the application software with the approval from the controlling office/ department.

J. Virus Protection

The IS auditors should verify whether:

(a) Anti-virus software is loaded in the system.

(b) Anti-virus software is regularly updated to cover software updates against the latest viruses.

(c) All extraneous floppies are checked for virus including the floppies carried by the IS auditors.

System Effectiveness:

The IS auditors should verify whether:

(a) Computerized operations provide better customer service in terms of time and quality.

(b) Staff serves a larger number of customers during the day than prior to the introduction of online operations.

(c) Customer information is provided timely and accurately.

(d) The system reflects any improvement in the overall quality of products and services offered.

(e) System has improved the tasks accomplishment capacity of its users by enabling them to be more productive.

(f) Users are satisfied with the performance of the system.

(g) System is user friendly and takes less effort.

(h) The users are putting the software to frequent use, which requires less effort and is easier to use and the users are satisfied with the performance of the software.

System Efficiency:

The IS auditors should verify whether:

(a) Department/Office ensures the use of every computer asset.

(b) Department/Office utilizes every computer asset to its optimum capacity.

(c) Periodical maintenance of the hardware asset ensures its uninterruped service.

(d) The online operations help complete day's workload on the same day consuming less time than the time taken for the respective manual operations.

(e) The online operations provide accurate, complete and consistent data at each stage of processing.

(f) Department/Office takes consistency check of balances daily to aid in the detection of errors or fraud.

(g) Department/Office uses the hardware peripherals such as printers, nodes etc. efficiently.

Organisation and Administration:

The IS auditors should verify whether:

(a) There is an Information Systems Security Programme for the entire organisation, approved by the Board of Directors.

(b) There is a Corporate Information Systems Security Policy, well defined and documented and implemented including Information Systems Awareness Programme.

(c) There is an established hierarchy in the organisation with a Senior Executive in charge of the implementation of the Corporate Security Policy with Information Systems Security Officials at various levels in an Office.

(d) Identified System Administrator for each computerised Office / Department, as required.

(e) Job description for each level is prepared and implemented (including System Administrator).

(f) Training is imparted to all staff members in turn for better results and output.

(g) The entire staff is involved/motivated for working in the online environment.

(h) The department allots online jobs to staff members accessing performance parameters like willingness, aptitude, expertise, skill, experience and knowledge.

(i) Record is maintained showing details of the work assigned, period of assignment, rotation, training imparted, login name and acknowledgement obtained.

(j) Dual control aspect is implemented for the important online operations.

(k) The functions of initiating, authorizing, inputting, processing and checking of the data are separated to ensure that no person has complete control over a particular function. Therefore, abuse of that function is not possible without collusion between two or more individuals.

(l) Rotation of duties is carried out at regular intervals.

(m) System Administrator is supervised and controlled with respect to the creation of user ids at the Application Software level.

(n) There are at least 2 persons for key functions of online operations to take care of absenteeism.

(o) Department/Office ensures to bring up the servers into operation readiness sufficiently in advance before the commencement of the business hours.

(p) Computers are covered to keep them free from dust, rain water, etc.

(q) Clear communication from the Management of the organisation to the effect that each member of the staff is responsible for maintaining security in the organisation, as per the Security Policy.

9

CHAPTER

OPERATING SYSTEM

Structure:

9.1 INTRODUCTION

An operating system is a software program that loads automatically and controls just about everything on your computer. Here's what an operating system does:

- **Controls Your Computer's Hardware:** Windows controls the different devices of your computer system. It's what makes your printer print, what makes graphics and text appear on your monitor, and what makes your mouse point and click.
- **Runs Your Computer's Programs:** An operating system is what runs all your programs. Without an operating system, your word processor, Web browser (Internet), and games wouldn't work. An operating system lets your programs talk to your hardware, so, for example, your word processor can print things for the printer.
- **Organizes Files:** An operating system stores information in files and folders on your computer's local disk, just like you store files and folders in a filing cabinet.

An operating system is like an orchestra conductor who makes sure all the parts of your computer — your hardware and programs work together. Operating systems have been around for a long time — here's a brief history of the various operating systems out there:

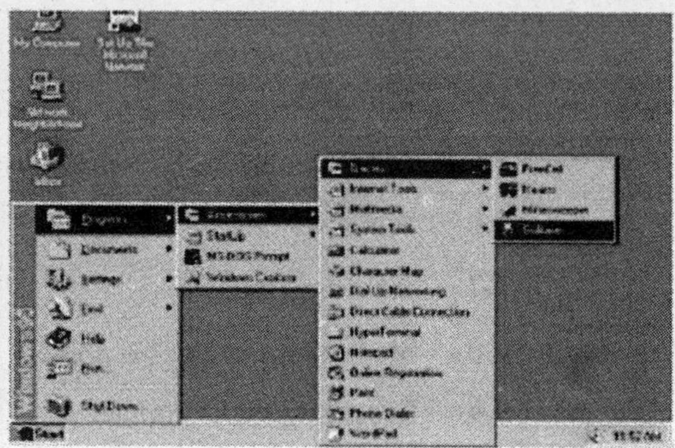

9.2 TYPES OF OPERATING SYSTEM

Operating System	*Released*	*Description*
MS-DOS	1980	MS-DOS stands for Microsoft Disk Operating System. MS-DOS was one of the earliest PC operating systems that displayed boring lines of text on the screen instead of icons and pictures. You performed tasks in MS-DOS by typing text commands. MS-DOS file names could only be eight characters long.
Windows 3.1	1992	Windows 3.1 was the first *successful* operating system *for the PC* that featured a GUI (Graphical User Interface) that used easy to use pictures instead of hard to remember MS-DOS commands. Technically speaking, Windows 3.1 was not a true operating system, since it still required MS-DOS to operate.
Windows 95	1995	The incredibly successful successor to Windows 3.1, Windows 95 was a true operating system (no more MS-DOS). It featured long file names, better performance, and a greatly improved interface.
Windows 98	1998	Very similar with Windows 95, Windows 98 included several new and improved features. More importantly, Windows 98 came with support for many of the new hardware devices out there.

Windows ME	2000	Windows ME was the successor to Windows 98. ME stands for *Millennium Edition* or *Mistake Eternal*, depending on who you talk to. Windows ME was very similar to Windows 95 and 98 but it included new multimedia features, new utilities and lots of new bugs.
Windows NT	1993	Windows NT (stands for *New Technology*) was a powerful 32-bit operating system that was faster, more secure, and much more stable than Windows 95 or 98. Windows NT was designed for use in large companies where stability and security were especially important.
Windows 2000	2000	Windows 2000 was the successor to Windows NT. Windows 2000 includes the best features of Windows 98 (easy Plug and Play hardware installation) and Windows NT (security and stability). Windows 2000 is still widely used in many businesses.
Windows XP Home	2001	Windows XP (stands for eXPerience — huh?) Home is designed for home and consumer computing and is the successor to Windows ME. Windows XP has the same technology found in Windows NT and 2000, so it's much more stable than earlier versions of Windows.
Windows XP Professional	2001	Windows XP Professional is the business edition of Windows and is the successor to Windows NT and Windows 2000.
Windows CE / Pocket PC	Varies	Windows CE (stands for Consumer Electronics) is the operating system made by Microsoft used to power handheld computers or PDAs (Personal Data Assistants).
Palm OS®	Varies	The Palm OS is another operating system that can be found on handheld computers or PDAs.
UNIX	Varies	UNIX is an older, very powerful operating system that can run on a computer, mainframe, or network. UNIX features great performance, security, and reliability.
Linux	Varies	Linux is a newer UNIX-base operating system that is available for FREE on the Internet. Linux is becoming a popular alternative to Microsoft Windows.
Mac OS X	2001	Mac OS X is the latest operating system for Macintosh computers.

When the computer starts, it starts the operating system that takes the control of the machine. An Operating System is a set of programs that help in controlling and managing the Hardware and the Software resources of a computer system. A good operating system should have the following features:

1. Help in the loading of programs and data from external sources into the internal memory before they are executed.
2. Help programs to perform input/output operations, such as:
   - Print or display the result of a program on the printer or the screen.
   - Store the output data or programs written on the computer in storage device.
   - Communicate the message from the system to the user through the VDU.
   - Accept input from the user through the keyboard or mouse.

Computer software can be divided into two main categories: application software and system software. "An Application **software** consists of the programs for performing tasks particular to the machine's utilization. Examples of application software include spreadsheets, database systems, desktop publishing systems, program development software, and games." Application software is generally what we think of when someone speaks of computer programs. This software is designed to solve a particular problem for users.

On the other hand, **System Software** is more transparent and less noticed by the typical computer user. This software "provides a general programming environment in which programmers can create specific applications to suit their needs. This environment provides new functions that are not available at the hardware level and performs tasks related to executing the application program." **System software** acts as an interface between the hardware of the computer and the application software that users need to run on the computer. The diagram below illustrates the relationship between application software and system software.

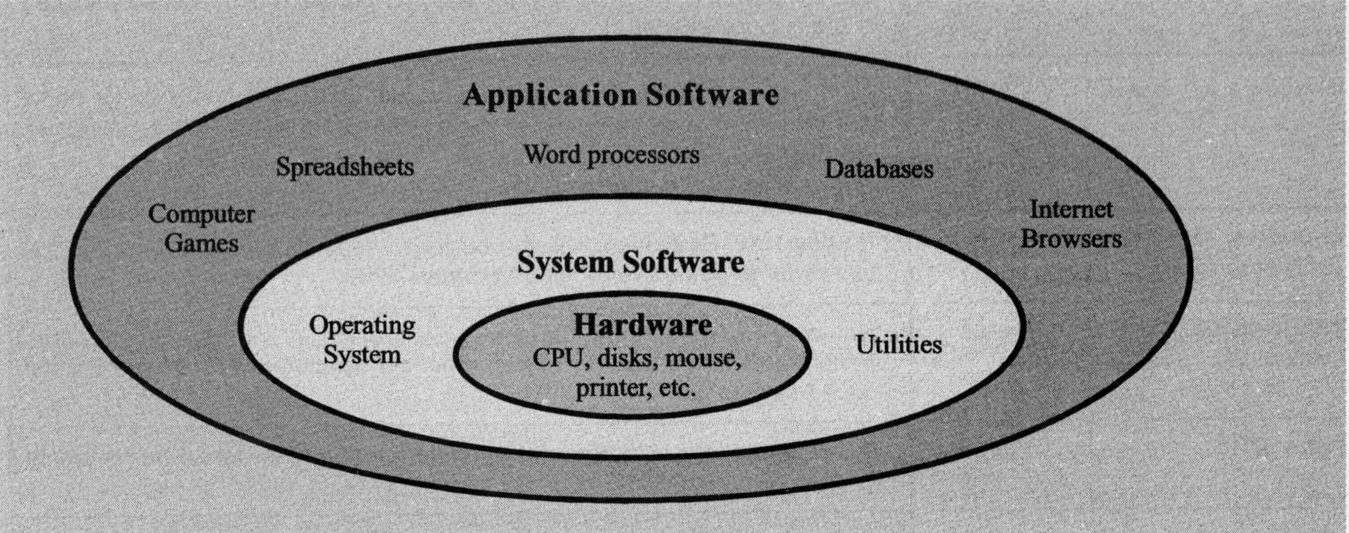

Conceptual View of a Computer System

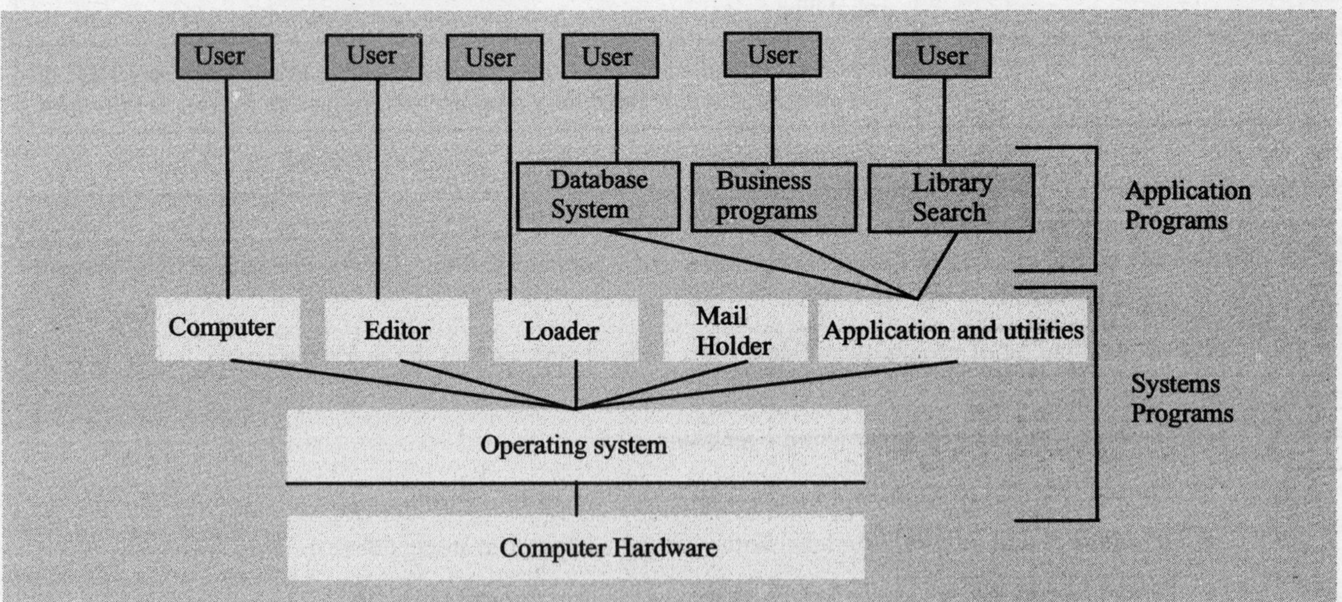

The central processing unit (CPU) is located on chips inside the system unit. The CPU is the brain of the computer. This is the place where the computer interprets and processes information.

The operating system is the first component of the systems programs that interests us here. Systems programs are programs written for direct execution on computer hardware in order to make the power of the computer fully and efficiently accessible to applications programmers and other computer users. Systems programming is different from application programming because it requires an intimate knowledge of the computer hardware as well as the end users' needs. Moreover, systems programs are often large and more complex than application programs, although that is not always the case. Since systems programs provide the foundation upon which application programs are built, it is most important that systems programs are reliable, efficient and correct.

9.3 DEFINITION

In a computer system the hardware provides the basic computing resources. The applications programs define the way in which these resources are used to solve the computing problems of the users. The operating system controls and coordinates the use of the hardware among the various systems programs and application programs for the various users.

The basic resources of a computer system are provided by its hardware, software and data. The operating system provides the means for the proper use of these resources in the operation of the computer system. It simply provides an environment within which other programs can do useful work.

We can view an operating system as a resource allocator. A computer system has many resources (hardware and software) that may be required to solve a problem: CPU time, memory space, file storage space, input/output devices etc.

The operating system acts as the manager of these resources and allocates them to specific programs and users as necessary for their tasks. Since there may be many, possibly conflicting, requests for resources, the operating system must decide which requests are allocated resources to operate the computer system fairly and efficiently. An operating system is a control program. This program controls the execution of user programs to prevent errors and improper use of the computer.

Operating systems exist because they are a reasonable way to solve the problem of creating a usable computing system. The fundamental goal of a computer system is to execute user programs and solve user problems.

The primary goal of an operating system is a convenience for the user. Operating systems exist because they are supposed to make it easier to compute with an operating system than without an operating system. This is particularly clear when you look at operating system for small personal computers.

A secondary goal is the efficient operation of computer system. This goal is particularly important for large, shared multi-user systems. Operating systems can solve this goal. It is known that sometimes these two goals, convenience and efficiency, are contradictory.

While there is no universally agreed definition of the concept of an operating system, we offer the following as a reasonable starting point:

A computer's operating system (OS) is a group of programs designed to serve two basic purposes:

1. To control the allocation and use of the computing system's resources among the various users and tasks, and.

2. To provide an interface between the computer hardware and the programmer that simplifies and makes feasible the creation, coding, debugging, and maintenance of application programs.

Specifically, we can imagine that an effective operating system should accomplish all of the following:

- Facilitate creation and modification of program and data files through an editor program,

- Provide access to compilers to translate programs from high-level languages to machine language,
- Provide a loader program to move the compiled program code to the computer's memory for execution,
- Provide routines that handle the intricate details of I/O programming,
- Assure that when there are several active processes in the computer, each will get fair and non-interfering access to the central processing unit for execution,
- Take care of storage and device allocation,
- Provide for long-term storage of user information in the form of files, and
- Permit system resources to be shared among users when appropriate, and be protected from unauthorized or mischievous intervention as necessary.

Though systems programs such as editor and translators and the various utility programs (such as sort and file transfer program) are not usually considered part of the operating system, the operating system is responsible for providing access to these system resources.

9.4 MS-DOS (MICROSOFT DISK OPERATING SYSTEM)

Windows is a graphical operating system in which you use a mouse to select icons on the screen. MS-DOS is a command line operating system in which you type commands.

Entering DOS

From the Start menu choose Programs Æ MS-DOS Prompt

Moving around

Use the *cd* command (change directory) to go to a particular folder.

Examples:

cd c:\	to the top level of the c-drive
cd c:\windows\desktop	to the desktop level
cd ..	the folder one level up
cd *foldername*	to the folder within the current folder

Other commands

dir	See the contents of the current folder
dir | more	Use "| more" to see one screenful at a time
programname	Run the program "programname"
program | more	Run *program* and see output by screens
program > file.txt	Run *program* and send output to *file.txt*
<ctrl>-C	Recover if DOS freezes
exit	Return to Windows

Some course material on the Teaching Network may still use the command line operating system called DOS (Disk Operating System). This requires the user to type specific commands at a prompt.

You may also need to use this system, for example, when changing your password, and you can enter DOS by choosing 'MS-DOS Prompt' from the Public menu on the taskbar.

Command Format

Commands can be typed in response to the network DOS prompt:

G:\>

Commands may be typed in upper or lower case. Here, they are specified in upper case to distinguish them from other input.

Commands have a particular format. Some can be used simply by typing the command name only, as in:

DIR

which displays a listing of files in the current directory.

Parameters

Many commands can take extra information called parameters to make them more specific, For example, the COPY command can have a parameter specifying a file to be copied and a parameter specifying a file to which the copy is to be made. So the command would look like this:

COPY *filea fileb*

In this case, *filea* would be the name of a file to copy from and *fileb* would be the name of a file to copy to.

Parameters can sometimes be omitted in which case a default action will apply.

Options

Commands can also be qualified by the use of options. Options are preceded by a / sign. A simple example of the use of an option is with the DIR command. DIR can be qualified by /P or /W. Thus, the commands:

DIR

DIR /W

DIR /P

result in listings presented in a different format as detailed later.

9.5 SOME USEFUL DOS COMMANDS

COPY

Make a copy of a file or merge files together.

COPY *original-file destination-file*

where *original-file* and *destination-file* are file names, separated by a space.

The command can be used to merge several files into one file since the *original-file* parameter can be a list of filenames separated by the + symbol.

For example:

COPY file1 + file2 file3

would copy file1 and file2 into file3.

Note that the file names used in the copy command must include the file extension if it exists. So if you were copying a fortran program called first, for example, you would need to include the .for extension in the file name.

DEL

Delete a file.

DEL *filename*

where *filename* is the name of the file to be deleted. You are asked to confirm that you really want to delete the file. Note that the name must include the file extension.

The amount of space on a disk is limited and it is necessary periodically to tide up unwanted files. It is possible to use a '*' character in a filename to match any sequence of characters. This feature is very useful when deleting unwanted files with identical extensions. For example, when developing programs,

DEL *.obj

will delete every binary (.obj) file in the current directory. Since an .obj file can always be recreated from the original source program, it is usually unnecessary to keep it.

DIR

Obtain a list of the files stored in a directory. If used without options this command will give a list of files in the current directory, including any extension (e.g., for), and their size.

If used with the option /P, that is:

DIR /P

The same information will be displayed page by page with the message:

strike a key when ready at the end of each page.

If it is used with the /W option, i.e. :

DIR /W

the listing is of names and extensions only and in a more compact format across the page.

DISKCOPY

Take a security copy of your working disk. It is very important to have a second copy of our programs and data in case you lose your disk or it becomes unreadable for some reason. Use the DISKCOPY command as follows:

DISKCOPY A: A:

where A: denotes the drive the disks will be loaded into. When a copy of your disk is generated in the computer's memory, the computer tells you to remove the first or source disk and insert the disk, which is to become the copy (the target disk). Insert the target disk and press ENTER. If the second disk is not formatted it will be formatted automatically. The source disk should be write protected using the tab in the corner in case you mistake it for the target disk.

LIST

Obtain a printed listing of a file.

LIST *filename*

where *filename* is the file to be printed. If the printer is busy, or if you don't need a printed copy, you can use the TYPE command to view a file on the screen.

You could also use an editor such as DOS Edit to display a file, in which case, as a bonus, you would then be in a position to correct any errors you might notice. Remember that the file name must include the file extension. So if you want to print your Pascal program called first you would need to use:

LIST first.pas

RENAME

Change the name of a file. This command can be abbreviated to REN:

REN *oldname newname*

where *oldname* is the file to be renamed and *newname* is the name it is to be given. Note that files on drives other than the current drive can be referred to by prefixing the filename by the relevant drive letter, for example:

A:*filename*

where the \ refers to the 'root' directory of the drive. Filenames can also include directories separated by the \ character as in:

A:*dir1dir2**filename***

TYPE

View a file on the screen.

TYPE *filename*

where filename is the name of the file to be displayed on the monitor screen. If you are looking at a long file, you will need to press the PAUSE key to stop continuous scrolling. Press the space bar to continue scrolling when you have read the screen.

FORMAT

To format a floppy disk, place the disk in the floppy drive and type:

FORMAT A:

Note that by default the disk will be formatted to hold about 1.44 megabytes of data.

Warning: formatting will destroy any data on the disk so only do this once!

DOS COMMAND LISTING

In the following section, alternative options are separated by the '!' character. Arguments are optional unless in italics. 'cwd' stands for 'Current Working Directory.'

DOS Conventions

DOS commands are not case sensitive. Some commands have switches; these must be preceded by a forward slash (/). Pathnames may be preceded by a drive letter as in 'X:pathname' and if no drive or pathname is given the current directory is assumed.

The Commands

ATTRIB +!-r +!-a *pathname*

display, or set!clear Read-only or

Archive attribute

BREAK on!off

display, or turn on!off increased level of ^C detection

CHDIR (CD) path

display, or change working directory

CHKDSK pathname (A: drive only)

check disk or file logical structure

/f - fixproblems encountered

/v - verbose; displays filespecs

CLS

clear screen

COMMAND path cttydev

run nested CLI from path with I/O device cttydev

/e:# - set environment size #

/p - do not invoke another CLI

/c command - run command and then enter

COPY pathname pathname

or

COPY *pathname* + *pathname*

copy or concatenate files

/v - verify writes

/a!b - preceding and all subsequent files are ascii!

binary (* filenames in source(s) and target are matched one-to-one.)

CTTY device

change MS-DOS I/O device

DATE dd-mm-yy

display and/or set date (numerical country-dependent format)

DEL ! ERASE *pathname*

delete file(s) - prompts if pathname is *.*

DIR pathname

display directory - filename and/or ext default to *

/p - paginate

/w - multi-column

DISKCOPY drive: drive:

copy disk sector-by-sector rather than file-by-file

EXIT

exit nested CLI

FIND "*string*" pathname

find and display lines containing string in file

/v - lines NOT containing string

/c - count lines only

/n - display line numbers also

FORMAT *drive*: **(A: drive only)**

/1 - single sided

/4 - use double rather than high density (40 tracks)

/8 - use 8 sectors of each track

/n:xx - specifies xx sectors per track

/t:yy - specifies yy tracks

/v - prompt for volume label, up to 11 characters

/f:720 - format at 720 kb

LABEL drive: label (A: drive only)

display, or edit volume label - 11 characters excluding most specials

MKDIR (MD) path

make directory

MODE

interactively configure various options

MORE

paginates screen output

e.g. type filename | more

PATH path;path;...

display or set command search path(s) to be used after cwd

PATH;

resets default to cwd only

PROMPT string

Characters (each prefixed by $) mean:

$=$, t=time, d=date, p=cwd, v=version, n=drive,

g=>, l=<, b=!, _=CRLF, s=leading space, e=ESC (for ANSI driver)

RENAME (REN)*pathname pathname*

rename file(s) within a drive - wildcards are matched one-to-one

RMDIR (RD) path

remove empty directory

SET variable = text

display all, set or clear MS-DOS variable - accessed as % variable %

SHARE

enable networked multi-access file locking

/f:nbytes - nbytes per file, need about 20 bytes per file, default 2048

/l:nlocks - nlocks per file, default 20

SORT pathname pathname

sort lines of file alphabetically, ignoring case, to file or stdout; reads stdin by default

/r - reverse order

/+n - on n'th character in each line, default is first

SUBST drive: path (A: drive only)

display substitutions, or substitute path by virtual drive

SYS *drive*: **(A: drive only)**

copy hidden MS-DOS .sys files from default drive

TIME hours:minutes

display and/or set time using 24-hour format

TYPE *pathname*

output contents of a file, with tab spacing of 8

VER

display MS-DOS version

VERIFY on!off

display, or set!clear disk write verification

VOL drive:

display disk volume label

XCOPY *pathname* **pathname**

copy directory tree

/a!m - if archive bit set ! also clears in source

/d:date- modified on or after date only

/s!e - copy subdirectories if not empty ! even if empty

/p - prompt

/v - verify

/w - wait for keypress

If renamed to MCOPY it determines automatically whether target is file or directory.

ON-LINE COMMAND HELP

Full details of all DOS commands can be seen by following the command with the switch /? For example,

DIR /?

gives a listing of all DIR options.

COMMAND EDITING

DOS commands are stored in a template and previous commands can be recalled, character by character enabling editing as required. The template is accessed by the following keys:

F1	-	get next character from template
F2 C	-	get characters up to but excluding character C
F3	-	get remaining characters from template
del	-	skip one character in template
F4 C	-	skip characters up to but excluding character C
ESC	-	clear command line
INS	-	toggle overwriting of template
F5	-	copy command to template for re-editing
F6	-	put ^Z in new template

The arrow keys may also be used to recall the previous command.

BATCH FILE COMMANDS

All DOS commands may be used in batch files. Additionally, the following commands are useful for more advanced batch processes.

Arguments for batch files are accessed as '%1' to '%9'.

ECHO on!off!message

display echo status, turn echoing on!off (default on)

or display message

FOR % %C IN (SET of items) DO command

C is any character other than 0-9, SET, e.g., list of files

GOTO LABEL

LABEL is any line of text, usually preceded by colon (:) in first column, which makes MS-DOS ignore it other than as a label. Terminates if label not found

IF ERRORLEVEL *number command*

command executed if previous command returned exit code >= number

IF *string1* == *string2* **command**

command executed if strings match may be negated by NOT before condition

IF EXIST *filename command*

command executed if file exists may be negated by NOT before condition

PAUSE comment

comment displayed only if echo on

REM comment

remark - ignored by MS-DOS

SHIFT

shift arguments - allows access to more than 9

SPECIAL CHARACTERS

Several special characters may be used when referring to directories and files:

\	=	root directory or a directory separator
.	=	current directory
..	=	parent directory

Wildcard characters may be used in filenames or extensions:

?	=	any character
*	=	any tail or extension
X:	-	switches to current working directory (cwd) on drive X.

FILE COMPARISON UTILITY

The FC command enables comparison of two files:

FC *pathname1 pathname2*

compare two files, or two wildcarded sets of files

/a	-	abbreviate output of ASCII comparison
/b	-	force binary comparison (byte-by-byte)
/c	-	ignore case
/L	-	force ASCII comparison (line-by-line)
/Lb#	-	use line buffer of # lines

/n - display line numbers in ASCII mode

/t - do not expand tabs - default expands to spacing of 8

/w - compress white space (tabs and spaces) to single space (leading or trailing white space always ignored)

/# - # lines must match to re-synchronize else regarded different (default is 2)

I/O CONTROL

DOS input and output may be controlled by the following control key sequences. (^ = the CTRL key).

^C - abort current command

^H - destructive backspace

^J - linefeed - physical newline to input long lines

^N - toggle copying of terminal output to printer

^P - toggle redirection of terminal output to printer

^S - suspend/restart terminal output

^X - cancel current line, and output \-CR-LF

^Z - end of file

I/O REDIRECTION

Input and output from commands or programs can be redirected by using the following symbols:

> send output to...

>> append output to...

< take input from...

| pipc output to next input

For example:

pipe output from command a to input of command b:

command a | command b

send a directory listing to file filename:

DIR > filename

Using the DOS Editor

DOS includes a full-screen editor invoked by the EDIT command (with or without a filename). To use this editor type:

EDIT (*filename*)

The editor provides pull-down menus, operated by the keyboard or mouse, and a help facility. Note that any changes made to a file overwrites the original, no backup is created.

9.6 WINDOWS OS

9.6.1 The Main Section

This part of the key board is very much like an old-fashioned typewriter. Additional keys such as ctrl, and the F (unction) keys allow many more signals to be sent to the PC

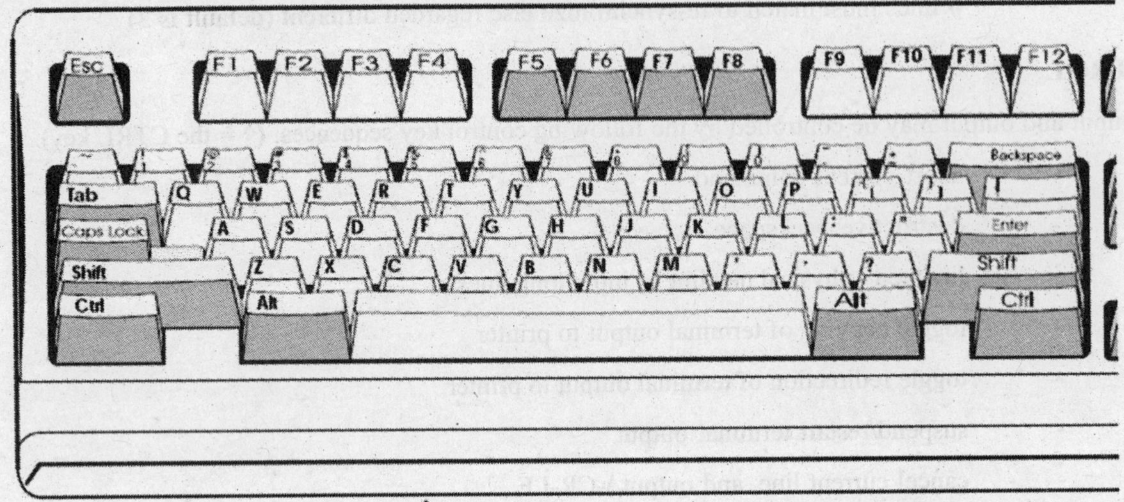

Shift is often denoted by ⇑ The main Enter key is often called Return and denoted by ↵

Backspace is often denoted by ←

9.6.2 The Special Keys

This part of the key board provides keys for moving around documents and also a numeric or accountants keypad.

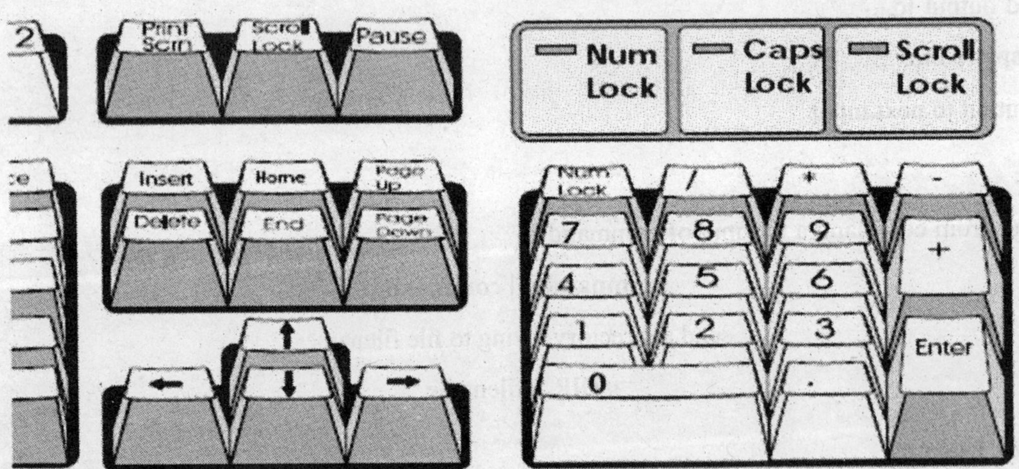

9.6.3 The Mouse

The mouse controller is a very important part of the system. Don't be put-off if you cannot get it to perform the way you want first time, it will take a little bit of practice to master it, the more you use it, the easier it becomes. To use the mouse, hold it in your hand and move it across a flat surface. An arrow shaded cursor õwill move across the computer screen in the same direction you move the mouse.

Apart from moving the pointer on the screen, a mouse will have two and sometimes three buttons on it. These are used for sending commands to the computer.

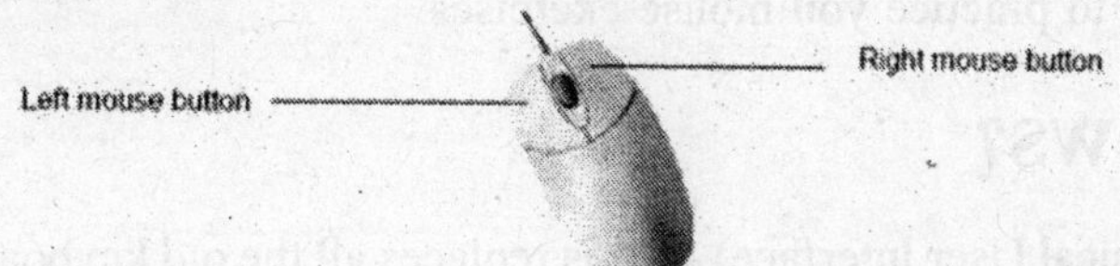

After moving the mouse to an item on the screen, there are basically four functions which can be performed with the mouse buttons:

1. Single click — press and release the left button immediately; used to select items
2. Double click — same as a single but press twice and release in rapid succession.
3. Click and drag — press the left button and hold; used to drag items around the screen.
4. Right click — press and release the right mouse button; used to bring up short-cut menus.

The mouse pointer will give a lot of information if you know how to interpret it. Observe the mouse as you move it over certain items, it will change from time to time letting you know when you can perform certain functions.

Here are some possible mouse pointer shapes and their meanings:

	Normal Select	
	Help Select	
	Working in Background	
	Busy	
	Precision Select	
	Text Select	
	Handwriting	
	Unavailable	
	Vertical Resize	
	Horizontal Resize	
	Diagonal Resize 1	
	Diagonal Resize 2	
	Move	
	Alternate Select	

TIPS

Try playing some of the games that come with windows when you have some free time, these are very mouse intensive and a good way for you to practice you mouse exercises.

9.7 WHAT IS WINDOWS?

Windows is a GUI (Graphical User Interface) — this replaces all the old keyboard commands and functions with a user-friendly screen. There different versions of Windows (as discussed earlier), which include Windows 95, Windows 98, Windows Millennium Edition (ME) and Windows XP.

Included with the Windows operating system are some useful accessories, which include WordPad, Notepad and MS Paint. Although these applications (programs) are very basic in their facilities, they can be used to accomplish several tasks that users would like to perform on a computer. For more demanding user, alternative programs such as Microsoft Office or Lotus Office, can be installed which will fulfill the needs of even the most demanding users.

Windows Minimum Hardware Requirements

Windows ME	Windows 98	Windows 95
• Processor: Pentium or equivalent, 150Mhz • Memory: 32MB RAM • Hard Disk: between 200 MB and 550MB disk space • Drive: CD-ROM or DVD-ROM drive	• Processor: 486DX, 66 Mhz (Pentium recommended) • Memory: 16MB RAM • Hard Disk: between 165 MB and 355MB disk space • Drive: 3 ½" high density floppy disk drive	• Processor: 386DX or higher (486 recommended) • Memory: 4MB RAM • Hard Disk: between 50 MB and 55MB disk space • Drive: 3 ½" high density floppy disk drive
Windows 2000	**Windows XP**	
• Processor: 133 Mhz (Pentium recommended • Memory: 64MB RAM (128 recommended) • Hard Disk: 2 GB space, with 650 MB free • Drive: CD-Rom	• Processor: 233 Mhz (Pentium 300 recommended • Memory: 64MB RAM (128 recommended) • Hard Disk: 1.5 GB space • Drive: CD-Rom • SVGA	

Special Reminder on Different Windows Versions

It is important to note that the basic functionalities among the different Windows versions remain the same. However, there will be slight differences in the appearance of the various screens and application windows. For example, Windows ME will have a more "Internet browser-based look" than Windows 95. The screen shots in these notes are based on Windows 98, and so may vary on different versions of Windows.

Starting the Computer

To start the computer, use the switch to power on the computer. Note that, the monitor may also need to be powered on. Once the computer has completely started, the desktop screen will be displayed.

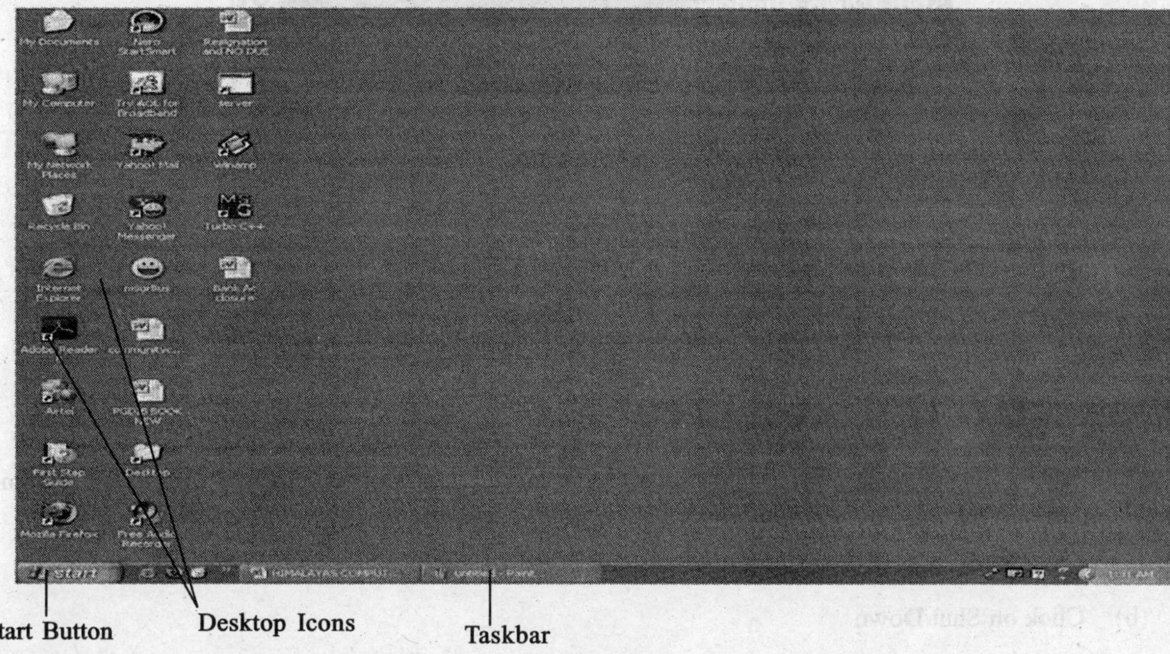

9.8 SHUTTING DOWN THE COMPUTER

This procedure must be used to shut down the computer, as the computer tidies its system and files used. In most cases, this will automatically power off the computer, so there is need to use the power button to switch off the machine. However, the monitor must be switched off using the power button.

1. Click on the Start Button
2. Click on Shut Down
3. Select the option to Shut Down the computer
4. Then click OK

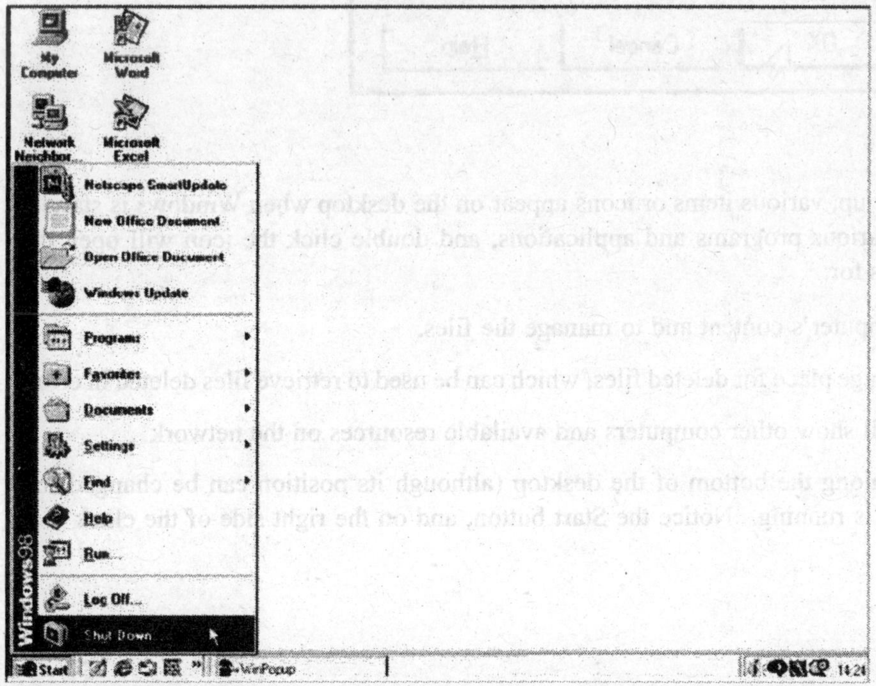

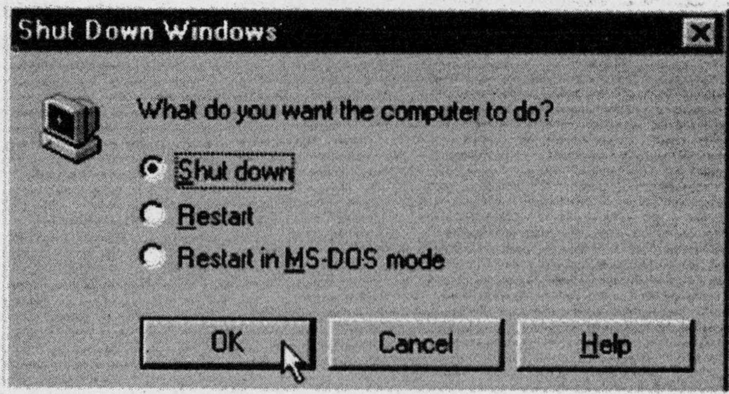

9.9 RESTARTING THE COMPUTER

At times, it is necessary to restart the computer, after system settings have been changed or if new programs have been installed.

(a) Click on the Start Button

(b) Click on Shut Down

(c) Select the option to start

(d) Then click OK

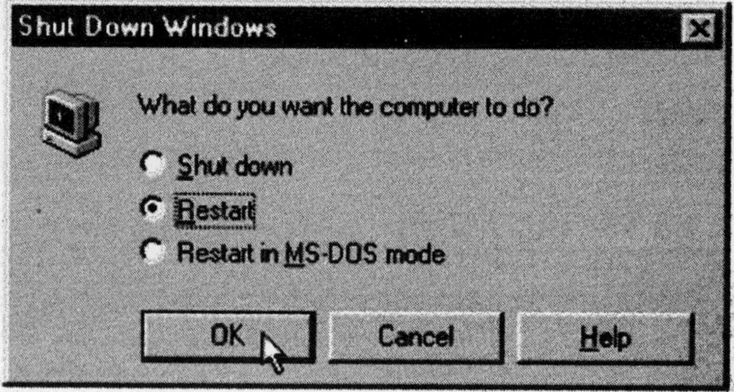

9.10 THE DESKTOP

Depending on how the computer is set up, various items or icons appear on the desktop when Windows is started. These icon points to, or are shortcuts to various programs and applications, and double click the icon will open the application. For example, there will be icons for:

- My computer — to see the computer's content and to manage the files.
- Recycle Bin — a temporary storage place for deleted files, which can be used to retrieve files deleted in error.
- Network Neighbourhood — will show other computers and available resources on the network

THE TASKBAR is the bar running along the bottom of the desktop (although its position can be changed) by default, it is always visible when Windows is running. Notice the Start button, and on the right side of the clock it is displayed.

When you click the Start Button, you see a menu that contains everything you need to begin using Windows. If you want to start a program, point to programs. Following is an overview of each command:

1. Programs — Displays a list of programs you can start
2. Documents — Displays a list of documents that have been recently opened
3. Settings — Displays a list of system components for which you can change settings
4. Find — Enables you to find a folder, file, or shared computer

Run — Starts a program or opens a folder when you type a command. This is most often used to install new programs.

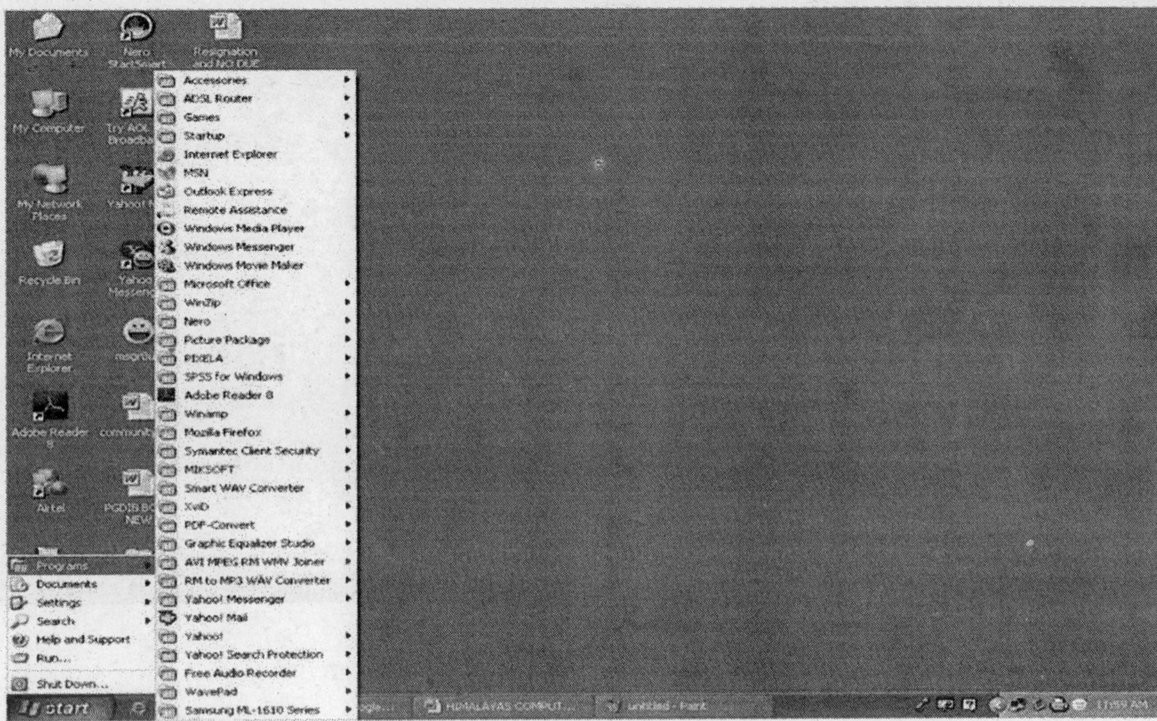

9.11 CONTROL PANEL

The control panel is used to change the computer's hardware and software settings. Care should be exercised when using Control Panel options, as altering settings without understanding the changes can result in loss of files, or even damage to the computer.

1. Click on the Start button
2. Move-up the menu that has appeared to settings
3. Note the arrow/triangle which points right, hold the mouse over this arrow until another menu appears
4. Move across to this other menu and select control panel

My Documents
Nero StartSmart
Resignation and NO DUE
My Computer
Try AOL for Broadband
server
My Network Places
Yahoo! Mail
Winamp
Recycle Bin
Yahoo! Messenger
Turbo C++
Internet Explorer
msgrBus
Bank Ac closure
Adobe Reader 8
Authorisation
Airtel
PGDIB BOOK NEW
Programs
Documents
Settings
Control Panel
Search
Help and Support
Run...
Shut Down...
Provides options for you to customize the appearance and functionality of your computer, add or remove programs, and set up network connections and user accounts.
start
untitled - Paint
12:03 PM

CHAPTER

10 MICROSOFT OFFICE 2010

Structure:

- 10.1 Microsoft Office
- 10.2 Starting Word 2010
- 10.3 Create a New Document
- 10.4 Editing a Document
- 10.5 Formatting Text
- 10.6 Handling the Tables in Word
- 10.7 Use of the Different Tools
- 10.8 Page Formatting
- 10.9 Saving the Document
- 10.10 Print Documents
- 10.11 Mail Merge 2010
- 10.12 Microsoft Excel
- 10.13 Microsoft PowerPoint
- 10.14 Ms Project
- 10.15 Database Management System (Overview)
- 10.16 Microsoft Access
- 10.17 Microsoft Word 2010 Shortcut Keys

10.1 MICROSOFT OFFICE

Microsoft Office 2010 provides features that help IT administrators configure, validate, deploy, and protect Office installations in their organizations. Microsoft Office 2010 is a productivity suite for Microsoft Windows, and the successor to Microsoft Office 2007. Office 2010 includes extended file format support, user interface updates, and a changed user experience. A 64-bit version of Office 2010 is available, although not for Windows XP or Windows Server 2003.

Office 2010 marks the debut of free online versions of Word, Excel, PowerPoint, and OneNote, which work in the web browsers Internet Explorer, Firefox, Chrome and Safari, but not Opera. Office Starter 2010, a new edition of Office, replaced the low-end home productivity software, Microsoft Works. Microsoft's update to its mobile productivity suite, Office Mobile 2010, will also be released for Windows Phones running Windows Mobile 6.5 and Windows Phone 7. In Office 2010, every application features the ribbon, including Outlook, OneNote, Publisher, InfoPath, SharePoint Workspace (previously known as Groove), and the new Office Web Applications.

Microsoft Office 2010 Specification to Install

- Developer(s): Microsoft
- Initial release: June 15, 2010 (2010-06-15)
- Stable release: Service Pack 1 (14.0.6023.1000)
- Operating system:
  - (i) Windows 7
  - (ii) Windows Server 2008
  - (iii) Windows Vista with Service Pack 1
  - (iv) Windows Server 2003 R2
  - (v) Windows XP with Service Pack 3 (32-Bit only)
- Platform: Intel x86 32-bit and 64-bit

Available in English, Arabic, Simplified Chinese, Traditional Chinese, Czech, Danish, Dutch, Finnish, French, German, Greek, Hebrew, Hindi, Hungarian, Italian, Japanese, Korean, Lithuanian, Norwegian (Bokmål), Polish, Portuguese (Brazil), Portuguese (Portugal), Romanian, Russian, Slovak, Slovenian, Spanish, Swedish, Thai, Turkish, and Ukrainian.

New and Efficient Features in Office 2010

The following features are highlights of Office 2010.

Fluent User Interface

The Office 2010 Fluent user interface (UI) lets you support users more efficiently. It contains updates to the ribbon and a new backstage view that displays the details of files and functionalities, even letting you create a custom UI, all within the XML schema. The ribbon organizes commands in a more usable way by presenting them as a set of tabs. Each contextual tab represents a task area relevant to a particular Office product. The ribbon is improved in Office 2010 and is included in all Office 2010 applications.

Backstage View

The Microsoft Office Backstage view in Office 2010 replaces the Microsoft Office Button of the 2007 Microsoft Office system. The Backstage view enables you to create a custom UI, similar to within the ribbon, and to add elements such as workflow or task information that is specific to an organization's needs. The Backstage view is available in all Office 2010 applications, and replaces the **File** menu of earlier Microsoft Office versions.

Silverlight

Microsoft Silverlight is a technology that works in the browser and on the desktops that brings many Microsoft Office experience to life with amazing video, animations and interactivity. Microsoft recommends installing Microsoft Silverlight along with Office to improve the information worker user experience with Office 2010. Specifically, Microsoft Silverlight enables better online experience with Office Online, powers the Office 2010 interactive guides (available with Office 2010), improves the user experience of Office SharePoint 2010, improves the performance of Office Web Companion applications and help with the process of uploading Office document to cloud services.

File Formats

Microsoft Office 2003 introduced a format based on extensible markup language (XML) that enabled you to understand the details of a document. The 2007 Office system made XML the default file format so that you could easily work with your documents. The data that was contained in the XML file listed the content in a document, and the description included any settings that were needed for the document to work within the application. In addition to supporting about 20 different document formats including XML Paper Specification (XPS), Portable Document Format (PDF) 1.5, PDF/A and Open Document Format (ODF) v1.1. Office 2010 continues to support XML.

The XML format provides advantages such as easier data mining and content reuse; faster document creation from different data sources; reduction of the size of Excel, PowerPoint, and Word files; and improved data recovery of corrupted files.

ODF users can save documents in version 1.1 of the ODF for Word, Excel and PowerPoint. Users can open, edit and save files in the OpenDocument Text (*.odt), OpenDocument Spreadsheet (*.ods), and OpenDocument Presentations (*.odp) formats.

Edition Comparison

Five editions of Office 2010 suites are available — three user versions and two business versions.

Differences between Microsoft Office Versions

Within each application, Office 2010 has improved functionality in many areas. When the 2007 Microsoft Office system was released, a significant difference from Office 2003 was the introduction of the ribbon in the user interface (UI). The UI changed from a collection of menus and toolbars to a single ribbon mechanism. The Office 2010 suites maintain the ribbon and have some new features.

The following table describes the differences in UI basics between Office 2010, the Office 2007 system, and Office 2003.

UI Element	Office 2010	Office 2007	Office 2003
Menus and tabs	The ribbon replaces menus and toolbars across all products of Office 2010 and can be fully customized.	The ribbon replaces menus and toolbars in Access 2007, Office Excel 2007, PowerPoint 2007, Word 2007, and parts of Outlook 2007.	Menus and toolbars only are available.
Task panes	Groups of commands on the ribbon and the ability to customize.	Groups of commands on the ribbon and the ability to customize.	Basic task pane.
Quick Access Toolbar (QAT)	Fully customizable.	Introduced in 2007.	Not available.
Backstage view	More tools outside the document viewing window.	Limited tools that can be accessed through the Microsoft Office Button.	Limited tools on the File menu

Digital signatures	Found in the Backstage view under Information about Document/Protect Document.	Formatted with XMLDSig, found under File/Finalize Document/Signatures.	Found under Tools/Options/Security/Digital Signatures.
Smart Art	Improved from the 2007 version.	Design tools available in all Microsoft Office applications.	Not available.
Open Formats (*.odt) Open Document Text	Included in this version.	Added in 2007 Office system Service Pack 2 (SP2).	Not available.
Windows Live Writer integration	Blog posting options available in the application.	Not available.	Not available.
Spelling checker	The spelling checker is now integrated with automatic correction.	Basic spelling checker.	Basic spelling checker.
Paste Preview	A live preview before you commit to Paste. Avoids having to use the Undo button.	Paste, Undo, Paste.	Basic Paste capabilities.
Print	The Backstage combines Print with Print Preview, Page Layout and other print options.	Microsoft Office Button, Print with limited printing tools spread across several commands.	Basic Print option on the File menu.
Sparklines	A miniature chart inserted into text or embedded in a spreadsheet cell to summarize data.	Dynamic charts and chart types.	Three-dimensional (3-D) charting.
E-mail Essentials	Conversation, Cleanup, Ignore Thread, and Mail Tips for when a person is out of the office or if e-mail is sent to a group.	Not available.	Not available.
Photo editing tools	Available in these applications: (Word 2010, Excel 2010, PowerPoint 2010, Outlook 2010, and Microsoft Publisher 2010).	Limited functionality.	Limited functionality.
Video in Microsoft PowerPoint	Video triggers and controls.	Not available.	Not available.

10.2 STARTING WORD 2010

To start Microsoft Office Word 2010 click on the start button, choose all programs and click once on Microsoft office and then click Microsoft Office Word 2010. By keeping the cursor on the word itself, the message will display below as to create and edit professional-looking documents such as letters, papers, reports and booklets by using Microsoft Office Word.

The Microsoft Word window appears and your screen looks similar to the one shown here.

For changing the color of the windows ribbon, go to file menu and click it, in that options button will appear below. While click options button, then Word options window will open. Under the User Interface options, color scheme will be shown. You can choose your color of window ribbon like sliver, blue and black. The default color of the windows ribbon will open in the silver color only.

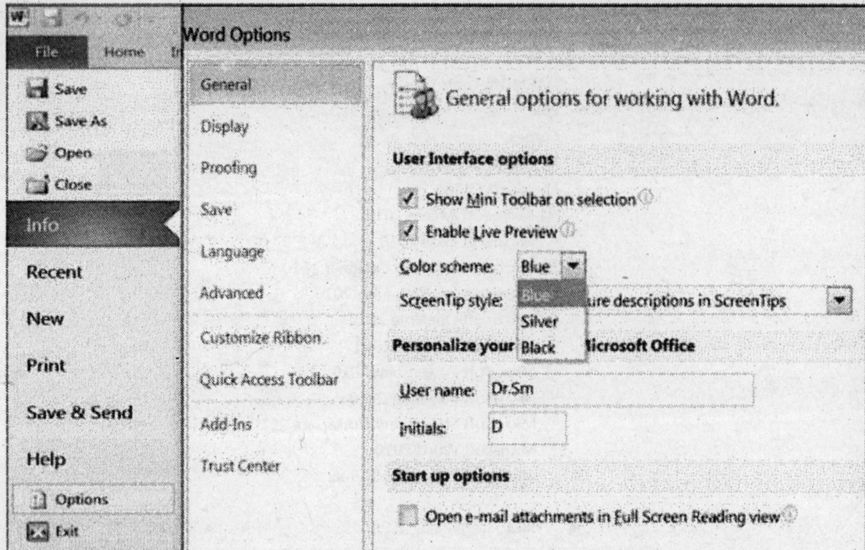

Screen Layout Menus

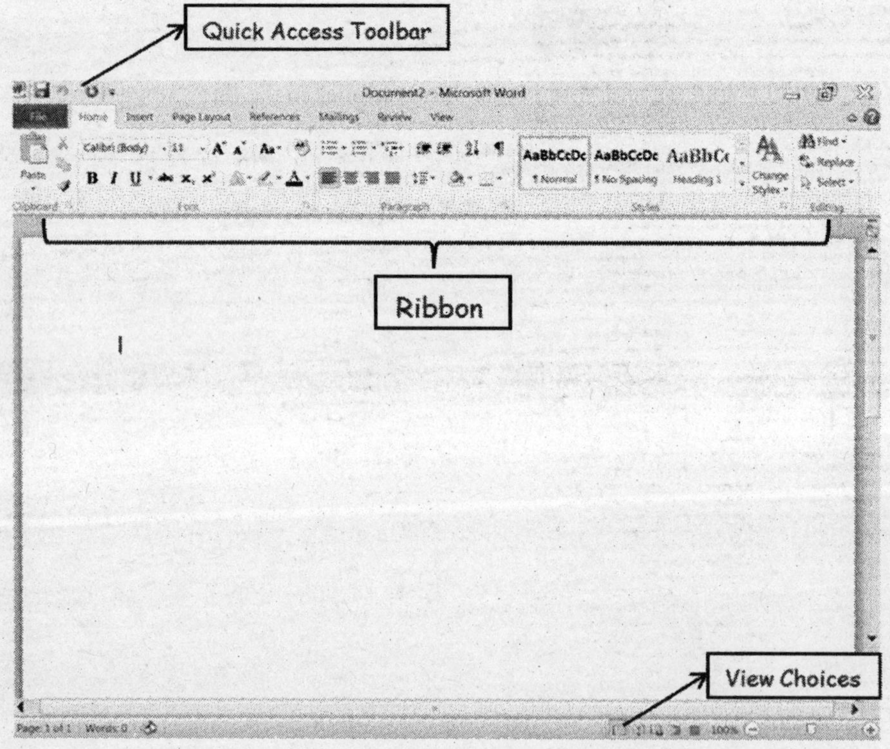

When you begin to explore Word 2010, you will notice three features that you should remember as you work within Word 2010: the Quick Access Toolbar, the Ribbon and view choices. The functions of these three features will be more fully explored below.

The Quick Access Toolbar

In the **upper left corner** – to the right of the Microsoft Office word - you will see an area called the **Quick Access Toolbar** (image on left). This area is quite handy as it currently contains several of the most used buttons in Office applications – Save, Undo, Redo, Print and Print Preview. You can customize this toolbar by adding and removing as many Quick Access button choices as you desire.

To Add Commands to the Quick Access Toolbar

- ❖ Click the **arrow** to the right of the Quick Access toolbar.
- ❖ Select the **command** you wish to add from the drop-down list. It will appear in the Quick Access toolbar.

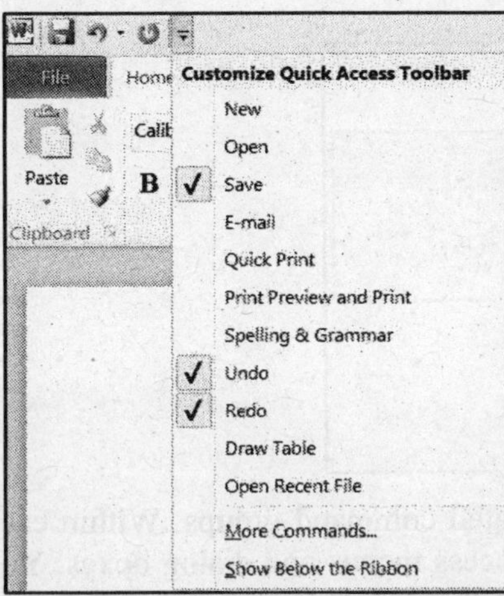

The Save, Undo, and Redo commands appear by default in the Quick Access toolbar. You may wish to add other commands to make using specific Word features more convenient for you.

The Title Bar

Next to the Quick Access toolbar is the Title bar. The Title bar displays the title of the document on which you are currently working. Word names the first new document you open Document1. As you open additional new documents, Word names them sequentially. When you save your document, you assign the document a new name.

Document1 - Microsoft Word

The Ribbon

The Ribbon is the panel at the top portion of the document. It has eight tabs: File, Home, Insert, Page Layout, References, Mailings, Review, and View that contain many new and existing features of Word 2010. Each tab is divided into groups. The groups are logical collections of features designed to perform functions that you will utilize in developing or editing your Word document. Commonly used features are displayed on the Ribbon, to view additional features within each group, click on the arrow at the bottom right of each group.

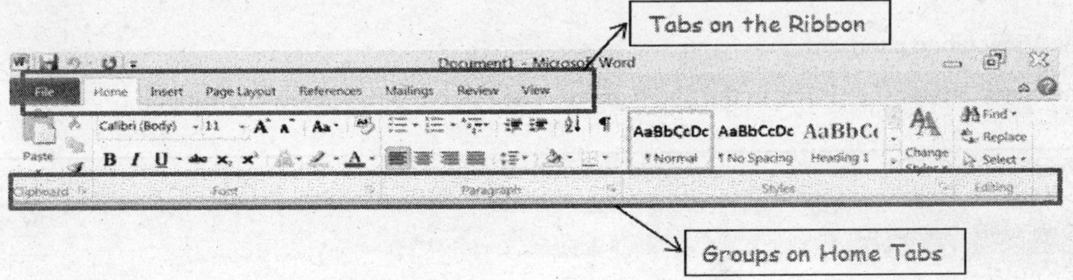

Each of the tabs contains the following tools:

- ❖ **File:** Save, Save As, Open, Close, Info, Recent, New, Print, Save & Send, Help, Options and Exit.
- ❖ **Home:** Clipboard, Font, Paragraph, Styles, and Editing.
- ❖ **Insert:** Pages, Tables, Illustrations, Links, Header & Footer, Text, and Symbols.

- **Page Layout:** Themes, Page Setup, Page Background, Paragraph and Arrange.
- **References:** Table of Contents, Footnote, Citation & Bibliography, Captions, Index, and Table of Authorities
- **Mailings:** Create, Start Mail Merge, Write & Insert Fields, Preview Results and Finish.
- **Review:** Proofing, Language, Comments, Tracking, Changes, Compare and Protect.
- **View:** Document Views, Show, Zoom, Window and Macros.

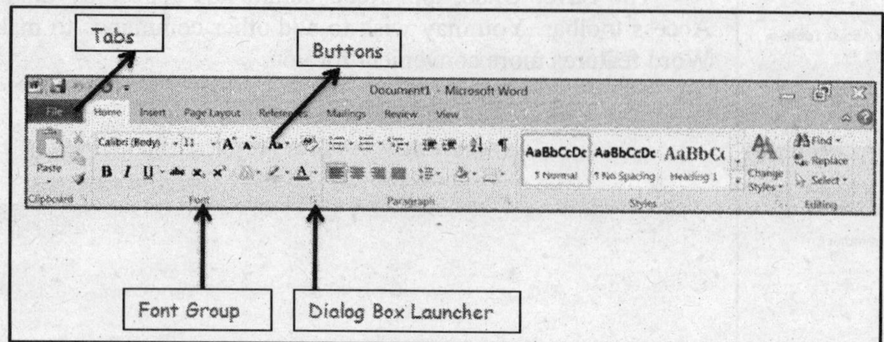

At the top of the Ribbon are several tabs; clicking a tab displays several related command groups. Within each group are related command buttons. You click buttons to issue commands or to access menus and dialog boxes. You may also find a dialog box launcher in the bottom-right corner of a group. Clicking the dialog box launcher gives you access to additional commands via a dialog box.

The Ruler

The ruler is found below the Ribbon. It is shown in the window below.

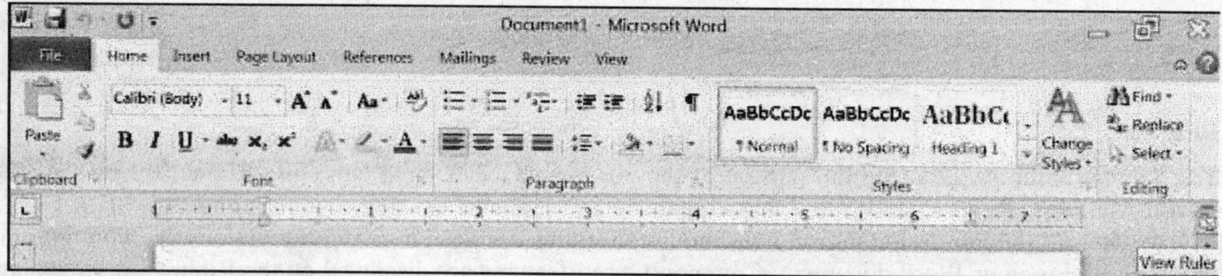

You can use the ruler to change the format of your document quickly. If your ruler is not visible, follow the steps listed here:

1. Click the View tab to choose it
2. Click the check box next to Ruler in the Show group. The ruler appears below the Ribbon

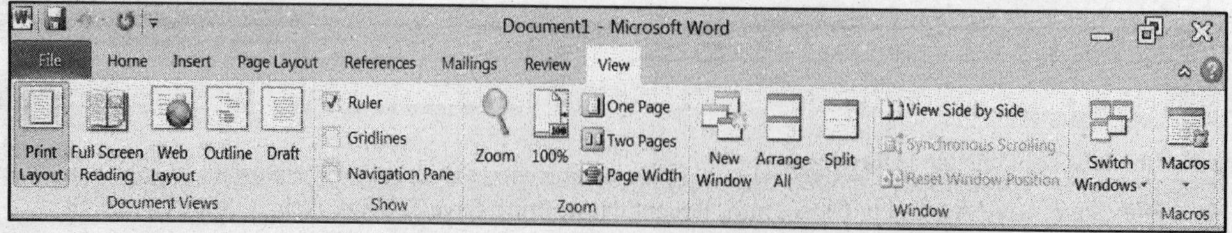

To Display or Hide the Ruler

Click the **View Ruler** icon over the scrollbar. The **View Ruler** icon works as a toggle button to turn the ruler on and off.

The Text Area

Just below the ruler is a large area called the text area. You type your document in the text area. The blinking vertical line in the upper-left corner of the text area is the cursor. It marks the insertion point. As you type, your text displays at the cursor location. The horizontal line next to the cursor marks the end of the document.

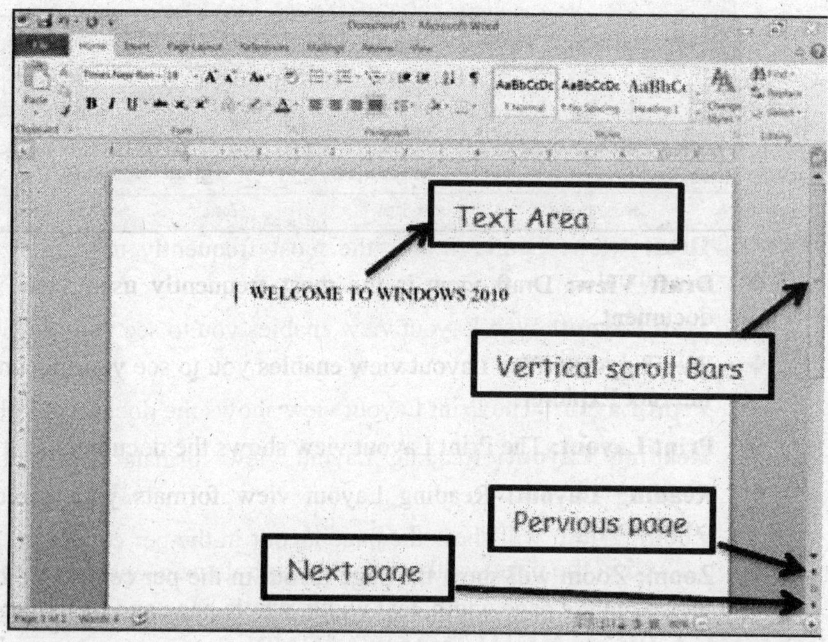

The vertical scroll bars enable you to move up, down, and across your window simply by dragging the icon located on the scroll bar. The vertical scroll bar is located along the right side of the screen. There are two buttons below the vertical scroll bar. The top is button is used to go to the **pervious page (ctrl + page up)** and down button is for **next page (ctrl + page down)**.

The Status Bar

The Status bar appears at the very bottom of your window and provides such information as the current page and the number of words in your document. You can change what displays on the Status bar by right-clicking on the Status bar and selecting the options you want from the Customize Status Bar menu. You click a menu item to select it. You click it again to deselect it. A check mark next to an item means it is selected.

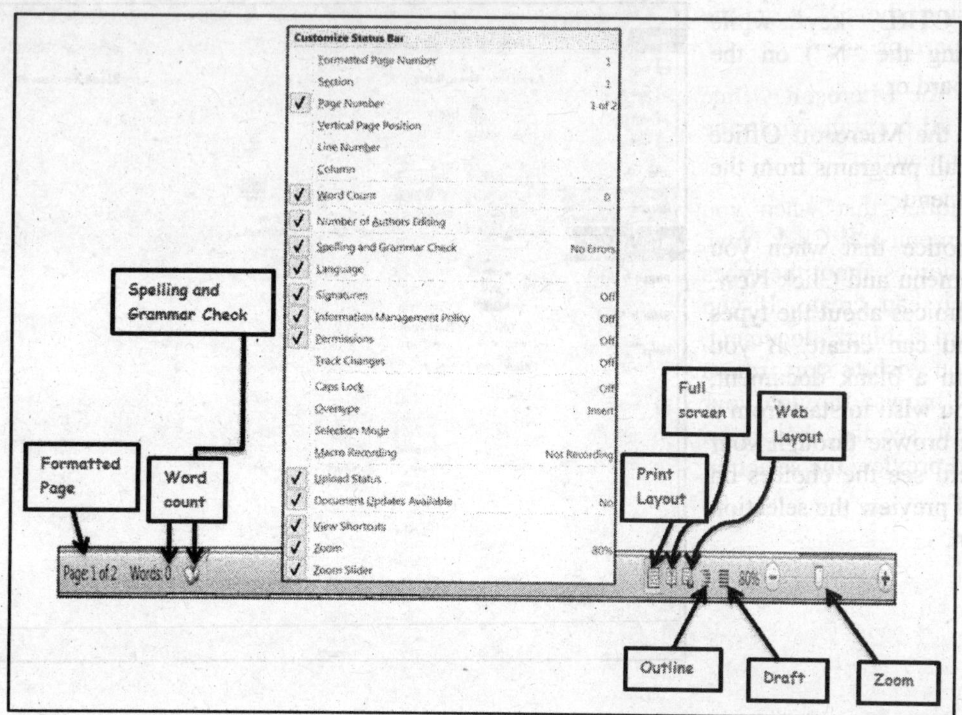

In the status bar on the left corner, you can see the Formatted Page, Word Count, Spelling and Grammar Check. In the right side, you can view Print Layout, Full Screen, Web Layout, Outline, Draft and Zoom buttons.

View Tab

Click the View tab.

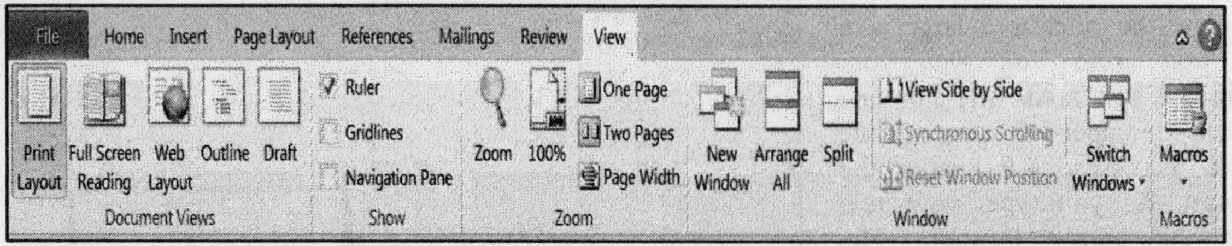

- ❖ **Draft View:** Draft view is the most frequently used view. You use Draft view to quickly edit your document.
- ❖ **Web Layout:** Web Layout view enables you to see your document as it would appear in a browser such as Internet Explorer.
- ❖ **Print Layout:** The Print Layout view shows the document as it will look when it is printed.
- ❖ **Reading Layout:** Reading Layout view formats your screen to make reading your document more comfortable.
- ❖ **Zoom:** Zoom will show the page layout in the per cent (e.g.: 200%, 100% and 75%) and page can be also viewed in the page width, text width, whole page and many pages.

10.3 CREATE A NEW DOCUMENT

There are several ways to create new documents. They are:

- ❖ Click the File menu and Click **New** or
- ❖ Press CTRL + N (Depress the CTRL key while pressing the "N") on the keyboard or
- ❖ Open the Microsoft Office from all programs from the start menu.

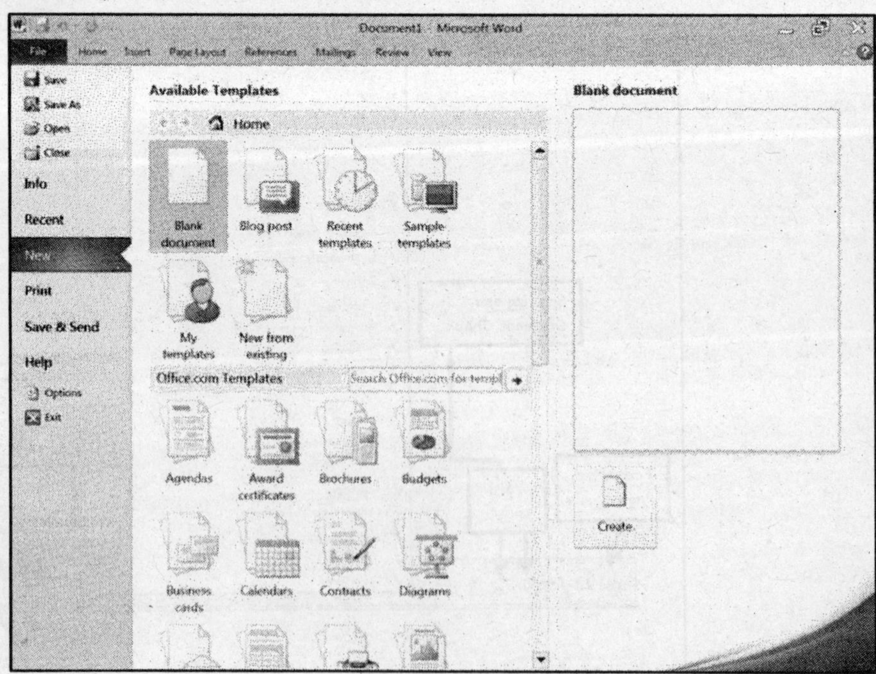

You will notice that when you click on the File menu and Click **New**, you have many choices about the types of documents you can create. If you wish to start from a blank document, click **Blank**. If you wish to start from a template you can browse through your choices on the left, see the choices on centre screen, and preview the selection on the right screen.

Opening an Existing Document

- ❖ Click the **File Menu** and Click **Open,** or
- ❖ Press **CTRL + O** (Depress the CTRL key while pressing the "O") on the keyboard, or
- ❖ You can view the recently used document by clicking the **Recent** button from the **File Menu.** It will show the all recent documents used and recent place of the documents present in the folder of your computer hard disk.

Below that window on the left side, there is check box named as Quick asses this number of Recent document, if you click that it also show number the recent document used that you enter the box and right side there button named as Recover unsaved document it will recover your unsaved word document from the program files.

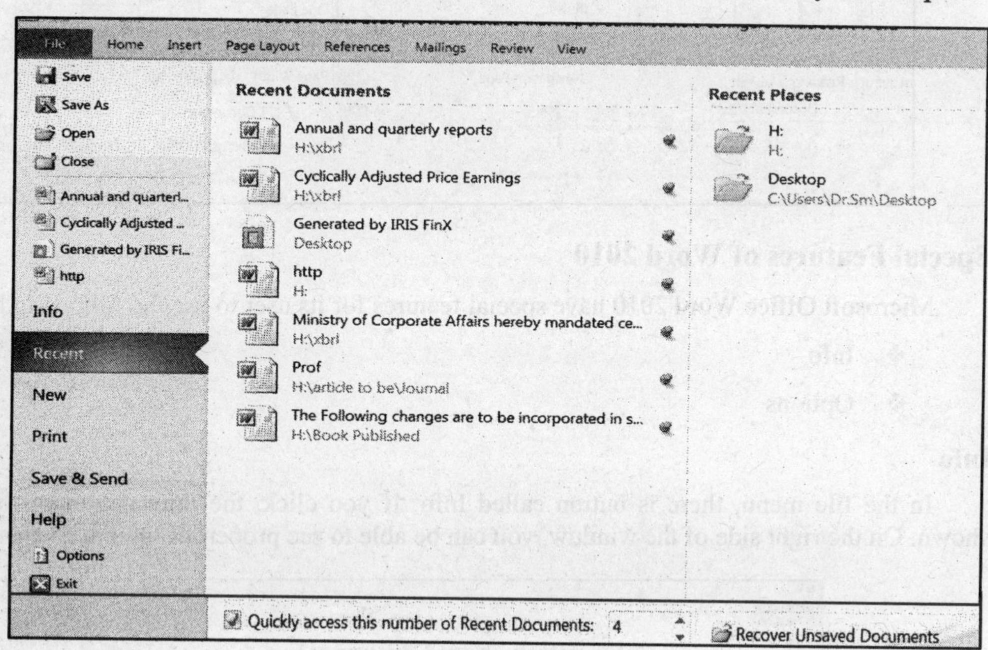

Saving a Document

- ❖ Click the **File Menu** and Click **Save** or **Save As** (remember, if you're sending the document to someone who does not have Office 2010, you will need to click the **Save As,** and Click **Word 97-2003 Document** to save), or
- ❖ Press CTRL + S (Depress the CTRL key while pressing the "S") on the keyboard, or
- ❖ Click the **File** icon on the Quick Access Toolbar.

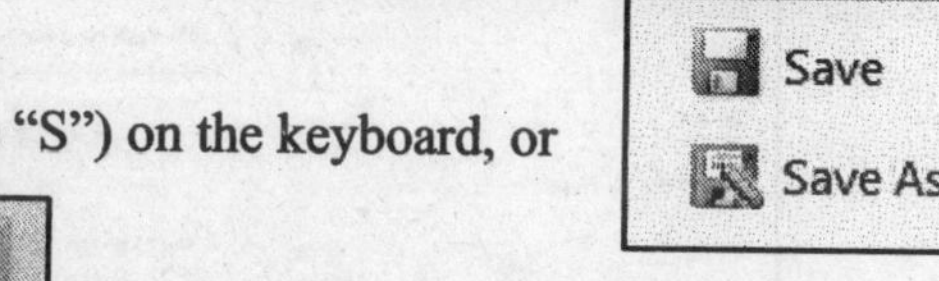

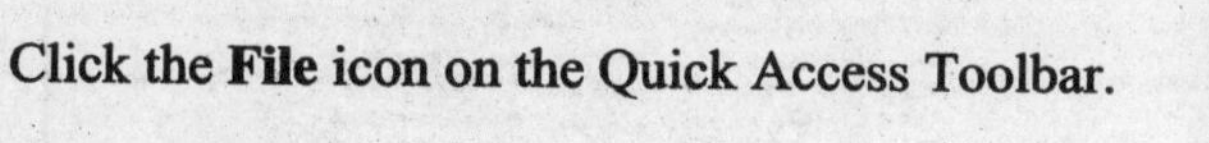

Renaming Documents

To rename a Word document while using the program:

- ❖ Right-click the document name with the mouse and select **Rename** from the shortcut menu
- ❖ Type the new name for the file and press the **ENTER** key

Working on Multiple Documents

Several documents can be opened simultaneously if you are typing or editing multiple documents at once. All open documents will be listed in the **View Tab** of the Ribbon when you click on Switch Windows. The current document has a checkmark beside the file name. Select another open document to view it.

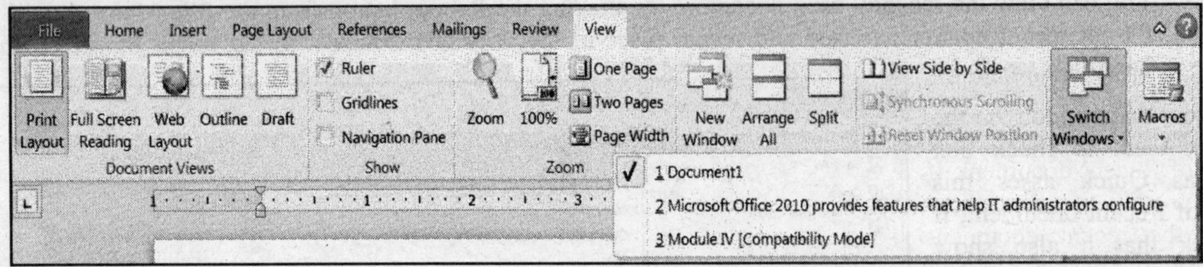

Special Features of Word 2010

Microsoft Office Word 2010 have special features for its user to use the following buttons:

- Info
- Options

Info

In the file menu, there is button called Info. If you click, the information of that particular document will be shown. On the right side of the window, you can be able to see properties on that particular document.

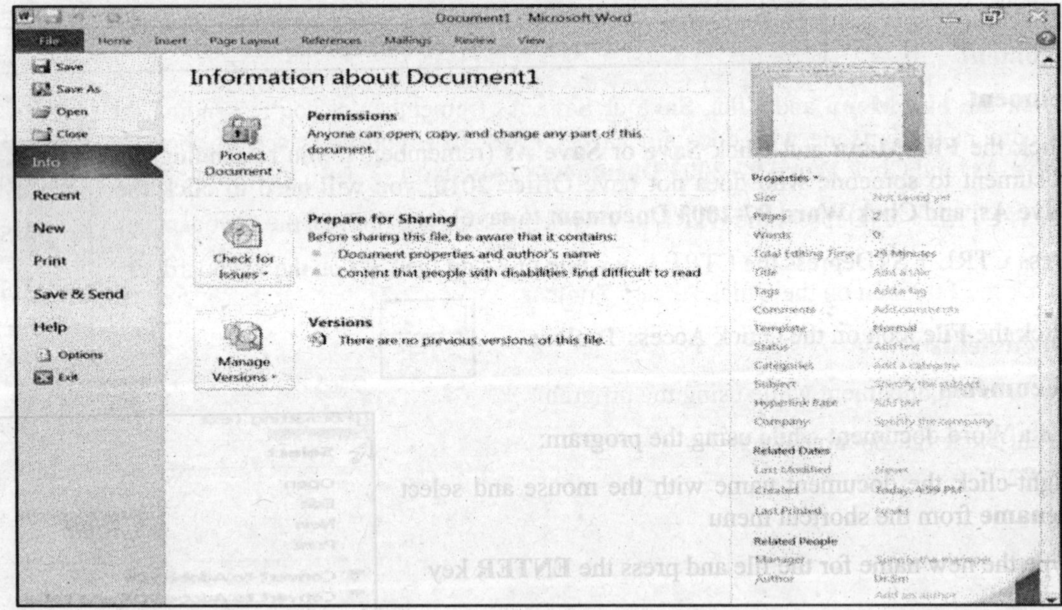

In the Info window, there are three information given, they are Permission, Prepare for sharing and Versions.

Permissions

Anyone to open, copy and change any part of the document. If you want your document to be protected from other user, then click the protect document button. It will show the following options to protect your document.

(i) **Mark as Final:** It shows to the reader that document is final and it can be read-only.

(ii) **Encrypt with password:** It indicates that the document is protected and it requires password to open.

(iii) Restrict Editing: It controls, restrict the user to make changes in the document and it allows user to make changes in a selection of styles in limit formatting, to editing the document according to the editing restrictions and there is option for the user to edit freely on the select part of the document.

(iv) Digital Signature: Ensure the integrity of the document by adding an invisible digital signature.

Prepare for Sharing

Before sharing the file, you should be aware by checking the following issues in the document.

(i) Inspect document: It will check the document for hidden properties or personal information of the document.

(ii) Check accessibility: The document content should check that disabilities people shouldn't find difficult to read.

(iii) Check compatibility: The features should check before sharing whether read has earlier versions of Word.

Versions

Versions help to manage the browse to recover recent copies of unsaved documents and also to delete all unsaved recent copies.

Properties

Properties of the document can be viewed and edited in the word with the help of two options.

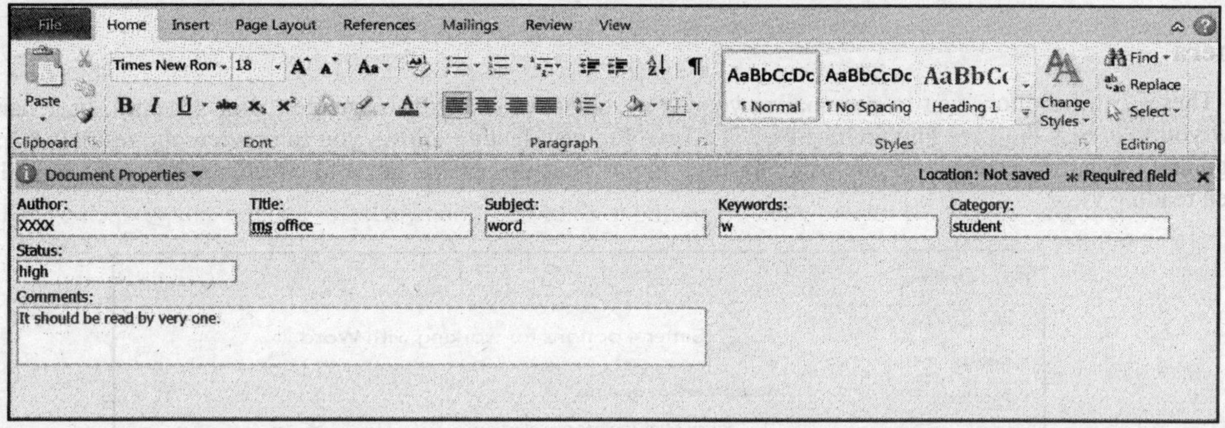

Show the document panel: Properties can be edited by you in the document panel above the document.

Advanced properties: Info window reveal the details of the document. It documents the following information like Size, Pages, Words, Total Editing Tim, Title, Tags, Comments, Template, Status, Categories, Subject, Hyperlink Base, Company, Last Modified, Created, Last Printed, Manager, Author and Last Modified By.

Customize the Word Environment

Word 2010 offers a wide range of customizable options that allow you to make Word work the best for you. To access these customizable options:

- ❖ Click the File Menu
- ❖ Click Options

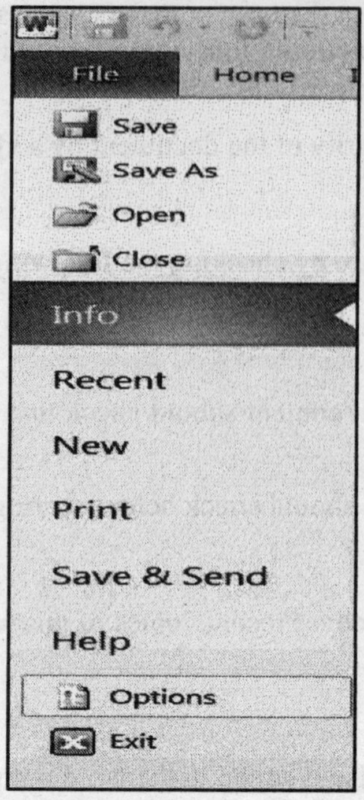

General

These features allow you to personalize your work environment with language, color schemes, user name and allow you to access the Live Preview feature. The Live Preview feature allows you to preview the results of applying design and formatting changes without actually applying it. Start-up options helps to attachments to open e-mail in full screen reading view.

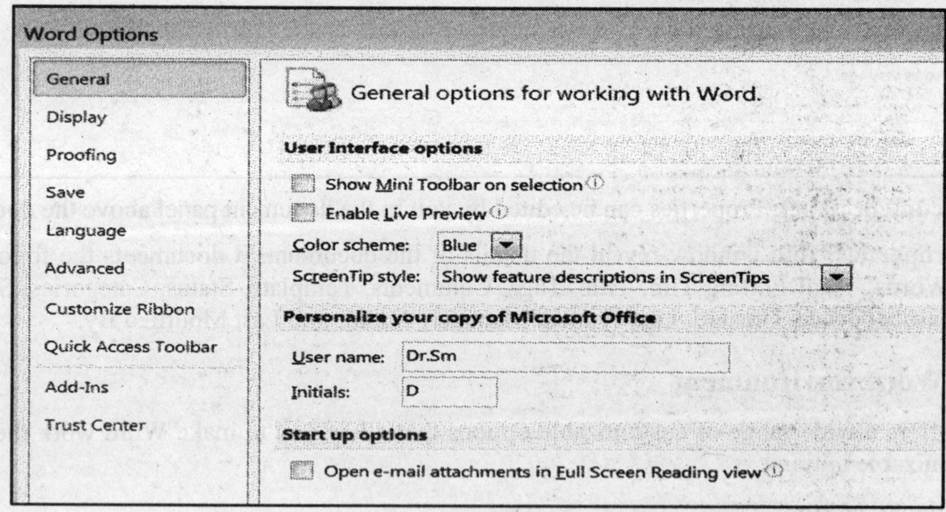

Display

This feature allows you to modify how the document content is displayed on the screen and when printed. You can opt to show or hide certain page elements.

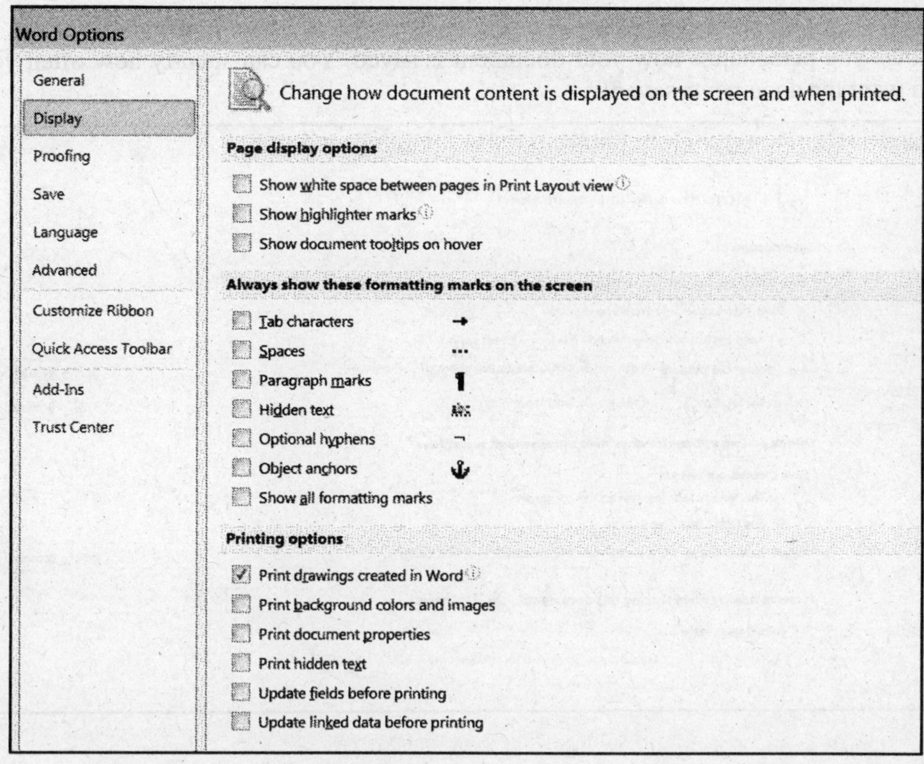

Proofing

This feature allows you personalize how Word corrects and formats your text. You can customize autocorrection settings and ignore certain words or errors in a document.

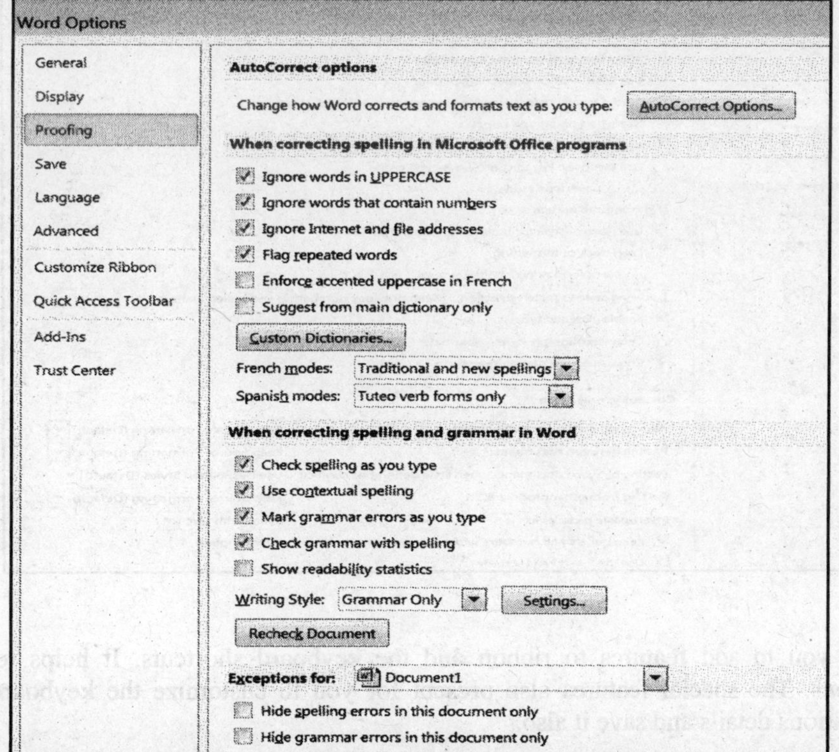

Save

This feature allows you personalize how your document is saved. You can specify how often you want auto save to run and where you want the documents saved.

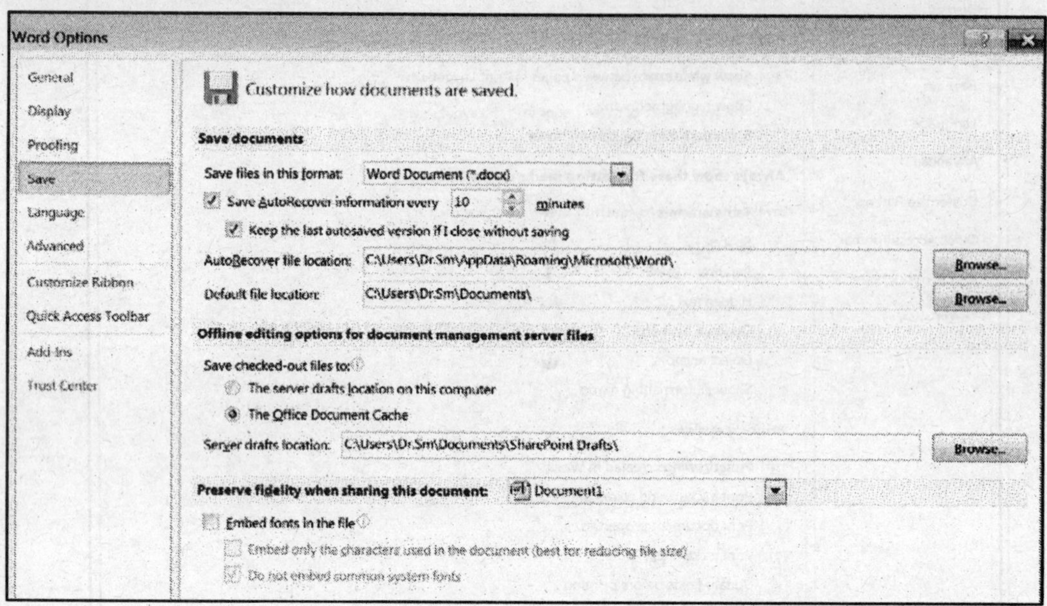

Advanced

This feature allows you to specify options for editing, copying, pasting, displaying, printing and saving.

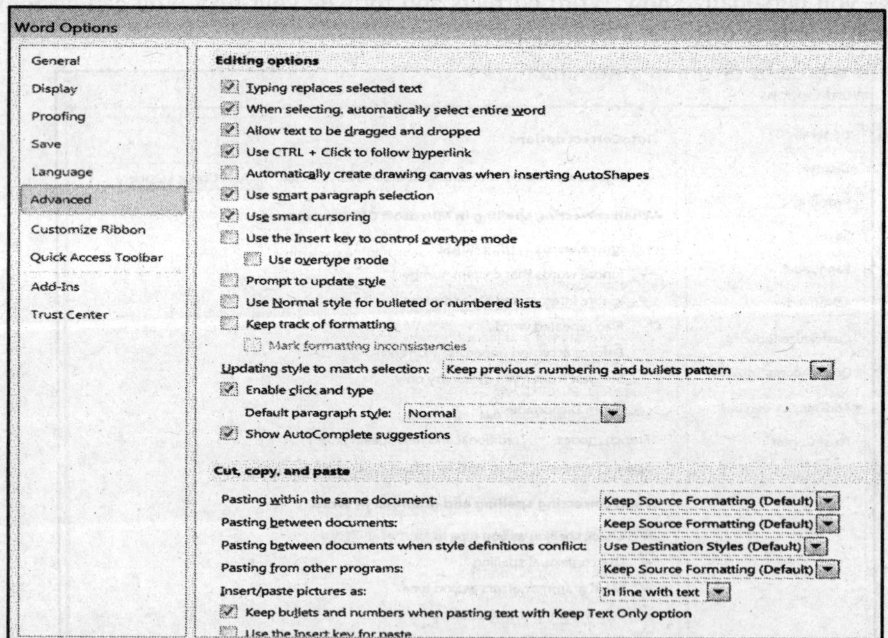

Customize Ribbon

Customize allows you to add features to ribbon and the keyboard shortcuts. It helps to add or remove the commands in the ribbons. The special features also present for you to customize the keyboard shortcuts. You can import/export customizations details and save it also.

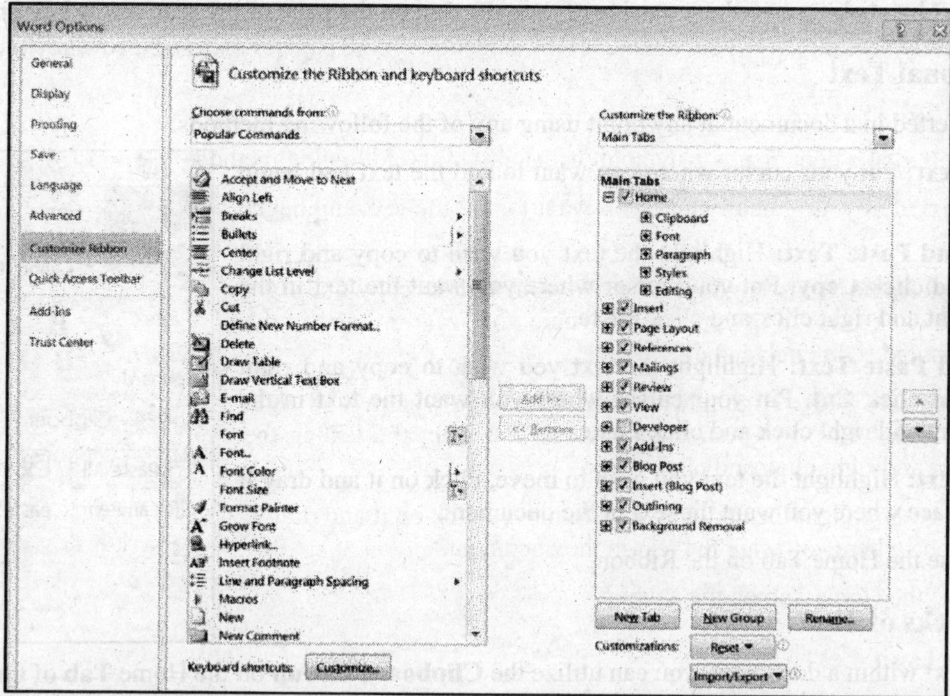

10.4 EDITING A DOCUMENT

Typing and Inserting Text

To enter text, just start typing! The text will appear where the blinking cursor is located. Move the cursor by using the arrow buttons on the keyboard or positioning the mouse and clicking the left button. The keyboard shortcuts listed below are also helpful when moving through the text of a document:

Move Action	**Keystroke**
Beginning of the line	**HOME**
End of the line	**END**
Top of the document	**CTRL+HOME**
End of the document	**CTRL+END**

Selecting Text

To change any attributes of text, it must be highlighted first. Select the text by dragging the mouse over the desired text while keeping the left mouse button depressed, or hold down the SHIFT key on the keyboard while using the arrow buttons to highlight the text. The following table contains shortcuts for selecting a portion of the text:

Selection	**Technique**
Whole word	**double-click within the word**
Whole paragraph	**triple-click within the paragraph**
Several words or lines	**drag the mouse over the words, or hold down SHIFT while using the arrow keys**
Entire document	**choose Editing | Select | Select All from the Ribbon, or press CTRL+A**

Deselect the text by clicking anywhere outside of the selection on the page or press an arrow key on the keyboard.

Inserting Additional Text

Text can be inserted in a document at any point using any of the following methods:

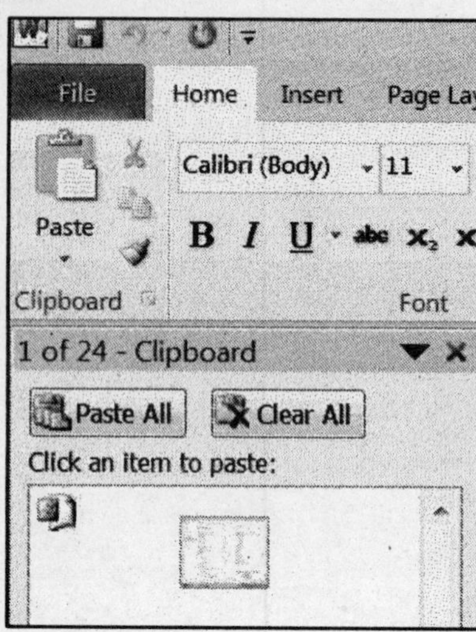

- ❖ **Type Text:** Put your cursor where you want to add the text and begin typing.
- ❖ **Copy and Paste Text:** Highlight the text you wish to copy and right click and click **Copy**. Put your cursor where you want the text in the document and right click and click **Paste**.
- ❖ **Cut and Paste Text:** Highlight the text you wish to copy and right click and click **Cut**. Put your cursor where you want the text in the document and right click and click **Paste**.
- ❖ **Drag Text:** Highlight the text you wish to move, click on it and drag it to the place where you want the text in the document.

You can also use the Home Tab on the Ribbon.

Rearranging Blocks of Text

To rearrange text within a document, you can utilize the **Clipboard Group** on the Home **Tab** of the Ribbon.

Insert picture of clipboard group labelled

- ❖ **Move Text:** Cut and Paste or Drag as shown above
- ❖ **Copy Text:** Copy and Paste as above or use the Clipboard group on the Ribbon
- ❖ **Paste Text:** Ctrl + V (hold down the CTRL and the "V" key at the same time) or use the Clipboard group to Paste, Paste Special, or St Default Paste

Deleting Blocks of Text

Use the **BACKSPACE** and **DELETE** keys on the keyboard to delete text. Backspace will delete text to the left of the cursor and Delete will erase text to the right. To delete a large selection of text, highlight it using any of the methods outlined above and press the **DELETE** key.

Search and Replace Text

To find a particular word or phrase in a document:

- ❖ Click **Find** on the **Editing Group** on the Ribbon
- ❖ To find and replace a word or phrase in the document, click **Replace** on the **Editing Group** of the Ribbon

Undo Changes

To undo changes:

- ❖ Click the **Undo Button** on the Quick Access Toolbar

10.5 FORMATTING TEXT

Styles

A style is a format enhancing tool that includes font typefaces, font size, effects (bold, italics, underline, etc.), colors and more. You will notice that on the Home Tab of the Ribbon, you have several areas that will control the style of your document: Font, Paragraph, and Styles.

Change Font Typeface and Size

To change the font typeface:

- ❖ Click the **arrow** next to the font name and choose a font

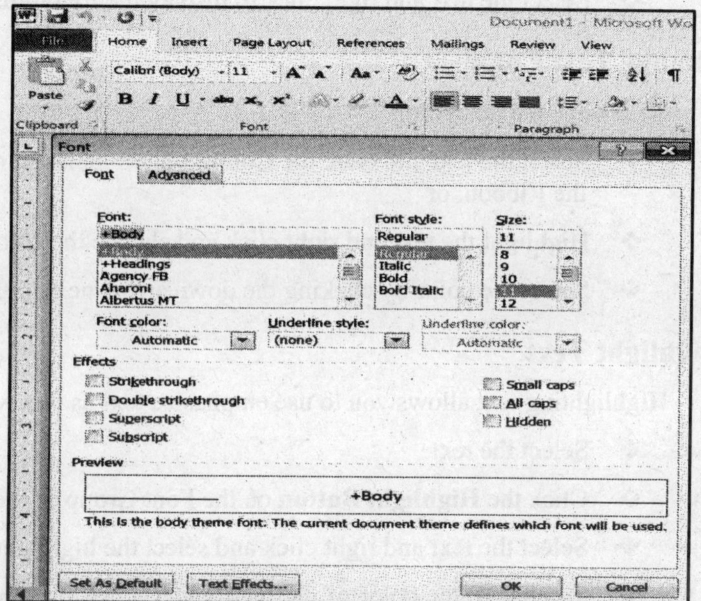

- ❖ Remember that you can preview how the new font will look by highlighting the text, and hovering over the new font typeface.

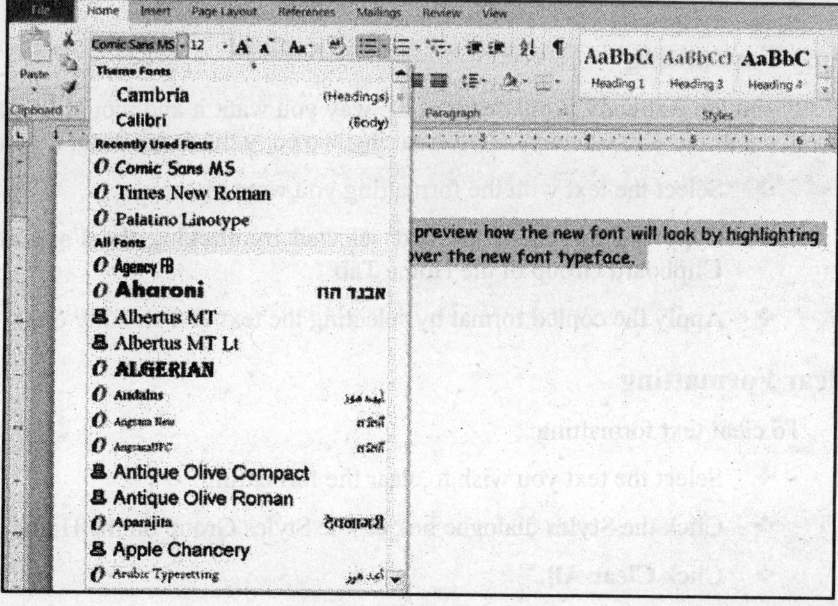

To change the font size:

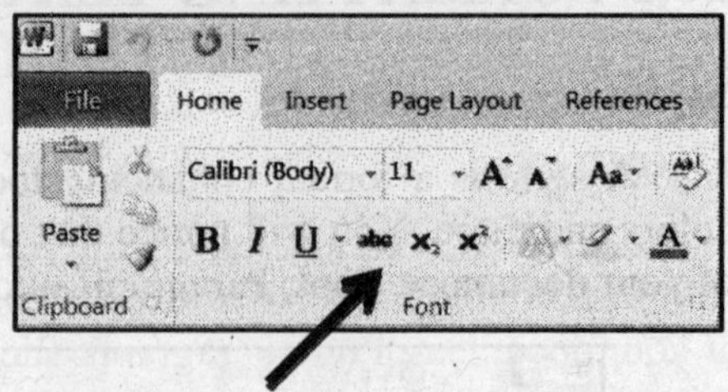

- ❖ Click the **arrow** next to the font size and choose the appropriate size, or
- ❖ Click the **increase** or **decrease** font size buttons

Font Styles and Effects

Font styles are predefined formatting options that are used to emphasize text. They include: Bold, Italic, and Underline. To add these to text:

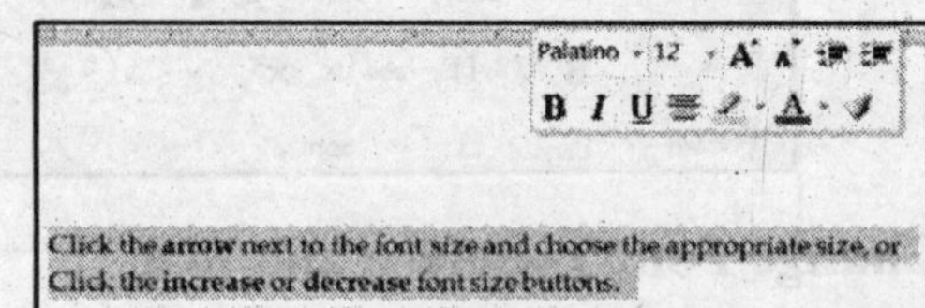

- ❖ Select the text and click the **Font Styles** included on the Font Group of the Ribbon, or
- ❖ Select the text and right click to display the font tools

Change Text Color

To change the text color:

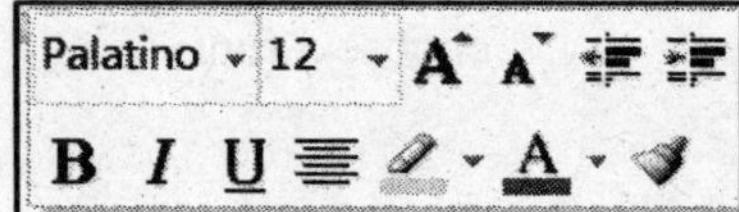

- ❖ Select the text and click the **Colors** button included on the Font Group of the Ribbon, or
- ❖ Highlight the text and right click and choose the colors tool.
- ❖ Select the color by clicking the down arrow next to the font color button.

Highlight Text

Highlighting text allows you to use emphasize text as you would if you had a marker. To highlight text:

- ❖ Select the text
- ❖ Click the **Highlight Button** on the Font Group of the Ribbon, or
- ❖ Select the text and right click and select the highlight tool
- ❖ To change the color of the highlighter, click on down arrow next to the highlight button

Copy Formatting

If you have already formatted text the way you want it and would like another portion of the document to have the same formatting, you can copy the formatting. To copy the formatting, do the following:

- ❖ Select the text with the formatting you want to copy
- ❖ Copy the format of the text selected by clicking the **Format Painter** button on the Clipboard Group of the Home Tab
- ❖ Apply the copied format by selecting the text and clicking on it

Clear Formatting

To clear text formatting:

- ❖ Select the text you wish to clear the formatting
- ❖ Click the **Styles** dialogue box on the Styles Group on the Home Tab
- ❖ Click **Clear All**

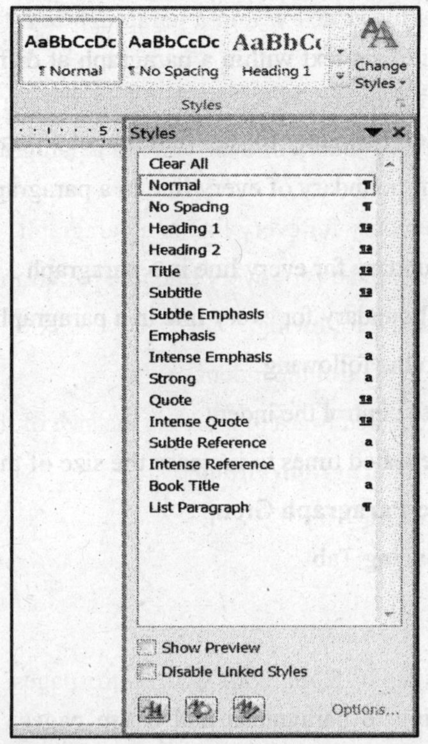

Formatting Paragraphs

Formatting paragraphs allows you to change the look of the overall document. You can access many of the tools of paragraph formatting by clicking the **Page Layout** Tab of the Ribbon or the **Paragraph** Group on the Home Tab of the Ribbon.

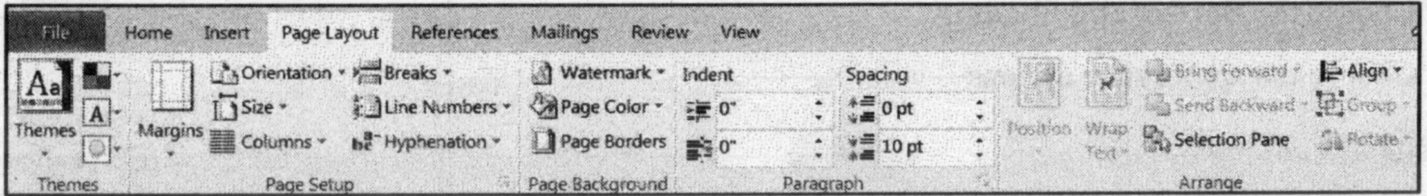

Change Paragraph Alignment

The paragraph alignment allows you to set how you want text to appear. To change the alignment:

❖ Click the Home Tab

❖ Choose the appropriate button for alignment on the Paragraph Group.

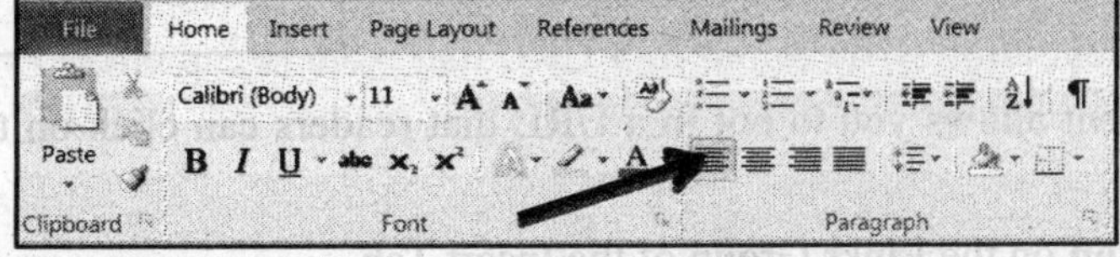

- **Align Left:** The text is aligned with your left margin
- **Center:** The text is centered within your margins
- **Align Right:** Aligns text with the right margin
- **Justify:** Aligns text to both the left and right margins

Indent Paragraphs

Indenting paragraphs allows you to set text within a paragraph at different margins. There are several options for indenting:

- **First Line:** Controls the left boundary for the first line of a paragraph
- **Hanging:** Controls the left boundary of every line in a paragraph except the first one
- **Left:** Controls the left boundary for every line in a paragraph
- **Right:** Controls the right boundary for every line in a paragraph

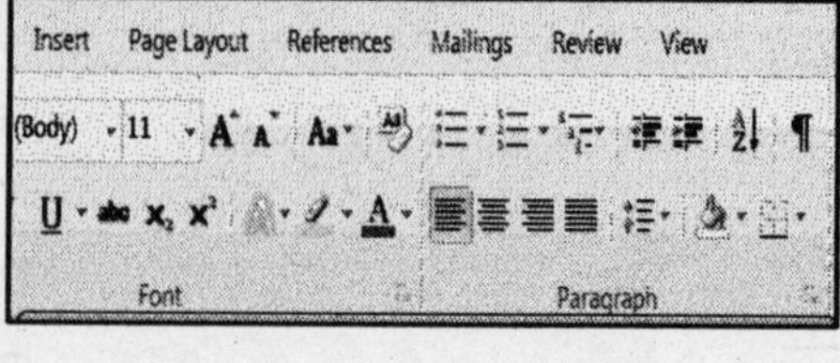

To indent paragraphs, you can do the following:

- Click the **Indent** buttons to control the indent
- Click the **Indent** button repeated times to increase the size of the indent
- Click the dialog box of the **Paragraph** Group
- Click the **Indents and Spacing** Tab
- Select your indents

Add Borders and Shading

You can add borders and shading to paragraphs and entire pages. To create a border around a paragraph or paragraphs:

- Select the area of text where you want the border or shading
- Click the **Borders** Button on the Paragraph Group on the Home Tab
- Choose the **Border and Shading**
- Choose the appropriate options

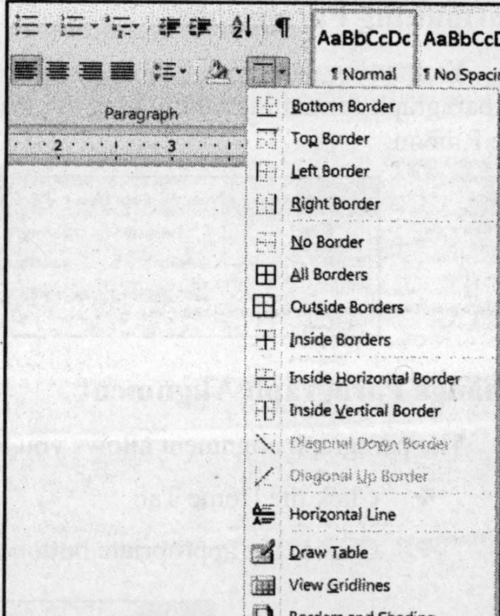

Create Links

Creating links in a Word document allows you to put in a URL that readers can click on to visit a web page. To insert a link:

- Click the **Hyperlink Button** on the Links Group of the Insert Tab
- Type in the text in the "Text to Display" box and the web address in the "Address" box

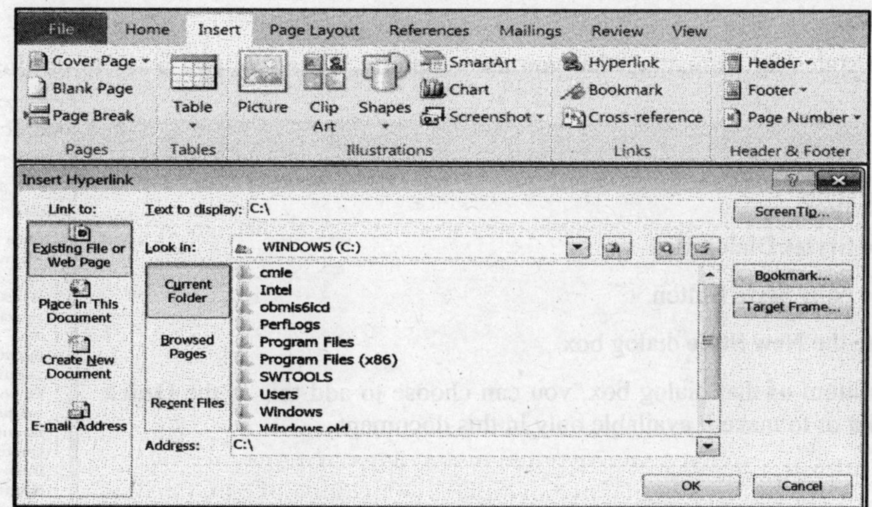

Change Spacing between Paragraphs and Lines

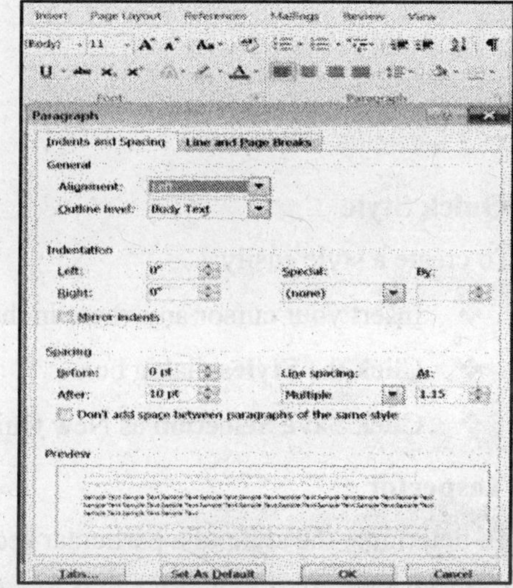

You can change the space between lines and paragraphs by doing the following:

- ❖ Select the paragraph or paragraphs you wish to change
- ❖ On the Home Tab, click the **Paragraph** Dialog Box
- ❖ Click the **Indents and Spacing** Tab
- ❖ In the **Spacing** section, adjust your spacing accordingly

Styles

The use of Styles in Word will allow you to quickly format a document with a consistent and professional look. Styles can be saved for use in many documents.

Apply Styles

There are many styles that are already in Word ready for you to use. To view the available styles, click the **Styles** dialog box on the Styles Group in the Home Tab. To apply a style:

- ❖ Select the text
- ❖ Click the **Styles** Dialog Box
- ❖ Click the **Style** you choose

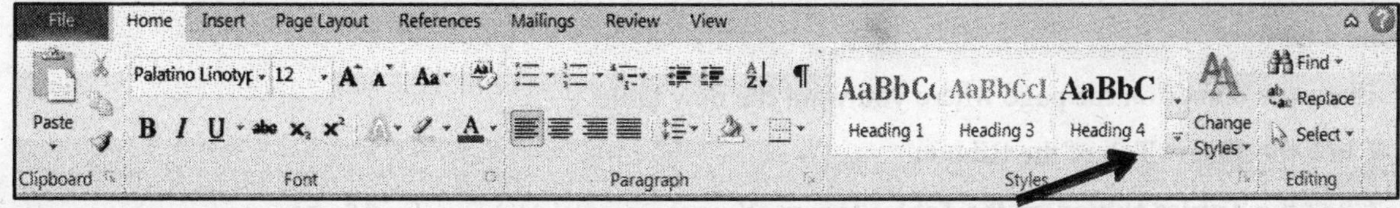

Creating New Styles

You can create styles for formatting that you use regularly. There are two ways to do this: New Styles or New Quick Styles.

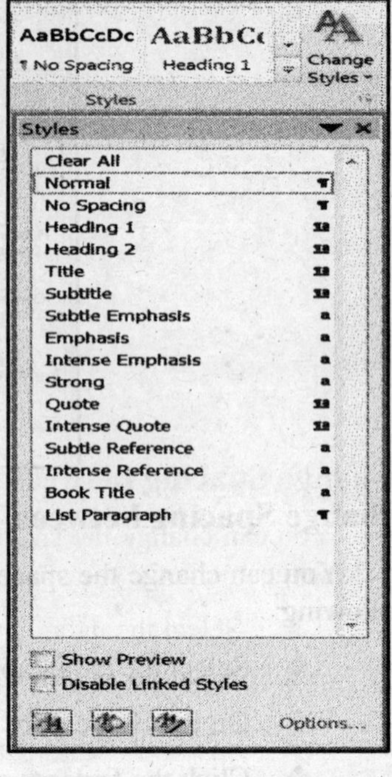

New Styles

To create a new style:

- ❖ Click the **Styles** Dialog Box
- ❖ Click the **New Style** Button
- ❖ Complete the **New Style** dialog box
- ❖ At the bottom of that dialog box, you can choose to add this to the **Quick Style List** or to make it available only in this document

New Quick Style

To create a style easily:

- ❖ Insert your cursor anywhere in the chosen style
- ❖ Click the **Styles** dialog box
- ❖ Click **Save Selection** as New Quick Style

Style Inspector

To determine the style of a particular section of a document:

- ❖ Insert cursor anywhere in the text that you want to explain the style
- ❖ Click the **Styles Drop Down** Menu
- ❖ Click the **Style Inspector** Button

10.6 HANDLING THE TABLES IN WORD

Adding Tables

Tables are used to display data in a table format.

Create a Table

To create a table:

- ❖ Place the cursor on the page where you want the new table
- ❖ Click the **Insert** Tab of the Ribbon
- ❖ Click the **Tables** Button on the Tables Group. You can create a table one of four ways:

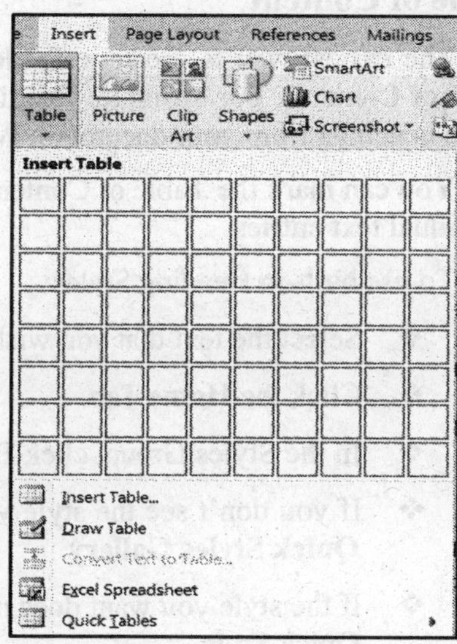

- Highlight the number of row and columns
- Click **Insert Table** and enter the number of rows and columns
- Click the **Draw Table**, create your table by clicking and entering the rows and columns
- Click **Quick Tables** and choose a table

Enter Data in a Table

Place the cursor in the cell where you wish to enter the information. Begin typing.

Modify the Table Structure and Format a Table

To **modify** the structure of a table:

❖ Click the table and notice that you have two new tabs on the Ribbon: **Design and Layout**. These pertain to the table design and layout

❖ On the Design Tab, you can choose: **Table Style Options**

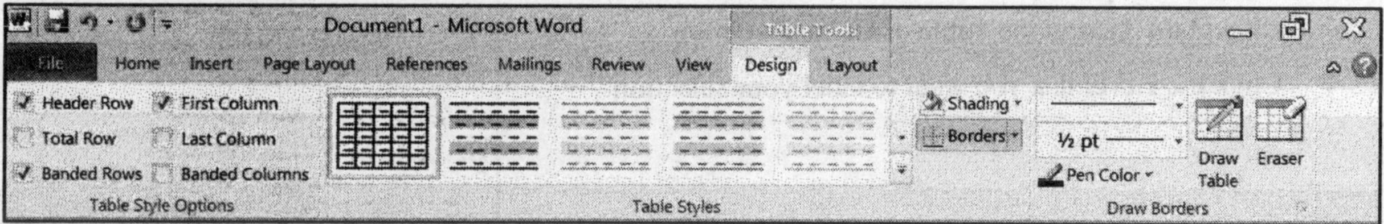

❖ Table Styles

❖ Draw Borders

To **format** a table, click the table and then click the **Layout** Tab on the Ribbon. This Layout tab allows you to:

❖ **View Gridlines and Properties** (from the Table Group)

❖ **Insert Rows and Columns** (from the Rows & Columns Group)

❖ **Delete the Table, Rows and/or Columns** (from the Rows & Columns Group)

❖ **Merge or Split Cells** (from the Merge Group)

❖ **Increase and Decrease cell size** (Cell Size Group)

❖ **Align text within the cells and change text directions** (Alignment Group)

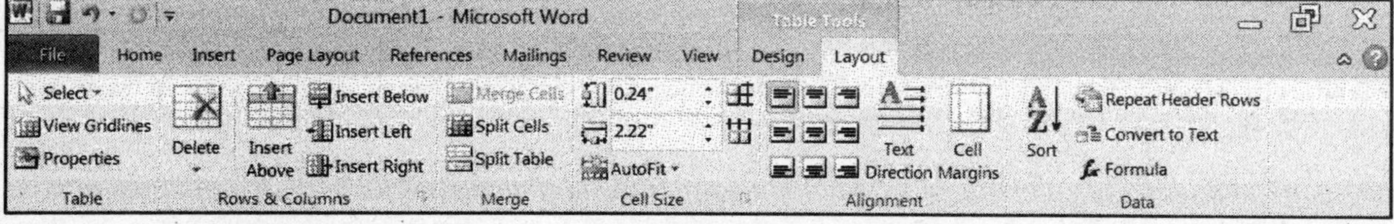

Table of Content

The easiest way to create a **Table of Contents** is to utilize the **Heading Styles** that you want to include in the Table of Contents. For example: Heading 1, Heading 2, etc. based on the content of your document. When you add or delete headings from your document, Word updates your **Table of Contents**.

You can mark the Table of Contents entries in one of the two ways: by using built-in heading styles or by marking individual text entries.

To use built-in Heading Styles:

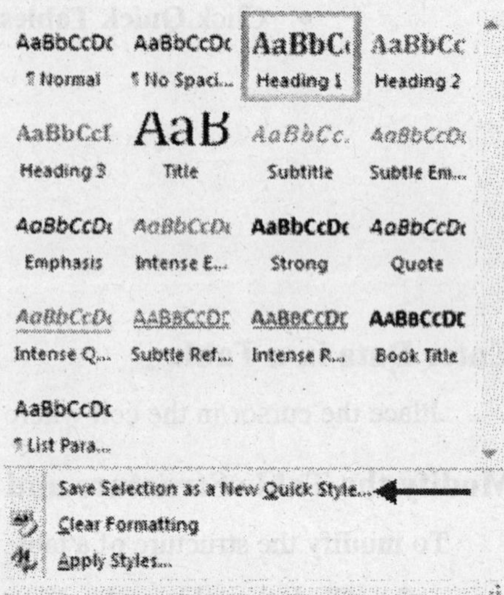

- ❖ Select the text that you wish to be the heading
- ❖ Click the **Home** Tab
- ❖ In the Styles Group, click **Heading 1** (or the appropriate heading)
- ❖ If you don't see the style you want, click the arrow to expand the **Quick Styles Gallery**
- ❖ If the style you want does not appear, click **Save Selection** as New Quick Style

To mark Individual Entries:

- ❖ Select the text you wish to make a heading
- ❖ Click the **References** Tab
- ❖ Click **Add Text** in the Table of Contents Group
- ❖ Click the **Level** that you want to label your selection

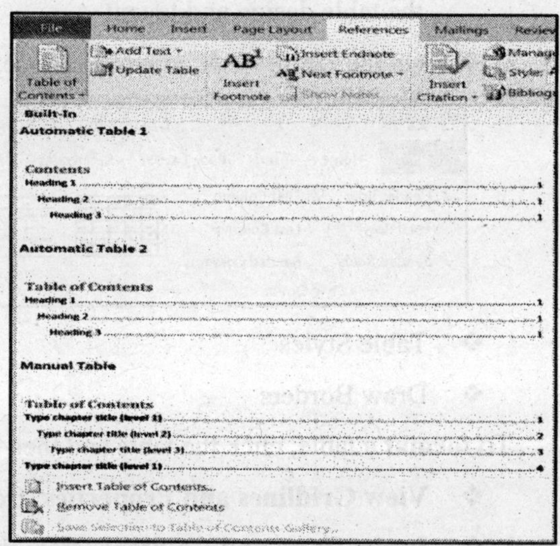

Create a Table of Contents

To create the table of contents:

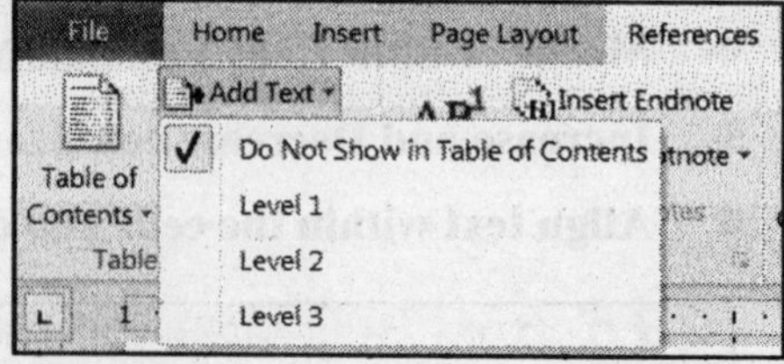

- ❖ Put your cursor in the document where you want the Table of Contents
- ❖ Click the **References** Tab
- ❖ Click the **Table of Contents** button

Update Table of Contents

If you have added or removed headings or other table of contents entries, you can update by:

- ❖ Apply headings or mark individual entries as directed above
- ❖ Click the **References** Tab in the Ribbon
- ❖ Click **Update Table**

Delete Table of Contents

To delete a table of contents:

- ❖ Click the **References** Tab on the Ribbon
- ❖ Click **Table of Contents**
- ❖ Click **Remove Table of Contents**

10.7 USE OF THE DIFFERENT TOOLS

Graphics

Word 2007 allows you to insert special characters, symbols, pictures, illustrations, and watermarks.

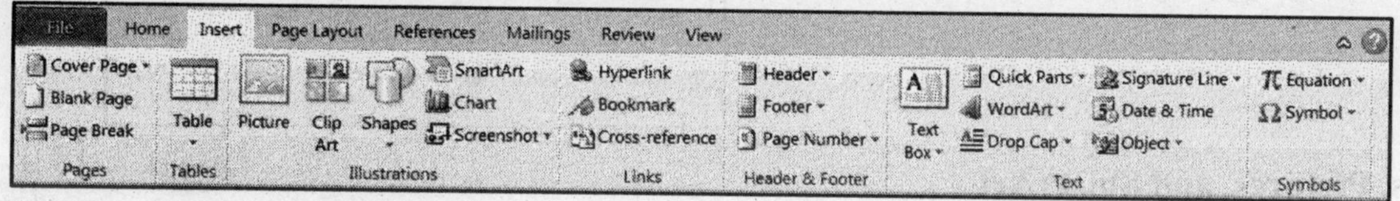

Symbols and Special Characters

Special characters are punctuation, spacing, or typographical characters that are not generally available on the standard keyboard. To insert symbols and special characters:

- ❖ Place your cursor in the document where you want the symbol
- ❖ Click the **Insert** Tab on the Ribbon
- ❖ Click the **Symbol** button on the Symbols Group
- ❖ Choose the appropriate symbol

Equations

Word 2010 also allows you to insert mathematical equations. To access the mathematical equations tool:

- ❖ Place your cursor in the document where you want the symbol
- ❖ Click the **Insert** Tab on the Ribbon
- ❖ Click the **Equation** Button on the Symbols Group
- ❖ Choose the appropriate equation and structure or click Insert New Equation
- ❖ To edit the equation, click the equation and the **Design** Tab will be available in the Ribbon

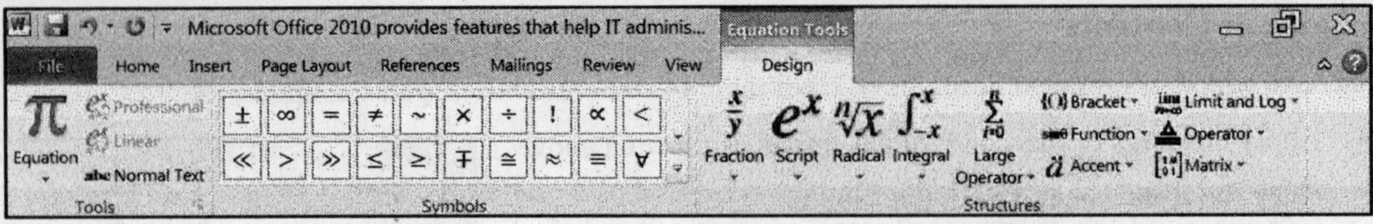

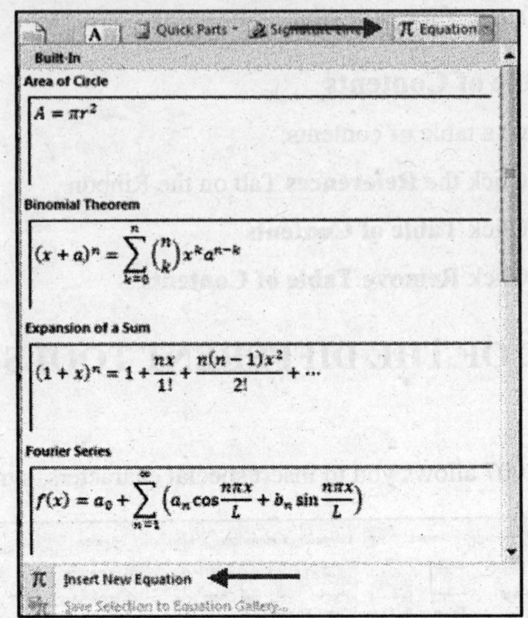

Illustrations, Pictures, and SmartArt

Word 2010 allows you to insert illustrations and pictures into a document. To insert **illustrations:**

- Place your cursor in the document where you want the illustration/picture
- Click the **Insert** Tab on the Ribbon
- Click the **Clip Art** Button
- The dialog box will open on the screen and you can search for Clip Art
- Choose the illustration you wish to include

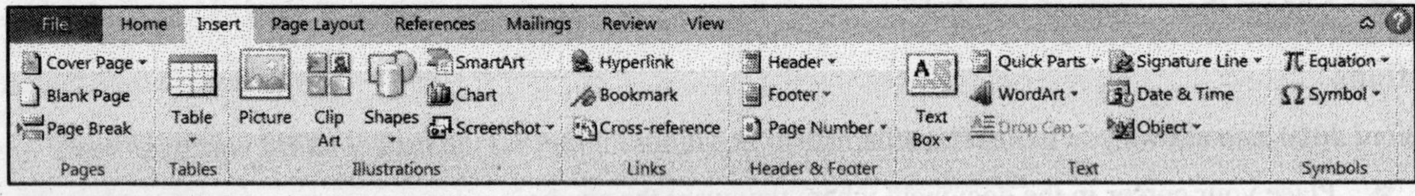

To insert a **picture**:

- Place your cursor in the document where you want the illustration/picture
- Click the **Insert** Tab on the Ribbon
- Click the **Picture** Button
- Browse to the picture you wish to include
- Click the **Picture**
- Click **Insert**

Smart Art is a collection of graphics you can utilize to organize information within your document. It includes timelines, processes, or workflow.

To insert SmartArt:

- ❖ Place your cursor in the document where you want the illustration/picture
- ❖ Click the **Insert** Tab on the Ribbon
- ❖ Click the **SmartArt** button
- ❖ Click the **SmartArt** you wish to include in your document
- ❖ Click the arrow on the left side of the graphic to insert text or type the text in the graphic

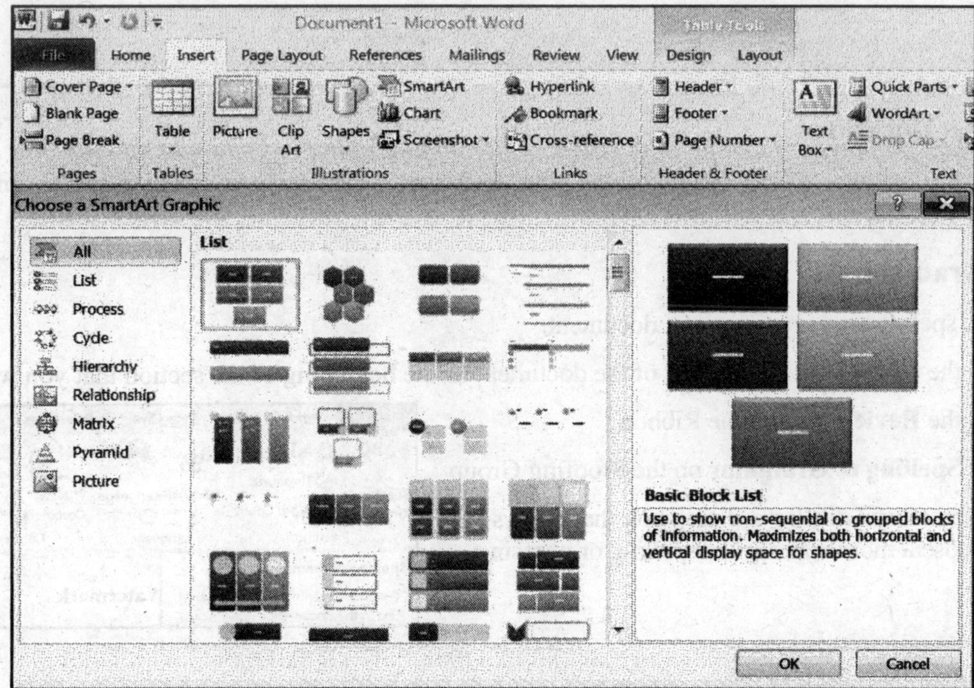

Resize Graphics

All graphics can be resized by clicking the image and clicking one corner of the image and dragging the cursor to the size you want the picture.

Watermarks

A watermark is a translucent image that appears behind the primary text in a document. To insert a watermark:

- ❖ Click the **Page Layout** Tab in the Ribbon
- ❖ Click the **Watermark** Button in the Page Background Group
- ❖ Click the **Watermark** you want for the document or click **Custom Watermark** and create your own watermark
- ❖ To remove a watermark, follow the steps above, but click **Remove Watermark**

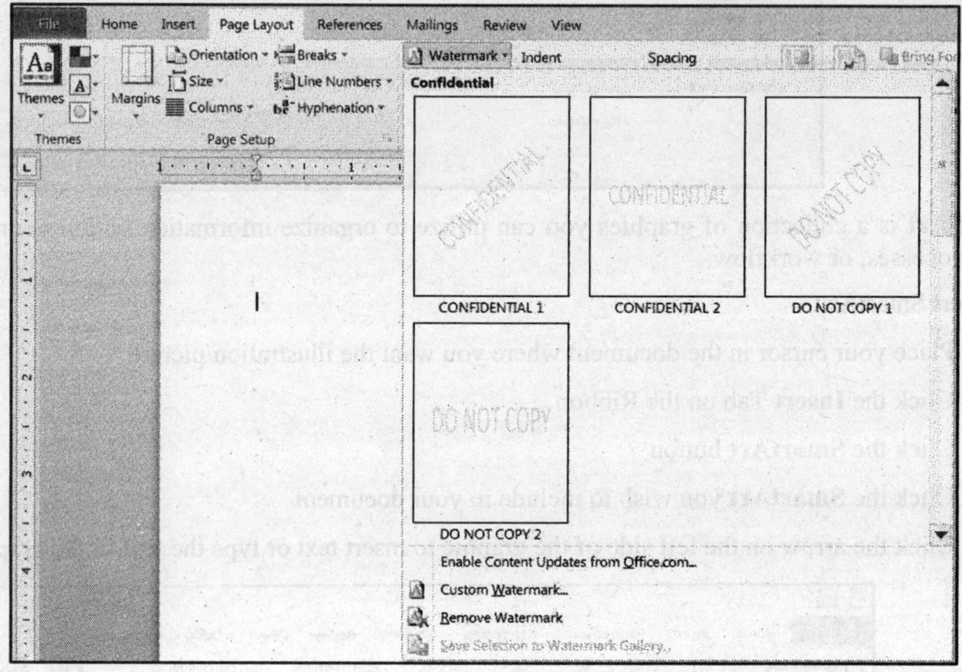

Proof Reading a Document

There are many features to help you proofread your document. These include: Spelling and Grammar, Thesaurus, AutoCorrect, Default Dictionary, and Word Count.

Spelling and Grammar

To check the spelling and grammar of a document:

- ❖ Place the cursor at the beginning of the document or the beginning of the section that you want to check
- ❖ Click the **Review** Tab on the Ribbon
- ❖ Click **Spelling & Grammar** on the Proofing Group
- ❖ Any errors will display a dialog box that allows you to choose a more appropriate spelling or phrasing

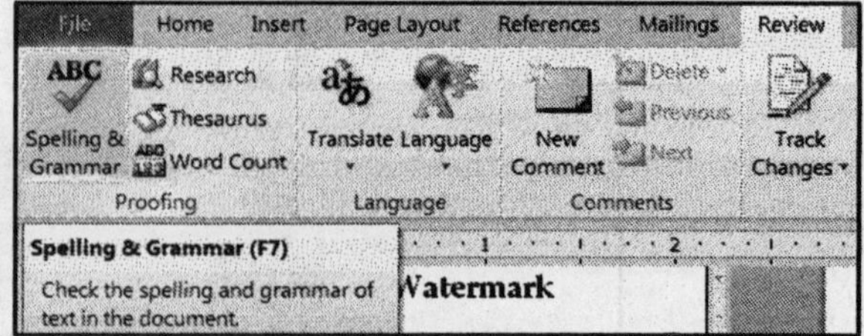

If you wish to check the spelling of an individual word, you can right click any word that has been underlined by Word and choose a substitution.

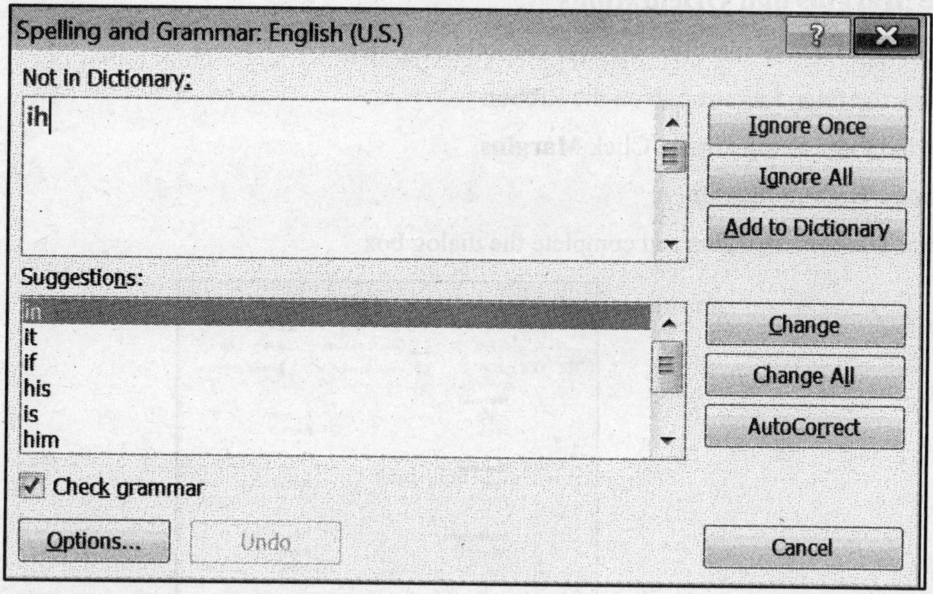

Thesaurus

The Thesaurus allows you to view synonyms. To use the thesaurus:

- Click the **Review** Tab of the Ribbon
- Click the **Thesaurus** Button on the Proofing Group
- The thesaurus tool will appear on the right side of the screen and you can view Word options

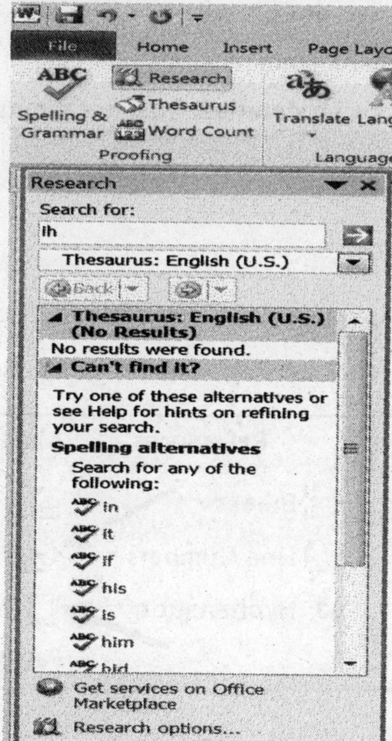

10.8 PAGE FORMATTING

Modify Page Margins and Orientations

The page margins can be modified through the following steps:

- Click the **Page Layout** Tab on the Ribbon
- On the **Page Setup** Group, Click **Margins**
- Click a **Default Margin**, or
- Click **Custom Margins** and complete the dialog box

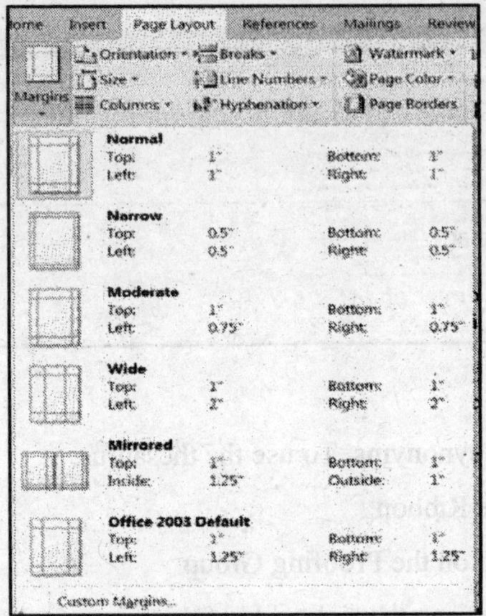

To change the Orientation, Size of the Page, or Columns:

- Click the **Page Layout** Tab on the Ribbon
- On the Page Setup Group, Click the **Orientation, Size,** or **Columns drop-down menus**
- Click the appropriate choice

Apply a Page Border and Color

To apply a page border or color:

- Click the **Page Layout** Tab on the Ribbon
- On the Page Background Group, click the **Page Colors** or **Page Borders drop-down menus**

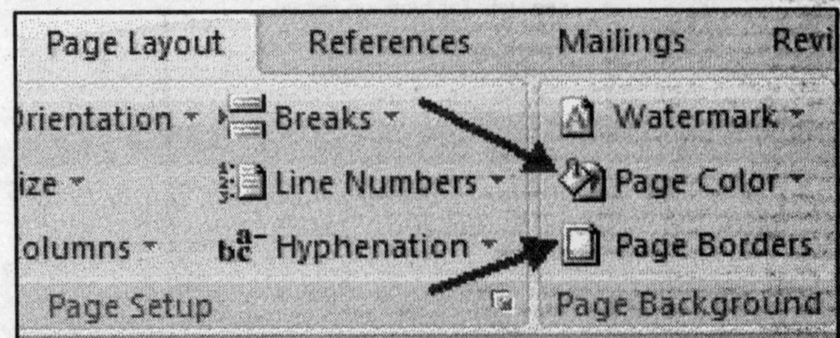

Insert Common Header and Footer Information

To insert Header and Footer information such as page numbers, date, or title, first, decide if you want the information in the header (at the top of the page) or in the Footer (at the bottom of the page), then:

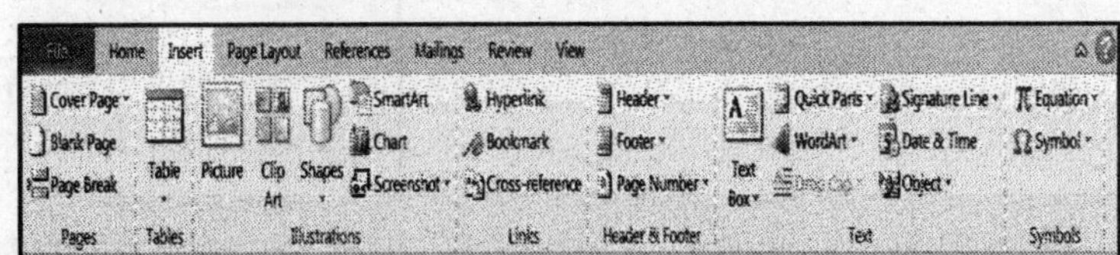

- Click the **Insert** Tab on the Ribbon
- Click **Header or Footer**
- Choose a style
- The **Header/Footer Design** Tab will display on the Ribbon
- Choose the information that you would like to have in the header or footer (date, time, page numbers, etc.) or type in the information you would like to have in the header or footer

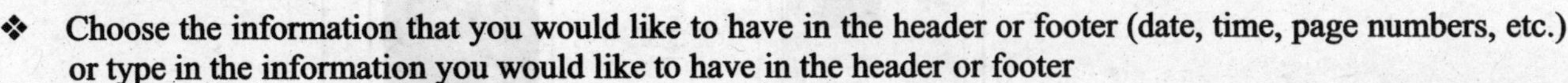

Create a Page Break

To insert a page break:

- Click the **Page Layout** Tab on the Ribbon
- On the **Page Setup** Group, click the **Breaks Drop-down Menu**
- Click **Page Break**

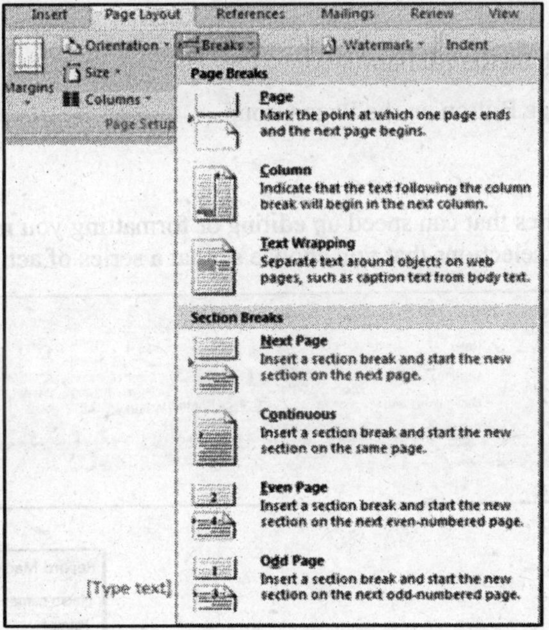

Insert a Cover Page

To insert a cover page:

- Click the **Insert** Tab on the Ribbon
- Click the **Cover Page** Button on the Pages Group
- Choose a style for the cover page

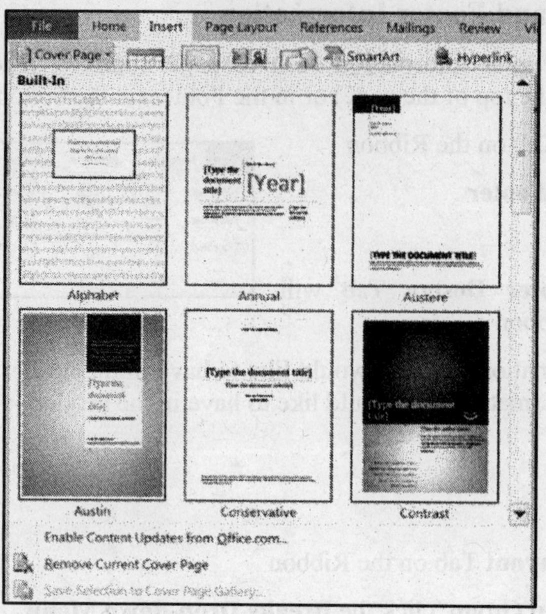

Insert a Blank Page

To insert a blank page:

- ❖ Click the **Insert** Tab on the Ribbon
- ❖ Click the **Blank Page** Button on the Page Group

Macros

Macros are advanced features that can speed up editing or formatting you may perform often in a Word document. They record sequences of menu selections that you choose so that a series of actions can be completed in one step.

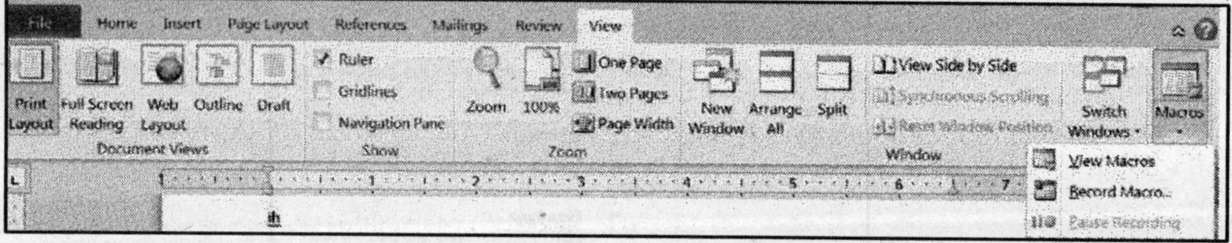

Recording a Macro

To record a Macro:

- ❖ Click the **View** Tab on the Ribbon
- ❖ Click **Macros**
- ❖ Click **Record Macro**
- ❖ Enter a name (without spaces)
- ❖ Click whether you want it assigned to a **button** (on the Quick Access Toolbar) or the **keyboard** (a sequence of keys)

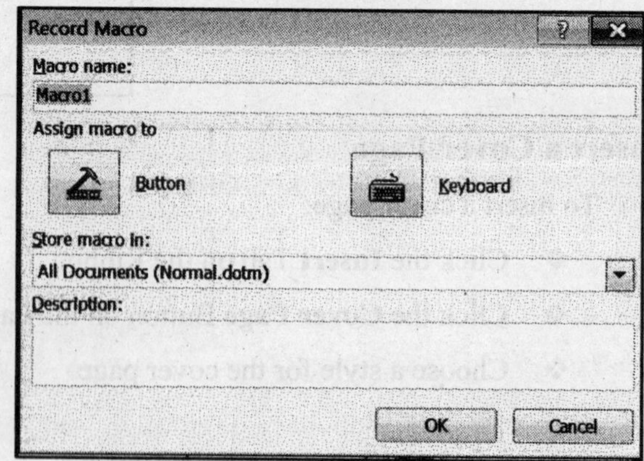

To assign the macro a **button** on the Quick Access Toolbar:

- ❖ Click Button
- ❖ Under the Customize Quick Access Toolbar, select the document for which you want the Macro available
- ❖ Under Choose Commands: Click the Macro that you are recording
- ❖ Click Add
- ❖ Click OK to begin Recording the Macro
- ❖ Perform the actions you want recorded in the Macro
- ❖ Click on Macros
- ❖ Click on Stop Recording Macros

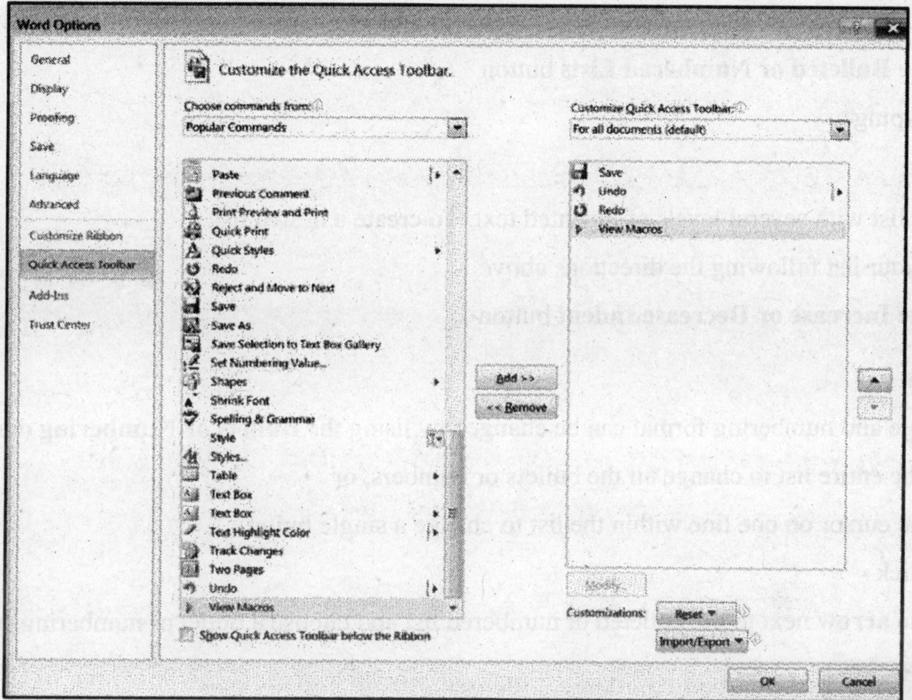

Running a Macro

Running a macro depends on whether it's been added to the Quick Access Toolbar or if it's been given a Keyboard Shortcut.

- ❖ To run a Macro from the Quick Access Toolbar, simply click the **Macro Icon**
- ❖ To run a Macro from the Keyboard shortcut, simply **press the keys** that you have programmed to run the Macro

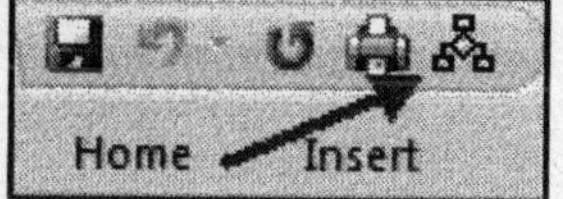

Lists

Lists allow you to format and organize text with numbers, bullets, or in an outline.

Bulleted and Numbered Lists

Bulleted lists have bullet points, numbered lists have numbers, and outline lists combine numbers and letters depending on the organization of the list.

To **add** a list to existing text:

❖ Select the text you wish to make a list

❖ From the Paragraph Group on the Home Tab, Click the **Bulleted or Numbered Lists** button

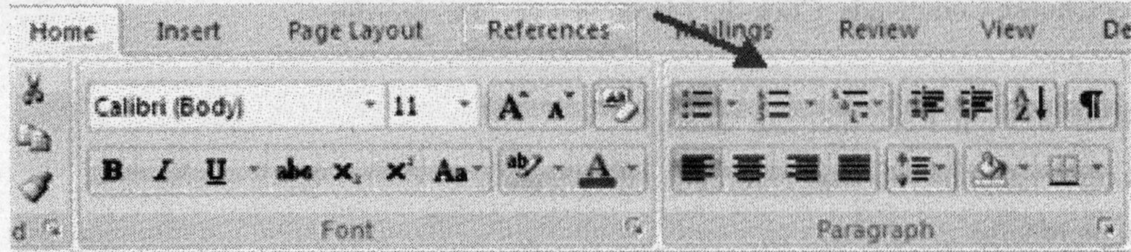

To **create** a new list:

❖ Place your cursor where you want the list in the document

❖ Click the **Bulleted or Numbered Lists** button

❖ Begin typing

Nested Lists

A nested list is list with several levels of indented text. To create a nested list:

❖ Create your list following the directions above

❖ Click the **Increase or Decrease Indent** button

Formatting Lists

The bullet image and numbering format can be changed by using the **Bullets or Numbering** dialog box.

❖ Select the entire list to change all the bullets or numbers, or

❖ Place the cursor on one line within the list to change a single bullet

❖ Right click

❖ Click the **arrow** next to the bulleted or numbered list and choose a bullet or numbering style

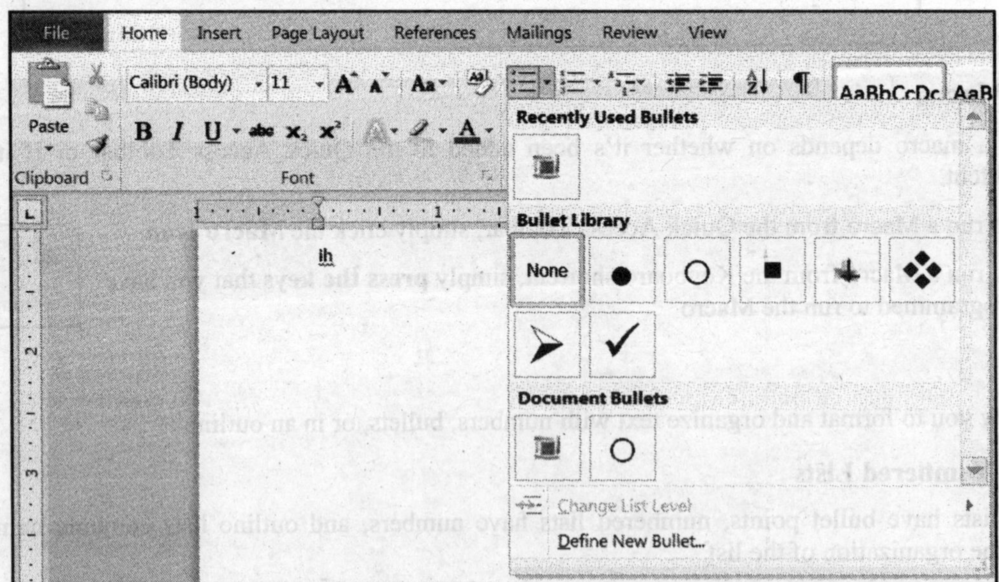

References and Citations

Word 2010 offers great tools for citing sources, creating a bibliography, and managing the sources. The first step to creating a reference list and citations in a document is to choose the appropriate style that you will be using for formatting the citations and references.

Style

To choose a publishing style:

- ❖ Click the **References** Tab on the Ribbon
- ❖ Click the drop-down box next to **Style** in the Citations & Bibliography Group
- ❖ Choose the appropriate style

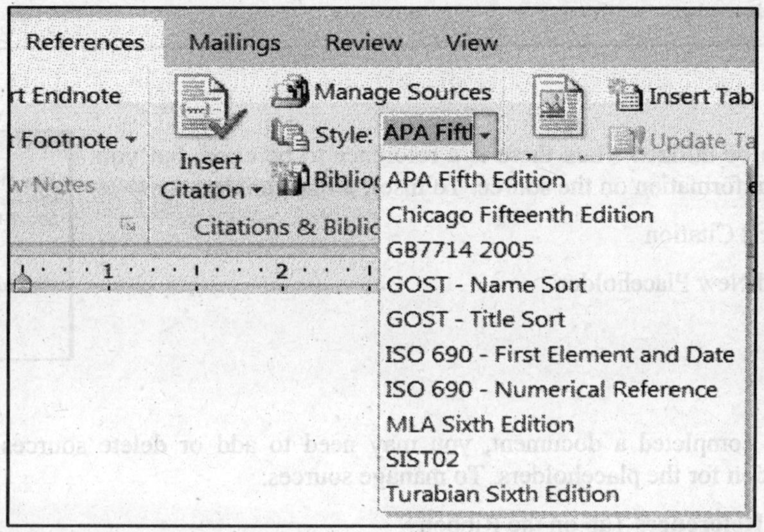

Citations

To insert a citation in the text portion of your document:

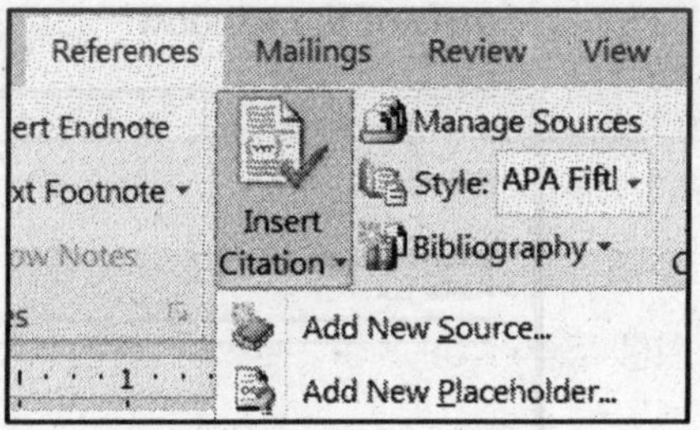

- ❖ Click the **References** Tab on the Ribbon
- ❖ Click the **Insert Citation** Button on the Citations & Bibliography Group
- ❖ If this is a new source, click **New Source**
- ❖ If you have already created this source, it will in the drop-down list and you can click on it
- ❖ If you are creating a **New Source**, choose the **type of source** (book, article, etc.)
- ❖ Complete the **Create Source Form**
- ❖ If you need additional fields, be sure to click the **Show All Bibliography Fields** check box
- ❖ Click **OK**

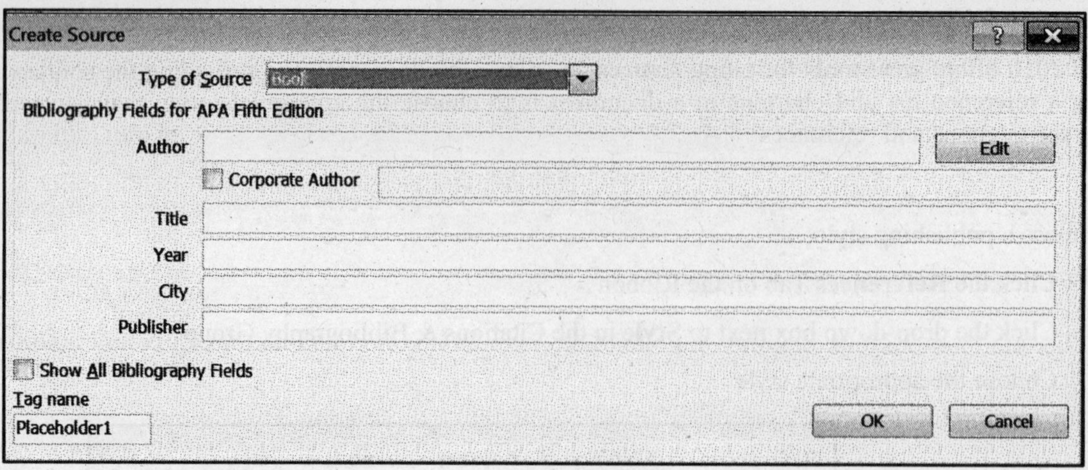

Placeholders

Placeholders can be utilized when there is a reference to be cited, but you do not have all of the information on the source. To insert a Placeholder:

- ❖ Click Insert Citation
- ❖ Click Add New Placeholder

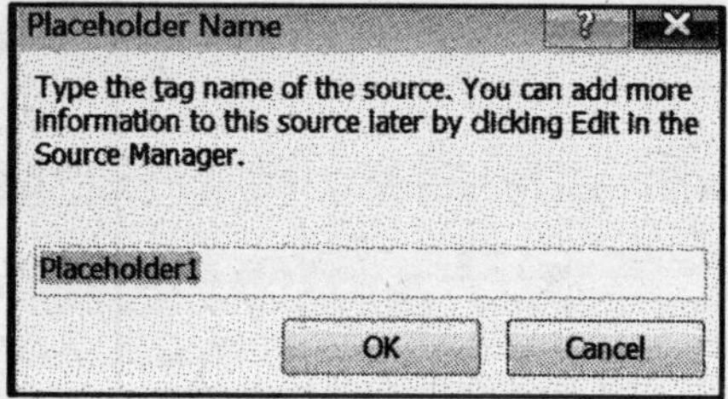

Manage Sources

Once you have completed a document, you may need to add or delete sources, modify existing sources, or complete the information for the placeholders. To manage sources:

- ❖ Click the **References** Tab on the Ribbon
- ❖ Click the **Manage Sources** Button on the Citations & Bibliography Group
- ❖ From this menu you can **Add, Delete, and Edit Sources** (note, you can preview the source in the bottom pane of the window

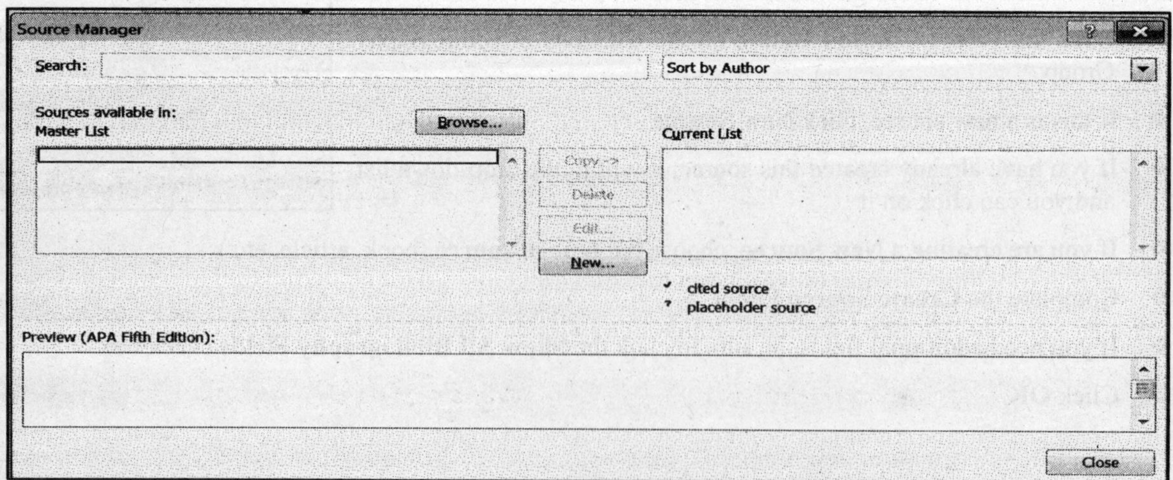

Bibliography

To add a Bibliography to the document:

- ❖ Place the cursor in the document where you want the bibliography
- ❖ Click the **References** Tab on the Ribbon
- ❖ Click the **Bibliography** Button on the Citations & Bibliography Group
- ❖ Choose **Insert Built-in Bibliography/Works Cited** or **Insert Bibliography**

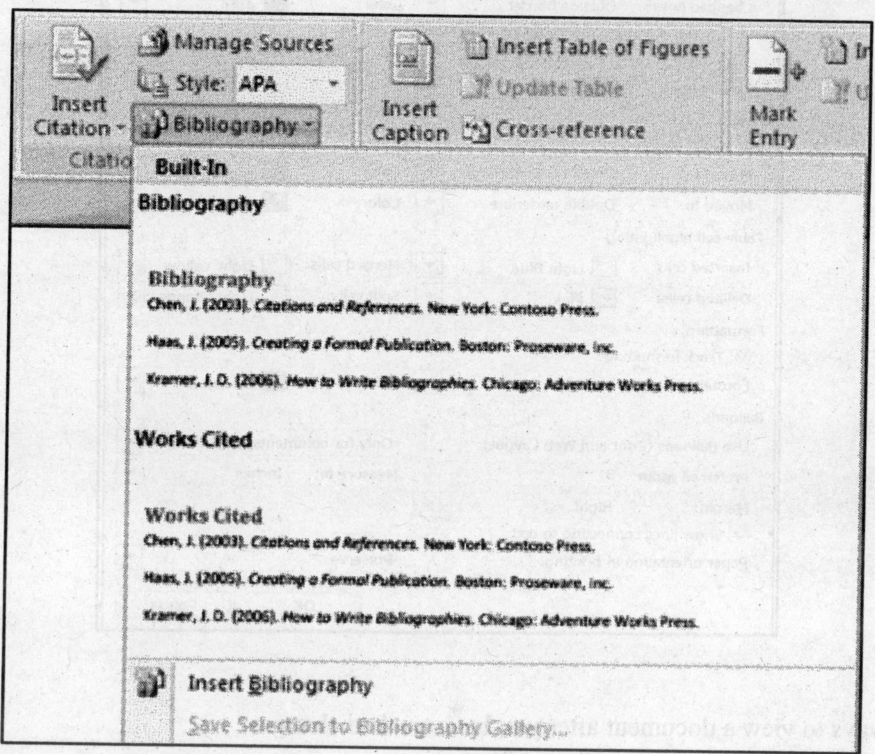

Insert Footnote

Some types of academic writing utilize footnotes. To insert a footnote:

- ❖ Click the **References** Tab on the Ribbon
- ❖ Click **Insert Footnote** (or Insert Endnote depending on your needs)
- ❖ Begin typing the footnote

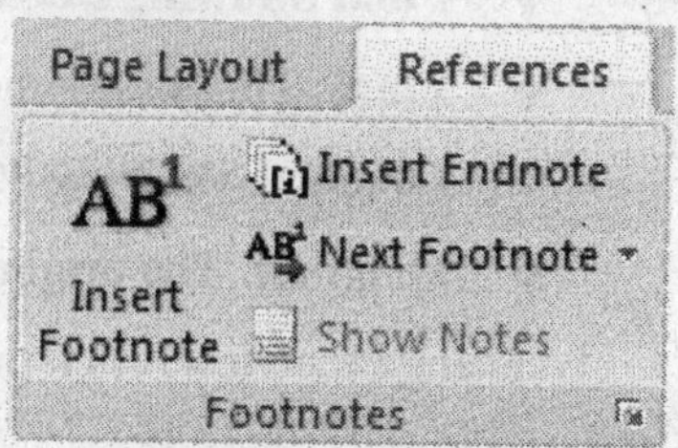

Track Changes

Track Changes is a great feature of Word that allows you to see what changes have been made to a document. The tools for track changes are found on the Reviewing tab of the Ribbon.

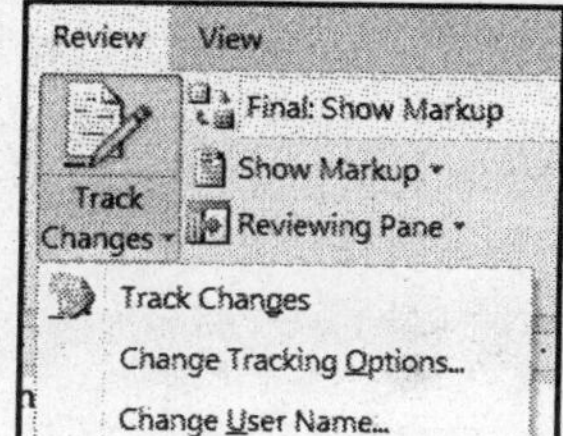

Begin Track Changes

To keep track of the changes you'll be making to a document, you must click on **Track Changes** icon. To start Tracking Changes:

❖ Click **Review** Tab on the Ribbon

❖ Click **Track Changes**

❖ Make the changes to your document and you will see any changes you have made

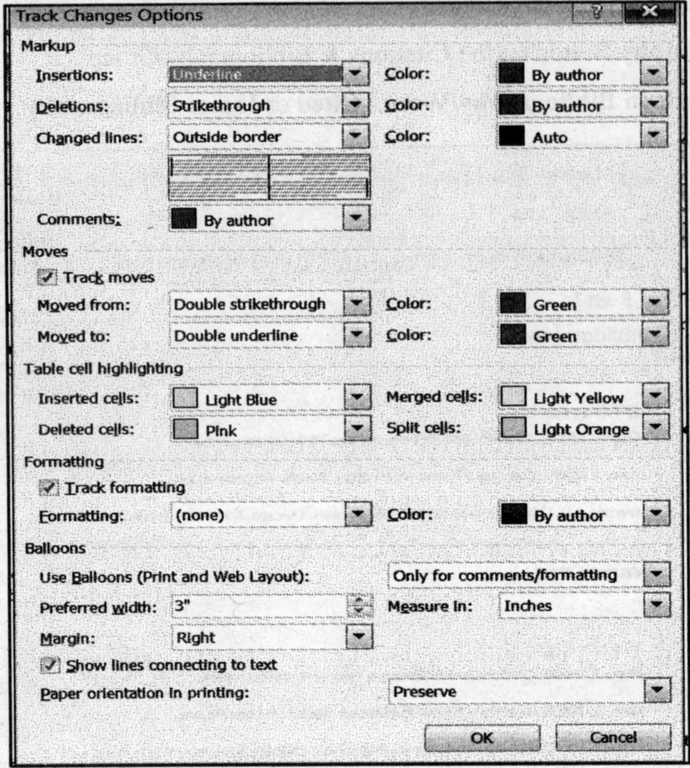

Document Views

There are four ways to view a document after you have tracked changes:

❖ **Final Showing Markup:** This shows the document with the changes displayed

❖ **Final:** This shows the changed document, without the changes displayed

❖ **Original Showing Markup:** The original document with the changes displayed

❖ **Original:** The original document without any changes

To change the view, click the appropriate choice in the Tracking Group of the Review Tab on the Ribbon.

The **Show Markup** feature allows you to view different items (comments, formatting, etc.) and choose to view different authors' comments.

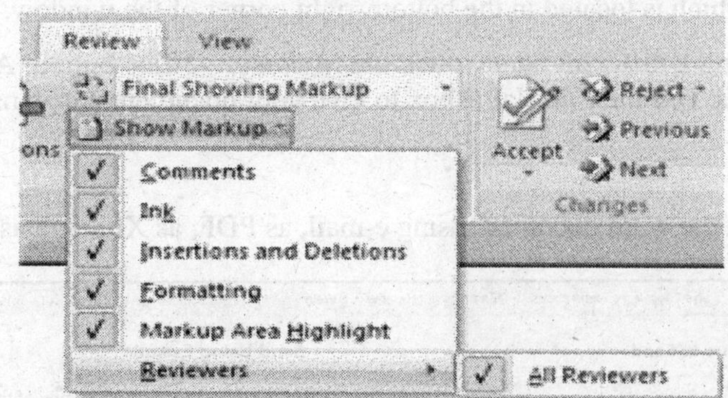

Accept or Reject Changes

When you view the changes in a document, you can either choose to accept or reject the changes. This allows you to review the document by each change to accept or reject each change.

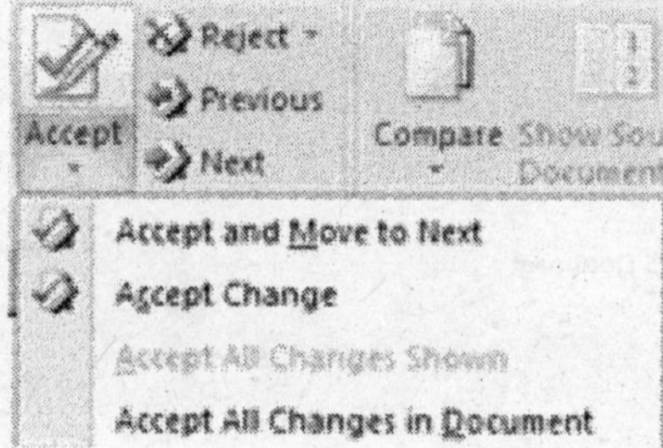

Comments

The New Comments icon also lets you add comments to the document. To add a new comment, put your cursor where you would like to add the comment and click on New Comment.

10.9 SAVING THE DOCUMENT

Save a File and Close Word

You must save your documents if you wish to recall them later. You can use the Save option on the File menu, to save a document. You can also save a document by typing Ctrl + S. The first time you save a document, the Save As dialog box appears. Use the Save as dialog box to locate the folder in which you want to save your document and to give your document a name. After you have saved your document at least once, you can save any changes you make to your document simply by clicking the Save after you click the File menu.

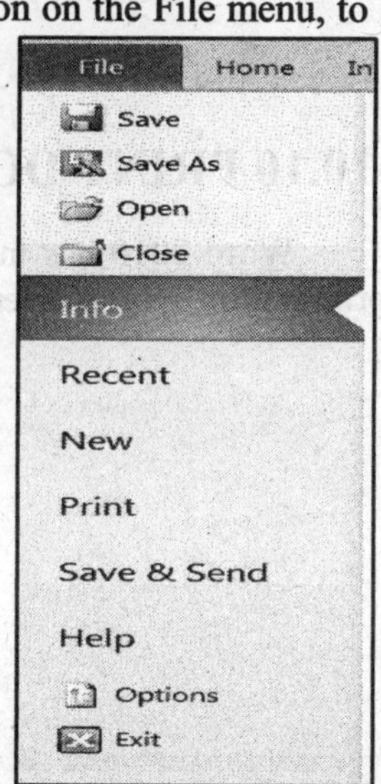

Save a File

1. Click the File Tab. A menu appears
2. Click Save. The Save As dialog box appears if you are saving your document for the first time
3. Specify the correct folder in the Save In box
4. Name your document by typing Lesson Two in the File Name box
5. Click Save

6. Click Exit Word, which is located in the bottom-right corner of the window. Word closes

To save the document using a different name, click the Microsoft Office button. A menu appears. Click Save As. The Save As dialog box appears. Use the File Name box to give your document a new name.

Save & Send

It helps you save and send the word document using e-mail, as PDF, as XPS and as Internet Fax.

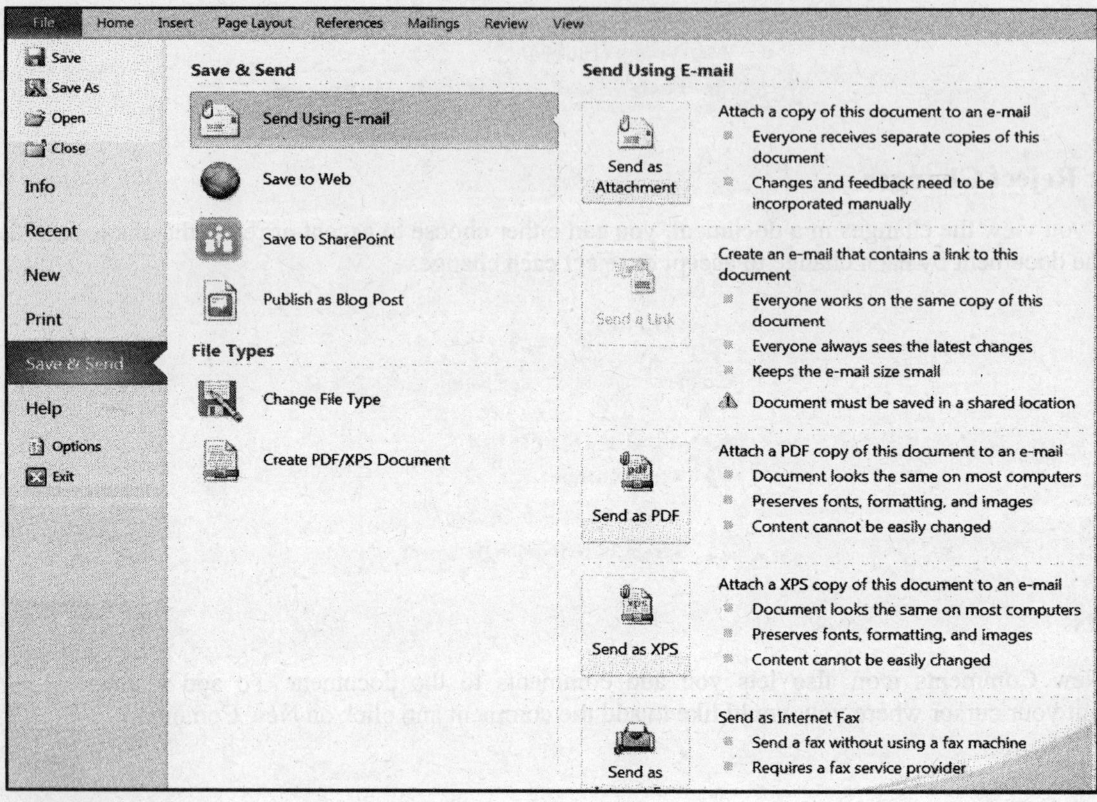

Close a Document

To close a document:

- ❖ Click the File Tab
- ❖ Click Exit

10.10 PRINT DOCUMENTS

Word 2010 has included many options for you to take print of your document. Click the File tab and click the print button. You can see the print screen.

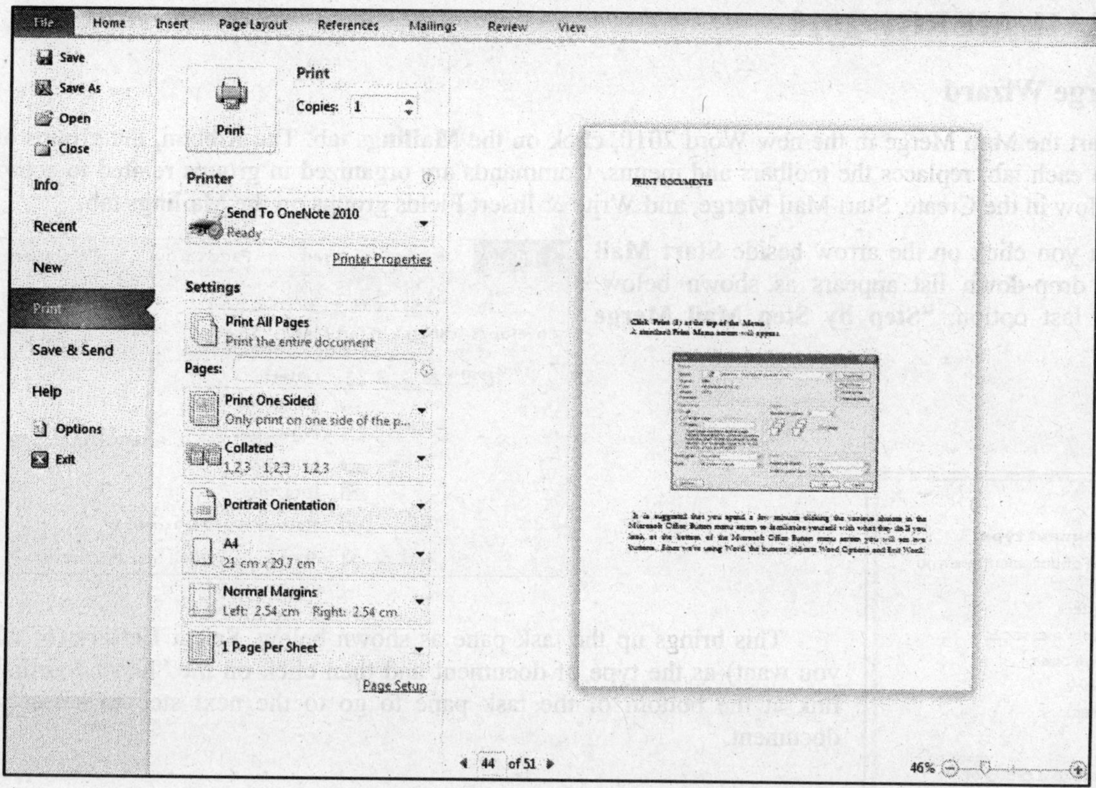

In the screen, you have the option like to print number of copies, selection of printer to take print and settings.

Settings

In settings, there are different options like Print All Pages, Print One Sided, Collated, Portrait Orientation, Page size, Margins and Page Per Sheet.

- **Print All Pages:** Print the entire document.
- **Print Selection:** Only print the select content in the document.
- **Print Current Page:** Only print the current page.
- **Print Custom Range:** Enter specific pages or sections to print.

Document properties setting helps you to take print document like table properties, values, list of markup only and list of styles used in document. You can also take print by only odd and even pages.

The pages have following options:

- **Print one sided:** It will only print on one side of the page.
- **Manually print on both sides:** It will reload paper when prompted to print the second side.
- **Collated:** It will order the page like 1,2,3 1,2,3 and 1,2,3 to print.
- **Uncollated:** It will unordered the page like 1,1,1 2,2,2 and 3,3,3 to print.

You **can** take printout in portrait and landscape orientation of the document. You can also change the document size like Letter, Tabloid, Legal, Executive, A3, A4, B4 (JIS), B5 (JIS), Envelope#10, Envelope monarch and more paper size. Margin can be set to take print of the document in Normal, Narrow, Moderate, Wide and Mirrored. You can customize margin according to document, another option in the settings is the Page Per Sheet. It takes print as 1, 2, 4, 6, 8 and 16 pages per sheet.

10.11 MAIL MERGE 2010

Mail Merge Wizard

To start the Mail Merge in the new Word 2010, click on the **Mailings** tab. The Ribbon, the groups of commands you see on each tab, replaces the toolbars and menus. Commands are organized in groups related to activities such as you see below in the Create, Start Mail Merge, and Write & Insert Fields groups on the Mailings tab.

When you click on the arrow beside **Start Mail Merge**, a drop-down list appears as shown below. Select the last option, **"Step by Step Mail Merge Wizard."**

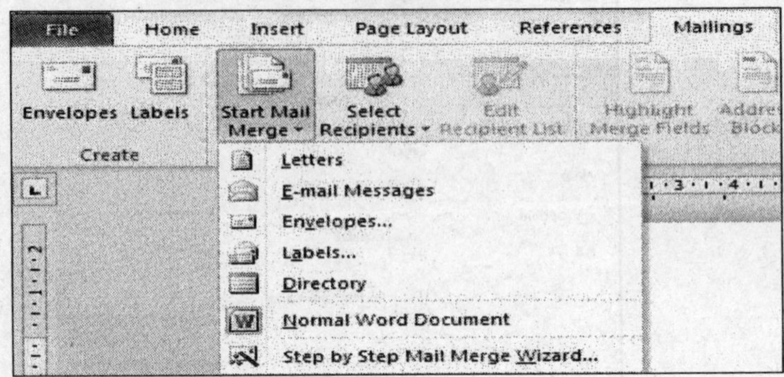

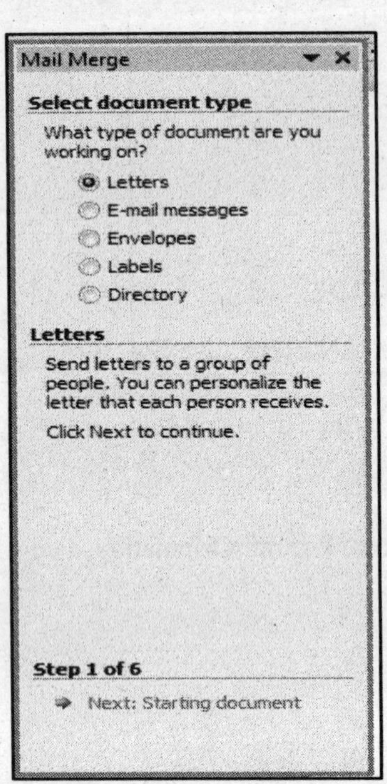

This brings up the task pane as shown below. Select **Letters** (or whatever type you want) as the type of document and then click on the "Next: Starting document" link at the bottom of the task pane to go to the next step to select your starting document.

Selecting a Template

You have options to use the current document you have open, to select a template, or to browse to an existing document not open. For this practice, select "Start from a template." This brings up a link you click on to "Select template."

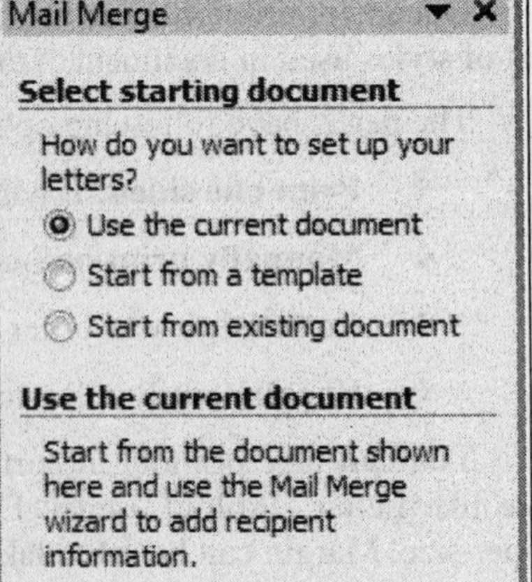

This opens the "Select Template" dialog box shown. Select the "Letters" tab and choose "Oriel Merge Letter." Click on OK.

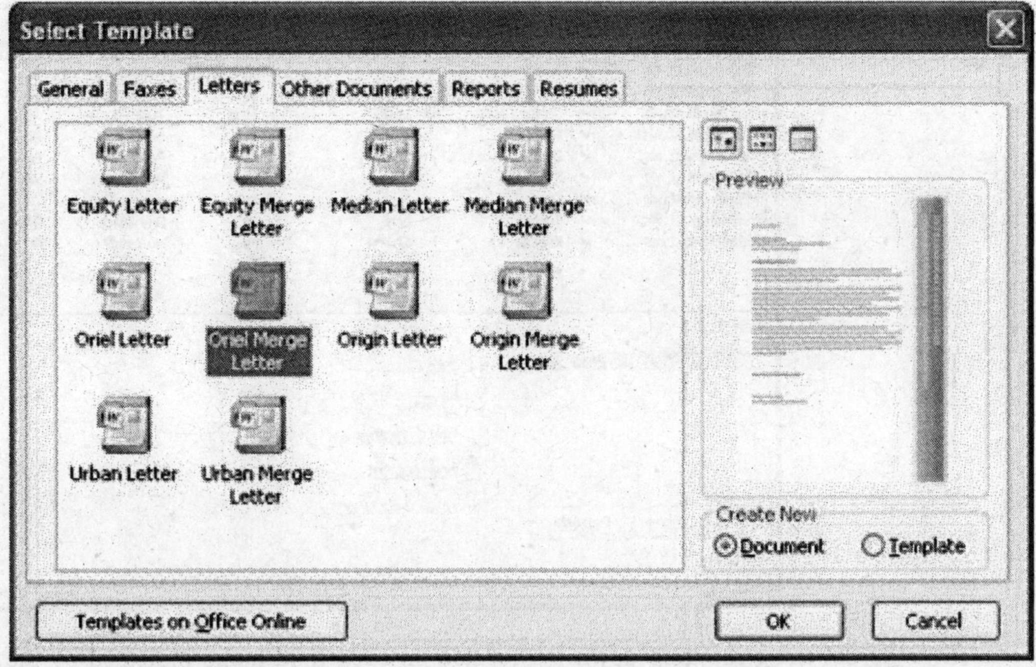

This takes you to Step 3 in the Mail Merge process in which you "Select recipients."

Selecting Recipients

Select "Use an existing list" and click on the "Browse" link. Locate and open the file containing your data source.

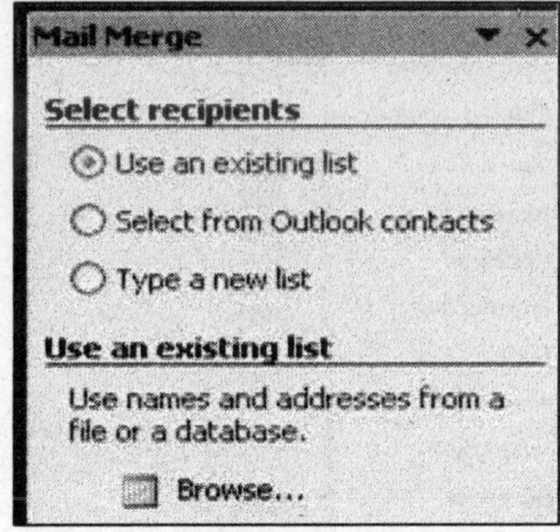

This opens the following dialog box in which you select the table (the named range defined within Excel) containing the mail merge recipients info you want to pull into the merge fields in your document.

Make sure to check the box indicating that the "First row of data contains column headers" so that the field labels (Last Name, First Name, Address1, etc.) on your spreadsheet won't be mistaken for data.

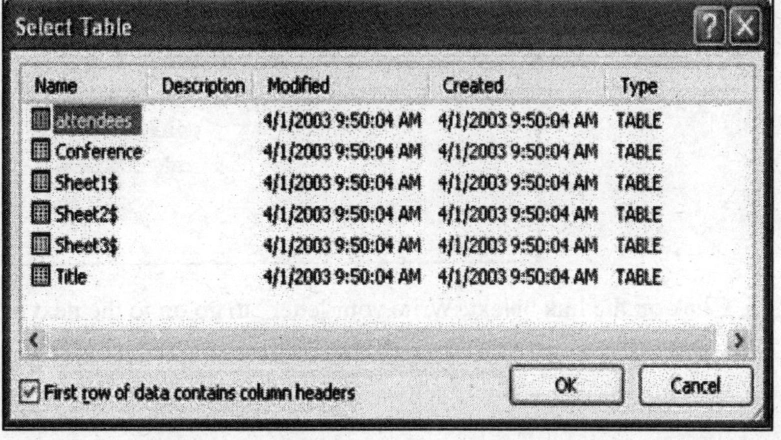

This opens the **Mail Merge Recipients** dialog box shown below. Here, you can select which recipients to include or deselect by unchecking the check box by the name.

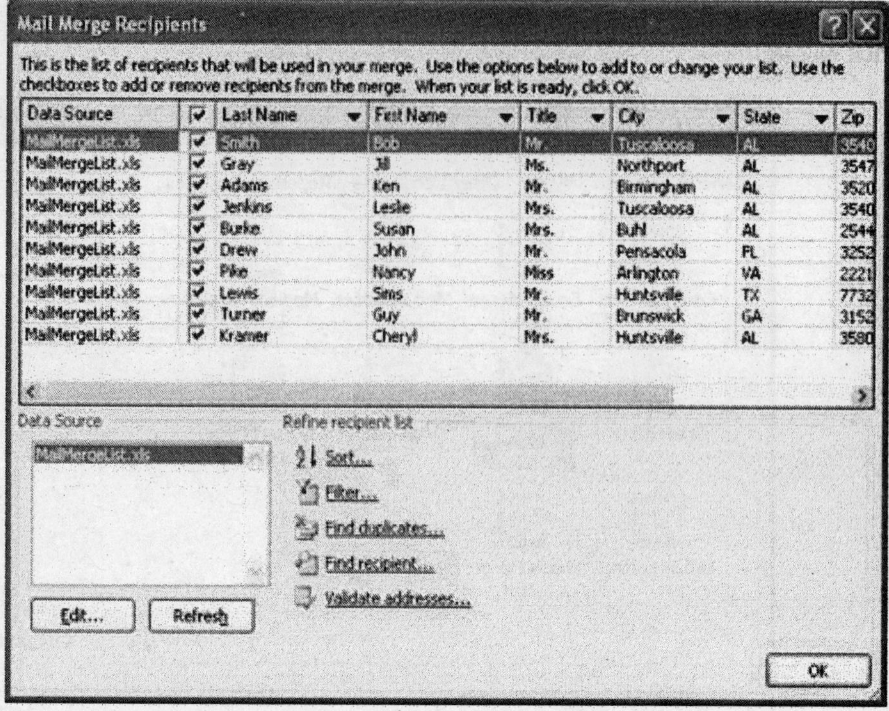

You can sort and filter the list using the drop-down list located on each field name indicated by the triangular black arrow. Note there are also links to Sort and Filter or Find Duplicates and recipients in the "Refine recipient list" section.

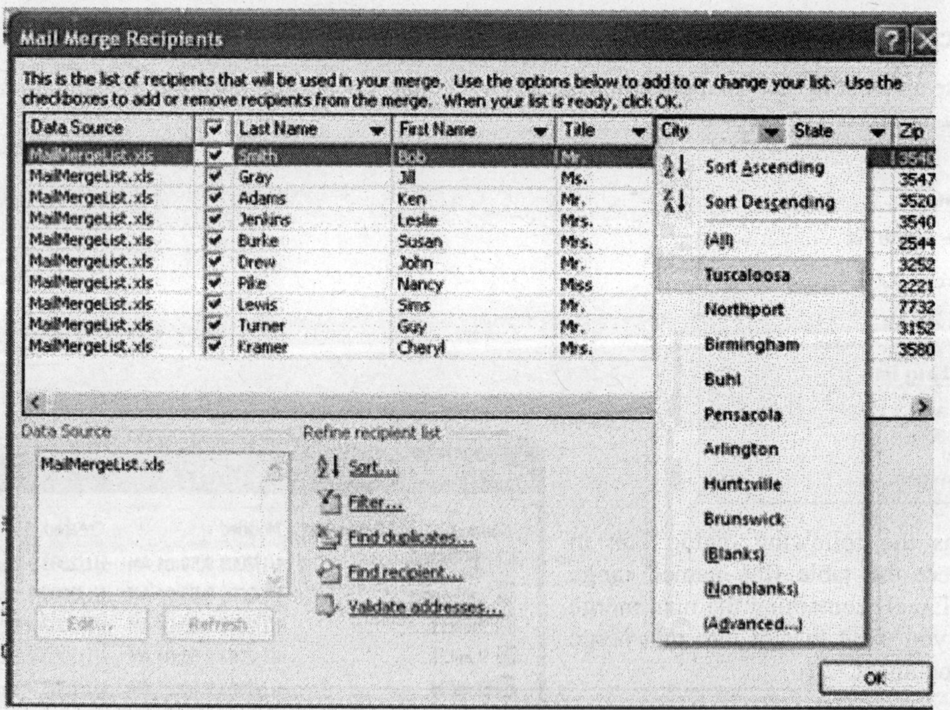

Click on the link "Next: Write your letter" to go on to the next step to edit the mail merge template letter content.

Inserting Merge Fields

Notice that the Address Block and Greeting Line fields are already inserted into this template letter. If you weren't using a preformatted mail merge letter, you would just simply click on the links on the right to insert the Address block, Greeting line, or more items (more merge fields). You also have these same options on the Mailings toolbar at the top—you don't have to use the wizard each time you do a mail merge. Pick the date and replace the letter content with your own and then go on to the next step to preview your letters by clicking on the link at the bottom of the task pane.

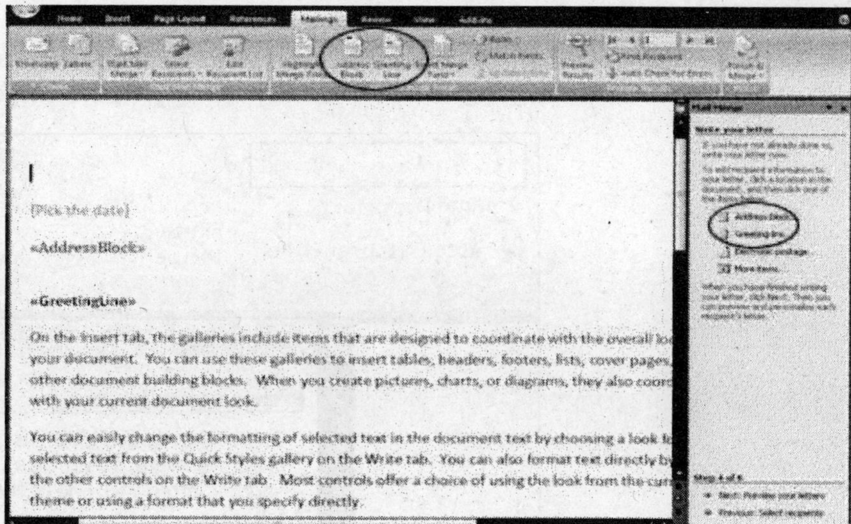

Matching Fields

When you click on the Address block link, the following dialog box appears in which you can choose the format of the address. Also, you can click on the **Match Fields** button to match the missing address field (the Match Fields button is also on the Mailings tab in the "Write and Insert Fields" grouping).

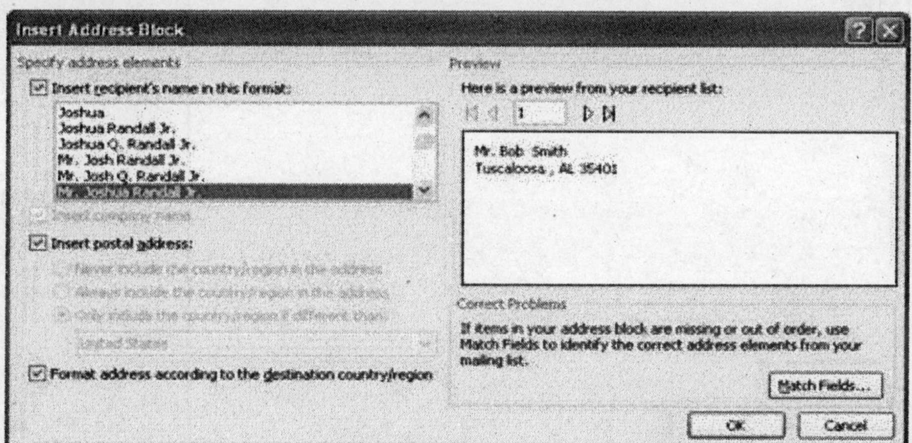

Clicking on the **Match Fields** button brings up the following dialog box. Use the Address 1 drop-down list to select the Street field name from the Excel spreadsheet.

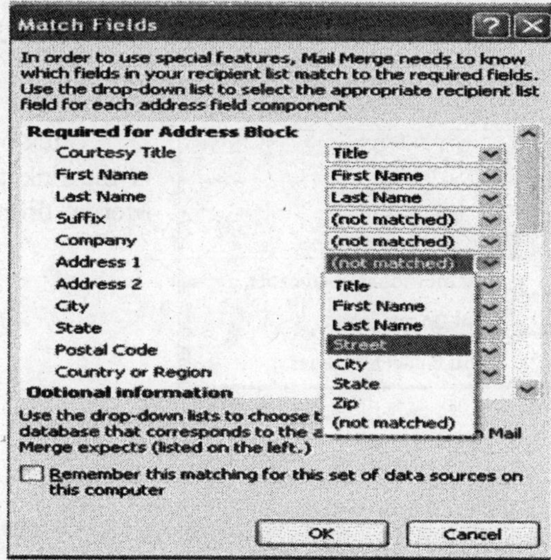

Previewing Results

You have buttons on both the Preview Results group on the Mailings ribbon as well as the task pane to look at different recipient info before going on to the next step to complete the merge.

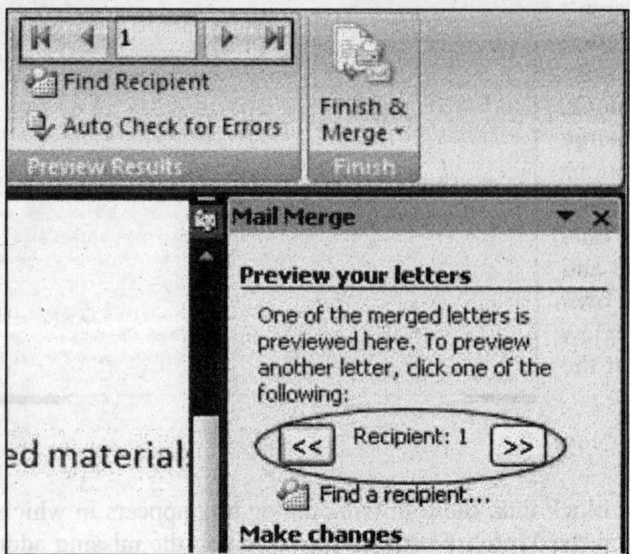

Completing the Merge

When you click on the link, "Next: Complete the merge," the following appears:

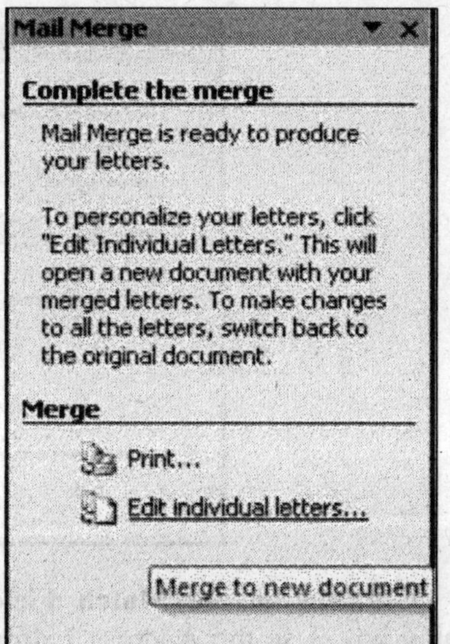

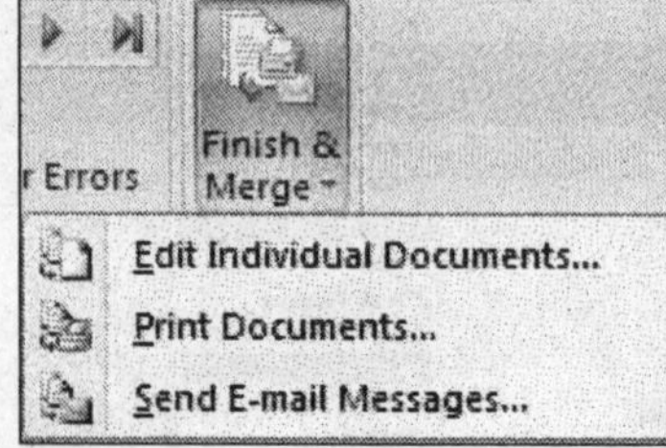

Click on the link "Edit individual letters" which you can see from the screen tip is the link to "Merge to new document." This is also a button on the "Finish & Merge" drop-down list on the Mailings Ribbon.

The Print link on the Task Pane or Print Documents on the Ribbon drop-down list allows you to merge directly to the printer. When you click on the link to edit the letters, the following dialog box appears:

You can choose whether to merge all or selected records. Click OK and then a new merged document entitled Letters1 is created. It contains the individual letters for each recipient. If you look at the status bar, you will see that it indicates multiple letters.

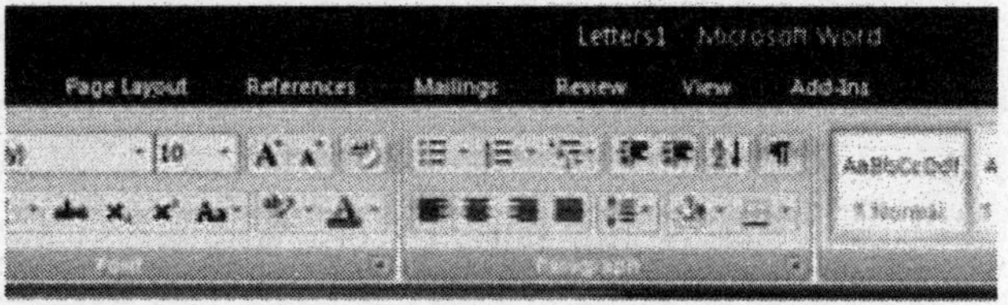

Saving

Save your work by clicking on the File menu.

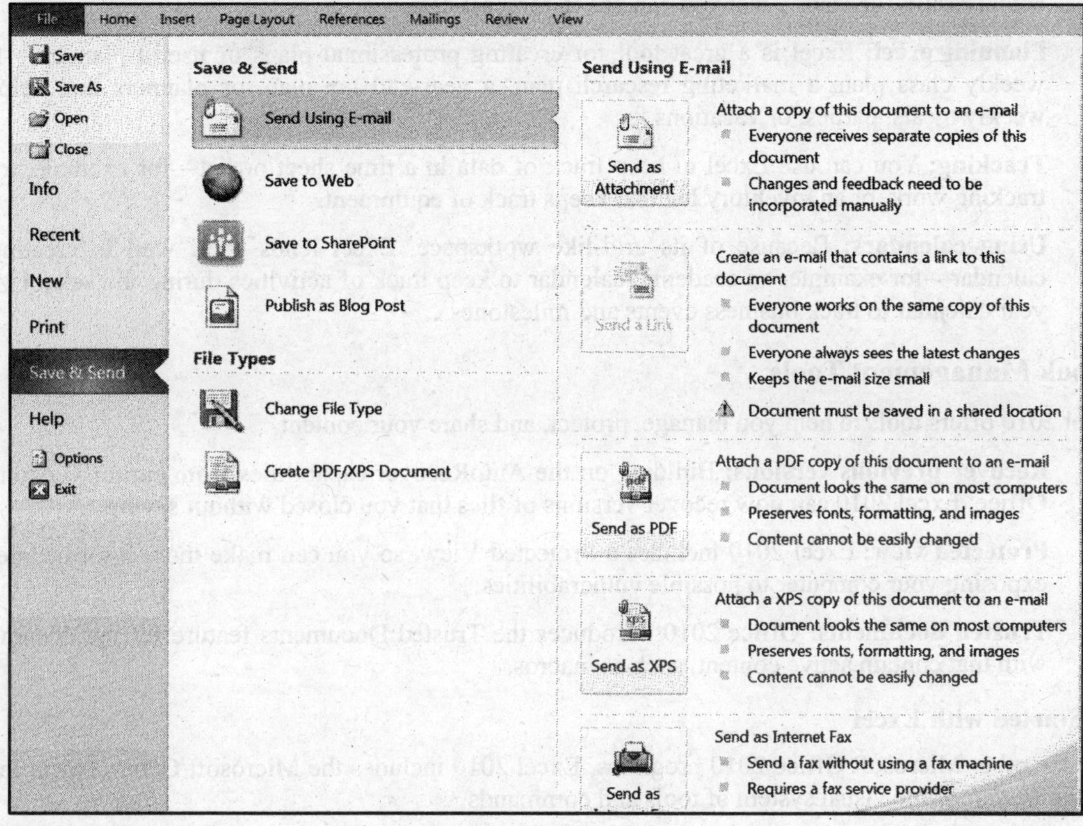

Select "Save As" to view the new options for saving in different formats.

The new "default" file format is .docx, a new file format for Word documents. It is one of the new Office XML formats. You also have the option to save in the Word 97-2003 format so that your file is compatible with those versions and can be opened in them.

10.12 MICROSOFT EXCEL

Ms Excel

Microsoft Excel (full name Microsoft Office Excel) is a spreadsheet application written and distributed by Microsoft for Microsoft Windows and Mac OS X. You can use Excel to create and format workbooks (a collection of spreadsheets) in order to analyze data and make more informed business decisions. Specifically, you can use Excel to track data, build models for analyzing data, write formulas to perform calculations on that data, pivot the data in numerous ways, and present data in a variety of professional looking charts.

Common Scenarios for using Excel Include:

- **Accounting:** You can use the powerful calculation features of Excel in many financial accounting statements—for example, a cash flow statement, income statement, or profit and loss statement.
- **Budgeting:** Whether your needs are personal or business related, you can create any type of budget in Excel—for example, a marketing budget plan, an event budget, or a retirement budget.
- **Billing and sales:** Excel is also useful for managing billing and sales data, and you can easily create the forms that you need—for example, sales invoices, packing slips, or purchase orders.
- **Reporting:** You can create various types of reports in Excel that reflect your data analysis or summarize your data—for example, reports that measure project performance, show variance between projected and actual results, or reports that you can use to forecast data.
- **Planning excel:** Excel is a great tool for creating professional plans or useful planners—for example, a weekly class plan, a marketing research plan, a year-end tax plan, or planners that help you organize weekly meals, parties, or vacations.
- **Tracking:** You can use Excel to keep track of data in a time sheet or list—for example, a time sheet for tracking work, or an inventory list that keeps track of equipment.
- **Using calendars:** Because of its grid-like workspace, Excel lends itself well to creating any type of calendar—for example, an academic calendar to keep track of activities during the school year, or a fiscal year calendar to track business events and milestones.

Workbook Management Tools

Excel 2010 offers tools to help you manage, protect, and share your content.

- **Recover previous versions:** Building on the AutoRecover capabilities from earlier versions of Microsoft Office, Excel 2010 can now recover versions of files that you closed without saving.
- **Protected view:** Excel 2010 includes a Protected View, so you can make more informed decisions before exposing your computer to possible vulnerabilities.
- **Trusted documents:** Office 2010 introduces the Trusted Documents feature for the documents you work with that contain active content, such as macros.

Getting Started with Excel

Like the other Microsoft Office 2010 programs, Excel 2010 includes the Microsoft Office Fluent interface, which consists of a customizable visual system of tools and commands.

Improved Ribbon

In Excel 2010, however, you can create your own tabs and groups and rename or change the order of the built-in tabs and groups.

Microsoft Office Backstage View

A new addition in Microsoft Office 2010 programs, the Backstage view is the latest innovation in the Microsoft Office Fluent user interface and a companion feature to the ribbon. Accessible by clicking the **File** menu, the Backstage view is where you open, save, print, share, and manage your files and set your program options.

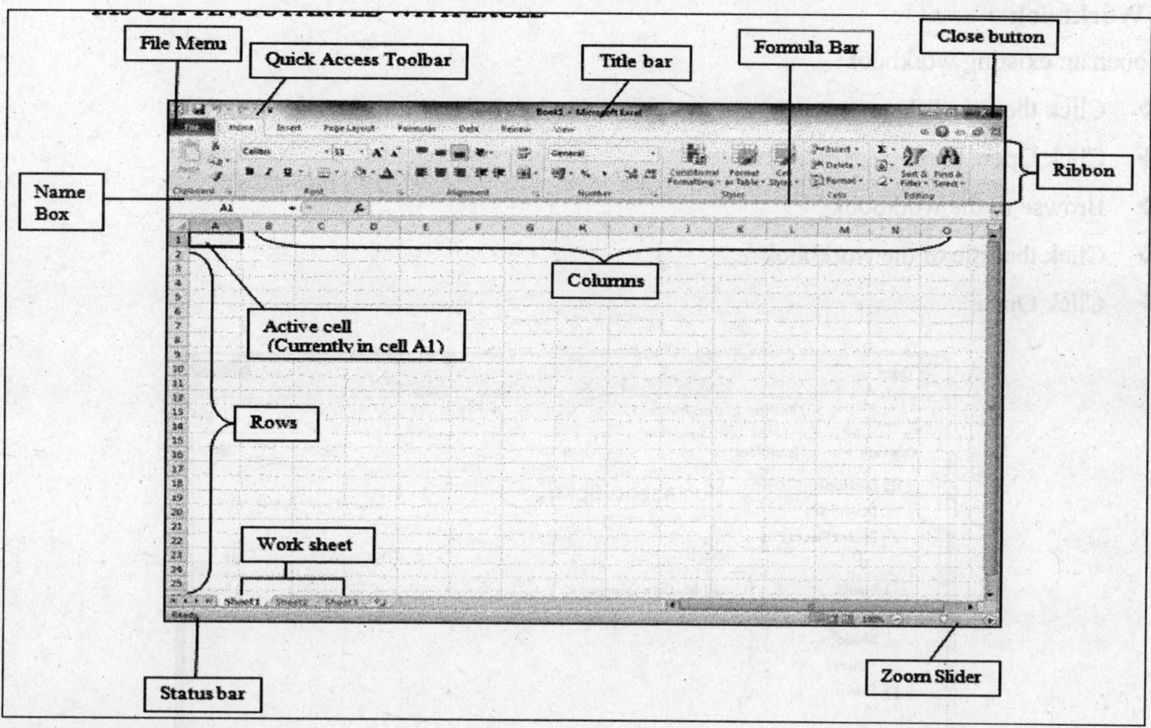

Working with Excel

Create a Workbook

To create a new Workbook:

- Click the **File Tab**
- Click **New**
- Choose **Blank Document**
- Under Available Templates, double-click **Blank Workbook** (Keyboard **shortcut** – CTRL + N)

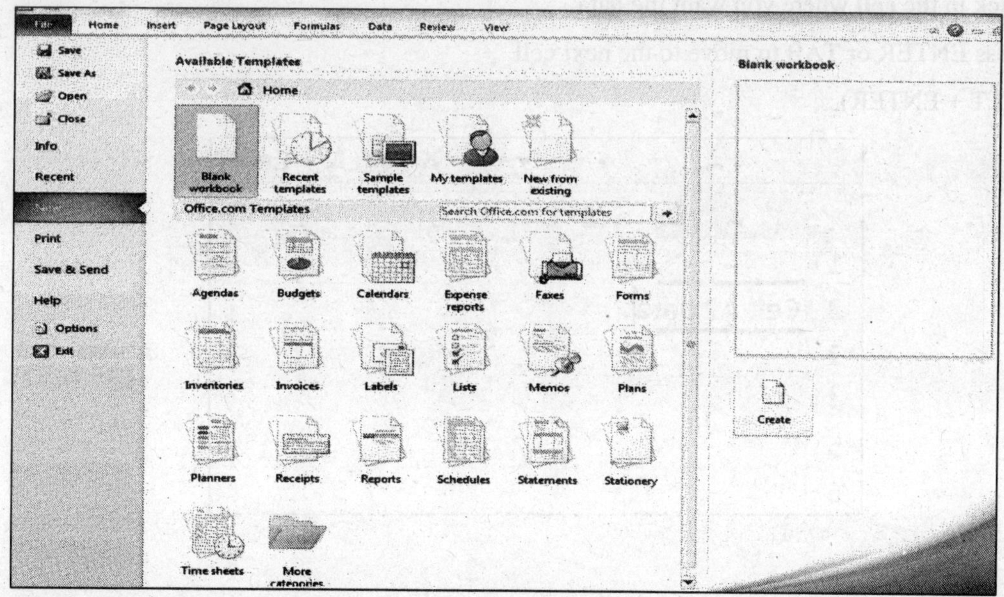

Open a Workbook

To open an existing workbook:

- ❖ Click the File Tab
- ❖ Click Open
- ❖ Browse to the workbook
- ❖ Click the title of the workbook
- ❖ Click Open

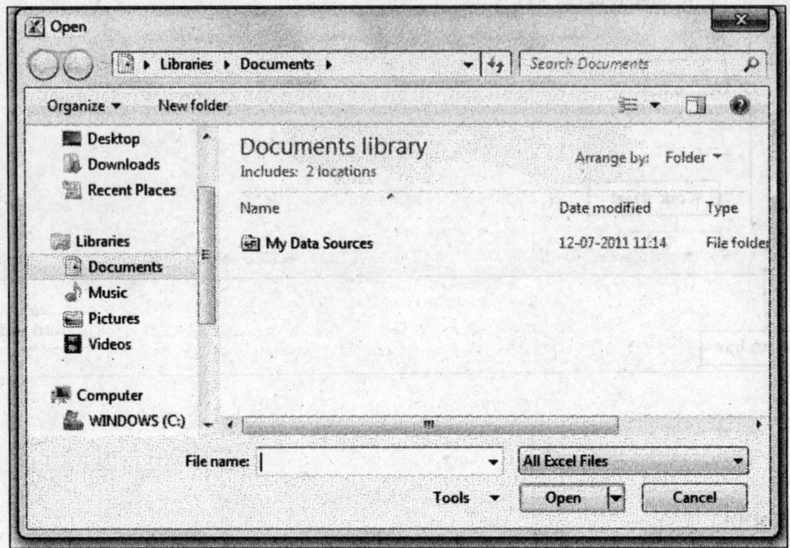

Entering Data

There are different ways to enter data in Excel: in an active cell or in the formula bar.

To enter data in an active cell:

- ❖ Click in the **cell** where you want the data
- ❖ Press ENTER or TAB to move to the next cell
- ❖ (ALT + ENTER).

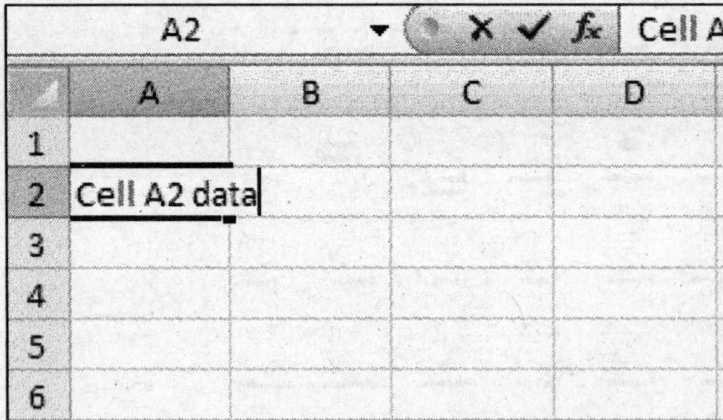

To enter data into the formula bar:

- ❖ Click the cell where you would like the data
- ❖ Place the cursor in the Formula Bar
- ❖ Type in the data

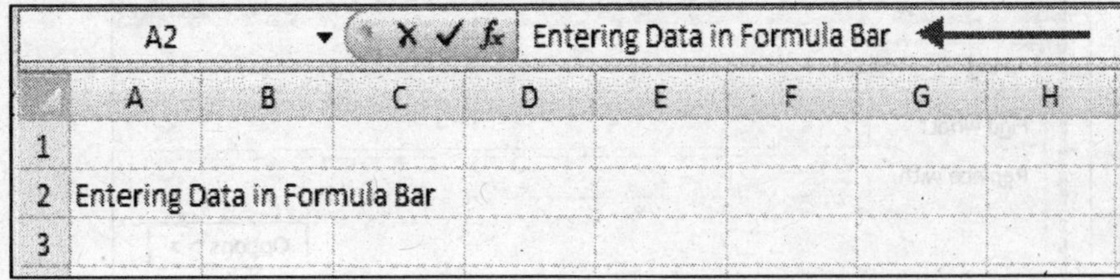

Modifying a Worksheet

Insert Cells, Rows, and Columns

To insert cells, rows, and columns in Excel:

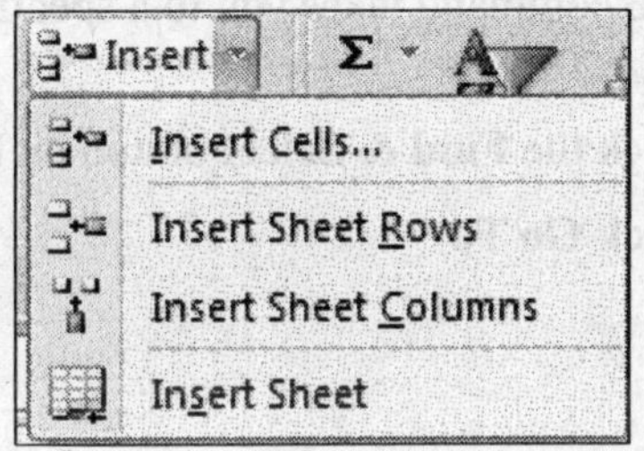

- ❖ Place the cursor in the row below where you want the new row, or in the column to the left of where you want the new column
- ❖ Click the **Insert** button on the **Cells** group of the **Home** tab
- ❖ Click the appropriate choice: **Cell, Row, or Column**

Delete Cells, Rows and Columns

To delete cells, rows, and columns:

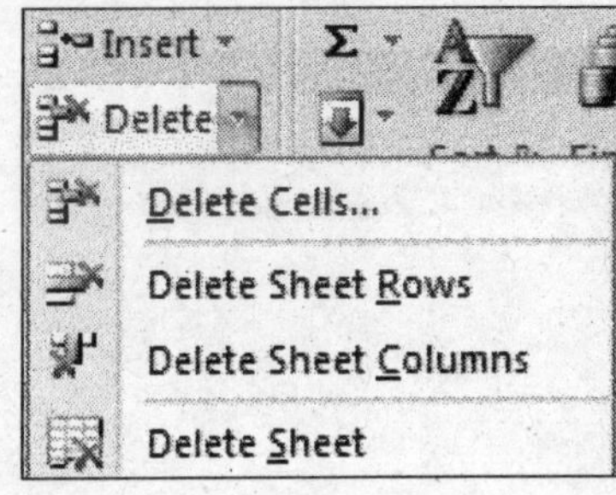

- ❖ Place the cursor in the cell, row, or column that you want to delete
- ❖ Click the **Delete** button on the **Cells** group of the **Home** tab
- ❖ Click the appropriate choice: **Cell, Row, or Column**

Find and Replace

To find data or find and replace data:

- ❖ Click the **Find & Select** button on the **Editing** group of the **Home** tab
- ❖ Choose **Find** or **Replace**
- ❖ Complete the **Find What** text box
- ❖ Click on **Options** for more search options

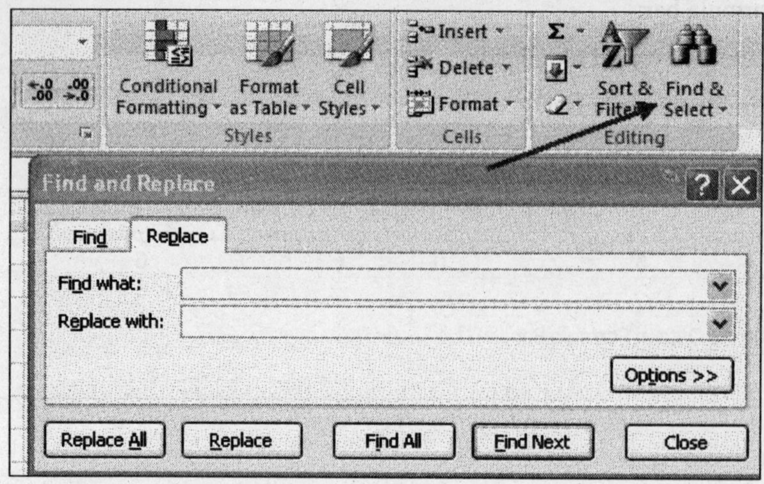

Go To Command

The Go To command takes you to a specific cell either by cell reference (the Column Letter and the Row Number) or cell name.

- ❖ Click the **Find & Select** button on the **Editing** group of the **Home** tab
- ❖ Click **Go To**

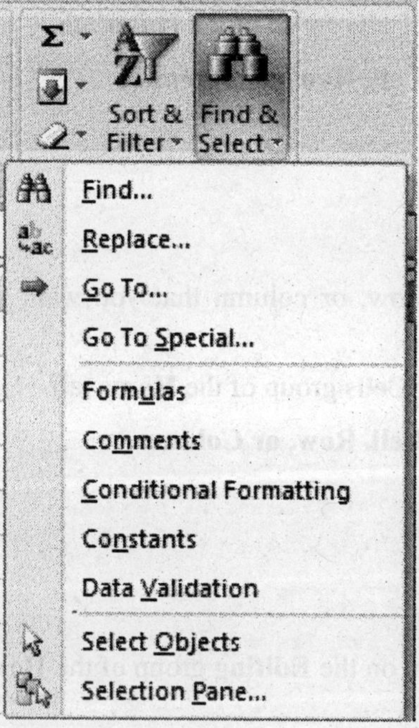

Spell Check

To check the spelling:

- ❖ On the **Review** tab, click the **Spelling** button

Performing Calculations

Excel Formulas

A formula is a set of mathematical instructions that can be used in Excel to perform calculations. Formals are started in the formula box with an = sign.

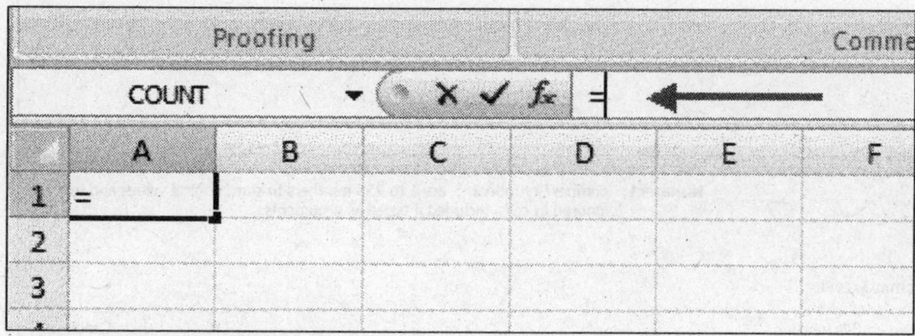

There are many elements to and Excel formula.

❖ **References:** The cell or range of cells that you want to use in your calculation

❖ **Operators:** Symbols (+, –, *, /, etc.) that specify the calculation to be performed

❖ **Constants:** Numbers or text values that do not change

❖ **Functions:** Predefined formulas in Excel

To create a basic formula in Excel:

❖ Select the **cell** for the formula

❖ Type = (the equal sign) and the **formula**

❖ Click **Enter**

Calculate with Functions

A function is a built-in formula in Excel. A function has a name and arguments (the mathematical function) in parentheses. Common functions in Excel:

❖ **Sum:** Adds all cells in the argument

❖ **Average:** Calculates the average of the cells in the argument

❖ **Min:** Finds the minimum value

❖ **Max:** Finds the maximum value

❖ **Count:** Finds the number of cells that contain a numerical value within a range of the argument

To calculate a function:

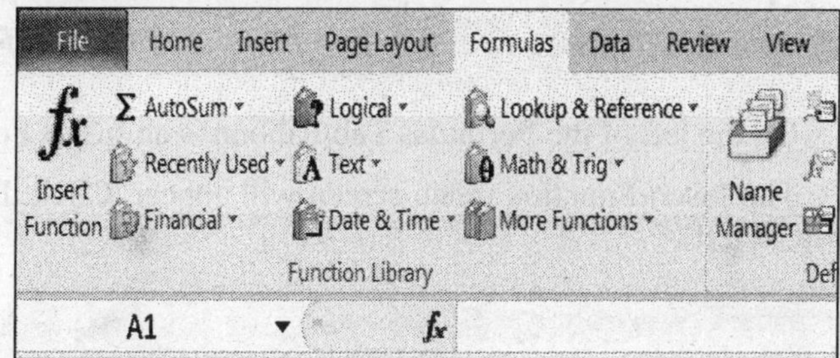

❖ Click the **cell** where you want the function applied

❖ Click the **Insert Function** button

❖ Choose the function

❖ Click **OK**

❖ Complete the Number1 box with the first cell in the range that you want calculated

❖ Complete the Number2 box with the last cell in the range that you want calculated.

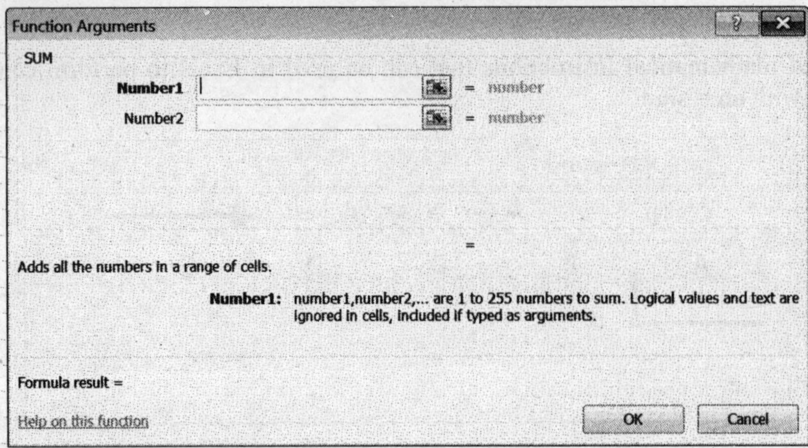

Function Library

The function library is a large group of functions on the Formula Tab of the Ribbon. These functions include:

❖ **AutoSum:** Easily calculates the sum of a range

❖ **Recently Used:** All recently used functions

❖ **Financial:** Accrued interest, cash flow return rates and additional financial functions

❖ **Logical:** And, If, True, False, etc.

❖ **Text:** Text based functions

❖ **Date & Time:** Functions calculated on date and time

❖ **Math & Trig:** Mathematical Functions

Functions

There are a number of **formulas built into Excel,** like **Sum**. These formulas are called **Functions.**

Look at the top of your Excel screen and click on the Formulas Tab. The Formulas Ribbon will display.

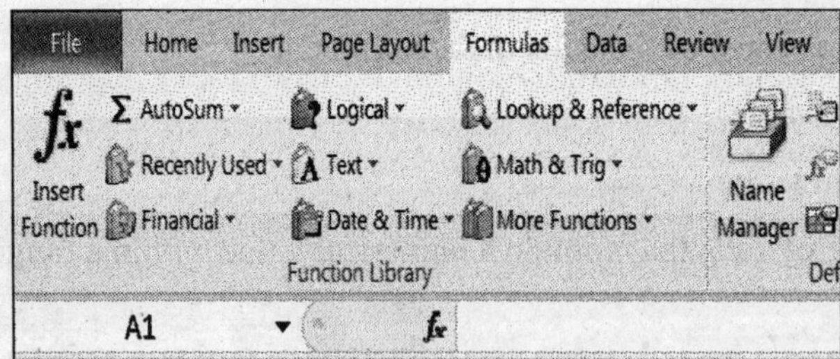

On the left of the Formulas Tab/Ribbon is an Insert Function button. Click the Insert Function button.

The Insert Function menu screen will appear. Click the small down arrow to the right of or select a category: (see arrow at left).

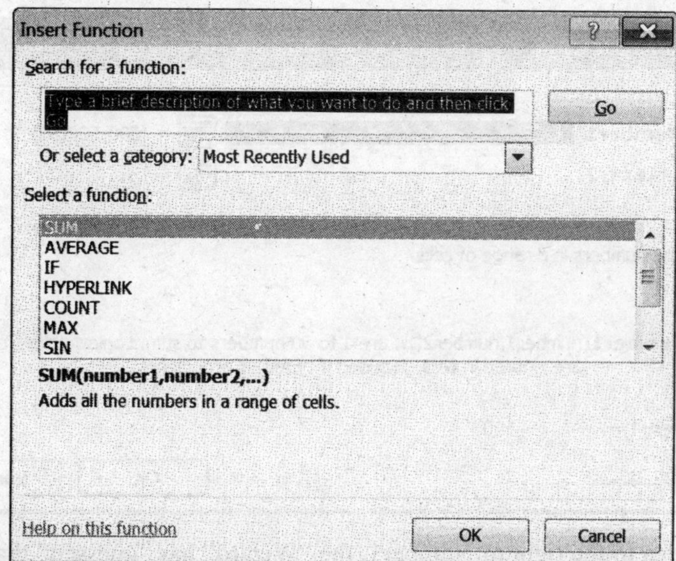

In the drop-down menu that appears, you can see that there are all kinds of formulas (functions) that come with Excel spreadsheet (e.g., statistical, mathematical, financial, etc.). Instead of having to go to math, financial, or statistical tables in a book, you can enter data from your spreadsheet into the formulas and receive answers.

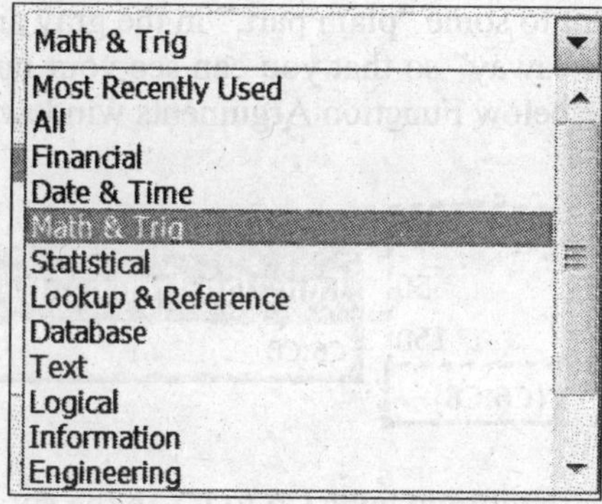

Click All in the **drop-down menu.**

The **Select a function menu** will look like the **image below.**

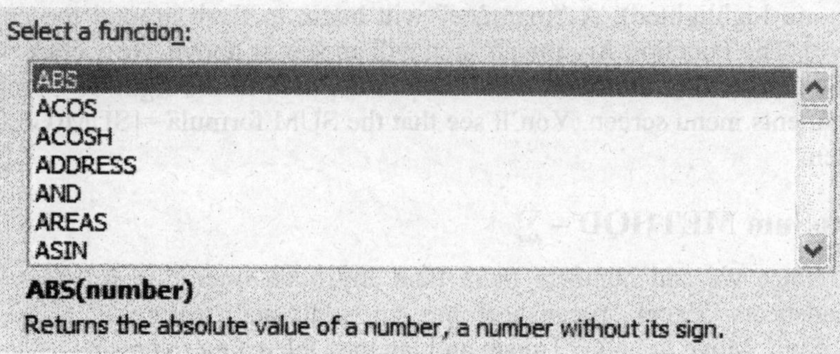

Look at all the functions (formulas). Use the elevator bar on the right side of the Select a function menu screen to move down the list until you see SUM. Click SUM.

Then **click OK.**

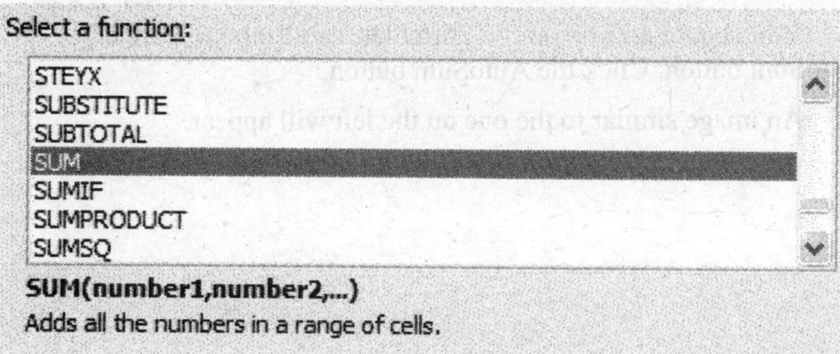

The **Function Arguments** menu screen will still be on the screen.

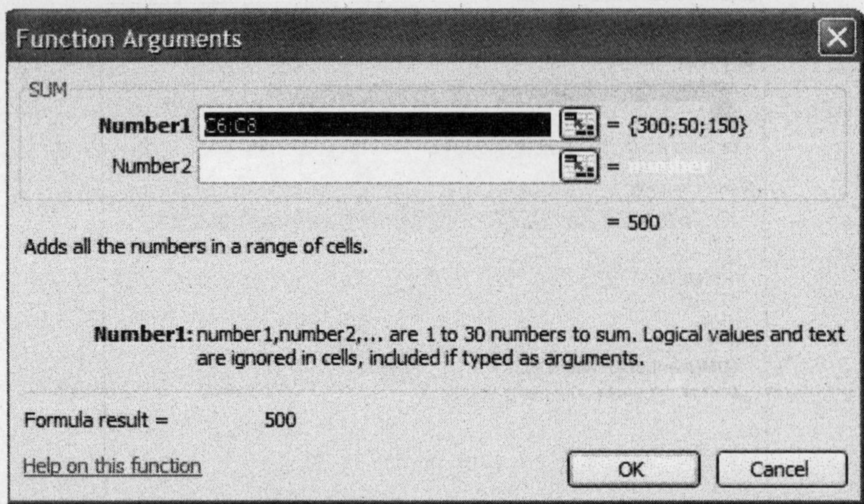

As you can see, in the area to the right of Number1, the "Wizard" has "guessed" that you want to add the numbers in the range C6 to C8 - (C6:C8). Now that you are becoming skilled with Excel, we'll try something special. Carefully, point to some "plain part," in the gray area above. Click and hold down the left mouse button, and drag the above SUM box "away" so that you can see your numbers in C column cells. When you have done this, release the mouse button. The below Function Arguments window will appear.

Highlight cells C6 to C8 in the spreadsheet (click-on C6, hold down the left mouse button, and drag until the three cells are highlighted). A "marquee" will begin to flash around the cells, indicating they are highlighted (left arrow above). The Function Arguments area will appear as above. Now click the small button on the right of the cell (see right arrow above). The numbers will show in the area to the right of Number 1. Click OK at the bottom of the Function Arguments menu screen. You'll see that the SUM formula =[SUM(C6:C8)] shows in the formula area at the top of the screen.

AutoSum METHOD – ∑

Since we add numbers more than any other operation in spreadsheets, Excel spreadsheet has an additional feature – AutoSum. Move to cell C9 again and tap the Delete key to erase your last formula.

You should still be on the Formulas Tab/Ribbon. Notice ∑ AutoSum button. Click the AutoSum button.

An image similar to the one on the left will appear.

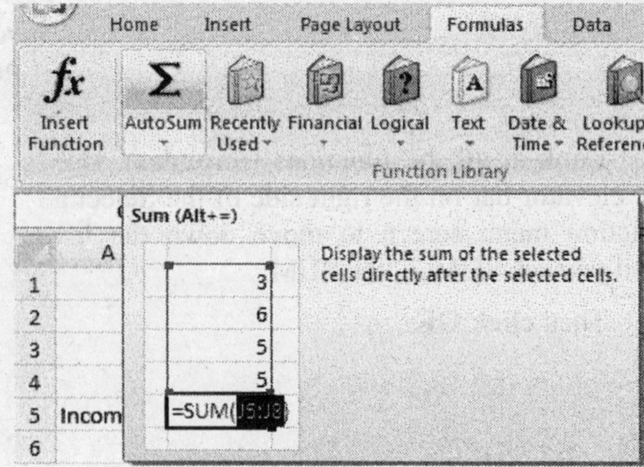

Click ∑ Sum

Reference Operators

By using functions, you can quickly and easily make many useful calculations, such as finding an average, the highest number, the lowest number, and a count of the number of items in a list. Microsoft Excel has many functions that you can use.

Using Reference Operators

To use functions, you need to understand reference operators. Reference operators refer to a cell or a group of cells. There are two types of reference operators: *range* and *union*.

A range reference refers to all the cells between and including the reference. A range reference consists of two cell addresses separated by a colon. The reference A1:A3 includes cells A1, A2, and A3. The reference A1:C3 includes cells A1, A2, A3, B1, B2, B3, C1, C2, and C3.

A union reference includes two or more references. A union reference consists of two or more numbers, range references, or cell addresses separated by a comma. The reference A7, B8: B10, C9, 10 refers to cells A7, B8 to B10, C9 and the number 10.

Understanding Functions

Functions are prewritten formulas. Functions differ from regular formulas in that you supply the value but not the operators, such as +, –, *, or /. For example, you can use the SUM function to add. When using a function, remember the following:

- ❖ Use an equal sign to begin a formula.
- ❖ Specify the function name.

Enclose arguments within parentheses. Arguments are values on which you want to perform the calculation. For example, arguments specify the numbers or cells you want to add.

Use a comma to separate arguments.

Here is an example of a function:

= SUM(2,13,A1,B2:C7)

In this function:

- ❖ The equal sign begins the function.
- ❖ SUM is the name of the function.
- ❖ 2, 13, A1, and B2:C7 are the arguments.
- ❖ Parentheses enclose the arguments.
- ❖ Commas separate the arguments.

After you type the first letter of a function name, the AutoComplete list appears. You can double-click on an item in the AutoComplete list to complete your entry quickly. Excel will complete the function name and enter the first parenthesis.

Functions

The SUM function adds argument values.

- ❖ Open Microsoft Excel.
- ❖ Type **12** in cell B1.
- ❖ Press Enter.

- Type **27** in cell B2.
- Press Enter.
- Type **24** in cell B3.
- Press Enter.
- Type = **SUM(B1:B3)** in cell A4.
- Press Enter. The sum of cells B1 to B3, which is 63, appears.

B4 =SUM(B1:B3)

	A	B	C	D	E
1		12			
2		27			
3		24			
4		63			
5					
6					

Format Worksheet

- Move to cell A4.
- Type the word **Sum**.
- Select cells B4 to C4.
- Choose the Home tab.
- Click the down arrow next to the Borders button.
- Click Top and Double Bottom Border.

	A	B	C	D
1		12	150	
2		27	85	
3		24	65	
4	Sum	63	300	
5				
6				

Calculate an Average

You can use the AERAGE function to calculate the average of a series of numbers.

- Move to cell A6.
- Type **Average**. Press the right arrow key to move to cell B6.
- Type =**AVERAGE(B1:B3)**.
- Press Enter. The average of cells B1 to B3, which is 21, appears.

B6 =AVERAGE(B1:B3)

	A	B	C	D	E	F
1		12	150			
2		27	85			
3		24	65			
4	Sum	63	300			
5						
6	Average	21				
7						

Calculate an Average with the AutoSum Button

In Microsoft Excel, you can use the AutoSum button Σ to calculate an average.

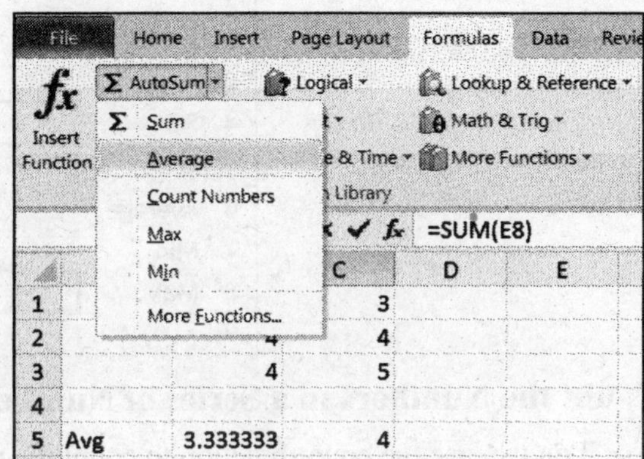

- ❖ Move to cell B1.
- ❖ Choose the Home tab.
- ❖ Click the down arrow next to the AutoSum button Σ.
- ❖ Click Average.
- ❖ Select cells C1 to B3.
- ❖ Press Enter. The average of cells C1 to C3, which is 4, appears.

B5 =AVERAGE(B1:B3)

	A	B	C	D	E	F
1		2	3			
2		4	4			
3		4	5			
4						
5	Avg	3.333333	4			
6						

Find the Lowest Number

You can use the MIN function to find the lowest number in a series of numbers.

- ❖ Move to cell A7.
- ❖ Type **Min**.
- ❖ Press the right arrow key to move to cell B7.
- ❖ Type = **MIN(B1:B3)**.
- ❖ Press Enter. The lowest number in the series, which is 12, appears.

B7 =MIN(B1:B3)

	A	B	C	D	E	F
1		12	150			
2		27	85			
3		24	65			
4	Sum	63	300			
5						
6	Average	21	100			
7	Min	12				
8						
9						

Note: You can also use the drop-down button next to the AutoSum button Σ to calculate minimums, maximums, and counts.

Find the Highest Number

You can use the MAX function to find the highest number in a series of numbers.

- ❖ Move to cell A8.
- ❖ Type **Max**.
- ❖ Press the right arrow key to move to cell B8.
- ❖ Type = **MAX(B1:B3).**
- ❖ Press Enter. The highest number in the series, which is 27, appears.

B8 ▾ fx =MAX(B1:B3)

	A	B	C	D	E	F
1		12	150			
2		27	85			
3		24	65			
4	Sum	63	300			
5						
6	Average	21	100			
7	Min	12				
8	Max	27				
9						

Count the Numbers in a Series of Numbers

You can use the count function to count the number of numbers in a series.

- ❖ Move to cell A9.
- ❖ Type Count.
- ❖ Press the right arrow key to move to cell B9.
- ❖ Choose the Home tab.
- ❖ Click the down arrow next to the AutoSum button Σ ▾.
- ❖ Click Count Numbers. Excel places the count function in cell C9 and takes a guess at which cells you want to count. The guess is incorrect, so you must select the proper cells.
- ❖ Select B1 to B3.
- ❖ Press Enter. The number of items in the series, which is 3, appears.

B9 ▾ fx =COUNT(B1:B3)

	A	B	C	D	E	F
1		12	150			
2		27	85			
3		24	65			
4	Sum	63	300			
5						
6	Average	21	100			
7	Min	12				
8	Max	27				
9	Count	3				
10						
11						

Create Headers and Footers

You can use the Header & Footer button on the Insert tab to create headers and footers. A header is text that appears at the top of every page of your printed worksheet. Footer is text that appears at the bottom of every page of your printed worksheet. When you click the Header & Footer button, the Design context tab appears and Excel changes to Page Layout view. A context tab is a tab that only appears when you need it. Page Layout view structures your worksheet so that you can easily change the format of your document. You usually work in Normal view.

You can type in your header or footer or you can use predefined headers and footers. To find predefined headers and footers, click the Header or Footer button or use the Header & Footer Elements group's buttons. When you choose a header or footer by clicking the Header or Footer button, Excel centers your choice. The table shown here describes each of the Header & Footer Elements group button options.

Header & Footer Elements	
Button	**Purpose**
Page Number	Inserts the page number.
Number of Pages	Inserts the number of pages in the document.
Current Time	Inserts the current time.
File Path	Inserts the path to the document.
File Name	Inserts the file name.
Sheet Name	Inserts the name of the worksheet.
Picture	Enables you to insert a picture.

Both the header and footer areas are divided into three sections: left, right, and center. When you choose a Header or Footer from the Header & Footer Elements group, where you place your information determines whether it appears on the left, right, or center of the printed page. You use the Go To Header and Go To Footer buttons on the Design tab to move between the header and footer areas of your worksheet.

Insert Headers and Footers

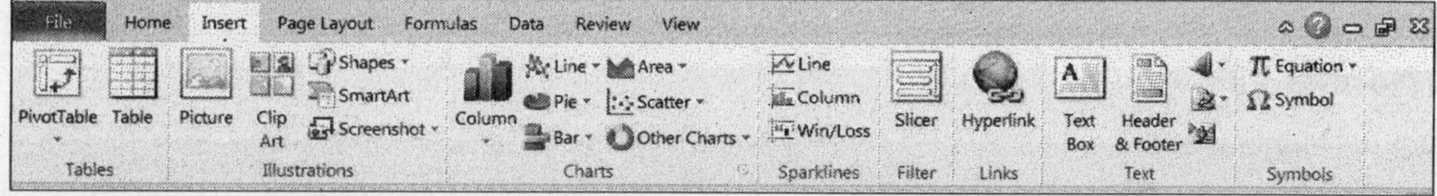

❖ Choose the Insert tab.

❖ Click the Header & Footer button in the Text group. Your worksheet changes to Page Layout view and the Design context tab appears. Note that your cursor is located in the center section of the header area.

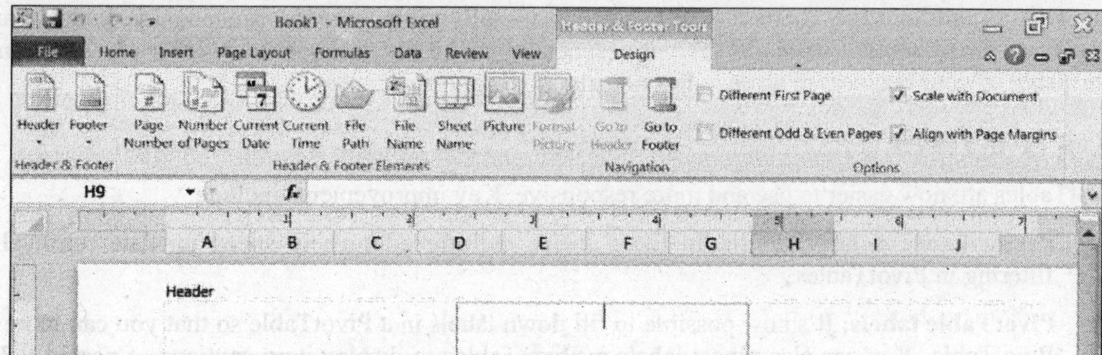

❖ Click the right side of the header area.

❖ Click Page Number in the Header & Footer Elements group. When you print your document, Excel will place the page number in the upper-right corner.

❖ Click the left side of the Header area.

- ❖ Type your name. When you print your document, Excel will place your name in the upper-left corner.
- ❖ Click the Go To Footer button. Excel moves to the footer area.
- ❖ Click the Footer button. A menu appears.
- ❖ Click the path to your document. Excel will place the path to your document at the bottom of every printed page.

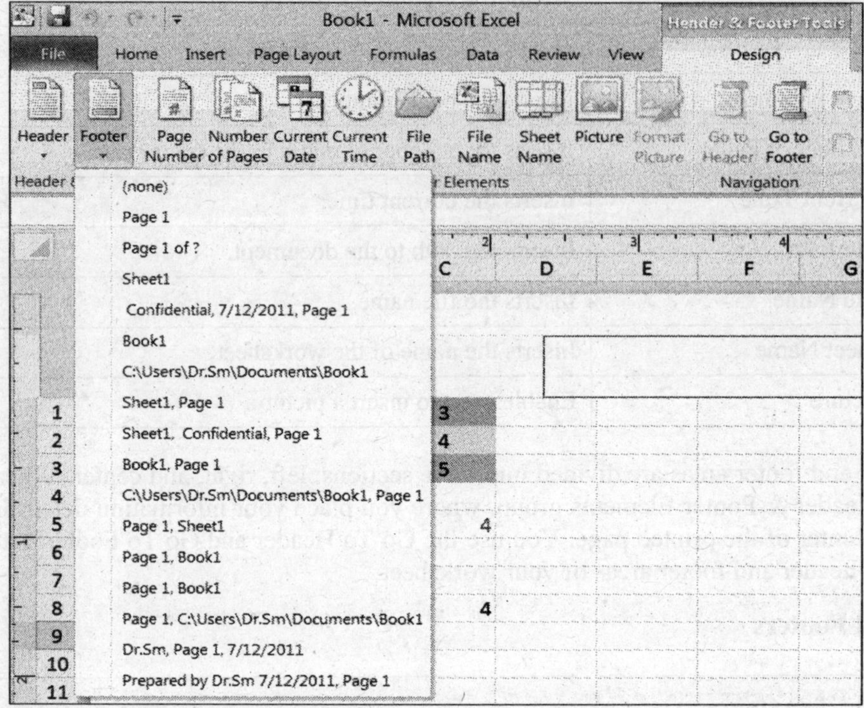

Return to Normal View

To return to Normal view:

- ❖ Choose the View tab.
- ❖ Click the Normal button in the Workbook Views group.

Sparklines

You can use sparklines tiny charts that fit in a cell to visually summarize trends alongside data. Because sparklines show trends in a small amount of space, they are especially useful for dashboards or other places where you need to show a snapshot of your business in an easy-to-understand visual format.

Improved PivotTables

PivotTables are now easier to use and more responsive. Key improvements include:

- ❖ **Performance enhancements:** In Excel 2010, multithreading help speed up data retrieval, sorting, and filtering in PivotTables.
- ❖ **PivotTable labels:** It's now possible to fill down labels in a PivotTable so that you can more easily use the PivotTable. You can also repeat labels in PivotTables to display item captions of nested fields in all rows and columns.
- ❖ **Enhanced filtering:** You can use slicers to filter data in a PivotTable with the click of a button and to quickly see which filters are applied without having to open additional menus.

- **Write-back support:** In Excel 2010, you can change values in the OLAP PivotTable Values area and have them written back to the Analysis Services cube on the OLAP server.
- **Show values As feature:** The Show Values As feature includes a number of new, automatic calculations, such as % of Parent Row Total, % of Parent Column Total, % of Parent Total, % Running Total, Rank Smallest to Largest, and Rank Largest to Smallest.
- **PivotChart improvements:** It's easier to filter data directly in a PivotChart report and to reorganize the chart's layout by adding and removing fields.

Slicers

New in Excel 2010, slicers offer a highly visual way to filter the data in PivotTables. Once you insert a slicer, you use buttons to quickly segment and filter the data to display just what you need. In addition, when you apply more than one filter to your PivotTable, you no longer have to open a list to see which filters are applied to the data. You can make slicers match your workbook formatting and easily reuse them in other PivotTables, PivotCharts, and cube functions.

Charts

Charts allow you to present information contained in the worksheet in a graphic format. Excel offers many types of charts including: Column, Line, Pie, Bar, Area, Scatter and more. To view the charts available click the Insert Tab on the Ribbon.

Create a Chart

To create a chart:

- Select the **cells** that contain the data you want to use in the chart
- Click the **Insert** tab on the Ribbon
- Click the type of **Chart** you want to create

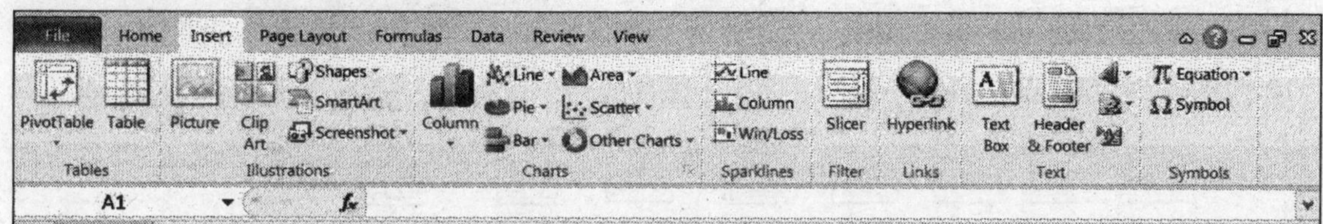

Modify a Chart

Once you have created a chart, you can do several things to modify the chart.

To move the chart:

- Click the **Chart** and **Drag** it another location on the same worksheet, or
- Click the **Move Chart** button on the **Design** tab
- Choose the desired location (either a new sheet or a current sheet in the workbook)

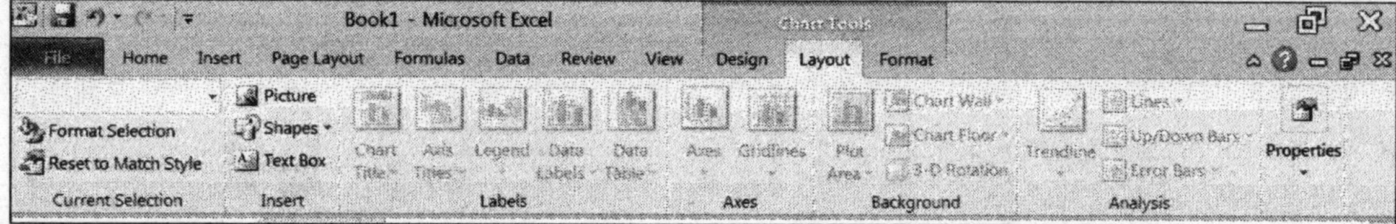

To change the data included in the chart:

- Click the **Chart**

❖ Click the **Select Data** button on the **Design** tab

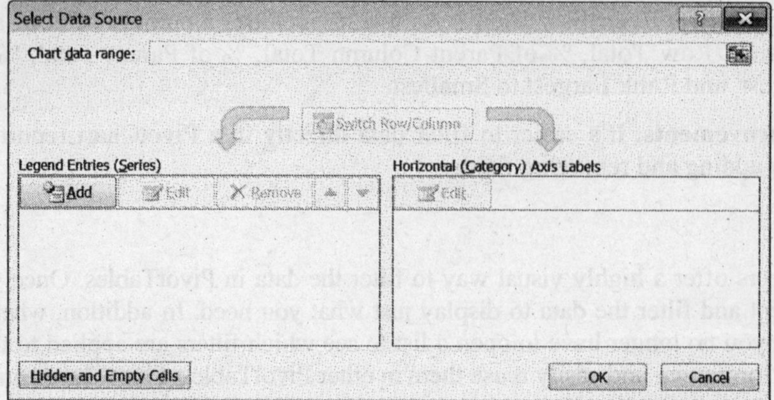

To reverse which data are displayed in the rows and columns:

❖ Click the Chart

❖ Click the Switch Row/Column button on the Design tab

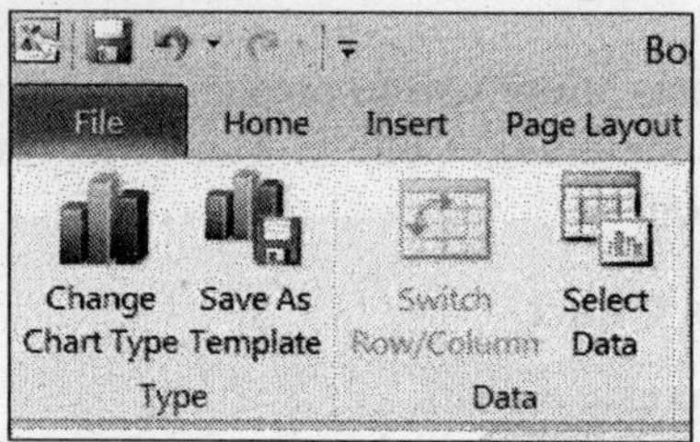

To modify the labels and titles:

❖ Click the Chart

❖ On the **Layout** tab, click the **Chart Title** or the **Data Labels** button

❖ Change the **Title** and click **Enter**

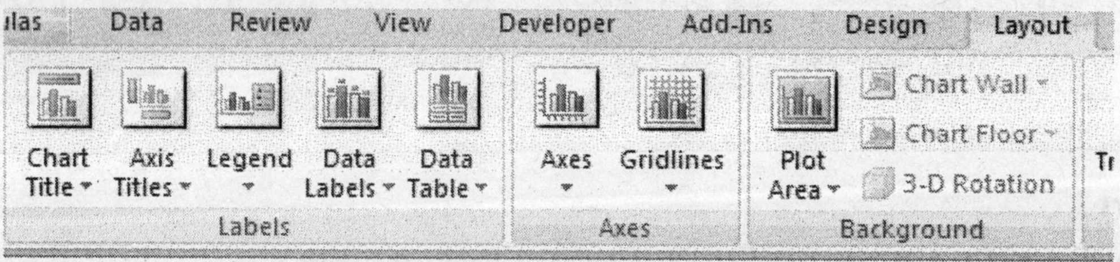

Chart Tools

The Chart Tools appear on the Ribbon when you click on the chart. The tools are located on three tabs: design, layout, and format.

Within the **Design** tab, you can control the chart type, layout, styles, and location. Within the **Layout** tab, you can control inserting pictures, shapes and text boxes, labels, axes, background, and analysis.

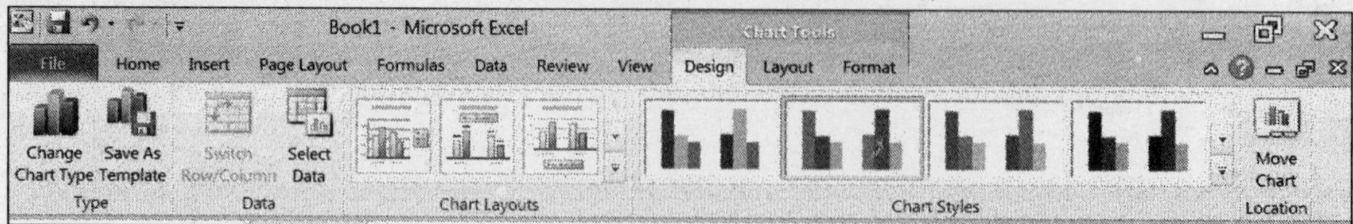

Within the **Format** tab, you can modify shape styles, word styles and size of the chart.

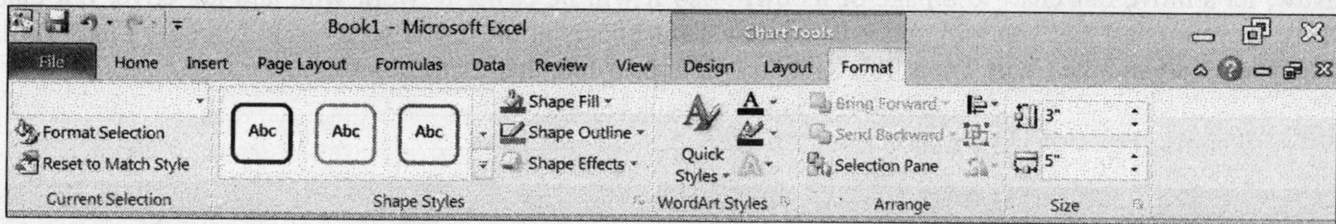

Copy a Chart to Word

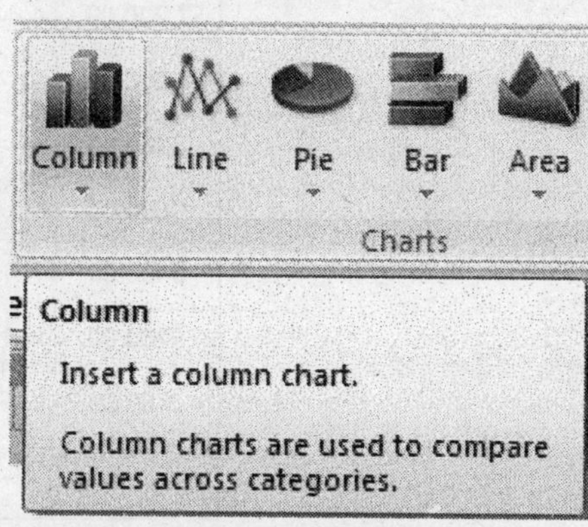

- ❖ Select the **chart**
- ❖ Click **Copy** on the **File** tab
- ❖ Go to the **Word** document where you want the chart located
- ❖ Click **Paste** on the **File** tab

We'll use a Column Chart. Move your cursor over Column and an image like the one on the right will appear.

Click the **Column button** and you'll see an image like the one on the left. As you can see there all kinds of Column Charts. We'll begin with a simple two dimension **2-D Column** chart. You'll be able to change this later, if you desire – to another Column Chart of one of the other selections.

Click on the 2-D Column chart indicated by the arrow on the left.

As soon as you click, because you highlighted your data, an image similar to the one below will appear. Don't worry that the Chart is covering your data – we'll take care of that in a minute.

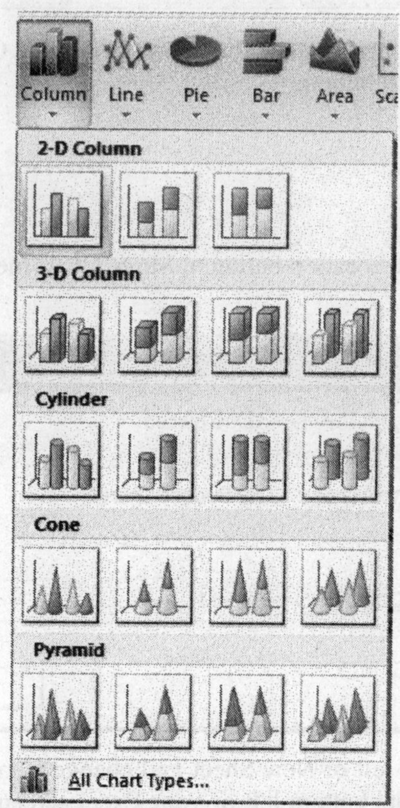

Now, let's move our chart to a page of its own – so it will be easier to work with and not cover our data. Click anywhere on your chart and you will notice that a new Tab appears at the top of your Excel screen – Chart Tools. Click the Chart tools Tab and the Chart Tools Tab/Ribbon will appear like the image below.

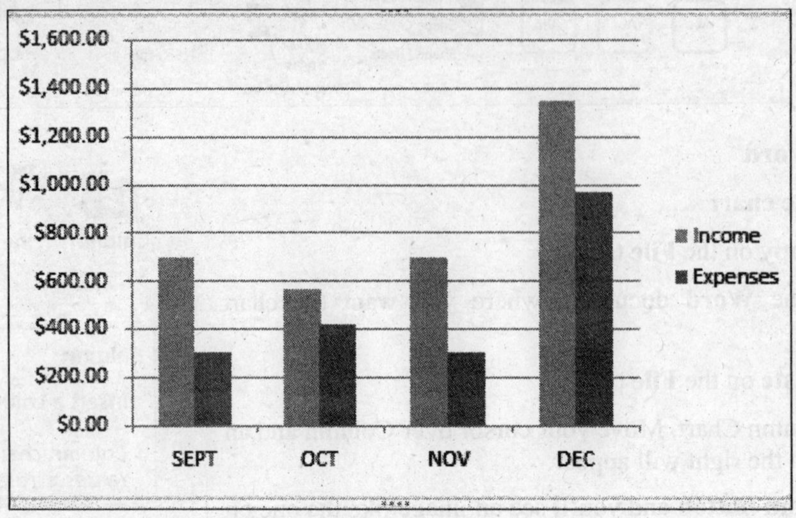

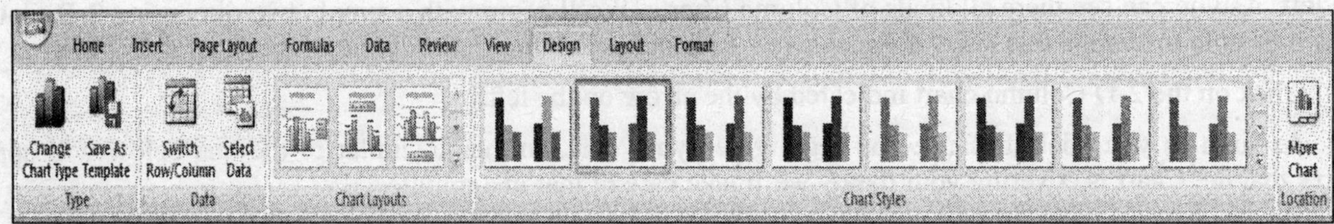

Notice, on the right end of the Chart Tools Tab/Ribbon is a Move Chart Location button. Click the Move Chart Location button.

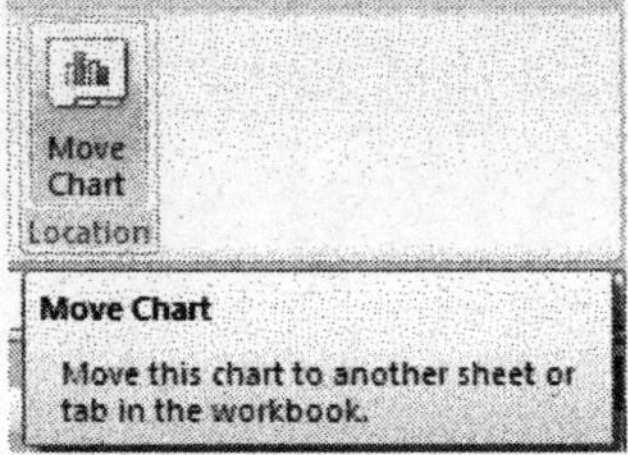

When you click the Move Chart Location button, a Move Chart menu screen will appear (like the image below).

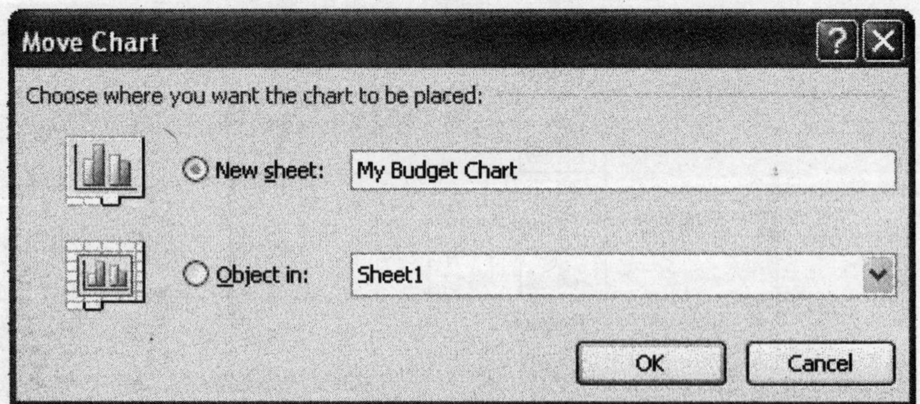

Click on the small circle to the left of New Sheet and change Chart 1 to My Budget Chart – as indicated above. Then click the OK button. Look at the bottom left of your Excel screen. You will see a new Tab – My Budget Chart! Your data is on Sheet1. We'll rename it when we have finished working with our chart.

You should be on you're My Budget Chart Tab. If not, click this tab. Your chart should now fill the Excel screen. Click in one of the outside corners of your chart.

Chart Styles

A **Chart Styles menu screen** (similar to the one **below**) will **appear**. You can **click** the various choices as you desire. Each time you click, you're My Budget Chart will change to the Style you chose.

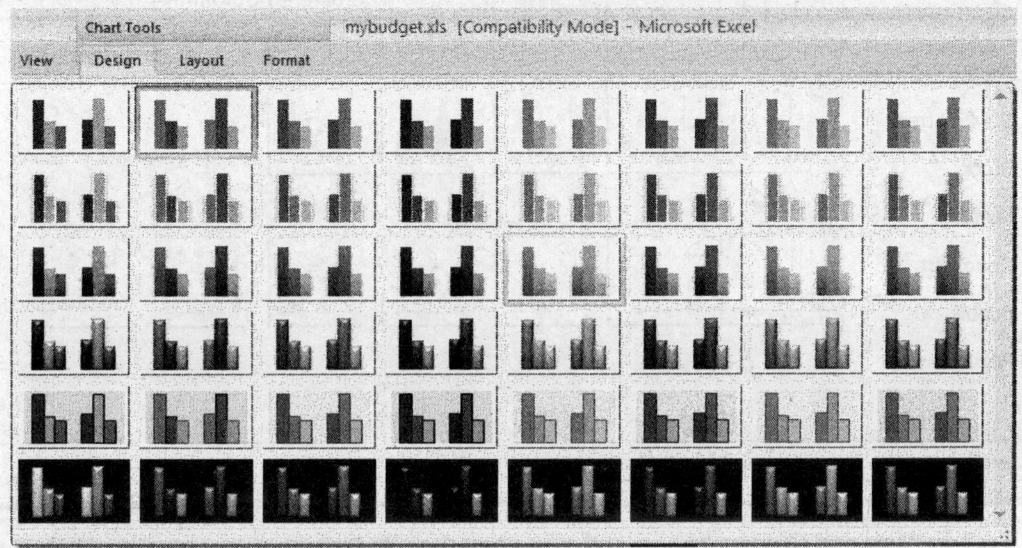

If you don't like the Chart Styles, you can use the Undo Arrow (in the Quick Access Toolbar) to remove them. A note – as you choose different Chart Types, you will see the Chart Styles menu (above) change to that new Chart Type.

We'll show you another way to enhance the colors of your bars in a moment.

If you would like to change your Chart Type – look in the upper left corner of the Chart Tools Ribbon. You'll see a Change Chart Type button.

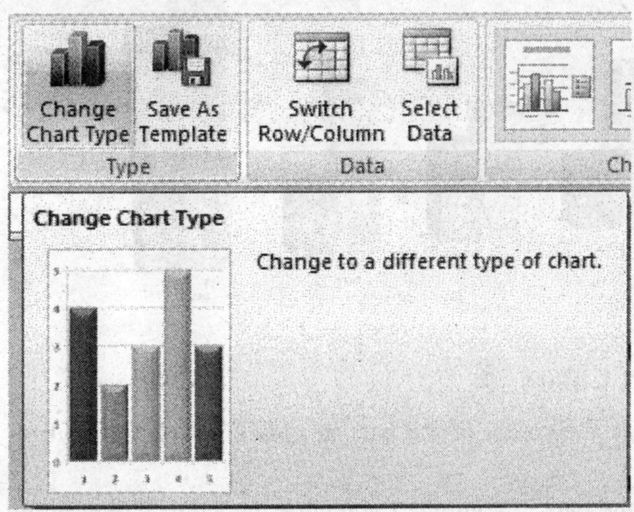

Click the Change Chart Type button.

A Change Chart Type menu screen (below) will appear. Currently it is "on" our 2-D Column Chart. We'll change it to a 3-D Clustered Column chart next.

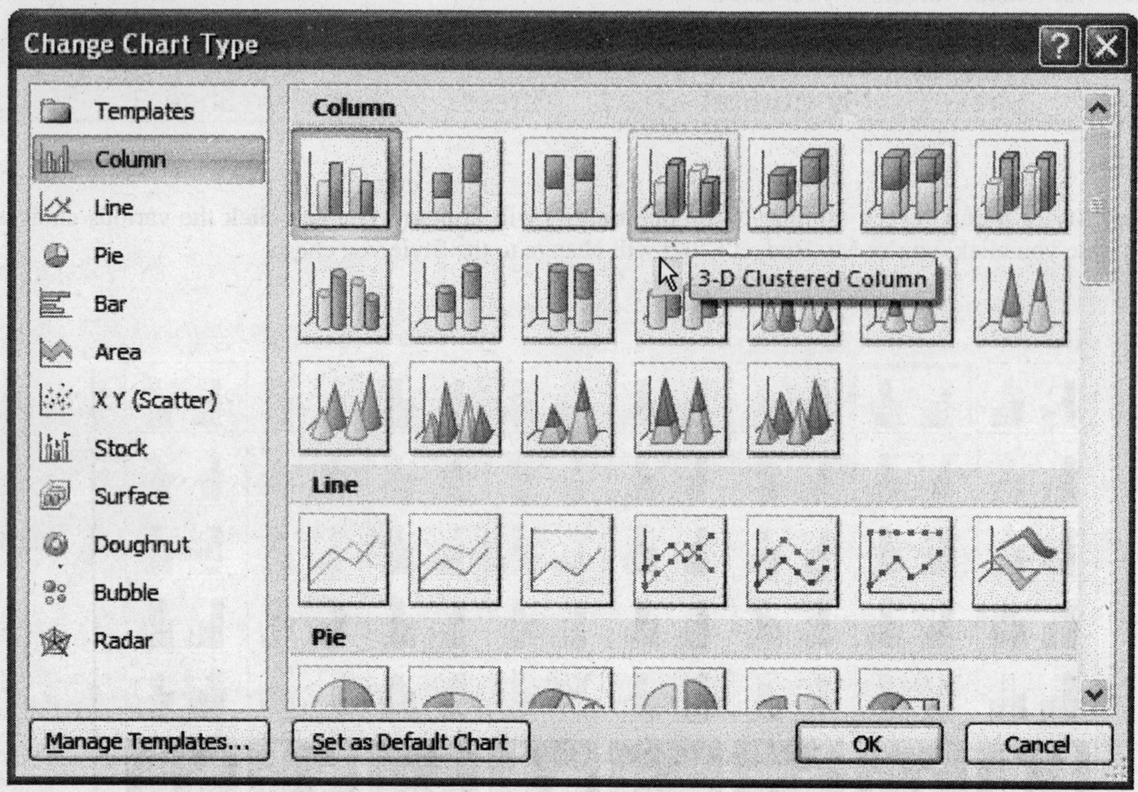

We'll click the 3-D Clustered Column choice and then click the OK button. As soon as we click the OK button, our entire chart changes to a 3-D Chart.

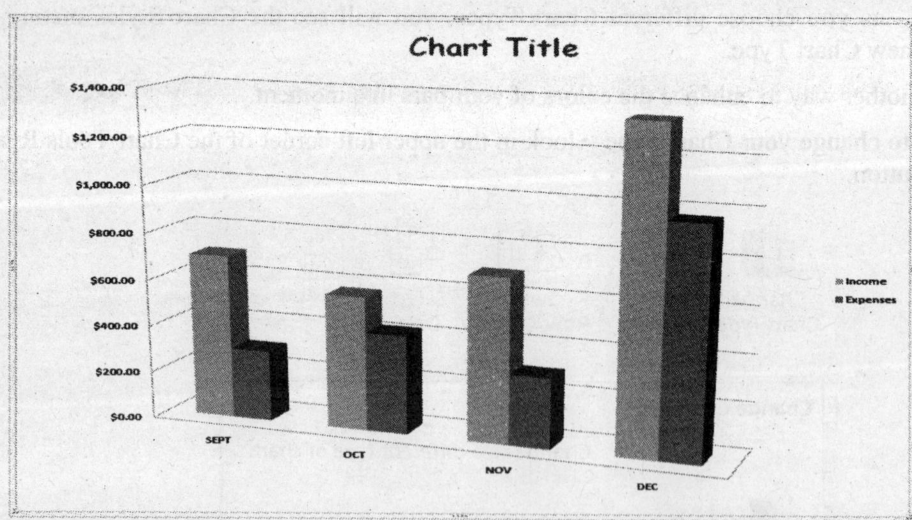

Another Way to Change Chart Colors

You saw how you could change the colors of the bars in your chart (Chart Styles). Here is the second way to change colors.

Move your cursor over one of the bars in your chart and click the RIGHT mouse button. When the pop-up menu appears, click the Format Data Series… selection.

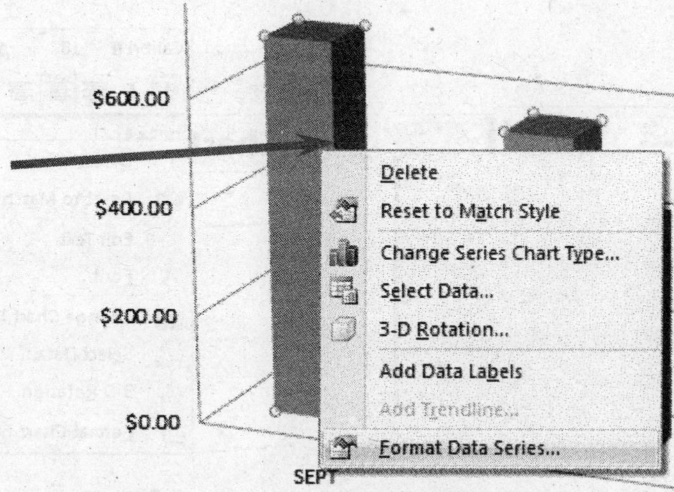

A Format Data Series menu screen (like the one below) will appear "over" your chart. In our original chart, the Income bars were blue. You think green would be a better color for our Income bars. So, you clicked the Fill choice on the left. When the Fill menu appeared on the right, we clicked the small circle to the left of Solid fill and then clicked the down-arrow on the right side of the Color button. Then we clicked the green color choice. As soon as you clicked, our Income bars changed to green.

Notice the other choices in the Fill menu area. Experiment with the other choices as you desire. You can really get some neat effects with Gradient and Picture or texture fill.

When you are **finished,** click the **Close** button.

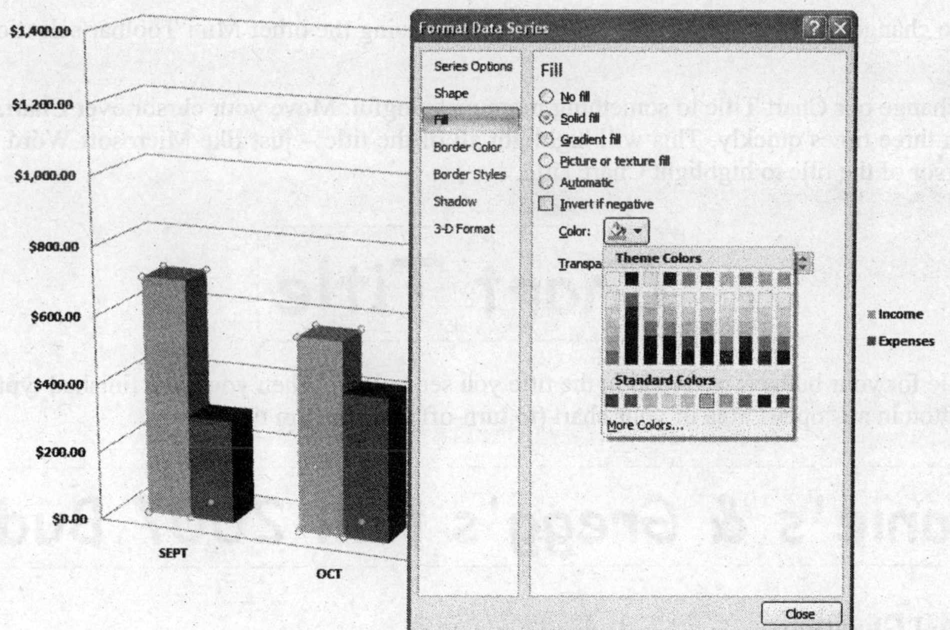

Changing Text

To change text in Excel 2010 you need to click on the text, the Legend, or the axis on which the text is located.

We RIGHT clicked on our Chart Title and two menus appeared. The upper menu is another new, great feature in Excel 2010. It's called the Mini Toolbar. The lower menu is the standard menu that appeared previously.

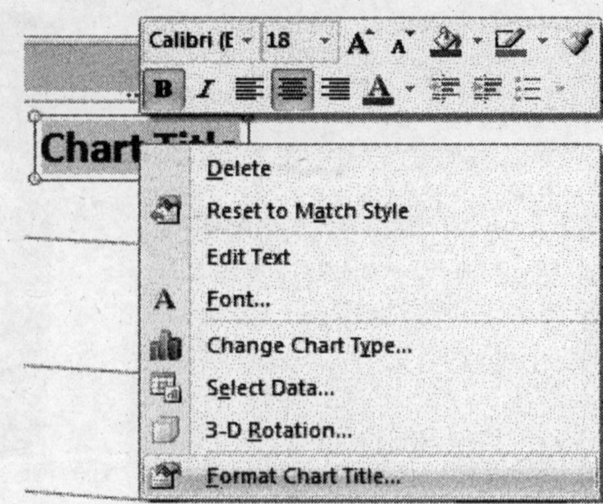

We clicked the down arrow to the right of Calibri and a drop-down menu of font choices appeared. We moved down the list and clicked-on Comic Sans MS. You move down the menu and choose a font you like.

As soon as we clicked our font choice, our Chart Title changed to that font.

You can also change the Font size, Bold, Color, and more using the other Mini Toolbar selections. Experiment as you desire.

Now we'll change our Chart Title to something more meaningful. Move your cursor over Chart Title and click the left mouse button three times quickly. This will highlight all of the title – just like Microsoft Word. Or, you can click and drag your cursor of the title to highlight Chart Title.

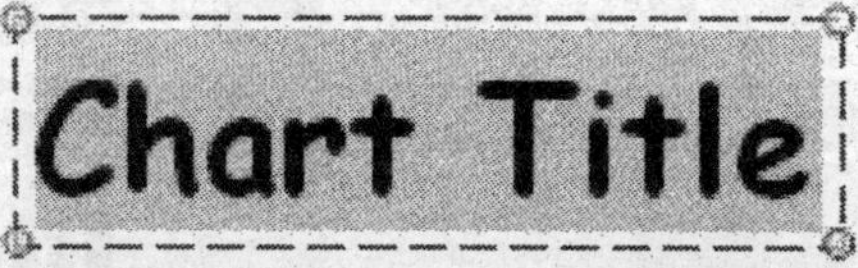

Type in a title for your budget, we typed in the title you see below. When you have finished typing your title, click the left mouse button in an "open" area of your chart (to turn-off and confirm the title).

Janie's & Gregg's Fall 2007 Budget

Some Additional Charting

Excel 2010 have new feature called sparklines. It has three buttons. They are line, column and win/loss. This will be useful for seeing the share price movement in the stock market.

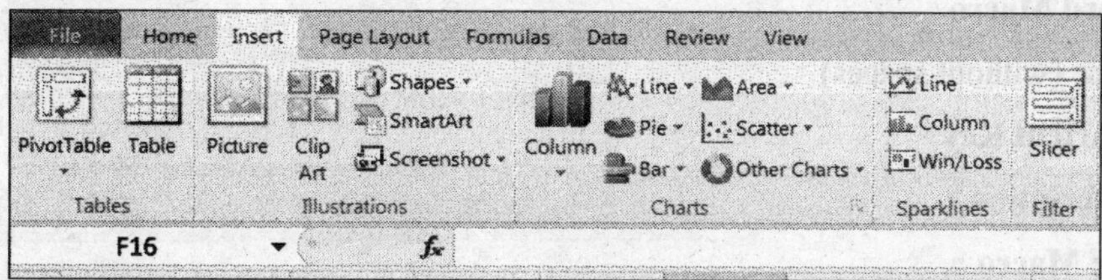

Design of Sparkline enables to edit data and it show the Sparkline in following point they are high, low, first, last, negative and markers.

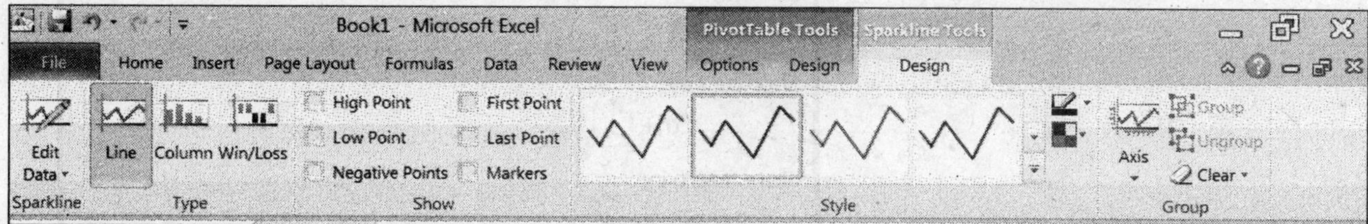

Below screen shows the Sparkline line, column and win/loss diagram. You can also change the design color of Sparkline.

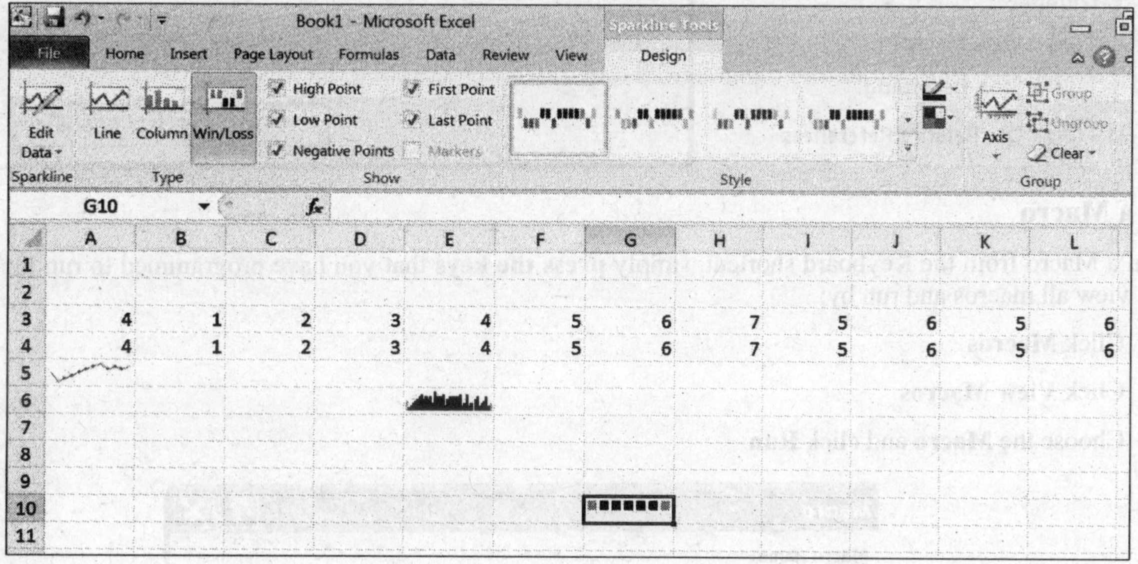

Macros

Macros are advanced features that can speed up editing or formatting you may perform often in an Excel worksheet. They record sequences of menu selections that you choose so that a series of actions can be completed in one step.

Recording a Macro

To record a Macro:

- Click the **View** tab on the Ribbon
- Click **Macros**

- Click **Record Macro**
- Enter a name (without spaces)
- Enter a **Shortcut Key**
- Enter a **Description**
- Perform the **Macro**
- Click **Marcos**
- Click **Stop Recording**

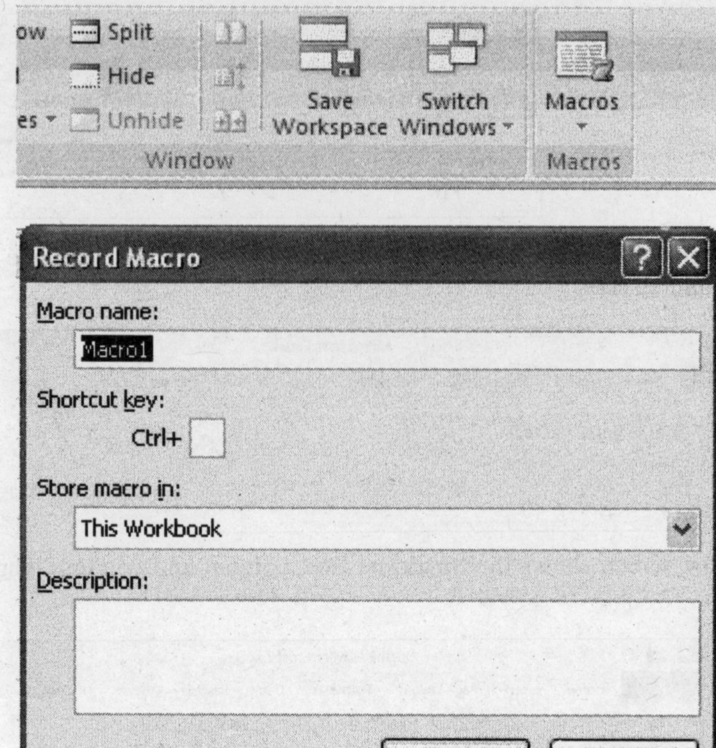

Running a Macro

To run a Macro from the Keyboard shortcut, simply **press the keys** that you have programmed to run the Macro. Or you can view all macros and run by:

- Click **Macros**
- Click **View Macros**
- Choose the **Macro** and click **Run**

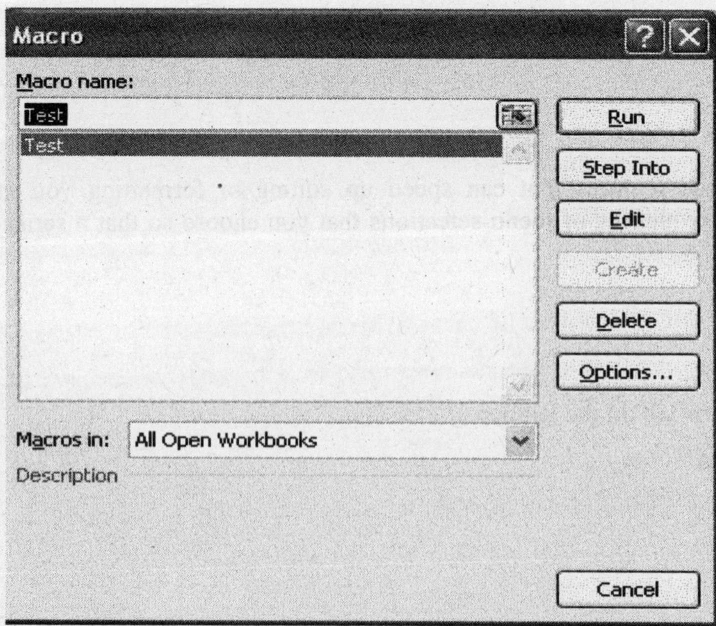

Sort and Filter

Sorting and Filtering allow you to manipulate data in a worksheet based on given set of criteria.

Basic Sorts

To execute a basic descending or ascending sort based on one column:

- ❖ Highlight the cells that will be sorted
- ❖ Click the **Sort & Filter** button on the **Home** tab
- ❖ Click the **Sort Ascending** (A-Z) button or **Sort Descending** (Z-A) button

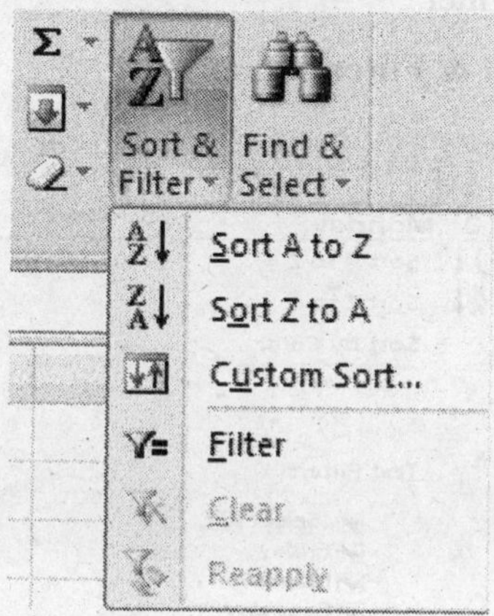

Custom Sorts

To sort on the basis of more than one column:

- ❖ Click the **Sort & Filter** button on the **Home** tab
- ❖ Choose which column you want to sort by first
- ❖ Click **Add Level**
- ❖ Choose the next column you want to sort
- ❖ Click **OK**

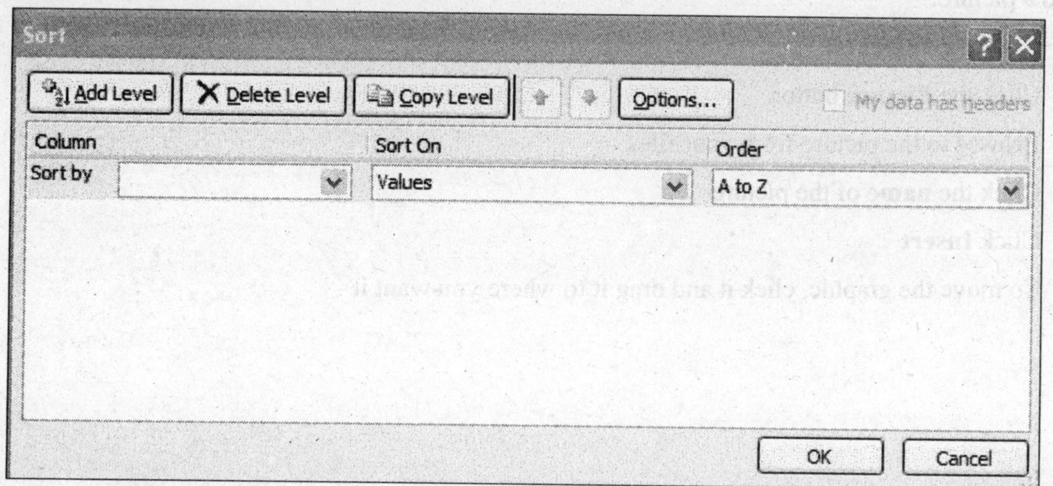

Filtering

Filtering allows you to display only data that meets certain criteria. To filter:

- ❖ Click the column or columns that contain the data you wish to filter
- ❖ On the **Home** tab, click on **Sort & Filter**
- ❖ Click **Filter** button
- ❖ Click the **Arrow** at the bottom of the first cell
- ❖ Click the **Text Filter**
- ❖ Click the **Words** you wish to Filter
- ❖ To clear the filter click the **Sort & Filter** button
- ❖ Click **Clear**

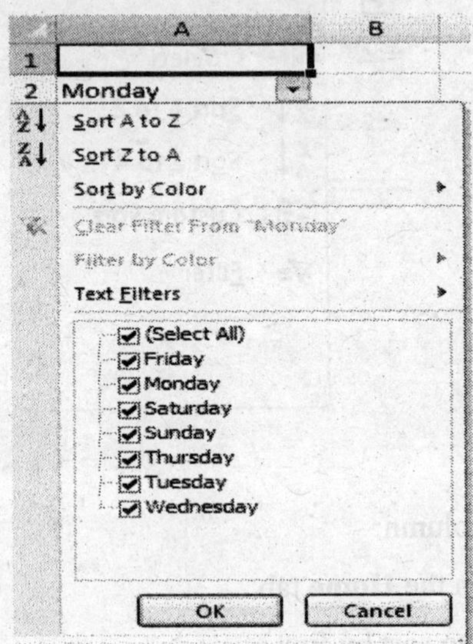

Graphics

Adding a Picture

To add a picture:

- ❖ Click the **Insert** tab
- ❖ Click the **Picture** button
- ❖ Browse to the picture from your files
- ❖ Click the **name** of the picture
- ❖ Click **Insert**
- ❖ To move the graphic, click it and drag it to where you want it

Adding Clip Art

To add Clip Art:

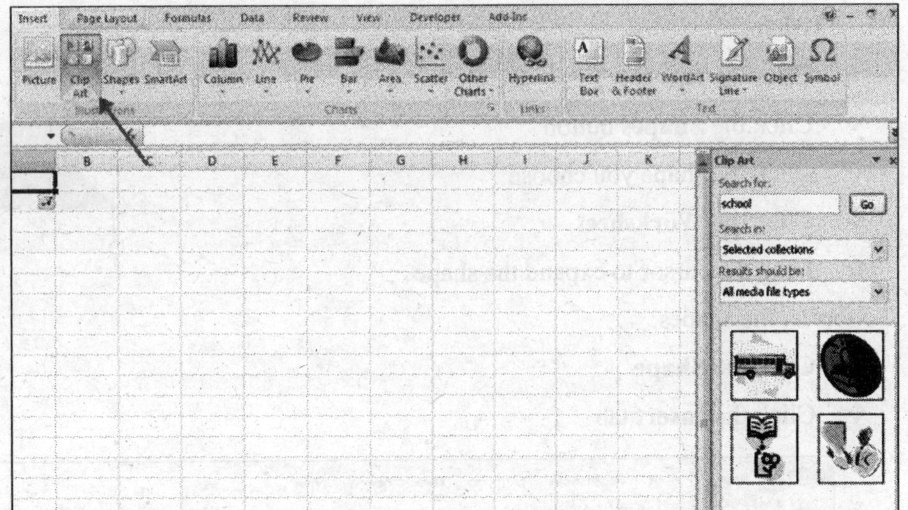

- Click the **Insert** tab
- Click the **Clip Art** button
- Search for the clip art using the search **Clip Art** dialog box
- Click the **clip art**
- To move the graphic, click it and drag it to where you want it

Editing Pictures and Clip Art

When you add a graphic to the worksheet, an additional tab appears on the Ribbon. The Format tab allows you to format the pictures and graphics. This tab has four groups:

- **Adjust:** Controls the picture brightness, contrast, and colors
- **Picture Style:** Allows you to place a frame or border around the picture and add effects

- **Arrange:** Controls the alignment and rotation of the picture
- **Size:** Cropping and size of graphic

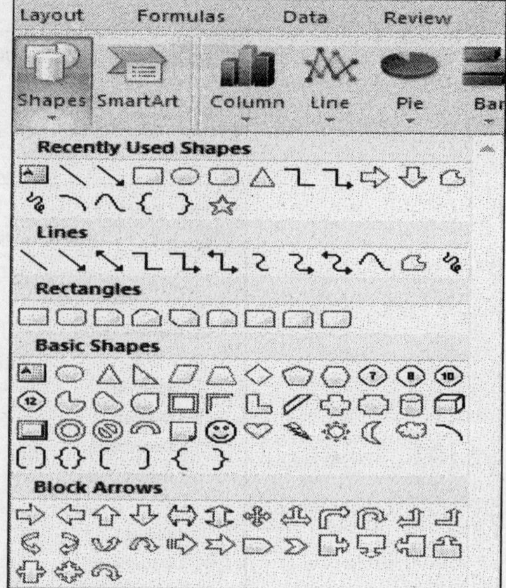

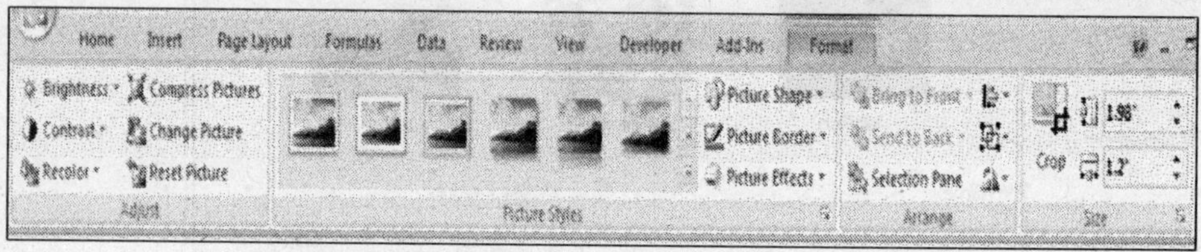

Adding

Shapes

To add Shape:

- Click the **Insert** tab
- Click the **Shapes** button
- Click the shape you choose
- Click the **Worksheet**
- Drag the cursor to expand the shape

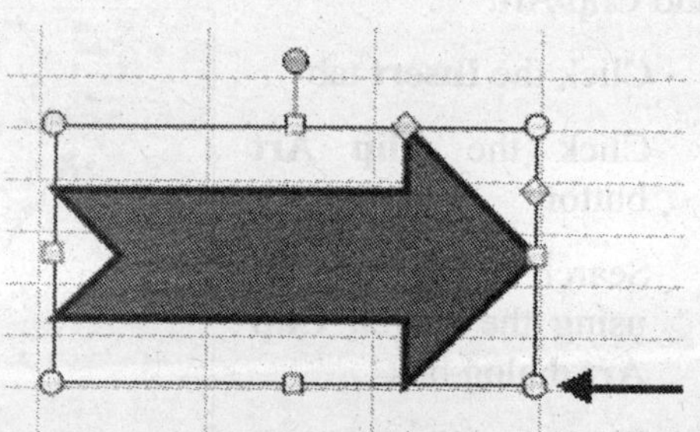

To format the shapes:

- Click the **Shape**
- Click the **Insert** tab

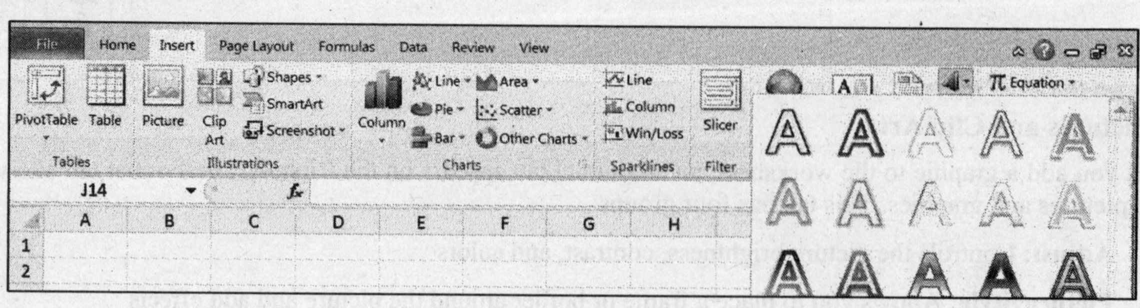

Adding SmartArt

SmartArt is a feature in Office 2007 that allows you to choose from a variety of graphics, including flow charts, lists, cycles, and processes. To add SmartArt:

- ❖ Click the **Insert** tab
- ❖ Click the **SmartArt** button
- ❖ Click the **SmartArt** you choose
- ❖ Select the **SmartArt**
- ❖ Drag it to the desired location in the worksheet

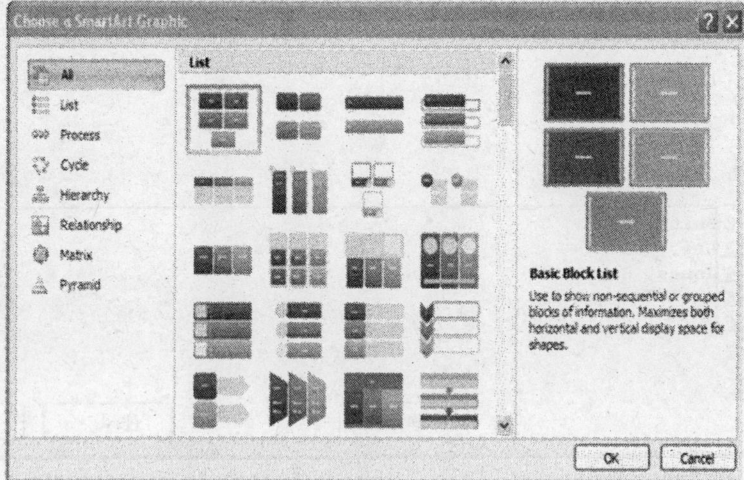

To format the SmartArt:

- ❖ Select the **SmartArt**
- ❖ Click either the **Design** or the **Format** tab
- ❖ Click the **SmartArt** to add text and pictures

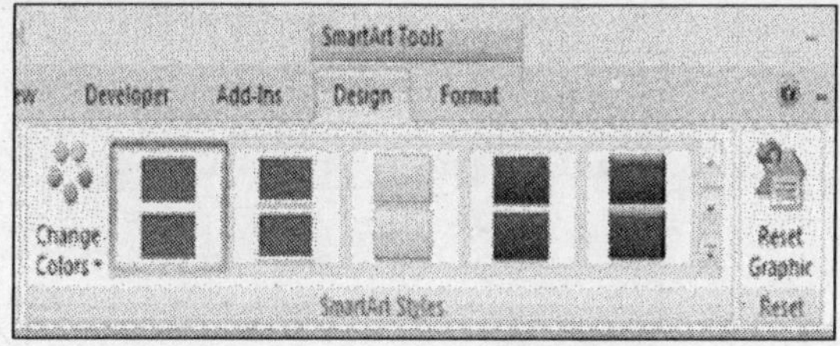

Formatting a Worksheet

Convert Text to Columns

Sometimes you will want to split data in one cell into two or more cells. You can do this easily by utilizing the Convert Text to Columns Wizard.

- ❖ Highlight the column in which you wish to split the data
- ❖ Click the **Text to Columns** button on the **Data** tab
- ❖ Click **Delimited** if you have a comma or tab separating the data, or click fixed widths to set the data separation at a specific size

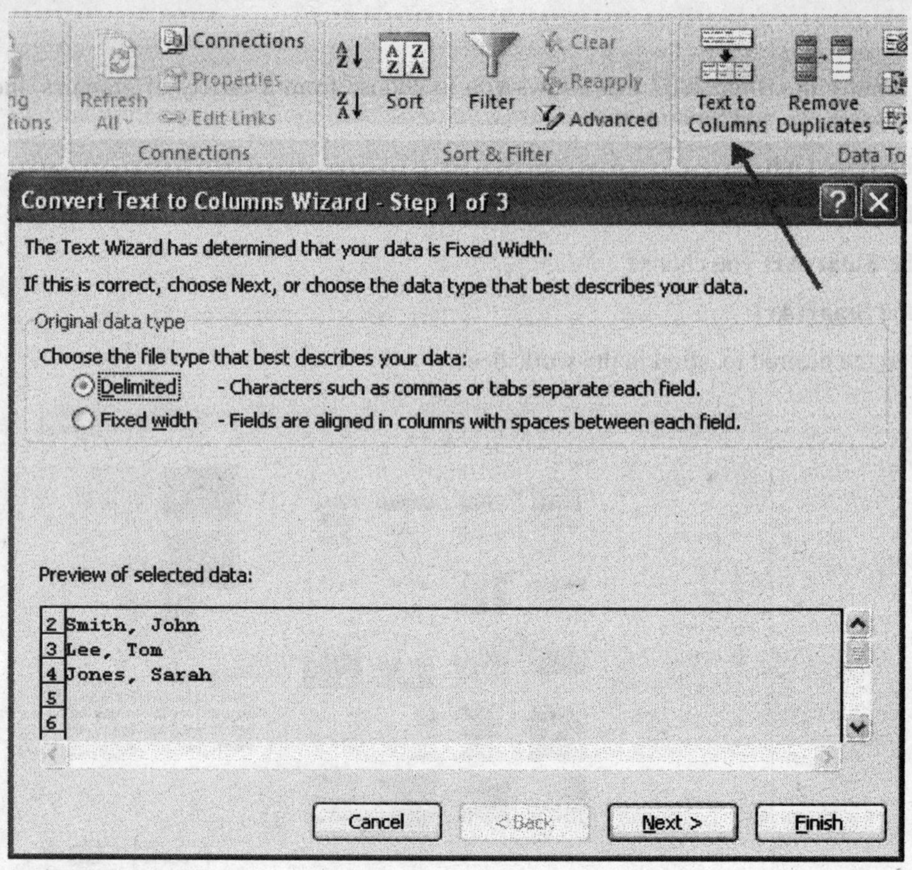

Modify Fonts

Modifying fonts in Excel will allow you to emphasize titles and headings. To modify a font:

- ❖ Select the cell or cells that you would like the font applied
- ❖ On the **Font** group on the **Home** tab, choose the font type, size, bold, italics, underline, or color

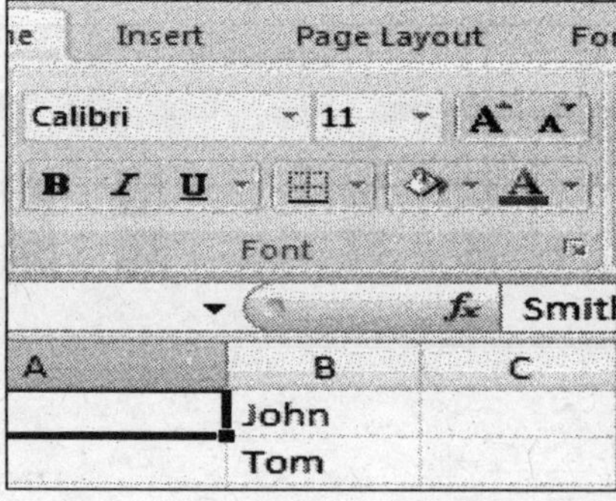

Format Cells Dialog Box

In Excel, you can also apply specific formatting to a cell. To apply formatting to a cell or group of cells:

- ❖ Select the cell or cells that will have the formatting
- ❖ Click the **Dialog Box** arrow on the **Alignment** group of the **Home** tab

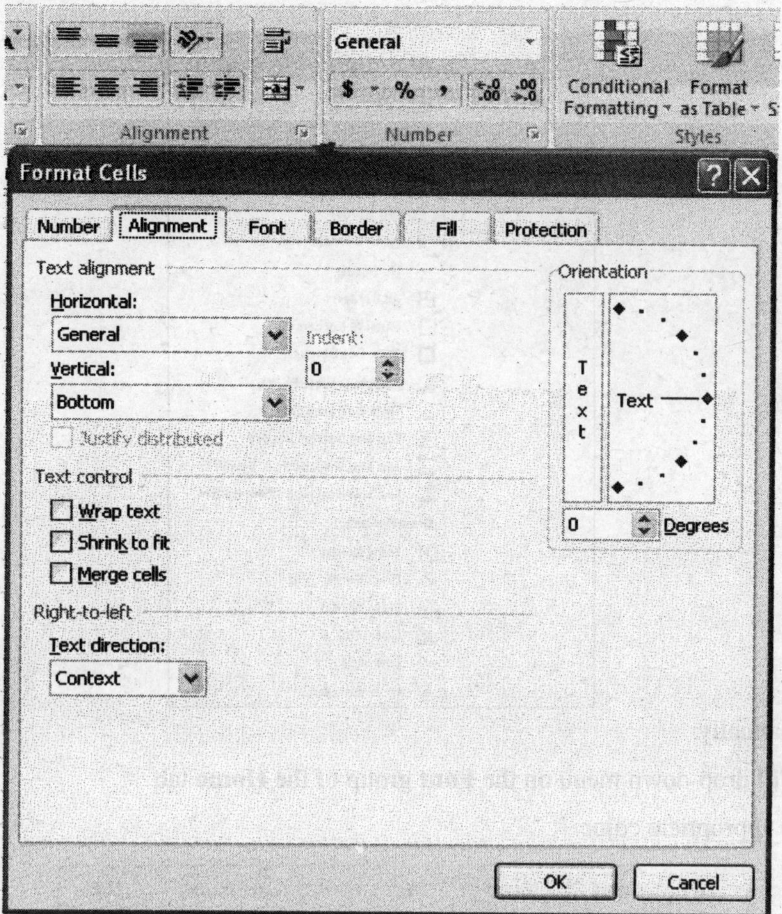

There are several tabs on this dialog box that allow you to modify properties of the cell or cells.

- **Number:** Allows for the display of different number types and decimal places
- **Alignment:** Allows for the horizontal and vertical alignment of text, wrap text, shrink text, merge cells and the direction of the text
- **Font:** Allows for control of font, font style, size, color, and additional features
- **Border:** Border styles and colors
- **Fill:** Cell fill colors and styles

Add Borders and Colors to Cells

Borders and colors can be added to cells manually or through the use of styles. To add borders manually:

- Click the **Borders** drop-down menu on the **Font** group of the **Home** tab
- Choose the appropriate border

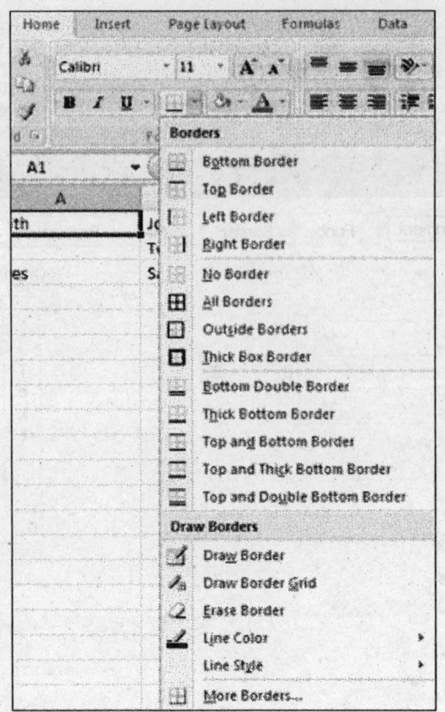

To apply colors manually:

- ❖ Click the **Fill** drop-down menu on the **Font** group of the **Home** tab
- ❖ Choose the appropriate color

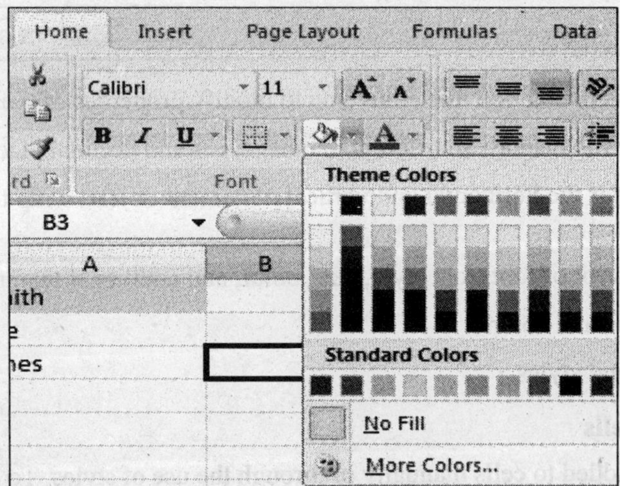

To apply borders and colors using styles:

- ❖ Click **Cell** Styles on the **Home** tab
- ❖ Choose a style or click **New Cell Style**

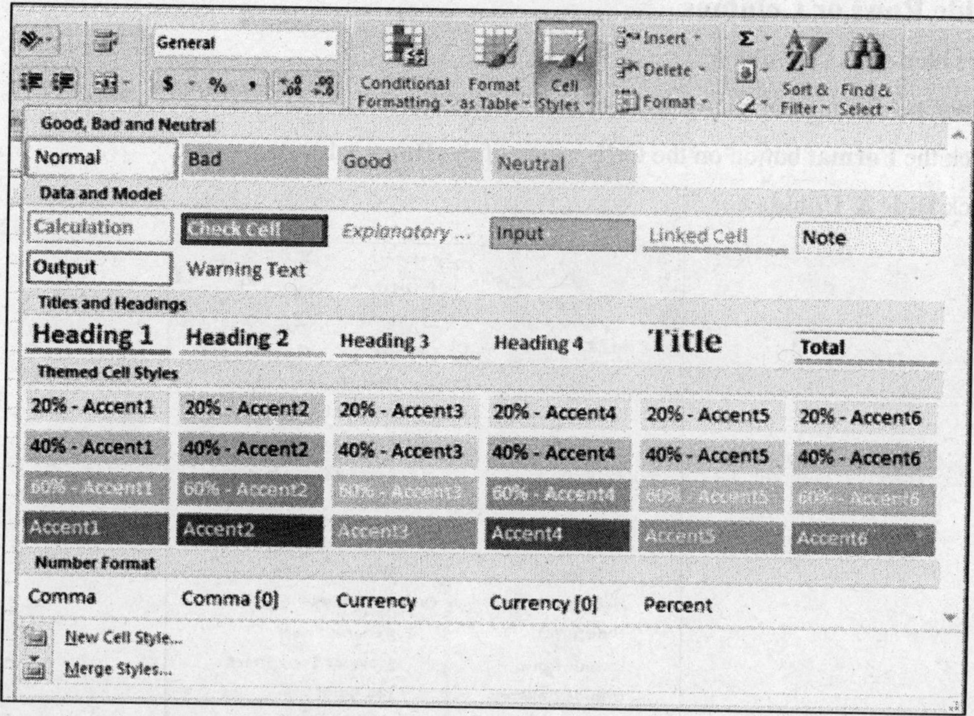

Change Column Width and Row Height

To change the width of a column or the height of a row:

- ❖ Click the **Format** button on the **Cells** group of the **Home** tab
- ❖ Manually adjust the height and width by clicking **Row Height** or **Column Width**
- ❖ To use **AutoFit** click **AutoFit Row Height** or **AutoFit Column Width**

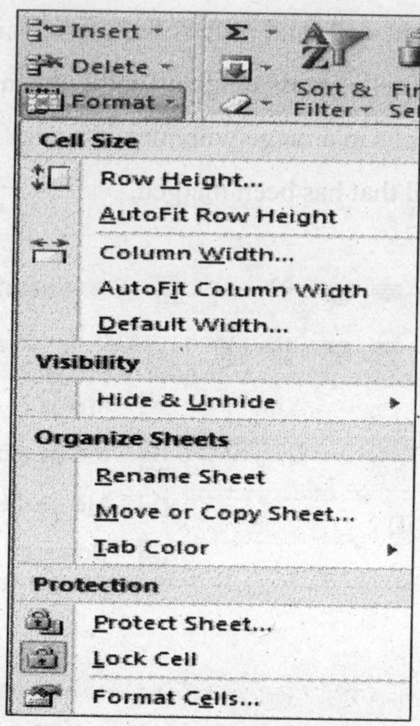

Hide or Unhide Rows or Columns

To hide or unhide rows or columns:

- ❖ Select the row or column you wish to hide or unhide
- ❖ Click the **Format** button on the **Cells** group of the **Home** tab
- ❖ Click **Hide & Unhide**

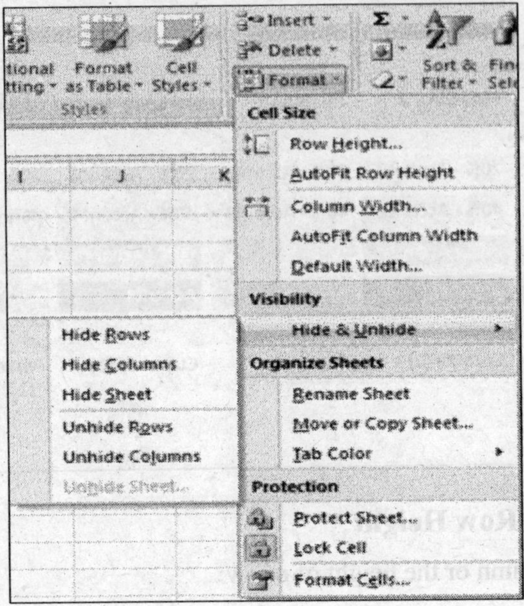

Merge Cells

To merge cells, select the cells you want to merge and click the **Merge & Center** button on the **Alignment** group of the **Home** tab. The four choices for merging cells are:

- ❖ **Merge & Center:** Combines the cells and centers the contents in the new, larger cell
- ❖ **Merge Across:** Combines the cells across columns without centering data
- ❖ **Merge Cells:** Combines the cells in a range without centering
- ❖ **Unmerge Cells:** Splits the cell that has been merged

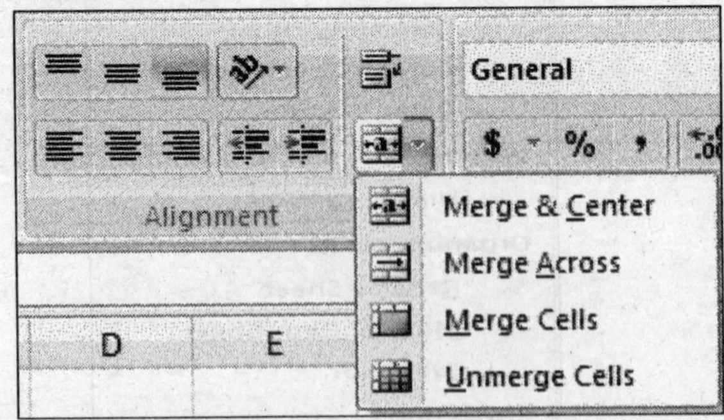

Align Cell Contents

To align cell contents, click the cell or cells you want to align and click on the options within the **Alignment** group on the **Home** tab. There are several options for alignment of cell contents:

- **Top Align:** Aligns text to the top of the cell
- **Middle Align:** Aligns text between the top and bottom of the cell
- **Bottom Align:** Aligns text to the bottom of the cell
- **Align Text Left:** Aligns text to the left of the cell
- **Center:** Centers the text from left to right in the cell
- **Align Text Right:** Aligns text to the right of the cell
- **Decrease Indent:** Decreases the indent between the left border and the text
- **Increase Indent:** Increase the indent between the left border and the text
- **Orientation:** Rotate the text diagonally or vertically

Developing a Worksheet

Format Worksheet Tab

You can rename a worksheet or change the color of the tabs to meet your needs. To rename a worksheet:

- Open the sheet to be renamed
- Click the **Format** button on the **Home** tab
- Click **Rename** sheet
- Type in a new name
- Press **Enter**

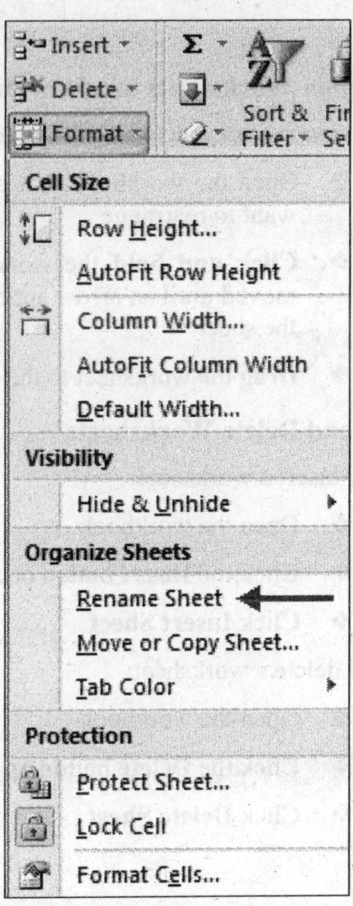

To change the color of a worksheet tab:

- ❖ Open the sheet to be renamed
- ❖ Click the **Format** button on the **Home** tab
- ❖ Click **Tab Color**
- ❖ Click the color

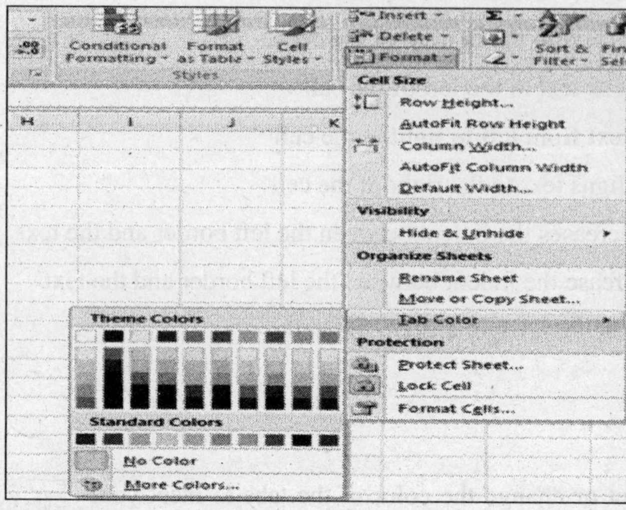

Reposition Worksheets in a Workbook

To move worksheets in a workbook:

- ❖ Open the workbook that contains the sheets you want to rearrange
- ❖ **Click and hold** the worksheet tab that will be moved until an arrow appears in the left corner of the sheet
- ❖ **Drag** the worksheet to the desired location

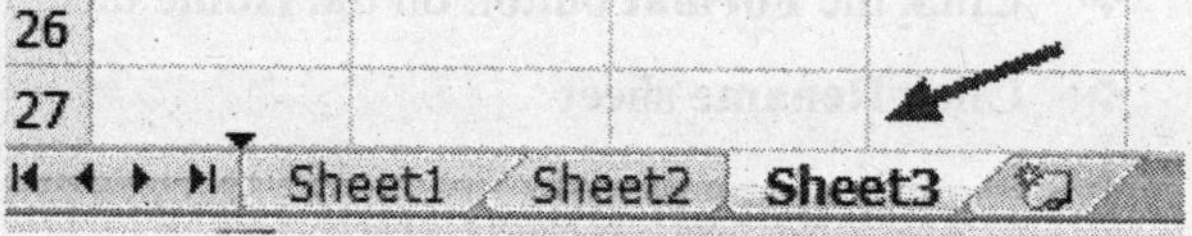

Insert and Delete Worksheets

To insert a worksheet:

- ❖ Open the workbook
- ❖ Click the **Insert** button on the **Cells** group of the **Home** tab
- ❖ Click **Insert Sheet**

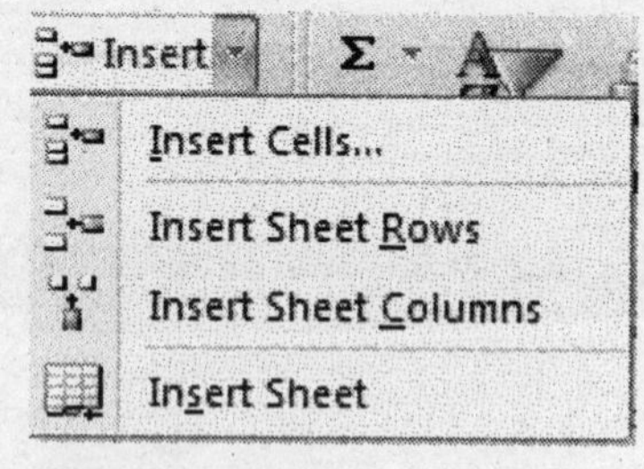

To delete a worksheet:

- ❖ Open the workbook
- ❖ Click the **Delete** button on the **Cells** group of the **Home** tab
- ❖ Click **Delete Sheet**

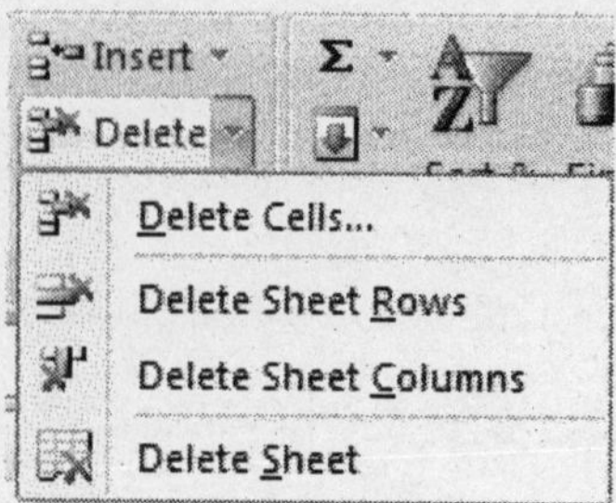

Copy and Paste Worksheets

To copy and paste a worksheet:

❖ Click the tab of the worksheet to be copied

❖ **Right click** and choose **Move** or **Copy**

❖ Choose the desired position of the sheet

❖ Click the check box next to **Create a Copy**

❖ Click **OK**

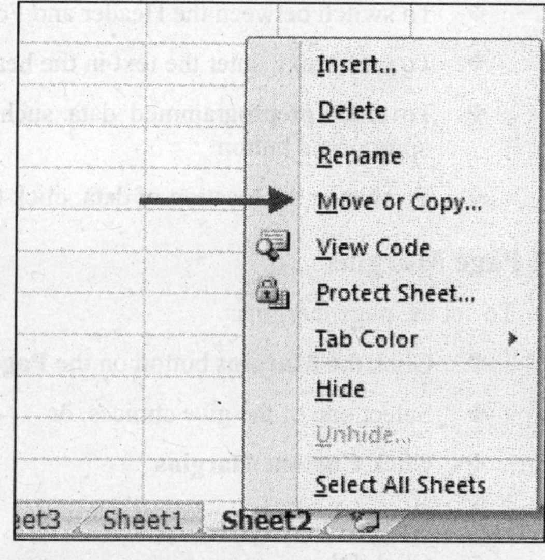

Printing

Set Print Titles

The print titles function allows you to repeat the column and row headings at the beginning of each new page to make reading a multiple page sheet easier to read when printed. To print titles:

❖ Click the **Page Layout** tab on the Ribbon

❖ Click the **Print Titles** button

❖ In the **Print Titles** section, click the box to select the rows/columns to be repeated

❖ Select the row or column

❖ Click the **Select Row/Column Button**

❖ Click OK

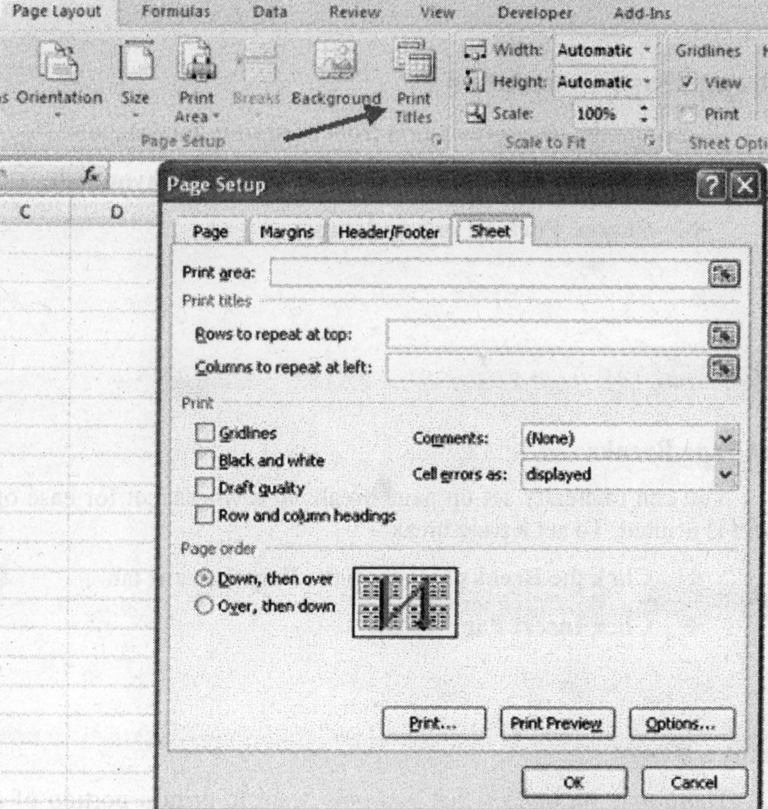

Create a Header or Footer

To create a header or footer:

❖ Click the **Header & Footer** button on the **Insert** tab

❖ This will display the **Header & Footer Design Tools Tab**

- ❖ To switch between the Header and Footer, click the **Go to Header** or **Go to Footer** button
- ❖ To insert text, enter the text in the header or footer
- ❖ To enter preprogrammed data such as page numbers, date, time, file name or sheet name, click the appropriate button
- ❖ To change the location of data, click the desired cell

Set Page Margins

To set the page margins:

- ❖ Click the **Margins** button on the **Page Layout** tab
- ❖ Select one of the give choices, or
- ❖ Click **Custom Margins**
- ❖ Complete the boxes to set margins
- ❖ Click **Ok**

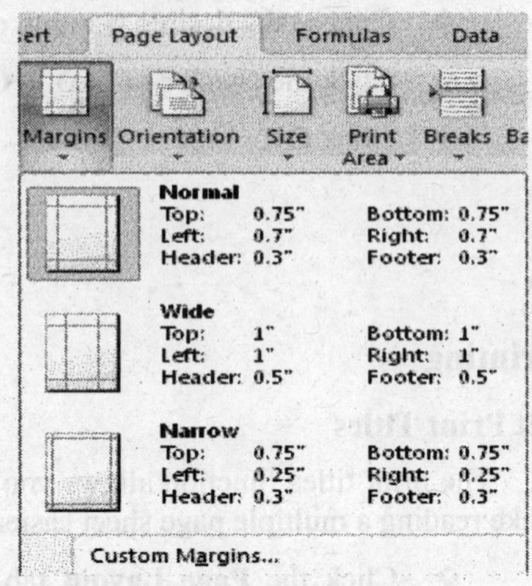

Change Page Orientation

To change the page orientation from portrait to landscape:

- ❖ Click the **Orientation** button on the **Page Layout** tab
- ❖ Choose **Portrait** or **Landscape**

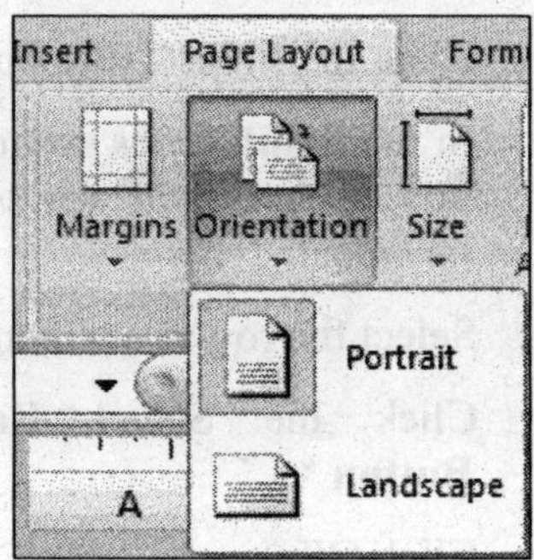

Set Page Breaks

You can manually set up page breaks in a worksheet for ease of reading when the sheet is printed. To set a page break:

- ❖ Click the **Breaks** button on the **Page Layout** tab
- ❖ Click **Insert Page Break**

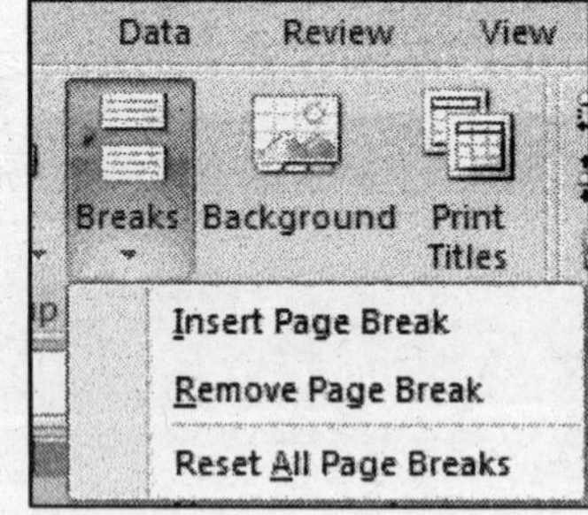

Print a Range

There may be times when you only want to print a portion of a worksheet. This is easily done through the Print Range function. To print a range:

- ❖ Select the area to be printed
- ❖ Click the **Print Area** button on the **Page Layout** tab
- ❖ Click Select **Print Area**

Layout

Split a Worksheet

You can split a worksheet into multiple resizable panes for easier viewing of parts of a worksheet. To split a worksheet:

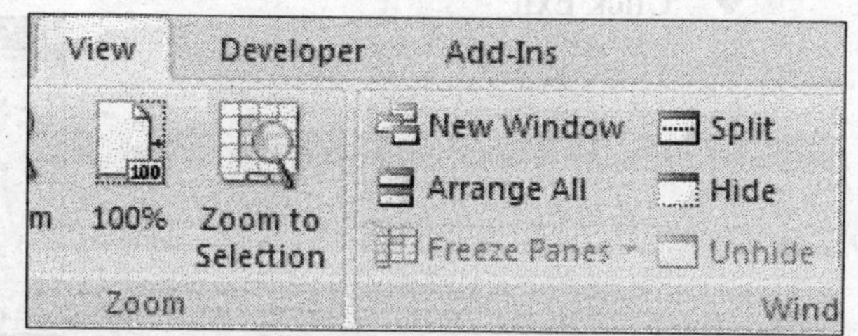

- ❖ Select any cell in center of the worksheet you want to split
- ❖ Click the **Split** button on the **View** tab
- ❖ Notice the split in the screen, you can manipulate each part separately

Freeze Rows and Columns

You can select a particular portion of a worksheet to stay static while you work on other parts of the sheet. This is accomplished through the Freeze Rows and Columns Function. To freeze a row or column:

- ❖ Click the **Freeze Panes** button on the View tab
- ❖ Either select a section to be frozen or click the defaults of top row or left column
- ❖ To unfreeze, click the **Freeze Panes** button
- ❖ Click **Unfreeze**

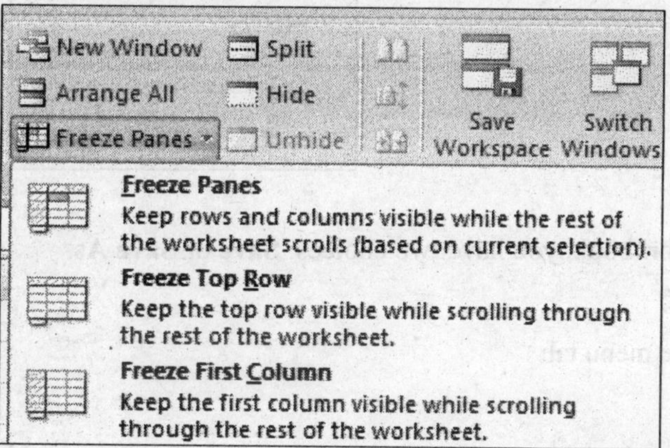

Hide Worksheets

To hide a worksheet:

- ❖ Select the tab of the sheet you wish to hide
- ❖ **Right-click** on the tab
- ❖ Click **Hide**

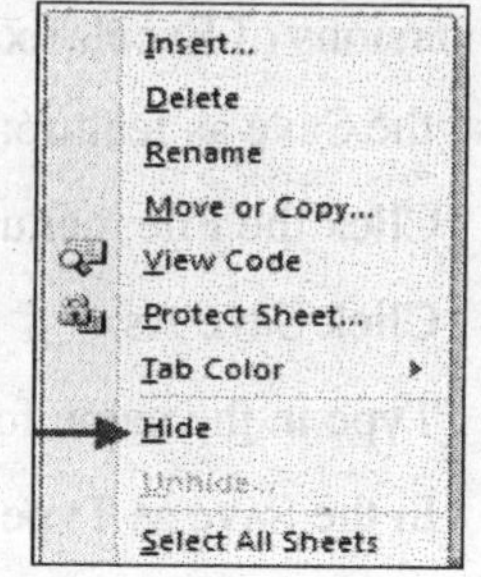

To unhide a worksheet:

- ❖ **Right-click** on any worksheet tab
- ❖ Click **Unhide**
- ❖ Choose the worksheet to unhide

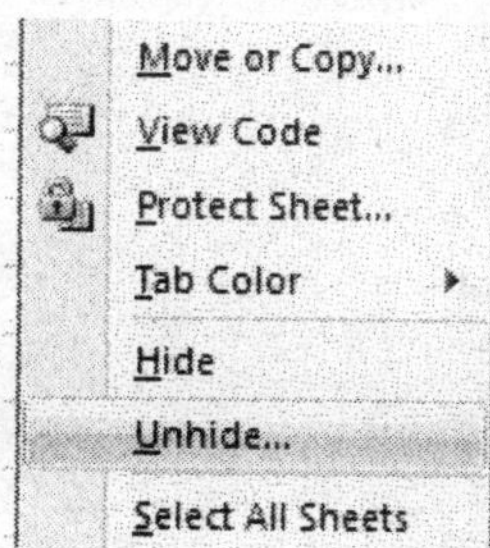

Closing a Microsoft Excel Worksheet

- ❖ Click File menu tab
- ❖ Click Exit

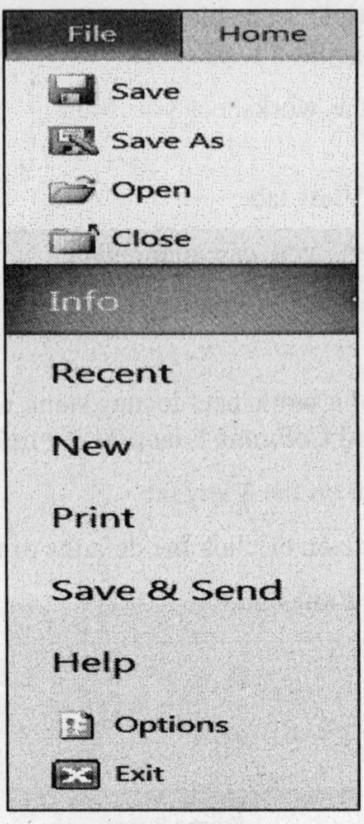

Save a Workbook

When you save a workbook, you have two choices: **Save** or **Save As.**

To save a document:

- ❖ Click the File menu tab
- ❖ Click Save

You may need to use the Save As feature when you need to save a workbook under a different name or to save it for earlier versions of Excel. Excel 2010 has office compability to save the file Excel 2007 and Excel 97-2003 Format.

To use the Save as feature:

- ❖ Click the File menu tab
- ❖ Click Save As
- ❖ Type in the name for the Workbook
- ❖ In the Save as Type box, choose Excel 97-2003 Workbook

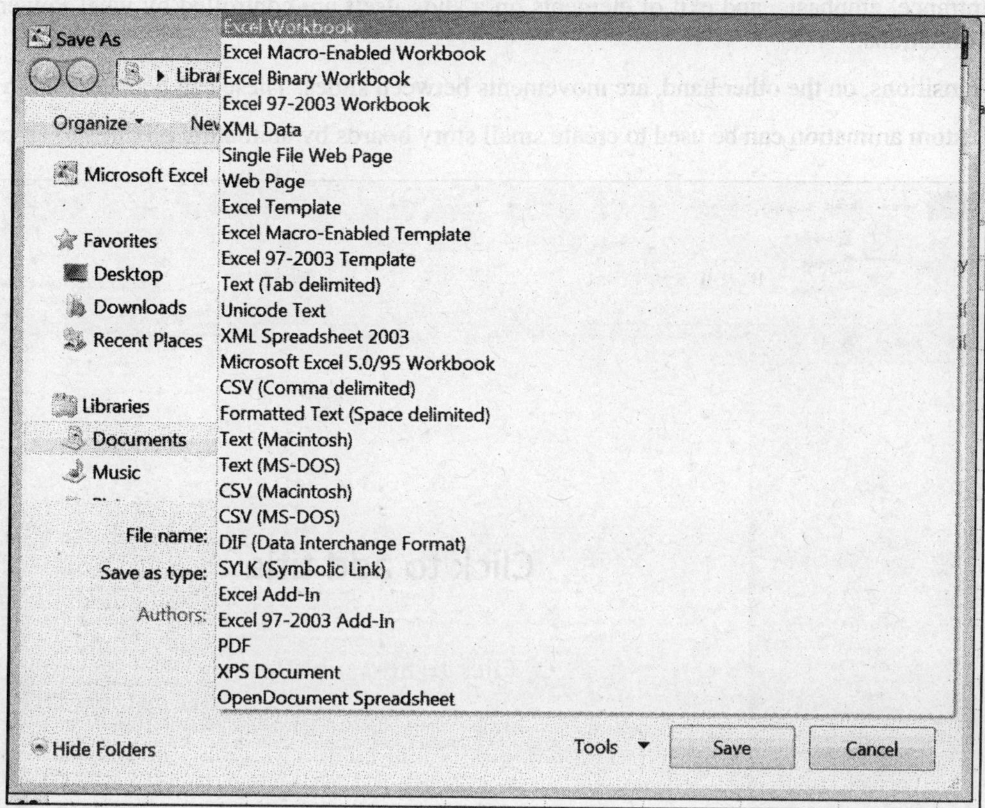

10.13 MICROSOFT POWERPOINT

Microsoft PowerPoint

Microsoft PowerPoint is a presentation program by Microsoft. It is part of the Microsoft Office Suite, and runs on Microsoft Windows and Apple's Mac OS X operating system. PowerPoint is used by business people, educators, students, and trainers. From Microsoft Office 2003 to 2008 for Mac, Microsoft revised the branding to emphasize PowerPoint's place within the Office Suite, calling it Microsoft Office PowerPoint instead of just Microsoft PowerPoint. The current versions are Microsoft PowerPoint 2010 for Windows and Microsoft Office PowerPoint 2008 for Mac.

The original version of this program was created by Dennis Austin and Thomas Rudkin of Forethought Inc. originally designed for the Macintosh Computer, the initial release was called "Presenter". In 1987, it was renamed to "PowerPoint" due to problems with trademarks, the idea for the name coming from Robert Gaskins.

Operation

PowerPoint presentations consist of a number of individual pages or "slides". The "slide" analogy is a reference to the slide projector, a device that can be seen as obsolete, within the context of widespread use of PowerPoint and other presentation software. Slides may contain text, graphics, movies, and other objects, which may be arranged freely on the slide. PowerPoint, however, facilitates the use of a consistent style in a presentation using a template or "Slide Master".

The presentation can be printed, displayed live on a computer, or navigated through at the command of the presenter. For larger audiences, the computer display is often projected using a video projector. Slides can also form the basis of webcasts.

PowerPoint provides three types of movements:

- ❖ Entrance, emphasis, and exit of elements on a slide itself are controlled by what PowerPoint calls Custom Animations.
- ❖ Transitions, on the other hand, are movements between slides. These can be animated in a variety of ways.
- ❖ Custom animation can be used to create small story boards by animating pictures to enter, exit or move.

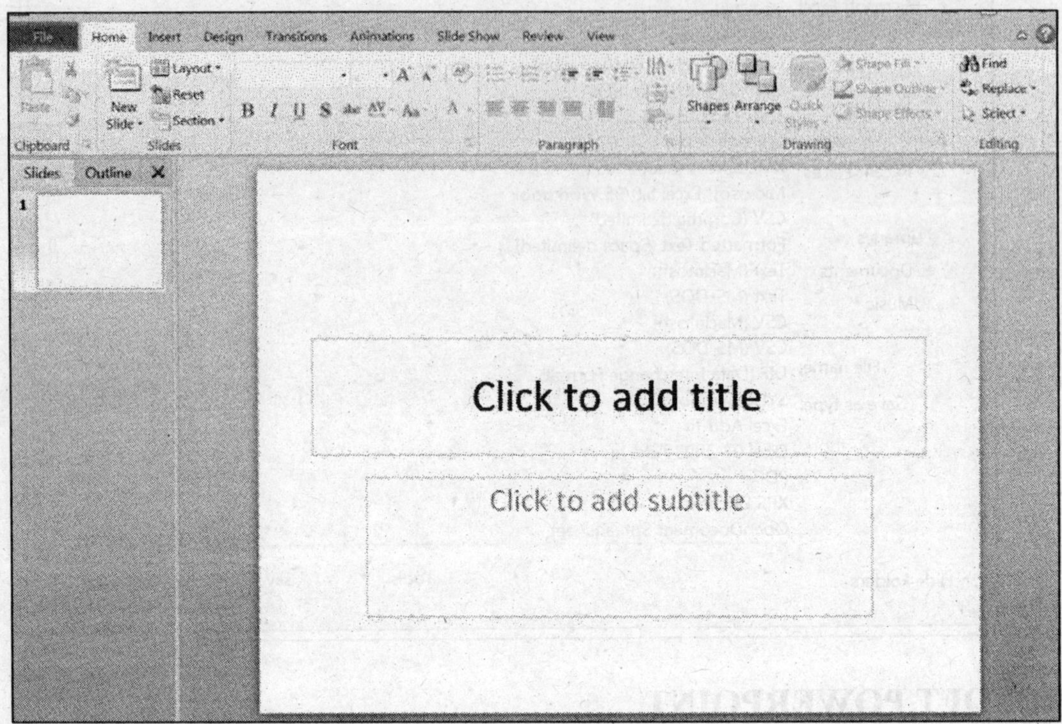

Starting PowerPoint

Getting started with PowerPoint 2010, you will notice that there are many similar features to previous versions. You will also notice that there are many new features that you'll be able to utilize. There are three features that you should remember as you work within PowerPoint 20107: File Menu Tab, the Quick Access Toolbar, and the Ribbon. The function of these features will be more fully explored below.

Presentations

A presentation is a collection of data and information that is to be delivered to a specific audience. A PowerPoint presentation is a collection of electronic slides that can have text, pictures, graphics, tables, sound and video. This collection can run automatically or can be controlled by a presenter.

File Menu Tab

The File Menu Tab many of the functions that were located in the File menu of older versions of PowerPoint. This button allows you to create a news presentation, open an existing presentation, save and save as, print, save & send, or close.

Ribbon

The ribbon is the panel at the top portion of the document. It has seven tabs: Home, Insert, Design, Animations, Slide Show, Review and View. Each tab is divided into groups. The groups are logical collections of features designed to perform function that you will utilize in developing or editing your PowerPoint slides.

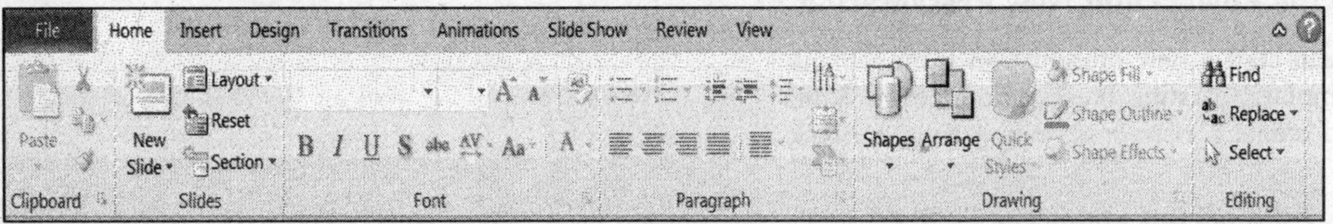

Commonly utilized features are displayed on the Ribbon. To view additional features within each group, click the arrow at the bottom right corner of each group.

- **Home:** Clipboard, Slides, Font, Paragraph, Drawing, and Editing
- **Insert:** Tables, Illustrations, Links, Text, and Media Clips
- **Design:** Page Setup, Themes, Background
- **Animations:** Preview, Animations, Transition to this Slide
- **Slide Show:** Start Slide Show, Set Up, Monitors
- **Review:** Proofing, Comments, Protect
- **View:** Presentation Views, Show/Hide, Zoom, Window, Macros

Quick Access Toolbar

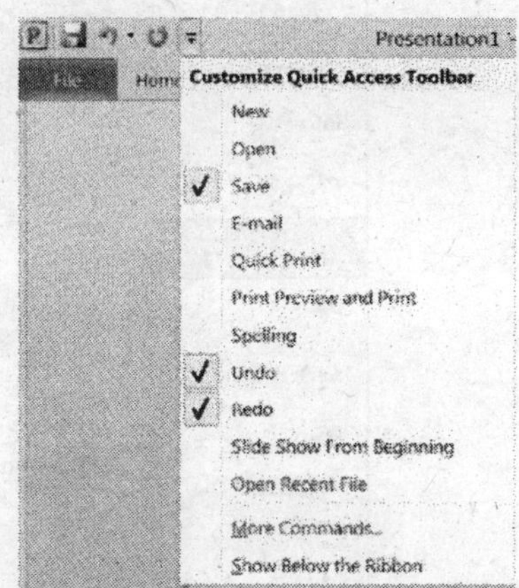

The **quick access toolbar** is a customizable toolbar that contains commands that you may want to use. You can place the quick access toolbar above or below the ribbon. To change the location of the quick access toolbar, click on the arrow at the end of the toolbar and click **Show below the Ribbon**.

You can also add items to the quick access toolbar. Right click on any item in the Office Button or the Ribbon and click Add to Quick Access Toolbar and a shortcut will be added.

Mini Toolbar

A new feature in Office 2010 is the Mini Toolbar. This is a floating toolbar that is displayed when you select text or right-click text. It displays common formatting tools, such as Bold, Italics, Fonts, Font Size and Font Color.

Navigation

Navigation through the slides can be accomplished through the Slide Navigation menu on the left side of the screen. Also, an outline appears from materials that have been entered in the presentation. To access the outline, click the outline tab.

Slide Views

Presentations can be viewed in a variety of manners. On the View tab, the Presentation Views group allows you to view the slides as Normal, Slide Sorter, Notes Page, Slide Show, Slide Master, Handout Master, and Notes Master.

Creating the PowerPoint New Presentation

You can start a new presentation from a blank slide, a template, existing presentations, or a Word outline. To create a new presentation from a blank slide:

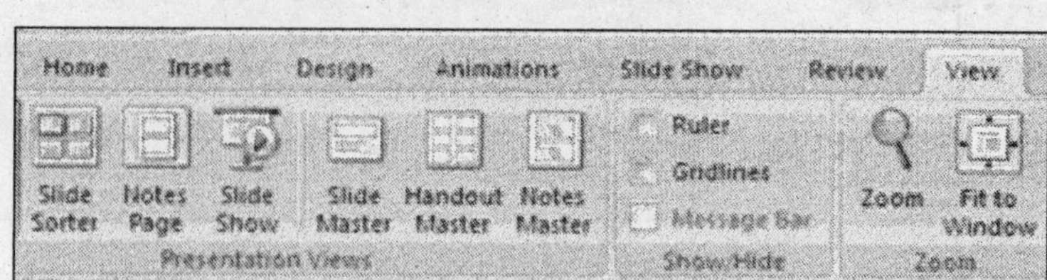

- ❖ Click the **File Menu Tab**
- ❖ Click **New**
- ❖ Click **Blank Presentation**

To create a new presentation from a template:

- ❖ Click the **File Menu Tab**
- ❖ Click **New**
- ❖ Click **Installed Templates or Browse through Microsoft Office Online Templates**
- ❖ Click the template you choose

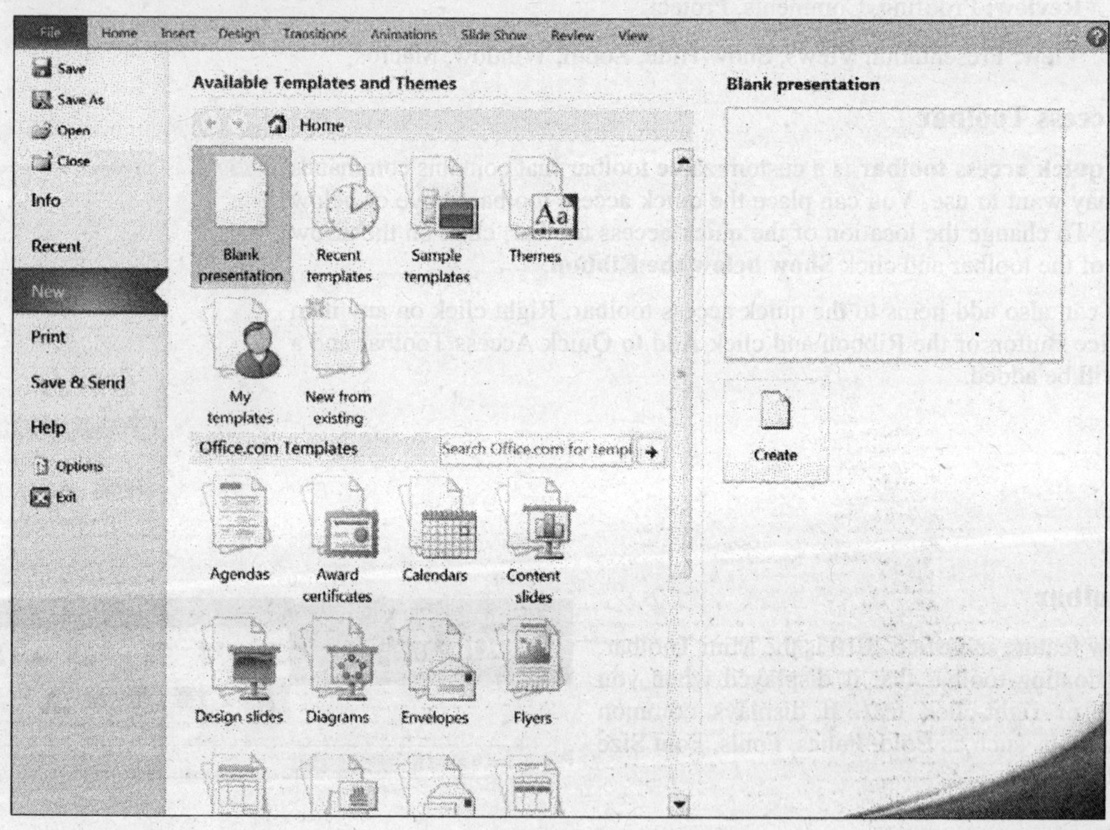

To create a new presentation from an existing presentation:

- ❖ Click the Microsoft Office Button
- ❖ Click New
- ❖ Click New from Existing
- ❖ Browse to and click the presentation

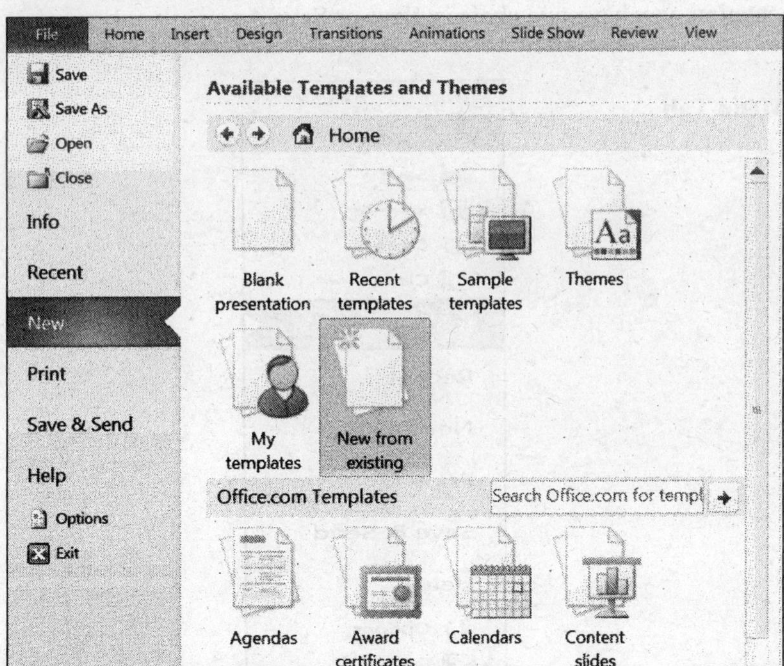

To create a new presentation from a Word outline:

- ❖ Click the slide where you would like the outline to begin
- ❖ Click **New Slide** on the **Home** tab

- ❖ Click **Slides from Outline**
- ❖ Browse and click the Word Document that contains the outline

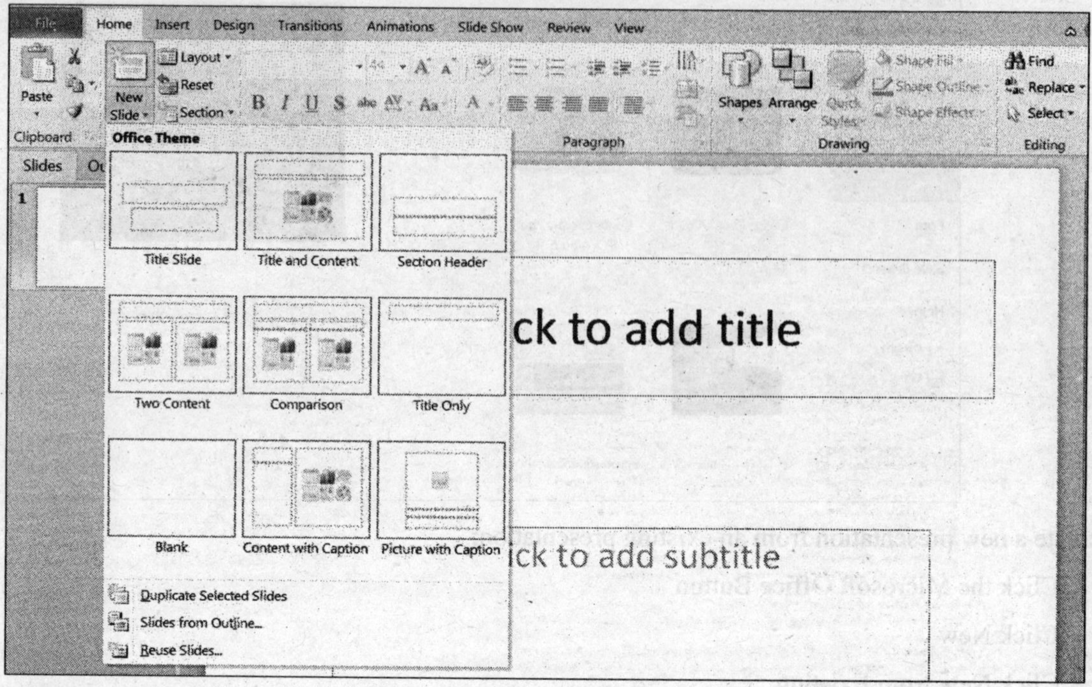

Save a Presentation

When you save a presentation, you have two choices: Save or Save As.

To save a document:

- ❖ Click the **File Menu Tab**
- ❖ Click **Save**

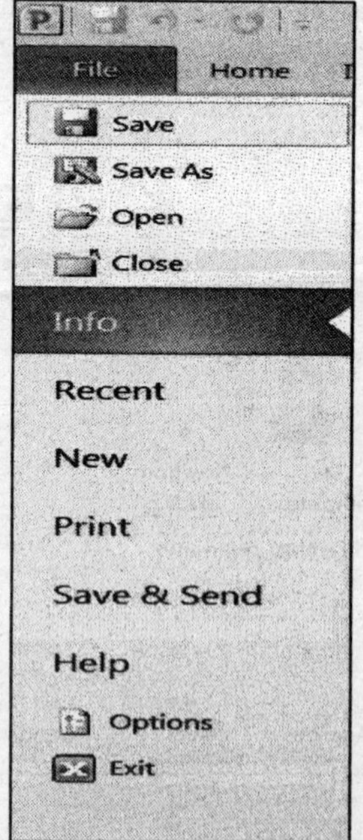

You may need to use the **Save As** feature when you need to save a presentation under a different name or to save it for earlier versions of PowerPoint. Remember that older versions of PowerPoint will not be able to open PowerPoint 2010 presentation unless you save it as a PowerPoint 97-2003 Format. To use the **Save As feature:**

- Click the **File Menu Tab**
- Click **Save As**
- Type in the name for the Presentation
- In the **Save as Type** box, choose **Excel 97-2003 Presentation**

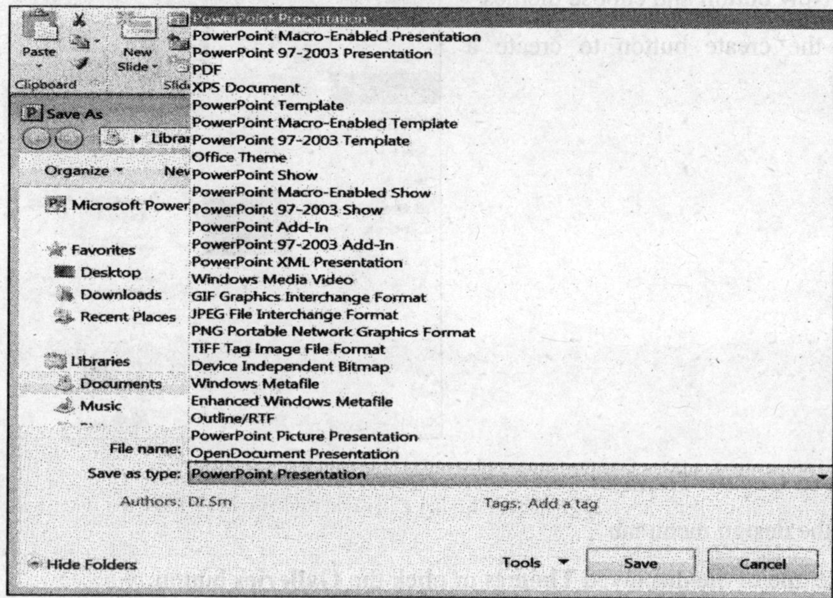

Add Slides

There are several choices when you want to add a new slide to the presentation: Office Themes, Duplicate Selected Slide, or Reuse Slides.

To create a new slide from Office Themes:

- Select the slide immediately **BEFORE** where you want the new slide
- Click the **New Slide** button on the **Home** tab
- Click the slide choice that fits your material

To create a slide as a duplicate of a slide in the presentation:

- Select the slide to duplicate
- Click the **New Slide** button on the **Home** tab
- Click **Duplicate Selected Slides**

To create a new slide from another presentation:

- Select the slide immediately BEFORE where you want the new slide
- Click the **New Slide** button on the Home tab
- Click **Reuse Slides**
- Click **Browse**
- Click **Browse File**
- Locate the slide show and click on the slide to import

Themes

Themes are design templates that can be applied to an entire presentation that allows for consistency throughout the presentation. To add a theme to a presentation:

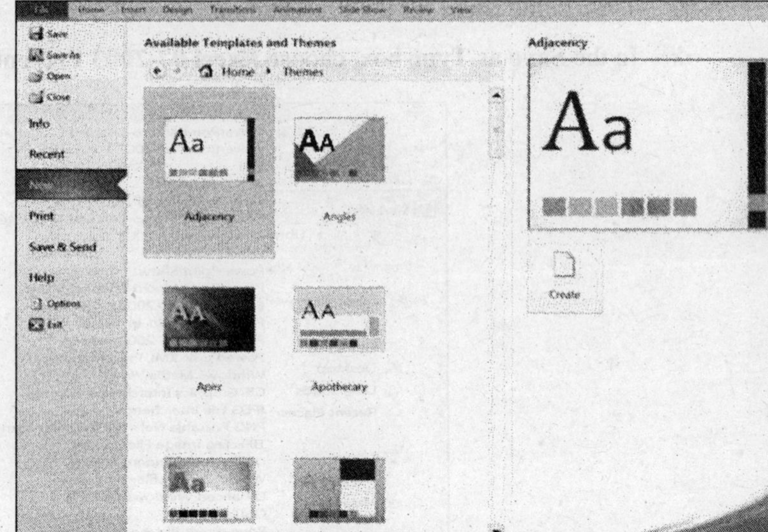

- Click the File Menu Tab
- Click New button and choose themes
- Click the create button to create a theme

Another Method to Create Themes:

- Click the design menu tab
- Choose one of the displayed **Themes** or click the **Galleries** button

To apply new colors to a theme:

- Click the **Colors** drop-down arrow
- Choose a color set or click **Create New Theme Colors**

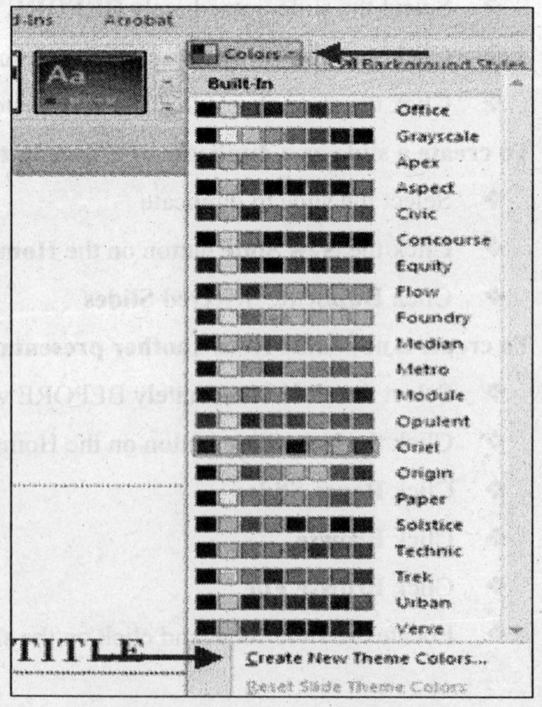

To change the background style of a theme:

- ❖ Click the Background Styles button on the Design tab

Working with Content Enter Text

To enter text:

- ❖ Select the **slide** where you want the text
- ❖ Click in a **Textbox** to add text

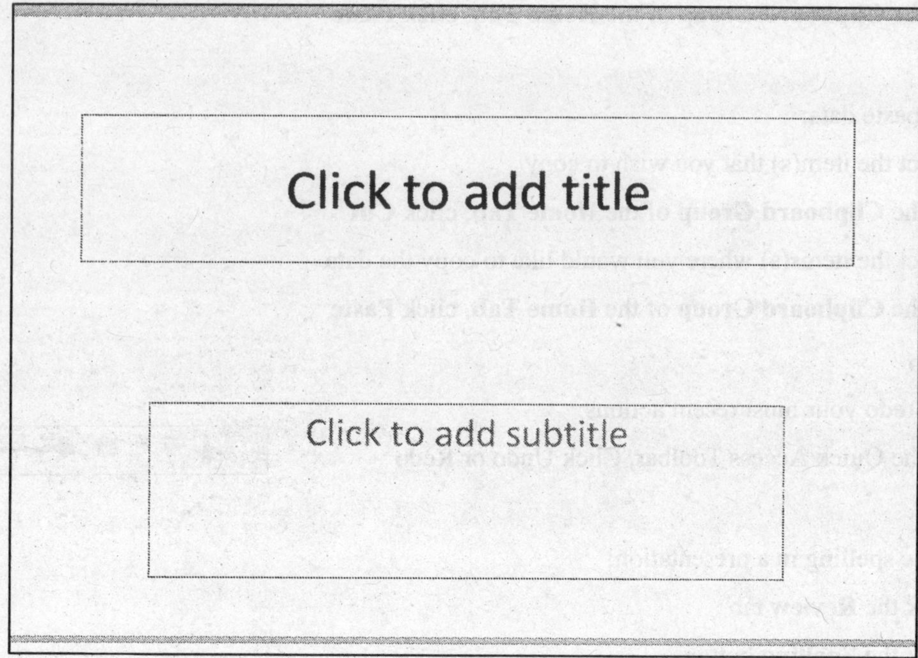

To add a text box:

- ❖ Select the **slide** where you want to place the text box
- ❖ On the **Insert** tab, click **Text Box**
- ❖ Click on the slide and drag the cursor to expand the text box

❖ Type in the text

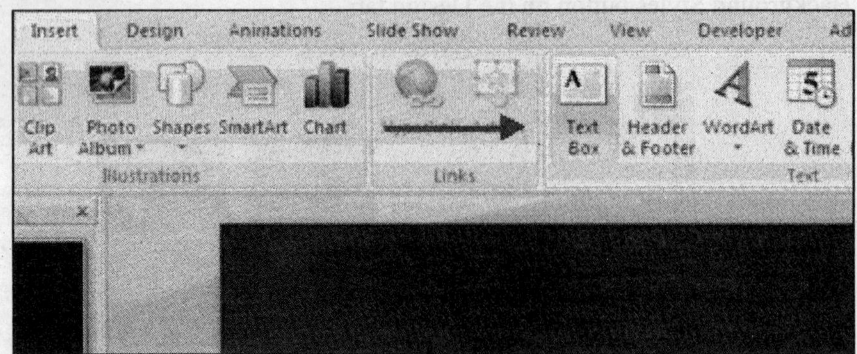

Select Text

To select the text:

❖ Highlight the text

This is the text to highlight

Copy and Paste

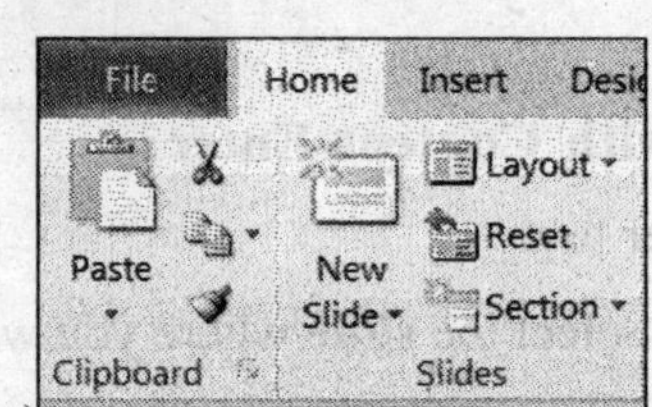

To copy and paste data:

❖ Select the item(s) that you wish to copy

❖ On the **Clipboard Group** of the **Home Tab**, click **Copy**

❖ Select the item(s) where you would like to copy the data

❖ On the **Clipboard Group** of the **Home Tab**, click **Paste**

Cut and Paste

To cut and paste data:

❖ Select the item(s) that you wish to copy

❖ On the **Clipboard Group** of the **Home Tab**, click **Cut**

❖ Select the items(s) where you would like to copy the data

❖ On the **Clipboard Group** of the **Home Tab**, click **Paste**

Undo and Redo

To undo or redo your most recent actions:

❖ On the Quick Access Toolbar, Click Undo or Redo

Spell Check

To check the spelling in a presentation:

❖ Click the **Review** tab

❖ Click the **Spelling** button

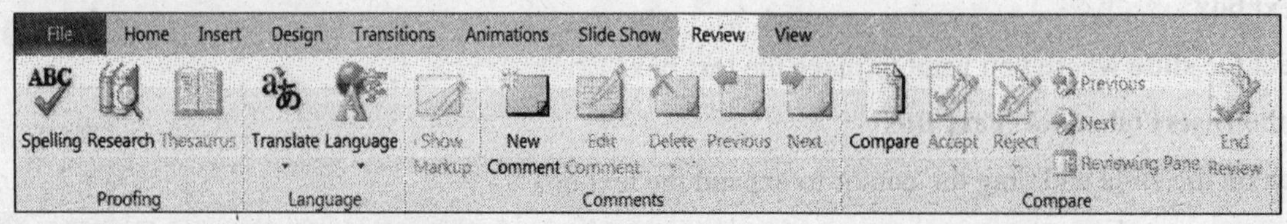

Formatting Text

Change Font Typeface and Size

To change the font typeface:

- ❖ Click the **arrow** next to the font name and choose a font.
- ❖ Remember that you can preview how the new font will look by highlighting the text, and hovering over the new font typeface.

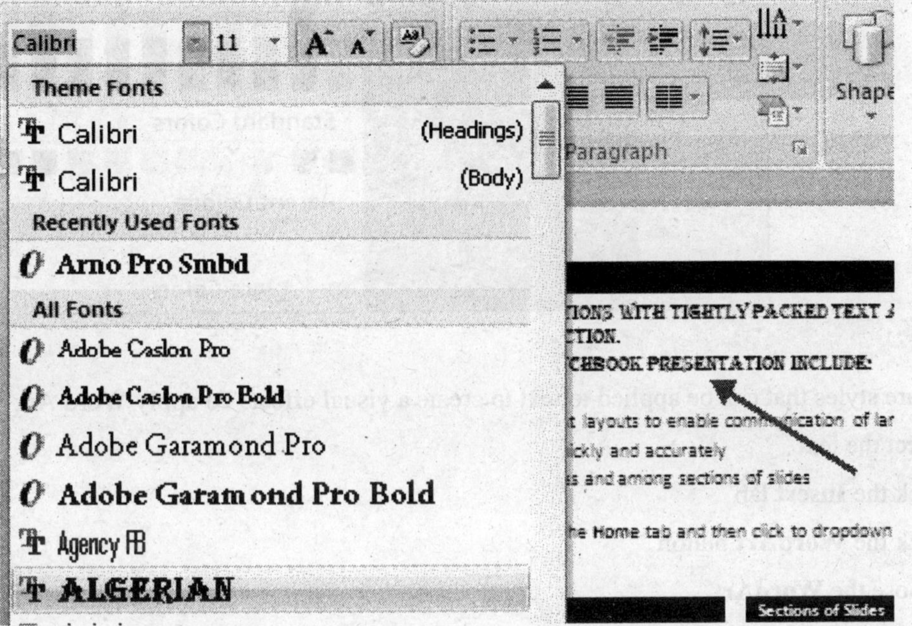

To change the font size:

- ❖ Click the **arrow** next to the font size and choose the appropriate size, or
- ❖ Click the **increase or decrease** font size buttons.

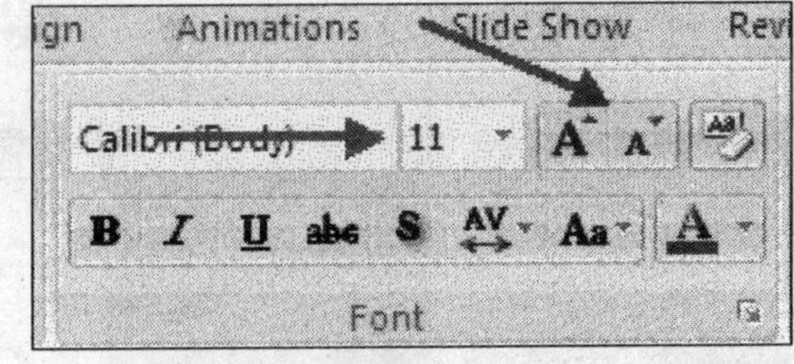

Font Styles and Effects

Font styles are predefined formatting options that are used to emphasize text. They include: Bold, Italic, and Underline. To add these to text:

- ❖ Select the text and click the **Font Styles** included on the Font group of the Home tab or
- ❖ Select the text and right click to display the font tools

Change Text Color

To change the text color:

- ❖ Select the text and click the **Colors** button included on the Font Group of the Ribbon, or
- ❖ Highlight the text and right click and choose the colors tool.
- ❖ Select the color by clicking the down arrow next to the font color button.

WordArt

WordArt are styles that can be applied to text to create a visual effect. To apply Word Art:

- ❖ Select the text
- ❖ Click the **Insert** tab
- ❖ Click the **WordArt** button
- ❖ Choose the **WordArt**

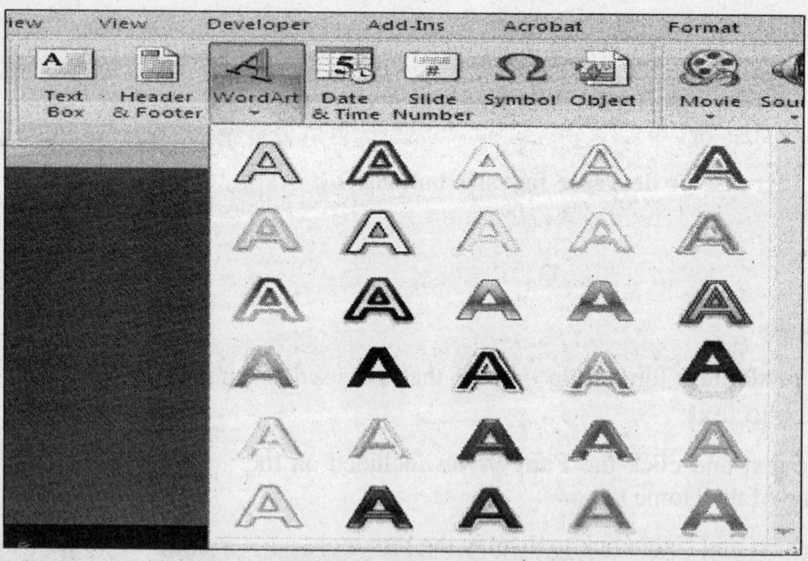

To modify the styles of WordArt:

- ❖ Select the WordArt
- ❖ Click the Format tab for the Drawing Tools
- ❖ Click the **WordArt Fill** button, the **WordArt Outline** button, or the **Text Effects** button

Change Paragraph Alignment

The paragraph alignment allows you to set how you want text to appear. To change the alignment:

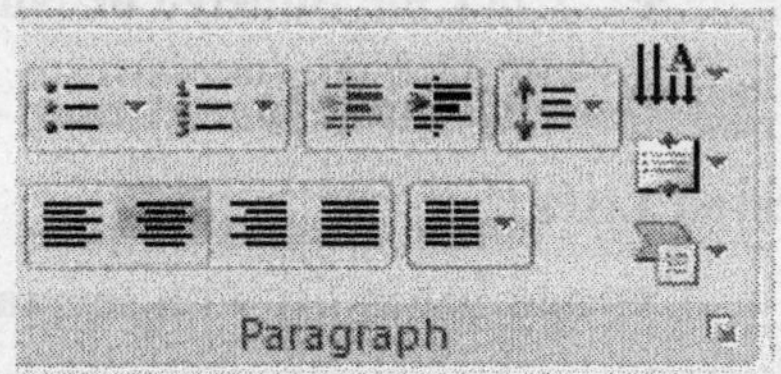

- ❖ Click the **Home Tab**
- ❖ Choose the appropriate button for alignment on the Paragraph Group.
  - **Align Left:** The text is aligned with your left margin
  - **Center:** The text is centered within your margins
  - **Align Right:** Aligns text with the right margin
  - **Justify:** Aligns text to both the left and right margins.

Indent Paragraphs

To indent paragraphs, you can do the following:

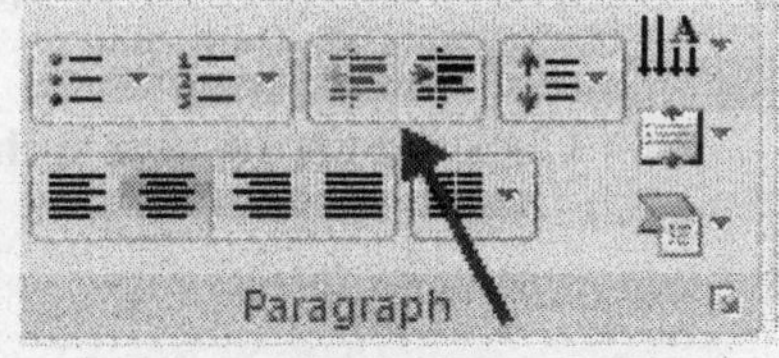

- ❖ Click the **Indent** buttons to control the indent.
- ❖ Click the **Indent** button repeated times to increase the size of the indent.

Text Direction

To change the text direction:

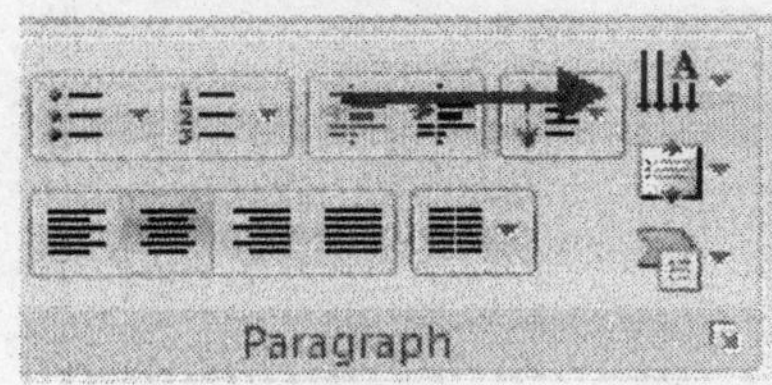

- ❖ Select the text
- ❖ Click the Text Direction button on the Home tab
- ❖ Click the selection

Adding Content

Resize a Textbox

To resize a textbox:

- ❖ Click on the **textbox**
- ❖ Click the corner of the box and drag the cursor to the desired size

Click to add subtitle

Bulleted and Numbered Lists

Bulleted lists have bullet points, numbered lists have numbers, and outline lists combine numbers and letters depending on the organization of the list.

To add a list to existing text:

❖ Select the text you wish to make a list

❖ Click the **Bulleted or Numbered Lists** button

To create a new list:

❖ Place your cursor where you want the list in the document

❖ Click the **Bulleted or Numbered Lists** button

❖ Begin typing

Nested Lists

A nested list is list with several levels of indented text. To create a nested list:

❖ Create your list following the directions above

❖ Click the **Increase or Decrease Indent** button

Formatting Lists

The bullet image and numbering format can be changed by using the **Bullets or Numbering** dialog box.

❖ Select the entire list to change all the bullets or numbers, or Place the cursor on one line within the list to change a single bullet.

❖ Click the **arrow** next to the bulleted or numbered list and choose a bullet or numbering style.

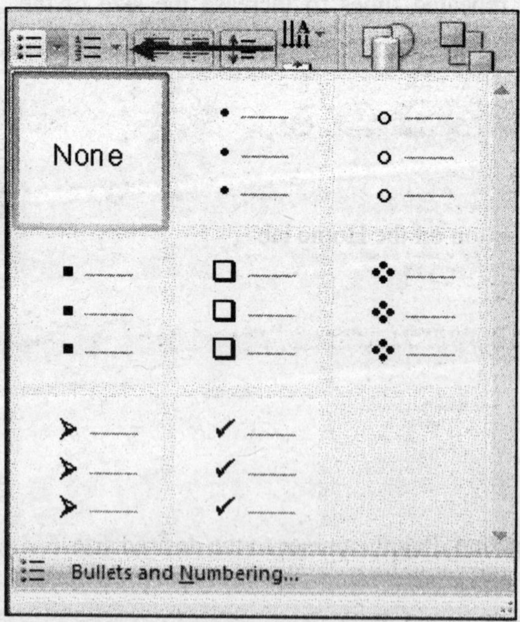

Adding Video

Video clips can be added to the presentation.

To add a video clip:

❖ Click the **Movie** button on the Insert tab

❖ Choose **Movie from File** or **Movie from Clip Organizer**

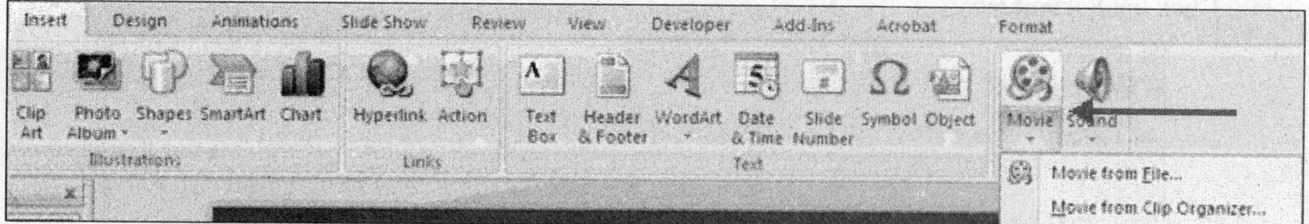

To edit the video options:

❖ Click the movie icon

❖ Click the **Format** tab

Adding Audio

Audio clips can be added to the presentation. To add an audio clip:

❖ Click the **Audio** button on the Insert tab

❖ Choose **Sound from File, Sound from Clip Organizer**, **Play CD Audio Track**, or **Record Sound**

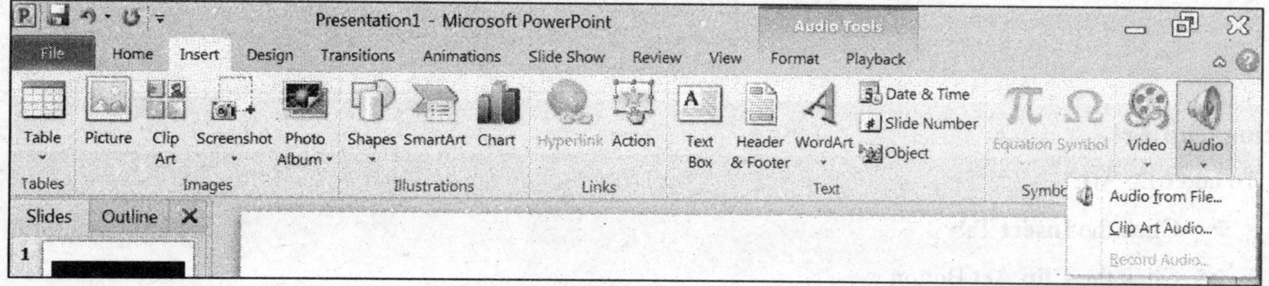

To edit the audio options:

❖ Click the audio icon

❖ Click the **Format** tab

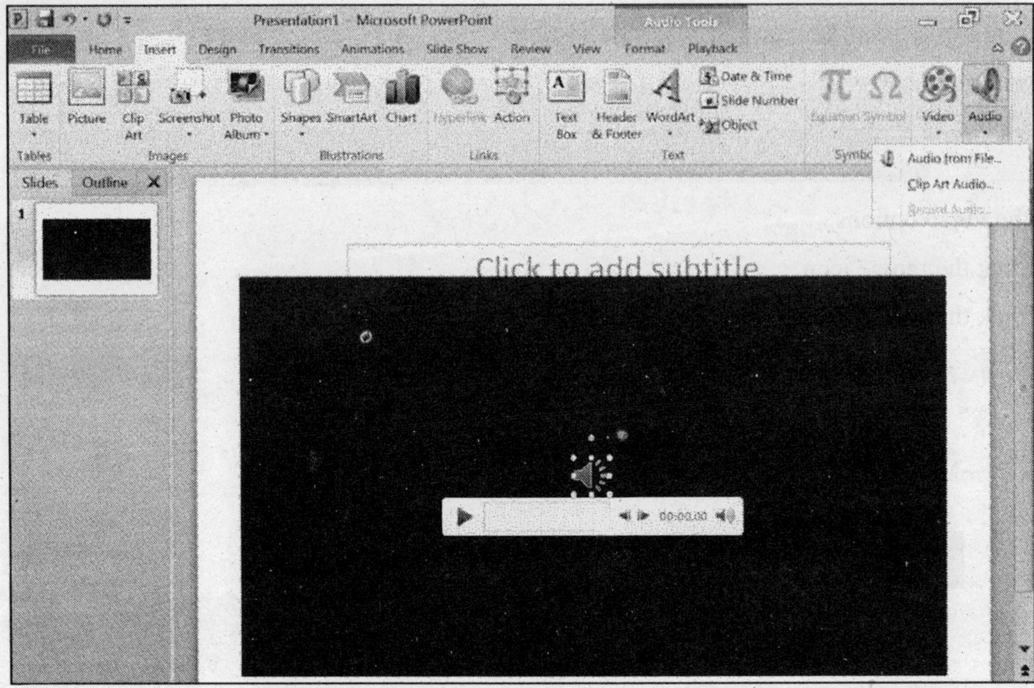

Graphics

To add a picture:

❖ Click the **Insert** Tab

❖ Click the **Picture** Button

❖ Browse to the picture from your files

❖ Click the **name** of the picture

❖ Click **insert**

❖ To move the graphic, click it and drag it to where you want it

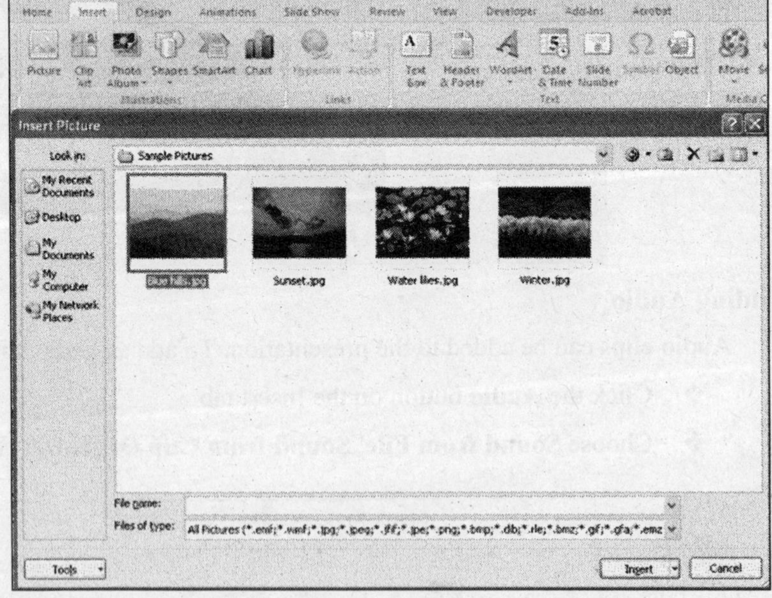

Adding Clip Art

To add Clip Art:

❖ Click the **Insert** Tab

❖ Click the **Clip Art** Button

❖ Search for the clip art using the search Clip Art dialog box

❖ Click the **Clip Art**

❖ To move the graphic, click it and drag it to where you want it

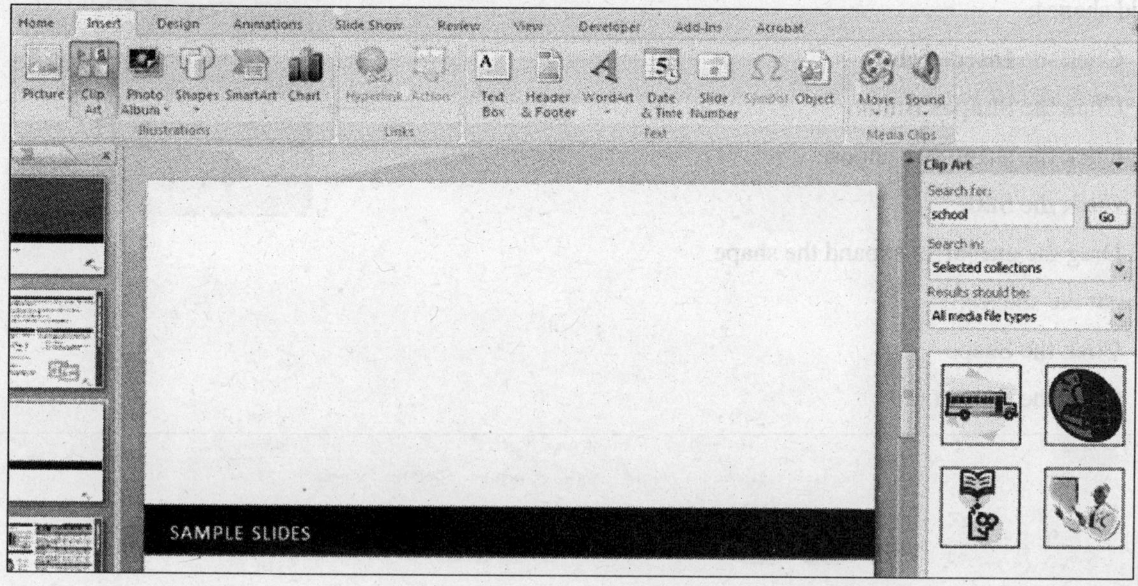

Editing Pictures and Clip Art

When you add a graphic to the presentation, an additional Tab appears on the Ribbon. The Format Tab allows you to format the pictures and graphics. This tab has four groups:

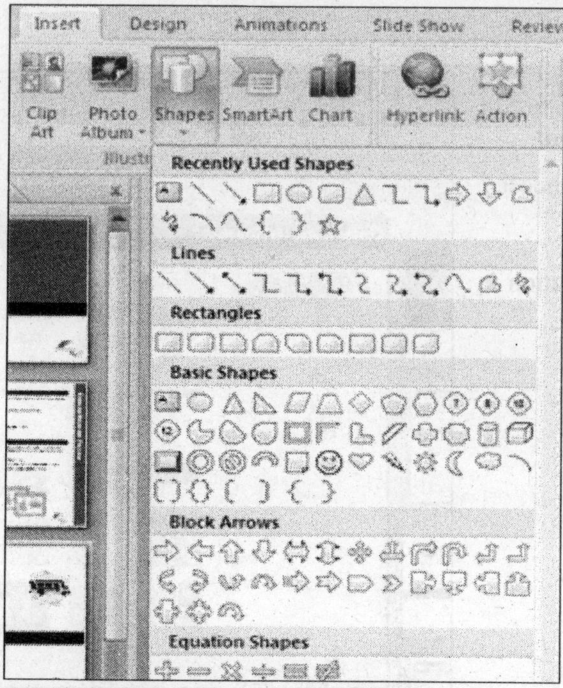

❖ **Adjust:** Controls the picture brightness, contrast, and colors

❖ **Picture Style:** Allows you to place a frame or border around the picture and add effects

- **Arrange:** Controls the alignment and rotation of the picture
- **Size:** Cropping and size of graphic

Adding a Shape

To add shapes:

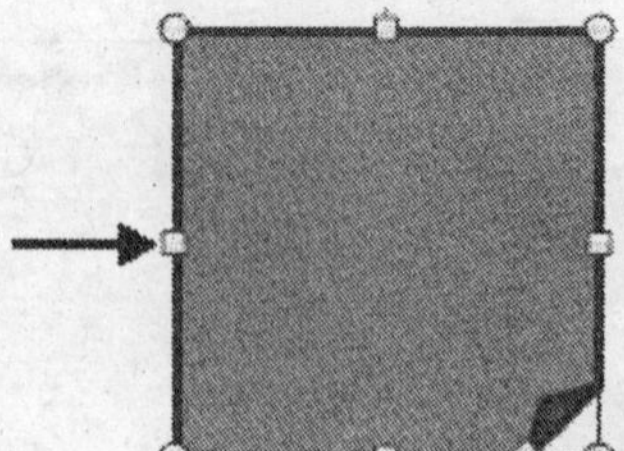

- Click the **Insert** Tab
- Click the **Shapes** Button
- Click the shape you choose
- Click the **Slide**
- Drag the **cursor** to expand the shape

To format the shapes:

- Click the Shape
- Click the Format tab

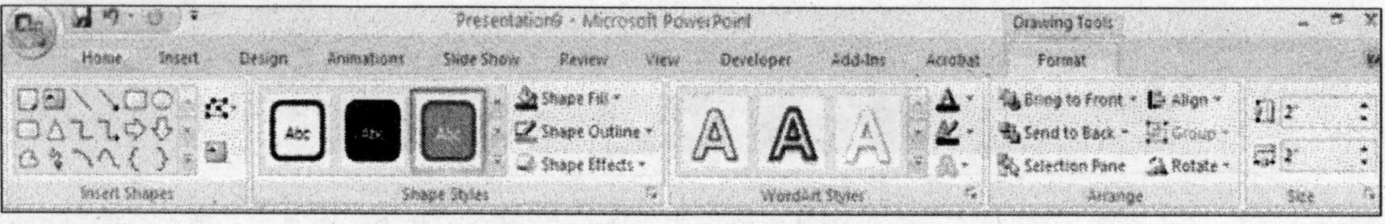

Adding SmartArt

SmartArt is a feature in Office 2010 that allows you to choose from a variety of graphics, including flow charts, lists, cycles, and processes.

To add SmartArt:

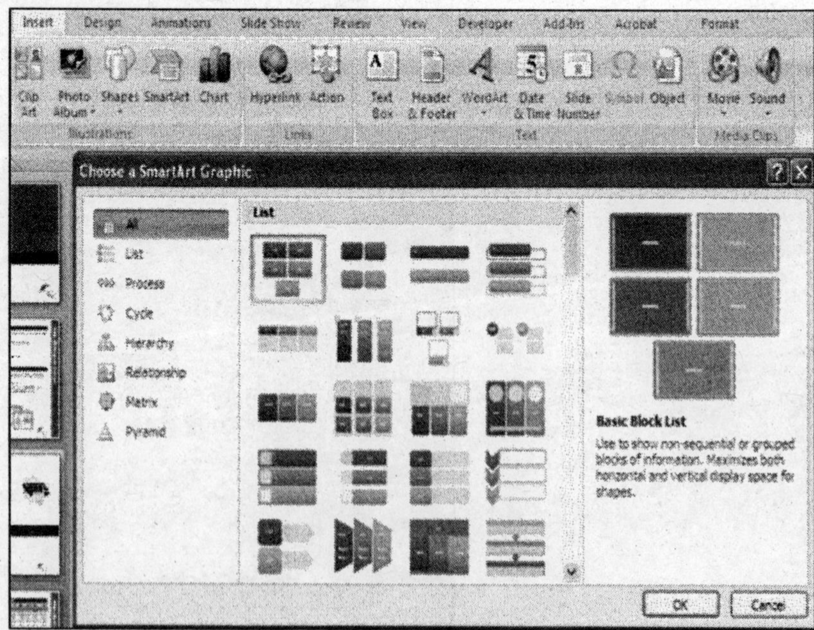

- Click the **Insert** Tab
- Click the **SmartArt** Button
- Click the **SmartArt** you choose
- Click the **SmartArt**
- Drag it to the desired location in the slide

To format the SmartArt:

- ❖ Click the **SmartArt**
- ❖ Click either the **Design** or the **Format** tab
- ❖ Click the **SmartArt** to add text and pictures.

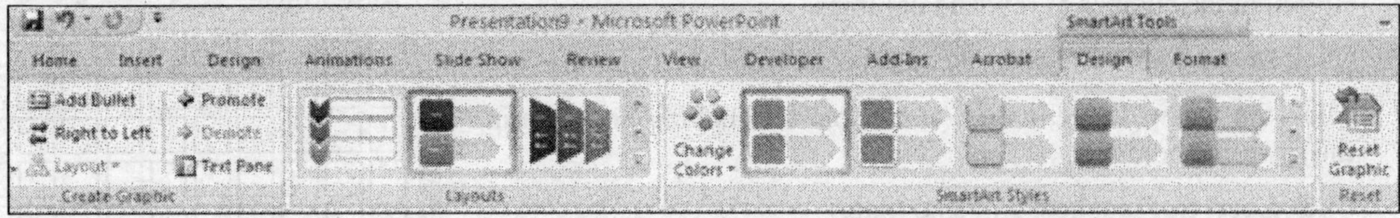

Adding a Photo Album

The photo album feature is new in PowerPoint 2007 and allows you to easily create a photo album to share pictures.

To create a photo album:

- ❖ Click the Photo Album button on the Insert tab
- ❖ Click New Photo Album
- ❖ Click File/Disk to add pictures to the photo album
- ❖ Move the pictures up and down in the order of the album but clicking the up/down arrows

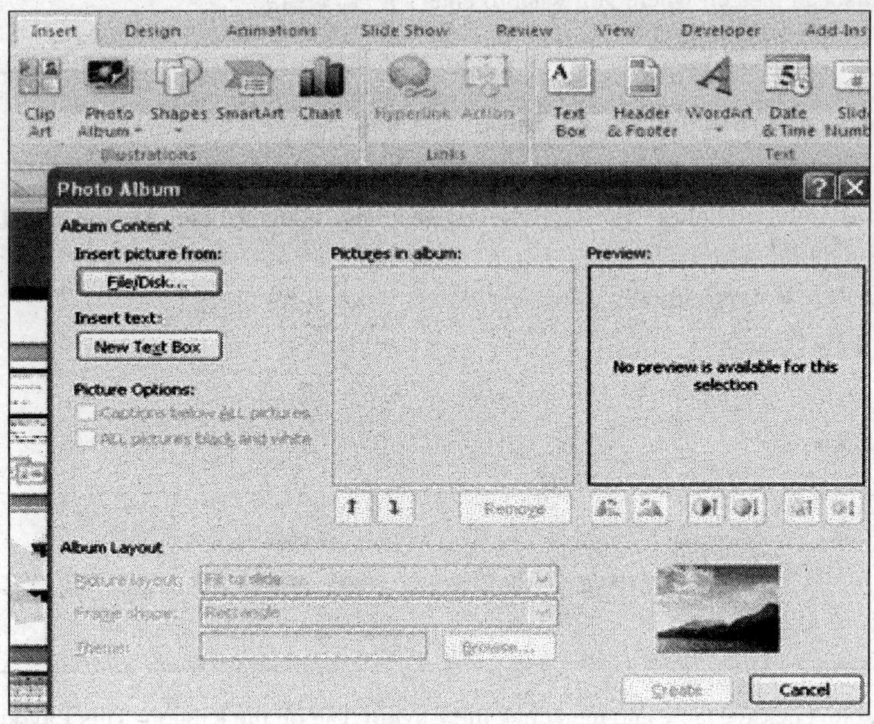

Tables

Tables are used to display data in a table format.

Create a Table

To create a table:

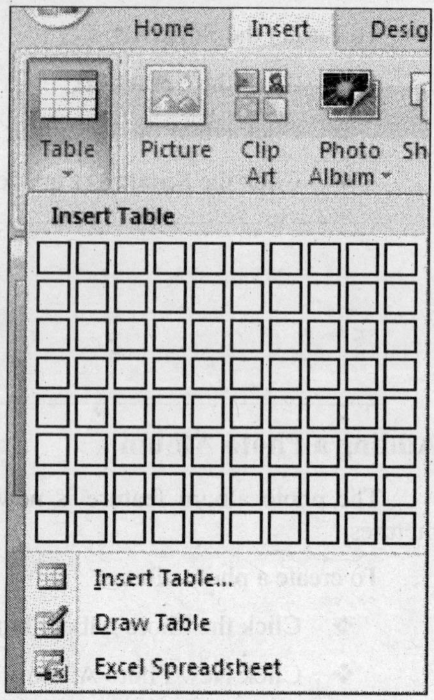

- ❖ Place the cursor on the page where you want the new table
- ❖ Click the **Insert** Tab of the Ribbon
- ❖ Click the **Tables** Button on the Tables Group.

You can create a table one of four ways:

- ❖ Highlight the number of row and columns
- ❖ Click **Insert Table** and enter the number of rows and columns
- ❖ Click the **Draw Table**, create your table by clicking and entering the rows and columns
- ❖ Click **Excel Spreadsheet** and enter data

Enter Data in a Table

Place the cursor in the cell where you wish to enter the information. Begin typing.

Modify the Table Structure and Format a Table

To modify the structure of a table:

- ❖ Click the table and notice that you have two new tabs on the Ribbon: **Design and Layout**. These pertain to the table design and layout.

On the Design Tab, you can choose:

- ❖ Table Style Options
- ❖ Table Styles
- ❖ Draw Borders

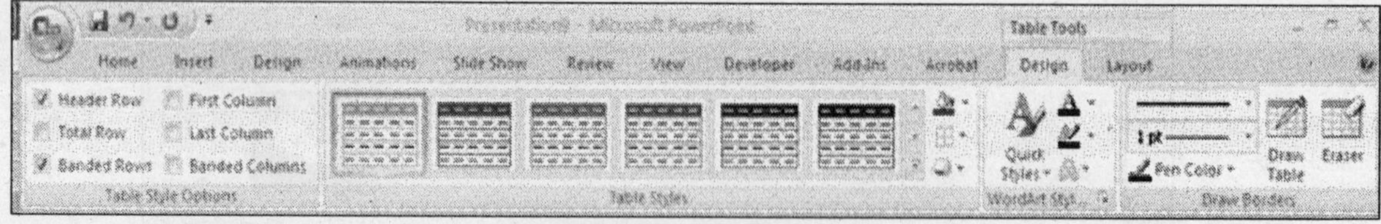

To format a table, click the table and then click the **Layout** Tab on the Ribbon. This Layout tab allows you to:

- ❖ **View Gridlines** and **Properties** (from the Table Group)
- ❖ **Insert Rows** and **Columns** (from the Rows & Columns Group)

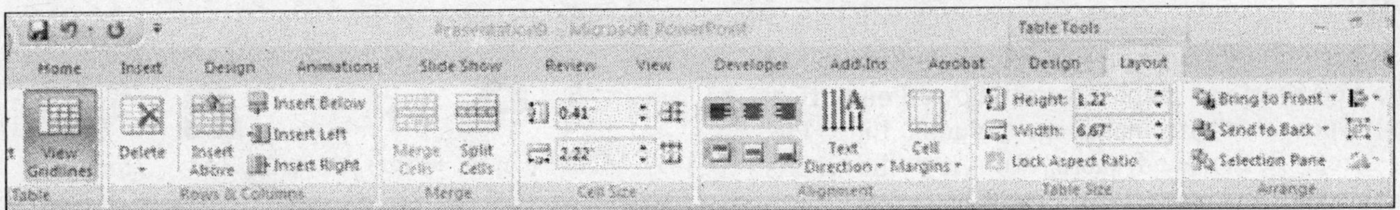

- ❖ **Delete** the Table, Rows and/or Columns (from the Rows & Columns Group)
- ❖ **Merge** or **Split** Cells (from the Merge Group)
- ❖ Increase and decrease **cell size** (Cell Size Group)
- ❖ **Align text** within the cells and change text directions (Alignment Group)

Insert a Table from Word or Excel

- ❖ Open the Word document or Excel worksheet
- ❖ Select the **chart**
- ❖ Click **Copy** on the Home tab
- ❖ Go to the **PowerPoint** document where you want the chart located
- ❖ Click **Paste** on the Home tab

Screenshot

PowerPoint2010 has special features like screenshot, it helps you take screenshot any window and paste in PowerPoint slide.

To open Screenshot window:

- ❖ Click Insert Menu Tab
- ❖ Click the Screenshot button
- ❖ It will show the available window in the screen to paste in the slide

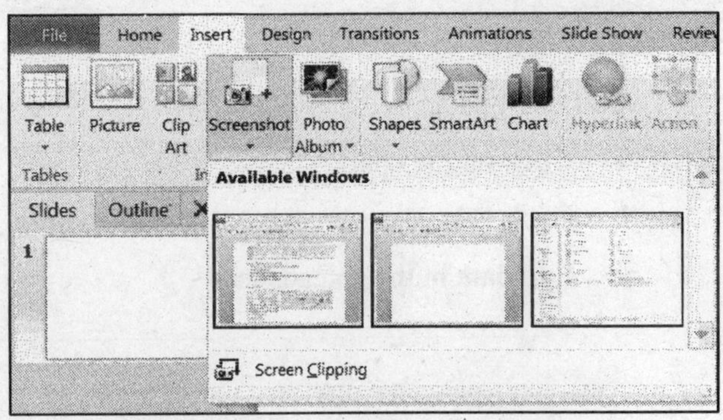

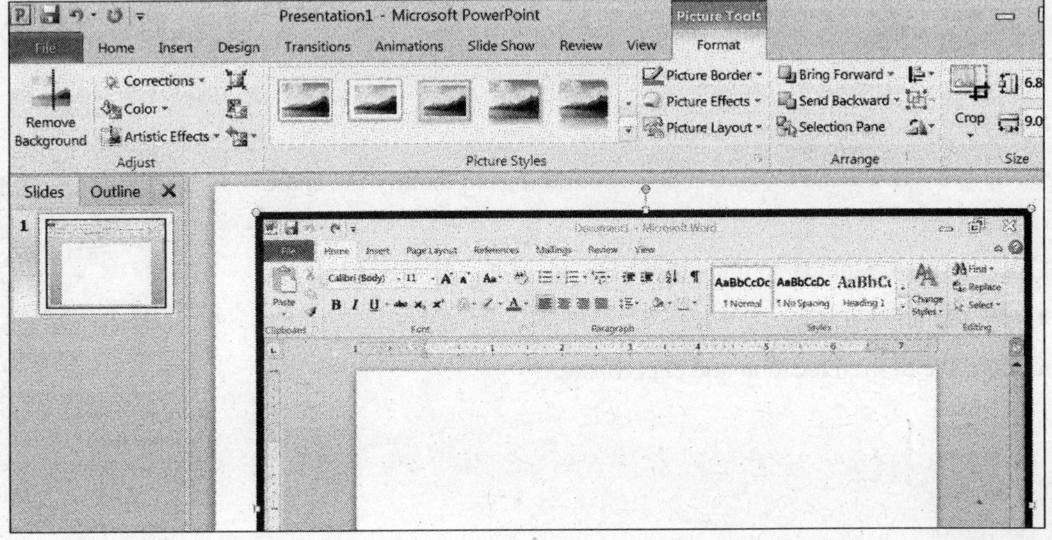

Charts

Charts allow you to present information contained in the worksheet in a graphic format. PowerPoint offers many types of charts including: Column, Line, Pie, Bar, Area, Scatter and more. To view the charts available click the Insert Tab on the Ribbon.

Create a Chart

To create a chart:

- ❖ Click the Insert tab on the ribbon
- ❖ Click the type of Chart you want to create
- ❖ Insert the **Data** and **Labels**

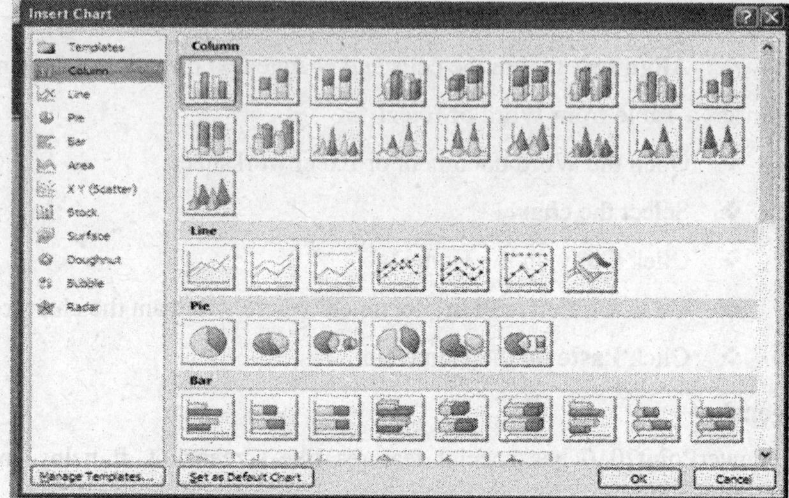

Edit Chart Data

To edit chart data:

- ❖ Click on the chart
- ❖ Click **Edit Data** on the Design tab
- ❖ Edit data in the spreadsheet

Modify a Chart

Once you have created a chart, you can do several things to modify the chart.

To move the chart:

- ❖ Click the **Chart** and Drag it another location on the same slide, or
- ❖ **Copy** it to another slide
- ❖ Choose the desired location and click **Paste**

To modify the chart size:

❖ Click the **Chart**

❖ Click on any of the corners and drop and drag to resize

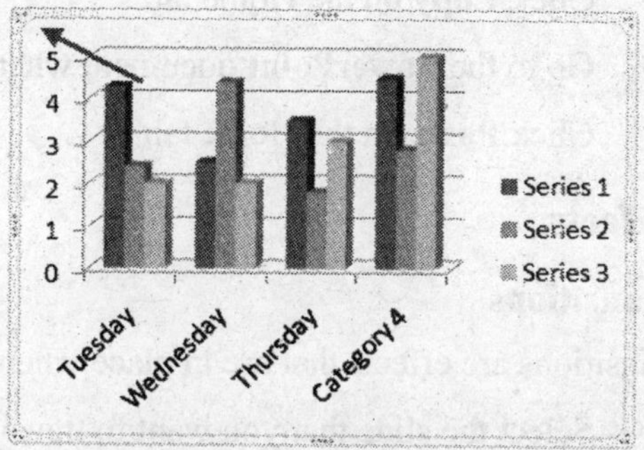

To modify the labels and titles:

❖ Click the chart

❖ Click the Layout tab

❖ Choose the appropriate label to change

Chart Tools

The Chart Tools appear on the Ribbon when you click on the chart. The tools are located on three tabs: Design, Layout and Format.

Within the Design tab you can control the chart type, layout, styles, and location.

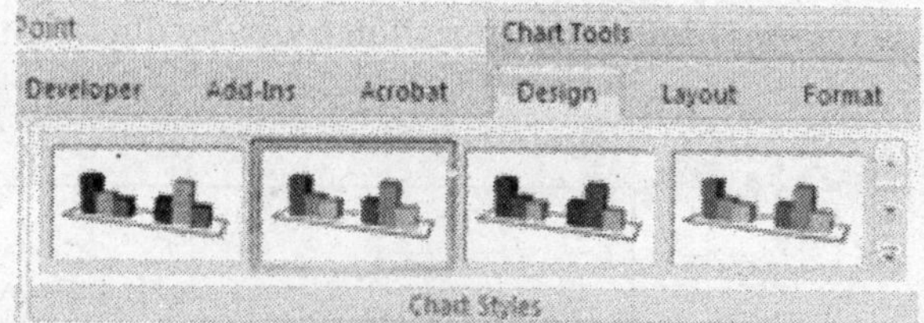

Within the Layout tab, you can control the insertion of pictures, textboxes, and shapes, labels, backgrounds, and data analysis.

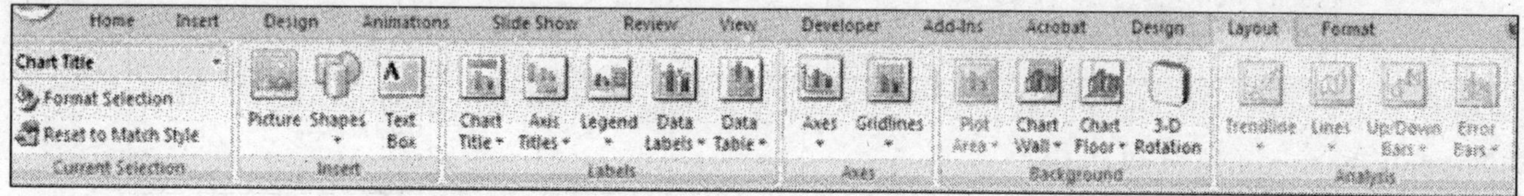

Within the Format tab, you can adjust the Fill Colors and Word Styles.

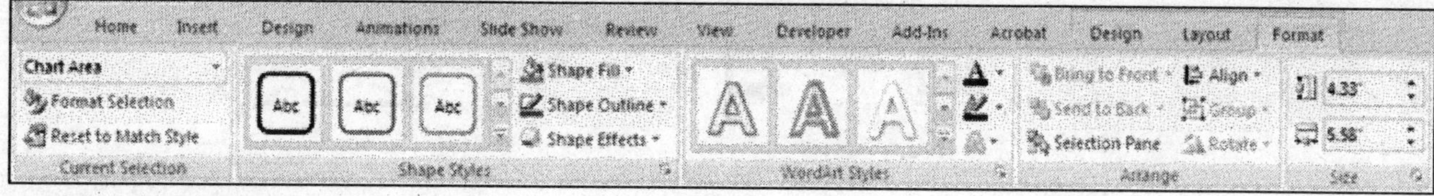

To paste a Chart from Excel:

❖ Open the Excel worksheet

❖ Select the **chart**

- Click **Copy** on the Home tab
- Go to the **PowerPoint** document where you want the chart located
- Click **Paste** on the Home tab

Slide Effects

Slide Transitions

Transitions are effects that are in place when you switch from one slide to the next. To add slide transitions:

- Select the slide that you want to transition
- Click the **Animations** tab
- Choose the appropriate animation or click the **Transition** dialog box

To adjust slide transitions:

- Add sound by clicking the arrow next to **Transition Sound**
- Modify the transition speed by clicking the arrow next to **Transition Speed**

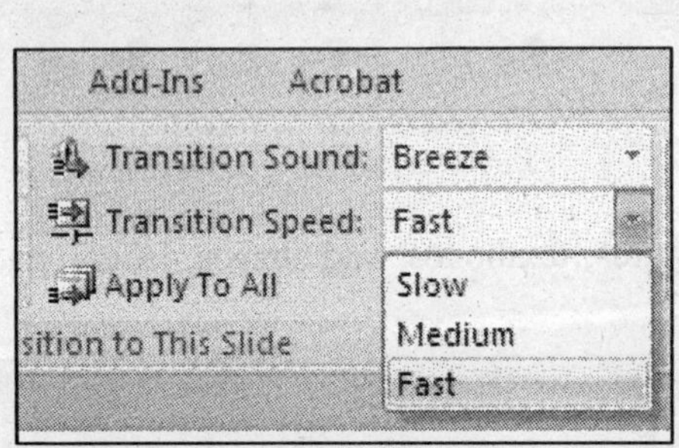

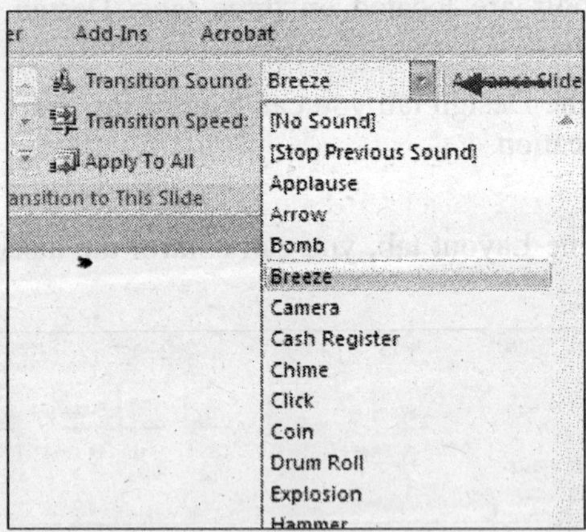

To apply the transition to all slides:

- Click the **Apply to All** button on the **Animations** tab

To select how to advance a slide:

- Choose to Advance on Mouse Click, or
- Automatically after a set number of seconds

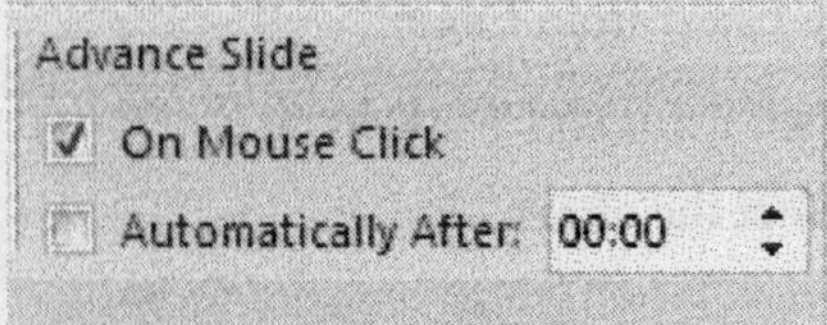

Slide Animation

Slide animation effects are predefined special effects that you can add to objects on a slide.

To apply an animation effect:

- ❖ Select the object
- ❖ Click the **Animations** tab on the Ribbon
- ❖ Click **Custom Animation**
- ❖ Click **Add Effect**
- ❖ Choose the appropriate effect

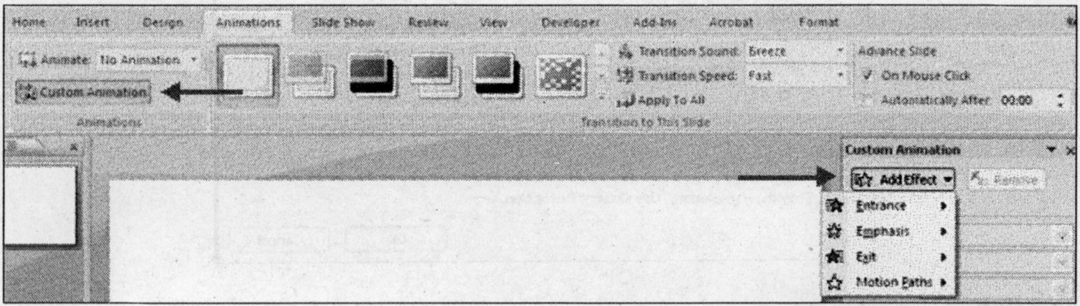

Animation Preview

To preview the animation on a slide:

- ❖ Click the **Preview** button on the **Animations** tab

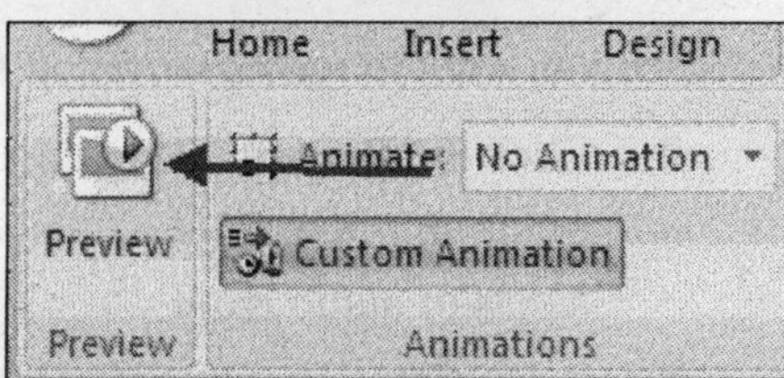

Slide Show Options

The Slide Show tab of the ribbon contains many options for the slide show. These options include:

- ❖ Preview the slide show from the beginning
- ❖ Preview the slide show from the current slide
- ❖ Set up Slide Show

Set Up Slide Show

This option allows you to set preferences for how the slide show will be presented. The options include:

- ❖ Whether the show will run automatically or will be presented by a speaker
- ❖ The looping options
- ❖ Narration options
- ❖ Monitor resolutions

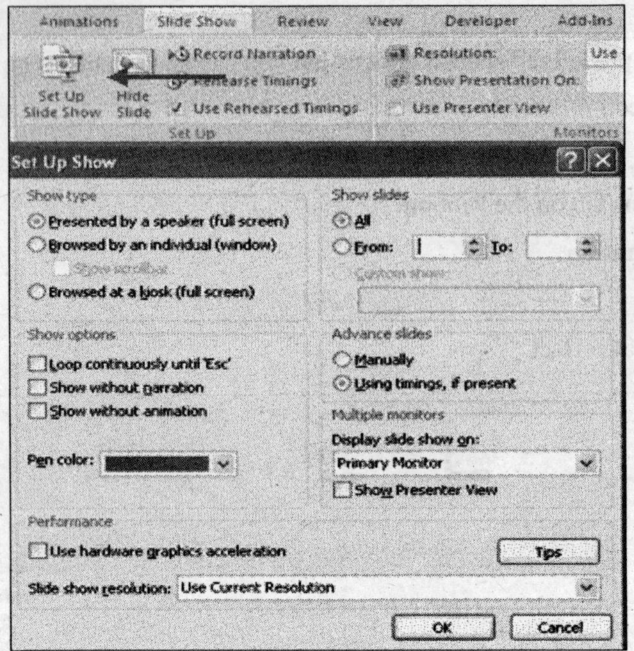

Record Narration

When you want to record narration for the slides:

❖ Click the **Record Narration** button

❖ Click **Set Microphone Level** to check the levels of audio input

❖ Click **OK** to record the narration

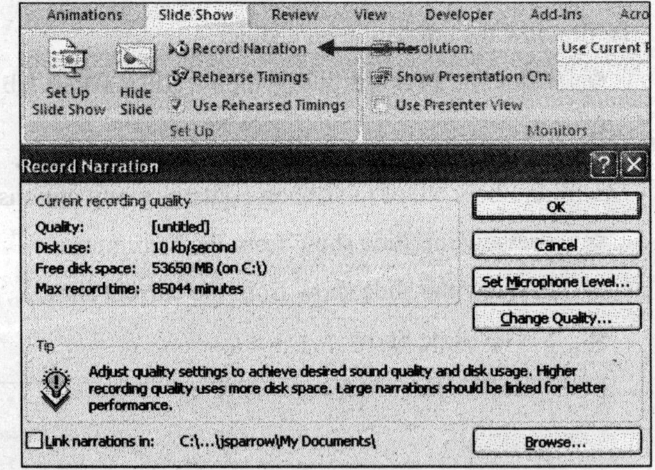

Rehearse Timings

Use Rehearse Timings to rehearse the timings of slide with audio.

❖ Click the Rehearse Timings button

❖ Practice speaking and advance the slides as you would in the presentation

❖ When you have completed this click through the end of the slide

❖ Choose whether or not to keep this timing or to retry

Printing

Create Speaker Notes

Speaker Notes can be added to allow you to create notes for each slide. To add speaker notes:

- ❖ Select the slide
- ❖ Click **View**
- ❖ Click **Note Pages**
- ❖ Click the **Click to add Notes** section of the screen
- ❖ Type in the **Notes** for that slide

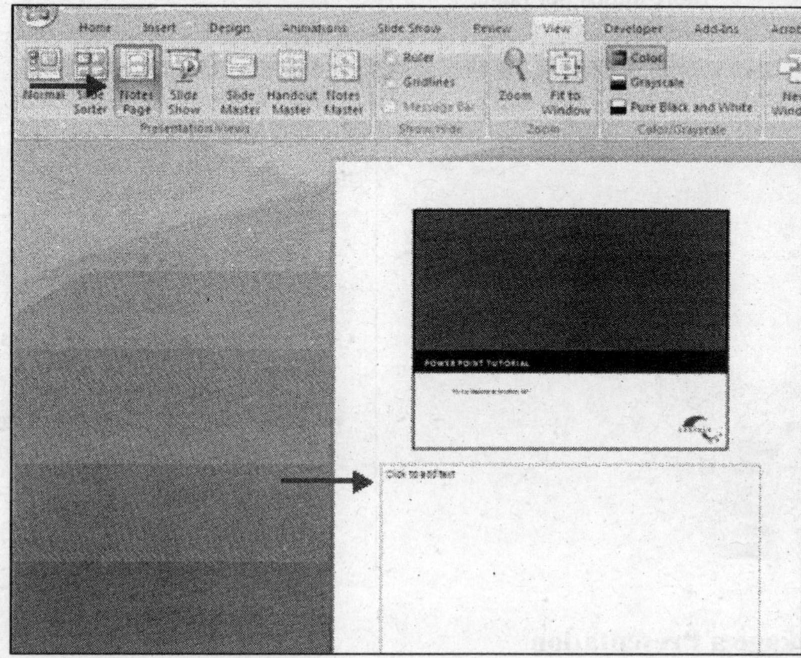

Print a Presentation

PowerPoint 2010 has new features for printing a presentation.

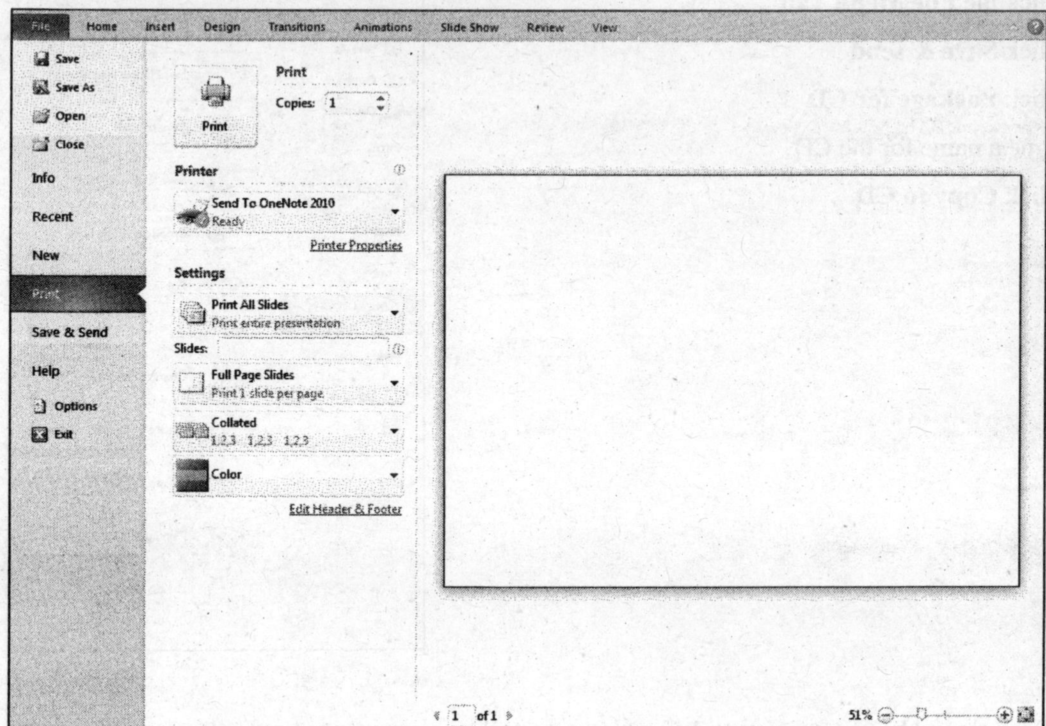

They are:

❖ **Print Layout:** These are slides that you would see print layout in full page slides, notes pages and outline.

❖ **Handouts:** 1, 2, 3 per page, 4, 6, 9 slides in horizontal and 4, 6, 9 slides in vertical. This option allows for more slides per page.

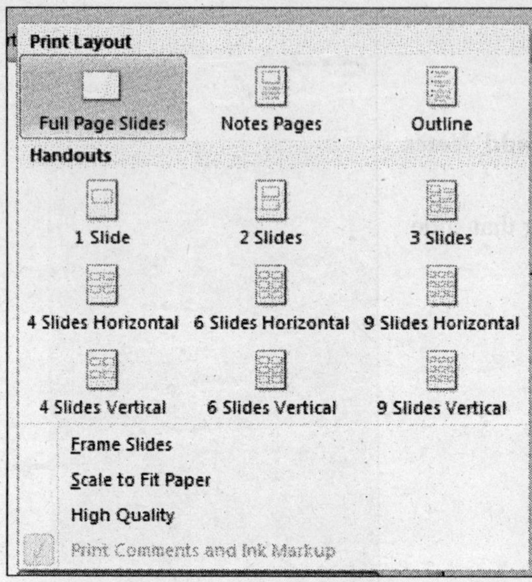

Package a Presentation

There are times when you want to package a presentation with all of the additional files attached as well. To package a presentation for CD:

❖ Click the **File Menu Tab**

❖ Click **Save & send**

❖ Click **Package for CD**

❖ Type a name for the CD

❖ Click **Copy to CD**

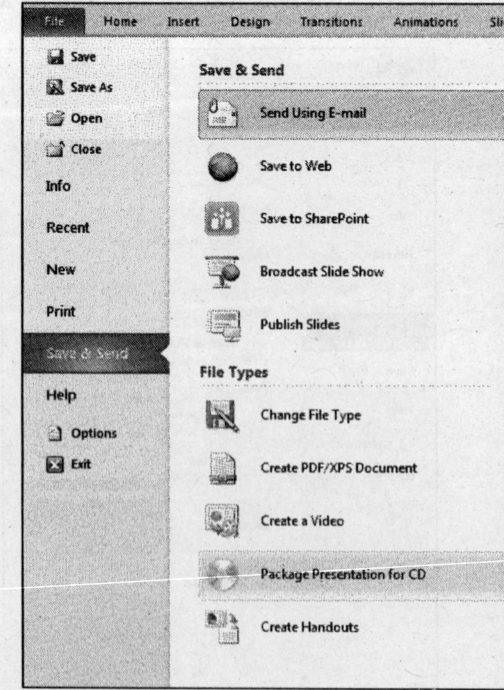

Design Tips

❖ Slides should be of a consistent design throughout the presentation

❖ Use graphics and pictures when possible

- ❖ Remove unnecessary information and graphics
- ❖ Use contrasting background and text colors
- ❖ Keep the number of fonts used in the presentation to 3
- ❖ Keep the fonts consistent throughout the presentation

Presentation Tips

- ❖ Identify the critical information for your presentation
- ❖ Use no more than 6 bullets per page
- ❖ Bullets should be short ideas, not complete sentences (these should be your talking points)
- ❖ To start the Slide Show, Click **Slide Show** on the **Presentation Views** group on the **View** tab
- ❖ Use the arrow keys to move forward or backward in a presentation
- ❖ Press the **Escape (Esc)** key to end the slide show
- ❖ A pen tool is available for drawing on the screen with the mouse. Press **CTRL + P** or click the right mouse button at any time and a popup window will appear. Choose **Pen** and the pointer will change to a pen that allows you to draw freehand on the screen using the mouse. Press the **E** key to erase all pen strokes. Press **CTRL + A** to disable the pen feature and revert the pen back to a pointer arrow.
- ❖ If you would like to use the pen to draw on a blank screen during a presentation, press the **B** or **W** keys, or select **Screen/Black Screen** from the popup menu and the screen will turn black. Press **B** or **W** again or choose **Next** from the popup menu to return to the presentation when you are finished drawing.
- ❖ To hide the pointer and button from the screen, press the **A** key.
- ❖ Be sure to preview the slide show using a projector if one will be used during the presentation. Words or graphics that are close to the edge of the screen may be cut off by the projector.

10.14 MS PROJECT

Ms Project

Microsoft Project is brimming with features to help you manage any kind of project, but you have to know something about project management to make those features sing. If your boss hands you a project to manage and you ask what she means by "project" and "manage".

Project management helps you deliver the right results on time, within budget, and without going into crisis mode. When a project falters, project management techniques also help you get it headed back in the right direction. But before it even begins, a project has to make it through a selection process. Just like a major-league baseball player waiting for a good pitch before he swings, you'll learn what to look for in potential projects.

The project concludes by covering the one skill that no project manager can afford to ignore: gaining and maintaining the support of project stakeholders—the folks who care about the project's success. You'll learn how to identify stakeholders and their expectations, and how to keep them on board so they're ready and willing to pitch in when the project needs their help.

What's So Special about Projects?

Projects come in all shapes and sizes, from learning how to set the date and time on a digital watch to designing and building a timepiece so powerful that you need a Ph.D. to operate it.

Definition: A project is a unique endeavour with clear-cut objectives, a starting point, an ending point, and, usually, a budget.

Unique is the most important word in that definition because every project is different in some way. Assembling reinforcing steel on site for different buildings, built on different topography, during different weather conditions, constitute different projects. The building designs, site conditions, and weather make every construction job unique, even if the buildings are cookie-cutter copies. On the other hand, a crew that cuts and bends concrete reinforcing bars performs the same work every day, typically called *operations*, even if the dimensions of the rebars vary.

Clear-cut objectives are necessary if you want any hope of reaching the end, staying within budget, and making customers happy. Whether you call them specific, quantifiable, or unambiguous, objectives define what the project is supposed to accomplish so everyone knows when it's done.

Budgets play a role in most projects, because few people consider money irrelevant. In addition to achieving the objectives within the desired timeframe, you also have to keep the price tag within an acceptable range.

Project Management

Project management is the art of balancing project objectives against the constraints of time, budget, and quality. Achieving that balance requires skill, experience, and a boatload of techniques.

Beginners sometimes think of project management as building a sequence of tasks, but those in the know recognize that project management starts *before* a project officially begins, and doesn't end for a while after the project's objectives are achieved. There's no one way to manage projects, but most methodologies cover the following five phases:

Getting Started

Often called initiating, the first phase of project management is short but important. It's your only opportunity to get the project off to a good start. In this phase, you answer questions like "Why are we doing this project?" and "Do we really want to do it?" The initial attempts to describe the purpose of a project may produce vague results like "Launch a website to improve customer service."

A project needs buy-in from an executive sponsor and the stakeholders to survive challenges like contradictory objectives, resource shortages, funding issues, and so on. What's more, you, the project manager, need official support, too, so everyone knows the extent of your authority.

Planning

This phase, which detail with the objectives to achieve, the work to perform, who's going to do that work when, and how much the whole thing will cost. Moreover, you set out the rules of the game, including how people will communicate with each other, who has to approve what, how you manage changes and risks, and so on.

Performing the Project

Also referred to as *executing*, this part of project management lasts a long time, but it boils down to following the plan. As the project manager, you keep the project team working on the right things at the right times would be enough, because things would always run according to plan. In the *controlling* phase, you measure project performance against the plan, decide what to do if the project is off track, make the necessary adjustments, and then measure again.

Gaining Closure

Like personal relationships, projects need closure. Before you can call a project complete, you have to tie up loose ends like closing out contracts, transitioning resources to their new assignments, and documenting the overall project performance. The *closing* phase is when you ask for official acceptance that the project is complete—your sign that your job is done.

MS Project 2010 Window

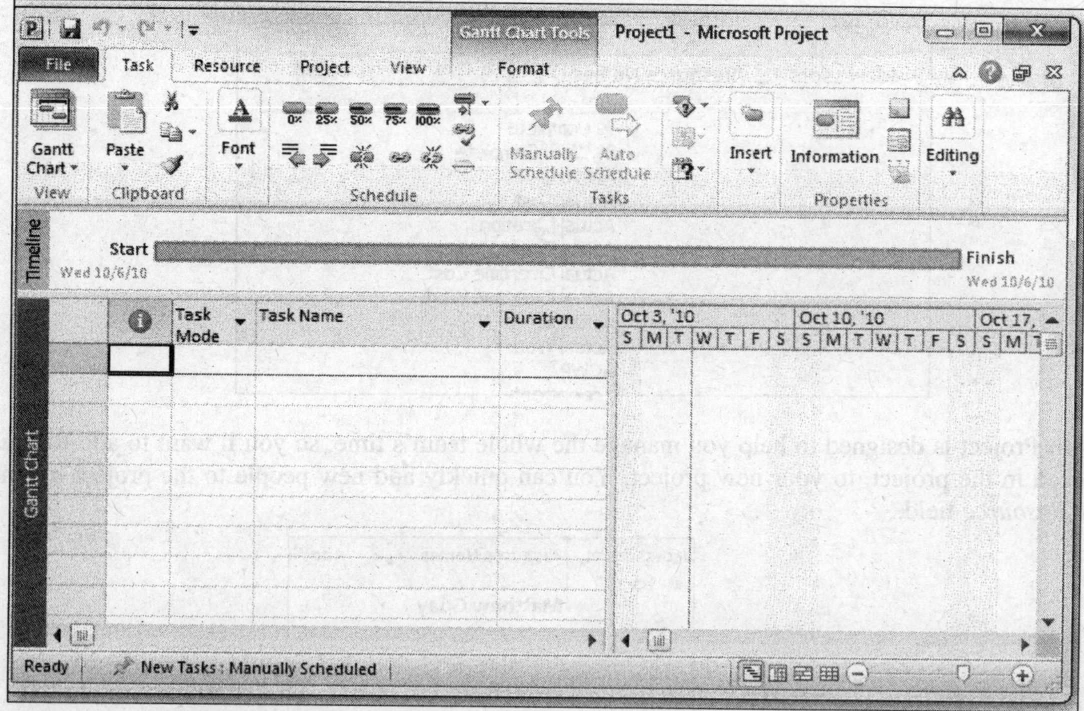

Getting Started with a Project

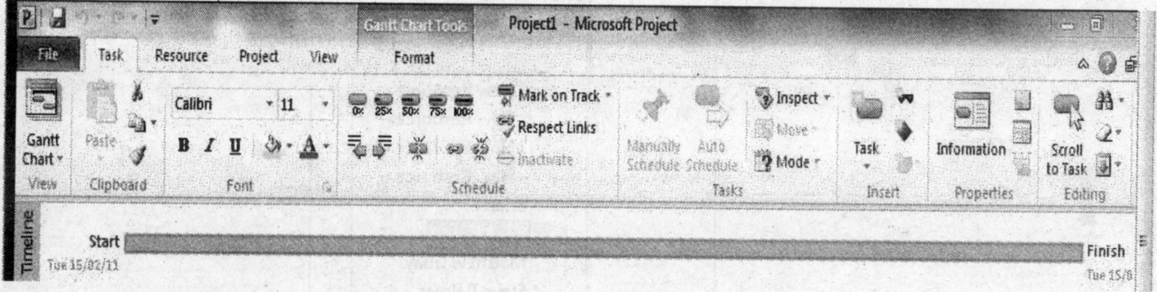

Manage Your Projects in Microsoft Project

When you first start Project, you'll notice that it's immediately ready for you to start entering tasks. Simply enter a task name, duration, start and finish times, and any other details you need. Your new tasks will show up automatically in the Gantt chart on the right, where you can drag the tasks to change the start and finish times.

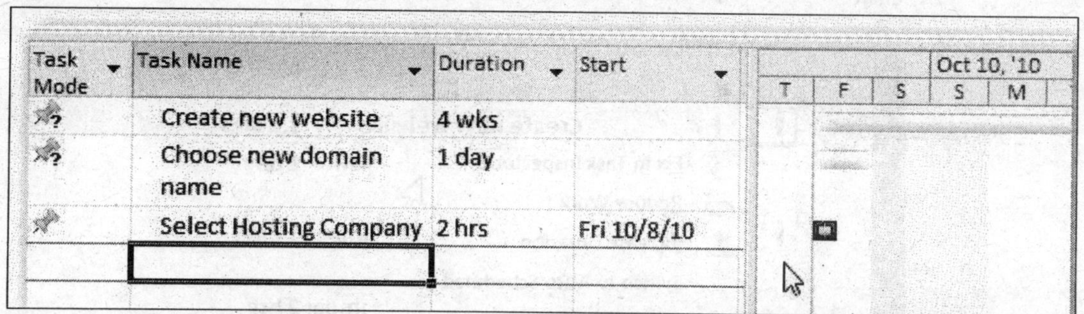

It includes a wide variety of fields you can add to tasks so you can keep track of all important aspects. Choose the things most important for this project.

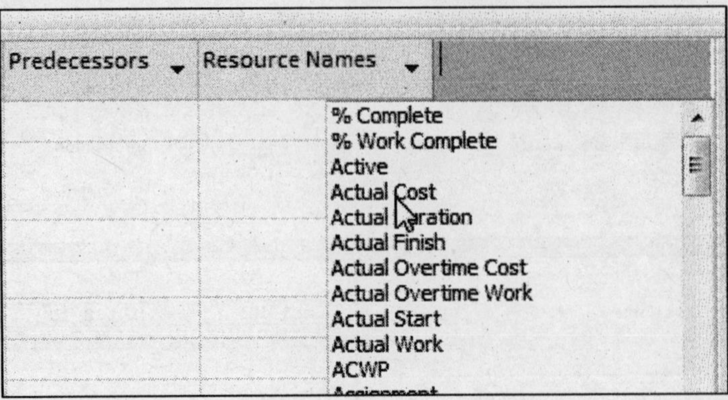

Microsoft Project is designed to help you manage the whole team's time, so you'll want to add Resources, or the people involved in the project, to your new project. You can quickly add new people to the project by entering their names in the *Resource* field.

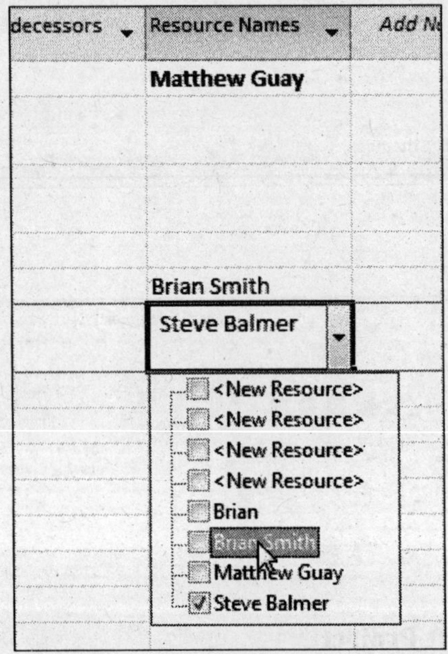

Now, select the *Resources* tab on the top ribbon, and click the *Details* button. This will open a details pane about your resources, where you can add the individual's rate per hour, available time to work on the project, and more.

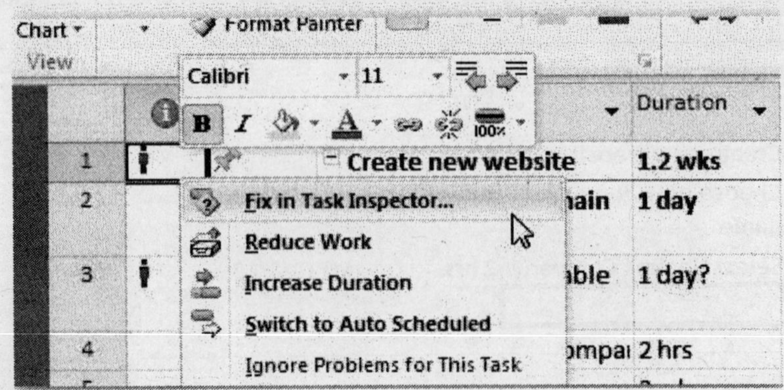

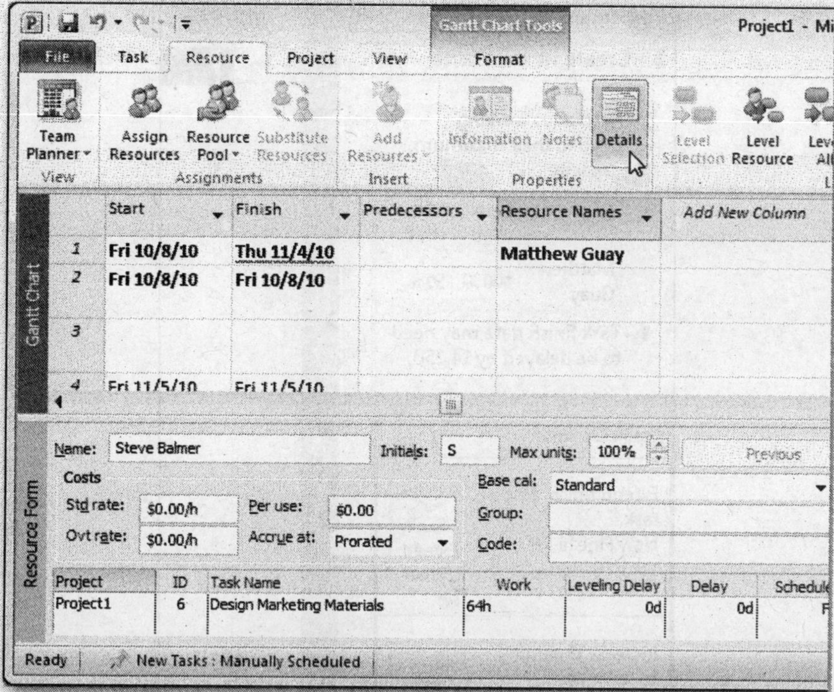

The Resource tab also lets you add resources, including material and cost resources. You can also import people into your project from your Active Directory or Address Book.

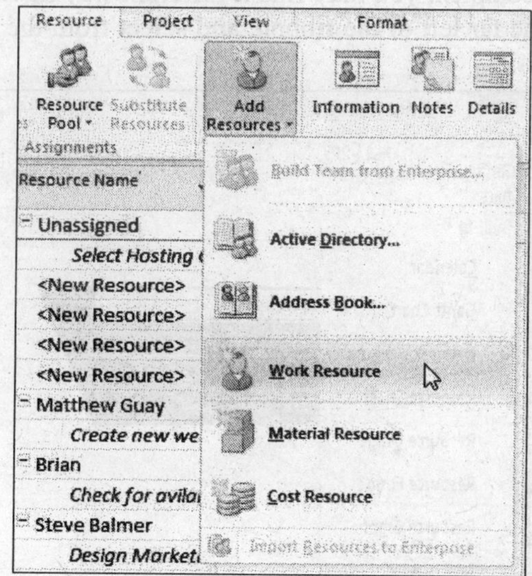

Once you've added everyone's rates and available times, you may notice some conflicts highlighted in red on your tasks. Right-click on the task to see some solutions, or select *Fix in Task Inspector* to get more insight on how to solve the problems.

The Task Inspector helps you see what conflicts the employee or other resource may have, and will give you options to extend the deadline, add more people on the task, and more. These features can help you manage your company without accidentally overscheduling anyone.

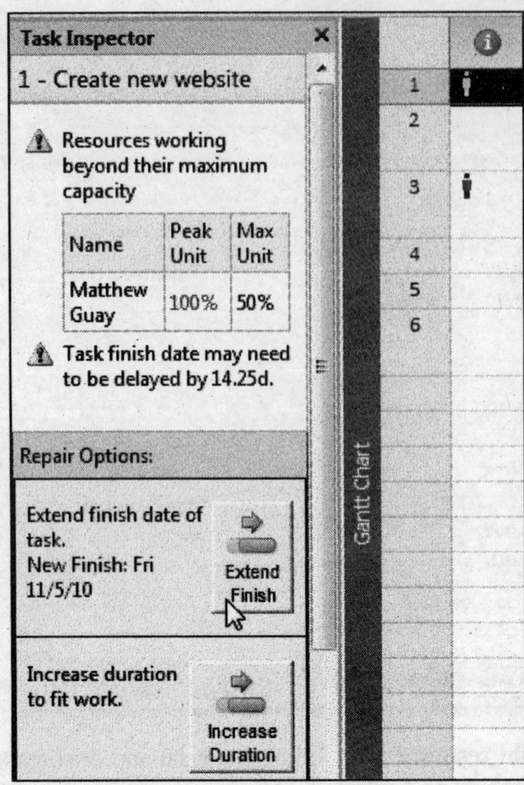

As your projects grow more complex, you may find a different way to view your project which would be helpful. Simply click the chart button on the far left of the ribbon, and select from the wide range of built-in views, sheets, and reports you can use for your project.

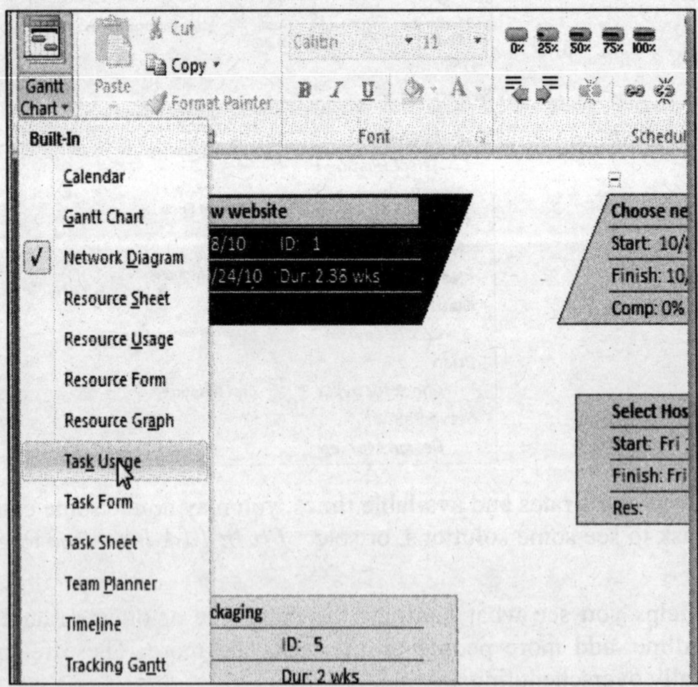

Large projects can become unwieldy on their own, so at some point, you'll need to decide to split tasks into new projects. Microsoft Project lets you keep everything together, still, even if you need to move it into a new project file. From the *Project* tab, you can link various projects together or create a subproject to keep everything in order.

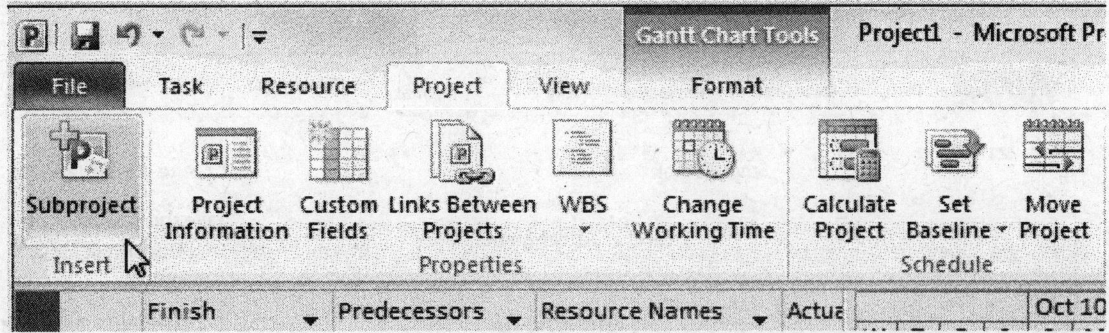

You can also fully customize how your project looks from the ribbon, complete with various graphics styles for your Gantt charts.

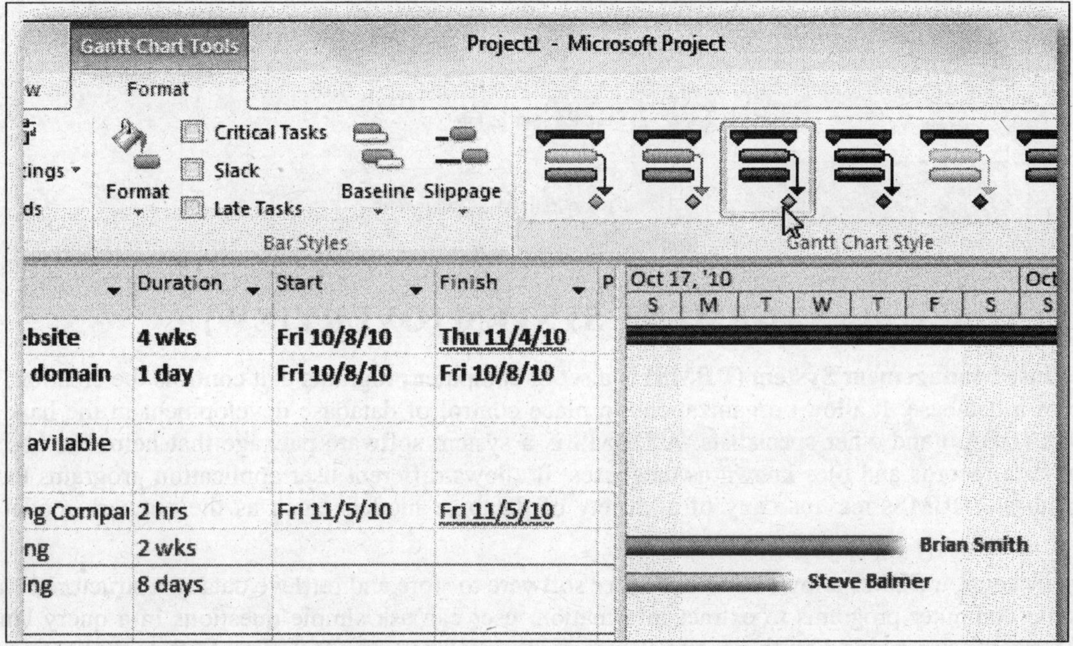

Project offers a wide range of reports you can generate about your projects, including costs, workload, and more. Note that you'll have to enter all the available information in your tasks to make sure your reports are as accurate as possible.

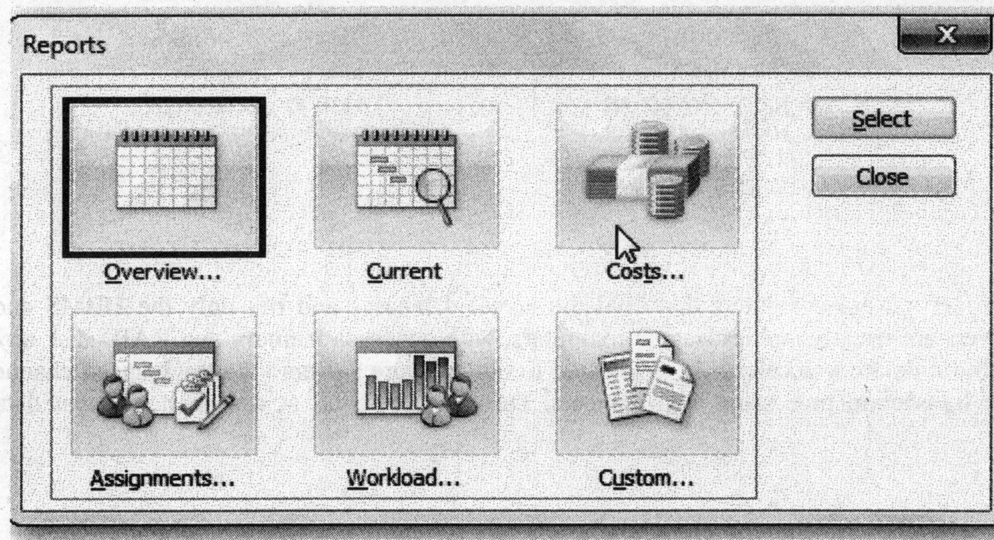

Then, you can share your project details with your team in PDF format so everyone can use it whether they have Project or not.

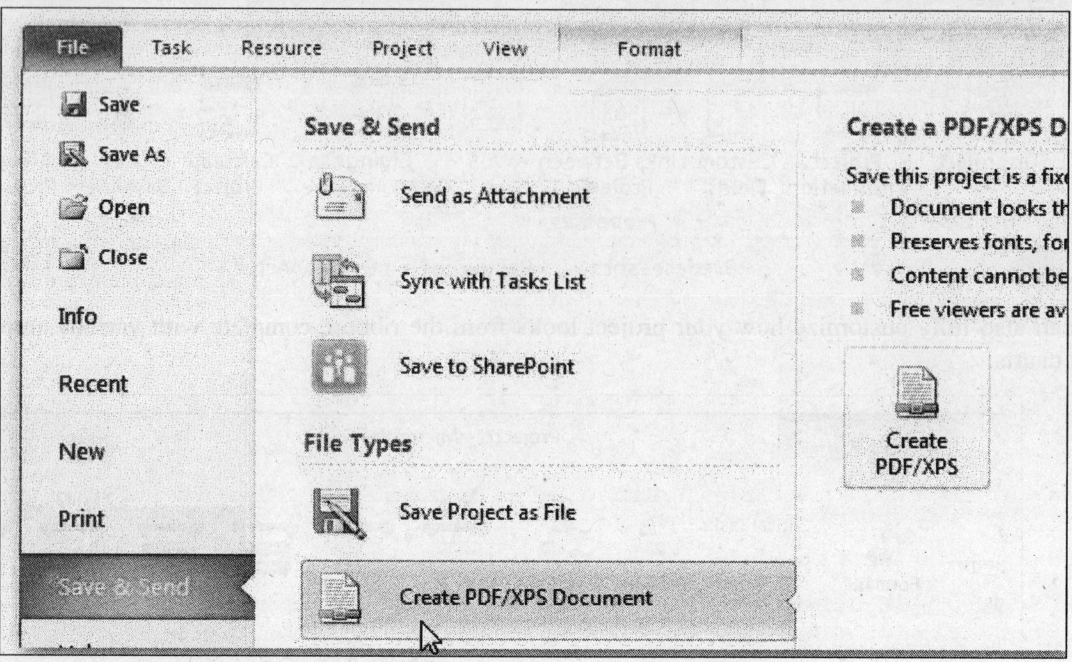

10.15 DATABASE MANAGEMENT SYSTEM (OVERVIEW)

A **Database Management System (DBMS)** is a set of computer programs that controls the creation, maintenance, and the use of a database. It allows organizations to place control of database development in the hands of database administrators (DBAs) and other specialists. A DBMS is a system software package that helps the use of integrated collection of data records and files known as databases. It allows different user application programs to easily access the same database. DBMSs may use any of a variety of database models, such as the network model or relational model.

In large systems, a DBMS allows users and other software to store and retrieve data in a structured way. Instead of having to write computer programs to extract information, user can ask simple questions in a query language. Thus, many DBMS packages provide Fourth-generation programming language (4GLs) and other application development features. It helps to specify the logical organization for a database and access and use the information within a database. It provides facilities for controlling data access, enforcing data integrity, managing concurrency, and restoring the database from backups. A DBMS also provides the ability to logically present database information to users.

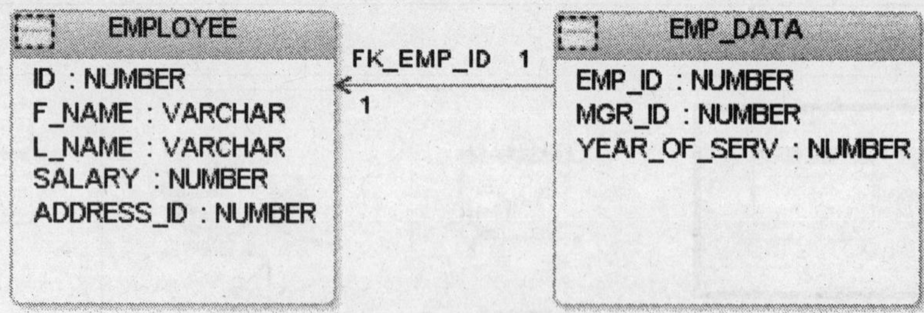

Database servers are computers that hold the actual databases and run only the DBMS and related software. Database servers are usually multiprocessor computers, with generous memory and RAID disk arrays used for stable storage. Hardware database accelerators, connected to one or more servers via a high-speed channel, are also used in large volume transaction processing environments. DBMSs are found at the heart of most database applications.

DBMSs may be built around a custom multitasking kernel with built-in networking support, but modern DBMSs typically rely on a standard operating system to provide these functions.

DBMS Building Blocks

A DBMS includes four main parts: modeling language, data structure, database query language, and transaction mechanisms:

Components of DBMS

- **DBMS Engine** accepts logical request from the various other DBMS subsystems, converts them into physical equivalents, and actually accesses the database and data dictionary as they exist on a storage device.
- **Data Definition Subsystem** helps user to create and maintain the data dictionary and define the structure of the files in a database.
- **Data Manipulation Subsystem** helps user to add, change, and delete information in a database and query it for valuable information. Software tools within the data manipulation subsystem are most often the primary interface between user and the information contained in a database. It allows user to specify its logical information requirements.
- **Application Generation Subsystem** contains facilities to help users to develop transaction-intensive applications. It usually requires that user perform a detailed series of tasks to process a transaction. It facilitates easy-to-use data entry screens, programming languages, and interfaces.
- **Data Administration Subsystem** helps users to manage the overall database environment by providing facilities for backup and recovery, security management, query optimization, concurrency control, and change management.

Modeling Language

A data modeling language to define the schema of each database hosted in the DBMS, according to the DBMS database model. The five most common types of models are:

- Hierarchical model
- Network model
- Relational model
- Multidimensional model
- Object model

Hierarchical Model: The hierarchical model was used in early mainframe DBMS. Records' relationships form a treelike model. This model is simple but non-flexible because the relationship is confined to a one-to-many relationship. IBM's IMS system and the RDM Mobile are examples of a hierarchical database system with multiple hierarchies over the same data. RDM Mobile is a newly designed embedded database for a mobile computer system.

Network Model: The network model consists of more complex relationships. Unlike the hierarchical structure, it can relate to many records and accesses them by following one of the several paths. In other words, this structure allows for many-to-many relationships.

Relational Model: The relational model is the most commonly used today. It is used by mainframe, midrange and microcomputer systems. It uses two-dimensional rows and columns to store data. The tables of records can be connected by common key values. While working for IBM, E.F. Cod designed this model in 1970. The model is not easy for the end-user to run queries with because it may require a complex combination of many tables.

Multidimensional Model: The multidimensional model is similar to the relational model. The dimensions of the cube looking model have data relating to elements in each cell. This model gives a spreadsheet like view of data. This model is easy to maintain because records are stored as fundamental attributes, the same way they're viewed and the structure is easy to understand. Its high performance has made it the most popular database structure when it comes to enabling online analytical processing (OLAP).

Object Model: The object-oriented model has the ability to handle graphics, pictures, voice and text, types of data, without difficultly unlike the other database structures. This model is popular for multimedia web-based applications. It was designed to work with object-oriented programming languages such as Java.

Data Structure

Data structures (fields, records, files and objects) optimized to deal with very large amounts of data stored on a permanent data storage device (which implies relatively slow access compared to volatile main memory).

Database Query Language

A database query language and report writer allows users to interactively interrogate the database, analyze its data and update it according to the user's privileges on data. It also controls the security of the database. Data security prevents unauthorized users from viewing or updating the database. Using passwords, users are allowed access to the entire database or subsets of it called *subschemas*. For example, an employee database can contain all the data about an individual employee, but one group of users may be authorized to view only payroll data, while others are allowed access to only work history and medical data.

If the DBMS provides a way to interactively enter and update the database, as well as interrogate it, this capability allows for managing personal databases. However, it may not leave an audit trail of actions or provide the kinds of controls necessary in a multi-user organization. These controls are only available when a set of application programs are customized for each data entry and updating function.

Transaction Mechanism

A database transaction mechanism ideally guarantees ACID properties in order to ensure data integrity despite concurrent user accesses (concurrency control), and faults (fault tolerance). It also maintains the integrity of the data in the database. The DBMS can maintain the integrity of the database by not allowing more than one user to update the same record at the same time. The DBMS can help prevent duplicate records via unique index constraints; for example, no two customers with the same customer numbers (key fields) can be entered into the database.

DBMS Topics

External, Logical and Internal View

Traditional View of Data

A database management system provides the ability for many different users to share data and process resources. But as there can be many different users, there are many different database needs. The question now is: How can a single, unified database meet the differing requirement of so many users?

A DBMS minimizes these problems by providing two views of the database data: an external view (or user view), logical view (or conceptual view) and physical (or internal) view. The user's view, of a database program, represents data in a format that is meaningful to a user and to the software programs that process those data.

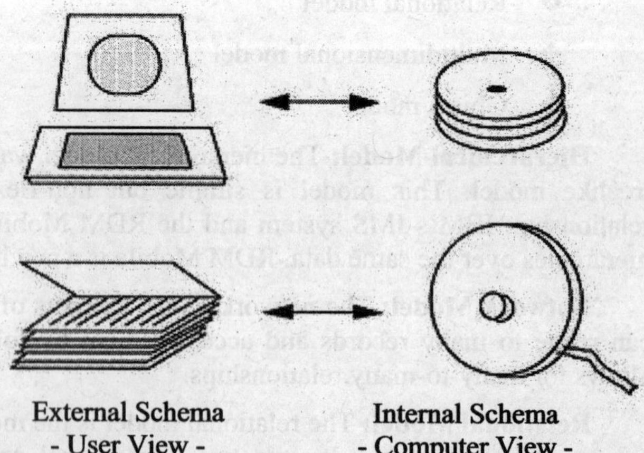

One strength of a DBMS is that while there is typically only one conceptual (or logical) and physical (or internal) view of the data, there can be an endless number of different external views. This feature allows users to see database information in a more business-related way rather than from a technical, processing viewpoint. Thus, the logical view refers to the way user views data, and the physical view to the way the data are physically stored and processed.

DBMS Features and Capabilities

Alternatively, and especially in connection with the relational model of database management, the relation between attributes drawn from a specified set of domains can be seen as being primary. For instance, the database might indicate that a car that was originally "red" might fade to "pink" in time, provided it was of some particular "make" with an inferior paint job. Such higher creative relationships provide information on all of the underlying domains at the same time, with none of them being privileged above the others.

- **Query ability:** Querying is the process of requesting attribute information from various perspectives and combinations of factors. A database query language and report writer allow users to interactively interrogate the database, analyze its data and update it according to the user's privileges on data.
- **Backup and replication:** Copies of attributes need to be made regularly in case primary disks or other equipment fails. A periodic copy of attributes may also be created for a distant organization that cannot readily access the original. DBMS usually provide utilities to facilitate the process of extracting and disseminating attribute sets. When data is replicated between database servers, so that the information remains consistent throughout the database system and users cannot tell or even know which server in the DBMS they are using, the system is said to exhibit replication transparency.
- **Rule enforcement:** Often one wants to apply rules to attributes so that the attributes are clean and reliable. For example, we may have a rule that says each car can have only one engine associated with it (identified by Engine Number). If somebody tries to associate a second engine with a given car, we want the DBMS to deny such a request and display an error message. However, with changes in the model specification such as, in this example, hybrid gas-electric cars, rules may need to change. Ideally, such rules should be able to be added and removed as needed without significant data layout redesign.
- **Security:** Often, it is desirable to limit who can see or change which attributes or groups of attributes. This may be managed directly by individual, or by the assignment of individuals and privileges to groups, through the assignment of individuals and groups to roles which are then granted entitlements.
- **Computation:** There are common computations requested on attributes such as counting, summing, averaging, sorting, grouping, cross-referencing, etc. Rather than have each computer application implement these from scratch, they can rely on the DBMS to supply such calculations.
- **Change and access logging:** Often one wants to know who accessed what attributes, what was changed, and when it was changed. Logging services allow this by keeping a record of access occurrences and changes.
- **Automated optimization:** If there are frequently occurring usage patterns or requests, some DBMS can adjust themselves to improve the speed of those interactions. In some cases, the DBMS will merely provide tools to monitor performance, allowing a human expert to make the necessary adjustments after reviewing the statistics collected.
- **Meta-data repository:** Meta-data is data describing data. For example, a listing that describes what attributes are allowed to be in data sets is called "meta-information". The meta-data is also known as data about data.

Current Trends

Database management is no longer limited to "monolithic entities". Many solutions have developed to satisfy individual needs of users. Development of numerous database options has created flexible solutions in database management.

Today, there are several ways database management has affected the technology world as we know it. Organizations' demand for directory services has become an extreme necessity as organizations grow. Businesses are now able to use directory services that provided prompt searches for their company information. Mobile devices are not only able to store contact information of users but have grown to bigger capabilities. Mobile technology is able to cache large information that is used for computers and is able to display it on smaller devices.

Web searches have even been affected with database management. Search engine queries are able to locate data within the World Wide Web. Retailers have also benefited from the developments with data warehousing. These companies are able to record customer transactions made within their business. Online transactions have become tremendously popular with the e-business world. Consumers and businesses are able to make payments securely on company websites. None of these current developments would have been possible without the evolution of database management. Even with all the progress and current trends of database management, there will always be a need for new development as specifications and needs grow.

As the speeds of consumer internet connectivity increase, and as data availability and computing become more ubiquitous, database are seeing migration to web services. Web-based languages such as XML and PHP are being used to process databases over web-based services. These languages allow databases to live in "the cloud".

10.16 MICROSOFT ACCESS

Microsoft Access

A database is an organized collection of records. Telephone and address books are examples of paper databases. With Access, you can create a computerized database. For example, you can use Access to organize the students who attend a school, the courses they take, and the instructors who teach them. After you create an Access database, you can search it, manipulate it, and extract information from it.

To begin, start Access 2010. Your screen will look similar to the one shown here.

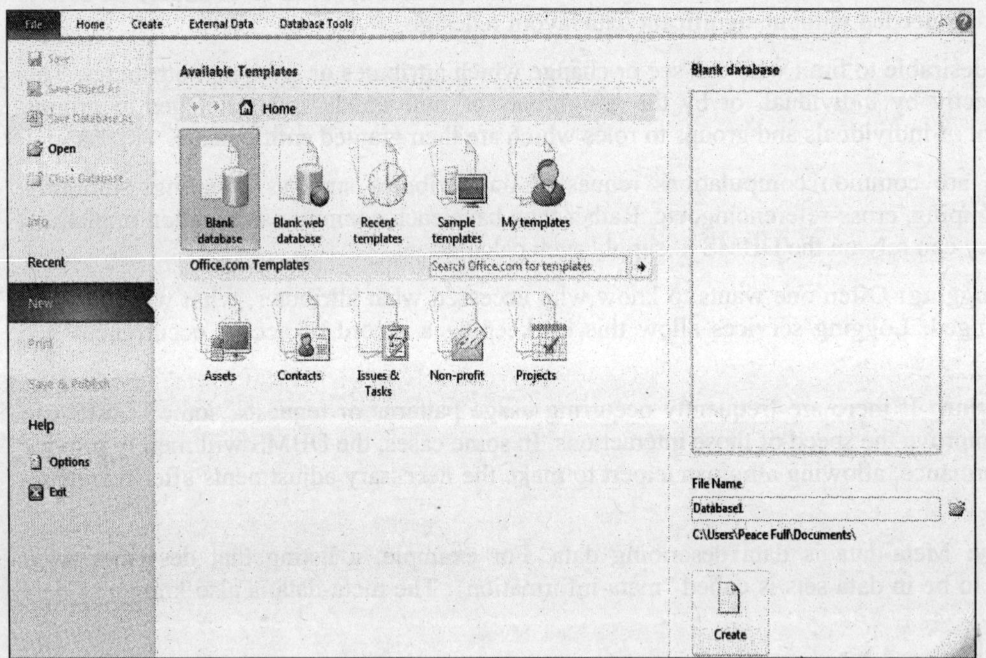

The File Menu

When you click file menu button, a menu appears. You can use the menu to create a new file, open an existing file, save a file, and perform many other tasks.

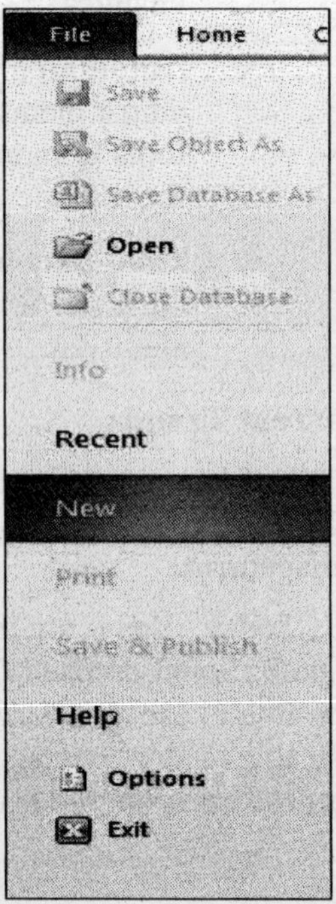

The Quick Access Toolbar

Next to the Microsoft Office button is the Quick Access toolbar. The Quick Access toolbar provides you with access to commands you frequently use. By default, Save, Undo, and Redo appear on the Quick Access toolbar. You use Save to save an object, Undo to roll back an action you have taken, and Redo to reapply an action you have rolled back.

The Title Bar

The Title bar is located at the top in the center of the Access window. The Title bar displays the name of the database on which you are currently working.

Access Objects

To view or hide the objects on the Navigation pane:

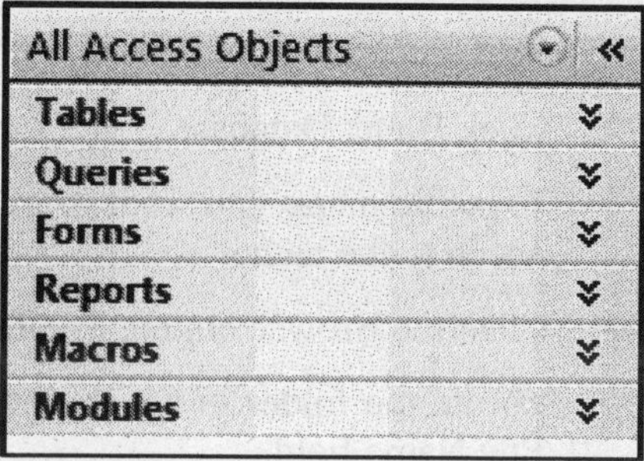

- ❖ You click the double down-arrows to view objects. The double down-arrows change to double up-arrows.
- ❖ You click the double up-arrows to hide objects. The double up-arrows change to double down-arrows.

As stated earlier, the Navigation pane stores the objects in your database: tables, queries, forms, reports, macros, and modules. Objects always display with an icon to the right. The icon tells you the object type: table, query, form, report, macro, and module.

Objects	
Tables	In Access, data is stored in tables. A table is a set of columns and rows, with each column referred to as a field. Each value in a field represents a single type of data. Each row of a table is referred to as a record.
Queries	You use queries to retrieve specific data from your database and to answer questions about your data. For example, you can use a query to find the names of the employees in your database who live in a particular state.
Forms	Forms give you the ability to choose the format and arrangement of fields. You can use a form to enter, edit, and display data.
Reports	Reports organize or summarize your data so you can print it or view it onscreen. You often use reports when you want to analyze your data or present your data to others.
Macros	Macros give you the ability to automate tasks. You can use a macro to add functionality to a form, report, or control.
Modules	Like macros, modules give you the ability to automate tasks and add functionality to a form, report, or control. Macros are created by choosing from a list of macro actions, whereas modules are written in Visual Basic for Applications.

You double-click an object to open the object. You right-click an object to view a menu of options. You can use the menu to do such things as open objects, rename objects, and delete objects. Objects that are open appear on tabs. Right-click a tab to view a menu of options you can perform, such as save the object, close the object, or change the view.

Create a Database

When you start Access, the Getting Started with Microsoft Office Access screen appears. You can use this screen to create a database. Within a database, you can do such things as enter data, create reports, and retrieve data. You can create a blank database or you can use one of the templates provided by Microsoft. When you use a template, Access creates forms you can use to enter data, reports you can use to retrieve data, and more. You can modify the forms, reports, and other objects to suit your needs. This tutorial will teach you how.

The following templates are included with Access: Assets, Contacts, Events, Faculty, Issues, Marketing Projects, Projects, Sales Pipeline, Students, and Tasks. Other templates are available online. Each template creates a database related to the title. For example, the Faculty template creates a faculty database that includes tables, queries, forms, and reports related to faculty. In Access, you use tables to store data, queries to retrieve data, forms to enter data, and reports to display data.

- ❖ Start Access.
- ❖ Click Blank Database.
- ❖ Type the name you want to give your database in the File Name field. Access will automatically append accdb to the name.
- ❖ Click the Browse button. The File New Database window appears.
- ❖ Locate the folder in which you want to store your database. Note that the name of the file appears in the File Name field.
- ❖ Click OK.
- ❖ Click the Create button. Access creates the database and opens a datasheet with the Table Tools available to you.

To use a template to create a database:

- ❖ Start Access. The Getting Started with Microsoft Office Access screen appears.
- ❖ Click Local Templates. Icons representing local templates appear in the center of the window.
- ❖ Click the icon for the template you want to use.
- ❖ Click the Browse button. The File New Database window appears.
- ❖ Locate the folder in which you want to store your database.
- ❖ Click OK.
- ❖ Click Create. Access creates and opens your database.
- ❖ Open the Navigation pane. Access displays the tables, queries, forms, reports and other objects related to the database you selected. You may wish to display the objects by type.

Creating Microsoft Access Tables

Tables are the foundation of an Access database. Access stores data in tables.

Understanding Tables

A table is a set of columns and rows. Each column is called a field. Within a table, each field must be given a name and no two fields can have the same name. Each value in a field represents a single category of data. For example, a table might have three fields: Last Name, First Name, and Phone Number. The table consists of three columns: one for last name, one for first name, and one for phone number. In every row of the table, the Last Name field contains the last name, the First Name field contains the first name, and the Phone Number field contains the phone number. Each row in a table is called a record.

Table1 | Table1 | Table1

ID	Item	First N	Last N	E-mail Address	Home Phon	Mobile Ph	Location	Address	City
1	Student	somu	sundar	somu@gmail.com	0432-2490560	09875624300	Pondy	34, New main r	Pondy
2	student	thiyagu	nataraj	thiyagu_tu@gmail.com	0422-2545896	09752638425	Coimbatore	234/34, west lc	Coimbatore
3	student	Raj	vadu	raj@ynmail.com	0431-2758452	08556245620	Trichy	89,gandhi stree	Trichy
4	student	vinu	raj	vuni_rty@rediffmail.com	011-52896333	0256387963	singapore	eastr costal are	Singu
5	faculty	thomas	raj	thom@yahoo.com		0944463285	Mumbai	35,dhadhar stre	Mumabi

To add fields to a table:

- ❖ Click the Add New Field column label.
- ❖ Activate the Datasheet tab.
- ❖ Click Rename in the Fields & Columns group.
- ❖ Type the field name.
- ❖ Press Enter. Access creates the field.
- ❖ Type the next field name. Access creates the field. Continue until you have created all of the fields in your table.
- ❖ Press Enter without entering a field name to end your entries.

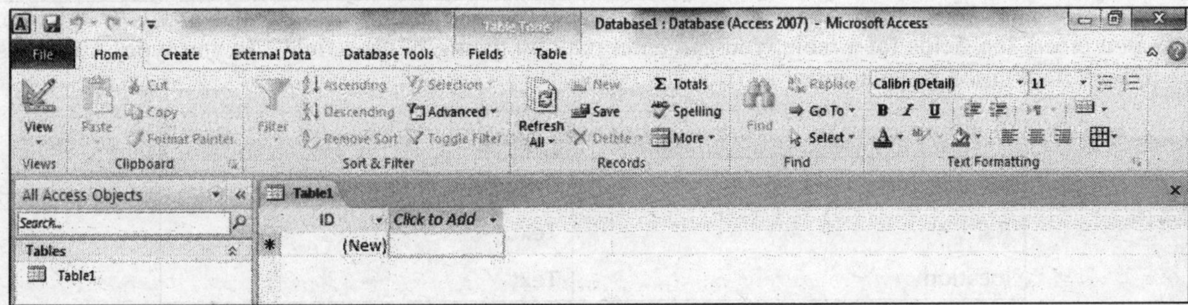

Name and Save a Table

After you create a table, you must name and save it.

- ❖ Click the Save button on the Quick Access toolbar. The Save As dialog box appears.
- ❖ Type the name you want to give your table.
- ❖ Click OK. Access names your table.

Understanding Data Types

In Access, you use data types to specify the type of data each field can capture. A field with a data type of text can store alphabetic characters and numbers. Generally speaking, you cannot perform mathematical calculations by using a text field. For example, you can use a text field to store a street address.

Data Types	Use	Notes
Text	Alphanumeric data. Used for text and for numbers that are not used in mathematical calculations. Used for names, addresses, and other relatively short pieces of text. Can store up to 255 characters.	
Memo	Long text. Used for long pieces of text, such as notes and long descriptions. Can store up to 64,000 characters.	
Number	Numeric data. Used for numbers you want to use in mathematical calculations.	If you are working with currency, use the currency type.
Date/Time	Used for dates and times.	
Currency	Used for currency.	Prevents rounding during calculation.
AutoNumber	Unique sequential numbers or random numbers automatically inserted when you create a record. Used to create a primary key.	
Yes/No	Logical data. Used when only one of two values is valid. Yes/No, True/False, etc.	
Hyperlink	Used to store hyperlinks.	
Attachment	Used to store attachments.	
OLE Object	Used to attach an OLE object such as a Word document, Excel spreadsheet, or PowerPoint presentation.	

After you create the fields for a table, you can enter data by typing in each field. As you type, Access assigns a data type to each field based on your entry.

Assigned Data Types

Sample Entry	Data Type Assigned
Raj	Text
location	Text
www.gmail.com	Number, Long Integer
10,000	Number, Long Integer
10,000.99	Number, Double
10000.999	Number, Double
01/01/2009 The date and time formats recognized are those of your user locale.	Date/Time
January 1, 2009	Date/Time
12:10:33	Date/Time
12:30 am	Date/Time
16:50	Date/Time
100.50	Number, Double

25.00%	Number, Double
1.23E+02	Number, Double

Explicitly Assign Data Types and Formats

You may want to change the data type Access assigned to a field, or you may want to explicitly assign a data type to each field. You can do so by choosing the Datasheet tab and then selecting the proper option in the Data Type field in the Data Type and Formatting group.

Some data types allow you to select the formatting you want. By formatting, you determine how data in a field displays. For example, if you choose a data type of number and a format of Euro, any number you enter will appear with a Euro sign in front.

Windows regional settings enable you to display information such as dates, times, and currency that match the standards or language used in the country in which you live. For example, if you live in the United States, the currency setting uses a dollar sign.

Regional Settings for English (United States)	
Number	123,456,789.00
Currency	$123,456,789.00
Time	3:39:44 PM
Short Date	7/28/2008
Long Date	Monday, July 28, 2008

Use the Windows Control panel's Regional and Language options to view or change regional settings.

	Data Types	
Data Type	**Format**	**How Numbers Display**
Number	General Number	As typed.
	Currency	Uses thousands separator. Follows regional settings.
	Euro	Uses currency format with Euro symbol.
	Fixed	Displays at least one digit. Follows regional settings.
	Standard	Uses thousands separator. Follows regional setting.
	Percent	Converts entry to percent.
	Scientific	Uses scientific notation.
Currency	General Number	As typed.
	Currency	Uses thousands separator. Follows regional settings.
	Euro	Uses currency format with Euro symbol.
	Fixed	Displays at least one digit. Follows regional settings.
	Standard	Uses thousands separator. Follows regional setting.
	Percent	Converts entry to percent.
	Scientific	Uses scientific notation.

Date/Time	General Date	Date values display as numbers and time values as hours, minutes, and seconds followed by AM or PM. Follows regional settings.
	Long Date	Uses the Long Date format specified in your Windows regional settings.
	Medium Date	Uses dd/mmm/yy, using the date separator specified in your Windows regional settings.
	Short Date	Uses the Short Date format specified in your Windows regional settings.
	Long Time	Uses hours, minutes, and seconds followed by AM or PM. Uses the separator specified in the Time setting in your Windows regional settings.
	Medium Time	Displays hours and minutes followed by AM or PM. Uses the separator specified in the Time setting in your Windows regional settings.
	Short Time	Uses hours and minutes. Uses the separator specified in the Time setting in your Windows regional settings.
Yes/No		Yes/No True/False On/Off

To explicitly assign a data type or format to a field:

- ❖ Click the field label for the field to which you want to assign a data type.
- ❖ Activate the Datasheet tab.
- ❖ Click the down-arrow next to the Data Type field and then choose a data type.
- ❖ Click the down-arrow next to the Format field and then choose a format. Access assigns a data type and format to the field you selected.

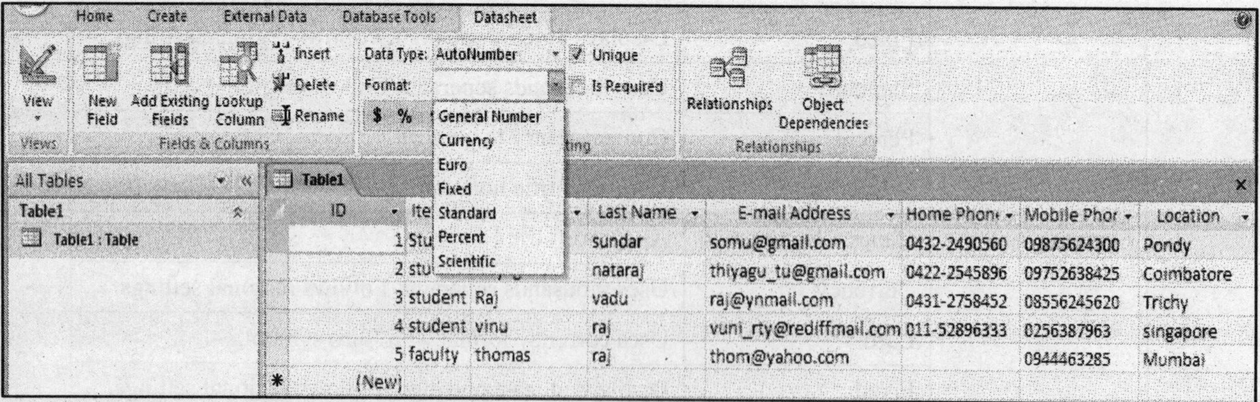

Understanding Design View

Access provides several ways to view the objects in your database. You can use Design view to create or modify an Access table. You can use the View button on the Home tab or the Table Design button on the Create tab to change to Design view. Using Design view is the preferred method for creating a table because it provides you with the most options and enables you to precisely define your table. In addition to selecting a data type, you can set all of the following options in Design view.

Design View Options		
Field Property	**Data Type**	**Comments**
Field Size	Text	Enables you to restrict the number of characters stored in a text field to 0 to 255 characters. The default is 255.
	Number	Enables you to select the type of number stored in a field.
	Number Types	*Values Stored*
	Byte	0 to 255 (No fractions)
	Decimal	–9.999... × 1027 through +9.999... × 1027
	Integer	–32,768 to + 32,767 (No fractions)
	Long Integer	–2,147,483,648 to + 2,147,483,647
	Single	–3.4 × 1038 to + 3.4 × 1038 numeric floating point values. Up to seven significant digits.
	Double	–1.797 × 10308 to + 1.797 × 10308 1038 numeric floating point values. Up to fifteen significant digits.
	Replication ID	Globally Unique Identifier (GUID). Used by Access to establish a unique identifier for replication.
Format	Number	Determines how numbers display. When you use the currency, fixed, standard, and percent formats. Access follows the settings specified in Regional Settings in the Windows Control Panel for negative amounts, decimal and currency symbols, and decimal places.
Currency Number	General Number	Displays as typed.
	Currency	Uses thousands separator. Follows regional setting.
	Euro	Uses currency format with Euro symbol.
	Fixed	Displays one digit. Follows regional settings.
	Standard	Uses thousands separator. Follows regional settings.
	Percent	Converts entry to percent.
	Scientific	Uses scientific notation.
Date/Time	General Date	Displays date and time.

		Example: 01/02/99, 06:28:21 PM
	Long Date	Displays Day of Week and Date Example: Saturday, January 02, 1999
	Medium Date	Example: 02-Jan-99
	Short Date	Example: 01/02/99
	Long Time	Example: 6:28:21 PM
	Medium Time	Example: 6:28 PM
	Short Time	Example: 18:28
Text and Memo	@	Text character required.
	&	Text character not required.
	<	Changes all characters to lowercase.
	>	Changes all characters to uppercase.
Yes/No	Yes/No	If the Lookup Display Control is a text box, displays Yes/No.
	True/False	If the Lookup Display Control is a text box, displays True/False.
	On/Off	If the Lookup Display Control is a text box, displays On/Off.
Decimal Places	Determines number of decimal places Access displays.	Auto. Number of decimals displayed depends on the format setting.
		0-15. Used with format property. Determines the number of digits that display to the right of the decimal point.
Input Mask	Special characters used to control the values the user can input.	
Caption	Field name displayed on forms.	
Default Value	Sets the value that appears in the field by default when a record is created.	
Validation Rule	Sets the requirements for user input.	
Validation Text	Text for error messages that are sent when validation rules are broken.	
Required	Specifies whether the field is required or not.	Yes: Required No: Not Required
Allow Zero Length	Determines whether a zero-length field is a valid entry.	Yes: Is valid No: Not valid
Index	Specifies whether an index should be created in a field. Indexes speed up queries.	Yes: Create index. No: Do not create index.

To use Design view to create a new table:

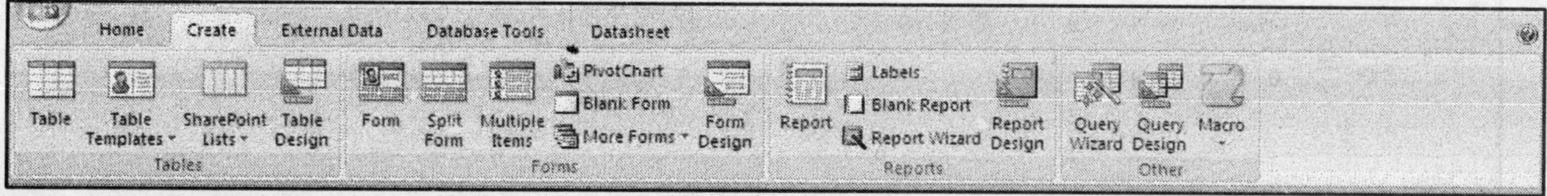

- ❖ Activate the Create tab.
- ❖ Click Table Design in the Tables group. Access changes to Design view and the Table Tools become available.
- ❖ Type the first field name in the Field Name field.
- ❖ Press the Tab key.
- ❖ Click the down-arrow that appears when you click in the Data Type field and then select a data type.
- ❖ Click Primary Key if the column you created is a primary key. A small key appears next to the field name.
- ❖ Press the Tab key.
- ❖ Type a description. The description is optional.
- ❖ Press the Tab key. Access moves to the Field Name field.
- ❖ Repeat steps 3 through 10 until you have created all of your fields.

Sorting, Filtering, and Creating Relationships

You can sort Access data so you can view records in the order you want to view them, and you can filter data so you only see the records you want to see.

Sort a Table

By sorting, you can put a column of information in alphabetical, numerical, or date order. You can sort in ascending order (alphabetical from A to Z, lowest number to highest number, earliest date to latest date) or descending order (alphabetical from Z to A, highest number to lowest number, latest date to earliest date). You can also sort within a sort. For example, you can sort by state and then sort within each state by city. When sorting within a sort, perform the innermost sort first. For example, if you are sorting by state and then city, sort the city first and then sort by state.

Filter a Table

- ❖ Click the column label for the column you want to filter.
- ❖ Activate the Home tab.
- ❖ Click the Filter button. A menu appears.
- ❖ Uncheck the items you do not want to appear, making sure only the items you want are checked.
- ❖ Click OK. Access filters your data and displays the word Filtered at the bottom of the window.

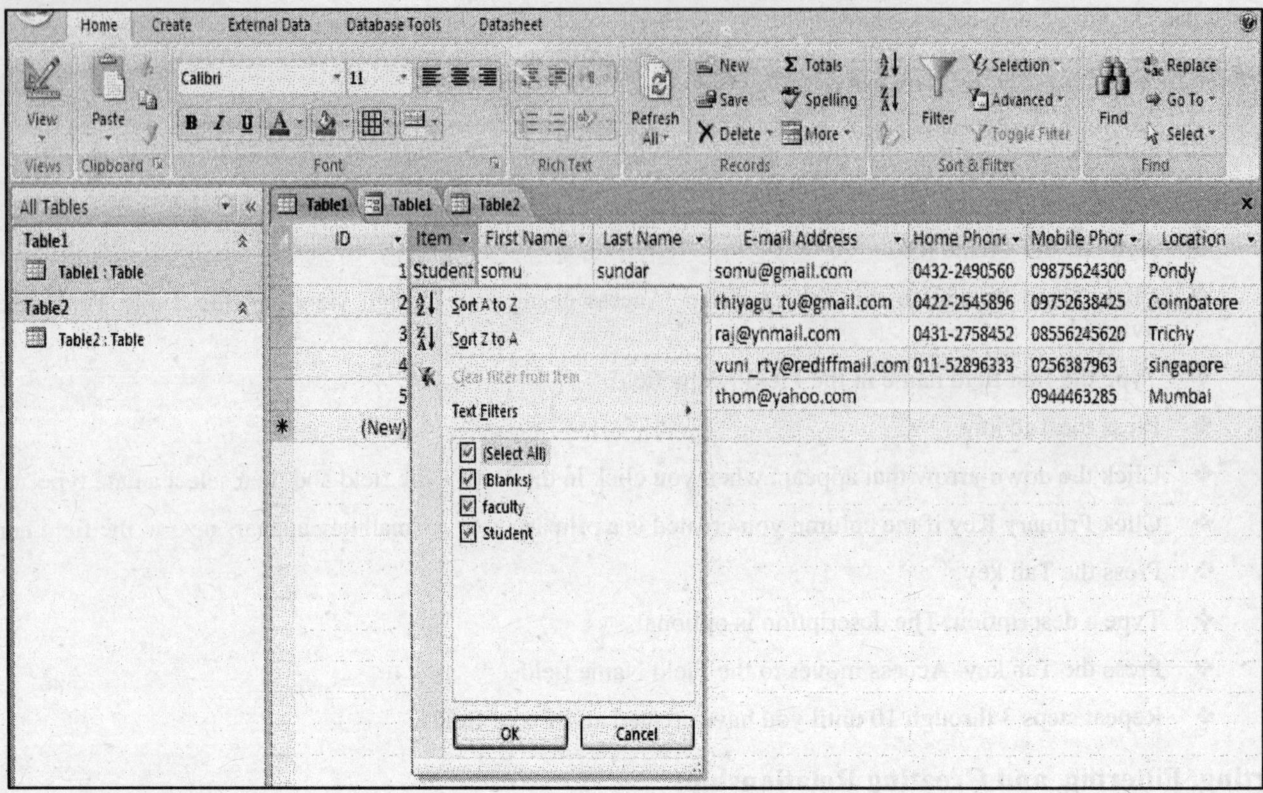

Apply a Specialized Filter

In addition to simply searching for a specific value, you can apply several specialized filters. For example, you can find all of the records that do not equal the value you specify or you can find all of the records that fall between two dates. The following are lists of specialized filters.

Text Filters	
Equals	Finds every record in the table where the field's value equals the value you enter.
Does Not Equal	Finds every record in the table where the field's value does not equal the value you enter.
Begins With	Finds every record in the table where the field's value begins with the value you enter.
Does Not Begin With	Finds every record in the table where the field's value does not begin with the value you enter.
Contains	Finds every record in the table where the field's value contains the value you enter.
Does Not Contain	Finds every record in the table where the field's value does not contain the value you enter.
Ends With	Finds every record in the table where the field's value ends with the value you enter.
Does Not End With	Finds every record in the table where the field's value does not end with the value you enter.

Number Filters	
Equals	Finds every record in the table where the field's value equals the value you enter.
Does Not Equal	Finds every record in the table where the field's value does not equal the value you enter.
Less Than	Finds every record in the table where the field's value is less than the value you enter.
Greater Than	Finds every record in the table where the field's value is greater than the value you enter.
Between	Finds every record in the table where the field's value is between the values you enter.

Date Filters	
Equals	Finds every record in the table where the field's value equals the date you enter.
Does Not Equal	Finds every record in the table where the field's value does not equal the date you enter.
Before	Finds every record in the table where the field's value is before the date you enter.
Greater Than	Finds every record in the table where the field's value is greater than (comes after) the date you enter.
Between	Finds every record in the table where the field's date is between the dates you enter.
All Dates in a Period	Finds every record in the table where the field's date is in the period you enter.

Format a Table

You can use the features in the Font group on the Home tab to apply a variety of formats to your table.

Format a Table	
Button	**Function**
Arial	Apply a font to all of the data in a table.
10	Apply a font size to all of the data in a table.
B	Bold all of the data in a table.
I	Italicize all of the data in a table.
U	Underline all of the data in a table.
	Left-align a column.
	Right-align a column.
	Center a column.

	Change the font color.
	Change the background color. By default, the background color is white.
	Change the gridlines. Gridlines separate columns and rows. This option allows you to display gridlines for columns only (vertical), gridlines for rows only (horizontal), gridlines for both columns and rows, or no gridlines at all.
	Change the alternating color. For example, on a datasheet, you can have every other row appear in an alternating color.

To bold, italicize, or underline:

- ❖ Place the cursor anywhere within the table.
- ❖ Activate the Home tab.
- ❖ Click the button for the format you want to apply. Access applies the format.

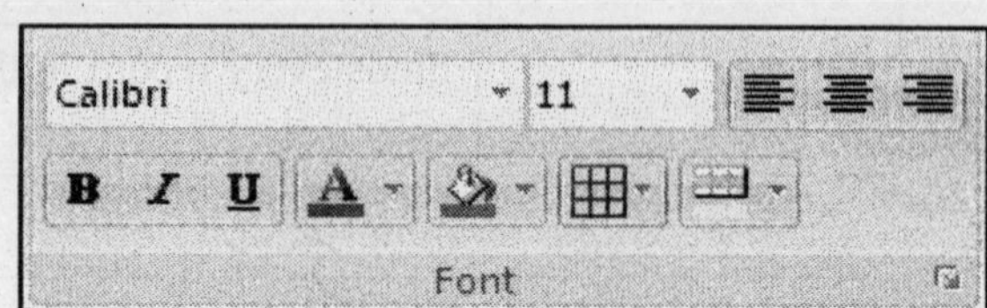

To left-align, right-align, or center:

- ❖ Place the cursor anywhere within the column you want to left-align, right-align, or center.
- ❖ Activate the Home tab.
- ❖ Click the button for the format you want to apply. Access applies the format.

To change the font, font size, or gridlines:

- ❖ Place the cursor anywhere within the table.
- ❖ Activate the Home tab.
- ❖ Click the down-arrow to the right of the option you want to apply. A menu appears.
- ❖ Select the option you want. Access changes the font, font size, or gridlines.

To change the font color, background color, or alternating color:

- ❖ Place the cursor anywhere within the table.
- ❖ Activate the Home tab.
- ❖ Click the down-arrow to the right of the option you want to apply. A menu of colors appears.
- ❖ Select the color you want. Access changes the font color or the alternating color.

To change the view:

- ❖ Open the form.
- ❖ Activate the Format tab.
- ❖ Click the down-arrow under the View button. A menu appears.
- ❖ Click the view you want.

Modify a Form

After you create a form, it opens in Layout view, where you can modify it.

To change the size of a field:

- ❖ Click a side of the field and drag to change the width of the field.

- ❖ Click the top or bottom of a field and drag to change the height of a field.

To move a datasheet:

- ❖ Click the datasheet to select it.
- ❖ Click and drag the four-sided arrow in the upper-right corner to move the datasheet.

To resize a datasheet:

- ❖ Click the datasheet to select it.
- ❖ Click a side of the datasheet and drag to change the width.
- ❖ Click the top or bottom of the datasheet and drag to change the height.

To apply an AutoFormat:

The AutoFormat option on the Format tab enables you to apply formats quickly, such as background colors, field colors, field label colors, and fonts.

- ❖ Activate the Format tab.
- ❖ Click AutoFormat. The AutoFormat menu appears.
- ❖ Click the format you want to apply.

To change a form title:

When you create a form, by default, Access uses the form name as the title. You can change the title.

- ❖ Activate the Format tab.
- ❖ Click the Title button.
- ❖ Type the new title.

To add the date and time:

You can easily add the date and time to your form.

- ❖ Activate the Format tab.
- ❖ Click the Date and Time button. The Date and Time dialog box appears. Select the date and time format you want. The date and time appear on your form.

Change Fonts and Formats

You can use options on the Format tab to manually apply individual formats to your report. However, before you can apply a format to a field or field label, you must select it. To select a field or field label, click it. To select multiple items, hold down the Shift key and then click each item you want to select. A box surrounds selected items.

Change Fonts and Formats		
Button	**Shortcut Key**	**Function**
Layout View—Format Tab, Font Group		
Arial		Apply a font the current selection
10		Set the size of the font for the current selection.
B	Ctrl + B	Bold the current selection.
I	Ctrl + I	Italicize the current selection.

U	Ctrl + U	Underline the current selection.
	Ctrl + L	Left-align the selection.
	Ctrl + R	Right-align the selection.
	Ctrl + C	Center the selection.
		Change the font color.
		Change the background color.
		Change the alternating color. For example, you can have every other row on a datasheet appear in an alternating color.
	Layout View—Format Tab, Formatting Group	
Standard		Apply a Number format
$		Use a currency symbol.
%		Change to percent.
,		Use thousand separators.
		Increase decimal places.
		Decrease decimal places.
	Layout View—Format Tab, Gridlines Group	
		Add gridlines.
		Change the weight of gridlines.
		Change the style of gridlines.
		Change the color of gridlines.
	Layout View—Format Tab, Controls Group	
		Add a logo.
		Add or change a title.
		Add a date and time.
		Set line thickness.
		Set line style.
		Set line color.

Creating Reports

Reports organize and summarize data for viewing online or for printing. A detail report displays all of the selected records. You can include summary data such as totals, counts, and percentages in a detail report. A summary report does not list the selected records but instead summarizes the data and presents totals, counts, percentages, or other summary data only. Access has several report generation tools that you can use to create both detail and summary reports quickly. This lesson teaches you how to create reports.

Use the Report Button

The Report button creates a simple report that lists the records in the selected table or query in a columnar format.

To use the Report button:

- ❖ Open the Navigation pane.
- ❖ Click the table or query on which you want to base your report.

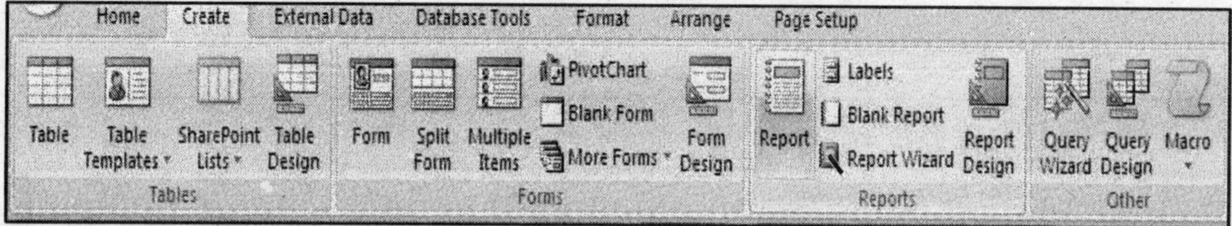

- ❖ Activate the Create tab.
- ❖ Click the Report button in the Reports group. Access creates your report and displays your report in Layout view. You can modify the report.

Print a Report

Often, the people who use Access data only see a printed report. In Print Preview, you can see exactly how your report will look when printed, you can make changes to it, and you can print it. To print, click the Print button in the Print group. The Print dialog box opens and you can select your print options.

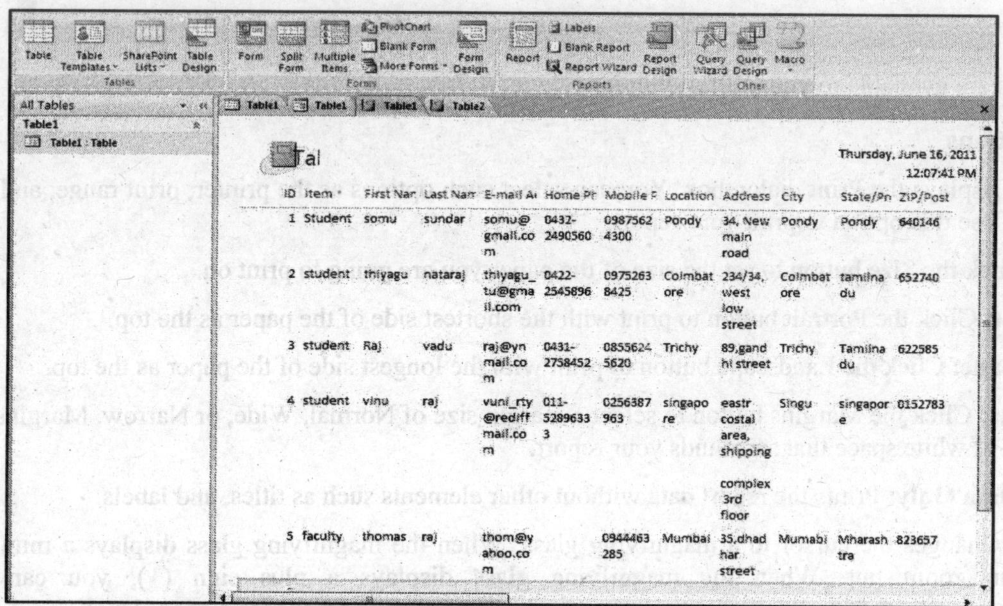

To change to Print Preview:

❖ Activate the File menu tab.

❖ Click the button the print.

❖ Click the print preview button.

❖ Click Print Preview. Access changes to Print Preview.

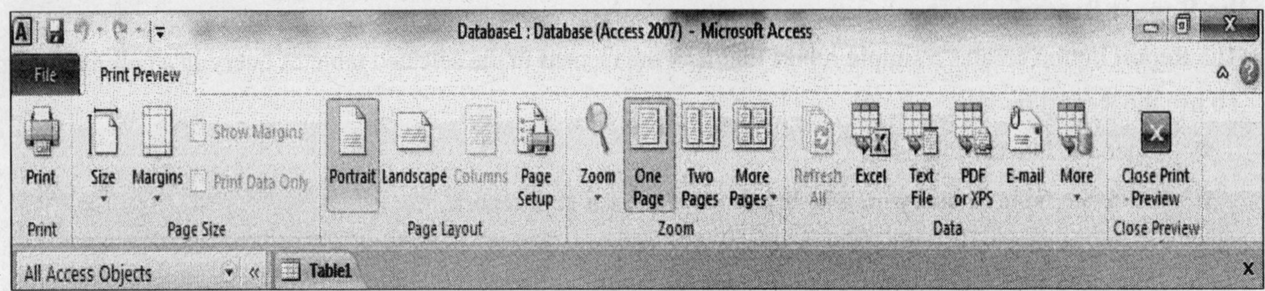

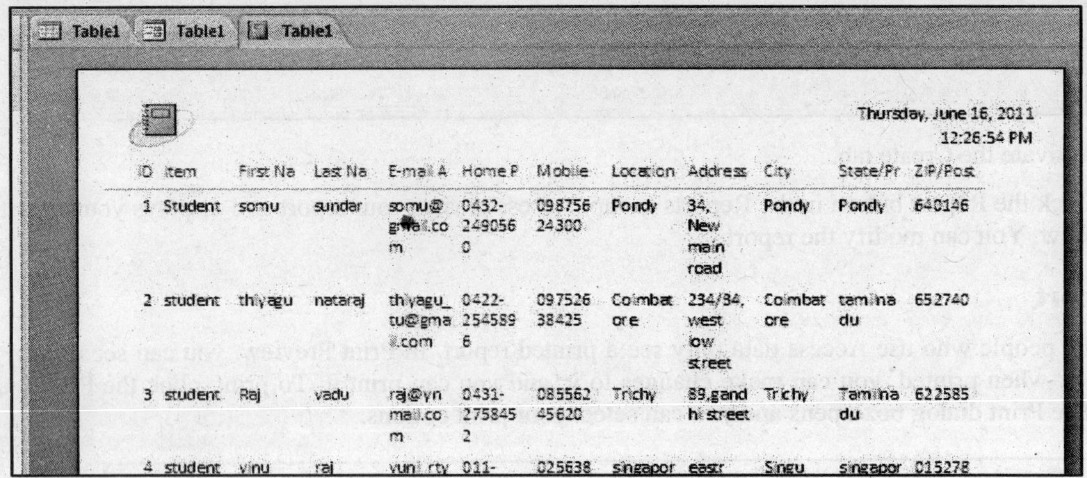

Thursday, June 16, 2011
12:26:54 PM

ID	Item	First Na	Last Na	E-mail A	Home P	Mobile	Location	Address	City	State/Pr	ZIP/Post
1	Student	somu	sundar	somu@gmail.com	0432-2490560	09875624300	Pondy	34, New main road	Pondy	Pondy	640146
2	student	thiyagu	nataraj	thiyagu_tu@gmail.com	0422-2545896	09752638425	Coimbatore	234/34, west low street	Coimbatore	tamilnadu	652740
3	student	Raj	vadu	raj@ynmail.com	0431-2758452	08556245620	Trichy	89,gandhi street	Trichy	Tamilnadu	622585
4	student	vinu	raj	yuni.rty	011-	025638	singapor	eastr	Singu	singapor	015278

Several options are available to you in Print Preview.

Print Preview Options

❖ **Print:** Displays the Print dialog box. You can select such options as the printer, print range, and number of copies. Use this option to print your report.

❖ **Size:** Click the Size button to set the size of the paper you are going to print on.

❖ **Portrait:** Click the Portrait button to print with the shortest side of the paper as the top.

❖ **Landscape:** Click the Landscape button to print with the longest side of the paper as the top.

❖ **Margins:** Click the Margins button to select a margin size of Normal, Wide, or Narrow. Margins define the amount of white space that surrounds your report.

❖ **Print Data Only:** Prints the report data without other elements such as titles, and labels.

❖ **Zoom:** Changes the cursor to a magnifying glass. When the magnifying glass displays a minus sign (–), you can zoom out. When the magnifying glass displays a plus sign (+), you can zoom in. Click the down-arrow under the Zoom button to display a menu and choose a zoom level.

❖ **One Page:** Displays one page of the report in the Access window.

- ❖ **Two Pages:** Displays two pages of the report in the Access window.
- ❖ **More Pages:** Displays a menu from which you can choose the number of page you want to display.

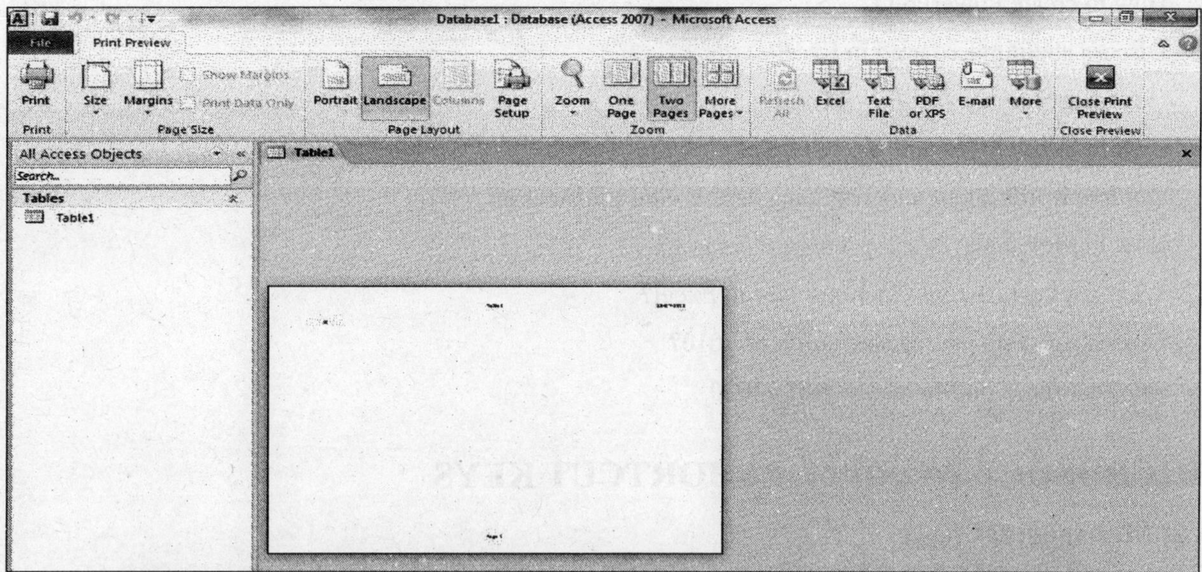

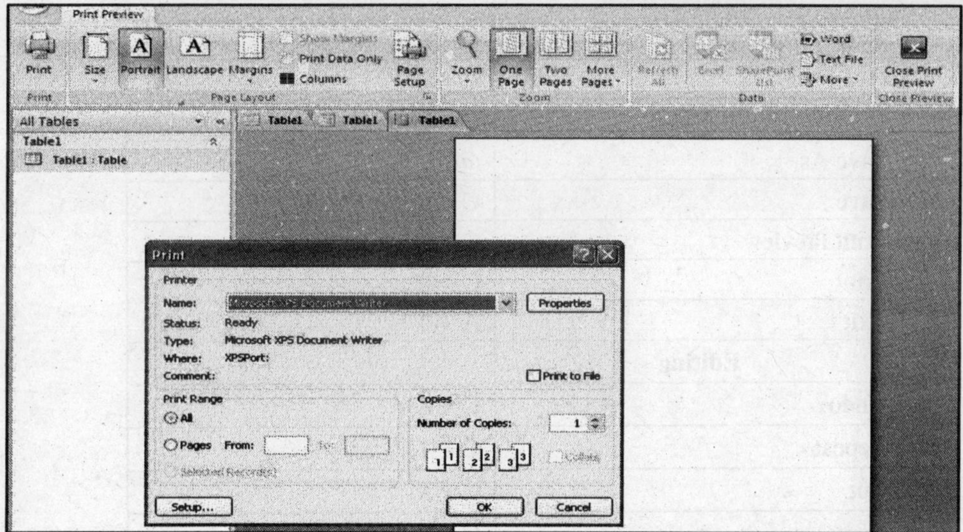

QUESTIONS

1. How Word can be created in the using Ms Word?
2. Explain about handling the table and graphics in Word?
3. Explain about database management?
4. What do you mean by mail merge?
5. How Excel can be customized and work in the worksheet?
6. Explain the performing calculation in Excel.
7. How can chart can be created and run slide in Ms PowerPoint?

8. Explain the project management and its uses.
9. How to format a worksheet in Excel?
10. How to create PowerPoint?
11. Discuss about macro used in Excel.
12. How charts are used in PowerPoint?
13. How to create Microsoft Access tables?
14. Say few words about understanding design views in Access.
15. How to format and develop a worksheet in Excel?
16. What are the different functions used in Excel?
17. Discuss special features used in Word 2010?
18. Say few words on Microsoft Office 2010.

10.17 MICROSOFT WORD 2010 SHORTCUT KEYS

Document Management Keys

File Management	
New	C + N
Open	C + O
Close	C + W *or* C + 4
Save As	@
Save	C + S
Print Preview	C + 2
Print	C + P
Exit	A + 4 *
Editing	
Undo	C + Z
Repeat	C + Y
Cut	C + X
Copy	C + C
Paste	C + V
Select All	C + A
Find	C + F
Replace	C + H
Go To	C + G

Helpful Function Keys

Action	Key
Activate main menu	0 or A
Activate short cut menu	V + 0

Change letter case	V + 3
Close active document	C + 4
Close Word	A + 4 *
Extend selection mode	8
Go back to previous positions	V + 5
Go To	5
Help	1
Help pointer (context-sensitive)	V + 1
Insert AutoText entry	3
Maximize document window	C + 0
Maximize Word window	A + 0 *
Next document window	C + 6
Open	C + @
Previous document window	C + V + 6
Print (also C + P)	C + V + @
Repeat Find or Go To	V + 4
Repeat previous command	4
Save	V + @
Save As	@
Show fields on/off	A + 9 *
Spelling	7
Thesaurus	V + 7
Update selected field	9

Formatting Keys

Paragraph	Formatting
Center	C + E
Justify	C + J
Left align	C + L
Right align	C + R
Indent from left	C + M
Decrease indent from left	C + V + M
Create hanging indent	C + T
Decrease hanging indent	C + V + T
Single space lines	C + 1
Double space lines	C + 2
One-and-one-half space lines	C + 5
Add/close space B4 paragraph	C + 0(zero)
Return to normal formatting	C + Q
Character formatting	

Bold	C + B
Italics	C + I
Underline (continuous)	C + U
Word underline	C + V + W
Double underline	C + V + D
Font (Font dialog box)	C + V + F
Point size (Font dialog box)	C + V + P
Hidden	C + V + H
All caps	C + V + A
Small caps	C + V + K
Subscript	C + =
Superscript	C + +
Increase font size	C + V + >
Decrease font size	C + V + <
Increase by 1 point	C +]
Decrease by 1 point	C + [
Remove formatting	C + V + Z

Additional Handy Short cuts

Action	Key
Cancel	E
Begin new paragraph	J
Begin new page (break)	C + J
Begin new line (same paragraph)	V + J
Begin new column/split table	C + V + J
Insert non-breaking space	C + V + s
Insert non-breaking hyphen	C + V + -
Insert tab character (in table)	C + F
Show hidden screen characters	C + V + *

* Now that the A key is used to access the Word 2010 Ribbon, these short cuts work best when the keys are pressed simultaneously.

MICROSOFT ACCESS 2010

Navigation

To Move	Press
Next field to the right	TAB or RIGHT arrow
Next field to the left	SHIFT + TAB or LEFT arrow
Last (rightmost) field of the record	END

First field of the record	HOME
Current field in the next record	DOWN arrow
Current field in the previous record	UP arrow
Current field in the last record	CTRL + DOWN arrow
Current field in the first record	CTRL + UP arrow
Last field of the last record in the table	CTRL + END
First field of the first record in the table	CTRL + HOME
Specific record in a datasheet	F5 (then type record #)
Down one screen	PAGE DOWN
Up one screen	PAGE UP
Right one screen	CTRL + PAGE DOWN
Left one screen	CTRL + PAGE UP
Switch between the upper and lower portions of the Design	F6

Data Entry and Editing

To Move	Press
Insert the current date	CTRL + ; (semicolon)
Insert the current time	CTRL + : (colon)
Insert the value from the same field in the previous record	CTRL + ' (apostrophe) or CTRL + " (double quote)
Insert the default value for a field *(if defined in the table structure)*	CTRL + ALT + SPACEBAR
Add a new record	CTRL + + (plus sign)
Delete the current record	CTRL + - (minus sign)
Save changes to the current record	SHIFT + ENTER
Zoom	SHIFT + F2 or right-click on expression
Insert a new line in a field, a label, or zoom box	CTRL + ENTER
Toggle the value in a check box or option box	SPACEBAR
Open a combo box or list box	F4 or ALT + DOWN arrow
Type response in a yes/no field	0 for no, 1 for yes or spacebar to turn on/off
Delete the selection or character to the left of the insertion point	BACKSPACE
Select the current record or cancel the record selection	SHIFT + SPACEBAR
Select current column	CTRL + SPACEBAR
Select all records	CTRL + A
Copy	CTRL + C
Cut	CTRL + X
Paste	CTRL + V
Undo current field/current record	ESC
Undo last changes to saved record	CTRL + Z or ALT + BACKSPACE

Find (opens dialog box)	CTRL + F
Replace (opens dialog box)	CTRL + H
Find the next occurrence of the text in the Find or Replace dialog box when the dialog box is closed	SHIFT + F4
Switch between navigation mode (selected field) and editing mode	F2
Delete the selection or character to the right of the insertion point	DELETE

File Management

Short cut	Command
ALT+TAB	Switch to the next window.
ALT+SHFT+TAB	Switch to the previous window.
CTRL+W or CTRL+F4	Close the active window.
ALT+F5	Restore the size of the active window after you maximize it.
F6	Move to a task pane from another pane in the program window (clockwise direction). You may need to press F6 more than once.
SHFT+F6	Move to a task pane from another pane in the program window (counter clockwise direction).
CTRL+F6	When more than one window is open, switch to the next window.
CTRL+SHFT+F6	Switch to the previous window.
CTRL+F10	Maximize or restore a selected window.
PRINT SCREEN	Copy a picture of the screen to the clipboard.
ALT+PRINT SCREEN	Copy a picture of the selected window to the clipboard.

Create a new database	CTRL + N
Open a database	CTRL + O
Save a table	CTRL + S
Print a table	CTRL + P
Close database	CTRL + F4
Close Access	ALT + F4

MICROSOFT EXCEL 2010 KEYBOARD SHORT CUTS

CTRL+shift+(	Unhides any hidden rows within the selection
CTRL+shift+)	Unhides any hidden column within the selection
CTRL+shift+&	Applies the outline border to the selected cells
CTRL+shift_	Removes the outline border to the selected cells
CTRL+shift~	Applies the general number format in Microsoft Excel
CTRL+shift+$	Applies the currency format with two decimal places (negative numbers in parentheses).
CTRL+shift+%	Applies the percentage format with no decimal places.
CTRL+shift+#	Applies the Exponential number format with two decimal places.
CTRL+shift+@	Applies the Date format with the day, month, and year.

CTRL+shift+(	Applies the Time format with the hour and minute, and Am or Pm
CTRL+shift+!	Applies the Number format with two decimal places, thousands separator, and minus sign (-) for negative values.
CTRL+shift+*	Selects the current region around the active cell (the data area enclosed by blank rows and blank columns). In a Pivot Table, it selects the entire Pivot Table report.
CTRL+shift+:	Enter the current time
CTRL+shift+	Copies the value from the cell above the active cell into the cell or the Formula Bar
CTRL shift Plus ()	Displays the insert dialog box to insert blank cells in Microsoft Excel
CTRL+Minus(-)	Displays the delete dialog box to delete the selected cells
CTRL+;	Enters the current date
CTRL+'	Alternates between displaying cell values and displaying formulas in the worksheet
CTRL+'	Copies a formula from the cell above the active cell into the cell or the Formula Bar.
CTRL+1	Displays the Format Cells dialog box
CTRL+2	Applies or removes bold formatting
CTRL+3	Applies or removes italic formatting.
CTRL+4	Applies or removes underlining in Microsoft Excel.
CTRL+5	Applies or removes strikethrough.
CTRL+6	Alternates between hiding objects, displaying objects, and displaying placeholders for objects.
CTRL+8	Displays or hides the outline symbol
CTRL+9	Hides the selected rows.
CTRL 0	Hides the selected columns in Microsoft Excel.
CTRL+A	Selects the entire worksheet. If the worksheet contains data, CTRL+A selects the current region. Pressing CTRL+A a second time selects the current region and its summary rows. Pressing CTRL+A a third time selects the entire worksheet. When the insertion point is to the right of a function name in a formula, displays the function Arguments dialog box. CTRL+SHIFT+A inserts the argument names and parentheses when the insertion point is to the right of a function name in a formula.
CTRL+B	Applies or removes bold formatting.
CTRL+C	Copies the selected cells. CTRL+C followed by another CTRL+C displays the clipboard.
CTRL+D	Uses the fill Down command to copy the contents and format of the topmost cell of a selected range into cells below.
CTRL+F	Displays the find and replace dialog box, with the find tab selected. SHIFT+F5 also displays this tab while SHIFT+F4 repeats the last find action. CTRL+SHIFT+F opens the format cells dialog box with the font tab selected.
CTRL+G	Displays the Go To dialog box. F5 also displays this dialog box.
CTRL+H	Displays the Find and replace dialog box, with the Replace tab selected.
CTRL+I	Applies or removes italic formatting in Microsoft Excel.
CTRL +K	Displays the insert Hyperlink dialog box for selected existing hyperlinks.
CTRL+N	Creates a new, blank workbook.
CTRL+O	Displays the open dialog box to open or find a file. CTRL SHIFT O selects all cells that contain comments in Microsoft Excel.

SHORT CUT KEYS GENERAL KEYBOARD SHORT CUTS

CTRL+C	Copy
CTRL+X	Cut
CTRL+V	Paste
CTRL+Z	undo
DELETE	Delete
SHIFT+DELETE	Delete the selected item permanently without placing the item in the recycle Bin
CTRL while dragging an item	Copy the selected item
CTRL+Shift while dragging an item	create a short cut to the selected item
F2	Rename the selected item
CTRL+RIGHT ARROW	Move the insertion point to the beginning of the next word
CTRL+LEFT ARROW	Move the insertion point to the beginning of the previous word
CTRL+DOWN ARROW	Move the insertion point to the beginning of the next paragraph
CTRL+UP ARROW	Move the insertion point to the beginning of the next paragraph
CTRL+shift with any of the arrow key	Highlights a block of text
Shift with any of the arrow keys	Select more than one item in a window or on the desktop, or select text in a document
CTRL+A	Select all
F3	Search for a file or a folder
ALT+ENTER	View the properties for the selected item
ALT+F4	Close the active item, or quit the active Program
ALT+ENTER	Display the properties of the selected object
ALT+SPACEBAR	Open the short cut menu for the active window
CTRL+F4	Close the active document in programs that enable you to have multiple documents open simultaneously
ALT+TAB	Switch between the open items
ALT+ESC	Cycle through items in the order that they had been opened
F6	Cycle through the screen elements in a window or on the desktop
F4	Display the address bar list in My computer or windows Explorer
Shift+F10	Display the short cut menu for the selected item
ALT+SPACEBAR	Displays the system menu for the active window
CTRL+ESC	Display the start menu
ALT+Underlined letter in a menu name	Display the corresponding menu
Underlined letter in a cmnd name on an open menu	Perform the corresponding command
F10	Activate the menu bar in the active program
RIGHT ARROW	Open the next menu to the right, or open a submenu
LEFT ARROW	Open the next menu to the right, or close a submenu

F5	Update the active window
BACKSPACE	View the folder one level up in My computer or Windows Explorer
ESC	Cancel the current task
Shift when you insert a CD-ROM into the CD_ROM drive	Prevent the CD-ROM from automatically playing
CTRL+shift+ESC	Open Task Manager
DIALOG BOX KEYBOARD SHORT CUTS	
Info	If you press SHIFT+F8 in extended selection list boxes, you enable extended selection mode. In this mode, you can use an arrow key to move a cursor without changing the selection you can press CTRL+SPACEBAR or SHIFT+SPACEBAR to adjust the selection. To cancel extended selection mode, press SHIFT+F8 again. Extended selection mode cancels itself when you move the focus to another control
CTRL+TAB	Move forward through the tabs
CTRL+SHIFT+TAB	Move backward through the tabs
TAB	Move forward through the options
SHIFT+TAB	Move backward through the options
ALT+Underlined letter	Perform the corresponding command or select the corresponding option
ENTER	Perform the command for the active option or button
SPACEBAR	Select or clear the check box if the active Option is a check box
Arrow keys	Select a button if the active option is a group of option buttons
F1	Display Help
F4	Display the items in the active list
BACKSPACE	Open a folder one level up if a folder is selected in the save As or Open dialog box
MICROSOFT NATURAL KEYBOARD SHORT CUTS	
Windows Logo	Displays or hide the start menu
Windows Logo+Break	Displays the system properties dialog box
Windows Logo+B	Set focus on a notification
Windows Logo+D	Display the desktop
Windows Logo+M	Minimize all of the windows
Windows Logo+Shift+M	Open my computer
Windows Log+E	Search for a file or a folder
CTRL+Windows Logo+F	Search for computers
Windows Logo+F1	Display window help
Windows Logo+L	Lock the keyboard
Windows Logo+R	Open the run dialog box
Windows Logo+U	Open utility manager
ACCESSIBILITY KEYBOARD SHORT CUTS	
Right shift for eight seconds	Switch Filter keys either on or off
Left ALT+left shift+PRINT SCREEN	Switch High Contrast either on or off
Left ALT+left shift+NUM LOCK	Switch the Mouse keys either on or off

Shift five times	Switch the stick keys either on or off
Num LOCK for five seconds	Switch the Toggle keys either on or off
Windows Logo+U	Open utility manager
WINDOWS EXPLORER KEYBOARD SHORT CUTS	
END	Display the bottom of the active window
HOME	Display the top of the active window
NUM LOCK+Asterisk sign (*)	Display all of the subholders that are under the selected folder
NUM LOCK+Plus sign(+)	Display the contents of the selected folder
NUM LOCK+Minus sign(-)	Collapse the selected folder
LEFT ARROW	Collapse the current selection if it is expanded, or select the parent folder
RIGHT ARROW	Display the current selection if it is collapsed or selected the first subholder
SHORT CUT KEYS FOR CHARACTER MAP	
RIGHT ARROW	Move to the right or to the beginning of the next line
LEFT ARROW	Move to the left or to the end of the previous line
UP ARROW	Move up one row
DOWN ARROW	Move down one row
PAGE UP	Move up one screen at a time
PAGE DOWN	Move down one screen at a time
HOME	Move to the beginning of the line
END	Move to the end of the line
CTRL+HOME	Move to the first character
CTRL+END	Move to the last character
SPACEBAR	Switch between Enlarged and Normal mode when character is selected
MICROSOFT MANAGEMENT CONSOLE (MMC) MAIN WINDOW	
CTRL+O	Open a saved console
CTRL+N	Open a new console
CTRL+S	Save the open console
CTRL+M	Add or remove a console item
CTRL+W	Open a new window
F5	Update the content of all console windows
ALT+SPACEBAR	Display the MMC window menu
ALT+F4	Close the console
ALT+A	Display the Action menu
ALT+V	Display the View menu
ALT+F	Display the File menu
ALT+O	Display the Favourites menu
MMC CONSOLE WINDOW KEYBOARD SHORT CUTS	
CTRL+P	Print the current page or active pane

ALT+minus sign(-)	Display the window menu for the active console window
Shift+F10	Display the action short cut menu for the selected item
F1	Open the Help topic, if any, for the selected item
F5	Update the content of all console windows
CTRL+F10	Maximize the active console window
CTRL+F5	Restore the active console window
ALT+ENTER	Display the properties dialog box, if any, for the selected item
F2	Rename the selected item
CTRL+f4	Close the active console window. When a console has only one console window, this short cut closes the console
REMOTE DESKTOP CONNECTION NAVIGATION	
CTRL+ALT+END	Open the Microsoft windows NT security dialog box
ALT+PAGE UP	Switch between programs from left to right
ALT+PAGE DOWN	Switch between programs from left to right
ALT+INSERT	Cycle through the programs in most recently used order
ALT+HOME	Display the start menu
CTRL+ALT+BREAK	Switch the client computer between a window and a full screen
ALT+DELETE	Display the windows menu
CTRL+ALT+Minus sign (-)	Place a snapshot of the entire client window area on the terminal server clipboard and provide the same functionality as pressing ALT+PRINT SCREEN on a local computer
CTRL+ALT+Plus sign (+)	Place a snapshot of the entire client window area on the terminal server clipboard and provide the same functionality as pressing ALT+PRINT SCREEN on a local computer
MICROSOFT INTERNET EXPLORER NAVIGATION	
CTRL+B	Open the organize favourites dialog box
CTRL+E	Open the search bar
CTRL+F	Start the find utility
CTRL+H	Open the history bar
CTRL+I	Open the Favourites dialog box
CTRL+L	Open the Open dialog box
CTRL+N	Start another instance of the browser with the same web address
CTRL+O	Open the Open dialog box, the same as CTRL+L
CTRL+P	Open the Print dialog box
CTRL+R	Update the current web page
CTRL+W	Close the current window

11 CHAPTER

PUBLISHING ON THE WEB AND HTML

Structure:

11.1 WHAT IS AN HTML FILE?

HTML stands for Hyper Text Markup Language. It is a way to "markup" or enhances standard text files, so they can do many different things. Most HTML file display images, format the text, and used different font sizes among the regular text. Other HTML commands can divide the window into frames, call another computer program, or play music. Internet browsers like Netscape and Explorer read the HTML commands and handle them accordingly.

HTML stands for **H**yper **T**ext **M**arkup **L**anguage. An HTML file is a text file containing small **markup tags.** The markup tags tell the Web browser **how to display** the page. An HTML file must have an **htm** or **html** file extension. An HTML file can be created using a **simple text editor.**

11.2 WHAT DOES HTML LOOK LIKE?

HTML commands, or "tags", are simple words surrounded by angle brackets. The HTML tag looks like <HTML> Usually, tags come in pairs. The complementary tag for <HTML> is the same commands, but with a slash before it. It looks like </HTML>. This pairing is important. The main tag tells the browser that a command is beginning, while the complementary, or closing, tag, tells that a command is ending. This should be a bit clearer with an example.

11.3 LEARNING HTML

To create your HTML document you will be using a text editor. A text editor is a simple program that can only handle text. On the Mac, We'll use SimpleText. On the PC, We'll use Notepad.

For Mac: Open SimpleText.

It is under Programs::Word Processing::SimpleText 1.4

For PC: Open Notepad.

It is under Program::Accessories::Notepad (for the NT stations) or Program Manager::Tools::Notepad (for the 3.1 stations) A new document will open and you will want to save it on to your disk. In HTML, your main (home) document is usually called **index.html**. It is necessary that you end your files' name with **.html** when you save them.

Do You Want to Try It?

If you are running Windows, start Notepad.

If you are on a Mac, start SimpleText.

In OSX start TextEdit and change the following preferences: Open the "Format" menu and select "Plain text" instead of "Rich text." Then open the "Preferences" window under the "Text Edit" menu and select "Ignore rich text commands in HTML files." Your HTML code will probably not work if you do not change the preferences above!

Type in the following text:

```
<html>

<head>

<title>Title of page</title>
</head>

<body>
```

This is my first homepage. <b>This text is bold</b>

</body>

</html>

Save the file as "trial.htm."

Start your Internet browser. Select "Open" (or "Open Page") in the File menu of your browser. A dialog box will appear. Select "Browse" (or "Choose File") and locate the HTML file you just created — "mypage.htm" — select it and click "Open." Now you should see an address in the dialog box, for example "file:///D:/PUBLICATIONS/CA/CA%20 Book-Final/HTML%20Tags%20&%20Results/Trial.html." Click OK, and the browser will display the page.

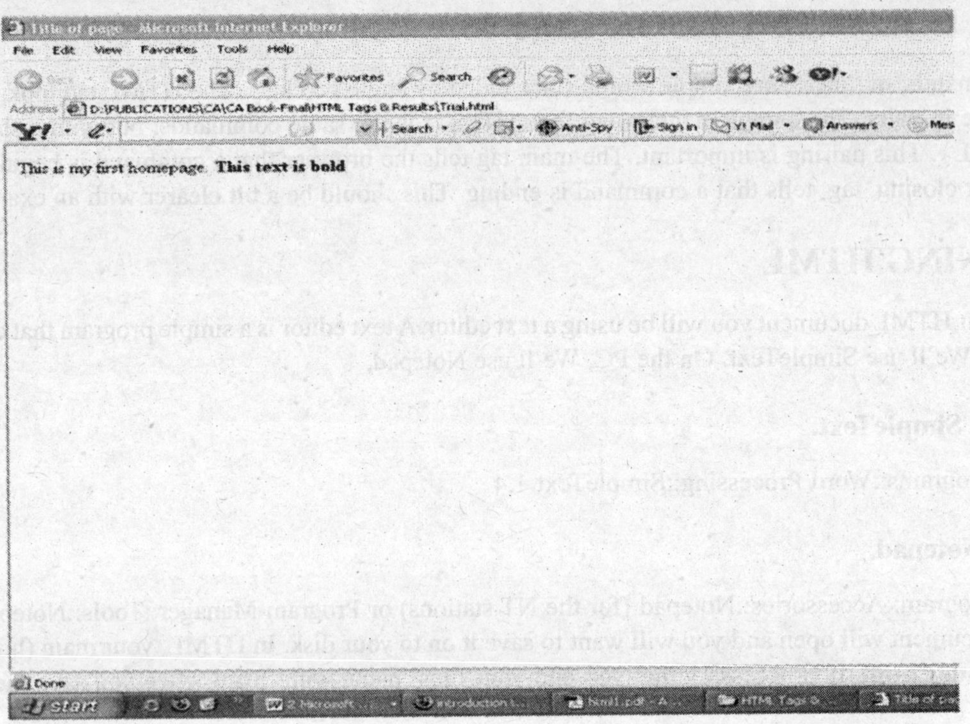

Example Explained

The first tag in your HTML document is <html>. This tag tells your browser that this is the start of an HTML document. The last tag in your document is </html>. This tag tells your browser that this is the end of the HTML document.

The text between the <head> tag and the </head> tag is header information. Header information is not displayed in the browser window.

The text between the <title> tags is the title of your document. The title is displayed in your browser's caption.

The text between the <body> tags is the text that will be displayed in your browser.

The text between the <b> and </b> tags will be displayed in a bold font.

HTM or HTML Extension?

When you save an HTML file, you can use either the .htm or the .html extension. We have used .htm in our examples. It might be a bad habit inherited from the past when some of the commonly used software only allowed three letter extensions.

With newer software we think it will be perfectly safe to use .html.

Note on HTML Editors

You can easily edit HTML files using a WYSIWYG (what you see is what you get) editor like FrontPage or Dream weaver, instead of writing your markup tags in a plain text file.

However, if you want to be a skilfull Web developer, we strongly recommend that you use a plain text editor to learn your primer HTML.

In the previous lesson, we had discussed about the concept of World Wide Web (WWW). Web page design is exciting and can provide an interesting challenge for anybody. In this lesson, we will introduce you to the concept of web page designing. You will come to know that with its rapid growth, Internet or web has given access to more and more users. However, each and every user accesses or uses the web in a different way than the other. As per statistics, more women and children are using the web and in different ways than the male users. The development of web page is for a specific audience. Hence, it is essential for a web designer to know who the audience are. For example, if you teach high school mathematics, your primary audience is your class and secondary audience are other students, colleagues, parents, and your local community.

With Internet and web pages both the organisation and the individual involved will gain mileage. For an organisation, this would provide (i) a low cost information distribution system, (ii) make database available for others to use, and maintain the security, (iii) collect information provided by others on Internet to expand and improve service to a target audience, and iv) provide low-cost training. On the other hand for an individual it would mean (i) get acquainted with new technology, (ii) learn new skills, (iii) receive low cost training and other information, and iv) get connected with other web creators with ease.

11.4 WEB PUBLISHING

When you browse the Internet you will come across quite often the word **home page**. Home page is the entry or starting point of a website. It is more or less in the format of the contents of a book or magazine. In other words, it is the welcome page of the website you are visiting, which in most cases gives an overview of what the website contains. One should not be surprised to see only one page in a website. Website can have one or more than one page, or a few long ones, depending on its design. But normally the website contains more than one page. Web pages vary in their look and content, but most of them follow a traditional book or magazine format. At the top of the page resides the master head or heading or banner graphic giving the main theme of the page. Then there is a list of items, such as subjects, with a brief description. The items listed are either hot or cold. When we say they are hot, it means they are linked to other pages within the same website or to other websites. These links are highlighted words in the body of the text, or in a list, or they can even be the images that link to other content. But how you will know the text is *hot* or *cold*. Usually the hot text appears in different colour from the rest of the text — usually in blue and underlined. When one moves the cursor over this text or graphics link, it will change from an arrow to a hand shape. And when you click on the hot text or image, you will be taken to the linked web page or website. Once you come back to a page with a link you have already visited, the hot text or hypertext words will appear in a different colour other than blue, so you know you have already visited there. But that does not prevent you from visiting the link again and again, you can certainly go there as many times, as you like. As the information and links are not static, don't feel surprised if the page looks different and the information has changed, when you visit a site, next time. The Internet is a dynamic medium of communication for displaying information. To encourage visitors to return to a site, it is very much required to change the look and feel of the web pages from time to time.

(a) **Planning Cycle:** Web planning involves a structured approach involving conceptualization of design and organizing the web developer and information resources required making the designing a reality. If the design is for a large and complex site, it is always advisable to note down all the planning, preferably in a notebook. This notebook can be used as a guide to deliver all the raw material needed for web designing such as: HTML, Java scripts, graphics, text, animation and icons, etc. You should also get ready with the policies and guidelines to be followed for developmental activities to give the websites a professional touch.

This requires careful planning. Create the sketch of the site, before the actual development work takes place. This will help to reduce the re-work while development is on. Basically this will act as a site roadmap to be followed by the web designer to create the actual websites. The most critical part a web page is its content. While working on content for a web page, it is necessary to take the target audience into consideration. Collect all the materials such as brochure, contact information, review, lessons, teaching material, quiz, FAQ's, photographs, etc. It is not necessary to use all of them in one go, but they will be handy when something needs to be changed.Once the conceptualization, collection of materials and creation of roadmap of the site is ready, it is time to decide how you are going to publish your site or how the web users will come to know about your site. Take the help of promotional Internet sites, professional organizations, etc.

(b) Design Cycle: Now let us look how user designs the web page from an information design perspective pointed view and not from a graphics design. Web page contents should not have more graphic page. In fact, the basic idea about a web page is information sharing enhanced by other elements such as graphics, animation, etc.

(c) Design Basics: Following are some basic steps to be followed while creating web pages.

- Create a Welcom/Index/first page of your website.
- Avoid use of heavy graphics in the first page from the user's point of view.
- Page should be descriptive and interactive both as per requirements.

Some minimum technical requirements might include

- Fast loading of pages
- Presentation with clarity and readability — with or without graphics
- Validation of the contents
- Easy and clear navigation
- Instruction on how to use the site.

Identify and address all potential problems such as

- Slow connections
- Physical constraints of the user such as sight or hearing impaired visitors
- Platform support
- Browser support, etc.

11.5 HTML (HYPERTEXT MARKUP LANGUAGE)

So far we have discussed the points you should be careful about while designing a web page. But what language we should use for creating web pages? HTML or Hyper Text Markup Language is used for creating web pages. Although HTML stands for HyperText Markup Language, it is not a programming language like Java. The basic function of the HTML is to describe the standard (—) how a browser should display text and multimedia elements such as graphics, animation, etc. It works on a limited number of tags and is not difficult to learn and use. Let us learn how it works.

How HTML works?

- The HTML is platform independent that is computer and computer operating system on which it is running. It means that HTML uses a small number of tags to create Web page. Any Web server regardless of their location and operating system can publish these web pages. These web pages can also be viewed or displayed by any Web browser regardless of the platform on which it is running.
- As we have discussed, HTML works on *tags*. These HTML tags control the page structure and the style sheet controls the details about page layout and their presentation. In other words, HTML style sheet provides consistency and creativity to create professional quality web pages.
- The basic structure of using tag is <tag_name> some text </tag_name>. For example, the tag for making text bold is <b> **this is bold** </b>. And when displayed in a browser it will be displayed, as **this is bold**.
- Web page is made up of two sections: head and body. Each of these sections is enclosed within a pair of <html> tags. The head section describes the page content while the body section defines the web page look and feel. Most of HTML tags are used in the body section, whereas the number of tags is limited in the head section. The standard web page structure in HTML is

```
<html>
<head>
<title>Title of the page is given here</title>
</head>
<body>
Web page contents goes here
</body>
</html>
```

11.6 GETTING STARTED WITH HTML

Before you actually start using HTML, you need certain things such as:

(a) **Text Editor:** To create an HTML document, a text editor is required. Any text editor, which can save the file in plain ASCII format, is good enough for creating HTML file. You can use right from MS-DOS editor "EDIT" to Microsoft Word for creating HTML document.

(b) **Web Browser:** After creating an HTML document, it is required to be viewed in a browser to see how it looks. There are several browsers available for viewing HTML documents such as Netscape Navigator, NCSA Mosaic, Microsoft Internet Explorer, Web Explorer, etc. But most popular among them are Microsoft Internet Explorer and Netscape Navigator. However, it is advisable to use at least two browsers to experiment with the look and feel of the developed web pages.

(c) **Graphics Tool:** Internet supports only GIF (Graphics File Format). Any other graphics file such as BMP, PCX, etc. needs to be converted in GIF format to be used in Internet. So you must use graphics software that is capable of creating GIF graphics file. There are a number of graphics packages available such as Adobe PhotoShop, Adobe Illustrator, etc., which support GIF file.

(d) **Content:** The actual contents of a web page are — all of the words, images, and links, which a web user can read and interact with. So all your content should be well documented and well researched before they are put in the web page. All graphics, Icons, etc. should be of correct impact.

(e) **Hyperlink:** Hyperlink is used to link between pages. A well-designed web page should have proper and meaningful links to other documents or web pages. The hyperlink can be a highlighted text in the document or images in the document.

11.7 USING HTML TAGS

The HTML document uses HTML tags, be it in the beginning of the document or end of it. These tags tell a Web browser where the HTML in the document begins and ends. The HTML document starts with a tag called <HTML> and ends with a tag </HTML>. i.e.:

<HTML>

<HTML>

</HTML>

The first tag <HTML> indicates the beginning of the HTML document and the last tag </HTML> indicates the end of the document. Within these two resides, the body of the HTML which defines the look and feel of the web page.

All the HTML tags end with the same tag name, but with a prefix of '/' with the tag name such as </HTML>.

(a) **Head:** The second tag in the HTML document is <HEAD>. This tag contains all header information about the document such as document title, author name, etc. It ends with </HEAD>.

(b) **Title:** This appears within the Head tag structure. This is where the title of the web page should be given, which will appear at the top of the browser's title bar, and also in the history list. The title of the document should be logically related to the content of the web page, and must be short but informative enough about the web page. As a norm, there should only be one title per document.

(c) **Body:** The actual work lies in the Body of the document. This appears after the Head tags. Between the Body tags, remains all the stuff that gets displayed in the browser window like all of the text, graphics, and links.

(d) **Headings:** As we know, the entire HTML document contains information that appears in different parts or section titles. There are a total of six levels of headings, from Heading 1 through Heading 6. They are marked as H1 for heading one and H6 for heading six. Heading 1 (H1) is "most important" and Heading 6 (H6) is "least important" in an HTML document. Given below are the structure of all six heading tags:

<H1>Heading 1</H1>

<H2>Heading 2</H2>

<H3>Heading 3</H3>

<H4>Heading 4</H4>

<H5>Heading 5</H5>

<H6>Heading 6</H6>

A heading in an HTML document always begins at the margin of a line. It also forces a line break at the end of the heading. In other words, there cannot be two headings on the same line.

(e) **Paragraphs:** Paragraphs are treated as the most basic structures in HTML. Presetting information in paragraphs is quite common in Web pages. Paragraph tags are <P> for beginning of the paragraph and </P> for the end. In other words, in HTML creation, the beginning of a paragraph is marked by <P>, and the end by </P>.

(f) **Lists:** As the name suggests, lists is the index of items to be appeared in a web page in a specific format. There are three types of lists, namely, Unordered, Ordered and Definition lists. Out of these three most widely used lists are Unordered and ordered list. Let us discuss them one by one.

(g) **Unordered lists:** While reading Microsoft Word you have known the 'Bullet List.' It is a list of items, where each listed item is preceded by a 'bullet' (a small black circle). In HTML, this bulleted list is termed as 'Unordered list.'

Unordered list starts with a tag <UL> and ends with a tags </UL>. Now all the items to be listed start with an HTML tag <LI>, which stands for "List Item." <LI> has a corresponding closing tag </LI>, but this closing tag is not compulsory to be given. There is no limitation to the number of list of items. Here is an example of Unordered List of items:

```
<UL>
<LI>Windows95
<LI>MS-DOS
<LI>Graphics
<LI>Animation
<LI>Internet
</UL>
```

And the result will be:

- Windows95
- MS-DOS
- Graphics
- Animation
- Internet

Almost anything can be put into a list item — line breaks, entire paragraphs, images, links, or even other lists.

(h) **Ordered lists:** In HTML, both unordered and ordered list looks similar and same set of rules applies to both of them. However, the differences between both of them is that instead of using <UL> and </UL>, an ordered list is contained within the tags <OL> and </OL> and the list items are preceded by numbers such as 1,2,3 and so on instead of a 'Bullet'. However, when an ordered list is displayed in a Web browser, it uses an automatically generated sequence of items.

Here is an example of Ordered List of items:

```
<OL>
<LI>Windows95
<LI>MS-DOS
<LI>Graphics
<LI>Animation
<LI>Internet
</OL>
```

And the result will be:

1. **Windows95**
2. **MS-DOS**
3. **Graphics**
4. **Animation**
5. **Internet**

As in the case of unordered list, almost anything can be put into a list item — line break, entire paragraphs, images, links, or even other lists. They can also be nested as unordered lists. Unordered lists can be nested in ordered lists, vice versa. For example:

```
<UL>
<LI>Rakesh
<LI>Harish
<LI>Manoj
<LI>Swati
<LI>Reena
<OL>
<LI>21 yrs.
<LI>20 yrs.
<LI>25 yrs.
<LI>19 yrs.
<LI>20 yrs.
</OL>
</UL>
```

This will result in

- **Harish**
- **Manoj**
- **Swati**
- **Reena**

1. **21 yrs.**
2. **20 yrs.**
3. **25 yrs.**
4. **19 yrs.**
5. **20 yrs.**

Character Style Tags

In addition to the above, there can also be character style tags used for bold, italics, underline, etc. They are sometimes called *forced style tags,* because their very nature forces a certain style on the character. The three most commonly used character style tags are:

(a) **Boldface:** This tag is used to make characters boldface. The tags used are <B> and </B>. And everything between <B> and </B> is **boldfaced**. For example,

<B> This is a Web Page</B> will result in **This is a Web Page**.

(b) **Italics:** HTML tags <I> and </I> are used to put the characters in Italics. Everything between <I> and </I> is *italicized.* For example,

<I> This is a Web Page</I> will result in *This is a Web Page.*

(c) **Underline:** As the name suggests, the Underline tags <U> and </U> are used to put character in underlined format. That means everything between <U> and </U> should be underlined. For example,

<U> This is a Web Page</U> will result in This is a Web Page.

The HTML Anchor or Links

As we have already discussed, a well-designed web page will have links to other pages and even to the outside world. These links can be a word within the text or an image in the document and they can appear anywhere in the HTML document. The links in HTML document starts with a tag <A> and ends with </A>. However, the <A> tags are not used alone, but this will contain attribute like HREF... HREF.

HREF stands for "Hypertext Reference", which indicates the location of the file to be linked to current page. The links are in the form of <A HREF="*URL or the address of the file*">, where *URL* is the location of the resource to which the file to be linked. For example, the National Open School Web server is at "http://www.nos.edu/". A sentence, which contained a link to that address, would look something like below:

For further information, please check out the <A HREF="http://www.nos.edu/">National Open School Web server</A>.

The words between <A> and </A> the open and close of the anchor ("National open School Web server") will be displayed as a hyperlink. Here is how it will look like National Open School Web server!_Clicking that link from a Web browser will load the National Open School Web server's main or index page.

(a) **IMG:** Till now we have discussed how to create and format text in an HTML document. Image also plays an important role in Web page creation. Images are inserted in Web documents using the IMG tag <IMG> and this tag has no closing tag such as </IMG>. However an <IMG> tag requires the location of the images file that is supposed to be placed in the document. This does not essentially mean that the said image file will be included in the HTML file. Visually, images are part of a Web page, but in reality an HTML file and any graphics it refers to are all separate files. All the referred graphics files are stored as individual files in the web server and they don't have to be in the same directory as the HTML document. But it is a good practice to put all the graphics files in a separate folder or directory preferably by images directory for easy location and manipulation.

But <IMG> tags alone do not help to place images in the HTML document. For <IMG> tags to work, you need another attribute called 'SRC'. This attribute, which stands for 'source' or 'source of this graphics' points to location of the graphics file. The source can either be a URL giving path for outside server or a path in the same server where the graphics file is stored. When this attribute is used along with <IMG> tags, a typical image tag will look like:

<IMG SRC="*URL/ path of graphic file*">

In other words, if there is a graphics file called 'welcome.gif' in NOS web server's graphics folder than the above image tags will look like

<IMG SRC=" http://www.nos.edu/graphics/welcome.gif">

The browser will put the graphic 'welcome if' wherever an image tag occurs in the document. Browser will treat this as another piece of text. Images can be placed almost anywhere within the body of the document, they can be between words, paragraphs, within paragraphs, in list items or even a link :

11.8 MULTIMEDIA

Multimedia is nothing but the processing and presentation of information in a more structured and understandable manner using more than one media such as text, graphics, animation, audio and video. Thus multimedia products can be an academic presentation, game or corporate presentation, information kiosk, fashion-designing, etc. Multimedia systems are those computer platforms and software tools that support the interactive uses of text, graphics, animation, audio, or motion video. In other words, a computer capable of handling text, graphics, audio, animation and video is called multimedia computer. If the sequence and timing of these media elements can be controlled by the user, then one can name it as Interactive Multimedia.

Different Media Elements

(i) **Text:** Inclusion of textual information in multimedia is the basic step towards development of multimedia software. Text can be of any type, may be a word, a single line, or a paragraph. The textual data for multimedia can be developed using any text editor. However, to give special effects, one needs graphics software which supports this kind of job. Even one can use any of the most popular word processing software to create textual data for inclusion in multimedia. The text can have different type, size, color and style to suit the professional requirement of the multimedia software.

(ii) **Graphics:** Another interesting element in multimedia is graphics. As a matter of fact, taking into consideration the human nature, a subject is more explained with some sort of pictorial/graphical representation, rather than as a large chunk of text. This also helps to develop a clean multimedia screen, whereas use of large amount of text in a screen makes it dull in presentation.

Unlike text, which uses a universal ASCII format, graphics does not have a single agreed format. They have different format to suit different requirement. Most commonly used format for graphics is BMP or bitmap pictures. The size of a graphics depends on the resolution it is using. A computer image uses *pixel* or *dots* on the screen to form itself. And these dots or pixel, when combined with number of colors and other aspects are called resolution. Resolution of an image or graphics is basically the pixel density and number of colors it uses. And the size of the image depends on its resolution. A standard VGA (Virtual Graphics Arrays) screen can display a screen resolution of 640 ? 480 = 307200 pixel. And a Super VGA screen can display upto 1024*768 = 786432 pixel on the screen. While developing multimedia graphics one should always keep in mind the image resolution and number of colors to be used, as this has a direct relation with the image size. If the image size is bigger, it takes more time to load and also requires higher memory for processing and larger disk-space for storage.

However, different graphics formats are available which take less space and are faster to load into the memory.

There are several graphics packages available to develop excellent images and also to compress them so that they take lesser disk-space but use higher resolution and more colors. Packages like Adobe PhotoShop, Adobe Illustrator, and Paint Shop Pro, etc. are excellent graphics packages. There is Graphics gallery available in CD's (Compact Disk) with readymade images to suit almost every requirement. These images can directly be incorporated into multimedia development.

(iii) Animation: Moving images have an overpowering effect on the human peripheral vision. Followings are few points for its popularity.

Showing Continuity in Transitions

Animation is a set of static state, related to each other with transition. When something has two or more states, then changes between states will be much easier for users to understand if the transitions are animated instead of being instantaneous. An animated transition allows the user to track the mapping between different subparts through the perceptual system instead of having to involve the cognitive system to deduce the **mappings.**

Indicating Dimensionality in Transitions

Sometimes opposite animated transitions can be used to indicate movement back and forth along some navigational dimension. One example used in several user interfaces is the use of zooming to indicate that a new object is "grown" from a previous one (e.g., a detailed view or property list opened by clicking on an icon) or that an object is closed or minimized to a smaller representation. Zooming out from the small object to the enlargement is a navigational dimension and zooming in again as the enlargement is closed down is the opposite direction along that dimension.

Illustrating Change Over Time

Since animation is a time-varying display, it provides a one-to-one mapping to phenomena that change over time. For example, deforestation of the rain forest can be illustrated by showing a map with an animation of the covered area changing over time.

Multiplexing the Display

Animation can be used to show multiple information objects in the same space. A typical example is client-side image maps with explanations that pop up as the user moves the cursor over the various hypertext anchors.

Enriching Graphical Representations

Some types of information are easier to visualize with movement than with still pictures. Consider, for example, how to visualize the tool used to remove pixels in a graphics application.

Visualizing three-dimensional Structures

As you know the computer screen is two-dimensional. Hence users can never get a full understanding of a three-dimensional structure by a single illustration, no matter how well designed. Animation can be used to emphasize the three-dimensional nature of objects and make it easier for users to visualize their spatial structure. The animation need not necessarily spin the object in a full circle — just slowly turning it back and forth a little will often be sufficient. The movement should be slow to allow the user to focus on the structure of the object.

You can also move three-dimensional objects, but often it is better if you determine in advance how best to animate a movement that provides optimal understanding of the object. This pre-determined animation can then be activated by simply placing the cursor over the object. On the other hand, user-controlled movements requires the user to understand how to manipulate the object (which is inherently difficult with a two-dimensional control device like the mouse used with most computers — to be honest, 3D is never going to make it big time in user interfaces until we get a true 3D control device).

Attracting Attention

Finally, there are a few cases where the ability of animation to dominate the user's visual awareness can be turned to an advantage in the interface. If the goal is to draw the user's attention to a single element out of several or to alert the user to updated information then an animated headline will do the trick. Animated text should be drawn by a one-time animation (e.g., text sliding in from the right, growing from the first character, or smoothly becoming larger) and never by a continuous animation since moving text is more difficult to read than static text. The user should be drawn to the new text by the initial animation and then left in peace to read the text without further distraction. One of the excellent software available to create animation is Animator Pro. This provides tools to create impressive animation for multimedia development.

Video

Beside animation there is one more media element, which is known as video. With latest technology it is possible to include video impact on clips of any type into any multimedia creation, be it corporate presentation, fashion design, entertainment games, etc.

The video clips may contain some dialogues or sound effects and moving pictures. These video clips can be combined with the audio, text and graphics for multimedia presentation. Incorporation of video in a multimedia package is more important and complicated than other media elements. One can procure video clips from various sources such as existing video films or even can go for an outdoor video shooting.

The entire video available are in analog format. To make it usable by computer, the video clips are needed to be converted into computer understandable format, i.e., digital format. Both combinations of software and hardware make it possible to convert the analog video clips into digital format. This alone does not help, as the digitised video clips take lots of hard disk space to store, depending on the frame rate used for digitization. The computer reads a particular video clip as a series of still pictures called *frames*. Thus video clip is made of a series of separate frames where each frame is slightly different from the previous one. The computer reads each frame as a bitmap image. Generally there are 15 to 25 frames per second so that the movement is smooth. If we take less frames than this, the movement of the images will not be smooth.

To cut down the space there are several modern technologies in windows environment. Essentially these technologies compress the video image so that lesser space is required. However, latest video compression software makes it possible to compress the digitized video clips to its maximum. In the process, it takes lesser storage space. One more advantage of using digital video is, the quality of video will not deteriorate from copy to copy as the digital video signal is made up of digital code and not electrical signal. Caution should be taken while digitizing the video from analog source to avoid frame droppings and distortion. A good quality video source should be used for digitization.

Currently, video is good for:

- Promoting television shows, films, or other non-computer media that traditionally have used trailers in their advertising.
- Giving users an impression of a speaker's personality.
- Showing things that move. For example, a clip from a motion picture. Product demos of physical products are also well suited for video.

Audio

Audio has a greater role to play in multimedia development. It gives life to the static state of multimedia. Incorporation of audio is one of the most important features of multimedia, which enhance the multimedia usability to its full potential. There are several types of sound, which can be used in multimedia. They are human voices, instrumental notes, natural sound and many more. All these can be used in any combination as long as they give some meaning to their inclusion in multimedia.

There are many ways in which these sounds can be incorporated into the computer. For example:

- Using microphone, human voice can directly be recorded in a computer.
- Pre-recorded cassettes can be used to record the sound into computer.
- Instrumental sound can also be played directly from a musical instrument for recording into the computer.

The sound transmitted from these sources is of *analog* nature. To enable the computer to process this sound, they need to be digitised. As all of us know that sound is a repeated pattern of pressure in the air and a microphone converts a sound wave into an electrical wave. The clarity of sound, the final output depends entirely on the shape and frequency of the sound wave. When digitised (recording into computer), the error in sound can be drastically reduced. Audio need to be converted into digital format to produce digitised audio in order to use them in multimedia. And these digitised sounds again can be re-converted into analog form so that the user can hear them through the speakers.

Musical Instrument Digitisation Interface or MIDI provides a protocol or a set of rules, using which the details of a musical note from an instrument is communicated to the computer. But MIDI data is not digitized sound. It is directly recorded into the computer from musical instruments, whereas digitised audio is created from the analog sound. The quality of MIDI data depends upon the quality of musical instrument and the sound system. A MIDI file is basically a list command to produce the sound. For example, pressing of a guitar key can be represented as a computer command. When the MIDI device processes this command, the result will be the sound from the guitar. MIDI files occupy lesser space as compared to the digitised audio and they are editable also.

The main benefit of audio is that it provides an exclusive channel that is separate from that of the display. Speech can be used to offer commentary or help without obscuring information on the screen. Audio can also be used to provide a sense of place or mood. Mood-setting audio should employ very quiet background sounds in order not to compete with the main information for the user's attention. Music is probably the most obvious use of sound. Whenever you need to inform the user about a certain work of music, it makes much more sense to simply play it than to show the notes or to try to describe it in words.

11.9 HTML EXERCISES

1. The use of line breaks

```
<html>
<body>
<p>
To break<br>lines<br>in a<br>paragraph,<br>use the br tag.
</p>
</body>
</html>
```

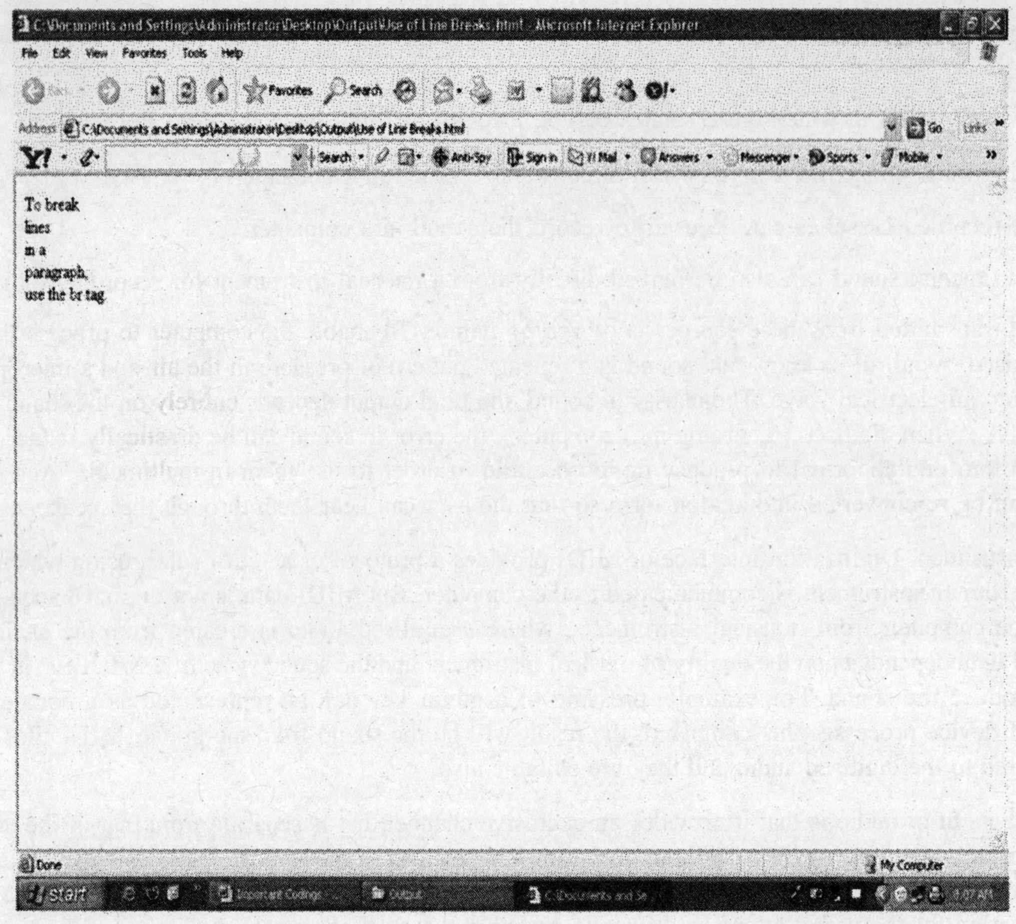

2. **Heading Tags**

```
<html>
<body>
<h1>This is heading 1</h1>
<h2>This is heading 2</h2>
<h3>This is heading 3</h3>
<h4>This is heading 4</h4>
<h5>This is heading 5</h5>
<h6>This is heading 6</h6>
<p>Use heading tags only for headings. Don't use them just to make something bold. Use other tags for that.</p>
</body>
</html>
```

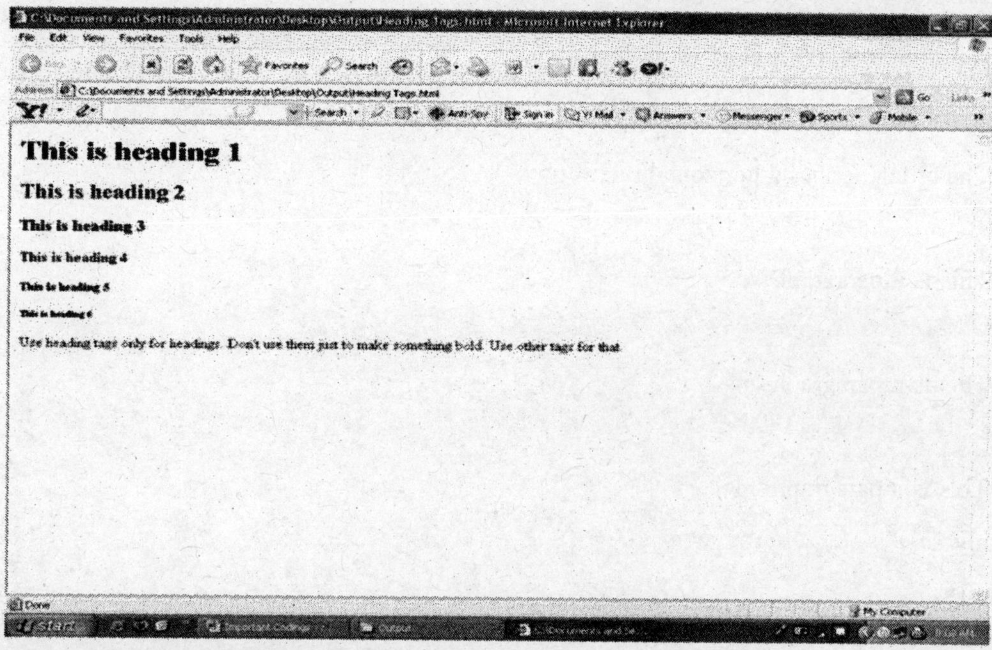

Use heading tags only for headings. Don't use them just to make something bold. Use other tags for that.

3. Center Aligned Heading

```
<html>
<body>
<h1 align="center">This is heading 1</h1>
<p>The heading above is aligned to the center of this page. The heading above is aligned to the center of this page. The heading above is aligned to the center of this page.</p>
</body>
</html>
```

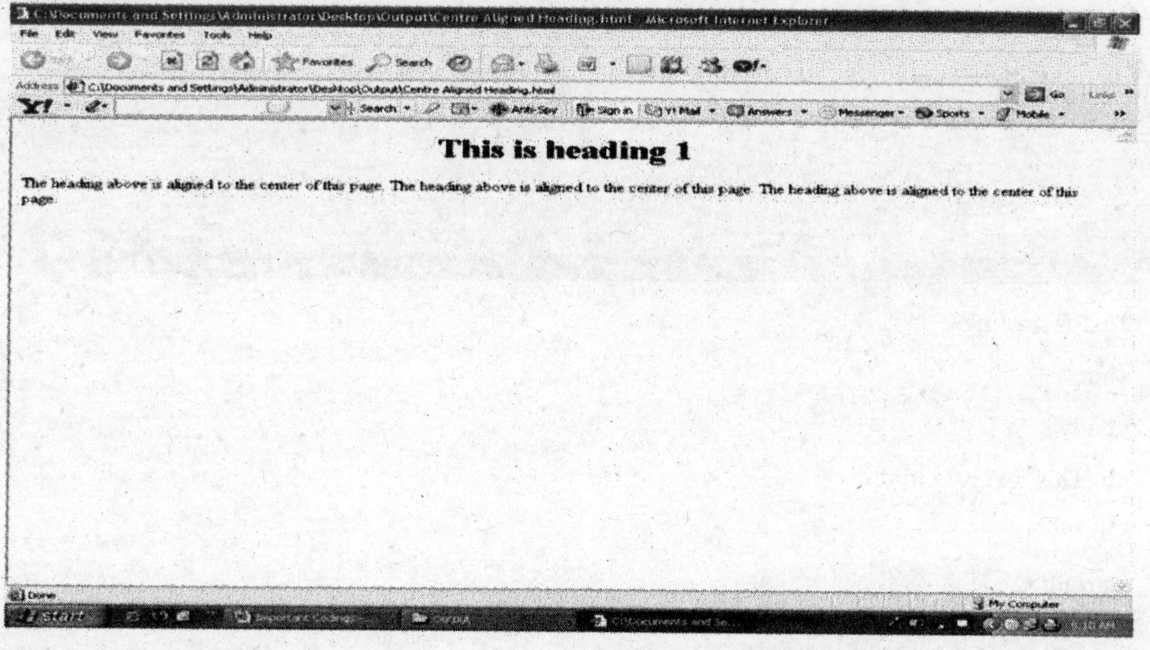

4. Insert a horizontal rule

```
<html>
<body>
<p>The hr tag defines a horizontal rule:</p>
<hr>
<p>This is a paragraph</p>
<hr>
<p>This is a paragraph</p>
<hr>
<p>This is a paragraph</p>
</body>
</html>
```

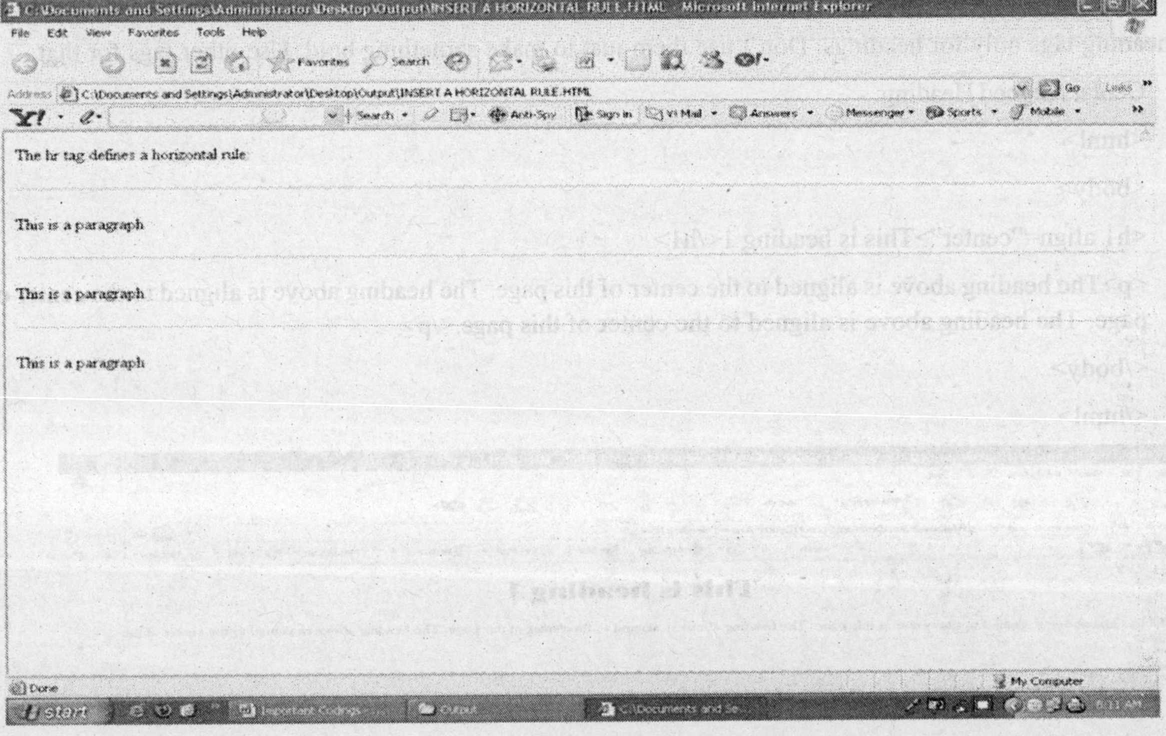

5. Text formating

```
<html>
<body>
<b>This text is bold</b>
<br>
<strong>
```

```
This text is strong
        </strong>
        <br>
        <big>
This text is big
        </big>
        <br>
        <em>
This text is emphasized
        </em>
        <br>
        <i>
This text is italic
        </i>
        <br>
        <small>
This text is small
        </small>
        <br>
This text contains
        <sub>
        subscript
        </sub>
        <br>
This text contains
        <sup>
        superscript
        </sup>
        </body>
        </html>
```

6. Text Direction

```
<html>
<body>
<p>
If your browser supports bi-directional override (bdo), the next line will be written from the right to the left (rtl):
</p>
<bdo dir="rtl">
Here is some Hebrew text
</bdo>
</body>
</html>
```

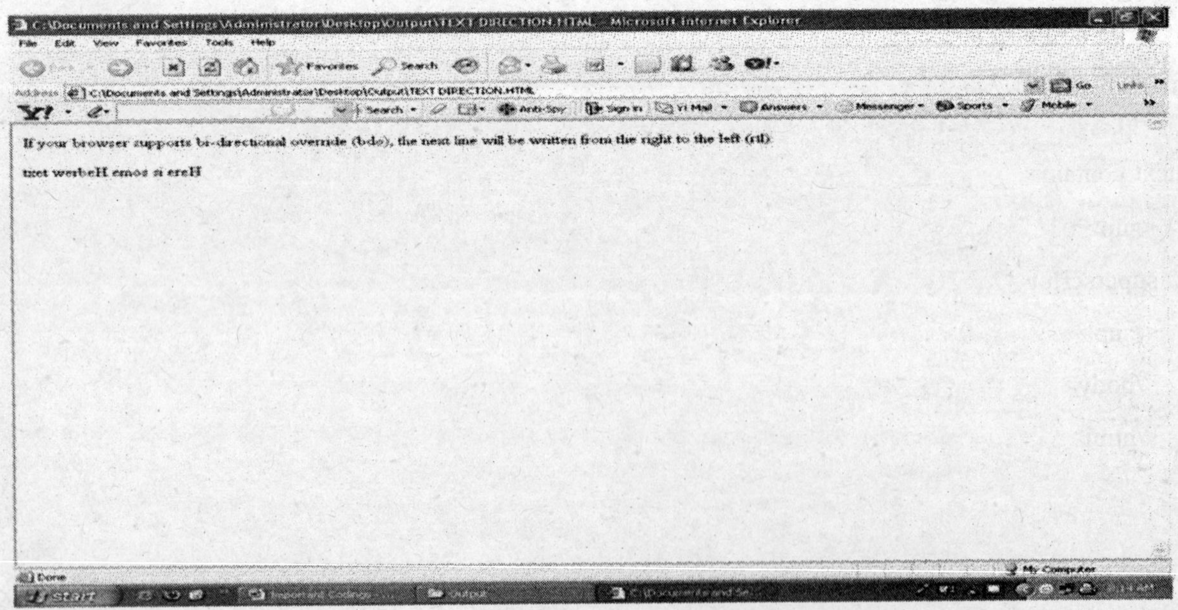

7. How to mark deleted and inserted text?

```
<html>
<body>
<p>
a dozen is
<del>twenty</del>
<ins>twelve</ins>
pieces
</p>
<p>
Most browsers will overstrike deleted text and underline inserted text.
</p>
<p>
Some older browsers will display deleted or inserted text as plain text.
</p>
</body>
</html>
```

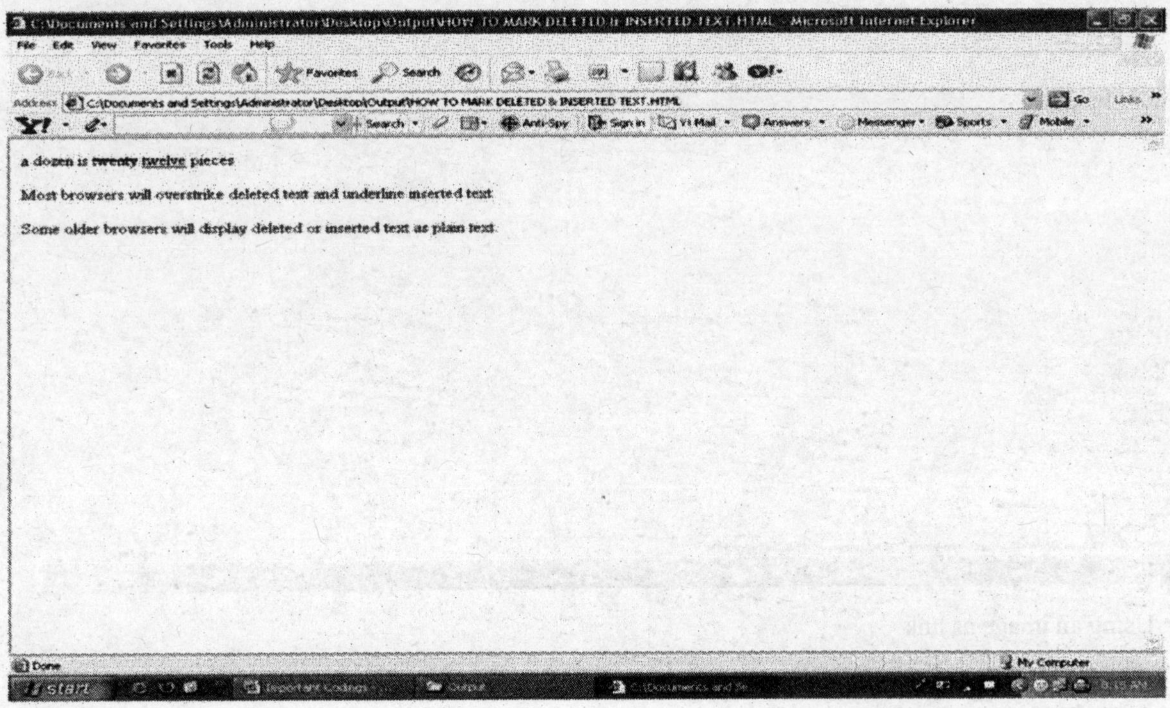

8. How to create hyperlinks ?

```
<html>
<body>
<p>
<a href="lastpage.htm">
This text</a> is a link to a page on this Web site.
</p>
<p>
<a href="http://www.microsoft.com/">
This text</a> is a link to a page on the World Wide Web.
</p>
</body>
</html>
```

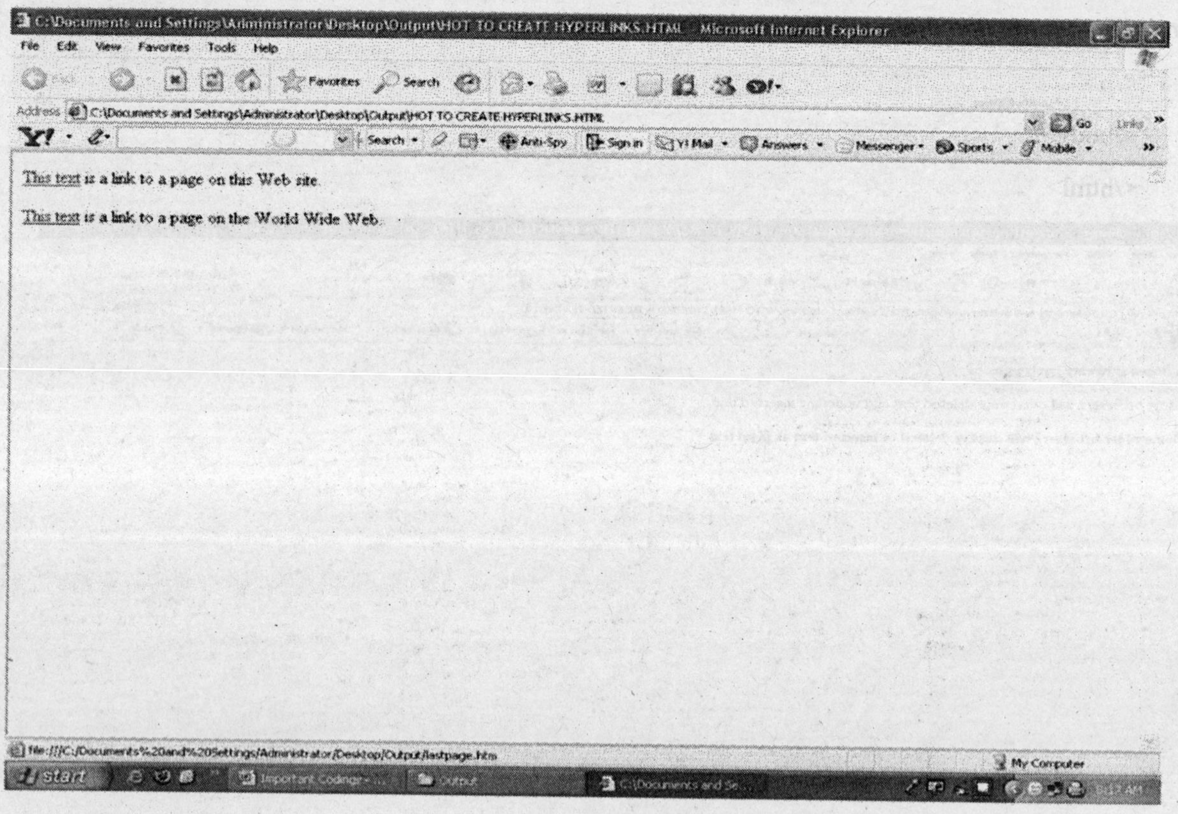

9. Using an image as link

```
<html>
<body>
<p>
```

You can also use an image as a link:

```
<a href="lastpage.htm">
<img border="0" src="buttonnext.gif" width="65" height="38">
</a>
</p>
</body>
</html>
```

10. How to create a vertical frameset with 3 different documents ?

```
<html>
<frameset cols="25%,50%,25%">
<frame src="frame_a.htm">
<frame src="frame_b.htm">
<frame src="frame_c.htm">
</frameset>
</html>
```

Output

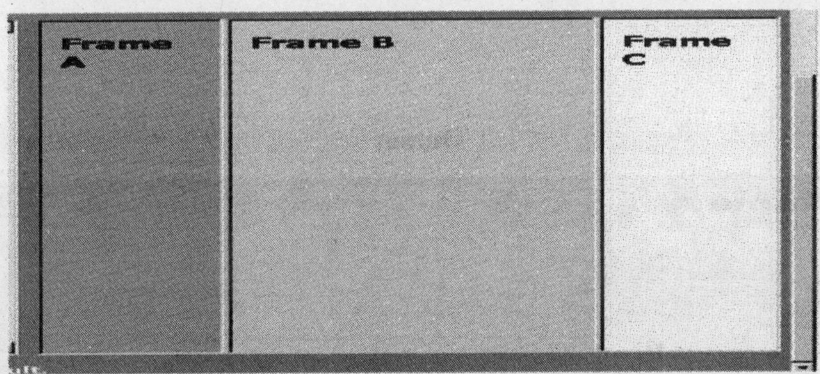

11. How to create a horizontal frameset with 3 different documents?

```
<html>
<frameset rows="25%,50%,25%">
<frame src="frame_a.htm">
<frame src="frame_b.htm">
<frame src="frame_c.htm">
</frameset>
</html>
```

Output

Frame A

Frame B

Frame C

12. How to mix a frameset in rows and columns?

```
<html>
<frameset rows=”50%,50%”>
<frame src=”frame_a.htm”>
<frameset cols=”25%,75%”>
<frame src=”frame_b.htm”>
<frame src=”frame_c.htm”>
</frameset>
</frameset>
</html>
```

Output

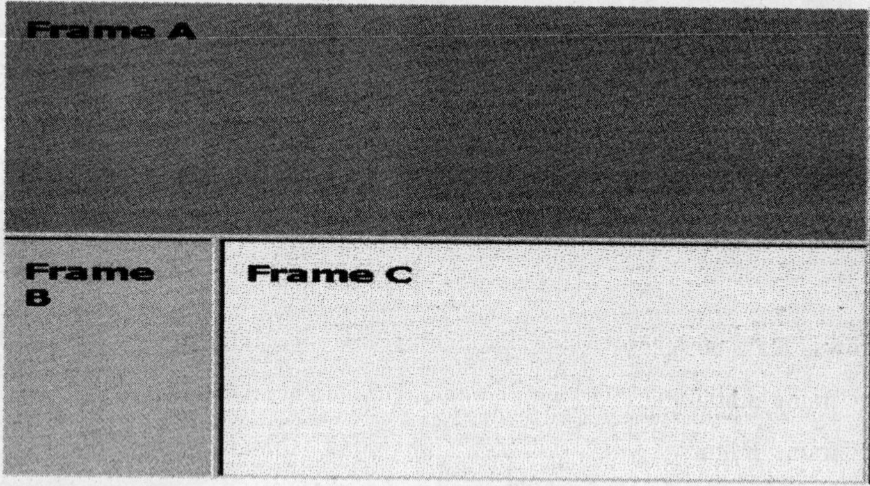

13. Simple tables

```
<html>
<body>
<p>
```

```
Each table starts with a table tag.
Each table row starts with a tr tag.
Each table data starts with a td tag.
</p>
<h4>One column:</h4>
<table border=”1">
<tr>
<td>100</td>
</tr>
</table>
<h4>One row and three columns:</h4>
<table border=”1">
<tr>
<td>100</td>
<td>200</td>
td>300</td>
</tr>
</table>
<h4>Two rows and three columns:</h4>
<table border=”1">
<tr>
<td>100</td>
<td>200</td>
<td>300</td>
</tr>
<tr>
<td>400</td>
<td>500</td>
<td>600</td>
</tr>
</table>
</body>
</html>
```

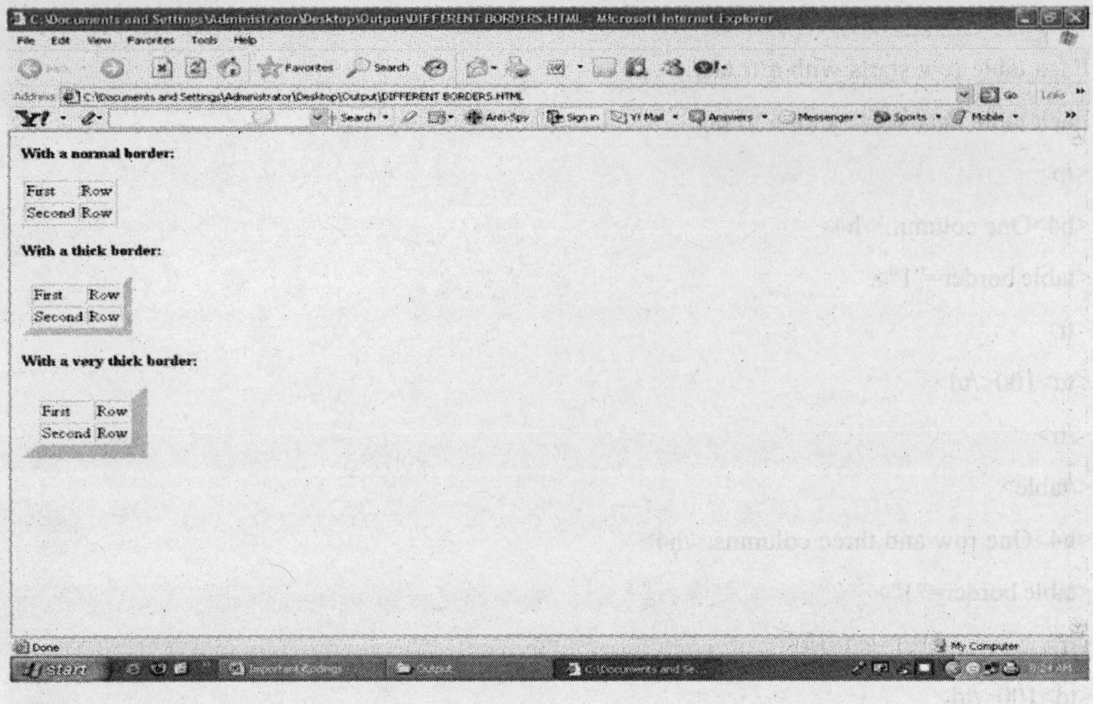

14. **Different table Borders**

```
<html>
<body>
<h4>With a normal border:</h4>
<table border="1">
<tr>
<td>First</td>
<td>Row</td>
</tr>
<tr>
<td>Second</td>
<td>Row</td>
</tr>
</table>
<h4>With a thick border:</h4>
<table border="8">
<tr>
<td>First</td>
<td>Row</td>
```

```
</tr>
<tr>
<td>Second</td>
<td>Row</td>
</tr>
</table>
<h4>With a very thick border:</h4>
<table border="15">
<tr>
<td>First</td>
<td>Row</td>
</tr>
<tr>
<td>Second</td>
<td>Row</td>
</tr>
</table>
</body>
</html>
```

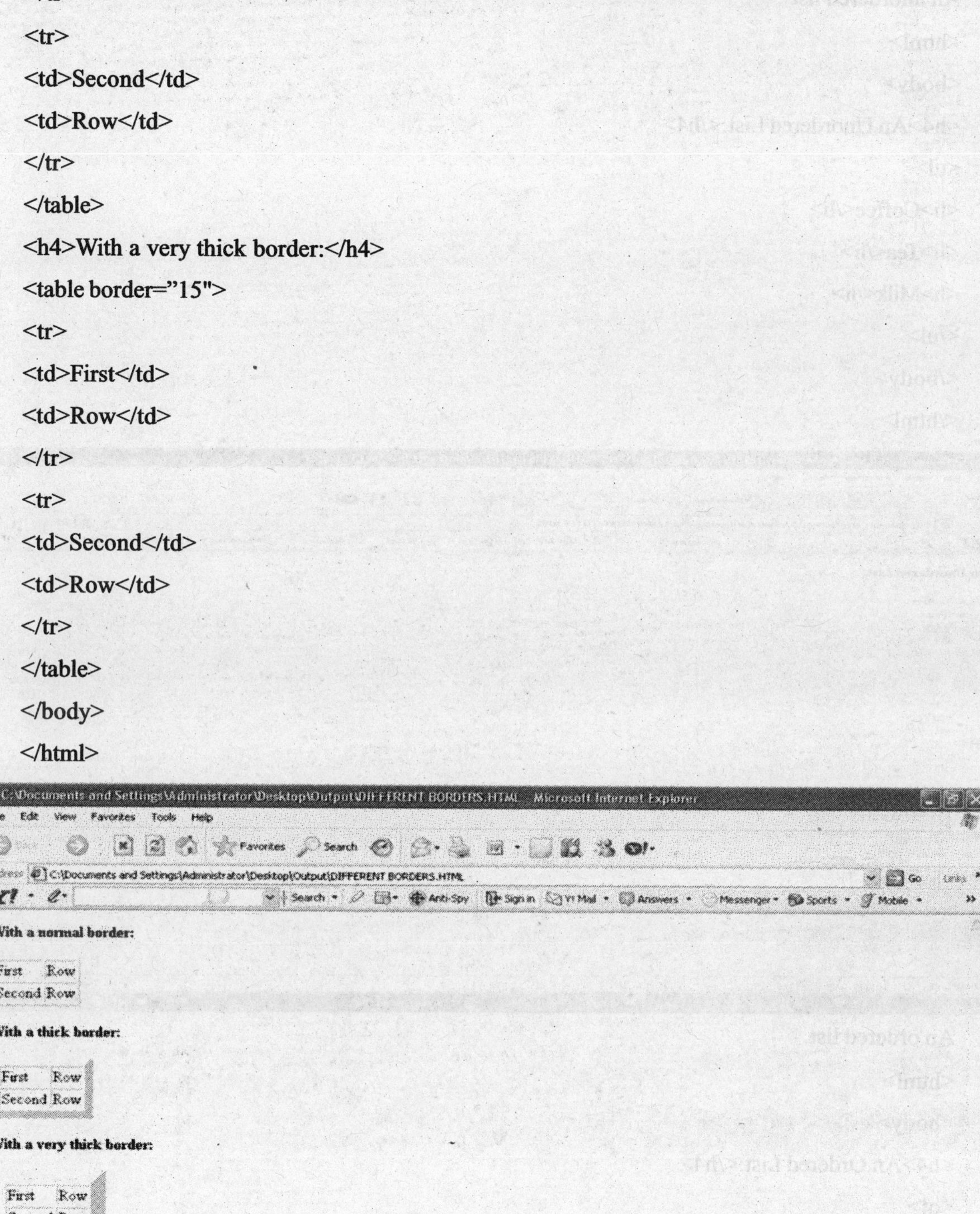

15. An unordered list

```
<html>
<body>
<h4>An Unordered List:</h4>
<ul>
<li>Coffee</li>
<li>Tea</li>
<li>Milk</li>
</ul>
</body>
</html>
```

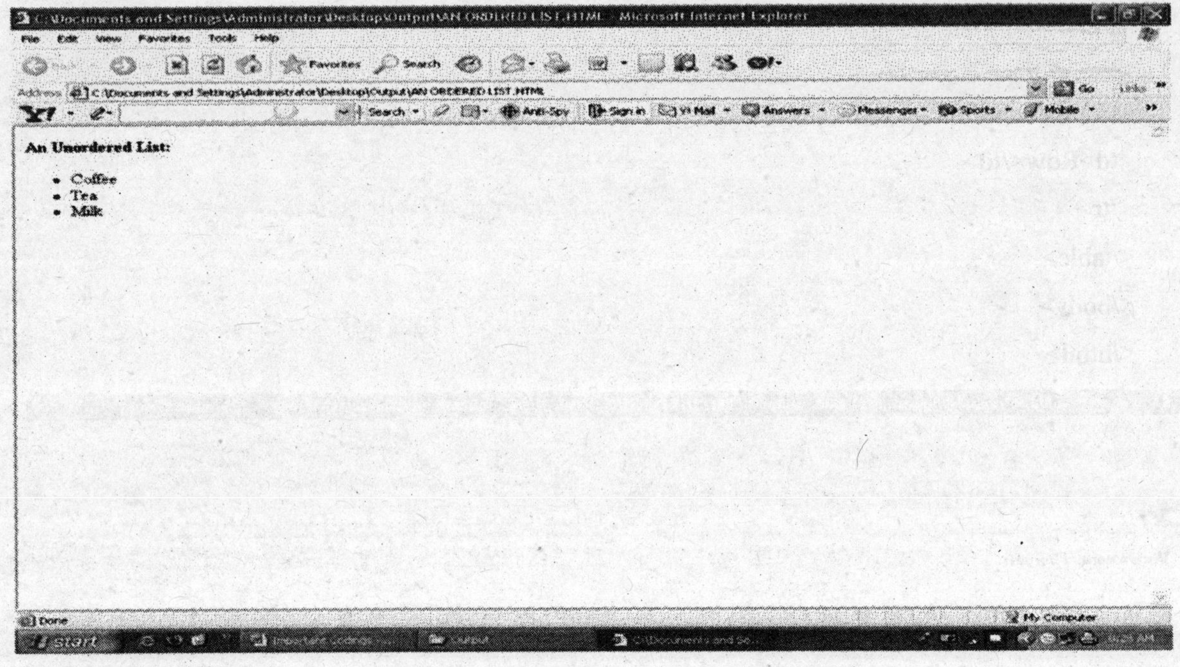

16. An ordered list

```
<html>
<body>
<h4>An Ordered List:</h4>
<ol>
<li>Coffee</li>
<li>Tea</li>
<li>Milk</li>
</ol>
</body>
</html>
```

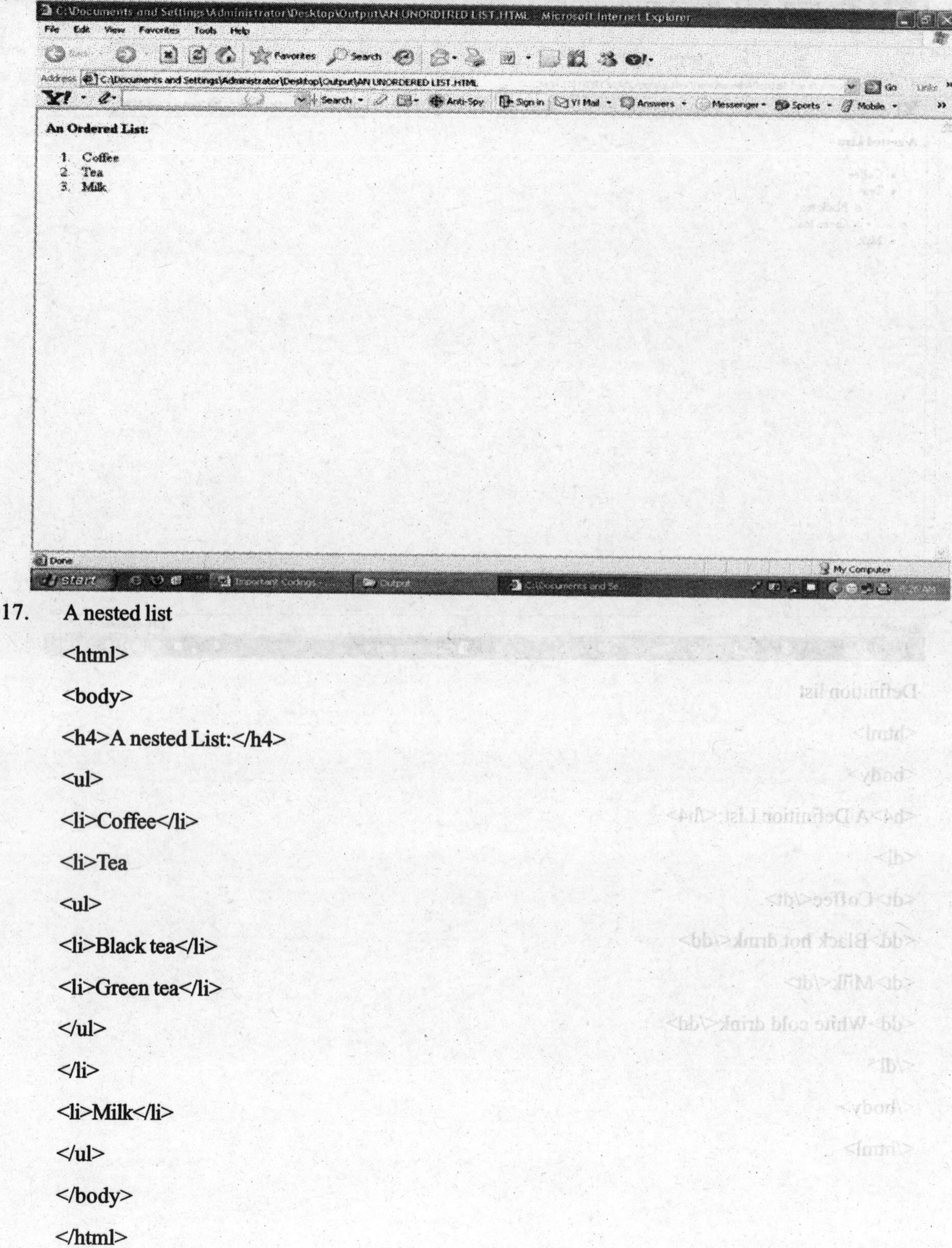

17. A nested list

```
<html>
<body>
<h4>A nested List:</h4>
<ul>
<li>Coffee</li>
<li>Tea
<ul>
<li>Black tea</li>
<li>Green tea</li>
</ul>
</li>
<li>Milk</li>
</ul>
</body>
</html>
```

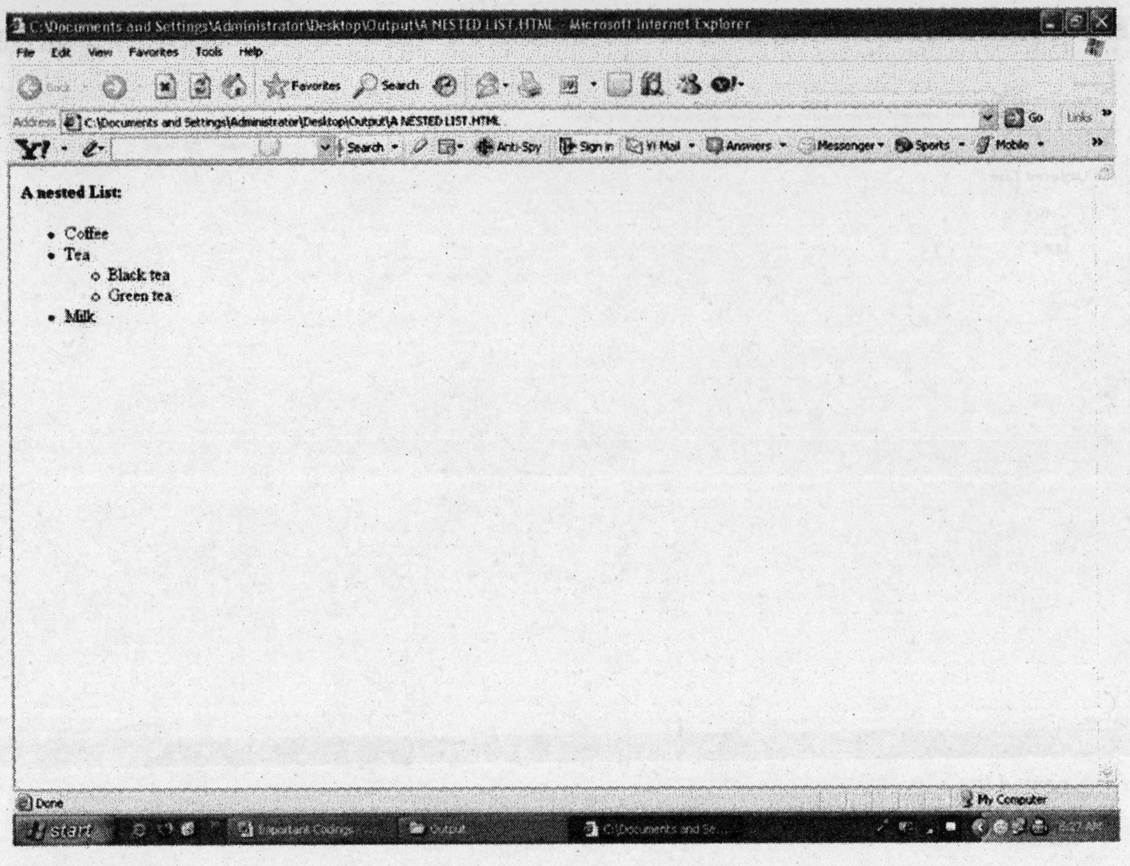

18. **Definition list**

```
<html>
<body>
<h4>A Definition List:</h4>
<dl>
<dt>Coffee</dt>
<dd>Black hot drink</dd>
<dt>Milk</dt>
<dd>White cold drink</dd>
</dl>
</body>
</html>
```

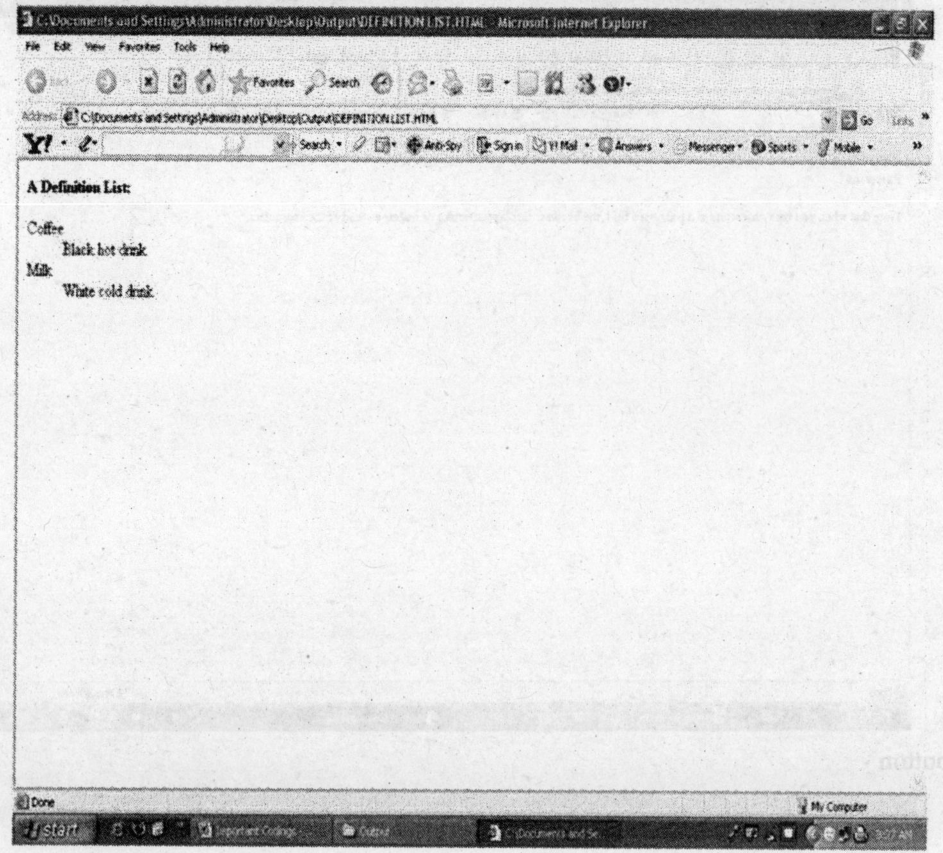

19. Password Fields

```
<html>
<body>
<form action="">
Username:
<input type="text" name="user">
<br>
Password:
<input type="password" name="password">
</form>
<p>
Note that when you type characters in a password field, the browser displays asterisks or bullets instead of the characters.
</p>
</body>
</html>
```

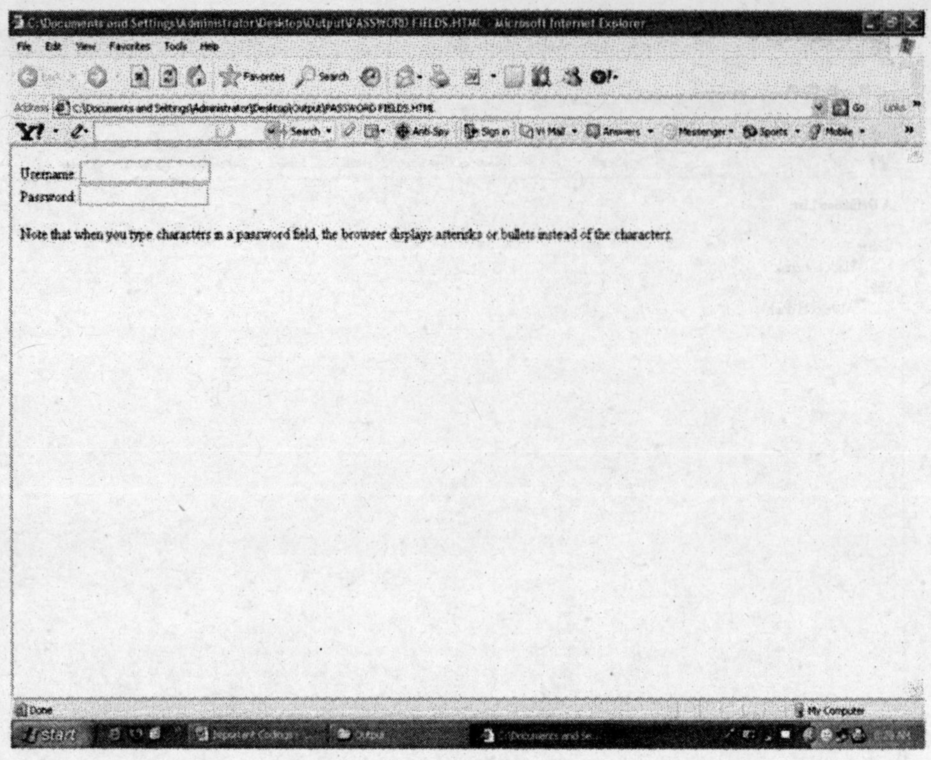

20. Radio button

```
        <html>
        <body>
        <form action="">
Male:
        <input type="radio" checked="checked"
        name="Sex" value="male">
        <br>
Female:
        <input type="radio"
        name="Sex" value="female">
        </form>
        <p>
```

When a user clicks on a radio-button, the button becomes checked, and all other buttons with the same name become unchecked

```
        </p>
        </body>
        </html>
```

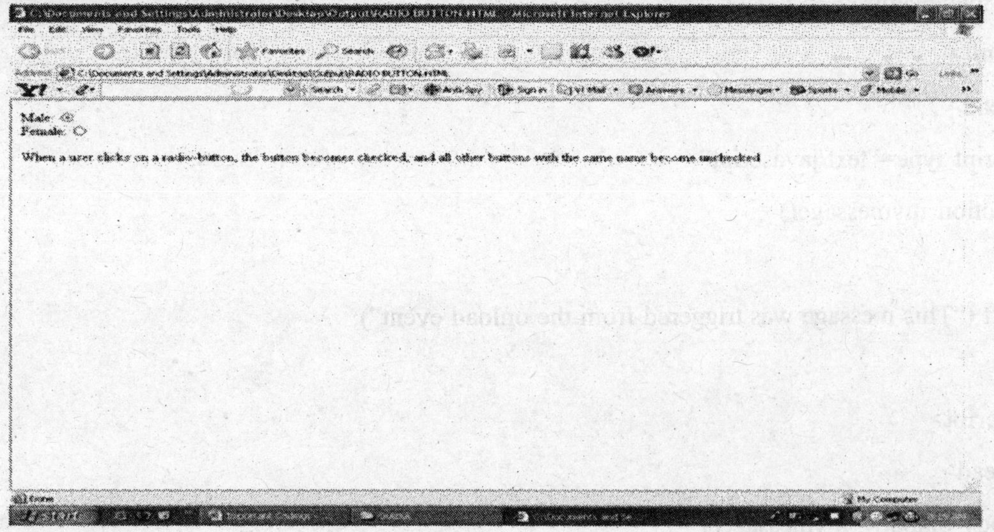

21. Drop-down options

```
<html>
<body>
<form action="">
<select name="cars">
<option value="volvo">Volvo</option>
<option value="saab">Saab</option>
<option value="fiat">Fiat</option>
<option value="audi">Audi</option>
</select>
</form>
</body>
</html>
```

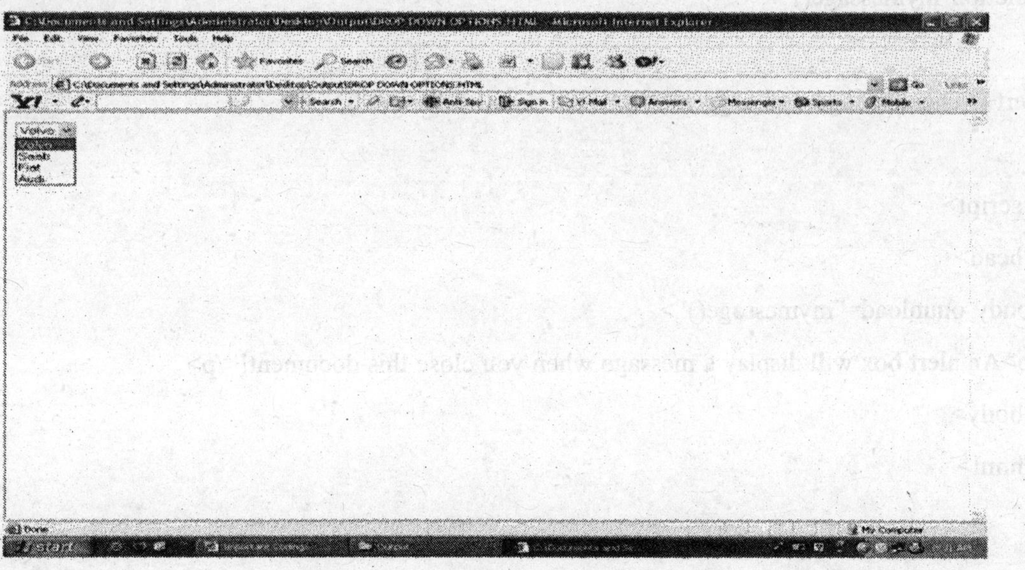

22. On load events

```
<html>
<head>
<script type="text/javascript">
function mymessage()
{
alert ("This message was triggered from the onload event");
}
</script>
</head>
<body onload="mymessage()">
</body>
</html>
```

Output

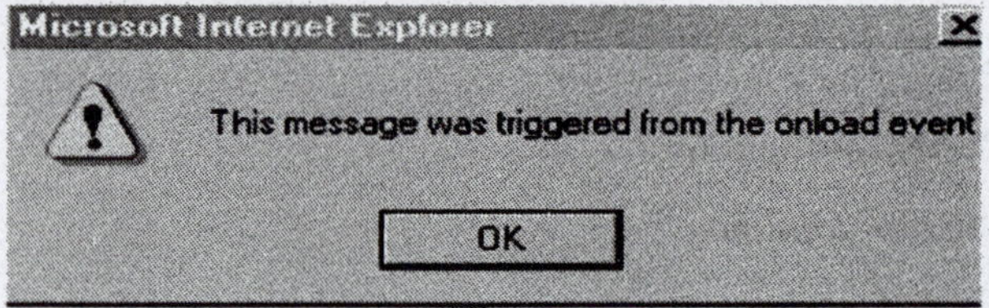

23. On unload

```
<html>
<head>
<script type="text/javascript">
function mymessage()
{
alert ("This message was triggered from the onunload event");
}
</script>
</head>
<body onunload="mymessage()">
<p>An alert box will display a message when you close this document!</p>
</body>
</html>
```

Output

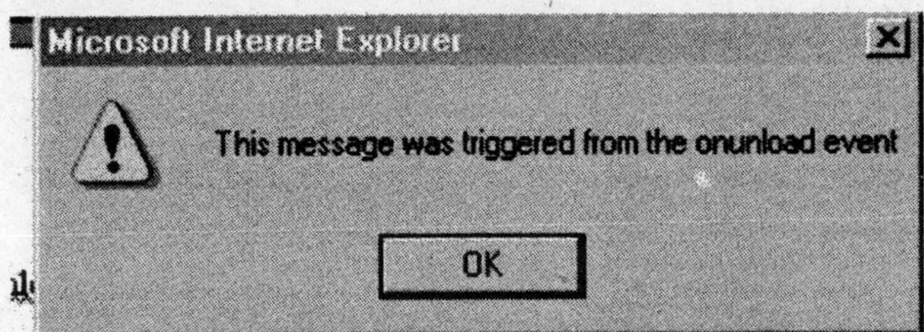

Javascript Codings

24. Write text with javascripts

```
<html>
<body>
<script type="text/javascript">
document.write("Hello World!");
</script>
</body>
</html>
```

25. Write HTML tags with javascripts

```
<html>
<body>
<script type="text/javascript">
document.write("<h1>This is a header</h1>");
</script>
</body>
</html>
```

26. Java Script in the body section

```
<html>
<head>
</head>
<body>
<script type="text/javascript">
document.write("This message is written by JavaScript");
</script>
</body>
</html>
```

27. Simple timing

```
<html>
<head>
<script type="text/javascript">
function timedMsg()
{
var t=setTimeout("alert ('5 seconds!')",5000);
}
</script>
</head>
<body>
<form>
<input type="button" value="Display timed alertbox!" onClick = "timedMsg()">
</form>
<p>Click on the button above. An alert box will be displayed after 5 seconds.</p>
</body>
</html>
```

28. Return the length of the string

```
<html>
<body>
<script type="text/javascript">
var txt="Anthony";
document.write(txt.length);
</script>
</body>
</html>
```

29. Birthday dish

```
<HTML>
<HEAD>
<TITLE>BEAUTIFUL B'DAY DISH</TITLE>
</HEAD>
<BODY bgColor=pink text=maroon><B>
<CENTER>B'DAY WISHES TO MY LOVELY FRIEND </CENTER></B>
<P align=left <H2><I><B>TO AKSHAYA</B> </I>
<H2></H2>
<P></P><FONTFACE="ARIAL">
```

```
<H1>
<CENTER>YOU'RE</H1>
<H3>ONE OF THOSE</CENTER><BR>
<CENTER>SPECIAL PEOPLE </CENTER><BR>
<CENTER>WHOSE SEEM TO HAVE A WAY</CENTER>
<CENTER>OF BRINGING CHEER AND GLADENESS</CENTER><BR>
<CENTER>TO OTHER DAY BY DAY....</CENTER><BR>
<CENTER>AND WHAT'S WHY </CENTER><BR>
<CENTER>IT'S SUCH A PLEASURE</CENTER><BR>
<CENTER>WHEN YOU HAVE A BIRTHDAY DUE </CENTER><BR>
<CENTER>TO WISH A REALLY SPECIAL DAY </CENTER><BR>
<CENTER>A HAPPY YEAR FOR YOU </CENTER></FONT>
<P ALIGN=RIGHT <H2> YOUR LOVING FRIEND DEEPA<H2> </p>
<MARQUEE direction=BOTTOM ?5? SIZE><B>***********HAVE A BEAUTIFUL
BIRTHDAY!*************</B></MARQUEE></H3></BODY></HTML>
```

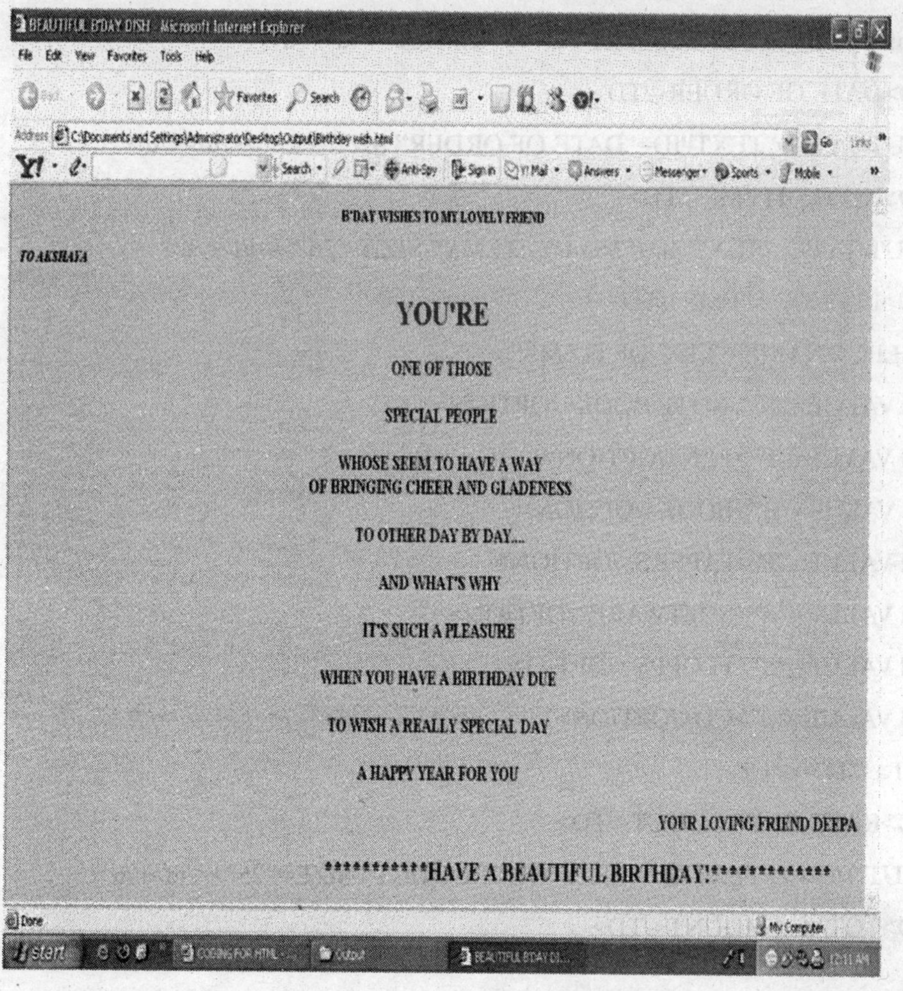

30. Purchasing order

```
<html>
<head>
<title>CUSTOMER DETAILS
</title>
<body BGCOLOR="MAROON">
<font size=18><center>PURCHASING ORDER</center></font>
<FORM METHOD="POST">
<table>
<tr>
<td>SNO</td>
<td><INPUT TYPE="INTEGER"ID="SNO" SIZE="25"></td></tr>
<tr><td>NAME</td>
<td><INPUT TYPE="TEXT"ID="NAME" SIZE="25"></td></tr>
<tr><td>ADDRESS</td>
<td><textarea name=ADDRESS  size="25"></textarea></td></tr>
<TR><TD>DATE OF ORDER</TD>
<td><INPUT TYPE="TEXT"ID="DATE OF ORDER" SIZE="25"></td></tr>
<TR><TD>NO OF ITEMS</TD>
<td><INPUT TYPE="TEXT"ID="NO OF ITEMS" SIZE="25"></td></tr>
<TR><TD>LIST OF ITEMS</TD>
<TD><SELECT NAME="LIST OF ITEMS">
<OPTION VALUE="N">NOTE BOOK</OPTION>
<OPTION VALUE="P">PEN</OPTION>'
<OPTION VALUE="B">BOOK</OPTION>
<OPTION VALUE="P">PAPERS</OPTION>
<OPTION VALUE="S">SOFTWARE</OPTION>
<OPTION VALUE="S">FLOPPY</OPTION>
<OPTION VALUE="S">CD</OPTION>
</SELECT></TD></TR>
<TR><TD>RATE OF PRODUCT</TD>
<td><INPUT TYPE="TEXT"ID="TATE OF PRODUCT" SIZE="25"></td></tr>
<TR><TD>TOTAL AMOUNT</TD>
```

```
<td><INPUT TYPE="TEXT"ID="TOTAL AMOUNT" SIZE="25"></td></tr>
</table>
<CENTER>
<INPUT TYPE=SUBMIT NAME=SUMIT VALUE=SUBMIT>
<INPUT TYPE=RESET NAME=RESET VALUE=CLEAR>
</CENTER>
</FORM>
</BODY>
</HEAD>
</HTML>
```

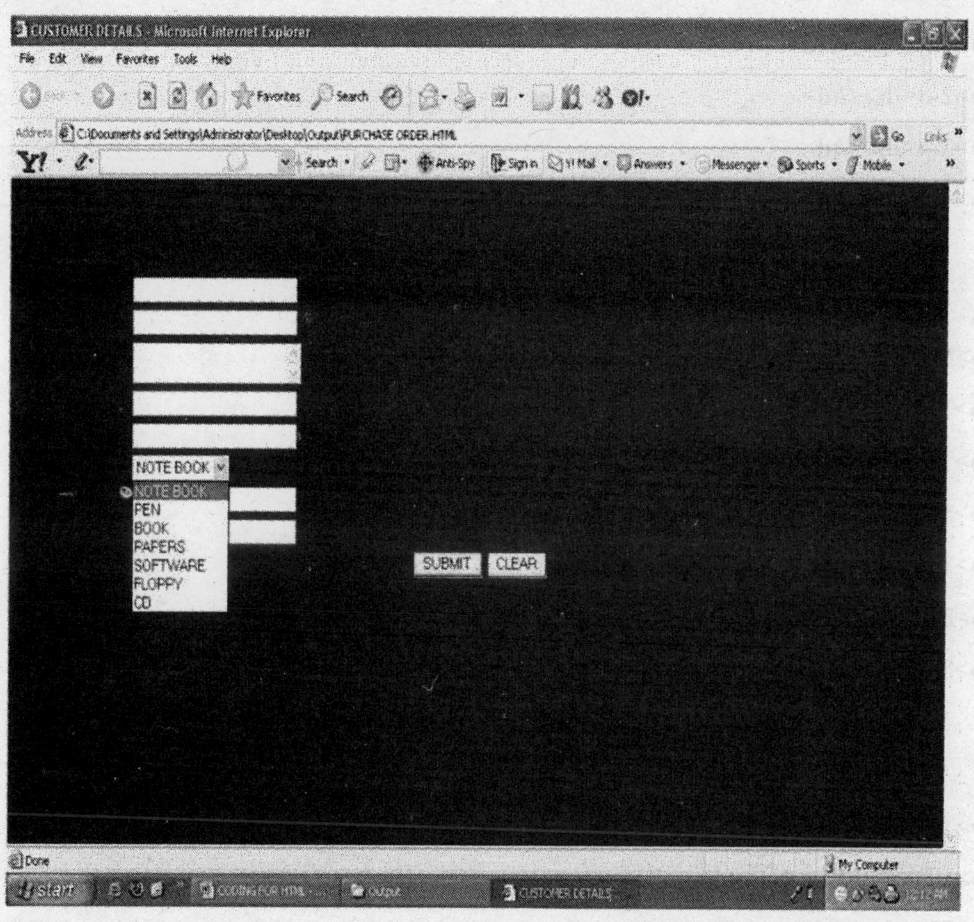

31. Time table

```
<html>
<head>
<title>CLASS TIMETABLE</title>
</head>
```

```
<center><h1>DEPARTMENT OF COMMERCE</p></font></center></h1>
<center><h2>BHARATHIAR UNIVERSITY</p></font></center></h2>
<center><h2>I.M.COM (FCA) TIME TABLE</font></center></h2>
<center><h3>2005-2006(even semester)<p></font></h3></center>
<table border=10 width="100%"bgcolor="lavender">
<body BGCOLOR="PINK">
<tr>
<td><b>Day</b></td>
<td><b>10-11</b></td>
<td><b>11-12</b></td>
<td><b>12-1</b></td>
<td><b>2-3</b></td>
<td><b>3-4</b></td>
<td><b>4-5</b></td>
</tr>
<tr>
<td><b>MONDAY</b></td>
<td><b>TEST</b></td>
<td><b>TEST</b></td>
<td><b>SE<P>(SM/MD)</b></td>
<td><b>VB<P>(SM)</b></td>
<td><b>Elective<p>(MM/MD)</b></td>
<td><b>Supportive</b></td>
</tr>
<tr>
<td><b>TUESDAY</b></td>
<td><b>VB<p>(SM)</b></td>
<td><b>FM</b></td>
<td><b>SE<P>(SM)</b></td>
<td><b>CMA<P>(PC)</b></td>
<td><b>CMA<p>(PC)</b></td>
<td><b>Elective<p>(MM/MD)</b></td>
```

```
</tr>
<tr>
<td><b>WEDNESDAY</b></td>
<td><b>SE<P>(MD)</b></td>
<td><b>VB<P>(SM)</b></td>
<td><b>Elective<p>(MM/MD)</b></td>
<td><b>FM</b></td>
<td><b>FM</b></td>
<td><b>Supportive</b></td>
</tr>
<tr>
<td><b>THURSDAY</b></td>
<td><b>CMA<P>(PC)</b></td>
<td><b>VB<P>(SM)</b></td>
<td><b>VB<P>(SM)</b></td>
<td><b>Elective<P>(MM/MD)</b></td>
<td><b>FM</b></td>
<td><b>SE<P>(SM)</b></td>
</tr>
<tr>
<td><b>FRIDAY</b></td>
<td><b>Elective<p>(MM/MD)</b></td>
<td><b>CMA<P>(PC)</b></td>
<td><b>CMA<P>(PC)</b></td>
<td><b>SE<P>(MD)</b></td>
<td><b>FM<p>(AVM)</b></td>
<td><b>Library</b></td>
</tr>
</body>
</html>
```

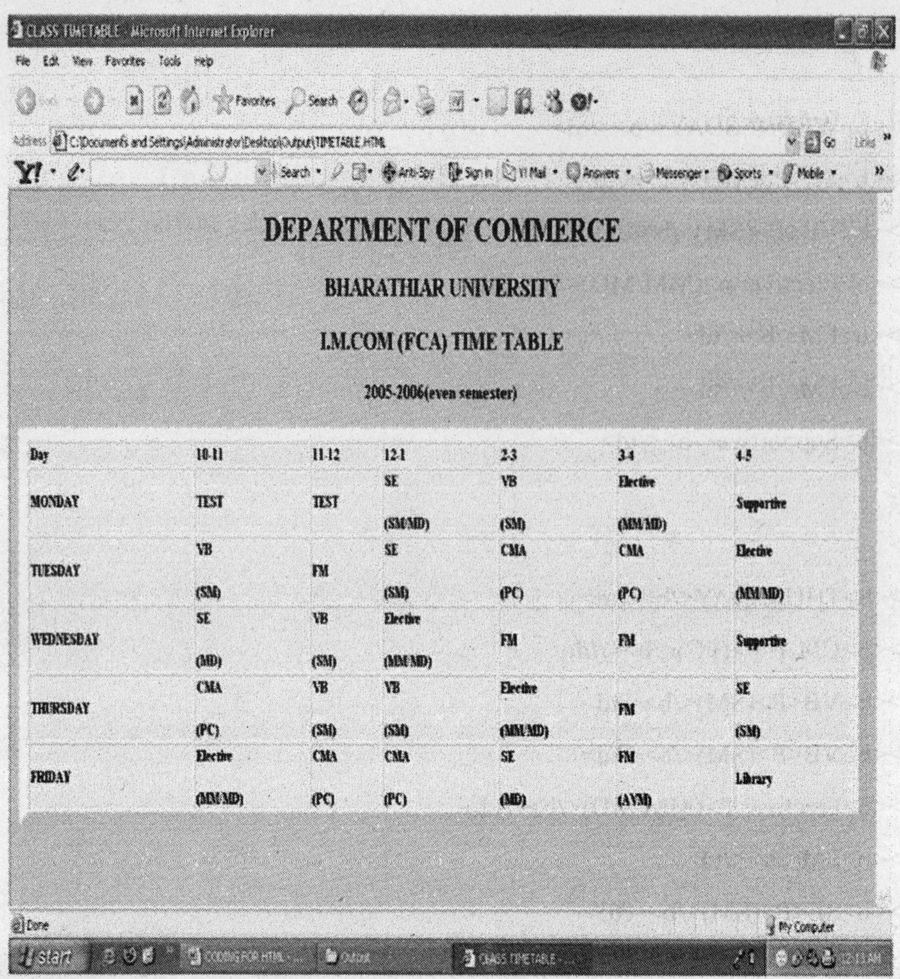

DEPARTMENT OF COMMERCE

BHARATHIAR UNIVERSITY

I.M.COM (FCA) TIME TABLE

2005-2006(even semester)

Day	10-11	11-12	12-1	2-3	3-4	4-5
MONDAY	TEST	TEST	SE (SM/MD)	VB (SM)	Elective (MM/MD)	Supportive
TUESDAY	VB (SM)	FM	SE (SM)	CMA (PC)	CMA (PC)	Elective (MM/MD)
WEDNESDAY	SE (MD)	VB (SM)	Elective (MM/MD)	FM	FM	Supportive
THURSDAY	CMA (PC)	VB (SM)	VB (SM)	Elective (MM/MD)	FM	SE (SM)
FRIDAY	Elective (MM/MD)	CMA (PC)	CMA (PC)	SE (MD)	FM (AYM)	Library

32. Product home page

```
<html>
<head><title>SRI HARI  DEPARTMENT STORES</TITLE>
<BODY BGCOLOR=”PINK”>
<H1><CENTER><MARQUEE>SRI HARI DEPARTMENT STORES</CENTER></MARQUEE>
<UL TYPE=.>
<LI><A HREF=”WEL.HTML”>WELCOME TO OUR DEPARTMENT STORE
<LI><A HREF=”PROD.HTML”> OUR PRODUCTS
<LI><A HREF=”SP.HTML”>SPECIAL OFFERS OF OUR DEPARTMENT
</UL>
<IMG SRC=”D:\cd\ANTONY\Logos\IATA.BMP”>
</BODY>
</HTML>
```

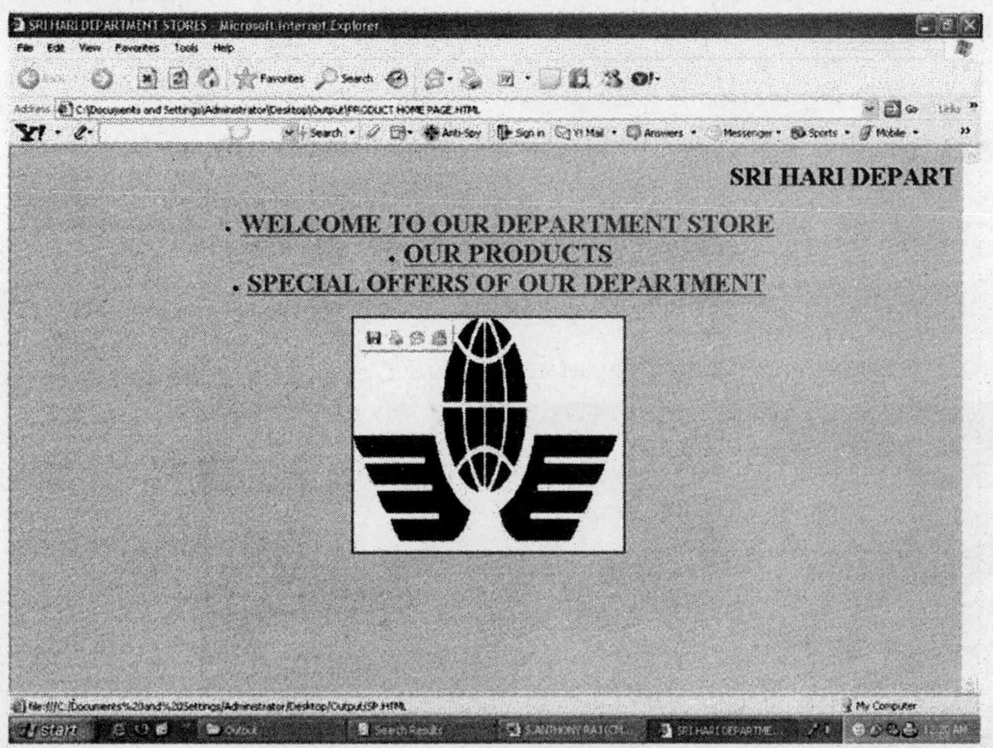

33. **Welcome page**

```
<HTML>
<HEAD>
<TITLE>WELCOME</TITLE>
<BODY BGCOLOR="PINK">
<P>
<CENTER><H1><FONT COLOR="GREEN">SRIHARI  DEPARTMENT STORES</CENTER></H1></
FONT>
<FONT STYLE="COMIC SANS MS"><UL TYPE=".">
<LI>YOU ARE WELCOME TO OUR HOME PAGE OF SRIHARI  DEPARTMENT STORES.
<LI>WE HAVE A WIDE VARIETY OF CHOICES OF COSMETICS,DRESS MATERIALS,GROCERS AND
LOTS MORE.
<LI>WE CATER TO YOUR NEEDS AND
<LI>WE CAN SURE U WILL HAVE PRIDE IN WITH OUR PRODUCTS.</FONT></UL>
<H2><MARQUEE=RIGHT>ENJOY THE SHOPPING IN SRIHARI DEPARTMENT STORES!!!</H2></
MARQUEE>
</P>
<IMG SRC="C:\WINNT\Web\Wallpaper\Paradise.jpg">
<H4>*****THANK YOU FOR VISITING OUR SITE COME AGAIN*****</H4>
```

```
<LI><A HREF=HOME.HTML>HOME
</BODY>
</HTML>
```

34. Product details

```
<HTML>
<HEAD><TITLE>OUR PRODUCTS</TITLE>
<BODY BGCOLOR="LAVENDER">
<CENTER><H1><FONT COLOR="BROWN">OUR PRODUCTS</H1></FONT>
<UL TYPE="*"><LI>PANTS<LI>T-SHIRTS<LI>CHILDREN WEARS<LI>SALVAR AND SAREES<LI>MODERN DRESS<LI>T-SHIRTS<LI>DHOTIES
</UL>
<MARQUEE direction="up"><IMG SRC="C:\WINNT\Web\Wallpaper\Windows 2000.jpg"></MARQUEE>
<LI><A HREF=HOME.HTML>HOME
</BODY>
</HTML>
```

35. Offers

```
<HTML>
<HEAD><TITLE>SPECIAL OFFERS OF OUR DEPARTMENT</TITLE>
<BODY BGCOLOR=”LAVENDER”>
<CENTER><H1><FONT COLOR=”AQUA”>OFFERS</H1></FONT>
<UL TYPE=”*”><LI>EXCELLENT COMPLIMENTS<LI>DISCOUNT 10% - 50%<LI>FUNNY GAMES DURING
FESTIVAL TIMES</UL>
<MARQUEE direction=”up”><F:\spss\Spss v10.05\Spss\Flags\SPAIN.BMP”></MARQUEE>
<LI><A HREF=HOME.HTML>HOME
</BODY>
</HTML>
```

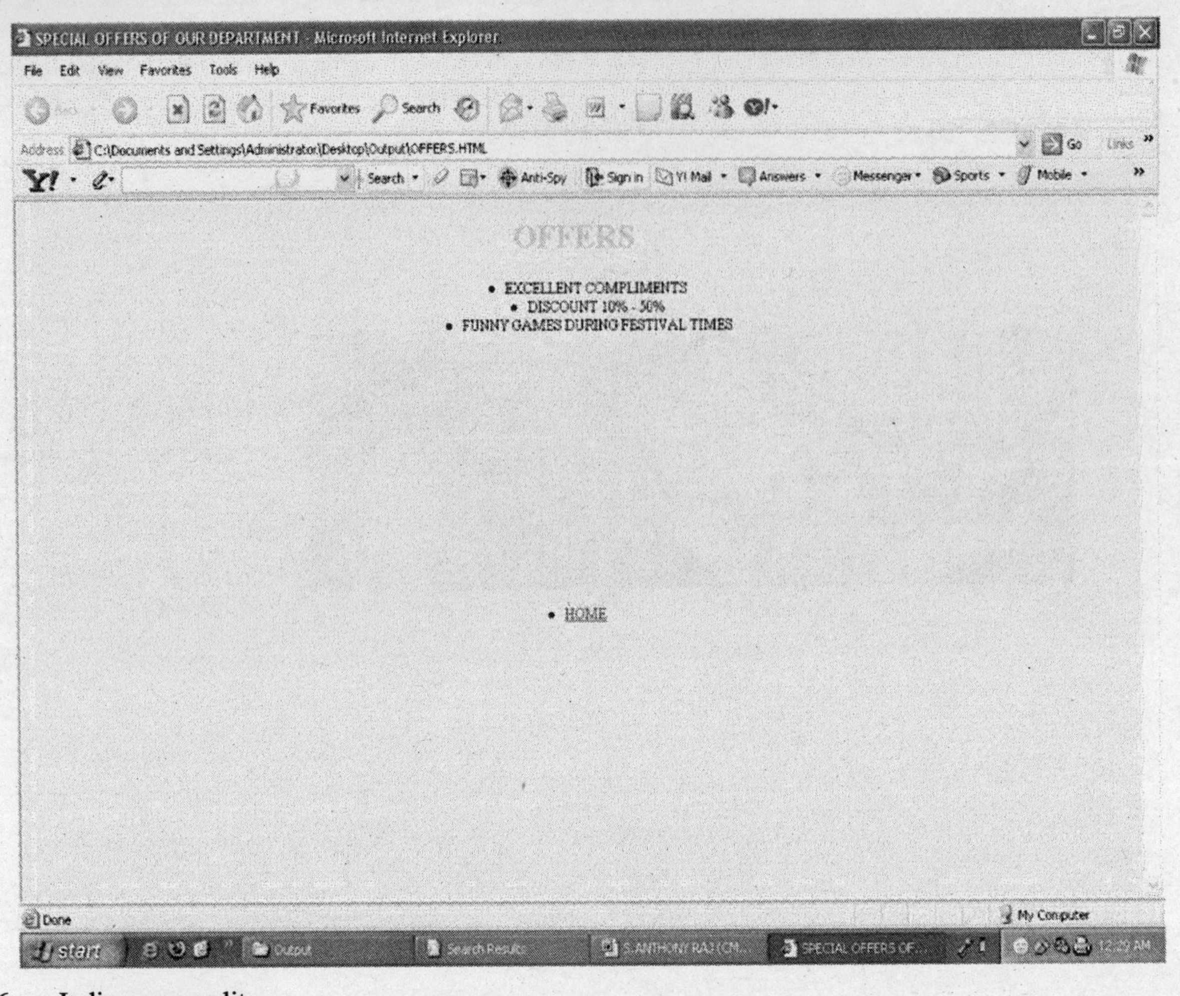

36. Indian personality

```
<HTML>
<HEAD>
<TITLE>MY FAVOURITE INDIAN PERSONALITY</TITLE></HEAD>
<BODY BGCOLOR ="MAROON" TEXT="WHITE">
<B> <CENTER><H2> THE FATHER OF OUR NATION </H2></CENTER> </B>
<CENTER><IMG SRC="D:\cd\ANTONY\Personalities\shivnadar.jpg"> </CENTER>
<P ALIGN="LEFT"><H2><B><center>BIOGRAPHY OF MAHATMA GANDHI</center ></
H2></B>
<A HREF="BIOGRAPHY.HTML">MAHATMA GANDHI
</BODY>
</HTML>
```

37. Greeting card

```
<Html>

<Head>

<Title>GREETING CARD</TITLE>

</HEAD>

<Body bgcolor="Aqua" text="maroon">

<b> <center><H3>BIRTHDAY WISHING</H3></center></b>

<p align="left"><h2><I>To USHA <br></I><H2></p>

<CENTER><IMG SRC="C:\Documents and Settings\All Users\Documents\My Pictures\Sample Pictures\Sunset.jpg" ></CENTER>

<FONT FACE="ARIAL"><CENTER><H5>YOU'RE<H5> ONE OF those <br><center> SPECIAL PEOPLE </CENTER> <BR> WHOSE SEEM TO HAVE A WAY <BR> OF BRINGING CHEER AND GLADNESS <BR> <CENTER>

<CENTER> TO OTHERS DAY BY DAY...<BR> AND THAT'S WHY <BR> IT'S SUCH A PLEASURE </ CENTER>

<BR> WHEN YOU HAVE A BIRTHDAY DUE <BR> <CENTER> TO WISH A REALLY SPECIAL DAY <BR> AND A HAPPY YEAR FOR YOU! </CENTER> </CENTER>
```

```
</FONT>
<MARQUEE DIRECTION="RIGHT" SIZE"4"><B>HAVE A BEAUTIFUL BIRTHDAY!</B></MARQUEE>
</BODY>
</HTML>
```

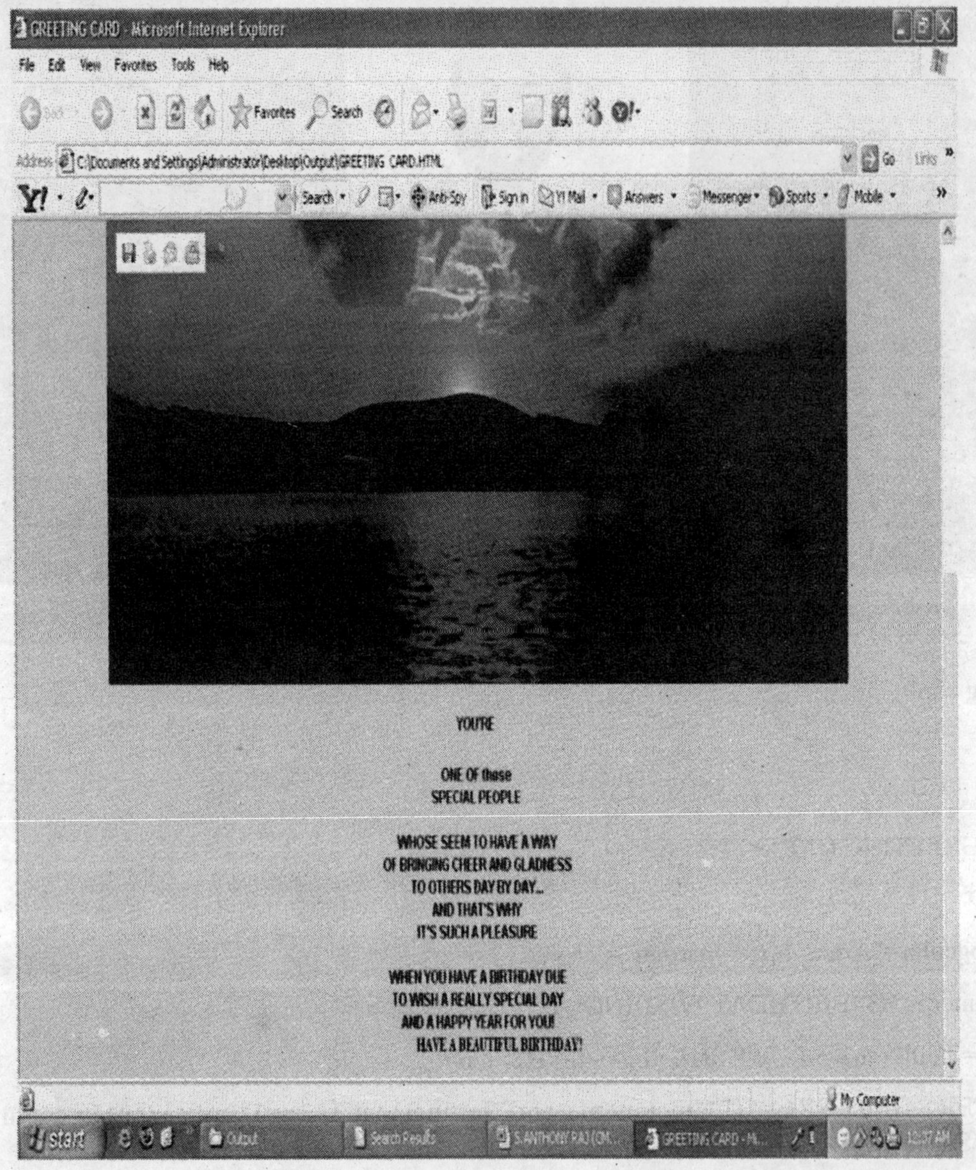

12

CHAPTER

ACCOUNTING PACKAGE — TALLY ERP 9

Structure:

12.1 SHORT CUT KEYS IN TALLY.ERP 9

Function Key Combination

Functions	Functionality	Availability
F1	To select a company	At all masters menu screen
F1	To select the Accounts Button	At the Accounting Voucher creation and alteration screen
F1 (ALT+F1)	To select the Inventory To view the detailed or condensed report	At the Inventory/Payroll Voucher creation and alteration screen In almost all the Reports
F1 (CTRL + F1)	To select Payroll Vouchers to alter	At the Accounting/Inventory voucher creation or alteration screen.
F2	To change the current date To select company inventory features	At almost all screens in TALLY.ERP 9 At the F11: Features screen
F3	To select the company To select Company Statutory and Taxation features	At almost all screens in TALLY.ERP 9 At F11: Features screen
F4	To select the Contra voucher	At Accounting/Inventory Voucher creation and alteration screen
F5	To select the Payment voucher	At Accounting/Inventory Voucher creation and alteration screen
F6	To select the Receipt voucher	At Accounting/Inventory Voucher creation and alteration screen
F7	To select the Journal voucher	At Accounting/Inventory Voucher creation and alteration screen
F8	To select the Sales voucher	At Accounting/Inventory Voucher creation and alteration screen
F8 (CTRL+F8)	To select the Credit Note voucher	At Accounting/Inventory Voucher creation and alteration screen
F9	To select the Purchase voucher	At Accounting/Inventory Voucher creation and alteration screen
F9 (CTRL+F9)	To select the Debit Note voucher	At Accounting/Inventory Voucher creation and alteration screen
F10	To select the Reversing Journal voucher	At Accounting/Inventory Voucher creation and alteration screen
F10 (Ctrl + F10)	To select the Memorandum voucher	At Accounting/Inventory/Payroll Voucher creation and alteration screen
F11	To select the Functions and Features screen	At almost all screens in TALLY.ERP 9
F12	To select the Configure screen	At almost all screens in TALLY.ERP 9

Special Key Combination

Functions	Functionality	Availability
ALT + 2	To Duplicate a voucher	At List of Vouchers – creates a voucher similar to the one where you positioned the cursor and used this key combination
ALT + A	To Add a voucher To Alter the column in columnar report	At List of Vouchers – adds a voucher after the one where you positioned the cursor and used this key combination. Alters the column in all the reports which can be viewed in columnar format
ALT + C	To create a master at a voucher screen (if it has not been already assigned a different function, as in reports like Balance Sheet, where it adds a new column to the report) To access Auto Value Calculator in the amount field during voucher entry	At voucher entry and alteration screens, at a field where you have to select a master from a list. If the necessary account has not been created already, use this key combination to create the master without quitting from the voucher screen. At all voucher entry screens in the amount field
ALT + D	To delete a voucher To delete a master To delete a column in any columnar report (if it has not been already assigned a different function, as explained above)	At Voucher and Master (Single) alteration screens. Masters can be deleted subject to conditions, as explained in the manual. All the reports screen which can be viewed in columnar format
ALT + E	To export the report in ASCII, Excel, HTML OR XML format	At all reports screens in TALLY.ERP 9
ALT + I	To insert a voucher To toggle between Item and Accounting invoice	At List of Vouchers – inserts a voucher before the one where you positioned the cursor and used this key combination. At creation of sales and purchase invoice
ALT + G	To select the Language Configuration	At almost all screens in TALLY.ERP 9
ALT + K	To select the Keyboard Configuration	At almost all screens in TALLY.ERP 9
ALT + O	To upload the report at your website	At all reports screens in TALLY.ERP 9
ALT + G	To select language for TALLY.ERP 9 Interface	At almost all screens of TALLY.ERP 9
ALT + M	To E-mail the report	At all reports screens in TALLY.ERP 9
ALT + N	To view the report in automatic columns	At all the reports where columns can be added
ALT + P	To print the report	At all reports screens in TALLY.ERP 9
ALT + R	To repeat the narration in different voucher type	At all Vouchers in TALLY.ERP 9
ALT + S	To bring back a line you removed using ALT + R	At all reports screens in TALLY.ERP 9

ALT + U	To retrieve the last line which is deleted using Alt + R	At all reports screens in TALLY.ERP 9
ALT+ V	From Invoice screen to bring Stock Journal screen	At Invoice screen > Quantity Field > Press Alt + V to select the Stock Journal.
ALT + X	To cancel a voucher in Day Book/List of Vouchers	At all voucher screens in TALLY.ERP 9
ALT + R	To repeat the narration in different voucher type	At almost all screens in TALLY.ERP 9.
CTRL + A	To accept a form – wherever you use this key combination, that screen or report gets accepted as it is	At almost all screens in TALLY.ERP 9, except where a specific detail has to be given before accepting
CTRL + B	To select the Budget	At Groups/Ledgers/Cost Centres/Budgets/Scenarios/Voucher Types/Currencies (Accounts Info) creation and alteration screen
CTRL + ALT + B	To check the Company Statutory details	At all the menu screens
CTRL + C	To select the Cost Centre To select the Cost Category	At Groups/Ledgers/Cost Centres/Budgets/Scenarios/Voucher Types/Currencies (Accounts Info) creation and alteration screen At Stock Groups/Stock Categories/Stock Items/Reorder Levels/Godowns/Voucher Types/Units of Measure (Inventory Info) creation/alteration screen
CTRL+ E	To select the Currencies	At Groups/Ledgers/Cost Centres/Budgets/Scenarios/Voucher Types/Currencies (Accounts Info) creation and alteration screen
CTRL + G	To select the Group	At Groups/Ledgers/Cost Centres/Budgets/Scenarios/Voucher Types/Currencies (Accounts Info) creation and alteration screen
CTRL + H	To view the Support Centre	At Almost all screens in TALLY.ERP 9
CTRL + I	To select the Stock Items	At Stock Group/Stock Categories/Stock Items/Reorder Levels/Godowns/Voucher Types/Units of Measure (Inventory Info) creation/alteration screen
Ctrl + Alt + I	To import statutory masters	At all menu screens
CTRL + K	To Login as Remote Tally.NET User	At Almost all screens in TALLY.ERP 9
CTRL + L	To select the Ledger To mark a Voucher as Optional	At Groups/Ledgers/Cost Centres/Budgets/Scenarios/Voucher Types/Currencies (Accounts Info) creation and alteration screen At the creation and alteration of Vouchers
CTRL + O	To select the Godowns	At Stock Groups/Stock Categories/Stock Items/Reorder Levels/Godowns/Voucher Types/Units of Measure (Inventory Info) creation/alteration screen
CTRL + Q	To abandon a form – wherever you use this key combination, it quits that screen without making any changes to it.	At almost all screens in TALLY.ERP 9.
CTRL + R	To repeat narration in the same voucher type	At creation/alteration of voucher screen

CTRL + Alt + R	Rewrite data for a Company	From Gateway of Tally screen
CTRL + S	Allows you to alter Stock Item master	At Stock Voucher Report and Godown Voucher Report
CTRL + U	To select the Units	At Stock Groups/Stock Categories/Stock Items/Reorder Levels/Godowns/Voucher Types/Units of Measure (Inventory Info) creation/alteration screen
CTRL + V	To select the Voucher Types To toggle between Invoice and Voucher	At Groups/Ledgers/Cost Centres/Budgets/Scenarios/Voucher Types/Currencies (Accounts Info) creation and alteration screen At creation of Sales/Purchase Voucher screen
CTRL + K	To login to Control Centre	At almost all screens of TALLY.ERP 9
CTRL + H	To access Support Centre. Wherein you can directly post your queries on the functional and technical aspects of Tally.ERP 9, Shopper and Tally. Developer.	At almost all screens of TALLY.ERP 9
Alt + Enter	To view the Voucher display	At Day Book and almost all Voucher Reports
Alt + S	To view Stock Query report	At all Voucher Creation and Alteration screens where inventory is applicable except Contra, Reversing Journal, Memorandum and Physical Stock Voucher

Special Key Combination

Functions	Functionality	Availability
ALT + 2	To Duplicate a voucher	At List of Vouchers – creates a voucher similar to the one where you positioned the cursor and used this key combination
ALT + A	To Add a voucher To Alter the column in columnar report	At List of Vouchers – adds a voucher after the one where you positioned the cursor and used this key combination. Alters the column in all the reports which can be viewed in columnar format
ALT + C	To create a master at a voucher screen (if it has not been already assigned a different function, as in reports like Balance Sheet, where it adds a new column to the report) To access Auto Value Calculator in the amount field during voucher entry	At voucher entry and alteration screens, at a field where you have to select a master from a list. If the necessary account has not been created already, use this key combination to create the master without quitting from the voucher screen. At all voucher entry screens in the Amount field
ALT + D	To delete a voucher To delete a master To delete a column in any columnar report (if it has not been already assigned a different function, as explained above)	At Voucher and Master (Single) alteration screens. Masters can be deleted subject to conditions, as explained in the manual. All the reports screen which can be viewed in columnar format

ALT + E	To export the report in ASCII, Excel, HTML OR XML format	At all reports screens in TALLY.ERP 9
ALT + I	To insert a voucher To toggle between Item and Accounting invoice	At List of Vouchers – inserts a voucher before the one where you positioned the cursor and used this key combination. At creation of sales and purchase invoice
ALT + G	To select the Language Configuration	At almost all screens in TALLY.ERP 9
ALT + K	To select the Keyboard Configuration	At almost all screens in TALLY.ERP 9
ALT + O	To upload the report at your website	At all reports screens in TALLY.ERP 9
ALT + G	To select language for TALLY.ERP 9 Interface	At almost all screens of TALLY.ERP 9
ALT + M	To E-mail the report	At all reports screens in TALLY.ERP 9
ALT + N	To view the report in automatic columns	At all the reports where columns can be added
ALT + P	To print the report	At all reports screens in TALLY.ERP 9
ALT + R	To repeat the narration in different voucher type	At all Vouchers in TALLY.ERP 9
ALT + S	To bring back a line you removed using ALT + R	At all reports screens in TALLY.ERP 9
ALT + U	To retrieve the last line which is deleted using Alt + R	At all reports screens in TALLY.ERP 9
ALT+ V	From Invoice screen to bring Stock Journal screen	At Invoice screen > Quantity Field > Press Alt + V to select the Stock Journal.
ALT + X	To cancel a voucher in Day Book/List of Vouchers	At all voucher screens in TALLY.ERP 9
ALT + R	To repeat the narration in different voucher type	At almost all screens in TALLY.ERP 9.
CTRL + A	To accept a form – wherever you use this key combination, that screen or report gets accepted as it is	At almost all screens in TALLY.ERP 9, except where a specific detail has to be given before accepting
CTRL + B	To select the Budget	At Groups/Ledgers/Cost Centres/Budgets/Scenarios/Voucher Types/Currencies (Accounts Info) creation and alteration screen
CTRL + ALT + B	To check the Company Statutory details	At all the menu screens
CTRL + C	To select the Cost Centre To select the Cost Category	At Groups/Ledgers/Cost Centres/Budgets/Scenarios/Voucher Types/Currencies (Accounts Info) creation and alteration screen At Stock Groups/Stock Categories/Stock Items/Reorder Levels/Godowns/Voucher Types/Units of Measure (Inventory Info) creation/alteration screen

CTRL+ E	To select the Currencies	At Groups/Ledgers/Cost Centres/Budgets/Scenarios/Voucher Types/Currencies (Accounts Info) creation and alteration screen
CTRL + G	To select the Group	At Groups/Ledgers/Cost Centres/Budgets/Scenarios/Voucher Types/Currencies (Accounts Info) creation and alteration screen
CTRL + H	To view the Support Centre	At Almost all screens in TALLY.ERP 9
CTRL + I	To select the Stock Items	At Stock Group/Stock Categories/Stock Items/Reorder Levels/Godowns/Voucher Types/Units of Measure (Inventory Info) creation/alteration screen
Ctrl + Alt + I	To import statutory masters	At all menu screens
CTRL + K	To Login as Remote Tally.NET User	At Almost all screens in TALLY.ERP 9
CTRL + L	To select the Ledger To mark a Voucher as Optional	At Groups/Ledgers/Cost Centres/Budgets/Scenarios/Voucher Types/Currencies (Accounts Info) creation and alteration screen At the creation and alteration of Vouchers
CTRL + O	To select the Godowns	At Stock Group/Stock Categories/Stock Items/Reorder Levels/Godowns/Voucher Types/Units of Measure (Inventory Info) creation/alteration screen
CTRL + Q	To abandon a form – wherever you use this key combination, it quits that screen without making any changes to it.	At almost all screens in TALLY.ERP 9.
CTRL + R	To repeat narration in the same voucher type	At creation/alteration of voucher screen
CTRL + Alt + R	Rewrite data for a Company	From Gateway of Tally screen
CTRL + S	Allows you to alter Stock Item master	At Stock Voucher Report and Godown Voucher Report
CTRL + U	To select the Units	At Stock Groups/Stock Categories/Stock Items/Reorder Levels/Godowns/Voucher Types/Units of Measure (Inventory Info) creation/alteration screen
CTRL + V	To select the Voucher Types To toggle between Invoice and Voucher	At Groups/Ledgers/Cost Centres/Budgets/Scenarios/Voucher Types/Currencies (Accounts Info) creation and alteration screen At creation of Sales/Purchase Voucher screen
CTRL + K	To login to Control Centre	At almost all screens of TALLY.ERP 9
CTRL + H	To access Support Centre. Wherein you can directly post your queries on the functional and technical aspects of Tally.ERP 9, Shopper and Tally. Developer.	At almost all screens of TALLY.ERP 9
Alt + Enter	To view the Voucher display	At Day Book and almost all Voucher Reports
Alt + S	To view Stock Query report	At all Voucher Creation and Alteration screens where inventory is applicable except Contra, Reversing Journal, Memorandum and Physical Stock Voucher

Special Key Combination

Functions	Functionality	Availability
ALT + 2	To Duplicate a voucher	At List of Vouchers – creates a voucher similar to the one where you positioned the cursor and used this key combination
ALT + A	To Add a voucher To Alter the column in columnar report	At List of Vouchers – adds a voucher after the one where you positioned the cursor and used this key combination. Alters the column in all the reports which can be viewed in columnar format
ALT + C	To create a master at a voucher screen (if it has not been already assigned a different function, as in reports like Balance Sheet, where it adds a new column to the report) To access Auto Value Calculator in the amount field during voucher entry	At voucher entry and alteration screens, at a field where you have to select a master from a list. If the necessary account has not been created already, use this key combination to create the master without quitting from the voucher screen. At all voucher entry screens in the Amount field
ALT + D	To delete a voucher To delete a master To delete a column in any columnar report (if it has not been already assigned a different function, as explained above)	At Voucher and Master (Single) alteration screens. Masters can be deleted subject to conditions, as explained in the manual. All the reports screen which can be viewed in columnar format
ALT + E	To export the report in ASCII, Excel, HTML OR XML format	At all reports screens in TALLY.ERP 9
ALT + I	To insert a voucher To toggle between Item and Accounting Invoice	At List of Vouchers – inserts a voucher before the one where you positioned the cursor and used this key combination. At creation of sales and purchase invoice
ALT + G	To select the Language Configuration	At almost all screens in TALLY.ERP 9
ALT + K	To select the Keyboard Configuration	At almost all screens in TALLY.ERP 9
ALT + O	To upload the report at your website	At all reports screens in TALLY.ERP 9
ALT + G	To select language for TALLY.ERP 9 Interface	At almost all screens of TALLY.ERP 9
ALT + M	To E-mail the report	At all reports screens in TALLY.ERP 9
ALT + N	To view the report in automatic columns	At all the reports where columns can be added
ALT + P	To print the report	At all reports screens in TALLY.ERP 9
ALT + R	To repeat the narration in different voucher type	At all Vouchers in TALLY.ERP 9
ALT + S	To bring back a line you removed using Alt + R	At all reports screens in TALLY.ERP 9
ALT + U	To retrieve the last line which is deleted using Alt + R	At all reports screens in TALLY.ERP 9
ALT+ V	From Invoice screen to bring Stock Journal screen	At Invoice screen > Quantity Field > Press Alt + V to select the Stock Journal.

ALT + X	To cancel a voucher in Day Book/List of Vouchers	At all voucher screens in TALLY.ERP 9
ALT + R	To repeat the narration in different voucher type	At almost all screens in TALLY.ERP 9.
CTRL + A	To accept a form – wherever you use this key combination, that screen or report gets accepted as it is	At almost all screens in TALLY.ERP 9, except where a specific detail has to be given before accepting
CTRL + B	To select the Budget	At Groups/Ledgers/Cost Centres/Budgets/Scenarios/Voucher Types/Currencies (Accounts Info) creation and alteration screen
CTRL + ALT + B	To check the Company Statutory details	At all the menu screens
CTRL + C	To select the Cost Centre To select the Cost Category	At Groups/Ledgers/Cost Centres/Budgets/Scenarios/Voucher Types/Currencies (Accounts Info) creation and alteration screen At Stock Groups/Stock Categories/Stock Items/Reorder Levels/Godowns/Voucher Types/Units of Measure (Inventory Info) creation and alteration screen
CTRL+ E	To select the Currencies	At Groups/Ledgers/Cost Centres/Budgets/Scenarios/Voucher Types/Currencies (Accounts Info) creation and alteration screen
CTRL + G	To select the Group	At Groups/Ledgers/Cost Centres/Budgets/Scenarios/Voucher Types/Currencies (Accounts Info) creation and alteration screen
CTRL + H	To view the Support Centre	At Almost all screens in TALLY.ERP 9
CTRL + I	To select the Stock Items	At Stock Groups/Stock Categories/Stock Items/Reorder Levels/Godowns/Voucher Types/Units of Measure (Inventory Info) creation and alteration screen
Ctrl + Alt + I	To import statutory masters	At all menu screens
CTRL + K	To Login as Remote Tally.NET User	At Almost all screens in TALLY.ERP 9
CTRL + L	To select the Ledger To mark a Voucher as Optional	At Groups/Ledgers/Cost Centres/Budgets/Scenarios/Voucher Types/Currencies (Accounts Info) creation and alteration screen At the creation and alteration of Vouchers
CTRL + O	To select the Godowns	At Stock Groups/Stock Categories/Stock Items/Reorder Levels/Godowns/Voucher Types/Units of Measure (Inventory Info) creation and alteration screen
CTRL + Q	To abandon a form – wherever you use this key combination, it quits that screen without making any changes to it.	At almost all screens in TALLY.ERP 9.
CTRL + R	To repeat narration in the same voucher type	At creation and alteration of voucher screen
CTRL + Alt + R	Rewrite data for a Company	From Gateway of Tally screen
CTRL + S	Allows you to alter Stock Item master	At Stock Voucher Report and Godown Voucher Report

CTRL + U	To select the Units	At Stock Groups/Stock Categories/Stock Items/Reorder Levels/Godowns/Voucher Types/Units of Measure (Inventory Info) creation and alteration screen
CTRL + V	To select the Voucher Types To toggle between Invoice and Voucher	At Groups/Ledgers/Cost Centres/Budgets/Scenarios/Voucher Types/Currencies (Accounts Info) creation and alteration screen At creation of Sales/Purchase Voucher screen
CTRL + K	To login to Control Centre	At almost all screens of TALLY.ERP 9
CTRL + H	To access Support Centre. Wherein you can directly post your queries on the functional and technical aspects of Tally.ERP 9, Shopper and Tally. Developer.	At almost all screens of TALLY.ERP 9
Alt + Enter	To view the Voucher display	At Day Book and almost all Voucher Reports
Alt + S	To view Stock Query report	At all Voucher Creation and Alteration screens where inventory is applicable except Contra, Reversing Journal, Memorandum and Physical Stock Voucher

12.2 STARTING UP WITH TALLY.ERP 9

Start Tally.ERP 9 using the following steps:

- Go to Start ▸ Programs ▸ Tally.ERP 9 ▸ Tally.ERP 9 icon.
- Double Click on the Tally.ERP 9 icon on the desktop.

The welcome screen, 'Tally.ERP 9 – Power of Simplicity' appears while the software loads. When the Tally.ERP 9 start-up screen appears, you are ready to explore Tally.ERP 9. The Tally.ERP 9 Start-up screen appears as:

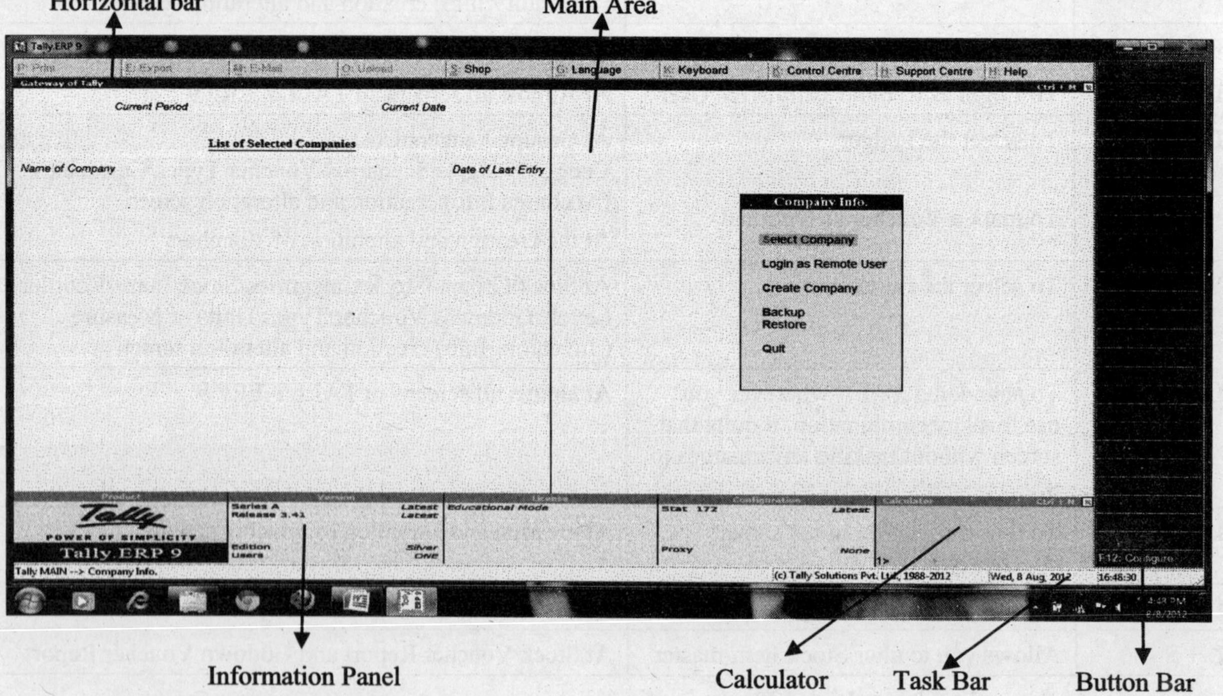

Tally.ERP 9 Screen Components

The Gateway of Tally screen is separated into six sections, namely Horizontal Button Bar, Main Area (Ctrl+M), Bottom Pane, Calculator Area (Ctrl+N), Task Bar and Button Bar.

The elements of the Gateway of Tally screen are explained as follows:

Horizontal Button Bar

The buttons can be seen in the Horizontal Button Bar. Print (Alt+P), Export (Alt+E), E-mail (Alt+M), Upload (Alt+O), Language (Ctrl+L), Keyboard (Ctrl+K), Control Centre (Ctrl+K), Support Centre (Ctrl+H) Help (Alt+H)

Gateway of Tally:

The Main Area is separated into two: (1) Left Hand side area, and (2) Right hand side area

1. **Left hand side area:** It provides information on Current Period, Current Date and List of Selected Companies (Name of the company and the date when last entry has been made).
2. **Right hand side area:** It shows the Company Information menu such as Select a Company, Create a Company, Back-up a Company or Restore a Company and so on.

Calculator Area Press [Ctrl + N] to activate the calculator. Calculator area is used for calculator functions. Any type of independent calculation can also be done using the calculator.

Switching between Screen Areas

When Tally.ERP 9 first loads, the Gateway of Tally.ERP 9 screen is displayed. To toggle between this and the Calculator/ODBC server area at the bottom of the screen, press Ctrl + N or Ctrl + M as indicated on the screen. A green bar highlights the active area of the screen.

Button Bar

The buttons are designed to make the work easier and faster and vary from one screen to another based on the screen functionality. They appear on the right hand side of the Tally.ERP 9 screen and the inactive buttons are with grey colour.

The following are some of the buttons and their functions which were discussed in the Short Cut Key Section also:

F1: Select Cmp – To select the Company from the List of Companies

F12: Configure – To access the configuration settings to manage the information entered in Tally.ERP 9. For example, you can access the General Configuration to set country specific defaults, before creating a company. Buttons where a character or function key is underlined indicates that you have to press underlined character or the function key along with [ALT] key. Buttons where a character or function key is double underlined indicates, you have to press the character or the function key along with [CTRL] key.

1. **F1: Use the short cut function key [F1] to select a company**
2. **F1: Select [ALT+F1] to shut a company**
3. **F8: Select [CTRL+F8] to select the Credit Note voucher**
4. **Ctrl+M: Select Ctrl+M to access the Gateway of Tally**
5. **Ctrl+N: Press Ctrl+N to access the Calculator frame**

12.3 MOUSE/KEYBOARD USAGES

While working with Tally.ERP, use the following conventions:

MOUSE or KEY BOARD USAGE

Actions	Particulars
Click	Press the left mouse button
Double Click	Press and release the left mouse button twice, without moving the mouse pointer off the item.
Choose	Position the mouse pointer on the item and click the left mouse button.
Select	Position the mouse pointer on the item and double click the left mouse button.
Press	Position the mouse pointer on the item and double click the left mouse button.
Fn	Press the function key
Fn	Press ALT + function key
Fn	Press CTRL + function key

Quitting Tally.ERP 9

The program from any Tally.ERP screen can be quitted, but Tally.ERP requires all screens to be closed before it shuts down.

To quit working on Tally.ERP the following methods should be followed:

Press Esc until you see the message 'Quit? Yes or No'? Press Enter or Y, or click on Yes to quit Tally.ERP.

- Alternatively, to exit without confirmation, press Ctrl+Q in the Gateway of Tally.ERP.
- You can also press Enter or Quit in the Gateway of Tally.ERP.

How to Create Company in Tally.ERP 9:

You can create a Company profile by using the following procedures:

1. Gateway of Tally.ERP Alter ▸ (Alt+F3)
2. Gateway of Tally.ERP ▸ Create Company (from opening screen)

Let us use the example to understand the process. SUDALAIANTO, registered under VAT, is in TAMILNADU, and provides Accounts Training all over INDIA and also deals in Purchase and Sale of Software and Hardware. The Company wants to maintain the Financial Year Accounts from 01-04-2012 to 31-03-2013. The Company details are given below:

(1) Company : SUDALAIANTO

(2) Address : Karunya University, Pondicherry

(3) State : Tamilnadu

(4) VAT TIN No. : 9876543210

(5) PAN : ASIPA3583A

(Permanent Account No.)

Create the Company using any one of the above processes. It provides the following screen.

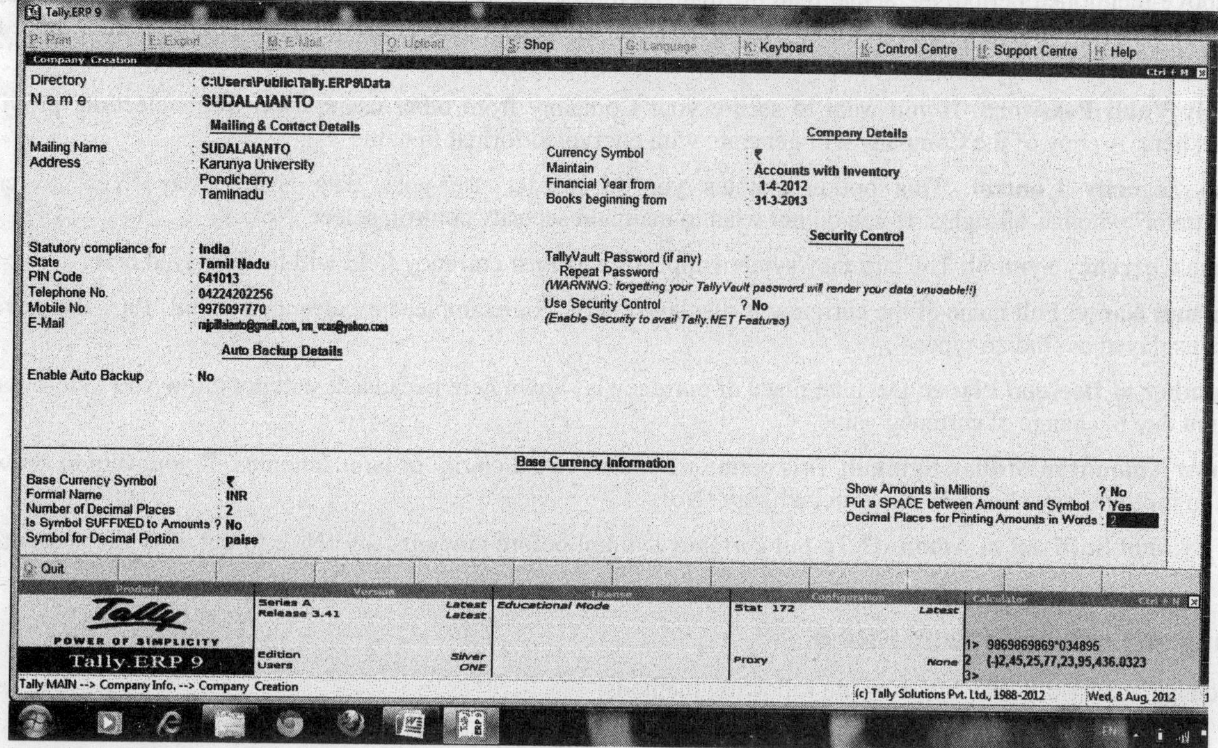

Finally, confirm company creation by pressing the ENTER key/"Y" key to accept all declaration for the Company. (Now you will be able to work with the Current Company)

To enter Company information, the following steps have to be followed:

Field Name Values — Directory

Specify the path where the Company data will be stored. The Default data directory of Tally.ERP 9 is C:\Tally.ERP 9\Data. If you want to keep your data in another location, you can specify the location; for example, if you want to keep your data in your 'D drive', specify the path D:\ or E:\

Name	***Enter Name of the Company.***
Mailing Address	***Address of the Company.***
State	***Select the State Name from the pop-up list.***
Pin Code	***Enter your city PIN code.***
E-mail Address	***Enter the E-mail Address of the Company.***

Currency Symbol

Currency symbol will be displayed in which the account books of the company are to be maintained. By default, it shows 'Rs.' as currency symbol.

Maintain the existing: Depending on the activity of the company, you can maintain the records in two ways: 1. Accounts only, and 2. Accounts with Inventory.

Financial Year From: Enter the Starting date of the Financial Year for which you are maintaining Company Accounts. However, it will never ask you to enter the Closing date of the Financial period like other software.

In Tally.ERP 9, you can maintain multiple accounting years in the same Company. For example, if you want to set up the financial period of a Company for the year 2012-2013, the Start date should be 01-04-2012.

Books Beginning From: Enter a date within the financial period on which books have been started. For example, In the above-mentioned period, the actual date of financial transaction begins on 01-04-2012; so in this field enter the date as 01-04-2012. Remember that this date can be the same as starting date of the financial period or later, only for a new Concern/Company.

Tally Vault Password: If you want to secure your Company from other users, even from selection, provide a password here. A copy of the Company will generate with encrypted format in name.

Use Security Control: This option enables you to restrict user-wise data access. Say 'Yes' to create 'administrator' who has all rights. If you do not wish to maintain security control, select 'No'.

Base Currency Symbol: The currency symbol appearing against currency field will be displayed here.

Formal Name: Full name of the currency is displayed here. For example, for currency symbol 'Rs.', the currency name is displayed as 'Indian rupees'.

Number of Decimal Places: Decimal place of currency is shown here because it will not allow you to lose part of an amount due to change of currency value.

Show Amount in Million Symbol: This option maintains visual clarity of large amounts. If you want to show the amount in millions, say 'Yes'. To show in lakh, say 'No'.

Is Symbol Suffixed to Amount? To put currency symbol before amounts say 'No'; to put after the amount, say 'Yes'.

Opening or Loading of Tally.ERP 9

You can load Tally.ERP by using the following methods:

1. Short cut stores on the Desktop
2. Start ▸ Program ▸Tally.ERP 9

The first screen is the "Gateway of Tally.ERP"

Gateway of Tally is the screen that appears on selecting a company. The Gateway of Tally menu differs based on the type of Company selected. An Accounts Only Company has a different Gateway of Tally menu from that of an Accounts-with-Inventory Company.

The Gateway of Tally menu of a company appears as shown below:

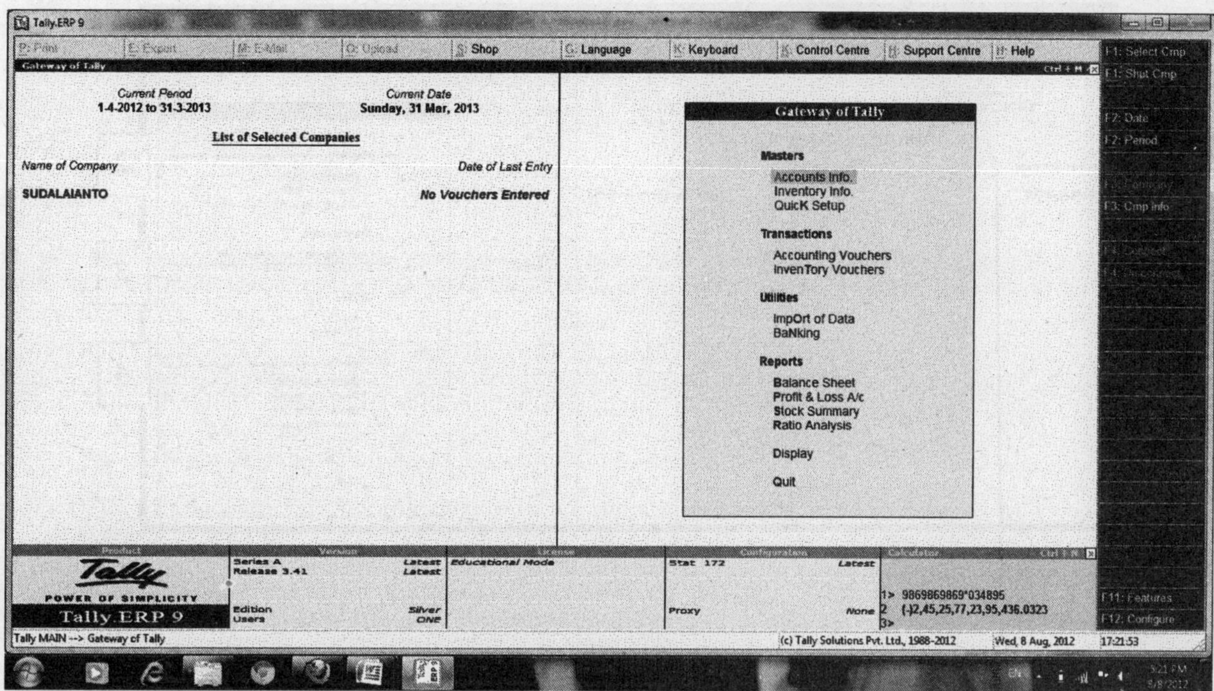

Main Area (Ctrl+M): The Main Area is separated into the following two areas:

1. Left hand side area
2. Right hand side area

The left hand side area in the Main Area provides information of Current Period, Current Date and List of Selected Companies and Date of Last Entry.

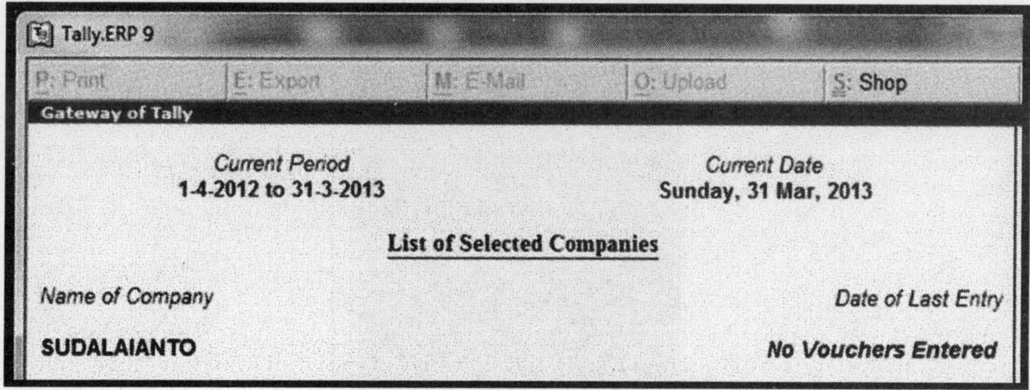

In the right hand side, you get more detailed information on the Company. The Company information menu consists of the following:

1. List of activated Company (Company already created)
2. Masters (for defining Ledger, Group, Subgroup, Inventory)
3. Transactions/Voucher Entry (Recording Transactions)
4. Reports (Viewing the Balance Sheet, P&L and other Reports)

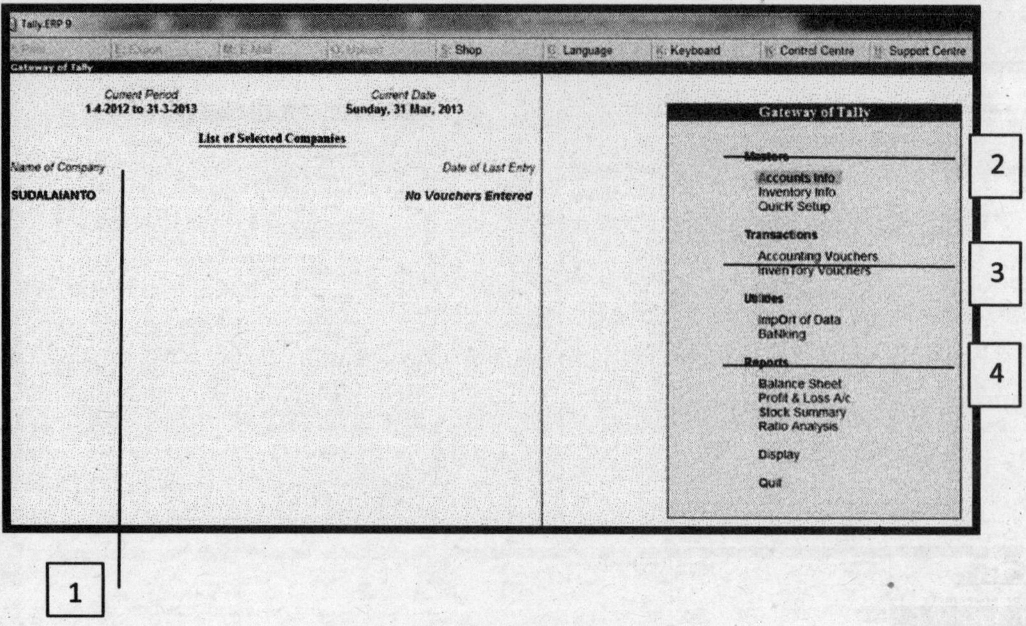

Button Bar:

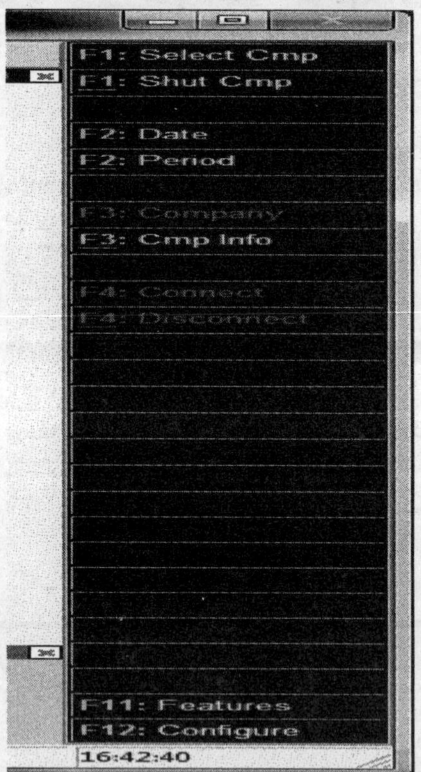

By using the buttons shown in the above figure you can access different utilities of Tally. For example, by pressing F1, you can select the company which has already been created in Tally.ERP 9. Similarly, F1, F2, F2, and F3 for selecting from the list, closing the activated company, change date, changing the financial period and entering the company related data can be performed.

Selection Procedure of Menu Options

The following procedures are followed to select the Menu options:

1. By double clicking the Left Mouse Button
2. By pressing Functional Ley
3. By pressing Highlighted character (It appears normally in Red and Bold)
4. By selecting UP/DOWN arrow keys and entering with Enter Key.

Modification of Company

You can Modify your Company at any time, and for any information given while creating the Company.

Go to Gateway of Tally

1. Select F3: Cmp Info. (ALT+F3) from the button bar
2. Select Alter and press Enter

Deletion of a Company

To delete a company, you have to load the company.

1. Select F3: Cmp Info. (ALT+F3) from the Gateway of Tally to proceed to the Company Information menu.
2. Select Alter and press Enter.
3. Select the company to be deleted. The Company Alteration screen is displayed.
4. Use Alt + D to delete. Tally.ERP 9 will prompt for a confirmation on deleting the company.
5. Press enter to delete the company.

Note: Deletion a company is irreversible and the company is permanently deleted from the system.

Shut (Close) a Company

You can shut a Company in Two ways – either using the button F1: Shut Cmp (Alt+F1) from Gateway of Tally.ERP OR by pressing Enter on Shut Company option from Company Information Menu (Alt+F3).

Company Selection

To select a Company click F1: "Select Company" button (or use F1 function key). By default it will show the list of existing companies with their names, company number and financial period. The screen appears as shown here:

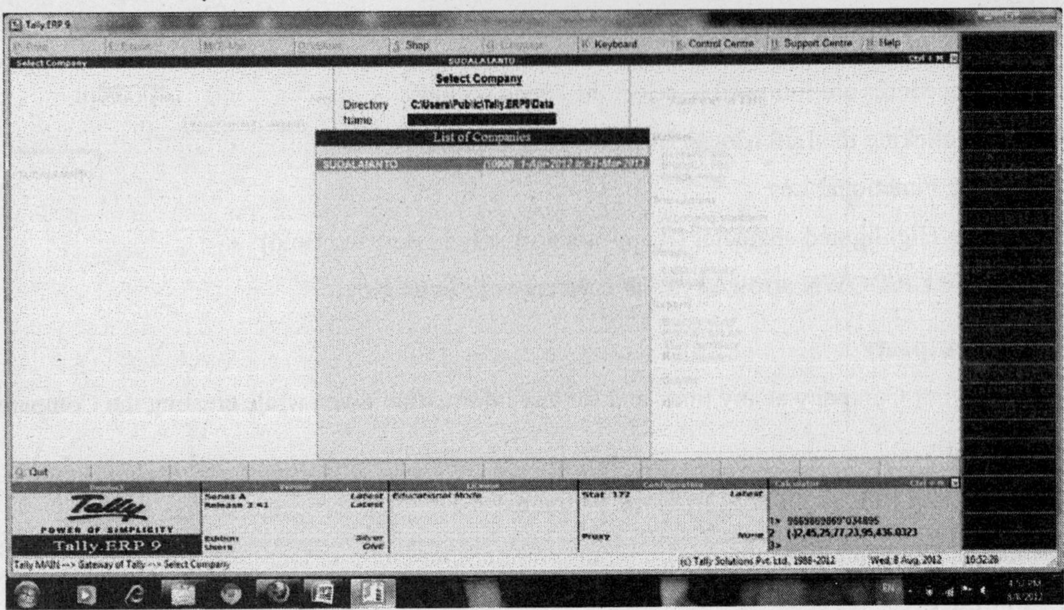

12.4 SET-UP OF ACCOUNTING MASTER IN TALLY.ERP 9

In this chapter, you will learn about setting up or the classification of accounts. The entire accounts group is classified into the following four entities: Asset, Liabilities, Income and Expenses. This unit also discusses about the Accounts info menu. This unit will then introduce to the modern way of accounting all financial entries, which are performed using ledgers or account heads. Groups are created so that ledger information can be classified based on their functions. Further groups will be subdivided into 28 predefined groups. You will also learn about ledgers and accounting vouchers in this unit.

Assets, Liabilities, Income and Expenses

The next process is setting up/classification of Accounts. The entire Accounts group is classified into four entities:

Contents of 'Accounts Info' Menu

The 'Accounts Info' menu consists of the following options:

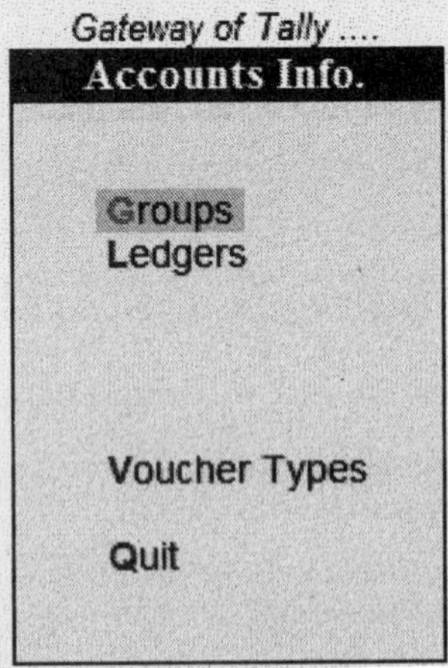

Groups: These are used for creation, modification and deletion of Groups

Ledgers: These are used for creation, modification and deletion of Ledgers

Voucher Types: These are used for defining different types of Voucher and Configuration

Quit: It is used to Return to Gateway Menu

After Configuration of the Features from F11 key the Accounts Info menu will look like as shown here.

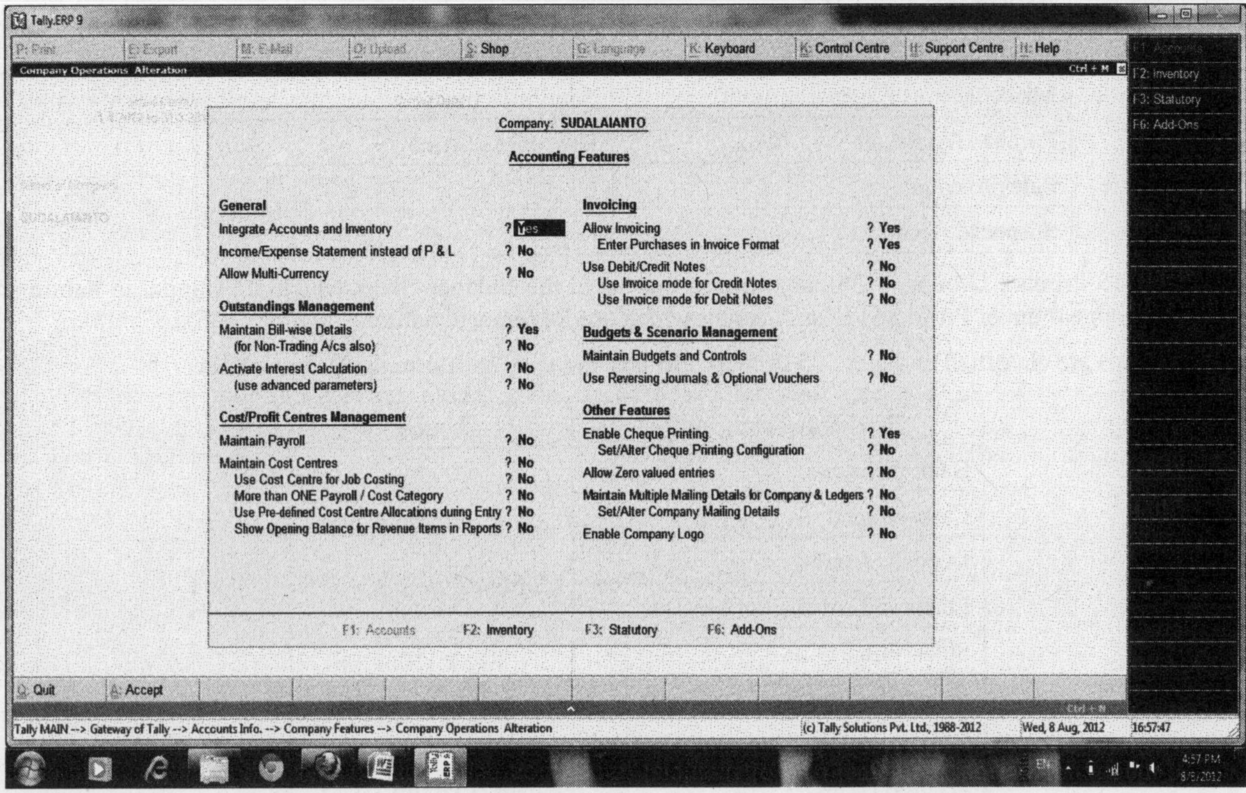

The Group

In the current way of accounting, all financial entries are performed using ledgers or account heads. It is advisable to Group/Classify ledger information based on their functions. Groups are helpful in classifying and identifying account heads based on their nature. Grouping helps in presenting summarized information. Regrouping of accounts is also permitted by Tally.ERP. At the highest level of grouping, accounts are classified into Assets, Liabilities, Income and Expenditure.

Groups by Default (Predefined Groups)

Tally.ERP 9 provides you with 28 predefined Groups to save you from unnecessary burden of creating frequently used Groups. Out of these 28 Groups, 15 are Primary Groups and 13 Subgroups. Subgroups are a part of the main group. There are 28 predefined Groups in Tally.ERP 9, out of which 15 are Primary Groups and 13 are Sub-groups.

15 Primary Groups	13 Subgroups
Branch/Divisions	Bank Accounts
Capital Account	Bank O/D Account
Current Assets	Cash in Hand
Current Liabilities	Deposits (Asset)
Direct Expenses	Duties and Taxes
Direct Incomes	Loans and Advances (Asset)

Fixed Asset	Provisions
Indirect Expenses	Reserves and Surplus
Indirect Incomes	Secured Loans
Investments	Stock-in-hand
Loans (Liability)	Sundry Creditors
Miscellaneous Expenses (Asset)	Sundry Debtors
Purchase Accounts	Unsecured Loans
Sales Accounts	
Suspense Accounts	

Out of the 15 Primary Groups, 9 Primary Groups appear in the Balance Sheet which are Capital in nature and 6 Primary Groups appear under Profit and Loss Account which are Revenue in nature.

13 Subgroups are classified under the 15 Primary Groups and they appear in the Balance Sheet.

Predefined subgroups	Under
Bank Accounts	Current Assets
Cash-in-hand	
Deposits (Asset)	
Loans and Advances (Asset)	
Stock-in-hand	
Sundry Debtors	
Bank Over Draft Account	Loans (Liability)
Secured Loans	
Unsecured Loans	
Duties and Taxes	Current Liabilities
Provisions	
Sundry Creditors	
Reserves and Surplus	Capital Account

Creating GROUP

For Single

Gateway of Tally.ERP ▸ Master ▸ Accounts Info ▸ Groups ▸ Create (Single)

1. Name Box : Enter the Name of the Group
2. Under : Specify the Groups under which it will be created.

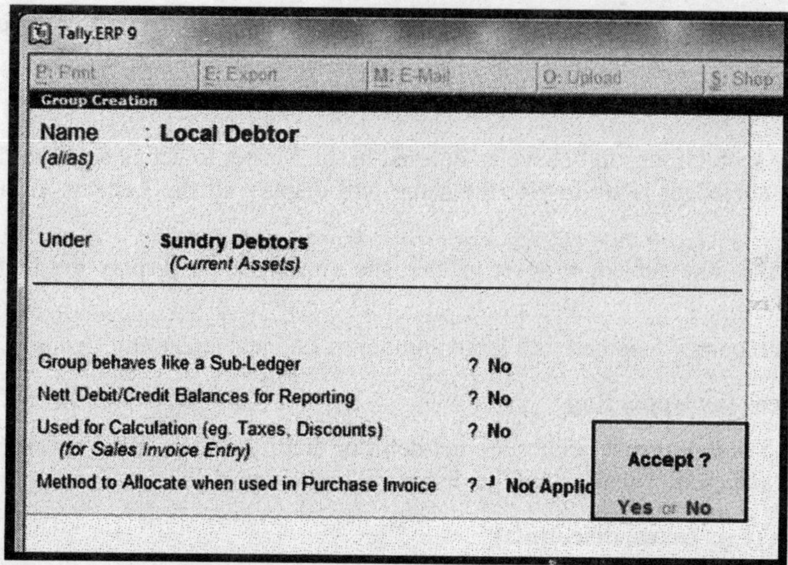

Creating a Group with Advanced Usage

Go to Gateway of Tally > Accounts Info > Groups > Create under Single Group > select F12 configure (Group Configuration) and enable Allow Advanced entries in Masters under Accounts Masters.

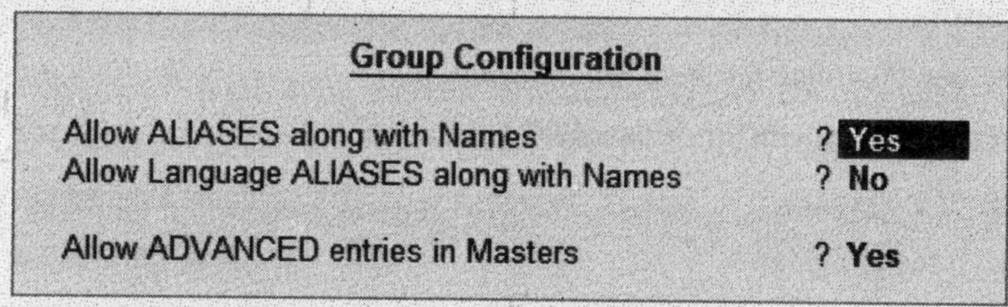

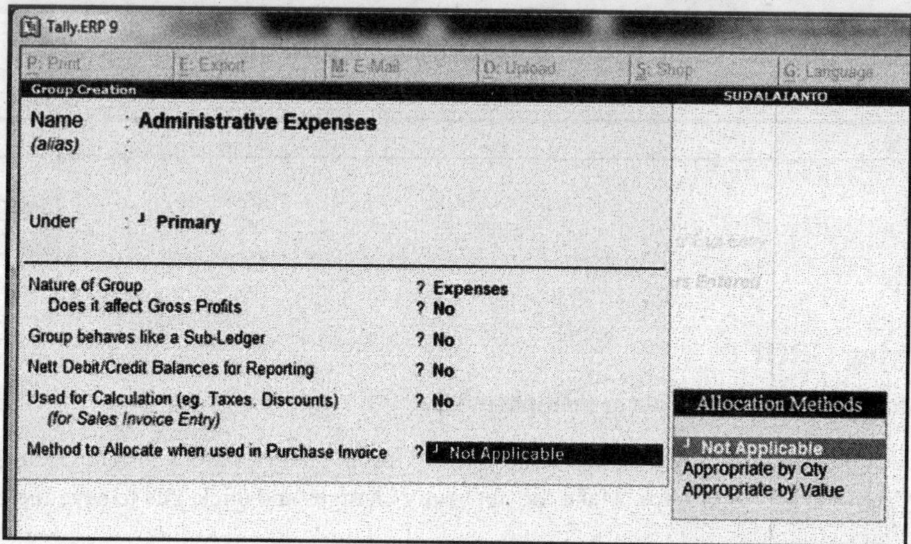

Does it affect gross profits: If a group (e.g., Administrative Expenses) is created under primary, you must select the appropriate option from the list whether it is an asset, liability, income or expenses. If you select an income or expenses you should specify whether it will affect the gross profits or not by suitably setting the option does it affect

Gross Profits? To Yes/No. If the option is selected as Yes, the Group will appear under Trading Account and if the option is selected as No, the Group will appear under Profit and Loss Account.

Group Behaves Like Subledger

This option will allow such Groups to behave as defined in the Master to act as equal to the behaviour of Ledger. When Group behaves like subledger is set to No, the same will display all the Ledgers Grouped under the same in detailed mode.

When the Group behaves like subledger is set to Yes, the same will not display the Ledgers grouped under the same in detailed mode.

The same is helpful in reports when there is a large number of Ledgers under any Group.

Nett Debit/Credit Balances for Reporting

Setting this option to Yes will display either the net debit or credit balance in the report (whichever is higher). If this is set to No, both debit and credit balances will be displayed in the report.

D—Used for Calculation (e.g., taxes, discounts)

Set this option to Yes if ledgers under this Group would have percentages for discounts/taxes to be used in invoice entry. This gets reflected while passing voucher entry in Invoice mode and for automatic calculations.

Method to allocate when used in purchase invoice: Select the appropriate allocation method from the list. This is used to allocate the expense of the item in the ratio of the quantity or value.

Creating Multiple Groups

To create a Multiple Group the following steps are followed:

Gateway of Tally ▸ Master ▸ Accounts Info ▸ Groups ▸ Create (Multiple)

1. Select the Name of the Group
2. Enter the Name of the Subgroup

Multi Group Creation SUDALAIANTO Ctrl + M

Under Group : **Sundry Debtors**

S.No.	Name of Group	Under
1.	**Local Debtors**	Sundry Debtors
2.	**Outside Debtors**	Sundry Debtors

Altering or Modifying GROUP

You can alter the Groups in Single mode or multiple mode.

Single mode: Go to Gateway of Tally ▸ Accounts Info. ▸ Group ▸ Alter (under Single Group) Select the Group that you wish to alter from the List of Groups. Make the necessary changes and click Yes to save the changes.

Multiple Mode: Go to Gateway of Tally ▸ Accounts Info. ▸ Group ▸ Alter (under Multi Groups)

Select the Group for which you want to alter from the List of Groups. In Multi Group Alteration screen, make the necessary changes and click Yes to save changes.

Permanently Deleting a GROUP

Go to Gateway of Tally ▸ Accounts Info ▸ Groups ▸ Single/Alter

The Delete function is performed through the single alteration mode. You cannot delete groups from the Multiple Alteration mode.

1. Select the Group to be deleted.
2. Press Alt+D to delete.

Displaying a GROUP

You can display the Groups in Single mode or Multiple mode.

Single Mode

Go to Gateway of Tally ▸ Accounts Info. ▸ Group ▸ Display (under Single Group)

Select the name of the Group from the List of Groups. You cannot make any changes in the Display mode.

Multiple Mode

Go to Gateway of Tally ▸ Accounts Info ▸ Group ▸ Display (under Multiple Group)

Select the Group from the List of Groups to display all the Groups under the selected Group or select All Items to display all Groups. The Multi Group Display screen lists Groups and the corresponding details of the Groups.

12.5 THE LEDGER

A ledger is the actual account head to which you identify a transaction and must be used in all Accounting Vouchers. Without a ledger we cannot record any transactions. Ex: Purchase, payments, sales, Receipts, etc., all these accounts heads are ledger accounts. All ledgers have to be classified into Groups. Classification of ledgers to the appropriate groups is very important. These Groups and ledgers are classified to Profit and Loss or Balance Sheet.

The creation and usage of Groups in Tally.ERP 9 has been explained earlier. Now you will learn how Tally.ERP 9 works with ledgers .

Gateway of Tally.ERP ▸ Master ▸ Accounts Info ▸ Ledger

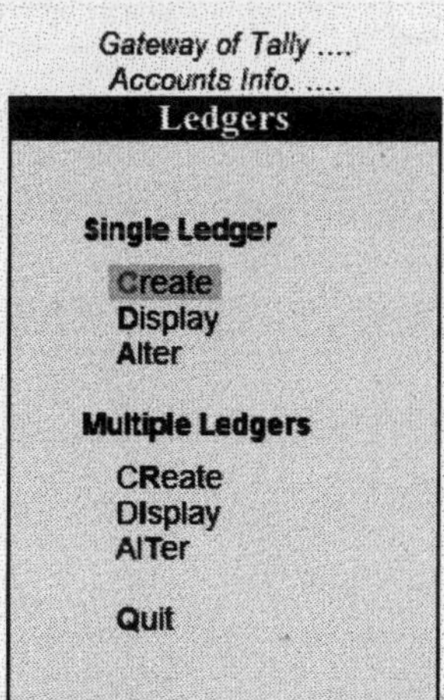

For Single Ledger

Create: It is to create or add any ledger under any parent Group

Display: It is to show the list of ledger already created

Alter: It is to Delete or Modify

(To use these menus one can use arrow keys or mouse clicks)

For Multiple Ledgers

Create: It is to create or add more than one ledger under primary or specific groups.

Display: It is to show the list of ledgers already created under specific groups.

Alter: It is to delete or modify the ledgers specified under any group.

(To use these menus one can use arrow keys or mouse clicks)

Predefined Ledgers in Tally.ERP 9

There are two predefined ledgers available in Tally.ERP 9, they are:

(i) Cash: This ledger is created under the Group Cash-in-hand. You can enter the opening balance as on the date of books beginning from. You can also alter the name and even delete the ledger.

(ii) Profit and Loss Account: This ledger is created under the Group Primary. Previous year's profit or loss is entered as the opening balance for this ledger. The balance entered here is treated as the opening profit/loss and shown in the Balance Sheet as opening balance of profit and loss account in the liabilities side. You cannot delete this ledger, but you can modify the same.

Creating a Single LEDGER

Gateway of Tally.ERP ▸ Master ▸ Accounts Info ▸ Ledger ▸ Create (Single)

1. Name Box: Enter the name of ledger; alias is used for short name.
2. Select the group under which the ledger will be created.
3. Enter the Opening Balance.

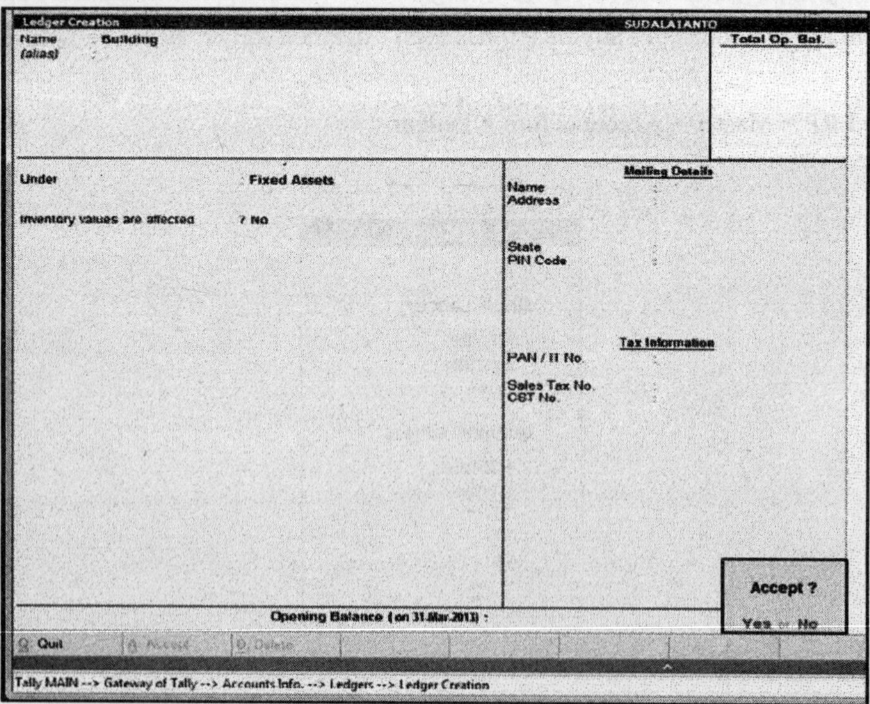

Configuring F12 (functional key): You can also configure your ledger creation as per your requirement by using 'F12'.

Name: Enter the name of the account. Tally.ERP 9 does not allow the entry of duplicate names. The uniqueness check is made here itself. Note that the punctuation and other non-relevant information are ignored by Tally.ERP 9 in its recognition of a name. Thus, CST, C.S.T. and C. S. T. are all considered as same. Tally.ERP 9 converts the first letter of all relevant words to upper case, which helps you; speed up data entry.

Alias: Enter an alias name if required. You can access the ledgers using the original name or the alias name.

Under: All accounts must be classified under their appropriate Groups. Select the Group under which the ledger is created from the list of Groups. (To create a new Group from this field press [ALT + C]). A wrong classification would affect the treatment of the ledger account in final statements and during voucher entry. You can, alter a ledger account to change its Group classification at any time.

Opening Balance: If yours is an existing company whose books you are entering into Tally.ERP 9, Opening Balance would be applicable in circumstances where the ledger is an asset or a liability and if it has a balance in the account as on the date of beginning of books in Tally.ERP 9. Tally.ERP 9 recognizes normal accounting principles of debit balances for assets and credit balances for liabilities. Revenue accounts normally do not have balances. Tally.ERP 9, however, permits you to give balances even for such accounts —

F12: Configure (Ledger)

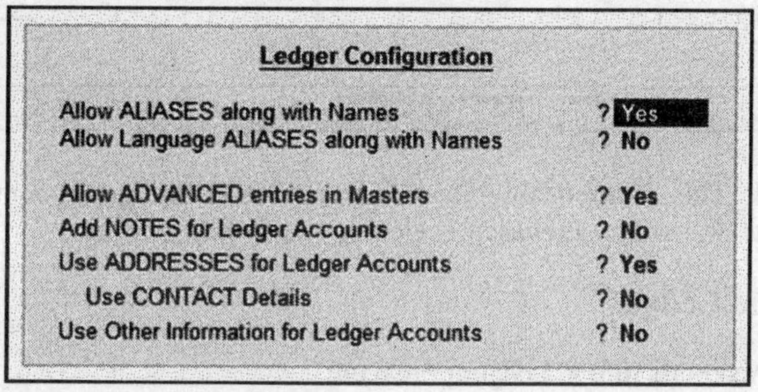

Ledger Configuration

Allow ALIASES along with Names	? Yes
Allow Language ALIASES along with Names	? No
Allow ADVANCED entries in Masters	? Yes
Add NOTES for Ledger Accounts	? No
Use ADDRESSES for Ledger Accounts	? Yes
Use CONTACT Details	? No
Use Other Information for Ledger Accounts	? No

Use of these features in Ledger Configuration:

1. Advanced entries master: This will allow you to enter the data much faster.
2. Additional information can be provided against any respective ledger, for example: Phone number of the party.
3. Address: This feature is useful at the time of party ledger creation.
4. Contact details: You can enter the name of the contact person.

Creating a Purchase/Sales Ledger

Go to Gateway of Tally ▸ Accounts Info ▸ Ledgers ▸ Create

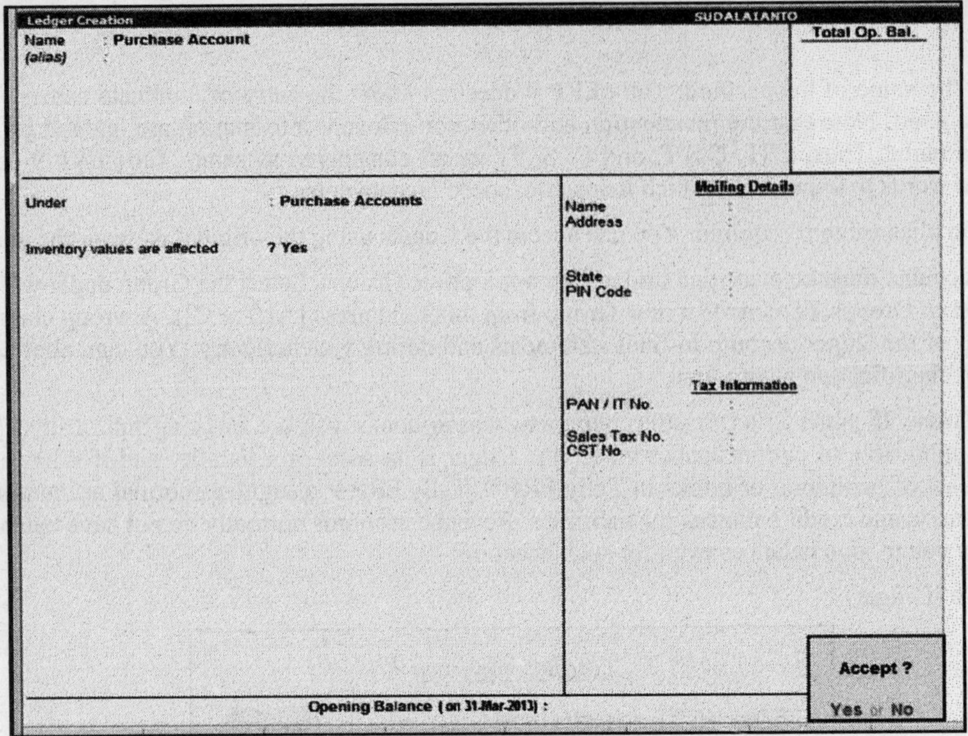

Inventory values affected: This is applicable for companies maintaining accounts with inventory. Inventory allocation is required for accounts like sales, purchase, receipt note, delivery note, etc.

Creating a Expenses/Income Ledger

Go to Gateway of Tally ▸ Accounts Info ▸ Ledgers ▸ Create

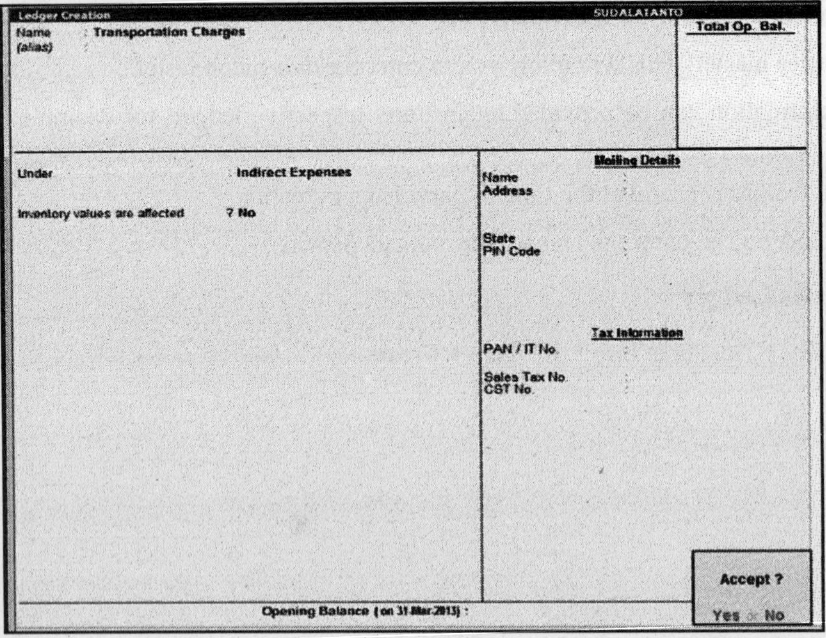

Inventory values affected: This is applicable for companies maintaining accounts with inventory. Inventory allocation is required for accounts like sales, purchase, receipt note, delivery note, etc. However, Tally.ERP 9 does not restrict you to particular accounts as you may have the need to affect inventory with accounts like customs duty, and perhaps, direct expenses related to purchases such as freight inwards.

Cost centres are applicable: Tally's concept of Cost Centres allows an additional dimension to a transaction.

You have set maintain Cost Centres to Yes in F11: Features: F1: Accounting Features, to get this option in the Ledger creation screen. If any of the transactions need to be allocated to any particular Cost Centre (Which involves this ledger) set this option to Yes.

Activate interest calculation: Set this option to Yes to enable Tally.ERP 9 to calculate interest automatically based on the interest rate and style of calculation specified for this ledger account.

Creating a Party Ledger

Go to Gateway of Tally▸ Accounts Info ▸ Ledgers ▸ Create

The Party Ledger account screen is displayed as shown:

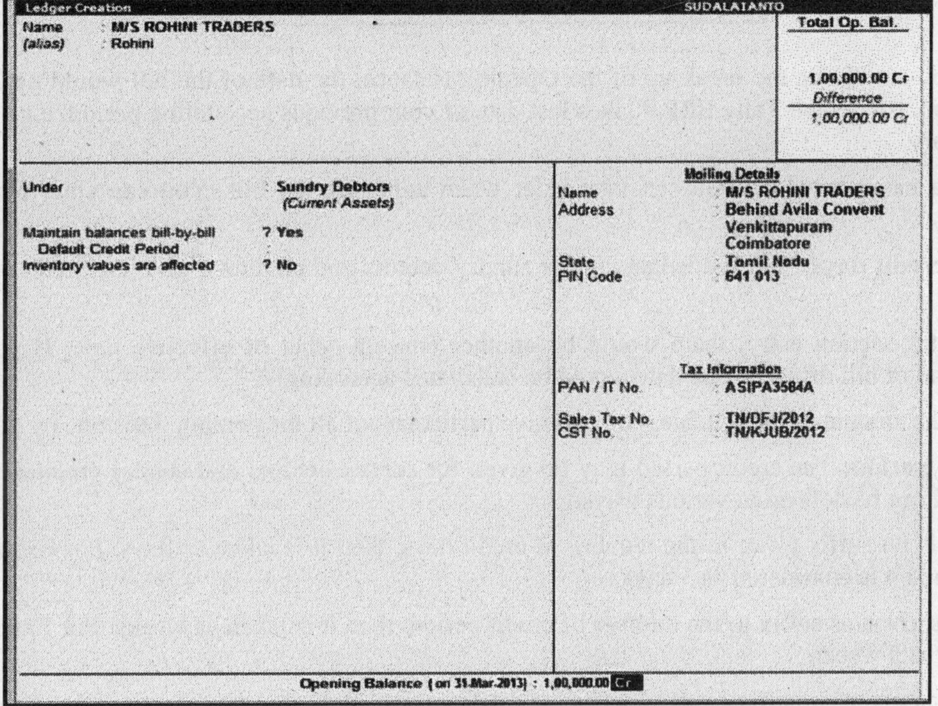

Maintain balances bill-by-bill: This option is applicable when you want the balances to be maintained bill-by bill or bill wise. Normally, this option is useful for ledgers falling under sundry debtors and sundry creditors. If you set this option to Yes, while entering the opening balance in the Opening Balance field at the end of ledger creation screen and press Enter, the bill-wise break-up screen of the ledger created is displayed as shown below:

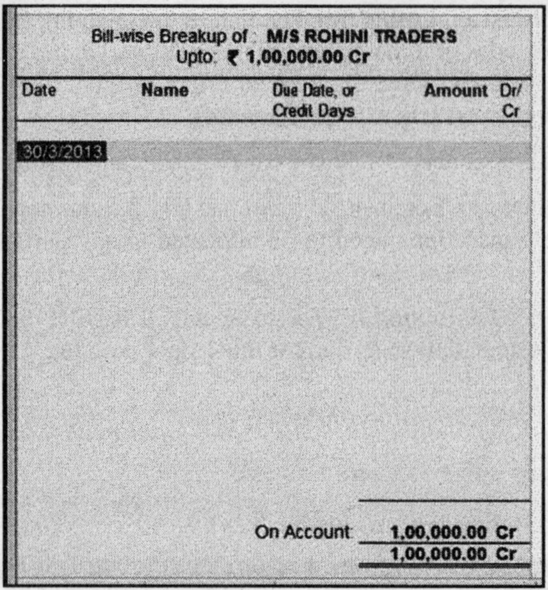

Date: Since you are giving the break-up of the Opening Balance, the date of the bill would naturally be prior to the accounting period. By default Tally.ERP 9 takes last date of your previous accounting period, e.g., 31 March, 2008. Change it, if necessary.

Name: Enter a name to which you can later refer when adjusting the bill. You can enter the bill number or document number.

Due date (or credit days): For the ledgers under sundry debtors and creditors, give the credit period or the date when the bill is due.

Note: During transaction entry, there would be another concept—that of effective date. If you opt for using effective dates instead of bill dates the due date would be calculated accordingly.

Amount: For the amount of the bill due, you can give particulars of all the pending bills one by one.

Default credit period: The credit period may be given for sundry debtors and sundry creditors. The number of credit days or period can be defined in various ways:

Days: If there is no suffix given to the number of credit days, then it is taken as days. For Example if you enter just the number 5, then it is considered as 5 days.

Weeks: If W is given as suffix to the number of credit period, then it is taken as weeks. For Example if you enter 5 W, then it is taken as 5 weeks.

Months: If M is given as suffix to the number of credit period, then it is taken as months. Example Ex: if you enter 5 M, then it is taken as 5 months.

Year: If Y is given as suffix to the number of credit period, then it is taken as year. For Example if you enter 5 Y, then it is taken as 5 years.

Inventory values affected: This is applicable for companies maintaining accounts with inventory. Inventory allocation is required for accounts like sales, purchase, receipt note, delivery note, etc. However, Tally.ERP 9 does not restrict you to particular accounts as you may have the need to affect inventory with accounts like customs duty, and perhaps, direct expenses related to purchases such as freight inwards.

Cost centres are applicable: Tally's concept of Cost Centres allows an additional dimension to a transaction. You have set to maintain Cost Centres to Yes in F11: features: F1: Accounting Features, to get this option in the ledger creation screen. If any of the transactions need to be allocated to any particular Cost Centre (Which involves this ledger) set this option to Yes. **Activate interest calculation:** Set this option to Yes to enable Tally.ERP 9 to calculate interest automatically based on the interest rate and style of calculation specified for this ledger account.

Use advanced parameters: The advanced parameters are particularly useful where interest rates change from time-to-time. Set this option to Yes to enable this.

Mailing details: is applicable only for party accounts like sundry debtors, creditors and branch divisions, branch/divisions, bank and Bank OCC A/c, loans and advances assets, loans and advances liabilities, secured and unsecured loans, etc. These are used in mailing outputs like statement of accounts.

Creating Bank Account

Go to Gateway of Tally ▸ Accounts Info ▸ Ledgers ▸ Create

The Bank account screen is displayed as shown:

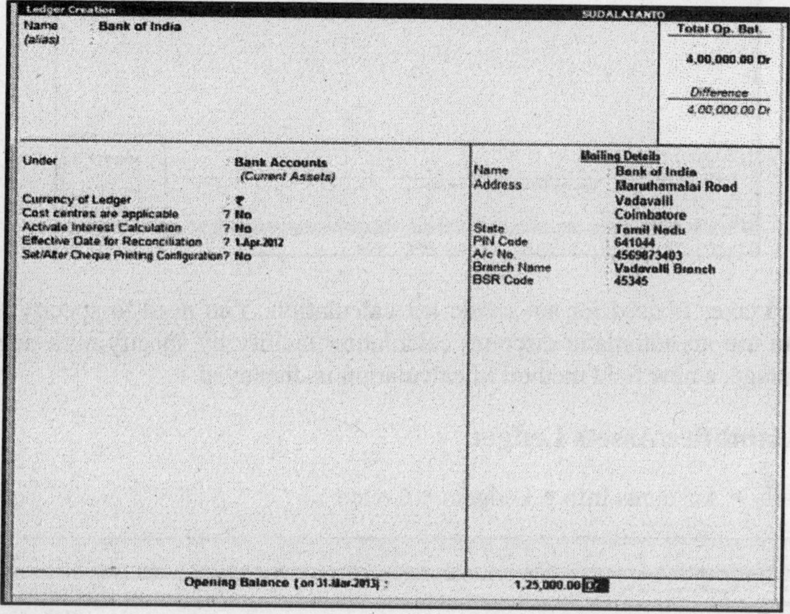

Effective date for Reconciliation option will appear when a ledger is created under Bank Account Group. Give the date of reconciliation on which you would like to reconcile the voucher.

Creating a Duty and Taxes Ledger

Gateway of Tally ▸ Accounts Info ▸ Ledgers ▸ Create

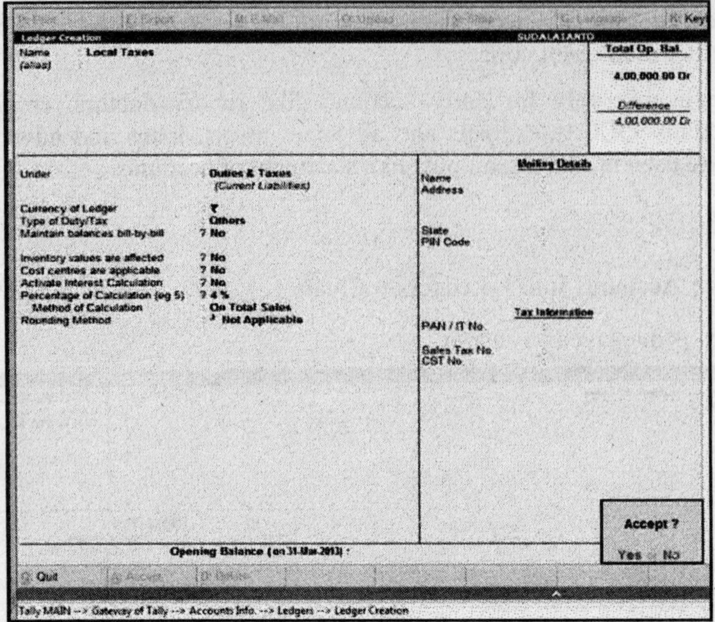

The Group duties and taxes is used for automatic tax calculation. You need to specify the rate of tax, e.g., 5%, 10%, 12.5%, etc. You can use an automatic discount calculation facility by specifying a negative percentage in this field. On entering a percentage, a new field method of calculation is displayed.

Creating a Current Liabilities/Assets Ledger

Go to Gateway of Tally ▸ Accounts Info ▸ Ledgers ▸ Create

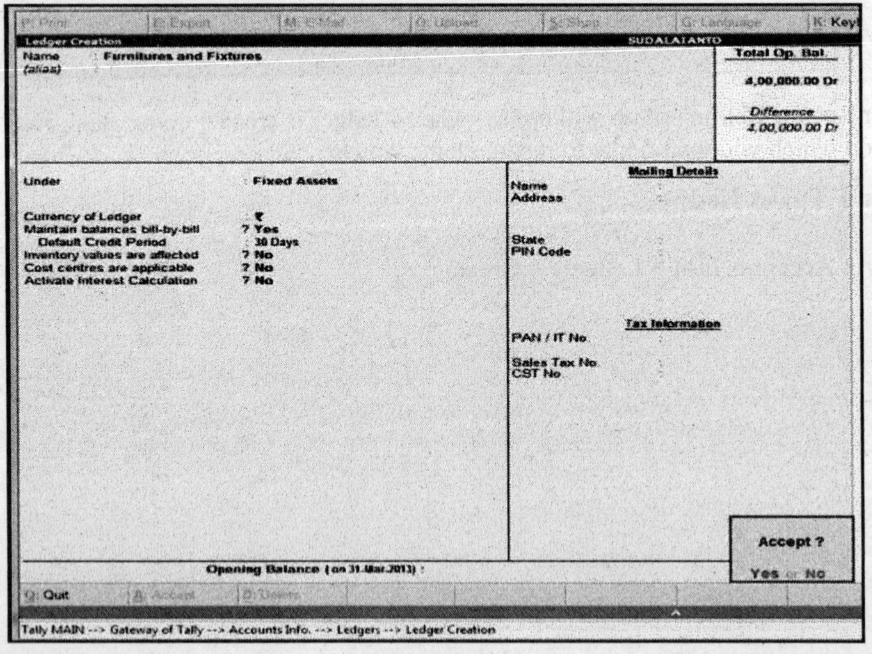

Creating a Multiple LEDGER

To create a Multiple Ledger the following steps have to be followed:

Gateway of Tally.ERP 9 ▸ Master ▸ Accounts Info ▸ Ledger ▸ Create (Multiple)

P: Print | E: Export | M: E-Mail | O: Upload | S: Shop | G: Language | K: Keyboard | K: Control Centre | H: Support Centre | H: Help

Multi Ledger Alteration SUDALAIANTO Ctrl + M

Under Group Fixed Assets For 31-Mar-2013

S.No.	Name of Ledger	Under	Opening Balance	Dr/Cr
1.	Building	Fixed Assets	6,50,000.00	Dr
2.	Furnitures and Fixtures	Fixed Assets	9,00,000.00	Dr
3.	Land	Fixed Assets	85,00,000.00	Dr
4.				

Display or Alter a Single Ledger Account

Information under Display and Alter is the same. Display option does not permit any modification. Alter option permits you to alter the information.

You are allowed to alter any information of the ledger master with the exception of the closing balance of a ledger account, if any, other than closing balance of accounts under the group Stock-in-hand.

Go to Gateway of Tally Accounts Info. Ledgers Display or Alter

Modification of account ledgers is possible under single ledger as well as multiple ledgers option. However, under multiple ledgers, all the fields are not available for alteration

Deleting a Single Ledger Account

You can delete the ledger if no vouchers have been created under this ledger.

Go to Gateway of Tally ▸ Accounts Info ▸ Ledgers ▸ Alter ▸ Press Alt+D

If you want to delete a ledger for which vouchers have been created, then you have to first delete all the vouchers from that ledger and then delete the ledger account. Tally.ERP does not allow deletion of accounts that have transactions. Therefore, should you wish to delete an account, which has transactions, you must first delete all its voucher entries.

EXERCISE

Create the following ledger account in the XYZ & Co:

- Building account
- Capital account
- Cash
- Cash account
- Commission paid account
- Commission received account
- Computer account
- Computer sales account
- Depreciation account
- John & Co.
- Machinery account
- Printer account
- Pinter purchase account
- Profit and loss account
- Ram agency account
- Rent paid account
- Rent received account
- Salary account
- Indian bank account
- Sales return account
- Wages account

Tally Solution

Step 1: Gateway of Tally → Master → Accounts Info →Ledger → Single/Multiple Ledger → Create You can Choose-Multiple Ledger→ Create

Step 2: Under Group: → All Item (select)

Step 3: Enter the given ledger account in the following way

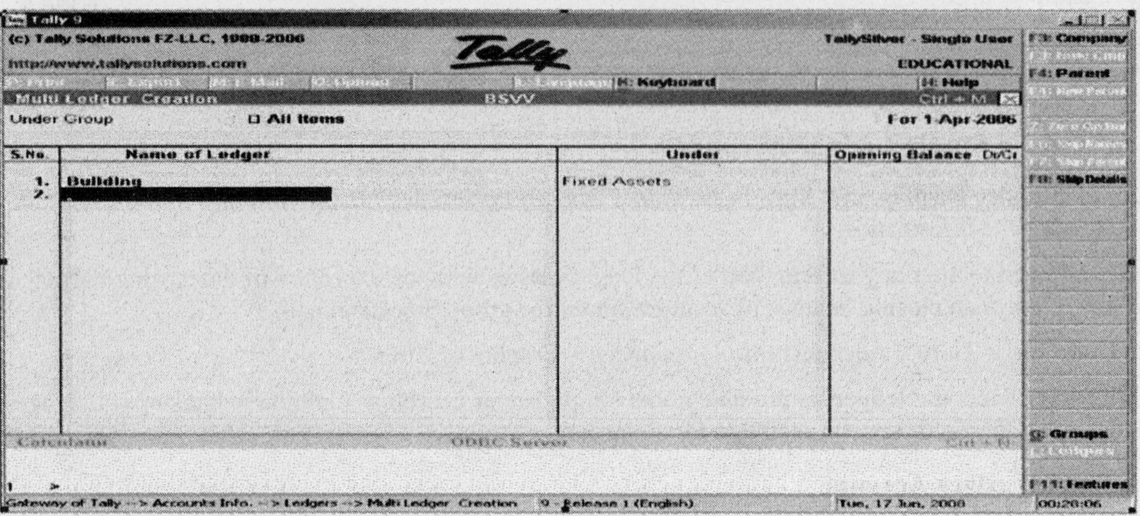

Step 4: After entered the ledger account accept the entered ledgers

Step 5: Now we can see the created ledger in the following format.

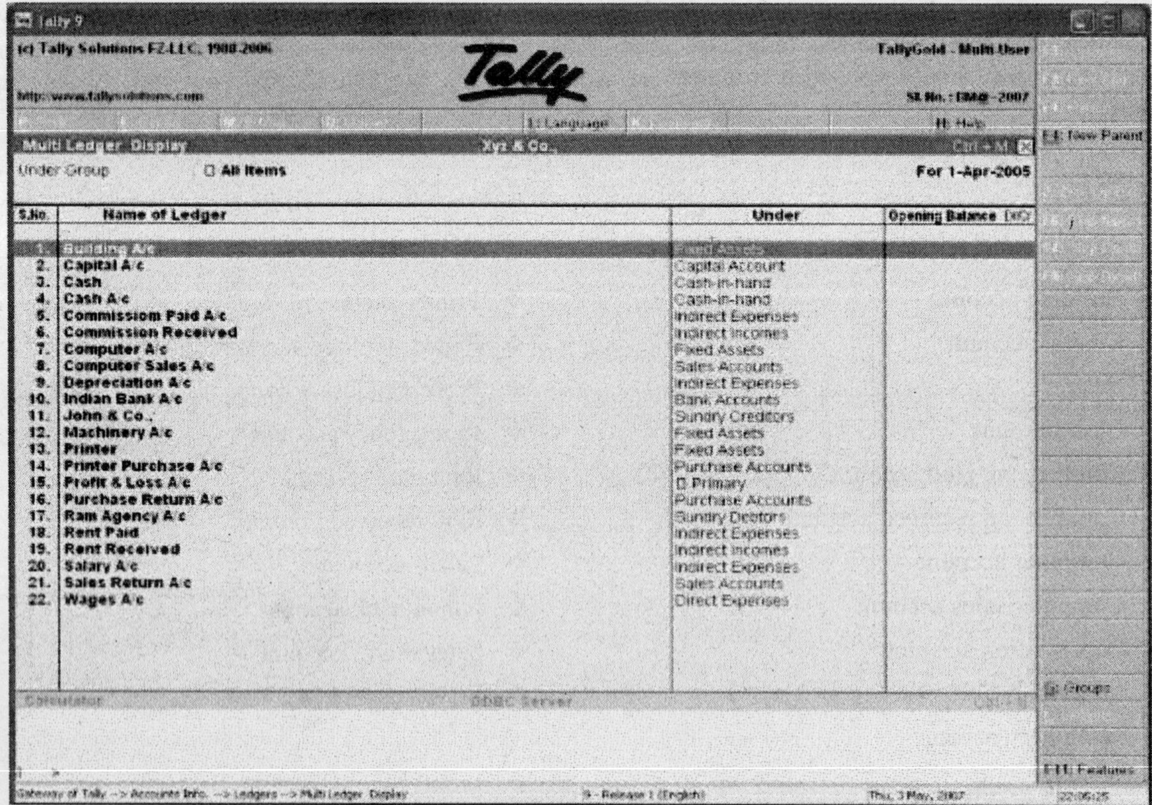

Tally Result

EXERCISE

Suppose if a Trial Balance is given/or Ledger A/c Balances are given.

	Rs.
Capital	49,000
Machinery	7,000
Wages	14,000
Sales	1,30,000
Purchase	94,000
Stock (Closing)	32,000

- ❖ Here, in this question, voucher entry is not required, because the final balances of ledger accounts are given.
- ❖ Hence, here, we have to create the ledger accounts and enter the balances.
- ❖ For Example: The first entry is Capital: Rs. 49,000
  - Go to Gateway of Tally → Accounts Information → ledgers →single Ledger →create
  - Now we can see the ledger creation screen.
  - Name: Enter the name of the ledger you wish to create
  - Alias: Give an alternative name for the ledger a/c (if necessary)
  - Under: Classify appropriate Group (Here, it is under Capital)
  - Opening Balance: Opening Balance/Previous Year Balance (Rs. 49,000)
  - Fill the other particulars if necessary.
- ❖ Hence, for the above illustration the ledger accounts are grouped as under:

❖ Capital	Under	Capital
Machinery	Under	Fixed Assets
Wages	Under	Direct Expenses
Sales	Under	Sales
Purchases	Under	Purchases
Stock	Under	Stock-in-hand

Trial Balance

After all ledgers under appropriate groups, we can see the Trial Balance through

- ❖ Gateway of Tally → Display →Trial Balance

Note: In Trial Balance Opening Stock is given the entry will be

- ❖ Accounts information/Ledgers/Create/Name (Stock) Understock-in-hand/Opening Balance (Opening Date) Amount (Say Rs. 9300 Dr).

Note: Closing Stock Given in Adjustments

- ❖ Accounts Information/Ledgers/Alter/Stock/Name/Stock/Understock-in-hand/opening Balance/opening Date — say Rs. 9,300 Dr. Closing Balance — (Same Date) say Rs. 7,500 Dr.

Here both are coming under Dr. and in the similar date. Now Go to P and L or B/S. You can see the correct answer.

After entering all entries we can see Profit and Loss A/C and Balance Sheet of a Company.

- Gateway of Tally → Profit and Loss A/C, or
- Gateway of Tally/Balance Sheet.

12.6 INVENTORY MASTER

The main concepts of trading activities are receipt of goods and delivery of goods. We generally call them purchase or sale activities. The trading items can be raw material, finished goods, semi-finished goods, etc. For better organization you can use the group and subgroup for classification of the trading item.

Functions in Inventory Info. Menu

Inventory information contains the inventory masters. Each master has **Create, Display** and **Alter** functions. These three functions are grouped under:

1. Single
2. Multiple

In **Single**, you can execute the function on one master. In **Multiple**, you can execute the function on multiple masters.

Functions

(a) **Create:** The Create option is used to create new masters. Any modification to the masters can be done only through the Alter mode.

(b) **Display:** The Display option is used to view the master information. Master information cannot be modified in Display mode.

(c) **Alter:** The Alter option allows you to view and make the necessary changes to the master information. This does not allow creation of masters. In Alteration mode, you can delete the master. [Press ALT+D for deletion]

Inventory Info Menu

Inventory can be created using the following options:

Go to Gateway of Tally ▸ Masters ▸Inventory Info

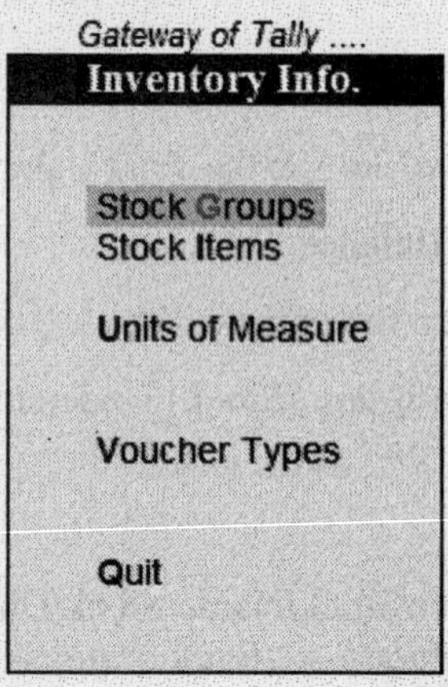

1. **Stock Group:** Create your group here, for example, raw materials, work-in-progress, finished goods, etc.
2. **Stock Items:** Create your stock items here, for example, TV, sound system, VCD, etc.
3. **Voucher Types**
4. **Unit of Measurement:** Create your measurement unit for items, for example, LTR. MTR, PCS, BOX, etc.
5. **Quit:** Exit from the menu. Before creating the inventory info menu we should know what stock groups, stock items and units of measurement are.

Items, Groups and Units

Stock Items: Stock items are the primary inventory entity, like ledgers. Usually it means item or product, which can be buying, selling or issue for production purpose. Each item is required to be accounted for, and receipt or issue needs to be created. In fact, you will create a stock ledger account for each item and Tally.ERP calls this account "Stock Item".

Stock Units: You can measure the stock item by units, like money is measured in currency. For example, Litres, Meters, Kilograms, Pieces, Box, Dozen, etc. Units can be classified under the following types:

1. **Single Units:** When only one unit is used for receipt and issue of stock items. Above-mentioned are all example of single units.
2. **Compound Units:** When two different types of units can be used for receipt and issue of the stock item is called compound unit. For example:

First Unit	Conversion Factor	Second Unit
Dozen	12	Pcs
Meter	1,000	Millimeters
Box	30	Pcs

Stock Group: As per requirement of the business numerous items can be created, but to generate a report on similar types of stock items you need the classification of stock items. This classification will help you to get stock report in an organized manner. For example, raw material, WIP, finished goods, hardware, software, electrical, electronics, etc.

Creating a Single Stock Group

From this screen you can create a single stock group as follows:

1. Gateway of Tally.ERP ▸ Inventory Info ▸ Single Stock Group ▸ Create.
2. Enter the name of the group.
3. Select the group under which this group will be classified.

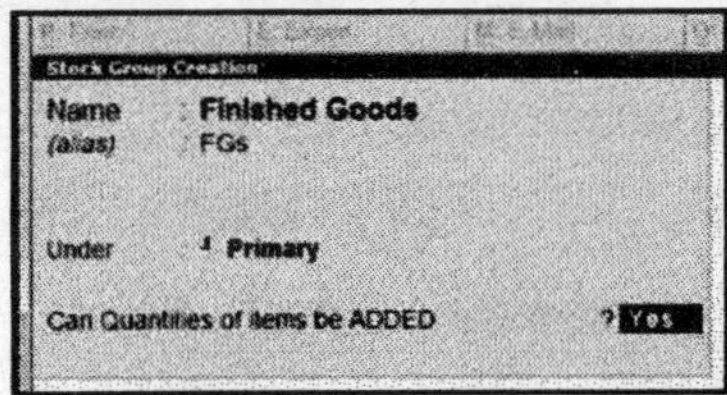

Under

Specify whether it is a primary group or a subgroup of another group, by selecting from the list. Press Alt+C to create a parent group, if you do not have it in the list.

Items to be added

This field pertains to information on measuring the units of the stock items that you would categorize under the stock group. The stock items categorised under the group should have similar units for them to be added up. You cannot add quantities in kgs to quantities in pcs. Any modifications such as name, change of parent group is possible here.

Modifying a Single Stock Group

Gateway of Tally.ERP ▸ Inventory Info ▸ Single Stock Group ▸ Alter

Displaying a Stock Group

Gateway of Tally.ERP ▸ Inventory Info ▸ Single Stock Group ▸ Display

Deleting a Single Stock Group

Gateway of Tally.ERP ▸ Inventory Info ▸ Single Stock Group ▸ Alter

For deleting a group from the list the key combination is ALT+D. Remember that the group should be empty, which means that no stock item is under this group.

Creating a Multiple Stock Group

1. Gateway of Tally.ERP 9 ▸ Inventory Info ▸ Multiple Stock Group ▸ Create.
2. Select/create the group (for creation press ALT+C).
3. Enter the name of the groups **For Example:** A sanitary fittings store has different types of fittings. **Fittings:** Toilet, bath, kitchen, urinals

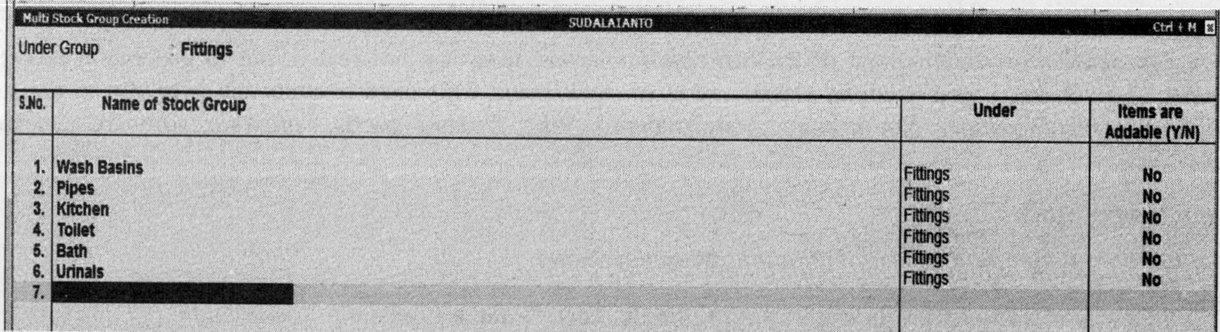

Items are Addable? (Y/N) You can select whether units of the stock items under stock group are to be added or not.

Creation of Stock Units

Gateway of Tally.ERP ▸ Inventory Info ▸ Units of Measure ▸ Create.

Alternation/Deletion of Stock Units

Gateway of Tally.ERP ▸ Inventory Info ▸ Units of Measure ▸ Alter

Key combination is ALT+D

Stock Items: After creation of groups and units of measurement you can create the Stock Item

Creation of Single Stock Item

Gateway of Tally.ERP ▸ Inventory Info ▸ Stock Item ▸ Create (single or multiple options)

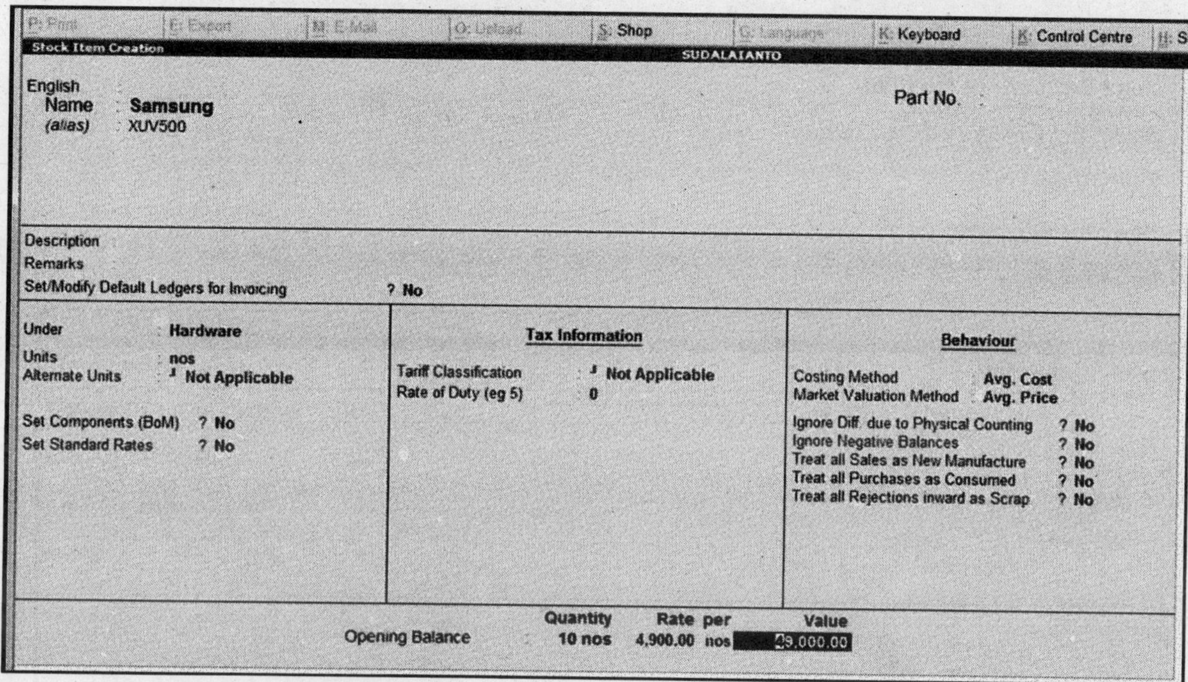

If you want to add any new group or any units in this list then press ALT+C for online creation by putting the cursor in the group or units option.

Configuration of Stock item (F12)

Inventory

Allow ADVANCED entries in Masters	? Yes
Use PART NUMBERS for Stock Items	? Yes
Use Description for Stock Items	? Yes
Use REMARKS for Stock Items	? Yes
Use ALTERNATE UNITS for Stock Items	? Yes
Allow Std. Rates for Stock Items	? Yes
Specify Default Ledger Allocation for Invoicing	? Yes
Allow Component list details (Bill of Materials)	? Yes
Use ADDRESSES for Godowns	? Yes

Configured stock item appears as follows:

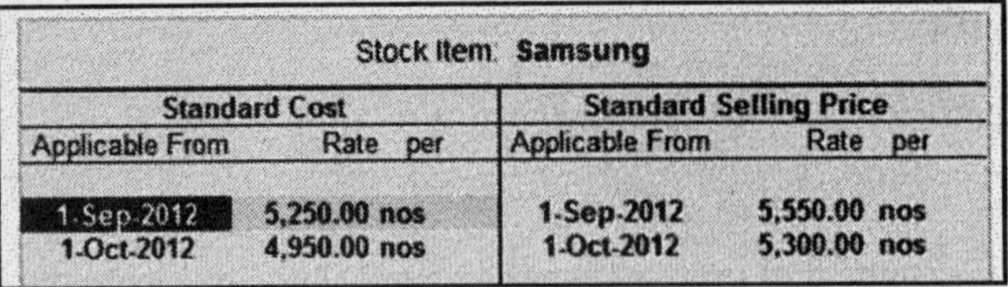

Stock Item: **Samsung**

Standard Cost			Standard Selling Price		
Applicable From	Rate	per	Applicable From	Rate	per
1-Sep-2012	5,250.00	nos	1-Sep-2012	5,550.00	nos
1-Oct-2012	4,950.00	nos	1-Oct-2012	5,300.00	nos

Creation of Multiple Stock Item

1. Gateway of Tally.ERP ▸ Inventory Info ▸ Stock Item ▸ Multiple Stock Items ▸ Create
2. Select the Group of the Product
3. Enter the name of the Item
4. Select the Category from the list.
5. Specify the Unit
6. Enter the Quantity
7. Enter the Rate

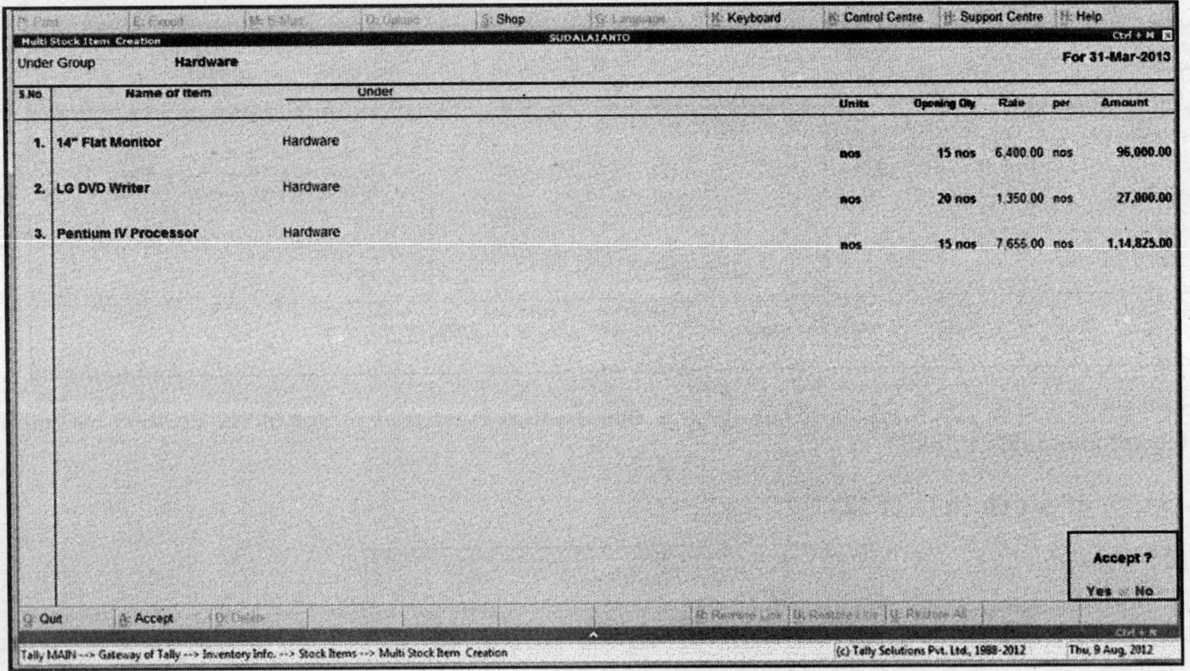

Multi Stock Item Creation

Under Group: **Hardware** — For 31-Mar-2013

S.No.	Name of Item	Under	Units	Opening Qty	Rate	per	Amount
1.	14" Flat Monitor	Hardware	nos	15 nos	6,400.00	nos	96,000.00
2.	LG DVD Writer	Hardware	nos	20 nos	1,350.00	nos	27,000.00
3.	Pentium IV Processor	Hardware	nos	15 nos	7,655.00	nos	1,14,825.00

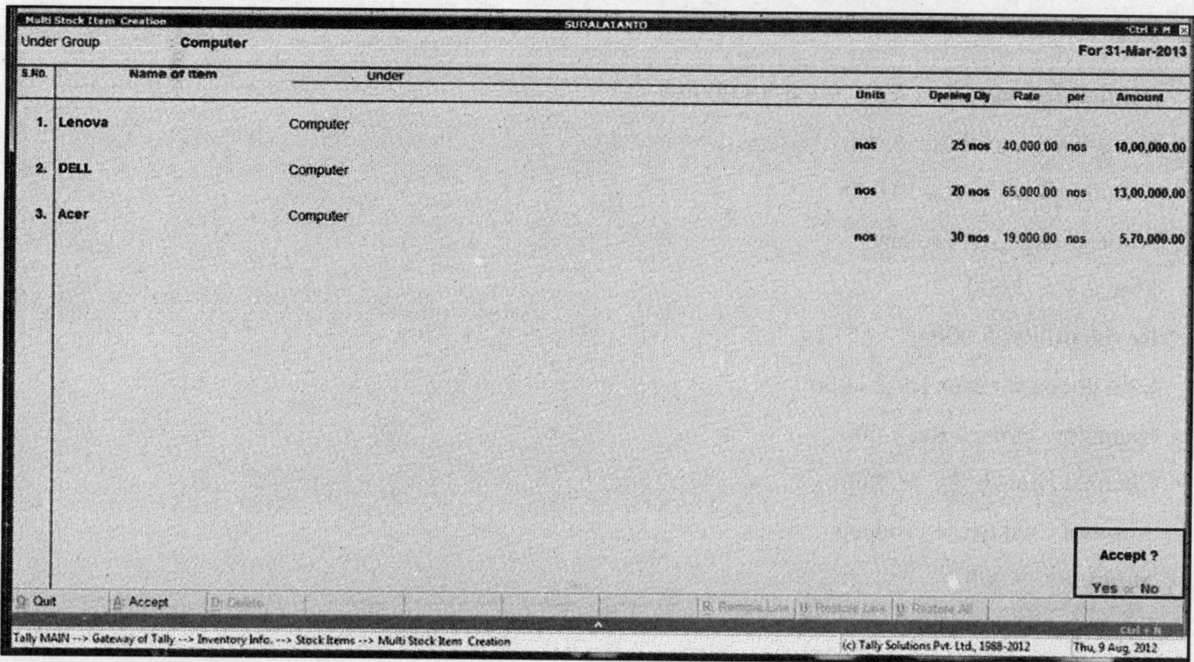

Modification and Deletion of Stock Item

Gateway of Tally.ERP ▸ Inventory Info ▸ Stock Item ▸ Single Alter

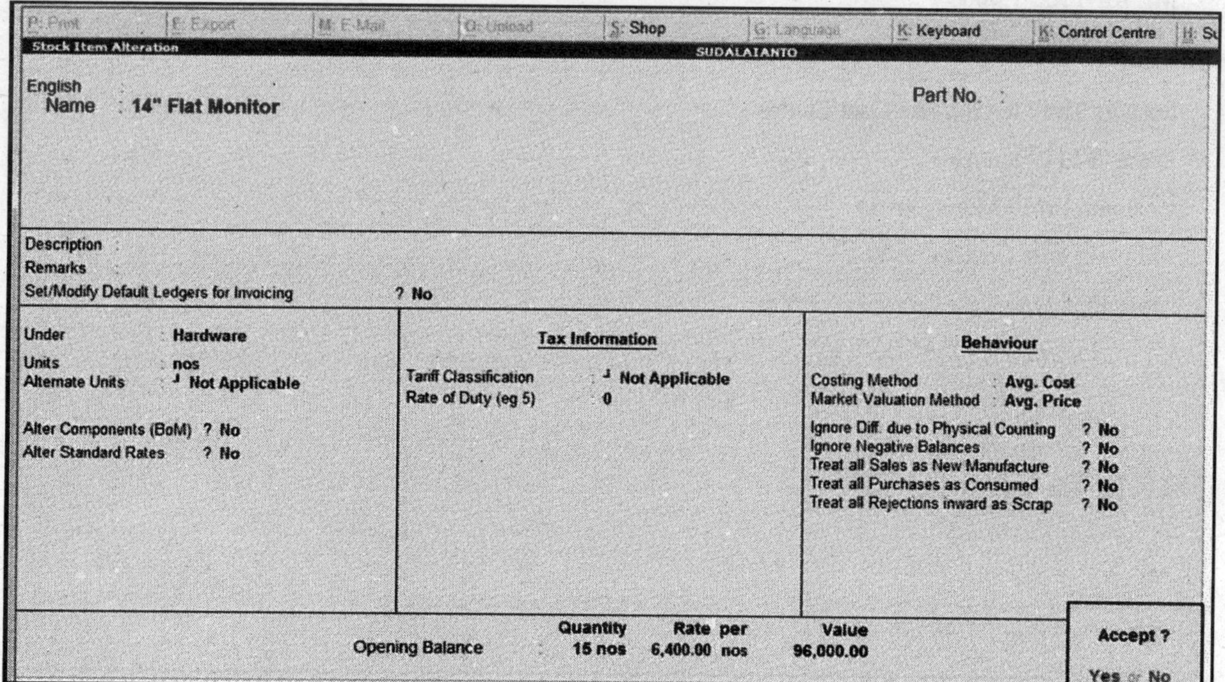

Key used to delete an item: ALT + D (If there is no Opening Quantity and/or No Transaction).

EXERCISE

1. Purchase goods From ABC & Co. 15,000

   Bangalore Branch Rs. 5,000

   Chennai Branchi Rs. 10,000

   Allocate the Cost Products

   Mouse Rs. 7,000

   Keyboard Rs. 5,000

2. Sold goods for cash Rs. 20,000

   Bangalore Branch Rs. 7,000

   Chennai Branch Rs. 13,000

   Allocate Cost to the Products

   Mouse Rs. 9,000

   Keyboard Rs. 11,000

3. Paid to ABC & Co. Rs. 15,000

4. Salary paid Rs. 3,000 to salesman

   Mr. Raj Rs. 1,600

   Mr. Ravi Rs. 1,400

Tally Solution

Step 1: Tally to Activate Cost Centre

Press "F11" Feature

Cost and Profit Management

Maintain cost Centers → Yes

More than One Cost Category → Yes

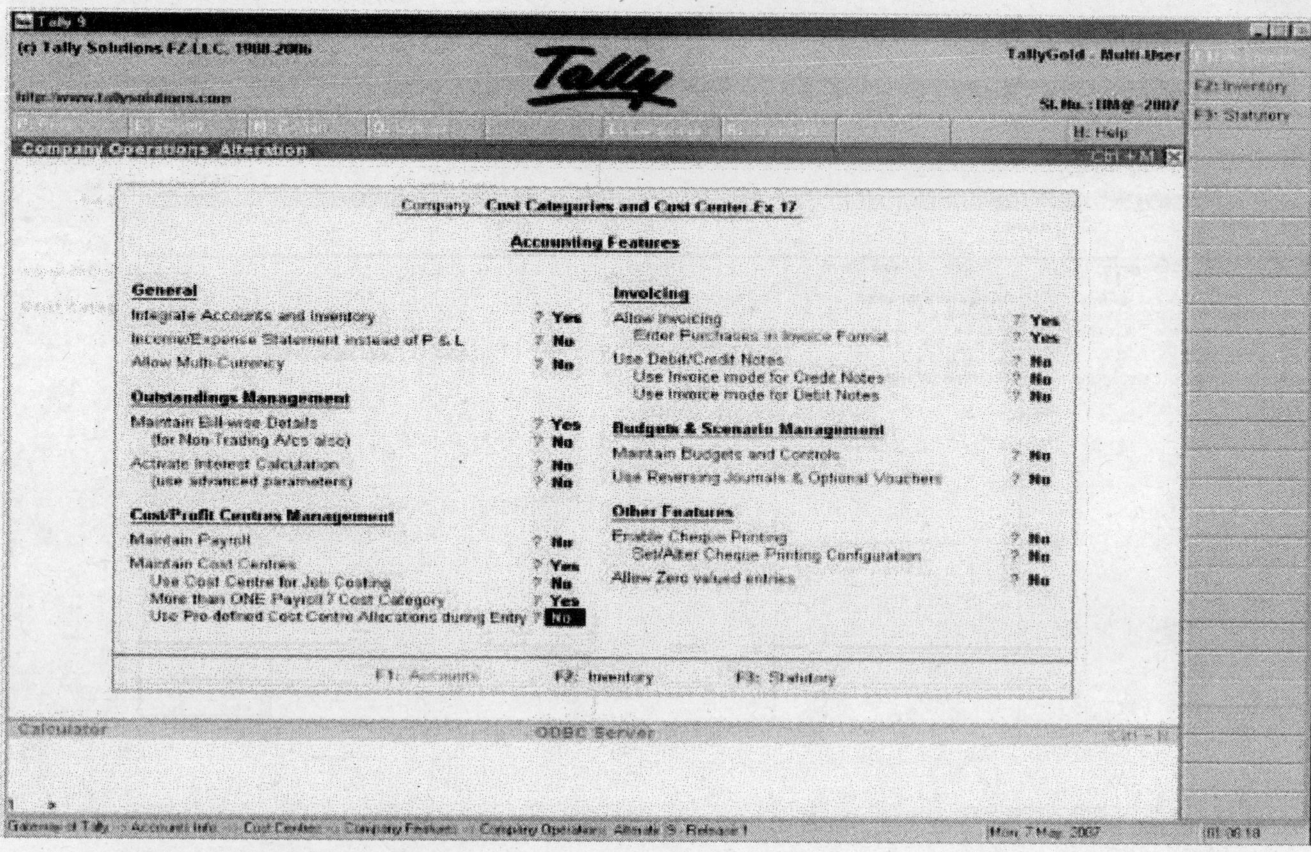

Step 2: To "Create Cost centre"

Gateway of Tally → Accounts Info → Cost Category Creat Single Cost Category

Name		Under
1. Bangalore Branch	— — —	Primary cost Category
2. Chennai Branch	— — —	"
3. Salesman	— — —	"

Display Multiple Cost Category

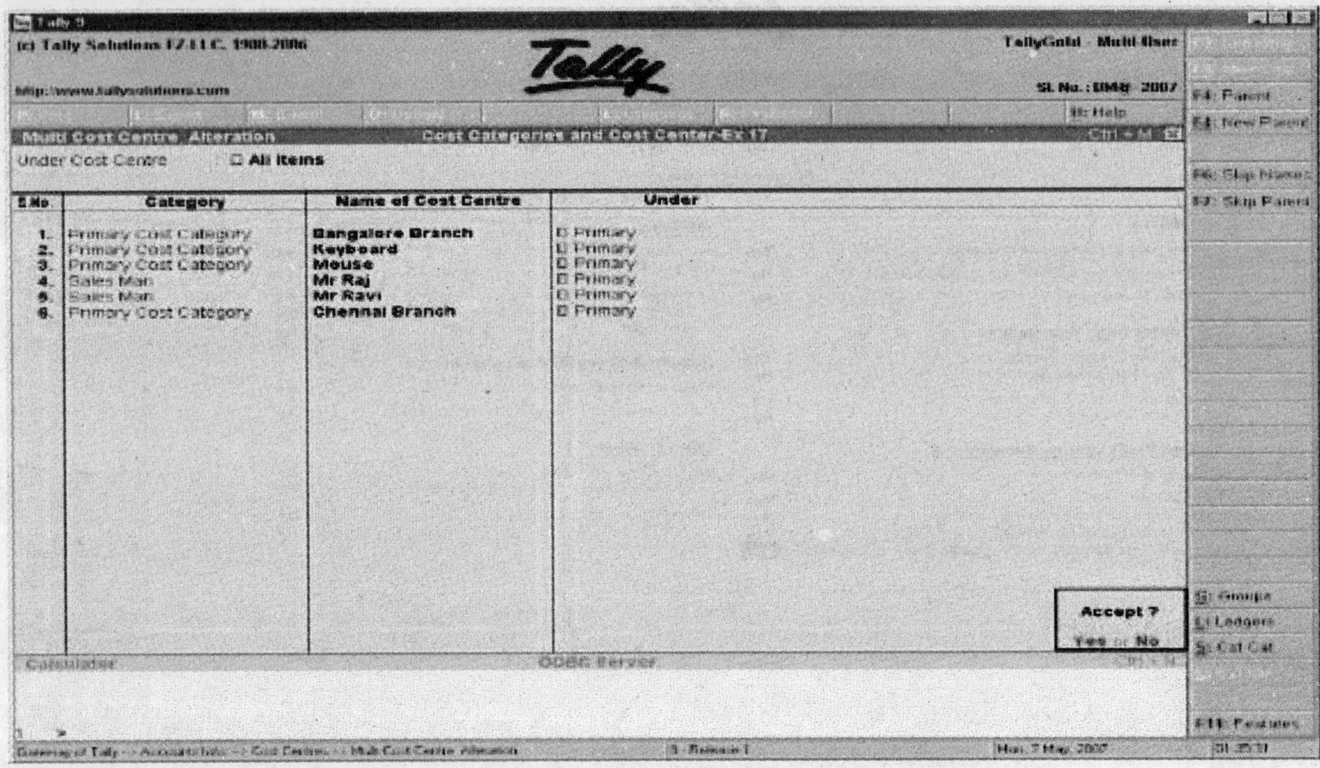

Gateway of Tally → Accounts Info → Cost Centre → Create → Multiple Cost Centre

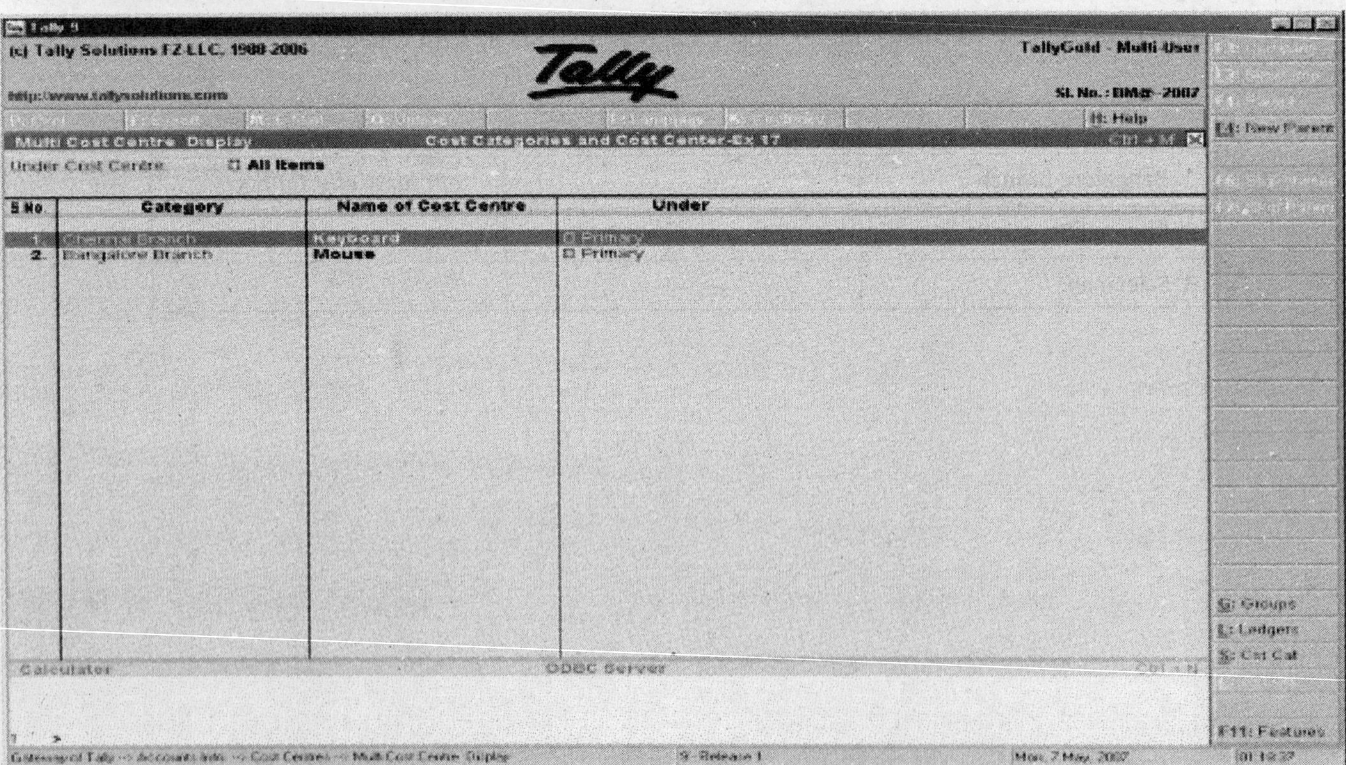

Step 3: Gateway of Tally → Accounts Info → Cost Centre → Create → Multiple Cost Centre

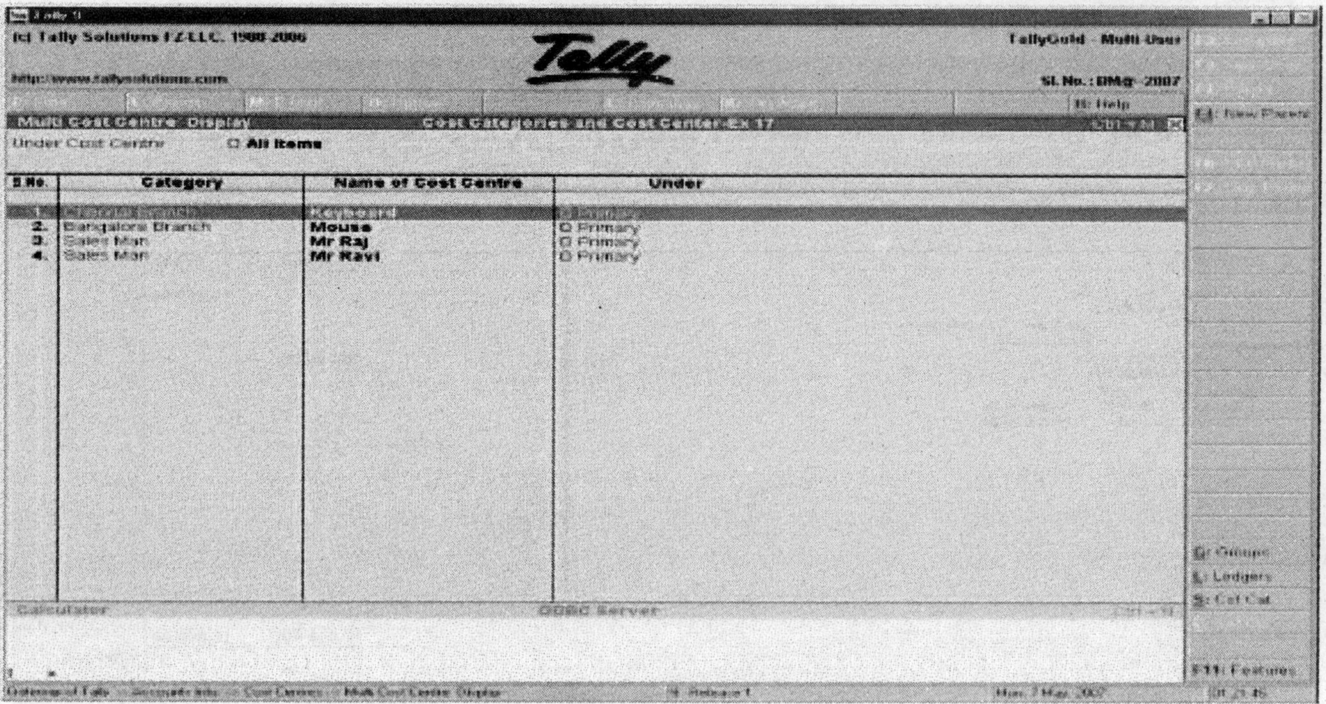

Step 4: Gateway of Tally → Accounting Info → Ledger → Create

To activate Cost Centre Yes

Cost Centre Are Applicable Yes

Sample Output in Tally

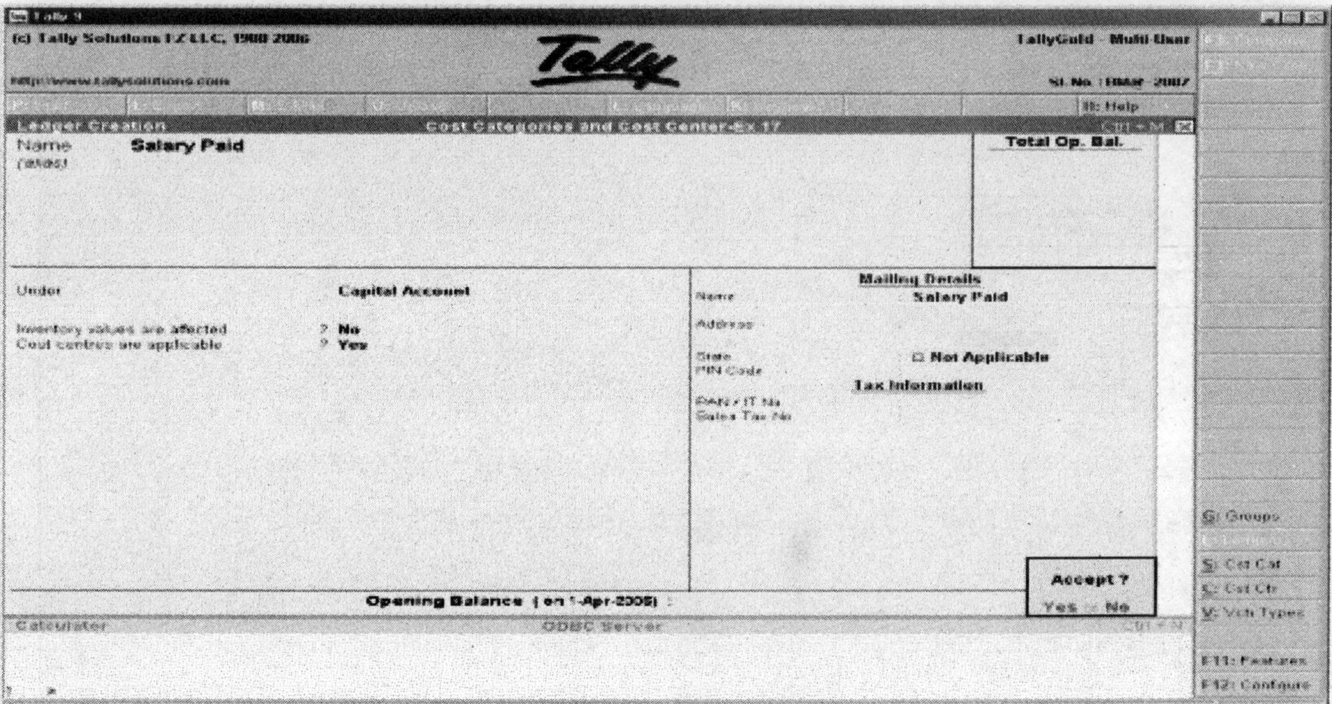

Voucher Entry

Press F9 Key → Purchase Voucher

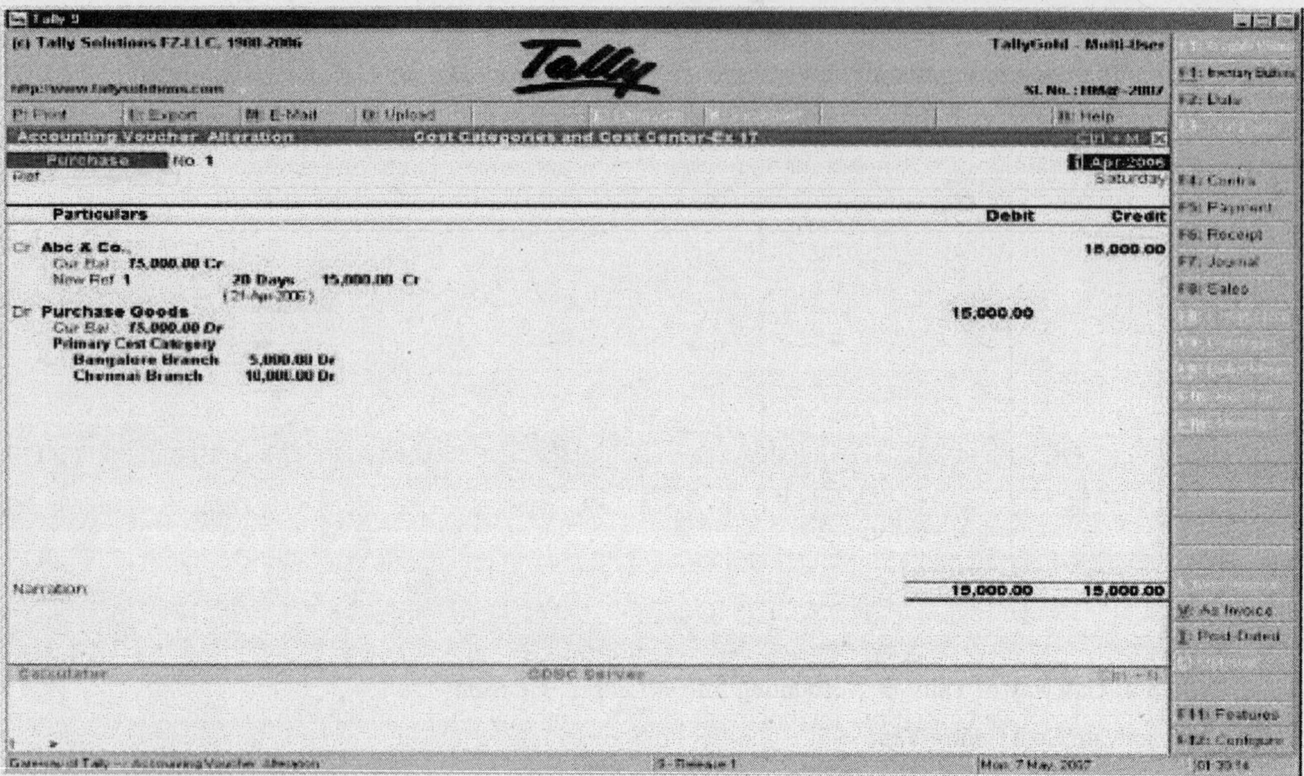

Sample II

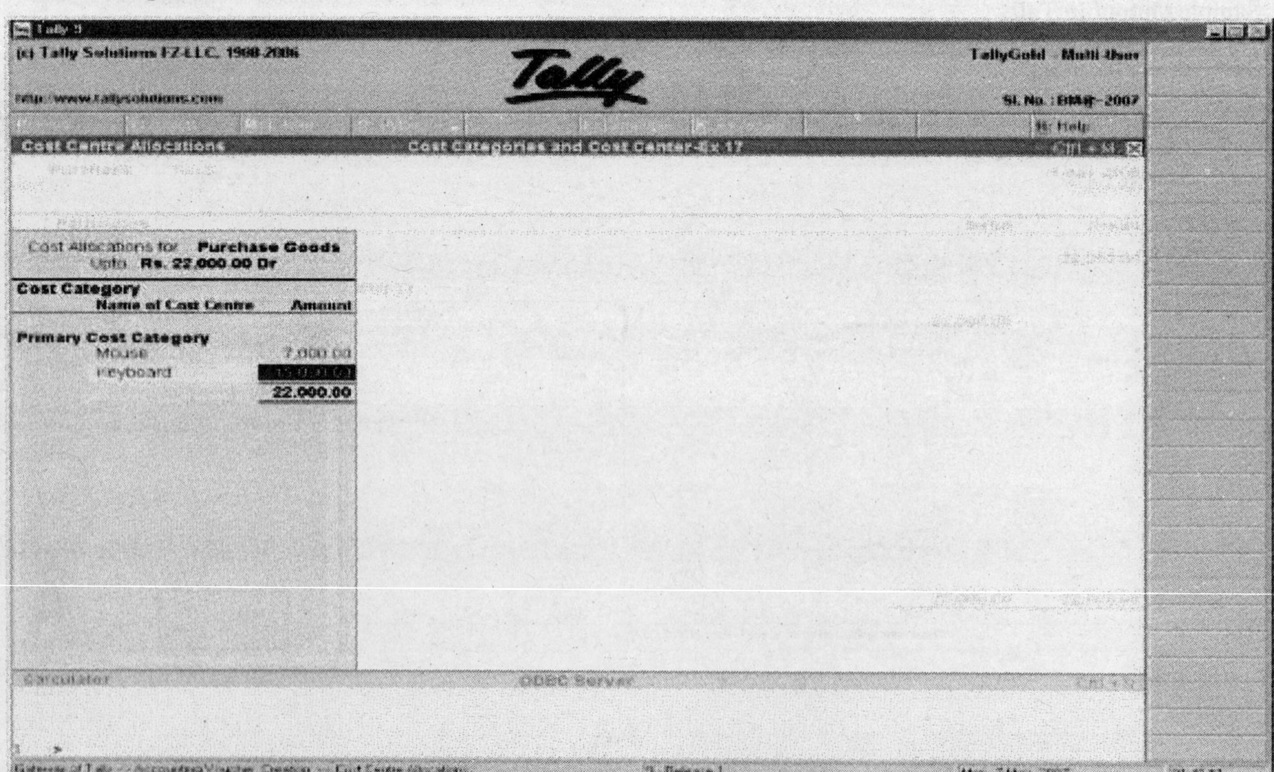

Sales Voucher (Press F8 key)

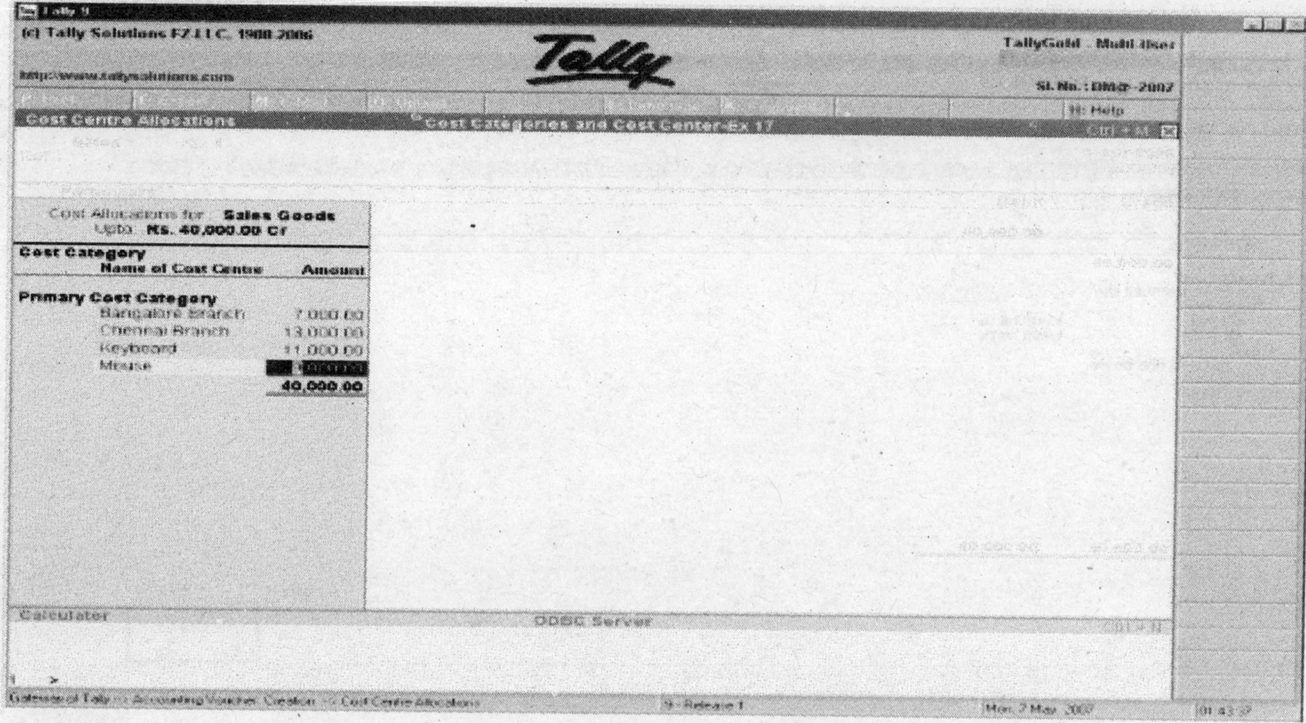

Entry

(c) Tally Solutions FZ-LLC, 1988-2006

Tally

TallyGold - Multi-User

Accounting Voucher Creation — Cost Categories and Cost Center-Ex 17

Sales No. 1 — 1-Apr-2006 Saturday

Ref:

Particulars	Debit	Credit
Dr **Cash**	40,000.00	
Cur Bal 40,000.00 Dr		
Cr **Sales Goods**		40,000.00
Cur Bal 40,000.00 Cr		
Primary Cost Category		
Bangalore Branch 7,000.00 Cr		
Chennai Branch 13,000.00 Cr		
Keyboard 11,000.00 Cr		
Mouse 9,000.00 Cr		
Narration:	40,000.00	40,000.00

Accept ?

Yes or No

Expenses a/c in Cost Centre

Gateway of Tally → Accounting Voucher → Payment (F5 key Press)

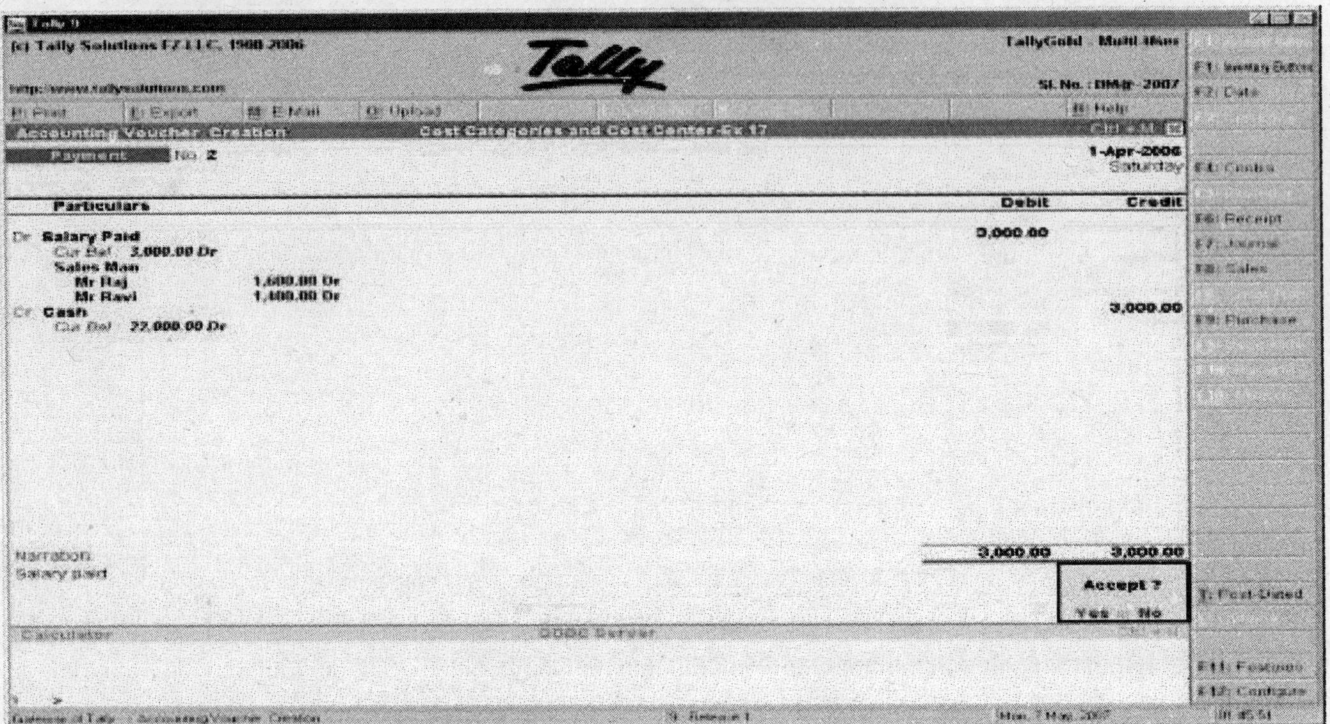

Output Result View in Tally

Display → Statement of a/c→ Cost Centre

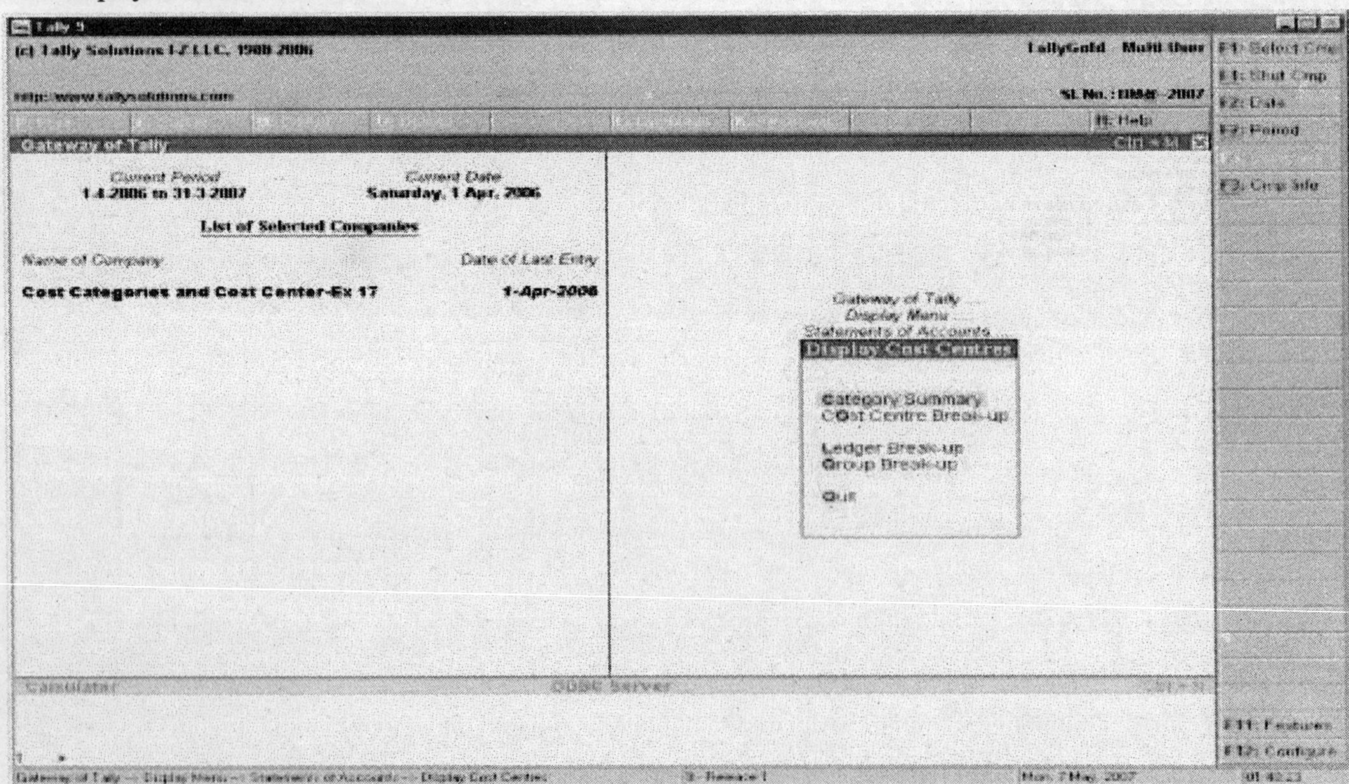

Output II (Cost Break-up)

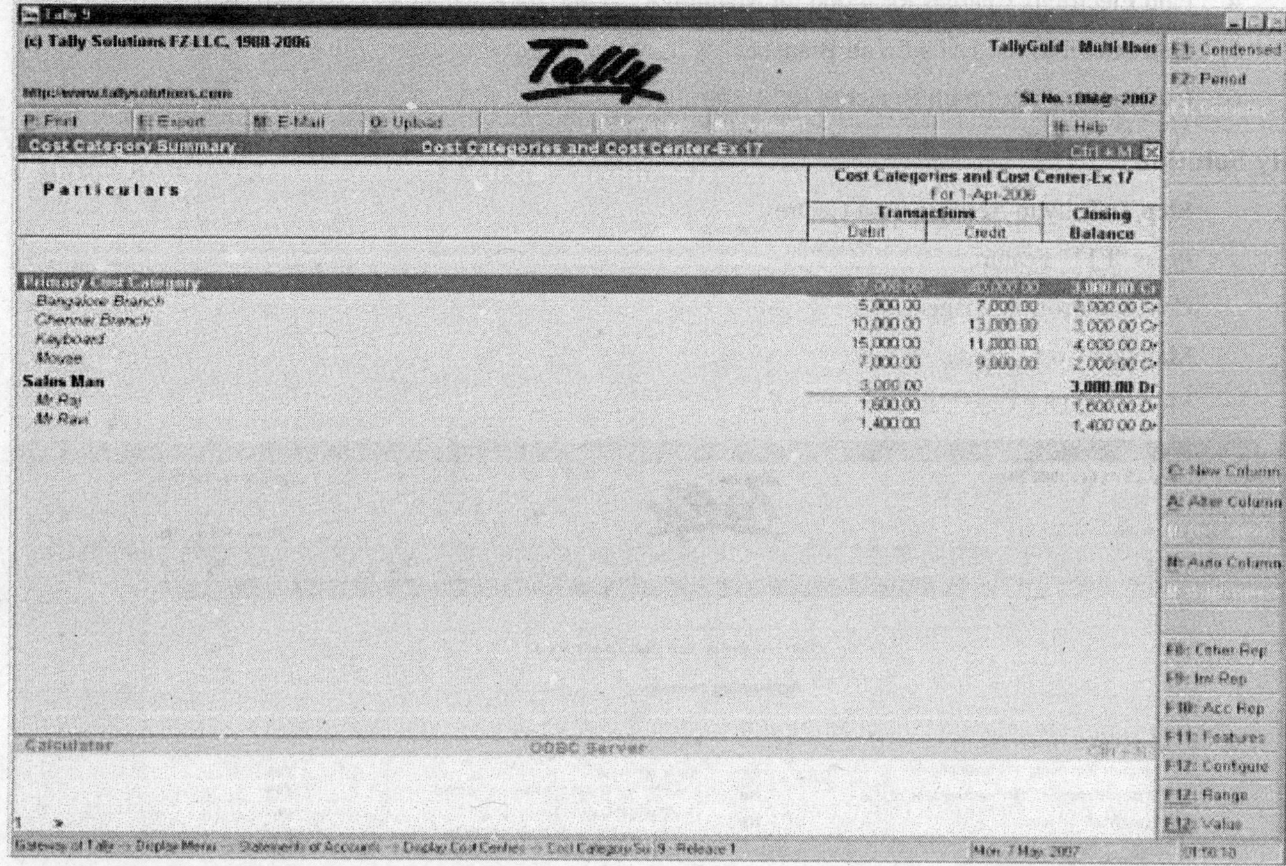

Particulars	Debit	Credit	Closing Balance
Primary Cost Category	37,000.00	40,000.00	3,000.00 Cr
Bangalore Branch	5,000.00	7,000.00	2,000.00 Cr
Chennai Branch	10,000.00	13,000.00	3,000.00 Cr
Keyboard	15,000.00	11,000.00	4,000.00 Dr
Mouse	7,000.00	9,000.00	2,000.00 Cr
Sales Man	3,000.00		**3,000.00 Dr**
Mr Raj	1,600.00		1,600.00 Dr
Mr Ravi	1,400.00		1,400.00 Dr

Inventory (Stock) Creation Exercise-III

Cost Category:

1. Chennai
2. Bangalore
3. Madurai

Cost Centre:

Marketing

Finance

Administration

1. Paid Salary to staff Rs. 1,05,000

   Chennai: 35,000 (Marketing 15,000: Finance: 10,000 Administration: 10,000)

   Bangalore: 35,000 (Marketing 15,000: Finance: 10,000 Administration: 10,000)

   Madurai: 35,000 (Marketing 15,000: Finance: 10,000 Administration: 10,000)

   Rs. 1,05,000

2. Paid rent for Madurai Rs. 7,500 For Chennai Rs. 8,000, for Bangalore Rs. 10,000

3. Paid for Stationery Rs. 3,500 for all Branches
4. Paid Electricity Charges Rs. 4,000 for Madurai Rs. 5,500 for Chennai Rs. 7,500 for Bangalore
5. Paid sales Tax Rs. 1,500 for all Branches
6. Paid Income Tax for all Branches Rs. 1,500

Tally Solution

Step 1: Tally to Activate Cost Centre

Press "F11" Feature

Cost and Profit Management

Maintain Cost Centres → Yes

More than One Cost Category → Yes

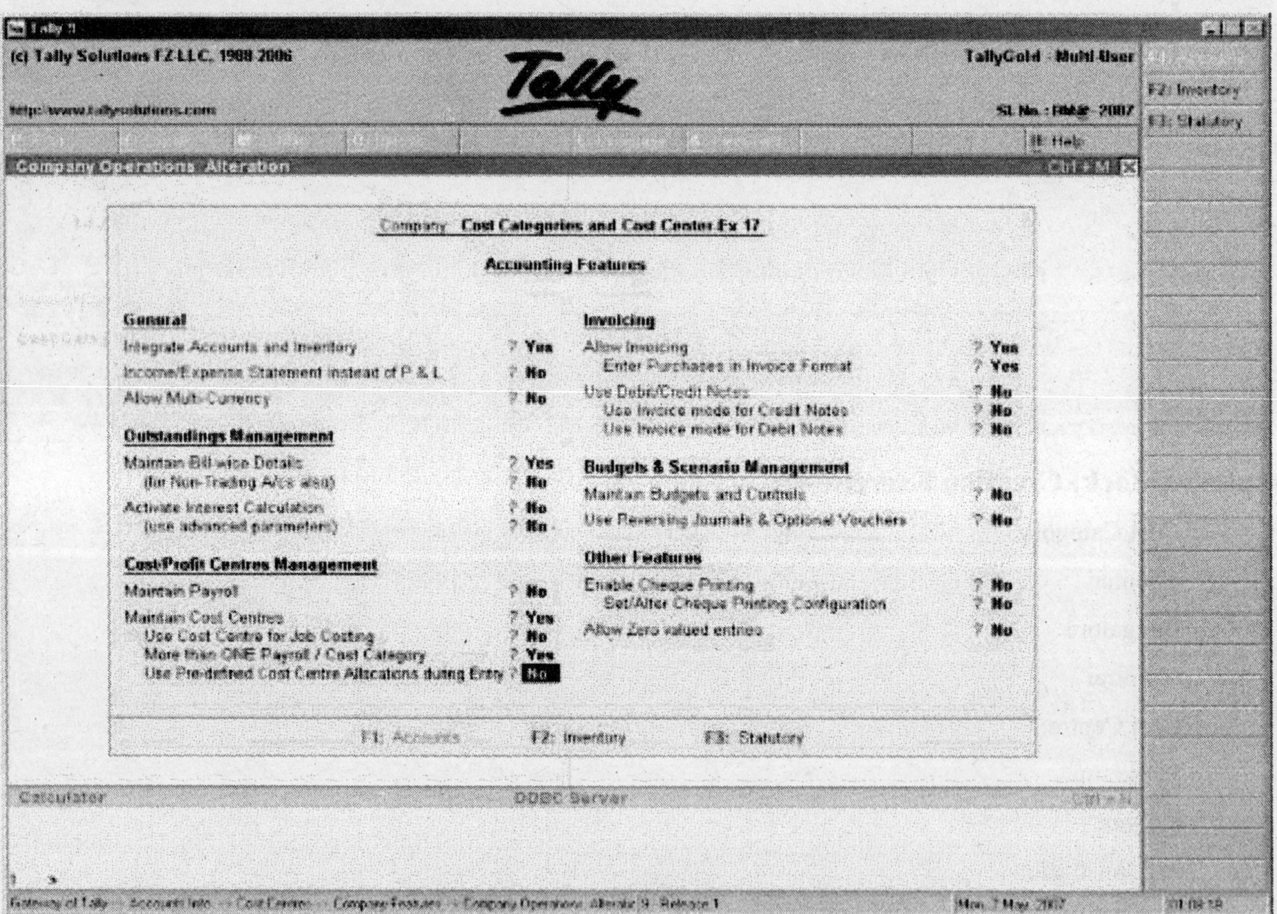

Step 2: To "Create Cost Centre"

Gateway of Tally → Accounts Info → Cost Category → Create → Single Cost Category

Name	Under
Chennai	Non-revenue Item → Yes, Revenue Item→ Yes
Bangalore	Non-revenue item → Yes, Revenue Item→ Yes
Madurai	Non-revenue item –"' → Yes, Revenue Item→ Yes

Display Multiple Cost Category

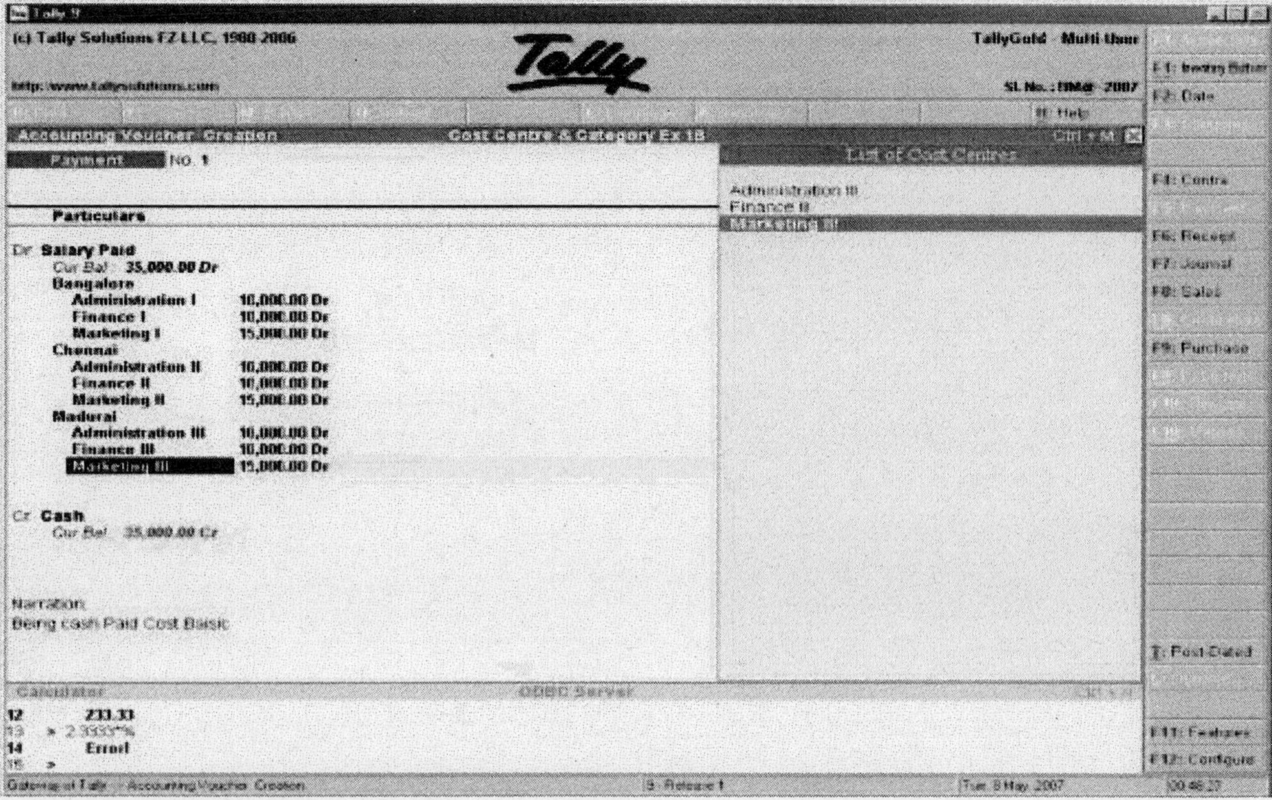

Voucher Entry Cost/Centre and Category

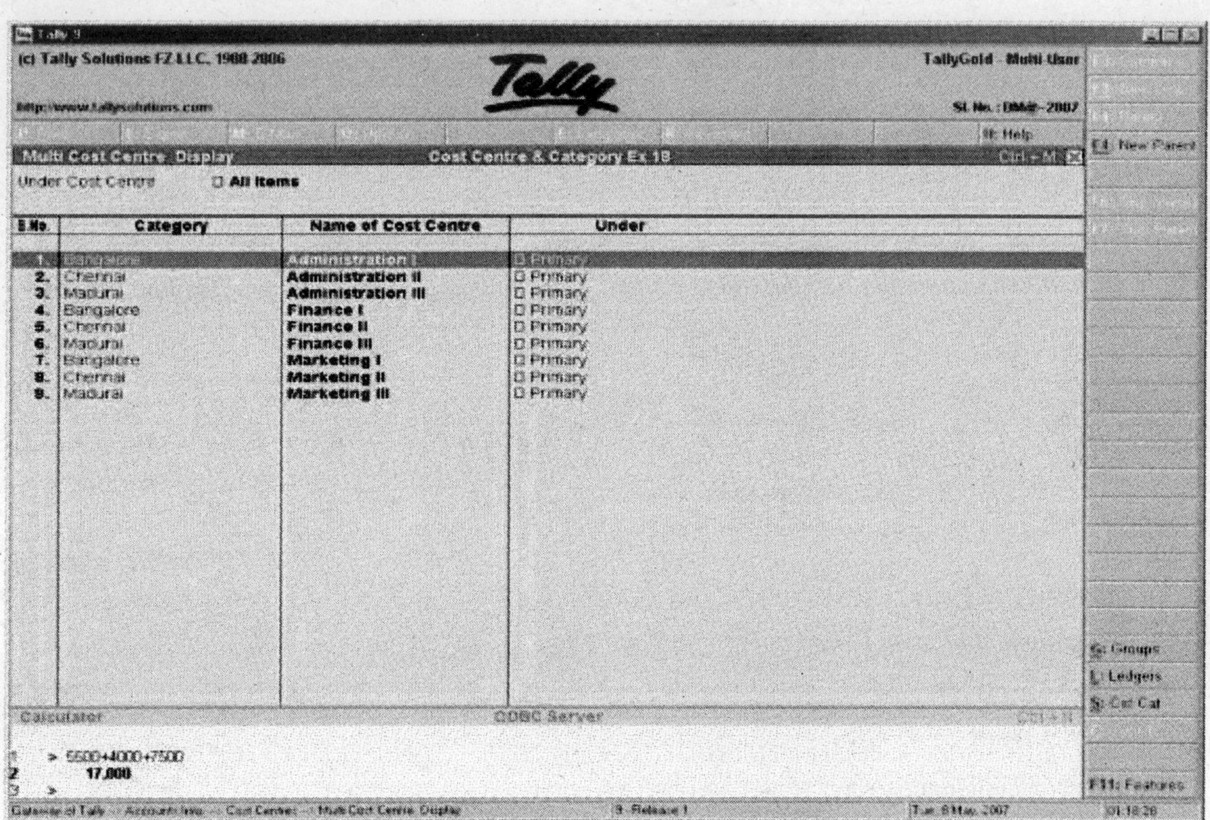

Step 3

Report: Display → Statement of Accounts → Cost Centre

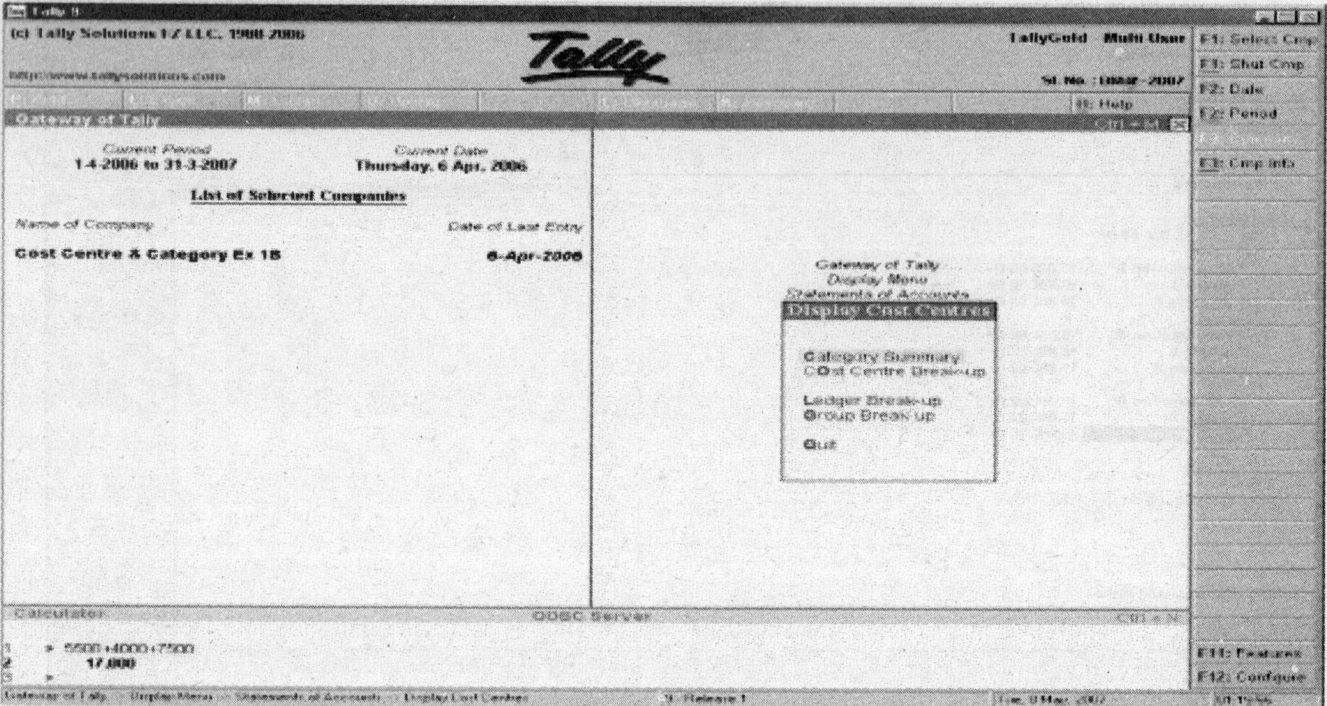

Output Result

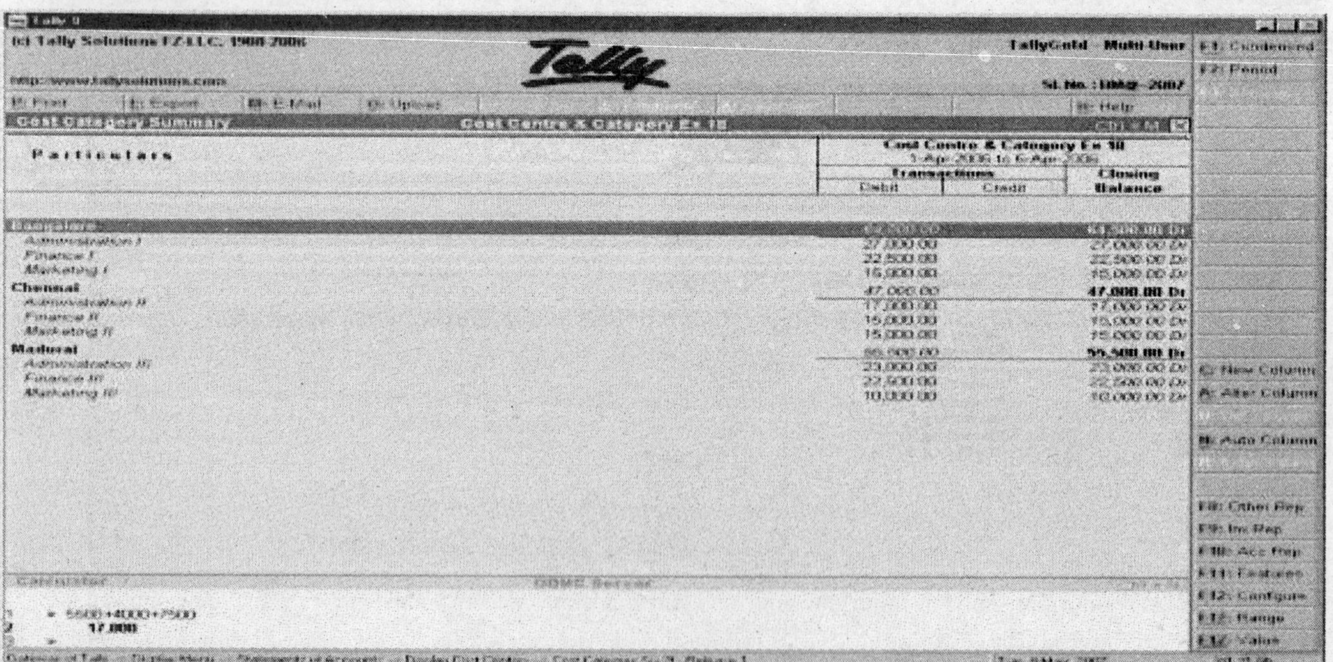

Step 4: Display Day Book Result

Display → Day Book

Change "F2 Date"

Press F 12 "Configuration Key"

Show Cost Centre Details Also → Yes

Press Alt +F1 (Details Information)

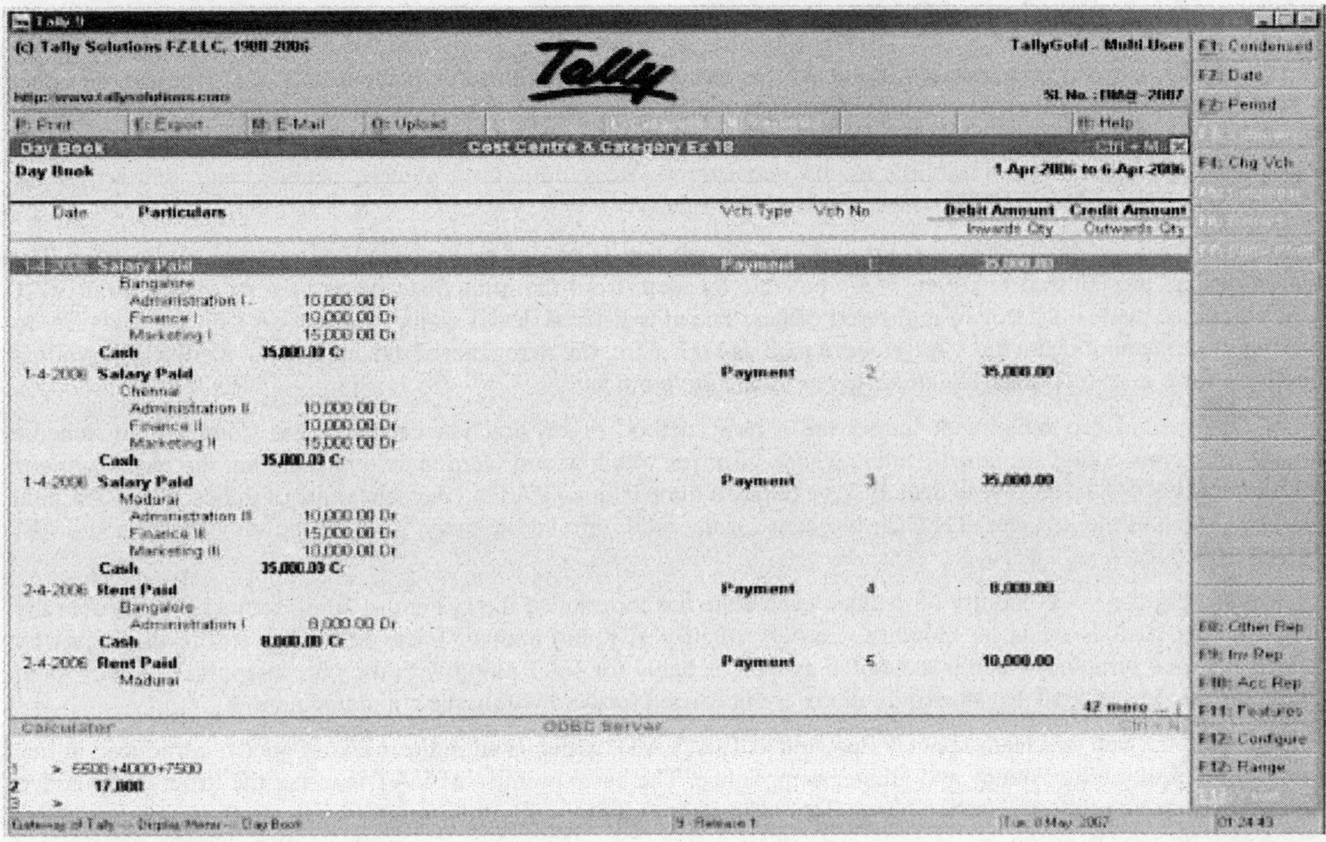

12.7 VAT (VALUE ADDED TAX) IN TALLY.ERP 9

The Concept of VAT is a very popular system of Taxation which emerged in European Countries. The VAT system is adopted by most of the countries to bring about user-convenience and transparency in the entire system of taxation. The working system of VAT is simple to follow, implement and administer.

VAT stands for Value Added Tax. In this system, the tax is levied on the value of the goods and charged at every level of value addition, i.e., on the value added portion of goods at each level.

The earlier system of taxation was allowing the levy of tax on tax. This ultimately lead to wrong assessment of Tax liability and tax evasion. The concept of VAT resolved the cascading effect of taxes resulting in prevention of tax evasions.

The VAT system levies tax on every level of value addition to the product or good. At the same time the tax paid for acquiring this product or good will be allowed as tax credit and can be used for payment of VAT at the time of selling the product or good to the immediate dealer. The net effect of tax will be only on the portion of value added by the seller. The following example clearly explains the flow of VAT system and its effect on the selling price.

Example: Mr. Sudalai Anto, a registered dealer purchased one good at Rs. 1,000 by paying 4% tax on it, i.e., Rs. 40. The tax paid by him can be claimed as input tax credit. On the good purchased, he did some value addition worth Rs. 500. The VAT liability after such value addition amounted to Rs. 60, i.e., 4% on Rs. 1,500. Since there is a credit of Rs. 40 on the initial purchase made, the same can be adjusted against Rs. 60. Only the balance amount of Rs. 20 needs to be paid to the department.

The tax paid on inputs purchases is termed as **Input Tax** and VAT payable on the goods after value addition is called as **Output Tax**. The input tax paid can be taken as Input Tax Credit and is popularly known as **ITC**. The VAT liability of the dealer will be arrived at as given below:

(a) VAT Payable = Output Tax – Input Tax

(b) If the tax paid on purchases (Input tax), is more than the tax payable (output tax), the same can be either carried forward to next return period or claimed as refund. The tax amount carried forward will be accounted as input tax credit for the next return period. In the subsequent periods, this credit can be utilized for payment of any liability to the department like output tax, interest, penalty, etc., subject to the provisions or restrictions as specified in VAT rules.

The Value Added Tax (VAT) is a type of indirect tax and is one of major source of revenue to the state. The registered dealers are allowed to collect VAT payable by them from the immediate buyer. They can claim the VAT paid on purchases made only from a registered dealer. The unregistered dealer cannot charge VAT on the invoices, so the buying dealer cannot claim the VAT amount paid as ITC. Also, the unregistered dealers are not eligible for availing concessions, for e.g., exemptions, which are given by the government.

The commercial tax department introduced a new method of levying tax called as the Composition Scheme especially after considering the small dealers whose turnover was low and were unable to maintain the records as per the requirements of VAT Act. These dealers have to pay a lump sum as VAT on the sale value of goods. The VAT paid will not be shown in the invoices. They can account for the total turnover and pay VAT on the same at the end of the return period.

For assessing the VAT liability of dealers, each state has introduced the system of filing returns for different tax periods. The tax periods could be monthly, quarterly, half-yearly and annual. Each dealer has to file the return by specifying the total turnover which is exempted as well as liable for VAT along with the purchases made and tax paid on it with the amount of VAT payable or input tax credit carried forward within the stipulated period.

In this chapter, you will learn about Value Added Tax (VAT), which is an indirect tax on goods, introduced in lieu of sales tax, to ensure transparency and greater compliance. The basic premise of VAT is to tax the 'true value' added to goods at each stage of the transaction chain. This ultimately reduces

- Tax paid to the government
- Cost/tax passed on to the consumer

VAT is a multi-point tax as against sales tax, which is a single-point tax. Under the sales tax regime, the 'Value' of goods to be taxed at each stage is computed as Basic Cost + Profit Margin + Sales Tax paid at earlier stages. VAT does away with the cascading effect of tax on tax by allowing a set-off for the input tax, that is, tax paid at earlier stages on purchases. It is an efficient, globally acceptable and easy-to-administer taxation system.

VAT in India

The Value Added Tax (VAT) is a type of indirect tax and is one of major source of revenue to the state. The VAT system was introduced in India by replacing the General Sales Tax laws of each state. Presently in India, out of 35 states and union territories, 33 are following this new system of sales taxation. The states/union territories which are yet to implement the VAT system are Andaman and Nicobar Islands and Lakshadweep.

The VAT system of taxation was adopted by Indian states and union territories in the year 2005 by replacing the General Sales Tax laws with New Value Added Tax Acts and the supporting Value Added Tax Rules for proper administration and collection of tax. Each state or union territory has its own methods to assess the tax liability and collection methods from the dealers who fall under the purview of VAT.

The administration of VAT system was undertaken by the Commercial Taxes Department of each state along with the Excise and other indirect taxes. For easy and quick assessment of taxation and prevention of tax evasion, the department has introduced the registration system. This registration system of VAT helps in identifying the assessees who come under purview of VAT and are liable to collect and pay VAT. For encouraging the registration process some benefits or concessions are given to the dealers.

The registered dealers are allowed to collect VAT payable by them from the immediate buyer. They can claim the VAT paid on purchases made only from a registered dealer. The unregistered dealer cannot charge VAT on the invoices, so the buying dealer cannot claim the VAT amount paid as ITC. Also, the unregistered dealers are not eligible for availing concessions, for e.g., exemptions, which are given by the government.

The commercial tax department introduced a new method of levying tax called as the **Composition Scheme** especially after considering the small dealers whose turnover was low and were unable to maintain the records as per the requirements of VAT Act. These dealers have to pay a lump sum as VAT on the sale value of goods. The VAT paid will not be shown in the invoices. They can account for the total turnover and pay VAT on the same at the end of the return period.

For assessing the VAT liability of dealers, each state has introduced the system of filing returns for different tax periods. The tax periods could be monthly, quarterly, half-yearly and annual. Each dealer has to file the return by specifying the total turnover which is exempted as well as liable for VAT along with the purchases made and tax paid on it with the amount of VAT payable or input tax credit carried forward within the stipulated period.

Terminologies in VAT

Term	Description
Input Tax	This is the tax paid on purchases
Output Tax	This is the tax charged on sales
Input Credit	The excess amount of input tax over output tax for the current period which is permitted to be set-off against output tax of subsequent periods is termed as input credit.
TIN	Tax Identification Number (TIN) is the registration number given by the department to the dealer at the time of registration. This needs to be quoted at all required places where the registration details are to be provided.
Tax Invoice	This is the sales invoice format issued by one registered dealer to another. Based on this invoice, the ITC can be claimed by the purchasing dealer.
Retail Invoice	The sales invoice format used for invoicing the exempted sales and the sales made to unregistered dealers is termed as retail invoice.
Registered Dealer	This term is used to identify a dealer who is registered either under voluntary registration or compulsory registration under the VAT Act. Such dealer can issue tax invoice and also claim the tax paid on purchases made from other registered dealers as input tax credit.
Unregistered Dealer	Dealers who are not registered under the VAT Act are called as Unregistered Dealers (URD). Such dealers cannot issue tax invoice. They can neither charge tax nor claim input tax credit.
Composite Dealer	Dealers with annual gross turnover not exceeding a certain threshold who can opt for a composition scheme whereby they will pay tax as a small percentage of their gross turnover.
Purchase Tax	The tax paid on goods purchased from unregistered dealers is liable to purchase tax. The purchase tax is treated as output VAT payable by the dealer as it is a liability. It has to be paid while making the payment towards VAT liability. Based on the rules and regulations, the input tax credit can be claimed on the payment made towards purchase tax.

Calculation of VAT

Example 1: The following transaction has been done by the Sudai-Anto Pvt. Ltd. Based on this transaction compute the VAT payable to the government.

1. Purchase from Rohini Infotech, 10 CDs of Antivirus Software @Rs. 1,000 each, VAT rate @ 4%.
2. Purchase from Harsh-Darsh India Ltd., 10 Apple Computers @40,000 each, however discount allowed @5%, Excise tax @16%, i.e., Rs. 60,800 and Educational Cess @2%, i.e., Rs. 600, VAT @4%.

3. Sale of 2 Antivirus CDs @Rs. 1,200 to Rajib Roy.
4. Sale of 2 Monitors @Rs. 4,500, VAT @4% to H. Goenka.

Solutions: For Purchase Amount

For Transaction 1: VAT payable to party on assessable value of Rs. 4,000 @ 4% Input VAT, Rs. 160.00

For Transaction 2: VAT payable to party on the assessable value of Rs. 44,680 @ 4% Input VAT, Rs. 1,787.20

Total of Input VAT (A) Rs. 1,947.20

For SALES

For Transaction 3: VAT payable to the govt. on assessable value of Rs. 2,400 @4% Output VAT, Rs. 96.00

For Transaction 4: VAT Payable on govt. on assessable value of Rs. 9,000 @ 4% Rs. 360.00

Total Output VAT (B) Rs. 456.00

Therefore, VAT Payable/Receivable (A – B) (Rs.1,491.20)

VAT on Tally.ERP 9

Let us take the above example and see how it works on Tally.ERP. The procedure for implementation of VAT in Tally.ERP is very simple. Follow the steps given below:

Step 1 Enabling VAT: Go to Gateway of Tally.ERP ▸ Accounts Info. ▸ F11: Features ▸ Statutory and Taxation. Set Enable Value Added Tax (VAT) and Set/Alter VAT Details to Yes

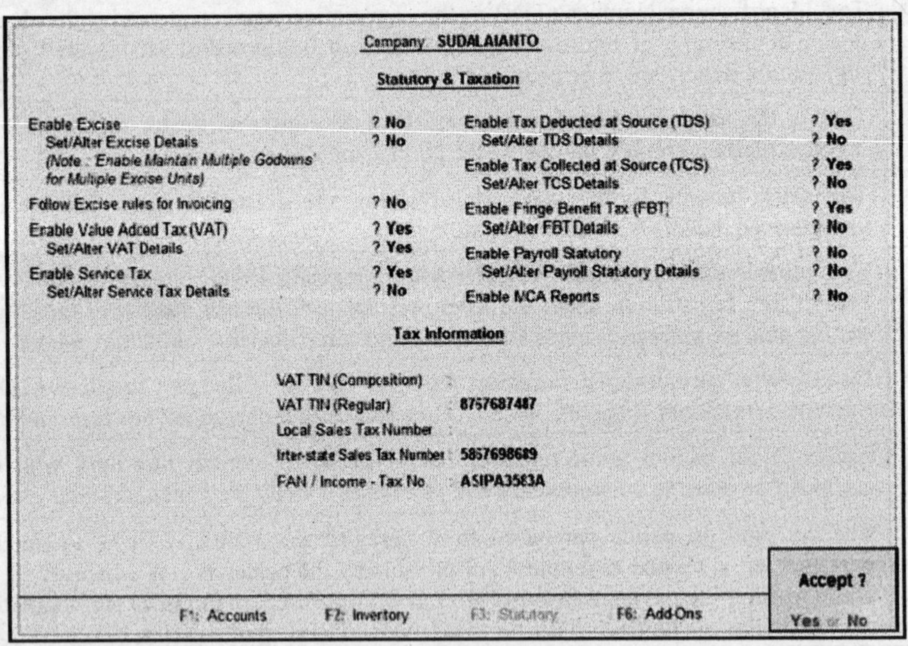

On enabling Set/Alter VAT Details to Yes, Tally.ERP will prompt with VAT Details Screen.

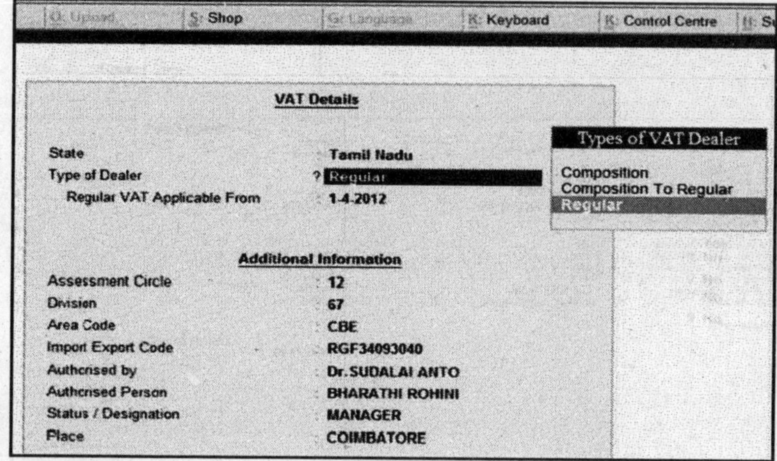

VAT Details:

- ❖ Select the State name.
- ❖ Set Type of Dealer? To Regular
- ❖ Enter the Regular VAT Applicable From date
- ❖ Accept the screen to save.

Step 2 Create the tax rate from ledger creation such as "Input VAT 4%" and "Output VAT 4%" under "Duties and Taxes". Create the ledger Input VAT 4%.

Gateway of Tally.ERP ▸ Master ▸ Accounts Info ▸ Single Ledger ▸ Create

At the time creation following things has to be specified in the respective ledgers such as:

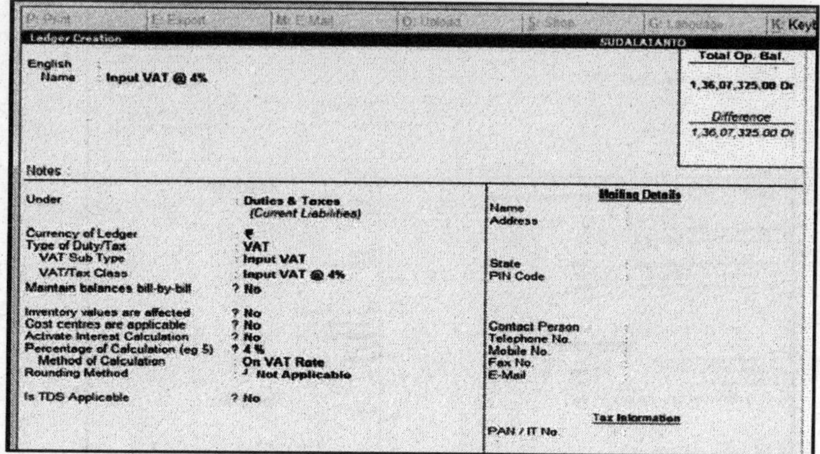

Step 3 Create the other Tax Ledger Output VAT 4%

Gateway of Tally.ERP ▸ Master ▸ Accounts Info ▸ Single Ledger ▸ Create

At the time of creation following things have to be specified in the respective ledgers such as:

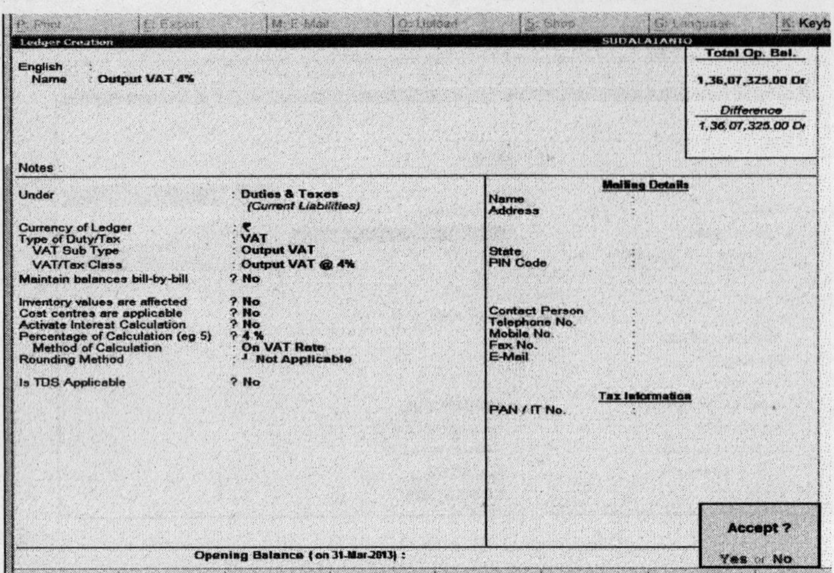

Step 4 Create the Purchase an Sales Ledger such as "Purchase @ 4%" and "Sales @ 4%

Gateway of Tally.ERP ▸ Master ▸ Accounts Info ▸ Single Ledger ▸ Create

Following things to be specified at the time of "Purchase @ 4%" Ledger creation:

(a) Used in VAT Returns = "Yes"

(b) VAT/Tax Classes = Purchase @ 4%

Following things to be specified at the time of "Sales @ 4% "Ledger creation:

(a) Used in VAT Returns = "Yes"

(b) VAT/Tax Classes = Sales @ 4%

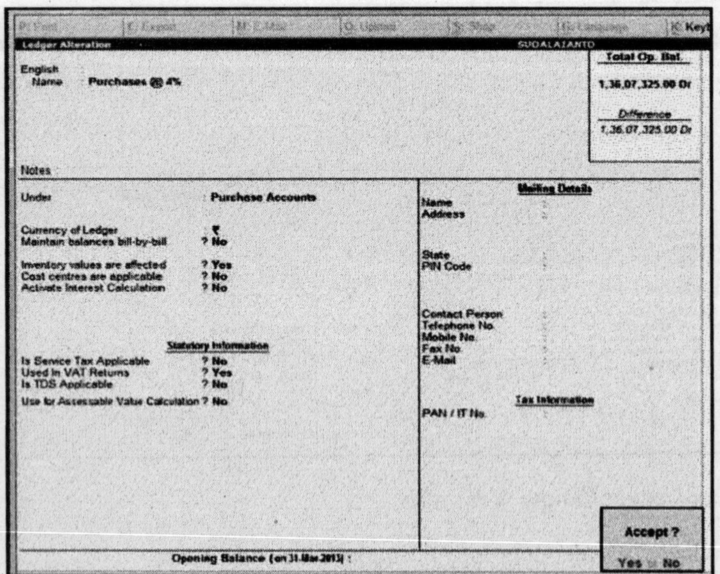

Like in the Purchase Ledger screen, select the required VAT/Tax classification in the Sales Ledger as well.

Go to Gateway of Tally.ERP ▸ Accounts Info ▸ Ledger ▸ Create/Alter

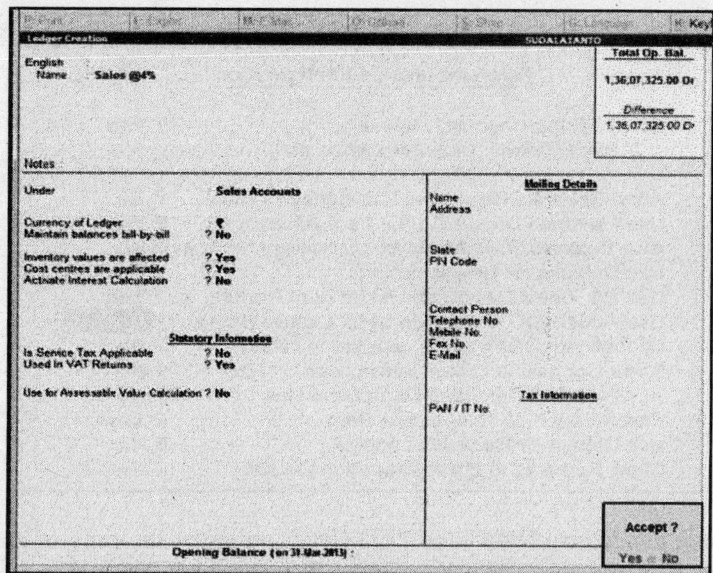

Used in VAT Return: Set this to Yes if you wish to select VAT/Tax class for this ledger. Tally.ERP gives the flexibility to the user to either have the classification selected in the Ledger Master tagged to all transactions (or) select different classifications each time during voucher entries. The rest of the ledger creation process is the same as in default Tally.ERP. In the above example we have selected a VAT class of 4%. The rest of the settings are the same as in default Tally.ERP.

Step 5 Create your respective Party Ledger (i.e., Sundry Creditors and Sundry Debtors).

Gateway of Tally.ERP ▸ Master ▸ Accounts Info ▸ Single Ledger ▸ Create

Under Sundry Creditor Group create the following Ledgers:

(a) Rohiniraj Infotech

(b) Sudalai Anto India

Under Sundry Debtor Group create the following Ledgers:

(a) Vinayakan Vidyasagar

(b) Dharshikha

(c) Harshika

Step- 6 Create your Product/Items for "Antivirus CD" and "Monitor".

Gateway of Tally.ERP ▸ Master ▸ Inventory Info ▸ Stock Item ▸ Create

Step- 7 Input the Transactions for Purchase in the Invoice Mode and configure the Voucher Entry Screen by using F12 key and set option "Use Common Ledger a/c for item allocation" as "Yes".

Gateway of Tally.ERP ▸ Accounting Voucher ▸ Purchase (F9)

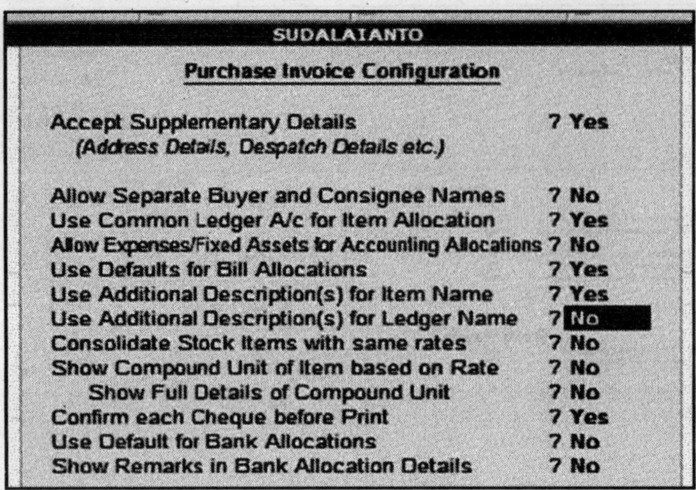

Create Other Ledgers such as "Excise Duty" and "ED Cess" online at the time of entry, set option VAT/Tax as "Other".

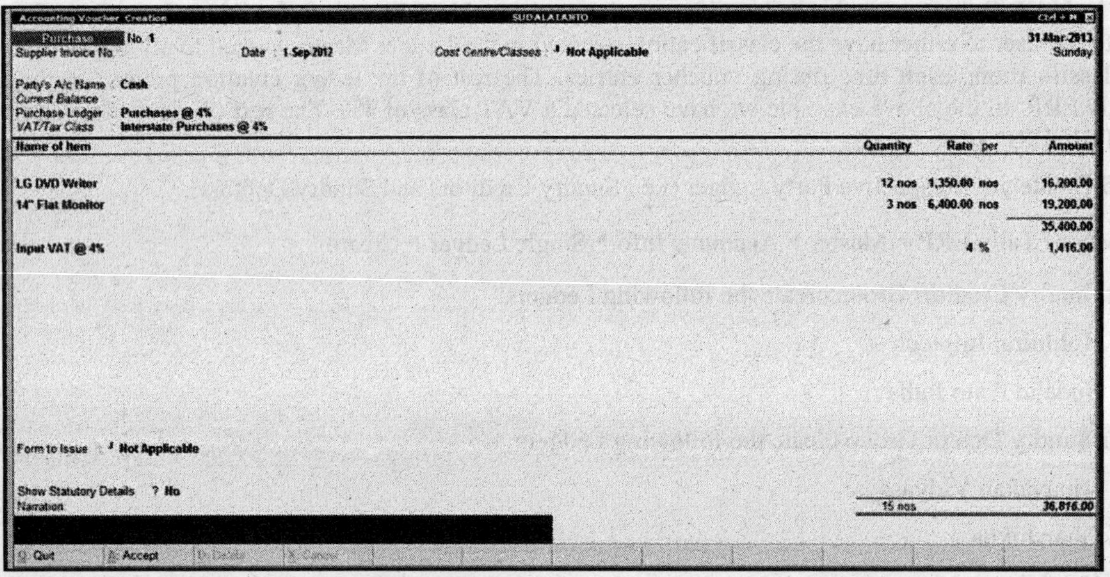

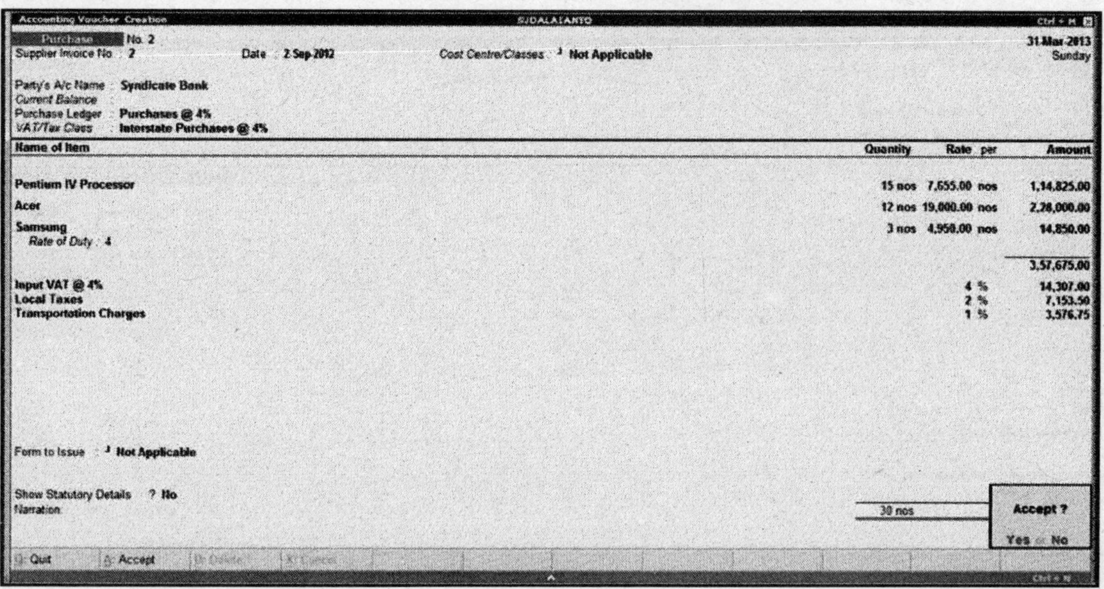

Step 8 Enter your Sales Transaction as given below:

Gateway of Tally.ERP ▸ Accounting Vouchers ▸ Sales (F8) (Invoice Mode)

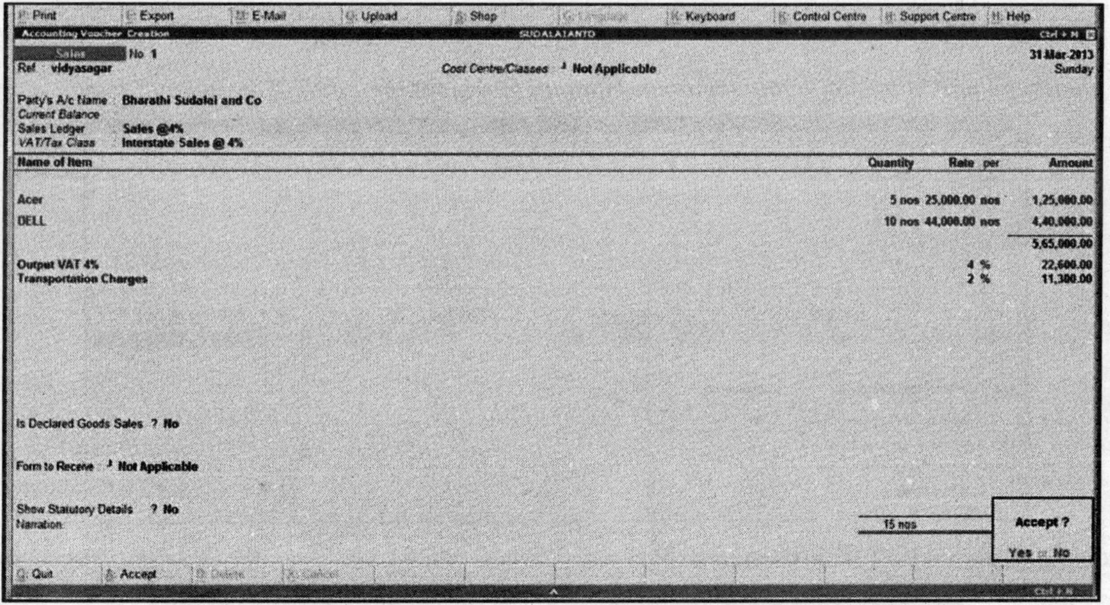

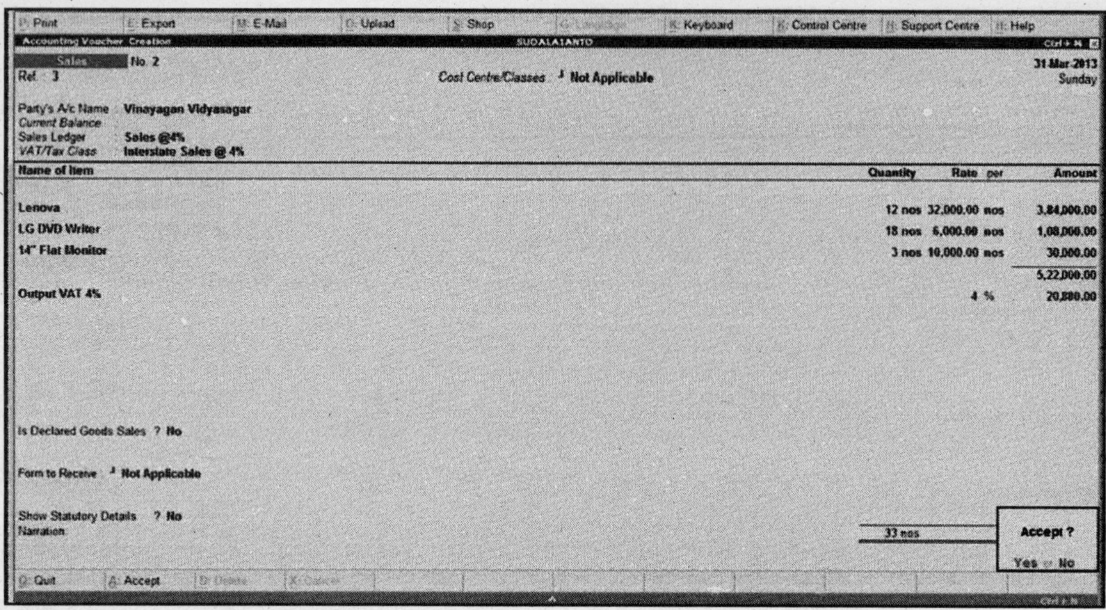

Creating a VAT Adjustment Class for Journal

To create a VAT Adjustment Class,

Go to Gateway of Tally ►Accounts Info. ► Voucher Types ► Alter ► Journal

In the Voucher Type Alteration screen, enter the Name of Class, for e.g., VAT Adjustment Class.

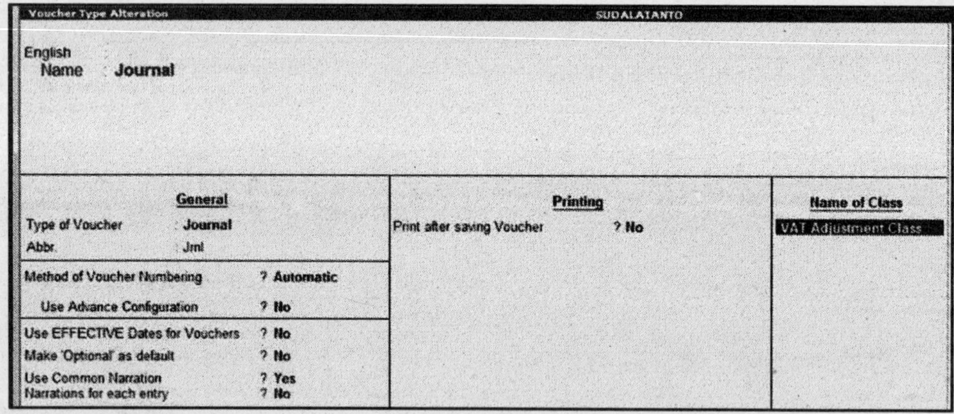

Set the 'Use Class for VAT Adjustments' to Yes.

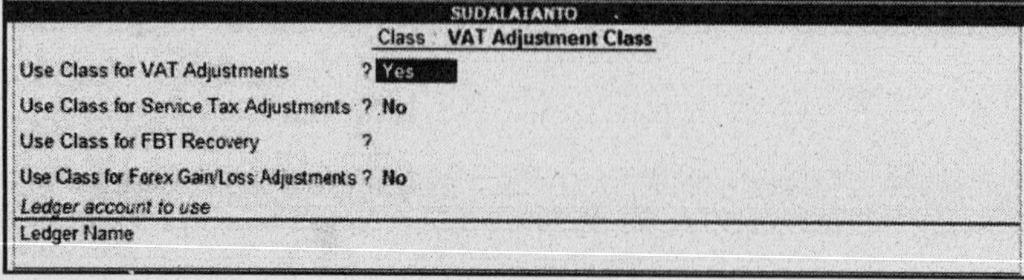

- ❖ Press Enter to go back to Voucher Type Alteration screen.
- ❖ Press Y or Enter to accept and save the screen.

How to compute VAT and Generate Report

Gateway of Tally.ERP ▸ Display Statutory Reports▸ VAT Computation

Particulars	Assessable Value	Tax Amount
Sales		
A. Output Tax		
CST @ 4%	10,87,000.00	43,480.00
Total Output Tax	10,87,000.00	43,480.00
Purchases		
Excess Input Credit Brought Forward		
Others (VAT Not Applicable)		
Interstate Purchases @ 4%	16,76,325.00	67,053.00
Total Input Credit	16,76,325.00	67,053.00
VAT Refundable/Carried Forward		23,573.00

Assessable Value: The assessable value is the sum of the total value of goods at which they are purchased and sold. This assessable value forms the value on which VAT is calculated.

Tax Amount: The total tax amount calculated on assessable value using the respective tax percentage is the tax amount.

VAT Computation – VAT and CST Details: You can configure the VAT computation screen to display all the VAT classifications and CST details by setting the options as given below in the F12: Configuration.

❖ Set Show All VAT Classifications to Yes

❖ Set Show CST Details to Yes

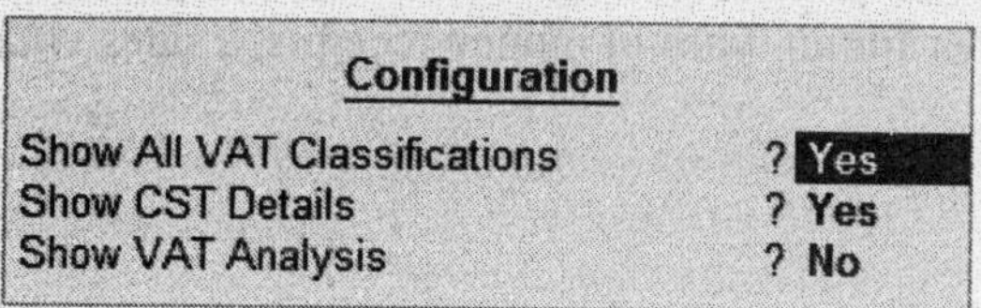

12.8 ACCOUNTING VOUCHERS IN TALLY.ERP 9

Accounting vouchers are used to record all accounts related transactions in Tally.ERP 9. You can selectively set the configuration for entry to allow only those features, which you require while entering vouchers.

Tally comprises of the following predefined vouchers, to suit different business requirements for recording various transactions. Tally also allows you to create user-defined vouchers (Voucher Types) as per your requirements.

❖ Contra Voucher

❖ Payment Voucher

❖ Receipt Voucher

❖ Journal Voucher

- ❖ Sales Voucher/Invoice
- ❖ Debit Note Voucher
- ❖ Credit Note Voucher
- ❖ Purchase Voucher/Invoice

Go to Gateway of Tally ▸ Display ▸ List of Accounts ▸ Ctrl + V [Voucher Types], you will be displayed the following screen

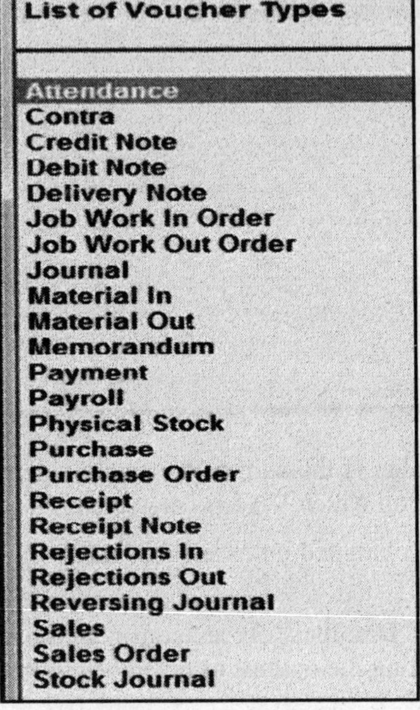

A voucher is the primary online document for recording transactions. Tally.ERP 9 provides 16 different predefined voucher formats. These are used for recording different types of transactions. A payment voucher is used for all types of payments, a receipt voucher for all types of money receipts, a sales voucher for recording sales transactions, and so on.

Types of Vouchers

Tally.ERP 9 is preprogrammed with a variety of accounting vouchers, each designed to perform a different job. Tally also allows you to create user-defined vouchers (Voucher Types) as per your requirements. The standard vouchers are:

- ❖ Payment Voucher
- ❖ Receipt Voucher
- ❖ Contra Voucher
- ❖ Sales Voucher
    - Sales Orders
    - Sales Vouchers/Invoices
    - Delivery Notes
    - Rejection In

❖ Purchase Voucher

- Purchase Orders
- Purchase Vouchers
- Goods Receipt Notes
- Rejection Out

❖ Journal Voucher

- Credit Notes
- Debit Notes
- Journal

❖ Memo Voucher

- Reversing Journal

❖ Stock Journal

❖ Physical Stock

Voucher Entry

This option allows you to configure the vouchers entries in Tally.ERP 9, both the Accounting and Inventory Vouchers can be configured from this menu for additional information.

Go to Gateway of Tally ▸ F12: Configure ▸ Voucher Entry. The Voucher Entry Configuration is shown below:

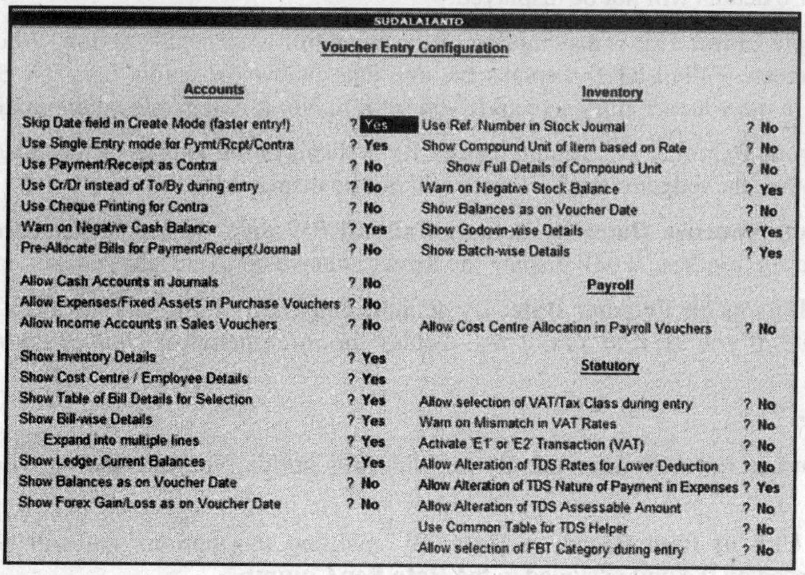

SUDALAIANTO

Voucher Entry Configuration

Accounts

Skip Date field in Create Mode (faster entry!)	? Yes
Use Single Entry mode for Pymt/Rcpt/Contra	? Yes
Use Payment/Receipt as Contra	? No
Use Cr/Dr instead of To/By during entry	? No
Use Cheque Printing for Contra	? No
Warn on Negative Cash Balance	? Yes
Pre-Allocate Bills for Payment/Receipt/Journal	? No
Allow Cash Accounts in Journals	? No
Allow Expenses/Fixed Assets in Purchase Vouchers	? No
Allow Income Accounts in Sales Vouchers	? No
Show Inventory Details	? Yes
Show Cost Centre / Employee Details	? Yes
Show Table of Bill Details for Selection	? Yes
Show Bill-wise Details	? Yes
Expand into multiple lines	? Yes
Show Ledger Current Balances	? Yes
Show Balances as on Voucher Date	? No
Show Forex Gain/Loss as on Voucher Date	? No

Inventory

Use Ref. Number in Stock Journal	? No
Show Compound Unit of item based on Rate	? No
Show Full Details of Compound Unit	? No
Warn on Negative Stock Balance	? Yes
Show Balances as on Voucher Date	? No
Show Godown-wise Details	? Yes
Show Batch-wise Details	? Yes

Payroll

Allow Cost Centre Allocation in Payroll Vouchers	? No

Statutory

Allow selection of VAT/Tax Class during entry	? No
Warn on Mismatch in VAT Rates	? No
Activate 'E1' or 'E2' Transaction (VAT)	? No
Allow Alteration of TDS Rates for Lower Deduction	? No
Allow Alteration of TDS Nature of Payment in Expenses	? Yes
Allow Alteration of TDS Assessable Amount	? No
Use Common Table for TDS Helper	? No
Allow selection of FBT Category during entry	? No

By default, the above configuration options are displayed in the Voucher Entry Configuration screen, which can be changed as per requirements. Depending upon the Company Features, options get added in **Voucher Entry Configuration**. For instance, if you enable **Allow Multi Currency** option in **F11: Accounting Features, Show Forex Gain/Loss as on Voucher Date** option gets added in Voucher Entry Configuration.

Skip Date Field in Creation Mode (for faster entry): By default, the cursor skips the date field during voucher creation. If you do not want to skip the date field then set this option to **No**.

Use Single Entry Mode for Payment/Receipt/Contra: By default, Tally.ERP 9 displays single entry mode for payment/receipt/contra entry. If you want to display it in double entry mode, then set this option to **No**.

Use Payment/Receipt as Contra: By enabling this option, you can enter contra in payment as well as receipt voucher.

Use Cr/Dr instead of To/By During Entry: By enabling this option, you can change **To/By** to **Cr/Dr** in the Voucher Entry screen.

Use Cheque Printing for Contra: By enabling this option, you can print the cheques from Contra Voucher itself while making the inter-bank transfers and cash withdrawals. The cheque printing option will appear for the Bank which is credited.

Warn on Negative Cash Balance: By default, Tally.ERP 9 displays a **Negative Cash balance warning Message**. If you set it to **No**, this error message will not be displayed.

Pre-allocate Bills for Payment/Receipt: By enabling this option, you can pre-allocate the bills before specifying the ledger amount.

Allow Cash Accounts in Journal: By enabling this option, you can select cash and also bank account in journal.

Allow Expenses/Fixed Assets in Purchase Voucher: By enabling this option, you can select the expenses and also Fixed Asset ledger in Purchase Voucher Entry.

Allow income accounts in Sales Voucher: By enabling this option, you can select the income ledger in sales voucher entry.

Show Inventory Details: By default, Tally.ERP 9 displays inventory details in the voucher entry screen. If you set it to **No**, the inventory details will not be displayed.

Show Table of Bill Details for Selection: By default, Tally.ERP 9 displays pending bills list of a ledger account in the voucher entry screen. If you set it to **No**, the pending bills list will not be displayed.

Show Bill-wise Details: By default, bill-wise details of a ledger account are displayed in the voucher entry screen. If you set it to **No**, bill-wise details will not be displayed.

Expand into Multiple Lines: This is a suboption of the show bill-wise details option. When you enter credit days in the bill-wise details screen, Tally.ERP 9 displays the due date below the credit days. By default, it displays both credit days and Due date in the voucher entry screen. If you set it to **No**, it will display only credit days.

Show Ledger Current Balance: By default, Tally.ERP 9 displays the ledger current balance up to last voucher entry date. If you set it to **No**, the ledger current balance will not be displayed.

Show Balance as on Voucher Date: By default, Tally.ERP 9 displays the ledger current balance up to last voucher entry date. If you set it to **Yes**, it will display the ledger balance up to current voucher entry date.

Show Forex Gain/Loss as on Voucher Date: By default, Tally.ERP 9 displays the forex gain/loss balance up to the last voucher entry date. If you set it to **Yes**, it will display the forex gain/loss balance up to current voucher entry date.

Inventory Vouchers

Use Reference Number in Stock Journal: By enabling this option, you can add the voucher reference field in stock journal also.

Show Compound Unit of Item Based on Rate: By enabling this option, you will be allowed to show the compound unit of item based on the unit provided in the **Rate Per Column**.

Show Full Details of Compound Unit: Enabling this option will display full details of compound unit in the **Quantity** field. If **kgs** is typed in rate **per** field, the quantity field will display as **12 Kgs.250 grms**.

Warn on Negative Stock Balance: By default, Tally.ERP 9 displays a warning message for negative stock balance. If you set it to **No**, the error message will not be displayed.

Honour Expiry Dates Usage for Batches: By default, Tally.ERP 9 displays expiry batches in the list of active batches during voucher entry. If you set it to **No**, expiry batches will not be displayed in the list of active batches.

Show Balances as on Voucher Date: By default, Tally.ERP 9 displays the stock item balance up to the last voucher entry date. If you set it to **Yes**, it will display the stock item balance up to current voucher entry date.

Show Godown-wise Details: This option is used only in the case of rejection in and rejection out vouchers. By default, Tally.ERP 9 displays the godown details in rejection in/out vouchers. If you set it to **No**, the godown details will not be displayed in rejection in/out vouchers.

Show Batch-wise Details: This option is used to display batch information pertaining to stock items during voucher entry. If you set it to **No**, the batch-wise details will not be displayed.

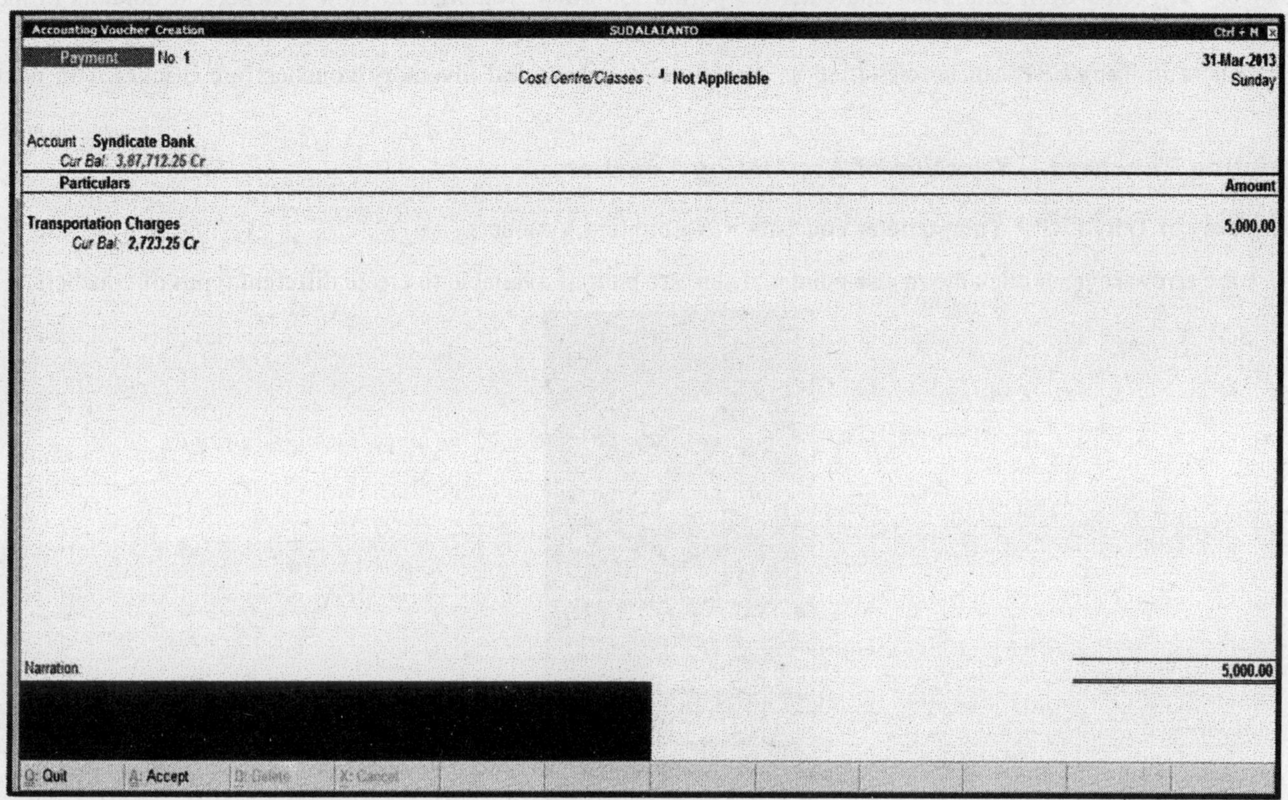

Voucher Entry Screen Components

Main Voucher Entry Area: The main voucher entry area is where you enter all your transactions. This area has fields for date, ledger name and amount as well as additional pop-up screens that are dependent on your voucher configuration and the nature of transaction you make.

Button Bar: The button bar area displays buttons that provide quick links to various functions and features of Tally.ERP 9. Buttons that are relevant to the current task are enabled and the other buttons are disabled.

Calculator Area: The calculator area provides a working space where you can enter any number of mathematical formulae for complex calculations. Press Ctrl+N to navigate to the calculator area and press Ctrl+M to toggle back to main voucher entry area.

"Press Alt+C to use calculator when at amount field."

Special Keys for Voucher Narration Field

ALT+R: Recalls the last narration saved for the first ledger in the voucher, irrespective of the voucher type.

CTRL+R: Recalls the last narration saved for a specific voucher type, irrespective of the ledger.

Checking the Accuracy of the Vouchers: To check the accuracy of the vouchers that you have entered:

Go to Gateway of Tally ▸ Display ▸ Day Book

Select **F2:** Period from button bar and enter the period for which you want to view vouchers. It defaults to the current date only but you may display all the transactions for a particular period.

Vouchers in Tally.ERP can be classified as Accounts Vouchers and inventory vouchers are discussed in next chapter.

Accounting Vouchers —Selection of Accounting Vouchers

Gateway of Tally.ERP ▸ Transactions/Vouchers ▸ Accounting Vouchers

Use the arrow keys, or click the mouse pointer. There are buttons available to create different types of vouchers.

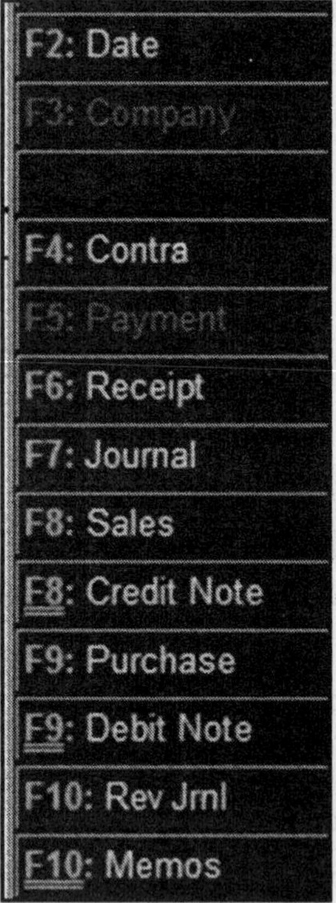

Contra Voucher (F4): The contra voucher can be passed using single entry mode or double entry mode. To toggle between single entry and double entry mode, we need to change the setting use single entry mode for Pymt/Rcpt/Contra **to** Yes/No **in** F12 configuration.

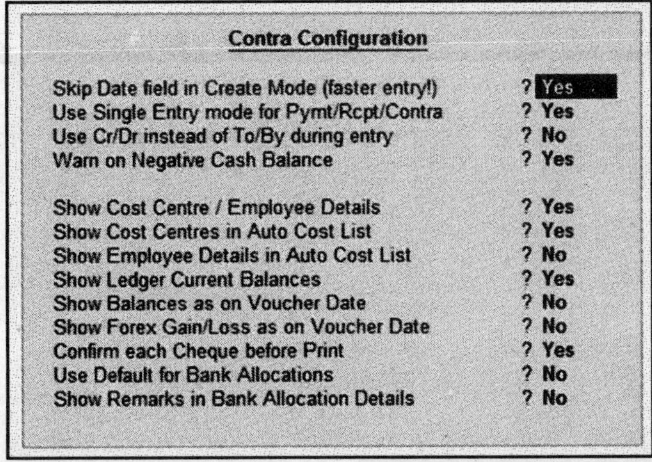

This voucher is used for fund transfers between cash and bank accounts only. Like fund transfer from one Bank/Cash account to another Bank/Cash account, Cash Deposit/Withdrawals into/from Bank.

Following steps will guide you to have Receipt Voucher creation screen.

Gateway of Tally.ERP ▸ Accounting Voucher ▸ Click on F4

Contra button present on the button panel to have the contra voucher creation screen. The following vouchers can be done through the contra vouchers:

1. Cash Deposited into Bank
2. Cash Withdrawal from the Bank
3. Funds Transfer from one Bank to another Bank
4. Cash Transfer to Petty Cash

   (i) Transaction: Cash Deposited Rs. 2,00,000 in the Bank of India (BoI)

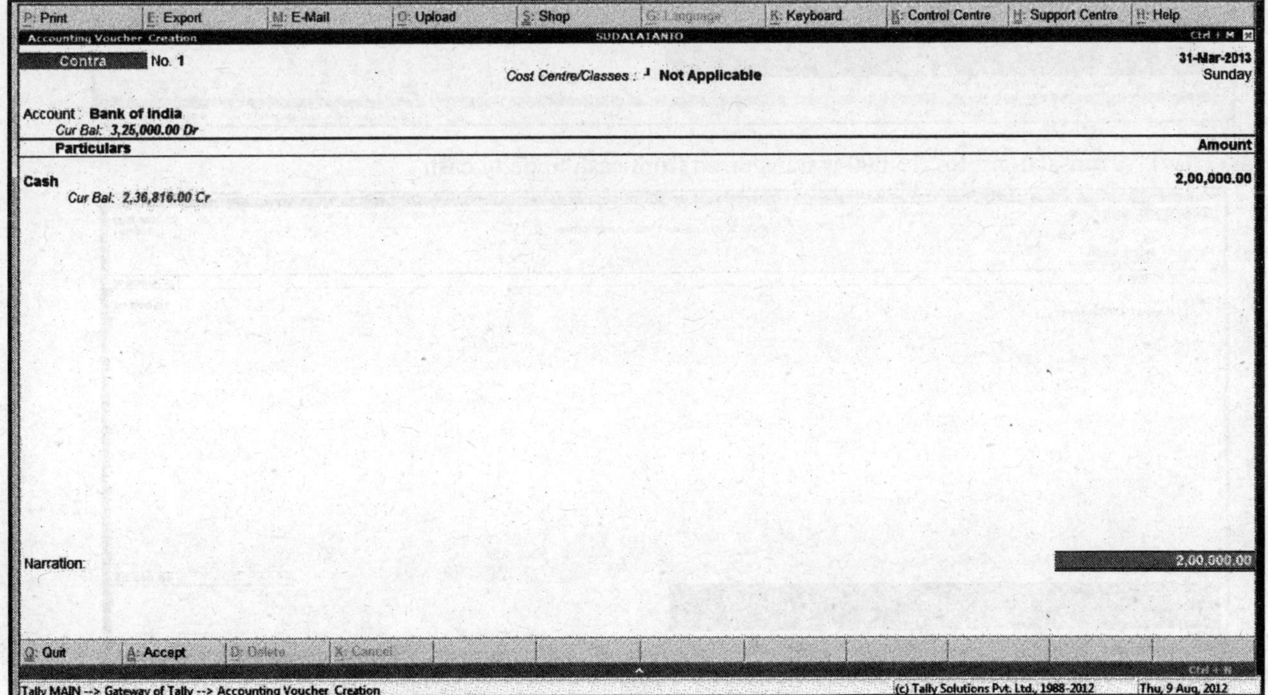

(ii) Transaction: Cash Withdrawal from the Bank Rs. 55,000

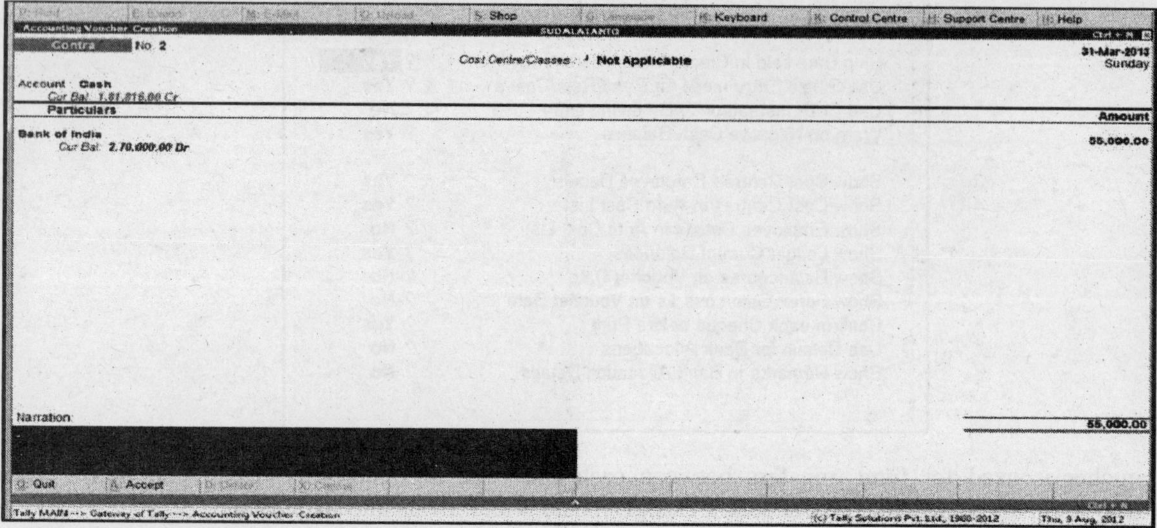

(iii) Transactions: Rs. 1,00,000 are transferred from Bank of India to Syndicate Bank

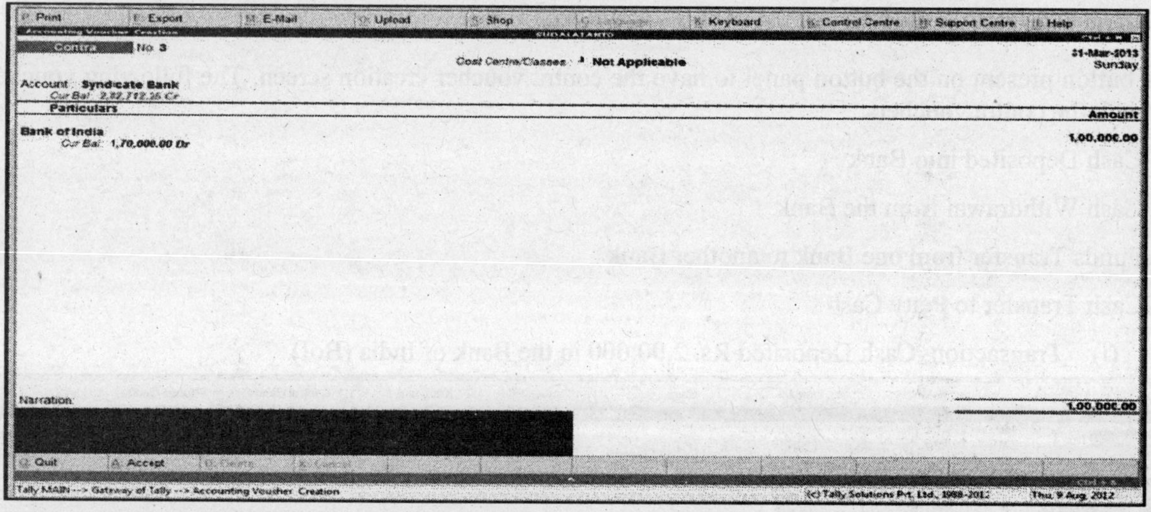

(iv) Transactions: Rs. 15,000 is transferred from cash to petty cash

Accounting Voucher Creation
SUDALAIANTO
Contra No. 4
Cost Centre/Classes : Not Applicable
31-Mar-2013
Sunday
Account : Petty Cash
Cur Bal: 15,000.00 Dr
Particulars
Amount
Cash
Cur Bal: 1,36,816.00 Cr
15,000.00
Narration:
15,000.00
Q: Quit
A: Accept
Tally MAIN --> Gateway of Tally --> Accounting Voucher Creation
(c) Tally Solutions Pvt. Ltd., 1988-2012
Thu 9 Aug, 2012

Payment Vouchers (F5): This voucher records all the payments made through Bank and Cash. It is also used for payment of fixed assets, purchases, dues to creditors, loans and advances given, payment of loans and advances given to you earlier.

Gateway of Tally.ERP ▸ Accounting Voucher ▸ Click on F5

Payment button present on the button panel to have the payment voucher creation screen. **Transactions:** Paid salary of Rs. 12,500 and office rent of Rs. 8,000 by cheque of Bank of India as on 2nd October, 2012.

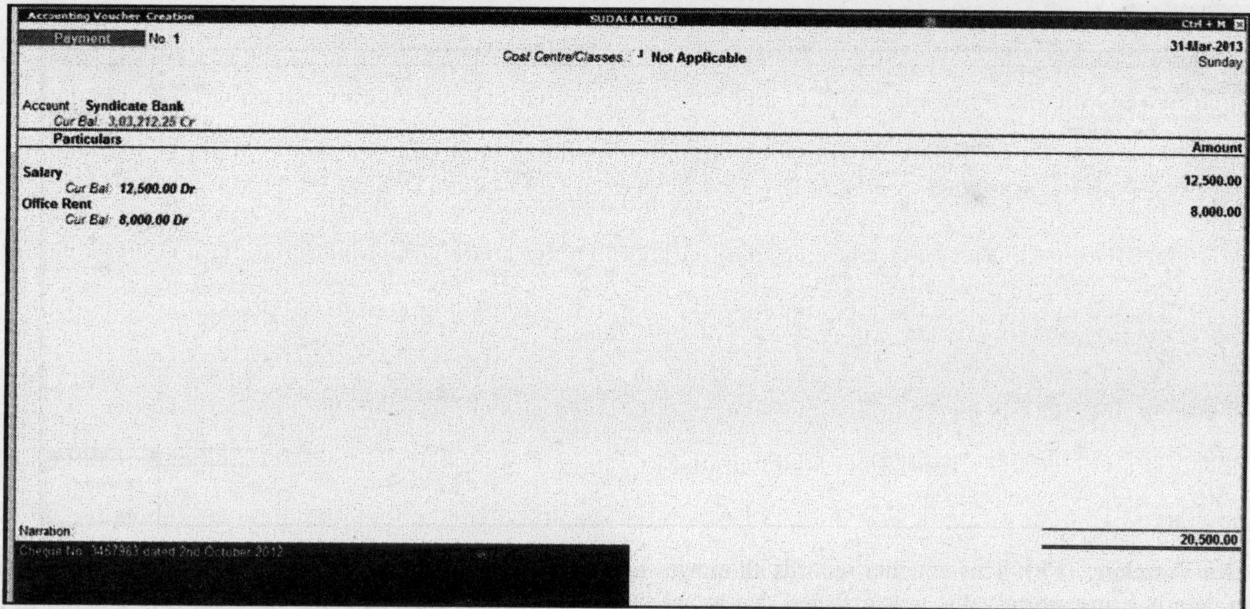

Receipt Voucher (F6): The purpose of these vouchers is to record all receipts into bank or cash accounts. Such receipt from debtors, any income, refund of loans or advances given earlier, sale of fixed assets, etc.

Gateway of Tally.ERP ▸ Accounting Voucher ▸ Click on F6

Receipt button present on the button panel to have the receipt voucher crea tion screen.

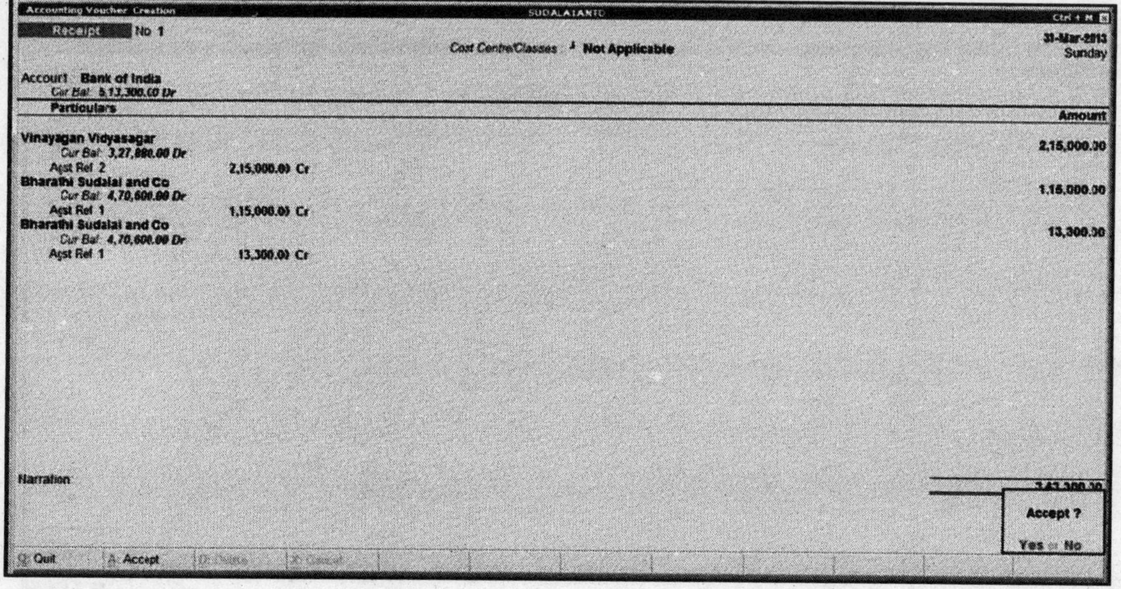

Journal Vouchers (F7): It is for adjustment between any two ledgers. No outside parties, like debtors, creditors, and branches/divisions are involved. These are for rectification entries in which as any kind of adjustment for non-cash or bank transactions are recorded here.

Gateway of Tally.ERP ▸ Accounting Voucher ▸ Click on F7

Journal Transactions: Depreciation charge on furniture Rs. 15,000

Sales Vouchers (F8): This voucher records all entries related to sales including cash and credit. You need to enter the item details if inventory value gets affected due to sales. The entries for cash sale are automatically entered in the cash book or bank book.

Gateway of Tally.ERP ▸ Accounting Voucher ▸ Click on F8

Sale Transactions: Sold the following items to M/s. Bharathi Sudalai and Co., on credit with VAT- 4%. Name of Items: Lenova (22 items/Rs. 32,000 each), Samsung (15 nos./Rs. 5,300 each), LG DVD Writer (22 nos./Rs. 6, 000 each) and DELL (21 nos./Rs. 44,000 each)

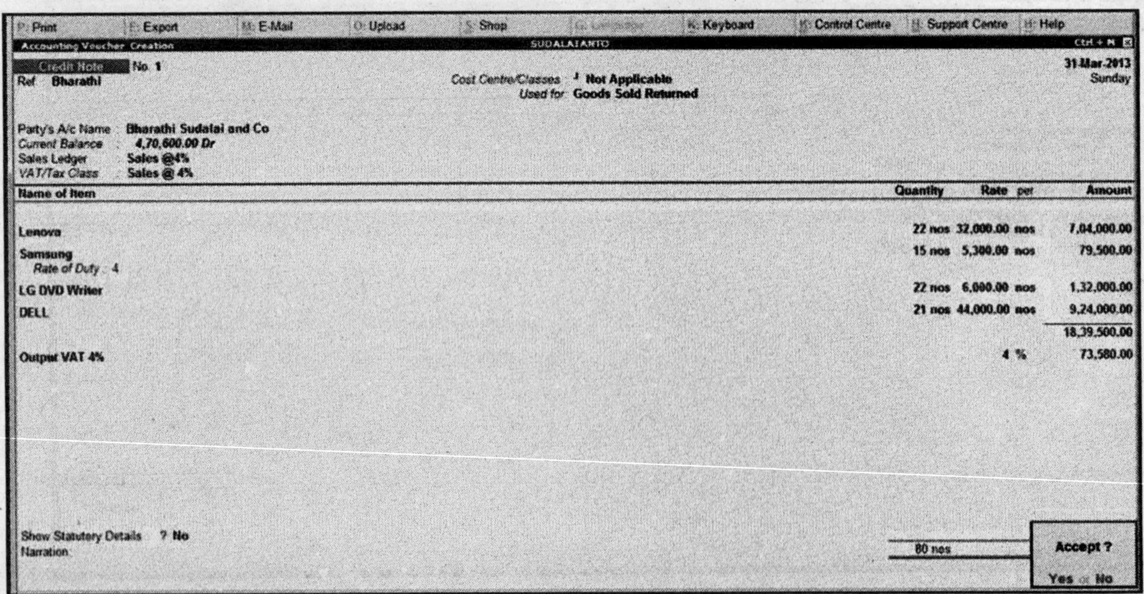

Credit Note Voucher (Ctrl + F8) – Sales Return

Credit note are used for giving credit to the party, for example, when a buyer returns the goods (SALE RETURN) or allows himself credit due to rate difference or discount or due to some adjustment. This voucher type will be available after configuration of F11 features.

Transaction: Goods returned by M/s. Bharathi Sudalai and Co., of the following items with VAT adjustment 4%. one DELL Computer and one LG DVD Writer.

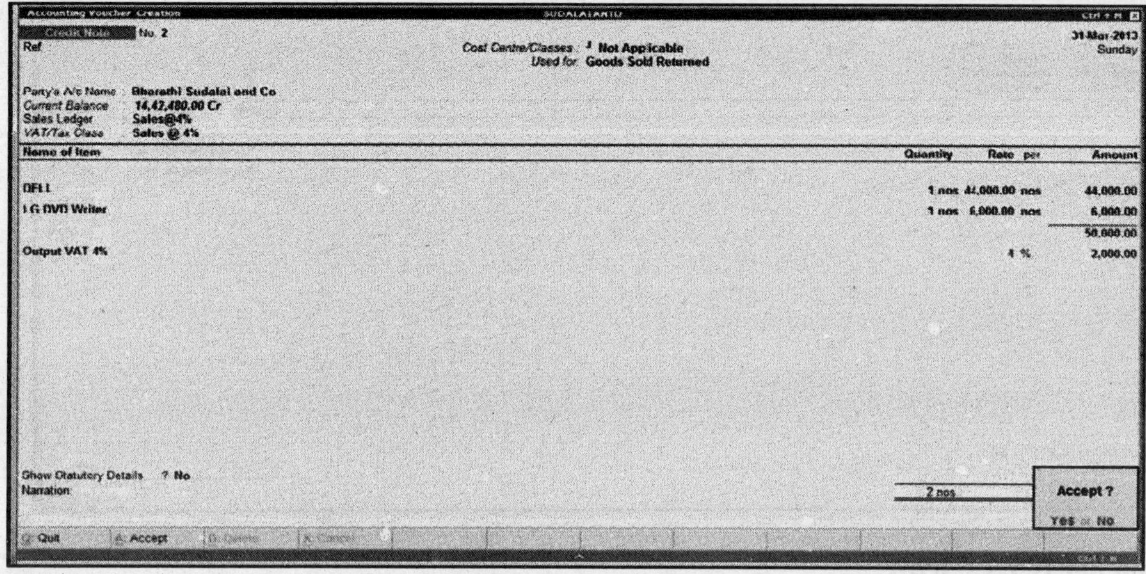

Purchase Vouchers (F9): This voucher records all entries related to purchase including cash and credit. You need to enter the item details if inventory value gets affected due to purchase. The entries for cash purchase are automatically entered in the cash book or bank book.

Gateway of Tally.ERP ▸ Accounting Voucher ▸ Click on F9

Purchase Transactions: Purchase the following items from M/s. Jehovah Jireh on credit with VAT- 4% with a trade discount of 7% Lenova-34 Items @ Rs. 40,000 each, DELL-50 items @ Rs. 65,000 each and Samsung – 25 items @ 4,950 each.

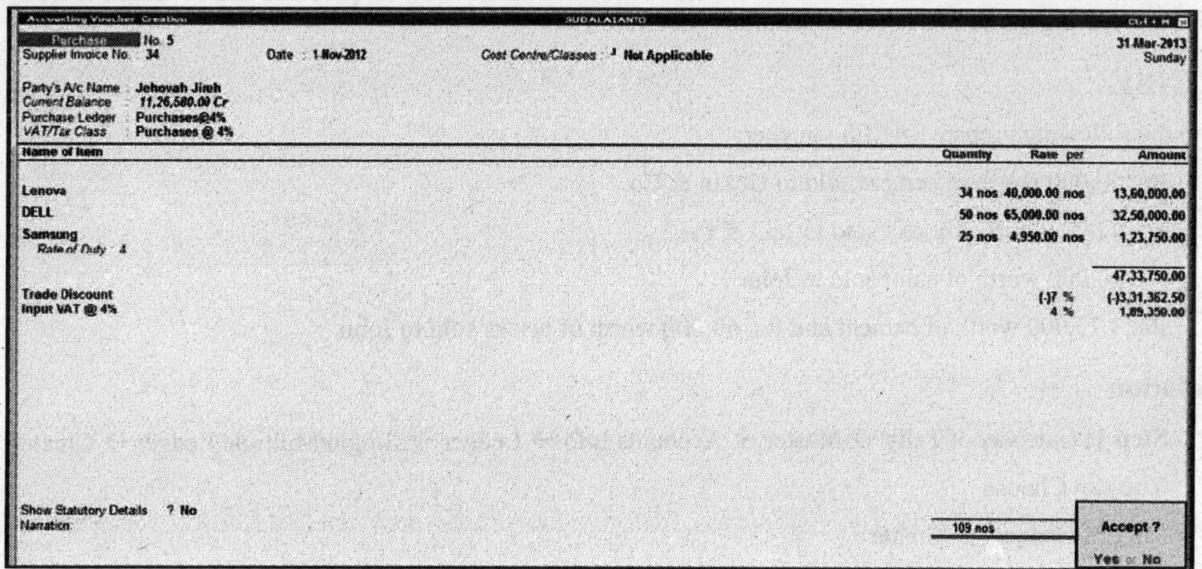

Debit Note Voucher (Ctrl + F9) – Purchase Return

Debit notes are used for debiting party accounts, for example, in case of purchase return or when your supplier has granted you credit due to different reasons. This voucher type will be available after configuration of F11 features.

Transaction: Following goods are returned to M/s. Jehovah Jireh: 4 DELL and 5 Samsung.

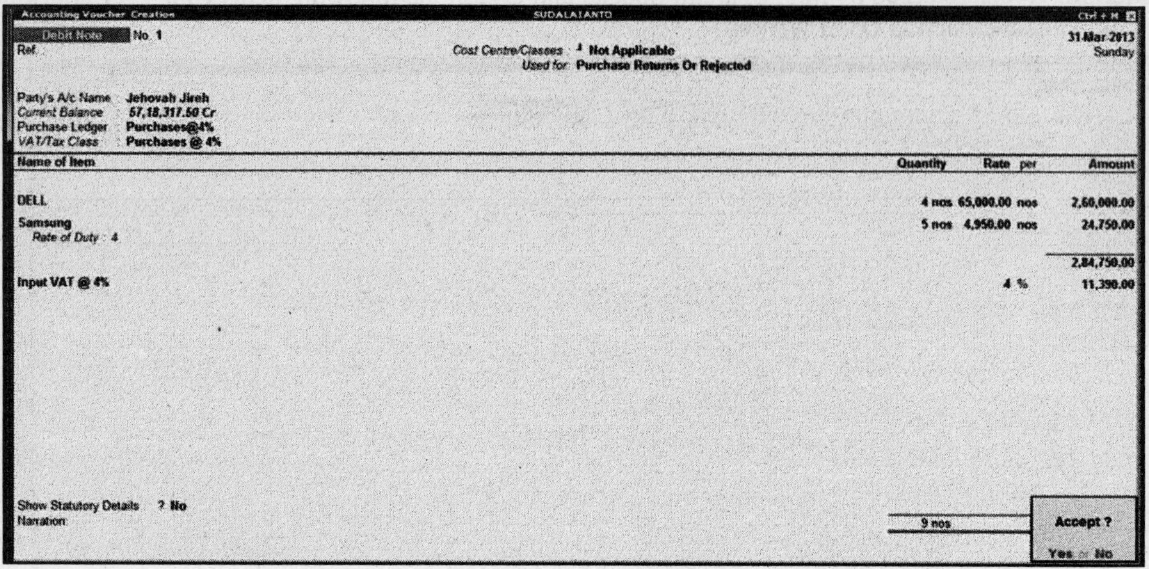

Memo Voucher (Ctrl + F10)

As the name implies, it is a non-accounting voucher whose entries do not affect your accounts at all. The entries in this voucher are not posted into ledgers, instead are stored in a separate memo register. A memo voucher can be converted into a regular voucher, to be included in your books of accounts.

Gateway of Tally.ERP ▸ Accounting Voucher ▸ Click on F10

This type of memo voucher, which can be used in many situations such as suspense accounts: In case, an employee takes an advance amount for his official purchase expenses. Till the expenses are incurred, the actual expenditure details cannot be worked out. A Memo Voucher can be entered for advance and can be turned to a payment voucher after receiving the details of the expenditure incurred.

EXERCISE

From the following prepare SALES voucher:

1. Rs. 50,000 worth of cement sold to Gokul & Co.
2. Rs. 4,000 worth of bricks sold to Jain & Co.
3. Rs. 10,000 worth of paint sold to John
4. Rs. 3,75,000 worth of cement and Rs. 60,000 worth of bricks sold to John

Tally Solution

Step 1: Gateway of Tally → Master → Accounts Info → Ledger → Single/Multiple Ledger → Create

You can Choose

Multiple ledgers → Create

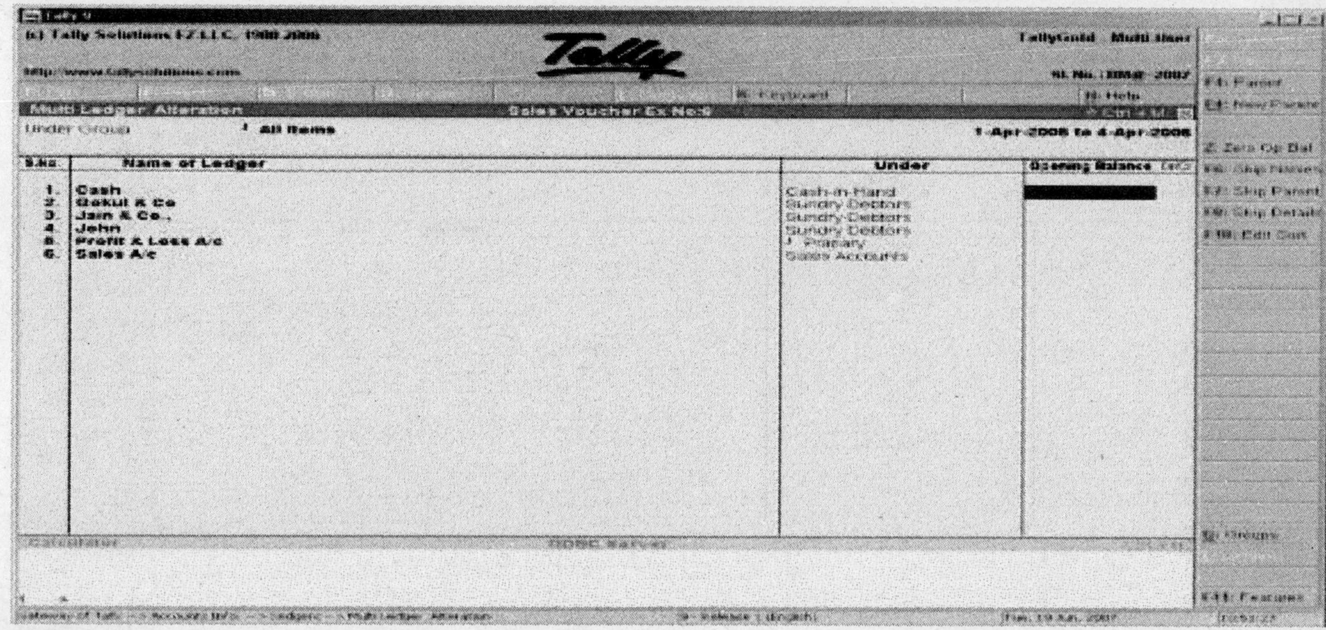

Step 2

Go to Gateway of Tally → Accounting Vouchers → Select F8: Sales.

Rules for Sales Entry

I. Credit Sales

The Receiver is –[Customer] [Debit]

The Giver is [Credit]

II. Cash Sales: [use Receipt Voucher F6 key]

Cash a/c	Dr.
What goes out	Cr.

Credit Sales

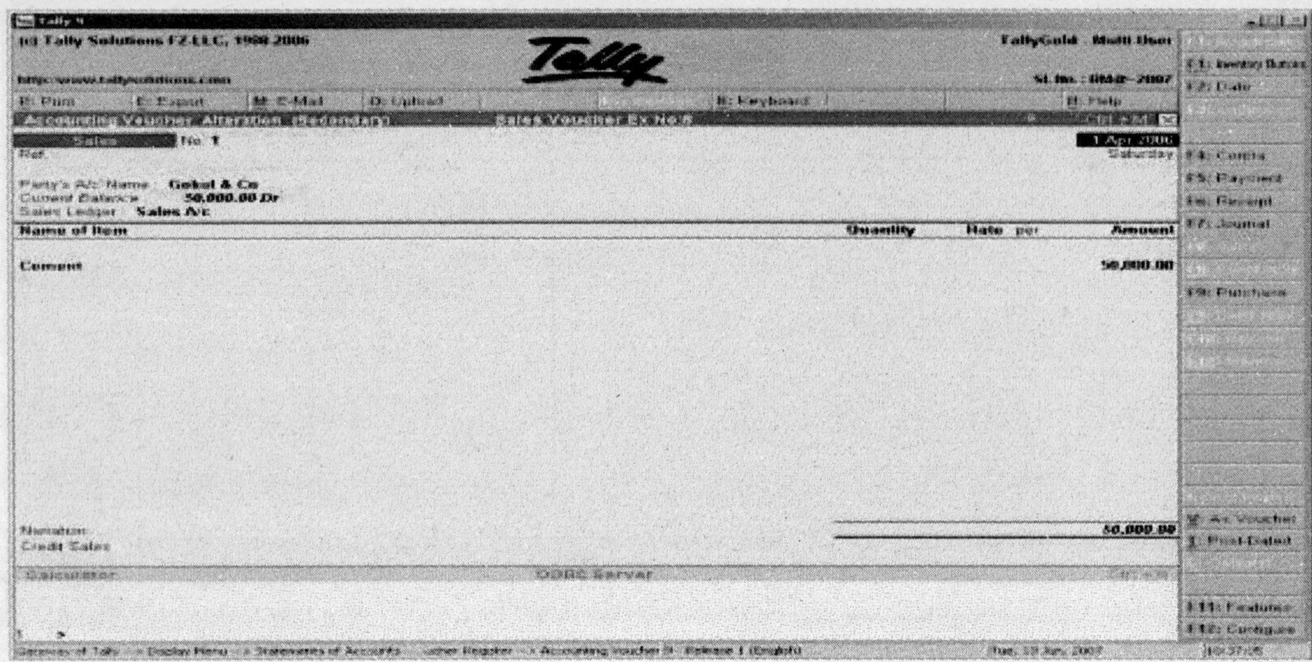

Despatch Details in Sales Invoice

Use F12 "configuration"

Accept Supplementary Details →Yes

(Address Details, Despatch Details, etc.,)

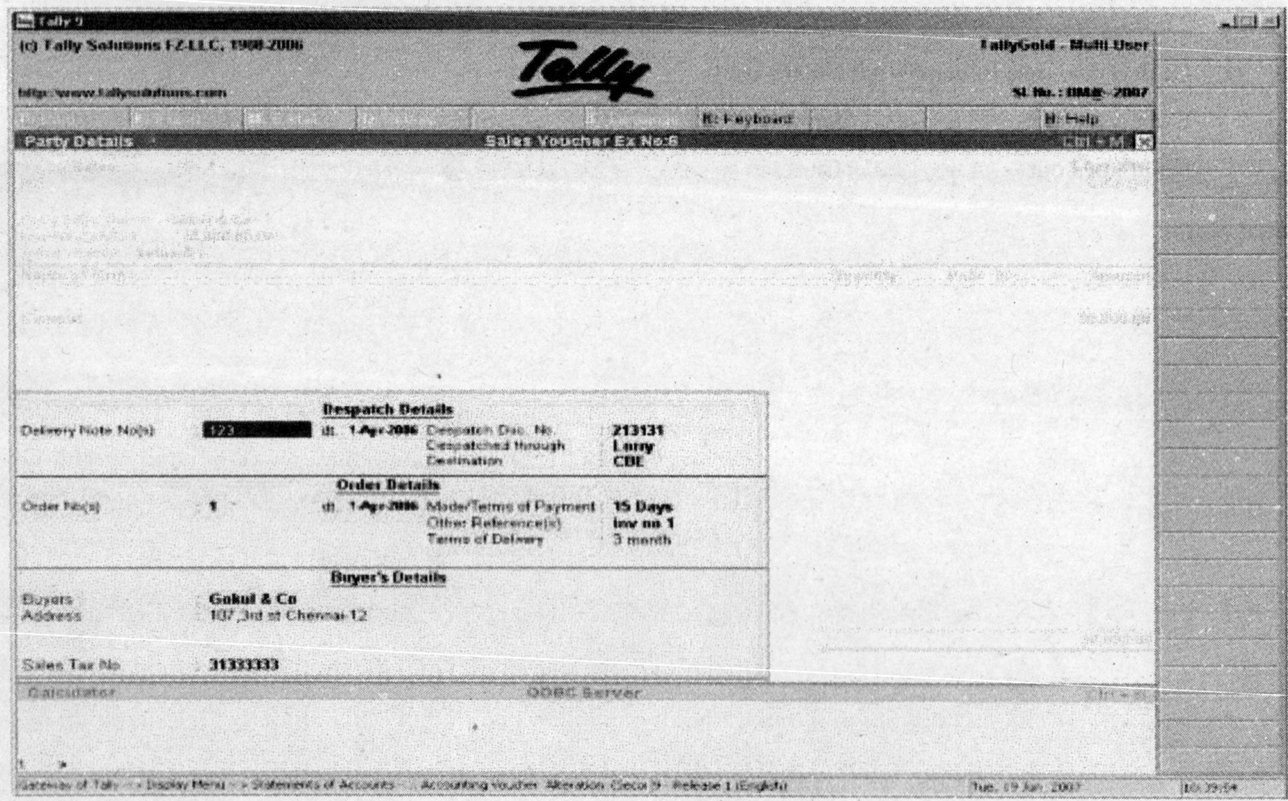

Accounting Voucher "Screen"

Press "**Ctrl+V**" — On Sales Entry Screen to view Sample Entry

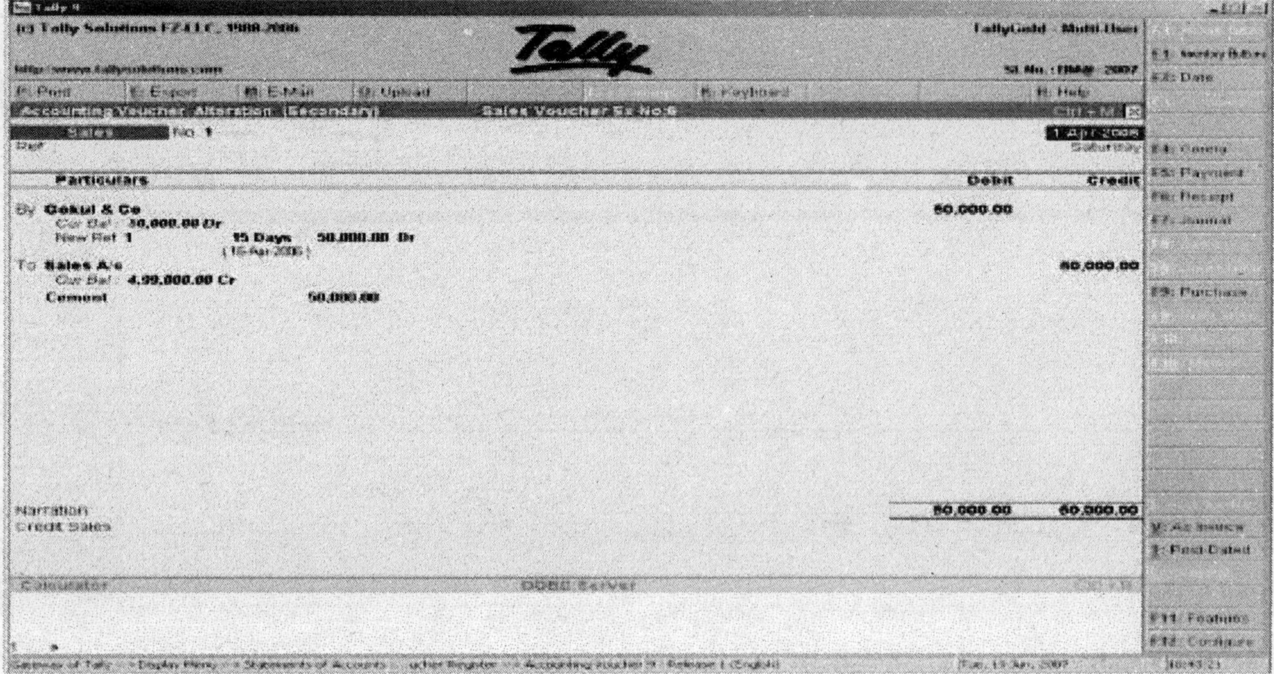

Note: Use F11 –Feature

Invoicing

Allow Invoicing

Enter Purchase in Invoice Format → **Yes**

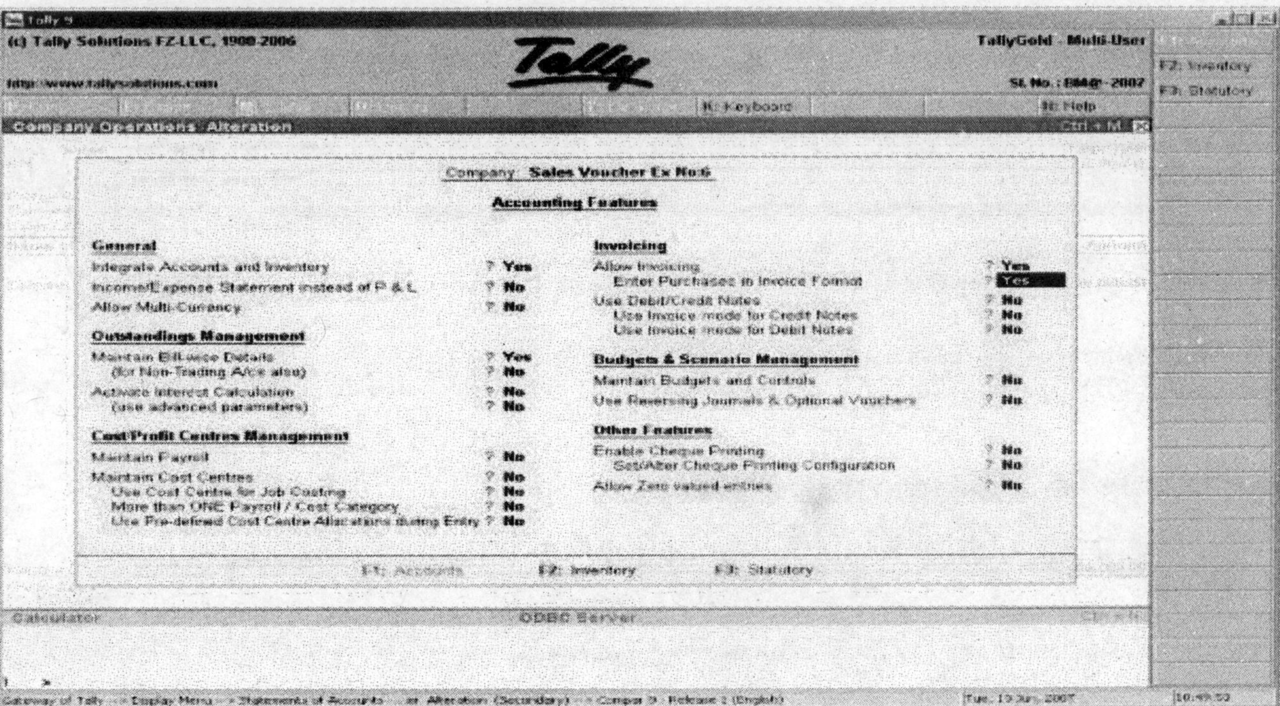

Sales Register

Display → Accounts Book → Sales Register — [Key Press "DAS"]

(c) Tally Solutions FZ LLC, 1988-2006
Tally
TallyGold - Multi-User
Sales Register
Sales Voucher Ex No:6
Particulars
Sales
Sales Voucher Ex No:6
1-Apr-2006 to 4-Apr-2006
Transactions
Debit
Credit
Closing Balance
April
May
June
July
August
September
October
November
December
January
February
March
Grand Total 4,99,000.00 4,99,000.00 Cr
Apr May Jun Jul Aug Sep Oct Nov Dec Jan Feb Mar

Extract Sales Entry

Display → Accounts Book → Sales Register — [Key Press "DAS"]

Press "Enter key"

Use F6 Key — Extract

Tally Display

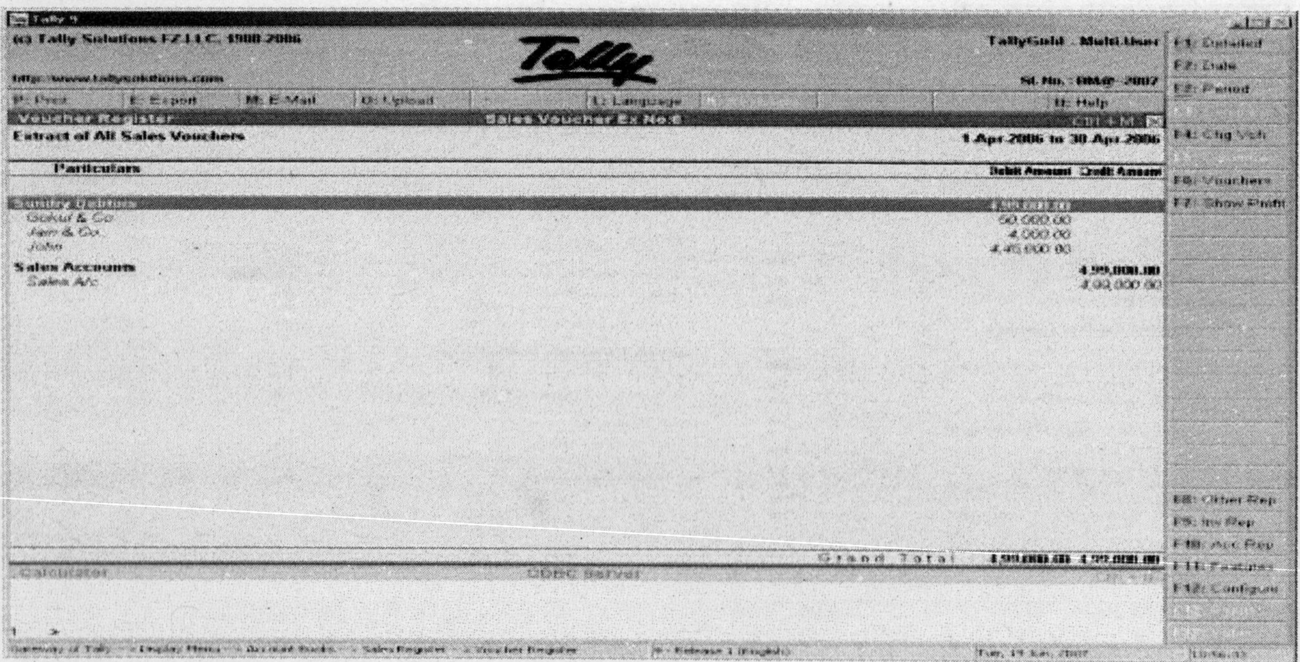

Sales Accounts Details

Display → A/c Books → Ledger → Sales a/c

Ledger Vouchers — Sales Voucher Ex No:6

Ledger: Sales A/c — 1-Apr-2006 to 4-Apr-2006

Date	Particulars		Vch Type	Vch No.	Debit	Credit
1-4-2006	Gokul & Co Cement Credit Sales	50,000.00	Sales	1		50,000.00
2-4-2006	Jain & Co., Bricks Credit Sales	4,000.00	Sales	2		4,000.00
3-4-2006	John Part Credit Sales	10,000.00	Sales	3		10,000.00
4-4-2006	John Cement Bricks Credit Sales	3,75,000.00 60,000.00	Sales	4		4,35,000.00
	Opening Balance					
	Current Total					4,99,000.00
	Closing Balance :					4,99,000.00

Sales Turnover in P and L A/c

Gateway of Tally → Reports → Profit and Loss A/c

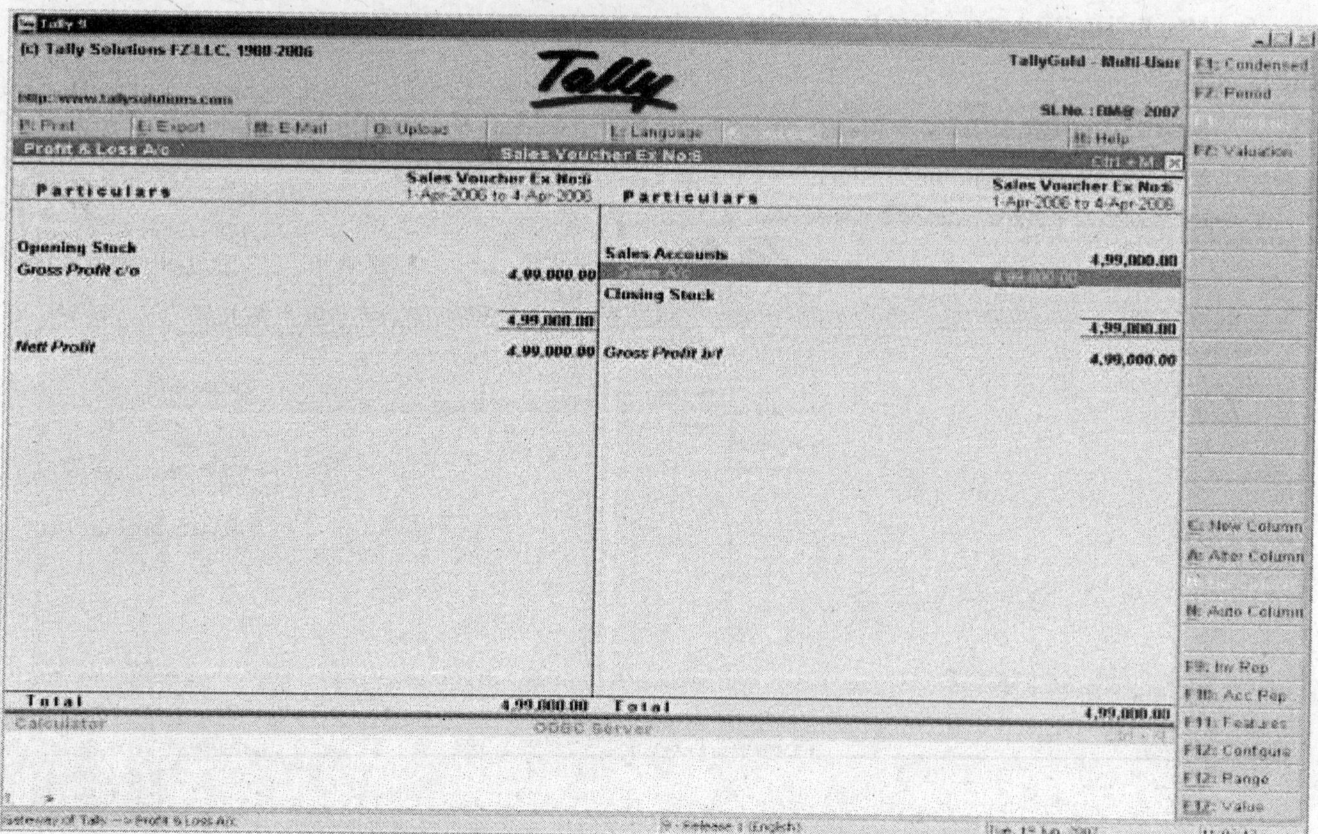

Purchase Voucher

Purchase Vouchers can now be created in invoice mode. You can enter the suppliers' invoices in the same way as they physically appear.

Set-up Invoice Mode Entry for Purchase Transactions

Select F11: Company Features.

Select F1: Accounting Features

Set the option 'Allow Invoicing' to Yes.

Enter Purchases in Invoice format? Set it to **Yes.**

Accept the screen using **Ctrl+A.**

Entry of Purchase vouchers in invoice mode

Select F9: Purchases — Select as invoice button or use ***"CTRL+V"***. This button is a toggle for Invoice and voucher modes. You may want to use the voucher mode for more complex entries

Purchase Voucher — Exercises

From the following prepare PURCHASE voucher

1. M/s. Ramco Cement supplied Rs. 2,00,000 worth of cement
2. M/s. Arasan & Co. supplied Rs. 75,000 worth of cement
3. Computer purchased worth Rs. 30,000 and printer purchased worth Rs. 5,000
4. Accounting software purchased Rs. 22,000 purchased from data systems
5. M/s. Indian Cement supplied Rs. 1,00,000 worth of goods.

Tally Solution

Step 1: Gateway of Tally → Master → Accounts Info → Ledger → Single/Multiple Ledger → Create

You can Choose – Multiple Ledgers → Create

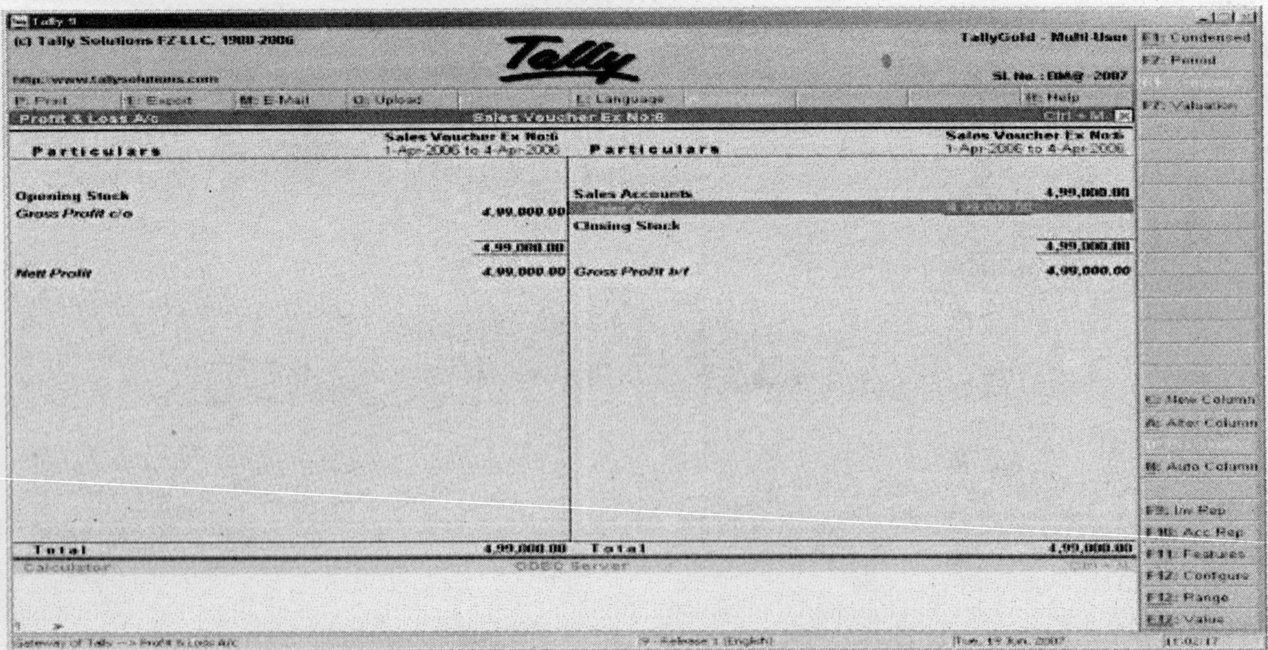

Step 2: Go to Gateway of Tally → Accounting Vouchers → Select F9: Purchases.

Rules for Entry

I. Credit Purchase:

What Comes in	Dr.
The Giver is [Suppliers]	Cr.

II. Cash Purchase: [use Payment Voucher F 5 –key]

Cash a/c	Cr.
What Comes in	Dr.

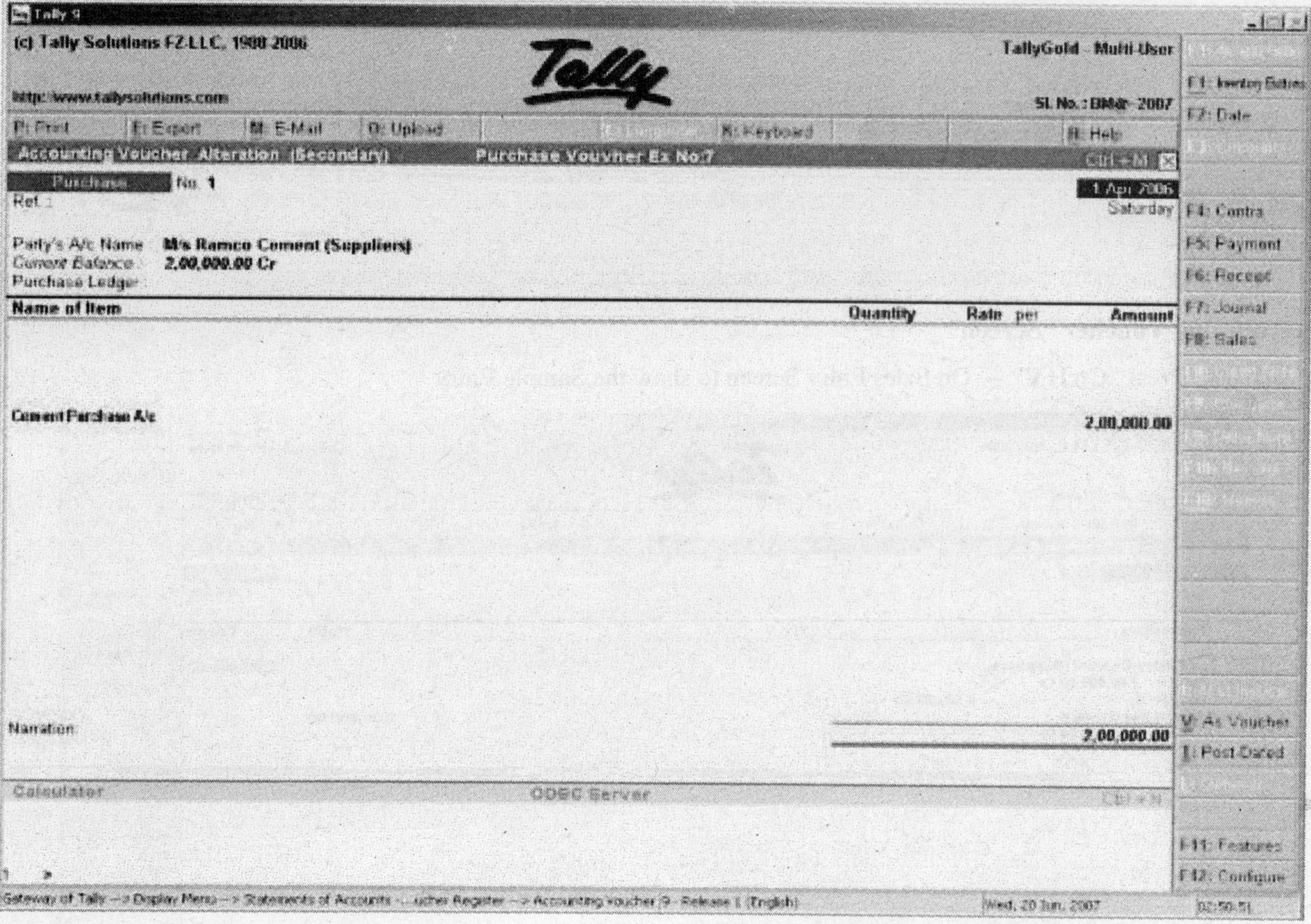

Model 2 — Enter the Suppliers Details

Use F12 "configuration"

Accept Supplementary Details →Yes

(Address Details, Despatch Details, etc.)

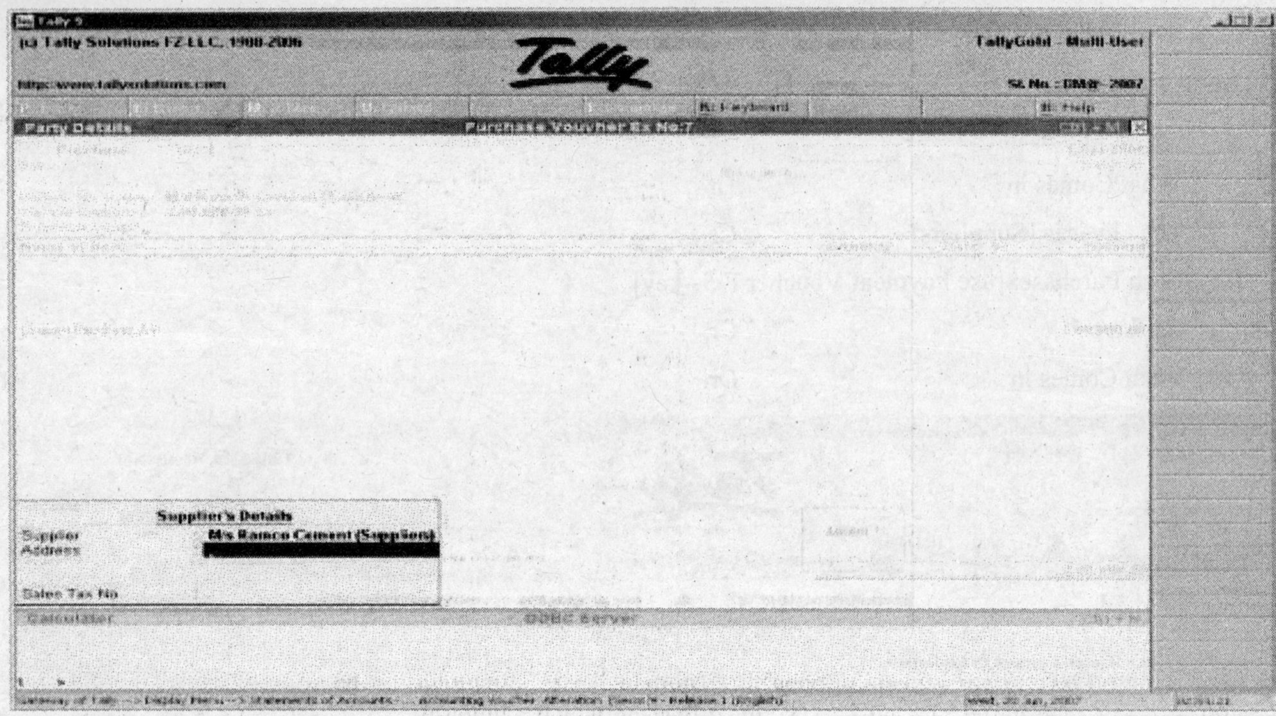

Accounting Voucher "Screen"

Press **"Ctrl+V"** — On Sales Entry Screen to show the Sample Entry

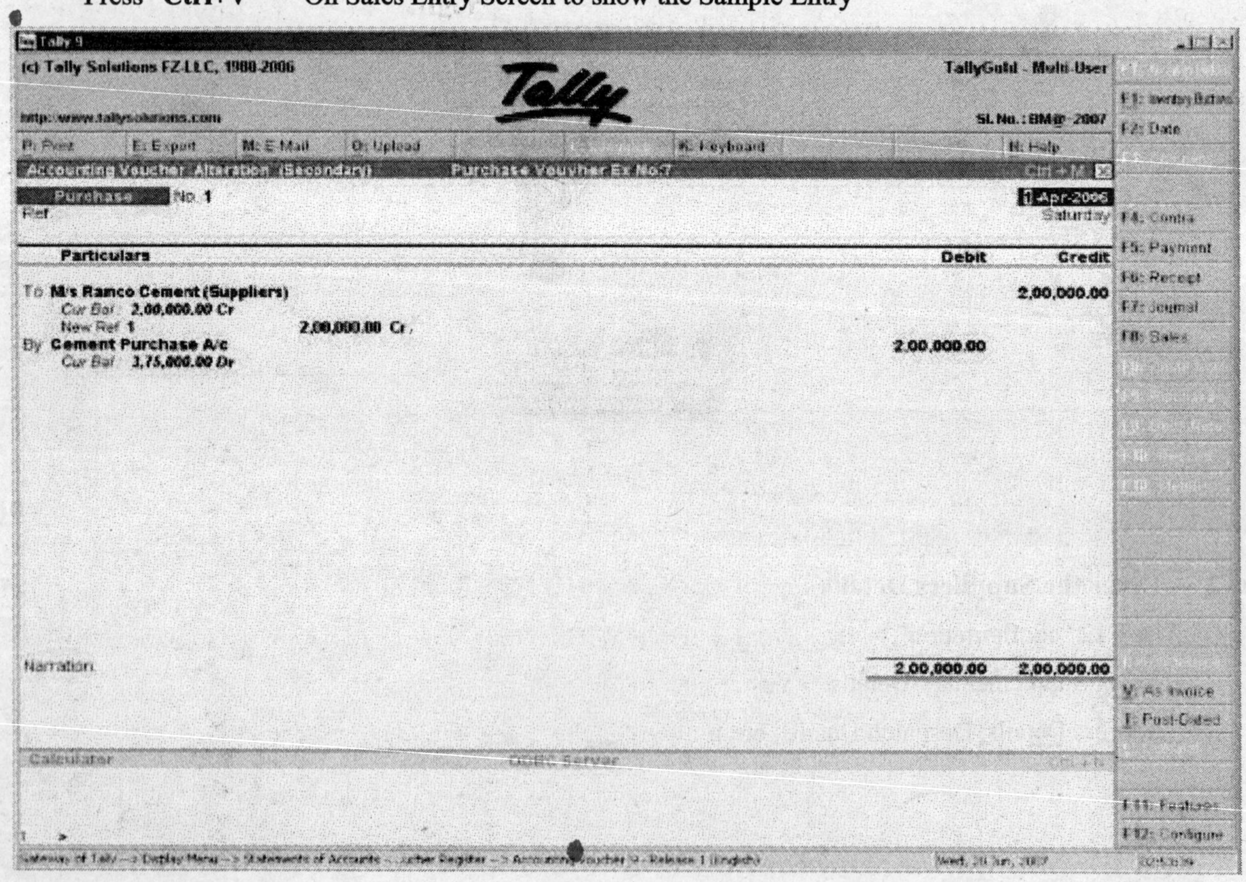

Note: Use F11 — Feature

Invoicing

To allow Invoicing —Enter Purchase in Invoice Format→**Yes**

Purchase Register

Display → Accounts Book → Purchase Register — [Key Press "DAP"]

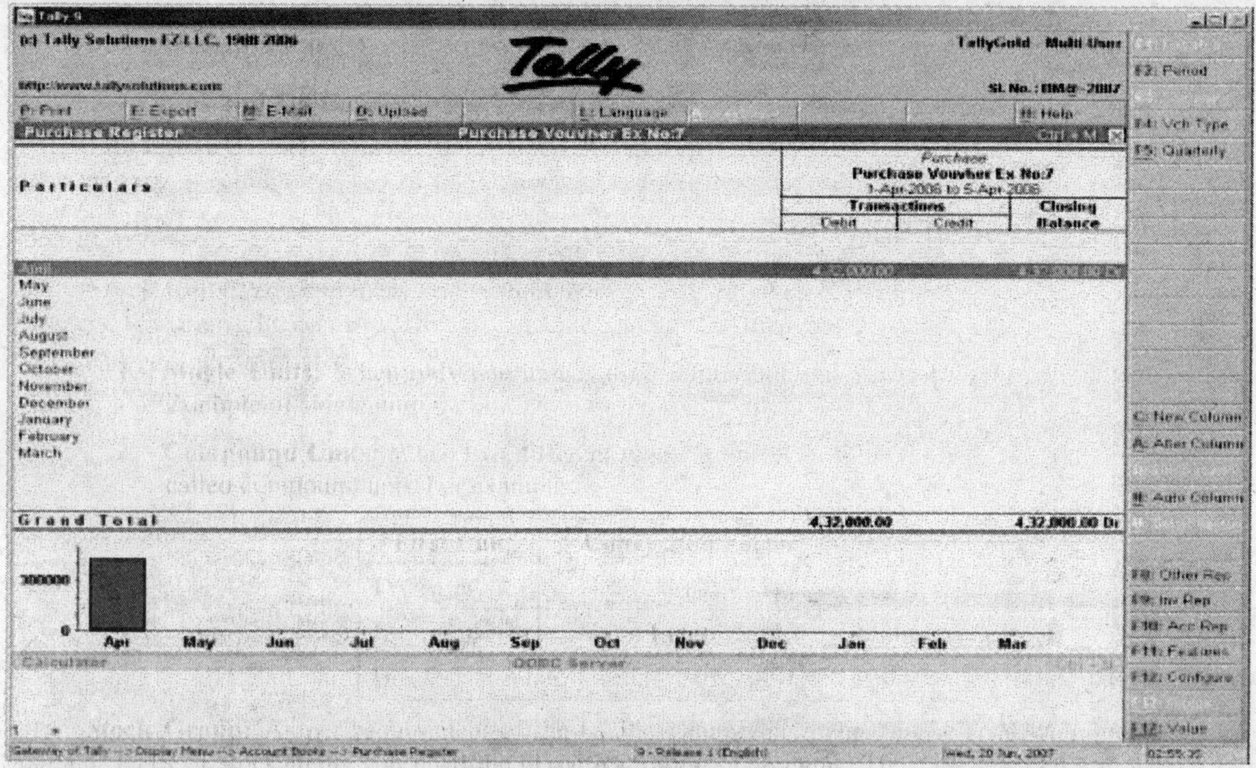

Press F4 Key to change Type of Sales, Journal Purchase

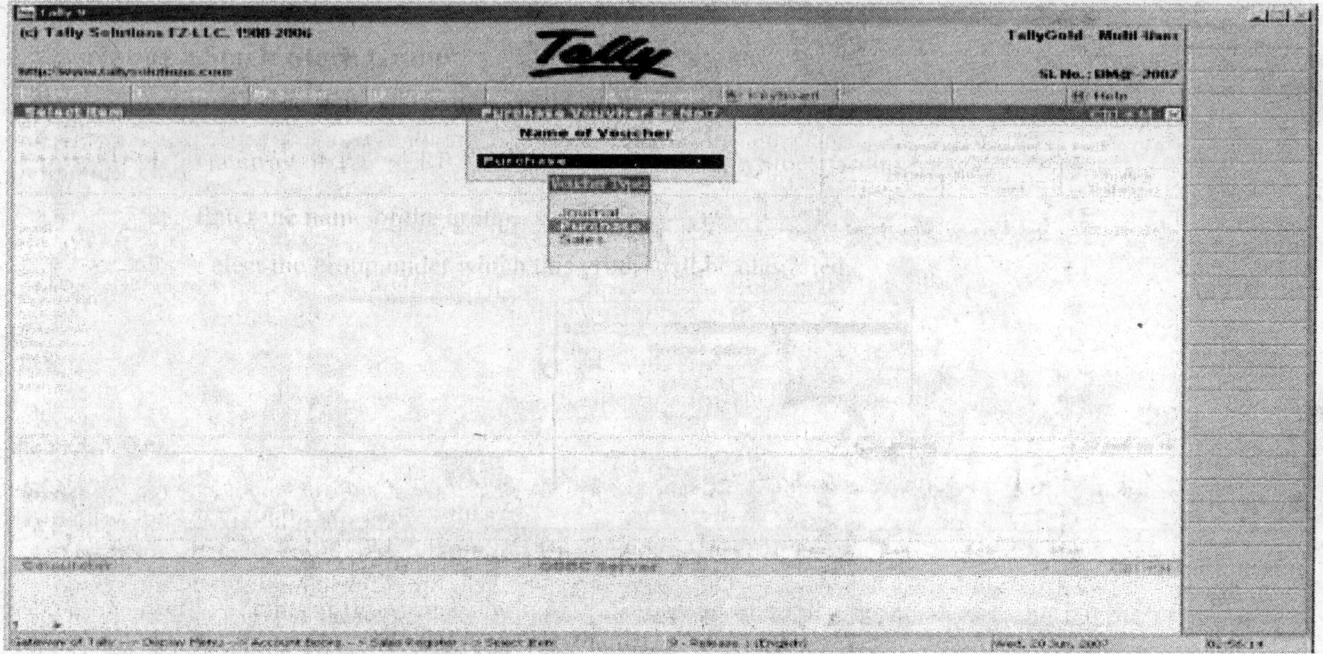

Extract Purchase Entry

Display → Accounts Book → Purchase Register — [Key Press "DAP"]

Press "Enter key"

Use F6 Key — Extract

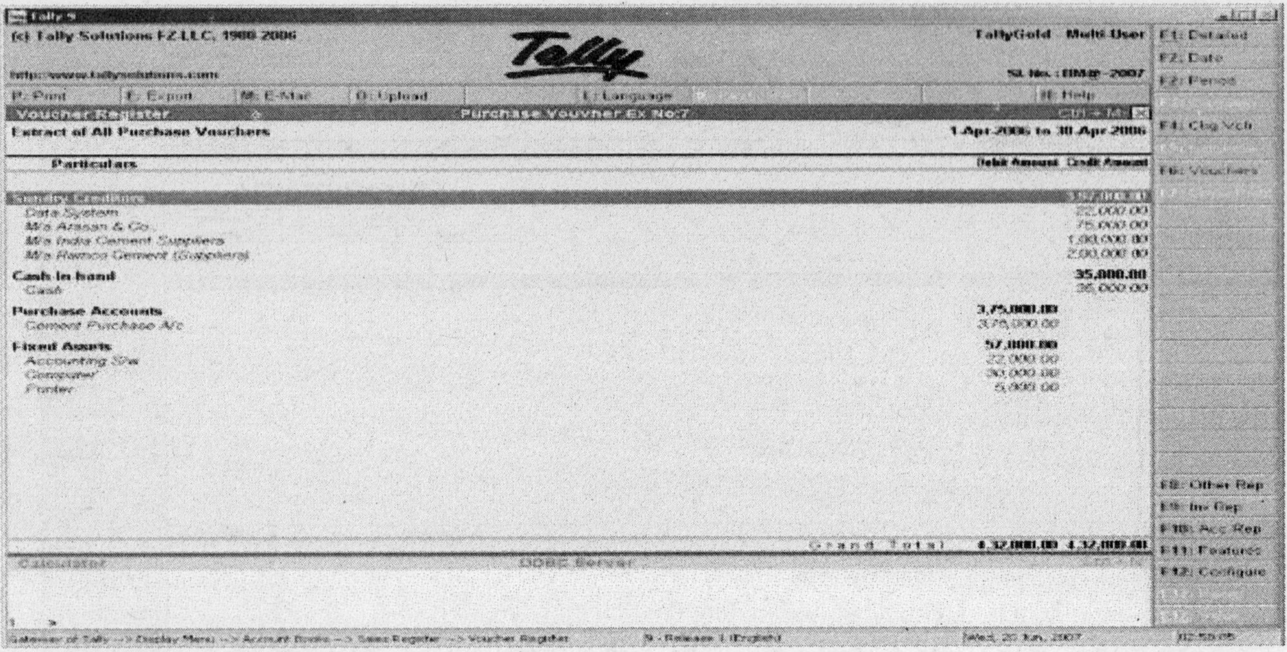

Purchase Accounts Details

Display → A/c Books → Ledger → Purchase A/c

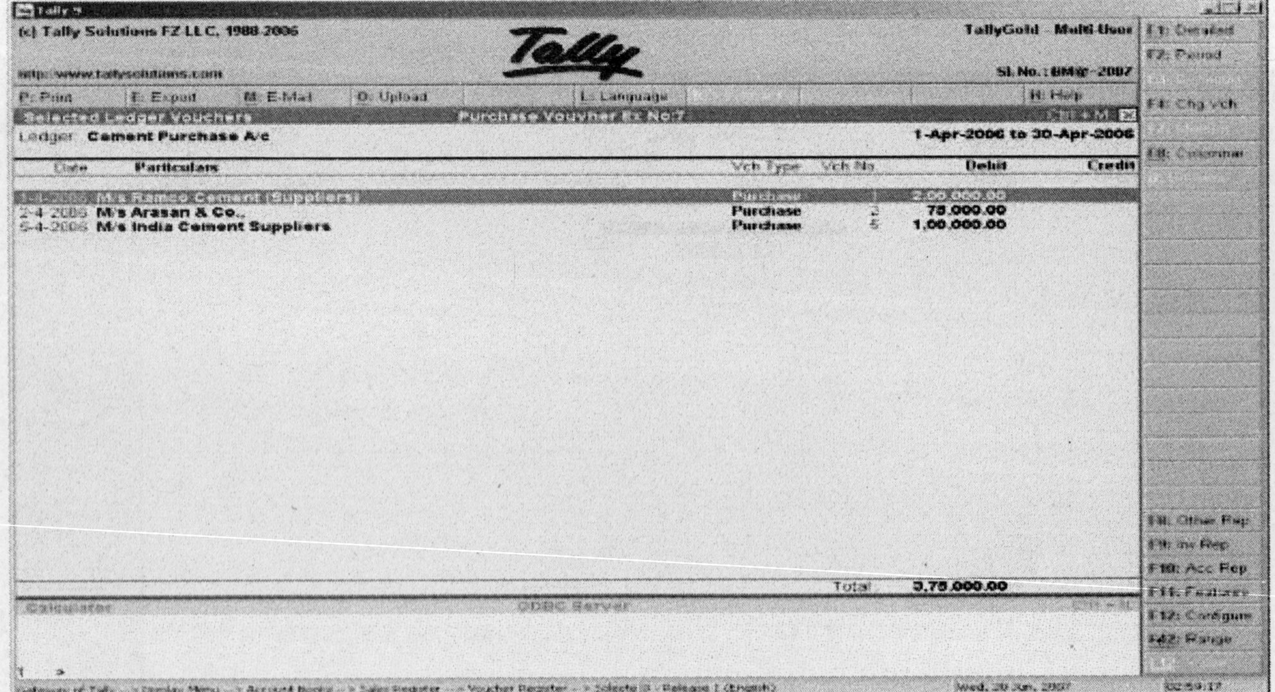

To View Purchase Turnover in P and L A/c

Gateway of Tally → Reports → Profit and Loss A/c

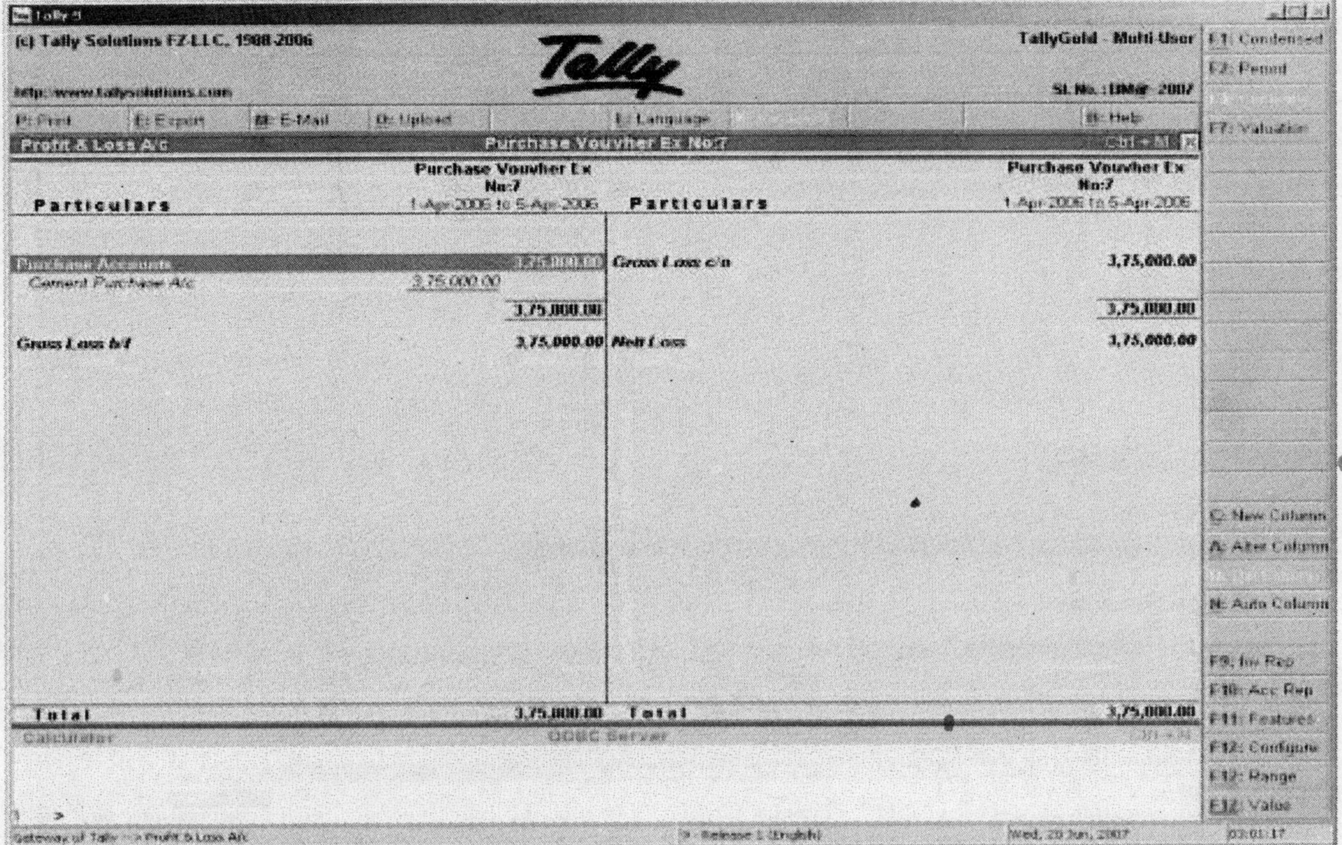

Journal, Debit Note, Credit Note Voucher

Meaning

Journal entries are used to adjust the debit and credit amounts without involving the cash or bank accounts. Hence, they are referred to as adjustment entries. To go to the Journal Entry Screen:

Go to Gateway of Tally → Accounting Vouchers

Click on F7: Journal on the button bar or press F7 key

Journal, Debit Note, Credit Note Voucher Exercises

From the following prepare journal voucher, debit note voucher and credit note voucher:

1. Depreciate Rs. 2,000 on machinery and Rs. 500 on building is to be entered.
2. M\s. Gokul returns the goods worth Rs. 500 as a damaged goods.
3. Rs. 1,200 worth goods purchased returned to M\s. Arasan due to late in delivery.
4. Purchased goods worth Rs. 500 returned to India Cement for excess supply.
5. Rs. 750 worth of goods sold returned back from Jain.

Setp 1: Gateway of Tally àMaster → Accounts Info → Ledger → Single/Multiple Ledger→ Create

Tally Display "Single/Multiple Ledger Creation window"

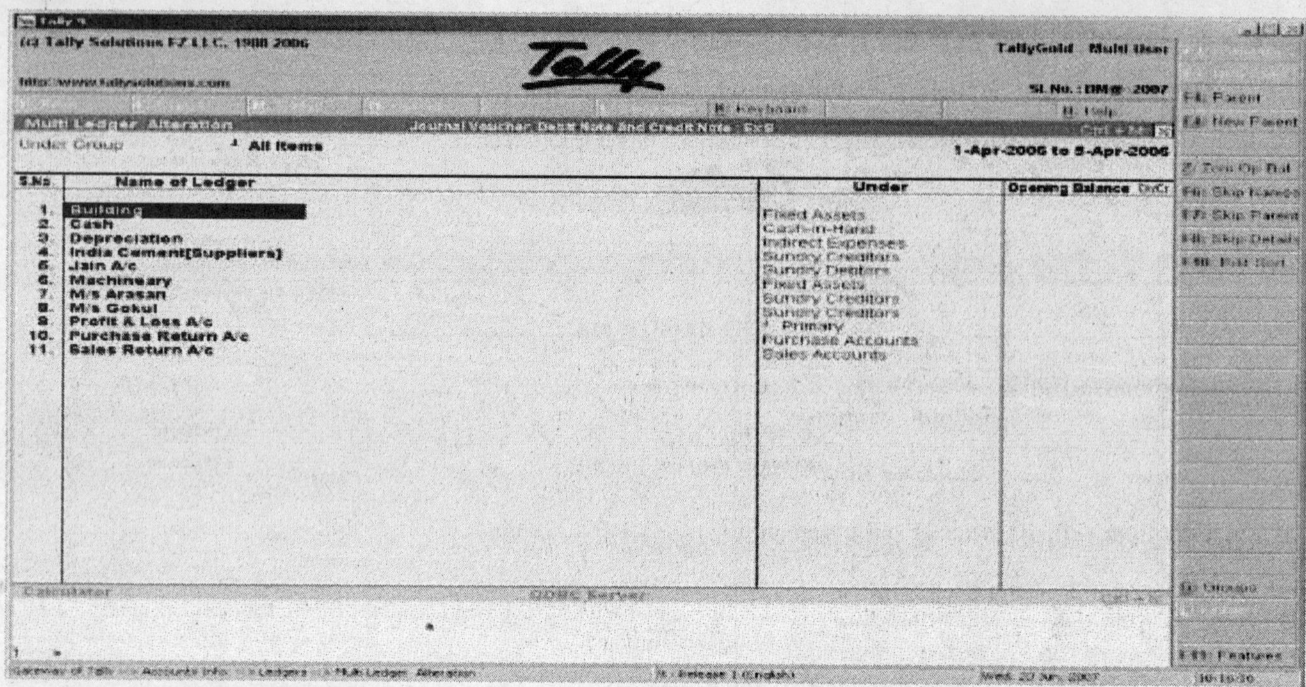

Journal Entry Screen

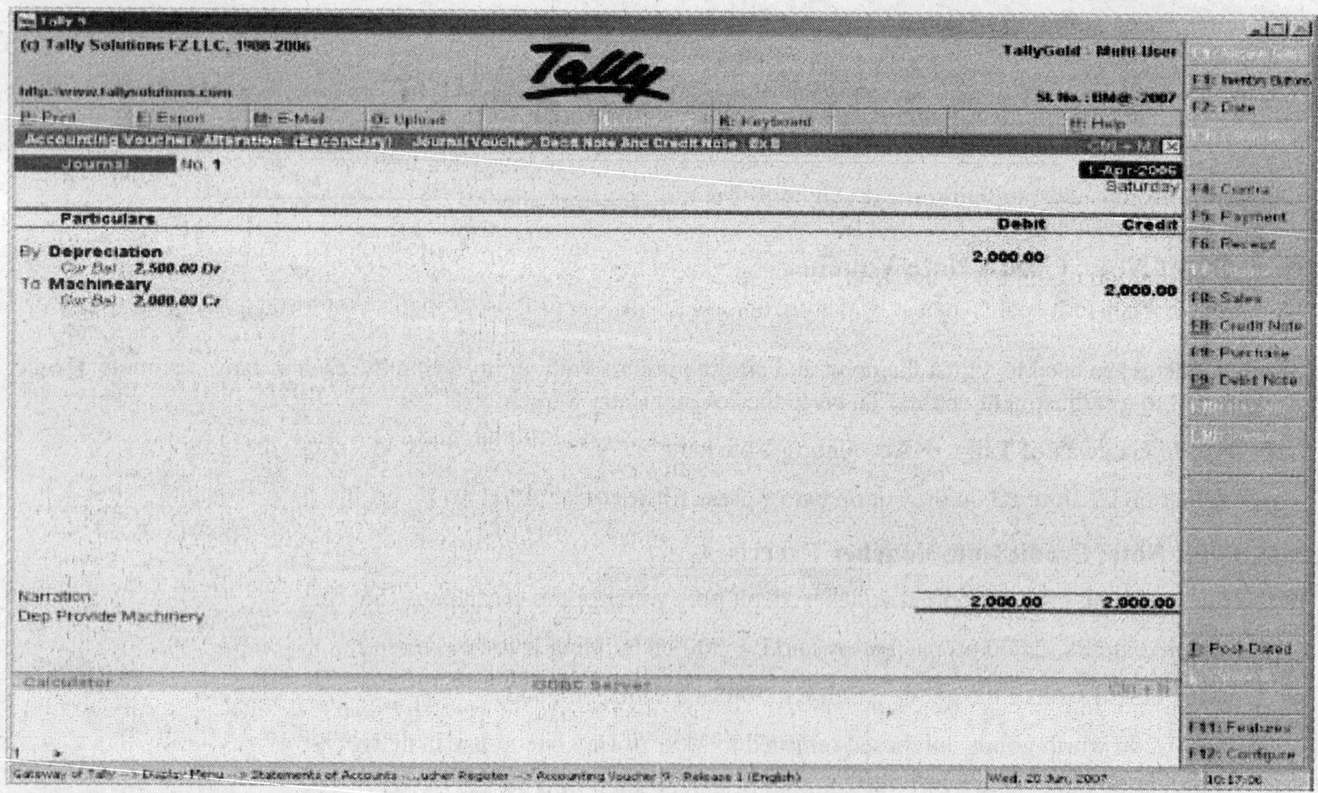

Cash Accounts in Journals

Journals are adjustment entries, which do not involve cash account and bank account. However, in many cases companies use journals to account for day-to-day transactions, where cash or bank accounts are required. To add this features:

Set Allow Cash Accounts in Journals to Yes in F12: Configuration.

Go to Gateway of Tally → Accounting Vouchers → **Select F7: Journal**

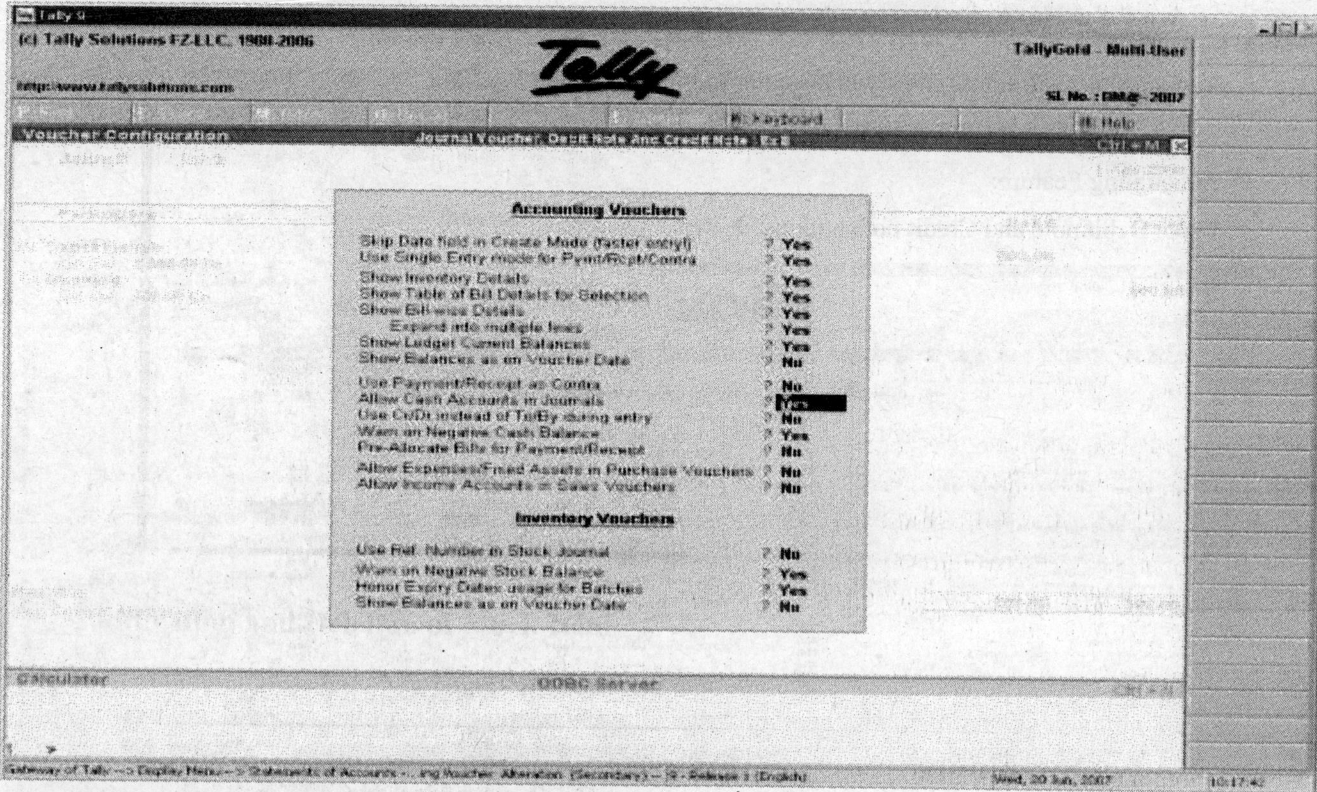

Journal Register

Gateway of Tally → Accounts Book → Journal Register

Debit Note Voucher

To record Purchase Returns entry you have to use the Debit Note Voucher

Credit Note Voucher

To record Sales Returns entry you have to use the Debit Note Voucher

Activate this Feature "Press F11 key"

Accounting Feature:

Make Debit note and Credit note options → Yes

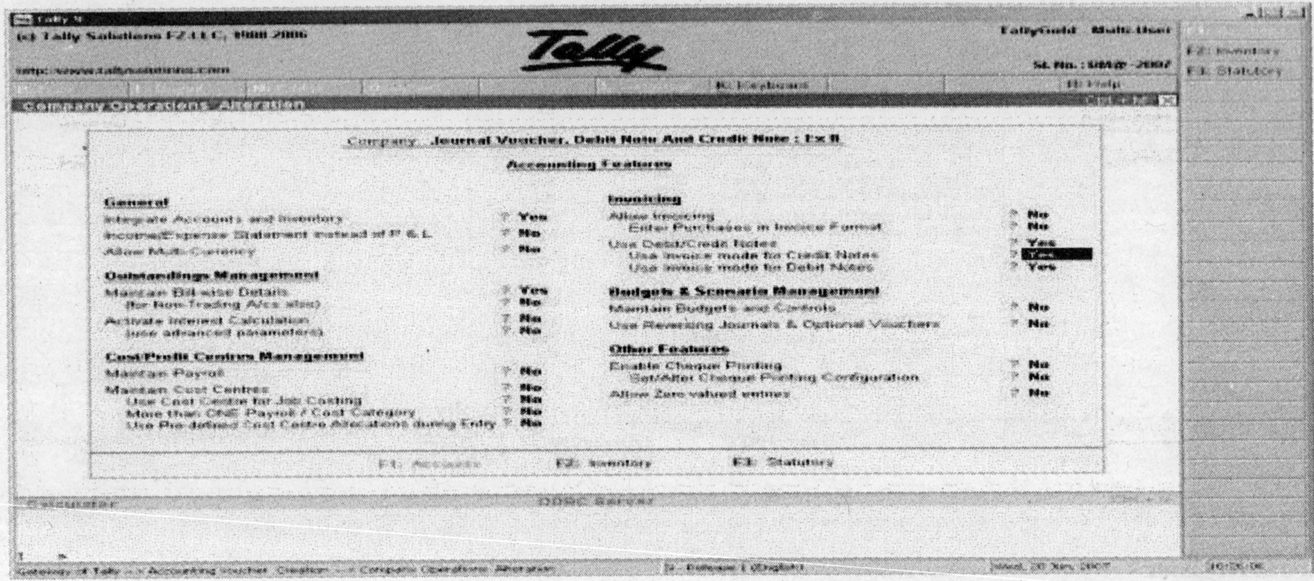

Voucher Entry — Credit Note

Gateway of Tally → Accounting Voucher → Enter

Press "Ctrl+F8" Key

Tally output

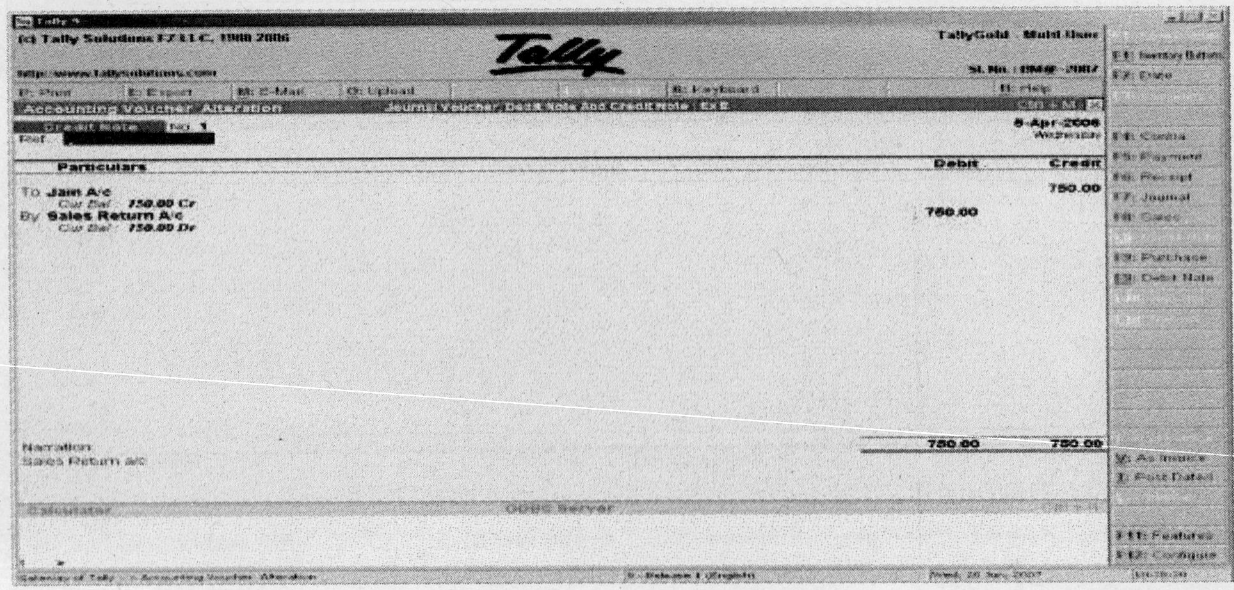

Voucher Entry — Debit note

Gateway of Tally → Accounting Voucher → Enter

Press "Ctrl+F9" Key

Tally output

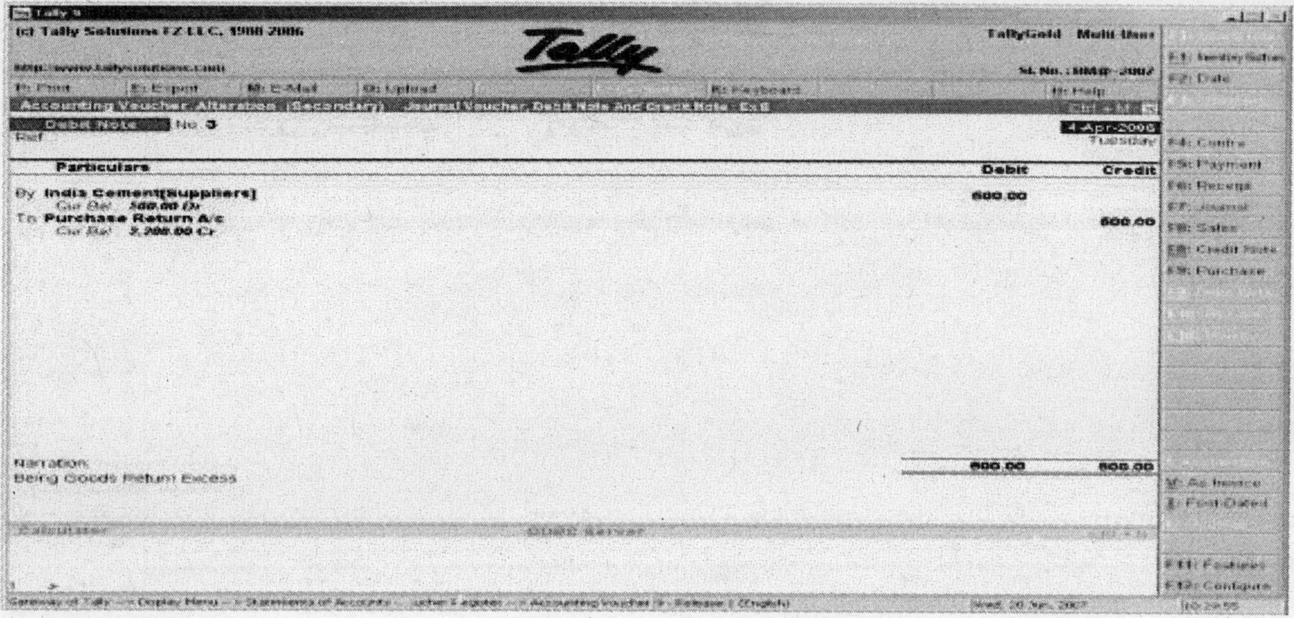

Debit Note Register

Gateway of Tally → Accounts Book → Journal Register → Enter

"Select Debit Note Register"

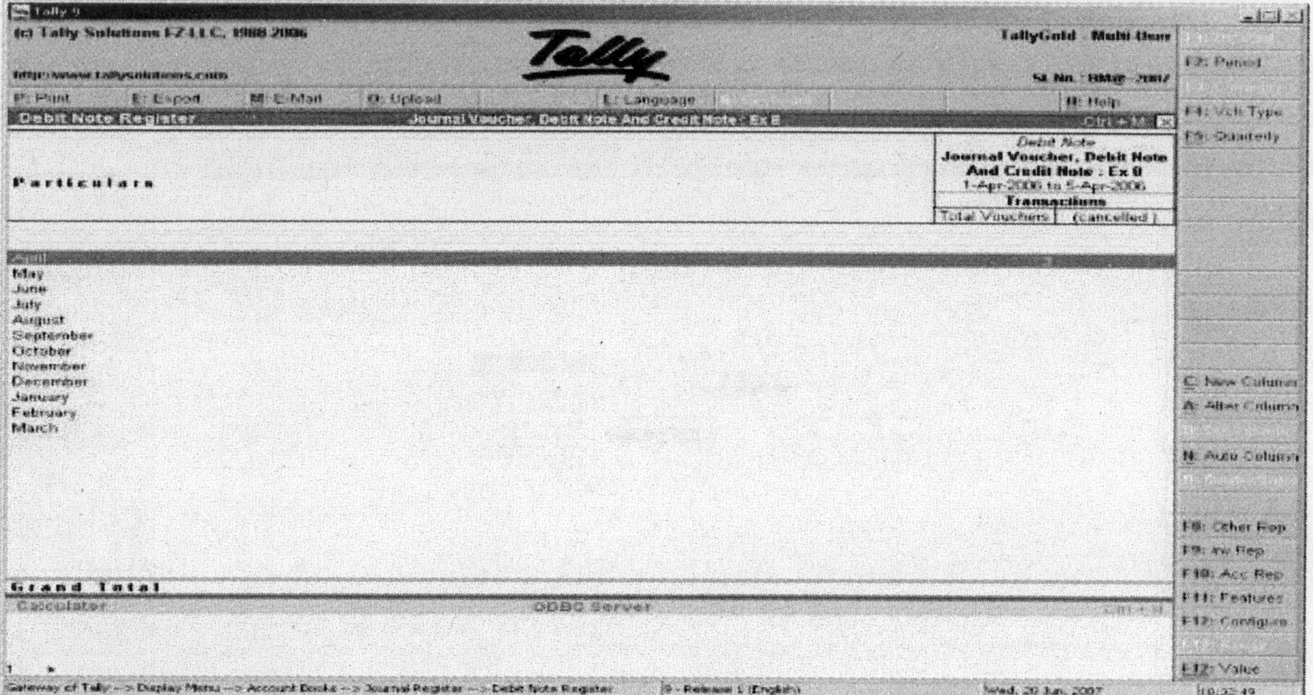

Credit Note Register

Gateway of Tally → Accounts Book → Journal Register → Enter

"Select Credit Note Register"

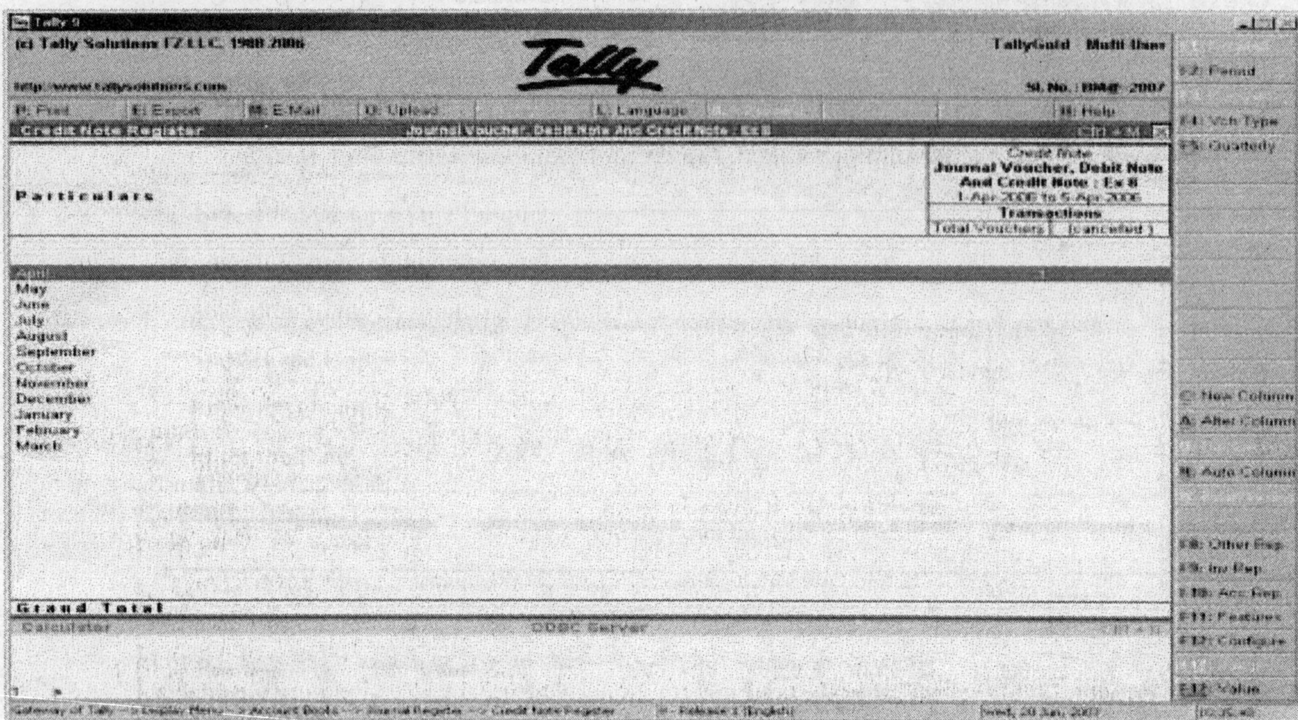

Note: *To u*se all register press F12 "Configuration key"

The Periodic Statement on monthly, quarterly, weekly, yearly basis is —

Tally output

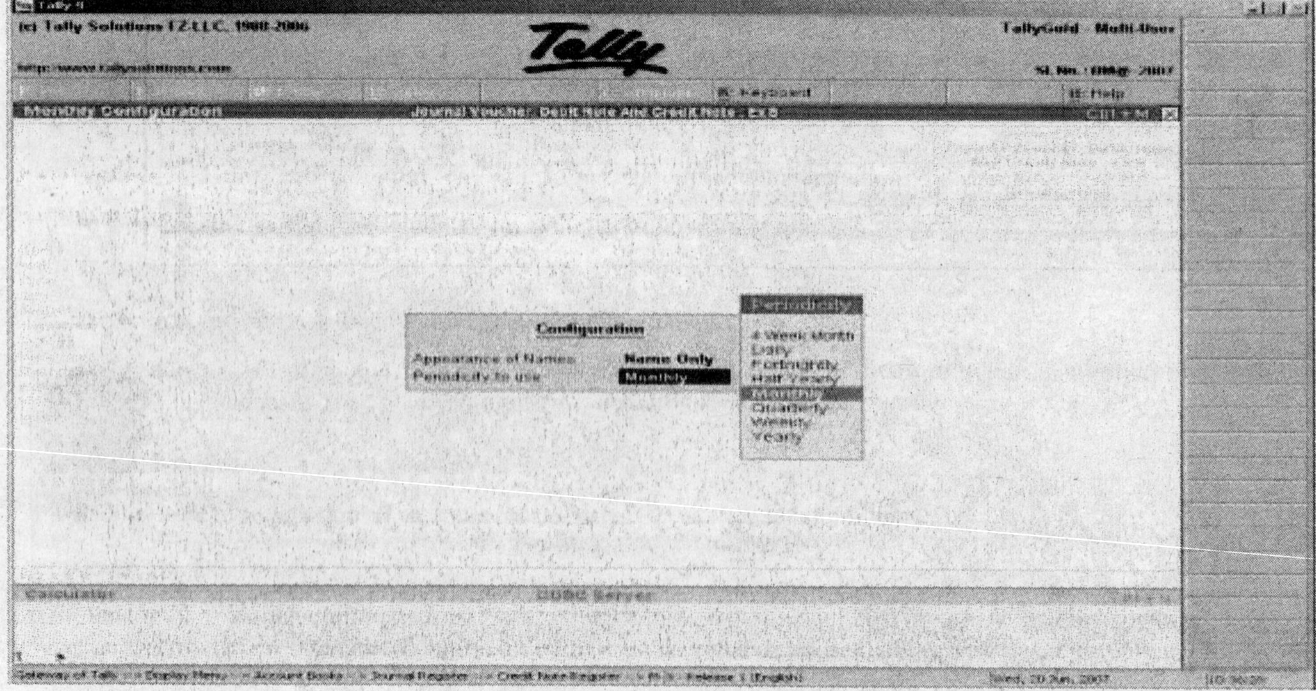

Journal Voucher — [F7 key]

Journal entries are used to adjust the debit and credit amounts without involving the cash or bank accounts. Hence, they are referred to as adjustment entries. To go to the Journal Entry Screen:

1. Go to Gateway of Tally → Accounting Vouchers
2. Click on F7: Journal on the Button Bar or press F7 key

For example, there may be entries made for interest accrued or interest to be paid. If a party is involved in such a transaction the entry will be:

1. Debit the Party
2. Credit the Interest Account

Journal Voucher Excercises:

1. Mr. Arunkumar started business with goods worth Rs. 15,000, cash Rs. 20,000 and building Rs. 17,000
2. Deposited Rs. 10,000 in Canara Bank.
3. Purchased goods from Kumar Rs. 5,000.
4. Sold goods to Ratna & Co Rs. 3,000.
5. Purchased furniture for Rs. 1,000.
6. Purchased a cycle for personal use Rs. 2,000 and given a cheque for it.
7. Commission received Rs. 250.
8. Purchased two furniture for Rs. 200 for cash.
9. Received a cheque from Ratna & Co. for Rs. 2,000.
10. Returned goods to Kumar Rs. 1,000.
11. Stationery purchased Rs. 20.
12. Paid to Kumar 3,800 by cheque and settled the amount.
13. Purchased electrical light for Rs. 300.
14. Rent given Rs. 500 and salary paid Rs. 1,000 by cheque.

Tally Solution

Step 1: Gateway of Tally → Master → Accounts Info → Ledger → Single/Multiple Ledger → Create

You can Choose

Multiple Ledgers → Create

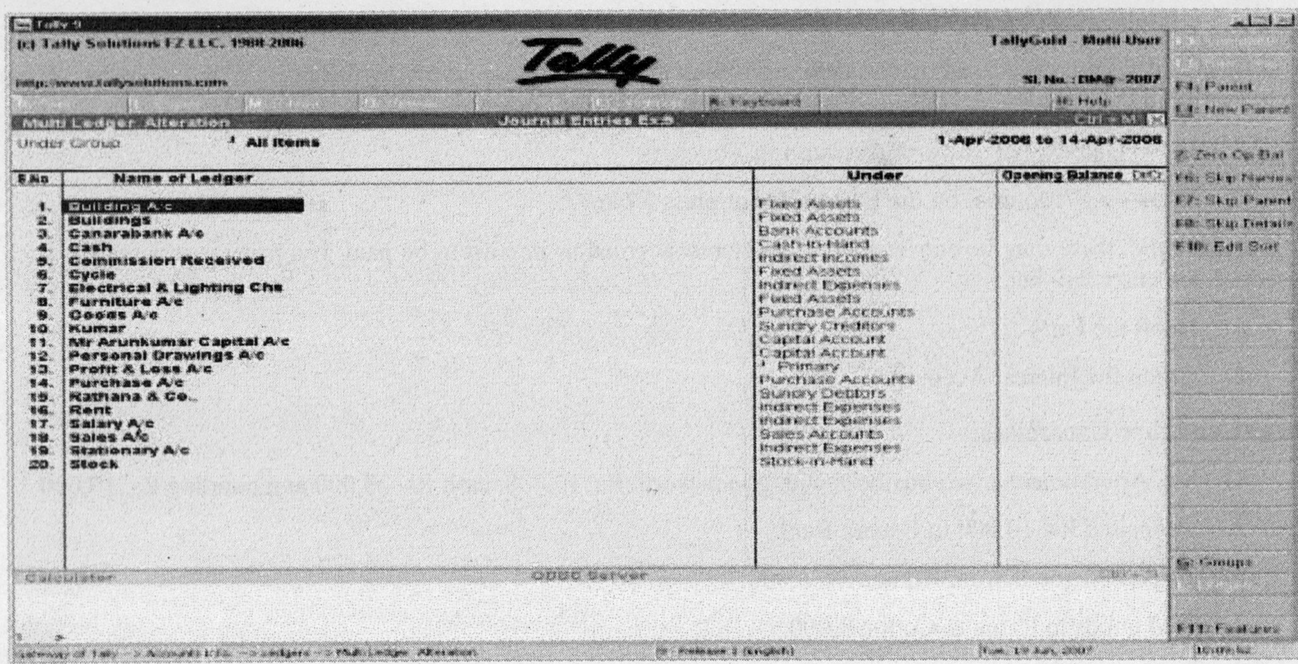

Voucher Entry

Gateway of Tally → Accounting Voucher → Feeding Voucher Entry

Journal Entry — Press "F7" key

Enter the "Voucher Entry"

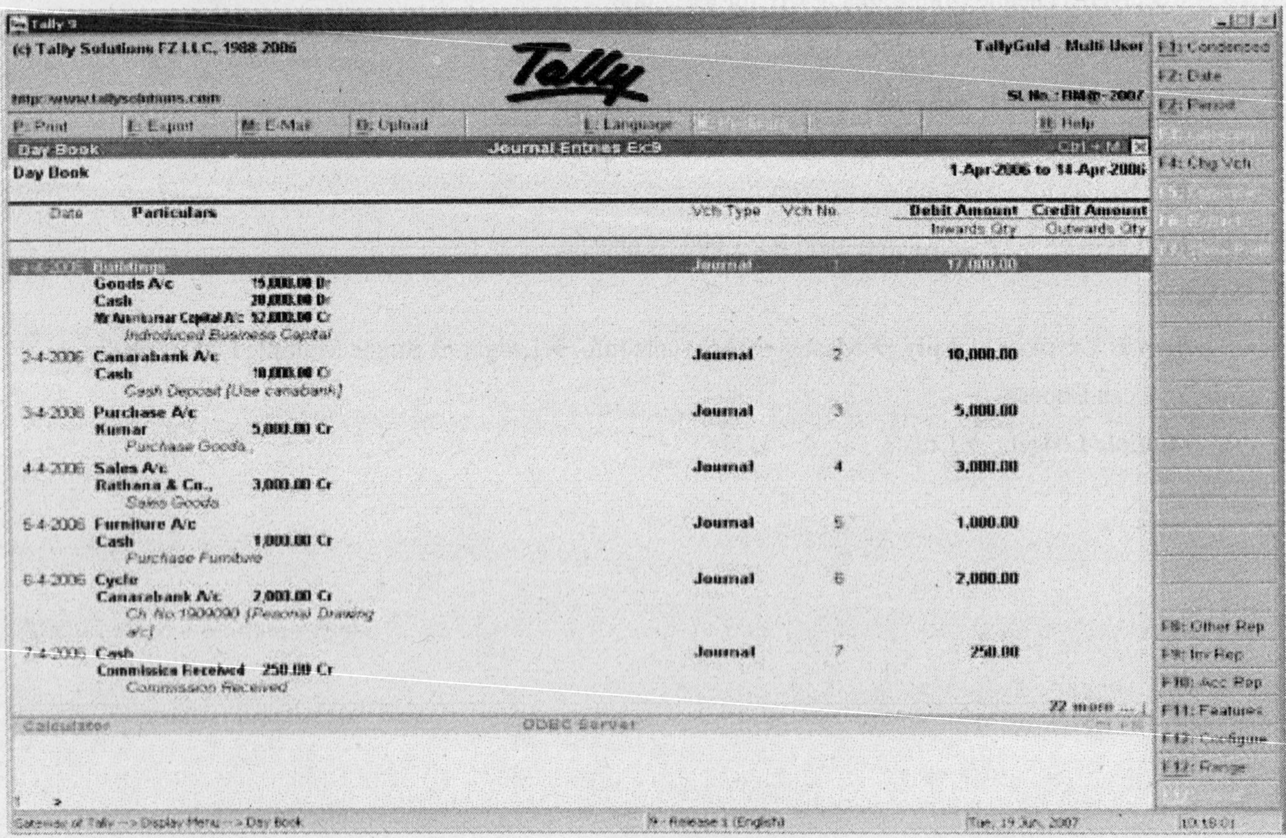

Page 2

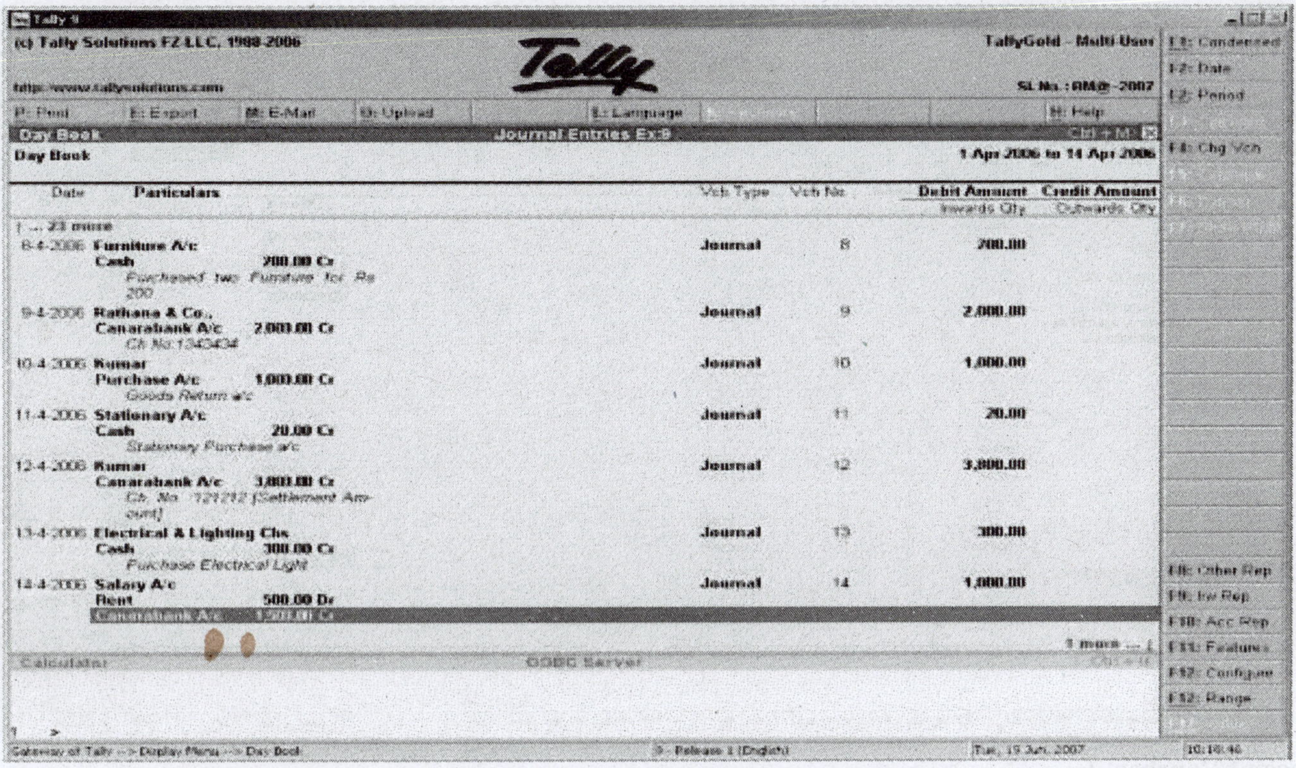

Use "**Configuration**" Press F12 Key to Use Cash Transaction in Journal

Setup "Configuration F12 Key" Allow Cash Accounts in Journals—Yes

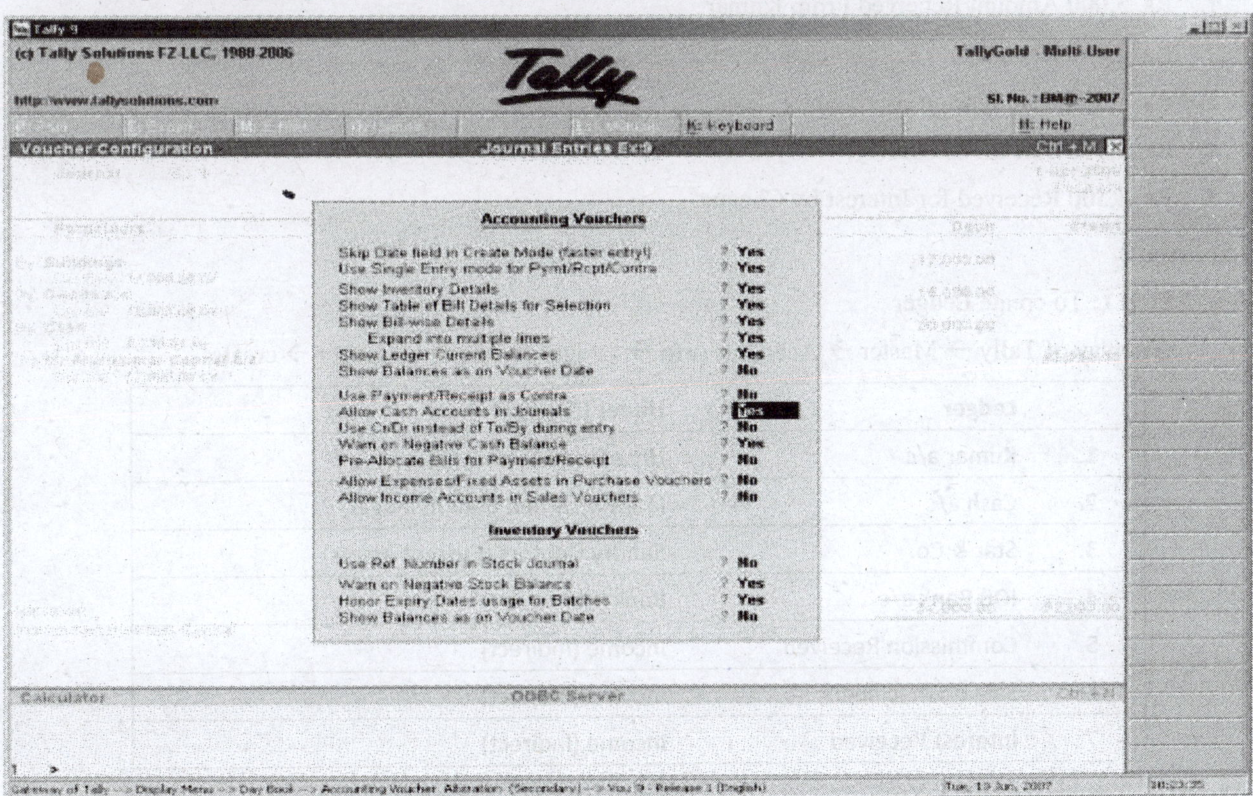

Model Journal Voucher

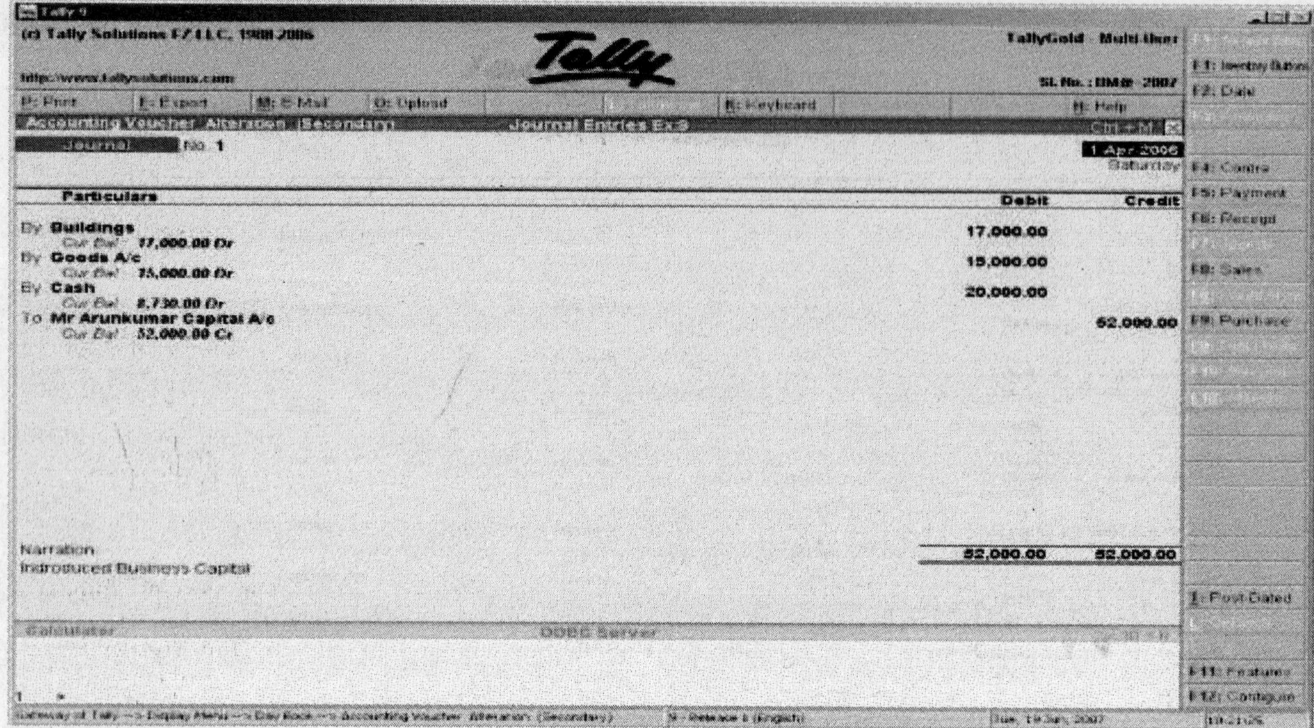

Receipt Voucher

Receipt Voucher Exercises:

1. Rs. 5,000 Amount Received From Kumar.
2. Rs. 2,000 Cheque and Rs. 500 cash Given By Star & Co.
3. Rs. 1,500 Commission received by Cash.
4. Rs. 1,000 Sale on machinery.
5. Rs. 2,500 Received for Interest by Cheque.

Tally Solutions

Step 1: To create Ledger

Gateway of Tally → Master → Accounts Info → Ledger → Multiple Ledger → create

	Ledger	Under (Group)
1.	Kumar a/c	Unsecured Loan
2.	Cash a/c	(Tally provided default ledger)
3.	Star & Co.	Sundry Debtors (Current assets)
4.	IOB Bank a/c	Bank a/c
5.	Commission Received	Income (Indirect)
6.	Sale on machinery	Income (Indirect)
7.	Interest Received	Income (Indirect)

Accept — Yes/No — Select Yes

Tally Output

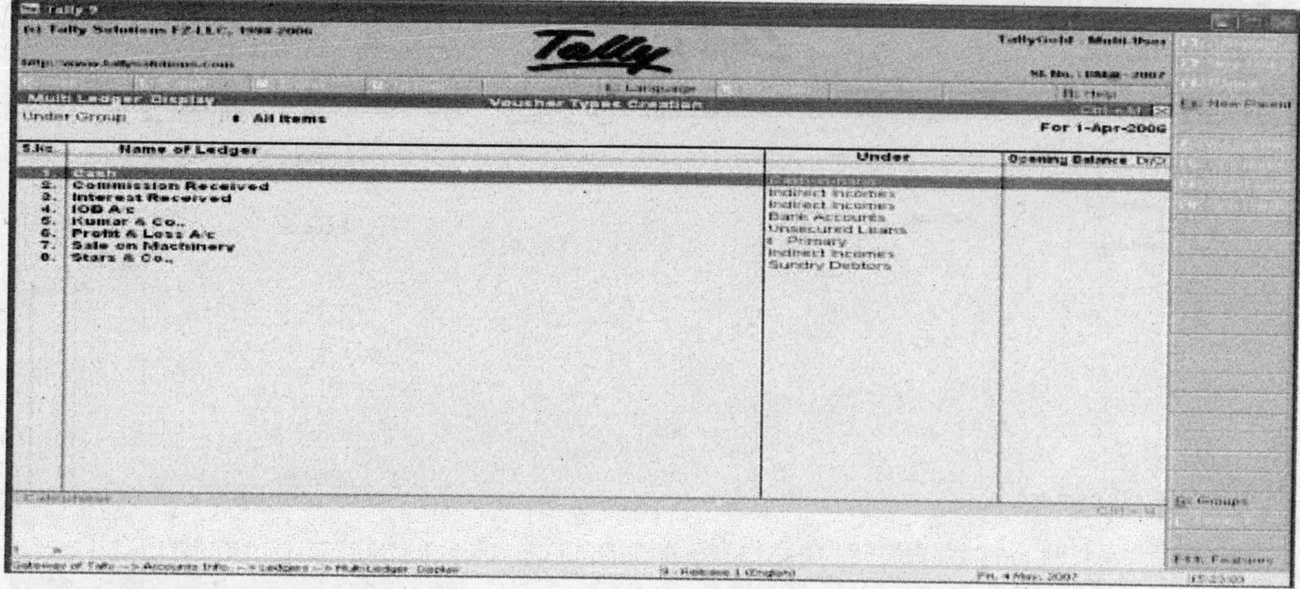

Step 2: Set up (Configuration)

Press F12 Configuration,.

Use single Entry Mode for Pymt/Rcpt/Contra? **No**

Save-Yes

Step 3: To Press → F6 key → Receipt Voucher → Rule for Voucher Entry:

What comes in Debit?

The Giver is Credit

Tally Sample Voucher Entry for Receipt:

I. Cash Receipt

II. Bank Receipt Entry

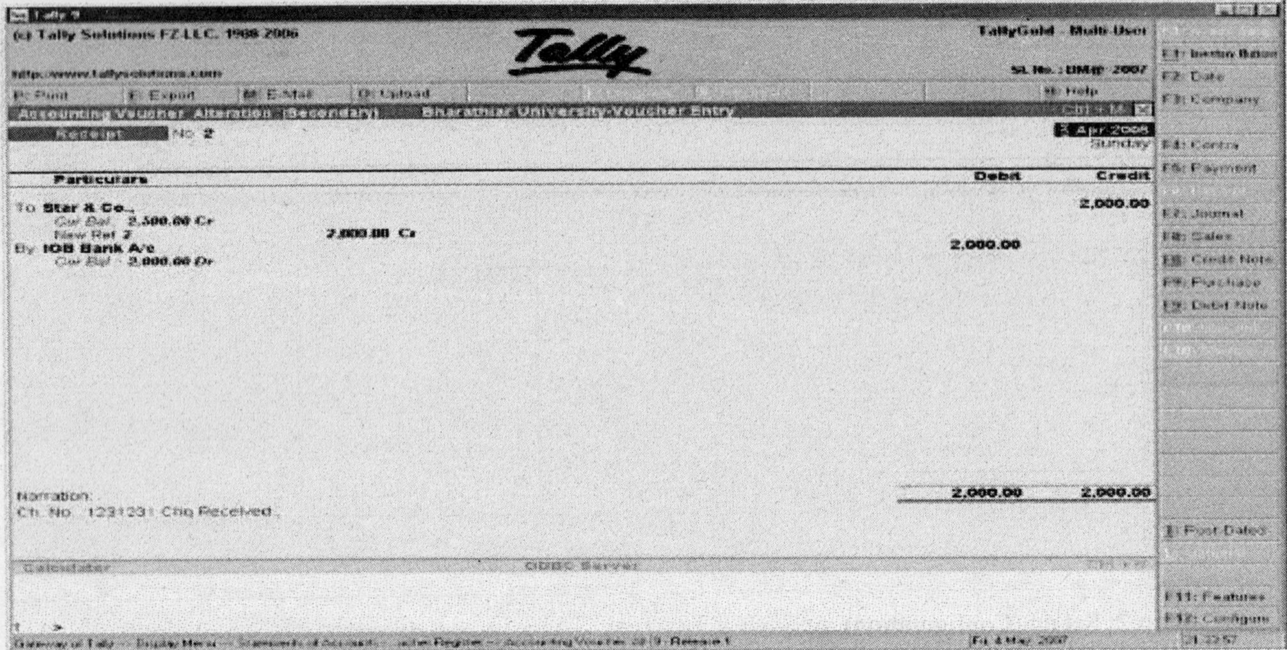

Tally Output Receipt Voucher:

Display →Statement of A/c → Statistics → Receipt → Select → Enter

Press Alt+F1 (Detailed Info)

Press "F 12" Key (Configuration)

Show Narration also **Yes**

Tally 9

(c) Tally Solutions FZ-LLC. 1988-2006 — Tally — TallyGold - Multi-User

http://www.tallysolutions.com — Sl. No. : BM@-2007

Voucher Register — Bharathiar University-Voucher Entry

List of Receipt Vouchers — 1-Apr-2006 to 30-Apr-2006

Date	Particulars	Vch Type	Vch No.	Debit Amount	Credit Amount
1-4-2006	Kumar Cash 5,000.00 Dr *Being Amount Rec Mr Kumar*	Receipt	1		5,000.00
2-4-2006	Star & Co., IOB Bank A/c 2,000.00 Dr *Ch. No. 1231231 Chq Received.*	Receipt	2		2,000.00
3-4-2006	Star & Co., Cash 500.00 Dr *Cash Received, Star & co.,*	Receipt	3		500.00
4-4-2006	Commission Received Cash 1,500.00 Dr *Comm Rec By Cash*	Receipt	4		1,500.00
4-4-2006	Sale of Machinery Cash 1,000.00 Dr *Sale of Machinery Amt Rec*	Receipt	5		1,000.00
5-4-2006	Interest Received Cash 2,500.00 Dr *Being Int. Rec.,*	Receipt	6		2,500.00

Gateway of Tally → Display Menu → Statements of Accounts → Statistics → Voucher Monthly Register → 9 - Release 1 — Fri, 4 May, 2007

EXERCISE

Payment Voucher

From the following transaction, prepare a Pvt. Voucher:

1. Rs. 4,500 paid for Bonus.
2. Rs. 2,000 cheque paid for Salaries.
3. Rs. 450 paid for Electric Charges.
4. Rs. 1,150 paid for Electricity Charges by Cheque.
5. Rs. 3,000 purchase on Furniture (Here Rs. 2,000 Canara Bank by Cheque and Rs. 1,000 paid by Cash).
6. Rs. 1,000 paid to M/s. Chitra & Co.

Tally Solution

Step 1: To create Ledger

Gateway of Tally → Master → Accounts Info → Ledger → Multiple Ledger → Create

	Ledger	Under (Group)
1.	Bonus a/c	Expenses (Indirect)
2.	Cash a/c	(Tally provide default ledger)
3.	Salaries Paid	Expenses (Indirect)
4.	Electricity Charges	Expenses (Indirect)
5.	Canara Bank a/c	Bank a/c
6.	Furniture a/c (Pur)	Fixed assets
7.	M/s. Chitra	Sundry Creditor

Accept

Yes/No — select yes

Tally Output

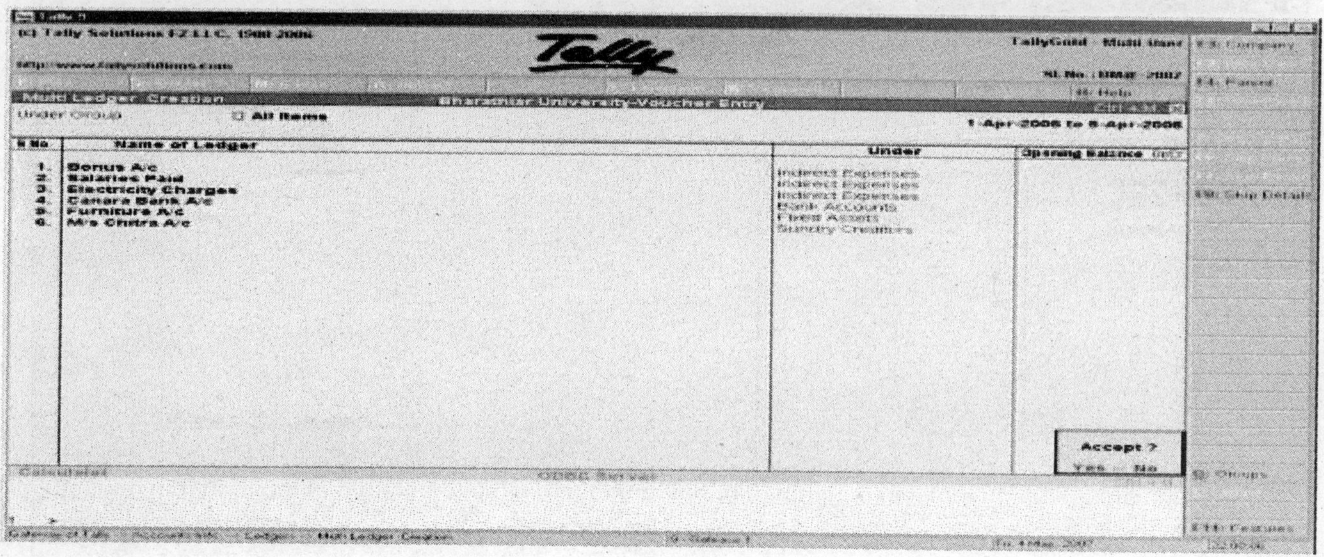

Step 2: To Press → F5 key → Payment Voucher

Rule for Voucher Entry:

All Expenses Loss	Debit
All Income and Gain	Credit

I. Tally Sample Voucher Entry for Payment

Tally 9

(c) Tally Solutions FZ-LLC, 1988-2006 | Tally | TallyGold . Multi User

http://www.tallysolutions.com | SL No. : RM@-2007

P: Print | E: Export | M: E-Mail | O: Upload | H: Help

Accounting Voucher Alteration (Secondary) | Bharathiar University-Voucher Entry | Ctrl + M

Payment No. 1 | 5-Apr-2006 Wednesday

Particulars	Debit	Credit
By **Bonus A/c**	4,500.00	
Cur Bal *4,500.00 Dr*		
To **Cash**		4,500.00
Cur Bal *3,550.00 Dr*		
Narration:	4,500.00	4,500.00

Being Bonus Paid Employee

F1: Inventory Buttons | F2: Date | F3: Company | F4: Contra | F5: Payment | F6: Receipt | F7: Journal | F8: Sales | F8: Credit Note | F9: Purchase | F9: Debit Note | T: Post Dated | F11: Features | F12: Configure

Calculator | ODBC Server | Ctrl + N

Gateway of Tally --> Display Menu --> Statements of Accounts --> ucher Register --> Accounting Voucher Alt | 9 : Release 1 | Fri, 4 May, 2007 | 22:08:50

II. Sample Voucher Entry (Cash and Bank Payment)

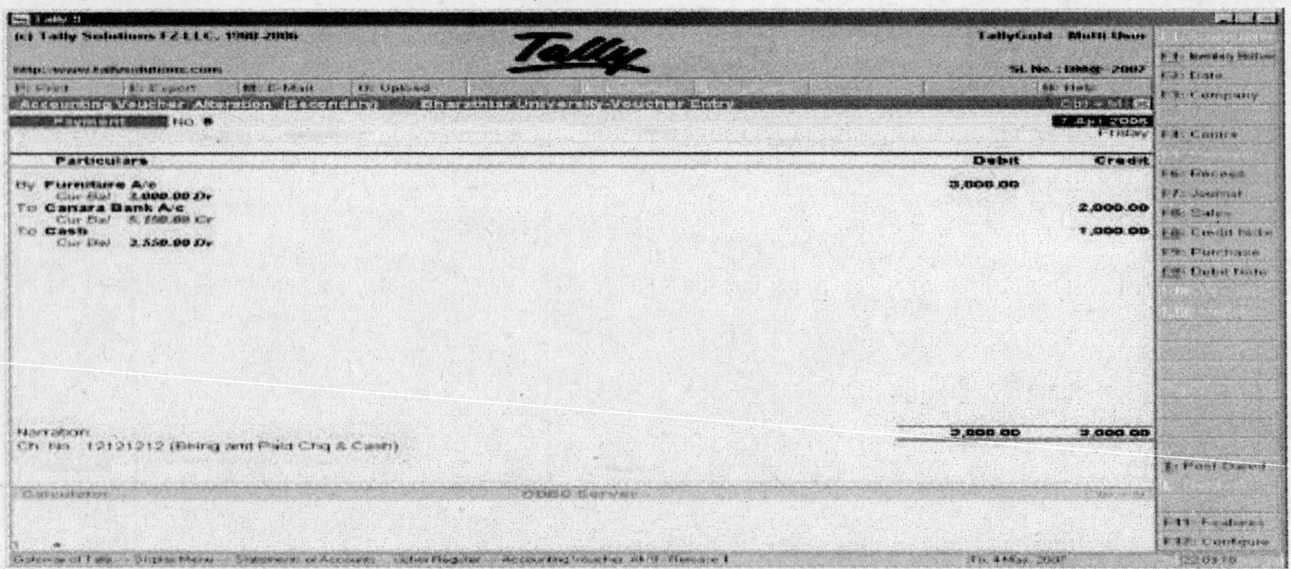

Tally Output Payment Voucher

Display → Statement of A/c → Statistics→ Payment → Select →Enter

Press Alt+F1 (Detailed Info)

Press "F12" Key (Configuration)

Show Narration also **Yes**

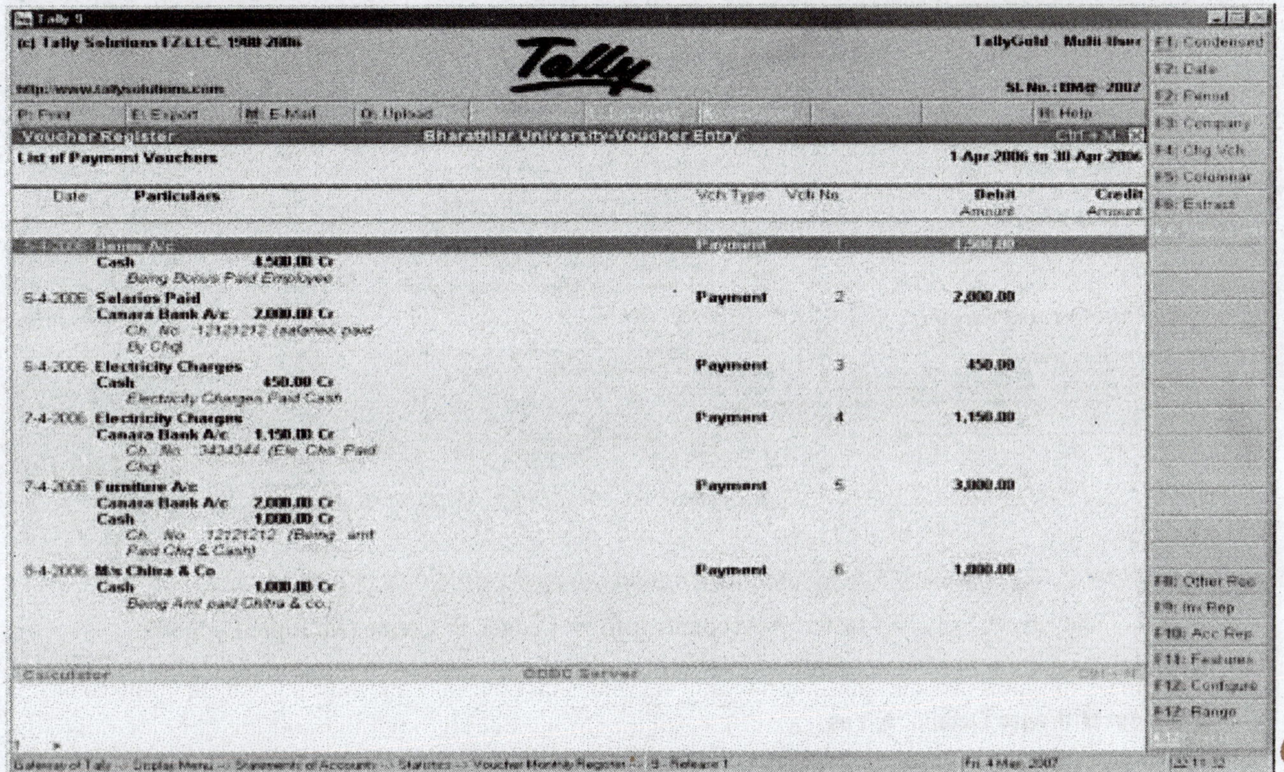

Maintain Bill-wise Details

EXERCISE

1. Raja Commenced with a Capital Rs. 10,000
2. Purchase goods from Kumar & Co. Rs. 15,000 paid three instalment within a five days gap,
3. Purchase goods for Cash Rs. 8,000
4. Sold goods to Rathna & Co. Rs. 20,000 amount to be paid in two instalments
5. Sold goods for cash Rs. 5,000
6. Received cash from Rathna & Co. Rs. 7,500
7. Paid to Kumar & Co. Rs. 7,500
8. Sold goods for cash Rs. 5,000

Tally Solution

Step 1: To Active F11 Features (Tally 9.0 Ver)

Outstanding Management

To Maintain Bill-wise Details → Yes

(Non-trading Also) Yes

Tally Output Display

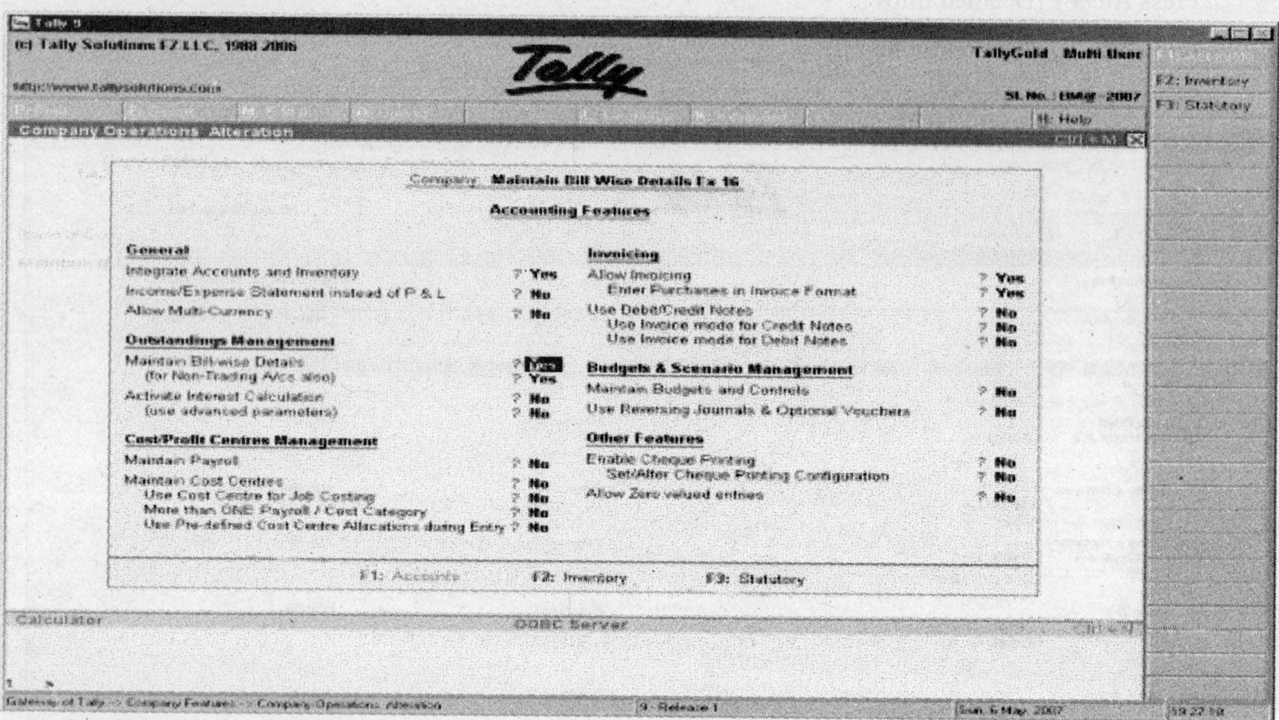

Step 2: Gateway of Tally → Master → Accounts Info → Ledger → Create (Multiple Ledgers)

Create Ledger With

Maintain Bill-wise Details → Yes

Show the following Display

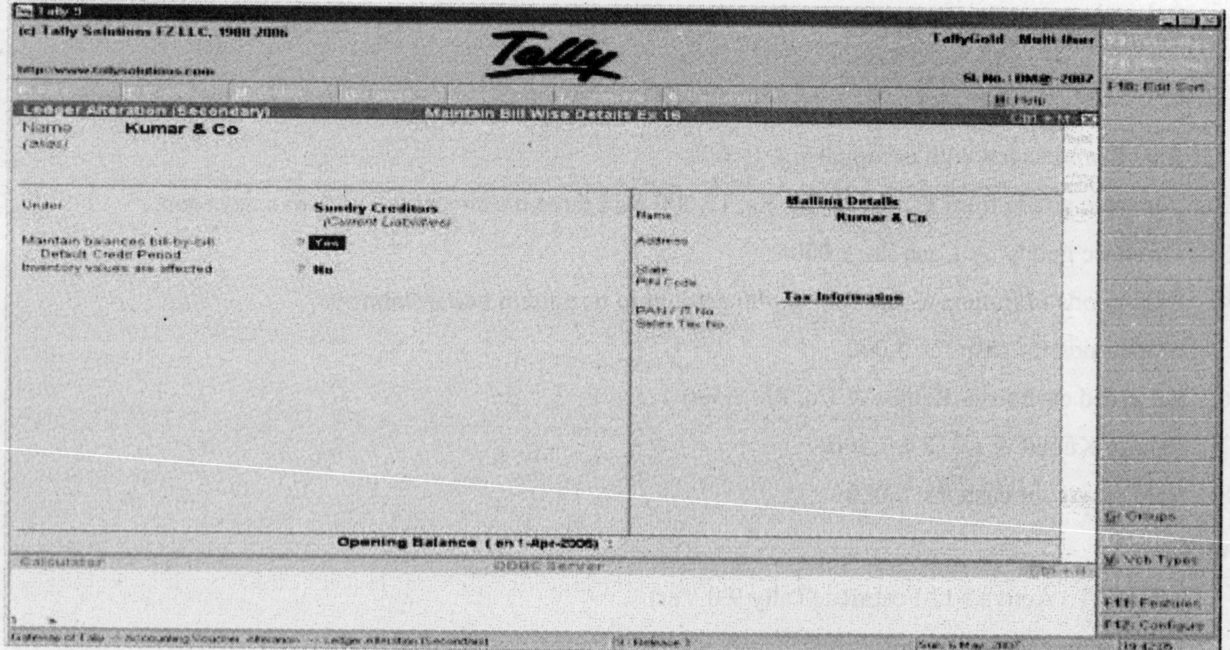

Tally Create Ledger (Output Display)

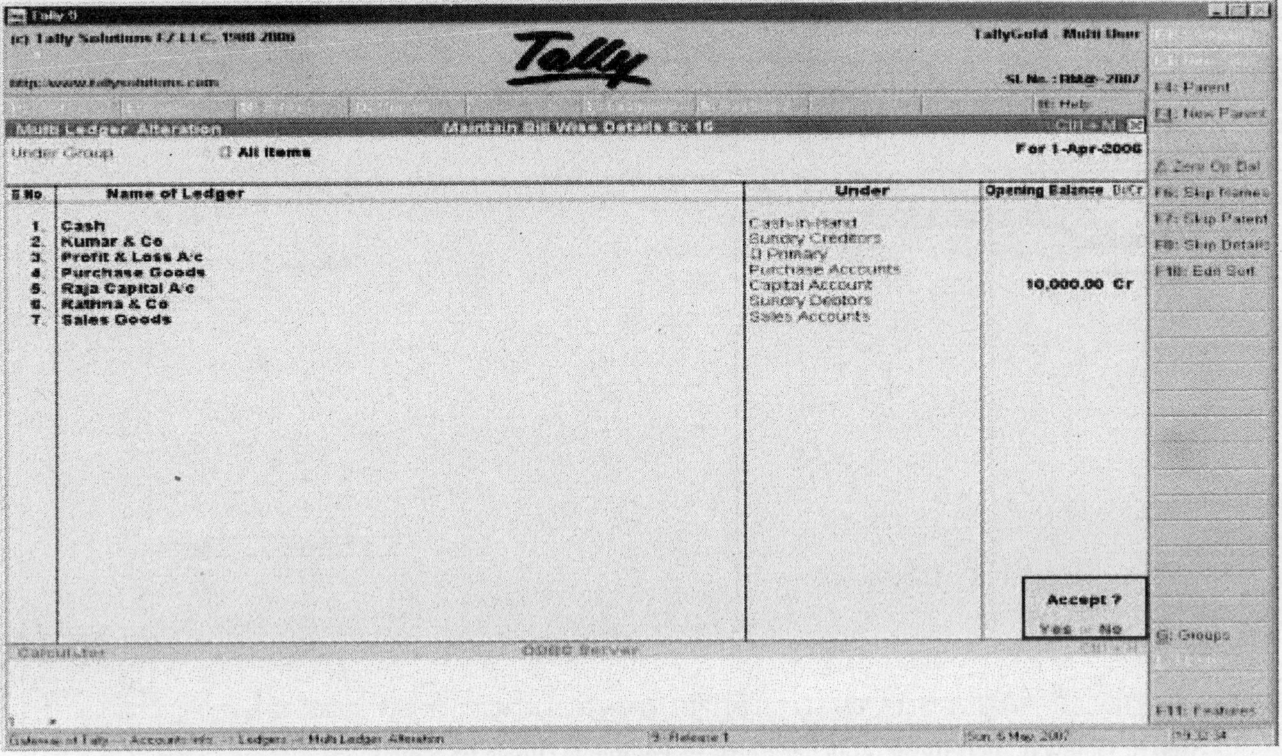

Step 3: Gateway of Tally → Accounting Voucher → Entry

Setup Configuration → Press F12 Keys

Show Bill-wise Details → Yes

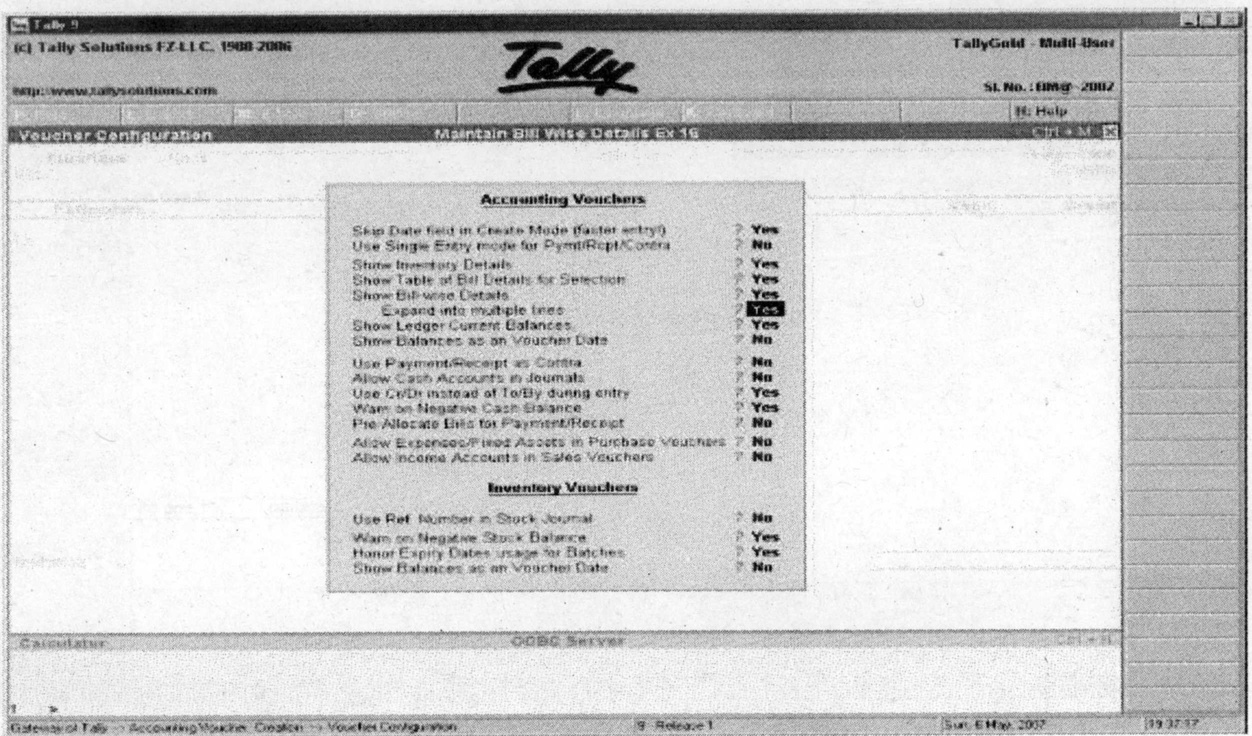

Step 4: Gateway of Tally → Voucher Entry → Receipts (Press F6 Keys)

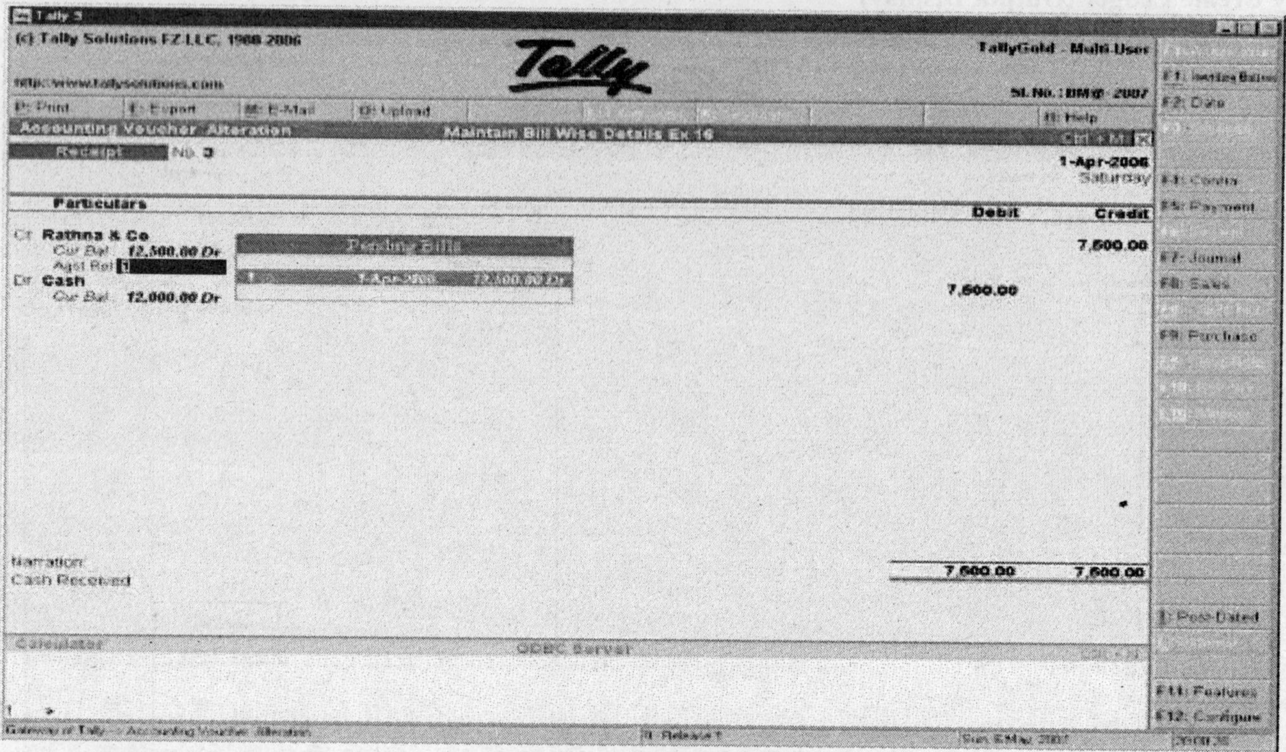

Step 5: Gateway of Tally → Voucher Entry → Payments (Press F5 Keys)

(c) Tally Solutions FZ-LLC, 1988-2006
Tally
TallyGold - Multi User
Accounting Voucher Alteration
Maintain Bill Wise Details Ex 16
Payment No. 2
1-Apr-2006
Saturday
Particulars
Debit
Credit
Dr Kumar & Co
Cur Bal: 7,500.00 Cr
Agst Ref
Pending Bills
Cr Cash
Cur Bal: 12,000.00 Dr
7,500.00
7,500.00
Narration:
Cash paid
7,500.00 7,500.00
F2: Date
F4: Contra
F6: Receipt
F7: Journal
F8: Sales
F9: Purchase
F11: Features
F12: Configure
Calculator
ODBC Server

Step 6: Gateway of Tally → Voucher Entry → Purchase (Press F9 Keys) →

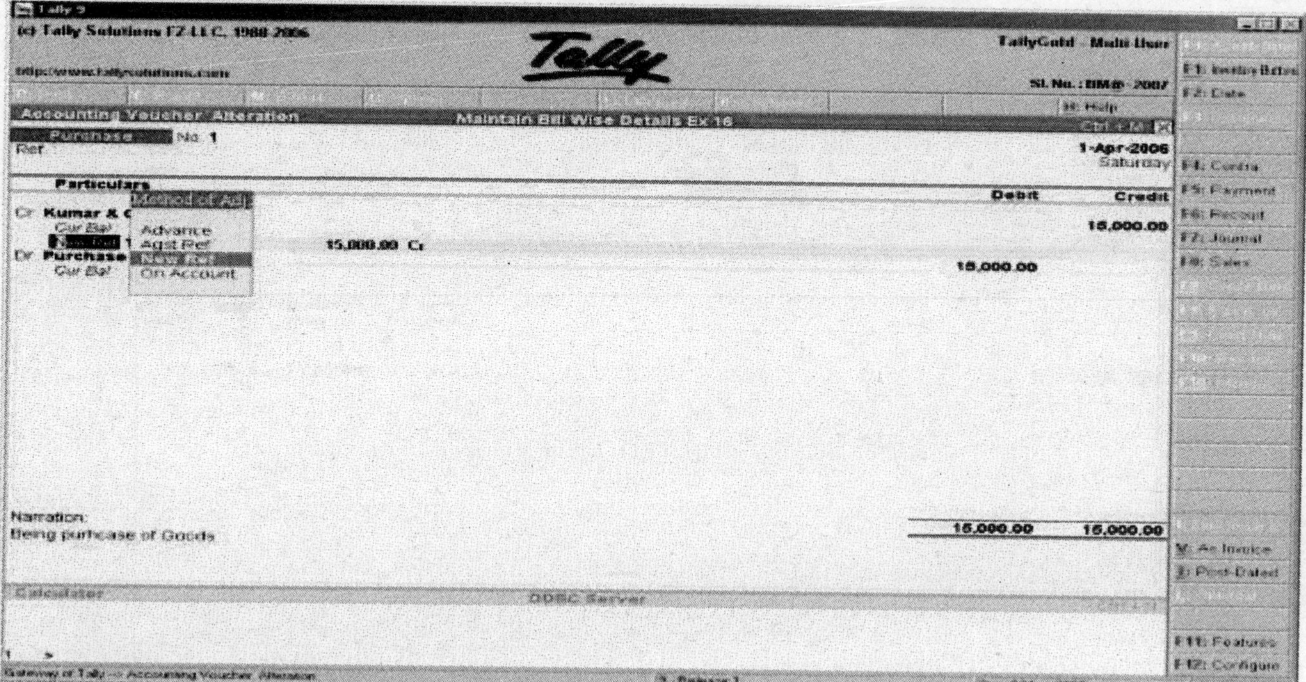

Show Output Display

Press F12 Keys Configuration Window Display

Bill-Wise Details → Yes

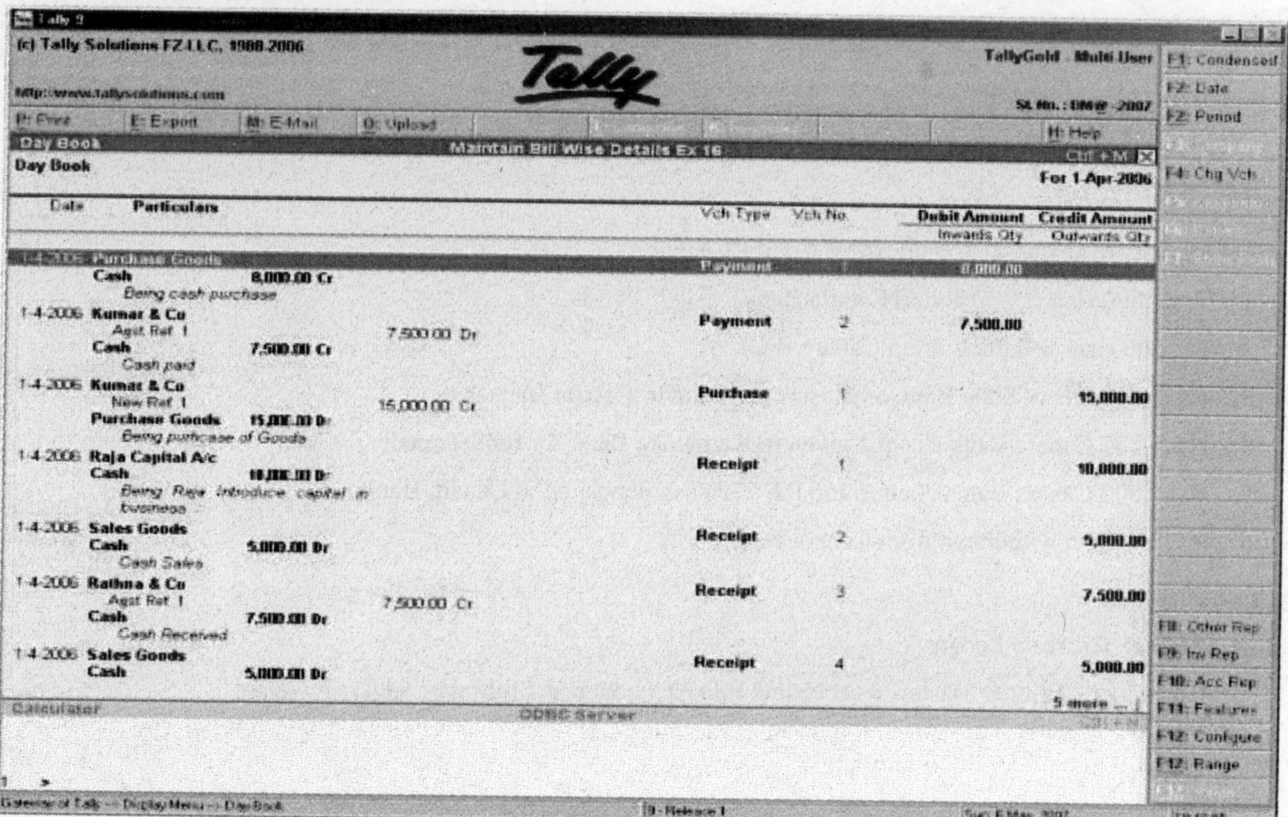

Steps 7: Show the Oustanding Display Screen

Gateway of Tally → Display → Statement of Accounts → Outstandins → Ledgers → Select

Show the Tally Display

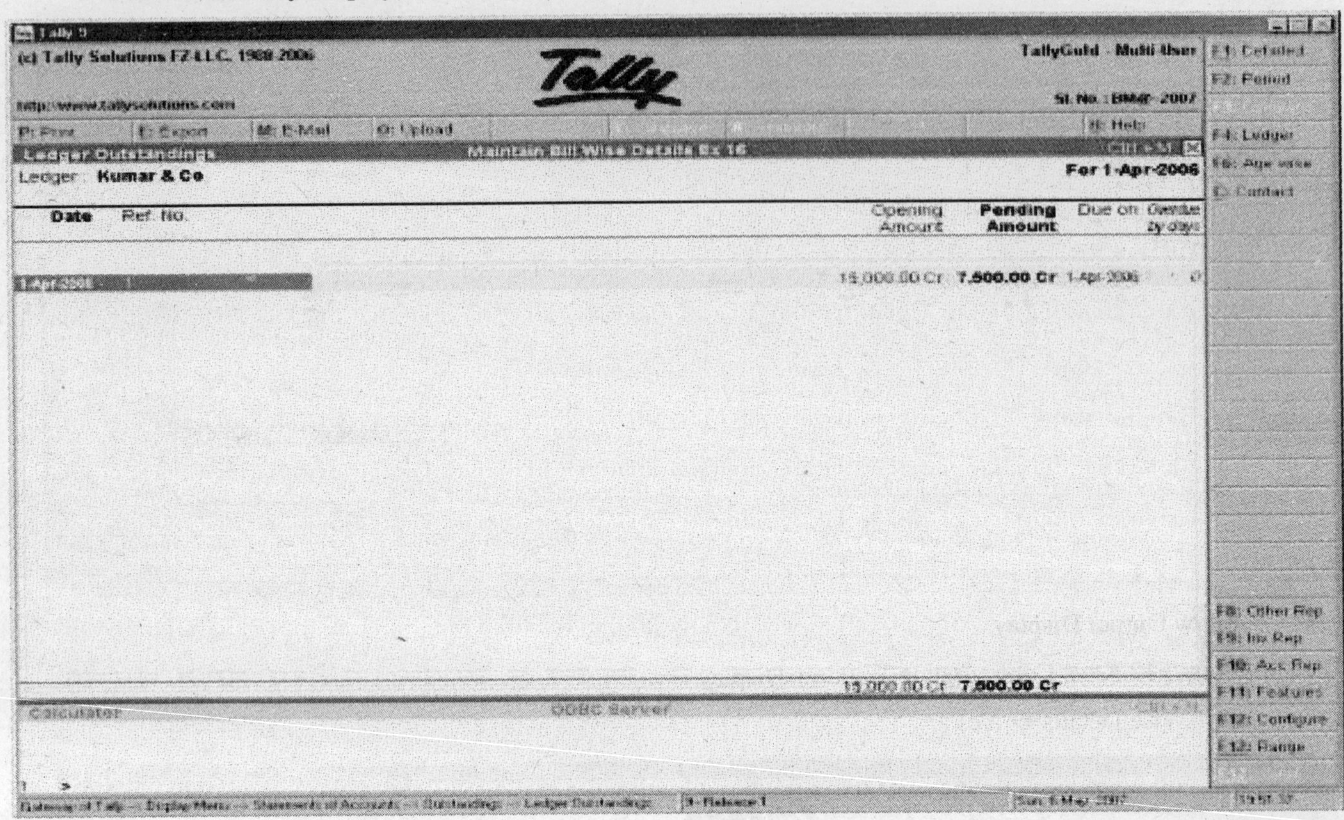

Contra Voucher - (F4) Key Use.

EXERCISE

From the following transaction prepare a Contra Voucher.

1. Rs. 2,500 Cash Deposit into Canara Bank.
2. Rs. 500 cash withdraw From Canara Bank.
3. Rs. 5,000 DD of State Bank of Mysore depositd to Canara Bank.
4. Rs. 1,500 Canara Bank Cheque given to Karnataka Bank for fund Transfer.
5. Rs. 1,000 Canara Bank Cheque and Rs. 750 cash deposited in Canara Bank.
6. Rs. 250 cash withdrawn from Canara Bank.

Tally Solution

Step 1: To create Ledger

Gateway of Tally →Master → Accounts Info → Ledger → Multiple Ledger → Create

	Ledger	Under (Group)
1.	Canara Bank A/c	Bank A/c (Current Assets)
2.	Cash A/c	(Tally provideedy default ledger)
3.	State Bank of Madurai (DD) -	Cash A/c
4.	Karnataka Bank a/c	Bank A/c

Accept

Yes/No — Select yes

Tally Output

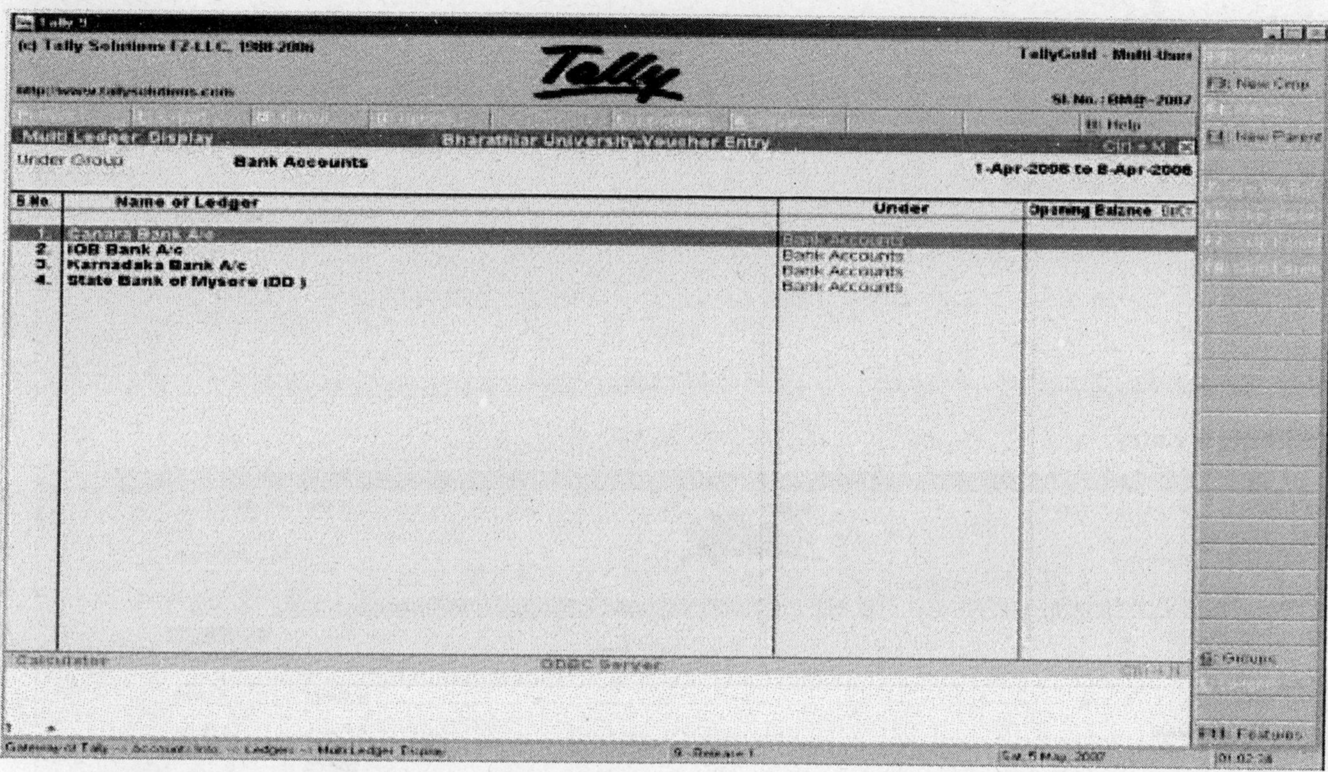

Step 2: To Press → F4 Key → Contra Voucher →

Rule for Voucher Entry:

I.	The Receiver is	Debit	
	What Goes out	Credit	(Deposit)
II.	The Giver is	Credit	
	What Comes in	Debit	(Withdraw)
III.	The Receiver is	Debit	
	The Giver is	Credit	(Bank Transfer)

I. Tally Sample Voucher Entry for Contra

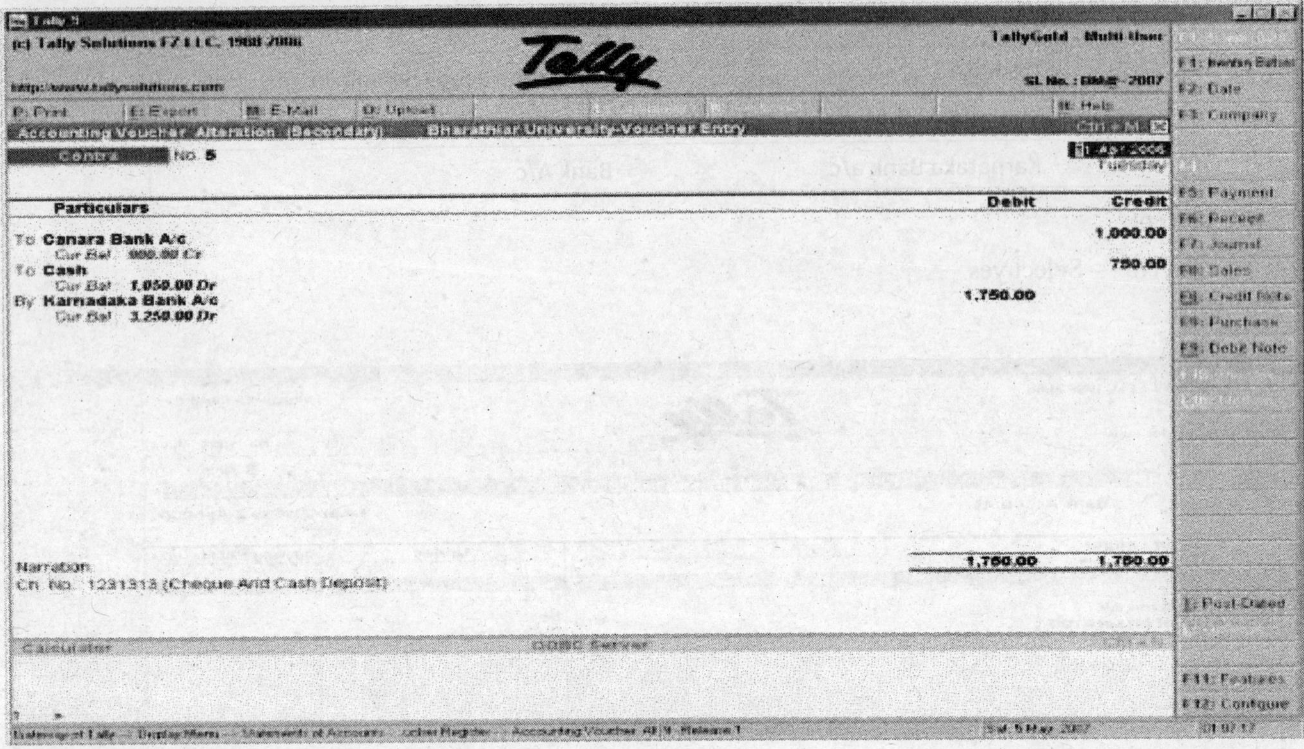

II. Withdraw Entry

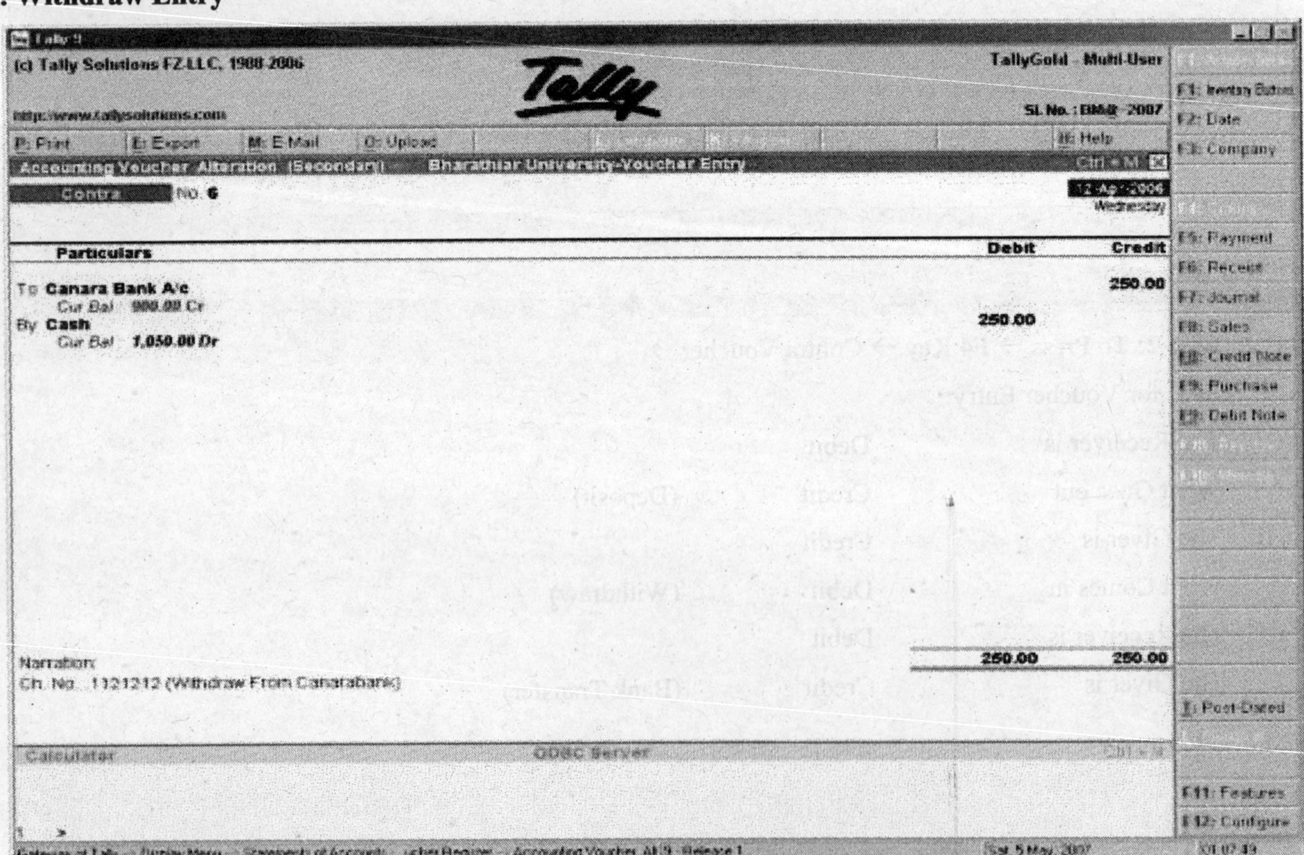

III. Fund Transfer

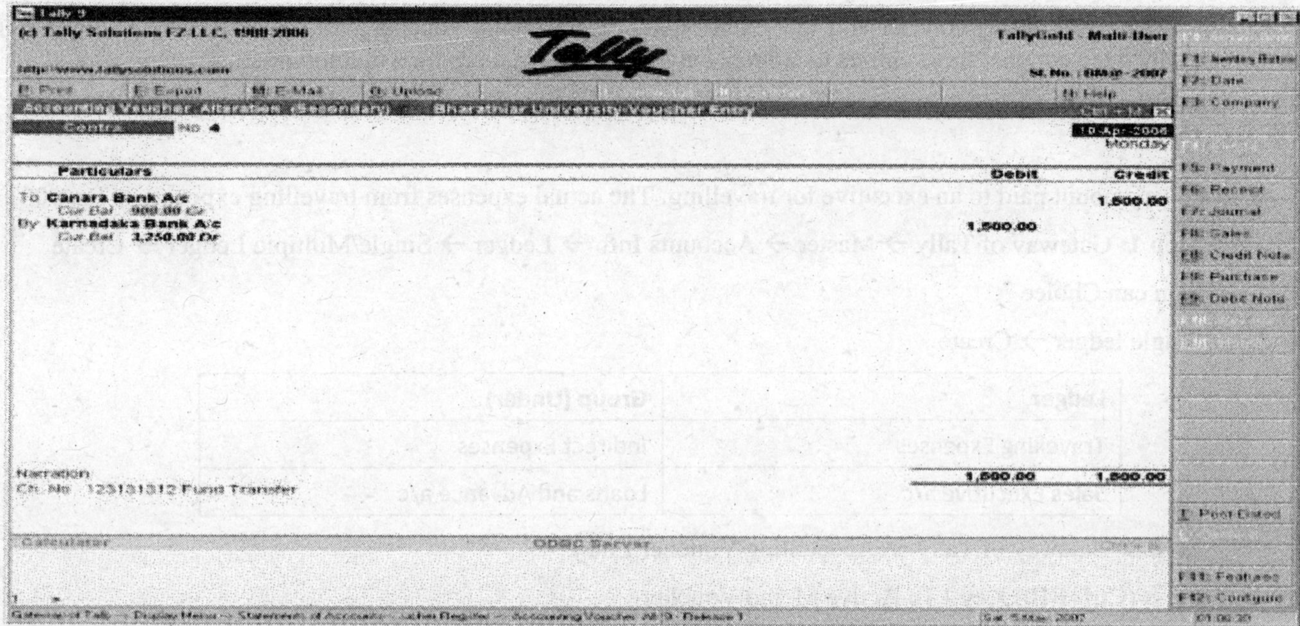

Tally Output

Contra Voucher

Display → Statement of A/c → Statistics → Contra → Select → Enter

Press Alt+F1 (Detailed Info) and Press "F12" Key (Configuration)

Show Narration also **Yes**

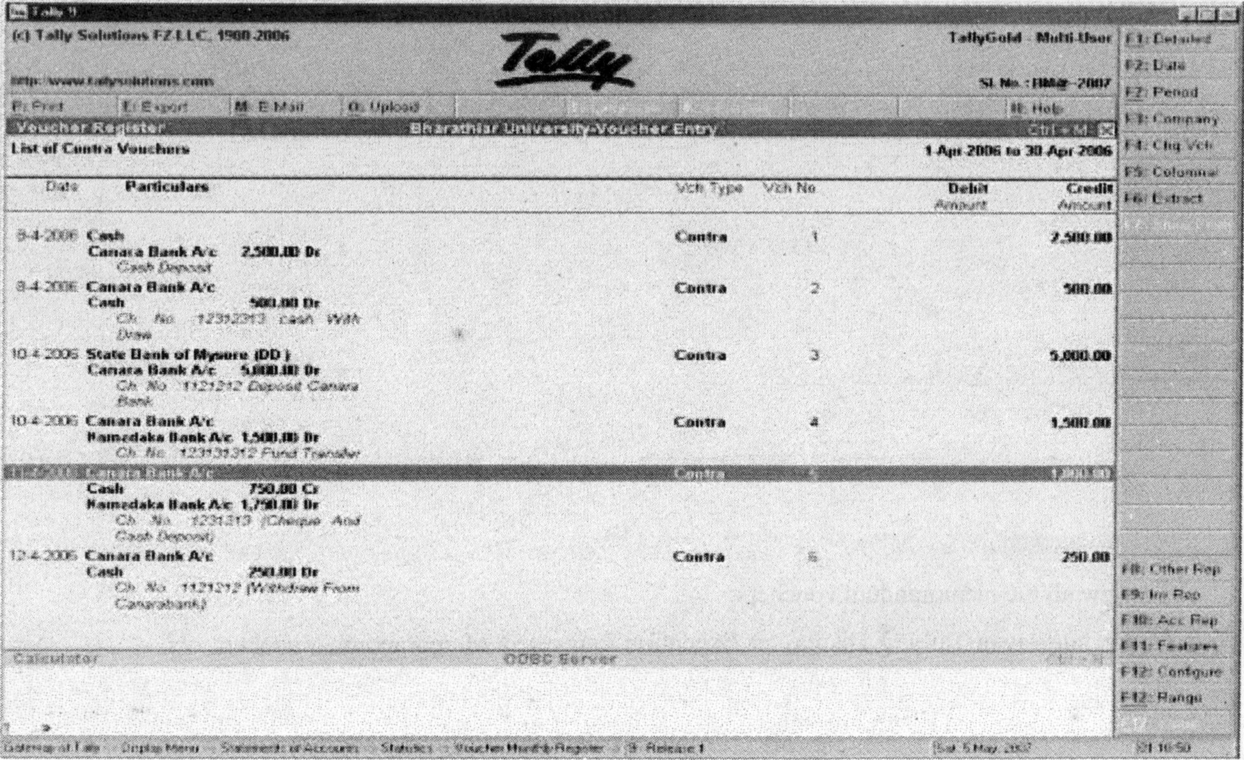

Memo Voucher

This is a **non-accounting** voucher and the entries made using memo voucher will not affect your accounts. In other words, tally does not post these entries to ledgers but stores them in a separate memorandum register.

EXERCISES

An advance amount paid to an executive for travelling. The actual expenses from travelling expenses is Rs. 500.

Step 1: Gateway of Tally → Master → Accounts Info → Ledger → Single/Multiple Ledger → Create

You can Choice

Single ledger → Create

Ledger	Group (Under)
Travelling Expenses	Indirect Expenses
Sales Executive a/c	Loans and Advance a/c

Step 2: Gateway of Tally → Accounting Voucher Entry

Press (Ctrl+F10) Key - To Active Memo Voucher

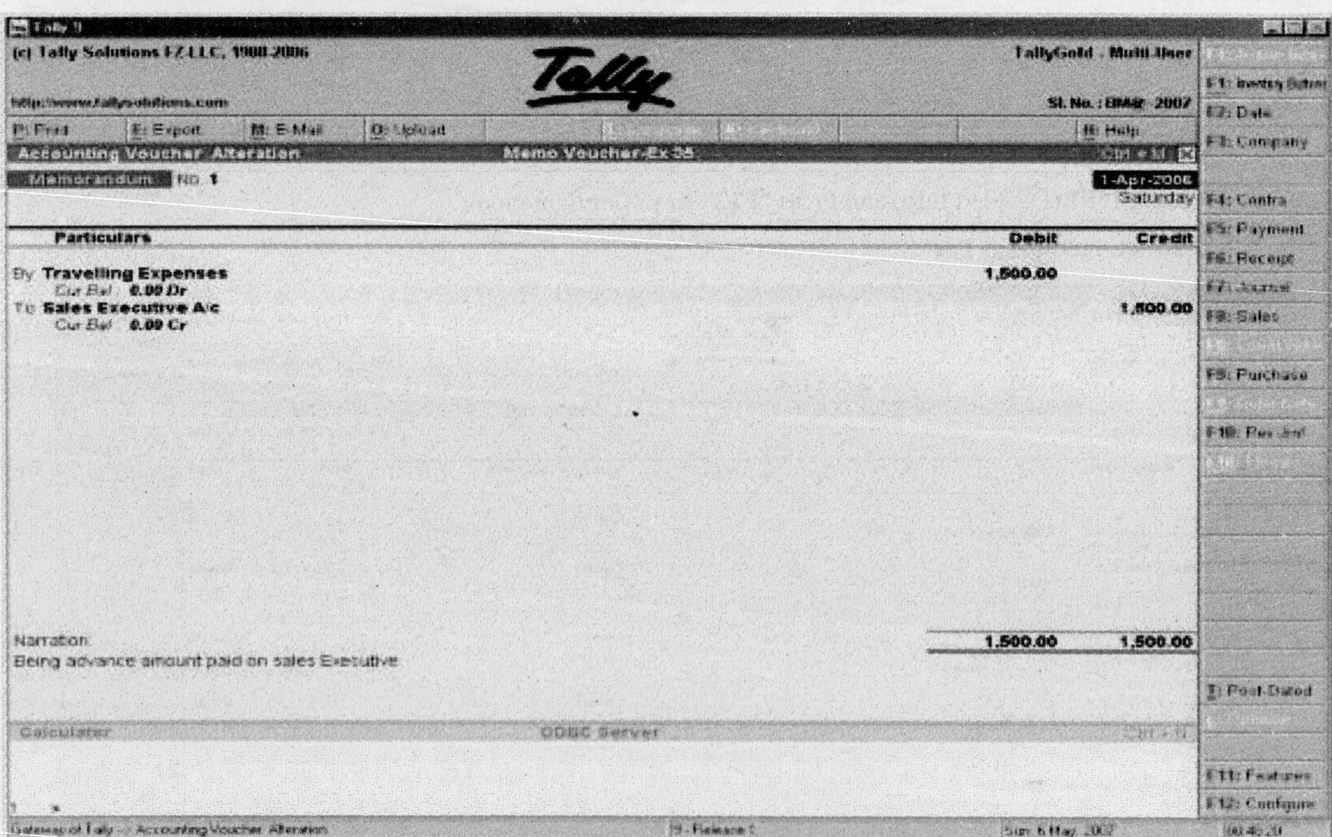

To view all the memorandum vouchers:

Go to Gateway of Tally → Display → Exception Reports → Memorandum Vouchers.

Tally Output

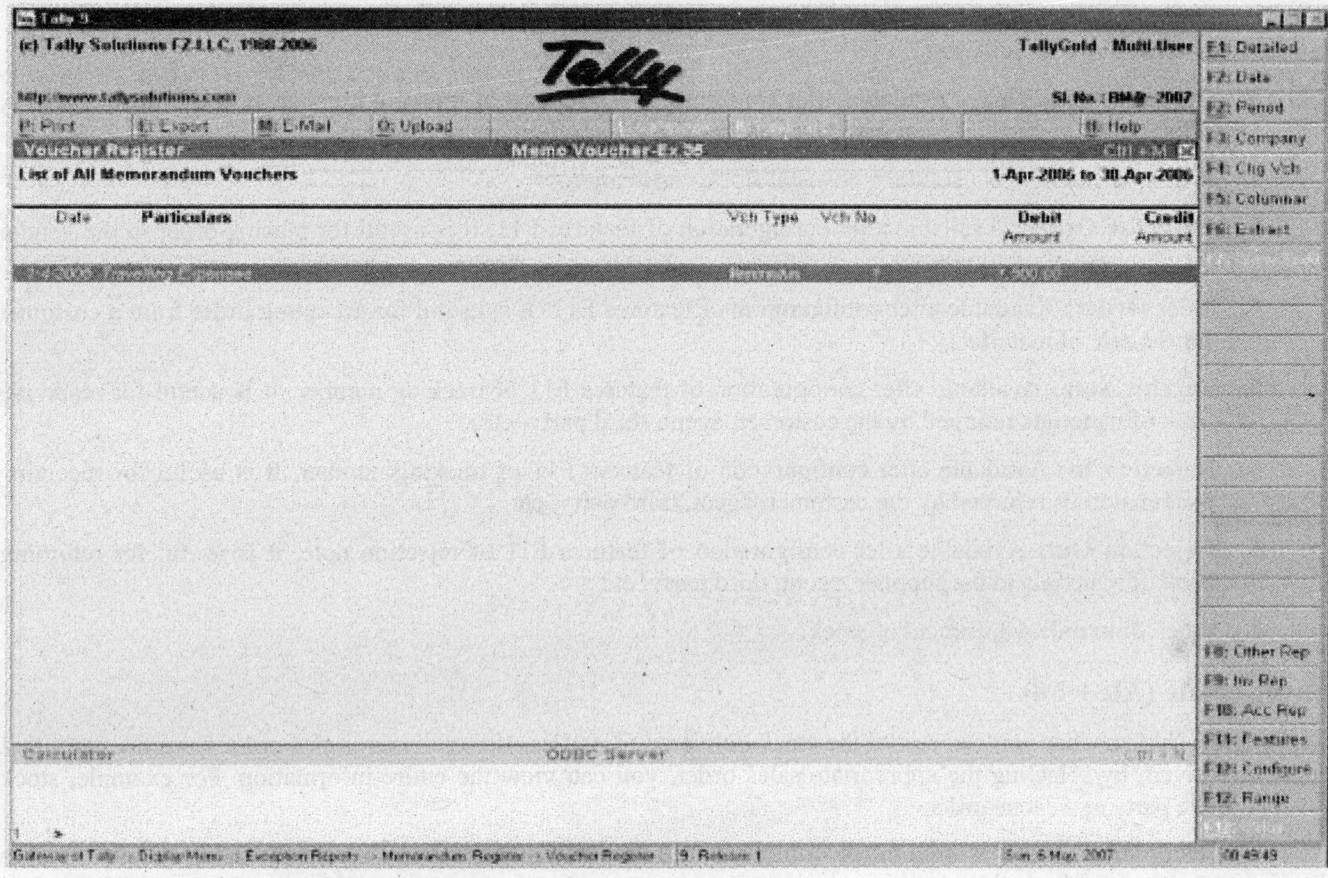

12.9 INVENTORY VOUCHERS USING TALLY.ERP 9

Accounting vouchers will update only accounts, but inventory vouchers will update both accounts and inventory. Inventory vouchers record the receipt and issue of goods/stock (movement of goods), the transfer of stock between locations and physical stock adjustments. If you have not integrated accounts with inventory, inventory vouchers will not have any impact on the Balance Sheet stock figures. The stock balances will be maintained separately. Set the option integrate accounts and inventory to Yes in F11: Features: F1: Accounting Features/Inventory Features.

Standard Vouchers

Tally.ERP 9 is preprogrammed with a variety of inventory vouchers, each designed to perform a different job. Some of them are available after configuration (F11). This voucher can be used in the following locations:

Company: SUDALAIANTO

Accouning Features

General	
Integrate Accounts and Inventory	? Yes
Income/Expense Statement instead of P & L	? Yes
Allow Multi-Currency	? Yes
Outstandings Management	
Maintain Bill-wise Details	? Yes
(for Non-Trading A/cs also)	? Yes
Activate Interest Calculation	? Yes
(use advanced parameters)	? Yes
Cost/Profit Centres Management	
Maintain Payroll	? Yes
Maintain Cost Centres	? Yes
Use Cost Centre for Job Costing	? Yes
More than ONE Payroll / Cost Category	? Yes
Use Pre-defined Cost Centre Allocations during Entry	? Yes
Show Opening Balance for Revenue Items in Reports	? No

Invoicing	
Allow Invoicing	? Yes
Enter Purchases in Invoice Format	? Yes
Use Debit/Credit Notes	? Yes
Use Invoice mode for Credit Notes	? Yes
Use Invoice mode for Debit Notes	? Yes
Budgets & Scenario Management	
Maintain Budgets and Controls	? Yes
Use Reversing Journals & Optional Vouchers	? Yes
Other Features	
Enable Cheque Printing	? Yes
Set/Alter Cheque Printing Configuration	? No
Allow Zero valued entries	? No
Maintain Multiple Mailing Details for Company & Ledgers	? Yes
Set/Alter Company Mailing Details	? No
Enable Company Logo	? Yes

Company: SUDALAIANTO

Inventory Features

General	
Integrate Accounts and Inventory	? Yes
Allow Zero valued entries	? No
Storage & Classification	
Maintain Multiple Godowns	? No
Maintain Stock Categories	? No
Maintain Batch-wise Details	? No
(set Expiry Dates for Batches)	? No
Use different Actual & Billed Qty	? No
Order Processing	
Allow Purchase Order Processing	? No
Allow Sales Order Processing	? No
Allow Job Order Processing (Note : Enables Maintain Multiple Godowns and Use Material in/Out)	? No

Invoicing	
Allow Invoicing	? Yes
Enter Purchases in Invoice Format	? Yes
Use Debit/Credit Notes	? Yes
Use Invoice mode for Credit Notes	? Yes
Use Invoice mode for Debit Notes	? Yes
Separate Discount column on Invoices	? No
Purchase Management	
Track additional costs of Purchase	? No
Sales Management	
Use Multiple Price Levels	? No
Other Features	
Use Tracking Numbers (Delivery/Receipt Notes)	? No
Use Rejection Inward/Outward Notes	? No
Use Material In/Out	? No
Use Cost Tracking for Stock Item	? No

Gateway of Tally.ERP 9 ▸ Inventory Voucher

Standard vouchers are as follows:

1. **Delivery Note:** This is available after configuring F11 feature of tracking number. It is useful for delivery of materials to customers, agents, third party or any other delivery of material.
2. **Physical Stock:** It is useful for physical stock verification.
3. **Purchase Order:** Available after configuration of features F11. It is useful for placing order to the vendor for purchase of materials.
4. **Sales Order:** Available after configuration of features F11. It is useful for accepting order from a customer for the sale of materials.
5. **Receipt Note:** Available after configuration of features F11 of tracking number. It is useful for receiving back of materials returned by the customer, agent, third party, etc.
6. **Rejection In:** Available after configuration of features F11 of tracking number. It is useful for receiving back materials returned by the customer, agent, third party, etc.
7. **Rejection Out:** Available after configuration of features F11 of rejection note, it is useful for returning back of materials to the supplier, agent, third party, etc.
8. **Stock Journal:** Adjustment of stock.

Delivery Note (Alt + F8)

By using this voucher you can record the stock delivered to parties. If there is any sales order from the party that has been received, by selecting the appropriate sales order, you can view the entire information. For example, stock delivered to the party against an order.

The delivery note voucher is used for recording goods delivered to a customer. To pass the delivery note voucher following steps can be followed:

Go to Gateway of Tally ▸ Inventory Vouchers

Press Alt+F8 or select the button F8: Delivery Note from the button bar.

SUDALAIANTO

Delivery Note Configuration

Accept Supplementary Details *(Address Details, Despatch Details etc.)*	? Yes
Allow Separate Buyer and Consignee Names	? Yes
Use Common Ledger A/c for Item Allocation	? Yes
Use Defaults for Bill Allocations	? Yes
Use Additional Description(s) for Item Name	? No
Use Pre-Closure order details	? No
Use Additional Description(s) for Ledger Name	? No
Consolidate Stock Items with same rates	? No
Show Compound Unit of Item based on Rate	? Yes
Show Full Details of Compound Unit	? No

Physical Stock Voucher (Alt + F10)

Physical stock voucher is used for recording the actual stock which is verified or counted. It could happen that the book stocks and the physical stock do not match. It is not unusual that the company finds a discrepancy between actual stock and computer stock figure.

To view the physical stock voucher, Go to Gateway of Tally ▸ Inventory Vouchers

Select the button F10 — Phys Stk from button bar or press Alt+F10.

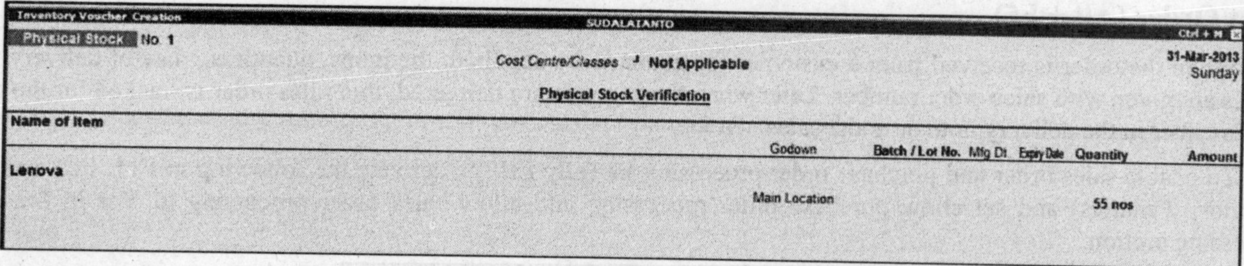

Inventory Voucher Creation — SUDALAIANTO — Ctrl + M

Physical Stock No. 1 — Cost Centre/Classes : Not Applicable — 31-Mar-2013, Sunday

Physical Stock Verification

Name of Item	Godown	Batch / Lot No.	Mfg Dt.	Expiry Date	Quantity	Amount
Lenova						
	Main Location				55 nos	

Physical stock quantity will be displayed as actual stock in the stock summary from the date of entry of the physical stock.

Purchase Order (Alt + F4): By using this voucher you can generate the purchase order register and keep track of records for orders placed to different parties.

Gateway of Tally.ERP ▸ Transactions ▸ Order Vouchers ▸ Purchase Order (Alt+F4)

Purchase Order: To enable Sales order and purchase order processing in Tally.ERP 9, activate the following in F11: Features (F2: Inventory Features)

Set allow purchase order processing and allow sales order processing to Yes in the order processing section.

Company: SUDALAIANTO

Inventory Features

General		Invoicing	
Integrate Accounts and Inventory	? Yes	Allow Invoicing	? Yes
Allow Zero valued entries	? Yes	Enter Purchases in Invoice Format	? Yes
Storage & Classification		Use Debit/Credit Notes	? Yes
Maintain Multiple Godowns	? Yes	Use Invoice mode for Credit Notes	? Yes
Maintain Stock Categories	? Yes	Use Invoice mode for Debit Notes	? Yes
Maintain Batch-wise Details	? Yes	Separate Discount column on Invoices	? Yes
(set Expiry Dates for Batches)	? Yes	**Purchase Management**	
Use different Actual & Billed Qty	? Yes	Track additional costs of Purchase	? Yes
Order Processing		**Sales Management**	
Allow Purchase Order Processing	? Yes	Use Multiple Price Levels	? No
Allow Sales Order Processing	? Yes	**Other Features**	
Allow Job Order Processing	? Yes	Use Tracking Numbers (Delivery/Receipt Notes)	? Yes
(Note: Enables Maintain Multiple Godowns and Use Material In/Out)		Use Rejection Inward/Outward Notes	? Yes
		Use Material In/Out	? Yes
		Use Cost Tracking for Stock Item	? Yes

P: Print | E: Export | M: E-Mail | O: Upload | S: Shop | G: Language | K: Keyboard | K: Control Centre | H: Support Centre | H: Help

Order Voucher Creation — SUDALAIANTO — Ctrl + M

Purchase Order No. 1 — Cost Centre/Classes : Not Applicable — 31-Mar-2013, Sunday

Party's A/c Name : M/s Rohini Bharadwaj Merchants
Current Balance : 2,08,000.00 Cr Credit Limit: 45,000.00 Cr
Purchase Ledger : Purchases@4%
VAT/Tax Class : Purchases @ 4%
Order No. : 1

Name of Item	Quantity Actual	Quantity Billed	Rate	per	Disc %	Amount
DELL	100 nos	100 nos	65,000.00	nos		65,00,000.00
Trade Discount			(-)5 %			(-)3,25,000.00
Input VAT @ 4%			4 %			2,60,000.00
	100 nos	100 nos				

Show Statutory Details ? No
Narration

Accept ? Yes or No

Sales Order (Alt + F5)

When the order is received from a customer for goods to be supplied, the items, quantities, date of delivery, etc., details are given with sales order number. Later when these goods are delivered, this sales order is tracked for the order details either in the delivery note or in the sales invoice.

To enable sales order and purchase order processing in Tally.ERP 9, activate the following in F11: Features (F2: Inventory Features) and set allow purchase order processing and allow sales order processing to Yes in the order processing section.

Order Processing	
Allow Purchase Order Processing	? Yes
Allow Sales Order Processing	? Yes

Sales order entry is exactly like the purchase order entry. Sales order details will also depend on configuration settings. To create a sales order,

Gateway of Tally.ERP ▸ Transactions ▸ Order Vouchers ▸ Sales Order (Alt+F5) or F5

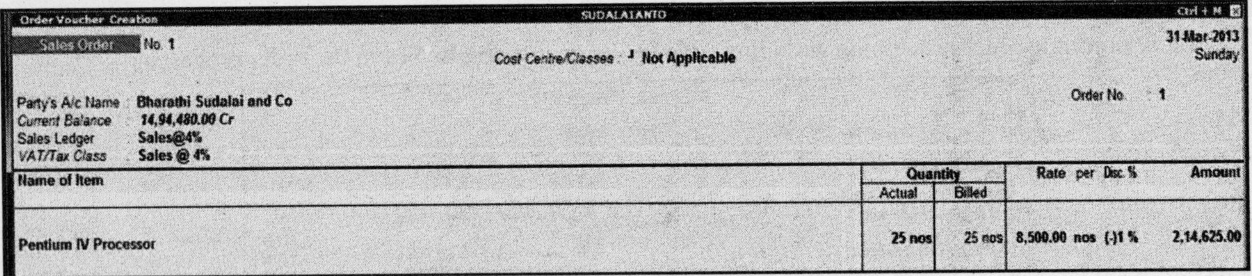

Viewing Sales/Purchase Order Position

To view the order position in Stock Summary:

Go to Gateway of Tally ▸ Stock Summary

- ❖ Press Alt + F1 (For detailed view)
- ❖ Press Alt + N ▸ Select Orders and Stock Details

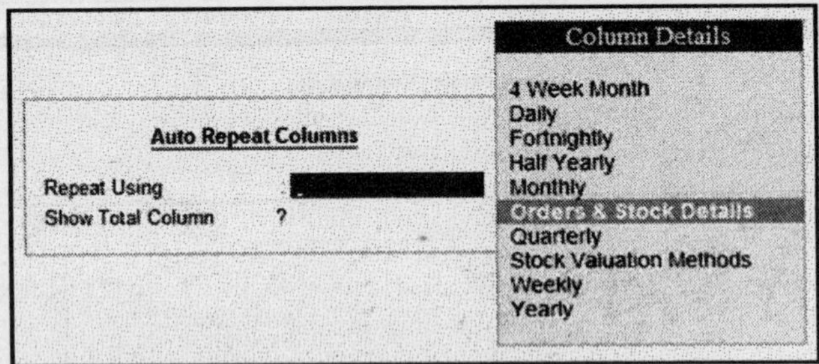

Stock Summary — SUDALAIANTO

Particulars	SUDALAIANTO 1-Apr-2012 to 31-Mar-2013 Stock details for Our Stock with us & Third Party			SUDALAIANTO 1-Apr-2012 to 31-Mar-2013 Sales Orders Outstanding			SUDALAIANTO 1-Apr-2012 to 31-Mar-2013 Saleable Stock			SUDALAIANTO 1-Apr-2012 to 31-Mar-2013 Purchase Orders Outstanding		
	Closing Balance			On Order			Closing Balance			On Order		
	Quantity	Rate	Value	Quantity	Rate	Value	Quantity	Rate	Value	Quantity	Rate	Value
												1 more ... →
Computer	183 nos	48,185.79	88,18,000.00				**183 nos**	**48,185.79**	**88,18,000.00**	**100 nos**	**65,000.00**	**65,00,000.00**
Acer	37 nos	19,000.00	7,03,000.00				37 nos	19,000.00	7,03,000.00			
DELL	91 nos	65,000.00	59,15,000.00				91 nos	65,000.00	59,15,000.00	100 nos	65,000.00	65,00,000.00
Lenova	55 nos	40,000.00	22,00,000.00				55 nos	40,000.00	22,00,000.00			
Hardware	**145 nos**	4,492.76	**6,51,450.00**	**26 nos**	8,585.00	**2,14,625.00**	**120 nos**	4,492.76	**5,39,131.03**			
14" Flat Monitor	15 nos	6,400.00	96,000.00				15 nos	6,400.00	96,000.00			
LG DVD Writer	47 nos	1,350.00	63,450.00				47 nos	1,350.00	63,450.00			
Pentium IV Processor	30 nos	7,655.00	2,29,650.00	25 nos	8,585.00	2,14,625.00	5 nos	7,655.00	38,275.00			
Samsung	53 nos	4,950.00	2,62,350.00				53 nos	4,950.00	2,62,350.00			
Grand Total	**328 nos**		**94,69,450.00**	**25 nos**		**2,14,625.00**	**303 nos**		**93,57,131.03**	**100 nos**		**65,00,000.00**

Viewing Purchase or Sales Order Outstanding

Go to Gateway of Tally ▸ Stock Summary ▸ Press F9 ▸ select Purchase or Sales Order

Receipt Note (Alt + F9)

By using receipt note you can record the stock received from the parties. If any purchase order has already been raised to the party, you may bring the entire information within this receipt note by selecting the appropriate purchase order. For example, stock received from the party against an order.

To view the Receipt Note Voucher:

Go to Gateway of Tally ▸ Inventory Vouchers

Press the button Alt+F9 or Select the button F9 — rcpt. Note from the Button Bar.

Under F12: Configure (Receipt Note Configuration) set the option Accept Supplementary Details to Yes.

SUDALAIANTO

Receipt Note Configuration

Accept Supplementary Details ? Yes
(Address Details, Despatch Details etc.)

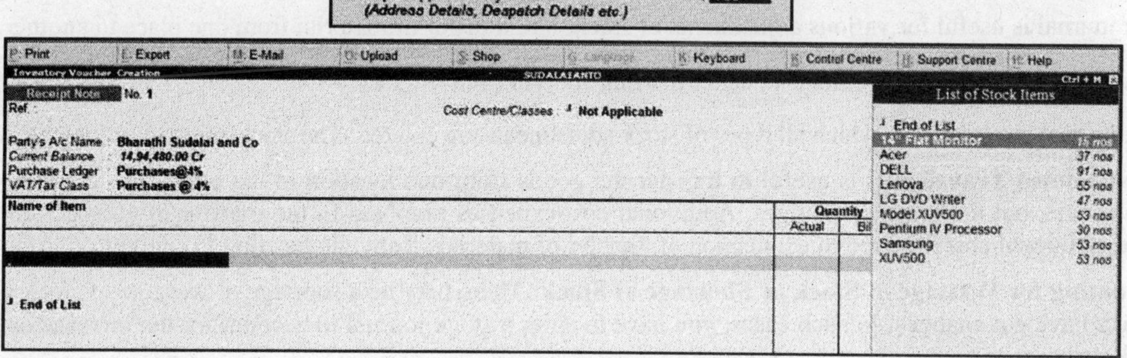

Rejection In (Ctrl + F6)

This voucher is used to record goods received back from a customer after rejection. For example, the company takes back items rejected by a customer into the stock.

To view the Rejections in Voucher:

Go to Gateway of Tally ▸ Inventory Vouchers

Press the Ctrl+F6 or select the button F6: Rej. In from the Button Bar

In Case M/s. Rohini Bharadwaj Merchants returns DELL (3 nos.) delivered by M/s. Sudalaian to

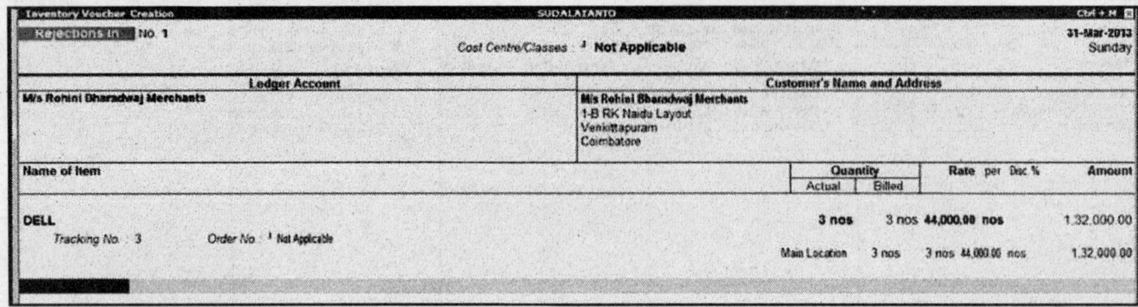

Rejection Out (Alt + F6)

This voucher is used to record goods returned back that were rejected by the company. For example, the company returns back those items that were rejected by a vendor.

To view Rejections out Voucher:

Go to Gateway of Tally ▸ Inventory Vouchers

Press Alt+F6 or Select the button F6 - Rej. Out from the Button Bar

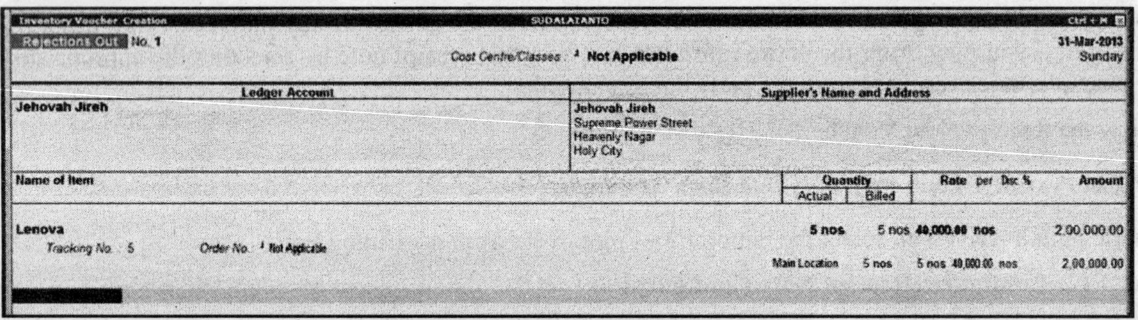

Stock Journal (Alt + F7)

Stock journal is useful for various adjustments of stock, like transfer of material from one place to another.

Gateway of Tally.ERP ▸ Inventory Voucher ▸ Stock Journal (Alt + F7)

Stock journal is a journal in which all types of stock adjustments are entered. The stock adjustment may be due to:

Inter-Godown Transfer: It is useful to transfer the goods from one location to the other. The quantity of stock remains the same, but the location changes. Additional cost/expenses involved in the transfer of goods. You can also account the additional cost incurred in connection of transfer of materials from one location to another.

Accounting for Wastage of Stock or Shortage of Stock: There may be a shortage or wastage of stock items, the quantity may have got changes. In such cases, you have to enter a stock journal to account for the increase or decrease in the stock item.

Manufacturing Process: If you are involved in the manufacturing process in which raw materials are consumed and finished goods are produced, then you can create a manufacturing journal voucher also.

To view the stock journal voucher,

Go to Gateway of Tally ▸ Inventory Vouchers

Press the buttons Alt + F7 or Select the button F7 - Stock Journal from the Button Bar

For example, the M/s. Sudalai Anto transfers Lenova from shop to godown which is referred as main location. To get the godown details enable the feature Maintain multiple godowns in F11: Features: F2: Inventory

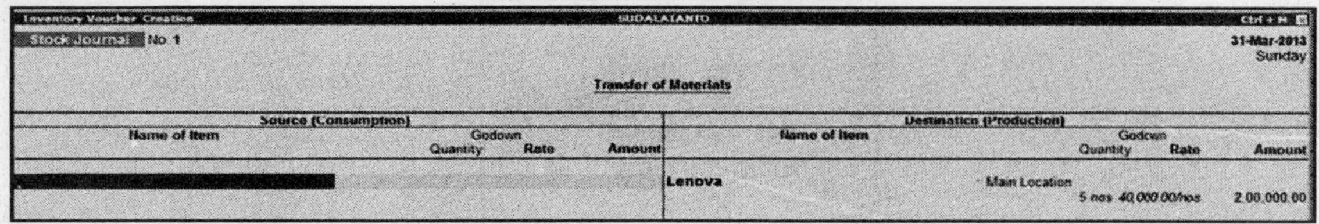

Shows the transfer of 5numbers of Lenova is sent to Godown from Shop

Additional Cost on Purchase in Stock Journal

To get the additional cost details in the stock journal voucher, enable track additional costs of purchase in F11: Features: F2: Inventory Features.

When there are some additional cost/expenses incurred, then you can account the same in the stock journal. After mentioning the quantity, rate and amount under destination (production), the 'Additional Cost Details' screen will be displayed. Enter the additional cost/expense incurred.

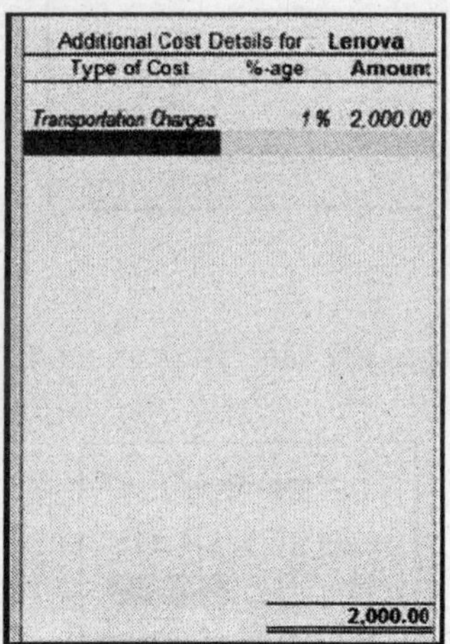

12.10 REPORTING IN TALLY.ERP 9

This chapter will explain the different types of inventory books, where you will learn to view group summary, stock transfers and physical stock register. It also describes in detail the different types of exception reports and how these are generated and used in Tally.ERP 9.

Features of Report generation in TALLY.ERP 9

Using the features of Tally.ERP 9, we can perform the following things:

- ❖ Modify reports
- ❖ Configure the balance sheet
- ❖ View the profit and loss account
- ❖ Define stock summary

- ❖ Know the purpose of a trial balance report
- ❖ List the transactions of a day book
- ❖ Create different types of books of account
- ❖ Clarify the exception reports available in Tally.ERP 9

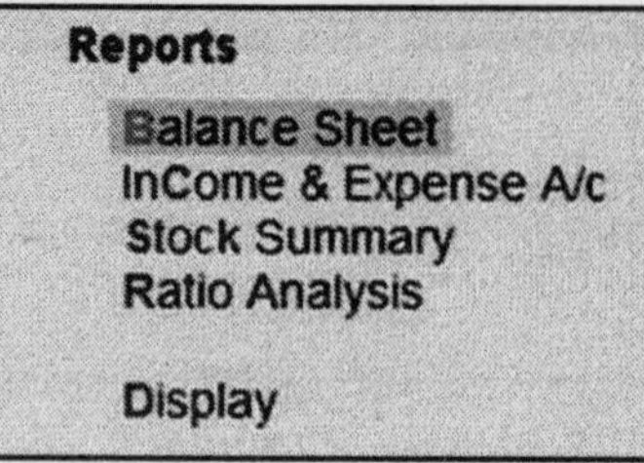

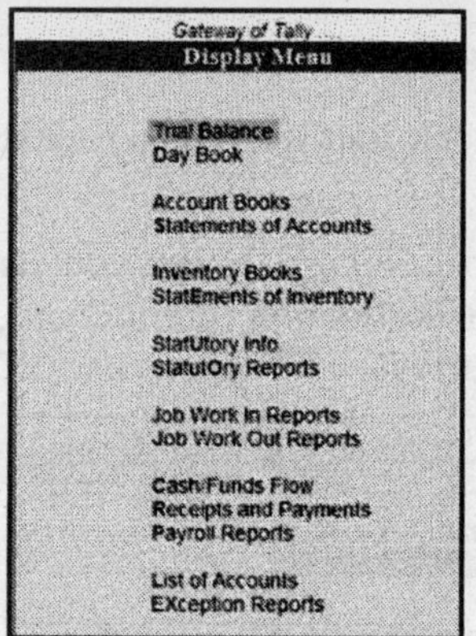

Modifying Reports

Once you have selected a report and its screen appears, you can modify the display to suit your requirements using the appropriate buttons on the button bar.

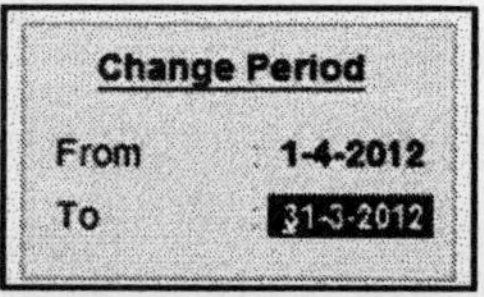

On selecting a report, the screen displays. Modify the display to suit your requirements using the appropriate buttons from the button bar. If you select the buttons using the keyboard, the conventions are:

F (n): Press the F (n) key

F (n): Press Alt + F (n)

F (n): Press Ctrl + F (n)

(Alt + F1) F1: Detailed/Condensed: Adds a further level of detail to the report, or condenses the report to a higher level of detail.

F2: Period: Enables you to change the period of the report by specifying new from/to dates.

F3: Company: If you have more than one company selected, this button enables you to change companies to display the new company data in the current screen format.

F4: to F10: The functions performed by these buttons vary from report-to-report.

F11: Company Features: This button is not related to displaying reports but to selecting options that affect voucher entry. The screen it displays must not be changed during training.

F12: Configure: This button is very relevant to displaying reports and enables you to define the report-specific options you wish to use. For example, depending on the report you are in, you can specify whether it should be in horizontal or vertical format, show percentages, show gross profit, show opening and/or closing balances, change the periodicity, change the sorting method, and so on.

F12: Range: This button enables you to filter the information you see displayed based on monetary value.

F12: Value: This button enables you to filter which vouchers you wish to be used in the calculations. For example, you can specify you only want vouchers having a narration containing the expression 'Sudalai Anto'.

New Column: This button enables you to add another column to the report to display comparable information for another company, or for a different period for the same company, all on the same screen.

Alter Column: This button enables you to alter the details of a new column you have previously created. You select the column to alter by positioning the cursor in it prior to selecting the button.

Del Column: You use this button to delete columns you no longer wish to see in the report. **Auto Column** — You use this button to add multiple columns to a report. You can also have a total column for the total of each item across all columns.

Balance Sheet: A Balance Sheet is a financial statement that reports a firm's financial position at a specific time. The term balance sheet implies that a report shows the balance between two figures. It shows a balance between the assets and liabilities of a firm and the owner's funds. The fundamental accounting equation applicable is therefore, Assets = Liabilities + Owner's Equity.

To view the Balance Sheet, Go to Gateway of Tally ▸ Balance Sheet

Balance Sheet — SUDALAIANTO — Ctrl + M

Liabilities		SUDALAIANTO as at 31-Mar-2013	
Capital Account			
Loans (Liability)			
Excess of Expenditure over Income		(-)32,492.63	0.24 %
Opening Balance			
Current Period	32,492.63		
Diff in Opening Balances		1,36,07,325.00	100.24 %
Total		1,35,74,832.37	100 %

Assets		SUDALAIANTO as at 31-Mar-2013	
Fixed Assets		1,00,50,000.00	74.03 %
Furnitures and Fixtures	15,000.00		
Building	6,50,000.00		
Furnitures and Fixtures	8,85,000.00		
Land	85,00,000.00		
Working Capital		35,24,832.37	25.97 %
Current Assets			
Closing Stock	98,66,071.62		
Sundry Debtors	(-)12,98,600.00		
Cash-in-hand	(-)1,81,816.00		
Bank Accounts	2,10,087.75		
Cash in Bank	2,50,000.00		
Stock	25,000.00		
	88,70,743.37		
Less: Current Liabilities			
Duties & Taxes	(-)2,84,266.50		
Sundry Creditors	56,30,177.50		
	53,45,911.00		
Total		1,35,74,832.37	100 %

Trial Balance: A trial balance is a summary of all ledger balances to check whether the figures are correct and balanced. Considering that the journal entries are error-free and posted correctly to the general ledger, the total of all debit balances should equal the total of all the credit balances. In Tally.ERP 9, the matching of the trial balance is a foregone conclusion since all voucher entries are in Debit-credit format and must balance at the entry point.

To view the Trial Balance,

Go to Gateway of Tally ▸ Display ▸Trial Balance

Trial Balance — SUDALAIANTO — Ctrl + M

Particulars	SUDALAIANTO 1-Apr-2012 to 31-Mar-2013 Closing Balance Debit	Credit
... 2 more		
Sundry Creditors		56,30,177.50
Fixed Assets	**1,00,50,000.00**	
Furnitures and Fixtures	15,000.00	
Building	6,50,000.00	
Furnitures and Fixtures	8,85,000.00	
Land	85,00,000.00	
Current Assets	**41,41,505.00**	**19,79,508.25**
Opening Stock	31,57,325.00	
Sundry Debtors	1,95,880.00	14,94,480.00
Cash-in-hand		1,81,816.00
Bank Accounts	5,13,300.00	3,03,212.25
Cash in Bank	2,50,000.00	
Stock	25,000.00	
Sales Accounts	**8,02,500.00**	**(-)1,32,000.00**
Sales Bills to Make		(-)1,32,000.00
Sales@4%	8,02,500.00	
Purchase Accounts	**61,25,325.00**	**3,31,362.50**
Purchases@4%	61,25,325.00	
Trade Discount		3,31,362.50
Indirect Expenses	20,500.00	7,723.25
Office Rent	8,000.00	
Salary	12,500.00	
Transportation Charges		7,723.25
Diff. in Opening Balances		1,36,07,325.00
Grand Total	**2,14,24,096.50**	**2,14,24,096.50**

In this view, each group is expressed as a percentage of the total of the Balance Sheet

Profit & Loss Account: To View Profit & Loss Account of M/S SudalaiAnto Limited

Go to Gateway of Tally.ERP ▸ Profit & Loss A/c

Press ALT+F1 for detailed Profit and Loss Account

Income & Expenditure Statement — SUDALAIANTO — Ctrl + H

Particulars		SUDALAIANTO 1-Apr-2012 to 31-Mar-2013
Trading Account :		
Sales Accounts		(-)9,34,500.00 100 %
Cost of Sales :		(-)9,14,784.12 97.89 %
Opening Stock	31,57,325.00	
Add: Purchase Accounts	57,93,962.50	
Less: Closing Stock	98,66,071.62	
	9,14,784.12	
Direct Expenses		
Gross Profit :		(-)19,715.88 (-)2.11 %
Income Statement :		
Indirect Expenses		12,776.75 1.37 %
Excess of Income over Expenditure :		(-)32,492.63 (-)3.48 %

Stock Summary: Stock Summary can be further configured to derive the following information.

1. **Stock Flow:** This can be viewed using the **F12: Configure** button on the Tally.ERP 9 screen. The flow of stock ranging from opening stock, goods inwards, goods outwards to the closing stock can be analyzed in terms of its quantity. It gives you an insight into the quantitative movement of each stock item. However, for reconciling the closing balance value, this report cannot be referred to, since the outward goods are valued at the sales price and not the cost price.

2. **Profitability and Consumption:** This can be viewed using the **F7: Show Profit** button on the screen. Stock Summary shows the profitability and consumption details for each stock item. This statement shows the quantity and value of the opening stock, inward goods, outward goods, closing stock and the value of consumption (using the cost method). This statement is used to reconcile the closing balance because here the closing value is derived by taking the consumption values instead of the outward goods at sales value.

Stock Flow

You can configure the Stock Summary Statement to display the flow of goods.

❖ Select **F12: Configure** while on the Stock Summary screen.

❖ Set the **configuration** as shown.

Stock summary is a statement of stock in hand on a particular date. The statement is undated with every transaction to provide stock position at any given time. Tally.ERP treats stock summary as one of the primary statements and makes it accessible directly from the Gateway of Tally.ERP. As with all Tally.ERP Reports, it can be drilled down and configured to view different details, as well as total flow of stock.

To view Stock Summary: Go to Gateway of Tally.ERP ▸ Stock Summary

Stock Summary — SUDALAIANTO — Ctrl + M

Particulars	SUDALAIANTO 1-Apr-2012 to 31-Mar-2013 Closing Balance		
	Quantity	Rate	Value
Computer	**191 nos**	*48,244.09*	**92,14,621.62**
Acer	*37 nos*	19,000.00	7,03,000.00
DELL	*94 nos*	65,000.00	61,10,000.00
Lenova	*60 nos*	40,027.03	24,01,621.62
Hardware	145 nos	4,492.76	6,51,450.00
14" Flat Monitor	*15 nos*	6,400.00	96,000.00
LG DVD Writer	*47 nos*	1,350.00	63,450.00
Pentium IV Processor	*30 nos*	7,655.00	2,29,650.00
Samsung	*53 nos*	4,950.00	2,62,350.00

Stock Flow (Opening-Inward-Outward-Closing)—Reconciliation: The stock summary statement can be configured to display the flow of goods. Select F12: Configure while in the stock summary screen. This statement shows the flow of stock: Opening Stock, Goods Inwards, Goods Outward and Closing Stock.

Configuration

- Show Quantities ? Yes
- Show Rates ? Yes
- Show Values ? Yes
- Show Opening Balance ? Yes
- Show goods inwards ? Yes
- Show goods outwards ? Yes
- Show Closing Balance ? Yes

Stock Summary — SUDALAIANTO — Ctrl + M

Particulars	SUDALAIANTO 1-Apr-2012 to 31-Mar-2013 Outwards						Closing Balance		
	Quantity	Rate	Value	Consumption	Gross Profit	Perc %	Quantity	Rate	Value
14" Flat Monitor	3 nos	*10,000.00*	30,000.00	19,200.00	10,800.00	36.00 %	15 nos	*6,400.00*	96,000.00
Main Location	3 nos	10,000.00	30,000.00	19,200.00	10,800.00	36.00 %	15 nos	6,400.00	96,000.00
Acer	5 nos	*25,000.00*	1,25,000.00	95,000.00	30,000.00	24.00 %	37 nos	*19,000.00*	7,03,000.00
Main Location	5 nos	25,000.00	1,25,000.00	95,000.00	30,000.00	24.00 %	37 nos	19,000.00	7,03,000.00
DELL	(-)15 nos	*44,000.00*	(-)6,60,000.00	9,75,000.00	3,15,000.00	(-)47.73 %	94 nos	*65,000.00*	61,10,000.00
Main Location	(-)15 nos	44,000.00	(-)6,60,000.00	9,75,000.00	3,15,000.00	(-)47.73 %	94 nos	65,000.00	61,10,000.00
Lenova	14 nos	*22,857.14*	(-)3,20,000.00	5,60,378.38	(-)8,80,378.38	275.12 %	60 nos	*40,027.03*	24,01,621.62
Main Location	14 nos	22,857.14	(-)3,20,000.00	5,60,378.38	(-)8,80,378.38	275.12 %	60 nos	40,027.03	24,01,621.62
LG DVD Writer	(-)5 nos	*6,000.00*	(-)30,000.00	6,750.00	(-)23,250.00	77.50 %	47 nos	*1,350.00*	63,450.00
Main Location	(-)5 nos	6,000.00	(-)30,000.00	6,750.00	(-)23,250.00	77.50 %	47 nos	1,350.00	63,450.00
Pentium IV Processor							30 nos	*7,655.00*	2,29,650.00
Main Location							30 nos	7,655.00	2,29,650.00
Samsung	(-)15 nos	5,300.00	(-)79,500.00	74,250.00	(-)5,250.00	6.60 %	53 nos	4,950.00	2,62,350.00
Main Location	(-)15 nos	5,300.00	(-)79,500.00	74,250.00	(-)5,250.00	6.60 %	53 nos	4,950.00	2,62,350.00
Grand Total	**(-)13 nos**		**(-)9,34,500.00**	**(-)3,81,421.62**	**(-)5,53,078.38**	**59.18 %**	**336 nos**		**98,66,071.62**

Day Book: The bay book lists all transactions made in a particular day and by default displays the last voucher entry date of a regular voucher. It could also be set up to list all the transactions made over a certain period. Transactions include all financial vouchers, reversing and memorandum journals as well as inventory vouchers.

In Tally.ERP 9, the day book is by default displayed for the current date (as on the last date of voucher entry). However, you may specify the required period, as per your requirements.

To view the day book, Go to Gateway of Tally ▸ Display ▸ Daybook

- Press **F2:** Period on the button bar or press the key Alt+F2
- Specify the required period

The day book for a specified period will display as shown:

Day Book SUDALAIANTO Ctrl + N

Day Book For 31-Mar-2013

Date	Particulars	Vch Type	Vch No	Debit Amount Inwards Qty	Credit Amount Outwards Qty
31-3-2013	Cash	Contra	1		2,00,000.00
31-3-2013	Bank of India	Contra	2		55,000.00
31-3-2013	Bank of India	Contra	3		1,00,000.00
31-3-2013	Salary	Payment	1	12,500.00	
	Cheque No: 3457983 dated 2nd October 2012				
31-3-2013	Vinayagan Vidyasagar	Receipt	1		2,15,000.00
31-3-2013	Depreciation	Journal	1	15,000.00	
31-3-2013	Bharathi Sudalai and Co	Credit Note	1		19,13,080.00
31-3-2013	Bharathi Sudalai and Co	Credit Note	2		52,000.00
31-3-2013	Jehovah Jireh	Debit Note	1	2,96,140.00	
31-3-2013	Bharathi Sudalai and Co Input VAT @ 4%	Sales	1	5,98,900.00	
31-3-2013	Vinayagan Vidyasagar	Sales	2	5,42,880.00	
31-3-2013	Cash	Purchase	1		36,816.00
31-3-2013	Syndicate Bank	Purchase	2		3,82,712.25
31-3-2013	M/s Rohini Bharadwaj Merchants	Purchase	3		2,08,000.00
31-3-2013	Jehovah Jireh	Purchase	4		11,26,580.00
31-3-2013	Jehovah Jireh	Purchase	5		45,91,737.50
31-3-2013	DELL	Delivery Note	1		
31-3-2013	DELL	Rejections In	1		(-)3 nos
31-3-2013	Lenova	Physical Stock	1	55 nos	
31-3-2013	Lenova	Stock Journal	1	5 nos	
31-3-2013	Bharathi Sudalai and Co	Sales Order	1	2,23,210.00	
31-3-2013	M/s Rohini Bharadwaj Merchants	Purchase Order	1		64,35,000.00

Books of Accounts: You can generate different types of books of accounts, which are needed daily for reporting purpose. The most common books of accounts are:

- Cash Book
- Petty Cash Book
- Bank Book
- Journal Book
- Ledger
- Purchase Register (including return).
- Sales Register (including return)
- Stock Summary
- Stock Flow
- Stock Item
- Balance Sheet
- Profit and Loss Account

- ❖ Trial Balance
- ❖ Day Book

Cash Book

Account books record individual transaction details that have been entered. Though the items are posted to different ledgers, Tally.ERP 9 brings together all the transactions of one category into books of account for viewing and printing. For example, the cash book records all transactions that affect cash.

Cash/Bank Summary

To display the cash/bank summary

Go to Gateway of Tally ▸ Display ▸ Account Books ▸ Cash/Bank Book(s)

The **Cash/Bank Summary** is displayed as shown:

Place the highlight bar over the figures for the month of May, press **Enter** to display the ledger vouchers screen. Note that all the vouchers for May are listed. Press **Alt + F2** to view the vouchers for the months of May and July.

The **ledger vouchers screen** is displayed as shown:

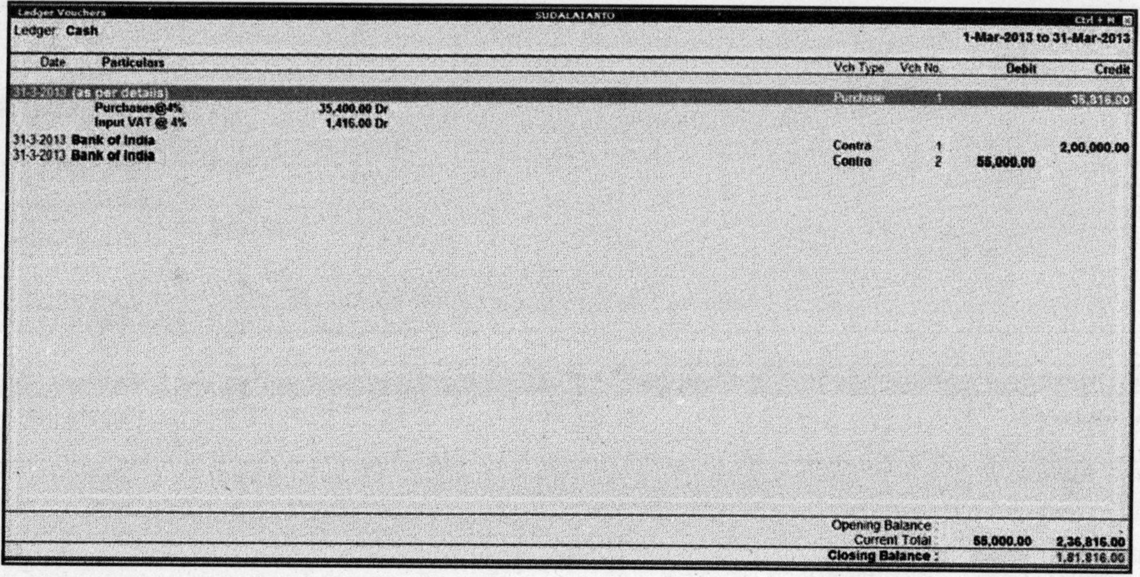

Bank Book

Tally.ERP 9 allows the facility to compare bank book with cash book or two or more banks by using the multi-columnar reporting facility. You can compare the information for multiple periods (year, month, or user defined period) for two or more banks on the same screen, instead of toggling between different periods/ledgers.

Use the New Column button to bring up the Cash book Monthly Summary.

Press New Column on the Button bar or ALT+C and change the Name of Ledger.

Based on the option selected in Tally.ERP 9 now displays comparisons as shown:

Gateway of Tally.ERP ▸ Reports ▸ Display ▸ Accounts Book ▸ Bank Book

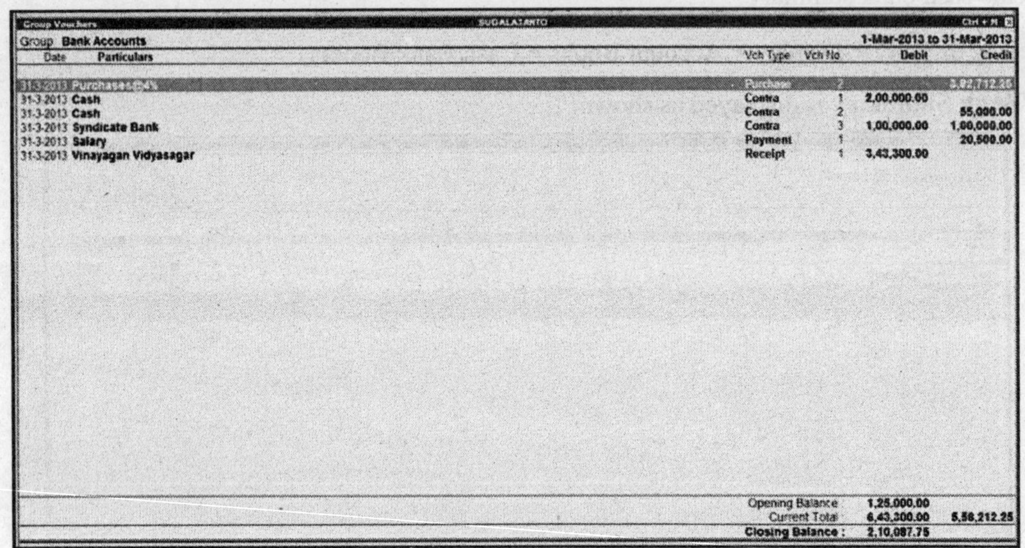

Journal Register: Journal register report displays all the journal vouchers that have been passed. To view journal register details

Go to Gateway of Tally ▸ Display ▸ Account Books ▸ Journal Register.

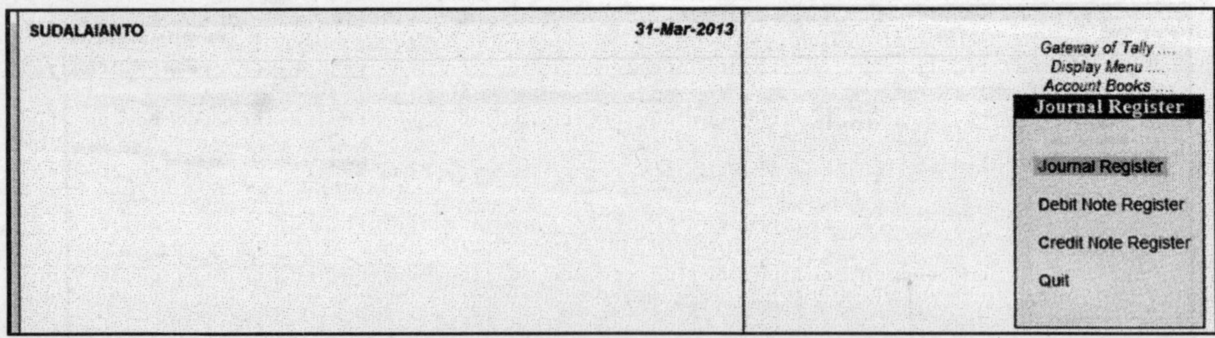

Voucher Register — SUDALAIANTO — Ctrl + N

List of All Journal Vouchers — 1-Mar-2013 to 31-Mar-2013

Date	Particulars		Vch Type	Vch No.	Debit Amount	Credit Amount
31-3-2013	Depreciation		Journal	1	15,000.00	
	Furnitures and Fixtures	15,000.00 Cr				

Ledger:

Gateway of Tally.ERP ▸ Reports ▸ Display ▸ Accounts Book ▸ Ledger

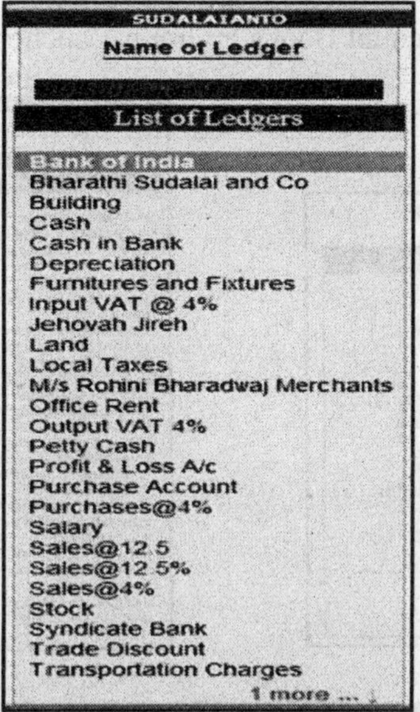

(Detailed transactions of a Ledger)

Group Summary

The group summary statement shows the closing balances of the accounts of a selected group for a specified period up to the current date. The default view is that of subgroups within a group.

To view group summary,

Go to Gateway of Tally ▸ Display ▸ Account Books ▸ Group Summary▸ Select a Group

In this example, select Group Indirect Expenses and press Enter.

The Group Summary screen is displayed as shown:

(Group summary of Sundry Creditors)

Group Voucher: Group voucher is a list of all vouchers having at least one ledger account entry belonging to the selected group. This statement is useful when you want to list all transactions for a particular group.

To view the Group Vouchers,

Go to Gateway of Tally ▸ Display ▸ Account Books ▸ Group Vouchers

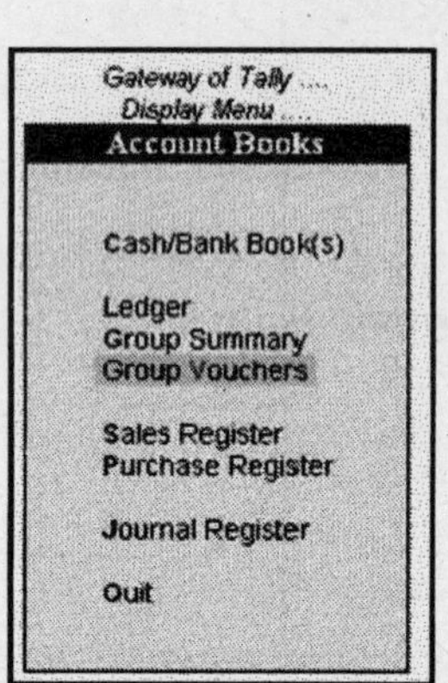

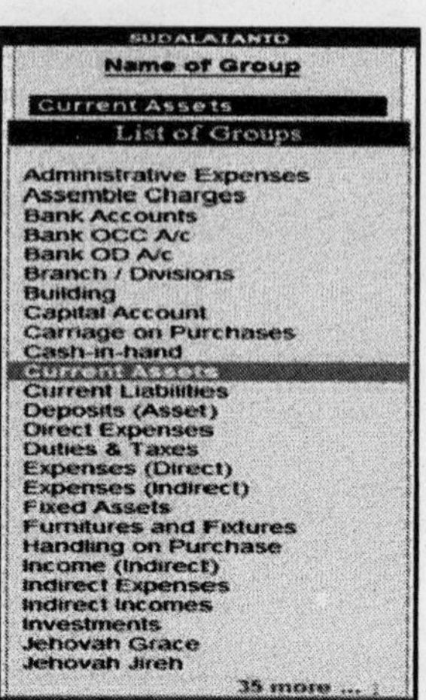

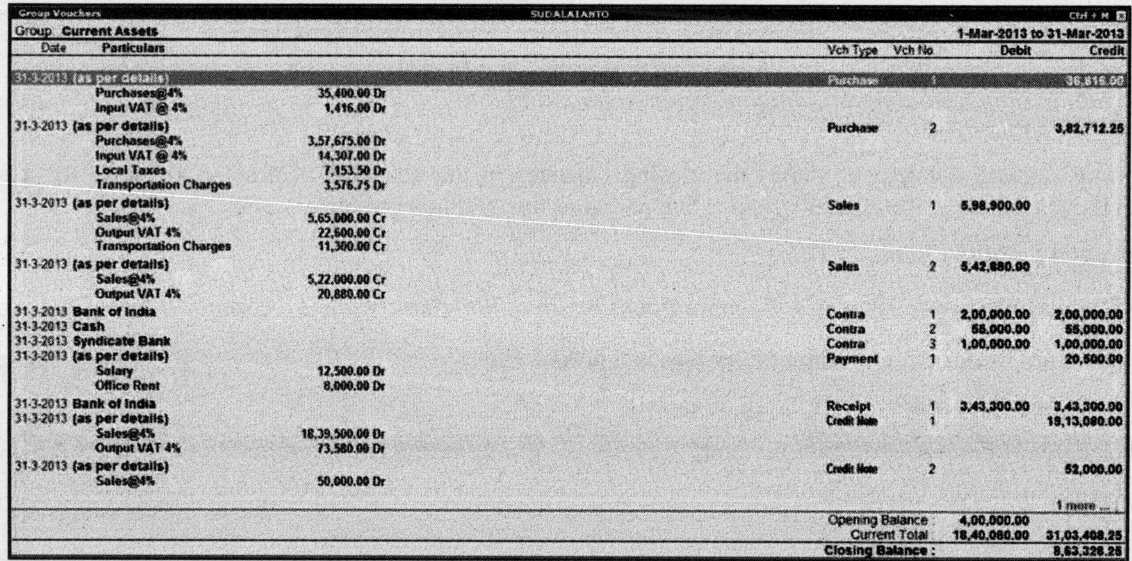
Group Vouchers — SUDALAIANTO — Ctrl + M

Group: Current Assets — 1-Mar-2013 to 31-Mar-2013

Date	Particulars		Vch Type	Vch No	Debit	Credit
31-3-2013	(as per details)		Purchase	1		36,816.00
	Purchases@4%	35,400.00 Dr				
	Input VAT @ 4%	1,416.00 Dr				
31-3-2013	(as per details)		Purchase	2		3,82,712.25
	Purchases@4%	3,57,675.00 Dr				
	Input VAT @ 4%	14,307.00 Dr				
	Local Taxes	7,153.50 Dr				
	Transportation Charges	3,576.75 Dr				
31-3-2013	(as per details)		Sales	1	5,98,900.00	
	Sales@4%	5,65,000.00 Cr				
	Output VAT 4%	22,600.00 Cr				
	Transportation Charges	11,300.00 Cr				
31-3-2013	(as per details)		Sales	2	5,42,880.00	
	Sales@4%	5,22,000.00 Cr				
	Output VAT 4%	20,880.00 Cr				
31-3-2013	Bank of India		Contra	1	2,00,000.00	2,00,000.00
31-3-2013	Cash		Contra	2	55,000.00	55,000.00
31-3-2013	Syndicate Bank		Contra	3	1,00,000.00	1,00,000.00
31-3-2013	(as per details)		Payment	1		20,500.00
	Salary	12,500.00 Dr				
	Office Rent	8,000.00 Dr				
31-3-2013	Bank of India		Receipt	1	3,43,300.00	3,43,300.00
31-3-2013	(as per details)		Credit Note	1		19,13,080.00
	Sales@4%	18,39,500.00 Dr				
	Output VAT 4%	73,580.00 Dr				
31-3-2013	(as per details)		Credit Note	2		52,000.00
	Sales@4%	50,000.00 Dr				
						1 more ...
			Opening Balance :		4,00,000.00	
			Current Total :		18,40,080.00	31,03,408.25
			Closing Balance :			8,63,328.25

Purchase Register: A purchase register displays the information on the periodic purchases of a business concern. Purchase register helps in analyzing the details of movement of purchased goods to various godowns, on the basis of which the stock movement at each godown is determined.

Go to Gateway of Tally ▸ Display ▸ Account books ▸ Purchase Register

The following screen is displayed.

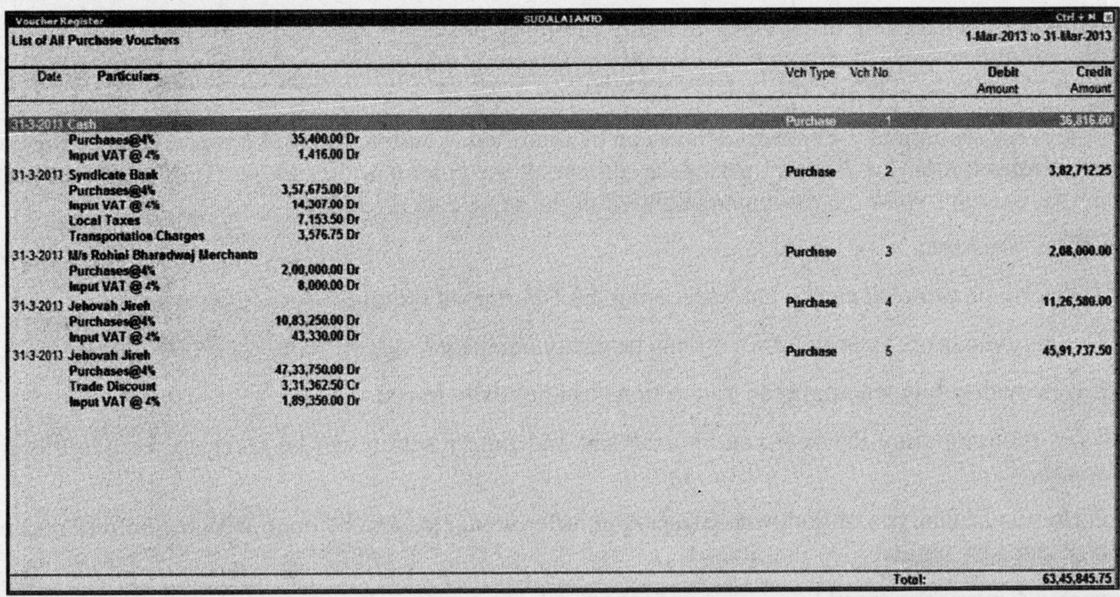

Voucher Register SUDALAIANTO Ctrl + N

List of All Purchase Vouchers 1-Mar-2013 to 31-Mar-2013

Date	Particulars		Vch Type	Vch No.	Debit Amount	Credit Amount
31-3-2013	Cash		Purchase	1		36,816.00
	Purchases@4%	35,400.00 Dr				
	Input VAT @ 4%	1,416.00 Dr				
31-3-2013	Syndicate Bank		Purchase	2		3,82,712.25
	Purchases@4%	3,57,675.00 Dr				
	Input VAT @ 4%	14,307.00 Dr				
	Local Taxes	7,153.50 Dr				
	Transportation Charges	3,576.75 Dr				
31-3-2013	M/s Rohini Bharadwaj Merchants		Purchase	3		2,08,000.00
	Purchases@4%	2,00,000.00 Dr				
	Input VAT @ 4%	8,000.00 Dr				
31-3-2013	Jehovah Jireh		Purchase	4		11,26,580.00
	Purchases@4%	10,83,250.00 Dr				
	Input VAT @ 4%	43,330.00 Dr				
31-3-2013	Jehovah Jireh		Purchase	5		45,91,737.50
	Purchases@4%	47,33,750.00 Dr				
	Trade Discount	3,31,362.50 Cr				
	Input VAT @ 4%	1,89,350.00 Dr				
			Total:			63,45,845.75

Purchase returns made during a year can also be traced. The parties to whom the purchase returns have been made and the causes thereof can be analyzed to draw conclusions on the supplier and the quality of purchases made.

A purchase register can be configured using the **Ctrl+F12: Value** button to view the following information.

- ❖ Actual Quantity
- ❖ Billed Quantity
- ❖ Date
- ❖ Bill Name
- ❖ Cost Centre
- ❖ Cost Category
- ❖ Voucher Number
- ❖ Narration
- ❖ Stock Item
- ❖ Godown Name

Configuration

Show Extract of Register	? No
Show Columnar Register	? No
Format	: Detailed
Show Narrations also	? No
Show Billwise Details also	? No
Show Cost Centre Details also	? No
Show Inventory Details also	? No
Show Bank Details also	? No
Show Forex Transactions	? No
Appearance of Names	: Name Only
Sorting Method	: Default

Sales Register: Sales register displays the monthly summary of sales transactions and closing balances. The list of transactions pertaining to each month can be viewed by selecting that month and viewing its details. Tally.ERP 9 permits you to change the display according to the information required.

The period of the report and the content details can be modified. Columnar periodic reports can be generated using **Alt+N: Auto Column** button for different periods as shown by the columnar details list. Tally.ERP 9 also allows you to compare similar data of two or more companies stored in the same data directory.

Uses of Sales Register:

- The periodic turnover can be analysed using the **F2: Period** button.
- The periodic taxes on such turnovers can be easily computed.
- Errors made while recording the transactions can be easily traced.
- Sales returns during the year can be analysed and timely action can be taken to remove the undesirable causes.
- Performance analysis of godown, salesperson, sales area, etc., can be done with the help of cost centre and cost category report

Sales register displays the monthly summary of sales made during the selected period.

To view Sales Register,

Go to Gateway of Tally ▸ Display ▸ Account books ▸ Sales Register

The **Sales Register** screen is displayed as shown:

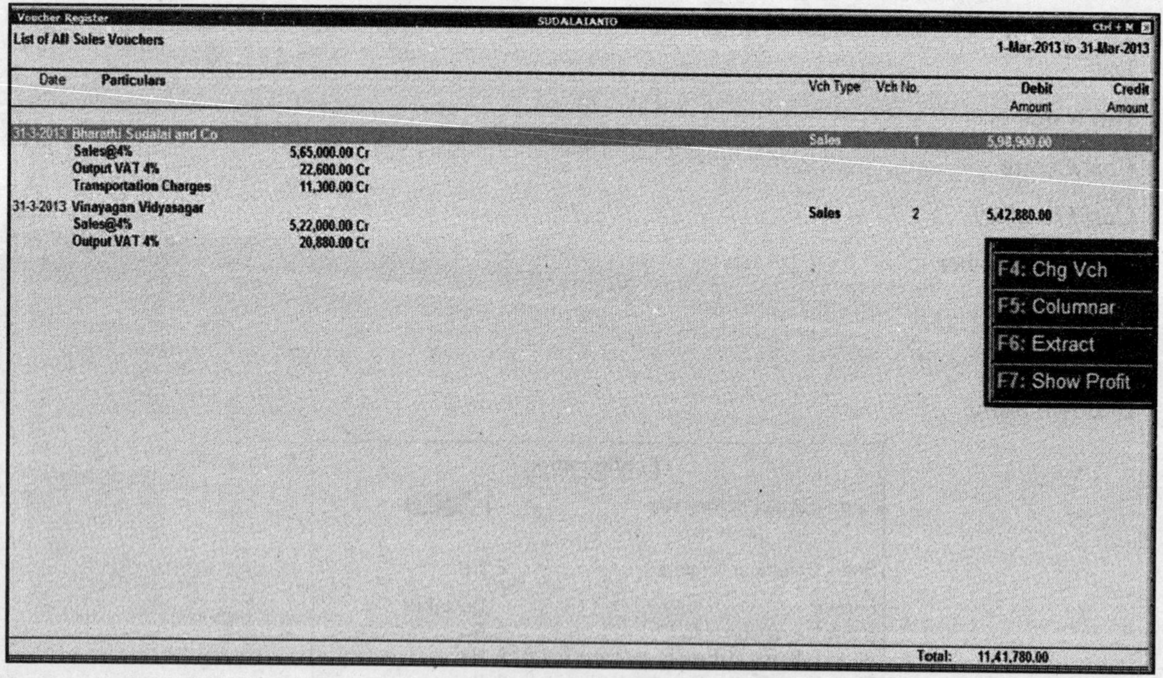

(Sales Register)

Press F5 and you will be displayed the below screen:

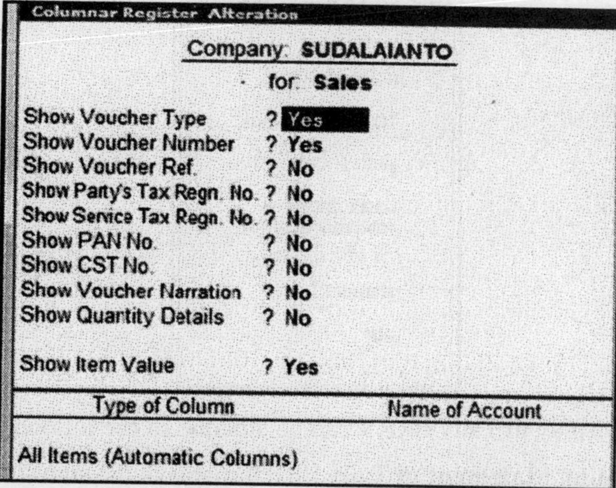

After the alteration, the following columnar Sales Registrar will be obtained.

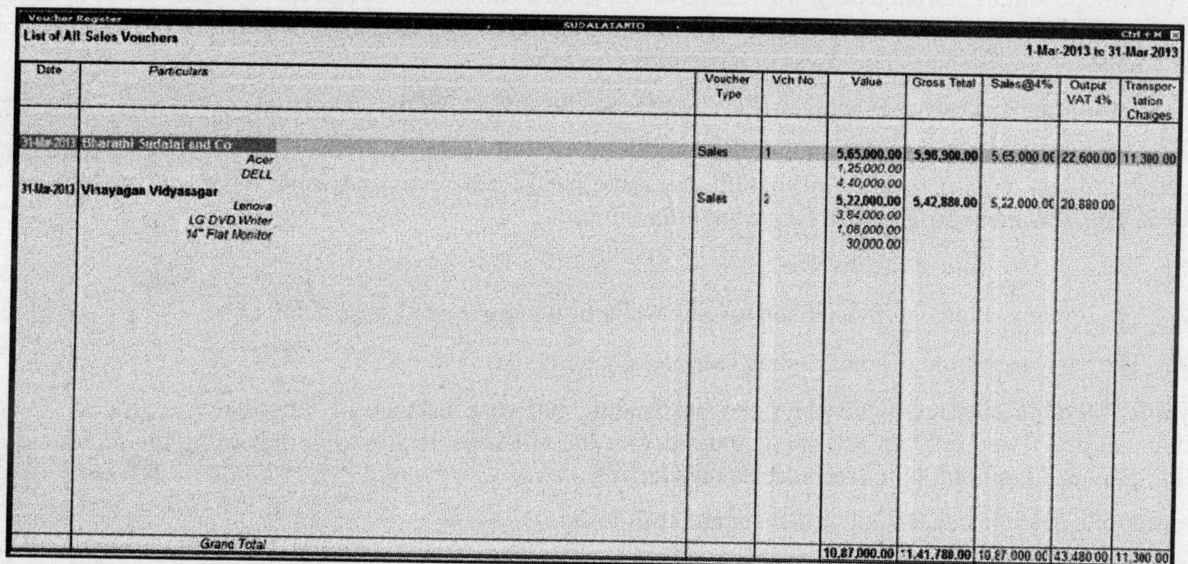

Voucher Register — SUDALAIANTO

List of All Sales Vouchers — 1-Mar-2013 to 31-Mar-2013

Date	Particulars	Voucher Type	Vch No.	Value	Gross Total	Sales@4%	Output VAT 4%	Transportation Chages
31-Mar-2013	Bharathi Sudalai and Co	Sales	1	5,65,000.00	5,98,900.00	5,65,000.00	22,600.00	11,300.00
	Acer			1,25,000.00				
	DELL			4,40,000.00				
31-Mar-2013	Vinayagan Vidyasagar	Sales	2	5,22,000.00	5,42,880.00	5,22,000.00	20,880.00	
	Lenova			3,84,000.00				
	LG DVD Writer			1,08,000.00				
	14" Flat Monitor			30,000.00				
	Grand Total			10,87,000.00	11,41,780.00	10,87,000.00	43,480.00	11,300.00

Statement of Accounts: Statements of accounts are derived from the transactions recorded in the books of accounts. In Tally.ERP 9, they are generated for cost centres and outstanding accounts. In Tally.ERP, statement of accounts pertains to cost centres and outstanding analysis. It is derived from individual transactions, but does not constitute a statutory requirement.

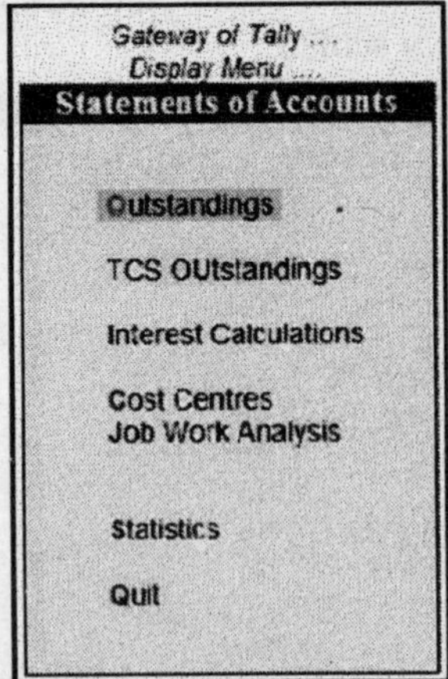

The Outstanding Statement Display in Tally.ERP 9 can be any one of the following:

Outstandings: The **Outstanding Statement** in Tally.ERP 9 displays the status of receivables and payables of the business concern. These are the two important components of the working capital of every business entity. Receivables form a major component of current assets, whereas payables from a component of current liabilities. Both determine the short-term liquidity and financial health of the company considerably. Therefore, effective control of the receivable and payable is a must for the financial soundness of a business concern.

The **Outstanding Statement Display** in Tally.ERP 9 can be any one of the following:

Receivables: This statement displays the sundry debtor's bill-wise balance till date. It is to be noted here that since this statement displays the information bill-by-bill, the same needs to be activated while recording the transactions in Tally.ERP 9. This statement provides the following information:

- The effective date of the invoice.
- The reference number given in the invoice while providing the bill-wise details.
- The party name and the outstanding balance of a particular invoice.

Payable: Payable outstanding displays the outstanding bill-wise balance of the sundry creditors. Again, this information can be viewed only on activating and entering the bill-wise details while recording the transactions. The information provided is similar to the receivables outstanding.

The uses of a payable outstanding statement are as follows:

- The pending party-wise bills and the number of days by which they are over-due can be viewed.
- The interest liability that is likely to arise can be estimated with the help of the number of days over-due.
- The credit period allowed by the party can be analysed and the need for arranging short-term funds can be evaluated.

Ledger: This summarises and displays the outstanding balance information with respect to each party. Thus, the bill status of a particular party account can be viewed with the help of this statement. Some of the uses of a ledger outstanding statement are:

- It displays information similar to the receivable and payable outstanding statements, but with respect to a particular party ledger. Thus, this statement can be put to a similar use as stated above.
- It facilitates the viewing of the address and contact details of the party selected, by using the **Alt + C** button.
- It can be used to generate reminder letters to be sent to the party specifying the details of outstanding bills. It is one of the very useful features in Tally.ERP 9 used with the Print Option.

Group: It displays a summarised view of the balances of all the ledgers under a particular group. For example, sundry debtors group will display all the party ledgers with their account balances. It can further be drilled down to each account to show the bill-wise outstanding for that account.

Some of the uses of a group outstanding statement are as follows:

- Summarised information can be viewed and analysed for each group.
- Another group can be displayed in a column using the **Alt+C**: New column button on the screen and comparisons can be made.
- Group details can be printed and submitted as a supporting schedule to the financial statements.
- The detailed break-up of parties under the chosen group and their pending balances can be viewed.

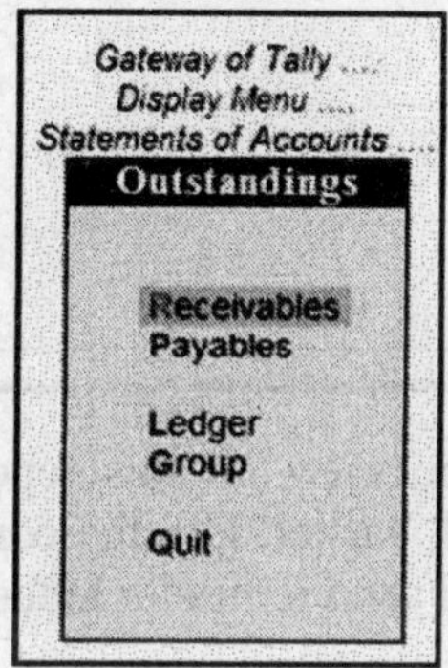

Receivable and payables are two important components of any organization's working capital. Receivable are current assets, whereas payables are current liabilities. They have a bearing on the short-term liquidity of the organization and can be used to effectively control the organization's financial health. Tally.ERP provides many reports and analysis to aid credit control.

Ledger-wise View of Outstanding Reports: Ledger-wise report in Tally.ERP displays the outstanding status of the bills of a particular party account.

To view the Single Ledger Outstanding Report,

Go to Gateway of Tally.ERP ▸ Display ▸ Statement of Accounts ▸ Outstanding ▸ Ledger Press ALT+F1 for details view. The Screen displays as below:

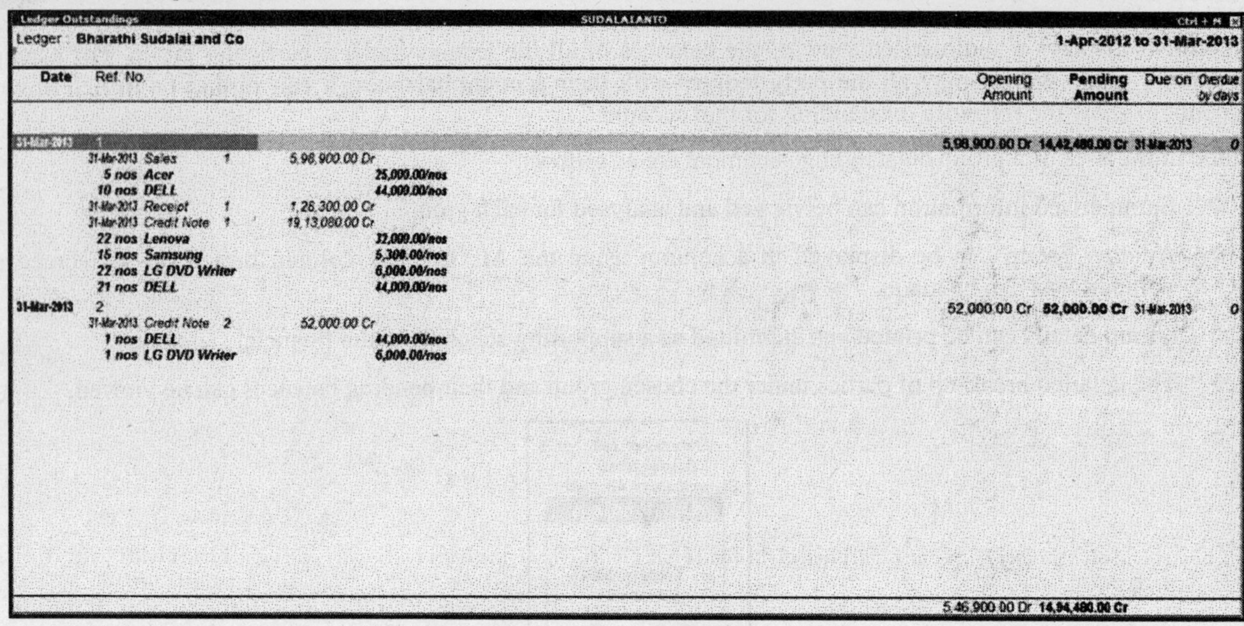

Ledger Outstandings SUDALAIANTO Ctrl + M

Ledger : **Bharathi Sudalai and Co** **1-Apr-2012 to 31-Mar-2013**

Date	Ref. No.				Opening Amount	Pending Amount	Due on	Overdue by days
31-Mar-2013	1				5,98,900.00 Dr	14,42,480.00 Cr	31-Mar-2013	0
	31-Mar-2013 Sales 1	5,98,900.00 Dr						
	5 nos Acer		25,000.00/nos					
	10 nos DELL		44,000.00/nos					
	31-Mar-2013 Receipt 1	1,26,300.00 Cr						
	31-Mar-2013 Credit Note 1	19,13,080.00 Cr						
	22 nos Lenova		32,000.00/nos					
	15 nos Samsung		5,300.00/nos					
	22 nos LG DVD Writer		6,000.00/nos					
	21 nos DELL		44,000.00/nos					
31-Mar-2013	2				52,000.00 Cr	52,000.00 Cr	31-Mar-2013	0
	31-Mar-2013 Credit Note 2	52,000.00 Cr						
	1 nos DELL		44,000.00/nos					
	1 nos LG DVD Writer		6,000.00/nos					
					5,46,900.00 Dr	14,94,480.00 Cr		

Use F12: Configure to further customize the view on this report. The age-wise analysis is the same for all receivable reports and has been discussed in detail, earlier. Use the contract button to view address and other contract details, by pressing ALT + C on the button bar, and send reminder letter.

Group (Outstanding): It displays a summarized view of the balances of all the ledgers under a particular group. For example, sundry debtors group will display all the party ledgers with their account balances. It can further be drilled down to each account to show the bill-wise outstanding for that account.

Some of the uses of a group outstanding statement are as follows:

- ❖ Summarized information can be viewed and analysed for each group.
- ❖ Another group can be displayed in a column using the Alt+C: New column button on the screen and comparisons can be made.
- ❖ Group details can be printed and submitted as a supporting schedule to the financial statements.
- ❖ The detailed break-up of parties under the chosen group and their pending balances can be viewed.

The group report displays the outstanding for a group of ledger accounts. It is a useful handout for managers of different group of customers or suppliers.

To view the Group-wise Outstanding Report,

Go to Gateway of Tally.ERP ▸ Display ▸ Statement of Accounts ▸ Outstanding ▸ Group ▸ Sundry Creditors

Select New Column (Alt + C) to view sundry debtors group in the same screen, to allow for comparison between sundry debtors and sundry creditors.

Group Outstandings — SUDALAIANTO — Ctrl + M

Particulars	Sundry Creditors SUDALAIANTO 1-Apr-2012 to 31-Mar-2013 Pending Bills		Sundry Debtors SUDALAIANTO 1-Apr-2012 to 31-Mar-2013 Pending Bills	
	Debit	Credit	Debit	Credit
Sales Bills to Make			(-)1,32,000.00	
Bharathi Sudalai and Co				14,94,480.00
Jehovah Jireh	2,96,140.00	57,18,317.50		
M/s Rohini Bharadwaj Merchants		2,08,000.00		
Vinayagan Vidyasagar			3,27,880.00	
Grand Total	2,96,140.00	59,26,317.50	1,95,880.00	14,94,480.00

Interest Calculations

Set show interest calculation to Yes in F11: Company Features –Accounting Features (F1) and set parameters in individual ledger accounts to view interest calculation reports. Interest is calculated on balances of accounts like Loans, and on overdue invoices.

Interest Receivable: Interest receivable is the amount due to be received from debtors or on deposits (for example, interest on bank deposits). To view Interest receivable:

Go to Gateway of Tally.ERP ▸ Display ▸ Statement of Accounts ▸ Interest Calculations ▸ Interest Receivable

❖ Press ALT + F2 to Change the Period

❖ Press ALT + F1 for detailed View.

❖ In F12: Configuration, Set Expand all levels in Detailed Format to YES.

Interest Payable: Interest Payable is the amount to be paid to creditors or on loans. To view the interest payable report,

Go to Gateway of Tally.ERP ▸ Display ▸ Statement of Accounts ▸ Interest Calculations ▸ Interest Payable

Cost Centers: A cost centres is a unit of an organization to which transactions (generally, revenue) cab be allocated. When only costs or expenses are allocated to these units, they are referred to as cost centres. Cost Centres are primarily performance reports.

Cost Category Summary: This report displays the summarized position of cost centre. You can drill down to the last vouchers. To view the cost centre summary report,

Go to Gateway of Tally.ERP ▸ Display ▸ Statement of Accounts ▸ Cost Centres ▸ Category Summary.

Group Break-up: The group break-up report displays the summaries information of all cost centres for the selected group. You can drill down till the voucher level. To view the group break-up,

Go to Gateway of Tally.ERP ▸ Display ▸ Statement of Accounts ▸ Cost Centres ▸ Group Break-Up.

❖ Select a Group: Indirect Expenses

❖ Press ALT + F1 to view detailed reports. The screen displays as shown:

Statistics: The statistics report displays the masters created and the number of vouchers types entered. You can step down to the transactions level from this report. To view statistics report.

Go to Gateway of Tally.ERP ▸ Display ▸ Statement of Accounts ▸ Statistics

P: Print | E: Export | M: E-Mail | O: Upload | S: Shop | G: Language | K: Keyboard | K: Control Centre | H: Support Centre | H: Help

Statistics — SUDALAIANTO — Ctrl + M

Types of Vouchers	SUDALAIANTO 1-Apr-2012 to 31-Mar-2013
Attendance	0
Contra	3
Credit Note	2
Debit Note	1
Delivery Note	1
Job Work In Order	0
Job Work Out Order	0
Journal	1
Material In	0
Material Out	0
Memorandum	0
Payment	1
Payroll	0
Physical Stock	1
Purchase	5
Purchase Order	1
Receipt	1
Receipt Note	0
Rejections In	1
Rejections Out	0
Reversing Journal	0
Sales	2
Sales Order	1
Stock Journal	1
Total	22

Types of Accounts	SUDALAIANTO 1-Apr-2012 to 31-Mar-2013
Groups	57
Ledgers	27
Cost Categories	1
Cost Centres	0
Stock Groups	10
Stock Categories	0
Stock Items	7
Godowns	1
Voucher Types	24
Units	1
Currencies	1
Budgets & Scenarios	0
Attendance/Production Types	0
Employee Groups	0
Employees	0
Tariff Classifications	0

Inventory Books—Inventory Group Summary: The group summary statement shows the closing balances of accounts under the selected group up to the current date. To view group summary,

Go to Gateway of Tally.ERP ▸ Display ▸ Inventory Books ▸ Group Summary ▸ Primary

In F12 configuration, set expand all levels in detailed format to Yes. Click F1 for Detailed

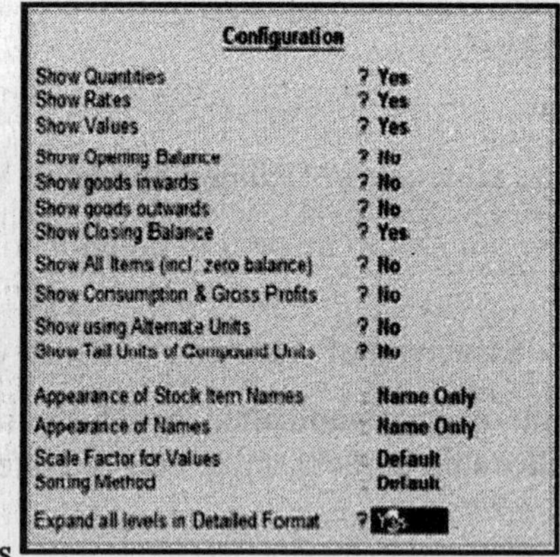

Stock Summary SUDALAIANTO Ctrl + N

Particulars	SUDALAIANTO 1-Apr-2012 to 31-Mar-2013 Closing Balance		
	Quantity	Rate	Value
Computer	191 nos	[illegible]	92,14,621.62
Acer	37 nos	19,000.00	7,03,000.00
Main Location	37 nos	19,000.00	7,03,000.00
DELL	94 nos	65,000.00	61,10,000.00
Main Location	94 nos	65,000.00	61,10,000.00
Lenova	60 nos	40,027.03	24,01,621.62
Main Location	60 nos	40,027.03	24,01,621.62
Hardware	**145 nos**	4,492.76	**6,51,450.00**
14" Flat Monitor	15 nos	6,400.00	96,000.00
Main Location	15 nos	6,400.00	96,000.00
LG DVD Writer	47 nos	1,350.00	63,450.00
Main Location	47 nos	1,350.00	63,450.00
Pentium IV Processor	30 nos	7,655.00	2,29,650.00
Main Location	30 nos	7,655.00	2,29,650.00
Samsung	53 nos	4,950.00	2,62,350.00
Main Location	53 nos	4,950.00	2,62,350.00
Grand Total	**336 nos**		**98,66,071.62**

Stock Transfers: Stock transfer displays the list of all the stock journal vouchers used in Tally.ERP 9 to make stock adjustments. For example, to record any increase or decrease in stock due to shortage, wastage of stock or to record inter-godown transfers of stock, assembling or disassembling.

It is used to reflect the status of godown-wise stock. It is optional to enter the details of rate or amount in the stock journal. Additional cost incurred during stock transfer can also be tracked. This adds up to the value of the stock but does not get reflected in the accounts.

To view Stock Transfer Register,

Go to Gateway of Tally ▸ Display ▸ Inventory Books ▸ Stock Transfers

This report displays entries made using stock journal vouchers. Press enter on the required month to display a voucher register. Where the voucher are listed date-wise.

To View Stock Transfer,

Go to Gateway of Tally.ERP ▸ Display ▸ Inventory Books ▸ Stock Transfers

Physical Stock Register: A physical stock voucher is used to record the actual stock of a particular stock item. In the inventory books, the actual balance of stock in hand as on the date of voucher entry is shown and the difference in stock is automatically added as inwards or outwards as the case may be. The cause of discrepancy can be recorded in the narration field of the physical stock journal voucher.

This register summarises the stock adjustments made during the reporting period. An analysis of the stock recorded in the register gives us an insight into the causes of discrepancies to ensure that timely action is taken.

To view Physical Stock Register,

Go to Gateway of Tally ▸ Display ▸ Inventory Books ▸ Physical Stock Register

Physical stock register is used to record actual stock available, i.e., stock found on conducting a stock check. It is not unusual to find a discrepancy between the actual stock and the computer recorded stock figure. Press Enter on the required month to display a voucher register, where the vouchers are listed date-wise.

Sales Order Book: Sales order is an order placed by a buyer for the purchase of goods. It consists of details such as date of sales order, party name, Vch Type, Vch No, Order Ref. No, Order amount. **Sales order book** displays a list of all sales orders.

From the Gateway of Tally ▸ Display ▸ Inventory Books ▸ Sales Order Book

Sales order book is a record of all sales orders made during a financial year.

Purchase Order Book: Purchase order book is a record of all purchase orders made during a financial year. To view the purchase order book,

Go to Gateway of Tally.ERP ▸ Display ▸ Inventory Books ▸ Purchase Order Book

Exception Reports: Exception reports are reports that track unusual transactions or balances. The different exception reports are:

Gateway of Tally.ERP ▸ Display ▸ Exception Reports

Negative Stock:

Gateway of Tally.ERP ▸ Display ▸ Exception Reports ▸ Negative Stock

This is a list of all stock items that have a negative balance at the end of the period of display.

Negative Ledgers:

Gateway of Tally.ERP ▸ Display ▸ Exception Reports ▸ Negative Ledgers

This is a list of ledger accounts that have obverse balances, i.e., balances that are opposite to the Nature of the account. For example, a creditor account has a debit balance and an asset account having a credit balance.

List of Memorandum Vouchers:

Gateway of Tally.ERP ▸ Display ▸ Exception Reports ▸ Memorandum Vouchers

List of Reversing Journals:

Gateway of Tally.ERP ▸ Display ▸ Exception Reports ▸ Journal Vouchers

This is a list of Reversing Journals entered during a period. Change the period as required.

List of Optional Vouchers:

Gateway of Tally.ERP ▸ Display ▸ Exception Reports ▸ Memorandum Vouchers

This is a list of vouchers marked as 'Optional' during a period. This list includes all types of vouchers that are marked 'Optional'.

Printing Reports: Reports and documents generated through Tally.ERP's extensive display capabilities can also be printed. Printing is possible in two ways:

Using the Print Button: You can choose to print directly from the screen currently displayed by selecting the button PRINT (top-most button on the right-hand side of the screen). This brings up the print configuration screen for the report and new button options on the right - hand side of the screen.

Multi-account printing: Principally geared towards printing the primary books of accounts, like the cash and bank books, account ledgers, sales and purchase registers, etc, without needing to select the accounts one at a time and pressing Alt+P. The facilities provide for printing one account at a time, All accounts, or all accounts in a selected group. Before printing, the date range and other selections may also be set up. Common printing options affect the printing of current selected reports. They are changed by selecting the appropriate button on the right hand side of the screen.

SYLLABUSES OF RELATED PAPERS IN THE COLLEGES AFFILIATED TO BHARATHIAR UNIVERSITY

BHARATHIAR UNIVERSITY

FOR B.COM. (CA) COURSE OFFERED BY AFFILIATED COLLEGES

FOR THE STUDENTS ADMITTED DURING THE ACADEMIC YEAR 2007-2008 ONWARDS

INTRODUCTION TO INFORMATION TECHNOLOGY

UNIT - I

Hardware and Software: Computer system – Importance of computers in business – Data and Information – Data processing – Data storage and data retrieval capabilities – Computer application in various areas of business – Computer related jobs in business.

UNIT - II

Types of computer system: Micro, Mini, Mainframe and Super computers, Analog, Digital and Hybrid computers, Business and Scientific computer systems. First, Second, Third and Fourth generation computers – Laptop or notebook computers – Data processing systems – batch, online and real time system – Time sharing – Multi Programming and multi processing system – Networking – Local area and wide area networks.

UNIT - III

Components of computer system – Input, Output and Storage device – Software system: Software and Application software – Programming language – Machine languag , Assembly language, High level language – Flowchart and Programme flowcharts – Steps in developing a computer Programme.

UNIT - IV

Operating system : DOS, Windows, UNIX, Window NT, Windows 98, E-Commerce, Internet, Intranet, Extranet, E-mail its uses and importance – World Wide Web – Mobile Computers.

UNIT - V

System Analysis and Design – Computer Based Information System – Transaction Processing – Office Automation – Management Information System. – Decision Support System – Expert System.

BHARATHIAR UNIVERSITY

FOR B.COM. COURSE OFFERED BY AFFILIATED COLLEGES

FOR THE STUDENTS ADMITTED DURING THE ACADEMIC YEAR 2007-2008 ONWARDS

COMPUTER APPLICATION IN BUSINESS

UNIT - I

Introduction to Computer: Introduction – Types and Characteristics of Computers – What Computer can do and can't do? Classification of Digital Computer System: Micro, Mini, Main, Super and Network Computers.

Anatomy of Digital Computer: Functions and components of a computer – CPU – Memory Units: RAM – ROM – PROM – EPROM – Flash Memory.

UNIT - II

Auxiliary Storage Devices: Introduction – Hard Disk – Floppy Disk – CD – ROM. Input Devices: Introduction – Keyboard – Mouse – Trackball – Joystick – Digitizing Tablet – Scanners – Digital Camera – MICR – OCR – OMR – Barcode Reader – Speech Input Devices – Touch Screen – Touch Pad – Light Pen.

Output Device: Introduction – Monitor – Classification of Monitor (Based on Color & Signals) – Printer – Plotter – Sound Cards & Speakers.

UNIT - III

Introduction to Software: Types of Software. Operating System: Introduction – Functions of an OS – Classification of OS.

Programming Languages: Introduction – Machine, Assembly and High-level languages – Types of High-level languages – Compilers and Interpreters.

UNIT - IV

Data Processing: Data vs. Information – File Processing – Database processing. Database Management System: History of Information – Quality of Information – Information Processing – Definition of Database & DBMS – Types of DBMS.

UNIT - V

Internet and World Wide Web: Introduction – About Internet – Internet Access – Internet Basics – Internet Addressing – WWW – Web Pages & HTML – Web browsers – Searching the Web.

Electronic Mail: Introduction – Use of E-Mail – Working of E-Mail – E-Mail Names and Addresses – Mailing Basics.

BHARATHIAR UNIVERSITY

FOR M.COM. COURSE OFFERED BY AFFILIATED COLLEGES

FOR THE STUDENTS ADMITTED DURING THE ACADEMIC YEAR 2007-2008 ONWARDS

INFORMATION TECHNOLOGY IN BUSINESS

UNIT - I

Hardware and software: Computer system – Importance of Computers in Business – Data and Information – Data Processing, Data Storage and Data Retrieval Capabilities – Computer applications in various areas of business – Computer related jobs in business – Recent developments in Hardware and Software – Laptop, Pen Drive, Mobile Computing, Blue tooth, Wireless Printers and Accessories, Broad brand.

UNIT - II

Types of Computer Systems – Micro, Mini, Mainframe and Super Computers – Analog, Digital and Hybrid Computers – Business and Scientific Computer Systems – First, Second, Third and Fourth Generation Computers – Laptops and Notebook Computers.

UNIT - III

Data processing system – Batch, Online and Real time system – Time sharing – Multi Programming and Multi Processing systems – Networking – Local areas and Wide area networks.

UNIT - IV

Components of computer system – Input, Output and Storage devices – Software – System Software and Application Software. Programming languages – Machine languages – Assembly languages – High level languages – Flow chart – System flow chart and Program flow charts – Steps in developing a computer program.

UNIT - V

E-Commerce – Internet – Intranet – Extranet – e-mails, its uses and importance – World Wide Web sites.

BHARATHIAR UNIVERSITY

FOR B.A. ENGLISH LITERATURE WITH COMPUTER APPLICATIONS COURSE OFFERED BY AFFILIATED COLLEGES

FOR THE STUDENTS ADMITTED DURING THE ACADEMIC YEAR 2007- 2008 ONWARDS

FUNDAMENTALS OF INFORMATION TECHNOLOGY

UNIT - I

Introduction to Computer systems: Introduction to Computers - Classification Digital Computer Systems – anatomy of digital Computer – Computer Architecture – Number Systems – Memory Units – Auxiliary Storage devices – Input / Output Devices. Computer Software and Software Development: Introduction to Computer Software – Operating Systems – Programming Languages – General Software features and tends.

UNIT - II

Database management systems: Data processing – Introduction to DBMS – Database Design. Telecommunications: Introduction to telecommunication – Computer Networks – Communications systems – Distributed systems

UNIT - III

Internet and intranet: Internet and WWW – Electronic Mail – Intranets. Multimedia and virtual Reality: Introduction to Multimedia – Multimedia tools – Introduction to Virtual reality

UNIT - IV

New Technologies in information technology: Electronic conference – Hyper media – data warehouses and data marts – data mining – on-line analytical processing (OLAP) – Geographic information systems (GIS).

UNIT - V

Applications of Information Technology: Computers in Business and Industries – computers in home – computers in education and training – computers in entertainment, science, medicine & engineering.

BHARATHIAR UNIVERSITY

FOR B.Sc. MATHS WITH CA COURSE OFFERED BY AFFILIATED COLLEGES

FOR THE STUDENTS ADMITTED DURING THE ACADEMIC YEAR 2007-2008 ONWARDS

SEMESTER: II CORE PAPER – IV

MS-OFFICE & LAB

UNIT - I

Microsoft Word: Word processing overview – creating and editing documents – formatting documents – working with header, footer and footnotes.

UNIT - II

Creating report and news letter – creating table and merging document – creating web page macros – keyboard shortcuts – menus – customs toolbars.

UNIT - III

Microsoft Excel: Spreadsheet overview – creating worksheet – managing and analyzing complex worksheet – creating charts creating form template – sharing data between application.

UNIT - IV

Microsoft Access: Database overview – creating database – modifying table and creating form filtering and querying tables – creating reports and mailing labels – sharing information between applications.

UNIT - V

Microsoft PowerPoint: Basics – using text-adding visual elements – charts and tables – drawing clipart – sounds – animation – apply time transitions to slides.

BHARATHIAR UNIVERSITY

FOR BBM WITH CA COURSE OFFERED BY AFFILIATED COLLEGES

FOR THE STUDENTS ADMITTED DURING THE ACADEMIC YEAR 2007-2008 ONWARDS

INTRODUCTION TO INFORMATION TECHNOLOGY

UNIT - I

Hardware and Software Computer Systems – importance of computers in business – data and information – data processing – data storage and data retrieval capabilities – computer applications in various areas of business – computer related jobs in business.

UNIT - II

Types of computer systems – Micro, Mini, Main frame and super computers – analogue, digital and hybrid computers – business and scientific computer systems – first, second, third and fourth generation computers – laptop or not book computers – data processing systems batch – online and real time systems – time sharing – multi programming and multi processing systems – net working – local area and wide area networks.

UNIT - III

Components of computer system – input, output and storage devices software system software and application software programming language machine language – assembly language – high level languages – flow chart and programme flow charts – steps in developing a computer programme.

UNIT - IV

Operating systems – Dos – windows – UNIX- windows NT – windows 198 E-commerce – IT Internet – intranet – e-mail its uses and importance – world wide web sites and Computers

UNIT - V

System analysis and design – computer based information system transaction processing – off automation – management information systems – decision support systems – expert system.

BHARATHIAR UNIVERSITY

FOR M.A., (CA) COURSE OFFERED BY AFFILIATED COLLEGES

FOR THE STUDENTS ADMITTED DURING THE ACADEMIC YEAR 2007-2008 ONWARDS

PAPER IV - MS WORD & POWERPOINT

UNIT - I

Introduction to common office tools and techniques – sharing information within MS office – word basics.

UNIT - II

Formatting text documents – working with header, footer and footnotes.

UNIT - III

Tabs – tables and sorting – graphics – templates writer tools – macros – keyboard shortcuts – menus – custom toolbars.

UNIT - IV

PowerPoint basics – using text – adding visual elements – charts and tables.

UNIT - V

Drawing – clipart – sounds – animation – apply time transitions to slides.

BHARATHIAR UNIVERSITY

FOR MBA COURSE OFFERED BY AFFILIATED COLLEGES

FOR THE STUDENTS ADMITTED DURING THE ACADEMIC YEAR 2007- 2008 ONWARDS

COMPUTER APPLICATIONS IN MANAGEMENT

MS OFFICE: Introduction to WORD, POWERPOINT and EXCEL.

WORD: Creating a new document with templates & Wizard – Creating own document – Opening/modifying a saved document – converting files to and from other document formats – Using keyboard short-cuts & mouse – Adding symbols & pictures to documents – headers and footers – Finding and replacing text – spell check and Grammar check – Formatting text – paragraph formats – adjusting margins, line space – character space – Changing front type, size – Bullets and numbering – Tables – Adding, editing, deleting tables – Working within tables – Adding, deleting, modifying rows and columns – merging & splitting cells.

EXCEL: Working with worksheets – cells – Entering, editing, moving, copying, cutting, pasting, transforming data – Inserting and deleting of cells, rows & columns – Working with multiple worksheets – switching between worksheets – moving, copying, inserting & deleting worksheets – Using formulas for quick Calculations – Working & entering a Formula – Formatting a worksheet – Creating and editing charts – elements of an EXCEL chart – Selecting data to a chart – Types of chart – chart wizard – Formatting chart elements – Editing a chart – Printing charts.

POWERPOINT: Creating new presentations – Auto content wizard – Using template – Blank presentation – Opening existing presentations – Adding, editing, deleting, copying, hiding slides – Presentations – Applying new design – Adding graphics – Using headers and footers – Animating text – Special effects to create transition slides – Controlling the transition speed – Adding sounds to slides – Using action buttons.

TALLY: Introduction and Installation, Required Hardware, Preparation for installation of Tally software, installation. Working in Tally: Opening new company, Safety of Accounts or Password, Characteristics, Making Ledger Accounts, Writing voucher, voucher entry, Making different types of vouchers, Correcting sundry debtors and sundry creditors accounts, Preparation of Trial Balance, Books of Accounts, Cash Book, Bank Books, Ledger Accounts, Group Summary, Sales Register and Purchase Register, Journal Register, Statement of Accounts & Balance Sheet.

PRACTICALS: Simple problems to be done in WORD, EXCEL and POWERPOINT using all the above-mentioned topics.

UNIVERSITY OF MADRAS

SYLLABUS FOR COMPUTER APPLICATIONS IN BUSINESS

UNIT - I

Word Processing: Meaning and role of Word Processing in Creating of Document ,Editing, Formatting and Printing Document, Using Tools Such as Spelling Check, Thesaurus, etc., in Word Processors (Ms Word), Electronic Spreadsheet Structure of Spreadsheet and its Applications to Accounting, financial, and Marketing functions of Business; Creating a dynamic / Sensitive worksheet; Concept of Absolute and Relative Cell reference; Using built-in functions; Goal Seeking and Solver Tools; Using graphics and formatting of Worksheet; Sharing Date With Other Desktop Applications; Strategies of Creating error-free worksheet (MS Excel)

UNIT - II

Programming Under a DBMS Environment: The Concept of Data BaseManagement System; Data field, Records, and Files, Sorting and Indexing Data; Searching Records. Designing Queries, and Reports; Linking of Data Files Understanding Programming Environment In DBMS; Developing Menu Driven Applications in Query Language (MS-Access).

UNIT - III

Electronic Data Interchange (EDI): Introduction to EDI Basics of EDI; EDI Standards; Financial EDI (FEDI) FEDI for International Trade Transaction; Applications of EDI, Advantages of EDI Future of EDI.

UNIT - IV

The Internet and Its Basic Concepts: Internet Concept, History Development in Indian: Technological Foundation of Internet; Distributed Computing; Client – Server Computing; Internet Protocol Suite; Application of Distributed Computing; Client Server Computing ; Internet Protocol Suite in The Internet Environment; Domain Name System (DNS); Generic Top-Level Domain (GTLD); Country Code Top Level Domain (cc TLD) — India ; — Allocation of Second Level Domains; IP Addresses, Internet Protocol; – Applications of Internet in Business Education, Governance, ETC.

UNIT - V

Information System Audit: Basic Idea of Information Audit; Difference With The Traditional Concepts of Audit; Conduct and Applications of Audit in Internet Environment.

PRACTICAL LISTS OF MS OFFICE AND TALLY (FOR THE COLLEGES AFFILIATED TO BHARATHIAR UNIVERSITY)

BHARATHIAR UNIVERSITY – COIMBATORE – 641 046.

B.COM. (CA) AND B.COM. (E-COMM.)

COMPUTER APPLICATIONS PRACTICALS I

SEMESTER – I

WORD

1. **Objective:** To know basic Typing and Formatting

   Requirement: Chairman's Speech / Auditor's Report / Minutes / Agenda

   Functions to be performed: Bold, Underline, Font Size, Style, Background Color Text Color, Line Spacing, Spell Check, Alignment, Bullets and Numbering.

   Output: Display and Printout.

2. **Objective:** To prepare an Invitation.

   Requirement: Invitation of the function / Cheques / Invoice / Account Sales

   Functions to be performed: Using Drawing Tool Bar, Clip Art, WordArt, Symbols, Borders and Shading – Design an Invitation.

   Output: Display and Printout.

3. **Objective:** To know the preparation of Table

   Requirement: Class Time Table / Result Analysis / Attendance Report / Consolidated Salary Statement.

   Functions to be performed: Inserting the Table – Alignment of Rows and Columns – Data Entry – Inserting and Deleting the Rows and Columns – Cell Alignment – Change of Table Format.

   Output: Display and printout.

4. **Objective:** To know the Mail Merge Operation.

   Requirement: Business Letters, List of Address

   Functions to be performed: Type the Letter – Type the Addresses – Perform the Mail Merge Operations.

   Output: Display and printout.

5. **Objective:** To know the wizard operations

   Requirement: Company Profile (Wizard) / Biodata (Template)

   Functions to be performed: Wizard and Template Operations

   Output: Display and printout.

EXCEL

1. **Objective:** To know the basic Mathematical and Logical Operations.

   Requirement: Students Roll No., Name, Marks (Minimum 5 Subjects for 10 Students)

   Functions to be performed: Data Entry – Total – Average – Result – Ranking using Logical functions.

   Output: Display and printout.

2. **Objective:** To know the Preparation of Final Accounts.

   Requirement: Trial Balance and Adjustments.

   Functions to be performed: Preparation of Trading and Profit and Loss Account and Balance Sheet in Tradition / New Format.

   Output: Display and printout.

3. **Objective:** To know the Preparation of Charts

   Requirement: Minimum 5 years Sales / Profit data of the Department / Branch

   Functions to be performed: Data Entry – Using Chart Wizard – Perform chart Options – copy the chart in another Sheet.

   Output: Display and printout.

4. **Objective:** To know the Preparation of Consolidated Salary Statement.

   Requirement: Employee Name, Employee Code, Basic Pay, Allowances and Perks, Details of Deductions for minimum 10 Employees.

   Functions to be performed: Data Entry – Calculate Allowances and Perks based on the Basic Pay – Calculation of Gross Pay, Deductions and the Net Pay.

   Output: Display and printout.

5. **Objective:** To know the Interest Calculations.

   Requirement: Name of the Customer, Details about them, Loan Amount, Period of Loan and Rate of Interest for minimum 10 Customers.

   Functions to be performed: Data Entry – Calculation of Interests – Using Functions – Presentation of Interest Report in suitable form.

   Output: Display and printout.

POWERPOINT

1. **Objective:** To know the strategies used introduce new product using custom animation in PowerPoint.

   Requirement: New product details – Name, Brand Name, Type of Product, Characteristics, Special Features, Price, Special Offer, etc.,

   Functions to be performed: Create Slides using animations, slide transition, etc.,

   Output: Slide Show and Hard Copy.

2. **Objective:** To know the Organization Structure and Draw the Same in PowerPoint.

Requirement: Organization details for 5 levels of hierarchy.

Functions to be performed: Blank Presentation using Organizational Chart.

Output: Slide Show and Hard Copy.

3. **Objective:** To know the News Presentation.

   Requirement: Headline news of a Particular Day.

   Functions to be performed: Type the News Headline and do Custom Animation.

   Output: Slide Show and Hard Copy.

4. **Objective:** To know the Presentation technique / methods using Wizard.

   Requirement: Details about a function / institution / department / organization.

   Functions to be performed: Type the details and prepare necessary slides using wizard.

   Output: Slide Show and Hard Copy.

5. **Objective:** To know the Seminar / Lecture Presentation methods using animation effects.

   Requirement: Key Points on a Particular Topic.

   Functions to be performed: Creation of different slides, changing background color, font color using word art etc.,

   Output: Slide Show and Hard Copy.

ACCESS

1. **Objective:** To know the DataBase and Table Creation using Design View.

   Requirement: Data about a Bank / Company / Customer / Employee / Supplier / Product.

   Functions to be performed: Create a DataBase using Blank Database option – Prepare Tables with minimum 6-7 fields – set a Primary Key – Enter 10 Records.

   Output: Display and printout.

2. **Objective:** To know the Query operations.

   Requirement: Table with Data.

   Functions to be performed: Creation of Database – Creation of Tables – Perform the Query Operations (Minimum 5 Queries).

   Output: Display and printout.

3. **Objective:** To know the Creation of Labels / Forms.

   Requirement: Data

   Functions to be performed: Creation of Database, Table – Enter the Data – Design the Labels / Forms.

   Output: Display and printout.

4. **Objective:** To know the generation of a Report about Customer / Supplier / Product / Employees etc.,

   Requirement: Data

Functions to be performed: Creation of Database, Table – Enter the Data – Generating Reports using Wizard.

Output: Display and printout.

5. **Objective:** To know the Asset Wizard.

   Requirement: Details of Assets of a Company.

   Functions to be performed: Enter details of 10 Assets using wizard.

   Output: Display and printout.

TALLY AND INTERNET

1. **Objective:** To know the preparation of accounts using accounting package.

   Requirement: Data about a company and its transactions for at least 15 transactions

   Functions to be performed: Creation of company, Ledger preparation, Voucher entry viewing reports

   Output: Display.

2. **Objective:** To know the creation of e-mail id

   Requirement: Personal Details about an individual

   Functions to be performed: Log on any e-mail service providers, website and enter the data

   Output: Display.

3. **Objective:** To know the use of search engine

   Requirement: Search engine.

   Functions to be performed: Log on any search engine website, enter the topic from the result and copy the material to MS word.

   Output: Display.

4. **Objective:** To visit any bank/stock exchange /company/college /Any University website and collect information.

   Requirement: Collect the website address.

   Functions to be performed: Log on the website and down load the materials

   Output: Display.

BHARATHIAR UNIVERSITY

FOR B.SC. MATHS WITH CA COURSE OFFERED BY AFFILIATED COLLEGES

FOR THE STUDENTS ADMITTED DURING THE ACADEMIC YEAR 2007-2008 ONWARDS

PRACTICAL LIST FOR MS-OFFICE

MS-WORD

1. Illustrate the mail merge concept to apply for a suitable job for at least 5 companies.
2. Using MS-word, perform the following:
   - Change the font size to 20
   - Change the font type to Garamond
   - Align the text to left, right, justify and center.
   - Underline the text.
   - Table manipulation.

MS-EXCEL

3. Built a worksheet to perform correlation and regression coefficient using formula and check the answer with built-in-functions.
4. Worksheet preparation for electricity bill preparation.
5. Draw graphs to illustrate class performance.

MS-POWER POINT

6. Prepare an organization chart for a college environment in PowerPoint.
7. Perform frame movement by inserting clipart to illustrate running of a car automatically.
8. Prepare a Power Point presentation with all the slide translation facilities.

MS-ACCESS

9. Perform sorting on name, place and pin code of students database and list them in the sorted order.
10. Using queries retrieve information from sales database which contains Trans-no, date, prod-id, prod-name qty, unit-price and region. List out records region wise, date-wise, product-wise.
11. Create mailing labels for employee database.

BHARATHIAR UNIVERSITY

FOR BBM CA COURSE OFFERED BY AFFILIATED COLLEGES

FOR THE STUDENTS ADMITTED DURING THE ACADEMIC YEAR 2007-2008 ONWARDS

PC SOFTWARE (MS-OFFICE & TALLY) PRACTICAL

LIST OF PRACTICALS

MS WORD

1. Type the text, check spelling and grammar, bullets and numbering list items, align the text to left, right, justify and centre.
2. Prepare a job application letter enclosing your bio-data.
3. Performing mail merger operation and preparing labels.
4. Prepare a neatly aligned, error free document, add header and footer also perform find replace operation and define bookmarks.
5. Prepare a document in newspaper column layout.
6. Demonstrate OLE concept by linking an excel worksheet into a work document.

MS EXCEL

7. Worksheet using formulas.
8. Worksheet Manipulation for electricity bill preparation.
9. Drawing graphs to illustrate class performance.
10. An excel worksheet contains monthly sales details of five companies.

MS ACCESS

11. Simple commands perform sorting on name, place and pin code of students database and Address printing using label format.
12. Pay roll processing.
13. Inventory control.
14. Screen designing for data entry.

MS POWER POINT

15. Prepare a Power Point presentation with at least three slides for Department inaugural function.
16. Draw an organisation chart with minimum three hierarchical levels.
17. Design an advertisement campaign with minimum three slides.
18. Insert an excel chart into a power point slide.

TALLY

19. Create a new company, voucher and ledger and record minimum 10 transactions and display the result.
20. Prepare a trial balance.
21. Prepare the Profit and Loss A/c
22. Prepare the Balance sheet.

BHARATHIAR UNIVERSITY

COMPUTER APPLICATIONS PRACTICAL LIST

FOR M.COM COURSE OFFERED BY AFFILIATED COLLEGES

FOR THE STUDENTS ADMITTED DURING THE ACADEMIC YEAR 2007- 2008 ONWARDS

COMPUTER APPLICATION PRACTICAL – I

MS WORD

1. Type a cost audit report and perform the following:
   (a) Right alignments, Bold the important words.
   (b) Center align the second paragraph and perform italics for the important words.
   (c) Change third paragraph into two column paragraph.
   (d) Insert page numbers at the bottom, Insert date, time and heading in the header section.
   (e) Character spacing for side headings.
2. Prepare a questionnaire (minimum 15 questions) in your area of specialization Marketing/ Finance / HR.
   - Use bullets and numbering
   - Check the spelling according to British
   - Use thesaurus replace a word
   - Use drop cap
3. Type a sample research report and perform the following functions:

   Insert symbols, caption, page break, justification of text, indent a text, rearrange paragraphs using mouse.
4. Type a published horizontal form of a balance sheet of a company and perform the following :
   - Tables: insert, delete rows and columns
   - Borders: top and bottom only
   - Auto format tables
   - Change backgrounds to differentiate heading of the table with others.
5. Identify an organization and prepare an organizational chart prevailing in that concern.
6. Prepare a table showing Employees Performance appraisal system, using the following for:
   - Use auto format for tables.
   - Change the text color of the headings.
   - Sort the employees in the alphabetical order.
   - Link the employees' address using hyperlink.
   - Merge two cells.

7. Using three column format type any 5 differences between Cost, Financial & Management Accounting.
8. Prepare a diagrammatic representation showing the Elements of Cost, using auto shapes.
9. Prepare an attractive Advertisement to create a demand for a particular Accounting Package by using 3D effects, Clip arts, Stars, Banners in Auto shapes.
10. Perform mail merge operation for sending notice to share holders for AGM.
11. Type your curriculum vitae and perform Template and indent the text.

MS POWER POINT

1. Draw diagram of different packing labels in MS Word and display it in PowerPoint.
2. Create contents of a sample research report on your area of specialization.
3. Prepare a PowerPoint Presentation for the following:

   (a) Product Advertisement, (b) Company Advertisement

Using hyperlink to all slides, different animation effect for text and pictures, fully automatic — timing 2 Minutes

MS EXCEL

1. Prepare a table showing the customer details of a bank. [Customer name, Nature of account, Account Number, Address, E-Mail ID] and Perform the following:
   - ➢ Delete the customer who had closed the A/c.
   - ➢ Insert a row in between the 1st and 2nd customer.
   - ➢ Insert a column in between Address and E-mail ID and Name it as Telephone Number
   - ➢ Hide the column 'Address'
2. Create a table of a company with the following details [Name of the employees, Name of the department, Net Pay, City Address]
   - ➢ Copy the production department employees in sheet number 2.
   - ➢ Copy the details of the employees staying in Coimbatore city.
   - ➢ Find the person who is getting a maximum salary.
3. Prepare payroll for the employees (10 employees) of an organization and count the number of employees who are getting the salary of more than Rs.10, 000/-. Calculate with the following components (DA, HRA, CCA, EPF, LIC) as a percentage of basic pay and sum the total basic pay, net pay of all employees.
4. Prepare an excel sheet under the main heading of assets and liabilities and perform the following:
   - ➢ Select a column and change the number format to Rupees and paise (0.00) format.
   - ➢ Change a particular range of cells font as bold
   - ➢ Select a row and hide it.
   - ➢ Use shortcut key and go to sheet 3 and select a cell.
   - ➢ Prepare a bin card for the issue and purchases made during the particular month use Auto format wizard.

5. Prepare a demand forecasting for a new Product Life Cycle of a given product, collect the details regarding sales, and profit of a product for the past 10 years fit it in a chart, and present it in power point.

6. Prepare a trend analysis of a product whose year and sales figures are given (10 years).

7. Prepare a break-even chart using Chart Wizard.

8. Collect EPS and Market price of the shares, NAV and Turnover of 10 different companies from the leading business dailies and enter in a table. Calculate the price earnings per share. Copy it into different sheets in the name of each company use copying, count function and statistical functions.

9. Find the correlation between demand and price of a product.

10. Create a table showing the following:

    (a) Years (Minimum 5 years)
    (b) Profit
    (c) Depreciation
    (d) Profit after Depreciation
    (e) Tax
    (f) Profit after tax
    (g) Cash Inflows
    (h) Cumulative cash inflows of a project and find its Payback Period.

11. Prepare Final account of a banking companies in the new format using excel.

MS ACCESS

1. Create a student's database Find Total, Average, Display list where average is greater than 60% and Retrieve the students according to the highest marks.

2. Collect and Create a database for maintaining the address of the policy holders of an Insurance company with the following constraints:

    (a) Policy Number should be the primary key.
    (b) Name should not be empty.
    (c) Maintain at least 10 records.
    (d) Retrieve the addresses of female policyholders whose residence is at Coimbatore.

3. Create a student's database using design view for students mark details:

    (a) Add at least 10 records.
    (b) Sortout the names in alphabetical order.
    (c) Find Total and Average
    (d) Display list where total is greater than 350.
    (e) Display list where marks are greater than 90 and total greater than 400.
    (f) Apply Sort option to display records.
    (g) Generate reports by using the above queries.

4. Collect pamphlets for 5 products and create product strategies in the MS ACCESS.

5. Using Access ledger Accounts Wizard, prepare the following accounts in the books of State Bank of India, Coimbatore.

(a) GAIL Limited

(b) Indian Oil Corporation

(c) Reliance Petro Chemicals

April 1 Opening balance in current account

A/C No.	Name of the A/C holder	Rs.
CA 250	Gail LTD	30000
CA 251	Indian oil corporation	40000
CA 252	Reliance Petro Chemicals	25000

April 2 Deposits received form GAIL Ltd. Rs. 4000

April 2 With drawls by Indian Oil Corpn. Rs. 10000

April 3 Reliance Petro Chemicals deposited a cheque issued by Hindustan Oils Rs. 10000.

April 3 GAIL issued a cheque for Rs. 20,000 to Indian Oil Corpn.

April 4 IOC encashed the cheque.

April 4 Insurance premium paid for Rs. 4000 as per standing instruction given by IOC.

April 5 Reliance Petro chemicals withdrawn Rs. 5000.

April 6 GAIL issued a cheque to IOC Rs.4000.

April 6 IOC deposited the cheque issued by GAIL.

April 7 Reliance deposited a cheque received from XYZ traders Rs. 5000.

You are required to prepare the general ledger of the bank and view individual accounts, Create accounts summary.

INTERNET

1. Connect the Internet through a browser.
2. Create an E-mail ID.
3. Send an e-mail to your friend and check mail inbox and other facilities in your mailbox.
4. Learn how to use search engines and list some of your search results.
5. Visit any of the stock exchanges website and collect the information regarding share price.
6. Visit www.rbi.com and download some information.
7. Visit the website of Commerce and Industries Ministry and collect some information about the trade policy.
8. Visit a website for an online marketing and write the procedures to place an order.
9. Discussion forums and E-groups.
10. Visit the website of National Informatics Centre go to the Ministry of Finance and collect information regarding Economic Survey and Union Budget.

COMPUTER APPLICATION PRACTICAL –II

III SEMESTER PRACTICAL LIST (TALLY)

TALLY

For the semester III, Practical classes are to be conducted for 6 hours per week.

Creating a Company

1. Create a Company with all relevant details including VAT options

Creating Ledger

2. Create the ledgers under appropriate predefined groups

Cash A/c	Computer sales A/c
Buildings A/c	Machinery A/c
Furniture A/c	Commission received A/c
Printer purchase A/c	Commission paid A/c
Rent received A/c	Salary A/c
Rent paid A/c	Indian Bank A/c
Wages A/c	Sales returns A/c
Capital A/c	Depreciation A/c
Purchase returns A/c	

John & Co. A/c (purchased goods from this company)

Ram Agency A/c (sold goods to this company)

3. Create vouchers and view profit and loss a/c and balance sheet for the following:

Hindustan Ltd. started the business on 01-04-….

1. Contributed capital by cash Rs. 2,00,000
2. Cash deposited in Indian bank Rs. 50,000
3. Credit purchases from Krishna traders Rs. 20000 invoice no. 12
4. Credit purchases from Pravin traders Rs. 20,000 invoice no. 12
5. Credit purchase from Krishna traders Rs. 20000 invoice no. 14
6. Credit purchase from Pravin traders Rs. 20,000 invoice no. 44
7. Returned goods to Krishna traders Rs. 5000 invoice no. 12
8. Returned goods to Pravin traders Rs. 5000 invoice no. 44
9. Credit sales to Ravi & Co. Rs. 50,000 inv no. 1
10. Credit sales to Kumar & Co. Rs. 50,000 inv no. 2

11. Cash sales Rs. 20,000 inv no. 3
12. Credit sales to Ravi & Co. Rs. 50,000 inv no. 2
13. Credit sales to Ravi & Co. Rs. 50000 inv no. 5
14. Goods returned by Ravi & Co. Rs. 5000 inv. no. 1
15. Goods returned by Kumar & Co. Rs. 5000 inv. no. 1
16. Payment made by cheque to Krishna Traders Rs. 30,000 ch no. 505580
17. Payment made by cheque to Pravin Traders Rs. 30,000 ch no. 505592
18. Received cheque from: Ravi & Co. and Kumar & Co. 75,000 each.

Payments Made by Cash

1. Paid to petty cash by cash Rs.1000
2. Furniture purchased Rs. 20000
3. Salaries paid Rs. 10000
4. Rent Rs. 4000
5. Electricity charges Rs. 3000
6. Telephone charges Rs. 3500
7. Cash purchases Rs. 5000

Payments made by Petty Cash

8. Conveyance Rs.150
9. Postage Rs.100
10. Stationery Rs.200
11. Staff welfare Rs.100
12. Stationery purchased from Sriram & Co. 1500 on credit
13. Depreciation on furniture 10%

4. Emerald & Co., started a business of home appliances from 1- 4....

1-4 received cash for capital 5,00,000

7-4 credit purchases from LG Limited invoice no. 123

Ovan	100 nos.	at Rs. 800
Mixies	100 nos.	at Rs. 1000
DVD player	100 nos.	at Rs. 1500
Fridge	100 nos.	at Rs. 2000

10-4 credit Sales to AMN invoice no 1

Oven	70 nos.	at Rs. 1000
Mixies	70 nos.	at Rs. 1500

DVD player 70 nos. at Rs. 2000

Fridge 70 nos. at Rs. 2500

+Tngst 4% ON Total Sales

10-4 Cash Sales invoice no. 2

Oven 10 nos. at Rs 1000

Mixies 10 nos. at Rs 1500

DVD player 10 nos. at Rs. 2000

Fridge 10 nos. at Rs. 2500

+Tngst 4% ON Total Sales

CASH discount 5%

15-4 Paid cheque to LG limited Rs. 2,00,000

15-4 Received cheque from AMN & Co. Rs. 3,00,000

Payment Made by Cash

Paid to petty cash Rs. 2000, Furniture Rs. 15,000, Salaries Rs. 10,000

Wages Rs. 7,000,Carriage inward Rs. 1500,

25-04 Payment made by petty cash

Conveyance Rs. 200, Postage Rs. 150, Stationery Rs. 150, Staff Welfare Rs. 200

30-4 Journal depreciate 10% on furniture:

Prepare Trading Profit and Loss Account and B/s

5. From the Balances of Ms. Kavitha, Prepare Trading And Profit And Loss A/C And Balance Sheet for the Year Ending

Stock	9,300	Misc income	200
Repairs	310	Purchases	15,450
Machinery	12,670	Purchase return	440
Furniture	1330	Sales return	120
Office expenses	750	Sundry creditors	12,370
Trading expenses	310	Advertisement	500
Land and buildings	15,400	Cash in hand	160
Bank charges	50	Cash at bank	5870
Capital	24,500	Sales	20,560
Loan	5,000	Sundry expenses	150
Closing stock	7580	Insurance	500
		Travelling expenses	200

Inventory Valuation

6. From the Information given below create unit of measurement, stock groups and stock items

Find the Stock Summary

Stock groups: 1. Magazine 2. Baby drinks 3. Cool drinks 4.dailynews paper 5. Hot drinks 6. Stationery 7. Vegetables

Stock items

Item	Qty	Rate	Units
Boost	25	80	nos.
Sports Star	20	15	nos.
Potato	260	30	kgs.
Star Dust	20	25	nos.
The Hindu	50	3.25	nos.
Tomato	150	15	kgs.
Fanta	10	25	lit.
Dinamalar	40	2,50	nos.
Coco	55	120	nos.
Horlicks	60	70	nos.
India Today	10	10	nos.
Lactogin	10	100	nos.

Maintain Billwise Details

7. Create bill wise details from the following

1. Ravi commenced business with a capital of Rs. 2,00,000
2. Purchased goods from Kumar & Co. Rs.15,000 paid in three instalments within 5 days gap
3. Purchased goods for cash Rs.8000
4. Sold goods to Ratna & Co. Rs. 20,000 amount to be paid in two instalments
5. Sold goods for cash for Rs .5000
6. Received cash from Ratna & Co. Rs. 75000
7. Paid to Kumar & Co. Rs. 7500
8. Sold goods for cash Rs. 5000

Consolidation of Accounts

8. Bharath Agencies, A Wholesaler Gives The Following Information:

Opening balances

Capital: 20,00,000	cash at bank:	10,00,000	
Cash in hand: 5,00,000	furniture:	5,00,000	

Bharath agencies are dealing in stationery. The selling prices are as follows;

Pen	Rs. 35 per dozen	pencil	Rs. 30 per dozen
Ink pens	Rs. 140 per dozen		

The following transactions taken on a particular date:

1. Purchased 100 dozens of pens from Ravana bros. @ Rs.25 per dozen for cash
2. Purchased 200 dozens of pencils from Gughan bros.@ Rs.21.50 per dozen for credit less discount of Rs 100
3. Sold 10 dozens of pens to Dharma bros. for cash
4. Sold 10 dozens of pens to Bema bros. for credit
5. Sold 50 dozens of pencils to Arjuna bros.
6. Purchased from Ravana bros. 50 dozens of ink pens @ Rs.120 and by cheque.

Prepare following statements using Ex-accounting packages:

- Stores ledger, Trading account, Income statement, Balance sheet
- Account summary. Ignore dates.

Foreign Gains/Loss

9. Calculate

01.01.2005 Purchased goods from U.K. supplier 1000 £

02.01.2005 Sold goods to U.S. buyer 1500

03.01.2005 Cash received from U.S. buyer 1500 (Selling rate Rs. 46/$)

04.02.2005 Paid cash to U.K. supplier 1000 (Selling rate Rs. 53/ £)

Dollar $:			Pound £:		
Std rate	- 1$	- 43 Rs.	Std rate	- 1 £	- 51 Rs.
Sales rate	- 1$	- 44 Rs.	Sales rate	- 1 £	- 50 Rs.
Buying rate	- 1$	- 42 Rs.	Buying rate	- 1 £	- 52 Rs.

10. Memo Voucher

An advance amount paid Rs. 1500 given to sales executive for travelling. The actual expenses for travelling expenses for the sales is Rs. 500

11. Cheque Printing

Print a cheque:

Company name on cheque: Wipro India Ltd.: name of the bank Indusind bank.

Width 168, height 76, starting location 116, distance from top 23.

12. Ratio Analysis

Enter the following details comment upon the short-term solvency position of the company:

Working capital Rs. 20560492

Cash 14500

Bank 18500

Debtors 518260

Creditors 429337

Sales 515252

Purchases 433310

Stock 125982

Net profit ...?

13. Interest Calulations

Cash deposited in Scotia Bank Rs. 1,00,000

Sold goods to Ganesh Rs. 25,000

31-12- cash deposited at Scotia Bank Rs. 50,000

Sold goods to Ganesh 50,000

Interest parameters rate 14% per 365 days year

14. Calculate Interest

Cash deposited in SBI 1,00,000 Rs.

1-12 purchased goods from suppliers Rs. 20,000

Deposited in SBI Rs. 50, 000

Purchased goods from suppliers Rs. 40,000

Interest parameters rate 16% per 365 days year

15. Display the interest calculations for the period 1-4 to 31-12

Opening balance

Ram & Co. Rs. 25,000

Krishna traders Rs. 20,000

Interest parameters rate 12% per 365 days year

Interest parameters rate 12% and 16% for sundry creditors per 365 days year

Purchased goods from Krishna for 25,000 (credit period 45 days)

Sold goods to Ram for Rs. 50,000 (credit period 30 days)

Paid to Krishna the amount plus interest

Received from Ram plus interest

16. Create stock items, stock groups, sales categories, godowns, units of measure

Stock	Category	Group	Godown	Unit of measure	Std. cost	Sell Price	Op. Qty.	Total Value
Intel Celeron	Processor	Celeron	Mumbai	Nos.	15000	20000	2	30000
Intel Premium III	Processor		Chennai	Nos.	20000	25000	3	60000
Tally Accounting	Silver	Tally	Chennai	Nos.	20000	22500	5	100000
Tally Accounting	Gold	Tally	Chennai	Nos.	42000	45000	5	21000
								400000

17. Using the above exercise create various vouchers including VAT calculation for the following:

Date	Transactions
9/4/2006	Intel Pentium III (3 Nos.) @ 25,000 delivered to Vijay & Co. from Madras Go down.
10/4/2006	10 Nos. of Intel Celeron @ 15000 per unit received from Jayaram and Co, and sent to Madras Godown.
12/4/2006	2 Nos. of Intel Premium III received from Vijay & Co. as it was not in a working position.
13/4/2006	2 Nos. of Intel Celeron returned to Jayaram & Co. from Madras Godown.
14/4/2006	Physical Stock verification shows Shortage of 1 No. Intel Pentium III.

18. Create the following Inventory vouchers with data from any cost accounting book.

(a) Purchase order (b) Sales order

(c) Rejection out (d) Rejection in

(e) Stock journal (f) Delivery note

(g) Receipt note (h) Physical stock

19. In addition to the above-mentioned lab exercises work out a problem from any advanced accountancy book with a minimum of 20 transactions and generate the tally reports in full.

BHARATHIAR UNIVERSITY

COMPUTER APPLICATIONS PRACTICAL LIST

FOR M.COM. (F&C) COURSE OFFERED BY AFFILIATED COLLEGES

FOR THE STUDENTS ADMITTED DURING THE ACADEMIC YEAR 2007-2008 ONWARDS

COMPUTER APPLICATION PRACTICAL – I

II SEMESTER PRACTICAL LIST (MS – OFFICE & INTERNET)

MS WORD

1. **Analyze the union budget and perform the following:**
   - (a) **Right alignment, bold the important words**
   - (b) **Centers align the second paragraph and perform italics for the important word.**
   - (c) **Change the third paragraph in to two column paragraph**
   - (d) **Insert page numbers at the bottom, insert data, time and heading in the header section, page break.**
2. **Identify a financial organization and prepare an organizational chart of that concern.**
3. **Prepare a chart showing the different elements of Indian financial system.**
4. **Type a cost audit report and perform the following:**
   - (a) **Use format tool bar, wizard and templates.**
   - (b) **Numbering and bullets.**
   - (c) **Create and apply styles to your documents.**
5. **Request a banker to open a current account for your business concern, using letter format.**
6. **Using mail merge send share allotment letter to the applicants for the share of a company.**
7. **Type your curriculum vitae and perform template and indent the text and take print out.**
8. **Prepare a questionnaire (minimum 15 questions in your area of specialization finance,**
   - ➢ **Use bullets and numbering**
   - ➢ **Check the spelling according to British**
   - ➢ **Use thesaurus too replaces a word**
   - ➢ **Use drop cap**
9. **Prepare a table on balance of payments by using auto format table.**
10. **Preparing a document by using special text effects highlight a particular part of your text. Set tab stops and leaders use bullets and numbers wherever necessary. Also use symbol character map and special character page.**
11. **Prepare a paper on a current topic which is relevant to your specialization following function is to be preformed:**
    - (a) **Use thesaurus command.**
    - (b) **Customize the spelling and grammar options**
    - (c) **Finding and replaying text it go to function**
    - (d) **Headers to footers, page numbers, section breaks, and columns and tablets.**
    - (e) **Use graphics for extra impact via inserting autoharps, line art object, and word art add a media clip in to your document.**

MS EXCEL

1. Prepare break-even chart using chart wizard.
2. Prepare a trend analysis of a product of your own choice with year and sale figures which are given.
3. Prepare an excel sheet under the main heading of capital and working capital as the column names and perform the following:
   - Select a column and change the number format rupees and Paise format
   - Change the particular range of cells font as bold,
   - Select a row hide it
   - Use short cut key and go to sheet 3 and select a cell
4. Prepare an excel sheet under the main heading of capital and working capital as the column names:

Capital	Working capital
Building 100000	Rent 15000
Software 15000	Salaries 15000
Ups 40000	Advertisement 20000
Telephone15000	Stationery 5000
Internet 20000	Electricity 3000

5. Determine the share price index and movements of 10 companies for 10 days from the newspapers by using the statistical functions of excel present it in a graphical form.
6. Prepare a bin card for purchases issues made during the year by using auto format wizard
7. Prepare a cost sheet with supporting evidence as to know cost per unit of product
   - ➢ Use formula function and built in functions.
   - ➢ Use pivot tables and charts
8. Determine correlation between demand and price of a product (minimum 10 entries).
9. Prepare a sales budget and perform the following:
   - Create a text box frame
   - Change the color line
   - Make it semi transparent
   - Change the height and width of the heading of the text box.
10. Using three column format type any five differences between financial management and cost accounting.
11. By using already prepared questionnaire (ms word) prepare a work sheet.
12. Collect earning per share and market price of the shares net assets value and turn over of ten different companies from the leading business dailies and enter in a table. Calculate the price earning per share. Copy it in to different sheets in the name of each and every company. Use copying, count functions and statistical functions.

MS ACCESS

1. Prepare a pay roll for employee's data base of an organization with the following details Employee Id, Employee Name, Date of birth, Department and designation Date of appointment, Basic pay, Dearness allowance, House rent allowance and Other deductions if any

- Create font for individual employees (pay slip)
- Create queries for different categories
- Create a report about the total salary distribution.

2. Draft the questionnaire among the students regarding the preference of the product
   - Create a master table an access for each and every question
   - Enter the collected data with help of queries
   - Identify the number of respondent in each and every category
   - Create a report with the help of queries
3. Through net collect share price of 5 companies from 5 different stock exchanges in India. Create a table access and enter the data. Create a font view for each compay's share.
4. Gather price quantity description for five products and enter in access table and create an invoice in form design view.
5. Gather the details regarding the receipt and payments for 6 months and by using a budget wizard. Prepare a cash budget.

MS POWER POINT

1. Gather Financial Details through Net Regarding five companies and presented in a slide show with animation and transitions (speed and sound).
2. Identify the different products, its process and collect different costs involved in each process and present it by inserting clip parts, text, table and a chart.
3. Collect data on recent development in foreign exchange in India. Create your presentation by adding text and object to slides. Use data, slide number of other text in a slide footer. You can add, delete or modify information in the footer area of all slides by using the slide master.
4. Create a professional looking organizational chart of a financial institution. Perform the following:
   - ➢ Choose a particular level and all levels and edit.
   - ➢ Change the color shadows and border options on selected boxes using the box menu.
   - ➢ Change the thickness and color of connecting lines using the lines menu

INTERNET

1. Create your e-mail id, learn search engines and browser
2. Send an e-mail to your superior by attaching the excel data which comprises details regarding the financial performance of the company.
3. Store your e-mail message by creating new folders, move mail between folders.
4. Visit any one of the stock exchange website and display the listed share price by using excel.
5. Visit NIC website go to ministry of finance and collect information regarding economic survey and union budget.
6. Download the NPV calculator and do NPV calculations.
7. Visit RBI website and collect necessary publications on financial areas.
8. Download the TT buying and TT selling rates.
9. Visit any one of the international capital market website and download the trend of the market and present the report.

COMPUTER APPLICATION PRACTICAL– II

III SEMESTER PRACTICAL LIST (TALLY)

TALLY

1. Create a Company with all the relevant details

Creating Ledgers

2. Create the ledgers under appropriate predefined groups

Cash A/c	Computer sales A/c
Buildings A/c	Machinery A/c
Furniture A/c	Commission received A/c
Printer purchase A/c	Commission paid A/c
Rent received A/c	Salary A/c
Rent paid A/c	Indian bank A/c
Wages A/c	Sales returns A/c
Capital A/c	Depreciation A/c
Purchase returns A/c	

John & Co. A/c (purchased goods from this company)

Ram agency A/c (sold goods to this company)

3. Voucher types

By using a minimum of 5 transactions for each of the following vouchers. Take transactions from any advanced accountancy book and prepare the following vouchers:

Receipt voucher, payment voucher, contra voucher, sales voucher, purchase voucher, debit note and credit note voucher.

4. Emerald & Co., started a business of home appliances from 1- 4

1-4 received cash for capital 5,00,000

7-4 credit purchases from BPL in no 123:

fridge	100 nos.	at Rs. 800
table fan	100 nos.	at Rs. 1000
mixies	100 nos.	at Rs. 1500
grinders	100 nos.	at Rs. 2000

10-4 credit sSales Ram electricals in no 1:

Fridge	70nos	at Rs 1000
Table fan	70nos	at Rs 1500
Mixies	70nos	at Rs 2000
Grinders	70nos	at Rs 2500

+TNGST 4% ON TOTAL SALES

10-4 Cash Sales in no 2:

Fridge	10nos	at Rs 1000
Table fan	10nos	at Rs 1500
Mixies	10nos	at Rs 2000
Grinders	10nos	at Rs 2500

+TNGST 4% ON TOTAL SALES

CASH discount 5%

15-4 Paid cheque to BPL Rs. 2,00,000

15-4 Received cheque from Kelvinator Rs. 3,00,000

Payment made by cash

Paid to petty cash Rs. 2000, Furniture Rs. 15,000,Salaries Rs. 10,000

Wages Rs. 7,000,Carriage inward Rs. 1500

25-04 **Payment made by petty cash**

Conveyance Rs. 200,Postage Rs. 150,Stationeries Rs. 150,Staff Welfare Rs. 200

30-4 Journal depreciate 10% on furniture:

Prepare Trading Profit and Loss Account and B/s

5. From the below create unit of measurement, stock groups and stokc items

Find the stock summary:

Stock groups: 1. magazine 2. baby drinks 3. cool drinks 4. dailynews paper 5. hot drinks 6. stationery 7. vegetables

Stock items:

Item	Qty	Rate	Units
Boost	25	80	nos
Sports Star	20	15	nos
Potato	260	30	kgs
Star Dust	20	25	nos
The Hindu	50	3.25	nos
Tomato	150	15	kgs
Fanta	10	25	lit
Dinamalar	40	2,50	nos
Coco	55	120	nos
Horlicks	60	70	nos
India Today	10	10	nos
Lactogin	10	100	nos

Maintain Billwise Details

6. Create billwise details

1. Raja commenced business with a capital of Rs. 10,000
2. Purchased goods from Kumar & Co. 15,000 Rs. Paid in three instalments within 5 days gap
3. Purchased goods for cash Rs. 8000
4. Sold goods to Ratna & Co. Rs. 20,000 amount to be paid in two instalment
5. Sold goods for cash for Rs. 5000
6. Received cash from ratna & Co. 7500
7. Paid to Kumar & Co. 7500
8. Sold goods for cash 5000

Consolidation of Accounts

7. Ram Agencies, A Wholesaler Gives The Following Information :

Opening balances :

Capital	: 20,00,000	cash at bank	: 10,00,000
Cash in hand	: 5,00,000	furniture	: 5,00,000

Ram agencies are dealing in trading of pens and pencils. The selling prices are as follows;

Pen	Rs. 35 per dozen	pencil	Rs. 30 per dozen
Ink pens	Rs. 140 per dozen		

The following transactions take place on a particular date:

1. Purchased 100 dozens of pens from Ravana bros. @ Rs. 25 per dozen for cash
2. Purchase 200 dozens of pencils from Gughan bros.@ Rs. 21.50 per dozen for credit less discount of Rs. 100
3. Sold 10 dozens of pens to Dharma bros. for cash
4. Sold 10 dozens of pens to Bema bros for credit
5. Sold 50 dozens of pencils to Arjuna bros.
6. Purchased from Ravana bros. 50 dozens of ink pens @ Rs.120 and by cheque.

Prepare following statements using Tally Accounting packages:

- Stores ledger, Trading account, Income statement, Balance sheet
- Account summary Ignore dates

8. Cost categories and Cost center

Nov 1: Purchased Goods from ABC & Co -15,000 Banglore branch-5,000, Chennai branch-10,000. Allocate the cost to the products:Mouse- 7000, Keyboard- 15,000

2. Sold Goods for Cash Rs. 20,000

   Banglore branch -7,000, Chennai branch -13,000

Allocate the cost to the products: Mouse -9000,Keyboard 11,000

3. Paid to ABC & Co. Rs. 15,000

4. Salary Paid 3000 Rs to Salesman

   Mr. Raj 1600

   Mr. Ravi 1400

9. Currencies

Calculate forex value

On 1-12-sold to foreign customer 100 bags of wheat at the rate of 25$ per bag (new ref. export 1 due dates 7 days)

On 15-12 received from foreign customer 2000 $ @ 39 per $ plus bank

Charge 50 $ std rate 35 per $ selling rate 36 $ buying rate 37 per $

On 1-12 the rates for pounds are as follows:

Std rate 50 per pound : selling rate 51 per pound : buying rate 52 per pound

On 12-12 purchased from foreign supplier 200 bags of wheat @ 5 pound per bag. The rupee was being traded at Rs. 52 per pound. Due days is 15 days

On 20-12 paid to the foreign supplier 1000 pounds at Rs. 53 per pound bank charges incurred was Rs. 2000

10. Foreign Gain/ Loss

01.01.2005 Purchased goods from U.K. supplier 1000 £

02.01.2005 Sold goods to U.S. buyer 1500

03.01.2005 Cash received from U.S. buyer 1500 (Selling rate rs.46/$)

04.02.2005 Paid cash to U.K. supplier 1000 (Selling rate Rs. 53/ £)

Dollar $:			Pound £:		
Std rate	- 1$	- 43 Rs.	Std. rate	- 1 £	- 51 Rs.
Sales rate	- 1$	- 44 Rs.	Sales rate	- 1 £	- 50 Rs.
Buying rate	- 1$	- 42 Rs.	Buying rate	- 1 £	- 52 Rs.

11. Ratio Analysis

Enter the following details comment upon the short-term solvency position of the company:

Working capital Rs. 3000492, Cash 14500, Bank 18500, Debtors 418260

Creditors 529337, Sales 715252, Purchases 403310, Stock 225982

Net profit?

12. Interest Calculations

Cash deposited in Canara bank Rs. 1,00,000

Sold goods to ganesh Rs. 25,000

31-12- cash deposited at canara bank Rs. 50,000

Sold goods to Ganesh 50,000

Interest parameters rate 16% per 365 days year

13. Calculate Interest

Cash deposited in SBI Rs.1,00,000

Purchased goods from suppliers Rs. 20,000 on 1st December

Deposited in SBI Rs.50,000

Purchased goods from suppliers Rs. 40,000

Interest parameters rate 16% per 365 days year

14. Create accounting vouchers for the following:

Date	Transaction	Amount
1/04/2004	Cash withdrawn from Indian Bank	10,000
2/04/2004	Office rent Paid by Cheque (ch.No:456797)	5000
2/04/2004	Telephone Bill paid by Cheque (ch No:456798)	2500
2/04/2004	Service Charge received from a customer Ramesh by Cash.	1000
2/04/2004	Hardware Sales made in cash.	25,000
5/04/2004	Salary paid to Mr.Siva by cheque (Ch No:3479289)	3000
6/04/2004	Conveyances Paid to Staff by Cash.	1000
6/04/2004	Electricity Bill paid by cash.	2500
7/04/2004	Software purchases made form Zee and co is the 10% local sales tax.	38,500
8/04/2004	Hardware sales made to Visa & Co.	26.000

BHARATHIAR UNIVERSITY

COMPUTER APPLICATIONS PRACTICAL LIST

FOR M.COM. (IB) COURSE OFFERED BY AFFILIATED COLLEGES

FOR THE STUDENTS ADMITTED DURING THE ACADEMIC YEAR 2007-2008 ONWARDS

COMPUTER APPLICATION PRACTICAL – I

II SEMESTER PRACTICAL LIST (MS – OFFICE & INTERNET)

MS OFFICE

MS WORD

1. Type your curriculum vitae using templates/wizards in MS Word.
2. Prepare a L/C in MS Word.
3. Prepare a Bill of Exchange.
4. Prepare a Quotation to various suppliers in order to purchase Raw materials: use mail merge.
5. Collect and prepare the certificate of origin.
6. Collect and prepare a pay slip.
7. Collect and prepare an invoice.
8. Collect and prepare a packing list.
9. Create a sample research reports (only on topics).
10. Draw a product lifecycle.
11. Draw an organizational chart in MS Word.
12. Prepare a minute for a meeting.
13. Draft a letter to various newspapers to display the press notes of the workshop conducted in your department: use mail merge.
14. Prepare a questionnaire for a survey.

MS EXCEL

1. Find the correlation between demand and supply.
2. Prepare an excel sheet under the main heading of assets and liabilities and perform the following:
   (a) Select a column and change the number format to rupees and paise format.
   (b) Change a particular range of cells font as bold.
   (c) Select key and go to sheet no.3 and select cell.
3. Calculate T Test and F Test for the data collected from any statistical book.
4. Create customs Exchange rate in Excel (buying rate and selling rate)
5. Take the sample data and draw a demand and supply curve and fix the price in Excel.

6. Draw a Break-even Chart with imaginary figures.
7. Draw an Indifference curve analysis.
8. Prepare a sales budget.
9. Prepare a market survey report for any product.
10. Estimate GDP and National income in Excel.

MS POWERPOINT

1. Prepare an agenda for an inauguration function of a one day seminar.
2. Draw a diagram of different packing labels and symbols in MS Word and display it in the power point.
3. Create an advertisement using PowerPoint.
4. Create a slide show of various activities of your department during the academic year.
5. Present using Power point the procedures involved in exporting a product.
6. List down the countries in the European union and also the currencies.

MS ACCESS

1. Create G8 countries (SAARC) trade data in access.
2. Create a database for countries cultural environment in access.
3. Create a database of major MNCs in India and their business using Access.
4. Display the details of softwares developed by any corporate in India and perform the following:
   (a) Display the details of the packages whose software costs exceed 20 thousand.
   (b) Display the details of the software that are developed in Tally.
   (c) What is a price of costliest software developed in accounting.
5. Create a table with the following fields and insert the values:
   (a) company name
   (b) proprietor
   (c) address
   (d) supplier's name
   (e) number of employees
   (f) GP percentage

Do the following:

(a) Display all the records of the company in ascending order with GP percentage.

(b) Display the name of the company whose supplier's name is TELCO

(c) Display the details of the company whose GP percentage is greater the 20

(d) Display the details of the company having employee ranging from 300 to 1000

(e) Display the name of the company whose supplier's name is TATA

6. Create a table named student in the following fields and insert the values:

(a) student name

(b) gender

(c) roll number

(d) department name

(e) address

(f) percentage

Calculate the following:

(a) Calculate the average percentage of the students

(b) Display the names of the students whose percentage is greater than 30

(c) Display the details of the student who got the highest percentage

(d) Display the details of the students whose percentage is 50 and 70

(e) Display the details of the students whose percentage is greater than the percentage of roll number 12CA01.

7. Create a table named product with the following fields:

(a) product number

(b) product name

(c) unit of measure

(d) quantity

(e) total amount

Do the following:

(a) Select the records whose unit of measurement is Kg

(b) Select the records whose quantity is greater than 10 and less than or equal to 20.

(c) Calculate the entire total amount by using sum operation.

(d) Calculate the number of records whose unit price is greater than 50 with count operation.

8. Create the table payroll with the following fields:

(a) Employee number

(b) Employee name

(c) Department

(d) Basic pay

(e) HRA

(f) DA

(g) PF

(h) Net pay

Calculate the following:

(a) Net pay.

(b) Arrange the records in ascending order according to the net pay.

(c) Display the details of the employees working in sales department.

(d) Select the details of the employees whose HRA is greater than 1000 and DA greater than 1000.

INTERNET

1. Discussions on various forums and E-groups.
2. Download the port areas in the map and display it in the Power Point.
3. Browse and collect the country profile. View as slide show.
4. Collect the various organizations assisting India's foreign trade and prepare a report.
5. Collect and prepare the containers' lists based on the commodity features.
6. Use Export 911.com and download any one export document.
7. Collect and prepare sailing routes and bunkering ports.
8. Download the information regarding storage factor of different commodities.
9. Download the shipping space in any of the leading ports in India and download the information regarding ship repair and construction.
10. Download the information regarding the different types of marine risks.
11. Download the information regarding ship schedule at different ports:

    (a) birth time

    (b) sailing time

    (c) arrival time and display it in Power point

COMPUTER APPLICATION PRACTICAL – II

III SEMESTER PRACTICAL LIST (TALLY)

TALLY

For the semester III, Practical classes are to be conducted for 6 hours per week.

Creating a Company

1. Create a Company with relevant details

2. Enter the following transactions and generate reports

Arun started the business on 1-4-

1. Received capital by cash Rs. 2,00,000
2. Cash deposited in Indian bank Rs. 50,000
3. Credit purchases from Krishna traders Rs. 20000 invoice no. 12
4. Credit purchases from Pravin traders Rs. 20,000 invoice no. 12
5. Credit purchase from Krishna traders Rs. 20000 invoice no. 14
6. Credit purchase from Pravin traders Rs. 20,000 invoice no. 44
7. Returned goods to Krishna traders Rs. 5000 invoice no. 12
8. Returned goods to Pravin traders Rs. 5000 invoice no. 44
9. Credit sales to Ravi & Co. Rs. 50,000 inv no. 1
10. Credit sales to Kumar & Co. Rs. 50,000 inv no. 2
11. Cash sales Rs. 20,000 inv no. 3
12. Credot sales to Ravi & Co. Rs. 50,000 inv no. 2
13. Credit sales to Ravi & Co. Rs. 50000 inv no. 5
14. Goods returned by Ravi & Co. Rs. 5000 omv no. 1
15. Goods returned by Kumar & Co. Rs. 5000 inv no. 1
16. Payment made by cheque to Krishna Traders Rs. 30,000 ch no. 302302
17. Payment made by cheque to Pravin Traders Rs. 30,000 ch no 116210

Received cheque from : Ravi & Co. and Kumar & Co. 75,000 Rs. each.

Payments made by cash

18. Paid to petty cash by cash Rs.1000
19. Furniture purchased Rs.20000
20. Salaries paid Rs. 10000
21. Rent Rs.4000

22. Electricity charges Rs.3000
23. Telephone charges Rs.3500
24. Cash purchases Rs. 5000

Payments made by petty cash:

25. Conveyance Rs.150
26. Postage Rs.100
27. Stationery Rs.200
28. Staff welfare Rs.100
29. Stationery purchased from Sriram & Co. Rs. 1500 on credit
30. Depreciation on furniture 10%

3. Royal Electricals started a business of Electricals items and home appliances from 1- 4

1-4 received cash for capital Rs. 5,00,000

7-4 credit purchases from govind electricals in no. 123:

Ceiling fan	100 nos.	at Rs. 800
Table fan	100 nos.	at Rs. 1000
Mixies	100 nos.	at Rs. 1500
Grinders	100 nos.	at Rs. 2000

10-4 credit Sales Ram electricals in no. 1:

Ceiling fan	70 nos.	at Rs. 1000
Table fan	70 nos.	at Rs. 1500
Mixies	70 nos.	at Rs. 2000
Grinders	70 nos.	at Rs. 2500

+TNGST 4% ON TOTAL SALES

10-4 Cash Sales in no 2:

Ceiling fan	10 nos.	at Rs. 1000
Table fan	10 nos.	at Rs. 1500
Mixies	10 nos.	at Rs. 2000
Grinders	10 nos.	at Rs. 2500

+TNGST 4% ON TOTAL SALES

CASH discount 5%

15-4 Paid cheque to Govind Electricals Rs. 2,00,000

15-4 Received cheque from Ram Electricals Rs. 3,00,000

Payment made by cash

Paid to petty cash Rs. 2000

Furniture Rs. 15,000

Salaries Rs. 10,000

Wages Rs. 7,000

Carriage inward Rs. 1500

25-04 Payment made by petty cash

Conveyance Rs. 200

Postage Rs. 150

Stationery Rs. 150

Staff Welfare Rs. 200

30-4 Journal depreciate 10% on furniture:

Prepare Trading Profit and Loss Account and Balance sheet.

From the Balances of Ms. Priya, prepare Trading and Profit and Loss A/C and Balance Sheet for the Year Ending....

Stock	9,300
Repairs	310
Machinery	12,670
Furniture	1330
Office expenses	750
Trading expenses	310
Land and buildings	15,400
Bank charges	50
Misc. income	200
Purchases	15,450
Purchase return	440
Sales return	120
Sundry creditors	12,370
Advertisement	500
Cash in hand	160
Cash at bank	5870
Sales	20,560
Sundry expenses	150

Insurance	500
Travelling expenses	200
Capital	24,500
Loan	5,000
Closing stock	7580

Inventory Valuation

4. From the below create unit of measurement, stock groups and stock items,Find the stock summary:

Stock groups: 1. Magazine 2. Baby drinks 3. Cool drinks 4.Daily news paper 5. Hot drinks 6. Stationery 7. Vegetables

Stock items:

Item	Qty	Rate	Units
Boost	25	80	nos
Sports Star	20	15	nos
Potato	260	30	kgs
Star Dust	20	25	nos
The Hindu	50	3.25	nos
Tomato	150	15	kgs
Fanta	10	25	lit
Dinamalar	40	2,50	nos
Coco	55	120	nos
Horlicks	60	70	nos
India Today	10	10	nos
Lactogin	10	100	nos

Maintain Billwise Details

5. Create Credit billwise details from the following:

1. Raja commenced business with a capital of Rs. 10,000
2. Purchased goods from Kumar & Co. Rs.15,000 Paid in three instalments within 5 days gap
3. Purchased goods for cash Rs. 8000
4. Sold goods to Ratna & Co. Rs. 20,000 amount to be paid in two instalment
5. Sold goods for cash for Rs. 5000
6. Received cash from Ratna & Co. Rs. 7500
7. Paid to Kumar & Co. Rs. 7500
8. Sold goods for cash Rs. 5000

6. Cost categories and Cost center

Nov 1: Purchased Goods from ABC & Co. Rs. 15,000

Banglore Branch Rs. 5,000

Chennai Branch Rs. 10,000

Allocate the cost to the products

Mouse Rs.7000

Keyboard Rs. 15,000

2. Sold Goods for Cash Rs. 20,000

Banglore Branch Rs. 7,000

Chennai Branch Rs. 13,000

Allocate the cost to the products

Mouse Rs. 9000

Keyboard Rs. 11,000

3. Paid to ABC & Co. Rs. 15,000

4. Salary Paid Rs. 3000 To Salesman

Mr. Raj Rs. 1600

Mr. Ravi Rs. 1400

Currencies

7. Calculate forex value

On 1-12-sold to foreign customer 100 bags of wheat at the rate of 25$ per bag (new ref. export 1 due dates 7 days)

On 15-12 received from foreign customer 2000 $ @ 39 per $ plus bank

Charge 50 $ std. rate 35 per $ selling rate 36 $ buying rate 37 per $

On 1-12 the rates for pounds are as follows

Std. rate 50 per pound: selling rate 51 per pound: buying rate 52 per pound

On 12-12 purchased from foreign supplier 200 bags of wheat @ 5 pound per bag. The rupee was being traded at Rs 52 per pound. Due days is 15 days

On 20-12 paid to the foreign supplier 1000 pounds at Rs. 53 per pound

bank charges incurred was Rs. 2000 Foreign gain/loss

8. Calculate foreign exchange gain or loss

01.01.2005

Purchased goods from U.K. supplier 1000 £

02.01.2005

Sold goods to U.S. buyer 1500

03.01.2005

Cash received from U.S. buyer 1500 (Selling rate Rs.46/$)

04.02.2005

Paid cash to U.K. supplier 1000 (Selling rate Rs. 53/ £)

Dollar $:			Pound £:		
Std rate	- 1$	- 43 Rs	Std rate	- 1 £	- 51 Rs
Sales rate	- 1$	- 44 Rs	Sales rate	- 1 £	- 50 Rs
Buying rate	- 1$	- 42 Rs	Buying rate	- 1 £	- 52 Rs

9. Memo Voucher

An advance amount paid Rs. 10000 given to sales executive for traveling. The actual expenses for traveling expenses for the sales is Rs. 5000

10. Cheque Printing

Print a cheque:

Company name on cheque: Bharathi: name of the bank State Bank of India.

Width 168, height 76, starting location 116, distance from top 23.

11. Interest Calculations

Cash deposited in Canara Bank Rs. 1,00,000

Sold goods to ganesh Rs. 25,000

31-12- cash deposited at canara bank Rs. 50,000

Sold goods to Ganesh 50,000

Interest parameters rate 16% per 365 days year

12. Display the interest calculations for the period 1-4 to 31-12

Opening balance

Ram & Co. Rs. 25,000

Krishna traders Rs. 20,000

Interest parameters rate 12% per 365 days year

Interest parameters rate 12% and 16% for sundry creditors per 365 days year

Purchased goods from Krishna for 25,000 (credit period 45 days)

Sold goods to Ram for Rs. 50,000 (credit period 30 days)

Paid to Krishna the amount plus interest

Received from Ram plus interest

BHARATHIAR UNIVERSITY

COMPUTER APPLICATIONS PRACTICAL LIST

FOR M.COM. (CA) COURSE OFFERED BY AFFILIATED COLLEGES

FOR THE STUDENTS ADMITTED DURING THE ACADEMIC YEAR 2007- 2008 ONWARDS

COMPUTER APPLICATION PRACTICAL –I

I SEMESTER PRACTICAL LIST (MS – OFFICE & SQL)

MS OFFICE

1. Type a document (like-Speech of a chairman in AGM, Budget speech of Finance Minister) and perform the following:
   - Right align and bold face
   - Center align and italics
   - Justify and center alignment
   - Also insert footnote and end note for the same.
   - Change a paragraph into two column paragraph
   - Insert page number at the bottom
   - Insert date, time and heading in the header section.
2. Using mail merge, send an invitation /notice (by creating the invitation/notice) for the following situation (at least 5 addresses to be entered) (any one of the following) :
   (a) For opening a new branch
   (b) Inauguration of ATM
   (c) Informing about new scheme or offer
3. Preparation of Table using MS word — Sales Analysis for a period of five years for three products
4. Using EXCEL prepare a table for (any one of the following):
   (a) Employees payroll
   (b) Sales data
   (c) Students marks and perform the following functions (Total, Average, Percentage, conditional sum and show the results in chart)
5. Prepare an Excel sheet and apply the following statistical functions to analyze the data (Any one of the following)
   (a) Mean, Median, Mode
   (b) Standard Deviation
   (c) Time Series

6. Prepare a questionnaire for a research problem by using MS WORD — use word art, reference, borders and shading and insert a table relevant to your research problem.

7. Prepare a PowerPoint presentation for (any one of the following):

   (a) Product Advertisement

   (b) Company Advertisement

   (c) Annual General Meeting (Minimum 5 slides)

Requirements

   (a) Using Hyperlink to all slides

   (b) Different animation effect for text and pictures

   (c) Fully automatic – timing – 2 minutes

8. Using Access prepare a table for (any one of the following) :

   (a) Pay Roll

   (b) Student record

   (c) Sales data

   (d) Address database of customers —

Requirements

(By using Design view/ Wizard view)

1. One of the fields should be Primary Key
2. Apply sort option to display records (at least three different methods of sorting)
3. Generate reports by using different queries.

COMPUTER APPLICATION PRACTICAL – II

II SEMESTER PRACTICAL LIST (TALLY & C++)

TALLY

1. By using Tally — Create Voucher & ledger with adjustments (using F11 and F12 keys).
2. Prepare Trial Balance, Profit & Loss A/C and Balance Sheet (With minimum of any 5 adjustments).
3. Prepare Inventory statement using (Calculate Inventory by using all methods)
   - (a) FIFO
   - (b) LIFO
   - (c) Simple Average method
   - (d) Weighted Average Method.
4. Prepare a fund flow statement and give your opinion.
5. Prepare a cash flow statement and present your view.
6. Analyze the performance of an organization by using Ratio (Minimum 5 Ratios are essential).

C++

7. Pay Roll calculation (Using simple program).
8. Find out EOQ, Minimum Level, Maximum Level, Re-order level (Using simple program).
9. Write a C++ program to calculate working capital using class and objects (member function should write inside and outside the class).
10. Program to calculate contribution, P/v Ratio, BEP and Margin of safety using Functions.
11. Calculate Simple Interest and compound interest using inline functions.
12. Calculate Depreciation — by using Constructors and Destructors.
13. Write a C++ program to calculate the sum and product of two complex numbers using operator overloading.
14. Write a C++ program to prepare cost sheet using inheritance.

COMPUTER APPLICATIONS PRACTICAL

(THERE IS NO UNIVERSITY PRACTICAL EXAMINATIONS)

PRACTICAL CLASSES SHOULD BE CONDUCTED DURING THE FOURTH SEMESTER

HTML

1. Using HTML create a web page to show the information of a Departmental Store.
2. Using HTML prepare a Resume of your own.
3. Using HTML create a video clipping.
4. Using HTML create a style sheet with border definition and font attributes.
5. Introduce a new product to the market and create web advertising.
6. Create a web page for your department — by using font effects, filters and linking within the page.

JAVA

7. Write a Java program to perform the following functions — sum, difference and product.
8. Write a Java program to calculate the Income Tax
9. Write a Java program to prepare budget.
10. Write a Java program for the properties of URL.
11. Write a Java Script program to calculate the Gross Profit and Net Profit using the Java Script Form Objects
12. Using Applets create a page for Arithmetic calculation.

BHARATHIAR UNIVERSITY

COMPUTER APPLICATIONS PRACTICAL LIST

FOR M.SC. (FCA) COURSE OFFERED BY AFFILIATED COLLEGES

FOR THE STUDENTS ADMITTED DURING THE ACADEMIC YEAR 2007- 2008 ONWARDS

COMPUTER APPLICATION PRACTICAL– I

I SEMESTER PRACTICAL LIST (MS – OFFICE C++ & SQL)

MS OFFICE

1. Type a document (like — Speech of a chairman in AGM, Budget speech of finance minister) and perform the following:
   - Right align and bold face
   - Center align and italics
   - Justify and center alignment
   - Also insert footnote and end note for the same.
   - Change a paragraph into two column paragraph
   - Insert page number at the bottom
   - Insert date, time and heading in the header section.
2. Using mail merge, send an invitation /notice (by creating the invitation/notice) for the following situation (at least 5 addresses to be entered)

   (Any one of the following):

   (a) For opening a new branch

   (b) Inauguration of ATM

   (c) Informing about new scheme or offer
3. Preparation of Table using MS word — Sales Analysis for a period of five years for three products
4. Using EXCEL prepare a table for (any one of the following):

   (a) Employees payroll

   (b) Sales data

   (c) Students' marks and perform the following functions:

   (Total, Average, Percentage, conditional sum and show the results in chart)
5. Prepare a PowerPoint presentation for (any one of the following):

   (d) Product Advertisement

   (e) Company Advertisement

   (f) Annual General Meeting (Minimum 5 slides)

Requirements

(a) Using Hyperlink to all slides

(b) Different animation effect for text and pictures

(c) Fully automatic – timing – 2 minutes

8. Using Access prepare a table for (any one of the following):

(d) Pay Roll

(e) Student record

(f) Sales data

(g) Address database of customers —

Requirements

(By using Design view/ Wizard view)

1. One of the fields should be Primary Key
2. Apply sort option to display records (at least three different methods of sorting)
3. Generate reports by using different queries.

COMPUTER APPLICATION PRACTICAL –II
III SEMESTER PRACTICAL LIST (TALLY, HTML AND JAVA)

TALLY

1. By using Tally — Create Voucher & ledger with adjustments (using F11 and F12 keys)
2. Prepare Trial Balance, Profit & Loss A/C and Balance Sheet (With minimum of any 5 adjustments)
3. Prepare Inventory statement using (Calculate Inventory by using all methods)
   (a) FIFO
   (b) LIFO
   (c) Simple Average method
   (d) Weighted Average Method.
4. Prepare a fund flow statement and give your opinion.
5. Prepare a cash flow statement and present your view.

HTML

6. Using HTML create a web page to show the information of a Departmental Store.
7. Using HTML prepare a Resume of your own.
8. Using HTML create a video clipping.
9. Using HTML create a style sheet with border definition and font attributes.
10. Introduce a new product to the market and create web advertising.
11. Create a web page for your department — by using font effects, filters and linking within the page.

BHARATHIAR UNIVERSITY

COMPUTER APPLICATIONS PRACTICAL LIST

FOR M.A. (CA) COURSE OFFERED BY AFFILIATED COLLEGES

FOR THE STUDENTS ADMITTED DURING THE ACADEMIC YEAR 2007-2008 ONWARDS

MA CA

LIST OF PRACTICAL (I SEMESTER)

MS WORD & POWERPOINT

1. Create a document containing 0.5" margin in all sides. Write a letter to the Collector, Coimbatore stating the pollution problems in the city.
2. Give a report of Movies impact on Society, and give header and footer and footnotes for that.
3. Prepare a bill for the items sold in a departmental store. Use Tables and change the background color of the unit price column.
4. Prepare slides for demonstrating one product form a company of your choice.
5. Prepare demonstration slides for a washing machine and add visual effects for each slide.